ACCOUNTING PRINCIPLES

ACCOUNTING PRINCIPLES

JERRY J. WEYGANDT Ph.D., C.P.A.
University of Wisconsin
Madison, Wisconsin

DONALD E. KIESO Ph.D., C.P.A.
Peat Marwick Professor of Accountancy
Northern Illinois University
DeKalb, Illinois

WALTER G. KELL Ph.D., C.P.A.
University of Michigan
Ann Arbor, Michigan

JOHN WILEY AND SONS
New York Chichester Brisbane
Toronto Singapore

Text and cover designer Madelyn Lesure
Copy editing supervisors Barbara Heaney and Josh Spieler
Photo researcher Alyssa Katz
Photo editor Stella Kupferberg
Illustrator John Balbalis, with the assistance of the Wiley Illustration Department
Front cover photographs: © Four By Five
Back cover photograph: © Allen Green/Photo Researchers

ISBN 0-471-03863-6

Printed in the United States of America

10 9 8 7 6 5 4 3 2

To our families
and especially our wives
Enid
Donna
Linda

ABOUT THE AUTHORS

Jerry J. Weygandt, Ph.D., CPA, is Professor of Accounting at the University of Wisconsin–Madison. He holds a Ph.D. in accounting from the University of Illinois. Articles by Professor Weygandt have appeared in the *Accounting Review, Journal of Accounting Research,* the *Journal of Accountancy,* and other professional journals. These articles have examined such financial reporting issues as accounting for price-level adjustments, pensions, convertible securities, stock option contracts, and interim reports. He is a member of the American Accounting Association, the American Institute of Certified Public Accountants, and the Wisconsin Society of Certified Public Accountants. He has served on numerous committees of the American Accounting Association and as a member of the editorial board of the *Accounting Review.* In addition, he is actively involved with the American Institute of Certified Public Accountants and has been a member of the Accounting Standards Executive Committee (AcSEC) of that organization. He has served as a consultant to a number of businesses and state agencies on financial reporting issues and currently is serving on an FASB task force that is examining the problems of "accounting for income taxes." Professor Weygandt recently received the Chancellor's Award for Excellence in Teaching; he has served as Secretary-Treasurer of the American Accounting Association.

Donald E. Kieso, Ph.D., CPA, received his doctorate in accounting from the University of Illinois. He has served as chairman of the Department of Accountancy and is currently the Peat Marwick Professor of Accountancy at Northern Illinois University. He has public accounting experience with Price Waterhouse & Co. (San Francisco and Chicago) and Arthur Andersen & Co. (Chicago) and research experience with the Research Division of the American Institute of Certified Public Accountants (New York). He has done postdoctorate work as a Visiting Scholar at the University of California at Berkeley and is a recipient of NIU's Teaching Excellence Award and the Executive MBA's Golden Apple Award. Professor Kieso is the author of other accounting and business books and is a member of the American Accounting Association, the American Institute of Certified Public Accountants, the Financial Executives Institute, and the Illinois CPA Society. Most recently he has served as a member of the Board of Directors of the Illinois CPA Society, the Board of Governors of the American Accounting Association's Administrators of Accounting Programs Group, the State of Illinois Comptroller's Commission, as Secretary-Treasurer of the Federation of Schools of Accountancy, and as Secretary-Treasurer of the American Accounting Association. Professor Kieso is currently serving as a member of the American Assembly of Collegiate Schools of Business Accounting Accreditation Standards Board, the Board of Directors and Executive Committee of Aurora University, and the Continuing Professional Education Committee of the Illinois CPA Society.

Walter G. Kell, Ph.D., CPA, received his doctorate in accounting from the University of Illinois. He is Professor of Accounting at the University of Michigan, where he has served as Chairman of the Department of Account-

ing. He also has served as the Chairman of the Accounting Department of Syracuse University. He has been an active member of the American Institute of Certified Public Accountants and has served on its Committee on Auditing Procedure (predecessor to the Auditing Standards Board) and Auditing Standards Advisory Council. He is a past president of the American Accounting Association. Professor Kell has been a consulting editor and co-editor of the *Accountant's Handbook* and is the co-author of an auditing textbook. He is a member of the Michigan Association of Certified Public Accountants and has served on its Committee on Accounting and Auditing Procedures and Board of Directors. In 1986 Professor Kell received the Association's Distinguished Service Award because of his significant contributions to the public accounting profession. Currently he is a member of the CPA Examination Review Board of the National Association of State Boards of Accountancy.

PREFACE

PURPOSE

Our objective in writing this textbook is to provide students with a solid conceptual and practical understanding of the discipline of accounting. We have, therefore, attempted to balance our coverage so that the conceptual discussion and procedural presentation are mutually reinforcing. The study of concepts develops an understanding of procedures, and the performance of procedures develops an understanding of the concepts. Individuals in business must act as well as think; therefore, we have given a balanced emphasis to the how and to the why.

Accounting Principles was written to be used in the first course in accounting. Designed for both majors and nonmajors, it can be used in a two-semester or a two- or three-quarter-course sequence. Coverage of the complete textbook will provide the student with a solid foundation for the study of additional areas in accounting and business. And, knowledge of the principles and procedures contained in this textbook should enable the student to make more informed business judgments and decisions.

GENERAL FEATURES

Accounting is an exciting and dynamic field of study. Unfortunately, the field is often portrayed as one involving only a set of rules or procedures to be followed. We have tried to avoid this approach. One of the main reasons why we decided to write an elementary textbook was to try to improve the pedagogical nature of teaching beginning accounting. In our view, an overemphasis on rules and procedures will only discourage students and leave them without a real understanding of how accounting can be used for making effective financial decisions.

To provide a textbook that is current, relevant, and interesting, we have emphasized certain features. These features are: (1) contemporary focus; (2) authoritative and professional content; (3) computer relevancy; (4) flexibility in coverage; and (5) increased managerial accounting coverage.

CONTEMPORARY FOCUS

Accounting continually changes as its environment changes. An up-to-date textbook therefore is a necessity. We believe that we have met that objective.

For example, in Chapter 19, the statement of cash flows, instead of the statement of changes in financial position, is discussed. By mid-1987, all companies complying with GAAP will be required to present a statement of cash flows as one of the primary financial statements in lieu of the previously required statement of changes in financial position. Therefore, to learn any other approach, such as the formerly popular working capital basis, has little value or applicability.

Similary, in Chapter 29, the new Tax Reform Act, the most sweeping federal tax legislation in more than 40 years, is covered. The Tax Reform Act dramatically lowers income tax rates, significantly broadens the tax base, and shifts the tax burden from individuals to corporations. The new tax law, rather than the old, is illustrated to ensure that the student will understand some of the basic tax rules that affect both individuals and corporations.

AUTHORITATIVE AND PROFESSIONAL CONTENT

Accounting is a practical discipline. This textbook therefore emphasizes how accounting is currently practiced. The concepts that underlie these practices are carefully explained so that students can understand why a particular rule or procedure is followed. As indicated earlier, textbooks often quote the rule or procedure with little attention to the why. In our view, this approach is inappropriate because it teaches students to memorize rules rather than to understand concepts.

Throughout the textbook we use the professional terminology as developed from the professional pronouncements of the FASB, AICPA, and SEC. Generally accepted accounting principles are discussed and illustrated throughout the textbook, where applicable.

COMPUTER RELEVANCY

It is important that students have some appreciation of the computer's use in accounting and business. We believe students should acquire this knowledge while learning accounting, not separately from accounting. To achieve this objective we have interspersed throughout the chapters a series of "computer notes" that discuss applications of the computer to accounting in particular and to business in general. These notes will help the students understand and appreciate how this important tool can be used in solving accounting problems. A sample computer note, illustrating the manner in which such notes are highlighted throughout this textbook, is shown below:

In computerized systems, the computer is programmed to flag these normal balance exceptions and to print out error or exception reports. In manual systems, careful visual inspection of the accounts is required to detect normal balance exceptions.

Substantial computer-related materials are also provided as part of the supplementary package of this textbook.

FLEXIBILITY OF COVERAGE

Our coverage is organized and designed to provide sufficient flexibility so that an instructor does not have to cover every topic in this textbook. Nine topics have been relegated to an Appendix so the instructor can more readily choose to cover or not to cover them. Material has been placed in an appendix for one or more reasons: (1) the procedure is little used; (2) the approach is highly procedural in nature; or (3) the subject is less essential if time is a constraint. Examples of appendix material are as follows:

Appendix 3-A Alternative Treatment of Prepaid Expenses and Unearned Revenues
This appendix covers the proper accounting for prepaid items when the initial entry is debited or credited to a nominal account.

Appendix 4-A Reversing Entries
It explains the purpose of reversing entries and illustrates how they can facilitate the accounting process.

Appendix 18-A International Accounting
Most businesses today engage in foreign trade, both importing and exporting goods. Thus, it is important that we understand the impact of exchange rates and how fluctuations in currencies affect financial statements.

Appendix 19-A Using a Work Sheet for Preparing the Statement of Cash Flows
This appendix illustrates the use of a work sheet in assembling and classifying data that will appear on the statement of cash flows.

Appendix 22-A Accounting Cycle for a Manufacturing Company
The accounting cycles of a manufacturing and a merchandising company are essentially the same. The differences, however, that exist in the use of a work sheet and in the preparation of closing entries are illustrated in this appendix.

In addition there are four other appendices which can be easily assigned or omitted, depending upon the emphasis to be given.

INCREASED MANAGERIAL ACCOUNTING COVERAGE

Unlike most traditional accounting principle textbooks that cover managerial accounting in seven or less chapters, this textbook includes nine chapters on managerial accounting. Our increased emphasis is in the following areas:

1. Expanded discussion of return on investment as it relates to segments of the business.
2. Additional material on flexible budgeting so that students can better understand why flexible budgets are so important in the decision-making process.
3. Complete and careful explanation of process costing.
4. Additional discussion of responsibility accounting and its role in performance evaluation.
5. Variable costing, highlighted with expanded rationale of its usefulness.

COMPLETE LEARNING PACKAGE

In addition to the general features of the textbook, some other qualitative aspects of the book are: (1) pedagogical features within each chapter; (2) extensive homework material; and (3) complete supplementary package.

PEDAGOGICAL FEATURES WITHIN EACH CHAPTER

Study Objectives

At the start of each chapter is a list of study objectives. These study objectives highlight the important concepts discussed in the chapter. At the end of the chapter is a summary of study objectives that provides an explanation of each study objective.

Demonstration Problems

At the start of the problem material, a demonstration problem and solution are provided. Unlike many textbooks that provide only a limited number of demonstration problems, if any at all, this textbook has a demonstration problem for every chapter.

Decision Cases

Each chapter has a decision case at the end of the problem material. The purpose of the decision case is to provide a less structured situation for the students to help them develop their decision-making skills.

Key Terms Highlighted

Each chapter has a list of key terms with a page reference indicating where that term is defined in the chapter. A complete glossary of all key terms appears at the end of the textbook in Appendix B.

Computer Notes

A discussion of the use of the computer in an accounting situation is discussed at least once in a chapter and in many chapters, more than once.

Liberal Use of Graphics, Diagrams, and Flow Charts

As often stated, a "picture is worth a thousand words." Throughout the textbook an abundance of graphics, diagrams, and flow charts make optimum use of the two-color format.

EXTENSIVE HOMEWORK MATERIAL

Because instructors often choose to emphasize different concepts and practices from semester to semester, and because different instructors emphasize

different points, we have provided a wide variety of homework material including questions, exercises, problems, and decision cases. In addition, an alternative problem set is included at the end of each chapter that can be used in alternating semesters or quarters if the instructor prefers. It should be noted that the homework material has been extensively checked to ensure accuracy and completeness.

SUPPLEMENTARY MATERIALS

For the Student

Student Study Guide. This valuable aid for students consists of a chapter review and review questions and exercises (true/false, multiple choice, matching, and short exercises) for each chapter. The Study Guide highlights and summarizes the material in the chapter and helps students measure progress and understanding by immediate feedback. Answers are included, and the incorrect answers to the true/false and multiple choice questions are explained.

Four Manual Practice Sets. College Hills Cycle Shop IA (narrative version) and IB (business papers version) are practice sets to be used after Chapter 7 of the textbook. Town City Furniture Galleries (Practice Set II) is a second financial practice set for use after Chapter 16 of the textbook. Lawn Pro Manufacturing Company (Practice Set III) is a managerial practice set for use after Chapter 22 of the textbook.

Computerized Practice Set IA. The computerized version of Practice Set IA for the IBM-PC includes a workbook, documentation, and a disk. Features of the computerized practice set include automatic posting of student entries to allow the student to concentrate on learning the principles involved. In addition, any journal entries entered in error are easily corrected by the computer; the computer will delete previous wrong postings and automatically correct them to reflect the proper data. The practice set also contains Lotus-type menus, which aid the student in building on previously learned computer skills.

Working Papers I and II. Working Papers I is provided for all problems in Chapters 1–14. These are partially filled in with headings and some preliminary data to save the students' time and act as a learning tool. Working Papers II provides similar information for Chapters 14–29.

Solving Accounting Exercises on the IBM-PC Microcomputer. Selected exercises from the textbook are set up for the students to solve on the computers. When errors are made there is a built-in review process to help students understand the concepts illustrated in the exercise.

Spreadsheet Software for Lotus 1-2-3. The package is keyed to the end-of-chapter problems in the textbook and is for use on the IBM-PC. The package provides the student with a wide selection of end-of-chapter problems and six

tutorial problems, as well as a section in the manual that trains the student in Lotus 1-2-3. The package includes ten preprogrammed templates for which the student identifies and enters relevant input data and evaluates the resulting output data; a number of partially completed templates test the student's accounting knowledge and developing computer skills. Eighty problems taken directly from the textbook are covered.

The Shoebox: A Computerized Accounting Practice Set for Use with BPI Systems General Accounting Program. This practice set, designed specifically to accompany the BPI General Accounting package, enables students to apply the concepts found in the General Accounting package. Workbook and data disk are included.

For the Instructor

Solutions Manual. Complete and accurate solutions to all questions, exercises, problems, and cases in the textbook are included.

Instructor's Manual. A comprehensive resource guide, this manual includes sample syllabi for two-semester, three-semester, and three-quarter use of the textbook, chapter by chapter outlines, lecture notes, and time and difficulty charts, including a short description of each problem for instructor assignment purposes.

Examination Book and Microtest. This collection of objective questions and problems for each chapter in the textbook with accompanying answers is also available in software format for IBM-PC and Apple II and compatibles. Microtest offers the professor a number of valuable options—the ability to generate a large number of test questions randomly from any chapter; easy question selection (professor can lock in desired question type and chapter number); and test previewing prior to printing. Examinations can be stored on a separate data disk (up to 38 for the IBM-PC and 18 for the Apple), and retrieved later for playback. Microtest also has the ability to generate multiple tests simultaneously, and is equipped with disk transfer capability, which enables the user to select questions from any portion of the testbank and from any disk. The machine will locate the questions and print out the test in one run.

Checklist of Key Figures. This is a listing of key figures for students to use to verify problem solutions.

Achievement Tests. These end-of-chapter and end-of-term tests are presented in a format to copy and distribute directly to students. Each test is available in two versions for make-up or second-year use.

Microstudy. Computerized Version of the Student Study Guide for the IBM-PC. Microstudy has been designed to reinforce the material and problems in the Study Guide. It offers the student both extensive review information and hundreds of self-testing questions from every chapter in the textbook. The student can select from a number of self-study options including:

Chapter Summaries; Chapter Learning Objectives; and Multiple Choice Questions. The multiple choice section of Microstudy goes well beyond most other computerized study programs in offering students explanations of why the wrong choices are not correct. In addition, all of the questions are automatically scrambled to avoid duplication of identical tests. Finally, Microstudy is easy to use. All of the major options can be triggered by simply pressing a numeric key.

Test Preparation Service. We provide a form from which the instructor selects the questions from Microtest that he or she wants on an exam, and we send one master exam within 24 hours of receipt of the form. If the instructor prefers, random selection from a number of chapters is possible.

Acetate Transparencies. Acetate transparencies are available for all exercises and problems in the textbook as well as a set of teaching transparencies selected from the illustrations in the textbook. All are in clear, dark type for good visibility.

BPI Software for IBM-PC and Compatibles.

General Accounting Educational Version. The Educational Version of the well-known, commercial BPI General Accounting package trains students in the basics of accounting. Features of the package include:

Three subsidiary ledgers: accounts payable, accounts receivable, and payroll.

Six special journals plus a general ledger to record each transaction.

Automatic posting of ledgers and automatic checkwriting.

Comprehensive financial reports.

BPI Self-Training Software Package. The Self-Training program is designed to teach students how to use the BPI General Accounting software. The disks explain the system's features; the computer keyboard; printing and understanding reports; and how to enter, create, and maintain data.

One set of the software (General Accounting and Self-Training packages) is free with the adoption of *Accounting Principles*. A site license is also available so that faculty members may make multiple disk copies.

ACKNOWLEDGMENTS

The authors acknowledge with gratitude the many individuals who helped with their comments and constructive criticisms. Special thanks are extended to the primary reviewers of our manuscript.

Susan B. Bennett
Sprinkle & Associates
Susan Beaumont
Northern Illinois University
Philip Blandford
Touche Ross & Co.
John Borke
University of Wisconsin–Platteville

Charles E. Boynton
University of Wisconsin
Jody F. Boynton
University of Wisconsin
Bruce P. Budge
University of Montana
Ron Burrows
University of Dayton
Lloyd Carroll
Manhattan Community College
Grant M. Clowery
University of Michigan
Robert Cox
Edison State College
Donald E. Edwards
University of Southwestern Louisiana
Tim A. Farmer
University of Wisconsin
Roy Fesmire
Peat, Marwick, Mitchell & Co.
James F. Gaertner
University of Texas–San Antonio
Steve Gilmour
Mount Mercy College
Robert A. Gruber
University of Wisconsin
Jerry Hamsmith
Aurora University
Robert Held
Harper Community College
James A. Hendricks
Northern Illinois University
Wayne Higley
Buena Vista College
Zaf Iqbal
California Polytechnic State University–San Luis Obispo
Kenneth R. Janson
Michigan Technological University
Douglas W. Kieso
Arthur Andersen & Co.
Carol Krenek
Aurora, Illinois
Catherine X. Larson
Middlesex Community College
Willard J. Lawrence
Austin Community College
Philip G. Montgomery
T. and B. Computing Inc.
Debra McGilsky
Northern Illinois University
Kathleen F. Oppenheimer
Western Connecticut State College
Lynn Paluska
Nassau Community College
James A. Patten
California State University
Timothy A. Pearson
University of Wisconsin
K. G. Radhakrishnan
Coopers & Lybrand
LaVonda Ramey
Schoolcraft College
George Ritchey
Harrisburg Area Community College
Gene Rozanski
Illinois State University
David L. Rozelle
Western Michigan University
Fred W. Schaeberle
Western Michigan University
James T. Schmid
Coopers & Lybrand
Kap Shin
Northern Illinois University
Elaine Simpson
St. Louis Community College
Dorothy Steinsapir
Middlesex County College
Sally Weber
Aurora University
James E. Wheeler
University of Michigan

We appreciate the exemplary support and professional commitment given us by our production manager, Donna R. Kieso, our word processing operators Mary Ann Benson, Vicki Worrell, Tracey Ruger, Debra J. Kieso, Heather Remmers, Nannette Kintner, Karen Robinson, and Barbara Hamsmith, and

by the production and editorial staffs of John Wiley & Sons, Inc., including Romayne Ponleithner and John Balbalis; and John Beresford and the staff of Allservice Phototypesetting. We especially thank our production manager, Suzanne Ingrao, and her staff, and our editor, Lucille Sutton, for their counsel on and commitment to this edition. In addition, a special debt of gratitude is expressed to our computer experts, Jiin-Feng Chen, James A. Patten, James H. Perkins, and Gregory Trompeter.

We appreciate the cooperation of the Financial Accounting Standards Board in permitting us to quote from their pronouncements. We also acknowledge permission from the Institute of Certified Management Accountants to adapt and use material from the Certificate in Management Accounting Examination (CMA). The business forms provided by Jack Eaker of Duplex Products Inc. add an appreciated measure of realism to our illustrations. We also thank PepsiCo, Inc. for permission to use excerpts from its 1985 Annual Report.

If this textbook helps teachers instill in their students an appreciation and understanding of financial and managerial accounting, if it encourages students to evaluate critically and understand basic accounting, and if it prepares students for more advanced study in business, then we will have attained our objective.

Suggestions and comments from users of *Accounting Principles* will be appreciated.

Madison, Wisconsin — Jerry J. Weygandt
DeKalb, Illinois — Donald E. Kieso
Ann Arbor, Michigan — Walter G. Kell

CONTENTS

CHAPTER OPENER PHOTO CREDITS

Chapter 1: Photo by Charlie Harrington. Courtesy Cornell University. *Chapter 2*: Photo by Stuart Bratesman. Courtesy Dartmouth News Service. *Chapter 3*: Courtesy News Bureau, University of Illinois, Urbana-Champaign. *Chapter 4*: Courtesy Nassau Community College, New York. *Chapter 5*: Courtesy Auburn University Bulletin, Alabama. *Chapter 6*: Courtesy Wayne State University, Michigan. *Chapter 7*: Courtesy University of Kansas. *Chapter 8*: Courtesy California State Polytechnic University, Pomona. *Chapter 9*: Barbara Rios/Photo Researchers. *Chapter 10*: Courtesy Austin Community College, Texas. *Chapter 11*: Photo by Robert Bishop. Courtesy Miami University, Ohio. *Chapter 12*: Courtesy University of California, Santa Cruz. *Chapter 13*: Courtesy Illinois State University. *Chapter 14*: Courtesy Macomb County Community College, Michigan. *Chapter 15*: Courtesy News Information Service, Southwest Texas State University. *Chapter 16*: Courtesy Pace University, New York. *Chapter 17*: Courtesy Information Services, North Carolina State University at Raleigh. *Chapter18*: Robert A. Isaacs/Photo Researchers. *Chapter 19*: Photo by Michael Mouchette. Courtesy University of New Mexico. *Chapter 20*: Frank Siteman/Stock, Boston. *Chapter 21*: Peter Menzel/Stock, Boston. *Chapter 22*: Courtesy Hofstra University, New York. *Chapter 23*: Courtesy St. Petersburg Junior College, Florida. *Chapter 24*: Courtesy Office of Public Affairs, Bentley College, Massachusetts. *Chapter 25*: Courtesy Iowa State University. *Chapter 26*: Courtesy Duke University. *Chapter 27*: Photo by Robert Daseler. Courtesy Claremont McKenna College, California. *Chapter 28*: F. W. Grunzweig/Photo Researchers. *Chapter 29*: Courtesy Boise State University.

CHAPTER 1

Cornell University

CHAPTER 1

CHARACTERISTICS AND BASIC CONCEPTS OF ACCOUNTING

STUDY OBJECTIVES

After studying this chapter, you should be able to:

1. Explain the meaning of accounting.
2. Determine the users and uses of accounting.
3. Know the major career paths of accountants.
4. Explain the meaning of generally accepted accounting principles and the cost principle.
5. Explain the meaning of the economic entity assumption and the monetary unit assumption.
6. Explain the meaning of assets, liabilities, and owner's equity.
7. Analyze the effect of business transactions on the basic accounting equation.
8. Prepare an income statement, owner's equity statement, and balance sheet.

The United States is rapidly changing from an industrial to an information society. For example, almost 90% of the new jobs created in the most recent decade were in information knowledge or service jobs.[1] As a result, it is not surprising to find that accounting is one of the fastest-growing professions and one of the most popular fields of study in colleges and universities. **The reason for this growth is quite simple—accounting is the financial informa-**

[1]John Naisbett, *Megatrends* (New York: Warner Books, Inc., 1982).

tion system that provides relevant financial information to every person who owns or uses economic resources or otherwise engages in economic activity.

Regardless of one's pursuits or occupation, the need for financial information is inescapable. Such common endeavors as earning a living, spending money, buying on credit, making investments, paying taxes—not to mention managing a business—involve receiving, using, or dispensing financial information. Accounting is engrained in our society and is vital to our economic system.

WHAT IS ACCOUNTING?

As a financial information system, accounting is the process of **identifying, measuring, recording,** and **communicating** the economic events of an organization (business or nonbusiness) to interested users of the information. The sale of goods to customers by J. C. Penney Company, the rendering of services to customers by American Telephone & Telegraph, and the payment of wages to employees by Ford Motor Company are examples of economic events. **Identifying involves observing activity and selecting those events that are (1) considered evidence of economic activity and (2) relevant to a particular business enterprise or organization.**

Once identified, the economic events (called transactions by accountants) must be measured in financial terms, that is, quantified in dollars and cents. If the event cannot be quantified in monetary terms, it is not considered part of the financial information system. The measurement function thereby eliminates some significant events (such as the appointment of a new company president) because they lack measurability in financial terms.

Once measured in dollars and cents, the events are recorded to provide a permanent history of the financial activities of the organization. **Recording consists of keeping a chronological diary of these measured events in an orderly and systematic manner.** In recording, the accountant also classifies and summarizes these events.

With the phenomenal growth in computers, more and more record keeping is being performed electronically. Businesses, small as well as large, are finding that through the use of the computer the entire recording process has become more efficient. However it is important to know the procedures used in a manual system to understand the operations a computer performs.

Throughout this textbook you will find computer notes highlighted like this. These notes are designed to show how computer technology is used in accounting and business.

All of this identifying, measuring, and recording activity is meaningless unless the information is **communicated** in some form to interested users. **The information is communicated through the preparation and distribution of accounting reports, the most common of which are called financial state-**

ments. To make the reported financial information meaningful, accountants describe and report the recorded data in a standardized manner and on a periodic basis. Information resulting from similar transactions is accumulated and reported in the aggregate. For example, all sales transactions of Apple Computer are accumulated over a certain period of time and reported as one amount in the financial statements of Apple Computer. By presenting the recorded data in this manner, the accounting process simplifies a multitude of transactions and renders a series of complex activities understandable and meaningful. The frequency of communicating varies according to the needs of the intended user of the data and the nature of the information reported. For example, the treasurer may request daily reports of cash, the sales manager may require weekly reports of sales, and the president may desire monthly reports on operations as a whole. In contrast, annual statements of financial position and results of operations may suffice for investors and governmental agencies.

A vital element in the communication process is the accountant's ability and responsibility to **interpret** the reported information. **Interpretation involves analyzing and explaining the uses, meaning, and limitations of reported data.** Through ratios, percentages, graphs, and charts, significant financial trends and relationships are reported to the users of financial reports.

The accounting process as discussed above may be diagrammed as follows:

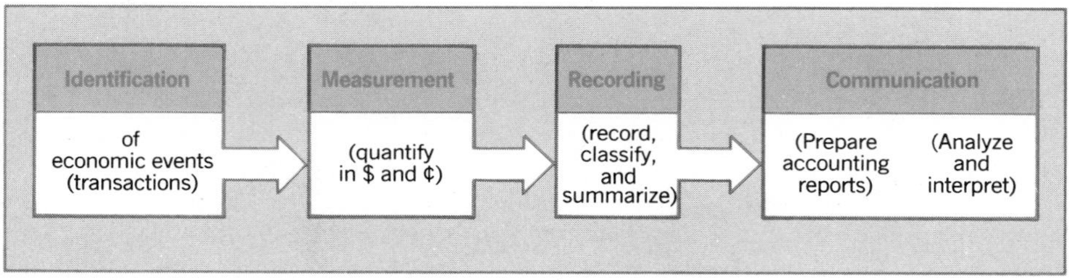

Accounting process

Accounting should be sensitive to the needs of the users of accounting information. As a consequence, we should know who these users are and something about their needs for information.

USERS AND USES OF ACCOUNTING DATA

Because it communicates financial information about a business enterprise, accounting is often called "the language of business." As indicated, the type and frequency of information that a specific user needs depend upon the kinds of decisions that the user makes. The differences in the decisions divide the users into two broad groups: (1) **internal users, those who manage the business (officers and other decision makers),** and (2) **external users, those outside the business who have either a present or potential direct financial interest (investors and creditors) or an indirect financial interest (taxing authorities, regulatory agencies, labor unions, customers, and economic planners).** The relationship of these users to the accounting process and to one another is diagrammed on the following page:

Users of accounting process

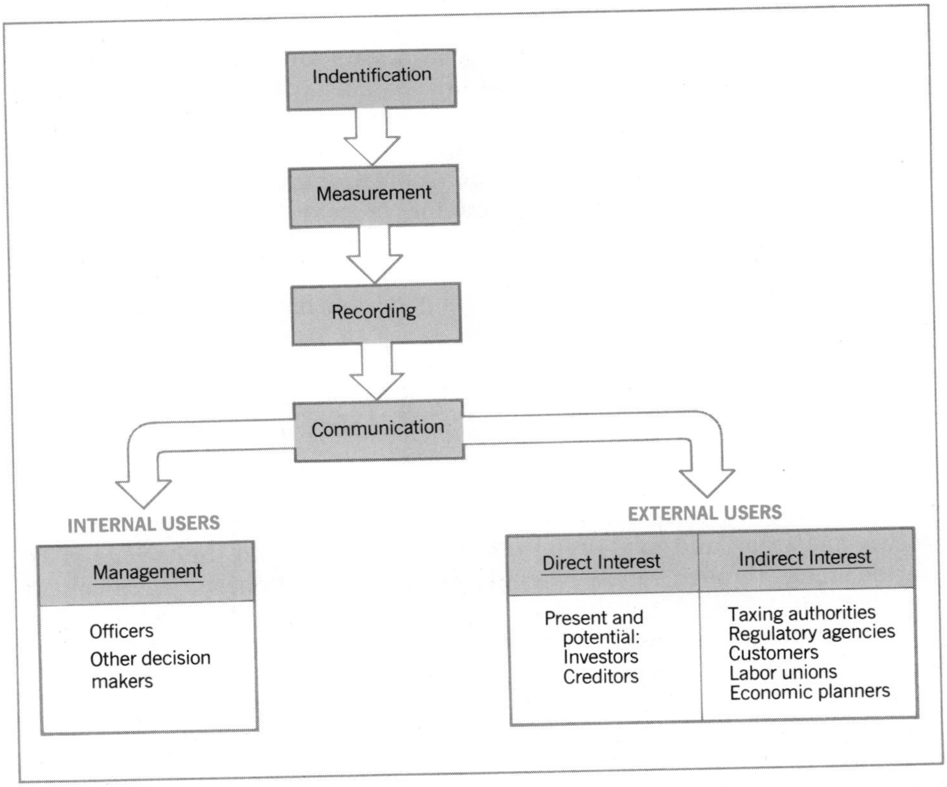

INTERNAL USERS

Management at all levels uses accounting information in planning, controlling, and evaluating business operations. To perform these functions managers need detailed information on a timely basis. For example, some questions asked by managers of a company might be:

Is cash sufficient to pay our debts?
Are customers paying their bills promptly?
What is the cost of manufacturing each unit of product?
What costs exceed budget?
Which product line is the most profitable?
How much money must be borrowed to expand the factory?

To assist management in these and other questions, accounting provides internal reports such as financial comparisons of operating alternatives, projections of income from new sales campaigns, and forecasts of cash needs for the next year. In addition, financial statements on the financial condition and results of operations of the entire business are prepared.

EXTERNAL USERS—DIRECT INTEREST

Investors (owners) judge the wisdom of buying, holding, or selling their financial interests on the basis of accounting data. **Creditors** (suppliers and

bankers) evaluate the risks of granting credit or loaning money to a particular business on the basis of the accounting information obtained about that business. Some of the questions asked by investors and creditors about a company might be:

Should an ownership interest be retained, increased, or decreased in this company?

Is the company earning satisfactory income?

How does the company compare in size and profitability with competitors?

Will the company be able to pay its debts as they come due?

Are interest payments and dividends protected by an adequate inflow of cash from operations?

EXTERNAL USERS—INDIRECT INTEREST

The information needs and the questions of the indirect financial interests vary considerably. **Taxing authorities** (such as the Internal Revenue Service) are interested in knowing if the company complied with the tax laws applicable to that business. **Regulatory agencies** (such as the Securities and Exchange Commission or the Federal Trade Commission) want to know if the company is operating within prescribed rules and reporting in accordance with regulatory requirements. **Customers** are interested in a company's financial strength as an indication of its ability to continue to honor product warranties and otherwise support its product lines. **Labor unions** want to know if the company has the ability to pay increased wages and benefits. **Economic planners** use accounting information to analyze and forecast economic activity.

The many and varied uses of accounting information clearly attest to its importance. Without accounting, our existing systems of production, investment, credit, and taxation would be seriously impaired.

BOOKKEEPING AND ACCOUNTING DISTINGUISHED

Bookkeeping and accounting are often considered to be one and the same. This confusion is understandable because the accounting process includes the bookkeeping function, but it also includes much more. **Bookkeeping** usually involves only the recording of economic events and therefore is just one part of the accounting process. **Accounting,** on the other hand, involves the entire accounting process, including identification, measurement, recording, and communication.

The bookkeeping function has often been performed by individuals with limited skills in accounting. As a result, it is not surprising that the continued increase in the use of computers by business enterprises has resulted in much of the detailed work that is part of the bookkeeping process being performed by machines.

THE ACCOUNTING PROFESSION

One question frequently asked by students of accounting is, "How will the study of accounting help me?" Perhaps the easiest way to answer that question is to provide some illustrations. For example, numerous studies confirm the fact that a strong background in accounting is extremely helpful in every business endeavor. One study indicated that many chief executive officers of the largest companies in the United States have a background in the accounting and finance area.[2]

It should be emphasized that a background in accounting is also helpful in many nonbusiness fields of interest. For example, governmental officials use accounting information to estimate how well programs are working and whether tax dollars are being spent efficiently. Members of the legal profession use accounting data in tax, fraud, and antitrust cases and in determining compliance with governmental regulation. Bankers and investment brokers use accounting information in making investment and other financial decisions. In short, a sound background in accounting will be extremely valuable to you, whatever field of study you ultimately select.

A second question often asked by students is, "What would I do if I became an accountant?" The answer is that accountants apply their expertise in three major areas—public accounting, private accounting, and not-for-profit accounting.

PUBLIC ACCOUNTING

In **public accounting,** the accountant offers expert service to the general public in much the same way that a doctor serves patients and a lawyer serves clients. The mark of excellence in public accounting is associated with a license to practice as a certified public accountant (CPA). Like his or her counterparts in medicine and law, the CPA must fulfill certain education and experience requirements and pass a rigorous examination. As a public accountant, an individual may perform one or more of the following services.

Auditing

A major portion of public accounting practice is involved with **auditing.** In this area, the CPA examines the financial statements of companies and expresses an opinion as to the fairness of presentation. A favorable opinion (commonly called an **unqualified** or **clean** opinion) means that the financial statements may be relied on by investors, creditors, and other interested parties in making decisions about the company.

Because the auditor is an independent contractor, the auditor is involved in a wide range of business situations. For example, one beginning auditor noted, "My assignments in my first year included such diverse enterprises as a large family-owned farming operation, a city government, an international plastics manufacturer, a land developer, a small newspaper, and a telephone company."

[2]John R. Linden, "Rising Corporate Stars: The Accountant as Chief Executive Officer," *The Journal of Accountancy* (September 1978).

Taxation

Another major area of public accounting is the field of **taxation.** The work performed by tax specialists include tax advice and planning, preparing tax returns, and representing clients before governmental agencies such as the Internal Revenue Service. Questions such as the following are often answered by the tax accountant:

1. What are the tax advantages of setting up a company in Switzerland?
2. How will the acquisition of a company affect the client's tax status?
3. How can estate planning minimize estate and inheritance taxes?

Management Consulting

Because public accountants have financial training and expertise, it is not surprising that they are asked for management advice. In fact, recent surveys indicate that the accounting profession does more consulting than any other professional group.[3] Financial planning and control and the development of appropriate accounting and computer systems are important areas of **management consulting.** Other areas are organizational design, financial forecasting, and mergers and acquisitions. Some questions addressed by management consultants are:

1. What type of security system should be employed in the data processing area?
2. How can hospitals continue to provide high-quality service in light of reduced governmental support?
3. What are the options open to a package delivery company threatened by electronic mail?

Management consulting ranges from the installation of basic accounting systems to helping companies determine whether they should use the space shuttle for high-tech research.

PRIVATE ACCOUNTING

Many accountants are employees of business enterprises. Often referred to as **private (or managerial) accountants,** they perform many different activities within the company. The controller, who supervises the accounting activities, is regarded as the principal accounting officer of the company. As indicated earlier, individuals well versed in the accounting discipline are frequently members of the top management team.

The private accountant may be involved in:

1. **Cost accounting**—determining the cost of producing a specific product.

[3]For example, *Forbes* magazine noted that seven of the largest management consulting companies are public accounting firms, and the largest management consulting company is a public accounting firm.

2. **Budgeting**—assisting management in quantifying its future goals concerning revenues, costs of goods sold, and operating expenses.
3. **General accounting**—recording daily transactions and preparing financial statements and related information.
4. **Accounting information systems**—designing both manual and computerized data processing systems.
5. **Tax accounting**—preparing the tax returns and engaging in tax planning for the company.
6. **Internal auditing**—reviewing the company's operations to determine its compliance with management policies and evaluating the efficiency of operations.

From the foregoing, it can be observed that within a specific company, private accountants perform as wide a variety of duties as the public accountant.

A certificate in management accounting (CMA) is awarded to individuals who demonstrate expertise in areas of management accounting by passing an examination covering accounting and related disciplines. In addition, a certificate in internal auditing (CIA) is issued to individuals who have demonstrated competence in this field.

NOT-FOR-PROFIT ACCOUNTING

The need for sound financial reporting and control by not-for-profit organizations such as governmental units, foundations, hospitals, unions, educational organizations, and charities is imperative. For example, the near bankruptcies of a number of our large cities, such as New York and Cleveland, demonstrate the need for sound financial information to avert these situations. In addition, the influence of not-for-profit organizations is very significant and continues to grow. It has been recently estimated that there are more than 500,000 not-for-profit organizations in the United States.

Governmental

Local, state, and federal governmental units have a high demand for individuals skilled in accounting. Users of governmental financial reports, such as legislators, citizens, employees, and creditors must have adequate financial information to measure the financial health and the efficiency of governmental units. As a result, many different types of governmental agencies employ accountants, including at the federal level the Internal Revenue Service, the General Accounting Office, and the Securities and Exchange Commission.

Nongovernmental

In addition to government, many other organizations such as the United Way, Ford Foundation, and Red Cross attempt to provide goods or services socially desirable and necessary. Donors to these organizations need information about how well the organization has met its objectives and whether continued support is justified. Managers and governing bodies of these organizations must make many decisions about the allocation of money. To support these

decisions, they need reports that compare budgeted and actual revenue and expenditures.

The following chart indicates the percentage of undergraduate accounting majors from the authors' schools that start their employment in a particular field. Note that the percentages vary across our schools; undoubtedly your school will vary somewhat from these percentages as well.

Accounting majors at authors' schools

	University of Wisconsin	Northern Illinois University	University of Michigan
Public accounting	72%	51%	70%
Private accounting	18	37	15
Not-for-profit accounting	0	6	2
Other	10	6	13

GENERALLY ACCEPTED ACCOUNTING PRINCIPLES

Every profession develops a body of theory consisting of principles, assumptions, definitions, concepts, or standards, and accounting is no exception. Just as a doctor follows certain standards in treating a patient's illness, an accountant follows certain standards in reporting financial information.

The accounting profession has attempted to develop a set of standards that is generally accepted and universally practiced. Its efforts have resulted in the adoption of a common set of rules and procedures called **generally accepted accounting principles (GAAP).** Generally accepted accounting principles, therefore, are those guidelines (standards) which indicate how to report economic events.

Two organizations are primarily responsible for establishing generally accepted accounting principles. The first, the **Financial Accounting Standards Board (FASB),** is a private organization that establishes broad reporting guidelines of general applicability as well as specific accounting rules. In addition, the **Securities and Exchange Commission (SEC),** a governmental agency, has the right to require that companies filing financial reports with them follow generally accepted accounting principles. In situations where no principles exist, the SEC often mandates that certain practices be employed. In general, the FASB and the SEC work hand in hand to assure that timely and useful financial principles are developed.

One important principle is the **cost principle,** which states that assets should be recorded at their cost. **Cost is the value exchanged at the time something is acquired.** At the time of acquisition, cost and fair market value are the same. In subsequent periods cost and fair market value may vary, but the accountant continues to use the cost amount. For example, at one time, Greyhound Corporation had 128 bus stations nationwide that cost approximately $200 million. The current market value of the stations is approximately $1 billion. Under the cost principle, the bus stations are recorded and reported at $200 million, not $1 billion. Until the bus stations are actually sold, market values are considered too subjective and therefore generally less reliable than cost.

Cost has an important advantage over other valuations: it is reliable. Cost is definite and verifiable. The values exchanged at the time something is acquired generally can be objectively measured. The characteristics of objectivity and verifiability are of great importance to those who use accounting information. To rely on the information supplied, users must know that the information is based on verifiable fact. By using cost as their basis for record keeping and reporting, accountants can best provide objective and verifiable data in their reports. Other generally accepted principles will be discussed in subsequent chapters.

ASSUMPTIONS

In developing generally accepted accounting principles, accountants must make certain basic assumptions. These assumptions provide a foundation for the accounting process. Two main assumptions are the **economic entity assumption** and the **monetary unit assumption.**

ECONOMIC ENTITY ASSUMPTION

An economic entity can be any organization or unit in society. It may be a business enterprise such as General Electric Company; a governmental unit such as the state of Ohio; a municipality such as Seattle; a school district such as St. Louis District 48; or a social organization such as a church (Southern Baptist), a fraternity (Theta Chi), or a sorority (Chi Omega). **The economic entity assumption states that economic events can be identified with a particular unit of accountability.** This assumption requires that the activities of the entity be kept separate and distinct from (1) the activities of its owner and (2) all other economic entities. To illustrate, if Sally Rider, owner of Sally's Boutique, charges any of her personal living costs as expenses of the Boutique, the economic entity assumption is violated. Similarly, the economic entity assumption assumes that the activities of McDonald's, Wendy's, and Burger King can each be segregated into separate economic entities for accounting purposes.

Although the economic entity assumption can be applied to any unit of accountability, we will generally discuss it in relation to a business enterprise, which may be organized as a proprietorship, partnership, or corporation.

Proprietorship

A business owned by one person is generally a **proprietorship.** The owner is often the manager/operator of the business. Small service-type businesses (barber shops, law offices, plumbing companies, and auto repair shops), farms, and small retail stores (antique shops, clothing stores, and jewelry stores) are often sole proprietorships. **Usually only a limited amount of money (capital) is necessary to start in business, and the owner receives any profits, suffers any losses, and is personally liable for all debts of the business.** Although there is no legal distinction between the business as an economic unit and the owner, the records of the business activities are kept

separate from the personal records and activities of the owner. Although sole proprietorships represent the largest number of businesses in the United States, they are typically the smallest in size and volume of business.

Partnership

A business owned by two or more persons associated as partners is a partnership. In most respects a partnership is similar to a sole proprietorship except that more than one owner is involved. When a partnership is created, there should be an agreement (written or oral) setting forth such terms as initial investment of each partner, duties of each partner, division of profits or losses, and settlement to be made upon death or withdrawal of a partner. Each partner generally has unlimited personal liability for the debts of the partnership. **Although the partnership, like a proprietorship, is not a separate legal entity, for accounting purposes the partnership affairs must be kept separate from the personal activities of the partners.** Partnerships are often used to organize small retail and service-type businesses, including professional practices (lawyers, doctors, and certified public accountants).

Corporation

A business organized as a separate legal entity under state corporation law and having ownership divided into transferable shares of stock is called a corporation. The holders of the shares (stockholders) **enjoy limited liability;** they are not personally liable for the debts of the corporate entity. The ease with which stockholders **may transfer all or part of their shares to other investors at any time** (i.e., sell their shares in the securities market) adds to the attractiveness of investing in a corporation. Because ownership can be transferred without dissolving the corporation, the corporation **enjoys an unlimited life.** While the combined number of proprietorships and partnerships in the United States is more than five times the number of corporations, the revenue produced by corporations is eight times greater. Most of the largest enterprises in the United States—for example, Exxon, General Motors, Sears Roebuck, and Pacific Gas and Electric—are corporations.

MONETARY UNIT ASSUMPTION

The monetary unit assumption requires that only transaction data capable of being expressed in terms of money be included in the accounting records of the economic entity. **Support for this assumption lies in the fact that the monetary unit is relevant, simple, and understandable.** Because money is the commonly used medium of exchange, this assumption enables accounting to quantify (measure) the economic event. The monetary unit assumption is vital to applying the cost principle discussed earlier. This assumption prevents such relevant information as the health of the owner, the quality of service, and the morale of employees from being included in the accounting records because they cannot be quantified in terms of money.

An important corollary to the monetary unit assumption is the added assumption that the unit of measure remains sufficiently constant over time. The assumption of a stable monetary unit has been seriously challenged

during the past two decades because of the significant decline in the purchasing power of the dollar. For example, what used to cost $1.00 in 1960, now costs approximately $3.50 in 1986, an increase of over threefold. In such situations, adding, subtracting, or comparing 1960 dollars with 1986 dollars is highly questionable. The profession has recognized this problem and encourages companies to disclose the effects of changing prices. A discussion on changing prices is provided in a later chapter.

ASSETS, LIABILITIES, AND OWNER'S EQUITY

In addition to principles and assumptions, accountants have identified a number of key components that form the content of financial statements. These components are categorized as follows: assets, liabilities, and owner's equity.[4]

ASSETS

Assets are defined as future economic benefits owned or controlled by a particular entity as a result of past transactions or events. To put it more simply, assets are the **things of value used by the business in its operations.** Thus, they are the economic resources used in carrying out such activities as production, consumption, and exchange. The common characteristic possessed by all assets is "service potential" or "future economic benefit," that is, the capacity to provide future services or benefits to the entities that use them. In a business enterprise, that service potential or future economic benefit eventually results in cash inflows to the enterprise.

For example, the enterprise Campus Pizza owns a delivery truck that provides economic benefits because it is used in delivering pizzas. Other assets of Campus Pizza are tables, chairs, juke box, cash register, oven, mugs and silverware, and, of course, cash. These are examples of tangible assets, assets that possess physical substance. Intangible assets represent nonphysical rights such as those granted by a patent, trademark, franchise, or copyright.

LIABILITIES

Liabilities are obligations arising from past transactions of the entity to transfer assets or services to other entities or individuals in the future. To put it more simply, **liabilities are existing debts and obligations.** For example, businesses of all sizes and degrees of success usually find it necessary to borrow money and to purchase merchandise on credit. Campus Pizza, for instance, purchases cheese, sausage, flour, and beverages on credit from suppliers; these obligations are called **accounts payable.** Additionally, Campus Pizza has a **mortgage payable** to Local Savings & Loan for the mortgage on its building and a **note payable** to First National Bank for the money borrowed to purchase its delivery truck. Campus Pizza may also have **wages payable** to

[4]The definitions that follow are adapted from "Elements of Financial Statements of Business Enterprises," *Statement of Financial Accounting Concepts No. 3* (Stamford, Conn.: FASB, 1980), par. 19.

employees, **sales and real estate taxes payable** to the local government, and **income taxes payable** to the federal government. Persons or entities to whom Campus Pizza owes money are called **creditors.**

It is important to recognize that most claims of creditors attach to total enterprise assets rather than to the specific assets provided by the creditor. In the event of nonpayment, creditors may legally force the liquidation of a business, in which case the law requires that creditor claims be paid before ownership claims.

OWNER'S EQUITY

The ownership claim on total assets is known as **owner's equity;** it is equal to total assets minus total liabilities. The assets of a business are supplied or claimed by either creditors or owners. Since the claims of creditors (liabilities) take precedence over ownership claims, the latter are often referred to as **residual equity.** In proprietorships, the principal subdivisions of owner's equity are capital, drawings, revenues, and expenses.

Capital

Capital is the term used to determine the owner's permanent investment in the business. **When an investment is made in the business, capital is increased.** It follows that total owner's equity increases as well.

Drawings

An owner may withdraw cash or other assets during the accounting period for personal use. These withdrawals could directly decrease capital. However, it is generally considered preferable to use a separate classification referred to as **drawings,** to determine the total withdrawals for the accounting period. **Drawings decrease total owner's equity.**

Revenues

Revenues represent cash or other asset inflows that have occurred as a result of the business's ongoing major operations during the period. Revenues may also be defined as amounts the business earns by providing its product or services to customers. **Revenues increase owner's equity;** they may take the form of an increase in an asset or a decrease in a liability. Revenues may arise from different sources, and they are identified by various names depending on the nature of the business. Campus Pizza, for instance, has two categories of sales revenues—pizza sales and beverage sales. Burlington Northern, Inc., classifies its revenues by business segment as follows: railroad, forestry, oil and gas, coal and minerals, and trucking. Other titles for and sources of revenue common to many businesses are: sales, fees, services, commissions, interest, dividends, royalties, and rent.

Expenses

Expenses are the cost of assets consumed or services used in the process of earning revenue. **Expenses are the decreases in owner's equity that result**

from operating the business. Expenses represent actual or expected cash outflows. Like revenues, expenses take many forms and are identified by various names depending on the type of asset consumed or service used. For example, Campus Pizza recognizes the following types of expenses: cost of ingredients (meat, flour, cheese, tomato paste, mushrooms, etc.); cost of beverages; wages expense; utility expense (electric, gas and water expense); telephone expense; delivery expenses (gas, repairs, license, etc.); supplies expenses (napkins, detergents, aprons, etc.); rent expense; interest expense; and property tax expense.

In summary, the principal sources (increases) of owner's equity are (1) investments by owners and (2) revenues from business operations. In contrast, reductions in owner's equity are a result of (1) withdrawals of assets by owners and (2) expenses. **Net income** results when revenues exceed expenses; conversely, a **net loss** occurs when expenses exceed revenues.

THE BASIC ACCOUNTING EQUATION

As explained above, enterprise assets are obtained from creditors and owners who have claims or equities in the total assets that are equal in amount to the resources they have provided. **Thus, assets must always equal the sum of creditor and ownership claims against the business.** The interdependence of these three components (assets, liabilities, and owner's equity) constitutes the basic accounting equation as follows:

Basic accounting equation

Assets = Liabilities + Owner's Equity

The basic equation may also be expressed as Assets = Equities, with equities defined as both creditor claims and owner's equities. The accounting equation applies to all economic entities regardless of size, nature of business, or form of business organization. Thus, it applies to a small proprietorship such as a corner grocery store as well as to a giant corporation such as AT&T. The equation provides the underlying framework for recording and summarizing the economic events of a business enterprise. Specific types of assets (cash, land), liabilities (accounts payable, wages payable), and owner's equity items may change with each economic event, but total assets must always equal total liabilities plus owner's equity.

TRANSACTIONS

Transactions are the economic events of the enterprise recorded by accountants. Transactions may be identified as external or internal transactions. **External transactions involve economic events between the company and**

some other enterprise or party. For example, for Campus Pizza the purchase of cooking equipment from a supplier, the payment of monthly rent to the landlord, and the sale of pizzas to customers are external transactions. **Internal transactions are economic events that occur entirely within one company.** The use of office supplies, or the use of ovens to bake pizza, illustrate this type of transaction for Campus Pizza.

It should be recognized that a company may carry on many activities that do not in themselves represent business transactions, such as hiring employees, answering the telephone, talking with customers, and placing an order for merchandise with a supplier. These activities, however, may eventually lead to a business transaction when the employee has earned wages or when the merchandise is delivered by the supplier.

Each transaction must be analyzed in terms of its effect on the components of the basic accounting equation. This analysis must also identify the specific items affected and the amount of the change in each item. Since the equality of the basic equation must be preserved, each transaction must have a dual effect on the basic components of the equation. For example, if an individual asset is increased, there must be a corresponding:

1. Decrease in another asset, or
2. Increase in a specific liability, or
3. Increase in owner's equity.

It follows that two or more items could be affected when an asset is increased. For example, as one asset is increased, another asset could decrease and a specific liability could increase. Note also that any change in an individual liability or ownership claim is subject to similar analysis.

ANALYSIS OF TRANSACTIONS

The analysis of transactions in terms of the basic accounting equation can be observed by studying the following examples of business transactions for a new computer programming business during its first month of operations.

Transaction (1). Investment by Owner. Ray Neal decides to open a computer programming service in a campus community. On September 1, 1987, he invests $15,000 cash in the business, which is named Softbyte. This transaction results in an equal increase in assets and owner's equity. In this case, there is an increase in the asset Cash, $15,000, and an equal increase in the owner's equity, R. Neal, Capital, $15,000. The effect of this transaction on the basic equation is:

	Assets	=	Liabilities	+	Owner's Equity	
	Cash	=			R. Neal, Capital	
(1)	+$15,000	=			+$15,000	Investment

Observe that the equality of the basic equation has been maintained. Note also that the source of the increase in owner's equity is indicated. Capital

investments by the owner do not represent revenues; they are excluded in determining net income.

Transaction (2). Purchase of Equipment for Cash. Computer equipment is purchased for $7,000 cash. This transaction results in an equal increase and decrease in total assets. The composition of assets, however, is changed: Cash is decreased $7,000, and the asset Equipment is increased $7,000. Both the specific effect of this transaction and the cumulative effect of the first two transactions are:

		Assets			=	Liabilities	+	Owner's Equity
								R. Neal,
		Cash	+	Equipment	=			Capital
	Old Bal.	$15,000						$15,000
(2)		−7,000		+$7,000				
	New Bal.	$ 8,000	+	$7,000	=			$15,000

Observe that total assets are still $15,000 and Neal's equity also remains at $15,000, the amount of his original investment.

Transaction (3). Purchase of Supplies on Credit. Softbyte purchases computer paper and other supplies expected to last several months from Acme Supply Company for $1,600. Acme Company agrees to allow Softbyte to pay this bill in October, a month later. This transaction is often referred to as a purchase on account or a credit purchase. Assets are increased by this transaction because of the expected future benefits of using the paper and supplies, and liabilities are increased by the amount due Acme Company. The asset Supplies is increased $1,600, and the liability Accounts Payable is increased by the same amount. The effect on the equation is:

		Assets					=	Liabilities	+	Owner's Equity
								Accounts		R. Neal,
		Cash	+	Supplies	+	Equipment	=	Payable	+	Capital
	Old Bal.	$8,000				$7,000				$15,000
(3)				+$1,600				+$1,600		
	New Bal.	$8,000	+	$1,600	+	$7,000	=	$1,600	+	$15,000

Total assets are now $16,600. This total is matched by a $1,600 creditor's claim and a $15,000 ownership claim.

Transaction (4). Services Rendered for Cash. Softbyte receives $1,200 cash from customers for programming services. This transaction represents the principal revenue-producing activity of Softbyte. Recall that revenue increases owner's equity. Both assets and owner's equity are then increased. In this case, Cash is increased $1,200, and R. Neal, Capital is increased $1,200. The new balances in the equation are:

		Assets					=	Liabilities	+	Owner's Equity	
		Cash	+	Supplies	+	Equipment	=	Accounts Payable	+	R. Neal, Capital	
	Old Bal.	$8,000		$1,600		$7,000		$1,600		$15,000	
(4)		+1,200								+1,200	Service Revenue
	New Bal.	$9,200	+	$1,600	+	$7,000	=	$1,600	+	$16,200	

The two sides of the equation balance at $17,800. Note that the source of the increase in owner's equity is indicated as service revenue. Service revenue is included in determining net income.

Transaction (5). Purchase of Advertising on Credit. Softbyte receives a bill for $250 from the *Daily News* for advertising the opening of its business but postpones payment of the bill until a later date. This transaction results in an increase in liabilities and a decrease in owner's equity. The specific items involved are Accounts Payable and R. Neal, Capital. The effect on the equation is:

		Assets					=	Liabilities	+	Owner's Equity	
		Cash	+	Supplies	+	Equipment	=	Accounts Payable	+	R. Neal, Capital	
	Old Bal.	$9,200		$1,600		$7,000		$1,600		$16,200	
(5)								+250		−250	Advertising Expense
	New Bal.	$9,200	+	$1,600	+	$7,000	=	$1,850	+	$15,950	

The two sides of the equation still balance at $17,800. Observe that owner's equity is decreased when the expense is incurred, and the specific cause of the decrease is noted. Expenses do not have to be paid in cash at the time they are incurred. When payment is made at a later date, the liability Accounts Payable will be decreased and the asset Cash will be decreased [see Transaction (9)]. The cost of advertising is considered an expense as opposed to an asset because the benefits have been used. This expense is included in determining net income.

Transaction (6). Services Rendered for Cash and Credit. Softbyte provides programming services of $3,500 for customers. Cash amounting to $1,500 is received from customers, and the balance of $2,000 is billed to customers on account. This transaction results in an equal increase in assets and owner's equity. Three specific items are affected: Cash is increased $1,500; Accounts Receivable is increased $2,000; and R. Neal, Capital is increased $3,500. The new balances are as follows:

		Assets				= Liabilities +	Owner's Equity	
		Cash	+ Accounts Receivable	+ Supplies	+ Equipment	= Accounts Payable	+ R. Neal, Capital	
(6)	Old Bal.	$ 9,200		$1,600	$7,000	$1,850	$15,950	
		+ 1,500	+ $2,000				+ 3,500	Service Revenue
	New Bal.	$10,700 +	$2,000 +	$1,600 +	$7,000	= $1,850	+ $19,450	

Note that owner's equity is increased when revenues are earned and that the source is indicated. The inflow of assets resulting from the earning of revenues does not have to be in the form of cash. When collections on account are received at a later date, Cash will be increased and Accounts Receivable will be decreased [see Transaction (10)].

Transaction (7). Payment of Expenses. Expenses paid in cash for September are store rent, $600, salaries of employees, $900, and utilities, $200. These payments result in an equal decrease in assets and owner's equity. Cash is decreased $1,700 and R. Neal, Capital is decreased by the same amount. The effect of these payments on the equation is:

		Assets				= Liabilities +	Owner's Equity	
		Cash	+ Accounts Receivable	+ Supplies	+ Equipment	= Accounts Payable	+ R. Neal, Capital	
(7)	Old Bal.	$10,700	$2,000	$1,600	$7,000	$1,850	$19,450	
		− 1,700					− 600	Rent Expense
							− 900	Salaries Expense
							− 200	Utilities Expense
	New Bal.	$ 9,000 +	$2,000	+ $1,600 +	$7,000	= $1,850	+ $17,750	

The two sides of the equation now balance at $19,600. Three lines are required in the analysis to indicate the types of expenses that have been incurred.

Transaction (8). Recognition of Supplies Used. A count of supplies on September 30 indicates that $400 of supplies have been used in developing software for clients. The cost of supplies used is an expense that decreases assets and owner's equity. Specifically, this transaction decreases the asset Supplies $400 and decreases R. Neal, Capital $400. The new balances in the equation are:

		Assets				= Liabilities +	Owner's Equity	
		Cash	+ Accounts Receivable	+ Supplies	+ Equipment	= Accounts Payable	+ R. Neal, Capital	
(8)	Old Bal.	$9,000	$2,000	$1,600	$7,000	$1,850	$17,750	
				− 400			− 400	Supplies Expense
	New Bal.	$9,000 +	$2,000	+ $1,200 +	$7,000	= $1,850	+ $17,350	

Here, as in previous examples, the cause of the decrease in owner's equity is indicated.

Transaction (9). Payment of Accounts Payable. Softbyte pays its *Daily News* advertising bill of $250 in cash. In analyzing the effect of this transaction, we must recall that the bill has previously been recorded in Transaction (5) as an increase in Accounts Payable and a decrease in owner's equity. Thus, this payment "on account" decreases both assets and liabilities. In this case, the asset Cash and the liability Accounts Payable are decreased by $250. The effect of this transaction on the equation is:

		Assets							=	Liabilities	+	Owner's Equity
		Cash	+	Accounts Receivable	+	Supplies	+	Equipment	=	Accounts Payable	+	R. Neal, Capital
	Old Bal.	$9,000		$2,000		$1,200		$7,000		$1,850		$17,350
(9)		−250								−250		
	New Bal.	$8,750	+	$2,000	+	$1,200	+	$7,000	=	$1,600	+	$17,350

Observe that the payment of a liability related to an expense that has previously been incurred does not affect owner's equity.

Transaction (10). Receipt of Cash on Account. The sum of $600 in cash is received from customers who have previously been billed for services in Transaction (6). This transaction does not change total assets, but it changes the composition of Softbyte's assets. Cash is increased $600 and Accounts Receivable is decreased $600. The new balances are:

		Assets							=	Liabilities	+	Owner's Equity
		Cash	+	Accounts Receivable	+	Supplies	+	Equipment	=	Accounts Payable	+	R. Neal, Capital
	Old Bal.	$8,750		$2,000		$1,200		$7,000		$1,600		$17,350
(10)		+600		−600								
	New Bal.	$9,350	+	$1,400	+	$1,200	+	$7,000	=	$1,600	+	$17,350

Note that a collection on account for services previously billed and recorded does not affect owner's equity.

Transaction (11). Withdrawal of Cash by Owner. Ray Neal withdraws $1,300 in cash from the business for his personal use. This transaction results in an equal decrease in assets and owner's equity. Thus, both Cash and R. Neal, Capital are decreased $1,300, as shown below:

		Assets							=	Liabilities	+	Owner's Equity	
		Cash	+	Accounts Receivable	+	Supplies	+	Equipment	=	Accounts Payable	+	R. Neal, Capital	
	Old Bal.	$9,350		$1,400		$1,200		$7,000		$1,600		$17,350	
(11)		−1,300										−1,300	Drawings
	New Bal.	$8,050	+	$1,400	+	$1,200	+	$7,000	=	$1,600	+	$16,050	

Observe that the effect of a cash withdrawal by the owner is the opposite of the effect of a capital investment by the owner. **Owner's drawings do not represent expenses.** Like owner's capital investment, they are not included in determining net income.

SUMMARY OF TRANSACTIONS

The transactions of Softbyte are summarized below to illustrate their cumulative effect on the basic accounting equation. The transaction number, the specific effects of the transaction, and the balances after each transaction are indicated. The illustration demonstrates a number of significant facts:

1. Each transaction must be analyzed in terms of its effect on:
   a. the three components of the basic accounting equation
   b. specific types (kinds) of items within each component.
2. The two sides of the equation must always be equal.
3. The causes of each change in the owner's claim on assets must be indicated in the owner's equity column.

Tabular summary

	Assets				= Liabilities +	Owner's Equity	
Transaction	Cash	+ Accounts Receivable	+ Supplies	+ Equipment	= Accounts Payable	+ R. Neal Capital	
(1)	+$15,000					+$15,000	Investment
(2)	−7,000			+$7,000			
	8,000 +			7,000 =		15,000	
(3)			+$1,600		+$1,600		
	8,000 +		1,600 +	7,000 =	1,600 +	15,000	
(4)	+1,200					+1,200	Service Revenue
	9,200 +		1,600 +	7,000 =	1,600 +	16,200	
(5)					+250	−250	Advertising Expense
	9,200 +		1,600 +	7,000 =	1,850 +	15,950	
(6)	+1,500	+$2,000				+3,500	Service Revenue
	10,700 +	2,000 +	1,600 +	7,000 =	1,850 +	19,450	
(7)	−1,700					−600	Rent Expense
						−900	Salaries Expense
						−200	Utilities Expense
	9,000 +	2,000 +	1,600 +	7,000 =	1,850 +	17,750	
(8)			−400			−400	Supplies Expense
	9,000 +	2,000 +	1,200 +	7,000 =	1,850 +	17,350	
(9)	−250				−250		
	8,750 +	2,000 +	1,200 +	7,000 =	1,600 +	17,350	
(10)	+600	−600					
	9,350 +	1,400 +	1,200 +	7,000 =	1,600 +	17,350	
(11)	−1,300					−1,300	Drawings
	$ 8,050 +	$1,400 +	$1,200 +	$7,000 =	$1,600 +	$16,050	

FINANCIAL STATEMENTS

Three financial statements are prepared from the summarized accounting data:

1. An **income statement** presents the revenues and expenses and resulting net income of a company for a specific period of time.
2. An **owner's equity statement** summarizes the changes in owner's equity for a specific period of time.
3. A **balance sheet** reports the assets, liabilities, and owner's equity of a business enterprise at a specific date.

Each statement provides management, owners, and other interested parties with relevant financial data. The financial statements of Softbyte and their interrelationships are illustrated on the following page. **Note that (1) net income shown on the income statement is added to the beginning balance of owner's capital in the owner's equity statement, and (2) owner's capital at the end of the reporting period shown in the owner's equity statement is reported on the balance sheet.**

A fourth statement, a **statement of cash flows,** is also prepared. It primarily summarizes information concerning the financing and investing activities of the company during the period. This statement will be discussed and illustrated in Chapter 19.

The format and content of each statement should be carefully examined. The essential features of each statement are briefly described below and on pages 22 and 23.

INCOME STATEMENT

The income statement for Softbyte is prepared from the data appearing in the owner's equity column of the transaction analysis above. The heading of the statement identifies the company, the type of statement, and the time period covered by the statement. Revenues are listed first, followed by expenses, and then net income (or net loss) is determined. Although practice varies considerably on this matter, for all homework problems list expenses in order of magnitude. Because the income statement summarizes the results of operations, it is often referred to as an **operating statement.** Alternative formats for the income statement will be considered in later chapters.

Note that investment and withdrawal transactions between the owner and the accounting entity are not included in the measurement of net income. For example, the withdrawal by Ray Neal of cash from Softbyte was not regarded as a business expense, as explained earlier. This type of transaction is considered a reduction of the owner's investment in the enterprise.

OWNER'S EQUITY STATEMENT

Data for the preparation of this statement are obtained from the owner's equity column of the transaction analysis for Softbyte and from the income statement. The heading of this statement identifies the company, the type of statement, and the time period covered by the statement. (The time period is

Financial statements and their inter-relationships

SOFTBYTE
Income Statement
For the Month Ended September 30, 1987

Revenues		
Service revenue		$4,700
Expenses		
Salaries expense	$900	
Rent expense	600	
Supplies expense	400	
Advertising expense	250	
Utilities expense	200	
Total expenses		2,350
Net income		$2,350 ①

SOFTBYTE
Owner's Equity Statement
For the Month Ended September 30, 1987

R. Neal, Capital, September 1	$15,000
Add: Net income	2,350 ①
	17,350
Less: Drawings	1,300
R. Neal, Capital, September 30	$16,050 ②

SOFTBYTE
Balance Sheet
September 30, 1987

Assets	
Cash	$ 8,050
Accounts receivable	1,400
Supplies	1,200
Equipment	7,000
Total assets	$17,650
Liabilities and Owner's Equity	
Liabilities	
Accounts payable	$ 1,600
Owner's Equity	
R. Neal, Capital	16,050 ②
Total liabilities and owner's equity	$17,650

the same as that covered by the income statement.) The beginning capital amount is shown on the first line of the analysis; net income is the amount shown on the income statement; and the owner's drawings are specifically identified in the owner's equity column. Neal's ending capital amount is then shown as the final amount on the statement. The information provided by this statement indicates the reasons why owner's equity has increased or decreased during the period.

BALANCE SHEET

The balance sheet for Softbyte is prepared from the column headings and the month-end data shown in the last line of the transaction analysis. The heading of a balance sheet must identify the company, the statement, and the date. Observe that the assets are listed at the top, followed by liabilities and owner's equity. In the illustration above, only one liability, accounts payable, was reported on the balance sheet. In most cases, there will be more than one liability. When two or more liabilities are involved, each should be listed and the total amount reported in the following manner.

Presentation of liabilities

Liabilities	
Notes payable	$10,000
Accounts payable	23,000
Salaries payable	18,000
Mortgage payable	40,000
Total liabilities	$91,000

The balance sheet provides an indication of the company's financial position at a particular time.

SUMMARY OF STUDY OBJECTIVES

1. Accounting is the process of identifying, measuring, recording, and communicating the economic events of an organization (business or nonbusiness) to interested users of the information.

2. The major users and uses of accounting are: (a) Management uses accounting information in planning, controlling, and evaluating business operations. (b) Investors (owners) judge the wisdom of buying, holding, or selling their financial interests on the basis of accounting data. (c) Creditors (suppliers and bankers) evaluate the risks of granting credit or loaning money to particular businesses on the basis of the accounting information obtained about those businesses. Other groups with an indirect interest are taxing authorities, regulatory agencies, customers, labor unions, and economists.

3. The major career paths in accounting are public accounting, private accounting, and not-for-profit accounting.

4. Generally accepted accounting principles are a common set of rules and procedures used by accountants. One important principle is the cost principle, which states that assets should be recorded at their cost.

5. The economic entity assumption states that economic events can be identified with a particular unit of accountability. The monetary unit assumption requires that only transaction data capable of being ex-

pressed in terms of money be included in the accounting record of the economic entity.

6. Assets are defined as future economic benefits owned or controlled by a particular entity as a result of past transactions or events. Liabilities are obligations arising from past transactions of the entity to transfer assets or services to other entities or individuals in the future. Owner's equity is the ownership claim on total assets. It is often referred to as residual equity.

7. The basic accounting equation is:

$$\text{Assets} = \text{Liabilities} + \text{Owner's Equity}$$

Each transaction must have a dual effect on the basic components of the equation.

8. An income statement presents the revenues and expenses of a company for a specified period of time. An owner's equity statement summarizes the changes in owner's equity that have occurred during a given period of time. A balance sheet reports the assets, liabilities, and owner's equity of a business at a specific date.

GLOSSARY

Accounting, p. 2
Assets, p. 12
Auditing, p. 6
Balance sheet, p. 21
Bookkeeping, p. 5
Capital, p. 13
Corporation, p. 11
Cost principle, p. 9
Drawings, p. 13
Economic entity assumption, p. 10
Expenses, p. 13
Financial Accounting Standards Board, p. 9
Generally accepted accounting principles (GAAP), p. 9
Income statement, p. 21
Liabilities, p. 12
Monetary unit assumption, p. 11
Net income, p. 14
Net loss, p. 14
Operating statement, p. 21
Owner's equity, p. 13
Owner's equity statement, p. 21
Partnership, p. 11
Private (or managerial) accounting, p. 7
Proprietorship, p. 10
Public accounting, p. 6
Revenues, p. 13
Securities and Exchange Commission, p. 9
Statement of cash flows, p. 21
Taxation, p. 7
Transactions, p. 14

DEMONSTRATION PROBLEM

Mary Malone opens her own law office on July 1, 1987. During the first month of operations, the following transactions occurred:

1. Invested $10,000 in cash in the law practice.
2. Paid $800 for July rent on office space.
3. Purchased office equipment on account, $3,000.
4. Rendered legal services to clients for cash, $1,500.
5. Received $700 cash from a client for services to be rendered in August.
6. Rendered legal services to client on account, $2,000.
7. Paid monthly expenses: salaries, $500; utilities, $300; and telephone, $100.

INSTRUCTIONS

(a) Prepare a tabular summary of the transactions.

(b) Prepare the financial statements at July 31 for Mary Malone, Attorney at Law.

SOLUTION TO DEMONSTRATION PROBLEM

(a)

Transaction	Assets: Cash	+ Accounts Receivable	+ Equipment	= Liabilities: Accounts Payable	+ Unearned Fees	+ Owner's Equity: Mary Malone, Capital	
(1)	+$10,000					+$10,000	Investment
(2)	−800					−800	Rent Expense
	9,200			=		9,200	
(3)			+$3,000	+$3,000			
	9,200	+	3,000 =	3,000	+	9,200	
(4)	+1,500					+1,500	Fees Earned
	10,700	+	3,000 =	3,000	+	10,700	
(5)	+700				+$700		
	11,400	+	3,000 =	3,000 +	700 +	10,700	
(6)		+$2,000				+2,000	Fees Earned
	11,400 +	2,000 +	3,000 =	3,000 +	700 +	12,700	
(7)	−900					−500	Salaries Expense
						−300	Utilities Expense
						−100	Telephone Expense
	$10,500 +	$2,000 +	$3,000 =	$3,000 +	$700 +	$11,800	

(b)

MARY MALONE
Attorney at Law
Income Statement
For the Month Ended July 31, 1987

Revenues		
Fees earned		$ 3,500
Expenses		
Rent expense	$800	
Salaries expense	500	
Utilities expense	300	
Telephone expense	100	
Total expenses		1,700
Net income		$1,800

MARY MALONE
Attorney at Law
Owner's Equity Statement
For the Month Ended July 31, 1987

Mary Malone, Capital, July 1	$10,000
Add: Net income	1,800
Mary Malone, Capital, July 31	$11,800

MARY MALONE
Attorney at Law
Balance Sheet
July 31, 1987

Assets

Cash	$10,500
Accounts receivable	2,000
Equipment	3,000
Total assets	$15,500

Liabilities and Owner's Equity

Liabilities	
Accounts payable	$ 3,000
Unearned fees	700
Total liabilities	3,700
Owner's Equity	
Mary Malone, Capital	11,800
Total liabilities and owner's equity	$15,500

QUESTIONS

1. Two students are discussing the possibility of entering business school. One student remarked that she had heard that the accounting field has grown substantially. Is she right? Discuss.

2. Describe the steps in the accounting process.

3. Two broad sets of users need accounting information. Identify these two sets of users and give examples of each.

4. Which is a broader term, bookkeeping or accounting? Explain.

5. Distinguish among public, private, and not-for-profit accounting.

6. Koehler Florist purchased land for $18,000 on December 10, 1987. At December 31, 1987, the land's value has increased to $20,000. What amount should be reported for land on Koehler's balance sheet at December 31, 1987? Explain.

7. What is the economic entity assumption?

8. What are the three basic forms of business organizations for profit-oriented enterprises.

9. Susan Huebner is the owner of a successful printing shop. Recently her business has been increasing, and Susan has been thinking about changing the organization of her business from a proprietorship to a corporation. Discuss some of the advantages Susan would enjoy if she were to incorporate her business.

10. What is the monetary unit assumption? What impact does inflation have on the monetary unit assumption?

11. What are the key components that form the content of financial statements?

12. Which of the following items are liabilities of Ace Retail Stores?

(a) Cash.
(b) Drawings.
(c) Accounts payable.
(d) Accounts receivable.
(e) Supplies.
(f) Equipment.

13. What is the basic accounting equation?

14. Can a business enter into a transaction in which only the left side of the basic accounting equation is affected? If so, give an example.

15. Do the following events represent business transactions? Explain your answer in each case.

(a) An employee is fired.
(b) The owner of the business withdraws cash from the business for personal use.
(c) Supplies are purchased on account.
(d) The owner of the company dies.

16. Listed below are some items found in the financial statements of Robert Morris, M.D. Indicate in which financial statement(s) the following items would appear.

(a) Cash.
(b) Robert Morris, Capital
(c) Wages payable.
(d) Advertising expense.
(e) Equipment.
(f) Service revenue earned.

17. In February of 1987, David Sticksup invested an additional $3,000 in his business, Sticksup Pharmacy, which is organized as a proprietorship. Dave's accountant, Jerome Shawn, recorded this receipt as an increase in cash and revenues. Is this treatment appropriate? Why or why not?

18. A company's net income appears directly on the income statement and the owner's equity statement, and it is included indirectly in the company's balance sheet. Do you agree? Explain.

19. Gomez Enterprises had a capital balance of $170,000 at the beginning of the period. At the end of the accounting period, the capital balance was $220,000.

(a) Assuming no additional investment or withdrawals during the period, what is the net income for the period?
(b) Assuming an additional investment of $30,000 but no withdrawals during the period, what is the net income for the period?

20. Indicate how the following business transactions affect the basic accounting equation.

(a) Invested cash in the business.
(b) Paid off an accounts payable.
(c) Paid cash for services performed.
(d) Purchased equipment for cash.

21. Summarized operations for the Morgenthaler Co. for the month of July are as follows:

Revenues earned: for cash $60,000; on account $70,000.

Expenses incurred: for cash $20,000; on account $30,000.

Indicate for Morgenthaler (a) the total revenues, (b) the total expenses, and (c) net income for the month of July.

EXERCISES

E1-1 Selected transactions for Daley Lawn Care Company are listed below:

1. Made cash investment to start business.
2. Paid monthly rent.
3. Purchased equipment on account.
4. Billed customers for services performed.
5. Withdrew cash for owner's personal use.
6. Made partial payment on equipment purchased in (3).
7. Received cash from customers billed in (4).
8. Incurred miscellaneous expenses on account.
9. Purchased additional equipment for cash.
10. Received cash from customers when service was rendered.

INSTRUCTIONS

List the number of the foregoing transactions and opposite each describe the effect of each transaction on assets, liabilities, and owner's equity. For example, the first answer would be: (1) Increase in assets and increase in owner's equity.

E1-2 A tabular analysis of the transactions made by Patricia Hammes and Co., a certified public accounting firm, for the month of August is shown below. Each increase and decrease in capital is explained.

	Cash	+ Accounts Receivable	+ Supplies	+ Office Equipment	= Accounts Payable	+ P. Hammes, Capital
1.	$10,000					$10,000 Investment
2.	− 900		$900			
3.	−2,000			$6,000	$4,000	
4.	1,200	$800				2,000 Fees
5.	−1,500				−1,500	
6.	− 500					− 500 Drawings
7.	− 600					− 600 Rent
8.	400	−400				
9.	− 700					− 700 Salaries
10.					300	− 300 Utilities

INSTRUCTIONS

(a) Describe each transaction that occurred for the month.

(b) Determine how much capital increased for the month.

(c) Compute the amount of net income for the month.

E1-3 The Schueler Computer Timeshare Company entered into the following transactions during May 1986.

1. Paid $3,500 cash for May rent on storage space.
2. Purchased additional computer terminals for $21,000 from Digital Equipment. Purchase was made on account.
3. Received $72,000 from customers for contracts billed in April.
4. Provided computer services to Mar Construction Company for $2,000.
5. Paid Northern States Power Co. $11,000 for energy usage in May.
6. Incurred wage expense of $7,000 for the last twelve days of May; however, the employees will not be paid until June 1.
7. D. Schueler invested an additional $22,000 in the business.
8. A new energy-efficient air-conditioning unit, with a useful life of nine years, was purchased for $6,500 on account.
9. Paid Digital Equipment for the terminals purchased in (2) above.
10. Rented computer time to an agency of the State of Minnesota for a fee of $6,000.

INSTRUCTIONS

Indicate with the appropriate letter whether each of the transactions above results in:

(a) an increase in assets and a decrease in assets.
(b) an increase in assets and an increase in owner's equity.
(c) an increase in assets and an increase in liabilities.
(d) a decrease in assets and a decrease in owner's equity.
(e) a decrease in assets and a decrease in liabilities.
(f) an increase in liabilities and a decrease in owner's equity.
(g) an increase in owner's equity and a decrease in liabilities.

E1-4 Presented below are the capital balances for Elayne Briggs that appeared on the balance sheet of Briggs' Gunsmith Shop on December 31, 1988 and December 31, 1987.

	December 31, 1988	December 31, 1987
Owner's Equity		
Elayne Briggs, Capital	$10,700	$11,000

INSTRUCTIONS

Assuming that during 1988 Elayne withdrew $12,000 from the company for her personal use and made an additional investment of $6,000 in the business, compute the 1988 net income for Briggs' Gunsmith Shop.

E1-5 Two items are omitted from each of the following summaries of balance sheet and income statement data for three proprietorships for the year 1987: Tomlin Co., Dienslake Enterprises, and Brandtmac, CPA.

	Tomlin Co.	Dienslake Enterprises	Brandtmac, CPA
Beginning of year:			
Total assets	$ 90,000	$110,000	(e)
Total liabilities	40,000	(c)	$ 50,000
Total owner's equity	(a)	70,000	80,000
End of year:			
Total assets	140,000	150,000	170,000
Total liabilities	60,000	60,000	70,000

Changes during year in owner's equity:			
Additional investment	(b)	10,000	20,000
Drawings	12,000	(d)	14,000
Total revenues	85,000	95,000	110,000
Total expenses	65,000	70,000	(f)

INSTRUCTIONS

Determine the missing amounts.

E1–6 The following information relates to the Newport Co. for the year 1987.

H. Newport, Capital, January 1, 1987	$60,000
H. Newport, Drawing during 1987	4,600
H. Newport, additional investment during 1987	10,000
Fees earned	40,000
Salaries expense	18,000
Advertising expense	1,400
Rent expense	6,000
Insurance expense	1,200
Supplies expense	2,400
Taxes expense	2,800
Utilities expense	3,200

INSTRUCTIONS

After analyzing the data, prepare an income statement and an owner's equity statement for the year ending December 31, 1987.

E1–7 Milt Sundstrom is the bookkeeper for James Company. Milt has been trying to get the balance sheet of James Company to balance. His balance sheet is as follows:

JAMES COMPANY
Balance Sheet
December 31, 1987

Assets		Liabilities	
Cash	$15,600	Accounts payable	$36,000
Supplies	6,800	Accounts receivable	(14,000)
Equipment	32,000	James, Capital	36,400
James, Drawing	4,000	Total liabilities and	
Total assets	$58,400	owner's equity	$58,400

INSTRUCTIONS

Prepare a correct balance sheet.

E1–8 Dan Garkey is the sole owner of Gark Park, a public camping ground near the Lake Mead National Recreation Area. Dan has compiled the following financial information as of December 31, 1987.

Revenues during 1987 – camping fees	$137,000
Revenues during 1987 – general store	38,000
Accounts payable	9,000
Cash on hand	4,500
Original cost of equipment	111,000
Current value of equipment	130,000
Notes payable	63,000

Operating expenses during 1987	141,000
Supplies on hand	4,000

INSTRUCTIONS

(a) Determine Dan Garkey's net income in Gark Park for 1987.

(b) Prepare a balance sheet for Gark Park as of December 31, 1987.

E1-9 Presented below is financial information related to the 1987 operations of the Disciple Islands Cruise Company.

Boat rental expense	$ 70,000
Property tax expense (on dock facilities)	14,000
Salaries expense	140,000
Advertising expense	3,000
Cash paid to purchase land for a parking lot	15,000
Miscellaneous expense	12,000
Ticket sales	220,000

INSTRUCTIONS

Prepare the 1987 income statement for the Disciple Islands Cruise Company.

E1-10 Presented below is information related to the single proprietorship of Mitchell Hago, D.D.S.

Dental fees earned	$340,000
Total expenses	215,000
Assets, January 1, 1987	45,000
Liabilities, January 1, 1987	22,000
Assets, December 31, 1987	52,000
Liabilities, December 31, 1987	31,000
Drawings	?

INSTRUCTIONS

Prepare the 1987 owner's equity statement for Mitchell Hago's dental practice.

PROBLEMS

P1-1 On April 1, Thomas Groves established the Groves Travel Agency. The following transactions were completed during the month:

1. Deposited $25,000 in the City Bank in the name of the agency.
2. Paid $300 cash for April office rent.
3. Purchased office equipment for $2,500, paying $1,000 cash and the balance on account.
4. Incurred $200 of advertising costs in the *Sun-Times*, payment to be made in May.
5. Paid $400 cash for office supplies.
6. Received $10,000 cash from customers for domestic flights booked; 93% of the fares is owed to the airlines, and 7% represents commissions earned.
7. Withdrew $400 cash for personal use by Groves.
8. Paid airlines amount due in transaction (6).
9. Paid $800 of balance due on equipment.

10. Booked international charter flight for alumni group, receiving $25,000 in cash; 90% of the fares is owed to the airlines, and 10% represents commissions earned.
11. Paid employees' salaries, $900.
12. Determined by physical count that $150 of office supplies have been used.

INSTRUCTIONS

(a) Prepare a tabular analysis of the transactions using the following column headings: Cash, Supplies, Office Equipment, Accounts Payable, and Thomas Groves, Capital.

(b) From an analysis of the column, Thomas Groves, Capital, compute the net income or net loss for April.

(c) If Groves had withdrawn $1,000 for personal use instead of $400 in transaction (7) above, what would be the change, if any, in (1) April net income or net loss, and (2) Thomas Groves, Capital balance, on April 30.

P1–2 Ann Atwood opened a law office, Ann Atwood, Attorney at Law, on July 1. On July 31, the balance sheet showed Cash $4,000, Fees receivable $1,500, Supplies $500, Office equipment $5,000, Accounts payable $4,200, and Ann Atwood, Capital, $6,800. During August the following transactions occurred:

1. Invested $1,000 additional cash in the law practice.
2. Collected $1,200 of fees receivable.
3. Paid $3,200 cash on accounts payable.
4. Earned fees of $4,600, of which $1,000 is paid in cash and the balance is due in September.
5. Purchased additional office equipment for $2,000, paying $400 in cash and the balance on account.
6. Paid salaries $500, rent for August $700, and miscellaneous expenses $200.
7. Used $100 of supplies in August.
8. Withdrew $500 in cash for personal use.
9. Received $750 from First National Bank on money borrowed on a note payable.
10. Incurred utility expenses for month on account, $150.

INSTRUCTIONS

(a) Prepare a tabular analysis of the August transactions beginning with July 31 balances. The column heading should be as follows: Cash + Fees Receivable + Supplies + Office Equipment = Notes Payable + Accounts Payable + Ann Atwood, Capital.

(b) Prepare an income statement for August, an owner's equity statement for August, and a balance sheet at August 31.

(c) If the owner's equity statement for July shows net income $2,500 and drawings $500, what was Atwood's initial capital investment?

(d) If Atwood had invested $5,000 on July 1 and her drawings were $700 in July, what was the combined net income for the law practice in the first two months?

P1–3 On June 1, Sue Tercek started Personalized Cosmetics Service, a company that provides individual skin care treatment to clients at their residence, by investing $20,000 cash in the business. Following are the assets and liabilities of the company at June 30 and the revenues and expenses for the month of June.

Cash	$10,000	Notes Payable	$10,000
Accounts Receivable	2,000	Accounts Payable	900
Fees Earned	5,000	Supplies Expense	1,200

Cosmetic Supplies	2,400	Gas and Oil Expense	700
Advertising Expense	300	Miscellaneous Expense	200
Automobile	18,000		

Sue made no additional investment in June, but withdrew $1,100 in cash for personal used during the month.

INSTRUCTIONS

(a) Prepare an income statement and owner's equity statement for the month of June and a balance sheet at June 30, 1987.

(b) Prepare an income statement and owner's equity statement for June assuming (1) cosmetic supplies on hand at June 30 were $2,000 and a total of $1,600 of supplies were used, and (2) $100 of the gas and oil expense was incurred for personal use.

P1-4 An inexperienced accountant prepared the following statements for Harris Auto Repair at the end of the first year of operations.

HARRIS AUTO REPAIR
Income Statement
December 31, 1987

Revenues:		
Repair service revenue		$60,000
Expenses:		
Salaries	$25,000	
Supplies	12,800	
Rent	7,200	
Utilities	5,000	
Advertising	1,000	
A. T. Harris, Drawings	3,000	
Total expenses		54,000
Net income		$ 6,000

HARRIS AUTO REPAIR
Balance Sheet
For Year Ended December 31, 1987

Assets		Liabilities	
Cash	$ 6,000	Notes payable	$ 5,000
Repair equipment	16,000	A. T. Harris, Capital	27,000
Delivery truck	10,000		
Total assets	$32,000	Total liabilities	$32,000

Additional analysis revealed the following:

1. Service revenue of $1,500 was earned but is uncollected and unrecorded at December 31.
2. A count of supplies showed that $2,200 is on hand at December 31.
3. Additional repair equipment of $1,800 purchased on account at the end of the year was not recorded.
4. The delivery truck is valued at cost. The market value of the truck at December 31 is $10,600.
5. Employee salaries of $2,000 were earned but unpaid and unrecorded at December 31.

INSTRUCTIONS

(a) Prepare an income statement for the year.

(b) Prepare an owner's equity statement for the year, assuming an initial capital investment of $21,000.

(c) Prepare a balance sheet at December 31.

P1-5 C. Renay organized the Renay Co. on March 1. The owner's equity column of the tabular summary for the month of March contained the following data:

Transaction	Amount	Description
(1)	$20,000	Investment
(4)	600	Rent expense
(6)	900	Fees earned
(8)	200	Advertising expense
(11)	500	Salaries expense
(12)	1,000	Fees earned
(15)	150	Utilities expense
(18)	200	Drawings
(20)	1,200	Fees earned
(22)	100	Repair expense
(24)	500	Advertising expense
(27)	200	Drawings
(29)	1,700	Fees earned
(32)	800	Salaries expense
(34)	400	Supplies expense
(36)	250	Utilities expense

All data were properly recorded except the following:

In transaction (20), $400 of the $1,200 recorded as fees earned represents a collection on account from clients billed in transaction (12).

In transaction (22), $50 of the repair expense was applicable to C. Renay's personal residence.

Transaction (24) includes the payment of advertising expenses incurred on account in transaction (8).

In transaction (36), $60 was applicable to repairs on business property.

INSTRUCTIONS

(a) Prepare an income statement for March.

(b) Prepare an owner's equity statement for March.

ALTERNATE PROBLEMS

P1-1A Bill's Barber Shop was started on May 1 by William Olsen. A summary of May transactions is presented below.

1. Deposited $15,000 in the Hudson Valley Bank in the name of the business.
2. Purchased office equipment for $3,000, paying $1,200 cash and the balance on account.
3. Paid $350 cash for May office rent.

4. Paid $450 cash for barber supplies.
5. Incurred $300 of advertising costs in the *Daily Reporter,* payment to be made in June.
6. Received $2,900 in cash from customers for haircuts.
7. Withdrew $500 for personal use by Olsen.
8. Used $120 of barber supplies.
9. Paid employee salaries $900.
10. Paid utility bills $140.
11. Paid miscellaneous expense $80.
12. Purchased additional office equipment for $2,300 cash.

INSTRUCTIONS

(a) Prepare a tabular analysis of the transactions, using the following column headings: Cash, Supplies, Office Equipment, Accounts Payable, and William Olsen, Capital.

(b) From an analysis of the column, William Olsen, Capital, compute the net income or net loss for May.

(c) If Olsen had withdrawn $1,100 for personal use instead of $500 in transaction (7) above, what would be the change in (1) May net income or net loss, if any, and (2) William Olsen, Capital balance, on May 31.

P1-2A Gerry Blacksmith opened a veterinary business in Paw Paw, Illinois on August 1. On August 31, the balance sheet showed Cash $8,000, Fees receivable $1,700, Supplies $600, Office equipment $6,000, Accounts payable $3,600, and G. Blacksmith, Capital $12,700. During September the following transactions occurred.

1. Invested $2,000 additional cash in the veterinarian business.
2. Paid $3,100 cash on accounts payable.
3. Collected $800 of fees receivable.
4. Purchased additional office equipment for $2,100, paying $600 in cash and the balance on account.
5. Earned fees of $3,900, of which $1,600 is paid in cash and the balance is due in October.
6. Used $350 of supplies in September.
7. Withdrew $600 for personal use.
8. Paid salaries $600, rent for September $800, and miscellaneous expense $300.
9. Incurred utility expenses for month on account, $170.
10. Received $8,000 from Hilldale Bank on money borrowed on a note payable.

INSTRUCTIONS

(a) Prepare a tabular analysis of the September transactions beginning with August 31 balances. The column headings should be as follows: Cash + Fees Receivable + Supplies + Office Equipment = Notes Payable + Accounts Payable + G. Blacksmith, Capital.

(b) Prepare an income statement for September, an owner's equity statement for September, and a balance sheet at September 30.

(c) If the owner's equity statement for August shows net income of $4,000 and drawings of $600, what was Blacksmith's initial capital investment?

(d) If Blacksmith had invested $10,000 on August 1 and his drawings were $900 in August, what was the combined net income for the veterinary practice in the first two months?

P1-3A On May 1, Matt Hamlin started Sunshine Flying School, a company that provides flying lessons to would-be pilots, by investing $40,000 cash in the business. Following are the assets and liabilities of the company on May 31, 1987, and the revenues and expenses for the month of May.

Cash	$ 6,000	Notes Payable	$35,000
Accounts Receivable	7,000	Rent Expense	1,400
Equipment	65,700	Repair Expense	400
Fees Earned	7,600	Fuel Expense	2,200
Advertising Expense	500	Insurance Expense	600
		Accounts Payable	2,800

Matt made no additional investment in May, but withdrew $1,600 in cash for personal use.

INSTRUCTIONS

(a) Prepare an income statement and owner's equity statement for the month of May and a balance sheet at May 31.

(b) Prepare an income statement and owner's equity statement for May assuming the following data is not included above: (1) $800 of fees were earned but unbilled at May 31, and (2) $300 of fuel expense was incurred but not paid.

(c) Prepare a balance sheet at May 31, 1987 using the data given in (b) above.

P1-4A Express Delivery Service is owned and managed by Jason Williams. Jason has recently purchased a personal computer, which he is trying to use to keep records and prepare financial statements for the business. As shown below, his first attempt includes several errors.

EXPRESS DELIVERY SERVICE
Income Statement
December 31, 1987

Revenues		
Delivery fees		$89,000
Expenses		
Supplies	$ 3,200	
Advertising	4,000	
Wages	31,000	
Rent	26,000	
J. Williams, Drawings	9,000	
Utilities	6,000	
Total expenses		79,200
Net income		$ 9,800

EXPRESS DELIVERY SERVICE
Balance Sheet
For the Year Ended December 31, 1987

Assets		Liabilities and Capital	
Accounts receivable	$14,000	Liabilities	
Cash	6,000	Accounts payable	$ 7,000
Equipment	25,000	Notes payable	3,000
Total assets	$45,000	Total liabilities	10,000
		Owner's Equity	
		J. Williams, Capital	35,000
		Total liabilities and capital	$45,000

1. A physical count showed that $1,200 of supplies are on hand at December 31.
2. Amounts owed by the company on account at December 31 totaled $1,600 for additional equipment. Neither the amount owed nor the additional equipment has been recorded.
3. Service revenue of $1,500 was earned but uncollected and unrecorded at December 31.
4. Employee wages of $1,700 were earned but unpaid and unrecorded at December 31.

INSTRUCTIONS

(a) Prepare an income statement for the year.

(b) Prepare an owner's equity statement for the year, assuming an initial capital investment of $25,200.

(c) Prepare a balance sheet at December 31.

P1-5A Presented below are the November 1987 transactions that affected the owner's equity account of the P. J. Welles Co.:

Transaction	Amount	Description
(7)	$ 800	Property tax expense
(9)	6,000	Fees earned
(10)	400	Supplies expense
(13)	4,000	Wage expense
(16)	300	Utilities expense
(18)	1,500	Rent expense
(19)	400	Advertising expense
(22)	4,000	Fees earned
(23)	800	Drawing, P. J. Welles
(25)	700	Repair expense
(27)	400	Auto expense
(31)	9,000	Fees earned
(32)	1,800	Drawing, P. J. Welles
(33)	4,000	Wage expense
(34)	300	Utilities expense

In reviewing the account, Mr. Welles realized that his new bookkeeper had made the following errors:

Transaction (7) was the payment of property taxes that had been recorded as a liability in October.

Transaction (16) was the payment of the October utility bill that already had been recorded.

Transaction (19) was a payment in advance for advertising in next month's trade journal.

Transaction (23) was actually a drawing of $1,000 by P. J. Welles.

Transaction (27) was recorded for work on Mr. Welles's family car.

A November 10 investment by Mr. Welles in the amount of $3,000 was not recorded.

INSTRUCTIONS

(a) Prepare an income statement for the month of November.

(b) Prepare a statement of owner's equity for November, assuming that Mr. Welles's beginning equity balance was $9,500 on November 1.

DECISION CASE

Jean and Joel Otten, local golf stars, opened the Parbuster Driving Range on March 1, 1987 by investing $10,000 of their cash savings in the business. A caddy shack was constructed for cash at a cost of $2,500 and $800 was spent on golf balls and golf clubs. The Ottens leased five acres of land at a cost of $1,000 per month and paid the first month's rent. During the first month, advertising costs totaled $600 of which $150 was unpaid at March 31, and $400 was paid to members of the high school golf team for retrieving golf balls. All fees from customers were deposited in the company's bank account. On March 15, Jean and Joel withdrew a total of $600 in cash for personal living expenses. A $100 utility bill was received on March 31 but it was not paid. On March 31, the balance in the company's bank account was $7,450.

Jean and Joel thought they had a pretty good first month of operations. However, their estimates of profitability ranged from a loss of $2,550 to net income of $500.

INSTRUCTIONS

(a) How did the Ottens conclude that the business operated at a loss of $2,550? Was this a valid basis to determine net income?

(b) How did the Ottens conclude that the business operated at a net income of $500? (Hint: prepare a balance sheet at March 31.) Was this a valid basis to determine net income?

(c) Without preparing an income statement, determine the actual net income for March.

(d) What were the fees earned in March?

CHAPTER 2

Dartmouth College

CHAPTER 2

THE RECORDING PROCESS

STUDY OBJECTIVES

After studying this chapter, you should be able to:

1. **Explain what an account is and how it helps in the recording process.**
2. **Define debits and credits and explain how they are used to record business transactions.**
3. **Distinguish between permanent (real) and temporary (nominal) accounts.**
4. **Identify the basic steps in the recording process.**
5. **Explain what a journal is and how it helps in the recording process.**
6. **Explain what a ledger is and how it helps in the recording process.**
7. **Explain what posting is and how it helps in the recording process.**
8. **Prepare a trial balance and explain its primary purposes.**

In Chapter 1, business transactions were analyzed in terms of the accounting equation, and the cumulative effects of these transactions were presented in tabular form. Imagine General Motors (GM) using that same tabular format to keep track of every one of its transactions! In a single day, GM probably engages in more than a hundred thousand business transactions. To record each transaction this way would be impractical, expensive, and unnecessary.

As a result, accountants have developed a set of procedures that make it possible to record the transaction data easily. To illustrate these procedures, an example of a manual accounting system is provided in this chapter so that each of the individual steps in the recording process can be easily understood.

Computerized and manual accounting systems basically parallel one another. Most of the procedures are handled by electronic circuitry in computerized systems and, thus, seem to occur invisibly. It is, therefore, necessary to illustrate and understand manual approaches for processing accounting data to fully comprehend how computerized systems operate.

THE ACCOUNT

An **account** is an individual accounting record of increases and decreases in specific asset, liability, and owner's equity items. For example, in Softbyte (discussed in Chapter 1) there would be separate accounts for Cash, Accounts Receivable, Accounts Payable, and so on. In its simplest form, an account consists of three parts: (1) the title of the account, (2) a left or debit side, and (3) a right or credit side. Because the alignment of these parts of an account often resembles the letter T, it is referred to as a **T account.** The basic form of an account is shown below.

Basic form of account

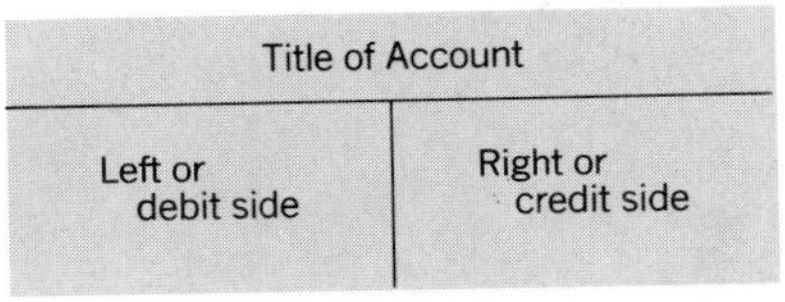

T Account

This form of account will be used often to explain basic accounting relationships.

DEBITS AND CREDITS

The terms **debit** and **credit** are synonymous with left and right respectively, and are commonly abbreviated as Dr. for debit and Cr. for credit.[1] These terms are used repeatedly in the recording process. For example, the act of entering an amount on the left side of an account is called **debiting** the account, and making an entry on the right side is **crediting** the account. Whenever the totals of the two sides of an account are compared, an account will have a **debit balance** if the total of the debit amounts exceeds the credits. Conversely, an account will have a **credit balance** if the credit amounts exceed the debits. The procedure of having debits on the left and credits on the

[1]These abbreviations come from the Latin words *debere* (Dr.) and *credere* (Cr).

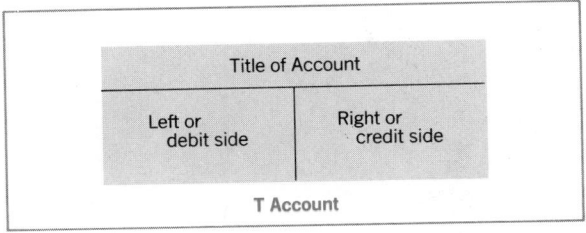

right is an accounting custom or rule. Accountants could function just as well if debits and credits were reversed. However, the custom of having debits on the left side of an account and credits on the right side (like the custom of driving on the right-hand side of the road) has been adopted in the United States. **This rule applies to all accounts.**

The procedure of recording debits and credits in an account can be understood by considering the effect of the cash transactions of Softbyte on the cash account. The data are taken from the cash column of the tabular summary on page 20 of Chapter 1.

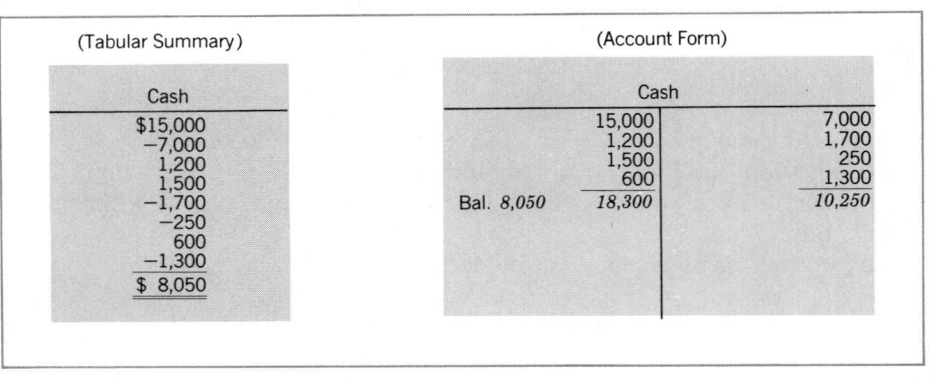

Tabular summary compared to account form

(Tabular Summary)

Cash
$15,000
−7,000
1,200
1,500
−1,700
−250
600
−1,300
$ 8,050

(Account Form)

	Cash	
	15,000	7,000
	1,200	1,700
	1,500	250
	600	1,300
Bal. *8,050*	*18,300*	*10,250*

Every positive item in the tabular summary represents a receipt of cash; every negative amount constitutes a payment of cash. However, in the account form the increases in cash are recorded as debits, and decreases in cash are recorded as credits. The arrangement of having increases on one side and decreases on the other helps in determining the totals of each side of the account and the balance in the account. In this example, total cash receipts are $18,300; total cash payments (disbursements) are $10,250; and there is an $8,050 ($18,300 − $10,250) debit balance in the cash account. The debit and credit totals (shown in italics here) are referred to as **footings**. The account balance (also in italics) is then shown on the appropriate side.

DEBIT AND CREDIT PROCEDURE

In Chapter 1 you learned the effect of a transaction on the basic accounting equation. It is important to recognize that each transaction must affect two or more accounts if the basic accounting equation is to remain in balance. In other words, there must be equal debit and credit entries in the accounts for each transaction. The equality of debits and credits provides the basis for the universally used double-entry system of recording transactions.

Under a **double-entry system** (sometimes referred to as double-entry bookkeeping), the dual (two-sided) effect of each transaction is recorded in appropriate accounts. This system provides a logical method for recording the transactions of a business enterprise and offers a means of proving the accuracy of the recording process. If every transaction is recorded with equal debits and credits, then the sum of all the debits to the accounts must equal the sum of all the credits.

Assets and Liabilities

In the illustration above, increases in cash (an asset) were entered on the left side, and decreases in cash were entered on the right side. It follows that if both sides of the basic equation (assets = liabilities + owner's equity) must be equal, then increases in liabilities must be entered on the right or credit side. Similarly, decreases in liabilities must be entered on the left or debit side. The effects that debit and credit entries have on assets and liabilities may be summarized as follows:

Debit and credit effect—assets and liabilities

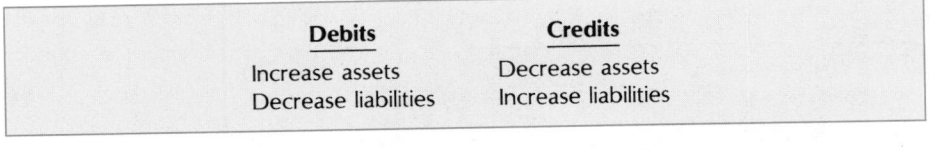

Debits	Credits
Increase assets	Decrease assets
Decrease liabilities	Increase liabilities

Debits to a specific asset account should exceed the credits to that account, and credits to a liability account should exceed debits to that account. Thus, asset accounts normally show debit balances, and liability accounts normally show credit balances.

The normal balances may be diagrammed as follows:

Normal balances—assets and liabilities

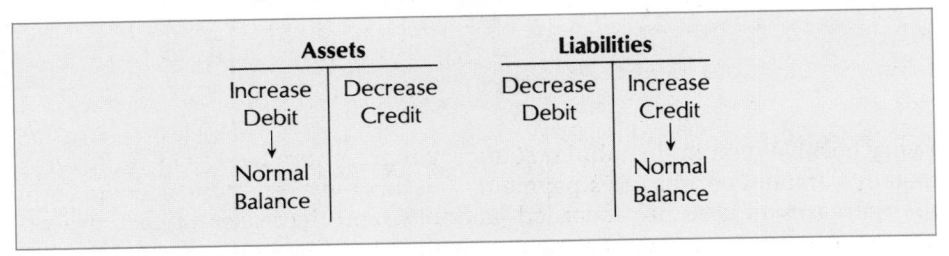

Assets		Liabilities	
Increase Debit ↓ Normal Balance	Decrease Credit	Decrease Debit	Increase Credit ↓ Normal Balance

An awareness of the normal balance in an account may help you when you are trying to trace errors. For example, a credit balance in an asset account such as Land and a debit balance in a liability account such as Wages Payable would indicate errors in recording. Occasionally, however, an abnormal balance may be correct. Accounts Receivable, for example, will have a credit balance if a customer overpays the balance due.

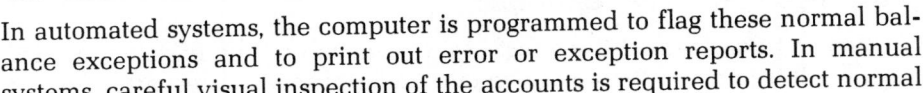

In automated systems, the computer is programmed to flag these normal balance exceptions and to print out error or exception reports. In manual systems, careful visual inspection of the accounts is required to detect normal balance problems.

Owner's Equity

As indicated in Chapter 1, owner's equity accounts comprise capital, drawings, revenues, and expenses. Each of these items is discussed below.

Capital. The capital account is used to determine the owner's permanent investment in the business. The capital account is increased by credits and decreased by debits. For example, when cash is invested in the business, cash

is debited and capital is credited. Conversely, owner's capital is debited when the owner's permanent investment in the business is reduced.

The rules of debit and credit for the owner's capital account are stated as follows:

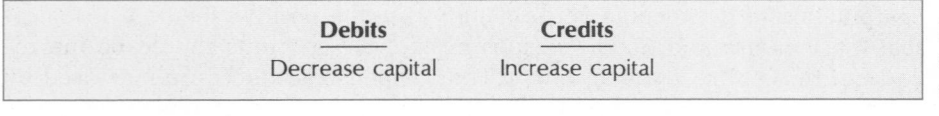

Debits	Credits
Decrease capital	Increase capital

Debit and credit effect—owner's capital

The normal balance in this account may be diagrammed as follows:

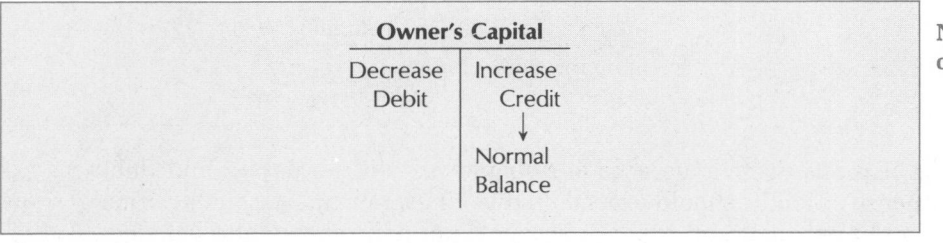

Owner's Capital	
Decrease Debit	Increase Credit ↓ Normal Balance

Normal balance—owner's capital

Drawings. An owner may withdraw cash or other assets during the accounting period for personal use. Withdrawals could be debited directly to owner's capital to indicate a decrease in capital. However, it is preferable to establish a separate account, referred to as the owner's drawing account, in order to determine the total withdrawals for the accounting period. **The drawing account is a subdivision of the owner's capital account. It is not an income statement account like revenue and expense.** Owner's drawing is increased by debits and decreased by credits. Normally, the drawing account will have a debit balance. The rules of debit and credit for the drawing account are stated as follows:

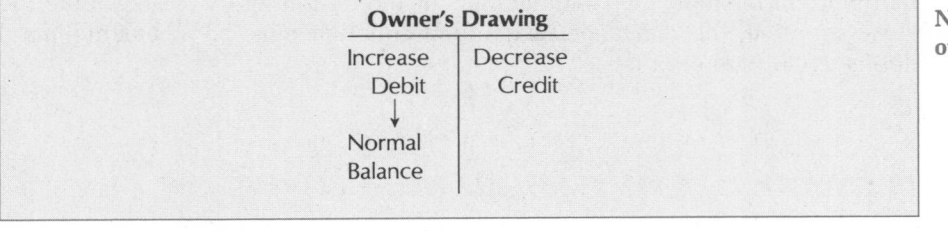

Debits	Credits
Increase owner's drawing	Decrease owner's drawing

Debit and credit effect—owner's drawing

The normal balance may be diagrammed as follows:

Owner's Drawing	
Increase Debit ↓ Normal Balance	Decrease Credit

Normal balance—owner's drawing

Observe that the effect of debits and credits and the normal balance of owner's drawing are exactly the reverse of those relating to owner's capital.

Revenues and Expenses

When revenues are earned, owner's capital is increased. Revenues are a subdivision of owner's capital which provides information as to why owner's

capital increased. Accordingly, the effect of debits and credits on revenue accounts is identical to their effect on owner's capital. Revenue accounts are increased by credits and decreased by debits.

On the other hand, expenses decrease owner's capital. As a result, expenses are recorded by debits. Since expenses are the negative factor in the computation of net income, and revenues are the positive factor, it is logical that the increase and decrease sides of expense accounts should be the reverse of those of revenue accounts. Thus, expense accounts are increased by debits and decreased by credits. The effect of debits and credits on revenues and expenses may be stated as follows:

Debit and credit effect—revenues and expenses

Debits	Credits
Decrease revenues	Increase revenues
Increase expenses	Decrease expenses

Credits to revenue accounts should exceed the debits, and debits to expense accounts should exceed credits. Thus, revenue accounts normally show credit balances and expense accounts normally show debit balances.

The normal balances may be diagrammed as follows:

Normal balances—revenues and expenses

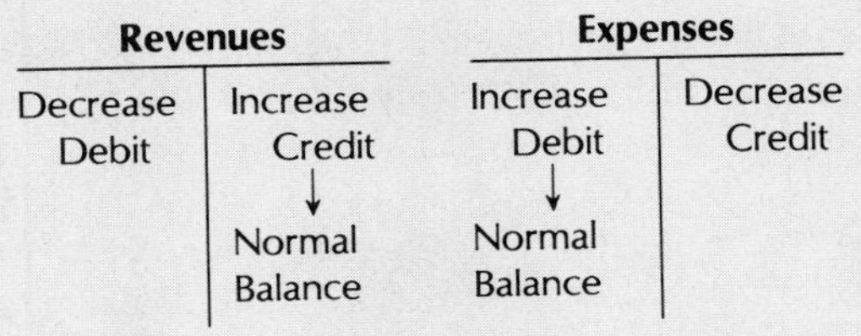

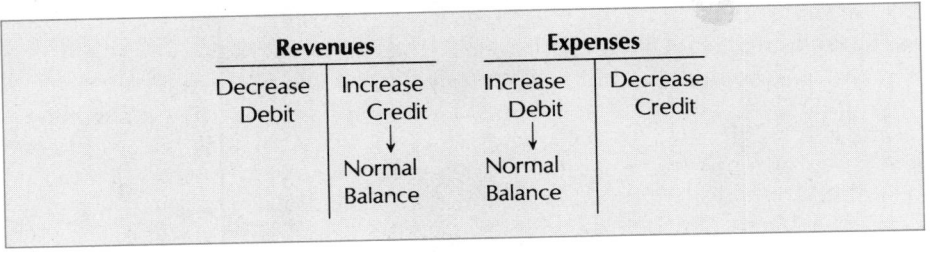

EXPANSION OF BASIC EQUATION

The basic accounting equation is: assets equal liabilities plus owner's equity. The diagram at the top of page 47 presents three equations that show (1) how the four owner's equity items (capital, drawings, revenues, and expenses) relate to the basic accounting equation, and (2) how the rules of debit and credit relate to an expanded basic equation. Study it carefully because it will help you understand the fundamentals of the double-entry system. Like the basic equation, the rearranged expanded equation must be in balance (total debits equal total credits).

PERMANENT AND TEMPORARY ACCOUNTS

As indicated earlier, the drawing, revenue, and expense accounts are subdivisions of owner's capital. These accounts are employed to provide additional information as to why the owner's capital increased or decreased during the period.

The drawing, revenue, and expense accounts are **temporary (nominal)** accounts. They are temporary because at the end of an accounting period their

Expanded basic equation

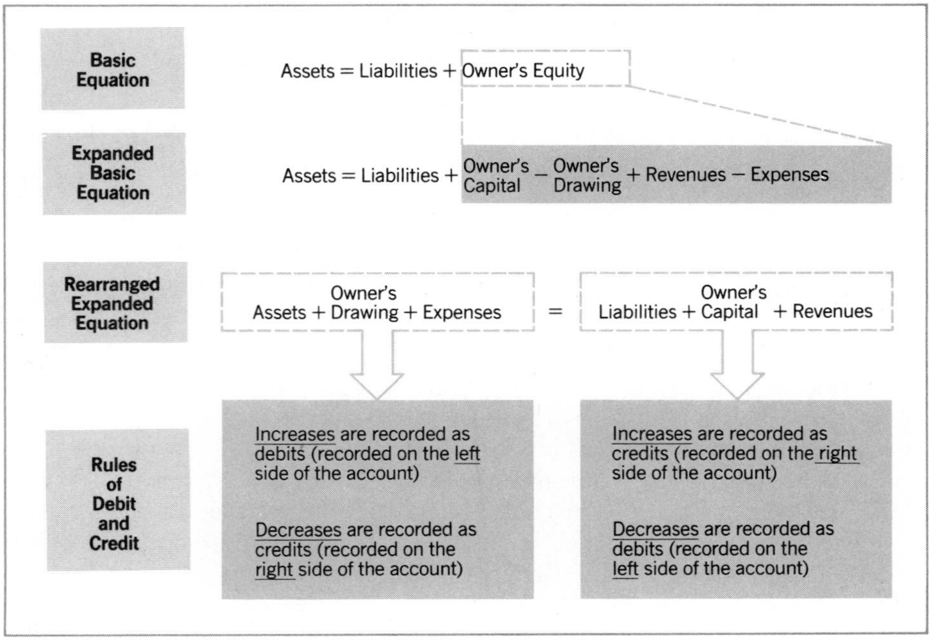

balances are transferred to the capital account. An accounting period may be a month, a quarter, or a year.

Conversely, the assets, liabilities, and owner's capital accounts are **permanent (real)** accounts. They are permanent because any balances in these accounts at the end of an accounting period are carried forward as the beginning balance of the next accounting period.

The following chart summarizes the four types of accounts affecting owner's equity and relates them to the temporary and permanent classifications just discussed.

Owner's equity accounts—temporary and permanent

Transactions Affecting Owner's Equity	Impact on Owner's Equity	Temporary Account	Permanent Account
Investment by Owner(s)	Increase		Capital
Withdrawal by Owner(s)	Decrease	Drawing	
Revenues Earned	Increase	Revenue	Capital
Expenses Incurred	Decrease	Expense	

The technique of transferring the temporary accounts to owner's capital is explained in a later chapter.

STEPS IN THE RECORDING PROCESS

It is possible to enter transaction information directly into the accounts. In practically every business, however, the basic steps in the recording process are:

1. Analyze each transaction in terms of its effect on the accounts.
2. Enter the transaction information in a journal (book of original entry).
3. Transfer the journal information to the appropriate accounts in the ledger (book of accounts).

The actual sequence of events begins with the occurrence of the transaction. Evidence of the transaction is obtained in the form of a business document, such as a sales slip, a check, a bill, or a cash register tape. This documentary evidence is analyzed to determine the effect of the transaction on specific accounts. When the analysis has been completed, the transaction is entered in the journal. Then the journal entry is transferred to the designated accounts in the ledger. The sequence of events in the recording process can be diagrammed as follows:

Recording process

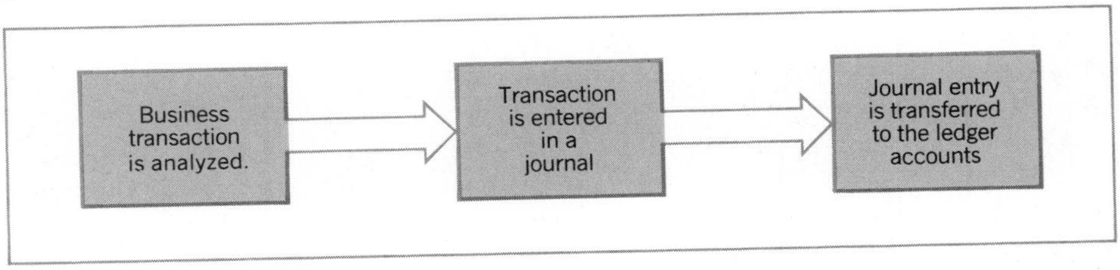

The basic steps in the recording process occur repeatedly in every business enterprise. The analysis of transactions has already been illustrated, and further examples of this step will be given in this and later chapters. The other steps in the recording process are explained and illustrated below.

THE JOURNAL

Transactions are initially recorded in chronological order in a **journal** before being transferred to the accounts. Thus, the journal is referred to as the book of original entry. The journal shows for each transaction the debit and credit effects on specific accounts. Companies may use various kinds of journals, but every company has a **general journal.** A general journal is the most basic form of journal. Typically, a general journal has two money columns, spaces for dates, account titles and explanations, and references, as illustrated on page 49. Whenever the term journal is used in this textbook without a modifying adjective, it will mean the general journal.

The journal makes several significant contributions to the recording process:

1. It discloses in one place the complete effect of a transaction.

2. It provides a chronological record of transactions.
3. It helps to prevent or locate errors because the debit and credit amounts for each entry can be readily compared.

You should realize that the recording phase is the most critical (and for most businesses the most expensive) point in the accounting process. In computerized systems, it is also the only place where you have to think. After the recording phase, your input and all further processing just boil down to file merging and report generation. Programmers and management information system types with good accounting backgrounds (such as they should gain from a good principles textbook) are better able to develop effective computerized systems.

JOURNALIZING

The procedure of entering transaction data in the journal is known as **journalizing.** Separate journal entries are made for each transaction. A complete entry consists of: (1) the date of the transaction, (2) the accounts and amounts to be debited and credited, and (3) a brief explanation of the transaction.

To illustrate the technique of journalizing, the first two transactions of Softbyte are journalized below. These transactions were: September 1, Ray Neal invested $15,000 cash in the business, and computer equipment was purchased for $7,000 cash.

Technique of journalizing

GENERAL JOURNAL J1

Date	Account Titles and Explanation	Ref.	Debit	Credit
1987				
Sept. 1	Cash		15,000	
	R. Neal, Capital			15,000
	(To record cash investment)			
1	Computer Equipment		7,000	
	Cash			7,000
	(To record purchase of equipment)			

The standard form and content of journal entries are as follows:

1. The date of the transaction is entered in the Date column. The date column should include the year, month, and day of the transaction.
2. The debit account title is entered first at the extreme left margin of the column headed Account Titles and Explanation. The credit account title is then entered and indented. The indentation decreases the possibility of switching the debit and credit amounts.
3. The amounts for the debits are recorded in the Debit (left) money col-

umn and the amounts for the credits are recorded in the Credit (right) money columns.

4. A brief explanation of the transaction is given.
5. A space is left between journal entries. The blank space separates individual journal entries and makes the entire journal easier to read.
6. The column entitled Ref. (which stands for reference) is left blank at the time the journal entry is made. The Reference column is used later when the journal entries are transferred to the ledger accounts. At that time, the ledger account number is placed in the Reference column to indicate where the amounts in the journal entry were transferred.

It is important to use correct and specific account titles in journalizing. Most accounts appear subsequently in the financial statements, and erroneous account titles lead to incorrect financial statements. Some flexibility exists initially in selecting account titles. The principal criterion is that each title must appropriately describe the content of the account. For example, the account title used for the cost of delivery trucks may be Delivery Equipment, Delivery Trucks, or Trucks. However, once a specific title has been chosen, all subsequent transactions involving the account should be recorded under the account title that was selected initially.[2]

If an entry requires only two accounts, one debit and one credit, it is referred to as a simple entry. For some transactions, however, it may be necessary to use more than two accounts in journalizing. Imagine, for example, the numerous accounts needed recently by General Electric to record the acquisition of all the assets and liabilities of RCA in what was one of the largest mergers ever completed. When three or more accounts are required in one journal entry, the entry is referred to as a **compound entry.** To illustrate, assume that on July 1, Butler Company purchases a delivery truck costing $14,000 by paying $8,000 cash and the balance at a later date. The entry is as follows:

Compound journal entry

GENERAL JOURNAL — J1

Date		Account Titles and Explanation	Ref.	Debit	Credit
1987					
July	1	Delivery Equipment		14,000	
		Cash			8,000
		Accounts Payable			6,000
		(Purchased truck for cash with balance on account)			

In a compound entry, it is important to determine that the total debit and credit amounts are equal. Also, the standard format requires that all debits be listed before the credits are listed.

[2]When specific account titles are given in homework problems, they should be used; when account titles are not given, you may select account titles that identify the nature and content of each account. The account titles used in journalizing should not contain explanations such as Cash Paid or Cash Received.

Computerized systems do not allow entries that are out of balance and are therefore "idiot proof" in this respect. When using a manual system, to avoid this type of mistake, you must be very careful when preparing journal entries.

THE LEDGER

The entire group of accounts maintained by a company is referred to collectively as the **ledger.** Companies may use various kinds of ledgers, but every company has a general ledger. A **general ledger** contains all the assets, liabilities, and owner's equity accounts. Whenever the term ledger is used in this textbook without a modifying adjective, it will mean the general ledger.

The ledger provides a means of accumulating in one place all the information about changes in specific account balances. A business can use a loose-leaf binder or card file for the ledger with each account kept on a separate sheet or card.

Computerized ledgers are almost universal in large businesses. Many small businesses also maintain their ledgers using microcomputers. The BPI supplement to this textbook is a popular example of such a system which you will find well worth your while to learn.

The ledger should be arranged in statement order beginning with the balance sheet accounts. First in order are the asset accounts, followed by liability accounts, owner's capital, drawings, revenues, and expenses. Each account is numbered for easier identification.

The information in the ledger provides management with the balances in various accounts. For example, the Cash account enables management to determine the amount of cash that is available to meet current obligations. Amounts due from customers and the amounts owed to creditors can be determined by examining the Accounts Receivable and Accounts Payable accounts, respectively.

STANDARD FORM OF ACCOUNT

The simple T-account form of an account is often very useful for illustration and analysis purposes because T accounts can be drawn so quickly. However, in practice, the account forms are much more structured. A form widely used in a manual system is illustrated below, using assumed data from the cash account of Antonio Company.

Three-column form of account

Cash — No. 10

Date	Explanation	Ref.	Debit	Credit	Balance
1987					
June 1			25,000		25,000
2				8,000	17,000
3			4,200		21,200
9			7,500		28,700
17				11,700	17,000
20				250	16,750
30				7,300	9,450

This form has three money columns, and the balance in the account is determined after each transaction. Thus, this form is often called the **three-column form of account.** By adding another money column to this form, it is possible to have two balance columns—one for a debit balance and one for a credit balance. You should note that the explanation space and reference columns are used to provide special information about the transaction.

POSTING

The procedure of transferring journal entries to the ledger accounts is called **posting. This phase of the recording process makes it possible to accumulate the effects of journalized transactions in the individual accounts.**

Posting involves the following steps:

1. In the ledger, enter the date, journal page, and debit amount shown in the journal in the appropriate columns of the account(s) debited.
2. In the reference column of the journal, write the account number to which the debit amount was posted.
3. In the ledger, enter the date, journal page, and credit amount shown in the journal in the appropriate columns of the account(s) credited.
4. In the reference column of the journal, write the account number to which the credit amount was posted.

These steps are diagrammed on the next page using the first journal entry of Softbyte. The circled numbers indicate the sequence of the steps.

Posting should be performed in chronological order. That is, all of the debits and credits of one journal entry should be posted before proceeding to the next journal entry. Under the journalizing procedures described in this chapter, postings should be made on a timely basis to insure that the ledger is up to date.[3]

[3]In homework problems, it will be permissible to journalize all transactions before posting any of the journal entries.

Illustration of posting

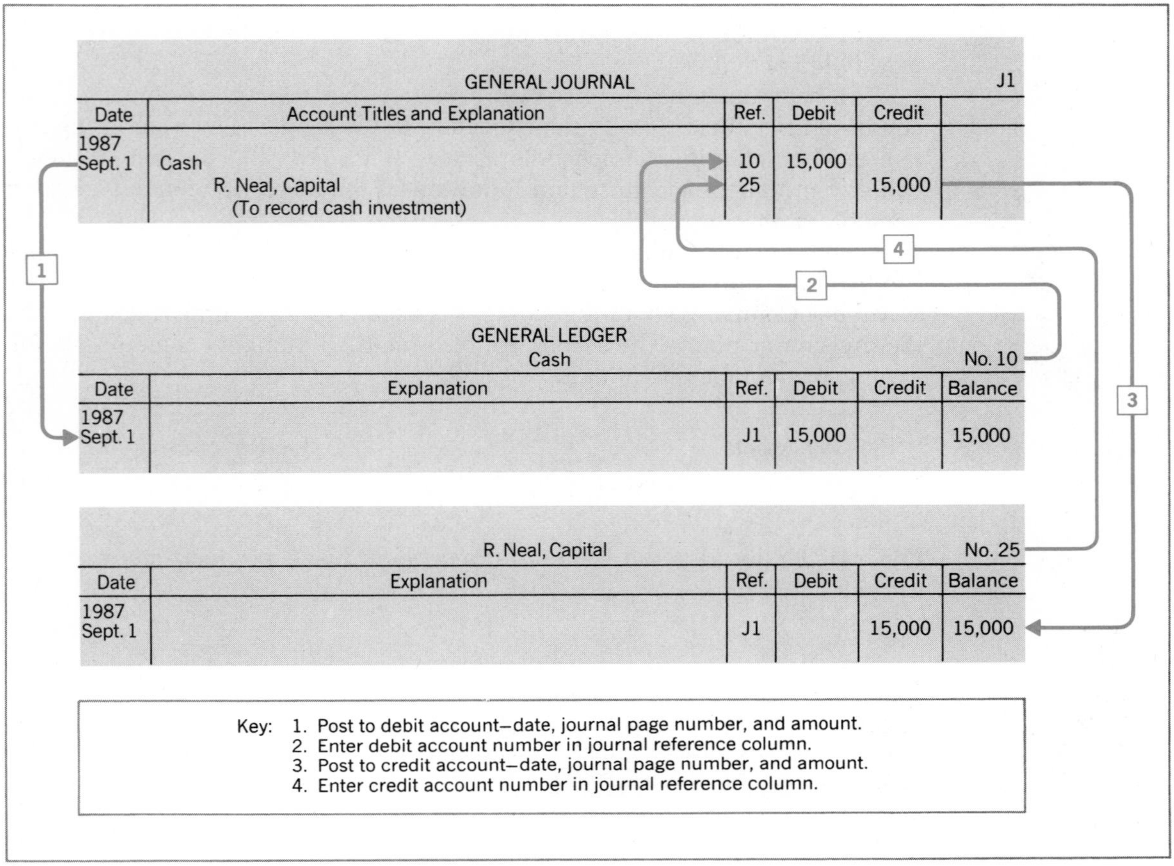

The reference column in the journal serves several purposes. The numbers in this column indicate the entries that have been posted. After the last entry has been posted, the journal reference column should be scanned to see that all postings have been made.

The reference column of a ledger account indicates the journal page from which the transaction has been posted. The explanation space of the ledger account is used infrequently because an explanation already appears in the journal. It generally is used only when detailed analysis of account activity is required.

CHART OF ACCOUNTS

The number and type of accounts used by an enterprise differ depending upon the size, complexity, and type of business involved. For example, the number of accounts depends on the amount of detail desired by management. As an illustration, the management of one company may desire one account for all types of utility expense, whereas another may keep separate expense accounts for each type of utility expenditure, such as gas, electricity, and water. Similarly, a single proprietorship like Softbyte will not have many

accounts compared with a corporate giant like Ford Motor Company. Softbyte may be able to manage and report its activities through the use of 20 to 30 accounts, while Ford requires thousands of accounts to keep track of its worldwide activities.

Most companies have a **chart of accounts** that lists the accounts and account numbers that identify their location in the ledger. The numbering system used to identify the accounts usually starts with the balance sheet accounts (permanent accounts) and follows with the income statement accounts (temporary accounts).

It should be noted that the numbering system used to identify the accounts can be quite sophisticated or relatively simple. For example, at Goodyear Tire & Rubber Company an 18-digit system is used. The first three digits identify the division or plant. The second set of three-digit numbers contains the following account classifications:

Numbering system for accounts

100–199 Assets	300–399 Revenues
200–299 Liabilities and Owner's Equity	400–599 Expenses

Other digits describe the location of a specific plant, product line, region of the country, etc.

Designing the chart of accounts is the necessary first step in computerized systems because it establishes the framework for the entire data base of accounting information.

In this and the next two chapters, we will be explaining the accounting for the proprietorship, Pioneer Advertising Agency (a service enterprise). Accounts 1–19 indicate an asset account is involved; 20–39 indicate liabilities; 40–49 indicate owner's equity accounts; 50–59, revenues; and 60–69, expenses. A partial chart of accounts for Pioneer Advertising Agency (C. R. Byrd, owner) identifying some of its accounts is as follows:

Partial chart of accounts

Pioneer Advertising Agency

Assets	Owner's Equity
1. Cash	40. C. R. Byrd, Capital
6. Fees Receivable	41. C. R. Byrd, Drawing
8. Advertising Supplies	**Revenues**
10. Prepaid Insurance	50. Fees Earned
15. Office Equipment	**Expenses**
Liabilities	60. Salaries Expense
25. Notes Payable	61. Advertising Supplies Expense
26. Accounts Payable	62. Rent Expense
28. Unearned Fees	63. Insurance Expense

Additional accounts for Pioneer Advertising will be used as needed in the following two chapters.

ILLUSTRATION OF RECORDING PROCESS

To illustrate the basic steps in the recording process, we will use the October transactions of the Pioneer Advertising Agency which has a month as its accounting period. A basic analysis and a debit-credit analysis precede the journalizing and posting of each transaction. Study these transaction analyses carefully. **The purpose of transaction analysis is first to identify the type of account involved, and then to determine whether a debit or a credit to the account is required.** You should always perform this type of analysis before preparing a journal entry. This analysis will help you understand the journal entries discussed in this chapter as well as more complex journal entries to be described in later chapters.

Keep in mind that every journal entry affects one or more of the following items: assets, liabilities, owner's capital, drawings, revenues, or expenses. By becoming skilled at transaction analysis, you will be able quickly to recognize the impact of any transaction on these six items. For simplicity, the T account form is used in the illustrations instead of the standard account form.

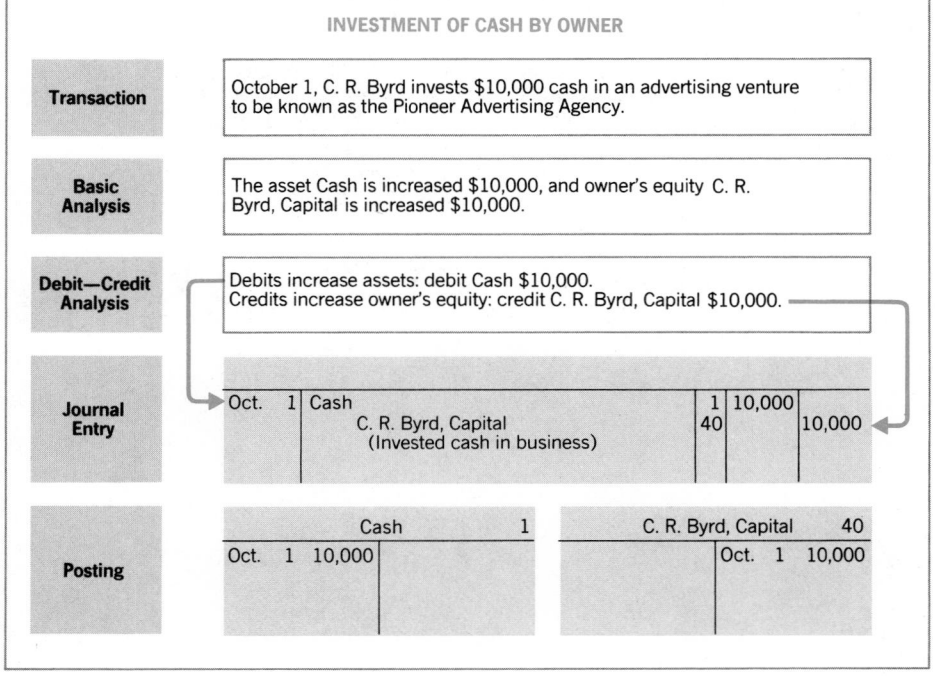

INVESTMENT OF CASH BY OWNER

Transaction	October 1, C. R. Byrd invests $10,000 cash in an advertising venture to be known as the Pioneer Advertising Agency.
Basic Analysis	The asset Cash is increased $10,000, and owner's equity C. R. Byrd, Capital is increased $10,000.
Debit—Credit Analysis	Debits increase assets: debit Cash $10,000. Credits increase owner's equity: credit C. R. Byrd, Capital $10,000.

Journal Entry

Oct.	1	Cash	1	10,000	
		C. R. Byrd, Capital	40		10,000
		(Invested cash in business)			

Posting

Cash 1	
Oct. 1 10,000	

C. R. Byrd, Capital 40	
	Oct. 1 10,000

PURCHASE OF OFFICE EQUIPMENT

Transaction

October 1, office equipment costing $5,000 is purchased by signing a three-month, 12%, $5,000 note payable.

Basic Analysis

The asset Office Equipment is increased $5,000, and the liability Notes Payable is increased $5,000.

Debit—Credit Analysis

Debits increase assets: debit Office Equipment $5,000.
Credits increase liabilities: credit Notes Payable $5,000.

Journal Entry

Oct.	1	Office Equipment	15	5,000	
		Notes Payable	25		5,000
		(Issued three-month, 12% note for office equipment)			

Posting

Office Equipment 15

Oct. 1 5,000	

Notes Payable 25

	Oct. 1 5,000

RECEIPT OF CASH FOR FUTURE SERVICE

Transaction

October 2, a $1,200 cash advance is received from R. Knox, a client, for advertising services that are expected to be completed by December 31.

Basic Analysis

The asset Cash is increased $1,200; the liability Unearned Fees is increased $1,200 because the service has not been rendered yet. That is, when an advance payment is received, an unearned fee or revenue (a liability) should be recorded in order to recognize the obligation that exists. Note also that although many liabilities have the word "payable" in their title, unearned fees are considered a liability even though the word payable is not used.

Debit—Credit Analysis

Debits increase assets: debit Cash $1,200.
Credits increase liabilities: credit Unearned Fees $1,200.

Journal Entry

Oct.	2	Cash	1	1,200	
		Unearned Fees	28		1,200
		(Received advance from R. Knox for future services)			

Posting

Cash 1

Oct. 1 10,000	
2 1,200	

Unearned Fees 28

	Oct. 2 1,200

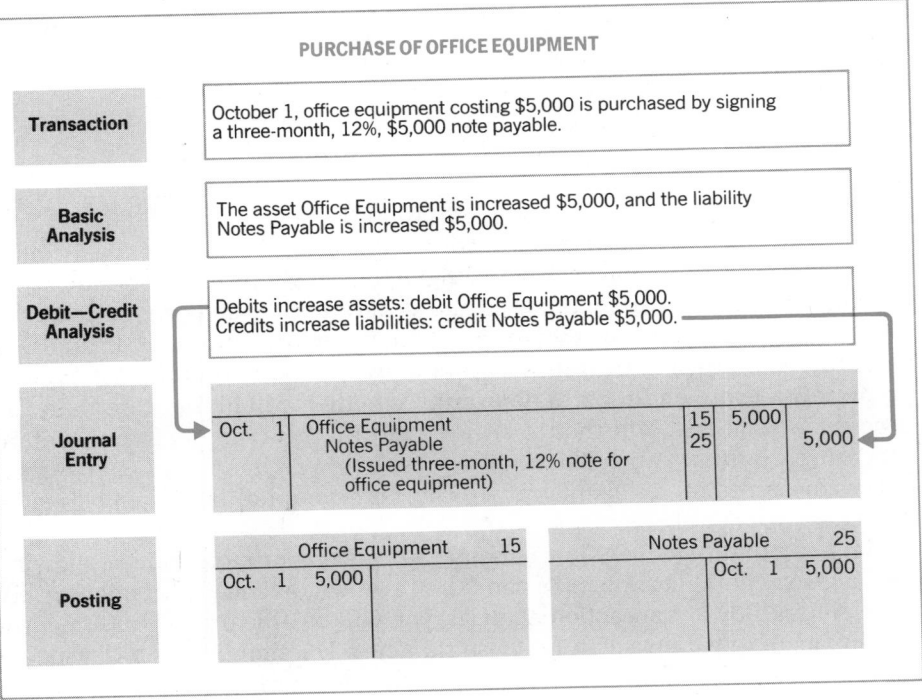

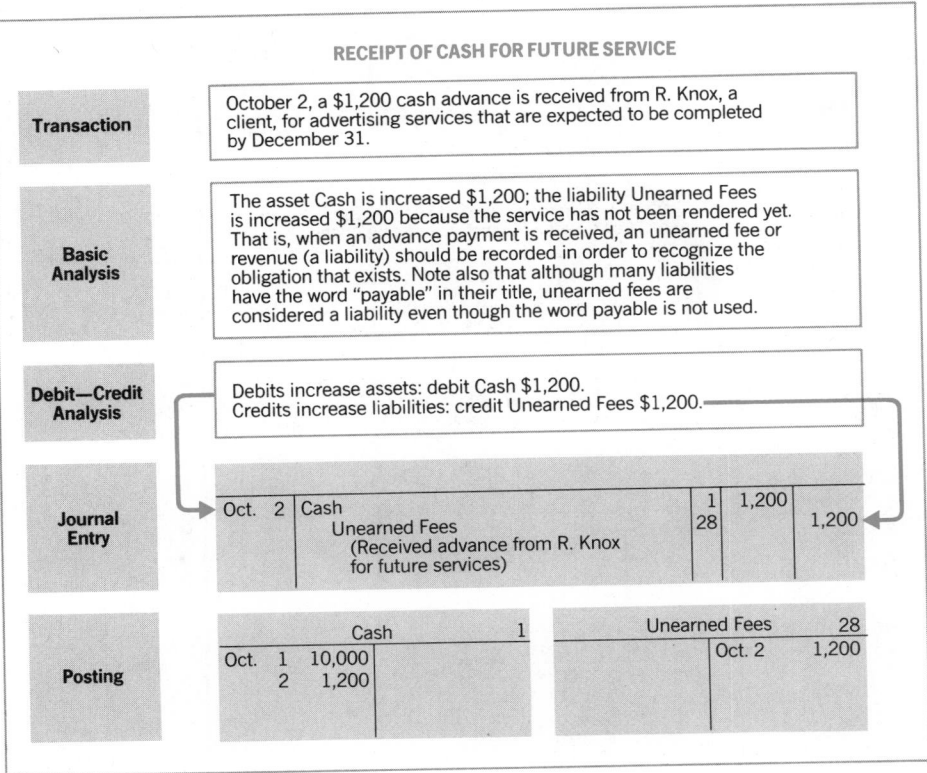

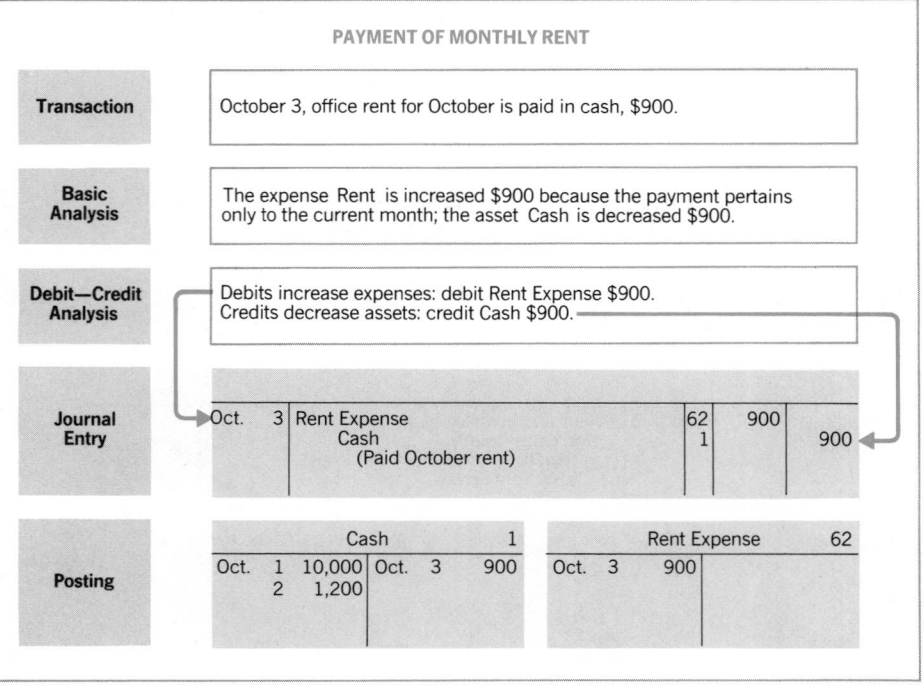

PAYMENT OF MONTHLY RENT

Transaction

October 3, office rent for October is paid in cash, $900.

Basic Analysis

The expense Rent is increased $900 because the payment pertains only to the current month; the asset Cash is decreased $900.

Debit—Credit Analysis

Debits increase expenses: debit Rent Expense $900.
Credits decrease assets: credit Cash $900.

Journal Entry

Oct.	3	Rent Expense	62	900	
		Cash	1		900
		(Paid October rent)			

Posting

Cash					1
Oct.	1	10,000	Oct.	3	900
	2	1,200			

Rent Expense					62
Oct.	3	900			

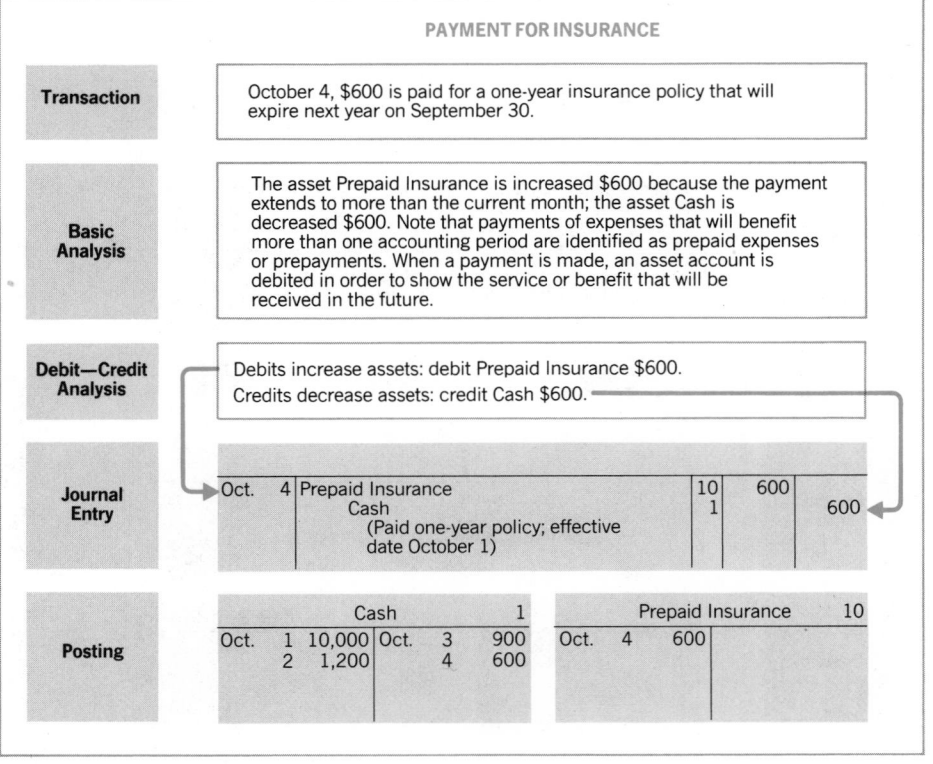

PAYMENT FOR INSURANCE

Transaction

October 4, $600 is paid for a one-year insurance policy that will expire next year on September 30.

Basic Analysis

The asset Prepaid Insurance is increased $600 because the payment extends to more than the current month; the asset Cash is decreased $600. Note that payments of expenses that will benefit more than one accounting period are identified as prepaid expenses or prepayments. When a payment is made, an asset account is debited in order to show the service or benefit that will be received in the future.

Debit—Credit Analysis

Debits increase assets: debit Prepaid Insurance $600.
Credits decrease assets: credit Cash $600.

Journal Entry

Oct.	4	Prepaid Insurance	10	600	
		Cash	1		600
		(Paid one-year policy; effective date October 1)			

Posting

Cash					1
Oct.	1	10,000	Oct.	3	900
	2	1,200		4	600

Prepaid Insurance					10
Oct.	4	600			

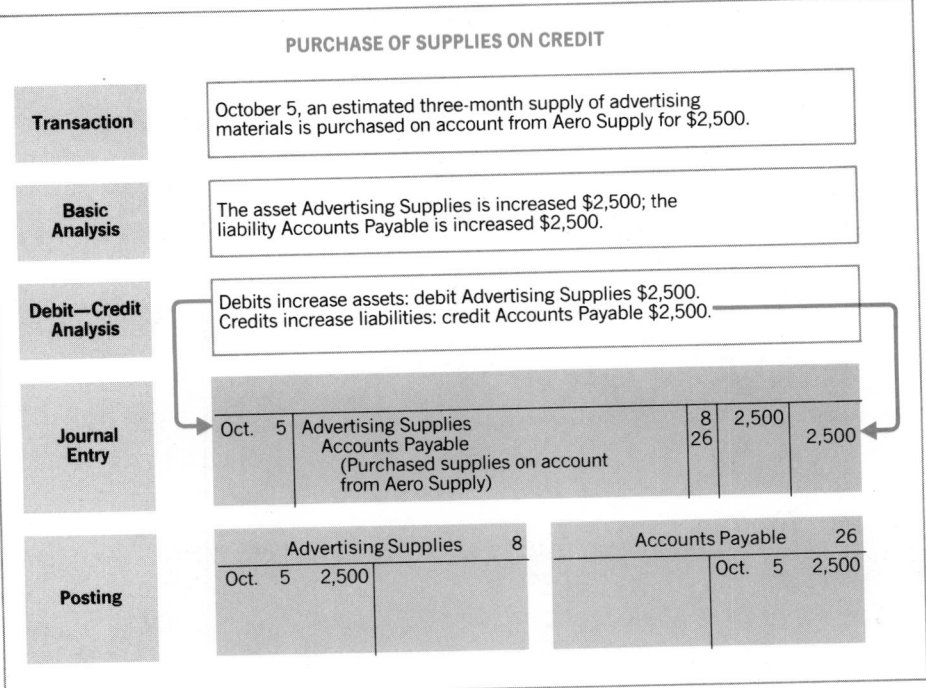

PURCHASE OF SUPPLIES ON CREDIT

Transaction

October 5, an estimated three-month supply of advertising materials is purchased on account from Aero Supply for $2,500.

Basic Analysis

The asset Advertising Supplies is increased $2,500; the liability Accounts Payable is increased $2,500.

Debit—Credit Analysis

Debits increase assets: debit Advertising Supplies $2,500.
Credits increase liabilities: credit Accounts Payable $2,500.

Journal Entry

Oct.	5	Advertising Supplies	8	2,500	
		Accounts Payable	26		2,500
		(Purchased supplies on account from Aero Supply)			

Posting

Advertising Supplies — 8

Oct. 5	2,500		

Accounts Payable — 26

		Oct. 5	2,500

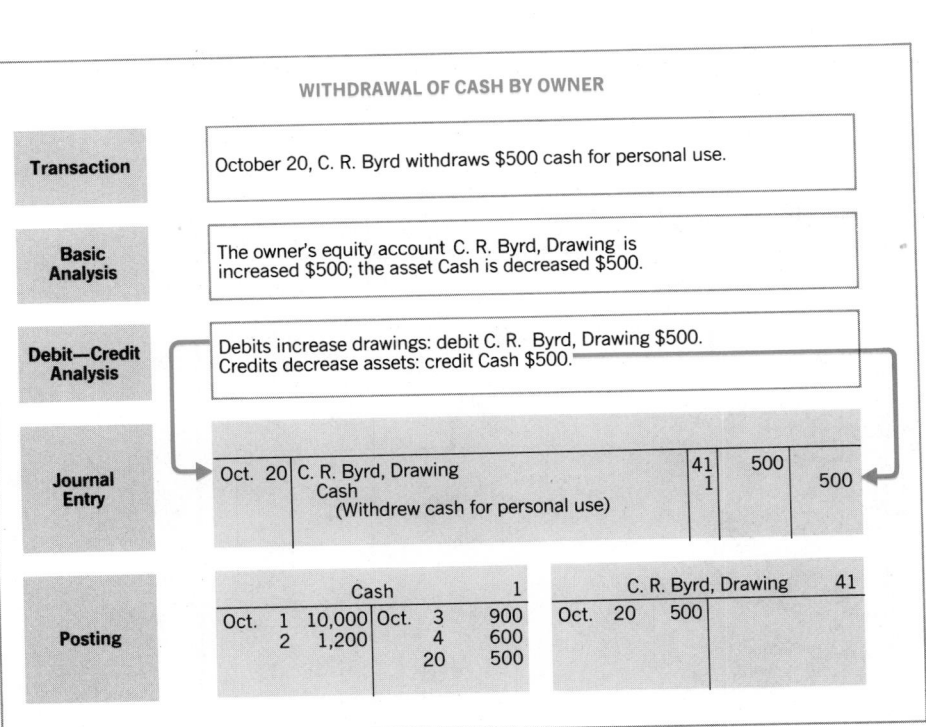

WITHDRAWAL OF CASH BY OWNER

Transaction

October 20, C. R. Byrd withdraws $500 cash for personal use.

Basic Analysis

The owner's equity account C. R. Byrd, Drawing is increased $500; the asset Cash is decreased $500.

Debit—Credit Analysis

Debits increase drawings: debit C. R. Byrd, Drawing $500.
Credits decrease assets: credit Cash $500.

Journal Entry

Oct.	20	C. R. Byrd, Drawing	41	500	
		Cash	1		500
		(Withdrew cash for personal use)			

Posting

Cash — 1

Oct. 1	10,000	Oct. 3	900
2	1,200	4	600
		20	500

C. R. Byrd, Drawing — 41

Oct. 20	500		

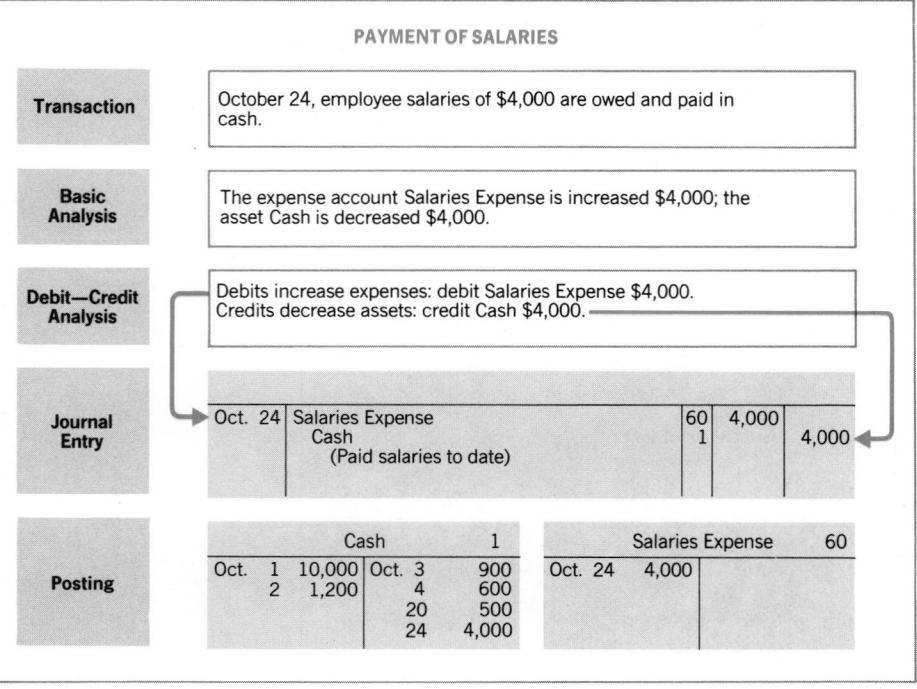

PAYMENT OF SALARIES

Transaction

October 24, employee salaries of $4,000 are owed and paid in cash.

Basic Analysis

The expense account Salaries Expense is increased $4,000; the asset Cash is decreased $4,000.

Debit—Credit Analysis

Debits increase expenses: debit Salaries Expense $4,000.
Credits decrease assets: credit Cash $4,000.

Journal Entry

Oct. 24	Salaries Expense	60	4,000	
	Cash	1		4,000
	(Paid salaries to date)			

Posting

Cash			1
Oct. 1	10,000	Oct. 3	900
2	1,200	4	600
		20	500
		24	4,000

Salaries Expense			60
Oct. 24	4,000		

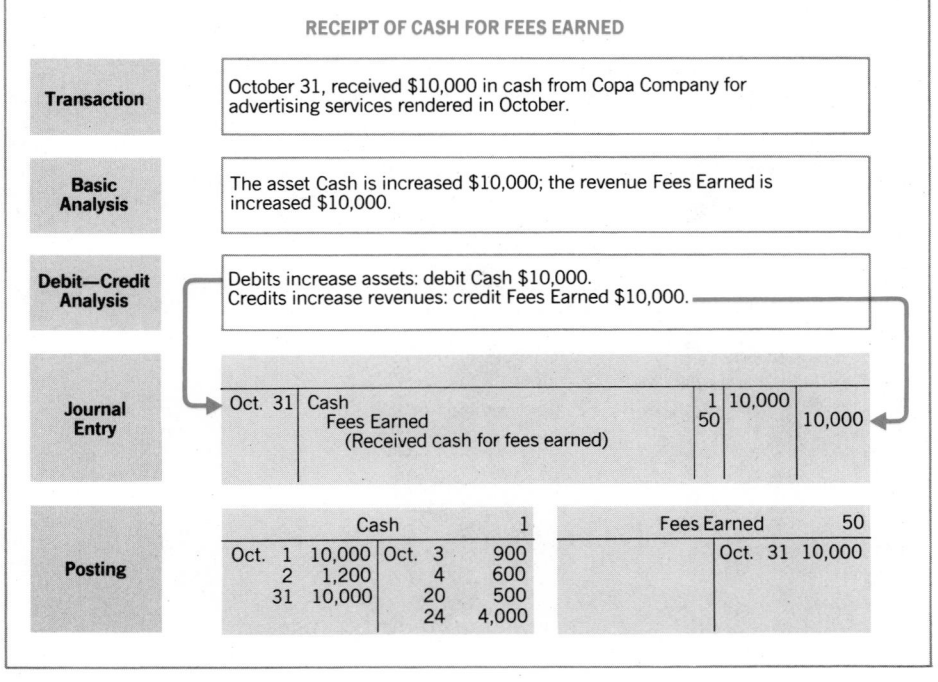

RECEIPT OF CASH FOR FEES EARNED

Transaction

October 31, received $10,000 in cash from Copa Company for advertising services rendered in October.

Basic Analysis

The asset Cash is increased $10,000; the revenue Fees Earned is increased $10,000.

Debit—Credit Analysis

Debits increase assets: debit Cash $10,000.
Credits increase revenues: credit Fees Earned $10,000.

Journal Entry

Oct. 31	Cash	1	10,000	
	Fees Earned	50		10,000
	(Received cash for fees earned)			

Posting

Cash			1
Oct. 1	10,000	Oct. 3	900
2	1,200	4	600
31	10,000	20	500
		24	4,000

Fees Earned			50
		Oct. 31	10,000

SUMMARY ILLUSTRATION OF JOURNALIZING AND POSTING

The journal and ledger for Pioneer Advertising Agency for the month of October are summarized below and on the next page.

GENERAL JOURNAL — Page J1

Date		Account Titles and Explanation	Ref.	Debit	Credit
1987					
Oct.	1	Cash	1	10,000	
		C. R. Byrd, Capital	40		10,000
		(Invested cash in business)			
	1	Office Equipment	15	5,000	
		Notes Payable	25		5,000
		(Issued three-month, 12% note for office equipment)			
	2	Cash	1	1,200	
		Unearned Fees	28		1,200
		(Received advance from R. Knox for future services)			
	3	Rent Expense	62	900	
		Cash	1		900
		(Paid October rent)			
	4	Prepaid Insurance	10	600	
		Cash	1		600
		(Paid one-year policy; effective date, October 1)			
	5	Advertising Supplies	8	2,500	
		Accounts Payable	26		2,500
		(Purchased supplies on account from Aero Supply)			
	20	C. R. Byrd, Drawing	41	500	
		Cash	1		500
		(Withdrew cash for personal use)			
	24	Salaries Expense	60	4,000	
		Cash	1		4,000
		(Paid salaries to date)			
	31	Cash	1	10,000	
		Fees Earned	50		10,000
		(Received cash for fees earned)			

THE TRIAL BALANCE

A **trial balance** is a list of accounts and their balances at a given time. Customarily, a trial balance is prepared at the end of an accounting period. The

Cash — No. 1

Date	Explanation	Ref.	Debit	Credit	Balance
1987					
Oct. 1		J1	10,000		10,000
2		J1	1,200		11,200
3		J1		900	10,300
4		J1		600	9,700
20		J1		500	9,200
24		J1		4,000	5,200
31		J1	10,000		15,200

Accounts Payable — No. 26

Date	Explanation	Ref.	Debit	Credit	Balance
1987					
Oct. 5		J1		2,500	2,500

Unearned Fees — No. 28

Date	Explanation	Ref.	Debit	Credit	Balance
1987					
Oct. 2		J1		1,200	1,200

Advertising Supplies — No. 8

Date	Explanation	Ref.	Debit	Credit	Balance
1987					
Oct. 5		J1	2,500		2,500

C. R. Byrd, Capital — No. 40

Date	Explanation	Ref.	Debit	Credit	Balance
1987					
Oct. 1		J1		10,000	10,000

Prepaid Insurance — No. 10

Date	Explanation	Ref.	Debit	Credit	Balance
1987					
Oct. 4		J1	600		600

C. R. Byrd, Drawing — No. 41

Date	Explanation	Ref.	Debit	Credit	Balance
1987					
Oct. 20		J1	500		500

Office Equipment — No. 15

Date	Explanation	Ref.	Debit	Credit	Balance
1987					
Oct. 1		J1	5,000		5,000

Fees Earned — No. 50

Date	Explanation	Ref.	Debit	Credit	Balance
1987					
Oct. 31		J1		10,000	10,000

Notes Payable — No. 25

Date	Explanation	Ref.	Debit	Credit	Balance
1987					
Oct. 1		J1		5,000	5,000

Salaries Expense — No. 60

Date	Explanation	Ref.	Debit	Credit	Balance
1987					
Oct. 24		J1	4,000		4,000

Rent Expense — No. 62

Date	Explanation	Ref.	Debit	Credit	Balance
1987					
Oct. 3		J1	900		900

accounts are listed in the order in which they appear in the ledger, with debit balances listed in the left column and credit balances in the right column. The totals of the two columns must be in agreement.

The primary purpose of a trial balance is to prove the mathematical equality of the accounting equation after all recorded transactions have been journalized and posted. Under the double-entry system the equation will be in balance if the sum of the debit account balances equals the sum of the credit account balances. **A trial balance facilitates the discovery of errors in journalizing and posting. It also is useful in the preparation of financial statements since it lists the balances in each ledger account.**

The procedure for preparing a trial balance consists of:

1. Listing the account titles and their balances.
2. Totaling the debit and credit columns.
3. Proving their equality.

The trial balance prepared from the ledger of Pioneer Advertising Agency is presented below:

Trial balance illustrated

PIONEER ADVERTISING AGENCY
Trial Balance
October 31, 1987

	Debit	Credit
Cash	$15,200	
Advertising Supplies	2,500	
Prepaid Insurance	600	
Office Equipment	5,000	
Notes Payable		$ 5,000
Accounts Payable		2,500
Unearned Fees		1,200
C. R. Byrd, Capital		10,000
C. R. Byrd, Drawing	500	
Fees Earned		10,000
Salaries Expense	4,000	
Rent Expense	900	
	$28,700	$28,700

Note that the total debits $28,700 equal the total credits $28,700.

LIMITATIONS OF A TRIAL BALANCE

A trial balance does not prove that all transactions have been recorded or that the ledger is correct. Numerous errors may exist even though the trial balance columns are in agreement. For example, the trial balance may balance even when (1) a transaction is not journalized, (2) a correct journal entry is not posted, (3) a journal entry is posted twice, (4) incorrect accounts are used in journalizing or posting, or (5) offsetting errors are made in recording the amount of a transaction. In other words, as long as equal debits and credits are posted, even to the wrong account or in the wrong amount, the total debits will equal the total credits.

LOCATING ERRORS

The procedure for preparing a trial balance is relatively simple. However, in manual systems if the trial balance does not balance, the process of locating an error can become time-consuming, tedious, and frustrating. The error(s) generally result from mathematical mistakes, incorrect postings, or simply transcribing the data incorrectly. Most accountants faced with a trial balance that does not balance determine the amount of the difference between the two columns of the trial balance. After this amount is known, the following steps are often helpful.

1. If the error is $1, $100, $1,000, re-add the trial balance columns and recompute the account balances.
2. If the error is divisible by two, scan the trial balance to see whether a balance equal to half the error has been entered in the wrong column.
3. If the error is divisible by nine, retrace the account balances on the trial balance to see whether they are incorrectly copied from the ledger. For

example, if a balance was $945 and it was listed as $954, a $9 error has been made. This is called a transposition error.

4. If the error is not divisible by two or nine, as, for example, $365, scan the ledger to see whether an account balance of $365 has been omitted from the trial balance, and scan the journal to see whether a $365 posting has been omitted.

In a computerized system, the trial balance is often only one column (no debit or credit columns), and the accounts have plus and minus signs associated with them. The final balance therefore is zero. Any errors that develop in a computerized system will undoubtedly involve the initial recording rather than some error in the posting or preparation of a trial balance.

USE OF DOLLAR SIGNS

Note that dollar signs do not appear in the journals or ledgers. Dollar signs are usually used only in the trial balance and the financial statements. Generally, a dollar sign is shown only for the first item in the column and for the total of that column. A single line is placed under the column of figures to be added or subtracted; the total amount is double underlined to indicate the final sum.

SUMMARY OF STUDY OBJECTIVES

1. An account is an individual accounting record of increases and decreases in specific asset, liability, and owner's equity items.

2. The terms debit and credit are synonymous with left and right. Assets, drawings, and expenses are increased by debits and decreased by credits. Liabilities, owner's capital, and revenues are increased by credits and decreased by debits.

3. Assets, liabilities, and owner's capital are considered permanent (real) accounts. Drawings, revenues, and expenses are considered temporary (nominal) accounts.

4. The basic steps in the recording process are: (a) analyze each transaction in terms of its effect on the accounts, (b) enter the transaction information in a journal, and (c) transfer the journal information to the appropriate accounts in the ledger.

5. The initial accounting record of a transaction is entered in a journal before the data are entered in the accounts. A journal (a) discloses

in one place the complete effect of a transaction, (b) provides a chronological record of transactions, and (c) prevents or locates errors because the debit and credit amounts for each entry can be readily compared.

6. The entire group of accounts maintained by a company is referred to collectively as a ledger. The ledger provides a means of accumulating in one place all the information about changes in specific account balances.

7. Posting is the procedure of transferring journal entries to the ledger accounts. This phase of the recording process makes it possible to accumulate the effects of journalized transactions in the individual accounts.

8. A trial balance is a list of accounts and their balances at a given time. A primary purpose of the trial balance is to prove the mathematical equality of the accounting equation after all recorded transactions have been journalized and posted.

GLOSSARY

Account, p. 42
Chart of accounts, p. 54
Compound entry, p. 50
Credit, p. 42
Debit, p. 42
Double-entry system, p. 43
Footings, p. 43
General journal, p. 48
General ledger, p. 51
Journal, p. 48
Journalizing, p. 49
Ledger, p. 51
Permanent (real) accounts, p. 47
Posting, p. 52
T-accounts, p. 42
Temporary (nominal) accounts, p. 46
Three-column form of account, p. 52
Trial balance, p. 60

DEMONSTRATION PROBLEM

Bob Sample opens the Campus Laundromat on September 1. During the first month of operations the following transactions occurred:

Sept. 1 Invested $20,000 cash in the business.
2 Paid $1,000 cash for store rent for the month of September.
3 Purchased washers and dryers for $25,000 paying $10,000 in cash and signing a $15,000 six-month 12% note payable.
4 Paid $1,200 for one-year accident insurance policy.
10 Received bill from the Daily News for advertising the opening of the laundromat, $200.
20 Withdrew $700 cash for personal use.
30 Determined that cash receipts for laundry fees for the month were $6,200.

INSTRUCTIONS

(a) Journalize the September transactions. (Use J1 for the journal page number.)
(b) Open ledger accounts and post the September transactions. Use assumed account numbers.
(c) Prepare a trial balance at September 30, 1987.

SOLUTION TO DEMONSTRATION PROBLEM

(a) General Journal J1

Date	Account Titles and Explanation	Ref.	Debit	Credit
1987				
Sept. 1	Cash	1	20,000	
	Bob Sample, Capital	40		20,000
	(Invested cash in business)			
2	Rent Expense	60	1,000	
	Cash	1		1,000
	(Paid September rent)			
3	Laundry Equipment	15	25,000	
	Cash	1		10,000
	Notes Payable	25		15,000
	(Purchased laundry equipment for cash and six-month 12% note payable)			
4	Prepaid Insurance	10	1,200	
	Cash	1		1,200
	(Paid one-year insurance policy)			
10	Advertising Expense	61	200	
	Accounts Payable	26		200
	(Received bill from Daily News for advertising)			
20	Bob Sample, Drawing	41	700	
	Cash	1		700
	(Withdrew cash for personal use)			
30	Cash	1	6,200	
	Fees Earned	50		6,200
	(Received cash for laundry fees earned)			

(b)

General Ledger

Cash — No. 1

Date	Explanation	Ref.	Debit	Credit	Balance
1987					
Sept. 1		J1	20,000		20,000
2		J1		1,000	19,000
3		J1		10,000	9,000
4		J1		1,200	7,800
20		J1		700	7,100
30		J1	6,200		13,300

Accounts Payable — No. 26

Date	Explanation	Ref.	Debit	Credit	Balance
1987					
Sept. 10		J1		200	200

Bob Sample, Capital — No. 40

Date	Explanation	Ref.	Debit	Credit	Balance
1987					
Sept. 1		J1		20,000	20,000

Prepaid Insurance — No. 10

Date	Explanation	Ref.	Debit	Credit	Balance
1987					
Sept. 4		J1	1,200		1,200

Bob Sample, Drawing — No. 41

Date	Explanation	Ref.	Debit	Credit	Balance
1987					
Sept. 20		J1	700		700

Laundry Equipment — No. 15

Date	Explanation	Ref.	Debit	Credit	Balance
1987					
Sept. 3		J1	25,000		25,000

Fees Earned — No. 50

Date	Explanation	Ref.	Debit	Credit	Balance
1987					
Sept. 30		J1		6,200	6,200

Notes Payable — No. 25

Date	Explanation	Ref.	Debit	Credit	Balance
1987					
Sept. 3		J1		15,000	15,000

Rent Expense — No. 60

Date	Explanation	Ref.	Debit	Credit	Balance
1987					
Sept. 2		J1	1,000		1,000

Advertising Expense — No. 61

Date	Explanation	Ref.	Debit	Credit	Balance
1987					
Sept. 10		J1	200		200

(c)

CAMPUS LAUNDROMAT
Trial Balance
September 30, 1987

	Debit	Credit
Cash	$13,300	
Prepaid insurance	1,200	
Laundry equipment	25,000	
Notes payable		$15,000
Accounts payable		200
Bob Sample, Capital		20,000
Bob Sample, Drawing	700	
Fees earned		6,200
Rent expense	1,000	
Advertising expense	200	
	$41,400	$41,400

QUESTIONS

1. What is meant by the terms "debit" and "credit"?
2. What is the standard form of an account?
3. What is the double entry system?

4. Is a credit balance favorable and a debit balance unfavorable? Discuss.

5. State the rules of debit and credit as applied to (a) asset accounts, (b) liability accounts, and (c) owner's equity accounts.

6. What is the normal balance for (a) Accounts Payable? (b) Cash? (c) Owner's Drawing? (d) Equipment? (e) Fee Revenue? (f) Wages Expense? (g) Owner's Capital?

7. Indicate whether each of the following accounts is an asset, a liability, or an owner's equity account and whether it would have a debit or credit balance: (a) Accounts Receivable, (b) Accounts Payable, (c) Equipment, (d) Owner's Drawing, (e) Supplies.

8. For the following transactions, indicate the account debited and the account credited:

(a) Supplies are purchased for cash.
(b) Cash is received on signing a note payable.
(c) Employees are paid wages.

9. Presented below are a series of accounts. Indicate whether these accounts will have (a) debit entries only, (b) credit entries only, (c) both debit and credit entries.

(1) Cash.
(2) Accounts Receivable.
(3) Owner's Drawing.
(4) Accounts Payable.
(5) Wages Expense.
(6) Fee Revenue.

10. For the accounts in question 9 above, which are (a) temporary (nominal) accounts; (b) permanent accounts?

11. (a) What are the basic steps in the recording process? (b) What are the advantages of using the journal in the recording process?

12. (a) When entering a transaction in the journal, should the debit or credit be written first? (b) What should be indented, the debit or credit?

13. Give an example of a compound entry.

14. (a) Can business transaction debits and credits be recorded directly in the ledger accounts? (b) What is the advantage of first recording transactions in the journal and then posting to the ledger?

15. The account number is entered as the last step in posting the amounts from the journal to the ledger. What is the advantage of this step?

16. Journalize the following business transactions.

(a) R. L. Cey invests $8,000 in the business.
(b) Office rent of $600 is paid for the month.
(c) Supplies of $6,000 are purchased on account.
(d) Cash of $5,500 is received for services rendered.

17. Is a chart of accounts important? Discuss.

18. What is a trial balance and what is its purpose?

19. Bart Hillery is confused about how accounting information flows through the accounting system. He believes the flow of information is as follows:

(a) Debits and credits posted to the ledger.
(b) Information entered in the journal.
(c) Business transaction occurs.

(d) Financial statements are prepared.
(e) Trial balance is prepared.
Indicate to Hillery the proper flow of the information.

20. Two students are discussing the use of a trial balance. They wonder whether the following errors, each considered separately, would prevent the trial balance from balancing.

(a) The bookkeeper debited Cash for $450 and credited Wages Expense for $450 for payment of wages.
(b) Equipment was recorded by a debit to Equipment for $8,000 and a credit to Cash for $6,000 and a credit to Accounts Payable for $3,000.
(c) Cash collected on account was debited to Cash for $800 and Fee Revenue was credited for $800.

What would you tell them?

EXERCISES

E2-1 Selected transactions for Ann Monroe, an interior decorator, in her first month of business, are as follows:

1. Invested cash in business.
2. Purchased supplies on account.
3. Billed customers for services performed.
4. Paid salaries of employees.
5. Received cash for services to be performed in future.
6. Paid creditor on account.
7. Withdrew cash for personal use of owner.
8. Received bill from utility company for utility service.

INSTRUCTIONS

For each transaction indicate (a) the basic type of account debited and credited (asset, liability, owner's equity); (b) the specific account debited and credited (cash, fees earned, etc.); (c) whether the specific account is increased or decreased; and (d) the normal balance of the specific account. Use the following format, in which transaction (1) is given as an example:

	Account Debited				Account Credited			
Trans-action	(a) Basic Type	(b) Specific Account	(c) Effect	(d) Normal Balance	(a) Basic Type	(b) Specific Account	(c) Effect	(d) Normal Balance
(1)	Asset	Cash	Increase	Debit	Owner's Equity	Monroe, Capital	Increase	Credit

E2-2 Selected journal entries from the journal of R. E. Sters' Century 22 real estate agency are presented on the next page:

Date	Account Titles and Explanation	Ref.	Debit	Credit
Aug. 10	Accounts Receivable		1,200	
	Commissions Earned			1,200
12	Office Equipment		3,000	
	Cash			1,400
	Notes Payable			1,600
15	Prepaid Insurance		600	
	Cash			600
17	Office Equipment		500	
	R. E. Sters, Capital			500
21	Notes Payable		800	
	Cash			800
25	Supplies Expense		200	
	Supplies			200
27	Cash		900	
	Commissions Earned			900
29	Cash		500	
	Accounts Receivable			500
31	Salaries Expense		1,000	
	Salaries Payable			1,000

INSTRUCTIONS

Identify each transaction by date and describe the transaction.

E2-3 The T accounts below summarize the ledger of Shaw Landscaping Company at the end of the first month of operations:

Cash No. 1			
4/1	7,000	4/15	600
4/12	900	4/25	500
4/29	400		
4/30	300		

Unearned Fees No. 28			
		4/30	300

Accounts Receivable No. 5			
4/7	1,200	4/29	400

R. A. Shaw, Capital No. 40			
		4/1	7,000

Supplies No. 8			
4/4	800		

Fees Earned No. 50			
		4/7	1,200
		4/12	900

Accounts Payable No. 26			
4/25	500	4/4	800
		4/20	100

Salaries Expense No. 60			
4/15	600		
4/30	600		

Salaries Payable No. 27			
		4/30	600

Miscellaneous Expense No. 61			
4/20	100		

INSTRUCTIONS

Prepare the complete general journal (including explanations) from which the postings were made.

E2–4 Presented below is information related to Arnold's Real Estate Agency:

Sept. 1 F. Arnold begins business as a real estate agent with a cash investment of $13,000.
2 Hires an administrative assistant.
3 Buys office furniture for $1,730, giving cash of $330 and a note for $1,400.
6 Sells a house and lot for B. Rollins; commission due from Rollins, $3,200 (not paid by Rollins at this time).
10 Receives a $140 commission for renting an apartment for the owner.
13 Pays office expenses of $70.
18 Buys an automobile from Randal Motors Co. to be used in the business, $12,000.
23 Receives a $1,500 check from B. Rollins to be applied to his account.
27 Pays $700 on the note indicated in the transaction of Sept. 3.
30 Pays the administrative assistant $960 in wages for September.
30 Withdraws $175 for personal use.

INSTRUCTIONS

Provide an analysis of each transaction above, indicating whether it increased or decreased assets, liabilities, and owner's equity and identify the accounts that increased or decreased in each case.

E2–5 Presented below is information related to H. J. Brennan's business:

1. H. J. Brennan invests $1,800 cash in a small welding business of which he is the sole proprietor.
2. Pays $900 for equipment.
3. Pays $220 rent to his landlord.
4. Purchases additional equipment on account from Stanek Co., $700.
5. Pays apprentice wages of $120.
6. Receives $180 from customers for welding done.
7. Bills J. Kronsnoble $295 for welding work done for him.
8. Pays electricity bill of $175.
9. Pays amount owed to Hendrick Co. by signing a $500 note and giving $200 in cash.
10. Pays one year insurance premium of $700 in advance.
11. Receives $295 from J. Kronsnoble.
12. Receives $175 from C. Schultz for work done same day.

INSTRUCTIONS

Analyze the above transactions and identify the accounts to be debited or credited in each case.

E2–6 J. A. Russell has the following transactions for the current year:

1. J. A. Russell opens an office as a financial advisor, investing office equipment valued at $4,500 and cash of $300.
2. Pays insurance in advance for six months, $1,800.
3. Receives advances from new clients, $2,900.
4. Purchases a new copy machine, $1,700.
5. Receives $500 from clients for advice.
6. Pays secretary $450.
7. Completes a major consulting engagement with a private corporation and bills client $3,800.

8. Purchases office supplies for $700 on account.
9. Pays for maintenance on new copy machine, $200.

INSTRUCTIONS

Name the accounts to be debited and credited for each of the above transactions.

E2-7 Presented below are a number of accounts for Johannes Company.

1. Salaries Payable
2. Supplies on Hand
3. Notes Payable
4. Earned Fees
5. Land
6. Accounts Receivable
7. Prepaid Insurance
8. Property Tax Payable
9. J. Johannes, Capital
10. J. Johannes, Drawing
11. Cash
12. Unearned Fees
13. Mortgage Payable
14. Equipment

INSTRUCTIONS

For each of the accounts above, indicate

(a) the normal balance of the account.
(b) whether it is a nominal (temporary) or real (permanent) account.
(c) whether it is an asset, liability, or owner's equity account.
(d) whether it appears in the balance sheet, income statement, owner's equity statement, or a combination of these statements.

E2-8 Presented below is the ledger for Highlight Co.

Cash			No. 1
10/1	3,000	10/4	400
10/10	350	10/12	1,500
10/10	4,000	10/15	250
10/20	600	10/30	3,010
10/25	2,000	10/31	450

J. Edwards, Capital			No. 40
		10/1	3,000
		10/25	2,000

Accounts Receivable			No. 5
10/6	800	10/20	600
10/20	740		

Service Revenue			No. 50
		10/6	800
		10/10	350
		10/20	740

Supplies			No. 20
10/4	400	10/31	140

Wages Expense			No. 60
10/31	450		

Furniture and Equipment			No. 21
10/3	2,000		

Supplies Expense			No. 61
10/31	140		

Notes Payable			No. 25
10/30	3,000	10/10	4,000

Rent Expense			No. 62
10/15	250		

Accounts Payable			No. 26
10/12	1,500	10/3	2,000

Interest Expense			No. 65
10/30	10		

INSTRUCTIONS

(a) Reproduce the journal entries for the transactions that occurred on October 1, 10, and 20 and provide explanations for each.

(b) Prepare a trial balance at October 31.

E2-9 The bookkeeper for Hardy's Equipment Repair made a number of errors in journalizing and posting, as described below:

1. A credit posting of $200 to Accounts Receivable was omitted.
2. A debit posting of $750 for Prepaid Insurance was credited to Prepaid Insurance.
3. A collection on account of $100 was journalized and posted as a debit to Cash $100 and a credit to Fees Earned $100.
4. A debit posting of $300 to Property Tax Expense was made twice.
5. A cash purchase of supplies for $250 was journalized and posted as a debit to Supplies $25 and a credit to Cash $25.
6. A debit of $456 to Advertising Expense was posted as $465.
7. A credit of $490 to Accounts Payable was posted as $49.
8. A cash purchase of equipment for $724 was journalized as a debit to Equipment and a credit to Notes Payable. The credit posting was made for $742.

INSTRUCTIONS

For each error, indicate (a) whether the trial balance will balance; if the trial balance will not balance, indicate (b) the amount of the difference, and (c) the trial balance column that will have the larger total. Consider each error separately. Use the following form, in which error (1) is given as an example.

Error	(a) In Balance	(b) Difference	(c) Larger Column
(1)	No	$200	debit

E2-10 The accounts in the ledger of the T&T Home Delivery Service contain the following balances on August 31, 1987:

Accounts Receivable	$ 6,642	Prepaid Insurance	$ 1,968
Accounts Payable	6,396	Rent Expense	492
Cash	23,567	Repair Expense	369
Delivery Equipment	39,360	Salaries Expense	4,428
Gas and Oil Expense	758	Salaries Payable	615
Insurance Expense	266	Service Revenue Earned	8,610
Miscellaneous Expense	157	T. Tyler, Drawing	718
Notes Payable	18,450	T. Tyler, Capital	44,654

INSTRUCTIONS

Prepare a trial balance with the accounts arranged in statement order.

PROBLEMS

P2-1 The Bogieless Miniature Golf and Driving Range was opened on April 1 by Jack Parr. The following selected events and transactions occurred during April:

April 1 Invested $60,000 cash in the business. deb. ₹ cash cred. ₹ capital

3 Purchased Lee's Golf Land for $35,000 cash. The price consists of land, $20,000, building, $9,000, and equipment, $6,000. (Make one entry.)

debit Land building & equip
Credit cash

5 Advertised the opening of the driving range and miniature golf course, paying $200 for newspaper ads and $400 for radio spots.
6 Paid $1,480 for a one-year insurance policy.
6 Hired three employees.
10 Purchased golf clubs and other equipment for $1,600 payable in 30 days.
17 Opening day for the driving range and miniature golf course.
17 Golf fee revenue of $800 in cash received.
19 Sold 100 coupon books for $12.00 each. Each book contains 10 coupons that enable the bearer to one round of miniature golf or to hit one bucket of golf balls.
25 Withdrew $500 cash for personal use.
30 Paid wages of $700 and miscellaneous expense $200. (Make one entry.)
30 Received $350 in cash for fees.

INSTRUCTIONS

Journalize the April transactions.

P2-2 Patrick Bausch is a licensed architect. During the first month of the operation of his business, the following events and transactions occurred.

Feb. 1 Invested $15,000 cash and equipment valued at $8,000 in the business.
2 Paid office rent for the month, $800.
3 Purchased architectural supplies on account, $250.
4 Hired a secretary-receptionist at a salary of $210 per week payable monthly.
6 Signed a contract to design a carport.
10 Completed blueprints on carport and billed client $900 for services. (Credit Fees Earned.)
11 Received $500 advance from R. Weld for the design of a new home.
17 Purchased a new automobile for $7,800 with personal funds. The automobile will be used exclusively for business purposes. (Use equipment account to record the purchase of the automobile.)
20 Received $750 cash for services completed and delivered to P. Donahue.
28 Paid secretary-receptionist for the month, $840.
28 Determined that $100 of supplies had been used.

INSTRUCTIONS

(a) Journalize the transactions in the general journal (omit explanations).
(b) Post to the ledger accounts, using assumed account numbers.
(c) Prepare a trial balance on February 28.

P2-3 The trial balance of Troy Laundry on September 30 is shown below:

TROY LAUNDRY
Trial Balance
September 30, 1987

Account No.		Debit	Credit
1	Cash	$ 7,500	
5	Accounts Receivable	1,200	
11	Supplies	1,700	
15	Equipment	8,000	
26	Accounts Payable		$ 4,000
28	Unearned Revenue		700
40	Jane Troy, Capital		13,700
		$18,400	$18,400

The October transactions were as follows:

Oct.	5	Received $800 cash from customers on account.
	7	Purchased additional equipment for $3,000, paying $3,000 in cash.
	10	Billed customers for services performed $2,400.
	15	Paid employee salaries $900.
	17	Discovered that $200 of customers' billings on October 10 had been paid for in advance and previously recorded in Unearned Revenue.
	20	Paid $1,600 to creditors on account.
	25	Overcharged a credit customer $100 on October 10.
	29	Withdrew $500 for personal use.
	30	Paid employees' salaries $900, utilities $600.
	30	Determined that $500 of supplies had been used.

INSTRUCTIONS

(a) Enter the opening balances in the ledger accounts as of October 1. Write "Balance" in the explanation space and insert a check mark (✓) in the reference column. Provision should be made for the following additional accounts: Jane Troy, Drawing, No. 41; Laundry Revenue, No. 50; Salaries Expense, No. 60; Utilities Expense, No. 61; and Supplies Expense, No. 63.

(b) Journalize the transactions.

(c) Post to the ledger accounts.

(d) Prepare a trial balance on October 31.

P2-4 The trial balance of Bruce Howat Co. as shown below does not balance.

BRUCE HOWAT CO.
Trial Balance
April 30, 1987

	Debit	Credit
Cash		$ 2,881
Accounts Receivable	$ 3,200	
Supplies	800	
Furniture and Equipment	2,600	
Accounts Payable		2,666
B. Howat, Capital		9,000
Fees Earned		2,350
Wages Expense	3,400	
Office Expense	940	
Totals	$10,940	$16,897

An examination of the ledger and journal reveals the following errors:

1. Each of the above listed accounts has a normal balance per the general ledger.
2. Cash received from a customer on account was debited for $650 instead of $560. (Accounts Receivable was also credited for $650.)
3. The purchase of a typewriter on account for $340 was recorded as a debit to Office Expense for $340 and a credit to Accounts Payable for $340.
4. Services were performed on account for a client, $890, for which Accounts Receivable was debited for $890 and Fees Earned was credited for $89.
5. A payment of $30 for telephone charges was entered as a debit to Office Expense for $30 and a debit to Cash for $30.
6. When the Fees Earned account was reviewed, it was found to total $2,360, not $2,350.

7. A debit posting to Wages Expense of $600 was omitted.
8. A payment on account for $260 was credited to Cash for $260 and credited to Accounts Payable for $206.
9. No one counted the inventory of Supplies to determine that only $500 of supplies were on hand April 30 and that $300 were used during April.

INSTRUCTIONS

Prepare a correct trial balance.

P2-5 The Moonglow Drive-In Theater, owned by Leo Thespin, will begin operations in May. The Moonglow will be unique in that it will show only triple features of sequential theme movies. As of April 30, the ledger of Moonglow showed: Cash $14,000, Land $42,000, Buildings (concession stand, projection room, ticket booth, and screen) $18,000, Equipment $16,000, Accounts Payable $12,000, and L. Thespin, Capital $78,000. During the month of May the following events and transactions occurred:

May 2 Acquired the three *Star Wars* movies (*Star Wars, The Empire Strikes Back,* and *The Return of the Jedi*) to be shown for the first three weeks of May. The film rental was $12,600; $4,000 was paid in cash and $8,600 will be paid on May 10.
3 Ordered the *Star Trek* trilogy to be shown the last 10 days of May. It will cost $400 per night.
9 Received $4,450 cash from admissions. (Credit Admissions Revenue.)
10 Paid balance due on *Star Wars* movies rental.
11 Sublet concession stand to M. Brewer for 15% of gross receipts payable monthly.
12 Paid advertising expenses $650.
15 Received $5,120 cash from admissions.
20 Received the *Star Trek* movies and paid the rental fee of $4,000.
21 Received $5,550 cash from admissions.
29 Paid salaries of $3,300 and miscellaneous expenses $750.
31 Received statement from N. Brewer showing gross receipts from concessions of $7,200 for May. Brewer paid one-half the balance due and will remit the remainder on June 5. (Credit Concession Revenue.)
31 Received $4,965 cash from admissions.

INSTRUCTIONS

(a) Post the beginning balances to the ledger. Insert a check mark (✓) in the reference column of the ledger for the beginning balance.
(b) Journalize the May transactions. Explanations are not needed.
(c) Post the May journal entries to the ledger. Assume that all entries are posted from page 1 of the journal. Use assumed account numbers.
(d) Prepare a trial balance on May 31.

ALTERNATE PROBLEMS

P2-1A The Wild Water World Park was started on March 1 by Ed Gill. The following selected events and transactions occurred during March.

March 1 Invested $70,000 cash in the business.
4 Purchased water slide equipment for $22,000.
8 Incurred advertising expense of $1,730 on account.

11	Paid wages to employees $900.
12	Hired office manager.
13	Paid $1,500 for a one-year insurance policy.
17	Withdrew $600 cash for personal use.
20	Received $700 in cash for fees.
23	Paid miscellaneous expense $400.
29	Purchased land for possible expansion purposes, paying $19,000 cash.
31	Received $900 in cash fees.

INSTRUCTIONS

Journalize the March transactions.

P2-2A Erin Suby is a licensed CPA. During the first month of operations of her business, the following events and transactions occurred.

April	1	Invested $32,000 cash and equipment valued at $11,000 in the business.
	2	Hired a secretary-receptionist at a salary of $230 per week payable monthly.
	3	Purchased supplies on account $700.
	7	Paid office rent of $550 for the month.
	11	Completed a tax assignment and billed client $1,100 for services rendered. (Use professional fees account.)
	12	Received $3,200 advance on a management consulting engagement.
	15	Purchased a new computer for $8,300 with personal funds. (The computer will be used exclusively for business purposes.)
	17	Received cash of $900 for services completed for H. Arnold Co.
	21	Paid insurance expense $110.
	30	Paid secretary-receptionist $920 for the month.
	30	A count of supplies indicated that $120 of supplies had been used.

INSTRUCTIONS

(a) Journalize the transactions in the general journal (omit explanations).
(b) Post to the ledger accounts, using assumed account numbers.
(c) Prepare a trial balance on April 30.

P2-3A The trial balance of B. Sterling Dry Cleaning on April 30 is shown below.

B. STERLING DRY CLEANERS
Trial Balance
April 30, 1987

Account No.		Debit	Credit
10	Cash	$14,532	
12	Accounts Receivable	5,536	
18	Supplies	4,844	
24	Equipment	25,950	
30	Accounts Payable		$14,878
33	Unearned Revenue		1,730
41	B. Sterling, Capital		34,254
		$50,862	$50,862

The May transactions were as follows:

May	6	Purchased additional equipment for $8,650, $2,000 cash and the balance on account.
	8	Collected $3,806 in cash on April 30 accounts receivable.

9 Paid employee salaries $2,076.
11 Received $4,325 in cash for services rendered, $2,700.
14 Paid November 30 creditors $8,650 on account.
17 Purchased supplies on account $554.
22 Billed customers for services rendered, $2,700.
30 Paid employee salaries $3,114, utilities $1,384, and repairs $692.
30 Received $2,595 from customers on account.
31 Determined that $1,038 of supplies had been used.
31 Withdrew $500 cash for personal use of owner.

INSTRUCTIONS

(a) Enter the opening balances in the ledger accounts as of May 1. Write "Balance" in the explanation space and insert a check mark (✓) in the reference column. Provision should be made for the following additional accounts: B. Sterling, Drawing, No. 42; Dry Cleaning Revenue, No. 50; Salaries Expense, No. 60; Utilities Expense, No. 61; Repair Expense, No. 62; and Supplies Expense, No. 63.

(b) Journalize the transactions.

(c) Post to the ledger accounts.

(d) Prepare a trial balance on May 31.

P2-4A The trial balance of the Creole Company shown below does not balance. Your review of the ledger reveals the following: (a) each account had a normal balance, (b) the debit footings in Prepaid Insurance, Accounts Payable, and Property Tax Expense were each understated $100, (c) transposition errors were made in Accounts Receivable and Fees Earned; the correct balances are $2,750 and $6,690, respectively, (d) a debit posting to Advertising Expense of $200 was omitted, and (e) a $1,000 cash drawing by the owner was debited to R. O. Creole, Capital, and credited to Cash.

CREOLE COMPANY
Trial Balance
April 30, 1987

	Debit	Credit
Cash	$ 5,400	
Accounts Receivable	2,570	
Prepaid Insurance	700	
Equipment		$ 8,000
Accounts Payable		4,500
Property Tax Payable	560	
R. O. Creole, Capital		11,700
Fees Earned	6,960	
Salaries Expense	4,200	
Advertising Expense	1,100	
Property Tax Expense		800
	$21,490	$25,000

INSTRUCTIONS

Prepare a correct trial balance.

P2-5A The Starlite Drive-In Theater is owned by Frances Hill. All facilities were completed on April 30. At this time, the ledger showed Cash $4,000, Land $12,000, Buildings (concession stand, projection room, ticket booth, and screen) $8,000, Equipment $6,000, Accounts Payable $2,000, Mortgage Payable $10,000, and Frances Hill, Capital $18,000. During May, the following events and transactions occurred.

May 2 Paid film rental of $600 on first movie.
3 Ordered two additional films at $400 each.
9 Received $1,200 cash from admissions. (Credit Admission Revenue.)
10 Made $2,000 payment on mortgage and $1,000 on accounts payable.
11 Sublet concession stand to R. Thoms for 15% of gross receipts payable monthly.
12 Paid advertising expenses $150.
20 Received one of the films ordered on May 3 and was billed $400.
25 Received $1,800 cash from admissions.
29 Paid salaries $1,300 and miscellaneous expenses $300.
31 Received statement from R. Thoms showing gross receipts of $1,200 for May. Thoms paid one-half of the balance due and will remit the remainder on June 5. (Credit Concession Revenue.)
31 Prepaid $500 rental on special film to be run in June.

INSTRUCTIONS

(a) Post the beginning balances to the ledger. Insert a check mark (✓) in the reference column of the ledger for the beginning balance.

(b) Journalize the May transactions. Explanations are not required.

(c) Post the May journal entries to the ledger. Assume that all entries are posted from page 1 of the journal. Use assumed account numbers.

(d) Prepare a trial balance on May 31.

DECISION CASE

Lana Lawton operates the Lawton Riding Academy on 10 acres of land purchased from her grandmother. Over the years, Lana has built a stable; a small building that contains an office, a reception area, and a lounge; and a riding corral. She also purchased saddles, bridles, and other riding equipment. Currently, the Academy owns 10 horses. To keep the horses, it is necessary to have feed and hay on hand at all times.

The Academy's primary sources of revenue are riding fees and lesson fees which are rendered on a cash basis. Lana also boards horses whose owners are billed monthly for boarding fees. In a few cases, boarders pay for stalls two or three months in advance of expected use.

The Academy employs a stable helper who receives an hourly wage and a woman who receives a monthly salary for running the office, keeping the books, and taking riding reservations. There usually is a small quantity of office supplies on hand. Lana gives all the riding lessons. At the end of each month, the mail usually brings bills for advertising, utilities, and telephone. Occasionally repairs are made to the stalls and the services of a veterinarian are required for the horses. Lana also carries fire and accident insurance on a two-year policy.

The Academy is Lana's sole source of income. Thus, she makes periodic withdrawals of cash for personal living expenses. To date, Lana has not had to obtain a bank loan for the Academy but she may do so in the future.

INSTRUCTIONS

Prepare a chart of accounts for the Lawton Riding Academy. Use 100 numbers for assets, 200 for liabilities, 300 for owner's equities, 400 for revenues, and 500 for expenses.

CHAPTER 3

University of Illinois

CHAPTER 3

ADJUSTING THE ACCOUNTS

STUDY OBJECTIVES

After studying this chapter, you should be able to:

1. **Explain the periodicity assumption.**
2. **Distinguish between the revenue recognition principle and the matching principle.**
3. **Prepare adjusting entries and know their purpose.**
4. **Identify the major types of adjusting entries.**
5. **Explain the meaning of depreciation.**
6. **Describe the nature and purpose of an adjusted trial balance.**

In the preceding chapter you learned the steps in the accounting cycle that pertain to the recording process. At this point you might think that we are ready to prepare financial statements from the trial balance, but additional steps in the accounting cycle still need to be performed. For example, during the past year, Pioneer Advertising purchased some supplies that are currently reported as an asset. The question is: What amount of the supplies purchased during the period should be reported as an expense? Similarly, office equipment that was purchased by Pioneer during the period is being used now. What portion, if any, of the equipment cost should be recognized as an expense of the current period? Before financial statements are prepared, these and other account balances must be adjusted. The purpose of this chapter is to explain and illustrate the different types of adjustments that accountants prepare. In addition, an adjusted trial balance and its role in preparing financial statements are illustrated.

PERIODICITY ASSUMPTION

No adjustments would be necessary if we waited to prepare financial statements until a company such as Pioneer terminated its operations. At the end of Pioneer's existence, we could readily determine its final balance sheet and the amount of lifetime income it earned. The following anecdote illustrates how easy it is to compute lifetime income.

A grocery store owner from the old country kept his accounts payable on a spindle, accounts receivable on a note pad, and cash in a cigar box. His daughter, having just passed the CPA exam, chided the father, "I don't understand how you can run your business this way. How do you know what your profits are?"

"Well," the father replied, "when I got off the boat forty years ago, I had nothing but the pants I was wearing. Today your brother is a doctor, your sister is a college professor, and you are a CPA. Your mother and I have a nice car, a well-furnished house, and a lake home. We have a good business and everything is paid for. So, you add all that together, subtract the pants, and there's your profit."

While the old grocer may be correct in his evaluation, in today's business environment all enterprises find it desirable, and necessary, to report the results of their activities more frequently. As a consequence, **accountants make the assumption that the economic life of a business can be divided into artificial time periods.** This assumption is referred to as the **periodicity** or **time period assumption.**

Because accountants divide continuous operations into arbitrary time periods, and because many transactions affect more than one time period, it is necessary to determine the relevance of each business transaction to specific accounting periods. This often involves estimates, and generally the shorter the time period (e.g., a quarter of a year or a month), the more difficult it becomes to determine the proper adjustments to be made.

Both small and large companies find it necessary to prepare financial statements on a periodic basis to assess their financial condition and results of operations. **Accounting time periods are generally a month, a quarter, or a year.** Monthly and quarterly time periods are often referred to as **interim periods.** Most large companies are required to prepare both interim (quarterly) and annual financial statements for their users.

Accounting time periods that are one year in length are referred to as **fiscal years.** Fiscal years usually begin with the first day of a month and end on the last day of a month, 12 months later. The accounting period most frequently used coincides with the **calendar year** (January 1 to December 31); there are many exceptions. To illustrate, examples of companies with other than a December 31 fiscal year-end are: Delta Air Lines, June 30; Walt Disney Productions, September 30; K mart Corp., January 31; and Dunkin' Donuts, Inc., October 31.

REVENUE AND EXPENSE RECOGNITION

The determination of the amount of revenues and expenses to be reported in a given accounting period can be difficult. Therefore, accountants have developed two general principles that help in this determination.

One of these principles is the revenue recognition principle. The **revenue recognition principle** dictates that revenue be recognized in the accounting period in which it is earned. Revenues are considered earned in a service enterprise when the service is performed. To illustrate, if the service is performed, the revenue should be recognized (when it is earned) even if the cash has yet to be received. In this case, a receivable should be reported as an asset. However, if cash is received in advance of the performance of the service, it is unearned revenue and should not be reported as revenue in the current period. In this case, the unearned revenue should be reported as a liability.

In recognizing expenses, accountants follow the approach of "let the expense follow the revenues." Thus, expense recognition is tied to revenue recognition. For example, the expense for labor is recognized not when the wages are paid, but when it is incurred. The expense is incurred when the work (service) actually makes its contribution to revenue. This practice is referred to as the **matching principle** because it **dictates that efforts (expenses) be matched with accomplishments (revenues) whenever it is reasonable and practicable to do so.**

NEED FOR ADJUSTING ENTRIES

Adjusting entries are made at the end of the accounting period to insure that revenues are recorded in the period in which they are earned, and that expenses are recognized in the period in which they are incurred. In short, **adjustments are needed to insure that the revenue recognition and matching principles are followed.** Adjustments also make it possible to report on the balance sheet the appropriate assets, liabilities, and owner's equity at the statement date and to report on the income statement the proper net income (or loss) for the period. A trial balance may not contain up-to-date and complete financial statement data for the following reasons:

1. Some events, such as the consumption of supplies and the earning of wages by employees, are not journalized daily because it is unnecessary and inexpedient to do so.
2. The expiration of some costs, such as building and equipment deterioration and rent and insurance, is not journalized during the accounting period because these costs expire with the passage of time rather than as a result of recurring daily transactions.
3. Some items, such as the cost of utility service, may be unrecorded because the bill from the utility company has not been received.

Adjusting entries are required every time financial statements are prepared. The preparation of adjusting entries is often an involved process that requires the services of a skilled accountant. An essential starting point is an analysis of each account in the trial balance to determine whether it is complete and correct for financial statement purposes. The analysis requires a thorough understanding of the company's operations and the interrelationship of accounts. In accumulating the adjustment data, it may be necessary to make inventory counts of supplies and repair parts. Also it may be desirable to prepare supporting schedules of insurance policies, rental agreements, and other contractual commitments. Adjustments are often prepared by the accountant in the next accounting period, although the entries are dated on the last day of the current accounting period.

TYPES OF ADJUSTING ENTRIES

Adjusting entries can be classified in the following categories:

Prepayments

1. **Prepaid Expenses.** Expenses paid in cash and recorded in an asset account before they are used or consumed.
2. **Unearned Revenues.** Revenues received and recorded as liabilities before they are earned.

Accruals

3. **Accrued Revenues.** Revenues earned but not yet received or recorded.
4. **Accrued Expenses.** Expenses incurred but not yet paid or recorded.

Specific examples of each type of adjustment are given in subsequent sections. Each example is based on the October 31 trial balance of Pioneer Advertising Agency, reproduced on page 85 from Chapter 2. Accordingly, the adjusting entries are dated as of October 31.

PREPAID EXPENSES—APPORTIONMENT OF RECORDED COSTS

Payments of expenses that will benefit more than one accounting period are identified as **prepaid expenses** or **prepayments.** When a cost is incurred, an asset acccount is debited to show the service or benefit that will be received in the future. Prepayments often occur in regard to insurance, supplies, advertising, and rent. In addition, prepayments are made when buildings and equipment are purchased.

Prepaid expenses expire either with the passage of time or through use and consumption. The expiration of these costs does not require daily recurring entries, which would be unnecessary and impractical. Accordingly, it is customary to postpone the recognition of such cost expirations until financial statements are prepared. At each statement date, adjusting entries are made to record the expenses applicable to the current accounting period and to show the unexpired costs in the asset accounts. **An asset-expense relation-**

Trial balance

PIONEER ADVERTISING AGENCY
Trial Balance
October 31, 1987

	Debit	Credit
Cash	$15,200	
Advertising Supplies	2,500	
Prepaid Insurance	600	
Office Equipment	5,000	
Notes Payable		$ 5,000
Accounts Payable		2,500
Unearned Fees		1,200
C. R. Byrd, Capital		10,000
C. R. Byrd, Drawing	500	
Fees Earned		10,000
Salaries Expense	4,000	
Rent Expense	900	
	$28,700	$28,700

ship exists with prepaid expenses. In the typical case, assets are overstated and expenses are understated prior to adjustment. **Thus, the prepaid expense adjusting entry results in a debit (increase) to an expense account and a credit (decrease) to an asset account.**

Supplies

Several different types of supplies are used in a business enterprise. For example, there are office supplies such as stationery, paper clips, and pencils, and store supplies such as paper bags, wrapping paper, and cash register tapes. Supplies are generally charged to an asset account when they are acquired. During the course of operations, supplies are depleted or entirely consumed. However, recognition of supplies used is deferred until the adjustment process when a physical inventory (count) of supplies is taken. The difference between the balance in the Supplies (asset) account and the cost of supplies on hand represents the supplies used (expense) for the period.

Pioneer Advertising Agency purchased advertising supplies costing $2,500 on October 5. The debit was made to the asset Advertising Supplies, and this account shows a balance of $2,500 in the October 31 trial balance. An inventory count at the close of business on October 31 reveals that $1,000 of supplies are still on hand. Thus, the cost of supplies used is $1,500 ($2,500 − $1,000), and the following adjusting entry is made:

Oct. 31	Advertising Supplies Expense	1,500	
	Advertising Supplies		1,500
	(To record supplies used)		

After the adjusting entry is posted, the two supplies accounts in T-account form show:

Accounts after adjustment

Advertising Supplies				Advertising Supplies Expense		
10/5	2,500	10/31	**1,500**	10/31	**1,500**	

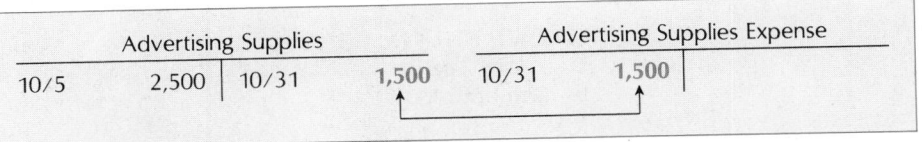

The asset account Advertising Supplies now shows a balance of $1,000, which is equal to the cost of supplies on hand at the statement date. In addition, Advertising Supplies Expense shows a balance of $1,500, which equals the cost of supplies used in October. If the adjusting entry is not made, October expenses will be understated and net income overstated by $1,500. Moreover, both assets and owner's equity will be overstated by $1,500 on the October 31 balance sheet.

Insurance

Most companies have fire and theft insurance on merchandise and equipment, personal liability insurance for accidents suffered by customers, and automobile insurance on company cars and trucks. The cost of insurance protection is determined by the payment of insurance premiums. The term and coverage are specified in the insurance policy. The minimum term is usually one year, but three- to five-year terms are available because lower annual premiums are obtainable under long-term policies. Insurance premiums normally are charged to the asset account Prepaid Insurance when paid. At the financial statement date it is necessary to debit Insurance Expense and credit Prepaid Insurance for the cost that has expired during the period.

On October 4, Pioneer Advertising Agency paid $600 for a one-year fire insurance policy. The effective date of coverage was October 1. The premium was charged to Prepaid Insurance when it was paid, and this account shows a balance of $600 in the October 31 trial balance. An analysis of the policy reveals that $50 ($600 ÷ 12) of insurance expires each month. Thus, the following adjusting entry is made:

Oct. 31	Insurance Expense	50	
	Prepaid Insurance		50
	(To record insurance expired)		

After the adjusting entry is posted, the accounts show:

Accounts after adjustment

Prepaid Insurance				Insurance Expense		
10/4	600	10/31	**50**	10/31	**50**	

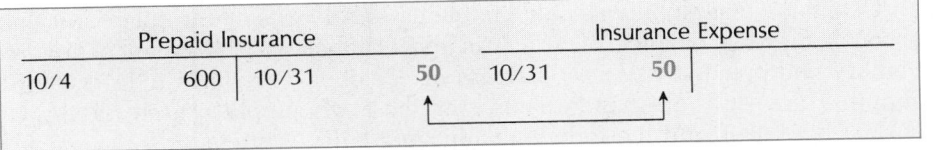

The asset Prepaid Insurance shows a balance of $550, which represents the unexpired cost applicable to the remaining eleven months of coverage. At the same time, the balance in Insurance Expense is equal to the insurance cost that has expired in October. If this adjustment is not made, October expenses will be understated by $50 and net income overstated by $50. Moreover, both assets and owner's equity also will be overstated by $50 on the October 31 balance sheet.

Depreciation

A business enterprise typically owns a variety of productive facilities such as buildings, equipment, and motor vehicles. These assets provide a service for a number of years. The term of service is commonly referred to as the **useful life** of the asset. Because an asset such as a building is expected to provide service for many years, its cost should be recorded as an asset, and not as an expense, in the year it is acquired. According to the matching principle, a portion of this cost should then be reported as an expense during each period of the asset's useful life. **Depreciation** is the process of allocating the cost of an asset to expense over its useful life in a rational and systematic manner.

From an accounting standpoint, the acquisition of productive facilities is viewed essentially as a long-term prepayment for services. The need for making periodic adjusting entries for depreciation is, therefore, the same as described above for other prepaid expenses; that is, to recognize the cost that has expired (expense) during the period and to report the unexpired cost (asset) at the end of the period.

In determining the useful life of a productive facility, consideration must be given to the primary causes of depreciation: actual use, deterioration due to the elements, inadequacy, and obsolescence. At the time an asset is acquired, the effects of these factors cannot be known with certainty, so they must be estimated. In computing depreciation it is also necessary to estimate the salvage value of the asset at the end of its useful life. Thus, you should recognize that depreciation is an estimate rather than a factual measurement of the cost that has expired.

Computation of Depreciation Expense. To compute depreciation expense, depreciable cost first must be computed. **Depreciable cost** is the total amount subject to depreciation. Depreciable cost is then divided by the asset's useful life to determine depreciation expense. To illustrate, assume that an asset costing $10,000 is expected to have a salvage value of $1,000 at the end of its 10-year useful life.[1] The computation of depreciation expense is as follows:

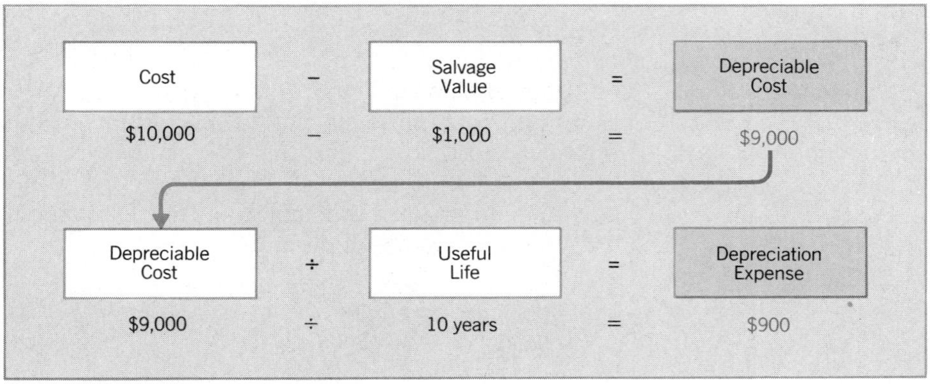

Formulas and computations for depreciation

Depreciation rates are often used in business. An asset with a 10-year life depreciates at the rate of 10% per year and an asset with a 4-year life depreci-

[1]The approach used here to depreciate the asset is the straight-line method. Other approaches are discussed in Chapter 10.

ates at the rate of 25% per year. When depreciation rates are used, the rate is applied to the depreciable cost of the asset. The formula for computing annual depreciation expense using a depreciation rate and the computation based on the preceding example are shown below:

Computation using depreciation rate

Depreciable Cost	×	Depreciation Rate	=	Depreciation Expense
$9,000	×	10%	=	$900

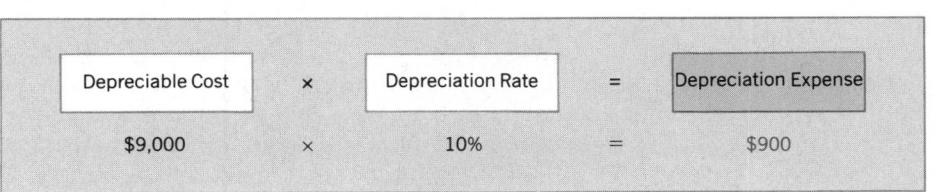

Pioneer Advertising Agency purchased office equipment for $5,000 on October 1. This equipment is expected to have a useful life of 10 years, and salvage value is estimated at $200. The depreciable cost of the office equipment is $4,800 ($5,000 − $200). The depreciation expense for October then is $40 ($4,800 ÷ 120 months), and the following adjusting entry is made:

Oct. 31	Depreciation Expense	40	
	Accumulated Depreciation—Office Equipment		40
	(To record monthly depreciation)		

After the adjusting entry is posted, the accounts show:

Accounts after adjustment

Office Equipment

10/1	5,000		

Accumulated Depreciation—Office Equipment

		10/31	40

Depreciation Expense

10/31	40		

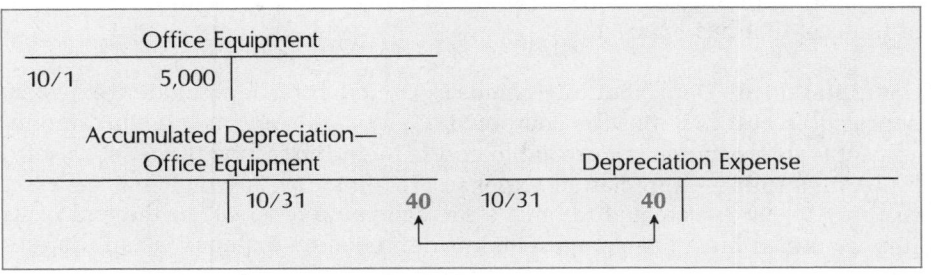

Statement Presentation. Accumulated Depreciation—Office Equipment is a **contra asset account.** This means that it is offset against Office Equipment on the balance sheet and that its normal balance is a credit. This account is used instead of crediting Office Equipment in order to permit disclosure of both the original cost of the equipment and the total cost that has expired to date. A title such as Allowance for Depreciation may also be used to identify this account. In the balance sheet, Accumulated Depreciation—Office Equipment is deducted from the related asset account as follows:

Balance sheet presentation

Office Equipment	$5,000	
Less: Accumulated Depreciation—Office Equipment	40	$4,960

The difference between the cost of any depreciable asset and its related accumulated depreciation is referred to as the **book value** of that asset. In the presentation above, the book value of the equipment at the balance sheet date is $4,960. It should be emphasized that the book value and the market value of

the asset are generally two different values. The reason is that depreciation is not a matter of valuation, but a means of cost allocation.

Note also that depreciation expense identifies the cost that has expired in October. As in the case of other prepaid adjustments, the omission of this adjusting entry would cause total assets, total owner's equity, and net income to be overstated and depreciation expense to be understated.

If additional equipment is involved, such as delivery or store equipment, or if the company has buildings, depreciation expense should be recorded on each of these items and related accumulated depreciation accounts established. These accumulated depreciation accounts would be described in the ledger as follows: Accumulated Depreciation—Delivery Equipment; Accumulated Depreciation—Store Equipment; and Accumulated Depreciation—Buildings.

UNEARNED REVENUES—APPORTIONMENT OF RECORDED REVENUES

Revenues received in advance of the accounting period in which they are earned are liabilities and are commonly titled **unearned revenues** or **revenues collected in advance.** Such items as rent, magazine subscriptions, and customer deposits for future service may result in unearned revenues. Airlines such as United, Texas Air, and Delta, for instance, treat receipts from the sale of tickets as unearned revenue until the flight service is provided. Unearned revenues are the counterpart to prepaid expenses. Indeed, unearned revenue on the books of one company is likely to be a prepayment on the books of the company that has made the advance payment. For example, if identical accounting periods are assumed, a landlord will have unearned rent revenue when a tenant has prepaid rent.

When the payment is received for services to be provided in a future accounting period, an unearned revenue (a liability) account should be credited to recognize the obligation that exists. Unearned revenues are earned through rendering service to a customer. During the accounting period it may not be practical to make daily recurring entries as the revenue is earned. In such cases, it is customary to delay the recognition of earned revenue until the adjustment process, when an adjusting entry is made to record the revenue that has been earned and to show the liability that remains. **A liability–revenue account relationship therefore exists with unearned revenues.** In the typical case, liabilities are overstated and revenues are understated prior to adjustment. Thus, **the adjusting entry for unearned revenues results in a debit (decrease) to a liability account and a credit (increase) to a revenue account.**

Pioneer Advertising Agency received $1,200 on October 1 from R. Knox for advertising services expected to be completed by December 31. The payment was credited to Unearned Fees, and this account shows a balance of $1,200 in the October 31 trial balance. When analysis reveals that $400 of those fees has been earned in October, the following adjusting entry is made:

Oct. 31	Unearned Fees	400	
	Fees Earned		400
	(To record fees earned)		

After the adjusting entry is posted, the accounts show:

Accounts after adjustment

Unearned Fees			
10/31	**400**	10/1	1,200

Fees Earned			
		10/31 Bal.	1,000
		31	**400**

The liability Unearned Fees now shows a balance of $800, which represents the remaining advertising services expected to be performed in the future. At the same time, Fees Earned shows total revenue earned in October of $1,400. If this adjustment is not made, revenues and net income will be understated by $400 in the income statement. Moreover, liabilities will be overstated and owner's equity will be understated by $400 on the October 31 balance sheet.

ACCRUED REVENUES—RECOGNITION OF UNRECORDED REVENUES

As indicated earlier, the second category of adjustments is accruals. In contrast to the prepayments explained above, both accounts involved in an accrued adjustment are **understated** prior to adjustment.

Revenues earned but unrecorded at the statement date are known as **accrued revenues** or **accrued receivables.** Accrued revenues may accumulate (accrue) with the passing of time, as in the case of interest and rent. Or they may result from services that have been performed but neither billed nor collected, as in the case of commissions and fees. The former are unrecorded because the earning of interest and rent does not involve daily transactions; the latter may be unrecorded because only a portion of the total service has been provided.

An adjusting entry is required to show the receivable that exists at the balance sheet date and to record the revenue that has been earned during the period. **An asset-revenue account relationship exists with accrued revenues.** Prior to adjustment both assets and revenues are understated. Accordingly, **an adjusting entry for accrued revenues results in a debit (increase) to an asset account and a credit (increase) to a revenue account.**

In October Pioneer Advertising Agency earned $200 in fees for advertising services that were not billed to clients before October 31. Because these services have not been billed, they have not been recorded. Thus, the following adjusting entry is made:

Oct. 31	Fees Receivable	200	
	Fees Earned		200
	(To accrue fees earned but not billed or collected)		

After the adjusting entry is posted, the accounts show:

Accounts after adjustment

Fees Receivable			Fees Earned		
10/31	**200**			10/31	1,000
				31	400
				31	**200**

The asset Fees Receivable shows that $200 is owed by clients at the balance sheet date. The balance of $1,600 in Fees Earned represents the total fees earned during the month ($1,000 + $400 + $200). If the adjusting entry is not made, assets and owner's equity on the balance sheet, and revenues and net income on the income statement, will all be understated.

In the next accounting period, the clients will be billed. When this occurs, the entry to record the billing should take into account the fact that $200 of fees earned in October have already been recorded in the October 31 adjusting entry. To illustrate, assume that bills totaling $3,000 are mailed to clients on November 10. Of this amount, $200 represents fees earned in October and recorded as Fees Earned in the October 31 adjusting entry. The remaining $2,800 represents fees earned in November. Thus, the following entry is made:

Nov. 10	Fees Receivable	2,800	
	Fees Earned		2,800
	(To record fees billed)		

This entry records the amount of fees earned between November 1 and November 10. The subsequent collection of fees from clients (including the $200 earned in October) will be recorded with a debit to Cash and a credit to Fees Receivable.

ACCRUED EXPENSES—RECOGNITION OF UNRECORDED EXPENSES

Expenses incurred but unrecorded at the statement date are called **accrued expenses** or **accrued liabilities.** Accrued expenses result from the same causes as accrued revenues. In fact, an accrued expense on the books of one company is an accrued revenue to another company. Interest, rent, taxes, and salaries are examples of accrued expenses.

Adjustments for accrued expenses are necessary to record the obligations that exist at the balance sheet date and to recognize the expenses that are applicable to the current accounting period. **A liability-expense relationship exists with accrued expenses.** Prior to adjustment both liabilities and expenses are understated. Therefore, **the adjusting entry for accrued expenses results in a debit (increase) to an expense account and a credit (increase) to a liability account.**

Accrued Interest

Pioneer Advertising Agency signed a three-month note payable in the amount of $5,000 on October 1. The note requires interest at an annual rate of 12%. The amount of the interest accumulation is determined by three factors: (1)

the face value of the note, (2) the interest rate, which is always expressed as an annual rate, and (3) the length of time the note is outstanding. In this instance, the total interest due on the $5,000 note at its due date three months hence is $150 ($5,000 × 12% × 3/12) or $50 for one month. The formula for computing interest and its applicability to Pioneer Advertising Agency for the month of October[2] are shown below:

Formula for computing interest

Face Value of Note	×	Annual Interest Rate	×	Time in Terms of One Year	=	Interest
$5,000	×	12%	×	1/12	=	$50

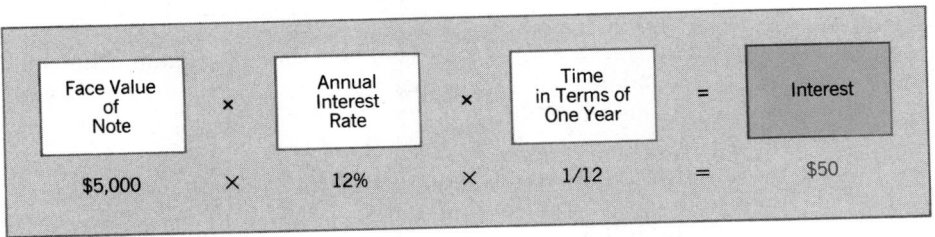

Observe in this case that the time period is expressed as a fraction of a year. The accrued expense adjusting entry at October 31 is as follows:

Oct. 31	Interest Expense	50	
	Interest Payable		50
	(To accrue interest on notes payable)		

After this adjusting entry is posted, the accounts show:

Accounts after adjustment

Interest Expense		Interest Payable	
10/31 50			10/31 50

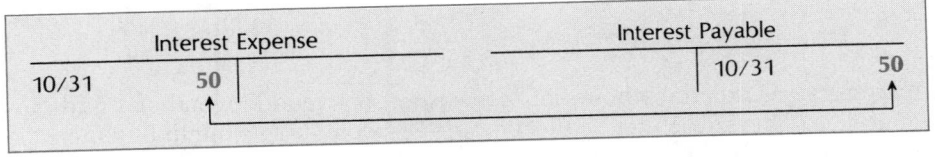

Interest Expense shows the interest charges applicable to the month of October. The amount of interest owed at the statement date is shown in Interest Payable. The Interest Payable account is used instead of crediting Notes Payable to disclose the two types of obligations (interest and principal) in the accounts and statements. If this adjusting entry is not made, liabilities and interest expense will be understated, and net income and total owner's equity will be overstated.

Accrued Salaries

Some types of services, such as insurance and rent, are paid for before they are used, whereas other types are paid for after the service has been performed. The services performed by employees is one that is paid for after performance. In the case of Pioneer Advertising, salaries were last paid on October 24 in the amount of $4,000 and will not be paid again until November. However, employees have performed services from October 25 to the end of October and have thus earned, but not received, compensation for that period of time. For the services performed October 25 through October 31, assume that the salaries owed total $1,200. These salaries represent an accrued expense and a related liability to Pioneer Advertising at October 31. This additional expense of $1,200 in October is debited to the Salaries Ex-

[2]The computation of interest will be discussed in more depth in later chapters.

pense account and credited to the Salaries Payable account by an adjusting entry as follows:

Oct. 31	Salaries Expense	1,200	
	Salaries Payable		1,200
	(To record accrued salaries)		

After this adjusting entry is posted, the accounts show:

Accounts after adjustment

Salaries Expense			Salaries Payable	
10/24	4,000		10/31	**1,200**
31	**1,200**			

After this adjustment, the balance in Salary Expense of $5,200 is the actual salary expense for October. The balance in Salaries Payable of $1,200 is the amount of the liability for salaries owed as of October 31. If the $1,200 adjustment for salaries is not recorded, Pioneer's expenses will be understated $1,200, and its liabilities will be understated $1,200.

If the accrued salaries are paid on November 1, the payment would be recorded as a debit to Salaries Payable for $1,200 and a credit to Cash for $1,200. An additional complication arises, however, if the next payment of salaries also includes salaries for November. To illustrate, assume that Pioneer Advertising pays $2,500 in salaries on November 8. Of this amount, $1,200 was recorded as Salaries Expense and Salaries Payable by means of the October 31 adjusting entry. The remaining $1,300 was earned between November 1 and November 8, and should be recognized as part of Salaries Expense for November. Thus, the following entry is made on November 8:

Nov. 8	Salaries Payable	1,200	
	Salaries Expense	1,300	
	Cash		2,500
	(To record November 8 payroll)		

This entry eliminates the liability for Salaries Payable that was recorded in the October 31 adjusting entry and records the proper amount of Salaries Expense for the period between November 1 and November 8.

SUMMARY OF BASIC RELATIONSHIPS

Pertinent data on each of the four basic types of adjusting entries are summarized on the next page. From an analysis of the adjusting entries shown in that summary, it can be seen that **each adjusting entry affects one balance sheet account and one income statement account.**

JOURNALIZING AND POSTING ADJUSTING ENTRIES

The journalizing and posting of adjusting entries for Pioneer Advertising Agency on October 31 are summarized on the next two pages. All adjustments

Summary of adjusting entries

Type of Adjustment	Account Relationship	Account Balances Before Adjustment	Adjusting Entry
1. Prepaid Expenses	Assets and Expenses	Assets Overstated Expenses Understated	Dr. Expenses Cr. Assets
2. Unearned Revenues	Liabilities and Revenues	Liabilities Overstated Revenues Understated	Dr. Liabilities Cr. Revenues
3. Accrued Revenues	Assets and Revenues	Assets Understated Revenues Understated	Dr. Assets Cr. Revenues
4. Accrued Expenses	Expenses and Liabilities	Expenses Understated Liabilities Understated	Dr. Expenses Cr. Liabilities

are identified in the ledger by the reference J2 because they are journalized on page 2 of the general journal. A center caption entitled Adjusting Entries may be inserted between the last transaction entry and the first adjusting entry to identify these entries. When reviewing the general ledger, you should note that the adjustments are highlighted in color.

GENERAL JOURNAL J2

Date	Account Titles and Explanation	Ref.	Debit	Credit
1987	Adjusting Entries			
Oct. 31	Advertising Supplies Expense	61	1,500	
	Advertising Supplies	8		1,500
	(To record supplies used)			
31	Insurance Expense	63	50	
	Prepaid Insurance	10		50
	(To record insurance expired)			
31	Depreciation Expense	65	40	
	Accumulated Depreciation—Office Equipment	15.1		40
	(To record monthly depreciation)			
31	Unearned Fees	28	400	
	Fees Earned	50		400
	(To record fees earned)			
31	Fees Receivable	6	200	
	Fees Earned	50		200
	(To accrue fees earned but not billed or collected)			
31	Interest Expense	64	50	
	Interest Payable	27		50
	(To accrue interest on notes payable)			
31	Salaries Expense	60	1,200	
	Salaries Payable	29		1,200
	(To record accrued salaries)			

GENERAL LEDGER

Cash — No. 1

Date	Explanation	Ref.	Debit	Credit	Balance
Oct. 1		J1	10,000		10,000
2		J1	1,200		11,200
3		J1		900	10,300
4		J1		600	9,700
20		J1		500	9,200
24		J1		4,000	5,200
31		J1	10,000		15,200

Fees Receivable — No. 6

Date	Explanation	Ref.	Debit	Credit	Balance
Oct. 31		J2	**200**		200

Advertising Supplies — No. 8

Date	Explanation	Ref.	Debit	Credit	Balance
Oct. 5		J1	2,500		2,500
31		J2		**1,500**	1,000

Prepaid Insurance — No. 10

Date	Explanation	Ref.	Debit	Credit	Balance
Oct. 4		J1	600		600
31		J2		**50**	550

Office Equipment — No. 15

Date	Explanation	Ref.	Debit	Credit	Balance
Oct. 1		J1	5,000		5,000

Accumulated Depreciation – Office Equipment — No. 15.1

Date	Explanation	Ref.	Debit	Credit	Balance
Oct. 31		J2		**40**	40

Notes Payable — No. 25

Date	Explanation	Ref.	Debit	Credit	Balance
Oct. 1		J1		5,000	5,000

Accounts Payable — No. 26

Date	Explanation	Ref.	Debit	Credit	Balance
Oct. 5		J1		2,500	2,500

Interest Payable — No. 27

Date	Explanation	Ref.	Debit	Credit	Balance
Oct. 31		J2		**50**	50

Unearned Fees — No. 28

Date	Explanation	Ref.	Debit	Credit	Balance
Oct. 1		J1		1,200	
31		J2	**400**		800

Salaries Payable — No. 29

Date	Explanation	Ref.	Debit	Credit	Balance
Oct. 31		J2		**1,200**	1,200

C. R. Byrd, Capital — No. 40

Date	Explanation	Ref.	Debit	Credit	Balance
Oct. 1		J1		10,000	10,000

C. R. Byrd, Drawing — No. 41

Date	Explanation	Ref.	Debit	Credit	Balance
Oct. 20		J1	500		500

Fees Earned — No. 50

Date	Explanation	Ref.	Debit	Credit	Balance
Oct. 31		J1		10,000	10,000
31		J2		**400**	10,400
31		J2		**200**	10,600

Salaries Expense — No. 60

Date	Explanation	Ref.	Debit	Credit	Balance
Oct. 24		J1	4,000		4,000
31		J2	**1,200**		5,200

Advertising Supplies Expense — No. 61

Date	Explanation	Ref.	Debit	Credit	Balance
Oct. 31		J2	**1,500**		1,500

Rent Expense — No. 62

Date	Explanation	Ref.	Debit	Credit	Balance
Oct. 3		J1	900		900

Insurance Expense — No. 63

Date	Explanation	Ref.	Debit	Credit	Balance
Oct. 31		J2	**50**		50

Interest Expense — No. 64

Date	Explanation	Ref.	Debit	Credit	Balance
Oct. 31		J2	**50**		50

Depreciation Expense — No. 65

Date	Explanation	Ref.	Debit	Credit	Balance
Oct. 31		J2	**40**		40

THE ADJUSTED TRIAL BALANCE

After all adjusting entries have been journalized and posted, another trial balance is prepared from the ledger accounts. This trial balance is called an **adjusted trial balance.** An adjusted trial balance shows the balances of all accounts, including those that have been adjusted, at the end of the account-

ing period. The purpose of an adjusted trial balance is to show the effects of all financial events that have occurred during the accounting period. The procedures for preparing an adjusted trial balance are identical to those described in Chapter 2 for preparing a trial balance.

An adjusted trial balance proves the equality of the total debit balances and the total credit balances in the ledger after all adjustments have been made. The proof provided by an adjusted trial balance, like the proof contained in a trial balance, extends only to the mathematical accuracy of the ledger. Because the accounts contain all data that are needed for financial statements, the adjusted trial balance provides the primary basis for the preparation of financial statements.

The adjusted trial balance for Pioneer Advertising Agency presented below has been prepared from the ledger accounts shown on page 95. To facilitate the comparison of account balances before and after adjustment, the adjusted data are arranged parallel to the trial balance, and the amounts affected by the adjusting entries are highlighted in color in the After Adjustment columns.

Trial balance and adjusted trial balance compared

PIONEER ADVERTISING AGENCY
Trial Balance
October 31, 1987

	Before Adjustment		After Adjustment	
	Dr.	Cr.	Dr.	Cr.
Cash	$15,200		$15,200	
Fees Receivable			**200**	
Advertising Supplies	2,500		**1,000**	
Prepaid Insurance	600		**550**	
Office Equipment	5,000		5,000	
Accumulated Depreciation — Office Equipment				$ **40**
Notes Payable		$ 5,000		5,000
Accounts Payable		2,500		2,500
Interest Payable				**50**
Unearned Fees		1,200		**800**
Salaries Payable				**1,200**
C. R. Byrd, Capital		10,000		10,000
C. R. Byrd, Drawing	500		500	
Fees Earned		10,000		**10,600**
Salaries Expense	4,000		**5,200**	
Advertising Supplies Expense			**1,500**	
Rent Expense	900		900	
Insurance Expense			**50**	
Interest Expense			**50**	
Depreciation Expense			**40**	
	$28,700	$28,700	$30,190	$30,190

FINANCIAL STATEMENTS FROM AN ADJUSTED TRIAL BALANCE

Financial statements can be prepared directly from an adjusted trial balance. The preparation of financial statements from the adjusted trial balance of Pioneer Advertising Agency and the interrelationship of data are presented in the following two exhibits. As shown in Exhibit I the income statement is prepared from the revenue and expense accounts; the owner's equity statement is derived from the owner's capital and drawing accounts and the net income or net loss shown in the income statement. As shown in Exhibit II the balance sheet is then prepared from the asset and liability accounts and the ending owner's capital balance as reported in the owner's equity statement.

Preparation of the income statement and owner's equity statement from the adjusted trial balance

Exhibit I

Pioneer Advertising Agency
Adjusted Trial Balance
October 31, 1987

Account	Debit	Credit
Cash	$15,200	
Fees Receivable	200	
Advertising Supplies	1,000	
Prepaid Insurance	550	
Office Equipment	5,000	
Accumulated Depreciation—Office Equipment		$ 40
Notes Payable		5,000
Accounts Payable		2,500
Interest Payable		50
Unearned Fees		800
Salaries Payable		1,200
C. R. Byrd, Capital		10,000
C. R. Byrd, Drawing	500	
Fees Earned		10,600
Salaries Expense	5,200	
Advertising Supplies Expense	1,500	
Rent Expense	900	
Insurance Expense	50	
Interest Expense	50	
Depreciation Expense	40	
	$30,190	$30,190

Preparation of the Income Statement From the Adjusted Trial Balance

Pioneer Advertising Agency
Income Statement
For the Month Ended October 31, 1987

Revenues		
Fees earned		$10,600
Expenses		
Salaries expense	$5,200	
Advertising supplies expense	1,500	
Rent expense	900	
Insurance expense	50	
Interest expense	50	
Depreciation expense	40	
Total expenses		7,740
Net income		$ 2,860

Preparation of the Owner's Equity Statement From the Adjusted Trial Balance

Pioneer Advertising Agency
Owner's Equity Statement
For the Month Ended October 31, 1987

C. R. Byrd, Capital, October 1	$10,000
Add: Net income	2,860
	12,860
Less: Drawings	500
C. R. Byrd, Capital, October 31	$12,360

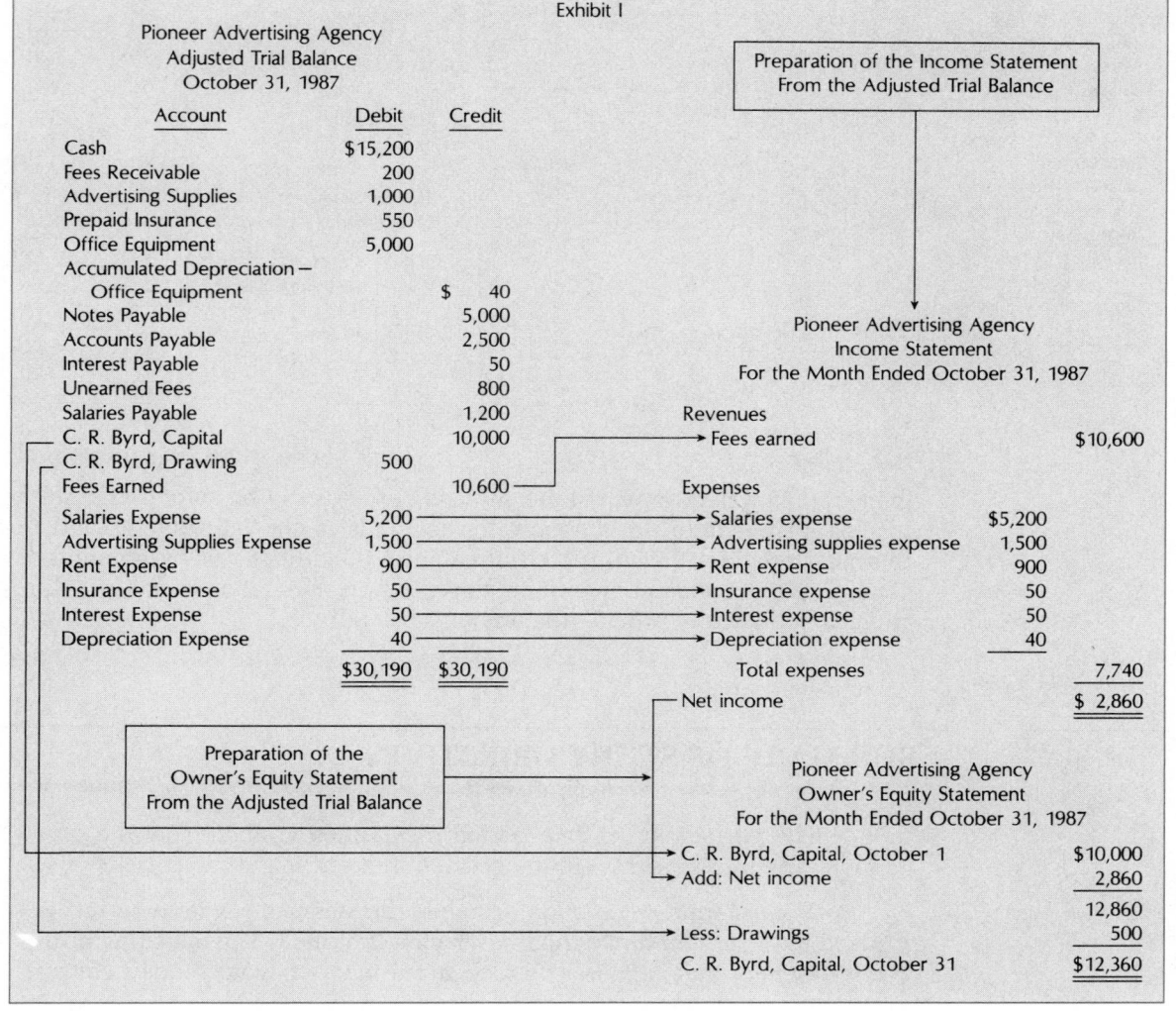

Preparation of the balance sheet from the adjusted trial balance

Exhibit II

Preparation of the Balance Sheet From the Adjusted Trial Balance

Pioneer Advertising Agency
Adjusted Trial Balance
October 31, 1987

Account	Debit	Credit
Cash	$15,200	
Fees Receivable	200	
Advertising Supplies	1,000	
Prepaid Insurance	550	
Office Equipment	5,000	
Accumulated Depreciation – Office Equipment		$ 40
Notes Payable		5,000
Accounts Payable		2,500
Interest Payable		50
Unearned Fees		800
Salaries Payable		1,200
C. R. Byrd, Capital		10,000
C. R. Byrd, Drawing	500	
Fees Earned		10,600
Salaries Expense	5,200	
Advertising Supplies Expense	1,500	
Rent Expense	900	
Insurance Expense	50	
Interest Expense	50	
Depreciation Expense	40	
	$30,190	$30,190

Pioneer Advertising Agency
Balance Sheet
October 31, 1987

Assets		
Cash		$15,200
Fees receivable		200
Advertising supplies		1,000
Prepaid insurance		550
Office equipment	$5,000	
Less: Accumulated Depreciation	40	4,960
Total assets		$21,910
Liabilities and Owner's Equity		
Liabilities		
Notes Payable		$ 5,000
Accounts Payable		2,500
Interest Payable		50
Unearned Fees		800
Salaries Payable		1,200
Total liabilities		9,550
Owner's Equity		
C. R. Byrd, Capital		12,360
Total liabilities and owner's equity		$21,910

Capital Balance at Oct. 31 from Owner's Equity Statement on page 97

In computer systems much of the adjusting process can be automated. All the accountant needs to do is supply the amounts of the adjustments and the computer provides the adjusted trial balance. In addition, where amounts are determined by calculations, as in depreciation and interest, software programs automatically provide the amounts as well.

SUMMARY OF STUDY OBJECTIVES

1. The periodicity or time period assumption assumes that the economic life of a business can be divided into artificial time periods.

2. The revenue recognition principle dictates that revenue be recognized in the accounting period in which it is earned. The matching principle dictates that expenses be recognized when they make their contribution to revenues.

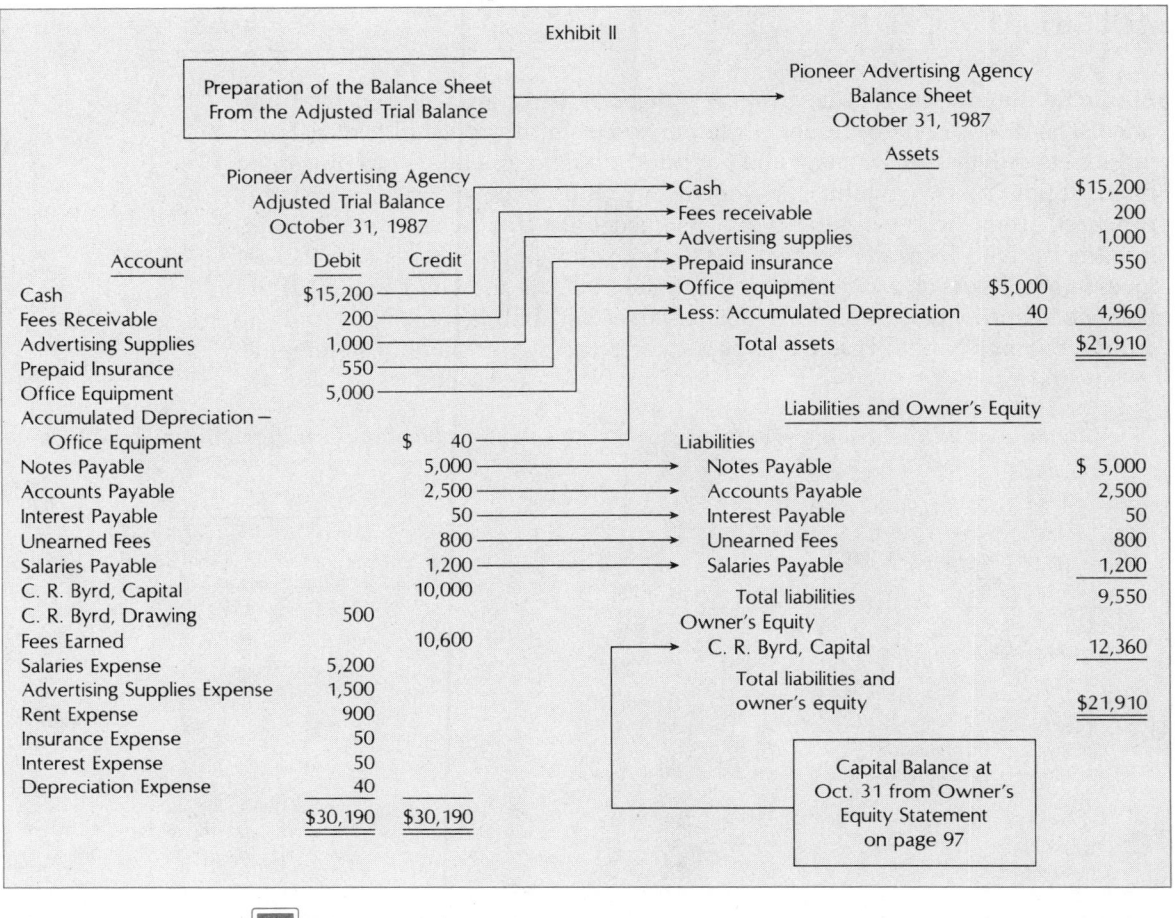

3. Adjusting entries are made at the end of an accounting period to insure that revenues are recorded in the period in which they are earned and that expenses are recognized in the period in which they are incurred.

4. The major types of adjusting entries are prepaid expenses, unearned revenues, accrued revenues, and accrued expenses.

5. Depreciation is the process of allocating the cost of an asset to expense over its useful life in a rational and systematic manner.

6. An adjusted trial balance is a trial balance that includes the balances of all accounts, including those that have been adjusted, at the end of an accounting period. The purpose of an adjusted trial balance is to show the effects of all financial events that have occurred during the accounting period.

APPENDIX 3–A

ALTERNATIVE TREATMENT OF PREPAID EXPENSES AND UNEARNED REVENUES

In our discussion of adjusting entries for prepaid expenses and unearned revenues we illustrated transactions for which the initial entries were made to balance sheet accounts. That is, in the case of prepaid expenses, the prepayment was debited to an asset account, and in the case of unearned revenue, the collection was credited to a liability account. Alternatively, at the time an expense is prepaid, it may be debited to an expense account, and at the time of a receipt for future services, it may be credited to a revenue account. The circumstances when such entries are justified and the different adjusting entries that may be required are described below. The alternative treatment of prepaid expenses and unearned revenues has the same effect on the financial statements as the procedures described in the chapter.

PREPAID EXPENSES

Prepaid expenses become expired costs either through the passage of time, as in the case of insurance, or through consumption, as in the case of advertising supplies. If at the time of purchase, the company expects to consume the supplies before the next financial statement date, **it may be more convenient to initially debit an expense account rather than an asset account.** Assume,

for example, that Pioneer Advertising expects that all of the supplies purchased on October 5 will be used before October 31. A debit of $2,500 to Advertising Supplies Expense rather than to the asset account, Advertising Supplies, on October 5 will eliminate the need for an adjusting entry on October 31, if all the supplies are used. At October 31, the Advertising Supplies Expense account will show a balance of $2,500, which is equal to the cost of supplies used between October 5 and October 31.

Assume, however that the company does not use up all the supplies, and an inventory of $1,000 of advertising supplies remains on October 31. In such a case, an adjusting entry is needed. Prior to adjustment:

1. The expense account, Advertising Supplies Expense, is overstated $1,000, and
2. The asset account, Advertising Supplies, is understated $1,000.

Thus, the following adjusting entry is made:

Oct. 31	Advertising Supplies	1,000	
	Advertising Supplies Expense		1,000
	(To record supplies inventory)		

After posting the adjusting entry, the accounts show:

Accounts after adjustment

Advertising Supplies				Advertising Supplies Expense			
10/31	**1,000**			10/5	2,500	10/31	**1,000**

After adjustment, the asset account, Advertising Supplies, shows a balance of $1,000, which is equal to the cost of supplies on hand at October 31. In addition, Advertising Supplies Expense shows a balance of $1,500, which is equal to the cost of supplies used between October 5 and October 31. If the adjusting entry is not made, expenses will be overstated and net income will be understated by $1,000 in the October income statement. Moreover, both assets and owner's equity will be understated by $1,000 on the October 31 balance sheet.

A comparative summary of the entries and accounts for advertising supplies is as follows:

Adjustment approaches—a comparison

Prepayment Initially Debited to Asset Account (Per Chapter)				**Prepayment Initially Debited to Expense Account (Per Appendix)**			
Oct. 5	Advertising Supplies	2,500		Oct. 5	Advertising Supplies Expense	2,500	
	Accounts Payable		2,500		Accounts Payable		2,500
Oct. 31	Advertising Supplies Expense	1,500		Oct. 31	Advertising Supplies	1,000	
	Advertising Supplies		1,500		Advertising Supplies Expense		1,000

After posting the entries, the accounts appear as follows:

Accounts after adjustment

(Per Chapter)

Advertising Supplies

10/5	2,500	10/31	1,500
Bal.	1,000		

Advertising Supplies Expense

10/31	1,500		

(Per Appendix)

Advertising Supplies

10/31	1,000		

Advertising Supplies Expense

10/5	2,500	10/31	1,000
Bal.	1,500		

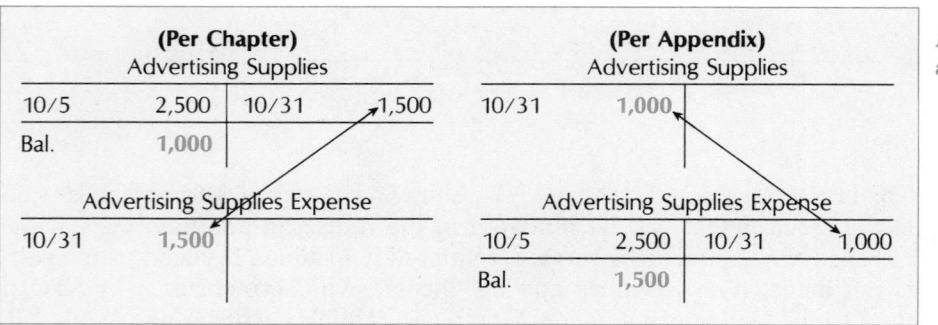

Note that the account balances under each alternative are the same at October 31; that is, Advertising Supplies $1,000, and Advertising Supplies Expense $1,500.

UNEARNED REVENUES

Unearned revenues become earned either through the passage of time, as in the case of unearned rent, or through rendering the service, as in the case of unearned fees. Like prepaid expenses, a revenue account may be credited when cash is received for future services and a different adjusting entry may be necessary.

To illustrate, assume when Pioneer Advertising received $1,200 in fees for future services on October 2 that the services were expected to be performed before October 31.[3] In such case, Fees Earned would be credited. If these fees are in fact earned before October 31, no adjustment is needed. However, if at the statement date, $800 of the services have not been provided, an adjusting entry is required. Prior to adjustment, the account relationships are:

1. The revenue account, Fees Earned, is overstated $800, and
2. The liability account, Unearned Fees, is understated $800.

Thus, the following adjusting entry is made:

Oct. 31	Fees Earned	800	
	Unearned Fees		800
	(To record unearned fees)		

[3]This example focuses only on the alternative treatment of unearned revenues. In the interest of simplicity, the entries to Fees Earned pertaining to the immediate earning of fees ($1,000) and the adjusting entry for accrued fees ($400) have been ignored.

After posting the adjusting entry, the accounts show:

Unearned Fees				Fees Earned			
		10/31	800	10/31	800	10/2	1,200

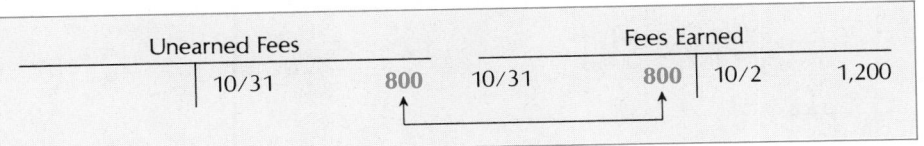

The liability account, Unearned Fees, shows a balance of $800, which is equal to the services that will be rendered in the future. In addition, the balance in Fees Earned equals the services rendered in October. If the adjusting entry is not made, both revenues and net income will be overstated by $800 in the October income statement. Moreover, liabilities will be understated by $800, and owner's equity will be overstated by $800 on the October 31 balance sheet.

A comparative summary of the entries and accounts for fees earned and unearned is as follows:

Adjustment approaches— A comparison

Unearned Revenue Initially Credited to Liability Account (Per Chapter)				Unearned Revenue Initially Credited to Revenue Account (Per Appendix)			
Oct. 2	Cash	1,200		Oct. 2	Cash	1,200	
	Unearned Fees		1,200		Fees Earned		1,200
Oct. 31	Unearned Fees	400		Oct. 31	Fees Earned	800	
	Fees Earned		400		Unearned Fees		800

After posting the entries, the accounts will show:

Accounts after adjustment

(Per Chapter)

Unearned Fees			
10/31	400	10/2	1,200
		Bal.	800

Fees Earned			
		10/31	400

(Per Appendix)

Unearned Fees			
		10/31	800

Fees Earned			
10/31	800	10/2	1,200
		Bal.	400

Note that the balances in the accounts are the same; that is, Unearned Fees, $800, and Fees Earned, $400.

SUMMARY OF ADDITIONAL ADJUSTMENT RELATIONSHIPS

Alternative adjusting entries necessitate additions to prepaid expenses and unearned revenues in the summary of basic relationships presented below. The additions are shown in color.

Summary of basic relationships for prepayments

Type of Adjustment	Account Relationship	Reason for Adjustment	Account Balances Before Adjustment	Adjusting Entry
1. Prepaid Expenses	Assets and Expenses	(a) Prepaid expenses initially recorded in asset accounts have been used.	Assets Overstated Expenses Understated	Dr. Expenses Cr. Assets
		(b) Prepaid expenses initially recorded in expense accounts have not been used.	Assets Understated Expenses Overstated	Dr. Assets Cr. Expenses
2. Unearned Revenues	Liabilities and Revenues	(a) Unearned revenues initially recorded in liability accounts have been earned.	Liabilities Overstated Revenues Understated	Dr. Liabilities Cr. Revenues
		(b) Unearned revenues initially recorded in revenue accounts have not been earned.	Liabilities Understated Revenues Overstated	Dr. Revenues Cr. Liabilities

Alternative adjusting entries are not applicable to accrued revenues and accrued expenses because no entries are made before these types of adjusting entries are made. Hence, the summary data shown on page 94 for these two types of adjustments remains unchanged.

GLOSSARY

Accrued expenses (liabilities), p. 91

Accrued revenues (receivables), p. 90

Adjusted trial balance, p. 95

Adjusting entries, p. 83

Book value, p. 88

Calender year, p. 82

Contra asset account, p. 88

Depreciable cost, p. 87

Depreciation, p. 87

Fiscal years, p. 82

Interim periods, p. 82

Matching principle, p. 83

Periodicity (time period) assumption, p. 82

Prepaid expenses, p. 84

Revenue recognition principle, p. 83

Unearned revenues, p. 89

Useful life, p. 87

DEMONSTRATION PROBLEM

Terry Thomas opens the Green Thumb Lawn Care Company on April 1. At April 30, the trial balance shows the following balances for selected accounts:

Prepaid Insurance	$ 3,600
Equipment	28,000
Notes Payable	20,000
Unearned Fees	4,200
Fees Earned	1,800

Analysis reveals the following additional data pertaining to these accounts:

1. Prepaid insurance is the cost of a two-year insurance policy, effective April 1.
2. The equipment was purchased on April 1. It is expected to have a useful life of four years with an estimated salvage value of $4,000.
3. The note payable is dated April 1. It is a six-months, 12% note.
4. Seven customers paid for the company's six month's lawn service package of $600 beginning in April. These customers were serviced in April.
5. Lawn services rendered other customers but not billed at April 30 totaled $1,500.

INSTRUCTIONS

Prepare the adjusting entries at April 30. Show computations.

SOLUTION TO DEMONSTRATION PROBLEM

General Journal — J2

Date	Account Titles and Explanation	Ref.	Debit	Credit
	Adjusting Entries			
Apr. 30	Insurance Expense		150	
	Prepaid Insurance			150
	(To record insurance expired: $3,600 ÷ 24 = $150 per month)			
30	Depreciation Expense		500	
	Accumulated Depreciation—Equipment			500
	(To record monthly depreciation: depreciable cost = $24,000 ($28,000 − $4,000); $24,000 ÷ 4 = $6,000 per year or $500 per month)			
30	Interest Expense		200	
	Interest Payable			200
	(To accrue interest on notes payable: $20,000 × 12% × 1/12 = $200)			
30	Unearned Fees		700	
	Fees Earned			700
	(To record fees earned: $600 ÷ 6 = $100; $100 per month × 7 = $700)			
30	Fees Receivable		1,500	
	Fees Earned			1,500
	(To accrue fees earned but not billed or collected)			

*Note: All **asterisked** Questions, Exercises, and Problems relate to material contained in the Appendix to each chapter.

QUESTIONS

1. Explain the periodicity assumption and indicate its importance to accounting.

2. What is meant by (a) an interim period? (b) a fiscal year?

3. Robert Conklin, a lawyer accepts a legal engagement in March, performs the work in April and is paid in May. If Conklin's law firm prepares monthly financial statements, when should it recognize revenue from this engagement? Why?

4. In completing the engagement in (3) above, Conklin incurs $1,000 of expenses in March, $2,000 in April and none in May. How much expense should be deducted from revenues in the month the revenue is recognized? Why?

5. Adjusting entries are required by the cost principle of accounting. Do you agree? Explain.

6. Why may a trial balance not contain up-to-date and complete financial information?

7. Distinguish between the two categories of adjusting entries and identify the types of adjustments applicable to each category.

8 What account relationship exists with prepaid expenses? What is the debit/credit effect of a prepaid expense adjusting entry?

9. Depreciation is a process of valuation that results in the reporting of the fair market value of the asset. Do you agree? Explain.

10. Explain the differences between depreciation expense and accumulated depreciation.

11. Crone Company purchases equipment for $13,000. The asset has a useful life of 8 years and an estimated salvage value of $1,000. Indicate how depreciation expense is computed.

12. What account relationships exist with unearned revenues? What is the debit/credit effect of an unearned revenue adjusting entry.

13. A company fails to recognize revenue earned but not yet received. Which of the following accounts are involved in the adjusting entry: (a) asset, (b) liability, (c) revenue, or (d) expense? For the accounts selected, indicate whether they would be debited or credited in the entry.

14. A company fails to recognize an expense incurred but not paid. Indicate which of the following accounts is debited and which is credited in the adjusting entry: (a) asset, (b) liability, (c) revenue, and (d) expense.

15. A company makes an accrued revenue adjusting entry for $800 and an accrued expense adjusting entry for $600. How much was net income understated prior to these entries? Explain.

16. On January 10, a company pays $3,200 for salaries of which $1,000 was reported as Salaries Payable on December 31. Give the entry to record the payment.

17. One half of the adjusting entry is given below. Indicate the account title for the other half of the entry.

(a) Prepaid Advertising is credited.
(b) Commissions Receivable is debited.
(c) Unearned Subscription Fees is debited.
(d) Salaries Expense is debited.
(e) Depreciation Expense is debited.
(f) Interest Earned is credited.

18. For each of the following items before adjustment, indicate the type of adjusting entry (prepaid expense, unearned revenue, accrued revenue, and accrued expense) that is needed to correct the misstatement. If an item could result in more than one type of adjusting entry, indicate each of the types.

(a) Liabilities are overstated.
(b) Assets are understated.
(c) Liabilities are understated.
(d) Expenses are understated.
(e) Assets are overstated.
(f) Revenue is understated.

19. An adjusting entry may affect more than one balance sheet or income statement account. Do you agree? Why or why not?

20. Why is it possible to prepare financial statements directly from an adjusted trial balance?

***21.** The Adler Company debits Supplies Expense for all purchases of supplies and credits Rent Revenue for all advanced rentals. For each type of adjustment, indicate the status of the accounts before adjustment and give the adjusting entry.

EXERCISES

E3-1 The Evans Company accumulates the following adjustment data at December 31.

1. Interest of $100 has accrued on a note payable.
2. Salaries of $800 are unpaid.
3. Prepaid insurance totaling $400 has expired.
4. An advance payment of rent from a tenant for $300 has been earned.
5. Store supplies of $250 have been used.
6. Fees earned but unbilled total $600.
7. Utility expenses of $175 are unpaid.
8. Fees of $260 collected in advance have been earned.

INSTRUCTIONS

For each of the foregoing items indicate:

(a) The type of adjustment (prepaid expense, unearned revenue, accrued revenue, or accrued expense).
(b) The account relationship (asset/revenue, liability/revenue, and so on).
(c) The account balances before adjustment.
(d) The adjusting entry.

Prepare your answer in tabular form, as shown on page 94.

E3-2 Selected accounts of the Coles Company are shown below:

Supplies

7/1 Bal.	900	7/31	500
7/10	300		

Salaries Payable

		7/31	1,200

Fees Receivable

7/31	400		

Unearned Fees

7/31	700	7/1 Bal.	1,500
		7/20	600

Salaries Expense

7/15	1,200		
7/31	1,200		

Fees Earned

		7/14	3,000
		7/31	700
		7/31	400

Supplies Expense

7/31	500		

INSTRUCTIONS

After analyzing the accounts, journalize (a) the July transactions and (b) the adjusting entries that were made on July 31. (Hint: July transactions were for cash.)

E3-3 The ledger of the Carlisle Company on March 31 of the current year includes the following selected accounts before adjusting entries have been prepared.

	Debit	Credit
Supplies	$ 2,400	
Prepaid Insurance	3,600	
Delivery Equipment	18,000	
Accumulated Depreciation		$ 7,200
Notes Payable		20,000
Unearned Rent Revenue		9,000
Rent Revenue		52,000
Wage Expense	14,000	
Interest Expense	-0-	

An analysis of the accounts shows the following:

1. Interest of $500 is accrued on the notes payable.
2. Supplies on hand total $600.
3. Insurance expires at the rate of $100 per month.
4. The delivery equipment depreciates $300 per month.
5. One-third of the unearned revenue was earned during the quarter.
6. Accrued wages at March 31 total $1,200.

INSTRUCTIONS

Prepare the adjusting entries at March 31, assuming that adjusting entries are made quarterly.

E3-4 On July 1, 1987, Bach Corp. pays $12,000 to the Maris Insurance Agency for a three-year property insurance contract. Both companies have fiscal years ending on December 31.

INSTRUCTIONS

(a) For Bach Corporation, prepare the entry on July 1 and the adjusting entries on December 31, 1987 and December 31, 1988.

(b) For Maris Insurance Agency, prepare the entry on July 1 and the adjusting entries on December 31, 1987 and December 31, 1988.

E3-5 Dr. Tim Tresh, D.D.S., opened a dental practice on January 1, 1987. During the first month of operations the following transactions occurred.

1. Purchased dental equipment for $80,000, paying $10,000 in cash and signing a $70,000, 12%, three-year note payable. The equipment is expected to last ten years and have a salvage value of $8,000 at the end of its useful life.
2. Purchased a one-year malpractice insurance policy for $6,000.
3. Purchased $1,500 of dental supplies. On January 31, determined that $400 of supplies were on hand.
4. Performed services for patients who had dental plan insurance. At January 31, $750 of such services was earned but not yet billed to the insurance companies.
5. Utility bills expected but not billed prior to January 31 totaled $650.

INSTRUCTIONS

Prepare the adjusting entries on January 31. (Omit explanations.)

E3-6 The income statement of Lee's Laundry for the month of July shows net income of $1,400 based on Fees Earned $5,200, Wages Expense $2,000, Supplies Expense $1,000, and Utilities Expense $800. In reviewing the statement, you discover the following:

1. Depreciation on equipment of $100 was omitted.
2. Accrued but unpaid wages at July 31 of $200 were not included.
3. Laundry services earned but unpaid and unrecorded totaled $600.
4. Insurance expired during July $400.
5. Utilities expense includes the payment of a $250 bill that was properly accrued on June 30.
6. Supplies expense includes $200 of supplies that are still on hand at July 31.

INSTRUCTIONS

Prepare a correct income statement for July.

E3-7 The balance sheets of Clarke Company include the following:

	12/31/87	12/31/86
Interest receivable	$2,400	$ -0-
Supplies	1,800	600
Wages payable	500	800
Unearned fees	-0-	1,500

The income statement for 1987 shows the following:

Interest revenue	$ 9,400
Supplies expense	4,000
Wages expense	26,000
Fees earned	52,000

INSTRUCTIONS

Determine the following for 1987:

(a) Cash received for interest.

(b) Cash paid for supplies.

(c) Cash paid for wages.

(d) Cash received for fees.

E3-8 A partial adjusted trial balance of the Millie Day Care Center at January 31, 1987 shows the following:

Adjusted Trial Balance	Debit	Credit
Supplies	$ 700	
Prepaid Insurance	1,500	
Equipment	30,000	
Accumulated Depreciation		$7,500
Salaries Payable		600
Unearned Fees		500
Supplies Expense	850	
Insurance Expense	300	
Depreciation Expense	250	
Salaries Expense	1,800	
Fees Earned		2,000

INSTRUCTIONS

Answer the following questions, assuming the year begins January 1:

(a) If the amount in Supplies Expense is the January 31 adjusting entry, and $600 of supplies was purchased in January, what was the balance in Supplies on January 1?

(b) If the amount in Insurance Expense is the January 31 adjusting entry, and the original insurance premium was for one year, what was the total premium and when was the policy purchased?

(c) If the equipment has a useful life of ten years and no salvage value, when was the equipment purchased?

(d) If $2,100 of salaries was paid in January, what was the balance in Salaries Payable at December 31, 1986?

(e) If $1,700 of fees was received in January for services performed in January, what was the balance in Unearned Fees at December 31, 1986?

***E3-9** At the Michele Company, prepayments are debited to expense when paid and unearned revenues are credited to revenue when received. During January of the current year, the following transactions occurred:

Jan. 2 Paid $2,400 for fire insurance protection for the year.

Jan. 10 Paid $1,500 for supplies.

Jan. 15 Received $4,000 in fees for services to be performed in the future.

On January 31, it is determined that $1,000 of the services has been earned and that there is $600 of supplies on hand.

INSTRUCTIONS

(a) Journalize and post the January transactions.
(b) Journalize and post the adjusting entries at January 31.
(c) Determine the ending balance in each of the accounts affected.

PROBLEMS

P3-1 The trial balance of Canyon Tours at the end of its first month of operations is presented below:

CANYON TOURS
Trial Balance
June 30, 1987

	Debit	Credit
Cash	$ 2,500	
Prepaid Insurance	7,200	
Office Equipment	1,800	
Buses	132,000	
Notes Payable		$ 60,000
Unearned Fees		10,000
Eldon Santo, Capital		67,500
Fees Earned		15,900
Salaries Expense	8,000	
Advertising Expense	700	
Gas and Oil Expense	1,200	
	$153,400	$153,400

Other data:

1. The insurance policy has a three-year term beginning June 1, 1987.
2. The office equipment was purchased on June 1. It will have no salvage value at the end of its five-year life.
3. Four used buses were purchased on June 1. Each bus is expected to have a salvage value of $3,000 at the end of its four-year life.
4. Interest of $600 accrues on the notes payable each month.
5. Deposits of $1,000 were received for advanced tour reservations from ten school groups. At June 30, three of these deposits have been earned.
6. Bus drivers are paid a total of $300 per day. At June 30, three days' salaries are unpaid.
7. A senior citizen's organization that had not made an advance deposit took a Canyon tour on June 30 for $1,200. This group has not been billed for the services rendered.

INSTRUCTIONS

(a) Journalize the adjusting entries at June 30, 1987.
(b) Prepare a partial ledger. Enter the trial balance amounts for each account that requires an adjustment and post the adjusting entries. (Use J2 as the posting reference.)
(c) Prepare an adjusted trial balance at June 30, 1987.

P3–2 The Mountain View Motel opened for business on May 1, 1987. Its trial balance on May 31 is as follows:

MOUNTAIN VIEW MOTEL
Trial Balance
May 31, 1987

	Debit	Credit
Cash	$ 2,500	
Prepaid Insurance	1,200	
Supplies	1,800	
Land	15,000	
Lodge	68,000	
Furniture	14,400	
Accounts Payable		$ 3,400
Advanced Rentals		3,300
Mortgage Payable		30,000
Carla Damon, Capital		62,000
Rent Revenue		8,100
Salaries Expense	2,700	
Utilities Expense	800	
Advertising Expense	400	
	$106,800	$106,800

Other data:

1. Insurance expires at the rate of $200 per month.
2. An inventory of supplies on May 31 shows that $150 of towels and linens is either missing or unfit for further use.
3. Annual depreciation rates are 5% on the lodge and 20% on furniture. At the end of its useful life, the lodge is expected to have a salvage value of $8,000 and the furniture is expected to have zero salvage value.
4. The mortgage interest rate is 12%. (The mortgage was taken out on May 1.)
5. Advanced rentals of $1,500 have been earned.
6. Salaries of $100 are accrued and unpaid at May 31.

INSTRUCTIONS

(a) Journalize the adjusting entries on May 31.
(b) Prepare an adjusted trial balance on May 31.
(c) Prepare an income statement and an owner's equity statement for the month of May and a balance sheet at May 31.

P3–3 The Brandt Co. was organized on July 1, 1987. Quarterly financial statements are prepared. The trial balance and adjusted trial balance on September 30 are shown below.

	Trial Balance		Adjusted Trial Balance	
	Dr.	Cr.	Dr.	Cr.
Cash	$ 6,700		$ 6,700	
Commissions Receivable	200		600	
Prepaid Rent	1,500		1,000	
Supplies	1,300		900	
Equipment	13,000		13,000	

	Trial Balance Dr.	Trial Balance Cr.	Adjusted Trial Balance Dr.	Adjusted Trial Balance Cr.
Accumulated Depreciation—Equipment				$ 375
Notes Payable		$ 3,000		3,000
Accounts Payable		1,510		1,510
Salaries Payable				500
Interest Payable				30
Unearned Rent		800		700
R. Brandt, Capital		14,000		14,000
R. Brandt, Drawing	600		600	
Commissions Earned		14,000		14,400
Rent Revenue		500		600
Salaries Expense	9,000		9,500	
Rent Expense	1,000		1,500	
Depreciation Expense			375	
Supplies Expense			400	
Utilities Expense	510		510	
Interest Expense			30	
	$33,810	$33,810	$35,115	$35,115

INSTRUCTIONS

(a) Journalize the adjusting entries that were made.

(b) Prepare an income statement and owner's equity statement for the three months ending September 30 and a balance sheet at September 30.

(c) Answer the following questions:

(1) What is the estimated useful life of the equipment, assuming a $1,000 salvage value? All of the equipment was purchased on July 1.

(2) If the note bears interest at 12%, how many months has it been outstanding?

P3-4 A review of the ledger of the Baldwin Company at December 31, 1987 produces the following data pertaining to the preparation of annual adjusting entries:

1. Prepaid Insurance, $9,000. The company has separate insurance policies on its buildings and its motor vehicles. Policy B4564 on the building was purchased on July 1, 1986 for $7,200. The policy has a term of three years. Policy A2958 on the vehicles was purchased on January 1, 1987 for $3,000. This policy has a term of two years.
2. Sales Commissions Payable, $0. Sales commissions are 3% of net sales, payable on the tenth day of the month following the sales. In 1987, $29,000 of sales commissions were paid, of which $3,000 applied to December 1986 net sales. Total net sales for 1987 were $950,000.
3. Unearned Subscription Revenue, $32,400. The company began selling magazine subscriptions in 1987 on an annual basis. The selling price of a subscription is $36. A review of subscription contracts reveals the following:

Subscription Date	Number of Subscriptions
October 1	200
November 1	300
December 1	400
	900

4. Notes Receivable, $40,000. This balance consists of a $25,000 note for six months at an annual interest rate of 12%, dated September 1, and a $15,000 three-month note at an annual interest rate of 10%, dated December 1.
5. Salaries Payable, $0. There are eight salaried employees. Salaries are paid every Friday for the current week. Five employees receive a salary of $500 each per week, and three employees earn $400 each per week. December 31 is a Wednesday. The employees do not work weekends. All employees worked the last three days of December.

INSTRUCTIONS

Prepare the adjusting entries at December 31, 1987.

P3-5 On November 1, 1987, the account balances of Locker Equipment Repair were as follows:

No.	Debits		No.	Credits	
10	Cash	$ 2,490	30	Accounts Payable	$ 1,900
12	Notes Receivable	1,000	31	Salaries Payable	400
13	Accounts Receivable	1,500	32	Customer Advances	200
14	Interest Receivable	10	19	Accumulated Depreciation	300
16	Supplies	1,300	40	R. Locker, Capital	12,500
18	Equipment	9,000			
		$15,300			$15,300

During November the following summary transactions were completed.

Nov. 8 Paid $900 for salaries due employees, of which $500 is for November.

10 Received $1,200 cash from customers on account and $1,400 cash for services performed during November.

15 Purchased equipment $2,000 and supplies $1,000 on account.

20 Paid cash on account $2,500, and November rent $250, salaries $700, and utilities $190.

27 Performed services on account and billed customers for services rendered $800.

29 Received $500 from customers for future service.

Adjustment data consist of:

1. Supplies on hand $1,600.
2. Accrued salaries payable $300.
3. Depreciation is at a monthly rate of 1% with no salvage value. (Hint: depreciate new equipment purchased for a half a month.)
4. Customers' advances earned $120.
5. The note was a three-month note dated October 1, 1987 with interest at 12%.

INSTRUCTIONS

(a) Enter the November 1 balances in the ledger accounts.
(b) Journalize the November transactions.
(c) Post to the ledger accounts using assumed account numbers for revenue and expenses.
(d) Prepare a trial balance at November 30.
(e) Journalize and post adjusting entries.
(f) Prepare an adjusted trial balance.
(g) Prepare an income statement and an owner's equity statement for November and a balance sheet at November 30.

***P3–6** The Miller Graphics Company was organized on January 1, 1987 by Nancy Miller. At the end of the first six months of operations, the trial balance contained the following accounts:

	Debits		Credits
Cash	$ 8,700	Notes Payable	$ 15,000
Fees Receivable	15,000	Accounts Payable	6,000
Supplies	1,000	Nancy Miller, Capital	25,000
Equipment	42,000	Graphic Fees Earned	52,800
Insurance Expense	1,800	Consulting Fees Earned	5,000
Salaries Expense	28,000		
Supplies Expense	1,500		
Advertising Expense	2,400		
Rent Expense	1,800		
Utilities Expense	1,600		
	$103,800		$103,800

Analysis reveals the following additional data:

1. All graphics fees are credited to Graphic Fees Earned when received. At June 30, $5,200 of fees has not been earned.
2. The $1,500 balance in Supplies Expense represents supplies purchased in January. The $1,000 balance in Supplies represents supplies purchased in May. At June 30, there was $1,300 of supplies on hand.
3. The note payable was issued on February 1. It is a 12%, 6-month note.
4. The balance in Insurance Expense is the premium on a one-year policy dated March 1, 1987.
5. Consulting fees are credited to revenue when received. At June 30, consulting fees of $1,100 are unearned.
6. Graphic fees earned but unbilled at June 30 total $2,000.
7. Depreciation is computed at the rate of 5% per year. Salvage value is expected to be 10% of cost. All equipment was purchased on January 1, except a $6,000 acquisition on May 1.

INSTRUCTIONS

(a) Journalize the adjusting entries at June 30.

(b) Prepare an adjusted trial balance.

(c) Prepare an income statement and statement of owner's equity for the six months ended June 30 and a balance sheet at June 30.

ALTERNATE PROBLEMS

P3–1A The Chapman Security Service began operations on January 1, 1987. At the end of Chapman's first year of operations, the trial balance shows the following:

CHAPMAN SECURITY SERVICE
Trial Balance
December 31, 1987

	Debit	Credit
Cash	$ 11,300	
Fees Receivable	2,200	
Prepaid Insurance	3,600	
Automobiles	52,000	
Notes Payable		$ 40,000
Unearned Fees		1,500
C. Chapman, Capital		15,000
Fees Earned		82,000
Salaries Expense	56,000	
Repair Expense	4,100	
Gas and Oil Expense	9,300	
	$138,500	$138,500

Other data:

1. Fees earned but unbilled $1,500 at December 31.
2. Insurance coverage began on January 1 under a two-year policy.
3. Automobiles are depreciated over a useful life of three years. Total salvage value is expected to be $7,000. All vehicles were purchased on January 1.
4. The note bears interest at 12% per year, assuming note dated January 1.
5. $500 of the unearned fees has been earned.
6. Drivers' salaries total $400 per day. At December 31, four days' salaries are unpaid.
7. Repairs to automobiles of $600 have been incurred, but bills have not been received prior to December 31. (Use Repairs Payable.)

INSTRUCTIONS

(a) Journalize the adjusting entries at December 31, 1987.

(b) Prepare a partial ledger. Enter the trial balance amounts for each account that requires an adjustment and post the adjusting entries. (Use J15 as the posting reference.)

(c) Prepare an adjusted trial balance at December 31, 1987.

P3-2A The Cannon Beach Resort opened for business on June 1 with eight air-conditioned units. Its trial balance on August 31 is as follows:

CANNON BEACH RESORT
Trial Balance
August 31, 1987

	Debit	Credit
Cash	$ 19,600	
Prepaid Insurance	4,500	
Supplies	2,600	
Land	20,000	
Cottages	120,000	
Furniture	16,000	
Accounts Payable		$ 4,500
Advanced Rentals		4,600

	Debit	Credit
Mortgage Payable		60,000
Tina Lee, Capital		100,000
Tina Lee, Drawing	5,000	
Rent Revenue		76,200
Salaries Expense	44,800	
Utilities Expense	9,200	
Repair Expense	3,600	
	$245,300	$245,300

Other data:

1. Insurance expires at the rate of $250 per month.
2. An inventory count on August 31 shows $400 of supplies on hand.
3. Annual depreciation rates were cottages (4%) and furniture (10%). Salvage value is estimated to be 10% of cost.
4. Advanced rentals of $4,000 were earned prior to August 31.
5. Salaries of $200 were unpaid at August 31.
6. Rentals of $800 were due from tenants at August 31.
7. The mortgage interest rate is 14% per year.

INSTRUCTIONS

(a) Journalize the adjusting entries on August 31 for the 3-month period June 1–August 31.

(b) Prepare an adjusted trial balance on August 31.

(c) Prepare an income statement and an owner's equity statement for the three months ending August 31 and a balance sheet as of August 31.

P3-3A The Gage Advertising Agency was founded by Thomas Gage in January of 1983. Presented below are both the adjusted and unadjusted trial balances as of December 31, 1987.

GAGE ADVERTISING AGENCY
Trial Balance
December 31, 1987

	Unadjusted		Adjusted	
	Dr.	Cr.	Dr.	Cr.
Cash	$ 6,000		$ 6,000	
Fees Receivable	18,000		19,000	
Art Supplies	8,000		5,000	
Prepaid Insurance	2,250		1,500	
Printing Equipment	57,000		57,000	
Accumulated Depreciation		20,000		26,000
Accounts Payable		4,000		4,000
Interest Payable		0		250
Notes Payable		5,000		5,000
Unearned Advertising Fees		6,000		4,000
Salaries Payable		0		800
T. Gage, Capital		32,500		32,500
T. Gage, Drawing	12,000		12,000	
Advertising Fees		58,000		61,000

	Unadjusted		Adjusted	
	Dr.	Cr.	Dr.	Cr.
Salaries Expense	11,000		11,800	
Insurance Expense			750	
Interest Expense	250		500	
Depreciation Expense			6,000	
Art Supplies Expense	6,000		9,000	
Rent Expense	5,000		5,000	
	$125,500	$125,500	$133,550	$133,550

INSTRUCTIONS

(a) Journalize the adjusting entries that were made.

(b) Prepare an income statement and a statement of owner's equity for the year ending December 31, 1987 and a balance sheet at December 31.

(c) Answer the following questions:

(1) If the useful life of equipment is 8.5 years, what is the expected salvage value?

(2) If the note has been outstanding five months, what is the annual interest rate on that note?

(3) If the company paid $11,700 in salaries in 1987, what was the balance in Salaries Payable on December 31, 1986?

P3-4A A review of the ledger of Sterns Company at December 31, 1987 produces the following data pertaining to the preparation of annual adjusting entries.

1. Prepaid Advertising, $13,200. This balance consists of payments on two advertising contracts. The contracts provide for monthly advertising in two trade magazines. The terms of the contracts are as follows:

Contract	Date	Amount	Issues
A650	May 1	$6,000	12
B974	Sept. 1	7,200	18

The first advertisement runs in the month in which the contract is signed.

2. Notes Payable, $70,000. There are two notes outstanding. A $40,000, 12%, one-year note was signed on June 1, and a $30,000, 10%, nine-month note was signed on November 1.

3. Unearned Rent Revenue, $305,000. The company began subleasing office space in its new building on November 1. Each tenant is required to make a $5,000 security deposit that is not refundable until occupancy is terminated. At December 31, the company had the following rental contracts that are paid in full for the entire term of the lease.

Date	Term (in months)	Monthly Rent	Number
Nov. 1	6	$5,000	3
Dec. 1	6	$7,500	4

4. Salaries Payable, $0. There are seven salaried employees. Payday for each month is on the fifth day of the following month. Four employees are paid salaries of $4,000 each per month, and three employees earn $3,000 each per month.

5. Sales Commissions Expense, $16,000. Salespersons are paid commissions equal to 2% of net sales payable on the tenth day of the month following the sales. Commis-

sions have been paid in full when due. In 1987, commission payments totaled $17,500, which includes commissions payable of $1,500 on December 31, 1986. Net sales were $860,000 in 1987.

INSTRUCTIONS

Prepare the adjusting entries at December 31, 1987. (Show all computations.)

DECISION CASE

The Happy Home Travel Court was organized on April 1, 1986 by Alice Adams. Alice was a good manager but a poor accountant. From the trial balance prepared by a part-time bookkeeper, Alice prepared the following income statement for the quarter that ended March 31, 1987.

HAPPY HOME TRAVEL COURT
Income Statement
For the Quarter Ended March 31, 1987

Revenues		
Travel court rental fees		$75,000
Operating expenses		
Advertising	$ 3,200	
Wages	28,800	
Utilities	900	
Telephone	500	
Repairs	3,000	
Total operating expenses		36,400
Net income		$38,600

Alice knew that something was wrong with the statement because net income had never exceeded $15,000 in any one quarter. Knowing that you are an experienced accountant, she asks you to review the income statement and other data.

You first look at the trial balance. In addition to the account balances reported above in the income statement, the ledger contains the following additional selected balances at March 31, 1987.

Supplies	$ 4,200	Accumulated Depreciation— Equipment	$ 3,000
Prepaid Insurance	7,200		
Equipment	25,000	Notes Payable	10,000

You then make inquiries and discover the following:

1. Travel court rental fees include advanced rentals for summer month occupancy $18,000.
2. There were $1,100 of supplies on hand at March 31.
3. Prepaid insurance resulted from the payment of a one-year policy on January 1, 1987.
4. The balance in Accumulated Depreciation—Equipment was depreciation for nine months in 1986. All the equipment was purchased when the travel court was started.

5. The mail on April 1, 1987 brought the following bills: advertising for week of March 24, $90; repairs made March 10, $240; and utilities, $150.
6. There are four employees who receive wages totaling $320 per day. At March 31, three days wages have been incurred but not paid.
7. The note payable is a three-month 10% note dated January 1, 1987.

INSTRUCTIONS

(a) Prepare a correct income statement for the quarter ended March 31, 1987.

(b) Explain to Alice the accounting principles that she did not recognize in preparing her income statement and their effect on her results.

CHAPTER 4

Nassau Community College, New York

CHAPTER 4

COMPLETION OF THE ACCOUNTING CYCLE

STUDY OBJECTIVES

After studying this chapter, you should be able to:

1. **Prepare a work sheet.**
2. **Explain the closing entries for a proprietorship.**
3. **Describe the content and purpose of a post-closing trial balance.**
4. **State the required steps in the accounting cycle.**
5. **Contrast the closing entries for a corporation with those of a proprietorship and a partnership.**
6. **Explain the approaches to preparing correcting entries.**
7. **Identify the sections of a classified balance sheet.**
8. **Discuss the analysis of a balance sheet.**

In Chapter 3 we illustrated the preparation of different types of adjustments that the accountant must prepare at the end of the accounting period to make the ledger accounts accurate and complete. The adjusting entries for Pioneer Advertising Agency were journalized, posted to the ledger, and an adjusted trial balance was prepared. Financial statements were then prepared directly from the adjusted trial balance. With so many details involved in these end-of-the-period accounting procedures, it is easy to make errors. Locating and correcting errors can cost much time and effort. One way to minimize errors in the records and to simplify the end-of-the-period procedures is to use a work sheet.

In this chapter, we will explain the role of the work sheet in accounting and the remaining steps in the accounting cycle, again using the Pioneer Advertising Agency as an example. Then we will consider (1) correcting entries, (2) classified balance sheets, and (3) fundamental relationships in analyzing a balance sheet.

USE OF A WORK SHEET

A **work sheet** is a multiple-column form that may be used in the adjustment process and in preparing financial statements. As its name suggests, the work sheet is a working tool or a supplementary device for the accountant. **A work sheet is not a permanent accounting record.** In small companies with relatively few accounts and adjustments a work sheet may not be needed. In large companies with numerous accounts and many adjustments it is almost indispensable.

The basic form of a work sheet and the procedure for preparing a work sheet are as follows:

Form and procedure for a work sheet

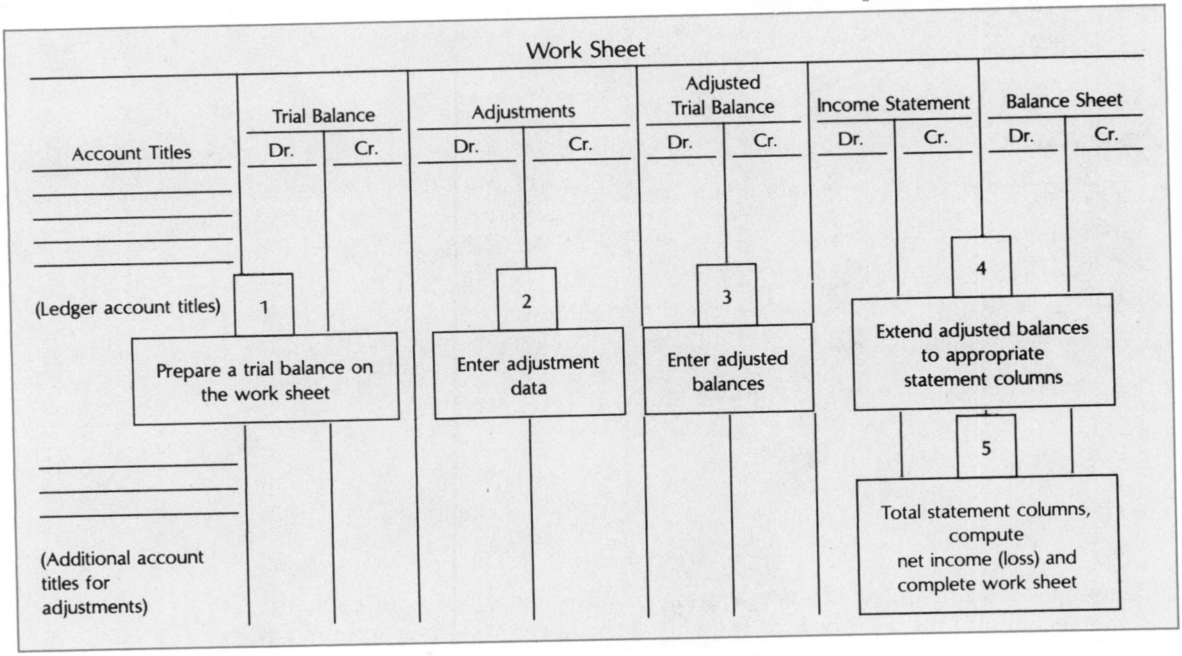

Each of the steps in preparing the work sheet must be performed in the prescribed sequence.

The use of a work sheet is an optional step in the accounting cycle. When a work sheet is used, financial statements are prepared from the work sheet. The adjusting entries that are entered in the work sheet columns are then journalized and posted after the financial statements have been prepared.

PREPARATION OF A WORK SHEET ILLUSTRATED

We will use the October 31 trial balance and adjustment data of Pioneer Advertising to illustrate the preparation of a work sheet. Each step of the process is described below.

Steps 1–3

The first three steps in preparing a work sheet are as follows:

Step 1. Prepare a trial balance on the work sheet. The account title space and trial balance columns are used to prepare a trial balance. The data for the trial balance are taken directly from the ledger accounts. The trial balance for Pioneer Advertising Agency is the same as the trial balance given on page 85.

Step 2. Enter the adjustments in the adjustment columns. When a work sheet is used, all adjustments are entered in the adjustment columns. In entering the adjustments, applicable trial balance accounts should be used. If additional accounts are needed, they should be inserted on the lines immediately below the trial balance totals. Each adjustment is indexed and keyed to facilitate the subsequent journalizing of the adjusting entry in the general journal. **It is important to recognize that the adjustments are not journalized until after the work sheet is completed and the financial statements have been prepared.**

The adjustments for Pioneer Advertising Agency are the same as the adjustments illustrated on page 94. They are keyed in the adjustment columns of the work sheet as follows:

(a) An additional account, Advertising Supplies Expense, is debited $1,500 for the cost of supplies used, and Advertising Supplies is credited $1,500.

(b) An additional account, Insurance Expense, is debited $50 for the insurance that has expired, and Prepaid Insurance is credited $50.

(c) Two additional accounts are needed; Depreciation Expense is debited $40 for the month's depreciation, and Accumulated Depreciation—Office Equipment is credited $40.

(d) Unearned Fees is debited $400 for fees earned, and Fees Earned is credited $400.

(e) An additional account, Fees Receivable, is debited $200 for fees earned but not billed, and Fees Earned is credited $200.

(f) Two additional accounts are needed; Interest Expense is debited $50 for accrued interest, and Interest Payable is credited $50.

(g) Salaries Expense is debited $1,200 for accrued salaries, and an additional account, Salaries Payable, is credited $1,200.

After all the adjustments have been entered, the adjustment columns are totaled and the equality of the column totals is established.

Step 3. Enter adjusted balances in the adjusted trial balance columns. The adjusted balance of an account is obtained by combining the amounts entered in the first four columns of the work sheet for each account. For example, the Prepaid Insurance account in the trial balance columns has a

$600 debit balance. When this is combined with the $50 credit in the adjustment columns, the result is a $550 debit balance recorded in the adjusted trial balance columns. **For each account on the work sheet, the amount in the adjusted trial balance columns is equal to the account balance that will appear in the ledger after the adjusting entries have been journalized and posted.** The balances in these columns are the same as those in the adjusted trial balance on page 96.

After the balances of all accounts have been entered in the adjusted trial balance columns, the columns are totaled and their equality is established. The agreement of the column totals facilitates the completion of the work sheet. Unless these columns are in agreement, the statement columns will not balance. The work sheet for Pioneer Advertising Agency after steps 1-3 is shown below.

Steps 1-3 in preparation of work sheet

PIONEER ADVERTISING AGENCY
Partial Work Sheet
For the Month Ended October 31, 1987

Account Titles	Trial Balance Dr.	Trial Balance Cr.	Adjustments Dr.	Adjustments Cr.	Adjusted Trial Balance Dr.	Adjusted Trial Balance Cr.	Income Statement Dr.	Income Statement Cr.	Balance Sheet Dr.	Balance Sheet Cr.
Cash	15,200				15,200					
Advertising Supplies	2,500			(a) 1,500	1,000					
Prepaid Insurance	600			(b) 50	550					
Office Equipment	5,000				5,000					
Notes Payable		5,000				5,000				
Accounts Payable		2,500				2,500				
Unearned Fees		1,200	(d) 400			800				
C. R. Byrd, Capital		10,000				10,000				
C. R. Byrd, Drawing	500				500					
Fees Earned		10,000		(d) 400 (e) 200		10,600				
Salaries Expense	4,000		(g) 1,200		5,200					
Rent Expense	900				900					
Totals	28,700	28,700								
Advertising Supplies Expense			(a) 1,500		1,500					
Insurance Expense			(b) 50		50					
Accum. Depreciation—Office Equipment				(c) 40		40				
Depreciation Expense			(c) 40		40					
Interest Expense			(f) 50		50					
Interest Payable				(f) 50		50				
Fees Receivable			(e) 200		200					
Salaries Payable				(g) 1,200		1,200				
Totals			3,440	3,440	30,190	30,190				
	Step 1		**Step 2**		**Step 3**					

Key to adjustments:
(a) Supplies Used; (b) Insurance Expired; (c) Depreciation Expensed; (d) Fees Earned; (e) Fees Accrued; (f) Interest Payable; (g) Salaries Accrued.

Steps 4-5

The last two steps in preparing a work sheet are as follows:

Step 4. Extend adjusted trial balance amounts to appropriate financial statement columns. This step involves the horizontal extension of amounts to the last four columns of the work sheet as shown on page 126. The adjusted balances of balance sheet accounts such as Cash and Notes Payable are entered in the balance sheet debit and credit columns, respectively. Similarly, the adjusted balances of expense and revenue accounts such as Salaries Expense and Fees Earned are entered in the appropriate income statement columns.

Step 5. Total the statement columns, compute the net income (or loss), and complete the work sheet. Each of the statement columns must be totaled. The net income or loss for the period is then found by computing the difference between the totals of the two income statement columns. If total credits exceed total debits, net income has resulted. In such a case, as illustrated on page 126, the words "net income" are inserted in the account title space, and the amount is entered in the income statement debit column and the balance sheet credit column. The debit amount balances the income statement columns and the credit amount balances the balance sheet columns. In addition, the credit in the balance sheet column indicates the increase in owner's equity resulting from net income. Conversely, if total debits in the income statement columns exceed total credits, a net loss has occurred. The amount of the net loss is entered in the income statement credit column and the balance sheet debit column.

After the net income or net loss has been entered, new column totals are determined for the four statement columns. The totals shown in the debit and credit income statement columns will be identical. The totals shown in the debit and credit balance sheet columns will also be identical. If either the income statement columns or the balance sheet columns are not equal after the net income or net loss has been entered, an error has been made in completing the work sheet. The completed work sheet for Pioneer Advertising Agency is shown on page 126.

FINANCIAL STATEMENTS FROM A WORK SHEET

After a work sheet has been completed, the statement columns contain all the data that are required for the preparation of financial statements. The income statement is prepared from the income statement columns, and the balance sheet and owner's equity statement are prepared from the balance sheet columns. The financial statements prepared from the work sheet for Pioneer Advertising Agency would be identical with the statements presented on 97 and 98 and are not repeated here.

A work sheet facilitates the preparation of financial statements because the statements can be prepared before the adjusting entries are journalized and posted. It is important to recognize that the completed work sheet is not a substitute for formal financial statements. Data in the statement columns are not arranged properly for financial statement purposes. For example, the contra asset account, Accumulated Depreciation, with its credit balance is listed with liabilities and owner's equity account balances. Moreover, the owner's drawing account with its debit balance is listed with the asset balances. The work sheet is essentially a working tool of the accountant and is not distributed to management and other parties.

Steps 4–5 in preparation of work sheet

PIONEER ADVERTISING AGENCY
Work Sheet
For The Month Ended October 31, 1987

Account Titles	Trial Balance Dr.	Trial Balance Cr.	Adjustments Dr.	Adjustments Cr.	Adjusted Trial Balance Dr.	Adjusted Trial Balance Cr.	Income Statement Dr.	Income Statement Cr.	Balance Sheet Dr.	Balance Sheet Cr.
Cash	15,200				15,200				15,200	
Advertising Supplies	2,500			(a) 1,500	1,000				1,000	
Prepaid Insurance	600			(b) 50	550				550	
Office Equipment	5,000				5,000				5,000	
Notes Payable		5,000				5,000				5,000
Accounts Payable		2,500				2,500				2,500
Unearned Fees		1,200	(d) 400			800				800
C. R. Byrd, Capital		10,000				10,000				10,000
C. R. Byrd, Drawing	500				500				500	
Fees Earned		10,000		(d) 400 (e) 200		10,600		10,600		
Salaries Expense	4,000		(g) 1,200		5,200		5,200			
Rent Expense	900				900		900			
Totals	28,700	28,700								
Advertising Supplies Expense			(a) 1,500		1,500		1,500			
Insurance Expense			(b) 50		50		50			
Accum. Depreciation—Office Equipment				(c) 40		40				40
Depreciation Expense			(c) 40		40		40			
Interest Expense			(f) 50		50		50			
Interest Payable				(f) 50		50				50
Fees Receivable			(e) 200		200				200	
Salaries Payable				(g) 1,200		1,200				1,200
Totals			3,440	3,440	30,190	30,190	7,740	10,600	22,450	19,590
Net Income							2,860			2,860
Totals							10,600	10,600	22,450	22,450

Steps 4 and 5

ADJUSTING ENTRIES FROM A WORK SHEET

A work sheet is not a journal, and it cannot be used as a basis for posting to ledger accounts. To adjust the accounts, it is necessary to journalize and post the adjustments to the ledger. The adjusting entries are prepared from the adjustment columns of the work sheet. Identification of the journal entries is facilitated by the reference letters in the adjustment columns and the key to the adjustments that appears at the bottom of the work sheet. Writing the key to the adjustments at the bottom of the work sheet is not required. As indicated previously, the journalizing and posting of adjusting entries follows the preparation of financial statements when a work sheet is used. The adjusting entries on October 31 for Pioneer Advertising Agency are the same as those illustrated on page 94.

The work sheet can be computerized using an electronic spreadsheet program. The LOTUS 1-2-3 supplement for this textbook is one of the most popular versions of such spreadsheet packages. With a program like LOTUS 1-2-3, you can produce any type of work sheet (accounting or otherwise) that you could produce with paper and pencil on a columnar pad. The tremendous advantage of an electronic work sheet over the paper and pencil version is the ability to change selected data and have the computer update the balance of your computations instantly. More specific applications of electronic spreadsheets will be noted as we proceed.

CLOSING THE BOOKS OF A PROPRIETORSHIP

In Chapter 2, we explained that revenue and expense accounts and the owner's drawing account are **temporary owner's equity accounts.** Because these accounts pertain only to a given accounting period, they are also called **nominal accounts.** In contrast, you will recall that balance sheet accounts are called **permanent** or **real accounts** because they are carried forward into future accounting periods. At the end of the accounting period, the balance in each nominal account is transferred to the permanent owner's equity account, Owner's Capital, through the preparation of closing entries. **Closing entries** formally recognize in the ledger the transfer of net income (or loss) and owner's drawings to owner's capital as shown in the owner's equity statement. These entries also produce a zero balance in each temporary account so they can be used to accumulate data in the next accounting period.

Journalizing and posting closing entries is a required step in the accounting cycle. This step is performed after financial statements have been prepared. In contrast to the steps in the cycle that you have already studied, closing entries are generally journalized and posted only at the end of a company's annual accounting period. This practice facilitates the preparation of annual financial statements because all temporary accounts will contain data for the entire year. In preparing closing entries, each income statement account could be closed directly to owner's capital, but this would result in excessive detail in the permanent owner's capital account. Accordingly, the revenue and expense accounts are closed to another temporary account, **Income Summary,** and only the net income (or loss) is transferred to owner's capital.

CLOSING ENTRIES

Closing entries are journalized in the general journal. A center caption entitled Closing Entries may be inserted in the journal between the last adjusting entry and the first closing entry to identify these entries. Then the closing entries are posted to the ledger accounts. Closing entries may be prepared directly from the adjusted balances in the ledger, from the income statement and balance sheet columns of the work sheet, or from the income and owner's

equity statements. Separate closing entries could be prepared for each nominal account, but the following four entries accomplish the desired result more efficiently:

1. Debit each revenue account for its balance, and credit Income Summary for total revenues.
2. Debit Income Summary for total expenses, and credit each expense account for its balance.
3. Debit Income Summary, and credit owner's capital for the amount of net income; conversely, credit Income Summary and debit owner's capital if a net loss exists.
4. Debit owner's capital for the balance in owner's drawing account and credit owner's drawing for the same amount.

The four entries are referenced in the diagram of the closing process shown below and in the journal entries on page 129. The posting of closing entries is illustrated on page 130.

Diagram of closing process—proprietorship

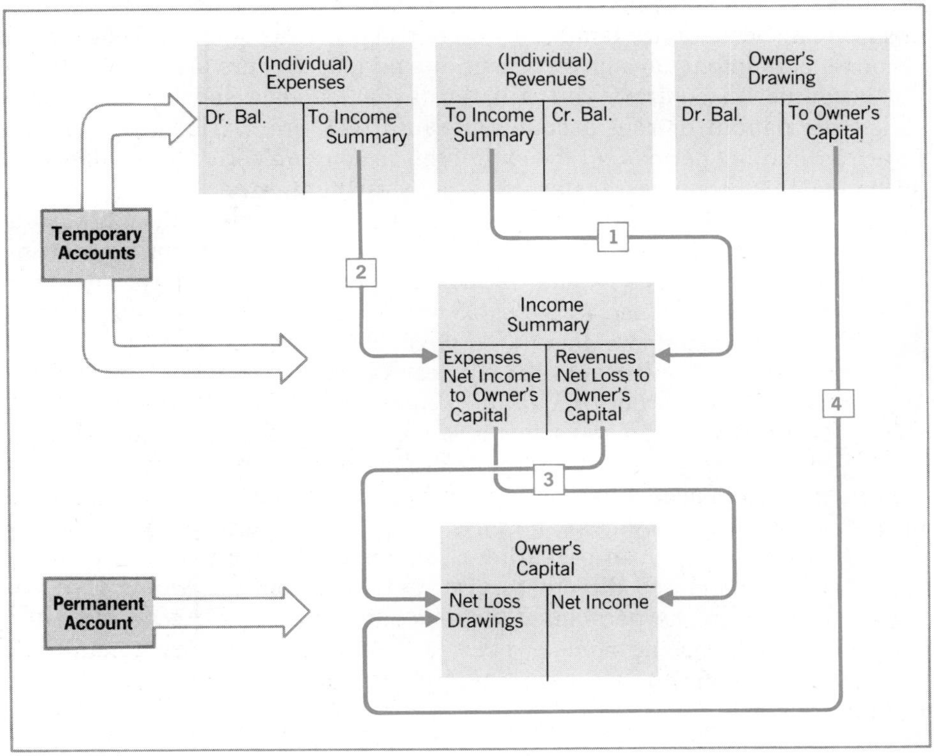

CLOSING ENTRIES ILLUSTRATED

As explained above, closing entries are generally prepared only at the end of a company's annual accounting period. However, to illustrate the journalizing and posting of closing entries, we will assume that Pioneer Advertising Agency closes its books monthly. The closing entries at October 31 are as follows:

GENERAL JOURNAL J3

Date	Account Titles and Explanation	Ref.	Debit	Credit
	Closing Entries			
	(1)			
Oct. 31	Fees Earned	51	10,600	
	Income Summary	49		10,600
	(To close revenue account)			
	(2)			
31	Income Summary	49	7,740	
	Salaries Expense	60		5,200
	Advertising Supplies Expense	61		1,500
	Rent Expense	62		900
	Insurance Expense	63		50
	Interest Expense	64		50
	Depreciation Expense	65		40
	(To close expense accounts)			
	(3)			
31	Income Summary	49	2,860	
	C. R. Byrd, Capital	40		2,860
	(To close net income to capital)			
	(4)			
31	C. R. Byrd, Capital	40	500	
	C. R. Byrd, Drawing	41		500
	(To close drawings to capital)			

In preparing closing entries, you should be careful to avoid (1) unintentionally doubling the revenue and expense balances rather than zeroing them, and (2) closing owner's drawing through the Income Summary account. Owner's drawings are not expenses and they are not a factor in determining net income.

POSTING OF CLOSING ENTRIES

The posting of the closing entries and the ruling of the accounts are illustrated on the following page. Note that all temporary accounts have zero balances. In addition, you should realize that the balance in owner's capital represents the total equity of the owner at the end of the accounting period. This balance will equal the amount reported for owner's equity on the balance sheet and the ending capital equity reported on the owner's equity statement as shown in the financial statements on page 97. The Income Summary account is used only in closing. No entries are journalized and posted to this account during the year.

If Pioneer Advertising Agency had incurred a net loss from operations for October, the debits to the Income Summary account would have exceeded the credits. Income Summary would then have to be closed with a credit to Income Summary and a debit to the owner's capital account for the amount of the net loss, thus reducing owner's equity.

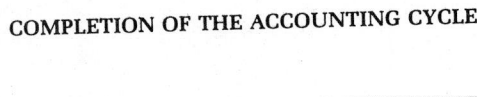

Posting of closing entries

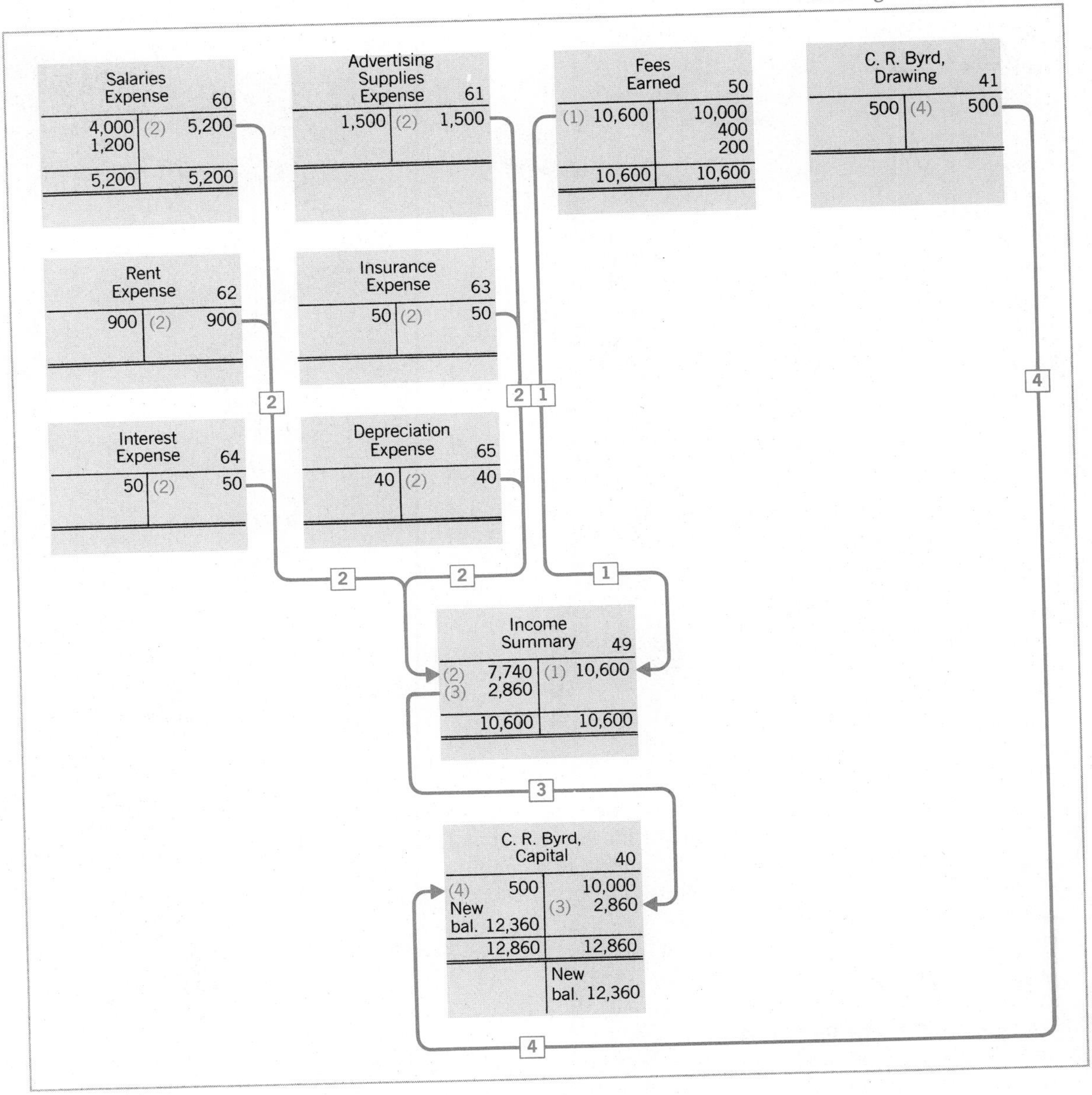

POST-CLOSING TRIAL BALANCE

After all closing entries have been journalized and posted, another trial balance, called a **post-closing trial balance,** is prepared. **The purpose of this trial balance is to prove the equality of the permanent account balances that are carried forward into the next accounting period.** Since all temporary accounts will have zero balances, the post-closing trial balance will contain only balance sheet accounts. The procedure for preparing a post-closing trial balance again consists entirely of listing the accounts and their balances.

These balances are the same as those reported in the company's balance sheet on page 98.

Post-closing trial balance

PIONEER ADVERTISING AGENCY
Post-Closing Trial Balance
October 31, 1987

	Debit	Credit
Cash	$15,200	
Fees Receivable	200	
Advertising Supplies	1,000	
Prepaid Insurance	550	
Office Equipment	5,000	
Accumulated Depreciation		$ 40
Notes Payable		5,000
Accounts Payable		2,500
Interest Payable		50
Unearned Fees		800
Salaries Payable		1,200
C. R. Byrd, Capital		12,360
	$21,950	$21,950

The post-closing trial balance is based on the following ledger balances:

LEDGER

Cash — No. 1

Date	Explanation	Ref.	Debit	Credit	Balance
Oct. 1		J1	10,000		10,000
2		J1	1,200		11,200
3		J1		900	10,300
4		J1		600	9,700
20		J1		500	9,200
24		J1		4,000	5,200
31		J1	10,000		15,200

Fees Receivable — No. 6

Date	Explanation	Ref.	Debit	Credit	Balance
Oct. 31		J2	200		200

Advertising Supplies — No. 8

Date	Explanation	Ref.	Debit	Credit	Balance
Oct. 5		J1	2,500		2,500
31		J2		1,500	1,000

Prepaid Insurance — No. 10

Date	Explanation	Ref.	Debit	Credit	Balance
Oct. 4		J1	600		600
31		J2		50	550

Office Equipment — No. 15

Date	Explanation	Ref.	Debit	Credit	Balance
Oct. 1		J1	5,000		5,000

Accumulated Depreciation—Office Equipment — No. 15.1

Date	Explanation	Ref.	Debit	Credit	Balance
Oct. 31		J2		40	40

Notes Payable — No. 25

Date	Explanation	Ref.	Debit	Credit	Balance
Oct. 1		J1		5,000	5,000

Accounts Payable — No. 26

Date	Explanation	Ref.	Debit	Credit	Balance
Oct. 5		J1		2,500	2,500

Interest Payable — No. 27

Date	Explanation	Ref.	Debit	Credit	Balance
Oct. 31		J2		50	50

Unearned Fees — No. 28

Date	Explanation	Ref.	Debit	Credit	Balance
Oct. 1		J1		1,200	
31		J1	400		800

Salaries Payable — No. 29

Date	Explanation	Ref.	Debit	Credit	Balance
Oct. 31		J2		1,200	1,200

C. R. Byrd, Capital — No. 40

Date	Explanation	Ref.	Debit	Credit	Balance
Oct. 1		J1		10,000	10,000
31		J3		2,860	12,860
31		J3	500		12,360

REVERSING ENTRIES—AN OPTIONAL STEP

Some accountants prefer to reverse certain adjusting entries at the beginning of a new accounting period. A **reversing entry**is made at the beginning of the next accounting period and is the exact opposite of the adjusting entry made in the previous period. **The preparation of reversing entries is an optional bookkeeping procedure that is not a required step in the accounting cycle.** Accordingly, we have chosen to cover this topic in Appendix 4-A at the end of the chapter.

SUMMARY OF THE ACCOUNTING CYCLE

The required steps in the accounting cycle are shown graphically on the following page. From the graphic you can see that the cycle begins with the analysis of business transactions and ends with the preparation of a post-closing trial balance. The steps in the cycle are performed in sequence and are repeated in each accounting period.

Steps 1–3 may occur daily during the accounting period, as explained in Chapter 2. Steps 4–7 are performed on a periodic basis, such as monthly, quarterly, or annually. Steps 8 and 9, closing entries, and a post-closing trial balance, are usually prepared only at the end of a company's **annual** accounting period.

There are two optional steps in the accounting cycle. A work sheet may be used in the preparation of adjusting entries and financial statements, as explained in this chapter. In addition, reversing entries may be journalized and posted, as explained in the appendix.

CLOSING ENTRIES FOR A PARTNERSHIP

There is good news and bad news about closing entries for a partnership. The good news is that closing the revenue and expense accounts to Income Summary is the same in a partnership as in a proprietorship. The bad news is that the balance in Income Summary must then be allocated to each partner's capital account on some equitable basis. In addition, each partner's drawing account must be closed to the partner's capital account.

To illustrate the closing entries for net income and partners' drawings, we will assume that the Goldy-Hahn partnership has net income of $36,000. The partners, Lisa Goldy and Amy Hahn, share income and loss equally. For the year, drawings were Goldy, $12,000 and Hahn, $15,000. The entries (for net income and the partners' drawings) are:

Dec. 31	Income Summary	36,000	
	Lisa Goldy, Capital		18,000
	Amy Hahn, Capital		18,000
	(To close net income to partners' capitals)		

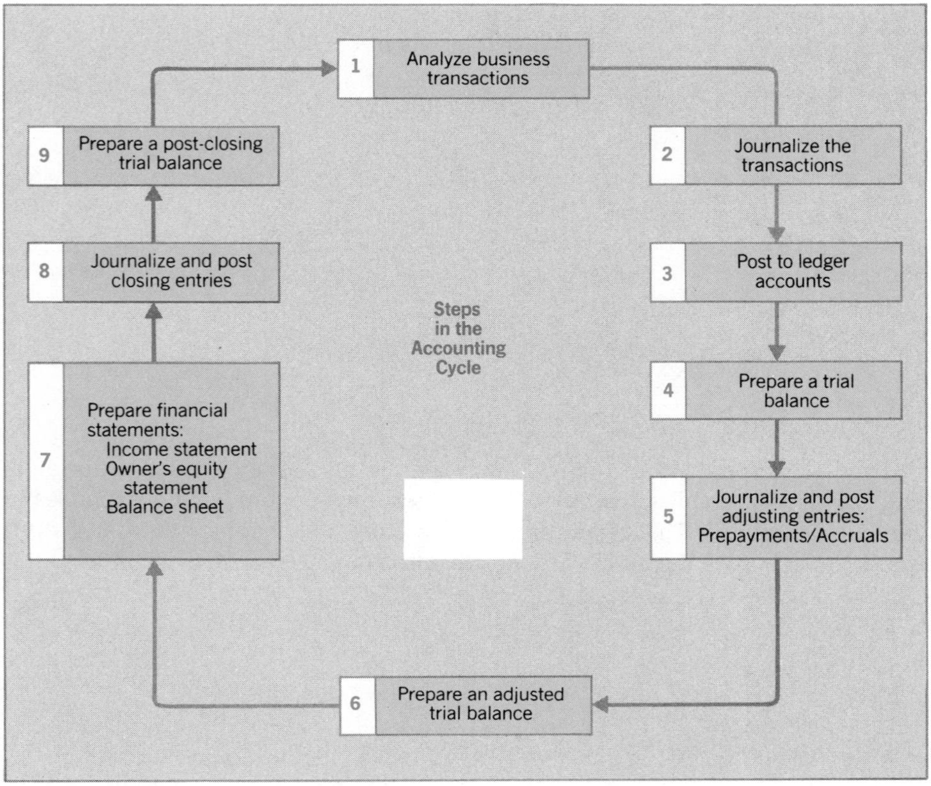

Accounting cycle

Dec. 31	Lisa Goldy, Capital	12,000	
	Amy Hahn, Capital	15,000	
	Lisa Goldy, Drawings		12,000
	Amy Hahn, Drawings		15,000
	(To close partners' drawings to partners' capitals)		

Accounting for partnerships is discussed further in Chapter 14.

CLOSING ENTRIES FOR A CORPORATION

Thus far, we have discussed only the owner's equity accounts for proprietorships and partnerships. Owners' equity in a corporation has the following distinctive features:

1. Two permanent accounts replace the owner's capital account.
   a. **Capital Stock** is used to record investments of capital in the business by owners, who are called **stockholders.**
   b. **Retained Earnings** is used to record the closing of all temporary owners' equity accounts.

2. A temporary account, **Dividends,** replaces the drawing account. This account is used to record distributions of earnings to stockholders.[1]

The effects of debits and credits and the normal balance of these accounts are summarized as follows:

Normal balances of owners' equity accounts—corporation

Account	Debit	Credit	Normal Balance
Capital Stock	Decrease (−)	Increase (+)	Credit
Retained Earnings	Decrease (−)	Increase (+)	Credit
Dividends	Increase (+)	Decrease (−)	Debit

Four closing entries are made for corporations as they are for proprietorships and partnerships. The first two entries close revenues and expenses to Income Summary. The remaining entries close net income (loss) and dividends to Retained Earnings. The entries are shown graphically below.

Diagram of closing process—corporation

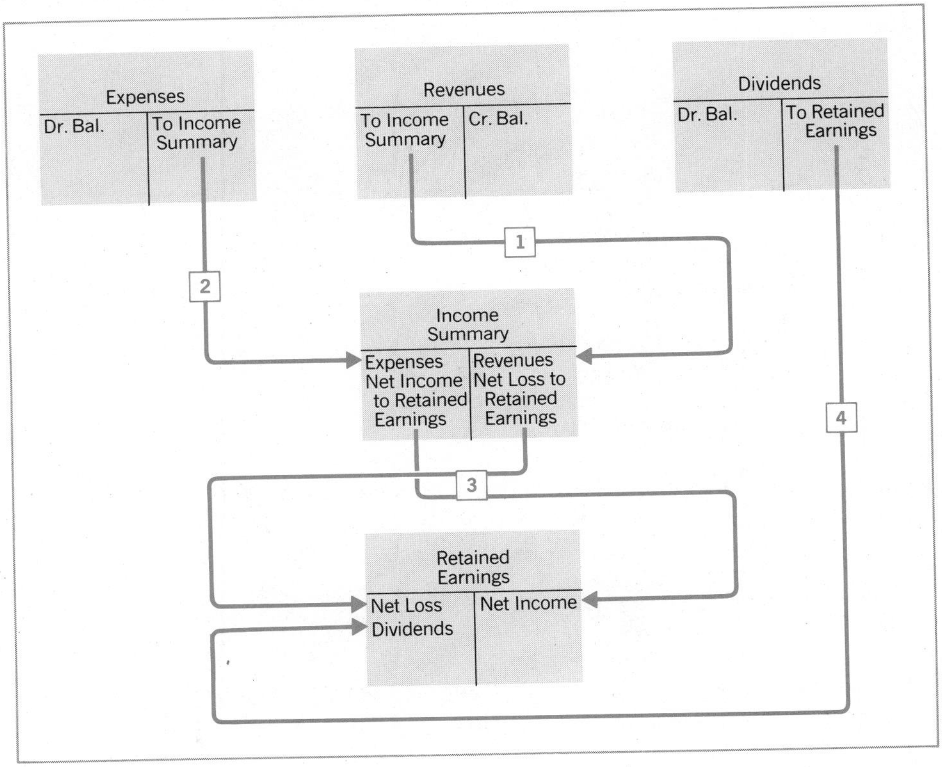

[1]In a corporation, owners are not permitted to withdraw corporate assets for personal use. However, as will be explained in Chapter 15, they are entitled to receive dividends from earnings when declared and paid by the corporation.

To illustrate the entries, we will assume the following for the Moore Corporation in 1987: retained earnings, January 1, $150,000; net income, $90,000 (revenues, $950,000 and expenses, $860,000); and dividends, $40,000. The closing entries are:

Dec. 31	Revenues (Individual accounts)	950,000	
	Income Summary		950,000
	(To close revenue accounts)		
31	Income Summary	860,000	
	Expenses (Individual accounts)		860,000
	(To close expense accounts)		
31	Income Summary	90,000	
	Retained Earnings		90,000
	(To close net income to retained earnings)		
31	Retained Earnings	40,000	
	Dividends		40,000
	(To close dividends to retained earnings)		

After posting, Income Summary and the new owners' equity accounts will show the following:

Corporation owners' equity accounts after closing

Temporary Accounts

Income Summary

Dec. 31	860,000	Dec. 31	950,000
31	90,000		
	950,000		950,000

Dividends

Bal.	40,000	Dec. 31	40,000

Real Account

Retained Earnings

Dec. 31	40,000	Jan. 1	150,000
New bal.	200,000	Dec. 31	90,000
	240,000		240,000
		New bal.	200,000

Note that the temporary accounts have zero balances. The balance in Retained Earnings represents the undistributed earnings of the company.

In a corporation, the **retained earnings statement** replaces the statement of owner's equity. The statement shows the change in Retained Earnings during the accounting period. Based on the foregoing data, this statement for the Moore Corporation is as follows:

Retained earnings statement

MOORE CORPORATION
Retained Earnings Statement
For the Year Ended December 31, 1987

Balance, January 1	$150,000
Add: Net income	90,000
	240,000
Less: Dividends	40,000
Balance, December 31	$200,000

For a corporation, the owner's equity section of the balance sheet is called stockholders' equity. If Moore Corporation has $1,000,000 of capital stock on December 31, 1987, the stockholders' equity section would show the following:

Stockholders' equity section

Stockholders' equity		
Capital stock	$1,000,000	
Retained earnings	200,000	
Total stockholders' equity		1,200,000

Much more will be said about this section in Chapters 15 and 16.

CORRECTING ENTRIES

Errors that occur in recording transactions should be corrected as soon as they are discovered by journalizing and posting **correcting entries.** You should recognize several significant differences between correcting entries and adjusting entries. Adjusting entries are an integral part of the accounting cycle, whereas correcting entries are unnecessary if the records are free of errors. **Adjustments are journalized and posted only at the end of an accounting period; in contrast, correcting entries are made whenever an error is discovered.** In addition, adjusting entries always affect at least one balance sheet account and one income statement account, whereas correcting entries may involve any combination of accounts in need of correction.

A useful approach to determining the correcting entry is to compare the incorrect entry with the correct entry. After comparison, a correcting entry is made to correct the accounts. This approach is illustrated below.

CASE 1 On May 10, a $50 cash payment on account by a customer is journalized and posted as a debit to Cash $50 and a credit to Fees Earned $50. The error is discovered on May 20, when the customer pays the remaining balance in full.

Comparison of entries

Incorrect Entry (May 10)			Correct Entry (May 10)		
Cash	50		Cash	50	
Fees Earned		50	Fees Receivable		50

A comparison of the incorrect entry with the correct entry reveals that the debit to Cash $50 is correct. However, the $50 credit to Fees Earned should have been credited to Fees Receivable. As a result, both Fees Earned and Fees Receivable are overstated in the ledger, and the following correcting entry is required:

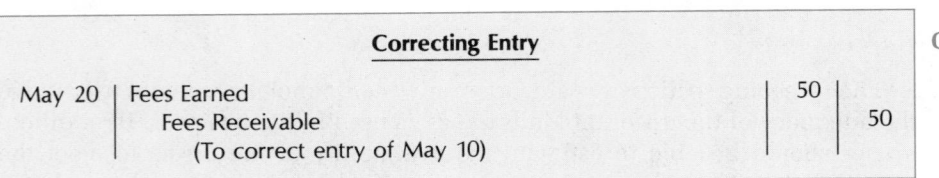

Correcting entry

Correcting Entry

May 20	Fees Earned	50	
	Fees Receivable		50
	(To correct entry of May 10)		

CASE 2 On May 18, office equipment costing $450 is purchased on account. The transaction was journalized and posted as a debit to Delivery Equipment $45, and a credit to Accounts Payable $45. The error is discovered on June 3, when the monthly statement for May is received from the creditor.

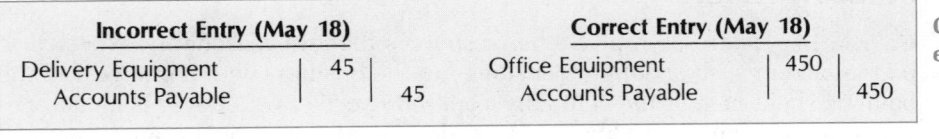

Comparison of entries

Incorrect Entry (May 18)			Correct Entry (May 18)		
Delivery Equipment	45		Office Equipment	450	
Accounts Payable		45	Accounts Payable		450

A comparison of the two entries shows that three accounts are incorrect. Delivery Equipment is overstated $45; Office Equipment is understated $450; and Accounts Payable is understated $405. The correcting entry is:

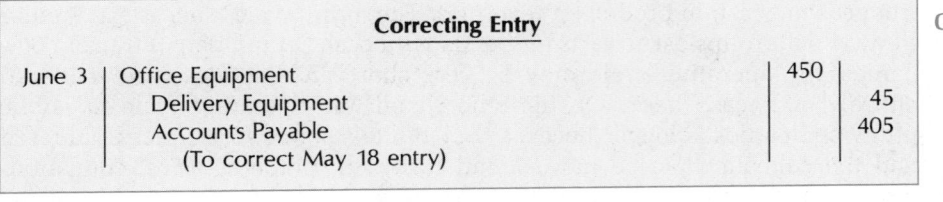

Correcting entry

Correcting Entry

June 3	Office Equipment	450	
	Delivery Equipment		45
	Accounts Payable		405
	(To correct May 18 entry)		

Instead of preparing a correcting entry, it is possible to reverse the incorrect entry and then prepare the correct entry. This approach will result in more entries and postings than a correcting entry, but it will accomplish the desired result.

CLASSIFIED FINANCIAL STATEMENTS

The financial statements illustrated up to this point were purposely kept simple. No attempt was made to classify the items other than as assets, liabilities, and owner's equity in the balance sheet, and as revenues and expenses in the income statement. **Financial statements, however, become more useful when the elements are classified into significant subgroups.** In this chapter we will introduce you to the primary balance sheet classifications. The classified income statement is presented in Chapter 5.

A **classified balance sheet** generally contains the following standard classifications:

Standard balance sheet classifications

Assets	Liabilities and Owner's Equity
Current Assets	Current Liabilities
Long-Term Investments	Long-Term Liabilities
Property, Plant, and Equipment	Owner's Equity
Intangible Assets	

The foregoing sections or categories help the financial statement user judge the adequacy of the different kinds of assets used in the business. In addition, a user should be able to estimate the availability of the assets to meet the various liabilities as they come due. A classified balance sheet also makes it easier to compare companies in the same industry, such as GM, Ford, and Chrysler in the automobile industry. Each of the categories is explained below, except for owner's equity, which has already been discussed.

CURRENT ASSETS

Current assets are cash and other resources that are reasonably expected to be realized in cash or sold or consumed in the business within one year of the balance sheet date or the company's operating cycle, whichever is longer. For example, accounts receivable are included in current assets because they will be realized in cash through collection within one year. In contrast, a prepayment such as supplies is a current asset because of its expected use or consumption in the business within one year.

The **operating cycle** of a company is the average time that is required to go from cash to cash in producing revenues. The term "cycle" suggests a circular flow, which in this case, starts and ends with cash. In municipal transit companies, the operating cycle may be very short since services are rendered entirely on a cash basis. On the other hand, the operating cycle in public utility companies is longer because they bill customers for services rendered and the collection period may extend for several months. Most companies have operating cycles of less than one year.

In a service enterprise, it is customary to recognize four types of current assets: (1) cash, (2) marketable securities such as U.S. government bonds held as a temporary (short-term) investment, (3) receivables (notes receivable, accounts receivable, and interest receivables), and (4) prepaid expenses (insurance and supplies). These items are listed in the order of liquidity, that is, according to their expected realization in cash. This arrangement is illustrated below in the following presentation of UAL, Inc. (United Airlines).

Current asset section

UAL, INC. (United Airlines)

Current assets (in thousands)	
Cash	$ 52,368
Marketable securities	389,862
Receivables	721,479
Aircraft fuel, spare parts, and supplies	178,840
Prepaid expenses	83,662
Total current assets	$1,426,211

A company's current assets are important in assessing the company's short-term debt-paying ability, as explained later in the chapter.

LONG-TERM INVESTMENTS

Like current assets, **long-term investments** are resources that can be realized in cash. However, the conversion into cash is not expected within one year or the operating cycle, whichever is longer. In addition, long-term investments are not intended for use or consumption within the business. This category, often just called Investments, normally includes stocks and bonds of other corporations. Deluxe Check Printers Incorporated reported the following in a recent balance sheet:

Long-term investment section

Deluxe Check Printers Incorporated

Long-term investments		
Investment in stock of Data Card Corporation	$20,468,000	
Other long-term investments	16,961,000	$37,429,000

PROPERTY, PLANT, AND EQUIPMENT

Property, plant, and equipment, often referred to as plant assets, are tangible resources of a relatively permanent nature that are being used in the business and not intended for sale. This category includes land, buildings, machinery and equipment, delivery equipment, and furniture and fixtures. Assets subject to depreciation should be reported at cost less accumulated depreciation. This practice is illustrated in the following presentation of Delta Airlines:

Property, plant, and equipment section

Delta Airlines, Inc.

Property, plant, and equipment (in thousands)			
Flight equipment	$3,985,796		
Less: Accumulated depreciation	1,713,059	$2,272,737	
Ground equipment	865,628		
Less: Accumulated depreciation	325,618	540,010	$2,812,747

INTANGIBLE ASSETS

Intangible assets are noncurrent resources that do not have physical substance. Their value to a company is generally derived from the rights or privileges granted by governmental authority. Intangible assets include patents, copyrights, and trademarks or trade names that give the holder exclusive right of use for a specified period of time.

In a recent balance sheet, Brunswick Corporation reported:

Intangible assets section

Brunswick Corporation

Intangible assets	
Patents, trademarks, and other intangibles	$10,460,000

CURRENT LIABILITIES

Current liabilities are obligations that are reasonably expected to be paid from existing current assets or through the creation of other current liabilities. As in the case of current assets, the time period for payment is one year or the operating cycle, whichever is longer. Current liabilities include (1) debts related to the operating cycle, such as accounts payable and wages and salaries payable, and (2) other short-term debts, such as bank loans payable, interest payable, taxes payable, and current maturities of long-term obligations. The arrangement of items within this section has evolved through custom rather than from a prescribed rule. Notes payable is usually listed first, followed by accounts payable, and then the other items are listed in any order. The current liability section adapted from a recent balance sheet of UAL, Inc. (United Airlines) is as follows:

Current liabilities section

UAL, INC. (United Airlines)

Current liabilities (in thousands)	
Notes payable	$ 297,518
Accounts payable	382,967
Current maturities of long-term obligations	81,525
Unearned ticket revenue	432,979
Salaries and wages payable	435,622
Taxes payable	80,390
Other current liabilities	240,652
Total current liabilities	$1,951,653

LONG-TERM LIABILITIES

Obligations expected to be paid after one year or from sources other than current assets or current liabilities are classified as **long-term liabilities (or long-term debt)**. Liabilities in this category include bonds payable, mortgages payable, long-term notes payable, lease liabilities, and obligations under employee pension plans. Many companies report long-term debt maturing after one year as a single amount in the balance sheet and show the details of the debt in the notes that accompany the financial statements. In a recent balance sheet, Consolidated Freightways Inc. reported:

Long-term liabilities section

Consolidated Freightways Inc.

Long-term liabilities (in thousands)	
Bank notes payable	$10,000
Mortgage payable	2,900
Bonds payable	53,422
Other long-term debt	9,597
Total long-term liabilities	$75,919

CLASSIFIED BALANCE SHEET ILLUSTRATED

An unclassified balance sheet of Pioneer Advertising Agency was presented on page 98. Using the same adjusted trial balance accounts for Pioneer at October 31, 1987, we can prepare the classified balance sheet shown below. For illustrative purposes, we have assumed that $1,000 of the notes payable are due currently and $4,000 are long-term.

Classified balance sheet

PIONEER ADVERTISING AGENCY
Balance Sheet
October 31, 1987

Assets		
Current assets		
Cash		$15,200
Fees receivable		200
Advertising supplies		1,000
Prepaid insurance		550
Total current assets		16,950
Property, plant, and equipment		
Office equipment	$5,000	
Less: Accumulated depreciation	40	4,960
Total assets		$21,910
Liabilities and Owner's Equity		
Current liabilities		
Notes payable		$ 1,000
Accounts payable		2,500
Interest payable		50
Unearned fees		800
Salaries payable		1,200
Total current liabilities		5,550
Long-term liabilities		
Notes payable		4,000
Total liabilities		9,550
Owner's equity		
C. R. Byrd, capital		12,360
Total liabilities and owner's equity		$21,910

The balance sheet is presented in **report form** with the assets shown above the liabilities and owner's equity. The balance sheet may also be presented in **account form** with the assets section placed on the left and the liabilities and owner's equity section on the right.

ANALYZING THE BALANCE SHEET

The analysis of the balance sheet should answer such questions as: Can the company pay existing current liabilities when they are due? Will the company be able to pay its long-term debt when it is due? What percentage of total

assets is being provided by creditors in comparison with the percentage provided by the owner? To illustrate the basic technique of analysis, we will focus only on the first question at this point. The relationship between current assets and current liabilities is critical in determining whether a company can pay its existing current liabilities when they are due. The relationships are expressed as a ratio, called the **current ratio,** and as a dollar amount, called **working capital.**

CURRENT RATIO

The **current ratio** is current assets divided by current liabilities. In Pioneer Advertising Agency, the ratio is 3.05:1 computed as follows:

Current ratio formula and computation

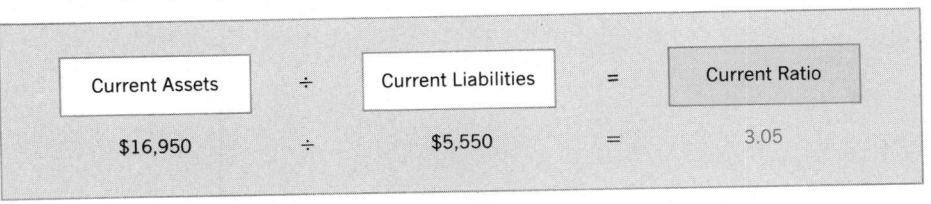

Current Assets	÷	Current Liabilities	=	Current Ratio
$16,950	÷	$5,550	=	3.05

This means that total current assets are more than three times greater than total current liabilities. It also indicates that current assets could be reduced by two-thirds and the company would still be able to meet existing current debts. This ratio is used by bankers, creditors, and agencies such as Dun & Bradstreet to determine whether the company is a good credit risk. In many cases, a ratio of 2:1 is considered to be the standard for a good credit rating. With its 3:1 ratio, Pioneer Advertising's short-term debt-paying ability appears to be very favorable.

From the foregoing, you might assume that the higher the current ratio, the better. This is not necessarily true. A very high current ratio may indicate that the company is holding more current assets than it currently needs in the business. It is possible, therefore, that the excess resources might be directed to more profitable investment opportunities.

WORKING CAPITAL

The excess of current assets over current liabilities is called **working capital.** In Pioneer Advertising, working capital is $11,400 as shown below.

Working capital formula and computation

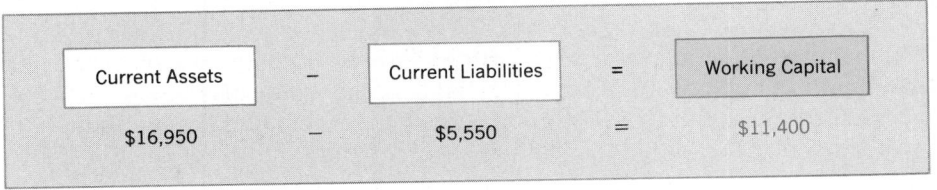

Current Assets	–	Current Liabilities	=	Working Capital
$16,950	–	$5,550	=	$11,400

The amount of working capital provides some indication of the company's ability to meet its existing current obligations.

Working capital is not as good an indicator of short-term debt-paying ability as the current ratio. The amount of working capital does not guarantee a satisfactory current ratio. This can be seen in the following example in which two companies (Henning and Frost) both have $200,000 of working capital.

Relationship of working capital to current ratio

	Henning Co.	Frost Co.
Total current assets (a)	$250,000	$1,200,000
Total current liabilities (b)	50,000	1,000,000
Working capital (a) − (b)	$200,000	$ 200,000
Current ratio (a) ÷ (b)	5:1	1.2:1

Although both companies have the same working capital, Henning Co. has a much higher current ratio and therefore appears to be in a much better position to pay its current liabilities.

SUMMARY OF STUDY OBJECTIVES

1. The steps in preparing a work sheet are: (a) prepare a trial balance on the work sheet, (b) enter the adjustments in the adjustment columns, (c) enter adjusted balances in the adjusted trial balance columns, (d) extend adjusted trial balance amounts to appropriate financial statement columns, and (e) total the statement columns, compute net income (or loss), and complete the work sheet.

2. In closing the books of a proprietorship, separate entries are made to close revenues and expenses to Income Summary, Income Summary to owner's capital, and owner's drawings to owner's capital.

3. A post-closing trial balance contains the balances in permanent accounts that are carried forward to the next accounting period. The purpose of this trial balance is to prove the equality of these balances.

4. The steps in the accounting cycle are: (a) analyze business transactions, (b) journalize the transactions, (c) post to ledger accounts, (d) prepare a trial balance, (e) journalize and post adjusting entries, (f) prepare an adjusted trial balance, (g) prepare financial statements, (h) journalize and post closing entries, and (i) prepare a post-closing trial balance.

5. The entries to close revenue and expense accounts in a corporation are the same as in a proprietorship and a partnership. However, Income Summary is then closed to Retained Earnings and the temporary account, Dividends, is also closed to Retained Earnings.

6. A useful approach to determining the correcting entry is to compare the incorrect entry with the correct entry. After comparison, a correcting entry is made to correct the accounts. Alternatively, instead of preparing a correcting entry, it is possible to reverse the incorrect entry and then prepare the correct entry.

7. In a classified balance sheet, assets are classified as current assets; long-term investments; property, plant, and equipment; or intangibles.

In addition, liabilities are classified as either current or long-term and there is also an owner's equity section.

8. The current ratio (current assets divided by current liabilities) and working capital (current assets less current liabilities) are helpful in assessing a company's ability to meet its current obligations when they are due.

APPENDIX 4–A

REVERSING ENTRIES

After the financial statements have been prepared and the books have been closed, it is often helpful to reverse some of the adjusting entries before recording the regular transactions of the next period. Such entries are called reversing entries. **A reversing entry is made at the beginning of the next accounting period and is the exact opposite of the adjusting entry made in the previous period.** The recording of reversing entries is an **optional** step in the accounting cycle which may be performed at the beginning of each accounting period.

The purpose of reversing entries is to simplify the recording of a subsequent transaction related to an adjusting entry. In Chapter 3, it may be recalled that the payment of salaries after an adjusting entry (page 93) resulted in two debits: one to Salaries Payable and the other to Salaries Expense. With reversing entries, the entire subsequent payment can be debited to Salaries Expense. The use of reversing entries does not change the amounts reported in the financial statements. It does, however, simplify the recording of subsequent transactions, because the subsequent transaction can be recorded as if the related adjusting entry had never been made.

ILLUSTRATION OF REVERSING ENTRIES

Reversing entries are most often used to reverse two types of adjusting entries: accrued revenues and accrued expenses. To illustrate the optional use of reversing entries for accrued expenses, we will use the salaries expense transactions for Pioneer Advertising Agency. The transaction and adjustment data are as follows:

1. October 24 (initial salary entry): $4,000 of salaries earned between October 1 and October 24 are paid.
2. October 31 (adjusting entry): Salaries earned between October 25 and October 31 are $1,200. These will be paid in the November 8 payroll.

3. November 8 (subsequent salary entry): Salaries paid are $2,500. Of this amount, $1,200 applied to accrued wages payable and $1,300 was earned between November 1 and November 8.

The comparative entries with and without reversing entries are as follows:

Comparative entries—not reversing vs. reversing

When Reversing Entries Are Not Used (Per Chapter)				When Reversing Entries Are Used (Per Appendix)			
Initial Salary Entry							
Oct. 24	Salaries Expense	4,000		Oct. 24	Salaries Expense	4,000	
	Cash		4,000		Cash		4,000
Adjusting Entry							
Oct. 31	Salaries Expense	1,200		Oct. 31	Salaries Expense	1,200	
	Salaries Payable		1,200		Salaries Payable		1,200
Closing Entry							
Oct. 31	Income Summary	5,200		Oct. 31	Income Summary	5,200	
	Salaries Expense		5,200		Salaries Expense		5,200
Reversing Entry							
Nov. 1	No entry is made.			Nov. 1	Salaries Payable	1,200	
					Salaries Expense		1,200
Subsequent Salary Entry							
Nov. 8	Salaries Payable	1,200		Nov. 8	Salaries Expense	2,500	
	Salaries Expense	1,300			Cash		2,500
	Cash		2,500				

The comparative entries show that the first three entries are the same whether or not reversing entries are used. The last two entries, however, are different. The November 1 **reversing entry** eliminates the $1,200 balance in Salaries Payable that was created by the October 31 adjusting entry. The reversing entry also creates a $1,200 credit balance in the Salaries Expense account. As you know, it is unusual for an expense account to have a credit balance, but the balance is correct in this instance because it anticipates that the entire amount of the first salary payment in the new accounting period will be debited to Salaries Expense. This debit will eliminate the credit balance, and the resulting debit balance in the expense account will equal the salaries expense incurred in the new accounting period ($1,300 in this example).

When reversing entries are made, all cash payments of expenses can be debited to the expense account. This means that on November 8 (and every payday) Salaries Expense can be debited for the amount paid without regard to the existence of any accrued salaries payable. Being able to make the same

entry each time simplifies the recording process in a manual accounting system. Similarly, computer processing is simplified because the computer does not have to be programmed to determine whether any accrued items exist.

The posting of the entries above with reversing entries is as follows:

Postings with reversing entries

Salaries Expense				Salaries Payable			
10/24 Paid	4,000	10/31 Closing	5,200	11/1 Reversing	**1,200**	10/31 Adjusting	1,200
31 Adjusting	1,200						
	5,200		5,200				
11/8 Paid	2,500	11/1 Reversing	**1,200**				

Reversing entries may also be made for accrued revenue adjusting entries. For Pioneer Advertising, the adjusting entry was: Fees Receivable (Dr) $200 and Fees Earned (Cr) $200. Thus, the reversing entry on November 1 is:

Nov.	1	Fees Earned	200	
		Fees Receivable		200
		(To reverse October 31 adjusting entry)		

When the accrued fees are collected, Cash is debited and Fees Earned is credited.

GLOSSARY

Classified balance sheet, p. 137
Closing entries, p. 127
Correcting entries, p. 136
Current assets, p. 138
Current liabilities, p. 140
Current ratio, p. 142
Income summary, p. 127
Intangible assets, p. 139
Long-term investments, p. 139
Long-term liabilities, p. 140
Operating cycle, p. 138
Post-closing trial balance, p. 130
Property, plant, and equipment, p. 139
Retained earnings statement, p. 135
Reversing entry, p. 132
Work sheet, p. 122
Working capital, p. 142

DEMONSTRATION PROBLEM

At the end of its first month of operations, the Watson Answering Service has the following trial balance:

WATSON ANSWERING SERVICE
August 31, 1987
Trial Balance

	Debit	Credit
Cash	$ 5,400	
Fees receivable	2,800	
Prepaid insurance	2,400	
Supplies	1,300	
Equipment	60,000	
Notes payable		$40,000
Accounts payable		2,400
Ray Watson, Capital		30,000
Ray Watson, Drawing	1,000	
Fees earned		4,900
Salaries expense	3,200	
Utilities expense	800	
Advertising expense	400	
	$77,300	$77,300

Other data consists of the following:

1. Insurance expires at the rate of $200 per month.
2. There are $1,000 of supplies on hand at August 31.
3. Monthly depreciation is $900 on the equipment.
4. Interest of $500 has accrued on the note payable in August.

INSTRUCTIONS

(a) Prepare a work sheet.
(b) Prepare a classified balance sheet assuming $35,000 of the notes payable are long-term.
(c) Journalize the closing entries.

SOLUTION TO DEMONSTRATION PROBLEM

(a)

WATSON ANSWERING SERVICE
Work Sheet
For the Month Ended August 31, 1987

Account Titles	Trial Balance		Adjustments		Adjusted Trial Balance		Income Statement		Balance Sheet	
	Dr.	Cr.	Dr.	Cr.	Dr.	Cr.	Dr.	Cr.	Dr.	Cr.
Cash	5,400				5,400				5,400	
Fees Receivable	2,800				2,800				2,800	
Prepaid Insurance	2,400			(a) 200	2,200				2,200	
Supplies	1,300			(b) 300	1,000				1,000	
Equipment	60,000				60,000				60,000	
Notes Payable		40,000				40,000				40,000

Account Titles	Trial Balance Dr.	Trial Balance Cr.	Adjustments Dr.	Adjustments Cr.	Adjusted Trial Balance Dr.	Adjusted Trial Balance Cr.	Income Statement Dr.	Income Statement Cr.	Balance Sheet Dr.	Balance Sheet Cr.
Accounts Payable		2,400				2,400				2,400
Ray Watson, Capital		30,000				30,000				30,000
Ray Watson, Drawing	1,000				1,000				1,000	
Fees Earned		4,900				4,900		4,900		
Salaries Expense	3,200				3,200		3,200			
Utilities Expense	800				800		800			
Advertising Expense	400				400		400			
Totals	77,300	77,300								
Insurance Expense			(a) 200		200		200			
Supplies Expense			(b) 300		300		300			
Depreciation Expense			(c) 900		900		900			
Accumulated Depreciation – Equipment				(c) 900		900				900
Interest Expense			(d) 500		500		500			
Interest Payable				(d) 500		500				500
Totals			1,900	1,900	78,700	78,700	6,300	4,900	72,400	73,800
Net Loss								1,400	1,400	
Totals							6,300	6,300	73,800	73,800

(b)

WATSON ANSWERING SERVICE
Balance Sheet
August 31, 1987

Assets

Current assets		
Cash		$ 5,400
Fees receivable		2,800
Prepaid insurance		2,200
Supplies		1,000
Total current assets		11,400
Property, plant, and equipment		
Equipment	$60,000	
Less: Accumulated depreciation – equipment	900	59,100
Total assets		$70,500

Liabilities and Owner's Equity

Current liabilities	
Notes payable	5,000
Accounts payable	2,400
Interest payable	500
Total current liabilities	7,900
Long-term liabilities	
Notes payable	35,000
Total liabilities	42,900
Owner's equity	
Ray Watson, Capital	27,600*
Total liabilities and owner's equity	70,500

*Ray Watson, Capital, $30,000 less drawings $1,000 and net loss $1,400.

(c)

Aug. 31	Fees Earned	4,900	
	Income Summary		4,900
	(To close revenue account)		

31	Income Summary	6,300	
	Salaries Expense		3,200
	Depreciation Expense		900
	Utilities Expense		800
	Interest Expense		500
	Advertising Expense		400
	Supplies Expense		300
	Insurance Expense		200
	(To close expense accounts)		
31	Ray Watson, Capital	1,400	
	Income Summary		1,400
	(To close net loss to capital)		
31	Ray Watson, Capital	1,000	
	Ray Watson, Drawing		1,000
	(To close drawings to capital)		

***Note:** All **asterisked** Questions, Exercises, and Problems relate to material contained in the Appendix to each chapter.

QUESTIONS

1. A work sheet is a permanent accounting record and its use is required in the accounting cycle. Do you agree? Explain.

2. The use of a work sheet affects two steps of the accounting cycle after preparing the trial balance. What steps are they and how are they affected by the work sheet?

3. What is the relationship, if any, between the amount shown in the adjusted trial balance column for an account and that account's ledger balance?

4. If a company's revenues are $122,000 and its expenses are $115,000, in which financial statement columns of the work sheet will the net income of $7,000 appear? When expenses exceed revenues, in which columns will the difference appear?

5. Why is it necessary to prepare formal financial statements when all of the data are in the statement columns of the work sheet?

6. Describe the nature of the Income Summary account and identify the four types of summary data that may be posted to this account.

7. What are the content and purpose of a post-closing trial balance?

8. Which of the following accounts would not appear in the post-closing trial balance?—Interest Payable, Equipment, Depreciation Expense, R. Jonas Drawing, Unearned Fees, Accumulated Depreciation—Equipment, and Fees Earned.

9. Distinguish between a reversing entry and an adjusting entry. Are reversing entries required?

10. List the three required steps in the accounting cycle in the sequence in which they are made that pertain to (a) journalizing, and (b) preparing trial balances.

11. How do the closing entries for a partnership differ from the closing entries for a proprietorship?

12. There is only one major difference between the closing entries for a corporation and the closing entries for a proprietorship. Do you agree? Explain.

13. For the year ended December 31, 1987, the Hanes Corporation has dividends $30,000, net income $110,000, and retained earnings, January 1, $180,000. Prepare the retained earnings statement.

14. How do correcting entries differ from adjusting entries?

15. What standard classifications are used in preparing a classified balance sheet?

16. Define current assets. What basis is used for arranging individual items within the current asset section?

17. What is meant by the term "operating cycle"?

18. Distinguish between long-term investments and property, plant, and equipment.

19. How do current liabilities differ from long-term liabilities?

20. The General Company has current assets of $30,000 and current liabilities of $12,000. What is its (a) working capital and (b) current ratio?

***21.** The Show Company prepares reversing entries. If the adjusting entry for interest payable is reversed, what type of an account balance will there be in Interest Payable and Interest Expense after the reversing entry is posted?

***22.** At December 31, accrued salaries payable totaled $1,500. On January 10, total salaries of $5,000 are paid. Give the January 10 entry and indicate the Salaries Expense account balance after the entry is posted. Assume that reversing entries are made at December 31.

EXERCISES

E4–1 Selected accounts from the ledger of the Menard Company are listed below with their unadjusted balances:

Prepaid Insurance	$ 4,200	Accumulated Depreciation	$ 6,000
Cash	9,400	Fees Earned	58,000
R. Menard, Drawing	3,000	Accounts Payable	2,900
Salaries Expense	24,000	R. Menard, Capital	28,000

Adjusting entries are required for (a) expired insurance $1,400, (b) accrued salaries payable $500, (c) accrued fees receivable $900, and (d) depreciation $2,400.

INSTRUCTIONS

Prepare a partial work sheet, adding additional accounts as needed.

E4-2 The adjusted trial balance columns of the work sheet for the Wieland Company are as follows:

WIELAND CO.
(Partial) Work Sheet
For the Month Ended April 30, 1987

	Adjusted Trial Balance		Income Statement		Balance Sheet	
Account Titles	Dr.	Cr.	Dr.	Cr.	Dr.	Cr.
Cash	12,312					
Marketable Securities	8,740					
Accounts Receivable	6,840					
Prepaid Rent	2,280					
Equipment	18,050					
Accumulated Depreciation		4,921				
Notes Payable		5,700				
Accounts Payable		5,472				
Wieland, Capital		34,960				
Wieland, Drawing	6,650					
Fees Earned		11,590				
Salaries Expense	6,840					
Rent Expense	760					
Depreciation Expense	171					
Interest Expense	57					
Interest Payable		57				
Totals	62,700	62,700				

INSTRUCTIONS

(a) Complete the work sheet.

(b) Prepare a classified balance sheet.

E4-3 The completed financial statement columns of the work sheet for the Geneva Company are shown below.

GENEVA COMPANY
Work Sheet
For the Year Ended December 31, 1987

	Income Statement		Balance Sheet	
	Dr.	Cr.	Dr.	Cr.
Cash			7,200	
Fees Receivable			6,500	
Prepaid Insurance			1,800	
Equipment			28,000	
Accumulated Depreciation				8,600
Accounts Payable				12,000
Salaries Payable				2,000
Ann Geneva, Capital				34,000
Ann Geneva, Drawing			7,200	
Fees Earned		41,000		
Salaries Expense	36,000			
Insurance Expense	1,200			
Depreciation Expense	2,800			

	Income Statement Dr.	Income Statement Cr.	Balance Sheet Dr.	Balance Sheet Cr.
Utilities Expense	3,700			
Repairs Expense	3,200			
Totals	46,900	41,000	50,700	56,600
Net Loss		5,900	5,900	
	46,900	46,900	56,600	56,600

INSTRUCTIONS

(a) Journalize the closing entries.

(b) Post the closing entries to Income Summary and to the drawing and capital accounts.

(c) Prepare a post-closing trial balance.

E4-4 For the month ending July 31, 1987, the income statement of the Oakdale Golf Club is as follows.

OAKDALE GOLF COURSE
Income Statement
For the Month Ended July 31, 1987

Revenues		
Green fees earned		$11,000
Golf lesson fees earned		900
Total revenues		11,900
Expenses		
Salaries expense	$4,200	
Maintenance expense	2,100	
Depreciation expense	1,500	
Miscellaneous expense	600	
Total expenses		8,400
Net income		$ 3,500

On July 1, the owner, R. A. Oker, had a capital balance of $18,200. During July, Oker withdrew $1,000 in cash for personal use.

INSTRUCTIONS

(a) Prepare closing entries at July 31.

(b) Post the closing entries and rule and balance the accounts.

E4-5 The adjusted trial balance of the Markhall Company, a partnership, at the end of its fiscal year on July 31, 1987 is as follows:

Debit Balances		Credit Balances	
Accounts Receivable	$ 7,780	Accounts Payable	$ 5,220
Cash	6,940	Accumulated Depreciation	5,400
Depreciation Expense	2,000	Commissions Earned	73,100
Equipment	35,900	C. A. Hall, Capital	18,400
C. A. Hall, Drawing	5,000	H. E. Mark, Capital	16,800
H. E. Mark, Drawing	4,000	Rent Earned	6,500
Rent Expense	12,000	Unearned Rent	1,800
Salaries Expense	48,700		$127,220
Utilities Expense	4,900		
	$127,220		

Hall and Mark share net income and net losses equally.

INSTRUCTIONS

(a) Prepare the closing entries.

(b) Post to Income Summary and the owners' drawing and capital accounts.

(c) Prepare a post-closing trial balance at July 31, 1987.

E4-6 The income statement for the Star Ice Skating Rink at the close of its fiscal year on March 31, 1987 is as follows:

STAR ICE SKATING RINK
Income Statement
For the Year Ended March 31, 1987

Revenues		
Skating fees earned		$76,000
Skating lesson fees earned		10,400
Total revenues		86,400
Expenses		
Salaries expense	$42,000	
Maintenance expense	12,600	
Depreciation expense	8,000	
Miscellaneous expense	1,500	
Total expenses		64,100
Net income		$22,300

The skating rink is organized as a corporation. During the year it paid a $10,000 dividend. On April 1, 1986, its ledger showed: Capital Stock $90,000 and Retained Earnings $36,000.

INSTRUCTIONS

(a) Prepare the closing entries.

(b) Post the closing entries to Income Summary, Dividends, and Retained Earnings.

(c) Prepare a retained earnings statement for the year.

E4-7 In the Strang Company, owned by R. Strang, the following errors were discovered after the transactions had been journalized and posted.

1. Repairs of $700 on the roof of Strang's personal residence paid for by the company were debited to Repairs Expense $700 and credited to Cash for $700.
2. Accrued salaries payable for the preceding year of $500 were paid in the current year. The payment was debited to Salaries Expense for $500 and credited to Cash for $500. (Strang Company does not prepare reversing entries).
3. A collection on account from a customer for $670 was recorded as a debit to Cash $760 and a credit to Fees Earned $760.
4. Store supplies of $1,500 were purchased on account. Store Equipment was debited for $1,500 and Notes Payable was credited for $1,500.

INSTRUCTIONS

Prepare the correcting entries, assuming the incorrect entry is not reversed. Omit explanations.

E4-8 The adjusted trial balance for France's Bowling Alley at December 31 contains the following accounts.

Debits		Credits	
Building	$124,800	W. O. France, Capital	$110,000
Accounts Receivable	13,520	Accumulated Depreciation – Building	45,600
Prepaid Insurance	4,680	Accounts Payable	12,480
Cash	21,840	Mortgage Payable	93,600
Equipment	62,400	Accumulated Depreciation – Equipment	18,720
Land	61,200	Interest Payable	2,600
Insurance Expense	780	Fees Earned	14,180
Depreciation Expense	5,360		
Interest Expense	2,600		
	$297,180		$297,180

INSTRUCTIONS

(a) Prepare a classified balance sheet; assume that $15,600 of the mortgage payable will be paid in the next operating cycle of France's Bowling Alley.

(b) Compute the amount of working capital and the current ratio. (Round to two decimals.)

E4-9 The following data are adapted from recent balance sheets of Consolidated Rail Corporation (Conrail). The data are arranged in alphabetical order. All dollar amounts are *in millions.*

Accounts payable	$ 54.9	Materials and supplies	161.0
Accounts receivable	494.2	Other current liabilities	486.3
Cash	296.0	Prepaid expenses	14.8
Current maturities of long-term debt	120.3	Wages and employee benefits payable	257.6
Marketable securities	550.0		

INSTRUCTIONS

(a) Prepare the current asset and current liability sections of the balance sheet. (Round to two decimals.)

(b) Compute the amount of working capital and the current ratio.

***E4-10** On December 31, the adjusted trial balance of the Chambers Talent Agency shows the following selected data:

Commissions Receivable	$3,000	Commissions Earned	$95,000
Interest Expense	7,800	Interest Payable	2,000

Analysis shows that adjusting entries were made for (a) $3,000 of commissions earned but not billed, and (b) $2,000 of accrued but unpaid interest.

INSTRUCTIONS

(a) Prepare the closing entries for the temporary accounts at December 31.

(b) Prepare the reversing entries on January 1.

(c) Enter the adjusted trial balance data in the four accounts. Post the entries in (a) and (b) and rule and balance the accounts.

(d) Prepare the entries to record (1) the collection of the accrued commissions on January 10, and (2) the payment of all interest due ($2,500) on January 15.

(e) Post the entries in (d) to the temporary accounts.

PROBLEMS

P4-1 The trial balance of Jaenike Roofing at March 31, 1987 is as follows:

JAENIKE ROOFING
Trial Balance
March 31, 1987

	Debit	Credit
Cash	$ 1,700	
Fees Receivable	2,600	
Roofing Supplies	1,100	
Equipment	6,000	
Accumulated Depreciation – Equipment		$ 1,200
Accounts Payable		1,100
Unearned Fees		300
R. T. Jaenike, Capital		7,000
R. T. Jaenike, Drawing	600	
Fees Earned		3,000
Salaries Expense	500	
Miscellaneous Expense	100	
	$12,600	$12,600

Other data:

1. A physical count reveals only $520 of roofing supplies on hand. → used up $580 debit supplies expense credit supplies
2. Equipment is depreciated at a rate of $120 per month. → debit depreciation expense credit Accum. depreciation
3. Unearned fees amounted to $100 on March 31.
4. Accrued salaries are $500.

INSTRUCTIONS

(a) Enter the trial balance on a work sheet and complete the work sheet, assuming that the adjustments relate only to the month of March.

(b) Prepare an income statement and owner's equity statement for the month of March and classified balance sheet at March 31.

(c) Journalize the closing entries. → Zero balancing of income statement accounts

(d) Prepare a post-closing trial balance.

P4-2 J. S. Rider is a dentist. Selected data from three trial balances at the end of the current year are presented below with the accounts arranged in alphabetical order.

	Trial Balances		
	Unadjusted	Adjusted	Post-closing
Accounts Payable	$ 1,535	$ 1,535	
Accounts Receivable	2,900	______	$ 2,900
Accumulated Depreciation	______	______	2,700
Cash	______	______	5,200
Dental Supplies	______	800	______
Depreciation Expense	______	900	______
Equipment	20,000	______	______
Fees Earned	______	19,400	______
Interest Expense	35	______	______
Interest Payable	______	______	25

	Trial Balances		
	Unadjusted	Adjusted	Post-closing
Notes Payable	5,000	____	____
Rent Expense	____	3,600	____
J. S. Rider, Capital	____	16,700	____
J. S. Rider, Drawing	4,000	____	____
Salaries Expense	____	5,000	____
Salaries Payable	____	500	____
Supplies Expense–Dental	____	2,200	____
Unearned Fees	400	____	200
Utilities Expense	1,400	____	____

Adjustments were made in this period to record supplies used, depreciation expense, interest accrued, unearned fees earned, and salaries accrued.

INSTRUCTIONS

(a) Prepare a work sheet (filling in the blank spaces with amounts) with the accounts arranged in financial statement order. (Note: The column totals for the trial balances are: Unadjusted $44,635, adjusted $46,060, and post-closing $28,900.) No additional accounts need to be added.

(b) Prepare an income statement and owner's equity statement for the year and a classified balance sheet at December 31.

(c) Journalize the adjusting entries.

(d) Journalize the closing entries.

P4-3 Gram's Apartment Management Services began business this year. Gram's rents space in its own office building, as well as managing rental properties for the actual owners. The trial balance and adjusted trial balance columns of the work sheet on December 31, 1987, the end of its first year of operations, are as follows:

GRAM COMPANY
Work Sheet
For the Year Ended December 31, 1987

Account Titles	Trial Balance		Adjusted Trial Balance	
	Dr.	Cr.	Dr.	Cr.
Cash	8,300		8,300	
Marketable Securities	4,200		4,200	
Accounts Receivable	23,600		23,600	
Prepaid Insurance	3,100		1,600	
Land	55,000		55,000	
Building	107,000		107,000	
Equipment	48,000		48,000	
Accounts Payable		13,400		13,400
Unearned Fees		1,000		800
Mortgage Payable		100,000		100,000
P. J. Gram, Capital		120,000		120,000
P. J. Gram, Drawing	20,000		20,000	
Fees Earned		99,100		99,300
Interest Earned		500		700

Salaries Expense	32,000		32,000	
Advertising Expense	17,000		17,000	
Utilities Expense	11,000		11,000	
Miscellaneous Expense	4,800		4,800	
Totals	334,000	334,000		
Interest Receivable			200	
Insurance Expense			1,500	
Depreciation Expense—Building			2,500	
Accumulated Depreciation—Building				2,500
Depreciation Expense—Equipment			3,900	
Accumulated Depreciation—Equipment				3,900
Interest Expense			12,000	
Interest Payable				12,000
Totals			352,600	352,600

INSTRUCTIONS

(a) Prepare a complete 10-column work sheet.

(b) Prepare an income statement and owner's equity statement for the year and a classified balance sheet. (Note: $10,000 of the mortgage payable is due for payment next year.)

(c) Prepare the closing entries, assuming the adjusting entries have been journalized and posted.

(d) Prepare a post-closing trial balance.

(e) Compute the working capital and the current ratio. (Round to two decimals.)

P4-4 Wilma Smith, CPA, was retained by Howell TV Repair to prepare financial statements for April 1987. Smith accumulated all the ledger balances per Howell's records and found the following:

HOWELL TV REPAIR
Trial Balance
April 30, 1987

	Debit	Credit
Cash	$ 5,600	
Accounts Receivable	3,200	
Supplies	800	
Equipment	10,600	
Accumulated Depreciation		$ 1,350
Accounts Payable		2,100
Salaries Payable		500
Unearned Fees		890
R. Howell, Capital		13,900
Fees Earned		5,450
Salaries Expense	3,700	
Miscellaneous Expense	290	
	$24,190	$24,190

Wilma Smith reviewed the records and found the following errors:

1. Cash received from a customer on account was recorded as $650 instead of $560.
2. The purchase, on account, of a typewriter costing $340 was recorded as a debit to supplies and a credit to accounts payable for $340.
3. Services were performed for a client on account, $890, for which cash was debited $890 and Unearned Fees was credited for $890.
4. A payment of $30 for advertising expense was entered as a debit to Miscellaneous Expense $30 and a credit to Cash $30.
5. The first salary payment this month was for $1,900, which included $500 of salaries payable on March 31. The payment was recorded as a debit to Salaries Expense $1,900 and a credit to Cash $1,900.
6. A cash payment of repair expense on equipment for $68 was recorded as a debit to Equipment $86 and a credit to Cash $86.

INSTRUCTIONS

(a) Prepare an analysis of each error showing (1) the incorrect entry, (2) the correct entry, and (3) the correcting entry.

(b) Prepare a correct trial balance.

(c) Prepare a post-closing trial balance, assuming that (1) the only adjusting entry is for depreciation on equipment of $120, and (2) closing entries have been journalized and posted. (Hint: Compute the net income for the month.)

P4–5 Emery Air Freight is one of the leading overnight air-cargo transportation companies. The following data are adapted from a recent adjusted trial balance. All dollar amounts are in thousands of dollars.

Debits		Credits	
Accounts Receivable	$ 97,345	Accounts Payable	$ 69,108
Aircraft	80,627	Accumulated Depreciation	48,268
Aircraft Supplies	2,520	Bank Loans	25,000
Airport Facilities	60,367	Bonds Payable	25,000
Cash	3,494	Capital Stock	40,000
Estimated Tax Refunds Receivable	16,700	Lease Contracts Payable	57,864
Equipment	37,529	Other Long-term Debt	17,496
Land	8,220	Retained Earnings	78,476
Investments	36,266	Taxes Payable	3,897
Patents	16,753	Wages Payable	5,963
Prepaid Expenses	11,251		
	$371,072		$371,072

Analysis of the accounting records reveals the following additional data (again in thousands of dollars):

1. Investments consist of short-term marketable securities $1,337, long-term investments in bonds $11,734, and long-term investments in stock $23,195.
2. Settlement of the tax refund is expected in May, 1988.
3. Accumulated depreciation pertains to three depreciable assets: Aircraft $22,600, Equipment $9,700, and Airport Facilities $15,968.
4. The bank loans, lease contracts, and bonds payable are long-term except for $20,000 of bonds expected to be paid from current assets in 1988.

INSTRUCTIONS

(a) Prepare a classified balance sheet, assuming that the adjusted trial balance related to 1987.

(b) Compute the amount of working capital and the current ratio.

(c) Comment on the company's short-term debt-paying ability, assuming that at December 31, 1986 current assets were $92,434 and current liabilities were $72,272 (in thousands of dollars).

ALTERNATE PROBLEMS

P4-1A Rita Valentine began operations as a private investigator on January 1, 1987. The trial balance at March 31 is as follows:

VALENTINE COMPANY
Trial Balance
March 31, 1987

	Debit	Credit
Cash	$12,600	
Accounts Receivable	5,420	
Prepaid Insurance	2,400	
Supplies	1,050	
Equipment	30,000	
Notes Payable		$10,000
Accounts Payable		12,350
R. Valentine, Capital		20,000
R. Valentine, Drawing	600	
Fees Earned		13,620
Salaries Expense	1,200	
Travel Expense	1,300	
Rent Expense	1,200	
Miscellaneous Expense	200	
	$55,970	$55,970

Other data:

1. Supplies on hand total $720.
2. Depreciation is $375 per quarter.
3. The note payable was issued January 2. It is a 12%, 6-month note.
4. Insurance expires at the rate of $150 per month.
5. Fees earned but unbilled at March 31 total $750.

INSTRUCTIONS

(a) Enter the trial balance on a work sheet and complete the work sheet.

(b) Prepare an income statement and owner's equity statement for the quarter and a classified balance sheet at March 31.

(c) Journalize the closing entries.

(d) Prepare a post-closing trial balance.

P4-2A Vicki Gregory is a veterinarian who owns and operates Vicki's Vets. Selected data from three trial balances at the end of the current year are presented below with the accounts arranged in alphabetical order.

	Trial Balances		
	Unadjusted	Adjusted	Post-closing
Accounts Payable	$ 5,900	$ 5,900	$ 5,900
Accumulated Depreciation	7,700	______	______
Advertising Expense	______	7,400	-0-
Boarding Fees Earned	______	16,100	______
Cash	9,200	______	______
Depreciation Expense	______	2,100	______
Equipment	24,000	______	24,000
Vicki Gregory, Capital	______	47,000	______
Vicki Gregory, Drawing	11,000	______	______
Medical Fees Earned	______	68,700	______
Medical Fees Receivable	1,400	______	2,700
Medical Supplies	______	______	10,000
Prepaid Advertising	______	______	1,000
Prepaid Rent	14,000	______	______
Rent Expense	______	12,000	______
Supplies Expense	______	26,000	______
Unearned Boarding Fees	______	7,900	______
Utilities Expense	______	11,000	______
Wages Expense	37,000	______	______
Wages Payable	______	______	1,200

Adjustments were made in this period to record accrued medical fees, supplies used, rent expense, advertising expense, depreciation expense, wages accrued, and boarding fees earned.

INSTRUCTIONS

(a) Prepare a work sheet (filling in the blank spaces with amounts) with the accounts arranged in financial statement order. (Note: The column totals for the trial balances are: unadjusted $152,000, adjusted $156,600, and post-closing $48,900.) No additional accounts need be added.

(b) Prepare the income statement and owner's equity statement for the year and the balance sheet at December 31, 1987.

(c) Journalize the adjusting entries.

(d) Journalize the closing entries.

P4-3A Dreamland Amusement Park is owned by Harris Conlin. Its fiscal period ends on September 30. Selected data from the September 30 work sheet are presented below:

DREAMLAND AMUSEMENT PARK
Work Sheet
For the Year Ended September 30, 1987

	Trial Balance		Adjusted Trial Balance	
	Dr.	Cr.	Dr.	Cr.
Cash	12,400		12,400	
Marketable Securities	25,000		25,000	
Prepaid Insurance	31,900		3,900	
Supplies	18,600		1,200	
Land	80,000		80,000	
Equipment	120,000		120,000	

	Trial Balance		Adjusted Trial Balance	
	Dr.	Cr.	Dr.	Cr.
Accumulated Depreciation		36,200		43,000
Accounts Payable		14,600		14,600
Unearned Admission Revenue		2,700		0
Mortgage Payable		50,000		50,000
H. Conlin, Capital		109,700		109,700
H. Conlin, Drawing	14,000		14,000	
Admission Revenue		276,000		278,700
Interest Earned		2,500		3,700
Salaries Expense	109,000		109,000	
Repair Expense	32,500		32,500	
Advertising Expense	7,400		7,400	
Utilities Expense	16,900		16,900	
Property Taxes Expense	18,000		21,000	
Interest Expense	6,000		12,000	
Totals	491,700	491,700		
Interest Receivable			1,200	
Insurance Expense			28,000	
Supplies Expense			17,400	
Interest Payable				6,000
Depreciation Expense			6,800	
Property Taxes Payable				3,000
Totals			508,700	508,700

INSTRUCTIONS

(a) Prepare a complete 10-column work sheet.

(b) Prepare an income statement and owner's equity statement for the year and a classified balance sheet. (Note: $10,000 of the mortgage payable is due for payment in the next fiscal year.)

(c) Prepare the closing entries, assuming the adjusting entries have been journalized and posted.

(d) Prepare a post-closing trial balance.

(e) Compute the working capital and current ratio. (Round to two decimals.)

P4-4A Len Myers, CPA, was asked by Lois Haynes to review the accounting records and to prepare the financial statements for her sewing shop. The company's inexperienced, part-time bookkeeper has accumulated the following trial balance.

BITS N PIECES
Trial Balance
May 31, 1987

	Debit	Credit
Cash	$ 3,530	
Accounts Receivable	1,400	
Supplies	1,100	
Equipment	12,000	
Accumulated Depreciation—Equipment		$ 2,400
Accounts Payable		2,890
Unearned Fees		630
Lois Haynes, Capital		12,000

	Debit	Credit
Lois Haynes, Drawing	1,000	
Fees Earned		2,500
Utilities Expense	200	
Advertising Expense	90	
Rent Expense	800	
Miscellaneous Expense	300	
	$20,420	$20,420

Len Myers reviewed the records and found the following errors.

1. Cash paid on accounts payable of $680 was recorded as a debit to Accounts Payable $860 and a credit to Cash $860.
2. The purchase of supplies on account for $250 was debited to Equipment $250 and credited to Accounts Payable $250.
3. Sewing done for a customer on account for $125 was debited to cash $215 and credited to Fees Earned $215.
4. Lois withdrew cash of $1,000 for personal expenses, and the bookkeeper debited Miscellaneous Expense for $100 and credited Cash $100.
5. The April advertising bill of $50, included in Accounts Payable on April 30, was paid in May. In the May entry, Advertising Expense was debited $50 and Cash was credited $50.
6. A cash payment of repair expense on equipment for $163 was recorded as a debit to Equipment $136 and credited to Cash $136.

INSTRUCTIONS

(a) Prepare an analysis of each error showing (1) the incorrect entry, (2) the correct entry, and (3) the correcting entry.

(b) Prepare a correct trial balance.

(c) Prepare a post-closing trial balance, assuming:

(1) There were two adjusting entries: (a) depreciation $150 and (b) supplies used $300.

(2) Closing entries have been journalized and posted. (Hint: Compute the net income for the month.)

P4-5A The Soo Line Corporation owns and operates the Soo Line Railroad, the tenth largest rail system in the United States, and several motor transportation companies.

The following data (in thousands of dollars) are adapted from a recent adjusted trial balance.

Debits		Credits	
Accounts Receivable	$112,967	Accounts Payable	$ 150,077
Cash	32,157	Accrued Expenses Payable	15,079
Investments	12,071	Accumulated Depreciation	334,281
Materials and Supplies	46,753	Bonds Payable	32,939
Prepaid Expenses	10,596	Capital Stock	156,887
Railroad Rights-of-Way	7,013	Dividends Payable	2,847
Railroad Track Components	930,877	Leases Payable	60,902
Transportation Equipment	320,052	Notes Payable	216,935
		Other Liabilities	282,578
		Retained Earnings	150,991
		Wages Payable	68,970
	$1,472,486		$1,472,486

Analysis of the accounting records reveals the following additional data (again in thousands of dollars).

1. Accumulated depreciation pertains to two depreciable assets: Railroad Track Components $223,861 and Transportation Equipment $110,420.
2. Investments consist of stock in the Morgan Corporation of $8,436 and other long-term investments that are expected to be held indefinitely.
3. Other liabilities consist of (a) other current liabilities $15,486, (b) long-term debt of $22,471 expected to be paid in 1988 from existing current assets, and (c) other long-term debt.
4. The bonds payable, leases payable, and notes payable are long-term liabilities.

INSTRUCTIONS

(a) Prepare a classified balance sheet, assuming that the adjusted trial balance related to 1987.

(b) Compute the amount of working capital and the current ratio.

DECISION CASE

The Beale Janitorial Service was started two years ago by Pat Beale. Because business has been exceptionally good, Pat decided on July 1, 1987 to expand operations by acquiring an additional truck and hiring two more assistants. To finance the expansion, Pat obtained on July 1, 1987, a $25,000, 10% bank loan, payable $10,000 on July 1, 1988 and the balance on July 1, 1989. The terms of the loan require the borrower to have $10,000 of working capital and a minimum current ratio of 1.8:1 at December 31, 1987. If these terms are not met, the bank loan will be refinanced at 15% interest.

At December 31, 1987, the accountant for Beale Janitorial Service prepared the following balance sheet:

BEAL JANITORIAL SERVICE
Balance Sheet
December 31, 1987

Assets		
Current assets		
Cash		$ 6,500
Accounts receivable		9,000
Janitorial supplies		4,200
Prepaid insurance		4,800
Total current assets		24,500
Property, plant, and equipment		
Cleaning equipment	$22,000	
Delivery trucks	34,000	56,000
Total assets		$80,500
Liabilities and Owner's Equity		
Current liabilities		
Notes payable		$10,000
Accounts payable		2,500
Total current liabilities		12,500

Long-term liability	
Notes payable	15,000
Total liabilities	27,500
Owner's equity	
Pat Beale, Capital	53,000
Total liabilities and owner's equity	$80,500

Pat presented the balance sheet to the bank's loan office on January 2, 1988 confident that the company had met the terms of the loan. The loan officer was not impressed. She said, "We need financial statements audited by a CPA."

A CPA was engaged and immediately realized that the balance sheet had been prepared from a trial balance and not from an adjusted trial balance. The adjustment data at the balance sheet date consisted of the following:

1. Earned but unbilled janitorial services were $1,800.
2. Janitorial supplies on hand were $2,500.
3. Prepaid insurance was a 3-year policy dated January 1, 1987.
4. December expenses incurred but unpaid at December 31, $250.
5. Interest on the bank loan was not recorded.
6. The amounts for plant assets were net of accumulated depreciation on January 1, 1987 of $4,000 for cleaning equipment and $5,000 for delivery trucks. Depreciation for 1987 was $4,000 for cleaning equipment and $8,000 for delivery trucks.

INSTRUCTIONS

(a) Prepare a correct balance sheet.

(b) Were the terms of the bank loan met? Explain.

CHAPTER 5

Auburn University, Alabama

CHAPTER 5

ACCOUNTING FOR MERCHANDISING OPERATIONS

STUDY OBJECTIVES

After studying this chapter, you should be able to:

1. Identify the components in measuring net income in a merchandising company.
2. Explain the entries pertaining to sales revenues.
3. Enumerate the accounts in recording merchandise purchases.
4. State the steps in determining the cost of goods sold.
5. Describe the content of the income statement for a merchandising company.
6. Explain how the merchandising accounts are closed.
7. Identify the features of a classified income statement.
8. Describe important relationships in analyzing an income statement.

In previous chapters, service enterprises were used to explain and illustrate the accounting cycle. Whether it be a professional sports team (Los Angeles Dodgers), a health spa (Vic Tanney), an airline (American Airlines), or a tax return preparation office (H & R Block), these businesses have one thing in common—they charge a fee for the services they perform. In this chapter, we are going to explain and illustrate another type of enterprise called a **merchandising** or **trading** concern. These enterprises buy and sell goods rather than perform services to earn a profit. Merchandising companies that purchase and sell directly to consumers such as K mart, Sears, Krogers, and Toys

R Us are called **retailers.** In contrast, merchandising companies that sell to retailers are known as **wholesalers** such as McKesson & Robbins (drugstores) and United Stationers (office supply stores).

Although the steps in the accounting cycle for a merchandising company are the same as the steps for a service enterprise, you must be sure to understand the additional accounts and entries required in recording merchandising transactions and the proper financial statement presentation of these accounts. The following discussion applies to both retail and wholesale enterprises. Later in the chapter, we will illustrate a classified income statement and explain the basic approach to analyzing an income statement.

INCOME MEASUREMENT IN A MERCHANDISING COMPANY

The process of measuring net income for a merchandising company is conceptually the same as for a service enterprise; that is, net income (loss) results from the matching of expenses with revenues. In a merchandising company, the primary source of revenues is the sale of merchandise, often referred to simply as sales revenue or sales. Expenses are divided into two categories: (1) the cost of goods sold and (2) operating expenses.

The **cost of goods sold** is the total cost of merchandise sold during the period. This expense is directly related to the revenue realized from the sale of the goods. The difference between sales and the cost of goods sold is called the **gross profit** (or gross margin) on sales. For example, when a pocket calculator costing \$15 is sold for \$25, the gross profit is \$10. Merchandising companies customarily report gross profit on sales in the income statement. After gross profit has been calculated, operating expenses are deducted to determine net income (loss). The income measurement process for a merchandising company may be diagrammed as follows:

Income measurement process for a merchandising company

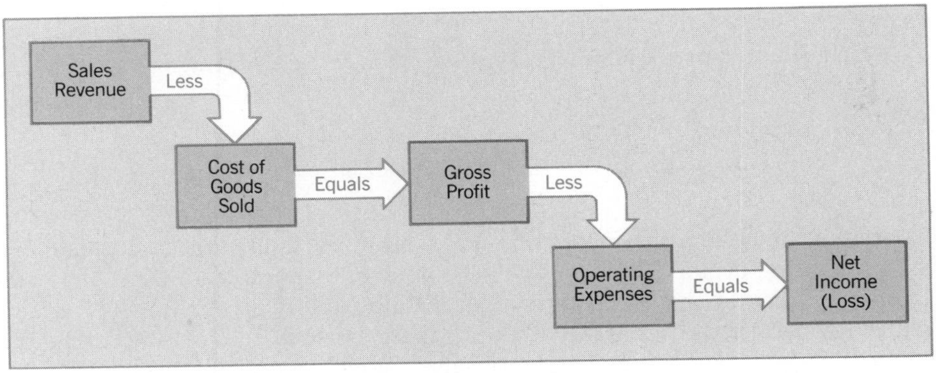

The operating expenses of a merchandising company include many of the expenses found in a service enterprise. Hence, attention in this chapter is focused primarily on the recording of sales revenues and the related cost of goods sold that produce gross profit.

SALES REVENUE

In accordance with the **revenue recognition principle,** sales revenues, like service revenues, are recorded when earned. Typically, this occurs when the goods are transferred from the seller to the buyer. At this point, the sale transaction is completed and the sales price is established.

Sales may be made on the basis of credit or for cash. Department stores such as J. C. Penney and Sears have a significant amount of both types of sales. Grocery stores such as Safeway and A&P normally have cash sales. Every sales transaction should be supported by a **business document** that provides written evidence of the sale. **Cash register tapes** provide evidence of cash sales, whereas a **sales invoice,** as illustrated below, provides support for credit sales. The original copy of the invoice is for the customer, and one copy is retained by the seller for use in recording the sale. The invoice shows the date of sale, customer name, total sales price, and other relevant information.

INVOICE NO. 731

Highpoint Electronic, Inc.
27 Circle Drive
Harding, Michigan 48281

SOLD TO
Firm Name: Chelsea Video Inc.
Attention Of: James Hoover, Purchasing Agent
Address: 125 Main Street
City: Chelsea State: Illinois Zip: 60915

Date 5/4/87 | Salesperson Malone | Terms 2/10, n/30 | Freight FOB Sh.Pt. -Collect

Catalogue No.	Description	Quantity	Price	Amount
X572Y9820	Printed Circuit Board-prototype	1	2,300	$2,300
A2547Z45	Production Model Circuits	5	300	1,500
			TOTAL	$3,800

IMPORTANT: ALL RETURNS MUST BE MADE WITHIN 10 DAYS

To record a sale, an asset account is debited, and the revenue account, Sales, is credited. The Cash account is debited for cash sales, and Accounts

Receivable is debited for credit sales. To illustrate a sale on credit, the following entry is made by Highpoint Electronics for the sales invoice shown on page 169.

May	4	Accounts Receivable	3,800	
		Sales		3,800
		(To record credit sale per invoice #731)		

As indicated by this entry, sales revenues can be recorded before cash is actually collected. For credit sales, the amount due may not be collected until the next period. Therefore, the sales revenues earned during a particular period may be significantly different from the cash collected from sales during that same period.

To illustrate a sale for cash, assume that the cash register total for cash sales on May 4 is $6,210. The entry, therefore, is:

May	4	Cash	6,210	
		Sales		6,210
		(To record daily cash sales)		

Merchandising companies may use more than one sales account. For example, Highpoint Electronics may have separate sales accounts for its sales of television sets, video cassette recorders, and microwave ovens. Because sales is the principal source of revenue for a merchandising company, the amount and trend of sales are of critical importance to management, creditors, and other interested parties. An increase in sales from the preceding year or month signifies a growing business and often leads to higher net income, whereas an unfavorable trend may suggest lower future earnings.

SALES RETURNS AND ALLOWANCES

A customer may be dissatisfied with the merchandise received because the goods are (1) damaged or defective, (2) of inferior quality, or (3) not in accord with the customer's specifications. In such cases, the customer may return the goods to the seller for credit if the sale was made on credit, or for a cash refund if the sale was originally for cash. This transaction is known as a **sales return.** Alternatively, the customer may elect to keep the merchandise if the seller is willing to grant an allowance (deduction) from the selling price. This transaction is known as a **sales allowance.** Sales returns and sales allowances are combined into one account, Sales Returns and Allowances, for accounting purposes.

Upon approval of the customer's request for a sales return or allowance, the seller normally prepares a business document known as a **credit memorandum.** The credit memorandum illustrated on page 171 relates to the sales invoice shown on page 169.

The original copy of the credit memorandum is sent to the customer as notification that the request for a sales return or allowance has been granted. A copy of the credit memorandum is retained by the seller as evidence of the transaction. The seller's entry to record a credit memorandum involves a debit to the Sales Returns and Allowances account and a credit to Accounts Receivable, as shown on the next page:

CREDIT-CM126

Highpoint Electronic, Inc.

27 Circle Drive
Harding, Michigan 48281

Firm Name: Chelsea Video Inc.

Attention Of: James Hoover, Purchasing Agent

Address: 125 Main Street

City: Chelsea State: Illinois Zip: 60915

Date 5/8/87	Salesperson Malone	Invoice No. 731	Invoice Date 5/4/87	Approved Reid

Catalogue No.	Description	Quantity	Price	Amount
A2547Z45	Production Model Circuits (Inoperative)	1	300	$300

Cash Refund ☐ Credit Account ☒ Other

May	8	Sales Returns and Allowances	300	
		Accounts Receivable		300
		(To record allowance for damaged goods per credit memorandum CM126)		

When a credit memorandum pertains to a cash sale, a cash refund is normally made. In such case, Sales Returns and Allowances is debited and Cash is credited.

Sales Returns and Allowances is a **contra revenue account** to Sales. The normal balance of this account is a debit. A contra account is used, instead of debiting Sales, to disclose the amount of sales returns and allowances in the accounts and in the income statement. Disclosure of this information is important to management, because excessive returns and allowances suggest inferior merchandise, inefficiencies in filling orders, errors in billing customers, and mistakes in delivery or shipment of the goods. Moreover, a debit directly to Sales would obscure the relative importance of sales returns and allowances as a percentage of sales, and it could distort comparisons between total sales in different accounting periods.

SALES DISCOUNTS

The terms of a credit sale may include an offer of a cash discount, called a **sales discount,** to the customer for prompt payment of the balance due. This incentive is advantageous to both parties. The purchaser obtains a cash saving. The seller is able to convert the accounts receivable into cash earlier and the company's normal operating cycle is shortened. The credit terms specify the amount and time period for the cash discount, as well as the length of time in which the purchaser is expected to pay the full invoice price. In the sales invoice on page 169, credit terms are 2/10, n/30, which is read "two-ten, net thirty." This means that a 2% cash discount may be taken on the invoice price (less any returns or allowances) if payment is made within 10 days of the invoice date (the discount period); otherwise, the invoice price less any returns or allowances is due 30 days from the invoice date. Alternatively, the discount period may extend to a specified number of days following the month in which the sale occurs. For example, 1/10 EOM (end-of-month) means that a 1% discount is available if the invoice is paid within the first 10 days of the next month.

When the seller elects not to offer a cash discount for prompt payment, credit terms will specify only the maximum time period for paying the balance due. For example, the time period may be stated as n/30, n/60, or n/10 EOM.

The seller debits Sales Discounts when cash discounts are taken by customers. To illustrate, assume Chelsea Video Inc. pays the balance due of $3,500 (Sales $3,800 less sales returns and allowances $300) on May 14, the last day of the discount period. The cash discount is $70 ($3,500 × 2%), and the amount of cash paid by Chelsea is $3,430 ($3,500 − $70). Assuming the payment is received by Highpoint Electronics on May 15, the entry is:

May 15	Cash	3,430	
	Sales Discounts	70	
	Accounts Receivable		3,500
	(To record collection within 2/10, n/30 discount period)		

Sales Discounts is also a contra revenue account, and its normal balance is a debit. This account is used, instead of debiting Sales, to disclose the amount of cash discounts taken by customers.

STATEMENT PRESENTATION

As contra revenue accounts, sales returns and allowances and sales discounts are deducted from sales in the income statement. The revenue section of the income statement based on assumed data for Highpoint Electronics is as follows:

PARTIAL INCOME STATEMENT		
Sales revenues		
Sales		$480,000
Less: Sales returns and allowances	$12,000	
Sales discounts	8,000	20,000
Net sales		$460,000

Statement presentation of sales revenues section

This presentation discloses the significant aspects of the company's principal revenue producing activities.

COST OF GOODS SOLD

As you learned earlier in this chapter, the second factor in measuring net income in a merchandising company is the cost of goods sold. The cost of goods sold may be determined each time a sale occurs or at the end of an accounting period. To make the determination when the sale occurs, a company must use a **perpetual inventory system.** Under this system, detailed records of the cost of each inventory item are maintained. For example, a Ford dealership will have separate inventory records for each Escort, Tempo, Taurus, and Thunderbird. When a car is sold, its cost is obtained from the inventory records. Perpetual inventory systems have traditionally been used by companies that sell high unit-value items such as furniture, television sets, and large home appliances. Much more will be said about perpetual inventory systems in Chapter 9.

When cost of goods sold is determined only at the end of an accounting period, a company is said to be using a **periodic inventory system.** This system is widely used by companies such as F. W. Woolworth, True Value hardware stores, and Rexall drugstores that sell thousands of low unit-value items. A periodic inventory system does not require detailed accounting records. Unless there is a specific statement to the contrary, a periodic inventory system will be assumed in this textbook.

To determine the cost of goods sold under a periodic inventory system, it is necessary to (1) record the purchases of merchandise for resale, (2) determine the cost of goods purchased during the accounting period, and (3) determine the cost of goods on hand at the beginning and end of the accounting period.

RECORDING PURCHASES OF MERCHANDISE

When merchandise is purchased for resale to customers, the temporary account, Merchandise Purchases, or simply Purchases, is debited for the cost of the goods. Note, however, that all purchases are not debited to Purchases. Purchases of supplies, equipment, and similar items should be debited to specific asset accounts rather than to Purchases, because these assets are acquired for use and not for resale.

Like sales, purchases may be made for cash or on account (credit). Every purchase should be supported by business documents that provide written evidence of the transaction. The purchase is normally recorded by the purchaser when the goods are received from the seller. Each cash purchase should be supported by a canceled check or cash register receipt indicating the items purchased. Cash purchases are recorded by a debit to Purchases and a credit to Cash. Each credit purchase should be supported by a **purchase invoice** indicating the total purchase price and other relevant information. The purchaser does not prepare a separate purchase invoice. Instead, the copy of the sales invoice sent by the seller becomes a purchase invoice to the buyer. The entry by Chelsea Video Inc. for the invoice shown on page 169 is:

May	4	Purchases	3,800	
		Accounts Payable		3,800
		(To record goods purchased on account, terms 2/10, n/30)		

Purchase Returns and Allowances

A sales return and allowance on the seller's books is recorded as a **purchase return and allowance** on the books of the purchaser. The purchaser often initiates the request for a reduction of the balance due through the issuance of a **debit memorandum.** The original debit memorandum is sent to the seller and one copy is retained by the purchaser. The information contained in a debit memorandum is similar to the information found in the credit memorandum on page 0–0. The entry by Chelsea Video Inc. based on the credit memorandum on page 171 is:

May	8	Accounts Payable	300	
		Purchase Returns and Allowances		300
		(To record allowance for damaged goods)		

Purchase Returns and Allowances represents a reduction in the cost of goods purchased for resale. It is a **contra account** to Purchases and its normal balance is a credit. The contra account is used instead of crediting Purchases in order to disclose both the dollar amount of returns and allowances and the percentage of gross purchases that have proven to be unsatisfactory. Excessive purchase returns and allowances may indicate inefficiencies in a company's purchasing procedures or the need to find more reliable suppliers.

Credit memorandums and debit memorandums derive their name from the action that the issuer intends to take on the accounts receivable or payable carried on its books. The purchaser sends a debit memorandum to indicate the intention to **debit** Accounts Payable and credit Purchase Returns and Allowances. Similarly, a seller issues a credit memorandum to indicate a debit to Sales Returns and Allowances and a **credit** to Accounts Receivable.

Purchase Discounts

To the seller, a cash discount granted to a customer is called a sales discount; the buyer calls this discount a **purchase discount.** Like a sales discount, a purchase discount is based on the invoice cost less returns and allowances, if

any. A contra account, Purchase Discounts, is credited for discounts that are taken. The entry to record the May 14 payment by Chelsea Video Inc. to Highpoint Electronics is as follows:

May 14	Account Payable	3,500	
	Purchase Discounts		70
	Cash		3,430
	(To record payment within discount period)		

Purchase Discounts represents a reduction in the cost of goods purchased for resale. As in the case of Purchase Returns and Allowances, Purchase Discounts is a contra account to Purchases, and its normal balance is also a credit.

A buyer usually should take all available discounts. For example, if Chelsea Video takes the discount, it pays $70 less in cash. Conversely, if it forgoes the discount and invests the $3,500 in a bank savings account for 20 days at 10% interest, it will earn only $19.44 in interest. The savings obtained by taking the discount is computed as follows:

Savings obtained by taking discount

Discount of 2% on $3,500	$70.00
Interest received on $3,500 (for 20 days at 10%)	19.44
Savings by taking the discount	$50.56

Alternatively, passing up the discount may be viewed as paying an interest rate of 2% for the use of $3,500 for 20 days. This is the equivalent of an annual interest rate of 36% (2% × 360/20). Obviously, it would be better for Chelsea Video to borrow at prevailing bank interest rates of 8–14% than to lose the discount.

To facilitate taking purchase discounts, unpaid invoices should be filed by due dates. For example, Chelsea Video should have a file folder dated May 14 in which all bills to be paid on this date are filed. In addition to helping the purchaser remember the discount date, this procedure prevents early payment of bills and maximizes the time that available cash can be used for other business purposes.

In computerized systems the invoice due date can be entered at the time the purchase is recorded. With this information programmed into the system, checks can automatically be generated on the proper due dates.

Freight Costs

The sales agreement should indicate whether the seller or buyer is to pay the cost of transporting the goods to the buyer's place of business. When a common carrier such as a railroad, trucking company, or airline is used, the transportation company prepares a freight bill (often called a bill of lading) in accordance with the sales agreement. Freight terms are expressed as either

FOB shipping point or **FOB destination.** The letters FOB mean **free on board.** Thus, **FOB shipping point** means that goods are placed free on board the carrier by the seller, and the buyer must pay the freight costs. Conversely, **FOB destination** means that the goods are placed free on board at the buyer's place of business, and the seller must pay the freight. For example, the sales invoice on page 169 indicates that freight is FOB shipping point. Thus, the buyer (Chelsea Video, Inc.) must pay the freight charges.

When the purchaser directly incurs the freight costs, the account Freight-in (or Transportation-in) is debited. For example, if upon delivery of the goods on May 10, Chelsea Video, Inc., pays Acme Freight Company $150 for freight charges, the entry on Chelsea's books is:

May 10	Freight-in	150	
	Cash		150
	(To record payment of freight, terms FOB shipping point)		

Freight-in's normal balance is a debit, and it is an **adjunct account** to purchases, which means it is added to purchases. It is added because the cost of merchandise purchased should include any freight charges necessary to bring the goods to the purchaser. The use of a Freight-in account enables management to determine the materiality of these costs. If freight costs are significant, management may want to compare the cost of truck, rail, or air freight to find the least expensive alternative.

In contrast, freight costs incurred by the seller on outgoing merchandise are an operating expense to the seller. These costs are debited to Freight-out or Delivery Expense, not to a contra sales account. For example, if the freight terms in the invoice on page 169 had specified FOB destination and Highpoint Electronics had paid the $150 freight charges, the entry by Highpoint would be:

May 10	Freight-out	150	
	Cash		150
	(To record payment of freight on goods sold, FOB destination)		

When the freight charges are paid by the seller, the seller will usually establish a higher invoice price for the goods.

DETERMINING THE COST OF GOODS PURCHASED

In explaining the accounting for goods purchased for resale, we discussed the following accounts:

Normal balances cost of goods purchased accounts

Account	Normal Balance
Purchases	Debit
Purchase Returns and Allowances	Credit
Purchase Discounts	Credit
Freight-in	Debit

In determining the cost of goods purchased: (1) the accounts with credit balances are subtracted from purchases to produce **net purchases,** and (2) freight-in is then added to net purchases to produce **cost of goods purchased.** To illustrate, assume that Highpoint Electronics shows the following balances for the accounts above: Purchases, $325,000; Purchase Returns and Allowances, $10,400; Purchase Discounts, $6,800; and Freight-in, $12,200. Net purchases and cost of goods purchased are $307,800 and $320,000, respectively, as shown below:

Computation of cost of goods purchased

Purchases		$325,000
Less: Purchases returns and allowances	$10,400	
Purchase discounts	6,800	17,200
Net purchases		**307,800**
Add: Freight-in		12,200
Cost of goods purchased		**$320,000**

DETERMINING COST OF GOODS ON HAND

To determine the cost of inventory on hand, it is necessary to take a physical inventory. Taking a physical inventory involves:

1. Counting the units on hand for each item of inventory.
2. Applying unit costs to the total units on hand for each item of inventory.
3. Aggregating the costs for each item of inventory to determine the total cost of goods on hand.

A physical inventory should be taken at or near the balance sheet date. To enhance the accuracy of the inventory counts, many stores and warehouses suspend operations while inventory is being taken.

In computerized inventory systems, inventory taking is greatly simplified. Once the item counts have been entered, the computer takes over the chores of applying unit cost data to quantities, determining total inventory, and printing out meaningful inventory summaries.

The account, Merchandise Inventory, is used to record the cost of inventory on hand at the balance sheet date. This amount becomes the beginning inventory for the next accounting period. For Highpoint Electronics, the balance in Merchandise Inventory at December 31, 1986 is $36,000. This amount is also the January 1, 1987 balance in Merchandise Inventory. During 1987, **no entries are made to Merchandise Inventory.** At December 31, 1987, entries will be made to eliminate the beginning inventory and to record the ending inventory, which we will assume is $40,000. These entries are illustrated later in the chapter.

Only taking a physical inventory once a year is a real disadvantage because it is not possible to determine the amount of inventory losses during the

period. For example, a supermarket chain such as A&P may have inventory losses from spoilage of meats, fruits, and vegetables during the year. Furthermore, a department store like Macy's may have losses from shoplifting. Under a periodic inventory system, goods not on hand are assumed to be sold.

Inventory losses can be substantial. For example, shoplifting is the biggest crime in the United States with a cost of more than $18 billion annually, or 5% of retail sales, not including thefts by store employees. Shoplifting losses have led to the demise of many companies. For example, Dayton-Hudson closed its landmark store in downtown Detroit because of excessive shoplifting losses.

COMPUTING THE COST OF GOODS SOLD

The computation of the cost of goods sold also involves two steps. First, the cost of goods purchased is added to the cost of goods on hand at the beginning of the period (beginning inventory) to obtain the **cost of goods available for sale.** Second, the cost of goods on hand at the end of the period (ending inventory) is subtracted from the cost of goods available for sale to arrive at the cost of goods sold. For Highpoint Electronics the cost of goods available for sale and the cost of goods sold are $356,000 and $316,000, respectively, as shown below:

Computation of cost of goods sold

Beginning inventory	$ 36,000
Add: Cost of goods purchased	320,000
Cost of goods available for sale	**356,000**
Less: Ending inventory	40,000
Cost of goods sold	**$316,000**

GROSS PROFIT

From the graphic at the beginning of the chapter, you learned that cost of goods sold is deducted from sales revenue to determine **gross profit.** On the basis of the sales data presented on page 173 and the foregoing cost of goods sold, the gross profit for Highpoint Electronics is $144,000, computed as follows:

Computation of gross profit

Net sales	$460,000
Cost of goods sold	316,000
Gross profit	**$144,000**

A company's gross profit may also be expressed as a percentage by dividing the amount of gross profit by net sales. For Highpoint Electronics the gross profit rate is 31.3% ($144,000 ÷ $460,000). As in the case of sales, the amount and trend of gross profit are closely watched by management and other interested parties. The volume of sales and the amount of gross profit on each unit

sold are two factors that affect a company's gross profit percentage. For example, in a recent year, Sears, Roebuck reported a gross profit rate of 32%; Kroger, 24%; Walgreen Drugs, 30%; K mart, 27%; and McDonald's, 62%.

OPERATING EXPENSES

Operating expenses are the third component in measuring net income for a merchandising company. As indicated earlier, these expenses in a merchandising company are similar to those in a service enterprise. At Highpoint Electronics, operating expenses were $114,000. Net income is determined by subtracting operating expenses from gross profit. Thus, net income is $30,000 ($144,000 − $114,000).

INCOME STATEMENT FOR A MERCHANDISING COMPANY

The income statement for retailers and wholesalers contains three features that are not found in the income statement of a service enterprise. These features are: (1) a sales revenue section, (2) a cost of goods sold section, and (3) gross profit. Using assumed data for specific operating expenses, the income statement for Highpoint Electronics is as follows:

Income statement for a merchandising company

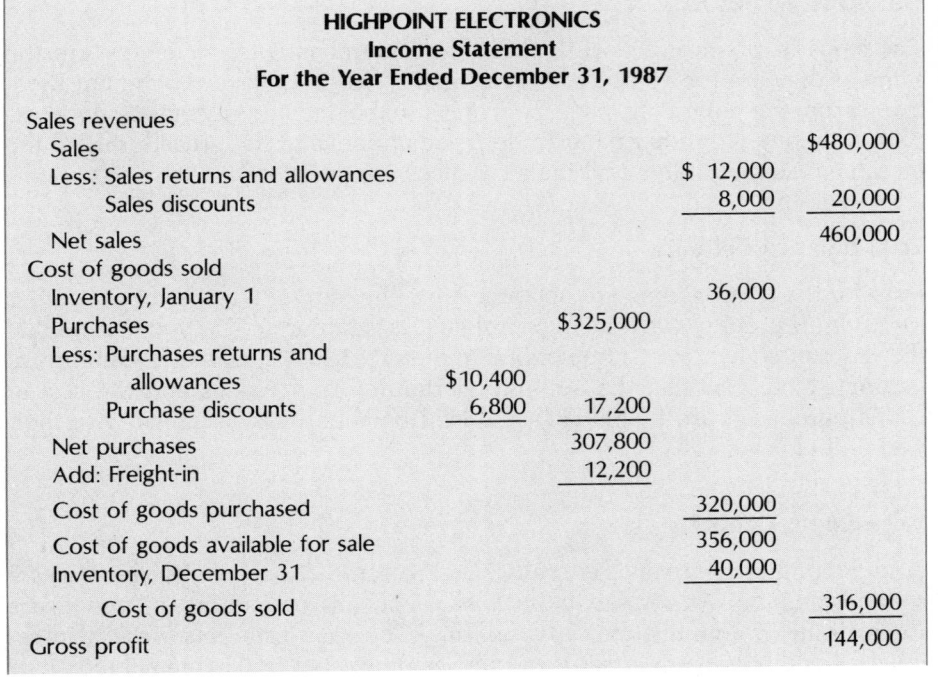

HIGHPOINT ELECTRONICS
Income Statement
For the Year Ended December 31, 1987

Sales revenues				
Sales				$480,000
Less: Sales returns and allowances			$ 12,000	
Sales discounts			8,000	20,000
Net sales				460,000
Cost of goods sold				
Inventory, January 1			36,000	
Purchases		$325,000		
Less: Purchases returns and allowances	$10,400			
Purchase discounts	6,800	17,200		
Net purchases		307,800		
Add: Freight-in		12,200		
Cost of goods purchased			320,000	
Cost of goods available for sale			356,000	
Inventory, December 31			40,000	
Cost of goods sold				316,000
Gross profit				144,000

Operating expenses		
Store salaries expense	45,000	
Rent expense	19,000	
Utilities expense	17,000	
Advertising expense	16,000	
Depreciation expense – store equipment	8,000	
Freight-out	7,000	
Insurance expense	2,000	
Total operating expenses		114,000
Net income		$ 30,000

ACCOUNTING CYCLE FOR A MERCHANDISING COMPANY

Up to this point, we have been primarily concerned with the measurement of net income in a merchandising company. We have also illustrated the basic entries in recording transactions relating to sales and purchases. It is now time to consider the remaining steps in the accounting cycle.

Each of the required steps in the cycle applies to a merchandising company, and a work sheet is again an optional step. To illustrate these steps, we will assume that Highpoint Electronics uses a work sheet.

USING A WORK SHEET

The steps in preparing a work sheet for a merchandising company are the same as they are for a service enterprise. The work sheet for Highpoint Electronics on the following page contains all the income statement data explained above plus other data. To help you understand the procedures, all the merchandising accounts and their balances are in color.

Trial Balance Columns

Data for the trial balance are obtained from the ledger balances at December 31, after all postings have been completed. It is important for you to note that the amount shown for Merchandise Inventory, $36,000, is the **beginning inventory.** Note also that the accounts pertaining to net sales and the cost of goods purchased are included in the trial balance in accordance with their normal balances.

Adjustment Columns

A merchandise company generally has the same types of adjustments as a service company. As you see in the work sheet, adjustments (a), (b), and (c) are for insurance, depreciation, and salaries. These adjustments were also required for Pioneer Advertising Agency, as illustrated in Chapters 3 and 4.

Conceptually, it can be argued that the change between the beginning and ending merchandise inventory balances should be shown on the work sheet as an adjustment. The adjustment would be similar to the adjustments for supplies in Pioneer Advertising. The alternative is to consider the change in inventories as part of the closing process. Both the adjusting entry approach and the closing entry approach are acceptable in accounting, and both approaches accomplish the same objective. We have elected to use the closing entry approach in this textbook. However, the adjusting entry approach is explained and illustrated in Appendix 5-A.

After all adjustment data are entered on the work sheet, the equality of the adjustment column totals is established, and the balances in all accounts are extended to the adjusted trial balance columns.

Work sheet for merchandising company

HIGHPOINT ELECTRONICS
Work Sheet
For the Year Ended December 31, 1987

	Trial Balance		Adjustments		Adjusted Trial Balance		Income Statement		Balance Sheet	
	Dr.	Cr.	Dr.	Cr.	Dr.	Cr.	Dr.	Cr.	Dr.	Cr.
Cash	9,500				9,500				9,500	
Accounts Receivable	16,100				16,100				16,100	
MERCHANDISE INVENTORY	**36,000**				**36,000**		**36,000**	**40,000**	**40,000**	
Prepaid Insurance	3,800			(a) 2,000	1,800				1,800	
Store Equipment	80,000				80,000				80,000	
Accumulated Depreciation		16,000		(b) 8,000		24,000				24,000
Accounts Payable		20,400				20,400				20,400
R. A. Lamb, Capital		83,000				83,000				83,000
R. A. Lamb, Drawing	15,000				15,000				15,000	
SALES		**480,000**				**480,000**		**480,000**		
SALES RETURNS AND ALLOWANCES	**12,000**				**12,000**		**12,000**			
SALES DISCOUNTS	**8,000**				**8,000**		**8,000**			
PURCHASES	**325,000**				**325,000**		**325,000**			
PURCHASE RETURNS AND ALLOWANCES		**10,400**				**10,400**		**10,400**		
PURCHASE DISCOUNTS		**6,800**				**6,800**		**6,800**		
FREIGHT-IN	**12,200**				**12,200**		**12,200**			
FREIGHT-OUT	**7,000**				**7,000**		**7,000**			
Advertising Expense	16,000				16,000		16,000			
Rent Expense	19,000				19,000		19,000			
Store Salaries Expense	40,000		(c) 5,000		45,000		45,000			
Utilities Expense	17,000				17,000		17,000			
Totals	616,600	616,600								
Insurance Expense			(a) 2,000		2,000		2,000			
Depreciation Expense			(b) 8,000		8,000		8,000			
Salaries Payable				(c) 5,000		5,000				5,000
Totals			15,000	15,000	629,600	629,600	507,200	537,200	162,400	132,400
Net Income							30,000			30,000
Totals							537,200	537,200	162,400	162,400

Financial Statement Columns

Examination of the work sheet shows that the extending of adjusted balances to the financial statement columns for a merchandising enterprise is the same as for a service enterprise. From the work sheet, you can see that all of the merchandising accounts in the adjusted trial balance columns are transferred to the income statement columns. For the sales revenue accounts, the balance in Sales is shown in the credit column, and the contra revenue accounts, Sales Returns and Allowances and Sales Discounts, are shown in the debit column. Similarly, the balances in Purchases and Freight-In are extended to the income statement debit column, and the contra purchase accounts, Purchase Returns and Allowances and Purchase Discounts, are extended to the credit column.

The work sheet procedures for the account, Merchandise Inventory, merit specific comment. The procedures are:

1. The adjusted balance, \$36,000, is extended to the income statement debit column so that it can be added in reporting cost of goods available for sale in the income statement.
2. The ending inventory, \$40,000, is added to the work sheet by an income statement credit and a balance sheet debit. The credit makes it possible to deduct ending inventory from the cost of goods available for sale in the income statement. The debit means the ending inventory can be reported as an asset on the balance sheet.

These two procedures are specifically illustrated below:

Presentation of inventories on work sheet

	Income Statement			Balance Sheet	
	Dr.	Cr.		Dr.	Cr.
Merchandise Inventory (1)	36,000	40,000 ←	(2)	→ 40,000	

In a merchandising company, all income statement column debits do not represent expenses. The exceptions are the contra revenue accounts. Similarly, all income statement column credits are not revenues. The exceptions are the contra purchase accounts and ending merchandise inventory.

PREPARING FINANCIAL STATEMENTS

As is true in a service enterprise, financial statements for a merchandising company are prepared from the financial statement columns of the work sheet. The income statement for Highpoint Electronics has already been illustrated.

The owner's equity statement is as follows:

Owner's equity statement

HIGHPOINT ELECTRONICS
Owner's Equity Statement
For the Year Ended December 31, 1987

R. A. Lamb, Capital January 1	$ 83,000
Add: Net income	30,000
	$113,000
Less: Drawings	15,000
R. A. Lamb, Capital December 31	$ 98,000

The classified balance sheet then is as follows:

Classified balance sheet

HIGHPOINT ELECTRONICS
Balance Sheet
December 31, 1987

Assets

Current assets		
Cash		$ 9,500
Accounts receivable		16,100
Merchandise inventory		40,000
Prepaid insurance		1,800
Total current assets		67,400
Property, plant, and equipment		
Store equipment	$80,000	
Less: Accumulated depreciation—store equipment	24,000	56,000
Total assets		$123,400

Liabilities and Owner's Equity

Current liabilities	
Accounts payable	$ 20,400
Salaries payable	5,000
Total current liabilities	25,400
Owner's equity	
R. A. Lamb, Capital	98,000
Total liabilities and owner's equity	$123,400

In the balance sheet, merchandise inventory is reported as a current asset immediately below accounts receivable. You will recall that items are listed under current assets in the order of liquidity. Merchandise inventory is less liquid than accounts receivable because the goods must first be sold and then collection must be made from the customer.

The normal operating cycle for a merchandising company ordinarily is longer than it is for a service company. Graphically, the cycle can be depicted as follows:

Operating cycle for a merchandising company

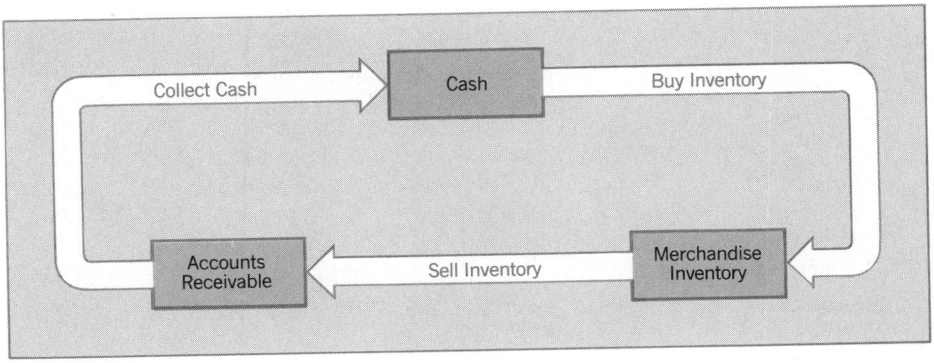

JOURNALIZING AND POSTING ADJUSTING ENTRIES

Adjusting entries are journalized from the adjustment columns of the work sheet. Because the journalizing and posting of the entries are the same as they are for a service enterprise, they are not illustrated.

JOURNALIZING AND POSTING CLOSING ENTRIES

For a merchandising company, like a service enterprise, all accounts that affect the determination of net income are closed to Income Summary. Data for the preparation of closing entries may be obtained from the income statement columns of the work sheet. In journalizing, all debit column amounts are credited, and all credit column amounts are debited. This means that to close the merchandise inventory, (1) the beginning inventory balance is debited to Income Summary and credited to Merchandise Inventory, and (2) the ending inventory balance is debited to Merchandise Inventory and credited to Income Summary. The two entries for Highpoint Electronics are:

	(1)		
Dec. 31	Income Summary	36,000	
	Merchandise Inventory		36,000
	(To close beginning inventory)		
	(2)		
31	Merchandise Inventory	40,000	
	Income Summary		40,000
	(To record ending inventory)		

After posting, the Merchandise Inventory and Income Summary accounts will show the following:

Relationship of inventory and income summary

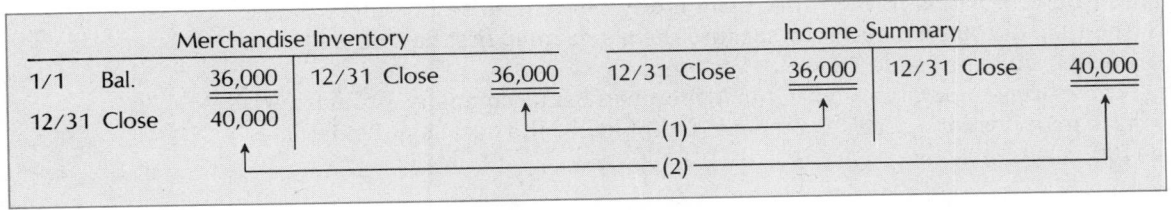

Merchandise Inventory					Income Summary			
1/1 Bal.	36,000	12/31 Close	36,000 (1)		12/31 Close	36,000 (1)	12/31 Close	40,000 (2)
12/31 Close	40,000 (2)							

It is more expedient, however, to include the closing of merchandise inventory into the regular closing entries, as shown below for Highpoint Electronics.

Dec. 31	**Merchandise Inventory (Dec. 31)**	**40,000**	
	Sales	480,000	
	Purchase Returns and Allowances	10,400	
	Purchase Discounts	6,800	
	Income Summary		537,200
	(To record ending inventory and close accounts with credit balances)		
31	Income Summary	507,200	
	Merchandise Inventory (Jan. 1)		**36,000**
	Sales Returns and Allowances		12,000
	Sales Discounts		8,000
	Purchases		325,000
	Freight-in		12,200
	Store Salaries Expense		45,000
	Rent Expense		19,000
	Freight-out		7,000
	Advertising Expense		16,000
	Utilities Expense		17,000
	Depreciation Expense		8,000
	Insurance Expense		2,000
	(To close beginning inventory and other income statement accounts with debit balances)		
31	Income Summary	30,000	
	R. A. Lamb, Capital		30,000
	(To transfer net income to capital)		
31	R. A. Lamb, Capital	15,000	
	R, A, Lamb, Drawing		15,000
	(To close drawings to capital)		

After the closing entries are posted, all temporary accounts will have zero balances. In addition, R. A. Lamb, Capital will have a credit balance of $98,000: beginning balance ($83,000) + net income ($30,000) – drawings ($15,000).

PREPARING THE POST-CLOSING TRIAL BALANCE

After the closing entries are posted, the post-closing trial balance is prepared. The only new account in the post-closing trial balance is merchandise inventory. The post-closing trial balance for Highpoint Electronics at December 31, 1987 is as follows:

Post-closing trial balance

HIGHPOINT ELECTRONICS
Post-Closing Trial Balance
December 31, 1987

	Debit	Credit
Cash	$ 9,500	
Accounts receivable	16,100	
Merchandise inventory	40,000	
Prepaid insurance	1,800	
Store equipment	80,000	
Accumulated depreciation		$ 24,000
Accounts payable		20,400
Salaries payable		5,000
R. A. Lamb, Capital		98,000
	$147,400	$147,400

SUMMARY OF MERCHANDISING ENTRIES

The daily recurring and closing entries for the merchandising accounts are summarized as follows:

Daily recurring and closing entries

Transactions	Daily Recurring Entries		
Selling merchandise to customers	Cash or Accounts Receivable	XX	
	Sales		XX
Granting sales returns or allowances to customers	Sales Returns and Allowances	XX	
	Cash or Accounts Receivable		XX
Receiving payment from customers within discount period	Cash	XX	
	Sales Discounts	XX	
	Accounts Receivable		XX
Purchasing merchandise for resale	Purchases	XX	
	Cash or Accounts Payable		XX
Paying freight costs on merchandise purchased; FOB shipping point	Freight-in	XX	
	Cash		XX
Paying freight costs on merchandise sold; FOB destination	Freight-out	XX	
	Cash		XX
Receiving purchase returns or allowances from suppliers	Cash or Accounts Payable	XX	
	Purchase Returns and Allowances		XX
Paying suppliers within discount period	Accounts Payable	XX	
	Purchase Discounts		XX
	Cash		XX

Events	Closing Entries		
Recording ending inventory and closing accounts with credit balances	Merchandise Inventory	XX	
	Sales	XX	
	Purchase Returns and Allowances	XX	
	Purchase Discounts	XX	
	Income Summary		XX
Closing beginning inventory and accounts with debit balances	Income Summary	XX	
	Merchandise Inventory		XX
	Sales Returns and Allowances		XX
	Sales Discounts		XX
	Purchases		XX
	Freight-in		XX
	Freight-out		XX

CLASSIFIED INCOME STATEMENT

The **classified income statement** shows significant relationships in the determination of net income. You will recall, for example, that the income statement for Highpoint Electronics contained three sections: sales revenues, cost of goods sold, and operating expenses. These sections pertain to the company's operating activity. Further, classification of the income statement is possible when a company (1) has nonoperating activities that result in income or loss, and (2) wishes to recognize subgroupings of operating expenses.

NONOPERATING SECTIONS

The nonoperating sections include (1) revenues and expenses that result from secondary or auxiliary operations and (2) gains and losses that are unrelated to the company's operations. There are two nonoperating sections: **Other Revenues and Gains** and **Other Expenses and Losses.** For a merchandising company these sections will typically include the following items.

Items reported in nonoperating sections

Other revenues and gains	Other expenses and losses
Interest revenue from notes receivable and marketable securities	Interest expense on notes and loans payable
Dividend revenue from investments in capital stock	Casualty losses from recurring causes such as vandalism and accidents
Rent revenue from subleasing a portion of the store	Losses from the sale or abandonment of property, plant, and equipment
Gain from the sale of property, plant, and equipment	Loss from strikes by employees and suppliers

The nonoperating sections are reported in the income statement immediately after the sections that pertain to the company's operating activities. These sections are illustrated below by adding data for Highpoint Electronics.

Income statement—nonoperating sections and operating expenses

HIGHPOINT ELECTRONICS
Income Statement
For the Year Ended December 31, 1987

Sales revenues				
Sales				$480,000
Less: Sales returns and allowances			$ 12,000	
Sales discounts			8,000	20,000
Net sales				460,000
Cost of goods sold				
Inventory, January 1			36,000	
Purchases		$325,000		
Less: Purchases returns and allowances	$10,400			
Purchase discounts	6,800	17,200		
Net purchases		307,800		
Add: Freight-in		12,200		
Cost of goods purchased			320,000	
Cost of goods available for sale			356,000	
Inventory, December 31			40,000	
Cost of goods sold				316,000
Gross profit				144,000
Operating expenses				
Selling expenses				
Store salaries expense		45,000		
Advertising expense		16,000		
Depreciation expense – store equipment		8,000		
Freight-out		7,000		
Total selling expenses			76,000	
Administrative expenses				
Rent expense		19,000		
Utilities expense		17,000		
Insurance expense		2,000		
Total administrative expenses			38,000	
Total operating expenses				114,000
Income from operations				**30,000**
Other revenues and gains				
Interest revenue		**3,000**		
Gain on sales of equipment		**600**	**3,600**	
Other expenses and losses				
Interest expense		**1,800**		
Casualty loss from vandalism		**200**	**2,000**	**1,600**
Net income				**$ 31,600**

Note that when these sections are included, the label **Income from Operations** (or Operating Income) is also added to clearly identify the results of operation. Within the nonoperating sections, items are generally reported at the net amount. Thus, if a company received a $1,000 insurance settlement on a $1,500 casualty loss, the loss would be reported at $500.

SUBGROUPING OF OPERATING EXPENSES

In larger companies, operating expenses are often subdivided by functional groupings. A common grouping is to distinguish between selling expenses and administrative expenses, as illustrated in the income statement on page 188. **Selling expenses** pertain to the expense associated with making sales; they include sales promotional expenses as well as expenses of completing the sale, such as delivery and shipping expenses. **Administrative expenses** (sometimes called general expenses) relate to such activities as personnel management, accounting, and store security.

The subgroupings aid in the control of expenses because responsibility for them can be assigned to a specific individual. When subgroupings are made, some expenses may have to be allocated. For example, if the store building is used for both selling and general functions, building expenses such as depreciation, utilities, and property taxes will need to be allocated.

SINGLE-STEP INCOME STATEMENT

The income statement for Highpoint Electronics shown on page 188 is considered to be a **multiple-step income statement** because numerous steps are involved before net income or net loss is reported. These steps include the determination of gross profit and income from operations. Many accountants, however, prefer an alternative form of income statement, known as a **single-step income statement.** The statement is so named because only one step, subtracting total expenses from total revenues, is required in determining net income or net loss. This form of income statement is extensively used in practice.

In a single-step statement, all data are classified under two categories: (1) **Revenues,** which includes both operating revenues and other revenues and gains, and (2) **Expenses,** which includes cost of goods sold, operating expenses, and other expenses and losses. A condensed single-step statement for Highpoint Electronics is illustrated below.

Single-step income statement

HIGHPOINT ELECTRONICS
Income Statement
For the Year Ended December 31, 1987

Revenues	
Net sales	$460,000
Interest revenue	3,000
Gain on sale of equipment	600
Total revenues	$463,600

Expenses		
Cost of goods sold	$316,000	
Selling expenses	76,000	
Administrative expenses	38,000	
Interest expense	1,800	
Casualty loss from vandalism	200	
Total expenses		432,000
Net income		$ 31,600

Detailed data have been omitted to facilitate your understanding of the form of the statement.

The primary reasons for using the single-step form are that (1) a company does not realize any type of profit or income until total revenues exceed total expenses, and (2) the distinction between operating and nonoperating activities is often arbitrary, and it may lead to incorrect interpretations by users of the income statement. For homework problems, the single-step form of income statement should only be used when it is specifically requested.

ANALYZING THE INCOME STATEMENT

The analysis of the income statement for a merchandising company should answer such questions as: Was the gross profit on sales sufficient to cover operating expenses? What proportion of net income was from operations? Were any operating expenses out of control?

The multiple-step income statement for Highpoint Electronics shows gross profit of $144,000, which was sufficient to produce income from operations of $30,000. Using net sales as 100%, it is also possible to determine the following as a percentage of net sales: gross profit, 31.3%; income from operations, 6.5%; and net income, 6.9%. The percentage relationships are often used for comparison with the results of prior years and with those of other companies in the same line of business.

One indication of whether any operating expenses are out of control is found in the relationship between expenses and net sales. For example, store salaries expense is approximately 9.8% ($45,000 ÷ $460,000) of net sales this year. If these salaries were only 7% of net sales last year, one may conclude that salaries are increasing too rapidly. Conversely, if salaries were 14% last year, it may suggest that this expense is under control this year.

From an owner's point of view, there is an important additional factor in assessing the adequacy of net income in a proprietorship. In measuring net income, the economic entity assumption of accounting prevents any recognition of either a salary expense to the owners for time worked or interest expense for capital invested in the business. In judging the adequacy of net income, the owner may want to implicitly recognize these two items. For example, R. A. Lamb may believe that he could earn a salary of $18,000 as a store manager. In addition, he may conclude that he could earn interest of

$9,000 by investing his capital in high-grade marketable securities. In such case, the **pure profit** from the business is only $3,000 ($30,000 − $18,000 − $9,000). This profit is often an important factor in deciding whether to continue in the business.

You should realize that conclusions based on a single year's results are hazardous at best. Certainly, future prospects would have a significant bearing on any decision to continue or to terminate the business. Further consideration is given to the analysis of income statements in later chapters.

SUMMARY OF STUDY OBJECTIVES

1. The components in measuring net income in a merchandising company are sales revenue, cost of goods sold, and operating expenses.

2. In recording sales revenues, entries are required for (a) cash and credit sales, (b) sales returns and allowances, and (c) sales discounts.

3. The accounts used in recording merchandise purchases and their normal balances are: Purchases (Debit), Purchase Returns and Allowances (Credit), Purchase Discounts (Credit), and Freight-In (Debit).

4. Computing cost of goods sold involves two steps: (a) beginning inventory is added to cost of goods purchased to obtain the cost of goods available for sale, and (b) ending inventory is subtracted from cost of goods available for sale to arrive at cost of goods sold.

5. The income statement for a merchandising company contains three sections: sales revenue, cost of goods sold, and operating expenses.

6. The merchandise accounts are closed through two entries: (1) the ending inventory is recorded and the accounts with credit balances are closed to Income Summary, and (2) the beginning inventory and accounts with debit balances are closed to Income Summary.

7. Classified income statements include the sections in (5) above plus (a) two nonoperating sections: other revenues and gains and other expenses and losses, and (b) the subgrouping of operating expenses as either selling or administrative expenses.

8. The gross profit rate and the percentage relationship of individual operating expenses to net sales are helpful in analyzing an income statement.

APPENDIX 5–A
ADJUSTING ENTRY METHOD FOR MERCHANDISE INVENTORY

As stated in this chapter, the change between the beginning and ending inventory balances may be made through adjusting entries rather than through closing entries. Some believe that changes in merchandise inventory should receive the same accounting treatment as changes in the cost of supplies on hand between two points in time. The adjusting entry method is just as acceptable as the closing entry method, and it accomplishes the same objective.

The adjusting entry method affects several steps in the accounting cycle, beginning with the use of a work sheet. These effects are explained and illustrated below, again using Highpoint Electronics as an example.

The adjusting entry method is used in most computerized systems since the programming logic involved is more straightforward. Some accountants favor this method in manual systems as well.

USING A WORK SHEET

In the work sheet on the following page, you will see two adjustments for merchandise inventory. Adjustment (d) for $36,000 transfers the beginning inventory to an Inventory Adjustment account that has been added to the work sheet. Adjustment (e) for $40,000 establishes the ending inventory from the Inventory Adjustment account. A credit balance of $4,000 results in the adjustment account in this case because the ending inventory is $4,000 higher than the beginning inventory. When the reverse is true, this account will have a debit balance. Inventory Adjustment is a **temporary account.** As will be shown shortly, this account receives entries only when adjusting and closing entries are being prepared. Inventory Adjustment will not appear in the trial balance or in the company's financial statements.

In the work sheet, as illustrated, the adjusted balance in Merchandise Inventory is extended to the balance sheet debit column, and the balance in Inventory Adjustment is included in the income statement credit column.

HIGHPOINT ELECTRONICS
Work Sheet
For the Year Ended December 31, 1987

	Trial Balance		Adjustments		Adjusted Trial Balance		Income Statement		Balance Sheet	
	Dr.	Cr.	Dr.	Cr.	Dr.	Cr.	Dr.	Cr.	Dr.	Cr.
Cash	9,500				9,500				9,500	
Accounts Receivable	16,100				16,100				16,100	
MERCHANDISE INVENTORY	36,000		(e)40,000	(d)36,000	40,000				40,000	
Prepaid Insurance	3,800			(a) 2,000	1,800				1,800	
Store Equipment	80,000				80,000				80,000	
Accumulated Depreciation		16,000		(b) 8,000		24,000				24,000
Accounts Payable		20,400				20,400				20,400
R. A. Lamb, Capital		83,000				83,000				83,000
R. A. Lamb, Drawing	15,000				15,000				15,000	
SALES		480,000				480,000		480,000		
SALES RETURNS AND ALLOWANCES	12,000				12,000		12,000			
SALES DISCOUNTS	8,000				8,000		8,000			
PURCHASES	325,000				325,000		325,000			
PURCHASE RETURNS AND ALLOWANCES		10,400				10,400		10,400		
PURCHASE DISCOUNTS		6,800				6,800		6,800		
FREIGHT-IN	12,200				12,200		12,200			
FREIGHT-OUT	7,000				7,000		7,000			
Advertising Expense	16,000				16,000		16,000			
Rent Expense	19,000				19,000		19,000			
Store Salaries Expense	40,000		(c) 5,000		45,000		45,000			
Utilities Expense	17,000				17,000		17,000			
Totals	616,600	616,600								
Insurance Expense			(a) 2,000		2,000		2,000			
Depreciation Expense			(b) 8,000		8,000		8,000			
Salaries Payable				(c) 5,000		5,000				5,000
INVENTORY ADJUSTMENT			(d)36,000	(e)40,000		4,000		4,000		
Totals			91,000	91,000	633,600	633,600	471,200	501,200	162,400	132,400
Net Income							30,000			30,000
Totals							501,200	501,200	162,400	162,400

PREPARING FINANCIAL STATEMENTS

In previous examples, complete financial statements have been prepared directly from the financial statement columns of the work sheet. Under the adjusting entry method, this is not true of the income statement because the income statement columns only show the **net change** in merchandise inventory. To ascertain the beginning and ending inventories, it is necessary to use the adjustment data that appear on either the Inventory Adjustment or Merchandise Inventory lines of the work sheet.

JOURNALIZING AND POSTING ADJUSTING ENTRIES

Under the adjusting entry method, the adjustments for merchandise inventory must be journalized and posted. The two entries are as follows:

		Debit	Credit
	(1)		
Dec. 31	Inventory Adjustment	36,000	
	Merchandise Inventory		36,000
	(To eliminate beginning inventory)		
	(2)		
31	Merchandise Inventory	40,000	
	Inventory Adjustment		40,000
	(To record ending inventory)		

After posting, the accounts will show:

Merchandise Inventory

Jan. 1	Bal.	36,000	Dec. 1	Adj.	36,000 (1)
Dec. 31	Adj.	40,000 (2)			

Inventory Adjustment

Dec. 31 Adj.	36,000 (1)	Dec. 31 Adj.	40,000 (2)

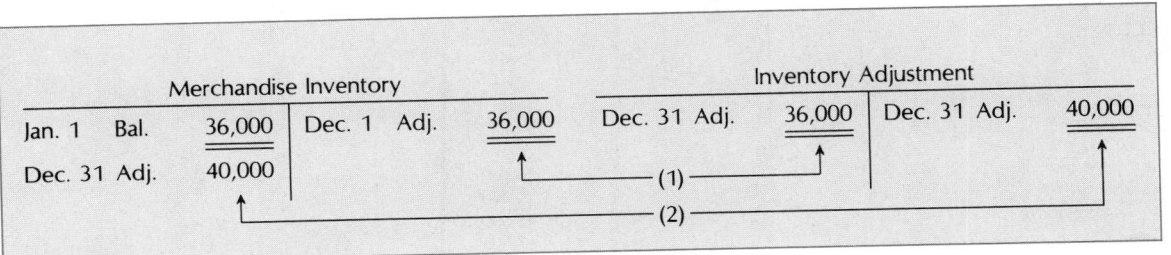

JOURNALIZING AND POSTING CLOSING ENTRIES

When the adjusting entry method is followed, two changes are required in preparing closing entries: (1) Merchandise Inventory is not closed, and (2) the Inventory Adjustment account must be closed. These changes affect the first two closing entries shown on page 185 as follows:

		Debit	Credit
Dec. 31	Sales	480,000	
	Purchase Returns and Allowances	10,400	
	Purchase Discounts	6,800	
	Inventory Adjustment	**4,000**	
	Income Summary		501,200
	(To close income statement accounts with credit balances and inventory adjustment)		
31	Income Summary	471,200	
	Sales Returns and Allowances		12,000
	Sales Discounts		8,000
	Purchases		325,000
	Freight-In		12,200
	Store Salaries Expense		45,000
	Rent Expense		19,000

	Freight-Out		7,000
	Advertising Expense		16,000
	Utilities Expense		17,000
	Depreciation Expense		8,000
	Insurance Expense		2,000
	(To close income statement accounts with debit balances)		

These entries produce a credit balance in Income Summary of $30,000 ($501,200 − $471,200), which equals the net income for the year reported for Highpoint Electronics under the closing entry method. After the first entry is posted, Inventory Adjustment will have a zero balance as shown below:

Inventory adjustment account

Inventory Adjustment					
Dec. 31	Adj.	36,000	Dec. 31	Adj.	40,000
31	Close	4,000			
		40,000			40,000

GLOSSARY

Adjunct account, p. 176

Administrative expenses, p. 189

Classified income statement, p. 187

Contra revenue account, p. 171

Cost of goods available for sale, p. 178

Cost of goods purchased, p. 177

Cost of goods sold, p. 168

Credit memorandum, p. 170

Debit memorandum, p. 174

FOB destination, p. 176

FOB shipping point, p. 176

Gross profit, p. 168

Income from operations, p. 189

Multiple-step income statement, p. 189

Net purchases, p. 177

Other expenses and losses, p. 187

Other revenues and gains, p. 187

Periodic inventory system, p. 173

Perpetual inventory system, p. 173

Purchase invoice, p. 174

Sales invoice, p. 169

Selling expenses, p. 189

Single-step income statement, p. 189

DEMONSTRATION PROBLEM

The adjusted trial balance columns of the work sheet for the year ended December 31, 1987 for the Dykstra Company are as follows:

Debit		Credit	
Cash	14,500	Accumulated Depreciation	18,000
Accounts Receivable	11,100	Notes Payable	25,000
Merchandise Inventory	32,000	Accounts Payable	10,600
Prepaid Insurance	2,500	Gene Dykstra, Capital	81,000
Store Equipment	95,000	Sales	520,000
Gene Dykstra, Drawing	12,000	Purchase Returns and Allowances	9,600
Sales Returns and Allowances	6,700	Purchase Discounts	7,200
Sales Discounts	5,000	Interest Revenue	2,500
Purchases	352,000		673,900
Freight-in	8,400		
Freight-out	7,600		
Advertising Expense	12,000		
Store Salaries Expense	56,000		
Utilities Expense	18,000		
Rent Expense	24,000		
Depreciation Expense	9,000		
Insurance Expense	4,500		
Interest Expense	3,600		
	673,900		

INSTRUCTIONS

(a) Enter the adjusted trial balance data on a work sheet. Complete the work sheet assuming that ending merchandise inventory is $29,000.

(b) Prepare an income statement assuming the Dykstra Company does not use subgroupings for operating expenses.

SOLUTION TO DEMONSTRATION PROBLEM

(a)

DYKSTRA COMPANY
Work Sheet
For the Year Ended December 31, 1987

Account Titles	Adjusted Trial Balance Dr.	Adjusted Trial Balance Cr.	Income Statement Dr.	Income Statement Cr.	Balance Sheet Dr.	Balance Sheet Cr.
Cash	14,500				14,500	
Accounts Receivable	11,100				11,100	
Merchandise Inventory	32,000		32,000	29,000	29,000	
Prepaid Insurance	2,500				2,500	
Store Equipment	95,000				95,000	
Accumulated Depreciation		18,000				18,000
Notes Payable		25,000				25,000
Accounts Payable		10,600				10,600
Gene Dykstra, Capital		81,000				81,000

Account Titles	Adjusted Trial Balance Dr.	Adjusted Trial Balance Cr.	Income Statement Dr.	Income Statement Cr.	Balance Sheet Dr.	Balance Sheet Cr.
Gene Dykstra, Drawing	12,000				12,000	
Sales		520,000		520,000		
Sales Returns and Allowances	6,700		6,700			
Sales Discounts	5,000		5,000			
Purchases	352,000		352,000			
Purchase Returns and Allowances		9,600		9,600		
Purchase Discounts		7,200		7,200		
Freight-in	8,400		8,400			
Freight-out	7,600		7,600			
Advertising Expense	12,000		12,000			
Store Salaries Expense	56,000		56,000			
Utilities Expense	18,000		18,000			
Rent Expense	24,000		24,000			
Depreciation Expense	9,000		9,000			
Insurance Expense	4,500		4,500			
Interest Expense	3,600		3,600			
Interest Revenue		2,500		2,500		
Totals	673,900	673,900	538,800	568,300	164,100	134,600
Net Income			29,500			29,500
Totals			568,300	568,300	164,100	164,100

(b)

DYKSTRA COMPANY
Income Statement
For the Year Ended December 31, 1987

Sales revenues				
Sales				$520,000
Less: Sales returns and allowances			$ 6,700	
Sales discounts			5,000	11,700
Net sales				508,300
Cost of goods sold				
Inventory, January 1			32,000	
Purchases		$352,000		
Less: Purchase returns and allowances	$9,600			
Purchase discounts	7,200	16,800		
Net purchases		335,200		
Add: Freight-in		8,400		
Cost of goods purchased			343,600	
Cost of goods available for sale			375,600	
Inventory, December 31			29,000	
Cost of goods sold				346,600
Gross profit				161,700
Operating expenses				
Store salaries expense			56,000	
Rent expense			24,000	

Utilities expense	18,000	
Advertising expense	12,000	
Depreciation expense	9,000	
Freight-out	7,600	
Insurance expense	4,500	
Total operating expenses		131,100
Income from operations		30,600
Other revenues and gains		
Interest revenue	2,500	
Other expenses and losses		
Interest expense	3,600	1,100
Net income		$ 29,500

*Note: All **asterisked** Questions, Exercises, and Problems relate to material contained in the Appendix to each chapter.

QUESTIONS

1. What is the similarity and major differences between income measurement for a merchandising company and a service company?

2. Sales revenues are not earned until cash has been received. Do you agree? Explain.

3. Identify the three sales revenue accounts. For each account (a) classify it as revenue or contra revenue, and (b) indicate its normal balance.

4. A credit sale is made on July 6 for $800, terms 2/10, n/60. On July 8, $60 of goods are returned for credit. If the customer pays in full within the discount period, how much cash will be received by the seller?

5. Identify the accounts that are added or deducted from purchases to determine the cost of goods purchased. For each account, (a) classify it as either a contra account or an adjunct account, and (b) indicate its normal balance.

6. A purchase on account for $1,500 is made on July 7. On July 9, a $200 credit is granted by the supplier for damaged goods. How much cash will be paid if payment is made within the discount period and credit terms are 2/10, n/30?

7. Distinguish between FOB shipping point and FOB destination. Identify the freight terms that will result in a debit to Freight-In by the purchaser and a debit to Freight-Out by the seller.

8. In the following separate mini cases, identify the item(s) designated by letter.
(a) Purchases − X − Y = Net purchases.
(b) Cost of goods purchased − X = Freight-In.
(c) Beginning inventory + X = Cost of goods available for sale.
(d) Cost of goods available for sale − Cost of goods sold = X.
(e) Net sales − Cost of goods sold = X.

9. The Landon Company reports net sales $900,000 and cost of goods sold $720,000. What is the company's gross profit percentage?

10. Identify the distinguishing features of an income statement for a merchandising company.

11. The accounting cycle for a merchandising company is the same as for a service company. Do you agree? Why or why not?

12. Indicate the columns of the work sheet in which (a) the beginning merchandise inventory, and (b) the ending merchandise inventory will be shown.

13. Why is the normal operating cycle for a merchandising company likely to be longer than for a service company?

14. Prepare the closing entries for the merchandise inventory account, assuming a beginning inventory of $52,000 and an ending inventory of $47,000.

15. What merchandising account, or accounts, will appear in the post-closing trial balance?

16. Identify the sections of a classified income statement that relate to (a) operating activities, and (b) nonoperating activities.

17. Distinguish between the types of functional groupings of operating expenses. What problem is created by these groupings?

18. How does the single-step form of income statement differ from the multiple-step form?

19. What relationships may be used in assessing whether operating expenses are out of control?

20. Distinguish between the net income of a proprietorship and pure profit from the business.

***21.** What is the nature of the account, Inventory Adjustment? Is this account affected by adjusting entries, closing entries, neither adjusting nor closing entries, or both adjusting and closing entries?

***22.** Beginning inventory is $65,000 and ending inventory is $57,000. Assuming a work sheet is used with adjusting entries for merchandise inventory,

(a) What statement column will be used for the Inventory Adjustment amount?

(b) For Merchandise Inventory, what amount will be shown in the Adjustments credit column?

(c) For Inventory Adjustment, what amount will be shown in the Adjustments credit column?

EXERCISES

E5-1 The Sanders Company completed the following transactions in February.

Credit Sale			Sales Return		Date of
Date	Amount	Terms	Date	Amount	Collection
Feb. 2	$ 600	2/10, n/30	—	—	Feb. 8
Feb. 10	800	3/10, n/30	Feb. 13	$100	Feb. 17
Feb. 15	1,000	1/10, n/30	Feb. 18	200	Feb. 29

Credit Sale			Sales Return		Date of
Date	Amount	Terms	Date	Amount	Collection
Feb. 20	1,200	2/10, n/30	Feb. 22	200	Feb. 27
Feb. 24	1,500	1/10, n/30	Feb. 26	300	Feb. 28

INSTRUCTIONS

(a) Indicate the cash received for each collection. (Show computations.)

(b) Prepare the journal entry for (1) the February 10 sale, (2) the February 13 sales return, and (3) the February 17 collection.

E5-2 The trial balance of the Hanna Company shows the following data pertaining to sales at the end of its fiscal year December 31: Sales $976,000, Freight-Out $12,000, Sales Returns and Allowances $24,000, and Sales Discounts $18,000.

INSTRUCTIONS

(a) Prepare the sales revenue section of the income statement.

(b) Prepare separate closing entries for (1) sales, and (2) the contra revenue accounts.

E5-3 On May 10, Stone Company purchased $2,600 of merchandise from the Quary Company FOB shipping point, terms 3/10, n/30. Stone pays the freight costs of $150 on May 11. Damaged goods totaling $200 are returned to Quary for credit on May 12. On May 19, Stone pays Quary Company in full, less the purchase discount.

INSTRUCTIONS

(a) Prepare separate entries for each transaction.

(b) Prepare separate closing entries on May 31 for the purchase accounts with (1) debit balances, and (2) credit balances.

E5-4 The trial balance of the Berger Company on July 31 includes the following accounts: Merchandise Inventory $14,200, Purchases $112,400, Sales $160,000, Freight-In $4,000, Sales Returns and Allowances $3,000, Freight-Out $1,000, and Purchase Returns and Allowances $2,000. The ending merchandise inventory is $15,000.

INSTRUCTIONS

(a) Prepare a cost of goods sold section for the year ending July 31.

(b) Prepare the closing entries for the above accounts.

(c) Post the closing entries to Merchandise Inventory.

E5-5 In addition to the accounts in Exercise 4, above, assume that the trial balance of the Berger Company also shows Sales Discounts $5,000 and Purchase Discounts $6,000.

INSTRUCTIONS

(a) Insert the account balances in Exercises 4 and 5 in the appropriate financial statement columns of a work sheet. Present your answers in columnar form using four statement columns.

(b) Identify the merchandising account(s) that will appear in the post-closing trial balance.

E5-6 Financial information is presented below for four different companies.

	Lenore Cosmetics	Harris Grocery	Reynolds Distributors	Chambers Supply Co.
Sales	$80,000	c	$144,000	$100,000
Sales returns	a	$ 8,000	12,000	6,000
Net sales	76,000	92,000	132,000	g
Beginning inventory	14,000	d	40,000	24,000
Purchases	84,000	100,000	e	80,000
Purchase returns	6,000	10,000	8,000	h
Ending inventory	b	50,000	30,000	28,000
Cost of goods sold	64,000	70,000	f	72,000
Gross profit	12,000	22,000	20,000	i

INSTRUCTIONS

Determine the missing amounts. Show all computations.

E5-7 An inexperienced accountant for th Mayhew Company made the following errors in recording merchandising transactions.

1. A $50 purchase return was recorded as a debit to Accounts Payable $50 and a credit to Purchases $50.
2. A cash payment for $100 for freight on merchandise purchases was debited to Purchases $10 and credited to Cash $10.
3. A $100 refund to a customer for faulty merchandise was debited to Sales $100 and credited to Cash $100.
4. A $250 credit purchase of supplies was debited to Purchases $250 and credited to Cash $250.
5. A $50 sales discount was debited to Purchase Discounts.

INSTRUCTIONS

Prepare separate correcting entries for each error, assuming that the incorrect entry is not reversed. (Omit explanations.)

E5-8 In its income statement for the year ended December 31, 1987, Remlon Company reported the following condensed data.

Cost of goods sold	$989,000	Loss on sale of equipment	$ 2,000
Administrative expenses	435,000	Net sales	2,351,000
Interest expense	70,000	Selling expenses	693,000
Interest revenue	44,000		

INSTRUCTIONS

(a) Prepare a multiple-step income statement.

(b) Prepare a single-step income statement.

E5-9 The following information is obtained from the annual income statement of the Peggy Company.

Net income	$ 44,000	Gross profit	$160,000
Net sales	500,000	Income from operations	48,000

INSTRUCTIONS

(a) Compute the following as a percentage of net sales: gross profit, income from operations, and net income.

(b) Assuming the owner, Lois Peggy, could earn (1) a salary of $30,000 as the manager of another company, and (2) interest of $8,000 by investing her capital in marketable securities, determine the amount of pure profit earned by the company.

***E5-10** The Tyrone Company prepares adjusting entries for merchandise inventory at the end of the accounting period. On January 1 of the current year, the balance in Merchandise Inventory is $27,500 and the inventory on hand at December 31 is $31,700.

INSTRUCTIONS

(a) Determine the amount and the work sheet columns in which merchandise inventory and inventory adjustment will appear.
(b) Journalize and post the adjusting entries for the two accounts at December 31.
(c) Journalize the closing entry or entries at December 31 and post to the accounts in (b) above.

PROBLEMS

P5-1 The Day Hardware Store completed the following merchandising transactions in the month of March.

Mar. 1 Purchased merchandise on account from Ace Wholesale Supply $1,700, terms 2/10, n/30.
2 Sold merchandise on account $1,600, terms 2/10, n/30.
5 Received credit from Ace Wholesale Supply for merchandise returned $50.
9 Received collections in full, less discounts, from customers billed for $1,000 of sales on March 2.
10 Paid Ace Wholesale Supply in full, less discount.
12 Purchased merchandise for cash $1,400.
15 Received refund from supplier on cash purchase $130.
17 Purchased merchandise from Jackson Distributors $900, FOB shipping point, terms 3/10, n/30.
19 Paid freight on March 17 purchase $125.
24 Sold merchandise for cash $3,600.
25 Purchased merchandise for cash $2,500.
27 Paid Jackson Distributors in full, less discount.
29 Made refunds to cash customers for defective merchandise $80.
31 Sold merchandise on account $900, terms n/30.

INSTRUCTIONS

(a) Journalize the transactions. (Omit explanations.)
(b) Post to the merchandising accounts.
(c) Prepare an income statement through gross profit for the month of March, assuming ending inventory is $1,400, and no beginning inventory.

P5-2 Bill Murray, a former professional golf star, operates the pro shop at the Run Valley Golf Course. At the beginning of the current season the ledger of Murray's Pro Shop showed Cash $2,000, Merchandise Inventory $2,500, and B. Murray, Capital $4,500. The following transactions were completed during April.

Apr. 5 Purchased golf bags, clubs, and balls from Banta Co. $800, FOB shipping point, terms 2/10, n/60.
7 Paid freight on Banta purchase $30.
9 Received credit from Banta Co. for merchandise returned $50.
10 Sold merchandise to members $700, terms n/30.
12 Purchased golf shoes, sweaters, and other accessories from Peerless Sportswear $560, terms 1/10, n/30.
14 Paid Banta Co. in full.
17 Received credit from Peerless Sportswear for merchandise returned $60.
20 Made sales to members $400, terms n/30.
21 Paid Peerless Sportswear in full.
27 Granted credit to members for clothing that did not fit, $25.
30 Paid assistant's salary $200.
30 Received payments on account from members $600.

INSTRUCTIONS

(a) Journalize the April transactions. (Omit explanations.)

(b) Enter the beginning balances in the ledger accounts and post the April transactions.

(c) Prepare a trial balance on April 30.

(d) Prepare an income statement through gross profit, assuming merchandise inventory on hand at April 30 is $2,900.

P5-3 The trial balance of the Melvin Wholesale Distributors contained the following accounts at November 30, the end of the company's fiscal year.

MELVIN WHOLESALE DISTRIBUTORS
Trial Balance
November 30, 1987

	Debit	Credit
Cash	$ 24,200	
Accounts Receivable	46,800	
Merchandise Inventory	62,400	
Land	72,000	
Buildings	167,000	
Accumulated Depreciation – Building		$ 54,000
Equipment	83,500	
Accumulated Depreciation – Equipment		42,400
Accounts Payable		37,500
Customer Advances on Sales		4,800
Bank Loans Payable		50,000
Gary Melvin, Capital		217,800
Gary Melvin, Drawing	10,000	
Sales		786,100
Sales Discounts	4,600	
Purchases	625,100	
Purchase Discounts		11,200
Freight-in	12,400	
Salaries Expense	69,800	
Utilities Expense	7,400	
Repair Expense	5,900	
Gas and Oil Expense	9,200	
Insurance Expense	3,500	
	$1,203,800	$1,203,800

Adjustment data:

1. Merchandise inventory on hand at November 30, 1987, is $82,500.
2. Depreciation is $5,000 on buildings and $8,500 on equipment. (Both are administrative expenses.)
3. Interest of $6,000 is unpaid on the bank loans at November 30.
4. Customer advances totaling $2,500 have been earned.

Other data:

1. Salaries are 70% selling and 30% administrative.
2. Utilities expense, repair expense, and insurance expense are 100% administrative.
3. $10,000 of the bank loans are payable next year.
4. Gas and oil expense is a selling expense.

INSTRUCTIONS

(a) Enter the trial balance on a work sheet and complete the work sheet.
(b) Prepare a multiple-step income statement and owner's equity statement for the year, and a classified balance sheet at November 30, 1987.
(c) Journalize the adjusting entries.
(d) Journalize the closing entries.
(e) Prepare a post-closing trial balance.

P5-4 The Hampel Department Store is located in downtown Midland. During the past several years, net income has been declining because of suburban shopping centers. At the end of the company's fiscal year on October 31, 1987, the following accounts appeared in two of its trial balances.

	Trial Balances	
	Unadjusted	Adjusted
Accounts Payable	$ 43,310	$ 43,310
Accounts Receivable	20,770	20,770
Accumulated Depreciation—Delivery Equipment	15,680	19,600
Accumulated Depreciation—Store Equipment	32,300	41,800
Cash	6,350	6,350
Delivery Expense	8,200	8,200
Delivery Equipment	52,000	52,000
Depreciation Expense—Delivery Equipment		3,920
Depreciation Expense—Store Equipment		9,500
Freight-in	5,710	5,710
Harriet Hampel, Capital	87,200	87,200
Harriet Hampel, Drawing	15,000	15,000
Insurance Expense		4,500
Interest Expense	7,000	7,000
Interest Revenue	3,000	3,000
Merchandise Inventory	31,360	31,360
Mortgage payable, Due 1990	40,000	40,000
Prepaid Insurance	13,500	9,000
Property Tax Expense		2,500
Purchases	650,000	650,000
Purchase Discounts	7,000	7,000
Purchase Returns and Allowances	4,000	4,000
Rent Expense	19,600	19,600
Salaries Expense	120,000	120,000
Sales	869,000	869,000

	Trial Balances	
	Unadjusted	Adjusted
Sales Commissions Expense	8,000	12,000
Sales Commissions Payable		4,000
Sales Returns and Allowances	13,000	13,000
Store Equipment	125,000	125,000
Taxes Payable (Property)		2,500
Utilities Expense	6,000	6,000

Analysis reveals the following additional data:

1. Salaries expense is 70% selling and 30% administrative.
2. Insurance expense is 50% selling and 50% administrative.
3. Merchandise inventory on October 31, 1987 is $35,470.
4. Rent expense, utilities expense, and property tax expense are administrative expenses.

INSTRUCTIONS

(a) Prepare a multiple-step income statement, an owner's equity statement, and a classified balance sheet.

(b) Journalize the adjusting entries that were made.

(c) Journalize the closing entries that are necessary.

(d) Compute the following as a percentage of net sales: gross profit, income from operations, and net income.

(e) If total operating expenses were 24.2% of net sales in the preceding year, did management improve the control over these expenses? Explain.

P5-5 An inexperienced accountant prepared the following condensed income statement for the Burr Company, a retail firm that has been in business for a number of years.

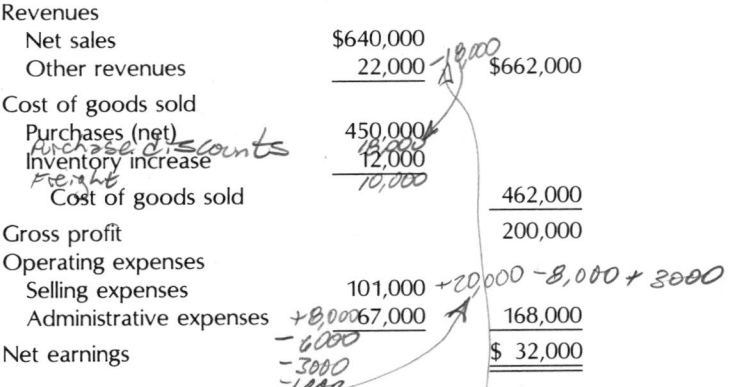

BURR COMPANY
Income Statement
For Year Ended December 31, 1987

Revenues		
Net sales	$640,000	
Other revenues	22,000	$662,000
Cost of goods sold		
Purchases (net)	450,000	
Inventory increase	12,000	
Cost of goods sold		462,000
Gross profit		200,000
Operating expenses		
Selling expenses	101,000	
Administrative expenses	67,000	168,000
Net earnings		$ 32,000

As an experienced, knowledgable accountant you review the statement and determine the following facts:

1. Net sales consists of sales $670,000, less delivery expense on merchandise sold $20,000, and sales returns and allowances $10,000.
2. Other revenues consist of purchase discounts $18,000, and rent revenue $4,000.

3. Net purchases includes purchases $440,000, and delivery costs on incoming merchandise $10,000.
4. The inventory did increase $12,000, which amounted to 20% of the beginning inventory.
5. Selling expenses consist of salespersons' salaries $68,000, depreciation on accounting equipment $8,000, advertising $19,000, and sales commissions $6,000. The commissions represent commissions paid. At December 31, $3,000 of commissions have been earned by salespersons, but have not been paid.
6. Administrative expenses consist of office salaries $24,000, owner's salary (drawing) $6,000, utilities $12,000, interest expense $1,000, and rent $24,000, which includes prepayments totaling $3,000 for the first quarter of 1988.

INSTRUCTIONS

(a) Prepare a correct detailed multiple-step income statement.
(b) Prepare a correct condensed single-step income statement.

***P5–6** The trial balance of United Global Enterprises at December 31, 1987 is shown below.

UNITED GLOBAL ENTERPRISES
Trial Balance
December 31, 1987

	Debit	Credit
Cash	$ 15,200	
Accounts Receivable	16,400	
Merchandise Inventory, January 1	29,600	
Prepaid Insurance	1,800	
Store Equipment	42,000	
Accumulated Depreciation – Store Equipment		$ 8,000
Accounts Payable		22,700
James Glow, Capital		50,300
Sales		238,000
Sales Returns and Allowances	3,600	
Sales Discounts	4,900	
Purchases	172,000	
Freight-in	2,900	
Purchase Returns and Allowances		1,400
Purchase Discounts		2,000
Salaries Expense	27,700	
Utilities Expense	6,300	
	$322,400	$322,400

Other data:

1. Merchandise inventory on hand, $32,100.
2. Insurance expired $1,200.
3. Depreciation expense, $4,000.
4. The company uses the adjusting entry method for merchandise inventory.

INSTRUCTIONS

(a) Enter the trial balance on a work sheet and complete the work sheet.
(b) Prepare the adjusting entries.

(c) Prepare the closing entries.

(d) Post the entries in (b) and (c) to Merchandise Inventory, Inventory Adjustment, and Income Summary. (Use T accounts.)

ALTERNATE PROBLEMS

P5-1A The Knight Distributing Company completed the following merchandising transactions in the month of June.

June 2 Purchased merchandise on account from Allied Wholesale Supply $2,700, terms 2/10, n/30.
4 Sold merchandise on account $2,600, FOB destination, terms 2/10, n/30.
5 Paid $50 freight on June 4 sale.
6 Received credit from Allied Wholesale Supply for merchandise returned $100.
10 Received collections in full, less discounts, from customers billed for $2,000 of sales on June 4.
10 Paid Allied Wholesale in full, less discount.
14 Purchased merchandise for cash $2,400.
16 Received refund from supplier on cash purchase $150.
18 Purchased merchandise from Janson Distributors $1,900, FOB shipping point, terms 3/10, n/30.
20 Paid freight on June 18 purchase $120.
23 Sold merchandise for cash $3,200.
25 Purchased merchandise for cash $3,500.
27 Paid Janson Distributors in full, less discount.
29 Made refunds to cash customers for defective merchandise $80.
30 Sold merchandise on account $900, terms n/30.

INSTRUCTIONS

(a) Journalize the transactions. (Omit explanations.)

(b) Post to the merchandising accounts.

(c) Prepare the income statement through gross profit for the month of June, assuming ending inventory is $5,700, and no beginning inventory.

P5-2A Teri Marrow, a former professional tennis star, operates the tennis shop at the Wivans Tennis Club. At the beginning of the current season, the ledger of Marrow's Tennis Shop showed Cash $2,500, Merchandise Inventory $2,700, and T. Marrow, Capital $5,200. The following transactions were completed during April.

Apr. 4 Purchased racquets and balls from Rako Co. $750 FOB shipping point, terms 2/10, n/30.
6 Paid freight on Rako purchase $40.
8 Sold merchandise to members $900, terms n/30.
10 Received credit of $50 from Rako Co. for a damaged racquet that was returned.
11 Purchased tennis shoes from All-Pro Sports, Inc. for cash, $300.
12 Paid Rako Co. in full.
13 Purchased tennis shirts and shorts from Classic Sportswear, $400, FOB shipping point, terms 1/10, n/60.
14 Received cash refund of $40 from All-Pro Sports, Inc. for damaged merchandise that was returned.
15 Paid freight on Classic Sportswear purchase $20.

16 Received $400 in cash from members in settlement of their accounts.
21 Paid Classic Sportswear in full.
27 Granted credit of $30 to members for tennis clothing that did not fit.
30 Sold merchandise to members $800, terms n/30.
30 Paid assistant's salary $250.

INSTRUCTIONS

(a) Journalize the April transactions. (Omit explanations.)
(b) Enter the beginning balances in the ledger accounts and post the April transactions.
(c) Prepare a trial balance on April 30.
(d) Prepare an income statement through gross profit, assuming merchandise inventory on hand at April 30 is $3,100.

P5-3A The trial balance of the Plaza Fashion Center contained the following accounts at December 31, the end of the company's fiscal year.

PLAZA FASHION CENTER
Trial Balance
December 31,1987

	Debit	Credit
Cash	$ 15,100	
Accounts Receivable	32,500	
Merchandise Inventory	58,000	
Store Supplies	5,500	
Store Equipment	65,000	
Accumulated Depreciation—Store Equipment		$ 18,000
Delivery Equipment	28,000	
Accumulated Depreciation—Delivery Equipment		6,000
Notes Payable		50,000
Accounts Payable		39,500
R. Fordham, Capital		90,000
R. Fordham, Drawing	12,000	
Sales		626,600
Sales Returns and Allowances	6,200	
Purchases	403,600	
Purchase Returns and Allowances		6,100
Purchase Discounts		3,700
Freight-in	12,800	
Salaries Expense	120,000	
Advertising Expense	16,400	
Utilities Expense	17,000	
Repair Expense	7,100	
Delivery Expense	16,700	
Rent Expense	24,000	
	$839,900	$839,900

Adjustment data:
1. Merchandise inventory on hand at December 31, 1987 is $52,400.
2. Store supplies on hand totaled $2,000.
3. Depreciation is $6,000 on the store equipment and $7,000 on the delivery equipment.

4. Interest of $8,000 is accrued on notes payable at December 31.

Other data:

1. Salaries expense is 80% selling and 20% administrative.
2. Rent expense and utilities expense are 90% selling and 10% administrative.
3. $30,000 of notes payable are due for payment next year.
4. Repair expense is 100% administrative.

INSTRUCTIONS

(a) Enter the trial balance on a work sheet and complete the work sheet.

(b) Prepare a multiple-step income statement and owner's equity statement for the year and a classified balance sheet as of December 31, 1987.

(c) Journalize the adjusting entries.

(d) Journalize the closing entries.

(e) Prepare a post-closing trial balance.

P5-4A The Swanson Department Store is located near the Villagedale shopping mall. At the end of the company's fiscal year on December 31, 1987, the following accounts appeared in two of its trial balances.

	Trial Balances	
	Unadjusted	Adjusted
Accounts Payable	$ 58,200	$ 58,200
Accounts Receivable	29,200	29,200
Accumulated Depreciation – Building	42,100	54,300
Accumulated Depreciation – Equipment	29,600	42,900
Building	210,000	210,000
Cash	21,700	21,700
Depreciation Expense – Building		12,200
Depreciation Expense – Equipment		13,300
Equipment	120,000	120,000
Freight-in	4,900	4,900
Insurance Expense		8,400
Interest Expense	3,000	6,000
Interest Payable		3,000
Interest Revenue	5,000	5,000
Merchandise Inventory	42,700	42,700
Mortgage Payable	50,000	50,000
Office Salaries Expense	32,000	32,000
Prepaid Insurance	9,600	1,200
Property Taxes Payable		4,800
Purchases	432,000	432,000
Purchase Discounts	12,000	12,000
Purchase Returns and Allowances	6,400	6,400
Sales Salaries Expense	76,000	76,000
Sales	598,000	598,000
Sales Commissions Expense	11,000	13,500
Sales Commissions Payable		2,500
Sales Returns and Allowances	8,000	8,000
Paul Swan, Capital	226,600	226,600
Paul Swan, Drawing	18,000	18,000
Taxes Expense (Property)		4,800
Utilities Expense	9,800	9,800

Analysis reveals the following additional data:

1. Merchandise inventory on December 31, 1987 is $61,400.
2. Insurance expense and utilities expense are 80% selling and 20% administrative.
3. $15,000 of the mortgage payable are due for payment next year.
4. Depreciation on the building and property tax expense are administrative expenses; depreciation on the equipment is a selling expense.

INSTRUCTIONS

(a) Prepare a multiple-step income statement, an owner's equity statement, and a classified balance sheet.

(b) Journalize the adjusting entries that were made.

(c) Journalize the closing entries that are necessary.

(d) Compute the following as a percentage of net sales: gross profit, income from operations, and net income.

(e) If total operating expense were 23.7% of net sales in the preceding year, did management improve its control over these expenses? Explain.

P5-5A A part-time bookkeeper prepared the following income statement for the Wurton Company for the year ending December 31, 1987.

WURTON COMPANY
Income Statement
December 31, 1987

Revenues		
Sales		$572,000
Less: Freight-in	$ 14,200	
Discounts	2,100	16,300
Net sales		555,700
Other revenues (net)		4,300
Total revenues		560,000
Expenses		
Purchases	440,000	
Selling expenses	106,000	
Administrative expenses	47,000	
Alan Wurton, Drawings	12,000	
Total expenses		605,000
Net decrease in owner's equity		$ 45,000

As an experienced, knowledgable accountant you review the statement and determine the following facts.

1. Sales includes $5,000 of deposits from customers for future sales orders.
2. Discounts consist of purchase discounts earned $7,200 and sales discounts granted $9,300.
3. Other revenues contains two items: interest expense $4,000 and gain on sale of plant assets $8,300.
4. Purchases includes freight-out $11,000 less purchase returns and allowances $7,500.
5. Ending merchandise inventory increased $15,000 from a beginning inventory of $33,000.
6. Selling expenses consist of sales salaries $74,000, advertising $18,000, depreciation on store equipment $7,500, and sales commissions expense $6,500. The commissions includes a $500 payment of accrued commissions payable at January 1, 1987.

7. Administrative expenses consist of office salaries $19,000, utilities expense $8,700, rent expense $15,000, and insurance expense $4,300. Insurance expense includes $1,200 of insurance applicable to 1988.

INSTRUCTIONS

(a) Prepare a correct detailed multiple-step income statement.

(b) Prepare a correct condensed single-step income statement.

DECISION CASE

Three years ago, Mary Kline and her brother-in-law Jim Kline opened Kline's Department Store. For the first two years, business was good but the following condensed income results for 1987 were disappointing.

KLINE'S DEPARTMENT STORE
Income Statement
For the Year Ended December 31, 1987

Net sales		$650,000
Cost of goods sold		520,000
Gross profit		130,000
Operating expenses		
Selling expenses	$80,000	
Administrative expenses	20,000	100,000
Net income		$ 30,000

Mary believes the problem lies in the relatively low gross profit rate of 20%. Jim believes the problem is that operating expenses are too high.

Mary believes the gross profit rate can be improved by making the following changes: (1) increase average selling prices by 15%; this increase is expected to lower sales volume so that total sales will increase only 5% and (2) buy merchandise in larger quantities and take all purchase discounts. These changes are expected to decrease cost of goods sold by 2%. Mary does not anticipate that these changes will have any effect on operating expenses.

Jim believes expenses can be cut by making the following changes: (1) cut 1987 sales salaries of $48,000 in half and give sales personnel a commission of 2% of net sales, and (2) reduce store deliveries to one day per week rather than twice a week; this change will reduce 1987 delivery expenses of $25,000 by 40%. Jim feels that these changes will not have any effect on net sales.

Mary and Jim come to you for help in deciding the best way to improve net income.

INSTRUCTIONS

(a) Prepare a condensed income statement for 1988 assuming (1) Mary's changes are implemented and (2) Jim's ideas are adopted.

(b) What is your recommendation to Mary and Jim?

(c) Prepare a condensed income statement for 1988 assuming both sets of proposed changes are made.

CHAPTER 6

Wayne State University, Michigan

CHAPTER 6

ACCOUNTING INFORMATION SYSTEMS: MANUAL AND ELECTRONIC DATA PROCESSING

STUDY OBJECTIVES

After studying this chapter, you should be able to:

1. **Identify the basic principles of accounting information system development.**
2. **Explain the major phases involved in the development of an accounting information system.**
3. **Describe the nature and purpose of a subsidiary ledger.**
4. **Explain how special journals are used in journalizing.**
5. **Indicate how a columnar journal is posted.**
6. **Identify the key points in comparing manual and computerized accounting systems.**

The accounting system of an organization transforms financial **data** into useful **information** that aids investors, creditors, managers, and other interested parties in making financial decisions. This system involves data collection, data processing, and information dissemination; it is often referred to as the **accounting information system.**

When an enterprise's operations become too complex or its transactions become too numerous to be handled efficiently by a manual accounting system, a computerized accounting system may be installed in its place. But, whether manual or computerized procedures are used to process the transaction data, some basic features and principles are applicable to both accounting information systems. The purpose of this chapter is to explain some of the

features that give an accounting information system, either manual or computerized, the flexibility to accommodate a multitude of transactions.

PRINCIPLES OF AN ACCOUNTING INFORMATION SYSTEM

In designing and developing an efficient and effective accounting information system (hereafter referred to simply as the accounting system), it is important that certain basic principles be followed. Some of these principles are:

1. **Cost awareness.** A major consideration in developing an accounting system is cost awareness. The system must be cost effective; that is, the benefits obtained from the information disseminated must outweigh the cost of providing it. For example, the value of each accounting report should be at least equal to the cost of producing it.
2. **Useful output.** To be useful, information must be understandable, relevant, reliable, timely, and accurate. When an accounting system is designed, consideration must be given to the needs and knowledge of the various users so that the system's output (reports and statements) will be useful. For example, some managers need daily or weekly reports of sales (sales managers) and production (factory supervisors). Others with differing responsibilities may need such reports only monthly or quarterly (vice-presidents).
3. **Flexible structure.** The accounting system should be able to accommodate a variety of users and changing information needs. When the environment changes as a result of technological advances, organizational growth, increased competition, government regulation, or changes in accounting principles, the accounting system should be sufficiently flexible to meet the resulting changes in the demands made upon it.

If the accounting system is cost effective, provides useful output, and has the flexibility to meet future needs, it can provide a valuable service and make a major contribution to both individual and organizational goals.

DEVELOPING AN ACCOUNTING SYSTEM

Good accounting systems do not just happen. They are carefully planned, designed, installed, managed, and refined. Generally, the development of an accounting system involves the following four phases:

1. **Analysis.** Analysis involves determining internal and external information needs, identifying sources of information and the need for controls, and studying alternatives. If an existing system is being analyzed, its strengths and weaknesses must be identified.

2. **Design.** For a new system, forms and documents must be designed; methods and procedures must be selected from alternatives; job descriptions must be prepared; controls must be integrated; reports must be formatted; and equipment must be selected. Successful systems design depends to a large extent upon the creativity, experience, and capabilities of the designer. Redesigning an existing system may involve only minor changes, a complete overhaul, or replacement of a manual system by a computerized system.
3. **Implementation.** Whether a new system is created or an existing system is revised, the plan and design have to be implemented. New or revised documents, procedures, reports, and processing equipment must be installed and made operational. Skilled personnel must be hired, trained, and closely supervised through a start-up or transition period.
4. **Follow-up.** After the new or revised system is operational, it must be evaluated and monitored for weaknesses and breakdowns. Furthermore, the effectiveness and efficiency of the system must be evaluated in relation to design and organizational objectives. Corrections in design or changes in implementation may be necessary. Both internal and external audit procedures provide feedback and follow-up assurances in regard to the soundness of the system.

The following diagram illustrates the relationship of these four phases in the life cycle of the accounting system:

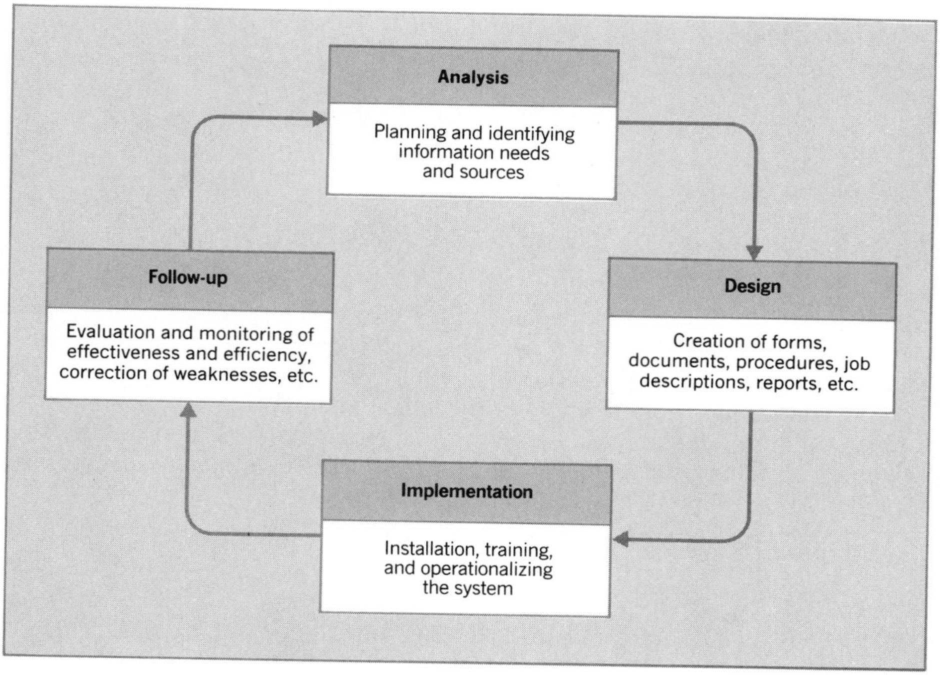

Phases in the development of an accounting system

These phases, which represent the life cycle of an accounting system, suggest that few systems remain the same forever. As experience and knowledge are obtained, and as technological and organizational changes occur, the accounting system may also have to grow and change.

In Chapter 2 you were introduced to the general journal/general ledger accounting system. Data processing using only a general journal and a general ledger is orderly and appears to be efficient. However, this type of system is best implemented when the volume of transactions is extremely low. To overcome the limitations of this simple system, accountants employ additional journals and ledgers to process large volumes of transactions. The remainder of this chapter is devoted to these additional journals and ledgers. Applications to manual systems are discussed in detail; applications to computerized systems are described briefly.

At this point you might ask, "Why cover manual accounting systems if the real world uses computerized systems?" Here is the answer.

- The design and structure of manual and computerized systems are essentially the same.
- Small businesses still abound and most of them begin operations with manual (or even shoe box) accounting systems with the successful ones eventually converting to computerized systems.
- Most students do not (at least not yet) have easy access to electronic data processing (EDP), and even if this was the case, the vast differences in protocol between different EDP hardware and software systems make manual systems much more practical for detailed study in your accounting textbook.

SECTION ONE—MANUAL DATA PROCESSING

In a **manual accounting system** each of the steps in the accounting cycle are performed by hand. For example, each accounting transaction is entered manually in the journal and posted manually to the ledger. To obtain the appropriate balance of an account in the ledger and to prepare a trial balance and financial statements, additional manual computations must be made. The following sections discuss how the manual processing system can be more efficiently used to process accounting data.

EXPANSION OF THE LEDGER—SUBSIDIARY LEDGERS

A business constantly needs detailed information about its dealings with individual customers and creditors. If a business has several thousand charge (credit) customers and the transactions with these customers are shown in only one account, Accounts Receivable, in the general ledger, it is virtually

impossible to determine the balance owed by an individual customer at a specific time. Similarly, details of transactions affecting a single creditor are needed from time to time, and a single Accounts Payable account in the general ledger cannot make this information available.

To provide this information, companies use a subsidiary ledger to keep track of individual balances. A **subsidiary ledger** is a group of accounts with a common characteristic (for example, all are customer accounts, that is, accounts receivable). The subsidiary ledger facilitates the recording process by freeing the general ledger from the details of individual balances. Thus, a typical merchandising enterprise has subsidiary ledgers containing accounts with customers (**accounts receivable** or **customers' ledger**) and creditors (**accounts payable or creditors' ledger**). The enterprise maintains a control account in the general ledger that summarizes the details in the accounts receivable and accounts payable ledgers. The summary account in the general ledger is called a **control account,** because the summary account controls the subsidiary ledger. **The general ledger control account balance must equal the composite balance of the individual accounts in the subsidiary ledger.**

As indicated, two common subsidiary ledgers are: (1) the accounts receivable ledger or customers' ledger, controlled by the general ledger account, Accounts Receivable; and (2) the accounts payable ledger or creditors' ledger, controlled by the general ledger account, Accounts Payable. In subsidiary ledgers, the individual accounts are usually arranged in alphabetical order.

An example of a control account and subsidiary ledger for Larson Enterprises is provided below.

Relationship between ledgers

ACCOUNTS RECEIVABLE SUBSIDIARY LEDGER

Aaron Co.

Date	Ref.	Debit	Credit	Balance
1987				
Jan 10		6,000		6,000
19			4,000	2,000

Branden Inc.

Date	Ref.	Debit	Credit	Balance
1987				
Jan 12		3,000		3,000
21			3,000	---

Caron Co.

Date	Ref.	Debit	Credit	Balance
1987				
Jan 20		3,000		3,000
29			1,000	2,000

GENERAL LEDGER

Accounts Receivable

Date	Ref.	Debit	Credit	Balance
1987				
Jan 31		12,000		12,000
31			8,000	4,000

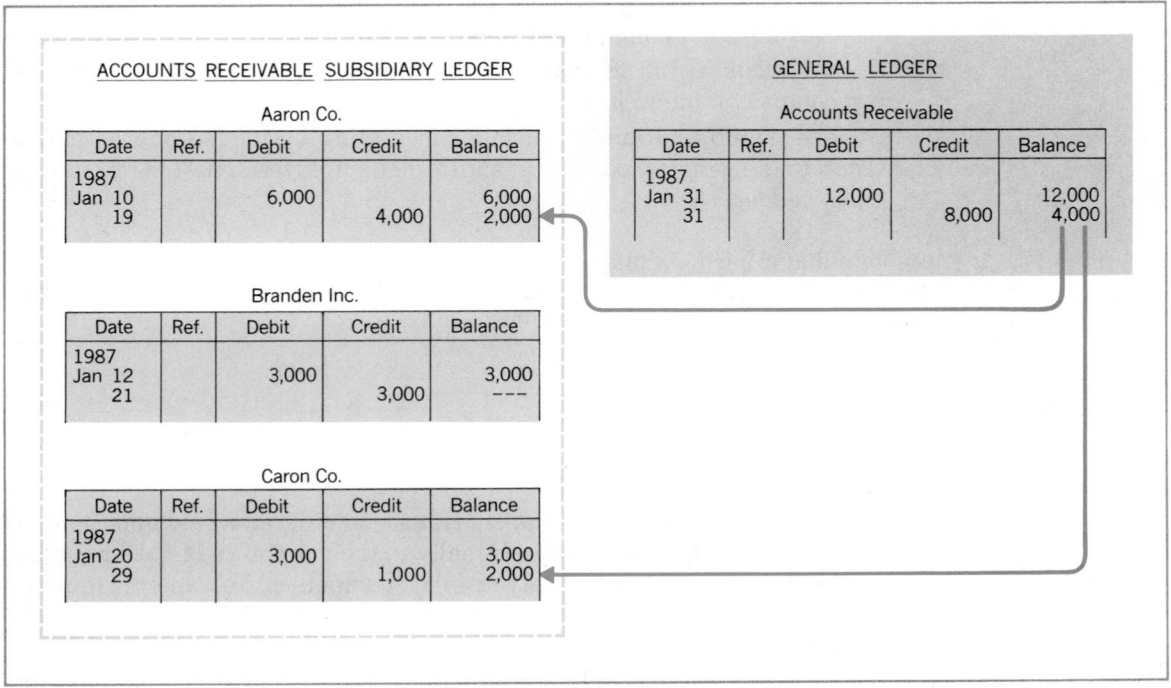

The explanation column in the accounts is not shown in this and subsequent illustrations because of space considerations.

The example is based on the following transactions:

Sales and collection transactions

Credit Sales			Collections on Account		
Jan. 10	Aaron Co.	$ 6,000	Jan. 19	Aaron Co.	$ 4,000
12	Branden Inc.	3,000	21	Branden Inc.	3,000
20	Caron Co.	3,000	29	Caron Co.	1,000
		$12,000			$ 8,000

The total debits and credits in Accounts Receivable in the general ledger are reconcilable to the detailed debits and credits in the subsidiary accounts. The balance of $4,000 in the accounts receivable control account agrees with the total of the balances in the individual accounts receivable accounts ($2,000 + $0 + $2,000) in the subsidiary ledger.

Note also in this example that postings to the control account are made in total at the end of the month, whereas each of the individual transactions is posted daily to the subsidiary ledger. Procedures used for posting entries to the subsidiary ledger and to the general ledger control account generally involve the use of special journals, discussed later in the chapter.

In summary, the advantages of using subsidiary ledgers are that they:

1. Show transactions affecting one customer or one creditor in a single account, thus providing necessary up-to-date information on specific account balances.
2. Free the general ledger of excessive details relating to accounts receivable and accounts payable. As a result, a trial balance of the general ledger does not contain vast numbers of individual account balances.
3. Help locate errors in individual accounts by reducing the number of accounts combined in one ledger and by using controlling accounts.
4. Make possible a division of labor in posting by having one employee post to the general ledger and a different employee(s) post to the subsidiary ledgers.

Note that a business may also use controlling accounts and subsidiary ledgers for other accounts such as inventory, equipment, and selling and administrative expenses.

EXPANSION OF THE JOURNAL—SPECIAL JOURNALS

So far you have learned to journalize transactions in a two-column general journal and post these entries individually to the general ledger. This procedure is satisfactory in only the very smallest companies. To expedite journalizing and posting transactions, most companies use special journals in addition to the general journal.

A **special journal** is used to group similar types of transactions, such as all sales of merchandise on account, or all cash receipts. The types of special journals used depends largely on the types of transactions that occur fre-

quently in a business enterprise. Most merchandising enterprises use the following journals to record transactions daily:

Sales journal—all sales of merchandise on account.
Cash receipts journal—all cash received (including cash sales).
Purchases journal—all purchases of merchandise on account.
Cash payments journal—all cash paid (including cash purchases).

If the transaction cannot be recorded in a special journal, it is recorded in the general journal. For example, if you had special journals only for the four types of transactions above, purchase returns and allowances or sales returns and allowances would be reported in the general journal. Similarly, correcting, adjusting, and closing entries are recorded in the general journal. Other types of special journals may be used in some situations. For example, where purchase returns and allowances or sales returns and allowances are frequent, special journals may be employed to record these transactions.

Special journals **permit greater division of labor** because several individuals can record entries in different journals at the same time. For example, one employee may be responsible for journalizing all cash receipts, and another for journalizing credit sales. In addition, the use of special journals **reduces the time necessary to complete the posting process.** When special journals are employed, monthly postings to some accounts may be substituted for daily postings, as will be illustrated later in the chapter.

As indicated later in this chapter, computerized accounting systems reduce the processing time even more. Humans are slow, error-prone, and limited in their abilities to process data. A computer can process hundreds of transactions in the time it may take a human to process one transaction.

SALES JOURNAL

The sales journal is used to record sales of merchandise on account. Cash sales of merchandise are entered in the cash receipts journal. Similarly, credit sales of assets other than merchandise are entered in the general journal.

JOURNALIZING CREDIT SALES

Each entry in the sales journal used here results in a debit to Accounts Receivable and a credit to Sales. Since each sale on account involves a debit to Accounts Receivable and a credit of equal amount to Sales, only one line is needed in this sales journal to record each transaction. All entries in a sales journal are made from sales invoices. Each invoice is prenumbered to insure that all invoices are journalized. To illustrate, assume that Karns Wholesale Supply has the following credit sales transactions:

Credit sales transactions

Date	Customer	Invoice No.	Amount	Date	Customer	Invoice No.	Amount
5/3	Abbot Sisters	101	$10,600	5/21	Abbot Sisters	105	$15,400
5/7	Babson Co.	102	11,350	5/24	Deli Co.	106	21,210
5/14	Carson Bros.	103	7,800	5/27	Babson Co.	107	14,570
5/19	Deli Co.	104	9,300				

The sales journal is illustrated below.

Journalizing sales journal

KARNS WHOLESALE SUPPLY
SALES JOURNAL

S1

Date		Account Debited	Invoice No.	Ref.	Accts. Receivable Dr. Sales Cr.
1987					
May	3	Abbot Sisters	101		10,600
	7	Babson Co.	102		11,350
	14	Carson Bros.	103		7,800
	19	Deli Co.	104		9,300
	21	Abbot Sisters	105		15,400
	24	Deli Co.	106		21,210
	27	Babson Co.	107		14,570
					90,230

Note that the reference (Ref.) column is not used in journalizing. It is used in posting the sales journal as explained below.

POSTING THE SALES JOURNAL

Postings from the sales journal are made **daily** to the individual accounts receivable in the subsidiary ledger and **monthly** to the general ledger, as shown on the next page.

A check mark (✓) is inserted in the reference posting column instead of an account number to indicate that the daily posting to the customer's account has been made. A check mark (✓) is used when subsidiary ledger accounts are not numbered.

In manual systems most files are alphabetical so there is, perhaps, little benefit in numbering accounts. In computerized systems, though, account numbering is essential. In today's information society, we are all numbers in many respects. We have social security numbers, drivers' license numbers, credit card numbers, etc. This can get burdensome, and to some respect dehumanizing, but the trade-off is in the efficiency of processing files under numerical control. It is far simpler to enter digits than account names. The problem of differentiating accounts with common names (i.e., Jones, Smith) is also greatly reduced with numerical referencing.

Posting the sales journal

Karns Wholesale Supply
Sales Journal

S1

Date		Account Debited	Invoice No.	Ref.	Accts. Receivable Dr. Sales Cr.
1987					
May	3	Abbot Sisters	101	√	10,600
	7	Babson Co.	102	√	11,350
	14	Carson Bros.	103	√	7,800
	19	Deli Co.	104	√	9,300
	21	Abbot Sisters	105	√	15,400
	24	Deli Co.	106	√	21,210
	27	Babson Co.	107	√	14,570
					90,230
					(4)/(60)

ACCOUNTS RECEIVABLE SUBSIDIARY LEDGER

Abbot Sisters

Date		Ref.	Debit	Credit	Balance
1987					
May	3	S1	10,600		10,600
	21	S1	15,400		26,000

Babson Co.

Date		Ref.	Debit	Credit	Balance
1987					
May	7	S1	11,350		11,350
	27	S1	14,570		25,920

Carson Bros.

Date		Ref.	Debit	Credit	Balance
1987					
May	14	S1	7,800		7,800

Deli Co.

Date		Ref.	Debit	Credit	Balance
1987					
May	19	S1	9,300		9,300
	24	S1	21,210		30,510

GENERAL LEDGER

Accounts Receivable — No. 4

Date		Ref.	Debit	Credit	Balance
1987					
May	31	S1	90,230		90,230

Sales — No. 60

Date		Ref.	Debit	Credit	Balance
1987					
May	31	S1		90,230	90,230

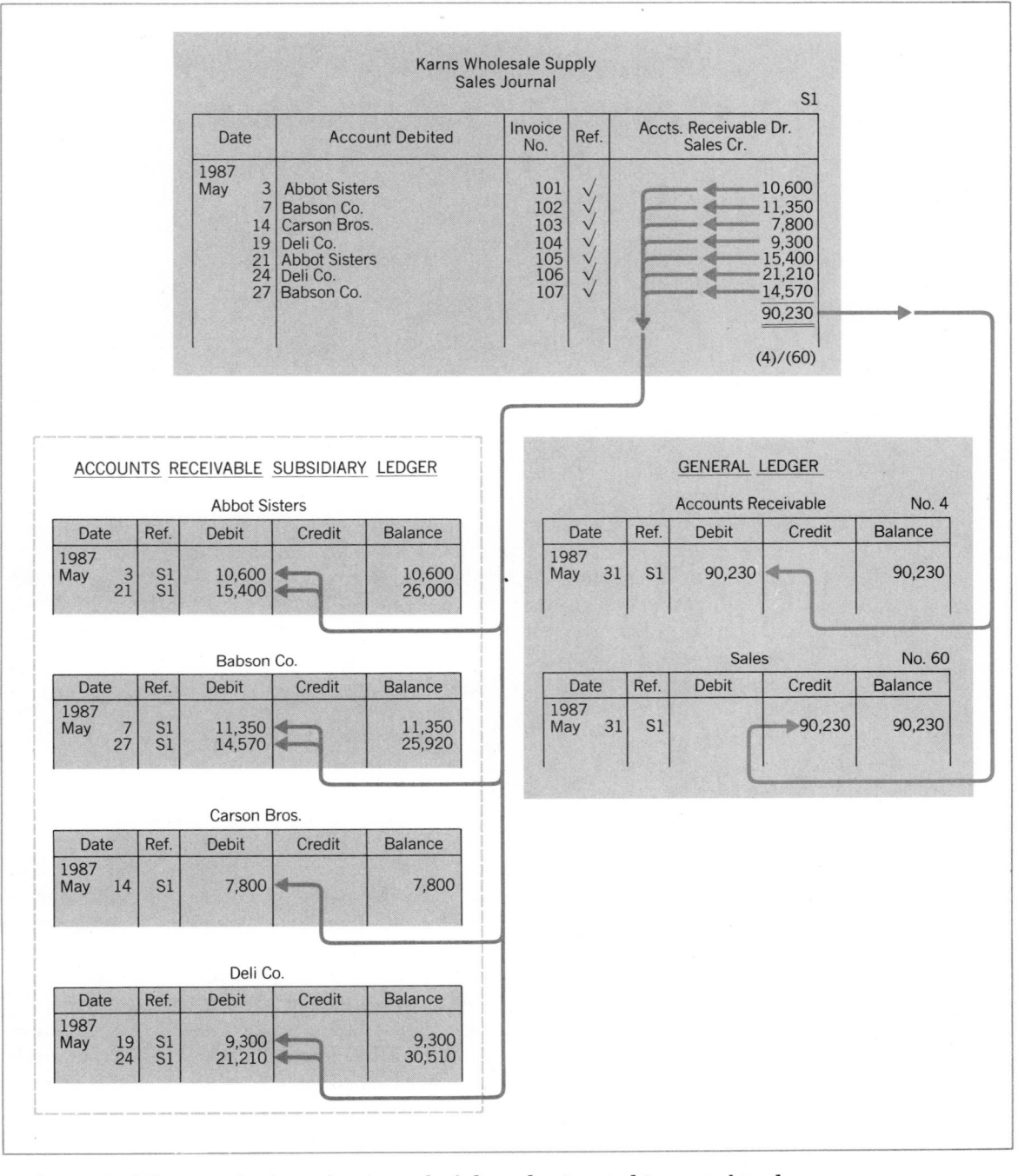

At the end of the month, the column total of the sales journal is posted to the general ledger—as a debit to Accounts Receivable (Account No. 4) and as a credit to Sales (Account No. 60). The insertion of the respective account numbers below the column total indicates that the postings have been made. In both the general ledger and subsidiary ledger accounts, the reference S1 indicates that the posting came from page 1 of the sales journal.

Proof of the accuracy of the postings of the sales journal is shown in the following tabulation.

Proving the postings of the sales journal

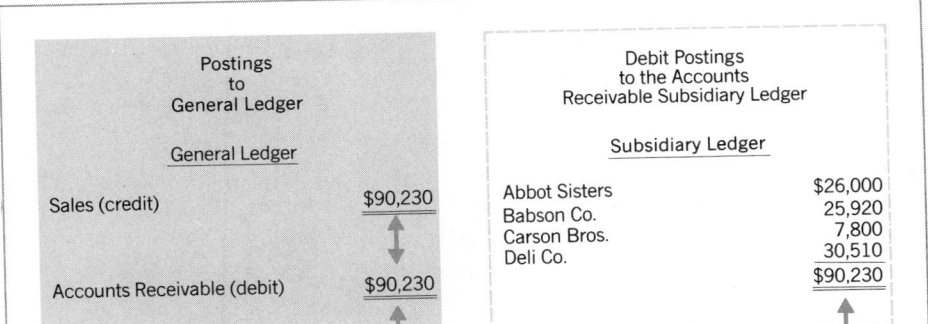

Postings to General Ledger

General Ledger	
Sales (credit)	$90,230
Accounts Receivable (debit)	$90,230

Debit Postings to the Accounts Receivable Subsidiary Ledger

Subsidiary Ledger	
Abbot Sisters	$26,000
Babson Co.	25,920
Carson Bros.	7,800
Deli Co.	30,510
	$90,230

If management wishes to record its sales by department, additional columns may be provided in the sales journal. For example, a department store may have columns for home furnishings, sporting goods, shoes, etc.

From the foregoing, it should be apparent that the use of a special journal to record sales on account has a number of advantages. First, the one-line entry for each sales transaction **saves time,** because it is not necessary to write out a debit to accounts receivable and a credit to sales for each transaction. Second, only totals are posted to the general ledger, rather than each individual entry, thus **saving posting time and reducing the possibilities of errors in posting.** And, finally, **a division of labor results,** because one individual can take responsibility for the sales journal.

CASH RECEIPTS JOURNAL

All receipts of cash are recorded in the cash receipts journal. The most common types of cash receipts are cash sales of merchandise and collections of accounts receivable. Many other possibilities exist, however, such as receipt of money from bank loans and cash proceeds from disposals of equipment, building, or land. As a result, a one-column cash receipts journal is not sufficient to accommodate all possible cash receipts transactions; therefore, a multiple-column cash receipts journal is used. Generally, a cash receipts journal includes debit columns for cash and sales discounts and credit columns for accounts receivable, sales, and "other" accounts. The other accounts category is used when the cash receipt does not involve a cash sale or a collection of accounts receivable. A five-column cash receipts journal is illustrated on the top of page 224. When a special journal has more than one column it is often referred to as a **columnar journal.**

Additional credit columns may be used if they significantly reduce postings to a specific account. For example, the cash receipts of a loan company, such as Household Finance, include thousands of collections from customers that

are credited to Loans Receivable and Interest Revenue. A significant saving in posting would result from using separate credit columns for Loans Receivable and Interest Revenue, rather than using the other accounts credit column for these amounts. In contrast, a retailer that has only one interest collection a month would not reduce its postings by using a separate column for interest revenue.

JOURNALIZING CASH RECEIPTS TRANSACTIONS

To illustrate the journalizing of cash receipts transactions, we will continue with the transactions of Karns Wholesale Company during the month of May. Collections from customers relate to the entries recorded in the sales journal on page 221. The entries in the cash receipts journal are based on the following cash receipts transactions:

May	1	D. A. Karns makes an investment of $5,000 in the business
	4	Cash sales of merchandise total $2,000
	7	Cash sales of merchandise total $1,900
	10	A check for $10,388 is received from Abbot Sisters in payment of invoice No. 101 for $10,600 less a 2% discount
	12	Cash sales of merchandise total $2,600
	17	A check for $11,123 is received from Babson Co. in payment of invoice No. 102 for $11,350 less a 2% discount
	20	Cash sales of merchandise total $2,500
	22	Cash is received by signing a note for $6,000
	23	A check for $7,644 is received from Carson Bros. in full for invoice No. 103 for $7,800 less a 2% discount
	28	A check for $9,114 is received from Deli Co. in full for invoice No. 104 for $9,300 less a 2% discount
	30	Cash sales of merchandise total $2,200

Further information about the columns in the cash receipts journal (see page 224) is as follows:

Debits:

1. **Cash.** The amount of cash actually received in each transaction is entered in this column; the column total indicates the total cash receipts for the month.
2. **Sales Discounts.** The Sales Discount column is included so that it is not necessary to enter sales discount items in the general journal. As a result, the collection of an accounts receivable within the discount period is expressed on one line in the appropriate columns of the cash receipts journal.

Credits:

3. **Accounts Receivable.** The Accounts Receivable column is used to record cash collections on account. The amount entered in this column is the amount to be credited to the individual customer's account.

Karns Wholesale Supply
Cash Receipts Journal

CR1

Date	Explanation	Accounts Credited	Ref.	Cash Dr.	Sales Discounts Dr.	Accounts Receivable Cr.	Sales Cr.	Other Accounts Cr.
1987								
May 1	Investment	D.A. Karns, Capital	50	5,000				5,000
4	Cash sales			2,000			2,000	
7	Cash sales			1,900			1,900	
10	Collection in full	Abbot Sisters	√	10,388	212	10,600		
12	Cash sales			2,600			2,600	
17	Collection in full	Babson Co.	√	11,123	227	11,350		
20	Cash sales			2,500			2,500	
22	Issued note	Notes Payable	20	6,000				6,000
23	Collection in full	Carson Bros.	√	7,644	156	7,800		
28	Collection in full	Deli Co.	√	9,114	186	9,300		
30	Cash sales			2,200			2,200	
				60,469	781	39,050	11,200	11,000
				(1)	(61)	(4)	(60)	(x)

ACCOUNTS RECEIVABLE SUBSIDIARY LEDGER

Abbot Sisters

Date	Ref.	Debit	Credit	Balance
1987				
May 3	S1	10,600		10,600
10	CR1		10,600	---
21	S1	15,400		15,400

Babson Co.

Date	Ref.	Debit	Credit	Balance
1987				
May 7	S1	11,350		11,350
17	CR1		11,350	---
27	S1	14,570		14,570

Carson Bros.

Date	Ref.	Debit	Credit	Balance
1987				
May 14	S1	7,800		7,800
23	CR1		7,800	---

Deli Co.

Date	Ref.	Debit	Credit	Balance
1987				
May 19	S1	9,300		9,300
24	S1	21,210		30,510
28	CR1		9,300	21,210

GENERAL LEDGER

Cash — No. 1

Date	Ref.	Debit	Credit	Balance
1987				
May 31	CR1	60,469		60,469

Accounts Receivable — No. 4

Date	Ref.	Debit	Credit	Balance
1987				
May 31	S1	90,230		90,230
31	CR1		39,050	51,180

Notes Payable — No. 20

Date	Ref.	Debit	Credit	Balance
1987				
May 22	CR1		6,000	6,000

D.A. Karns, Capital — No. 50

Date	Ref.	Debit	Credit	Balance
1987				
May 1	CR1		5,000	5,000

Sales — No. 60

Date	Ref.	Debit	Credit	Balance
1987				
May 31	S1		90,230	90,230
31	CR1		11,200	101,430

Sales Discounts — No. 61

Date	Ref.	Debit	Credit	Balance
1987				
May 31	CR1	781		781

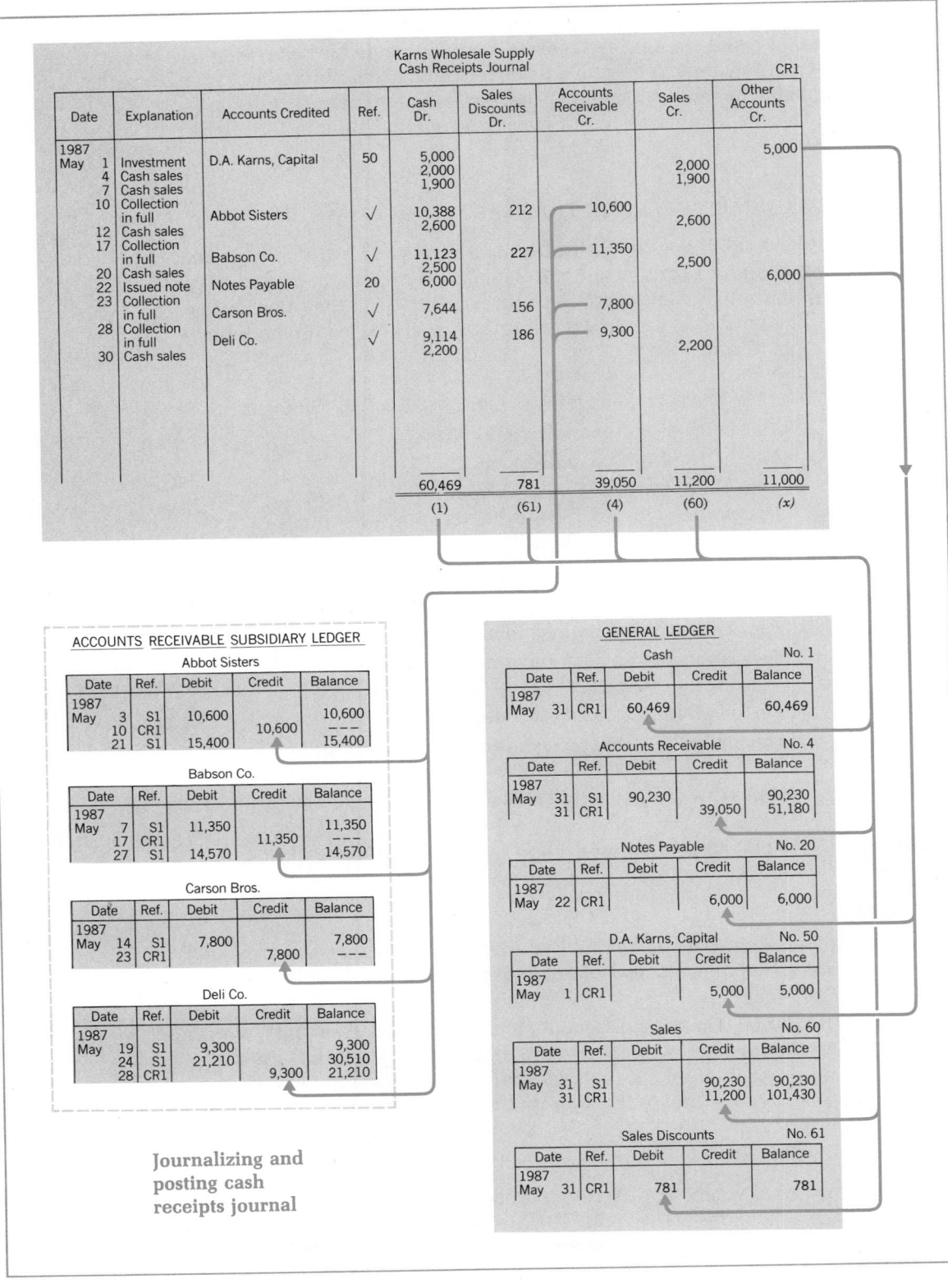

Journalizing and posting cash receipts journal

4. **Sales.** The Sales column records all cash sales of merchandise. Cash sales of plant assets, for example, are not reported in this column.
5. **Other Accounts.** The Other Accounts column, often referred to as the **sundry accounts column,** is used whenever the credit is other than to Accounts Receivable or Sales. For example, in the first entry, $5,000 is entered as a credit to D. A. Karns, Capital.

In a columnar journal, as in a single-column journal, only one line is needed for each entry. However, in contrast to a single-column journal, an explanation is given for each entry, and there must be equal debit and credit amounts for each line. When the collection from Abbot Sisters on May 10 is journalized, for example, three amounts are indicated. Note also that the Accounts Credited column is used to identify both general ledger and subsidiary ledger account titles. The former is illustrated in the May 1 entry for Karns' investment; the latter is illustrated in the May 10 entry for the collection in full from Abbot Sisters.

When the journalizing of a columnar journal has been completed, the amount columns are totaled, and the totals are balanced to prove the equality of debits and credits. The proof for Karns Wholesale Company is as follows:

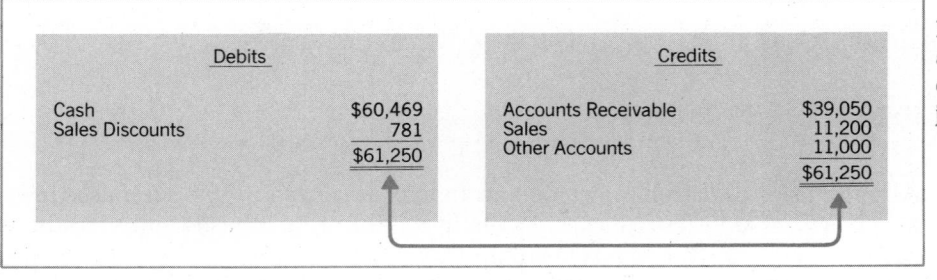

Proving the accuracy of the cash receipts journal

Debits		Credits	
Cash	$60,469	Accounts Receivable	$39,050
Sales Discounts	781	Sales	11,200
		Other Accounts	11,000
	$61,250		$61,250

Totaling the columns of a journal and proving the equality of the totals is called **footing and cross-footing** a journal.

POSTING THE CASH RECEIPTS JOURNAL

Posting a columnar journal involves the following procedures.

1. All column totals except the total for the Other Accounts column are posted once at the end of the month to the account title specified in the column heading, such as Cash or Accounts Receivable.
2. The total of the Other Accounts column is not posted. Instead, the individual amounts comprising the total are posted separately to the general ledger account specified in the Accounts Credited column. See, for example, the credit posting to D. A. Karns, Capital. The symbol (×) is inserted below the total to this column to indicate that the amount is not posted.
3. The individual amounts in a column, posted in total to a control account (Accounts Receivable, in this case), are posted daily to the subsidiary ledger account specified in the Accounts Credited column. See, for example, the credit posting of $10,600 to Abbot Sisters.

Therefore, cash is posted to account No. 1, accounts receivable to account No. 4, sales to account No. 60, and sales discounts to account No. 61. The symbol (CR) is used in the ledgers to identify postings from the cash receipts journal.

At the end of the month, the agreement of the balance of the accounts receivable control account with the sum of the customer balances in the subsidiary ledger can be proved as follows:

Reconciling accounts receivable subsidiary ledger to control account

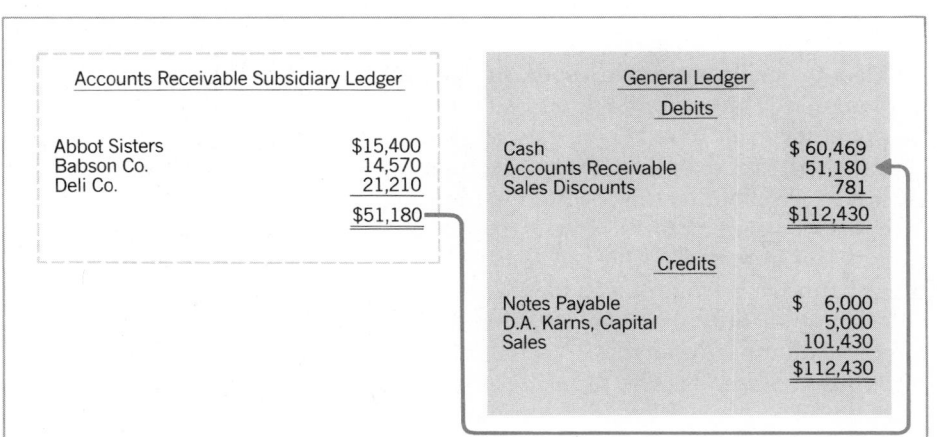

Accounts Receivable Subsidiary Ledger	
Abbot Sisters	$15,400
Babson Co.	14,570
Deli Co.	21,210
	$51,180

General Ledger	
Debits	
Cash	$ 60,469
Accounts Receivable	51,180
Sales Discounts	781
	$112,430
Credits	
Notes Payable	$ 6,000
D.A. Karns, Capital	5,000
Sales	101,430
	$112,430

PURCHASES JOURNAL

All purchases of merchandise on account are recorded in the purchases journal. Each entry in this journal results in a debit to purchases and a credit to accounts payable. When a one-column purchases journal is used, other types of purchases on account and cash purchases cannot be journalized in the purchases journal. For example, credit purchases of equipment or supplies must be recorded in the general journal, and all cash purchases are entered in the cash payments journal. As illustrated later, where credit purchases for items other than merchandise are numerous, the purchases journal is often expanded to a multi-column format. The purchases journal for Karns Wholesale Company is shown on the top of page 228.

JOURNALIZING CREDIT PURCHASES OF MERCHANDISE

Entries in the purchases journal are made from purchase invoices. The journalizing procedure is similar to the procedures described earlier for a single-column sales journal. In contrast to the sales journal the purchases journal may not have an invoice number column, because invoices received from different suppliers will not be in numerical sequence. To assure that all purchase invoices are recorded, however, some companies consecutively number each invoice upon receipt and then provide for an internal document number column in the purchases journal.

The entries for Karns Wholesale Company are based on the following assumed transactions:

Credit purchases transactions

Date	Supplies	Amount	Date	Supplies	Amount
5/3	Wells Fargo Company	$10,800	5/19	Jasper Manufacturing Inc.	$17,500
5/6	Jasper Manufacturing Inc.	11,000	5/22	Wells Fargo Company	14,400
5/10	Eaton and Howe, Inc.	7,200	5/26	Fabor and Son	8,700
5/14	Fabor and Son	6,900	5/29	Eaton and Howe, Inc.	12,600

The single column purchases journal is shown on the top of the next page.

POSTING THE PURCHASES JOURNAL

The procedures for posting the purchases journal are similar to those described earlier for the sales journal. In this case, postings are made **daily** to the accounts payable ledger and **monthly** to Purchases and Accounts Payable in the general ledger, as shown on page 228. In the ledgers, however, the letter P is used in the reference column to show that the postings are from the purchases journal. Proof of the accuracy of the postings to both ledgers in this example (as in Karns Wholesale Company) is shown by the following tabulation:

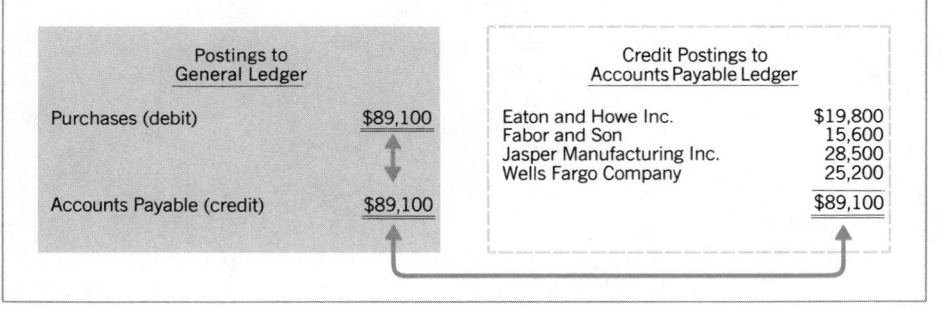

Proving the postings of the purchases journal

Postings to General Ledger	
Purchases (debit)	$89,100
Accounts Payable (credit)	$89,100

Credit Postings to Accounts Payable Ledger	
Eaton and Howe Inc.	$19,800
Fabor and Son	15,600
Jasper Manufacturing Inc.	28,500
Wells Fargo Company	25,200
	$89,100

EXPANSION OF THE PURCHASES JOURNAL

Some companies expand the purchases journal to include all types of purchases on account. Instead of one column for purchases and accounts payable, a multiple-column format is used. The multiple-column format usually includes a credit column for accounts payable and debit columns for purchases of merchandise, purchases of office supplies, purchases of store supplies, and other accounts. An example of a multiple-column purchases journal is illustrated on page 229 for Hanover Express Co. The posting procedures to be followed are similar to those used for posting the cash receipts journal illustrated earlier.

Journalizing and posting purchases journal

Karns Wholesale Supply
Purchases Journal

P1

Date	Account Credited	Terms	Ref.	Purchases Dr. Accounts Payable Cr.
1987				
May 3	Wells Fargo Company	n/60	√	10,800
6	Jasper Manufacturing Inc.	2/10, n/30	√	11,000
10	Eaton and Howe Inc.	3/10, n/30	√	7,200
14	Fabor and Son	1/10, n/30	√	6,900
19	Jasper Manufacturing Inc.	2/10, n/30	√	17,500
22	Wells Fargo Company	n/60	√	14,400
26	Fabor and Son	1/10, n/30	√	8,700
29	Eaton and Howe Inc.	3/10, n/30	√	12,600
				89,100
				(70)/(25)

ACCOUNTS PAYABLE SUBSIDIARY LEDGER

Eaton and Howe Inc.

Date	Ref.	Debit	Credit	Balance
1987				
May 10	P1		7,200	7,200
29	P1		12,600	19,800

Fabor and Son

Date	Ref.	Debit	Credit	Balance
1987				
May 14	P1		6,900	6,900
26	P1		8,700	15,600

Jasper Manufacturing Inc.

Date	Ref.	Debit	Credit	Balance
1987				
May 6	P1		11,000	11,000
19	P1		17,500	28,500

Wells Fargo Company

Date	Ref.	Debit	Credit	Balance
1987				
May 3	P1		10,800	10,800
22	P1		14,400	25,200

GENERAL LEDGER

Accounts Payable No. 25

Date	Ref.	Debit	Credit	Balance
1987				
May 31	P1		89,100	89,100

Purchases No. 70

Date	Ref.	Debit	Credit	Balance
1987				
May 31	P1	89,100		89,100

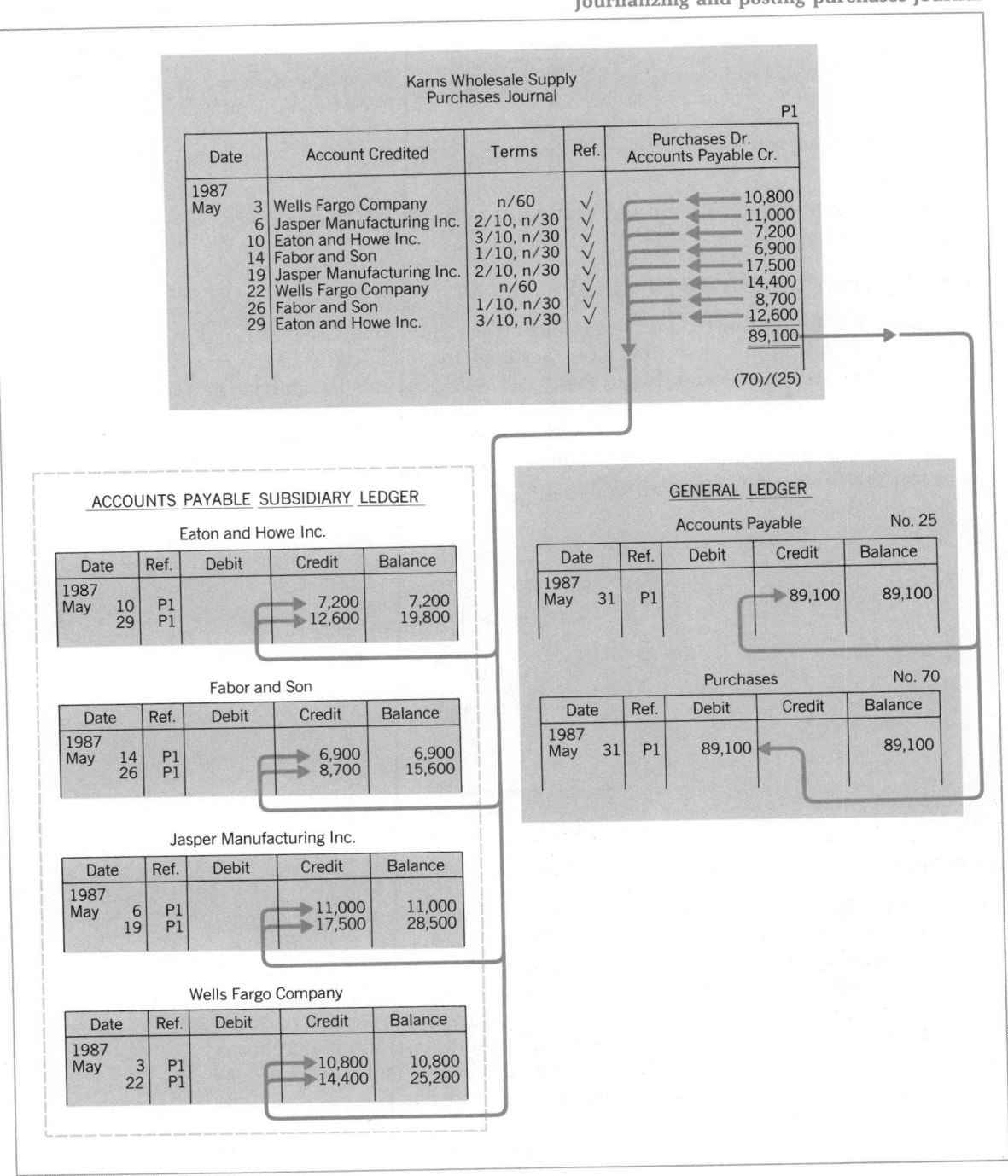

Columnar purchases journal

HANOVER EXPRESS CO.
PURCHASES JOURNAL P1

Date		Accounts Credited	Ref.	Accounts Payable Cr.	Purchases Dr.	Office Supplies Dr.	Store Supplies Dr.	Other Accounts Dr.		
								Account	Ref.	Amount
1987										
June	1	Signe Audio	✓	2,000		2,000				
	3	Wright Co.	✓	1,500	1,500					
	5	Orange Tree Co.	✓	2,600				Equipment	18	2,600
	30	Sue's Business Forms	✓	800			800			
				56,600	43,000	7,500	1,200			4,900

CASH PAYMENTS JOURNAL

All disbursements of cash are entered in a cash payments or cash disbursements journal. Entries in this journal are made from prenumbered checks. Because cash payments may be made for a variety of purposes, the cash payments journal has multiple columns. A five-column journal is shown on the top of page 230.

JOURNALIZING CASH PAYMENTS TRANSACTIONS

The procedures for journalizing transactions in this journal are similar to those described earlier for journalizing transactions in the cash receipts journal. For example, each transaction is entered on one line, and for each line there must be equal debit and credit amounts. The entries in the cash payments journal shown on page 230 are based on the following transactions for Karns Wholesale Company:

May 1 Check No. 101 for $1,200 is issued for the annual premium on a fire insurance policy.

3 Check No. 102 for $100 is issued in payment of freight when terms of purchase were FOB shipping point.

4 Check No. 103 for $300 is issued for store supplies.

8 Check No. 104 for $400 is issued for the purchase of merchandise.

10 Check No. 105 for $10,780 is sent to Jasper Manufacturing Inc. in payment of May 6 invoice for $11,000 less a 2% discount.

12 Check No. 106 for $10,800 is mailed to Wells Fargo Company in payment of May 3 invoice for $10,800.

Karns Wholesale Supply
Cash Payments Journal CP1

Date	Ck. No.	Explanation	Accounts Debited	Ref.	Other Accounts Dr.	Accounts Payable Dr.	Store Supplies Dr.	Purchase Discounts Cr.	Cash Cr.
1987 May 1	101	Pay annual premium	Prepaid Insurance	10	1,200				1,200
3	102	Pay freight	Freight-In	71	100				100
4	103	Purchase supplies					300		300
8	104	Buy merchandise	Purchases	70	400				400
10	105	Pay in full	Jasper Manufacturing Inc.	√		11,000		220	10,780
12	106	Pay in full	Wells Fargo Company	√		10,800			10,800
15	107	Purchase supplies					200		200
19	108	Pay in full	Eaton and Howe Inc.	√		7,200		216	6,984
23	109	Pay in full	Fabor and Son	√		6,900		69	6,831
28	110	Pay in full	Jasper Manufacturing Inc.	√		17,500		350	17,150
30	111	Withdraw cash	D.A. Karns Drawing	51	500				500
					2,200	53,400	500	855	55,245
					(x)	(25)	(12)	(72)	(1)

ACCOUNTS PAYABLE SUBSIDIARY LEDGER

Eaton and Howe Inc.

Date	Ref.	Debit	Credit	Balance
1987 May 10	P1		7,200	7,200
19	CP1	7,200		---
29	P1		12,600	12,600

Fabor and Son

Date	Ref.	Debit	Credit	Balance
1987 May 14	P1		6,900	6,900
23	CP1	6,900		---
26	P1		8,700	8,700

Jasper Manufacturing Inc.

Date	Ref.	Debit	Credit	Balance
1987 May 6	P1		11,000	11,000
10	CP1	11,000		---
19	P1		17,500	17,500
28	CP1	17,500		---

Wells Fargo Company

Date	Ref.	Debit	Credit	Balance
1987 May 3	P1		10,800	10,800
12	CP1	10,800		---
22	P1		14,400	14,400

GENERAL LEDGER

Cash No. 1

Date	Ref.	Debit	Credit	Balance
1987 May 31	CR1	60,469		60,469
31	CP1		55,245	5,224

Prepaid Insurance No. 10

Date	Ref.	Debit	Credit	Balance
1987 May 1	CP1	1,200		1,200

Store Supplies No. 12

Date	Ref.	Debit	Credit	Balance
1987 May 31	CP1	500		500

D.A. Karns, Drawing No. 51

Date	Ref.	Debit	Credit	Balance
1987 May 30	CP1	500		500

Accounts Payable No. 25

Date	Ref.	Debit	Credit	Balance
1987 May 31	P1		89,100	89,100
31	CP1	53,400		35,700

Purchases No. 70

Date	Ref.	Debit	Credit	Balance
1987 May 8	CP1	400		400
31	P1	89,100		89,500

Purchase Discounts No. 72

Date	Ref.	Debit	Credit	Balance
1987 May 31	CP1		855	855

Freight-In No. 71

Date	Ref.	Debit	Credit	Balance
1987 May 3	CP1	100		100

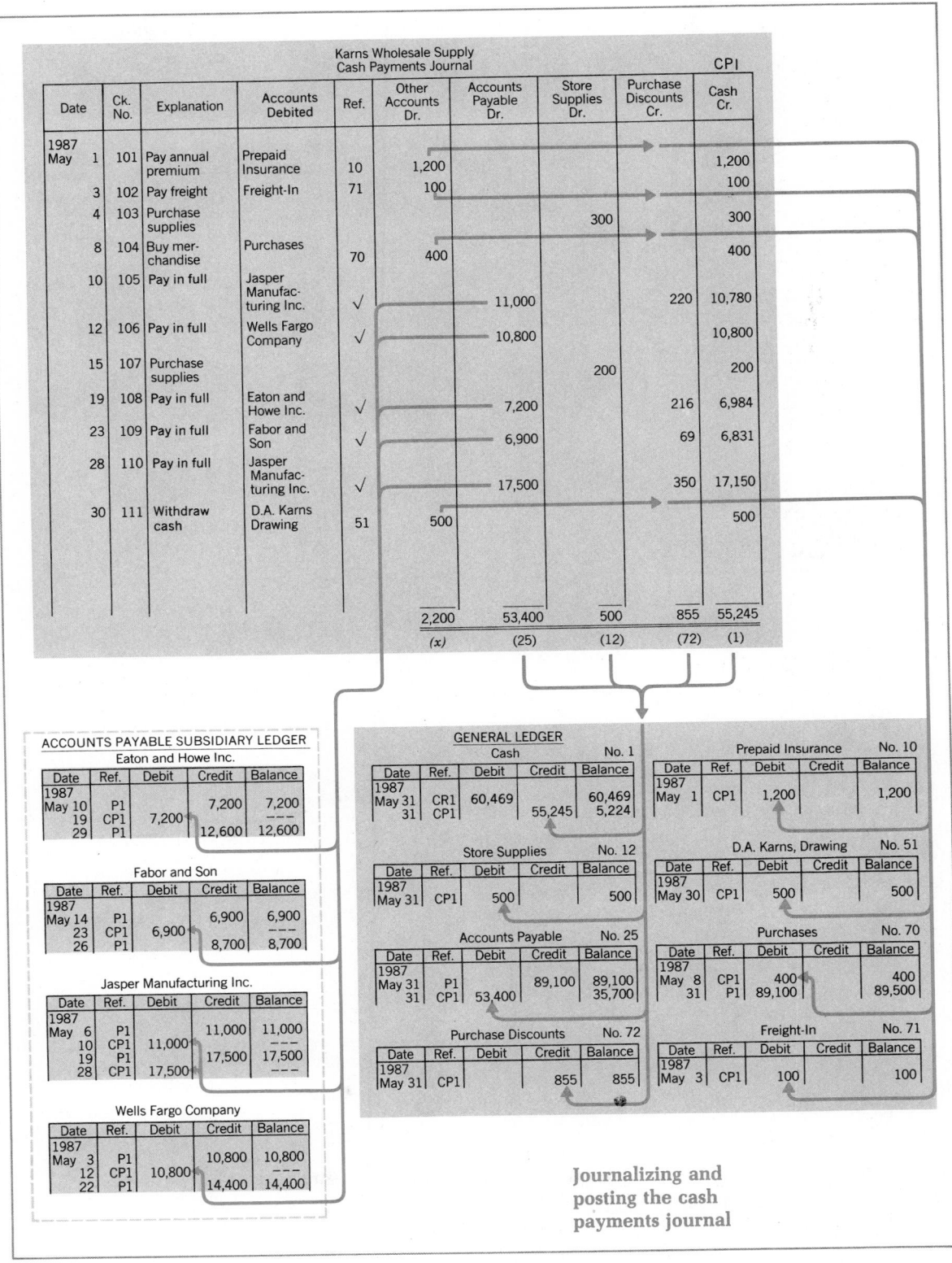

Journalizing and posting the cash payments journal

15 Check No. 107 for $200 is issued for store supplies.

19 Check No. 108 for $6,984 is mailed to Eaton and Howe, Inc. in payment of May 10 invoice for $7,200 less a 3% discount.

23 Check No. 109 for $6,831 is sent to Fabor and Son in payment of May 14 invoice for $6,900 less a 1% discount.

28 Check No. 110 for $17,150 is sent to Jasper Manufacturing Inc. in payment of May 19 invoice for $17,500 less a 2% discount.

30 Check No. 111 for $500 is issued to D. A. Karns as a cash withdrawal for personal use.

The symbol CP is used as the posting reference for this journal. Note that whenever an amount is entered in the Other Accounts column, a specific general ledger account must be identified in the Accounts Debited column. The entry for check No. 101 illustrates this situation. Similarly, a subsidiary account must be identified in the Accounts Debited column whenever an amount is entered in the Accounts Payable column, as, for example, the entry for check No. 105. However, when an amount is entered in the Store Supplies column, the Accounts Debited column needs no account title, because only the column total is posted at the end of the month. The entries for checks No. 103 and 107 are illustrative.

When the journalizing of a columnar journal has been completed, the amount columns are totaled. The totals are then balanced to prove the equality of debits and credits as follows:

POSTING THE CASH PAYMENTS JOURNAL

The procedures for posting the cash payments journal are similar to those described earlier for posting the cash receipts journal. Specifically, the amounts recorded in the Accounts Payable column are posted individually to the subsidiary ledger and in total to the control account. Store Supplies, Purchases, and Cash are posted only in total at the end of the month. When a transaction is recorded in the Other Accounts column, it is posted individually to the appropriate account(s) affected. No totals are posted for this column.

The posting of the cash payments journal is illustrated on page 230. Note that the symbol CP is used as the posting reference for this journal. After postings are completed, the equality of the debit and credit balances in the general ledger should be maintained. In addition, the control account balances should agree with the subsidiary ledger total balance. The agreement of these balances is shown on the top of the next page.

GENERAL JOURNAL

Special journals for sales, purchases, and cash substantially reduce the number of entries that are made in the general journal. **Only transactions that cannot be entered in a special journal are recorded in the general journal.** For example, the general journal may be used to record such transactions as

Reconciling accounts payable subsidiary ledger to control account

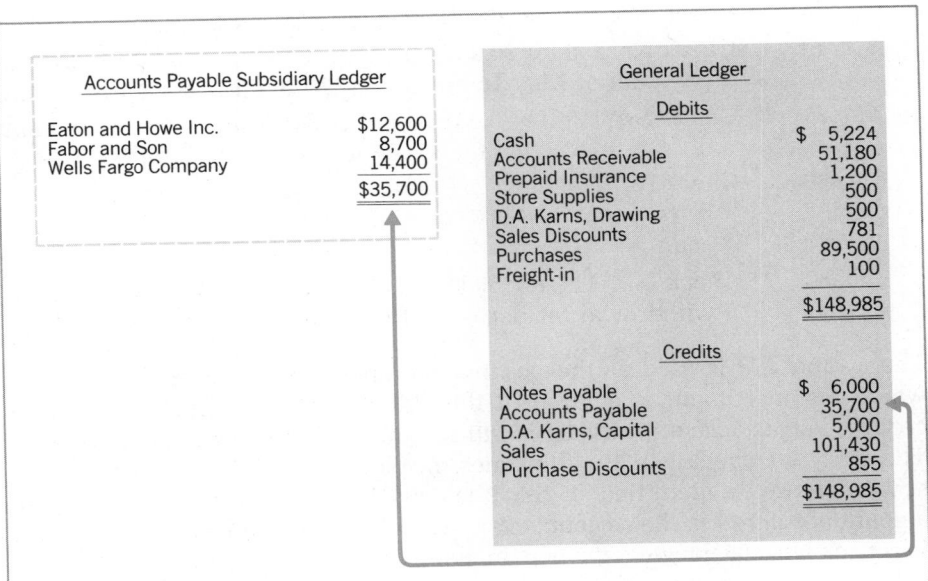

Accounts Payable Subsidiary Ledger

Eaton and Howe Inc.	$12,600
Fabor and Son	8,700
Wells Fargo Company	14,400
	$35,700

General Ledger

Debits

Cash	$ 5,224
Accounts Receivable	51,180
Prepaid Insurance	1,200
Store Supplies	500
D.A. Karns, Drawing	500
Sales Discounts	781
Purchases	89,500
Freight-in	100
	$148,985

Credits

Notes Payable	$ 6,000
Accounts Payable	35,700
D.A. Karns, Capital	5,000
Sales	101,430
Purchase Discounts	855
	$148,985

Journalizing and posting of general journal

Karns Wholesale Supply
General Journal
G1

Date	Accounts and Explanations	Ref.	Debit	Credit
1987				
May 31	Accounts Payable-Fabor and Son	25/√	500	
	Purchase Returns and Allowances	73		500
	(Received credit for returned goods)			

ACCOUNTS PAYABLE SUBSIDIARY LEDGER

Fabor and Son

Date	Ref.	Debit	Credit	Balance
1987				
May 14	P1		6,900	6,900
23	CP1	6,900		
26	P1		8,700	8,700
31	G1	500		8,200

GENERAL LEDGER

Accounts Payable No. 25

Date	Ref.	Debit	Credit	Balance
1987				
May 31	P1		89,100	89,100
31	CP1	53,400		35,700
31	G1	500		35,200

Purchase Returns and Allowances No. 73

Date	Ref.	Debit	Credit	Balance
1987				
May 31	G1		500	500

granting of credit to a customer for a sales return or allowance, receipt of credit from a supplier for purchases returned, acceptance of a note receivable from a customer, and purchase of equipment by issuing a note payable. In addition, correcting, adjusting, and closing entries are made in the general journal.

The form of the general journal remains the same. When control and subsidiary accounts are not involved, the procedures for journalizing and posting of transactions are identical with those described in earlier chapters. However, when control and subsidiary accounts are involved, two modifications of earlier procedures are required:

1. In journalizing, both the control and subsidiary accounts must be identified.
2. In posting, there must be a dual posting: once to the control account and once to the subsidiary account.

To illustrate, assume that on May 31, Karns Wholesale Supply returns $500 of merchandise for credit to Fabor and Son because of an error in filling its May 26 order. The entry in the general journal and the posting of the entry are shown in the graphic at the bottom of page 232.

Observe in the journal that two accounts are indicated for the debit and two postings are indicated in the reference column. One amount is posted to the control account and the other to the creditor's account in the subsidiary ledger.

KARNS WHOLESALE SUPPLY—A RECAP

Given the transaction information for the month of May, Karns' trial balance based on the general ledger data is as follows:

Trial balance

KARNS WHOLESALE SUPPLY
Trial Balance
May 31, 1987

	Debit	Credit
Cash	$ 5,224	
Accounts Receivable	51,180	
Prepaid Insurance	1,200	
Store Supplies	500	
Notes Payable		$ 6,000
Accounts Payable		35,200
D. A. Karns, Capital		5,000
D. A. Karns, Drawing	500	
Sales		101,430
Sales Discounts	781	
Purchases	89,500	
Freight-in	100	
Purchase Discounts		855
Purchase Returns and Allowances		500
	$148,985	$148,985

The schedule of the balances for accounts receivable and accounts payable is as follows:

Proving control accounts in trial balance

Accounts Receivable	
Abbot Sisters	$15,400
Babson Co.	14,570
Deli Co.	21,210
	$51,180

Accounts Payable	
Eaton and Howe, Inc.	$12,600
Fabor and Son	8,200
Wells Fargo Company	14,400
	$35,200

It follows that the total of the balances in the subsidiary ledgers for accounts receivable and accounts payable must agree with their control accounts as shown on the trial balance.

DIRECT POSTING TO SUBSIDIARY LEDGERS

Direct posting means posting subsidiary ledger accounts directly from a source document, rather than from a journal. In our earlier explanation of the sales journal, the entries were made from the prenumbered invoices. Postings to the accounts receivable subsidiary ledger were then made from the journal. Under direct posting, the invoice that provides the information for the sales journal entry is sent directly to the employee(s) responsible for maintaining the accounts receivable subsidiary ledger. The invoice is then used to post to the specific accounts receivable account. Direct posting facilitates the updating of subsidiary ledgers because subsidiary ledger clerks do not need access to the journals.

Direct posting illustrated

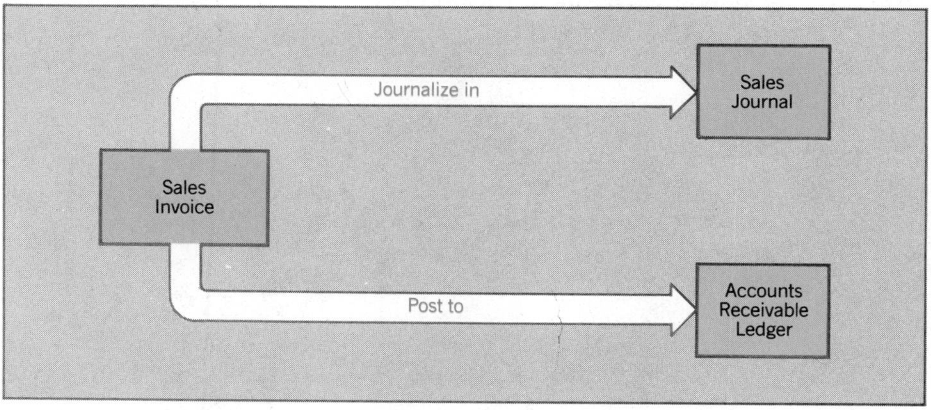

SECTION TWO—ELECTRONIC DATA PROCESSING

As in the case of a manual system, an **electronic data processing system** (also called a computerized or automated system) begins at the transaction level. In

computerized systems, journalizing is referred to as data entry and although data entry is much faster than journalizing, it still involves human input.

Data entry is the Garbage-In stage of the data processing acronym GIGO. Garbage-in is not automated, Garbage-out is automated. The real trick (and expensive part) of both manual and automated systems (either micros, minis, or main frames) is to get what you might call DIIO, that is, Data-In, Information-Out.

Once data have been entered into the computer each of the remaining steps in the accounting cycle are basically automated. In small micro systems some additional instructions must be entered into the computer to process the data, but once these simple chores are done, everything else is automated. In large computerized systems typical of the operations of financial institutions with automated teller machines, 99% of the processing is done automatically. After the data have been processed, the computer can almost instantly produce financial statements and a wide variety of reports. Later computer notes in this textbook will expand on these ideas.

ACCOUNTS RECEIVABLE—MANUAL SYSTEM vs. COMPUTERIZED SYSTEM

In the remainder of this chapter, we will discuss computerized systems. Computerized systems process data by electronic equipment that operates with little manual intervention. To develop an understanding of some of the advantages and the disadvantages of a computerized system, we will discuss a computerized system, using accounts receivable as an example. Other examples such as accounts payable, fixed assets, payroll, and inventory could be used. These applications are addressed briefly in subsequent chapters.

A computerized accounts receivable system closely resembles a manual accounts receivable system in concept, although it is quite different in appearance and operation. Computer files on disk or magnetic tape replace the sales journal, the cash receipts journal, the general ledger, and the accounts receivable subsidiary ledger used in a manual system. The accounts receivable computer files consist of two basic records: the **accounts receivable transaction file** and the **accounts receivable master file.**

The daily accounts receivable transaction file in a computerized system is comparable to the sales journal and the cash receipts journal in a manual system. It is a chronological record of every credit sale transaction and all collections from customers. The source documents for the computerized transaction record are the sales invoices and the checks from customers.

The accounts receivable master file in a computerized system is comparable to the accounts receivable subsidiary ledger in a manual system. It contains all of the permanent information about each customer, including account number, customer's name and address, balance due, credit limit, salesperson, sales territory, and any other data desired. The master file is

updated daily (or weekly or monthly in some firms) by a computer processing run that merges the daily accounts receivable transaction file with the accounts receivable master file to make current each customer's account balance; the result is a new updated accounts receivable master file. The following diagram illustrates this updating process:

Updating accounts receivable master file

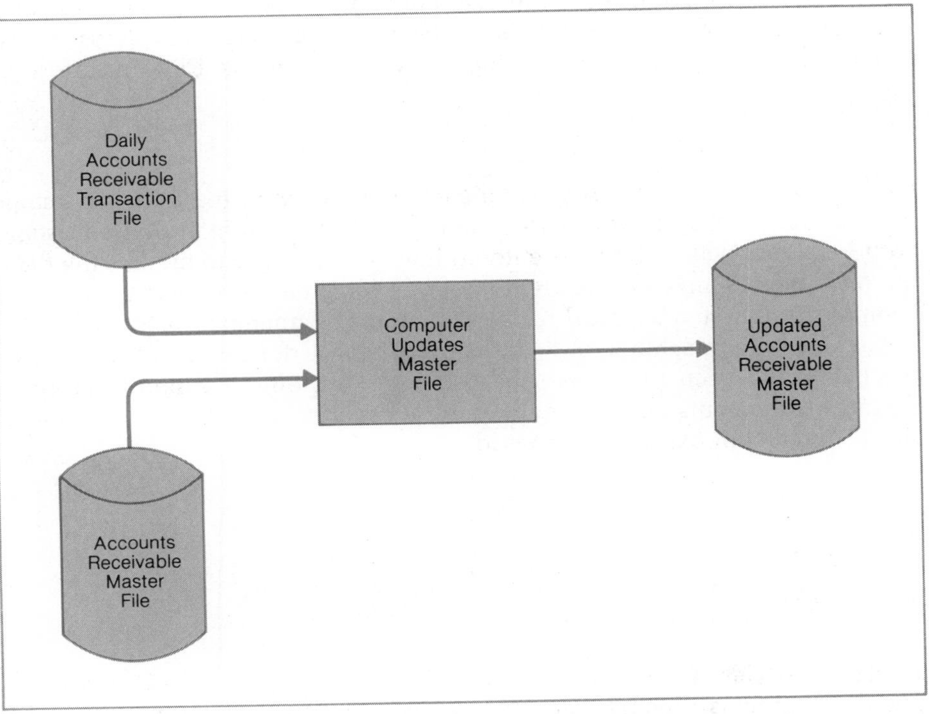

The daily accounts receivable transaction file can be printed out ("hard copy") in the form of a sales journal and a partial cash receipts journal (receipts from credit customers only). Printing out the accounts receivable master file provides an accounts receivable subsidiary ledger.

The source documents (sales invoices, credit memos, and so on) related to accounts receivable transactions are the same in both manual and computerized systems. However, the journalizing and posting functions are totally automated in a computerized system.

COMPARATIVE ADVANTAGES—MANUAL vs. COMPUTER

As we have shown, there are similarities and differences between manual and computerized accounts receivable accounting systems. But one should not conclude that computerized systems are always better than manual systems just because of their speed, accuracy, and capacity. Some key points to consider in evaluating and comparing manual and computerized systems are discussed on the following page.

COST CONSIDERATIONS

Only a few years ago, manual systems had a comparative cost advantage over computerized systems for small businesses. In a manual system, only a few bookkeepers and some accounting journals and ledgers are required, whereas computerized systems require processing and printing equipment and skilled operators. But today, with microcomputers widely available, as well as an abundance of user-friendly software packages, the manual system is losing its comparative cost advantage in even the smallest of businesses.

PROCESSING SPEED

Where the number of transactions is large, computerized accounts receivable systems have a real advantage. Thousands of transactions can be processed quickly by a computer, and high-speed printers can print reports at the rate of 20,000 lines per minute. But surprising lags in computer processing work still can occur. For example, if transactions are batched (held and processed later) and not processed until the end of the week or the end of the month, any sale made at the end of the period might not be keyed into the computer until the end of the next period—a lag of seven days on a weekly setup and a lag of four weeks on a monthly setup. This delay can be avoided by processing transactions daily or by using real-time processing systems in which data are processed as soon as received.

PROCESSING ERRORS

Unless a hardware failure occurs, the computer will not make a processing error. Both hardware and software controls generally ensure processing accuracy. Because error-prone humans perform the processing in a manual system, there is clearly a greater potential for processing errors in the manual system.

RESPONSIVENESS

Have you ever tried to call the computer to get your bill corrected? Errors and other problems are generally handled more swiftly and readily in a manual system than in a computerized system. For example, a bookkeeper is likely to have closer contact with the sales personnel and therefore may be more responsive to customer complaints. Also, an important psychological factor differentiates manual systems from computer systems. In a computerized system, customers become numbers, and customers generally prefer not to be treated as numbers; they like personalized relationships. The computer becomes a mechanical intermediary that neither recognizes individuality nor appreciates the customer's business; it never says, "Thank you!"

GENERATION OF ADDITIONAL REPORTS

A definite advantage of computerized systems is the ease with which additional reports can be prepared. Once the computer contains the data base, in this case, customer data and sales transactions, much useful information can be printed out in a matter of minutes. These include weekly or monthly sales reports, sales reports by salesperson or territory or product line, listings of overdue accounts, and reports on the average time to collect each customer's account.

Unfortunately, computer-related frauds have become a major concern. For example, the estimates of direct losses in one of the major computer fraud cases (the Equity Funding Insurance Company) ranged from $27 million to $200 million. On the basis of known cases, excluding Equity Funding, the average computer fraud loss is $650,000, compared with an average loss of only $19,000 resulting from other types of white-collar crime.

Preventing and detecting computer fraud represent a major challenge. One of the best ways for a company to minimize the likelihood of computer fraud is to have a good system of internal control. Internal control is discussed in the next chapter.

Although some tradeoffs exist between the efficiencies of computers and the personal responsiveness of manual systems, computer systems are gaining so significantly in popularity that one day manual accounting systems may become an endangered species.

SUMMARY OF STUDY OBJECTIVES

1. The basic principles in developing an accounting information system are cost awareness, useful output, and flexible structure.

2. The major phases in the development of an accounting information system are analysis, design, implementation, and follow-up.

3. A subsidiary ledger is a group of accounts with a common characteristic that facilitates the recording process by freeing the general ledger from details of individual balances.

4. A special journal is used to group similar types of transactions. In a special journal, only one line is used to record the transaction.

5. In posting a columnar journal

(a) all column totals except for the Other Accounts column are posted once at the end of the month to the account title specified in the column heading.

(b) the total of the Other Accounts column is not posted. Instead, the individual amounts comprising the total are posted separately to the general ledger account specified in the Accounts column.

(c) the individual amounts in a column posted in total to a control account are posted daily to the subsidiary ledger account specified in the Accounts column.

6. The key points in comparing manual and computerized accounting systems are (a) cost considerations, (b) processing speed, (c) processing errors, (d) responsiveness, and (e) generation of additional reports.

GLOSSARY

Accounting information system, p. 213

Accounts payable (creditors') ledger, p. 217

Accounts receivable (customers') ledger, p. 217

Accounts receivable master file, p. 235

Accounts receivable transaction file, p. 235

Cash payments journal, p. 219

Cash receipts journal, p. 219

Columnar journal, p. 222

Control account, p. 217

Direct posting, p. 234

Purchases journal, p. 219

Sales journal, p. 219

Special journal, p. 218

Subsidiary ledger, p. 217

DEMONSTRATION PROBLEM

The Emelia Company uses a five column cash receipts journal with columns for Cash (Dr.), Sales Discounts (Dr.), Accounts Receivable (Cr.), Sales (Cr.) and Other Accounts (Cr.). Cash receipts transactions for the month of July are as follows:

July 3 Cash sales total $5,800.
5 A check for $6,370 is received from the Jeltz Company in payment of invoice dated June 26 for $6,500 terms 2/10 n/30.
9 An additional investment of $5,000 in cash is made in the business by Betty Emelia, the proprietor.
10 Cash sales total $12,519.
12 A check for $7,275 is received from R. Eliot & Co. in payment of a $7,500 invoice dated July 3, terms 3/10 n/30.
15 A customer advance of $700 cash is received for future sales.
20 Cash sales total $15,472.
22 A check for $5,880 is received from Beck Company in payment of $6,000 invoice dated July 13, terms 2/10 n/30.
29 Cash sales total $17,660.
31 Cash of $200 is received on interest earned for July.

INSTRUCTIONS

(a) Journalize the transactions in the cash receipts journal.

(b) Contrast the posting of the Accounts Receivable and Other Accounts columns.

SOLUTION TO DEMONSTRATION PROBLEM

(a)

EMELIA COMPANY
Cash Receipts Journal

CR 1

Date	Explanation	Accounts Credited	Ref.	Cash Dr.	Sales Discount Dr.	Accounts Receivable Cr.	Sales Cr.	Other Accounts Cr.
7/3	Cash sales			5,800			5,800	
5	Collection in full	Jeltz Co.		6,370	130	6,500		
9	Additional investment	Betty Emelia, Capital		5,000				5,000
10	Cash sales			12,519			12,519	
12	Collection in full	R. Eliot & Co.		7,275	225	7,500		
15	Advance payment	Customer Advances		700				700
20	Cash sales			15,472			15,472	
22	Collection in full	Beck Co.		5,880	120	6,000		
29	Cash sales			17,660			17,660	
31	Collection of interest	Interest Revenue		200				200
				76,876	475	20,000	51,451	5,900

(b) The Accounts Receivable column total is posted as a credit to Accounts Receivable. The individual amounts are credited to the customers' accounts identified in the account credited column which are maintained in the accounts receivable subsidiary ledger.

The amounts in the other accounts column are only posted individually. They are credited to the account titles identified in the Accounts Credited column.

QUESTIONS

1. Walter Jones Company is considering changing its accounting system for its accounts receivable billing procedure. At present, the procedure is performed manually by two clerks. A consultant has recommended that a new computer and related software be purchased for $800,000. What basic principle of designing and developing an effective accounting system might be violated by this proposal?

2. In order to provide a valuable service and contribute to organizational goals and objectives, certain principles should be followed in the development of an accounting information system. Discuss these principles.

3. What are the phases of the life cycle of an accounting system?

4. Describe the relationship between a control account and a subsidiary account.

5. What is a subsidiary ledger? What are the advantages of using subsidiary ledgers?

6. When are postings normally made to (a) the subsidiary accounts, and (b) the general ledger control accounts?

7. Identify and describe the four specific journals discussed in the chapter. List an advantage of using each of these journals rather than using only a general journal.

8. Why would special journals used in different businesses not be identical in format?

Can you think of a business that would maintain a cash receipts journal but not include a column for accounts receivable?

9. D. Hopp Company uses special journals. A sale made on account to Joseph Weirich for $375 was recorded in a single-column sales journal. A few days later, Weirich returns $50 worth of merchandise for credit. Where should D. Hopp Company record the sales return? Why?

10. A $200 purchase of merchandise on account from Paulson Company was properly recorded in the purchases journal. When posted, however, the amount recorded in the subsidiary ledger was $20. How might this error be discovered?

11. The column total of a special journal is posted at month-end to only two general ledger accounts. One of these two accounts is Accounts Receivable. What is the name of this special journal? What is the other general ledger account to which the month-end total is posted?

12. The cash and the accounts receivable columns in the cash receipts journal were mistakenly overadded by $1,500 at the end of the month. (a) Will the customers' ledger agree with the Accounts Receivable control account? (b) Assuming no other errors, will the trial balance totals be equal?

13. In what journal would the following transactions be recorded? (Assume that a single column sales journal and a single column purchases journal are used.)

(a) Sales of merchandise on account.

(b) Collection of cash on account from a customer.

(c) Purchase of office supplies on account.

(d) Return of merchandise by a customer.

(e) Recording of depreciation expense for the year.

(f) Sales of merchandise for cash.

14. In what journal would the following transactions be recorded? (Assume that a single-column sales journal and a single-column purchases journal are used).

(a) Purchase of merchandise on account.

(b) Payment of cash on account due a supplier.

(c) Return of merchandise to a supplier.

(d) Cash received from signing a note payable.

(e) Investment of cash by the owner of the business.

(f) Closing of the expense accounts at the end of the year.

15. What transactions might be included in a multiple-column purchases journal that would not be included in a single-column purchases journal?

16. Give an example of a transaction in the general journal that causes an entry to be posted twice (i.e., to two accounts), one in the general ledger, the other in the subsidiary ledger. Does this affect the debit/credit equality of the general ledger?

17. Give some examples of appropriate general journal transactions for an organization using special journals.

18. What is direct posting?

19. What would be the major advantages of a computerized accounting system over a manual accounting system?

20. Distinguish between the accounts receivable master file and the accounts receivable transaction file.

EXERCISES

E6-1 Cliff Company uses both special journals and a general journal as described in this chapter. On April 30, after all monthly postings had been completed, the Accounts Receivable controlling account in the general ledger had a debit balance of $280,000 and the Accounts Payable controlling account had a credit balance of $89,000.

The May transactions recorded in the special journals are summarized below. No entries affecting accounts receivable and accounts payable were recorded in the general journal for May.

Sales journal	Total sales, $144,500
Purchases journal	Total purchases, $52,260
Cash receipts journal	Accounts Receivable column total, $121,000
Cash payments journal	Accounts Payable column total, $48,500

INSTRUCTIONS

(a) What is the balance of the Accounts Receivable control account after the monthly postings on May 31?

(b) What is the balance of the Accounts Payable control account after the monthly postings on May 31?

(c) What posting would be made of the column total of $144,500 in the sales journal?

(d) What posting would be made of the accounts receivable column total of $121,000 in the cash receipts journal?

E6-2 S. Comfort & Company uses both special journals and a general journal as described in this chapter. The company's bookkeeper made the following errors during June.

(a) Incorrectly added the credit entries in a supplier's account in the accounts payable subsidiary ledger. The total was listed as $1,470; it should have been $1,570.

(b) In the single-column sales journal, incorrectly added the entries for the month. Monthly total was listed as $48,760; it should have been $48,670.

(c) A remittance of $265 from customer J. W. Smith was correctly recorded in the cash receipts journal, but the amount was posted incorrectly to the account of customer J. Hamsmith.

(d) A purchase of merchandise on credit from D. Jensen Company for $1,100 was incorrectly entered in the purchases journal at $11,000.

INSTRUCTIONS

State how each of the errors above might be discovered.

E6-3 On September 1 the balance of the Accounts Payable controlling account in the general ledger of Donald MacArthur Company was $4,860. The creditors' subsidiary ledger contained account balances as follows: Palmer, $1,270; Harney, $870; Maxwell, $1,650; Burke, $1,070. At the end of September the various journals contained the following information:

Purchases journal: Purchases from Palmer, $1,200; from Harney, $1,050; from Maxwell, $1,080; from Burke, $1,150; from Hogan, $1,465.

Cash payments journal: Cash paid to Maxwell, $1,000; to Burke, $1,070; to Palmer, $2,446. (Palmer allowed MacArthur a $24 discount.)

General journal: An allowance from Hogan, $45; a return of merchandise to Harney, $60; and an entry to correct a $20 overcharge which Burke made on an invoice.

INSTRUCTIONS

(a) Set up control and subsidiary accounts, and enter the beginning balances. Do not construct the journals.

(b) Post the various journals. Post the items as individual items or as totals, whichever would be the appropriate procedure in the usual posting process.

(c) Prepare a list of creditors and prove the agreement of the controlling account with the subsidiary ledger.

E6-4 On November 1 the balance of the Accounts Receivable controlling account in the general ledger of Susan Sweeney Company was $9,680. The customer's subsidiary ledger contained account balances as follows: Bannister, $1,240; Crowley, $2,340; Dotson, $1,890; Seaver, $4,210. At the end of November the various journals contained the following information:

Sales journal: Sales to Seaver, $700; to Bannister, $1,850; to DeLeon, $880; to Dotson, $1,250.

Cash receipts journal: Cash received from Dotson, $1,510; from Seaver, $2,000; from DeLeon, $200; from Crowley, $1,600; from Bannister, $1,240.

General journal: An allowance is granted to Seaver, $90.

INSTRUCTIONS

(a) Set up control and subsidiary accounts and enter the beginning balances. Do not construct the journals.

(b) Post the various journals. Post the items as individual items or as totals, whichever would be the appropriate procedure.

(c) Prepare a list of customers and prove the agreement of the controlling account with the subsidiary ledger.

E6-5 The Cher Company uses the columnar cash journals illustrated in the text. In May, the following selected cash transactions occurred:

1. Made a refund to a customer for the return of damaged goods.
2. Purchased merchandise for cash.
3. Paid a creditor within the 2% discount period.
4. Received collection from customer after the 2% discount period had expired.
5. Paid freight on merchandise purchased.
6. Received cash due on a non-interest-bearing note receivable.
7. Paid cash for office equipment.
8. Received cash refund from supplier for merchandise returned.
9. Made cash sales.
10. Withdrew cash for personal use of owner.
11. Received an advance from a customer on June sales.
12. Received collection from customer within the 2% discount period.

INSTRUCTIONS

Indicate (a) the journal, and (b) the columns in the journal that should be used in recording each transaction.

E6–6 Walther Company has the following selected transactions during February:

Feb. 2 Purchased equipment costing $4,000 from Hampton Company, terms 2/10, n/30.
5 Received credit memorandum for $200 from Andrea Company for merchandise damaged in shipment.
7 Issud a credit memorandum for $300 to Frey Company for merchandise the customer returned.
10 Accepted Davis Company's $1,200 note receivable in settlement of the company's past due balance.

Walther Company uses a one-column purchases journal, the columnar cash journals used in the text, and a general journal.

INSTRUCTIONS

(a) Journalize the transactions in the general journal.
(b) Explain the postings to the control and subsidiary accounts.

E6–7 The general ledger of the D. Butkus Company contained the following Accounts Payable control account (in T account form). Also shown is the related subsidiary ledger.

General Ledger

Accounts Payable

Feb. 15	General Journal	9,000	Feb. 1	Balance	25,025
28	?	?	5	General Journal	155
			11	General Journal	660
			28	Purchases	14,700
			Feb. 28	Balance	9,240

Accounts Payable Ledger

Walters

	Feb. 28 Bal. 3,200

Elliot

	Feb. 28 Bal. ?

Zimmer

	Feb. 28 Bal. 5,000

INSTRUCTIONS

(a) Indicate the missing posting reference and amount in the control account and the missing ending balance in the subsidiary ledger.
(b) Indicate the amounts in the control account that were double-posted (i.e., posted to the control account and the subsidiary account).

E6–8 Selected accounts from the ledgers of the Raye Company at May 31 showed the following:

General Ledger

Store Equipment — No. 18

Date	Explanation	Ref.	Debit	Credit	Balance
May 1		G1	2,400		2,400

Purchases — No. 70

Date	Explanation	Ref.	Debit	Credit	Balance
May 31		P1	7,900		7,900

Freight-in — No. 71

Date	Explanation	Ref.	Debit	Credit	Balance
May 15		G1	200		200

Accounts Payable — No. 25

Date	Explanation	Ref.	Debit	Credit	Balance
May 31		P1		7,900	7,900
1		G1		2,400	10,300
15		G1		200	10,500
18		G1	100		10,400
25		G1	200		10,200

Purchase Returns and Allowances — No. 72

Date	Explanation	Ref.	Debit	Credit	Balance
May 18		G1		100	100
25		G1		200	300

Creditor's Ledger

Arlan Equipment Co.

Date	Explanation	Ref.	Debit	Credit	Balance
May 1		G1		2,400	2,400

Laura Co.

Date	Explanation	Ref.	Debit	Credit	Balance
May 14		P1		1,100	1,100
25		G1	200		900

Benton Co.

Date	Explanation	Ref.	Debit	Credit	Balance
May 3		P1		1,700	1,700
20		P1		900	2,600

Stacey Supply Co.

Date	Explanation	Ref.	Debit	Credit	Balance
May 12		P1		300	300
21		P1		400	700

Carlson Materials

Date	Explanation	Ref.	Debit	Credit	Balance
May 17		P1		1,200	1,200
18		G1	100		1,100
29		P1		2,300	3,400

Yates Transit

Date	Explanation	Ref.	Debit	Credit	Balance
May 15		G1		200	200

INSTRUCTIONS

From the data above prepare:

(a) the single-column purchases journal for May.

(b) any necessary general journal entries for May.

E6–9 Below are some typical transactions incurred by a Wrenwright company.

1. Sold land for cash.
2. Close income summary to owner's capital.
3. Payment to building contractor of balance due on completed office building.
4. Depreciation on building.
5. Depreciation on machinery.
6. Purchase of merchandise on account.
7. Purchase of office supplies for cash.
8. Payment of advertising expense.
9. Sales of merchandise on account.
10. Sales of merchandise for cash.
11. Return of merchandise purchased.
12. Sales discount given on goods sold.
13. Payment of employee wages.
14. Return of merchandise sold.
15. Payment of purchases on account in full
16. Collection on account from customers.

INSTRUCTIONS

For each transaction, indicate whether it would normally be recorded in a cash receipts journal, cash payments journal, single-column sales journal, single-column purchases journal, or general journal.

E6-10 Perry Products uses both special journals and a general journal as described in this chapter. Perry also posts customers' accounts in the accounts receivable subsidiary ledger directly from duplicate copies of the sales invoices. These postings for the most recent month are included in the subsidiary T accounts below.

Ecker

	Debit	Credit
Bal.	340	210
	180	

Jeltz

	Debit	Credit
Bal.	150	150
	190	

Nelson

	Debit	Credit
Bal.	-0-	145
	145	

Zartan

	Debit	Credit
Bal.	120	120
	180	
	160	

INSTRUCTIONS

Determine the correct amount of the end-of-month posting from the sales journal to the Accounts Receivable controlling account.

PROBLEMS

P6-1 Bowman Company's chart of accounts includes the following selected accounts:

1 Cash	52 Purchase Returns and Allowances
4 Accounts Receivable	60 Sales
11 Notes Receivable	61 Sales Discounts
27 Advances from Customers	65 Interest Revenue
40 A. J. Bowman, Capital	

On May 1 the customers' ledger of the Bowman Company showed the following balances: Bixby & Son, $2,100; Fowlett Co., $1,600; Grant Bros., $1,200; and Macon Co., $800. The May transactions involving the receipt of cash were as follows:

May 1 The owner, A. J. Bowman, invested additional cash in the business, $8,000.
3 Received check in full from Macon Co. less 2% cash discount.
6 Received check in full from Fowlett Co. less 2% cash discount.
7 Made cash sales of merchandise totaling $4,975.
9 Received check in full from Bixby & Son less 2% cash discount.
11 Received cash refund from a supplier for damaged merchandise, $200.
15 Made cash sales of merchandise totaling $5,200.
17 Collected $1,224 in settlement of $1,200 note receivable plus interest. (Assume no interest has been accrued.)
20 Received check from Grant Bros. in full for account, $1,200.
27 Received advances from customers for June sales deliveries, $600.

INSTRUCTIONS

(a) Journalize the transactions above in a five-column cash receipts journal with columns for Cash, Dr., Sales Discount, Dr., Accounts Receivable, Cr., Sales, Cr., and Other Accounts, Cr. Foot and crossfoot the journal.

(b) Insert the beginning balances in the Accounts Receivable control and subsidiary accounts and post the May transactions to these accounts.

(c) Prove the agreement of the control account and subsidiary account balances.

P6-2 The Dunmor Company's chart of accounts includes the following selected accounts:

1 Cash	41 V. Dunmor, Drawing
7 Prepaid Insurance	50 Purchases
12 Equipment	52 Purchase Discounts
21 Notes Payable	55 Interest Expense
22 Accounts Payable	

On June 1 the creditors' ledger of the Dunmor Company showed the following balances: R. Horn & Co., $3,000; G. Parlot, $2,250; R. Snyder, $1,000; and Wicks Bros., $1,500. The June transactions involving the payment of cash were as follows:

June 1 Purchased merchandise, check no. 11, $900.
3 Purchased store equipment, check no. 12, $1,200.
5 Paid Wicks Bros. balance due of $1,500, less 2% discount, check no. 13, $1,470.
9 Paid note payable of $2,000 plus interest of $40, check no. 14. (Assume no interest has been accrued.)
11 Purchased merchandise, check no. 15, $1,600.
15 Paid R. Snyder balance due of $1,000, less 3% discount, check no. 16, $970.
16 V. Dunmor, the owner, withdraws $500 cash for own use, check no. 17.
19 Paid G. Parlot in full for invoice no. 1245, $1,500 less 1% cash discount, check no. 18, $1,485.
25 Paid premium due on one year insurance policy, check no. 19, $2,400.
30 Paid R. Horn & Co. for invoice no. 832, $2,000, check no. 20.

INSTRUCTIONS

(a) Journalize the transactions above in a five-column cash payments journal with columns for Other Accounts, Dr., Accounts Payable, Dr., Purchases, Dr., Purchases Discounts, Cr., and Cash, Cr. Foot and rule the journal.

(b) Insert the beginning balances in the Accounts Payable control and subsidiary accounts and post the June transactions to these accounts.

(c) Prove the agreement of the control account and the subsidiary account balances.

P6-3 The chart of accounts of the Troy Company includes the following selected accounts:

15 Notes Receivable	51 Sales Returns and Allowances
16 Accounts Receivable	60 Purchases
18 Supplies	61 Freight-in
26 Equipment	62 Purchase Returns and Allowances
31 Accounts Payable	73 Advertising Expense
50 Sales	

In August the following selected transactions were completed. All purchases and sales were on account except as indicated.

Aug. 2 Purchased merchandise from Clyde Company, $6,000.
3 Received freight bill from Acme Freight on Clyde purchase, $300.
5 Sales were made to Devon Company, $1,500, Hendrix Bros., $2,500, and Nelles Company, $1,800.
8 Purchased merchandise from Ingalls Company, $7,000 and Lyle Company, $8,500.
10 Received credit on merchandise returned to Lyle Company, $300.
12 Accepted Higgins Company 60-day, 6% note on merchandise sold this date, $3,000.
15 Purchased supplies from Engle Supply, $800.
16 Purchased merchandise from Clyde Company, $3,500, and Ingalls Company $5,000.
17 Returned supplies to Engle Supply, receiving credit, $100. (Hint: Credit Supplies.)
18 Received freight bills on August 16 purchases from Acme Freight, $500.
20 Returned merchandise to Clyde Company receiving credit, $200.
23 Made sales to Hendrix Bros., $2,400, and Nelles Company, $1,900.
25 Received bill for advertising from Sable Advertising, $700.
26 Granted allowance to Nelles Company for merchandise damaged in shipment, $100.
28 Purchased a small adding machine from Engle Supply, $250. (Hint: Debit Equipment.)
29 Purchased store supplies from Engle Supply, $400.

INSTRUCTIONS

(a) Journalize the transactions above in a purchases journal with columns for Other Accounts, Purchases, Freight-in, Supplies, and Accounts Payable, a one-column sales journal, and a general journal.

(b) Post to both the general and subsidiary ledger accounts. (Assume that all accounts have zero beginning balances.)

(c) Prove the agreement of the control and subsidiary accounts.

P6-4 Selected accounts from the chart of accounts of Kelly Company are shown below.

1 Cash	50 Sales
15 Notes Receivable	54 Sales Discounts
16 Accounts Receivable	60 Purchases
18 Supplies	62 Purchase Returns and Allowances
22 Land	64 Purchase Discounts
24 Building	73 Advertising Expense
31 Accounts Payable	

During October, Kelly completed the following transactions:

Oct. 2 Purchased merchandise on account from Stieb Company, $11,500.
4 Sold merchandise on account to Alexander Co., $6,400. Invoice no. 204; terms 2/10, n/30.
5 Purchased supplies for cash, $75.
7 Made cash sales for the week totaling $8,640.
9 Paid in full the Stieb Company on account less a 2% discount.
10 Purchased merchandise on account from Hurst Corp., $3,400.
12 Received payment from Alexander Co. for invoice no. 204.
13 Issued a debit memorandum to Hurst Corp. and returned $200 worth of damaged goods.

14 Made cash sales for the week totaling $7,880.
16 Sold a parcel of land for $26,000 cash, the land's book value.
17 Sold merchandise on account to L. Boyton & Co., $4,350, invoice no. 205, terms 2/10, n/30.
18 Purchased merchandise for cash, $1,635.
21 Made cash sales for the week totaling $8,375.
23 Paid in full the Hurst Corp. on account for the goods kept. (no discount)
25 Purchased supplies on account from Frey Co., $210.
25 Sold merchandise on account to Green Corp., $6,220, invoice no. 206, terms 2/10, n/30.
25 Received payment from L. Boyton & Co. for invoice no. 205.
26 Purchased for cash a small parcel of land and a building on the land to use as a storage facility. The total cost of $30,000 was allocated $18,000 to the land and $12,000 to the building.
27 Purchased merchandise on account from Martin Co., $5,600.
27 Sold merchandise to Limbo Co., $1,500 and accepted a note for that amount.
28 Made cash sales for the week totaling $7,940.
30 Purchased merchandise on account from Stieb Company, $13,000.
30 Paid advertising bill for the month from the Gazette, $300.
30 Sold merchandise on account to L. Boyton & Co., $4,600. Invoice no. 207; terms 2/10, n/30.

Kelly Company uses the following journals:

1. Single-column sales journal.
2. Single-column purchases journal.
3. Cash receipts journal with columns for Cash Dr., Sales Discounts Dr., Accounts Receivable Cr., Sales Cr., and Other Accounts Cr.
4. Cash payments journal with columns for Other Accounts Dr., Accounts Payable Dr., Supplies Dr., Purchase Discounts Cr., and Cash Cr.
5. General journal.

INSTRUCTIONS

Using the selected accounts provided:

(a) Record, in the appropriate journals, the October transactions.
(b) Foot and crossfoot all special journals.
(c) Show how postings would be made by placing ledger account numbers and check marks as needed in the journals. (Actual posting to ledger accounts is not required.)

P6–5 Presented below are the sales and cash receipts journal for Hardy Co. for its first month of operations.

Sales Journal S1

Date	Account Debited	Ref.	Accounts Receivable Debit Sales Credit
Feb. 3	H. Dunlop		$ 3,000
9	R. Sandson		7,500
12	B. Sallie		9,000
26	L. Walker		6,000
			$25,500

Cash Receipts Journal CR1

Date	Explanation	Accounts Credited	Ref.	Cash Debit	Sales Discount Debit	Accounts Receivable Credit	Sales Credit	Other Accounts Credit
Feb. 1	Investment	B. Hardy, Capital		30,000				30,000
2	Cash sales			5,500			5,500	
6	Payment in advance	Advances from Customers		7,000				7,000
13	Collection in full	H. Dunlop		2,970	30	3,000		
18	Refund for damaged goods	Purchase Returns and Allowances		150				150
26	Collection in full	R. Sandson		7,500	—	7,500		
				53,120	30	10,500	5,500	37,150

In addition, the following transactions have not been journalized for February.

Feb. 2 Purchased merchandise on account from S. Healy for $900, terms 1/10, n/30.
7 Purchased merchandise on account from L. Held for $21,000, terms 1/10, n/30.
9 Paid cash of $700 for purchase of supplies.
12 Paid $891 to S. Healy in payment for $900 invoice, less 1% discount.
15 Purchased equipment for $6,000 cash.
16 Purchased merchandise on account from R. Landly, $2,200, terms 2/10, n/30.
17 Paid $20,790 to L. Held in payment of $21,000 invoice, less 1% discount.
20 Withdrew cash of $1,100 from business for personal use.
21 Purchased merchandise on account from J. Able for $6,300, terms 1/10, n/30.
28 Paid $2,200 to R. Landly in payment of $2,200 invoice.

INSTRUCTIONS

(a) Open the following accounts in the general ledger.

11 Cash	71 B. Hardy, Drawing
13 Accounts Receivable	100 Sales
22 Supplies	110 Sales Discounts
30 Equipment	120 Purchases
32 Accumulated Depreciation—Equipment	121 Purchase Discounts
50 Accounts Payable	122 Purchase Returns and Allowances
53 Advances from Customers	125 Supplies Expense
70 B. Hardy, Capital	127 Depreciation Expense

(b) Journalize the transactions that have not been journalized in a one-column purchases journal, and the cash payments journal similar to the one illustrated on page 230.

(c) Post to the accounts receivable and accounts payable subsidiary ledgers. Follow the sequence of transactions as shown in the problem.

(d) Post the individual entries and totals to the general ledger.

(e) Prepare a trial balance.

(f) Determine that the subsidiary ledgers agree with the control accounts in the general ledger.

(g) The following adjustments at the end of February are necessary.
1. A count of supplies indicates that $300 is still on hand.
2. Depreciation on equipment for February is $100.
3. $2,000 of the Advances from Customers is earned in February (Hint: Credit Sales).

Prepare the adjusting entries and then post the adjusting entries to the general ledger.

(h) Prepare an adjusted trial balance.

P6-6 The post-closing trial balance for Horicon Co. is as follows:

HORICON CO.
Post-Closing Trial Balance
December 31, 1987

	Debit	Credit
Cash	$ 35,750	
Notes Receivable	42,000	
Accounts Receivable	13,000	
Merchandise Inventory	18,000	
Equipment	6,450	
Accumulated Depreciation – Equipment		$ 1,500
Accounts Payable		35,000
S. Horicon, Capital		78,700
	$115,200	$115,200

The subsidiary ledgers contain the following information: (1) accounts receivable—R. Daniel $1,500; B. Jones $7,500; S. Lowe $4,000; (2) accounts payable—S. Lee $9,000; R. Manning $15,000; and D. Nankin $11,000.

The transactions for January 1988 are as follows:

Jan. 3 Sell merchandise to B. Senton, $1,200, terms 2/10, n/30.
5 Purchase merchandise from S. Warren, $2,000, terms 2/10, n/30.
7 Receive a check from S. Lowe, $3,000.
11 Pay freight on merchandise purchased, $175.
12 Pay rent of $900 for January.
13 Receive payment in full from B. Senton.
14 Post all entries to the subsidiary ledgers. Issues a credit memo to acknowledge receipt of damaged merchandise of $800 returned by R. Daniel.
15 Send D. Nankin a check for $10,890 in full payment of account, discount, $110.
17 Purchase merchandise from D. Lapeska, $1,600, terms 2/10, n/30.
18 Pay sales salaries of $2,100 and office salaries, $1,150.
20 Give R. Manning a 60 day note for $15,000 in full payment of accounts payable.
23 Total cash sales which amount to $9,000.
24 Post all entries to the subsidiary ledgers. Sells merchandise on account to B. Jones, $6,300, terms 1/10, n/30.
27 Send S. Warren a check for $850.
29 Receive payment on a note of $36,000 from S. Lava.
30 Return merchandise of $320 to D. Lapeska for credit. Post all journals to the subsidiary ledger.

INSTRUCTIONS

(a) Open general and subsidiary ledger accounts for the following:

100 Cash	400 Sales
110 Notes Receivable	403 Sales Discounts
120 Accounts Receivable	406 Sales Returns and Allowances
130 Merchandise Inventory	450 Purchases
140 Equipment	453 Purchase Discounts
141 Accumulated Depreciation—Equipment	456 Purchase Returns and Allowances
	457 Freight-in
190 Notes Payable	460 Rent Expense
200 Accounts Payable	510 Sales Salaries Expense
300 S. Horicon, Capital	520 Office Salaries Expense

(b) Record the January transactions in a single-column sales journal, a single-column purchases journal, a cash receipts journal as shown on page 224, a cash payments journal as shown on page 230, and a two-column general journal.

(c) Post the appropriate amounts to the general ledger.

(d) Prepare a trial balance at January 31, 1988.

(e) Determine whether the subsidiary ledgers agree with controlling accounts in the general ledger.

ALTERNATE PROBLEMS

P6-1A Patterson Company's chart of accounts includes the following selected accounts:

1 Cash	52 Purchase Returns and Allowances
4 Accounts Receivable	60 Sales
11 Notes Receivable	61 Sales Discounts
40 F. Patterson, Capital	65 Interest Revenue

On February 1 the customers' ledger of the Patterson Company showed the following balances: Hamilton, $1,250; Ilwan, $1,050; Midwest Co., $2,600; and Stone, $1,900. The February transactions involving the receipt of cash were as follows:

Feb. 1 The owner, F. Patterson, invested additional cash in the business, $5,000.
4 Received check for payment of account from Stone less 2% cash discount.
5 Received check for $520 in payment of invoice no. 307 from Midwest Co.
8 Made cash sales of merchandise totaling $5,375.
10 Received check for $700 in payment of invoice no. 309 from Hamilton.
11 Received cash refund from a supplier for damaged merchandise, $400.
17 Made cash sales of merchandise totaling $5,725.
20 Collected $2,025 in settlement of $2,000 note receivable plus interest.
23 Received check for $1,500 in payment of invoice no. 310 from Midwest Co.
26 Made cash sales of merchandise totaling $6,100.
27 Received check for payment of account in full from Ilwan.

INSTRUCTIONS

(a) Journalize the transactions above in a five-column cash receipts journal with columns for Cash, Dr., Sales Discount, Dr., Accounts Receivable, Cr., Sales, Cr., and Other Accounts, Cr. Foot and crossfoot the journal.

(b) Insert the beginning balances in the Accounts Receivable control and subsidiary accounts and post the February transactions to these accounts.

(c) Prove the agreement of the control account and subsidiary account balances.

P6-2A The Biltor Company's chart of accounts includes the following selected accounts:

1 Cash	41 L. Biltor, Drawing
7 Prepaid Insurance	50 Purchases
12 Equipment	52 Purchase Discounts
21 Notes Payable	55 Interest Expense
22 Accounts Payable	58 Repair and Maintenance Expense

On August 1 the creditors' ledger of the Biltor Company showed the following balances: Olson Company, $1,400; Palmer & Sons, $2,600; Rickler Bros., $1,200; and Player Company, $3,800. The August transactions involving the payment of cash were as follows:

Aug. 1 Purchased merchandise, check no. 63, $450.
3 Purchased store equipment, check no. 64, $600.
5 Paid Olson Company balance due of $1,400, less 2% discount, check no. 65, $1,372.
8 Paid note payable of $1,000 plus interest of $30, check no. 66.
10 Purchased merchandise, check no. 67, $2,050.
15 Paid Rickler Bros. balance due of $1,200, check no. 68.
16 L. Biltor, the owner, pays his personal insurance premium of $250, check no. 69.
19 Paid Palmer & Sons in full for invoice no. 610, $1,200 less 2% cash discount, check no. 70, $1,176.
24 Paid Gilbert Painters for painting the outside of the office building, check no. 71, $490.
29 Paid Player Company in full for invoice no. 264, $2,100, check no. 72.

INSTRUCTIONS

(a) Journalize the transactions above in a five-column cash payments journal with columns for Other Account Dr., Accounts Payable Dr., Purchases Dr., Purchase Discounts Cr., and Cash Cr. Foot and crossfoot the journal.

(b) Insert the beginning balances in the Accounts Payable control and subsidiary accounts and post the August transactions to these accounts.

(c) Prove the agreement of the control account and the subsidiary account balances.

P6-3A The chart of accounts of the Andrews Company includes the following selected accounts:

15 Notes Receivable	51 Sales Returns and Allowances
16 Accounts Receivable	60 Purchases
18 Supplies	61 Freight-in
26 Equipment	62 Purchase Returns and Allowances
31 Accounts Payable	73 Advertising Expense
50 Sales	

In May the following selected transactions were completed. All purchases and sales were on account.

May 1 Purchased merchandise from Logan Company, $5,000.
2 Received freight bill from Johnson Shipping on Logan purchase, $250.
3 Made sales to Grant Company, $1,200, and Franklin Bros., $1,900.
5 Purchased merchandise from Maxwell Company, $3,000.
8 Received credit on merchandise returned to Maxwell Company, $150.
10 Accepted Calvin Corporation 60 day, 6% note on merchandise sold this date, $2,000.
13 Purchased store supplies from Apollo Supply, $680.
15 Purchased merchandise from Logan Company, $3,500, and Sparky Company, $1,700.
16 Made sales to Jackson Company, $3,250, and Franklin Bros., $1,370.
18 Received bill for advertising from Nancy's Advertisements, $600.
21 Sales were made to Grant Company, $410, and Jeff Company, $2,100.
22 Granted allowance to Grant for merchandise damaged in shipment, $120.
24 Purchased merchandise from Maxwell Company, $2,560.
26 Purchased a small adding machine from Apollo Supply, $320.
28 Received freight bill from Johnson Shipping on Maxwell purchase of May 24, $280.
30 Sales were made to Jackson Company, $2,800.

INSTRUCTIONS

(a) Journalize the transactions above in a purchases journal (with columns for Other Accounts, Dr., Purchases, Dr., Freight-in, Dr., Supplies, Dr., and Accounts Payable, Cr.,) a one-column sales journal, and a general journal.

(b) Post to both the general and subsidiary ledger accounts. (Assume that all accounts have zero beginning balances.)

(c) Prove the agreement of the control and subsidiary accounts.

P6-4A Selected accounts from the chart of accounts of Dayton Company are shown below.

1 Cash	52 Sales Returns and Allowances
16 Accounts Receivable	54 Sales Discounts
18 Supplies	60 Purchases
26 Equipment	62 Purchase Returns and Allowances
31 Accounts Payable	64 Purchase Discounts
50 Sales	75 Salaries Expense

During January, Dayton completed the following transactions:

Jan. 3 Purchased merchandise on account from Bell Co., $8,800.
4 Purchased supplies for cash, $60.
4 Sold merchandise on account to Rose & Rose, $7,350, invoice no. 371, terms 1/10, n/30.
5 Issued a debit memorandum to Bell Co. and returned $300 worth of damaged goods.
6 Made cash sales for the week totaling $2,070.
8 Purchased merchandise on account from Law Co., $4,100.
9 Sold merchandise on account to Mays Corp., $5,200, invoice no. 372, terms 1/10, n/30.
11 Purchased merchandise on account from Berra Co., $2,300.

13 Paid in full the Bell Co. on account less a 2% discount.
13 Made cash sales for the week totaling $4,230.
15 Received payment from Mays Corp. for invoice no. 372.
15 Paid semi-monthly salaries of $12,200 to employees.
17 Received payment from Rose & Rose for invoice no. 371.
17 Sold merchandise on account to Amber Co., $1,100, invoice no. 373, terms 1/10, n/30.
19 Purchased equipment on account from Bennett Corp., $5,000.
20 Cash sales for the week totaled $2,000.
20 Paid in full the Law Co. on account less a 2% discount.
23 Purchased merchandise on account from Bell Co., $7,300.
24 Purchased merchandise on account from Griffey Corp., $4,490.
27 Made cash sales for the week totaling $3,830.
30 Received payment from Amber Co. for invoice no. 373.
31 Paid semi-monthly salaries of $12,200 to employees.
31 Sold merchandise on account to Rose & Rose, $6,710, invoice no. 374, terms 1/10, n/30.

Dayton Company uses the following journals:

1. Single-column sales journal.
2. Single-column purchases journal.
3. Cash receipts journal with columns for Cash Dr., Sales Discounts Dr., Accounts Receivable Cr., Sales Cr., and Other Accounts Cr.
4. Cash payments journal with columns for Other Accounts Dr., Accounts Payable Dr., Supplies Dr., Purchase Discounts Cr., and Cash Cr.
5. General journal.

INSTRUCTIONS

Using the selected accounts provided:

(a) Record, in the appropriate journal noted, the January transactions.
(b) Foot and crossfoot all special journals.
(c) Show how postings would be made by placing ledger account numbers and check marks as needed in the journals. (Actual posting to ledger accounts is not required.)

P6–5A Presented below are the purchases and cash payments journal for O'Laurel Co. for its first month of operations.

Purchases Journal P1

Date	Creditor	Ref.	Purchases Debit Accounts Payable Credit
July 4	T. Mooney		$ 5,800
5	S. Lindaur		7,080
11	S. Ritcher		4,320
13	W. Kuckkahn		17,300
20	D. Mannis		7,200
			$41,700
			120/50

Cash Payments Journal — CP1

Date	Explanation	Accounts Debited	Ref.	Other Accounts Debit	Store Supplies Debit	Accounts Payable Debit	Purchases Discounts Credit	Cash Credit
July 4					500			500
10	Payment in full	S. Lindaur	✓			7,080	71	7,009
11	Payment of rent for an entire year (July–June)	Prepaid Rent	15	4,200				4,200
15	Payment in full	T. Mooney	✓			5,800		5,800
19	Withdrawal	O'Laurel Drawing	71	1,500				1,500
21	Payment in full	W. Kuckkahn	✓			17,300	173	17,127
				5,700	500	30,180	244	36,136
				X	22	50	121	11

In addition, the following transactions have not been journalized for July.

July 1 The founder O'Laurel invests $50,000 in cash and $10,000 in equipment to start the business.
3 O'Laurel receives $3,900 as advances on future sales from customers.
6 O'Laurel ships $6,000 of merchandise to Hardy Co., terms 1/10, n/30.
7 Make cash sales totaling $3,500.
8 O'Laurel sells merchandise on account to D. Washburn, $3,300, terms, 1/10, n/30.
10 Sell merchandise on account to L. Lemansky, $4,700, terms 1/10, n/30.
13 Receive payment in full from D. Washburn.
16 Receive payment in full from L. Lemansky.
20 Receive payment in full from Hardy Company.
21 Sell merchandise on account to S. Kronsnoble, $2,600, terms, 1/10, n/30.
29 Return damaged goods to T. Mooney and received cash refund of $350.

INSTRUCTIONS

(a) Open the following accounts in the general ledger.

11 Cash
13 Accounts Receivable
15 Prepaid Rent
22 Store Supplies
30 Equipment
32 Accumulated Depreciation Equipment
50 Accounts Payable
53 Advances from Customers
70 O'Laurel, Capital
71 O'Laurel, Drawing

100 Sales
110 Sales Discounts
111 Sales Returns and Allowance
120 Purchases
121 Purchase Discounts
122 Purchase Returns and Allowances
125 Supplies Expense
126 Rent Expense
127 Depreciation Expense

(b) Journalize the transactions that have not been journalized in the single-column sales journal, and the cash receipts journal similar to the one illustrated on page 224 and the general journal.

(c) Post to the accounts receivable and accounts payable subsidiary ledgers. Follow the sequence of transactions as shown in the problem.

(d) Post the individual entries and totals to the general ledger.

(e) Prepare a trial balance.

(f) Determine whether the subsidiary ledgers agree with the controlling accounts in the general ledger.

(g) The following adjustments at the end of July are necessary.

1. A count of supplies indicates that $240 is still on hand.
2. Depreciation on equipment is $1,000 for July.
3. $3,500 of customer advances is earned in July. (Hint: Credit Sales.)
4. Recognize rent expense for July.

Prepare the necessary entries in the general journal. Post the entries to the general ledger.

(h) Prepare an adjusted trial balance.

DECISION CASE

Decker & Black is a wholesaler of small appliances and parts. Decker & Black is operated by two owners, Joe Decker and Ed Black. In addition, the company has one employee, a repair specialist, who is on a fixed salary. Revenues are earned through the sale of appliances to retailers (approximately 70% of total revenues), appliance parts to do-it-yourselfers (10%), and the repair of appliances brought to the store (20%). Appliance sales are made on both a credit and cash basis. Customers are billed on prenumbered sales invoices. Credit terms are always net/30 days. All parts sales and repair work are cash only.

Merchandise is purchased on account from the manufacturers of both the appliances and the parts. Practically all suppliers offer cash discounts for prompt payments, and it is company policy to take all discounts. Most cash payments are made by check. Checks are most frequently issued to suppliers, to trucking companies for freight on merchandise purchases, and to newspapers, radio, and TV stations for advertising. All advertising bills are paid as received. Joe and Ed each make a monthly drawing in cash for personal living expenses. The salaried repairman is paid twice monthly.

Decker & Black currently have a manual accounting system. However, the business is growing and some consideration is being given to an electronic data processing system.

INSTRUCTIONS

(a) Identify the special journals that Decker & Black should have in its manual system. List the column headings appropriate for each of the special journals.

(b) What control and subsidiary accounts should be included in Decker & Black's manual system? Why?

(c) Explain to Joe and Ed how a computerized accounts receivable system would work.

(d) Identify for Joe and Ed the key points they should consider in deciding whether to install a computerized system.

CHAPTER 7

University of Kansas

CHAPTER 7

INTERNAL CONTROL AND CASH

STUDY OBJECTIVES

After studying this chapter, you should be able to:

1. **Define internal control.**
2. **Identify the principles of internal accounting control.**
3. **Explain the applications of internal control to cash receipts.**
4. **Describe the applications of internal control to cash disbursements.**
5. **Indicate the control features of using a bank account.**
6. **Enumerate the steps in preparing a bank reconciliation.**
7. **Explain the operation of a petty cash fund.**

Could there be dishonest employees in the business that you own or manage? Unfortunately, the answer in some cases is Yes. For example, the financial press recently reported the following:

A bookkeeper in a small company diverted $750,000 of bill payments to a personal bank account over a three-year period.

A cracker jack shipping clerk with 28 years of service shipped $125,000 of merchandise to himself.

A computer operator embezzled $21 million from Wells Fargo Bank over a two-year period.

These situations emphasize the need for a good system of internal control.[1] This chapter explains the essential features of a good internal control system and describes their application to safeguarding of a company's cash. The applications include some cash controls with which you may already be familiar.

WHAT IS INTERNAL CONTROL?

Internal control has been defined as the plan of organization and all of the related methods and measures adopted within a business to:

1. **Safeguard its assets** from employee theft, robbery, and unauthorized use.
2. **Enhance the accuracy and reliability of its accounting data** by reducing the risk of errors in the accounting process.
3. **Promote operational efficiency** through employee training programs and quality control incentives.
4. **Encourage adherence to prescribed managerial policies** through periodic review and evaluation of employee performance.[2]

From this definition, it is customary to recognize two subdivisions of internal control: (1) **accounting controls** that relate to the first two objectives (safeguarding of assets and ensuring the accuracy and reliability of the accounting data), and (2) **administrative controls** that pertain to the last two objectives (operational efficiency and adherence to managerial policies). The distinction between accounting and administrative controls has been recognized by the Congress of the United States. Under the Foreign Corrupt Practices Act, all U.S. corporations subject to the jurisdiction of the Securities and Exchange Commission are required to maintain an adequate system of internal accounting control. Companies that fail to comply are subject to fines, and company officers may be imprisoned. Our interest in this chapter is in internal accounting control.

Good internal control must be designed into computerized systems. The design starting point is usually the preparation of flow charts that graphically depict each component of a firm's operations. The assembled flow charts serve as the basis for writing detailed programs. Several examples of flow charting are given in this chapter. Attempts to automate or improve accounting systems often fail due to the absence of such well documented procedures.

[1] Employee theft is estimated to total $40 billion annually, which is 1% of the Gross National Product.

[2] Auditing Standards Board, *Codification of Statements on Auditing Standards*, American Institute of Certified Public Accountants, New York, 1986, Auditing Section 320.09 (adapted).

PRINCIPLES OF INTERNAL ACCOUNTING CONTROL

To safeguard its assets and enhance the accuracy and reliability of its accounting data, a company follows specific control principles. Although accounting control measures adopted by a company vary with the size and nature of the business and with management's control philosophy, the following principles are applicable in most enterprises.

ESTABLISHMENT OF RESPONSIBILITY

An essential characteristic of internal control is the assignment of responsibility to specific individuals. **Control is most effective when only one person is responsible for a given task.** To illustrate, assume that the cash on hand at the end of the day in a Safeway supermarket is $10 short of the cash rung on the cash register. If only one person has operated the register, responsibility for the shortage can be assessed quickly. However, if two or more individuals have worked the register, it may be impossible to determine who is responsible for the error unless each person is assigned a separate cash drawer and register key.

SEGREGATION OF DUTIES

This principle (also identified as separation of functions or division of work) is indispensable in a system of internal control. **The rationale for segregation of duties is that the work of one employee should, without a duplication of effort, provide a reliable basis for evaluating the work of another employee.**

There are two common applications of this principle:

1. The responsibility for related activities should be assigned to different individuals.
2. The responsibility for establishing the accountability (keeping the records) for an asset should be separate from the physical custody of that asset.

Related Activities

Related activities arise in both the purchasing and selling areas. Related purchasing activities include ordering the merchandise, receiving the goods, and paying (or authorizing payment) for the merchandise. Related selling activities include making a sale, shipping (or delivering) the goods to the customer, and billing the customer. **When one individual is responsible for all of the related activities, the potential for errors and fraud is increased.** In purchasing, for example, orders could be placed with friends or with suppliers who give kickbacks. Similarly, only a cursory count and inspection may be made upon receiving the goods, which leads to errors and poor-quality merchandise. In addition, payment may be authorized without a careful review of the invoice and, even worse, fictitious invoices may be approved for payment. When the responsibility for ordering, receiving, and paying are assigned to different individuals or departments, the risk of such abuses is minimized.

That is, when different individuals perform different duties, they can check on each other's performance.

When one person is responsible for related sales transactions, a salesperson could make sales at unauthorized prices to increase sales commissions; a shipping clerk could ship goods to himself, as indicated at the beginning of the chapter; and a billing clerk could understate the amount billed for sales made to friends and relatives. These abuses are reduced when salespersons make the sale, shipping department employees ship the goods on the basis of the sales order, and billing department employees prepare the sales invoice after comparing the sales order with the report of goods shipped.

Accountability for Assets

If accounting is to provide a valid basis of accountability for an asset, the accountant should have neither physical custody of the asset nor access to it. Moreover, the custodian of the asset should not maintain or have access to the accounting records. **When one employee maintains the record of the asset that should be on hand, and a different employee has physical custody of the asset, the custodian of the asset is not likely to convert the asset to personal use.** The separation of accounting responsibility from the custody of assets is especially important for cash and inventories because these assets are very vulnerable to unauthorized use or misappropriation.

MECHANICAL AND ELECTRONIC EQUIPMENT AND DEVICES

The use of mechanical and electronic equipment enhances internal control. In executing transactions, equipment such as cash registers in stores, gasoline pumps in service stations, and coin machines in metro buses provide locked-in totals of transactions that have occurred. Moreover, these machines help to assure that every transaction is registered because the customer observes (or participates in) the use of the machine. Other examples include the use of time clocks to record time worked by employees and the use of check protectors that machine imprint the amount on a check.

In recording transactions, bookkeeping equipment and other electronic equipment have program controls and built-in equipment (hardware) controls that reduce the likelihood of both unintentional and intentional errors in the accounting records. Furthermore, machine and electronic equipment can be programmed to produce error and exception reports. In addition, machine and electronically produced records are usually less vulnerable to alteration than manually produced records.

Other devices used to safeguard assets are electronic burglar alarm systems to prevent unauthorized entry to stores and warehouses. In many department stores, including major companies such as Macy's, Baskin's, and Lord & Taylor, sensors are attached to garments in an effort to reduce losses from shoplifting. After a garment is purchased, the salesclerk removes the sensor from the garment. If the sensor is not removed, it will activate an alarm bell when the customer tries to leave the store.

INDEPENDENT INTERNAL VERIFICATION

Most systems of internal accounting control provide for independent internal verification, which involves the review, comparison, and reconciliation

Program controls may be developed to identify data having a value higher or lower than a predetermined amount (limit checks), to validate computations (arithmetic proofs), or to detect the improper order in processing (sequence checks).

A crucial consideration in programming computerized systems is building in controls that limit unauthorized or unintentional tampering. Entire books and movies have been produced with computer system tampering as a major theme. Most programmers would agree that tamper proofing and debugging programs are the most difficult and time-consuming phases of their jobs.

of information from two different sources. To obtain maximum benefit from the principle,

1. The verification should be made periodically or on a surprise basis.
2. The verification should be done by an employee who is independent of the personnel responsible for the information.
3. Discrepancies and exceptions should be reported to a management level that can take appropriate corrective action.

Independent internal verification is especially useful in comparing recorded accountability with existing assets. The reconciliation by an independent person of the cash balance per books with the cash balance per bank is a common example. The relationship between this principle and the segregation of duties principle is shown graphically below.

Comparison of recorded accountability with existing assets

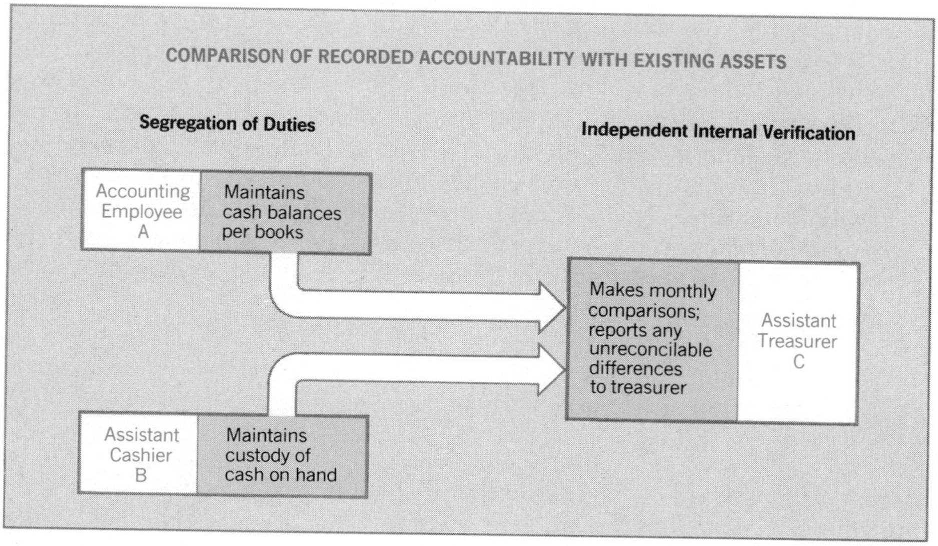

In large companies, independent internal verification is often assigned to internal auditors. **Internal auditors** are employees of the company who evaluate the effectiveness of the company's system of internal control on a

year-round basis. These individuals periodically review the activities of departments and individuals to determine compliance with prescribed internal controls.

PHYSICAL CONTROLS

Physical controls relate primarily to the safeguarding of assets. Such measures include safes in which to store cash before it is deposited, bank vaults for the deposit of cash, safety deposit boxes for the storage of valuable business papers, fences around storage areas, and locked warehouses for inventories. This principle also applies to the use of employee identification badges and plant security guards to prevent unauthorized entry during business hours, and outside security agencies to protect company property after business hours.

OTHER CONTROLS

Other control measures include the following:

1. **Prenumbered documents.** Prenumbering documents such as sales invoices and checks permits all documents in a related series to be sequentially accounted for. Prenumbering also helps to prevent a document from being recorded more than once. Thus, this control measure contributes directly to the accuracy and reliability of the accounting records.
2. **Bonding of employees who handle cash.** Bonding involves obtaining fidelity insurance protection against misappropriation of assets by dishonest employees. This measure contributes to the safeguarding of cash in two ways. First, the insured company may be prevented from hiring applicants who lack integrity because the insurance company carefully screens all individuals before adding them to the policy. Second, the bonded employees know that the insurance company will vigorously prosecute all offenders.
3. **Rotating employees' duties and requiring employees to take vacations.** These measures are designed to deter employees from attempting any thefts since they will not be able to permanently conceal their improper actions. Many bank embezzlements, for example, have been discovered when the perpetrator has been on vacation or assigned to a new position.

LIMITATIONS OF INTERNAL ACCOUNTING CONTROL

A company's system of internal accounting control is generally designed to provide reasonable, but not absolute, assurance that assets are properly safeguarded and that the accounting records are reliable. **The concept of reasonable assurance rests on the premise that the costs of establishing control procedures should not exceed their expected benefit.** To illustrate, consider shoplifting losses in retail stores. Such losses could be completely eliminated

by having a security guard stop and search customers as they leave the store. Store managers have concluded, however, that the cost and other negative effects of adopting such a procedure cannot be justified. Instead, stores have attempted to "control" shoplifting losses by less costly procedures such as: (1) posting signs saying, "We reserve the right to inspect all packages," and "All shoplifters will be prosecuted," (2) using hidden TV cameras and store detectives to monitor customer activity, and (3) using sensoring equipment at exits, as explained earlier.

It should also be recognized that the **human element** is an important factor in every system of internal accounting control. A good system can become ineffective as a result of employee fatigue, carelessness, and indifference. For example, a receiving clerk may not bother to count goods received, or may just "fudge" the counts. Moreover, **collusion** between two or more individuals to circumvent prescribed controls may significantly impair the effectiveness of a system. That is, a system of internal control is based on the premise that if different individuals perform different functions, their separate involvement will provide an adequate check. However, if a supervisor and a cashier collaborate to understate cash receipts, the system of internal control may be negated (at least in the short run). No system of internal control is perfect or infallible.

As noted in Chapter 6, computer fraud is a growing problem and it can occur on a grand scale. Computer fraud can be perpetrated almost invisibly and done with electronic speed. From the human aspect, stealing by tinkering with impersonal computer records seems far less criminal. Therefore, the moral threshold to commit computer fraud is far lower than in fraud involving person to person contact. Despite these problems, the cost and information benefits of computerized systems are irresistible.

NEED FOR CASH CONTROLS

Just as cash is the beginning of a company's operating cycle, it is usually the starting point for a company's system of internal accounting control. Cash is the one asset that is readily convertible into any other type of asset; it is easily concealed and transported; and it is highly desired. Because of these characteristics, cash is the asset most susceptible to improper diversion and use. Moreover, because of the large volume of cash transactions, numerous errors may occur in executing and recording cash transactions. To safeguard cash and to assure the accuracy of the accounting records for cash, effective internal control over cash is imperative.

WHAT IS CASH?

Cash consists of coins, currency (paper money), checks, money orders, and money on hand or on deposit in a bank or similar depository. The general

rule is that if the bank will accept it for deposit, it is cash. Items such as postage stamps and postdated checks (checks payable in the future) are not cash. Stamps are a prepaid expense, whereas the postdated checks are accounts receivable. Likewise, money market funds, certificates of deposit (CDs), and similar types of "short-term" paper that provide companies with an opportunity to earn interest on idle cash are not classified as cash. These securities cannot be converted into cash until specified maturity dates without incurring a significant penalty for early withdrawal. Thus, they are more appropriately classified as temporary investments. The accounting for temporary investments is discussed in Chapter 8.

Cash is usually listed first in the current asset section of the balance sheet because of its importance and its high liquidity. Cash restricted for a specific use such as the payment of specific long-term liabilities or the financing of a plant expansion program should be reported separately as a noncurrent asset.

Many companies have more than one bank account. For efficiency of operations and better control, national retailers like Wal-Mart Stores and K mart may have regional bank accounts. Similarly, a company such as Exxon with more than 150,000 employees may have a payroll bank account, as well as one or more general bank accounts. In addition, a company may maintain several bank accounts to have more than one bank line of credit that can be used to obtain short-term loans when needed.

INTERNAL ACCOUNTING CONTROL OVER CASH RECEIPTS

Cash receipts may result from a variety of sources such as cash sales; collections on account from customers; the receipt of interest, rents, and dividends;investments by owners; bank loans; and proceeds from the sale of noncurrent assets. The application of internal control principles to cash receipts transactions is as follows:

Application of internal control principles to cash receipts

Principle	Application to Cash Receipts
Establishment of responsibility	Only designated personnel such as cashiers and cashier department personnel should be authorized to handle or have access to cash receipts.
Segregation of duties	The duties of receiving cash, recording cash receipts transactions, and having custody of cash should be assigned to different individuals.
Mechanical and electronic equipment and devices	Cash registers should be used in executing cash receipts transactions.
Independent internal verification	Daily cash counts of register receipts should be made by cashier department supervisors; daily comparisons of total receipts and receipts de-

	posited in the bank should be made by the treasurer's office; and a reconciliation of bank and book balances should be made monthly.
Physical controls	Company safes and bank vaults should be used for the storage of cash, and access to storage areas should be limited to authorized personnel.
Other controls	All personnel who handle cash receipts should be bonded and be required to take vacations.

As might be expected, there is considerable variation in the application of these principles in different types of companies. Illustrative control measures for a retail store that has both over-the-counter and mail receipts are described below.

OVER-THE-COUNTER RECEIPTS

Control of over-the-counter receipts is centered on cash registers that are visible to customers.[3] When a cash sale occurs, the sale is "rung up" on a cash register with the amount clearly visible to the customer. This procedure prevents the cashier from ringing up a lower amount and pocketing the difference. The cashier registers a cash sale manually by punching the appropriate keys on the register or electronically by using electronic scanning equipment. The customer receives an itemized cash register receipt slip and is expected to count the change received. A cash register tape, which is locked into the register until removed by a supervisor or manager, accumulates the daily transactions and totals. When the tape is removed, the supervisor com-

Cash count sheet

CASH COUNT SHEET

Store No. 8	Date March 8, 1987
1. Opening cash balance	$ 50.00
2. Cash sales per tape (attached)	6,956.20
3. Total cash to be accounted for	$7,006.20
4. Cash on hand (see list)	6,996.10
5. Cash (short) or over	$ (10.10)
6. Ending cash balance	$ 50.00
7. Cash for deposit (Line 4-Line 6)	$6,946.10

Cashier J. Cruse   Supervisor M. Braun

[3]In supermarkets and variety stores such as K mart, cash registers are placed in check-out lines near the exit(s), whereas in Sears, Roebuck & Co. and J. C. Penney stores each department has its own cash register.

pares the total with the amount of cash in the register to determine whether all registered receipts are accounted for. The supervisor's findings are reported on a cash count sheet that is signed by both the cashier and supervisor. The count sheet used by Alrite Food Mart is shown on page 267.

The count sheets, register tapes, and cash are then given to the head cashier, who prepares a daily cash summary showing the total cash received and the amount from each source, such as cash sales and collections on account. The head cashier sends one copy of the summary to accounting for entry into the cash receipts journal. The other copy is sent to the treasurer's office for subsequent comparison with the daily bank deposit. Next, the head cashier prepares a deposit slip (see page 271) and makes the bank deposit. The total amount deposited should be equal to the total receipts on the daily cash summary to assure that all receipts have been placed in the custody of the bank. In accepting the bank deposit, the bank stamps (authenticates) the duplicate deposit slip, and sends this copy to the company treasurer who makes the comparison with the daily cash summary. The foregoing measures for cash sales are graphically illustrated below.

Executing over-the-counter cash sales

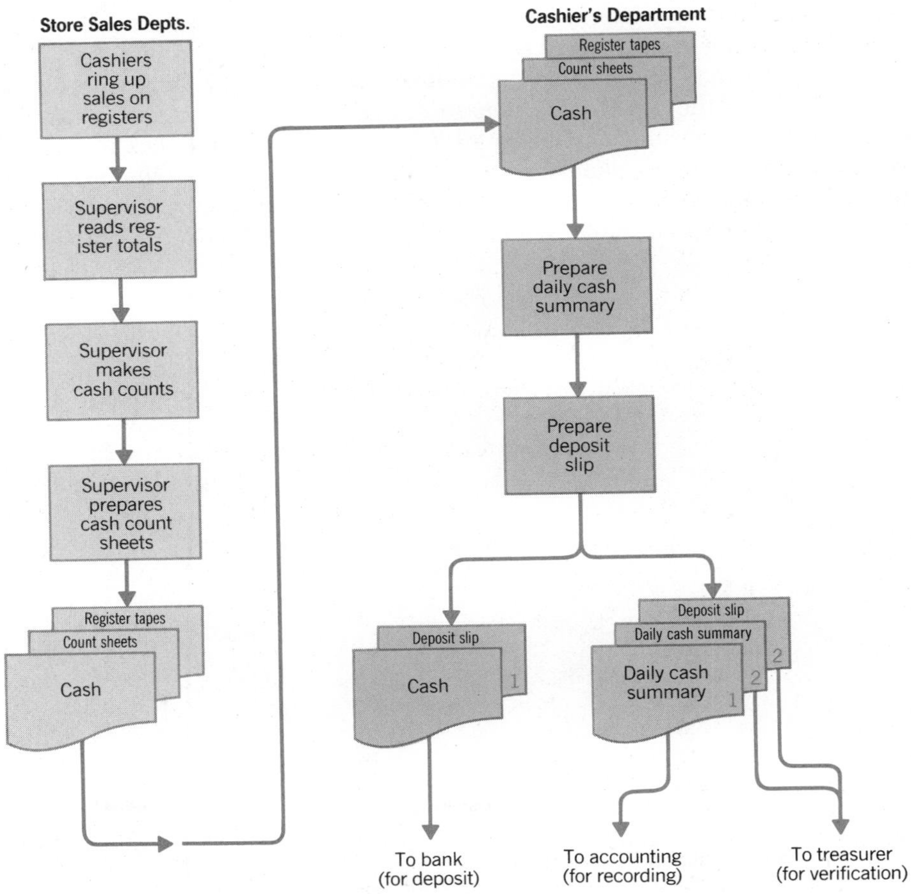

Cash Over and Short

Even though a company has good internal control over cash receipts, some unintentional errors may be made in making change. When the cash in the register at the time of the cash count does not agree with the total shown on the cash register tape, the difference is identified as cash over or cash short. In the cash count sheet shown earlier, there is a $10.10 cash shortage. The account **Cash Over and Short** is debited for a cash shortage and credited when cash is over. The entry, in general journal form, for the cash count sheet is:

Mar.	8	Cash	6,946.10	
		Cash Over and Short	10.10	
		Sales		6,956.20
		(To record daily cash sales)		

At the end of an accounting period, a debit balance in Cash Over and Short is reported in the income statement as Miscellaneous Expense, and a credit balance is reported as Miscellaneous Revenue.

MAIL RECEIPTS

As previously indicated, cash receipts result from a variety of sources. But mail receipts resulting from billings and credit sales are by far the most common way cash is received by the greatest variety of businesses and industries. All mail receipts should be received in the presence of two mail clerks. These receipts are generally in the form of checks or money orders and frequently are accompanied by a memo or a letter stating the purpose of the remittance. Each check should be promptly endorsed "For Deposit Only" by use of a company stamp. This restrictive endorsement reduces the likelihood that the check will be diverted to personal use. A list of the checks should be prepared showing the name of the issuer of the check, the purpose of the payment, and the amount of the check. Each mail clerk should sign the list to establish responsibility for the data. The originals of the list, checks, and memos are then sent to the cashier's department, where they are added to over-the-counter receipts in preparing the daily cash summary and in making the daily bank deposit. In addition, a copy of the list is sent to the treasurer's office for comparison with the total mail receipts shown on the daily cash summary to assure that all mail receipts have been included.

INTERNAL ACCOUNTING CONTROL OVER CASH DISBURSEMENTS

Disbursements may be made for a variety of reasons such as to pay expenses, liabilities, and dividends or to purchase assets. **It is generally recognized that more effective internal control over cash disbursements results when payments are made by check, except for incidental amounts that are paid out of**

petty cash.[4] Payment by check generally occurs only after specified control procedures have been followed. In addition, the "paid" check provides documentary proof of payment. The application of the principles of internal control to cash disbursements is as follows:

Application of internal control principles to cash disbursements

Principle	Application to Cash Disbursements
Establishment of responsibility	Only specified individuals such as the treasurer and assistant treasurer should be authorized to sign checks.
Segregation of duties	The duties of approving an item for payment and paying the item should be performed by different departments or individuals; check signers should not record cash disbursement transactions.
Mechanical and electronic equipment and devices	A checkwriter should be used to imprint the amount of the check in indelible ink.
Independent internal verification	Each check should be compared with the approved invoice before it is issued; bank and book balances should be reconciled monthly.
Physical controls	Blank checks should be stored in a safe, and access to the safe should be restricted to authorized personnel.
Other controls	Prenumbered checks should be used, and all checks in a series should be accounted for. After payment, the approved invoice should be stamped PAID to prevent it from being resubmitted for payment at a later date.

Most medium and large companies use a voucher system as part of their internal control over cash disbursements. A voucher system is an extensive network of approvals by authorized individuals acting independently to assure that all disbursements by check are proper. The essential features of a voucher system are explained in Appendix 7-A.

USE OF A BANK

The use of a bank contributes significantly to good internal control over cash. A company can safeguard its cash by using a bank as a depository and clearing house for checks received and checks written. Use of a bank minimizes the amount of currency that must be kept on hand. In addition, the use of a bank facilitates the control of cash because a double record is maintained of all bank transactions—one by the business and the other by the bank. The asset account Cash in Bank maintained by the depositor is the reciprocal of

[4]The operation of a petty cash fund is explained on pages 277–79.

the liability account for each depositor maintained by the bank. It should be possible to agree (or reconcile) these accounts at any time.

Opening a bank checking account is a relatively simple procedure. Typically, the bank makes a credit check on the new customer and the depositor is required to sign a **signature card.** The card should contain the signatures of each person authorized to sign checks on the account. The signature card is used by bank employees to validate signatures on the checks.

As soon as possible after an account is opened, the bank will provide the depositor with a book of serially numbered checks and deposit slips imprinted with the depositor's name and address. Each check and deposit slip is imprinted with both a bank and a depositor identification number in magnetic ink to permit computer processing of the transaction.

MAKING BANK DEPOSITS

Bank deposits should be made by an authorized employee, such as the head cashier. Each deposit must be documented by a deposit slip (ticket), as illustrated below.

Deposit ticket—front side

Deposit ticket—reverse side

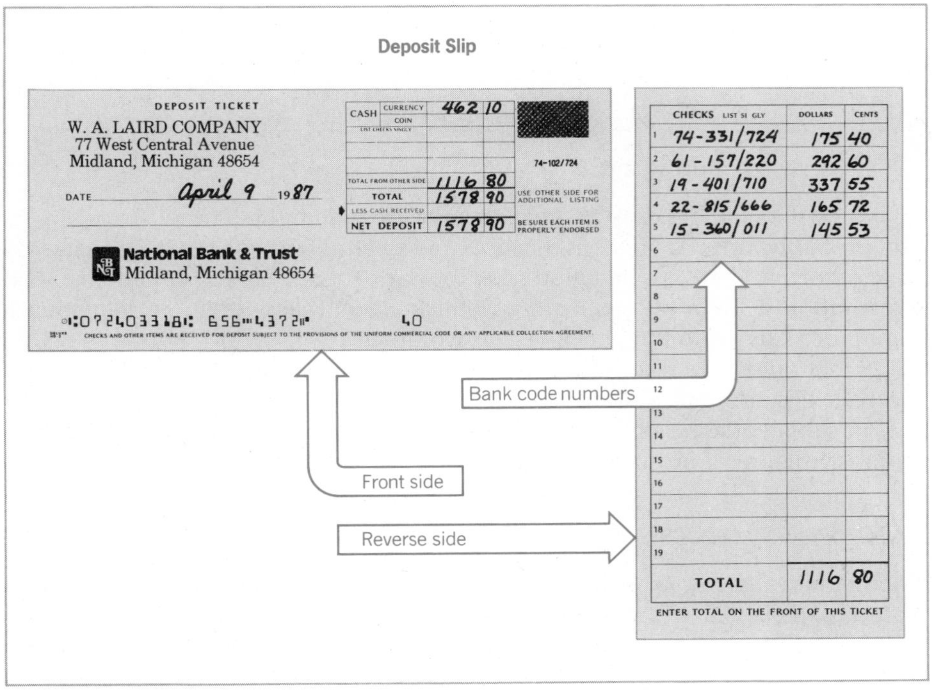

Deposit slips are prepared in duplicate. The original is retained by the bank; the duplicate, machine stamped by the bank to establish its authenticity, is retained by the depositor.

WRITING CHECKS

A **check** is a written order signed by the depositor directing the bank to pay a specified sum of money to a designated recipient. Thus, there are three parties to a check: the **maker** (or drawer) who signs the check, the **bank** (or payer)

Check

Remittance advice

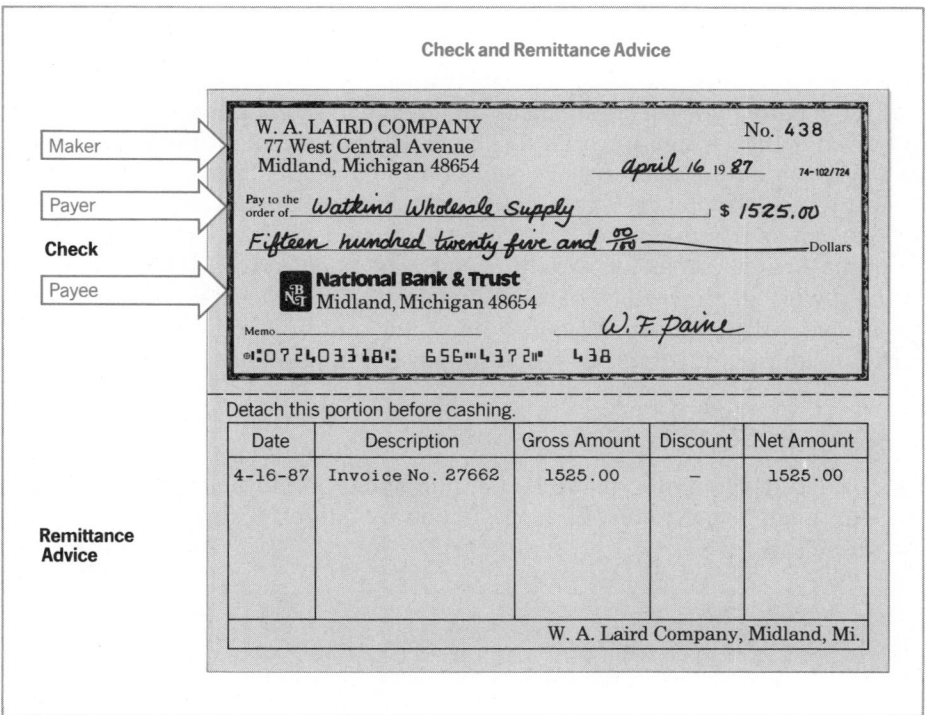

Check and Remittance Advice

Maker
Payer
Check
Payee
W. A. LAIRD COMPANY
77 West Central Avenue
Midland, Michigan 48654
No. 438
April 16 19 87
74-102/724
Pay to the order of Watkins Wholesale Supply
$ 1525.00
Fifteen hundred twenty five and 00/100 Dollars
National Bank & Trust
Midland, Michigan 48654
Memo
W. F. Paine
438

Detach this portion before cashing.

Remittance Advice

Date	Description	Gross Amount	Discount	Net Amount
4-16-87	Invoice No. 27662	1525.00	–	1525.00

W. A. Laird Company, Midland, Mi.

on which the check is drawn, and the **payee** to whom the check is payable. As you probably know, a check is a negotiable instrument that can be transferred to another party by endorsement. Each check should be accompanied by an explanation of its purposes. In many businesses, this is done by attaching a remittance advice to the check, as shown above.

For both individuals and businesses, it is important to know the balance in the checking account at all times. To keep the balance current, each deposit and check should be entered on running balance memorandum forms provided by the bank or on the check stubs contained in the checkbook.

BANK STATEMENTS

Each month the depositor receives a **bank statement** from the bank. As illustrated on page 273, the statement shows (1) checks paid and other debits that reduce the balance in the depositor's account, (2) deposits and other credits that increase the balance in the depositor's account, and (3) the account balance after each day's transactions. In some cases, the bank statement also contains additional sections for the depositor's savings and loan balances.

Included with the bank statement are the depositor's checks that have been paid. These checks are listed on the bank statements either in chronological order of payment or by check number sequence. Upon paying a check, the bank stamps the checks "paid"; "paid" checks are sometimes referred to as **canceled** checks. In addition, the bank includes memoranda explaining other debits and credits made by the bank to the depositor's account during the month.

Bank statement

Bank Statement

National Bank & Trust
Midland, Michigan Member FDIC

ACCOUNT STATEMENT

W. A. LAIRD COMPANY
77 WEST CENTRAL AVENUE
MIDLAND, MICHIGAN 48654

Statement Date/Credit Line Closing Date: April 30, 1987

ACCOUNT NUMBER: 324477

Balance Last Statement	Deposits and Credits		Checks and Debits		Balance This Statement
	No.	Total Amount	No.	Total Amount	
13,256 90	20	34,805 10	74	32,154 55	15,907 45

CHECKS AND OTHER DEBITS			DEPOSITS	DATE	BALANCE
292.77	185.79	513.80	4276.25	4-2	16540.79
644.95	2269.00	1737.60	2137.50	4-3	14026.74
94.20	810.75	352.80	1350.47	4-4	14119.46
919.42	3675.75	48.75	2035.95	4-5	11511.49
482.48	275.59	125.60 NSF	982.46	4-8	11610.28
623.00	1115.50	219.87	1578.90	4-9	11228.81
188.80	337.79	415.60	3475.23	4-10	13761.85
1226.00			1035.00 CM	4-11	13570.85
284.17	595.15	312.22	3710.15	4-27	17683.20
419.98	1525.00	1261.88	2720.18	4-28	17196.52
76.98	1572.76	776.65	1545.57	4-29	16315.70
781.70	10.00 SC	2146.00	2529.45	4-30	15907.45

Symbols: **CM** Credit Memo **DM** Debit Memo **EC** Error Correction **INT** Interest Earned **NSF** Not Sufficient Funds **SC** Service Charge

Reconcile Your Account Promptly

Debit Memorandum

Banks charge a monthly fee for the use of their facilities. Generally this occurs when the average monthly balance in a checking account is below a specified amount. The fee, called a **bank service charge,** is often identified on the bank statement by a code symbol such as SC, as shown above, and a debit memorandum explaining the charge is included with the bank statement. Separate debit memoranda may also be issued for other bank services such as the cost of printing checks, issuing traveler's checks, and wiring of funds to other locations. The symbol DM is often used for such charges.

A debit memorandum is used by the bank when a previously deposited customer's check "bounces" because of insufficient funds. In such case, the check is marked **NSF** (not sufficient funds) by the customer's bank, and the check is returned to the depositor's bank. The depositor's bank then debits the depositor's account, as shown by the symbol NSF on the bank statement above, and sends the NSF check and debit memorandum to the depositor as notification of the charge. The NSF check creates an accounts receivable for the depositor and reduces cash in bank.

Credit Memorandum

A depositor may ask the bank to collect its notes receivable. In such case, the bank will credit the depositor's account for the cash proceeds of the note, as illustrated on the bank statement by the symbol CM, and it will issue a credit memorandum to explain the entry.

RECONCILING THE BANK ACCOUNT

Because the bank and the depositor maintain independent records of the depositor's checking account, it might be presumed that the respective balances will always agree. In fact, the two balances are seldom the same at any given time, and it is necessary to reconcile (agree) the balance per books with the balance per bank. The lack of agreement between the two balances is due to:

1. **Time lags** that prevent one of the parties from recording the transaction in the same period.
2. **Errors** by either party in recording transactions.

Time lags occur frequently. For example, several days may elapse between the time a check is mailed to a payee and the date the check is paid by the bank. Similarly, when the depositor uses the bank's night depository for its deposits, there will be a difference of one day between the time the receipts are recorded by the depositor and the time they are recorded by the bank. A time lag also occurs whenever the bank mails a debit or credit memorandum to the depositor.

The incidence of errors depends on the effectiveness of the internal controls maintained by the depositor and the bank. Bank errors are usually infrequent. However, either party could inadvertently record a $450 check as $45 or $540. In addition, the bank might charge a check drawn by C. D. Berg to the account of C. D. Burg.

RECONCILIATION PROCEDURE

To obtain maximum benefit from a bank reconciliation, the reconciliation should be prepared by an employee who has no other responsibilities pertaining to cash. When the internal control principle of independent internal verification is not followed in preparing the reconciliation, cash embezzlements may escape unnoticed. For example, a cashier who prepares the reconciliation can embezzle cash and can conceal the embezzlement by misstating the reconciliation. Thus, the bank accounts would reconcile and the embezzlement would not be detected.

In reconciling the bank account, it is customary to reconcile the balance per books and balance per bank to their adjusted (correct or true) cash balances. The reconciliation schedule is divided into two sections, as shown on page 276. The starting point in preparing the reconciliation is to enter the balance per bank statement and balance per books on the schedule. The

following steps should reveal all the reconciling items that cause the difference between the two balances.

1. Compare the individual deposits on the bank statement with deposits in transit from the preceding bank reconciliation and with the deposits per company records or copies of duplicate deposit slips. Deposits not recorded by the bank represent **deposits in transit** and are added to the balance per bank.
2. Compare the paid (canceled) checks returned with the bank statement with checks outstanding from the preceding bank reconciliation and with the checks recorded by the company. Issued checks that have not been paid by the bank represent **outstanding checks** and are deducted from the balance per bank.
3. Note any **errors** discovered in the foregoing steps and list them in the appropriate section of the reconciliation schedule. For example, if a paid check for $195 was recorded by the depositor as $159, the $36 error is deducted from the balance per books.
4. Trace **bank memoranda** to the depositor's records. Any unrecorded memoranda should be listed in the appropriate section of the reconciliation schedule. For example, a $5.00 debit memorandum for bank service charges is deducted from the balance per books.

ILLUSTRATIVE BANK RECONCILIATION

The bank statement for the Laird Company on page 273 shows a balance per bank of $15,907.45 on April 30, 1987. On this date the balance of Cash in Bank per books is $11,269.45. From the foregoing steps, the following reconciling items are determined.

1. Deposit in transit: April 30 deposit.	$2,201.40
2. Outstanding checks: No. 462, $3,000.00; No. 467, $1,401.30; No. 470, $1,502.70.	5,904.00
3. Errors: Check No. 465 for $1,226.00 was correctly paid by the bank but was recorded for $1,262.00 by Laird Company.	36.00
4. Bank memoranda.	
a. Debit—NSF check from J. R. Baron for $125.60	125.60
b. Debit—Bank service charge, $10.00	10.00
c. Credit—Collection of note receivable for $1,000 plus interest $50 less bank collection fee, $15.00	1,035.00

The bank reconciliation is as follows:

LAIRD COMPANY
Bank Reconciliation
April 30, 1987

Balance per bank statement		$15,907.45
Add: Deposits in transit		2,201.40
		18,108.85
Less: Outstanding checks		
No. 462	$3,000.00	
No. 467	1,401.30	
No. 470	1,502.70	5,904.00
Adjusted balance per bank		**$12,204.85**
Balance per books		$11,269.45
Add: Collection of note receivable	$1,035.00	
Error in recording check No. 465	36.00	1,071.00
		12,340.45
Less: NSF check	125.60	
Bank service charge	10.00	135.60
Adjusted balance per books		**$12,204.85**

ENTRIES FROM BANK RECONCILIATION

Each reconciling item in determining the **adjusted balance per books** should be recorded by the depositor. If these items are not journalized and posted, the Cash in Bank account will not show the correct balance. The entries for the Laird Company on April 30 are as follows:

Collection of Note Receivable

This entry involves four accounts. Assuming that the interest of $50 has been accrued and the collection fee is charged to Miscellaneous Expense, the entry is:

Apr. 30	Cash in Bank	1,035.00	
	Miscellaneous Expense	15.00	
	Notes Receivable		1,000.00
	Interest Receivable		50.00
	(To record collection of notes receivable by bank)		

Book Error

An examination of the cash disbursements journal shows that check No. 465 was a payment on account to Andrea Company, a supplier. The correcting entry is:

Apr. 30	Cash in Bank	36.00	
	Accounts Payable—Andrea Company		36.00
	(To correct error in recording check No. 465)		

NSF Check

As indicated earlier, an NSF check becomes an account receivable to the depositor. The entry is:

Apr. 30	Accounts Receivable – J. R. Baron	125.60	
	Cash in Bank		125.60
	(To record NSF check)		

Bank Service Charge

Bank service charges are debited to Miscellaneous Expense because the charge is usually for a nominal amount. The entry is:

Apr. 30	Miscellaneous Expense	10.00	
	Cash in Bank		10.00
	(To record bank service charge)		

The foregoing entries could also be combined into one compound entry. If any bank errors are discovered in preparing the reconciliation, the bank should be notified so it can make the necessary corrections on its records.

PETTY CASH FUND

As you learned earlier in the chapter, better internal control over cash disbursements is possible when payments are made by check. However, using checks to pay such small amounts as those for postage due, employee lunches, and taxi fares is both impractical and a nuisance. A common way of handling such payments, while maintaining satisfactory control, is to use a petty cash fund. A **petty cash fund** is a cash fund used to pay relatively small amounts. The operation of a petty cash fund, often called an **imprest system,** involves (1) establishing the fund, (2) making payments from the fund, and (3) replenishing the fund.[5]

ESTABLISHING THE FUND

An essential step in establishing a petty cash fund is the appointment of a petty cash custodian who will be responsible for the fund. Also, the size of the fund must be determined. Ordinarily, the amount is expected to cover anticipated disbursements for a three- to four-week period. When the fund is established, a check payable to the petty cash custodian is issued for the stipulated amount. If the Laird Company decides to establish a $100 fund on March 1, the entry in general journal form is:

Mar. 1	Petty Cash	100.00	
	Cash in Bank		100.00
	(To establish a petty cash fund)		

[5]The term "imprest" means an advance of money for a designated purpose.

The check is then cashed and the proceeds are placed in a locked petty cash box or drawer. Most petty cash funds are established on a fixed amount basis. Moreover, no additional entries will be made to the Petty Cash account unless the stipulated amount of the fund is changed.

MAKING PAYMENTS FROM THE FUND

The petty cash fund custodian has the authority to make payments from the fund as long as the payments conform to prescribed management policies. Usually, management limits the size of expenditures that may be made and does not permit use of the fund for certain types of transactions, such as making loans to employees. Each payment from the fund must be documented on a prenumbered petty cash receipt (or petty cash voucher), as shown below. You should note that the signatures of both the custodian and the individual receiving payment are required on the receipt. If other supporting documents such as a freight bill or invoice are available, they should be attached to the petty cash receipt.

Petty cash receipt

LAIRD COMPANY
Petty Cash Receipt

No. 110 Date 5/6/87

Paid to Acme Express Agency Amount $18.00

For Collect Express Charges

CHARGE TO Freight-in

Approved Received Payment

L. A. Bird Custodian R. E. Meins

The receipts are kept in the petty cash box until the fund is replenished. As a result, the sum of the petty cash receipts and money in the fund should equal the established total at all times. This means that surprise counts can be made at any time by an independent person, such as an internal auditor, to determine whether the fund is being maintained intact. No entry is made when a petty cash payment is made. The accounting effects of each payment are recognized when the fund is replenished.

REPLENISHING THE FUND

When the money in the petty cash fund reaches a minimum level, the fund is replenished. The request for reimbursement is initiated by the petty cash custodian, who prepares a schedule (or summary) of the payments that have been made and sends the schedule, supported by petty cash receipts and other documentation, to the treasurer's office. The receipts and supporting documents are examined in the treasurer's office to determine that they were

proper payments from the fund. The treasurer then approves the request and a check is prepared to restore the fund to its established amount. At the same time, all supporting documentation is stamped "paid" so that it cannot be submitted again for payment.

To illustrate, assume that on March 15 the petty cash custodian requests a check for $87 and submits receipts showing postage, $44, freight-in, $18, office supplies, $20, and miscellaneous expenses, $5. The entry, in general journal form, to record the reimbursement check issued by Laird Company is:

Mar. 15	Postage Expense	44	
	Freight-in	18	
	Office Supplies Expense	20	
	Miscellaneous Expense	5	
	Cash in Bank		87
	(To replenish a petty cash fund)		

Note that the Petty Cash account is not affected by the reimbursement entry. Replenishment changes the composition of the fund by replacing the petty cash receipts with cash, but it does not change the balance in the fund.

It may be necessary in replenishing a petty cash fund to recognize a cash shortage or overage. To illustrate, assume the custodian had only $12 in cash in the fund in the example above. The request for reimbursement would, therefore, have been for $88, and Cash Over and Short would also have been debited for $1.00.

A petty cash fund should be replenished at the end of the accounting period regardless of the cash in the fund. Replenishment at this time is necessary in order to recognize the effects of the petty cash payments on the financial statements and to report the fund at its established amount on the balance sheet.

ELECTRONIC FUNDS TRANSFER (EFT)

To account for and control cash is an expensive and time-consuming process. For example, it was estimated recently that the cost to process a check through a bank system is from $0.55 to $1.00 and increasing. It is not surprising, therefore, that new approaches are being developed to transfer funds among parties without the use of paper (deposit tickets, checks, etc.). Such a procedure is called an **Electronic Funds Transfer (EFT)**. EFT may be defined as a disbursement system that uses wire, telephone, telegraph, or computer to transfer cash from one location to another. Examples of EFT are quite common. For example, the authors receive no formal payroll checks from their universities, which simply send magnetic tapes to the appropriate banks for deposit.

The development of EFT will continue. Already it is estimated that 80% of the total volume of bank transactions in the United States are performed using EFT. The computer technology is available to create a "checkless" society. The only major barriers appear to be the individual's concern for privacy and protection and certain legislative constraints. It should be noted that numerous safeguards have been built into EFT systems. However, the possibility of errors and fraud still exists because only a limited number of individuals are involved in the transfers, which may prevent appropriate segregation of duties.

SUMMARY OF STUDY OBJECTIVES

1. Internal control is the plan of organization and related methods and procedures adopted by a business to: safeguard assets, enhance the accuracy and reliability of its accounting data, promote operational efficiency, and encourage adherence to prescribed managerial policies.

2. The principles of internal accounting control are: establishment of responsibility, segregation of duties, mechanical and electronic equipment and devices, independent internal verification, physical controls, and other controls.

3. Internal controls over cash receipts include (a) designating only personnel such as cashiers to handle cash; (b) assigning the duties of receiving cash, recording cash, and custody of cash to different individuals; (c) using cash registers to execute cash receipts transactions; (d) making independent daily counts of register receipts, daily comparisons of total receipts with total deposits, and monthly reconciliation of bank and book balances; (e) using company safes and bank vaults to store cash, and limiting access to them to authorized personnel; and (f) bonding personnel that handle cash and requiring them to take vacations.

4. Internal controls over cash disbursements include: (a) only specified individuals such as the treasurer should be authorized to sign checks; (b) the duties of approving items for payment, paying the item, and recording the payment should be assigned to different individuals; (c) a checkwriter should be used in issuing checks; (d) each check should be compared with the approved invoice before it is issued, and bank and book balances should be independently reconciled monthly; (e) blank checks should be stored in a safe, and access to the safe should be restricted to authorized personnel; and (f) prenumbered checks should be used and accounted for, and after payment, the approved invoice should be stamped PAID.

5. A bank account contributes to good internal control by providing physical controls for the storage of cash, minimizing the amount of currency that must be kept on hand, and creating a double record of a depositor's bank transactions.

6. In reconciling the bank account, it is customary to reconcile the balance per books and balance per bank to their adjusted balances. The steps in determining the reconciling items are to ascertain deposits in transit, outstanding checks, errors by the depositor or the bank, and unrecorded bank memoranda.

7. In operating a petty cash fund, it is necessary to establish the fund, make payments from the fund, and replenish the fund.

APPENDIX 7–A

THE VOUCHER SYSTEM

The **voucher system** is an extensive series of prescribed control procedures designed to assure that every disbursement by check is a proper payment. The system begins with the authorization to incur the cost or expense. It ends with the issuance of a check for the liability incurred. The internal control principles of (1) establishment of responsibility, (2) segregation of duties, and (3) independent internal verification are essential in the voucher system.

Voucher systems are widely used in medium and large companies. In many of these cases, the system functions within an automated (electronic data processing) accounting system. Voucher systems are rarely found in small companies where the owner/manager can exercise personal surveillance over cash disbursements. The essential features of the voucher system for the Granger Company are explained below.

PREPARING THE VOUCHER

At the heart of the voucher system is the prenumbered voucher shown on page 282. A **voucher** is an authorization form prepared for each expenditure in a voucher system. The voucher itself may take the form of an envelope, folder, or packet. Vouchers are required for all types of cash disbursements except those made from petty cash. The voucher is prepared in the accounts (vouchers) payable department.

The starting point in preparing a voucher is to fill in the appropriate information about the liability on the face of the voucher from the vendor's invoice. Then the vendor's invoice is verified. Verification consists of establishing:

Voucher—front side

GRANGER COMPANY
Midland, Michigan

To J. B. Plain Co. — Voucher No. 126
45 State Street — Date June 1
Gary, Indiana — Due Date June 10

Attach invoice and supporting documents

Date	Inv. No.	Terms	Description	Amount
5/31	E46953	2/10 n/30	15 Doz. Drills	$600

Supporting Documents Examined	Prices and Terms Correct	Extensions and Footings on Invoice	Voucher Approved Correct
CRB	CRB	CRB	PRS

Face (Front) Side of Voucher

Voucher—reverse side

Account Distribution

Debit	Amount	
Purchases	600	00
Freight-in		
Store Supplies		
Advertising		
Delivery Expense		
Wages Payable		
Repairs		
Sundry		
Credit	**Amount**	
Vouchers payable	600	00
Distribution Approved	CRL	

Accounting Summary

Voucher recorded ______
Check recorded ______

Payment Summary

Date ______
Amount of invoice ______
Cash discount ______
Amount of check ______
Check number ______
Approved for payment ______

Reverse (Back) Side of Voucher

1. The agreement of the invoice with supporting documents, which generally consist of a copy of the purchase order sent to the vendor and a copy of the receiving report when the goods are received.
2. The correctness of prices and terms.
3. The accuracy of extensions and footings.

As each step in the verification is completed, the individual performing the control measure initials the voucher. After these steps are completed, the voucher is approved by a supervisor. The approved voucher, with attached supporting documents, is then ready to be recorded.

RECORDING THE VOUCHER

After the account distribution data on the back of the voucher are completed, the voucher is approved for entry by an accounting supervisor. The voucher is then journalized in the **voucher register** (or journal). As shown below, the voucher register is a columnar journal. The voucher register, which replaces the purchases journal described in Chapter 6, is used to record all types of expenditures. Under a voucher system, every payment by check is preceded by a credit to Vouchers Payable in the voucher register.

Vouchers are entered in numerical sequence, and all vouchers should be accounted for. After the voucher is entered, the accounting employee who journalized the voucher initials the accounting summary on the voucher. Procedures for posting the voucher register are similar to those described for a

Voucher register

GRANGER COMPANY
Voucher Register

			Payment					Other Accounts		
Date	Voucher No.	Payee	Date	Check No.	Vouchers Payable Cr.	Purchases Dr.	Freight-in Dr.	Dr.	Ref.	Title
1987										
June 1	126	J. B. Plain	June 9	464	600	600				
3	127	Aber Bros.	12	465	1,250	1,250				
5	128	C. R. Olsen	6	463	2,500			2,500	15	Equipment
8	129	A. K. Wilson	25	469	1,400	1,400				
9	130	Acme Frt. Co.	13	466	100		100			
14	131	R. E. Helms			400			400	8	Supplies
17	132	B. D. Hayes	26	470	1,500	1,500				
19	133	N C R. R.	20	467	90		90			
22	134	City Bank	23	468	3,000			3,000	28	Notes Payable
25	135	Daily News			200			200	72	Advertising Expense
27	136	P. T. Marr Co.			900	900				
30	137	E. M. Taylor			1,200	1,200				
					13,140	6,850	190	6,100		
					(26)	(62)	(63)	(X)		

columnar journal. Although the Voucher Payable account is used in recording, it is still customary to use the more familiar term, Accounts Payable, in the balance sheet.

FILING THE UNPAID VOUCHER

After the voucher is recorded, it is filed by date of payment in an unpaid voucher file (sometimes called a **tickler file**). This method of filing facilitates the payment of bills within due dates. At the end of the month, the balance in Voucher Payable is independently reconciled with the total vouchers in the tickler file. The balance should also equal the total of unpaid vouchers shown in the voucher register. The approving, recording, and filing of the voucher is shown graphically below:

Approving, recording, and filing a voucher

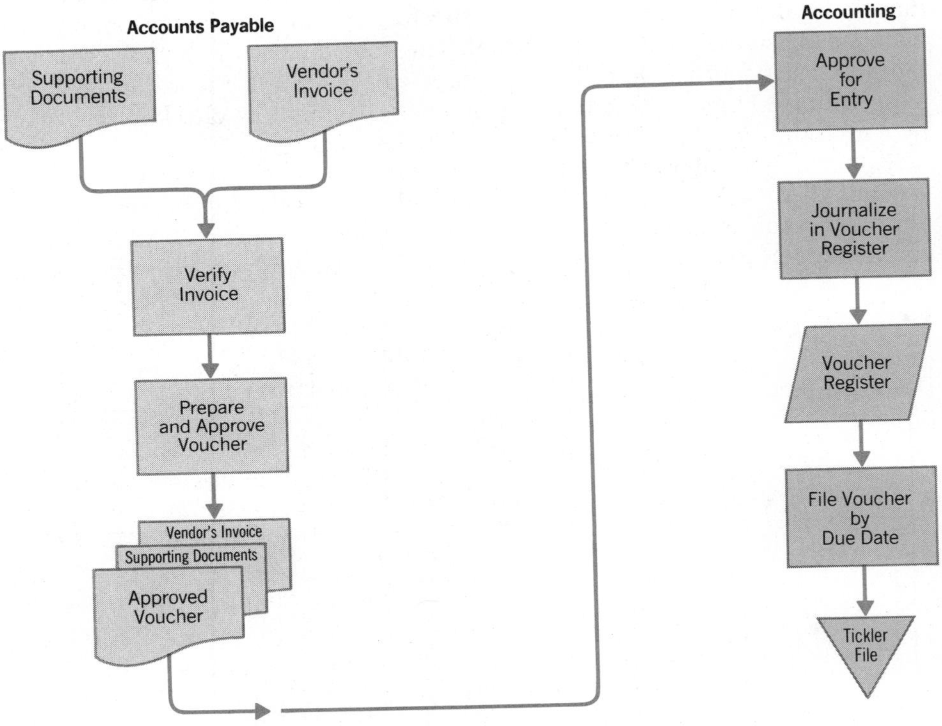

PAYING THE VOUCHER

On the due date, the voucher is removed from the tickler file and forwarded to cash disbursements. An authorized employee in cash disbursements reviews the voucher and, assuming everything is in order, approves the voucher for payment. The employee prepares (but does not sign) the check, inserts relevant data in the payment summary of the voucher, and transfers the unsigned check and voucher to the treasurer's office for signature.

In the treasurer's office, the authorized check signer signs the check after determining that proper approval has been given, and that all supporting documents are present. The check signer then

1. Mails the check to the payee.
2. Stamps (or marks) the voucher and supporting documents PAID to prevent them from being submitted again for payment.
3. Sends the "paid" voucher and a copy of the check to accounting.

The major advantage of a computerized voucher system, besides improved internal control over cash, is the management information that can be obtained by recording the voucher data in a data base format. Once in this form, the voucher data can be sorted in any fashion. Here are some examples:

Sort by amount (lump small items and highlight major accounts)
Sort by type of payable (merchandise, supplies, etc.)
Sort by payment due date (for check preparation)

In short, the arrays (sorts) are limited only by your imagination or management's needs.

RECORDING PAYMENT OF THE VOUCHER

Because all vouchers must be paid by check, the journal for recording checks is called a **check register** in a voucher system. As illustrated below, the check register contains just three money columns.

Check register

GRANGER COMPANY
Check Register

Date	Payee	Voucher No.	Check No.	Vouchers Payable Dr.	Purchase Discount Cr.	Cash Cr.
1987						
June 6	C. R. Olsen	128	463	2,500		2,500
9	J B. Plain	126	464	600	12	588
12	Aber Bros.	127	465	1,250	25	1,225
13	Acme Frt. Co.	130	466	100		100
20	N C R. R.	133	467	90		90
23	City Bank	134	468	3,000		3,000
25	A. K. Wilson	129	469	1,400		1,400
26	B. D. Hayes	132	470	1,500	30	1,470
				10,440	67	10,373
				(26)	(64)	(1)

After each check is recorded in numerical sequence, the check number and date of payment are also entered in the payment columns of the voucher register, and the accounting employee completes the accounting summary on the back of the voucher. The "paid" voucher is then filed alphabetically by vendor in a **paid voucher file.** The paying and recording payment of a voucher is graphically shown below.

Paying and recording payment of a voucher

PAYING AND RECORDING PAYMENT OF A VOUCHER

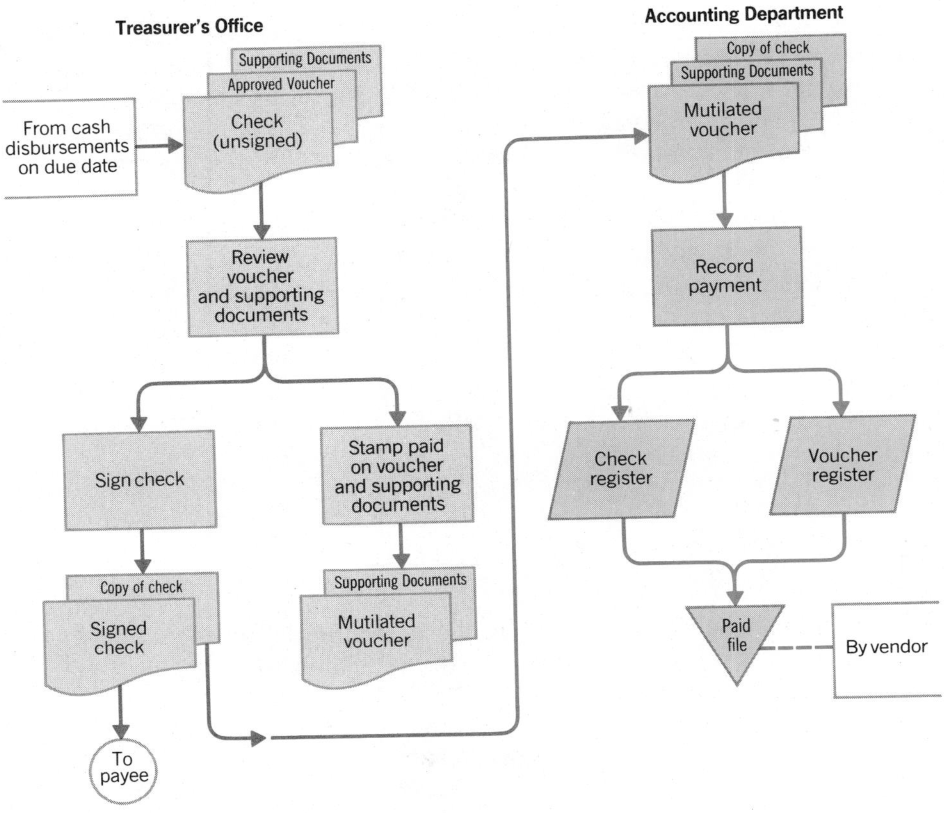

VOUCHERS AT THE NET AMOUNT DUE

Well-managed companies generally have a policy of taking all purchase discounts offered by suppliers. When such companies use a voucher system, they often establish the control procedure of preparing each voucher for the **net amount due.** Under this procedure, the failure to take a discount is considered to be an inefficiency that should be brought to management's attention. First, additional supervisory approval is required to pay the gross amount of the voucher, and the supervisor is expected to establish responsibility for the inefficiency. Second, purchase discounts lost are recognized separately in the accounts and financial statements.

To illustrate the entries under the net method, we will assume that Omar Company buys $5,000 of merchandise from the Adams Company when terms are 2/10, n/30. The entry in general journal form to record the net purchase of $4,900 ($5,000 − $100) is:

Purchases	4,900	
Vouchers Payable		4,900
(To record net cost of goods purchased)		

Because of a poor cash position, Omar does not pay this bill until after the discount period has lapsed. The entry to record the $5,000 payment is:

Vouchers Payable	4,900	
Discounts Lost	100	
Cash		5,000
(To record payment)		

Discounts Lost is reported under other expenses and losses in the income statement. This presentation permits purchases to be reported under cost of goods sold at the net invoice cost.

GLOSSARY

Accounting controls, p. 260
Administrative controls, p. 260
Bank service charge, p. 273
Bank statement, p. 272
Cash, p. 265
Cash over and short, p. 269
Check, p. 271
Check register, p. 285
Deposits in transit, p. 275
Electronic funds transfer, p. 279
Internal auditors, p. 263
Internal control, p. 260
NSF check, p. 273
Outstanding checks, p. 275
Petty cash fund, p. 277
Tickler file, p. 284
Voucher, p. 281
Voucher register, p. 282
Voucher system, p. 281

DEMONSTRATION PROBLEM

The Trillo Company's bank statement for May 1987 shows the following data:

Balance 5/1	$12,650	Balance 5/31	$14,280
Debit memorandum:		Credit memorandum:	
Nsf check	$ 175	Collection of note receivable	$ 505

The cash balance per books at May 31 is $13,319. Your review of the data reveals the following:

1. The NSF check was from Hup Co., a customer.
2. The note collected by the bank was a $500, three-month, 12% note. The bank charged a $10 collection fee. No interest has been accrued.
3. Outstanding checks at May 31 total $2,410.
4. Deposits in transit at May 31 total $1,752.
5. A Trillo Company check for $352 dated May 10 cleared the bank on May 25. This check, which was a payment on account, was journalized for $325.

INSTRUCTIONS

(a) Prepare a bank reconciliation at May 31.

(b) Journalize the entries required by the reconciliation.

SOLUTION TO DEMONSTRATION PROBLEM

(a)

TRILLO COMPANY
Bank Reconciliation
May 31, 1987

Balance per bank statement		$14,280
Add: Deposits in transit		1,752
		16,032
Less: Outstanding checks		2,410
Adjusted balance per bank		$13,622
Balance per books		$13,319
Add: Collection of note receivable		505
		13,824
Less: NSF check	$175	
Error in recording check	27	202
Adjusted balance per books		$13,622

(b)

May 31	Cash in Bank	505	
	Miscellaneous Expense	10	
	Notes Receivable		500
	Interest Revenue		15
	(To record collection of note by bank)		
31	Accounts Receivable	175	
	Cash in Bank		175
	(To record NSF check from Hup Co.)		
31	Accounts Payable	27	
	Cash in Bank		27
	(To correct error in recording check)		

*Note: All **asterisked** Questions, Exercises, and Problems relate to material contained in the appendix to each chapter.

QUESTIONS

1. There is more to internal control than preventing employee embezzlement. Do you agree? Explain.

2. Bonnie Baron is uncertain about the distinction between internal accounting control and internal administrative control. Explain the distinction to Bonnie.

3. In the corner grocery store, all sales clerks make change out of one cash register. Is this a violation of internal accounting control? Why?

4. Dee Demars is reviewing the principle of segregation of duties. What are the two common applications of this principle?

5. To obtain maximum benefit from the principle of independent internal verification, what practices should be followed?

6. There are two objectives of internal accounting control. Identify the objective served by (a) physical controls, and (b) prenumbered documents.

7. Management asks you, as the company accountant, to clarify the concept of reasonable assurance.

8. The controller of Glacier Company claims that the most important part of Glacier's system of internal control is the people who work for the company. Comment on this statement.

9. Badlands Manufacturing Inc. owns the following assets at the balance sheet date:

Cash in bank-savings account	$ 3,000
Cash on hand	850
Cash refund due from the IRS	1,000
Checking account balance	13,000
Postdated checks	500
Certificate of deposit	18,000

What amount should be reported as cash in the balance sheet?

10. What principle(s) of internal accounting control is (are) involved in making daily cash counts of over-the-counter receipts?

11. Benton Department Stores has just installed new electronic cash registers in its stores. How do cash registers improve internal control over cash receipts?

12. In the Allied Mail Order Company, two mail clerks open all mail receipts. How does this strengthen internal control?

13. To have maximum effective internal control over cash disbursements all payments should be made by check. Is this true? Explain.

14. The Hardy Company's internal controls over cash disbursements provide for the treasurer to sign checks imprinted by a checkwriter after comparing the check with the approved invoice. Identify the internal control principles that are present in these controls.

15. How do the principles of physical controls and other controls apply to cash disbursements?

16. The use of a bank contributes significantly to good internal control over cash. Is this true? Why?

17. Paul Penny is confused about the lack of agreement between the cash balance per books and the balance per the bank. Explain the causes for the lack of agreement to Paul and give an example of each cause.

18. Identify the specific objective of each of the four steps involved in preparing a bank reconciliation.

19. Millie Morz asks your help concerning an NSF check. Explain to Millie (a) what an NSF check is, (b) how it is treated in a bank reconciliation, and (c) whether it will require an adjusting entry per books.

20. The operation of a petty cash fund involves three activities. Identify the activities and indicate an internal control feature applicable to each activity.

21. When are journal entries required in the operation of a petty cash fund?

22. What is the essential feature of an electronic funds transfer (EFT) procedure?

***23.** What features of internal control are applicable to a voucher system?

***24.** (a) Identify the journals used in recording the issuance and payment of a voucher.
(b) Indicate the files maintained in a voucher system.

EXERCISES

E7-1 The following procedures are used in the Reardon Company for cash.

1. All counter receipts are registered by three clerks who use a cash register with a single cash drawer.
2. To minimize the risk of robbery, cash in excess of $100 is stored in an unlocked attache case in the stock room until it is deposited in the bank.
3. At the end of each day, the cash in the attache case is counted by the company accountant, who then deposits the amount intact in the bank.
4. Each week the owner gives the store manager 100 blank, unnumbered checks for making payments by check.
5. The store manager personally approves all payments before signing and issuing checks.
6. The company accountant prepares the bank reconciliation each month and reports any discrepancies to the owner.

INSTRUCTIONS

(a) For each situation, indicate the weakness in internal control, and the internal control principle that is violated.
(b) For each weakness, indicate the change in procedure that would result in good internal control.

E7-2 As a new staff auditor for the CPA firm of Rawlings, Spaulding and Bradsbey you have been assigned to review the internal controls over the cash receipts of the

Adirondak Company. Your review reveals the following: Most receipts arrive through the mail; while these receipts are promptly endorsed "For Deposit Only," no list of the checks is prepared by the person opening the mail. Furthermore, you determine that the mail is opened either by the cashier or by the employee who maintains the accounts receivable records.

INSTRUCTIONS

List the weaknesses in internal control over mail receipts and indicate your recommendations for improvement.

E7-3 The Yount Company has the following internal control procedures over cash receipts and cash disbursements.

1. All over-the-counter receipts are registered on cash registers.
2. Yount Company checks are prenumbered.
3. The bank statement is reconciled monthly by an internal auditor.
4. Receipts are stored in a safe prior to being deposited in the bank.
5. Daily comparisons of total receipts and deposited receipts are made by the treasurer's office.
6. Only cashiers may operate cash registers.
7. A checkwriter imprints amounts on company checks.
8. Daily cash counts are made by cashier department supervisors.
9. The duties of receiving cash, recording cash and custody of cash are assigned to different individuals.
10. Only the treasurer or assistant treasurer may sign checks.
11. Check signers are not allowed to record cash disbursement transactions.
12. Cashiers are required to take vacations.
13. Following payment, the approved invoice is stamped PAID.
14. The check signer must compare the check with the approved invoice prior to signing the check.
15. Blank checks are stored in a safe in the treasurer's office.

INSTRUCTIONS

Indicate the internal control principle that is applicable to each procedure.

E7-4 The following reconciling items are discovered in preparing the bank reconciliation for the Austin Company:

1. Outstanding checks.
2. Bank debit memorandum for service charges.
3. Deposit in transit.
4. Bank credit memorandum for collection of note for depositor by bank.
5. Book error in which an Austin Company check for $198.70 was recorded in the check register as $189.70.
6. Bank error in which a check written by Austern Company was charged to the Austin Company.
7. Bank debit memo for a customer's check returned because of insufficient funds (NSF).
8. Book error in which a deposit of $724.00 was recorded in the cash receipts journal as $742.00.

INSTRUCTIONS

(a) List the number of each reconciling item and indicate how the item should be shown on the bank reconciliation.

(b) Indicate the number of each reconciling item that will require an adjusting entry by Austin Company.

E7-5 The following information pertains to the Keanne Company.

1. Cash balance per books, July 31, $6,700.
2. July bank service charge not recorded by the depositor, $15.
3. Cash balance per bank, July 31, $5,312.
4. Deposits in transit, July 31, $3,100.
5. Note collected for depositor in July by the bank, $927 including $27 of interest revenue; no entry has been made by the depositor.
6. A July check written by the Kanere Company for $210 was incorrectly charged by the bank to the Keanne Company in July.
7. Outstanding checks, July 31, $1,028.
8. A $175 Keanne Company check for supplies which cleared the bank in July was recorded in the books at $157.

INSTRUCTIONS

(a) Prepare a bank reconciliation at July 31.

(b) Journalize the adjusting entries at July 31 on the books of the Keanne Company.

E7-6 The cash records of the Putnam Company show the following:

1. The June 30 bank reconciliation indicated that deposits in transit totaled $475. During July the general ledger account Cash in Bank shows deposits of $15,250, but the bank statement indicates that only $15,100 in deposits were received during the month.
2. The June 30 bank reconciliation also reported outstanding checks of $860. During the month of July, the Putnam Company books show that $16,000 of checks were issued, yet the bank statement showed that $16,100 of checks cleared the bank in July.
3. In September, deposits per the bank statement totaled $26,400, deposits per books were $25,200, and deposits in transit at September 30 were $2,300.
4. In September, cash disbursements per books were $22,900, checks clearing the bank were $24,000, and outstanding checks at September 30 were $2,000.

There were no bank debit or credit memoranda and no errors were made by either the bank or the Putnam Company.

INSTRUCTIONS

Answer the following questions:

(a) In situation (1), what were the deposits in transit at July 31?

(b) In situation (2), what were the outstanding checks at July 31?

(c) In situation (3), what were the deposits in transit at August 31?

(d) In situation (4), what were the outstanding checks at August 31?

E7-7 The information below relates to the Cash in Bank account in the ledger of Prescott Corporation:

Balance September 1 —$16,050—Cash deposited $62,000

Balance September 30—$17,920—Checks written $60,130

The September bank statement shows:

Balance, September 30	$16,644
Credit memorandum:	
Collection of note by bank including $18 of interest	$ 218
Debit memoranda:	
NSF check: J. Howe	$ 36
Bank service charge	$ 12

At September 30, deposits in transit amounted to $3,600 and outstanding checks totaled $2,154.

INSTRUCTIONS

(a) Prepare the bank reconciliation at September 30.

(b) Prepare the adjusting entries at September 30. Assume that the interest on the note has been accrued.

E7-8 The Glenco Company establishes a petty cash fund of $100 on September 1. During the first two weeks, the following transactions affecting this fund are completed:

Sept. 1 Issued check No. 625 for $100 to establish the petty cash fund.
2 Puchased stamps $40; petty cash ticket No. 1.
5 Reimbursed sales manager for gas used in his own car while on company business, $18.75; ticket No. 2.
8 Paid collect United Parcel Service bill for goods purchased for resale, $23.25; ticket No. 3.
13 Reimbursed office manager for dinner when working overtime, $12.50; ticket No. 4.
14 Replenished fund. Issued check No. 890 for expenditures to date.
15 Increased size of petty cash fund to $150 by issuing check No. 925.

INSTRUCTIONS

Journalize the entries that will result in postings to Petty Cash and Cash.

E7-9 The Brookens Company uses an imprest petty cash system. The fund was established on January 2 with a balance of $100. During January the following petty cash receipts were found in the petty cash box:

Date	Receipt No.	Amount	For	Date	Receipt No.	Amount	For
1/ 5	1	$35	Stamp Inventory	1/18	6	$21	Freight-in
7	2	18	Freight-in	21	7	42	Stamp Inventory
9	3	12	Miscellaneous Expense	23	8	16	Miscellaneous Expense
11	4	26	Office Supplies Expense	25	9	12	Office Supplies Expense
14	5	5	Miscellaneous Expense	29	10	6	Miscellaneous Expense

There was no cash over or short. The fund was replenished on January 15 and January 31. On January 31, the amount in the fund was increased to $150.

INSTRUCTIONS

Journalize the entries that pertain to the operation of the petty cash fund.

***E7-10** The Zenda Company uses a voucher system for cash disbursements. During June, the following transactions occurred. All purchases are subject to discount terms of 2/10, n/30.

Date	Voucher No.	Amount	For	Date	Check No.	Amount	For Voucher No.
June 1	610	$1,000	Rent	June 2	474	$1,000	610
5	611	8,500	Purchases	8	475	2,000	612
15	612	2,000	Wages	13	476	8,330	611
11	613	6,000	Purchases	16	477	5,000	614
15	614	5,000	Note payable	20	478	5,880	613
19	615	4,500	Purchases	30	479	2,000	617
27	616	3,600	Purchases				
30	617	2,000	Wages				

INSTRUCTIONS

(a) Assuming the vouchers are recorded at gross amounts, indicate (1) the balance in Vouchers Payable at June 30, and (2) the purchase discounts taken during the month.

(b) Assuming the vouchers for purchases are recorded at net amounts, indicate (1) the balance in Vouchers Payable at June 30, and (2) the purchase discounts lost during the month.

PROBLEMS

P7-1 Cinema II Theater is located in the Briarwood Mall. A cashier's booth is located near the entrance to the theater. Two cashiers are employed. One works from 1-5 p.m., the other from 5-9 p.m. Each cashier is bonded. The cashiers receive cash from customers and operate a machine that ejects serially numbered tickets. The rolls of tickets are inserted and locked into the machine by the theater manager at the beginning of each cashier's shift.

After purchasing a ticket, the customer takes the ticket to a doorperson stationed at the entrance to the theater lobby some 60 feet from the cashier's booth. The doorperson tears the ticket in half, admits the customer, and returns the ticket stub to the customer. The other half of the ticket is dropped into a locked box by the doorperson.

At the end of each cashier's shift, the theater manager removes the ticket rolls from the machine and makes a cash count. The cash count sheet is initialed by the cashier. At the end of the day, the manager deposits the receipts in total in a bank night deposit vault located in the mall. In addition, the manager sends copies of the deposit slip for recording and the initialed cash count sheets to the theater company treasurer for verification and to the company's accounting department. Receipts from the first shift are stored in a safe located in the manager's office.

INSTRUCTIONS

(a) Identify the internal control principles and their application to the cash receipts transactions of Cinema II Theater.

(b) If the doorperson and cashier decide to collaborate to misappropriate cash, what actions might they take?

P7-2 Leslie Office Supply Company recently changed its system of internal control over cash disbursements. The system includes the following features.

Instead of being unnumbered and manually prepared, all checks must now be prenumbered and written by using the new checkwriter purchased by the company. Before a check can be issued, each invoice must have the approval of Cindy Moore, the purchasing agent, and Ray Miller, the receiving department supervisor. Checks must be signed by either Frank Malzone, the treasurer, or Mary Arno, the assistant treasurer. Before signing a check, the signer is expected to compare the amounts of the check with the amounts on the invoice.

After signing a check, the signer stamps the invoice PAID and inserts within the stamp, the date, check number, and amount of the check. The "paid" invoice is then sent to the accounting department for recording.

Blank checks are stored in a safe in the treasurer's office. The combination to the safe is known only by the treasurer and assistant treasurer. Each month, the bank statement is reconciled with the bank balance per books by the assistant chief accountant.

INSTRUCTIONS

Identify the internal control principles and their application to cash disbursements of Leslie Office Supply Company.

P7-3 The November 30 bank reconciliation for the Wundel Company shows the following reconciling items: deposits in transit $100.00, and outstanding checks (No. 23, $400.00; No. 24, $180.00; No. 25, $175.00; and No. 26, $45.00).

During December the following checks and receipts were recorded:

Checks				Receipts
No. 29	$133.50	No. 33	$129.63	$543.00
No. 30	142.70	No. 34	145.55	352.00
No. 31	186.40	No. 35	155.00	120.00
No. 32	132.22	No. 36	167.32	150.00

The bank statement for December showed the following data together with cancelled checks and bank memoranda.

Checks and Other Debits		Deposits	Date	Balance
			12/1	$3,545.60
180.00	175.00	100.00	12/5	3,290.60
142.70	186.40	543.00	12/10	3,504.50
133.40		352.00	12/20	3,723.10
2.35 SC	155.00		12/27	3,565.75
90.00 NSF	129.63	120.00	12/30	3,466.12
		530.00 CM	12/31	3,996.12

Check No. 29 was actually written for $133.40 for payment on account. The debit memo, SC, is for bank service charges. The NSF check was from A. Wynn, a customer, in settlement of the balance due. No entry has been made by Wundel Company for

the NSF check. The credit memo designated as CM is for the collection of a $500 note receivable plus interest revenue of $30.

INSTRUCTIONS

(a) Determine the cash balance per books on December 1 after the November 30 bank reconciliation and appropriate adjusting entries have been made.

(b) Determine the cash balance per books on December 31 before the bank reconciliation.

(c) Prepare a bank reconciliation at December 31.

(d) Journalize the entries to adjust the cash balance per books to its correct amount. Assume that the interest on the note has not been accrued.

(e) Reproduce the Cash in Bank account per books for December.

P7-4 The Bay Company's bank statement from Valley National Bank at August 31 shows the following information:

Balance, August 1	$15,400	Bank credit memorandum:	
August deposits	74,000	Collection of note receivable	
Checks cleared in August	69,610	plus $60 interest	$2,060
Balance, August 31	21,838	Bank debit memorandum	
		Service charge	$12

A summary of the Cash in Bank account in the ledger for August shows: Balance, August 1, $16,900, receipts, $75,000, disbursements, $74,570, and balance, August 31, $17,330. Analysis reveals that the only reconciling items on the July 31 bank reconciliation were a deposit in transit for $3,000 and outstanding checks. In addition, you determine that there were two errors involving company checks drawn in August: (1) a check for $430 to a creditor on account that cleared the bank in August was journalized and posted for $400, and (2) a salary check to an employee for $275 was recorded by the bank for $285.

INSTRUCTIONS

(a) Prepare a bank reconciliation at August 31.

(b) Journalize the adjusting entries to be made by Bay Company at August 31. Assume the interest on the note has been accrued by the depositor.

(c) Reproduce the Cash in Bank account per books for August.

P7-5 The Patricia Company is a very profitable small business. It has not, however, given much consideration to internal control. For example, in an attempt to keep clerical and office expenses to a minimum, the company has combined the jobs of cashier and bookkeeper. As a result, Rob Rowen handles all cash receipts, keeps the accounting records, and prepares the monthly bank reconciliations.

The balance per the bank statement on October 31 was $15,550. Outstanding checks were: No. 62 for $116.25, No. 183 for $150, No. 284 for $253.25, No. 862 for $190.71, No. 863 for $206.80, and No. 864 for $145.28. Included with the statement was a credit memorandum of $100 indicating the collection of a note receivable for the Patricia Company by the bank on October 25. This memorandum has not been recorded by Patricia Company.

The company's ledger showed one cash account with a balance of $19,001.62. The balance included undeposited cash on hand. Because of the lack of internal controls, Rowen took for personal use all of the undeposited receipts in excess of $3,794.41. He then prepared the following bank reconciliation in an effort to conceal his theft of cash.

Balance per books, October 31		$19,001.62
Add: Outstanding checks		
No. 862	$190.71	
No. 863	206.80	
No. 864	$145.28	442.79
		19,444.41
Less: Undeposited receipts		3,794.41
Unadjusted balance per bank, October 31		15,650.00
Less: Bank credit memorandum		100.00
Balance per bank statement, October 31		$15,550.00

INSTRUCTIONS

(a) Prepare a correct bank reconciliation. (Hint: deduct the amount of the theft from the adjusted balance per books.)

(b) Indicate the three ways that Rowen attempted to conceal the theft and the dollar amount pertaining to each method.

(c) What principles of internal control were violated in this case?

P7-6 The Leary Company maintains a petty cash fund for small expenditures. The following transactions occurred over a two month period:

July 1 Established petty cash fund by writing a check on Metro Bank for $200.

15 Replenished the petty cash fund by writing a check for $193.80. On this date the fund consisted of $6.20 in cash and the following petty cash receipts: Freight-in $94.20, postage expense $41.40, office supplies expense $45.60, and miscellaneous expense $11.60.

31 Replenished the petty cash fund by writing a check for $191.00. At this date, the fund consisted of $9.00 in cash and the following petty cash receipts: Freight-in $84.10, charitable contributions expense $25.00, postage expense $27.80, and miscellaneous expense $54.10.

Aug. 15 Replenished the petty cash fund and increased the amount of the fund to $300 by writing a check for $278.00. On this date, the fund consisted of $22.00 in cash and the following petty cash receipts: Freight-in $72.40, office supplies expense $41.00, postage expense $44.00, and miscellaneous expense $20.00.

Aug. 31 Replenished petty cash fund by writing a check for $282.00. On this date, the fund consisted of $18 in cash and the following petty cash receipts: Postage expense $142.00, office supplies expense $92.60, and freight-in $47.40.

INSTRUCTIONS

(a) Journalize the petty cash transactions.

(b) Post to the Petty Cash account.

(c) What internal control features exist in a petty cash fund?

*__P7-7__ The Tastie Cookie Company uses a voucher system in which all vouchers are recorded at gross amounts. The voucher register has debit columns for purchases, freight-in, advertising expense, and other accounts. The following data are obtained from approved vouchers:

Date	Voucher No.	For	Payee	Amount
Sept. 2	101	Merchandise	Sugar Works	$1,800
5	102	Freight-in	Air Ease	150
8	103-5	Delivery equipment	OK Trucks	6,000

Date	Voucher No.	For	Payee	Amount
10	106	Advertising	Adams Advertising	200
12	107	Merchandise	Chip Corp.	1,500
13	108	Freight-in	Western RR	300
15	109	Petty cash	C. Johnson	50
17	110	Store equipment	Moritz Co.	3,000
21	111	Merchandise	Flour ETC	1,200
25	112	Advertising	Star Journal	100
26	113-4	Store equipment	Moritz Co.	3,000
27	115	Merchandise	Chip Corp.	1,000
30	116	Salaries payable	Payroll	1,475

Additional Data:

1. Vouchers Nos. 103–5 are for $2,000 each.
2. Voucher No. 109 is for replenishment of the petty cash fund. Petty cash expenditures were freight-in $15, advertising $25, and miscellaneous expenses $10.
3. Voucher No. 113 is for $1,200; Voucher No. 114 is for the balance due.
4. All purchases of merchandise are subject to cash discounts of 3/10, N/30. From the check stubs it is learned that the following vouchers were paid in September: Sept. 8, No. 103; Sept. 9, No. 101; Sept. 15, No. 109; Sept. 20, No. 107; Sept. 27, No. 113; and Sept. 30, No. 116. Checks were numbered consecutively beginning with Check No. 275.

INSTRUCTIONS

(a) Record the vouchers in the voucher register and the checks in the check register.
(b) Post to the Vouchers Payable account.
(c) Prepare a schedule of unpaid vouchers at September 30 and reconcile the schedule with the balance in Vouchers Payable.

ALTERNATE PROBLEMS

P7-1A The Harbough Company's system of internal control over cash includes the following procedures:

1. Cash is stored in a locked safe prior to being deposited daily in the bank.
2. The treasurer stamps each approved invoice PAID after signing the payment check.
3. Cash registers are used in ringing up cash sales.
4. An internal auditor reconciles the bank statement each month.
5. Mary Jones is designated as the petty cash custodian.
6. A cashier department supervisor makes daily cash counts of the cash registers.
7. Cashier department personnel are not allowed to journalize cash transactions.
8. Prenumbered checks are used.

INSTRUCTIONS

(a) Indicate the internal control principle applicable to each procedure.
(b) For each principle, give an example of an additional procedure that the Harbough Company should have for effective internal control over cash. Present your answers in tabular form with columns for Internal Control Principle and Additional Procedures.

P7-2A The data below relates to the general ledger cash accounts and checking account of Giles Products, Inc.

1. Ending balance per bank statement at March 31, 1987 was $11,985.
2. Included in the bank statement were the following documents:

   A credit memo to notify Giles of the collection of a $1,000 note and $120 interest revenue on the note. No interest has been accrued on the note.

   An NSF check in the amount of $75 made out to Giles by Robert Holworth, a customer.

   A debit memo indicating that the bank had reduced the Giles Products account by $2,000 in accordance with the terms of a note payable that was owed to the bank.
3. The bank statement indicated that the Giles Products account had been charged with a $25 service fee.
4. At the end of February the bank reconciliation had indicated that there were six checks outstanding. All of those checks cleared except number 1106 which was made out for $312.
5. Four checks were written in March which had not yet cleared the bank:

1179	$274	1182	$510
1180	$168	1183	$ 41

6. A comparison between the general ledger and the bank statement reveals deposits in transit totaling $1,200.
7. The ending balance per the general ledger showed a cash amount of $13,163.
8. In recording check 1160 an error was made. It was recorded for $4,000, yet the check was made out for $4,303. The check was written in payment of a creditor's balance.

INSTRUCTIONS

(a) Prepare a bank reconciliation for Giles Products, Inc. as of March 31, 1987.

(b) Prepare the adjusting journal entries required by the bank reconciliation.

P7-3A The April 30 bank reconciliation for the Narson Company shows the following reconciling items: deposit in transit $300.00 and outstanding checks (No. 113 $50.00, No. 114 $150.00, No. 115 $200.00, and No. 116 $75.00). During May the following checks and receipts were recorded:

Checks				Receipts
No. 120	$100.00	No. 124	$ 45.00	$628.00
121	$185.10	125	$ 49.25	$256.00
122	$215.30	126	$ 15.60	$485.00
123	$309.15	127	$409.00	$350.00

The bank statement for May showed the following data together with cancelled checks and bank memoranda:

Checks and Other Debits		Deposits	Date	Balance
			5/ 1	1,500.86
50.00	200.00	300.00	5/ 2	1,550.86
100.00	215.20	628.00	5/10	1,863.66
309.15		256.00	5/20	1,810.51
3.45 SC	49.25	485.00	5/27	2,242.81
80.00 NSF	15.60		5/30	2,147.21
		842.00 CM	5/31	2,989.21

Check No. 122 was actually written for $215.20 in payment of accounts payable. The debit memo, SC, is for the bank service charges. The NSF check was from Chien, a customer, in settlement of the balance due. No entry has been made by Narson Company for the NSF check. The credit memo designed as CM is for the collection of an $800 note receivable plus interest of $42 by the bank.

INSTRUCTIONS

(a) Determine the adjusted cash balance per books on May 1 from the April bank reconciliation.

(b) Determine the cash balance per books at May 31 before the bank reconciliation.

(c) Prepare a bank reconciliation at May 31.

(d) Journalize the entries to adjust the cash account per books for May. Assume the interest on the note has not been accrued.

(e) Reproduce the Cash in Bank account per books for May.

P7-4A The Coast Company maintains a checking account at the Harbor National Bank. At July 31, selected data from the ledger balance and the bank statement are as follows:

	Cash in Bank	
	Per Books	Per Bank
Balance, July 1	$18,300	$16,400
July receipts	80,000	
July credits		79,070
July disbursements	74,870	
July debits		70,015
Balance, July 31	$23,430	$25,455

Analysis of the bank data reveals that the credits consist of $76,000 of July deposits and a credit memorandum of $3,070 for the collection of a $3,000 note plus interest revenue of $70. The July debits per bank consist of checks cleared, $70,000 and a debit memorandum of $15 for bank service charges.

You also discover the following errors involving July checks: (1) a check for $320 to a creditor on account that cleared the bank in July was journalized and posted as $300, and (2) a salary check to an employer for $255 was recorded by the bank for $265.

The June 30 bank reconciliation contained only two reconciling items: deposits in transit $4,000, and outstanding checks.

INSTRUCTIONS

(a) Prepare a bank reconciliation at July 31.

(b) Journalize the adjusting entries to be made by Coast Company at July 31, 1987. Assume that the interest on the note has been accrued.

(c) Reproduce the Cash in Bank account for July.

P7-5A The cashier of the Stoner Company, Ann Adkins, is a busy person. She serves as the receptionist, cashier, and bookkeeper for the company. Ann is responsible for handling all cash receipts, recording cash transactions, and preparing the monthly bank reconciliation. As a result, internal control over cash is weak.

At August 31, the company's ledger showed one cash account with a balance of $20,230.82. This balance included undeposited cash on hand. Because of weakness in internal control, Ann took for personal use all of the undeposited receipts in excess of $4,108.24.

The balance per the bank statement at August 31 was $16,350.00. Outstanding checks were: No. 29 for $205.15, No. 159 for $487.59, No. 299 for $29.50, No. 501 for $89.32, No. 502 for $158.25, and No. 503 for $229.85. Included with this statement was a credit memorandum of $150 indicating collection of a note receivable for Stoner Company by the bank on August 25. This memo has not been recorded by Stoner Company.

In an attempt to conceal her theft, Ann Adkins prepared the following bank reconciliation:

Balance per books August 31		$20,230.82
Add: Outstanding checks		
No. 501	$ 89.32	
No. 502	158.25	
No. 503	129.85	377.42
		20,608.24
Less: Undeposited receipts		4,108.24
Unadjusted balance per bank, Aug. 31		16,500.00
Less: Bank credit memorandum		150.00
Balance per bank statement, Aug. 31		$16,350.00

INSTRUCTIONS

(a) Prepare a correct bank reconciliation. (Hint: Deduct the amount of the theft from the adjusted book balance.)

(b) Indicate the three ways that Ann Adkins used to conceal the theft and the dollar amount pertaining to each method.

(c) What principles of internal control were violated in this case?

*P7-6A The Pauly Company uses the net price method in its voucher system. On October 1, the unpaid voucher file shows the following vouchers for merchandise: No. 345 Hardy Co., $2,352; No. 346 McMay Co., $1,940; and No. 347 Roger Co., $2,910. During October the following transactions were completed:

Oct. 3 Issued check Nos. 201 and 202 in payment of Voucher Nos. 345 and 346 within the discount period.

4 Prepared Voucher No. 348 payable to Baker Co. for merchandise purchased, $2,000 terms 3/10, n/30.

5 Prepared Voucher No. 349 payable to Dart & Sons for store equipment, $1,500, terms n/30.

7 Issued Check No. 203 for $3,000 in payment of Voucher No. 347 because the discount period had elapsed.

9 Prepared Voucher No. 350 payable to Richard Bros. for store supplies, $700, terms n/30.

12 Issued Check No. 204 in payment of Voucher No. 348.

16 Prepared Voucher No. 351 payable to Hinkly Co. for merchandise purchased, $1,500, terms 1/10, n/30.

18 Prepared Voucher No. 352 for $450 as a cash drawing for owner Sue Pauly.

19 Issued Check No. 205 in payment of Voucher No. 352.

20 Prepared Voucher No. 353 payable to Easy Money Inc. for a 90-day, 10%, $3,000 note payable due on October 22.

21 Prepared Voucher No. 354 payable to Barber Inc. for merchandise purchased, $1,500, terms 2/10, n/30.

22 Issued Check No. 206 in payment of Voucher No. 353.

23 Prepared Voucher No. 355 payable to Lewis Bros. for store supplies, $600, terms n/30.

28 Issued Check No. 207 for $1,500 in payment of Voucher No. 351 after the discount period had elapsed.
29 Issued Check No. 208 in payment of Voucher No. 354.
30 Prepared Voucher No. 356 payable to Universal Insurance Co. for a 3-year auto insurance policy, $3,300.

INSTRUCTIONS

(a) Journalize the transactions in the Voucher Register with columns for Purchases Store Supplies, Other Accounts, and Vouchers Payable, and in the Check Register with a column for Purchase Discounts Lost.

(b) Post to Vouchers Payable.

(c) Prepare a schedule of unpaid vouchers at October 31 and reconcile the amount with the balance in Vouchers Payable.

DECISION CASE

The board of trustees of a local church is concerned about the internal accounting controls pertaining to the offering collections made at weekly services. They ask you to serve on a three-person audit team with the internal auditor of the university and a CPA who has just joined the church.

At a meeting of the audit team and the board of trustees you learn the following:

1. The church's board of trustees has delegated responsibility for the financial management and audit of the financial records to the finance committee. This group prepares the annual budget and approves major disbursements but is not involved in collections or record keeping. No audit has been made in recent years because the same trusted employee has kept church records and served as financial secretary for fifteen years. The church does not carry any fidelity insurance.
2. The collection at the weekly service is taken by a team of ushers who volunteer to serve one month. The ushers take the collection plates to a basement office at the rear of the church. They hand their plates to the head usher and return to the church service. After all plates have been turned in, the head usher counts the cash received. The head usher then places the cash in the church safe along with a notation of the amount counted. The head usher volunteers to serve for three months.
3. The next morning the financial secretary opens the safe and recounts the collection. The secretary withholds $150–$200 in cash, depending on the cash expenditures expected for the week and deposits the remainder of the collections in the bank. To facilitate the deposit, church members who contribute by check are asked to make their checks payable to "cash."
4. Each month, the financial secretary reconciles the bank statement and submits a copy of the reconciliation to the board of trustees. The reconciliations have rarely contained any bank errors and have never shown any errors per books.

INSTRUCTIONS

(a) Indicate the weaknesses in internal accounting control over the handling of collections.

(b) List the improvements in internal control procedures that you plan to make at the next meeting of the audit team for (1) the ushers, (2) the head usher, (3) the financial secretary, and (4) the finance committee.

(c) What church policies should be changed to improve internal accounting control?

CHAPTER 8

California State Polytechnic University–Pomona

CHAPTER 8

TEMPORARY INVESTMENTS AND SHORT-TERM RECEIVABLES

STUDY OBJECTIVES

After studying this chapter, you should be able to:

1. Explain the accounting for temporary investments.
2. Indicate the effects of using the lower of cost or market basis of valuation for marketable equity securities.
3. Enumerate the features of the allowance method of accounting for uncollectible accounts.
4. Distinguish between the bases used under the allowance method.
5. Describe the entries for recording credit card sales.
6. Compute the maturity date of, and interest on, notes receivable.
7. Explain when entries are required for notes receivable.
8. State the steps in discounting notes receivable.

In many companies, the first three current assets are cash, temporary investments, and short-term receivables. Collectively, these assets are often referred to as **short-term liquid assets** because these items are cash or can be quickly converted into cash. The ratio of short-term liquid assets to total current assets varies among companies. Recently, for example, at Eastman Kodak, these assets represented 54% of total current assets compared to 23% at Phillip Morris.

After studying the preceding chapter, you should have a good understanding of accounting for cash. In this chapter, we will explain and illustrate accounting for temporary investments and short-term receivables.

SECTION ONE—TEMPORARY INVESTMENTS

PURPOSE AND TYPES OF TEMPORARY INVESTMENTS

Many companies experience seasonal fluctuations in sales. A Cape Cod marina will have higher sales in the spring and summer than in the fall and winter, whereas the reverse will be true for an Aspen ski shop. Thus, at the end of their operating cycles, many companies may have cash on hand that is temporarily idle pending the start of another operating cycle. Until the cash is needed in operations, many companies invest the excess funds to earn interest and dividends. The relationship of temporary investments to the operating cycle is graphically depicted below:

Temporary investments and the operating cycle

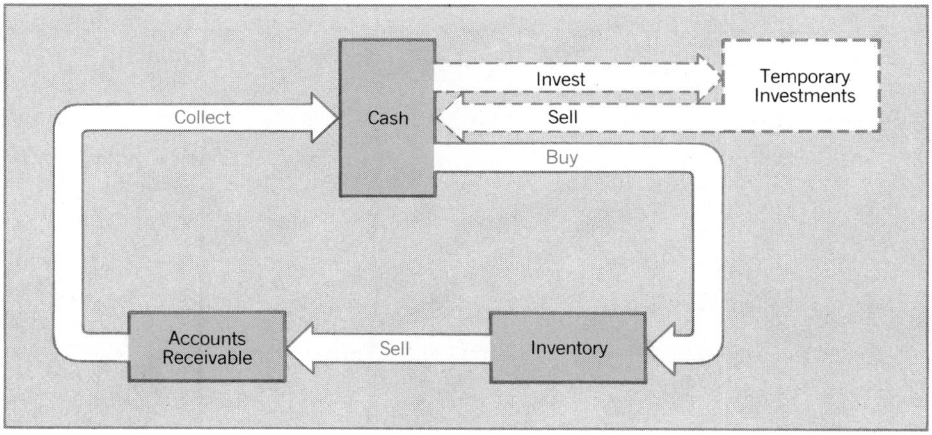

Both the funds invested and the revenue earned can be significant. In a recent balance sheet, Motorola reported $25 million in cash and $143 million in short-term investments. The investments earned annual interest of $15 million.

Temporary investments consist of (1) short-term paper[1], (2) marketable equity securities (capital stock), and (3) marketable debt securities (bonds). To be considered temporary (or short-term), the investment must be readily marketable and management should intend to convert the investment into cash within the next year or operating cycle, whichever is longer. An investment

[1]Short-term paper includes (1) certificates of deposits (CDs) issued by banks, (2) money market certificates issued by banks and savings and loan associations, (3) treasury bills issued by the U.S. government, and (4) commercial paper issued by corporations with good credit ratings.

that does not meet **both** criteria is classified as long-term. Long-term investments are discussed in Chapter 18.

READILY MARKETABLE

An investment is readily marketable when it can be sold easily whenever the need for cash arises. Short-term paper meets this criterion because it can be sold readily to other investors. Stocks and bonds traded on organized securities markets, such as the New York Stock Exchange, are readily marketable because they can be bought and sold daily. In contrast, there may be only a limited market for the securities issued by small corporations and no market for the securities of a closely held company.

INTENT TO CONVERT

Intent to convert means that management intends to sell the investment within the next year or operating cycle, whichever is longer. Generally, this criterion is satisfied when the investment is considered a resource that will be used whenever the need for cash arises. For example, an Aspen ski resort may invest idle cash during the summer months with the intent to sell the securities to buy supplies and equipment shortly before the next winter season. This investment is considered temporary even if lack of snow cancels the next ski season and eliminates the need to convert the securities into cash as intended.

ACCOUNTING FOR TEMPORARY INVESTMENTS

In accounting for temporary investments, entries are required to record (1) the acquisition, (2) interest and dividend revenue, and (3) the sale. At acquisition, the cost principle applies. Cost includes all expenditures necessary to acquire these investments, such as the price paid plus broker's fees, if any. The basic entries for marketable equity securities and marketable debt securities are illustrated below.

MARKETABLE EQUITY SECURITIES

Marketable equity securities are investments in the capital stock of corporations that are currently traded in the securities market.[2] When a company holds marketable securities of several different corporations, the group of securities is identified as an **investment portfolio.**

The starting point in accounting for these securities is cost. Assume, for example, that on July 1, 1987, Kuhl Corporation acquires 1,000 shares of Beal Corporation common stock at $40 per share plus broker's fees of $500. The entry for the purchase is:

[2] "Accounting for Certain Marketable Securities," *Statement of Financial Accounting Standards No. 12* (Stamford, Conn.: FASB, 1975).

July 1	Marketable Equity Securities	40,500	
	Cash		40,500
	(To record purchase of 1,000 shares of Beal Corporation common stock)		

Marketable Equity Securities is a general ledger control account. It is supported by a subsidiary ledger that contains separate accounts for each type of security purchased.

During the time the stock is held, entries are required for any dividends received. Thus, if a $2.00 per share dividend is received by Kuhl Corporation on December 31, the entry is:

Dec. 31	Cash	2,000	
	Dividend Revenue		2,000
	(To record receipt of a cash dividend)		

Dividend Revenue is reported under other revenues and gains in the income statement.

When securities are sold, the difference between the net proceeds from the sale and the cost of the securities is recognized as a gain or a loss. Assume, for instance, that Kuhl Corporation receives net proceeds of $39,500 on the sale of its Beal stock on February 10, 1988. Since the securities cost $40,500, a loss of $1,000 has been incurred. The entry to record the sale is:

Feb. 10	Cash	39,500	
	Loss on Sale of Marketable Equity Securities	1,000	
	Marketable Equity Securities		40,500
	(To record sale of Beal common stock)		

The loss account is reported under other expenses and losses in the income statement, whereas a gain on sale is shown under other revenues and gains.

MARKETABLE DEBT SECURITIES

Marketable debt securities are investments in government and corporation bonds that are currently traded in the securities market. Bonds usually pay interest semiannually. The accounting entries for marketable debt securities are basically the same as those for marketable equity securities. The principal differences are: (1) the account Marketable Debt Securities is used, and (2) both the accrual of interest and the receipt of interest payments must be recorded. These differences are illustrated below, assuming that Kuhl Corporation acquires 50 Doan Inc., $1,000 bonds on January 1, 1987 for $51,000 including brokerage fees. The entry to record the investment is:

Jan. 1	Marketable Debt Securities	51,000	
	Cash		51,000
	(To record purchase of 50 Doan Inc. bonds)		

The bonds pay interest of $3,000 semiannually. Thus, on July 1, the following entry results:

July	1	Cash	3,000	
		Bond Interest Revenue		3,000
		(To record receipt of interest on Doan Inc. bonds)		

VALUATION AT LOWER OF COST OR MARKET

During the time marketable equity securities are held, there may be significant fluctuations in the market value of the stock. The Dow-Jones Industrial Average of common stocks illustrates the volatile nature of stock prices. This average, which is based on the market prices of 30 large corporations, drops drastically during downturns in the economy and jumps dramatically during upturns. In the light of such fluctuations, how should marketable equity securities be valued at the balance sheet date? Valuation could be at cost, at market, or at the lower of cost or market. Market would seem to be the best basis because it represents the expected cash realizable value of the securities.

After considerable research and deliberation, the profession concluded that a marketable equity securities portfolio should be reported at the **lower of aggregate cost or market value determined at the balance sheet date.**[3] This approach is conservative because all losses are recognized, but gains are not. Under the lower of cost or market basis, the excess of aggregate cost over the market value of the portfolio is recorded through adjusting entries. Adjusting entries are required to recognize (1) unrealized losses and (2) recoveries of unrealized losses.

UNREALIZED LOSS

In recognizing a decline in value below cost, a **contra asset account** is used in the balance sheet, and an **unrealized loss account** is reported in the income statement. To illustrate, assume that Kuhl Corporation has the following portfolio of marketable equity securities at December 31, 1987:

Portfolio of marketable equity securities

Stock	Cost	Market Value
Beal common	$40,500	$39,200
Conwey common	18,000	20,000
Doram preferred	32,500	28,800
	$91,000	$88,000

Aggregate cost exceeds market value by $3,000 ($91,000 − $88,000). This decline in value is recorded by Kuhl Corporation through the following adjusting entry:

[3]*SFAS No. 12*, op. cit.

Dec. 31	Unrealized Loss on Valuation of Marketable Equity Securities	3,000	
	Allowance for Excess of Cost of Marketable Equity Securities Over Market Value		3,000
	(To record excess of aggregate cost over market value of marketable equity securities)		

The loss is considered to be **unrealized,** because it has not resulted from an exchange transaction between two parties; that is, none of the securities have actually been sold. In the income statement, the loss is reported under other expenses and losses. The allowance account is deducted from marketable equity securities in the current asset section of the balance sheet as shown below:

Presentation of aggregate cost in excess of market value

Marketable equity securities	$91,000	
Less: Allowance for excess of cost of marketable equity securities over market value	3,000	$88,000

It is important to recognize that the balance in the allowance account relates to the entire portfolio of securities. Separate allowances are not kept for each security. At each subsequent balance sheet date, the allowance account is adjusted to show the excess of aggregate cost over market value. Thus, if the aggregate market value of the portfolio above is $86,000 at December 31, 1988, the excess of the cost over market is $5,000 ($91,000 − $86,000). Accordingly, a $2,000 adjustment ($5,000 − $3,000) would be required.

RECOVERY OF UNREALIZED LOSS

If, instead, aggregate market value is $90,000 at December 31, 1988, there has been a $2,000 recovery of the $3,000 loss recognized previously. In this case, a recovery account is credited in the adjusting entry as follows:

Dec. 31	Allowance for Excess of Cost of Marketable Equity Securities Over Market Value	2,000	
	Recovery of Unrealized Loss on Valuation of Marketable Equity Securities		2,000
	(To record recovery in value of marketable equity securities)		

Note that the recovery account is also unrealized because the securities have not been sold. The recovery account is reported under other revenues and gains in the income statement. After this entry is posted, the balance in the allowance account is $1,000 ($3,000 − $2,000), which is the difference between cost ($91,000) and market value ($90,000).

It should be recognized that the credit balance in the allowance account can be reduced only as far as zero by subsequent recovery of market values. A debit balance in the account is not permitted, because it would result in the valuation of the portfolio in excess of cost.

SALE OF SECURITIES

When securities in the portfolio are sold, the securities account is credited for the cost of the shares and the balance in the allowance account is ignored. For example, if the Doram preferred stock is sold on March 1, 1989 for $34,000, the entry for the sale is:

Mar. 1	Cash	34,000	
	Marketable Equity Securities		32,500
	Gain on Sale of Marketable Equity Securities		1,500
	(To record sale of Doram preferred stock)		

At the next financial statement date, the balance in the allowance account is adjusted based on a comparison of the cost and market value of the securities contained in the investment portfolio at that time.

FINANCIAL STATEMENT PRESENTATION

Because of their high liquidity, temporary investments are listed immediately below cash in the current asset section of the balance sheet. The basis of valuation (cost or lower of cost or market) should be disclosed either in the body of the statement or in the accompanying notes. When aggregate cost is greater than market value, an allowance account is presented as shown earlier. If market value exceeds aggregate cost, the disclosure may be made in a parenthetical note as illustrated by the following presentation of Wm. Wrigley Jr. Company:

Presentation of market value in excess of aggregate cost

Marketable equity securities, at cost (market value, $13,240,000)	$2,636,000

The income statement effects of temporary investments are reported in the nonoperating section as follows:

Income statement presentation

Other revenues and gains	Other expenses and losses
Interest revenue	Loss on sale
Dividend revenue	Unrealized loss on valuation of marketable equity securities
Gain on sale of marketable equity securities	
Recovery of unrealized loss on valuation of marketable equity securities	

SECTION TWO—SHORT-TERM RECEIVABLES

TYPES OF SHORT-TERM RECEIVABLES

The familiar question in retail establishments: "Will that be cash or charge?" reminds us that our economy is heavily dependent on the use of credit. As a result, short-term receivables are a major component of current assets and an important factor in the normal operating cycle of many companies. Recently, for example, at General Mills, receivables represented 22% of current assets, whereas at Black & Decker they totaled 39%.

The term "receivables" refers to amounts due from individuals and other companies. Receivables are claims that are expected to be collected in cash. Receivables are frequently classified as (1) accounts, (2) notes, and (3) other.

Accounts receivable, also called trade receivables, are amounts owed by customers on account. They result from the sale of goods and services in the normal course of business operations (i.e., in trade). These receivables, which usually are the most significant type of claim held by a company, generally are expected to be collected within 30 to 60 days. This class of receivables also includes credit card receivables and installment accounts receivable.

Notes receivable represent claims that are evidenced by formal instruments of credit. The credit instrument normally requires the debtor to pay interest and extends for time periods of 60–90 days or longer.

Other receivables include nontrade receivables such as loans from company officers, advances to employees, and income taxes refundable.

CONTROLLING CREDIT RISK

In most businesses, the volume of sales could be significantly increased by extending credit to customers or by liberalizing a company's credit policies. However, unless effective control is maintained over credit sales, a company may find that some customers are unable or slow to pay the amount owed. In retail companies, losses from uncollectible accounts have increased from .06% to 1.1% of sales in the last decade. During this same period the average collection time for accounts receivable in manufacturing firms has risen from 33 to 43 days. The cost of carrying receivables for this length of time can be substantial if a company must resort to short-term borrowings to pay current obligations.

Credit reporting is a giant and important service industry. TRW, in Los Angeles, maintains a computerized data base on consumer credit records second to only the data base of the Social Security Administration.

Credit approval is usually the responsibility of the credit department, which should indicate its decision in writing. This decision is generally indicated on a copy of the sales invoice. In reaching its decision, the credit department investigates the short-term debt-paying ability of the customer. For a business customer, the credit department may review financial statements and obtain a credit rating from a local credit agency or from a national credit organization such as Dun & Bradstreet. For individual customers, the credit department requests relevant financial information such as salary, debts, savings, etc. On the basis of its findings, the credit department may authorize a line of credit up to a specified amount for each customer.

UNCOLLECTIBLE ACCOUNTS RECEIVABLE

Although each customer must satisfy the credit requirements of the seller before the credit sale is approved, inevitably some accounts receivable become uncollectible. Credit losses may be due to errors in judgment on the part of the seller or extenuating customer circumstances. For example, a company may be involved in a lengthy labor strike or be experiencing a decline in sales because of a major downturn in the economy. Similarly, individuals may be laid off from their jobs or be faced with unexpected hospital bills.

In accounting, credit losses are debited to Bad Debts Expense (or Uncollectible Accounts Expense). Such losses are considered a normal and necessary risk of doing business on a credit basis. In fact, from a management point of view, a reasonable amount of uncollectible accounts is evidence of a sound credit policy. When bad debts are abnormally low, there is reason to suspect that the company is losing profitable business by following a credit policy that is too strict. Of course, abnormally high bad debts are evidence of too liberal a credit policy.

There are two methods of accounting for uncollectible accounts: (1) the allowance method, and (2) the direct write-off method. Each of these methods is explained below.

ALLOWANCE METHOD

The allowance method is required when bad debts are material. Its essential features are:

1. Uncollectible accounts receivable are estimated and matched against sales in the same accounting period in which the sale occurred.
2. **Estimated uncollectibles** are debited to Bad Debts Expense and credited to Allowance for Doubtful Accounts through an adjusting entry at the end of each period.
3. **Actual uncollectibles** are debited to Allowance for Doubtful Accounts and credited to Accounts Receivable at the time the specific account is written off.

RECORDING ESTIMATED UNCOLLECTIBLES

To illustrate the allowance method, assume that Hampson Furniture has credit sales of $1,200,000 in 1987, of which $200,000 remain uncollected at December 31. The credit manager estimates that $12,000 of these sales will prove to be uncollectible. The adjusting entry to record the estimated uncollectibles is:

Dec. 31	Bad Debts Expense	12,000	
	Allowance for Doubtful Accounts		12,000
	(To record estimate of uncollectible accounts)		

Bad Debts Expense is reported as an operating expense (usually as a selling expense) in the income statement. Thus, the estimated uncollectibles are **matched** with sales in 1987 because the expense is recorded in the same year the sales are made. Allowance for Doubtful Accounts is a contra asset account that shows the portion of gross claims on customers that is expected to become uncollectible in the future. This account is not closed at the end of the fiscal year. It is deducted from Accounts Receivable in the current asset section of the balance sheet as follows:

Presentation of allowance for doubtful accounts

Accounts receivable	$200,000	
Less: Allowance for doubtful accounts	12,000	$188,000

The amount of $188,000 represents the expected **cash (or net) realizable value** of the accounts receivable at the statement date.

RECORDING THE WRITE-OFF OF AN UNCOLLECTIBLE ACCOUNT

When all appropriate means of collecting a past-due account have been exhausted and it is apparent that collection is impossible, the account should be written off. To prevent premature write-offs, each write-off should be approved in writing by authorized management personnel. Assume, for example, that the collection manager of Hampson Furniture authorizes the write-off of the $500 balance owed by R. A. Ware on March 1, 1988. The entry is:

Mar. 1	Allowance for Doubtful Accounts	500	
	Accounts Receivable—R. A. Ware		500
	(Write-off of R. A. Ware account)		

This is not an adjusting entry. Observe that Bad Debts Expense is not debited when the write-off occurs. Under the allowance method, every bad debt write-off is debited to the allowance account and not to Bad Debts Expense. A debit to Bad Debt Expense would be incorrect, because the expense is recognized when the adjusting entry is made for estimated bad debts. After posting, the general ledger accounts will show:

General ledger balances

Accounts Receivable				Allowance for Doubtful Accounts			
1/1/88 Bal.	200,000	3/1/88	500	3/1/88	500	1/1/88 Bal.	12,000

The write-off of the account reduces both Accounts Receivable and the Allowance for Doubtful Accounts. Cash realizable value, therefore, remains the same, as illustrated below.

Cash realizable value comparison

	Before Write-off	After Write-off
Accounts receivable	$200,000	$199,500
Allowance for doubtful accounts	12,000	11,500
Cash realizable value	$188,000	$188,000

RECOVERY OF AN UNCOLLECTIBLE ACCOUNT

Occasionally, a company collects from a customer after the account has been written off as uncollectible. Two entries are required to record the recovery of a bad debt: (1) the entry made in writing off the account is reversed to reinstate the customer's account, and (2) the collection is journalized in the usual manner. To illustrate, assume that R. A. Ware pays the amount due in full on July 1. The entries are:

1

July	1	Accounts Receivable—R. A. Ware	500	
		Allowance for Doubtful Accounts		500
		(To reverse write-off of R. A. Ware account)		

2

	1	Cash	500	
		Accounts Receivable—R. A. Ware		500
		(To record collection from R. A. Ware)		

Note that the recovery of a bad debt, like the write-off of a bad debt, affects only balance sheet accounts. The net effect of the two entries above is a debit to Cash and credit to Allowance for Doubtful Accounts for $500.

BASES USED FOR ALLOWANCE METHOD

In the preceding explanation, the amount of the expected uncollectibles was given. We will now consider the two bases that are used by companies to determine this amount. The bases are (1) percentage of sales, and (2) percentage of receivables. Both bases are generally accepted in accounting. The choice between the bases depends on the relative emphasis that management wishes to give to expenses and revenues on the one hand, and cash realizable value of the accounts receivable on the other, as illustrated on the next page.

As you can see from the graphic, the percentage of sales basis results in the best matching of expenses with revenues. In contrast, the percentage of receivables basis produces the best estimate of cash realizable value. Under both bases, it is necessary to determine the company's past experience with bad debt losses.

Comparison of bases of estimating uncollectibles

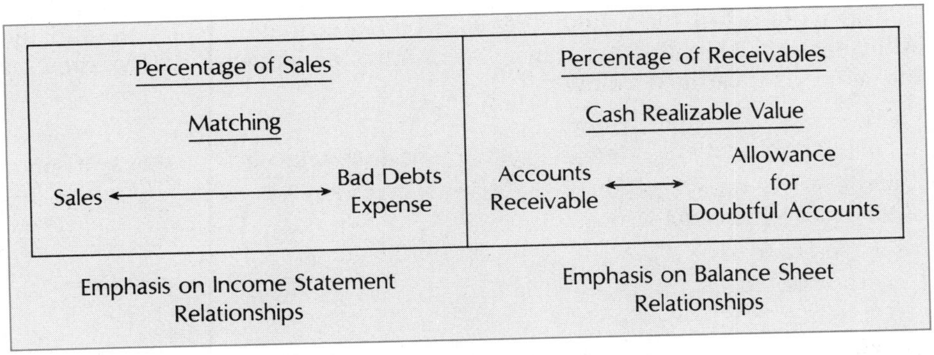

PERCENTAGE OF SALES

In the percentage of sales basis, management establishes a percentage relationship between the amount of credit sales and expected losses from uncollectible accounts. The percentage is based on past experience and anticipated credit policy. It is usually applied to either total credit sales or net credit sales of the current year.

In computerized accounts receivable systems, these relationships can be readily obtained from the data base of information on customer accounts. Such analysis is often referred to as a history search.

To illustrate, assume that Gonzalez Company elects to use the percentage of sales basis and concludes that 1% of net credit sales will become uncollectible. If net credit sales for 1987 are $800,000, the estimated bad debt expense is $8,000 (1% × $800,000), and the adjusting entry is:

Dec. 31	Bad Debts Expense	8,000	
	Allowance for Doubtful Accounts		8,000
	(To record estimated bad debts for year)		

This basis of estimating uncollectibles emphasizes the matching of expenses with revenues. As a result, Bad Debts Expense will show a direct percentage relationship to the sales base on which it is computed. When the adjusting entry is made, the existing balance in the Allowance for Doubtful Accounts is disregarded. The adjusted balance in this account should result in a reasonable approximation of the realizable value of the receivables. If actual write-offs differ significantly from the amount estimated, the percentage for future years should be modified.

PERCENTAGE OF RECEIVABLES

Under the percentage of receivables basis, the balance in the allowance account is derived from an analysis of individual customer accounts. To facilitate the analysis, a schedule (often called an **aging schedule**) is prepared in which customer accounts are classified by the length of time they have been

unpaid. Because of the emphasis on the time, the analysis is often called **aging the accounts receivable.**

The aging schedule is a further example of output that can be obtained from a computerized accounts receivable system. Manually, preparation of this schedule is an onerous and time consuming task. However, the schedule can be done in minutes on computer systems.

After the accounts are aged, the expected bad debt losses are determined by applying bad debt percentages based on past experience to the totals of each category. An aging schedule for the Dart Company is shown below.

Aging schedule

Customer	Total	Not Yet Due	Number of Days Past Due			
			1–30	31–60	61–90	Over 90
T. E. Adert	$ 600		$ 300		$ 200	$ 100
R. C. Bortz	300	$ 300				
B. A. Carl	450		200	$ 250		
O. L. Diker	700	500			200	
T. O. Ebbet	600			300		300
Others	36,950	26,200	5,200	2,450	1,600	1,500
	$39,600	$27,000	$5,700	$3,000	$2,000	$1,900
Estimated Percentage Uncollectible		2%	4%	10%	20%	40%
Total Estimated Bad Debts	$ 2,228	$ 540	$ 228	$ 300	$ 400	$ 760

Total uncollectibles ($2,228) is the amount of existing customer claims expected to become uncollectible in the future. Thus, this amount represents the **required balance** in Allowance for Doubtful Accounts at the balance sheet date. Accordingly, **the amount of the bad debt adjusting entry is the difference between the required balance and the existing balance in the allowance account.** If the trial balance shows Allowance for Doubtful Accounts with a credit balance of $528, an adjusting entry for $1,700 ($2,228 − $528) is necessary, as shown below:

Dec. 31	Bad Debts Expense	1,700	
	Allowance for Doubtful Accounts		1,700
	(To adjust allowance account to total estimated uncollectibles)		

After the adjusting entry is posted, the accounts of the Dart Company will show:

Bad debt accounts after posting

Bad Debts Expense			Allowance for Doubtful Accounts		
12/31	1,700			Bal.	528
				12/31	1,700
				Adj. Bal.	**2,228**

Occasionally the allowance account will have a **debit balance** prior to adjustment, because write-offs have exceeded previous provisions for bad debts. In such a case the debit balance is **added** to the required balance when the adjusting entry is made. Thus, if there had been a $500 debit balance in the allowance account before adjustment, the adjusting entry would have been for $2,728 ($2,228 + $500).

The percentage of receivables method will normally result in the best approximation of cash realizable value. This basis, however, will not result in the best matching of expenses with revenues if some customer's accounts are more than one year past due. Under such circumstances, bad debts expense for the current period would include amounts applicable to the sales of a prior period.

A variation in the percentage of receivables approach is to use only a single percentage based on the balance in accounts receivable. At J. C. Penney Company, for example, the Allowance for Doubtful Accounts is 2% of the balance in customers' accounts receivable, regardless of the age of the individual balances.

DIRECT WRITE-OFF METHOD

Under the direct write-off method, bad debt losses are not estimated and no allowance account is used. When an account is determined to be uncollectible, the loss is charged to Bad Debts Expense. Assume, for example, that Warden Co. writes off M. E. Doran's $200 balance as uncollectible on December 12. The entry is:

Dec. 12	Bad Debts Expense	200	
	Accounts Receivable — M. E. Doran		200
	(To record write-off of M. E. Doran account)		

When this method is used, Bad Debts Expense will show only actual losses from uncollectibles, and accounts receivable will be reported at its gross amount. Moreover, the expense is often recorded in a different period than the period in which the revenue was recorded. Thus, no attempt is made to match bad debt expense to sales revenues in the income statement or to show the cash realizable value of the accounts receivable in the balance sheet. **Consequently, the direct write-off method is not acceptable in accounting, unless bad debt losses are insignificant.**

Not GAAP

If a bad debt is recovered under the direct write-off method, the appropriate entry depends on the time the recovery occurs. When the write-off and recovery occur in the same accounting period, the write-off should be re-

versed and the collection should be recorded in the usual manner. However, if the recovery occurs in the following fiscal year, the customer's account is reinstated by a debit to Accounts Receivable and a credit to a nonoperating revenue account, Bad Debts Recovered. This account is credited, instead of Bad Debts Expense, because a credit to the expense account would understate actual bad debt expense in the current year. For example, if M. E. Doran pays in full on January 12 of a new accounting period, the entry is:

Jan. 12	Accounts Receivable – M. E. Doran	200	
	Bad Debts Recovered		200
	(To reverse write-off of M. E. Doran account)		

In addition, the collection is recorded in the regular manner as follows:

Jan. 12	Cash	200	
	Accounts Receivable – M. E. Doran		200
	(To record collection on account)		

Bad Debts Recovered is reported under other revenues and gains in the income statement.

OTHER TYPES OF ACCOUNTS RECEIVABLE

Many business enterprises have accounts receivable from credit card sales and from installment sales contracts. These two types of accounts receivable are explained below.

CREDIT CARD RECEIVABLES

In a recent year, the combined billings from Visa, MasterCard, American Express, and Sears, Roebuck & Co. credit cards totaled $160.5 billion.[4] When the sales made with other credit cards such as those issued by major oil companies and other retailers are combined, it is clear that credit card sales are important in our economy.

Credit cards are generally classified as either (1) **company** (or in house) cards such as the cards issued by Sears and Exxon or (2) **national** cards such as Visa, MasterCard, and American Express. Management policy determines the type of credit card a company will accept. For many years, Sears Roebuck only accepted its own cards. Now, however, it also accepts national credit cards.

Company Credit Cards

When a company issues credit cards, it must make its own credit investigation of each customer. Upon presentation of the card by a customer, sales clerks

[4]A billion dollars is a big number: A billion seconds ago—Pearl Harbor was attacked. A billion minutes ago—Caesar ruled Rome. A billion hours ago—Man was not yet upon the earth. But a billion dollars ago was yesterday in Washington. (Howard Jarvis)

are authorized to make the credit sale. In some companies, additional approval is required from the credit department when the sale exceeds a certain amount, such as $100. When the sale is made, the customer's name and credit card number are imprinted on the sales slip from the credit card and the customer is required to sign the slip. The sale is then rung up on the cash register and is subsequently recorded as a credit sale.

The company subsequently sends the customer a monthly statement of the transactions that have occurred and the balance due. If the customer fails to pay in full within a specified grace period (usually 25–30 days after the date of the statement), the computer automatically adds an interest charge to the balance due. Although interest rates vary, a common rate is 18% per year or 1.5% per month. When financing charges are added, the seller recognizes interest revenue. Revenue from this source is often very substantial.

National Credit Cards

In contrast to company credit cards, national credit cards are accepted in many retail establishments. Three parties are involved when national credit cards are used in making retail sales: (1) the credit card issuer, who is independent of the retailer, (2) the retailer, and (3) the customer. The major advantages of these cards to the retailer are:

1. The credit card issuer makes the credit card investigation of the customer.
2. The retailer does not have to maintain any individual customer accounts.
3. The retailer is not involved in the collection process, and the credit card issuer absorbs any losses from uncollectible accounts.
4. The retailer receives cash more quickly from the credit card issuer than it would from individual customers.

These advantages are partially offset by the fact that the credit card issuer usually charges a fee of from 2–6% of the invoice price for its services.

Sales resulting from the use of these cards are considered to be credit sales by the retailer, because the conversion of the sale into cash does not occur until the issuer remits the net amount to the seller. To illustrate, assume that the Four Seasons restaurant accepts an American Express card for a $300 dinner bill. The entry for the sale is:

Accounts Receivable — American Express	300	
Sales		300
(To record credit card sale)		

If the service fee is 5%, the cost of the credit card usage is $15. Thus, American Express will subsequently pay the restaurant $285 which is recorded as follows:

Cash	285	
Credit Card Service Expense	15	
Accounts Receivable — American Express		300
(To record redemption of credit card bill)		

Credit Card Service Expense is reported as a selling expense in the income statement.

Visa and MasterCard sales are handled a little differently. Many retailers consider Visa and MasterCard sales to be **cash sales.** These cards are issued by banks and upon receipt of credit sales slips from a retailer, the bank immediately adds the amount of the sales to the retailer's bank balance. Subsequently, the bank makes a monthly service charge deduction from the retailer's bank balance based on the total sales for the period.

INSTALLMENT ACCOUNTS RECEIVABLE

The sale of major home appliances and automobiles to individuals and the sale of major units of equipment to other companies often involve an installment sales contract. The installment contract is a formal document stating the terms of sale, the financing charges, and other information. In these contracts, credit terms usually provide for fixed periodic monthly payments of principal and interest by the purchaser for 24–48 months. The typical contract also provides for transfer of title to the purchaser when the sale is made.

In some cases, the seller may hold the installment contract and receive the monthly payments. For example, IBM reported $670 million of installment contracts receivable in a recent balance sheet. In other cases, the seller may be either unwilling or unable to hold the contract. It then is necessary for the seller to sell the contract to a bank, employee credit union, or a specifically created financing company. Ford Motor Company, for example, has Ford Motor Credit Corp. for financing sales made by Ford dealerships. Further consideration is given to installment contracts in Chapter 13.

NOTES RECEIVABLE

Credit may be granted on the basis of a formal credit instrument known as a promissory note. A **promissory note** is a written promise to pay a specified amount of money on demand or at a definite time. Promissory notes may be used (1) when the amount of the transaction and the credit period exceed normal limits, and (2) in settlement of an open account. Promissory notes are also used when individuals and companies loan or borrow money.

In a promissory note, the party making the promise is called the **maker**; the party to whom payment is to be made is called the **payee.** The payee may be specifically identified by name, or may be designated simply as the bearer of the note. In the note shown on the next page, Brent Company is the maker and Wilma Company is the payee. To the Wilma Company, the promissory note is a note receivable; to the Brent Company, the note is a note payable.

A note receivable gives the holder a stronger legal claim than an open account receivable. It is also more liquid because it can be readily discounted or sold to another party. Promissory notes are negotiable instruments, which means they can be transferred to another party by endorsement.

Promissory note

$1,000 Chicago, Illinois May 1, 1987

2 months after date We promise to pay

to the order of Wilma Company

One Thousand and no/100 -- dollars

for value received with interest at 12%

payable at City National Bank

No. 16

BRENT COMPANY

W. D. Hardy

Treasurer

DETERMINING THE MATURITY DATE

The due date of a promissory note may be stated in one of three ways.

1. On demand, thus: "On demand, I promise to pay. . . ."
2. On a stated date, thus: "On July 23, 1987, I promise to pay. . . ."
3. At the end of a stated period of time, thus:
   (a) "One year after date. . . ."
   (b) "Two months after date. . . ."
   (c) "Ninety days after date. . . ."

When the life of a note is expressed in terms of months, the due date is found by counting the months from the date of issue. For example, the maturity date of a 3-month note dated May 1 is August 1. A note drawn on the last day of a month matures on the last day of a subsequent month; that is, a July 31 note due in 2 months matures on September 30. When the due date is stated in terms of days, it is necessary to count the exact number of days to determine the maturity date. In counting, **the date the note is issued is omitted but the due date is included.** For example, the maturity date of a 60-day note dated July 17 is September 15, computed as follows:

Computation of maturity date

Term of note		60
July (31–17)	14	
August	31	45
Maturity date, September		15

COMPUTING INTEREST

As indicated in Chapter 3, the basic formula for computing interest on an interest-bearing note is:

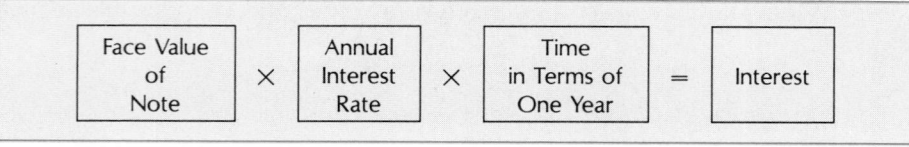

Formula for computing interest

Face Value of Note	×	Annual Interest Rate	×	Time in Terms of One Year	=	Interest

The interest rate specified on the note is an annual rate of interest. The time factor in the computation above expresses the fraction of a year that the note is outstanding. When the maturity date is stated in days, the time factor is the number of days divided by 365. When the due date is stated in months, the time factor is the number of months divided by 12. The computation of interest is illustrated below:

Computation of interest

Terms of Note	Interest Computation						
	Face	×	Rate	×	Time	=	Interest
\$ 730, 18%, 120 days	\$ 730	×	18%	×	120/365	=	\$ 43.20
\$1,000, 15%, 6 months	\$1,000	×	15%	×	6/12	=	\$ 75.00
\$2,000, 12%, 1 year	\$2,000	×	12%	×	1/1	=	\$240.00

ACCOUNTING FOR NOTES RECEIVABLE

To illustrate the basic entries for notes receivable, we will use the \$1,000, 2-month, 12% promissory note on page 322. Assuming that the note was in settlement of an open account, the entry for the receipt of the note by Wilma Company is:

May	1	Notes Receivable	1,000	
		Accounts Receivable – Brent Company		1,000
		(To record acceptance of Brent Company note)		

Observe that the note receivable is recorded at **face value.** No interest is recognized because none has accrued on the date of issue.

HONOR OF THE NOTE

A note is **honored** when it is paid in full at its maturity date. For each interest-bearing note, the amount due at maturity is the face value of the note plus interest for the length of time specified on the note. In this example, interest is \$20 (\$1,000 × 12% × 2/12), and the amount due, the **maturity value,** is \$1,020. To obtain payment, the holder (payee) must either present the note to the maker or to the maker's duly appointed agent, such as a bank. Assuming that Wilma Company presents the note to the Brent Company on July 1, the maturity date, the entries to record the collection are:

July	1	Cash	1,020	
		Notes Receivable		1,000
		Interest Revenue		20
		(To record collection of Brent Company note)		

Interest Revenue is reported under other revenues and gains in the income statement.

ACCRUAL OF INTEREST

In the preceding examples, we assumed that financial statements were not prepared during the time the note was held. Thus, there was no need to accrue interest on the note. However, if the Wilma Company prepares financial statements as of June 30, it would be necessary to accrue interest for the time the note was held. In this case the adjusting entry would be for two months interest or $20 as shown below:

June	30	Interest Receivable	20	
		Interest Revenue		20
		(To accrue two months' interest)		

When interest has been accrued, it is necessary to credit Interest Receivable at maturity. The entry to record the honoring of the Brent note on July 1 would be:

July	1	Cash	1,020	
		Notes Receivable		1,000
		Interest Receivable		20
		(To record collection of Brent Company note at maturity)		

In this case, Interest Receivable is credited because the receivable was established in the adjusting entry.

DISHONOR OF THE NOTE

A note is **dishonored** when it is not paid in full at maturity. When a note is dishonored, the maker generally does one of the following: (1) issues a new note for the maturity value of the dishonored note, (2) remits a partial cash payment and issues a new note for the unpaid balance due at maturity, or (3) refuses outright to make any settlement. The following entries for Wilma Company illustrate the entries that would be made by the holder under each circumstance, assuming interest revenue has not been accrued.

		Case 1—Brent Issues New Note for Old Note		
July	1	Notes Receivable (New)	1,020	
		Notes Receivable (Old)		1,000
		Interest Revenue		20
		(To record receipt of new note from Brent Company)		
		Case 2—Brent Pays $520 and Issues a New Note for Balance Due		
July	1	Cash	520	
		Notes Receivable (New)	500	
		Notes Receivable (Old)		1,000
		Interest Revenue		20
		(To record receipt of cash and new note from Brent Company)		

		Case 3—Brent Makes No Settlement		
July	1	Accounts Receivable – Brent Company	1,020	
		Notes Receivable		1,000
		Interest Revenue		20
		(To record dishonor of Brent Company note)		

In Case 3, the maturity value of the note is debited to Accounts Receivable, assuming the holder expects that collection will occur eventually. If there is no hope of collection, the maturity value of the note should be written off by debiting the Allowance for Doubtful Accounts.

DISCOUNTING NOTES RECEIVABLE

The holder of a note receivable may wish to obtain cash before the maturity date of the note. Instead of borrowing money through a bank loan, the holder may obtain cash by **discounting the note** at a bank. Three parties are involved when a note receivable is discounted at a bank: the holder (payee), the maker, and the bank. The payee discounts the note by endorsing it and transferring it to the bank, receiving cash proceeds equal to the discounted value of the note. Most notes are discounted "with recourse." This means that the payee is obligated to pay the maturity amount to the bank if the original maker fails to pay the note when it is due. Consequently, the holder (payee) is said to have a **contingent liability.**

In this case, the contingency is whether or not the maker will honor the note when it becomes due. If the note is honored, the payee will not have to pay it. Conversely, the contingent liability becomes an actual liability to the payee if the maker refuses to make any settlement of the note at the maturity date.

COMPUTING THE DISCOUNTED VALUE

The determination of the discounted value of a note and other data needed to record the transaction involves a series of steps. To illustrate, we will assume that C. T. Bohe's (the maker) $1,200, 10%, 4-month note dated July 1 is discounted by the Marion Company (holder and payee) on August 1 at the Corner National Bank at a bank discount rate of 12%. Marion has held the note since July 1. The steps and computation are as follows:

1. Determine the **maturity value** of the note by adding interest for the life of the note to the face value of the note.

Determining the maturity value

Life of Note:	7/1----------4 months----------11/1
Interest:	$1,200.00 × 10% × 4/12 = $40.00
Maturity Value:	$1,200.00 + $40.00 = $1,240.00

2. Determine the **bank discount** (the interest earned by the bank for discounting the note) by applying the bank discount rate to the maturity value of the note (Step 1) for the discount period.

Determining the bank discount

Discount Period:	8/1-------3 months-------11/1
Bank Discount:	$1,240.00 × 12% × 3/12 = **$37.20**

3. Determine the **cash proceeds** (discounted value) by subtracting the bank discount (Step 2) from the maturity value of the note (Step 1).

Determining the cash process

Cash Proceeds: $1,240.00 − $37.20 = **$1,202.80**

4. Determine the **book (carrying) value** of the note at the discount date by adding interest earned for the time the note was held to the face value of the note.

Determining the book value

Holding Period:	7/1---1 month---8/1
Interest Earned:	$1,200.00 × 10% × 1/12 = $10.00
Book Value:	$1,200.00 + $10.00 = **$1,210.00**

5. Determine the **interest expense** (or discount cost) by comparing the book value of the note (Step 4) with the cash proceeds of the note (Step 5).

Determining interest expense

Book value	$1,210.00
Cash proceeds	1,202.80
Interest expense	$ 7.20[5]

The computations can be summarized in the following schedule:

Discounting of a Note Receivable

Step	Computation	Amount
1	Maturity value ($1,200.00 + $40.00)	$1,240.00
2	Bank discount	(37.20)
3	Cash proceeds	1,202.80
4	Book value ($1,200 + $10.00)	1,210.00
5	Interest expense	$ 7.20

The entries for discounted notes receivable are explained below.

ENTRY AT DISCOUNT DATE

In recording the discounting of a note, Cash is debited for the cash proceeds determined in Step 3, Interest Expense is debited for the amount determined in Step 5, Interest Revenue is credited for the interest earned on the note

[5]When the book value is less than the discounted value, interest revenue results.

prior to discounting (Step 4), and Notes Receivable Discounted is credited for the face value of the note. The entry for the Marion Company is:

Aug.	1	Cash	1,202.80	
		Interest Expense	7.20	
		Interest Revenue		10.00
		Notes Receivable Discounted		1,200.00
		(To record discounting of Bohe note)		

Notes Receivable Discounted is credited rather than Notes Receivable in order to recognize Marion's contingent liability. Notes Receivable Discounted is a contra asset account that is reported on the balance sheet as a deduction from notes receivable. If the Marion Company has Notes Receivable of $20,000 and Notes Receivable Discounted of $1,200, the statement presentation in the current asset section is:

Notes receivable	$20,000	
Less: Notes receivable discounted	1,200	$18,800

Presentation of notes receivable discounted

Alternatively, the balance sheet presentation could show:

Notes receivable, $20,000, of which $1,200 have been discounted	$18,800

Alternative presentation of discounted note

Notes Receivable Discounted is not reported as a current liability. To do so would incorrectly indicate an actual liability and overstate both current assets and current liabilities.

ENTRIES AT MATURITY

When the maturity date is reached, disclosure of the contingent liability in the accounts is no longer necessary. Either the note will be (1) honored by the maker, which will release all parties, or (2) dishonored by the maker, and the payee will be required to pay the maturity value of the instrument. In either case, the contingent liability must be eliminated at the maturity date by debiting Notes Receivable Discounted and crediting Notes Receivable for the face value of the note. The entry for the Marion Company is:

Nov.	1	Notes Receivable Discounted	1,200.00	
		Notes Receivable		1,200.00
		(To remove contingent liability)		

If the note is honored, only the entry above is required. On the other hand, if the note is dishonored, an additional entry to recognize payment of the note by the discounter is necessary. In this example, Marion Company would have to pay the maturity value of the note ($1,240). In addition, the payment of a **protest fee** is usually required. This fee represents reimbursement to the holder (in this case, the holder is the bank) for the cost of obtaining an affidavit signed by a notary public that the maker has refused to pay the note. Assuming a protest fee of $10, the entry by Marion Company is:

Nov. 1	Accounts Receivable—C. T. Bohe	1,250.00	
	Cash		1,250.00
	(To record payment of maturity value of dishonored note, $1,240, plus protest fee, $10)		

The debit to accounts receivable is appropriate, because Marion Company has a claim on C. T. Bohe for the total amount due, and the note is no longer negotiable. This entry is based on the assumption that eventually Bohe will pay the amount due. If, instead, the amount is deemed to be uncollectible, the debit should be to Allowance for Doubtful Accounts.

FINANCIAL STATEMENT PRESENTATION OF RECEIVABLES

Short-term receivables are reported below temporary investments within the current asset section of the balance sheet. Each of the major types of receivables should be identified in the balance sheet or in the notes to the financial statements. Notes receivable are often listed first under receivables, because they can be quickly realized in cash through discounting. In addition, the contingent liability from discounting notes receivable should be disclosed. Both the gross amount of receivables and the allowance for doubtful accounts should be reported. The following example from a recent balance sheet from CPC International Inc. is illustrative of the current asset presentation of receivables.

Presentation of receivables

CPC International Inc.

Receivables (in millions)	
Notes receivable	$ 16.6
Accounts receivable	375.1
Other receivables	60.7
Total receivables	$452.4
Less: Allowance for doubtful accounts	10.5
Net receivables	$441.9

In the income statement, Bad Debts Expense and Credit Card Service Expense are reported as selling expenses in the operating expense section. Interest Expense is classified under other expenses and losses, and Interest Revenue and Bad Debts Recovered are shown under other revenues and gains.

SUMMARY OF STUDY OBJECTIVES

1. The accounting for temporary investments involves recording (a) the acquisition, (b) interest and dividend revenue, and (c) the sale.

2. Under the lower of cost or market basis of valuation, marketable equity securities are reported at the lower of aggregate cost or market value determined at the balance sheet date. The balance sheet will show a contra asset account for the excess of cost over market value. The income statement will show an unrealized loss account or a recovery of unrealized loss account.

3. The essential features of the allowance method of accounting for uncollectible accounts are: (a) uncollectible accounts are estimated and matched with sales in the period in which the sales occurred; (b) estimated uncollectibles are debited to Bad Debts Expense and credited to Allowance for Doubtful Accounts through an adjusting entry; and (c) actual uncollectibles are debited to Allowance for Doubtful Accounts and credited to Accounts Receivable.

4. Either the percentage of sales or the percentage of receivables basis may be used to estimate uncollectible accounts. The percentage of sales basis emphasizes the matching principle. The percentage of receivables basis emphasizes the cash realizable value of the accounts receivables. An aging schedule is frequently used with this basis.

5. Credit card sales are recorded in the same manner as credit sales. When the credit card holder does not pay the amount owed within a specified grace period, Accounts Receivable is debited and Interest Revenue is credited for the interest costs that are added to the unpaid balance.

6. The maturity date of a note must be computed unless the due date is specified or the note is payable on demand. For a note stated in months, the maturity date is found by counting the months from the date of issue. For a note stated in days, the number of days is counted, omitting the issue date and counting the due date. The formula for computing interest is face value times rate times time.

7. Entries for notes receivable are required for the acceptance of the note, the honoring of the note, the accrual of interest, the dishonoring of the note, and the discounting of the note.

8. The five steps in discounting notes receivable are to determine (a) maturity value, (b) bank discount, (c) cash proceeds, (d) book value, and (e) interest expense.

GLOSSARY

Aging of accounts receivable, p. 317

Dishonored note receivable, p. 324

Honored note receivable, p. 323

Investment portfolio, p. 307

Maker, p. 321

Marketable debt securities, p. 308

Marketable equity securities, p. 307
Payee, p. 321
Promissory note, p. 321
Protest fee, p. 327
Short-term liquid assets, p. 305
Temporary investments, p. 306

DEMONSTRATION PROBLEM

The DePino Company had the following selected transactions in 1987.

Jan.	16	Purchased for cash 600 shares of Sanmark common stock at $24 per share plus $1,200 brokers' fees. The shares are considered to be marketable equity securities.
Feb.	1	Accepted Juno's $2,000 six-month 12% note in settlement of account balance.
Apr.	1	Discounted the Juno note at City Bank. The bank discount rate was 15%.
July	1	Made American Express Company credit card sales totaling $6,700.
July	15	Received payment in full from American Express Company less 5% service charge.
Aug.	1	Received notice that Juno honored his note at maturity.
Sept.	1	Sold 100 shares of Sanmark common stock at $21 per share.
Oct.	1	Purchased 300 shares of Cey Company common stock at $27 per share plus $900 brokers' fees.

At December 31, the market values per share were: Sanmark common $20 and Cey common $31. The DePino Co. uses the percentage of sales basis to estimate bad debts. For 1987, credit sales totaled $1,400,000 and the bad debt percentage is 1%. At December 31, the balance in Allowance for Doubtful Accounts was $2,200.

INSTRUCTIONS

(a) Prepare the journal entries for the above transactions.
(b) Prepare the December 31 adjusting entries.

SOLUTION TO DEMONSTRATION PROBLEM

(a)

Date	Account	Debit	Credit
Jan. 16	Marketable Equity Securities	15,600	
	Cash		15,600
	(Purchased 600 shares of Sanmark common stock)		
Feb. 1	Notes Receivable	2,000	
	Accounts Receivable		2,000
	(Receipt of Juno's note in settlement of account balance)		
Apr. 1	Cash	2,014	
	Interest Expense	26	
	Notes Receivable Discounted		2,000
	Interest Revenue		40
	(Discounted Juno's note at bank discount rate of 15%)		

Date	Account	Debit	Credit
July 1	Accounts Receivable – American Express	6,700	
	Sales		6,700
	(Made credit card sales)		
15	Cash	6,365	
	Credit Card Service Expense	335	
	Accounts Receivable – American Express		6,700
	(Collection of credit card sales)		
Aug. 1	Notes Receivable Discounted	2,000	
	Notes Receivable		2,000
	(Record honoring of Juno's note)		
Sept. 1	Cash	2,100	
	Loss on Sale of Marketable Equity Securities	500	
	Marketable Equity Securities		2,600
	(Sale of 100 shares of Sanmark common stock)		
Oct. 1	Marketable Equity Securities	9,000	
	Cash		9,000
	(Purchase of 300 shares of Cey common stock)		

(b)

Date	Account	Debit	Credit
Dec. 31	Unrealized Loss on Valuation of Marketable Equity Securities	2,700	
	Allowance for Excess of Cost of Marketable Equity Securities over Market Value		2,700
	(To record excess of aggregate cost over market value of Marketable Equity Securities:		

	Cost	Market
Sanmark common	$13,000	$10,000
Cey common	9,000	9,300
	$22,000	$19,300

Date	Account	Debit	Credit
31	Bad Debts Expense	14,000	
	Allowance for Doubtful Accounts		14,000
	(To record estimated bad debts: $1,400,000 × 1% = $14,000)		

QUESTIONS

1. Roark Industries has excess cash. What types of securities may the company purchase as a temporary investment?

2. Kirby Wholesale Supply owns stock in Xerox Corporation, which it intends to hold indefinitely because of some negative tax consequences if sold. Should the investment in Xerox be classified as a temporary investment? Why?

3. Perez Construction Company invests $50,000 cash in the stock of a family-owned brick company. Should this investment be classified as a marketable equity security? Why?

4. To acquire Morgan Corporation stock, R. L. Duran pays $65,000 in cash plus $1,200 broker's fees. What entry should be made for this investment, assuming the stock is readily marketable?

5. Art Adler is confused about losses and gains on the sale of marketable equity securities. Explain to Art (a) how the gain or loss is computed, and (b) the statement presentation of the gains and losses.

6. Wendy Warner is the controller of D-Products, Inc. At December 31, 1987, the company's portfolio of marketable equity securities shows cost $74,000 and market $70,000. Indicate how Wendy would report these data in the financial statements prepared on December 31, 1987.

7. See (6) above. One year later, D-Products' investment portfolio shows cost $92,000 and market $91,000. What adjusting entry should Wendy make on December 31, 1988?

8. What are the essential features of the allowance method of accounting for bad debts?

9. Frank Frick cannot understand why cash realizable value does not decrease when an uncollectible account is written off under the allowance method. Clarify this point for Frank.

10. Distinguish between the two bases that may be used in estimating uncollectible accounts.

11. The Dugan Company has a credit balance of $2,000 in Allowance for Doubtful Accounts. The estimated bad debts expense under the percentage-of-sales basis is $4,100, and the total estimated uncollectibles under the percentage-of-receivables basis is $5,800. Prepare the adjusting entry under each basis.

12. How are bad debts accounted for under the direct write-off method? What are the disadvantages of this method?

13. The Hudson Company accepts both its own credit cards and national credit cards. What are the advantages of accepting both types of cards?

14. What are the distinctive features of installment accounts receivable?

15. Your roommate is uncertain about the advantages of a promissory note. Compare the advantages of a note receivable with those of an open accounts receivable.

16. How may the maturity date of a promissory note be stated?

17. Indicate the maturity date of each of the following promissory notes:

Date of Note	Terms
a. February 16	One year after date of note
b. March 31	Three months after date
c. June 10	Fifteen days after date
d. July 1	Sixty days after date

18. Compute the missing amounts for each of the following notes:

	Principal	Annual Interest Rate	Time	Total Interest
a.	$20,000	10%	3 years	?
b.	$75,000	?	5 months	$4,375
c.	?	12%	73 days	$156
d.	$50,000	11%	?	$1,375

19. The Mayo Company dishonors a note at maturity. What actions by Mayo may occur with the dishonoring of the note?

20. The discounted value of a notes receivable is derived from a series of steps. Identify the steps in the sequence in which they occur.

21. Tim Tyler is uncertain about notes receivable discounted. Explain to Tim why this account should be used and when entries involve this account.

22. The Petron Company has accounts receivable, notes receivable, and installment accounts receivable. How should the receivables be reported on the balance sheet?

EXERCISES

E8-1 The Myrna Company had the following transactions pertaining to marketable securities:

Feb. 1	Purchased 800 shares of ABC common stock for cash at a market price of $8,200 plus $600 broker's fees.
Apr. 1	Purchased 10 Sperry, Inc. bonds for $10,000 plus $500 broker's fees.
July 1	Received cash dividends of $1.00 per share on ABC common stock.
Sept. 1	Sold 300 shares of ABC common stock at a market price of $3,900 less broker's fees of $200.
Oct. 1	Received semiannual bond interest of $700.
Dec. 31	Sold 200 shares of ABC common stock at a market price of $2,100 less broker's fees of $100.

INSTRUCTIONS

Journalize the transactions.

E8-2 At December 31, 1987, the portfolio of current marketable equity securities for the Cárdenas Corporation consisted of the following securities:

	Cost	Market
Pinson Corporation	$17,500	$13,000
Tolan and Helms, Inc.	12,500	15,000
Maloney Consolidated, Inc.	23,000	22,500
	$53,000	$50,500

Additional information

1. Cárdenas Corporation held no securities on December 31, 1986.
2. On March 15, 1988, the investment in Pinson Corp. was sold for $16,700, net of broker's fees.

3. On July 31, 1988, the investment in Tolan and Helm's, Inc. was sold for $14,500, net of broker's fees.
4. On December 31, 1988, only Maloney Consolidated, Inc. was held. Its market value was $21,000.

INSTRUCTIONS

(a) Prepare the adjusting entry at December 31, 1987, to report the securities at the lower of cost or market.

(b) Journalize the 1988 transactions.

(c) Prepare the adjusting entry at December 31, 1988, to report the securities at the lower of cost or market.

E8–3 Rojas, Groat, and Allen, a toy manufacturer in Philadelphia, has very uneven cash flows because it receives big Christmas orders in the summer. Since the company receives nearly 60% of its annual cash receipts between June and September, it has a large surplus of cash to invest in short-term marketable equity securities. At December 31, 1987, the company's investment portfolio contains the following information.

Investment	Cost	Market
Short Industries	$17,000	$20,000
Callison and Co.	6,000	8,000
Bunning, Inc.	28,000	19,000
White Corp.	12,000	11,000
	$63,000	$58,000

INSTRUCTIONS

(a) Prepare the entry at December 31, 1987, to adjust the Allowance for Excess of Cost of Marketable Equity Securities over Market Value, assuming that the unadjusted balance in the allowance account is (1) $1,000, and (2) $7,000.

(b) Show the financial statement presentation at December 31, 1987, of the marketable equity securities and related gains/losses under each assumption in (a) above.

E8–4 The ledger of the Amy Company at the end of the current year shows Accounts Receivable $70,000, Sales $820,000, and Sales Returns and Allowances $20,000.

INSTRUCTIONS

(a) If the Allowance for Doubtful Accounts has a credit balance of $600 in the trial balance, journalize the adjusting entry at December 31 assuming bad debts are expected to be (1) 1% of net sales, and (2) 10% of accounts receivable.

(b) If the Allowance for Doubtful Accounts has a debit balance of $300 in the trial balance, journalize the adjusting entry at December 31, assuming bad debts are expected to be (1) .75% of net sales and (2) 8% of accounts receivable.

E8–5 Evers Company has accounts receivable of $87,400 at March 31. An analysis of the accounts shows the following:

Month of Sale	Balance, March 31
March	$64,000
February	12,700
December and January	8,300
November and October	2,400
	$87,400

Credit terms are 2/10, n/30. At March 31, there is a $1,200 credit balance in Allowance for Doubtful Accounts prior to adjustment. The company uses the percentage-of-receivables basis for estimating uncollectible accounts.

In recent months there has been a downturn in the economy. Thus, the company president and credit manager have differing views regarding the company's bad debts. Their estimates are as follows:

	Estimated Percentage Uncollectible	
Age of Accounts	President	Credit Manager
Current	2.0%	1.5%
1–30 days past due	10.0%	7.0%
31–90 days past due	30.0%	25.0%
Over 90 days	50.0%	40.0%

INSTRUCTIONS

(a) Determine the total bad debts estimated by each individual.

(b) Prepare the adjusting entry at March 31 for each estimate.

E8–6 Sloan Company uses the direct write-off method of accounting for bad debts. On October 1, 1987, it has two past-due accounts receivable: C. Wingly $450 and J. Jamric $300. The two accounts are written off as uncollectible on October 10 and October 31, respectively. Sloan Company's fiscal year ends on November 30.

INSTRUCTIONS

(a) Prepare the journal entries to record the write-off of the uncollectible accounts.

(b) Prepare the journal entries to record the recovery of the bad debt losses, assuming that Wingly pays the balance due on November 25 and Jamric pays in full on December 15.

(c) Explain the major weaknesses of the direct write-off method.

E8–7 Allied Stores accepts both its own and national credit cards. During 1987, the following selected summary transactions occurred.

Jan. 15	Made Allied Stores credit card sales for $14,200.
20	Made American Express credit card sales totaling $2,400.
30	Received payment in full from American Express less a 5% service charge.
Feb. 10	Received collections of $9,200 on Allied credit card sales.
15	Added finance charges of 1.5% to $5,000 of Allied Stores credit card balances.

INSTRUCTIONS

(a) Journalize the transactions.

(b) Indicate the statement presentation of the financing charges and the credit card service expense.

E8–8 The Cey Company has the following notes receivable.

Date of Note	Face	Term	Interest
March 1	$2,000	6 months	12%
March 31	3,600	3 months	13%
May 4	1,825	60 days	9%
September 30	2,400	73 days	10%

INSTRUCTIONS

(a) Compute the maturity date and maturity value of each note.

(b) Prepare the entry (or entries) at maturity for each note, assuming no interest has been accrued and that the:
1. March 1 note is honored.
2. March 31 note is dishonored, and the issuer issues a new note for the maturity value of the old note.
3. May 4 note is dishonored, and the issuer pays $1,000 in cash plus the accrued interest and issues a new note for the balance due on the old note.
4. September note is dishonored, and the issuer makes no settlement. (Assume that future settlement is possible.)

E8–9 The Jessel Company discounted the following notes receivable in May.
1. Binker Company $5,000 12% four-months note dated April 1. This note was received on April 1 and was discounted on May 1 at a bank discount rate of 12.5%.
2. Witt Company $6,000 10% three-months note dated March 10. This note was received on March 10 and was discounted on May 10 at a bank discount rate of 9%.

INSTRUCTIONS

Compute the amounts for each of the steps involved in discounting a note receivable. (Round to two decimals.)

E8–10 On June 1, Raun Company accepts Welker, Inc.'s $1,800, three-month, 12% note on account. The note is discounted at 12% on July 1.

INSTRUCTIONS

(a) Journalize the acceptance and discounting of the note.

(b) Journalize the entries at the maturity date of the note, assuming that:
1. The note is honored.
2. The note is dishonored and Raun Company pays the note and a protest fee of $15. Raun Company expects Welker eventually to pay the note.

PROBLEMS

P8–1 At December 31, 1987, the end of its first year, the Reed Company's portfolio of marketable equity securities consisted of the following:

Security	Cost	Market Value
1,000 shares LTZ, Common	$ 64,200	$ 61,700
800 shares IBF, Common	33,600	35,200
500 shares CRT, Preferred	12,500	10,500
	$110,300	$107,400

In its financial statements, the company correctly reported the securities at the lower of aggregate cost or market value.

In 1988, the following transactions occurred:

Mar. 1 Sold 400 shares of LTZ, common at $60 per share less broker's fees of $800.

July 1 Purchased 700 shares of MYP, common at $50 per share plus broker's fees of $1,000.

Sept. 1 Sold one-half of the shares of IBF, common at $50 per share less broker's fees of $500.

Dec. 1 Received cash dividends of $1.00 per share on LTZ, common and $2.00 per share on MYP, common.

On December 31, 1988, market values of the securities in the portfolio were LTZ, common $36,600; IBF, common $18,000; MYP, common $36,500; and CRT, preferred $10,845.

INSTRUCTIONS

(a) Journalize the 1987 adjusting entry to show the lower of aggregate cost or market valuation.

(b) Journalize the 1988 transactions.

(c) Journalize the 1988 adjusting entry to show the lower of aggregate cost or market valuation.

(d) Indicate the presentation of the securities in (1) the balance sheet at December 31, 1988, and (2) the income statement for 1988.

P8-2 An analysis of the customers' ledger of the Fritz Company at December 31, 1987, reveals the following data concerning specific customers.

Customers	Unpaid Invoices: Dates and Amounts		
Aber	10/5, $ 500;	12/4, $600	
Bohr	9/15, $ 900;	11/10, $800	
Case	11/5, $ 700;	11/30, $300	
Datz	8/15, $1,000		
Glas	9/27, $ 400;	10/27, $500;	11/27, $600
Howe	11/4, $ 200;	12/10, $700	
Mann	7/20, $ 600		
Owen	10/15, $ 900;	11/6, $300	

In addition, summary data on other customers show total claims $49,000, of which $31,700 is not yet due; $8,100 is 1–30 days past due; $6,100 is 31–60 days past due; $1,700 is 61–90 days past due; and $1,400 is over 90 days past due. It is estimated that the percentage of uncollectible accounts will double for each age category, beginning with 2% for accounts not yet due. All sales are billed n/30.

At December 31, the unadjusted balance in Allowance for Doubtful Accounts is a credit of $1,200.

INSTRUCTIONS

(a) Prepare an aging schedule.

(b) Journalize and post the adjusting entry for bad debts at December 31, 1987.

(c) Journalize and post to the allowance account the following 1988 events and transactions.

1. March 1, a $900 customer balance originating in 1987 is judged uncollectible.
2. May 1, a check for $900 is received from the customer whose account was written off as uncollectible on March 1.

(d) Journalize the adjusting entry for bad debts on December 31, 1988, assuming that the unadjusted balance in Allowance for Doubtful Accounts is a debit of $800 and the aging schedule indicates that total estimated bad debts will be $3,460.

P8-3 Bad debt data of the Willis Company for a three-year period are summarized below:

	1984	1985	1986
Credit Sales	$400,000	$450,000	$500,000
Bad Debt Write-offs			
1984 Sales	3,000	6,000	
1985 Sales		3,700	5,500
1986 Sales			4,900
Bad Debt Recoveries			
1984 Sales	200	800	
1985 Sales		100	400
1986 Sales			300

The company has used the direct write-off method of accounting for uncollectible accounts. As of January 1, 1987, the company decides to estimate its bad debts on the basis of net bad debt losses (write-offs less recoveries) on 1984 sales to total credit sales for 1984. In 1984, the percentage of net bad debt losses to total credit sales was 2%. All accounts receivable from credit sales are collected or deemed uncollectible by December 31 of the year following the sale. Bad debt recoveries of prior years' sales were applicable to write-offs made in the year of sale.

INSTRUCTIONS

(a) Journalize the entries made each year by the company for write-offs and recoveries under the direct write-off method.

(b) Journalize the entries that would have been made each year for write-offs, recoveries, and the December 31 adjustment if the company had used the allowance method and the percentage of sales basis.

P8-4 The Dalton Company closes its books monthly. On June 30, selected ledger account balances are

Notes Receivable	$33,800.00
Notes Receivable Discounted	9,800.00
Accounts Receivable — Dalton Charge Customers	52,500.00
Interest Receivable	88.77

Notes receivable include the following:

Date	Maker	Face	Term	Interest
May 16	Renna Co.	$6,000	60 days	12%
May 21	Alder Inc.	5,000	60 days	12%
May 25	Dorn Co.	4,800	2 months	11%
June 30	MJH Corp.	9,600	6 months	12%
June 30	Nemo Co.	8,400	3 months	10%

The Alder note was discounted at the bank at 12% on June 1, and the Dorn note was discounted at 15% on the day it was received. Interest receivable pertains to the Renna note. During July the following transactions were completed.

July 2 Received payments on account from Dalton charge customers, $16,800. This total includes $410 of finance charges billed in June.
5 Made sales of $6,200 on Dalton credit cards.
14 Made sales of $900 on American Express credit cards. The credit card service charge is expected to be 5%.
15 Collected Renna Co. note in full.
16 Added $315 to Dalton charge customer balances for finance charges on unpaid balances.

20 Received check from American Express in settlement of July 14 sales less 5%.
21 Received notice that Alder note has been honored by the maker.
22 Made sales of $5,700 on Dalton credit cards.
25 Received notice that the Dorn note has been dishonored. Paid bank maturity value plus a $10 protest fee. (Assume that Dorn is expected to pay in the future. Use Accounts Receivable – Other.)
27 Made sales of $600 on American Express credit cards.
30 Discounted the MJH Corp. note at 12%.

INSTRUCTIONS

(a) Journalize the July transactions and the July 31 adjusting entry for accrued interest receivable. (Round to two decimals.)

(b) Enter the balances at July 1 in the receivable accounts and post the entries to all of the receivable accounts.

(c) Show the balance sheet presentation of the receivable accounts at July 31.

P8-5 On January 1, 1987, Ricko Company had Accounts Receivable $54,200 and Allowance for Doubtful Accounts $4,700. Ricko Company prepares financial statements annually. During the year the following selected transactions occurred.

Jan. 5 Sold $5,000 of merchandise to Hubbard Company, terms n/30.
Feb. 2 Accepted a $5,000 four-month 12% promissory note from Hubbard Company for balance due.
Feb. 12 Sold $6,000 of merchandise to Gage Company and accepted Gage's $6,000 two-month 10% note for the balance due.
Mar. 1 Collected $27,400 in cash from customers on account and granted $4,100 of sales discounts for prompt payments.
Mar. 26 Sold $4,000 of merchandise to Gagnon Co., terms n/10.
Apr. 5 Accepted a $4,000 three-month 12% note from Gagnon Co. for balance due.
Apr. 12 Collected Gage Company note in full.
June 2 Hubbard Company remits $1,000 cash plus accrued interest and signs a new 4-month 12% note for the balance due on February 2 note.
July 5 Gagnon Co. dishonors its note of April 5. It is expected that Gagnon will eventually pay the amount owed.
July 15 Sold $2,000 of merchandise to Hoff Inc. and accepted Hoff's $2,000 3-month 12% note for the amount due.
Aug. 15 Discounted the Hoff note at Metro Trust Bank at a discount rate of 12%.
Sept. 20 Accepted Hawker Corporation's $8,000 4-month 12% note in settlement of past-due balance on account.
Oct. 15 Received notice that the Hoff Inc. note had been dishonored. Paid bank the maturity value of the note plus a protest fee of $20. Hoff Inc. is bankrupt, and there is no hope of future settlement.
Dec. 20 Discounted the Hawker Corporation note at the Century Bank at a discount rate of 12%.

INSTRUCTIONS

Journalize the transactions above.

ALTERNATE PROBLEMS

P8-1A At December 31, 1987, at the end of its first year, the Hart Company's portfolio of marketable securities consisted of the following:

Security	Cost	Market Value
1,200 shares of RHF, Common	$124,800	$120,950
750 shares of DWK, Common	52,750	54,000
400 shares of BGT, Preferred	19,400	17,600
	$196,950	$192,550

In its financial statements, the company correctly reported the securities at the lower of aggregate cost or market value.

In 1988, the following transactions occurred:

Mar. 1 Sold 500 shares of RHF, common at $101 per share less broker's fees of $1,500.

July 1 Purchased 600 shares of CCM, common at $45 per share plus broker's fees of $800.

Sept. 1 Sold 300 shares of DWK, common at $73 per share less broker's fees of $600.

Dec. 1 Received cash dividends of $1.50 per share on RHF, common and $2.00 per share on CCM, common.

On December 31, 1988, market values of the securities in the portfolio were RHF, common $69,900; DWK, common $32,500; CCM, common $28,200; and BGT, preferred $18,000.

INSTRUCTIONS

(a) Journalize the 1987 adjusting entry to show the lower of aggregate cost or market valuation.

(b) Journalize the 1988 transactions.

(c) Journalize the 1988 adjusting entry to show the lower of aggregate cost or market valuation.

(d) Indicate the presentation of the securities in (1) the balance sheet at December 31, 1988, and (2) the income statement for 1988.

P8-2A An analysis of the customers' ledger of the Garfield Company at December 31, 1987, reveals the following data concerning specific customers.

Customers	Unpaid Invoices: Dates and Accounts		
Ewen	10/6, $ 500;	12/11, $450	
Fritz	9/18, $1,000;	11/10, $750	
Incha	11/5, $ 600;	11/30, $300	
Jackson	8/25, $1,100		
Kuster	9/20, $ 500;	10/18, $600;	12/4, $400
Louvre	11/4, $ 200;	11/15, $700	
Nara	7/29, $ 500		
Peters	10/20, $ 800;	11/6, $400	

In addition, summary data on other customers show total claims $45,000, of which $29,900 is not yet due; $7,250 is 1–30 days past due; $5,825 is 31–60 days past due; $1,525 is 61–90 days past due; and $500 is over 90 days past due. It is estimated that the percentage of uncollectible accounts will double for each age category, beginning with 2% for accounts not yet due. All sales are billed n/30.

At December 31, the unadjusted balance in Allowance for Doubtful Accounts is a debit of $900.

INSTRUCTIONS

(a) Prepare an aging schedule.

(b) Journalize and post the adjusting entry for bad debts at December 31, 1987.

(c) Journalize and post to the allowance account the following 1988 events and transactions.
1. March 1, a $700 customer balance originating in 1987 is judged uncollectible.
2. May 1, a check for $700 is received from the customer whose account was written off as uncollectible on March 1.

(d) Journalize the adjusting entry for bad debts on December 31, 1988, assuming that the unadjusted balance in Allowance for Doubtful Accounts is a credit of $1,200 and the aging schedule indicates that total estimated bad debts will be $3,980.

P8-3A Bad debt data of Arnold Company for a three-year period are summarized below:

	1984	1985	1986
Credit Sales	$460,000	$500,000	$540,000
Bad Debt Write-offs			
1984 Sales	4,500	8,000	
1985 Sales		4,200	7,400
1986 Sales			5,200
Bad Debt Recoveries			
1984 Sales	300	700	
1985 Sales		200	400
1986 Sales			700

The company has used the direct write-off method of accounting for uncollectible accounts. As of January 1, 1987, the company decides to estimate its bad debts on the basis of net total bad debt losses on 1984 sales to total credit sales for 1984. In 1984, the percentage of net bad debt losses (write-offs less recoveries) to total credit sales was 2.5%. All accounts receivable credit sales are collected or deemed uncollectible by December 31 of the year following the sale. Bad debt recoveries of prior years sales were applicable to write-offs made in the year of sale.

INSTRUCTIONS

(a) Journalize the entries made each year by the company for write-offs and recoveries under the direct write-off method.

(b) Journalize the entries that would have been made each year for write-offs, recoveries, and the December 31 adjustment if the company had used the allowance method and the percentage of sales basis.

P8-4A The Mudger Company closes its books monthly. On September 30, selected ledger account balances are:

Notes Receivable	$37,400.00
Notes Receivable Discounted	11,200.00
Accounts Receivable—Mudger Charge Customers	54,700.00
Interest Receivable	221.92

Notes Receivable include the following:

Date	Maker	Face	Term	Interest
July 17	Hearns Co.	$ 9,000	90 days	12%
Aug. 16	Foran Inc.	6,000	60 days	12%
Aug. 25	Drexler Co.	5,200	2 months	12%
Sept. 30	MGH Corp.	10,200	6 months	10%
Sept. 30	Larson Co.	7,000	3 months	11%

The Foran note was discounted at the bank at 12% on September 1, and the Drexler note was discounted at 12% on the day it was received. Interest receivable pertains to the Hearns note. During October, the following transactions were completed.

Oct. 3 Received payments on account from Mudger charge customers, $17,200. This total includes $425 of finance charges billed in September.
7 Made sales of $5,900 on Mudger credit cards.
12 Made sales of $750 on American Express credit cards. The credit card service charge is expected to be 5%.
15 Collected Hearns Co. note in full.
17 Added $285 to Mudger charge customer balance for finance charges on unpaid balances.
19 Received check from American Express in settlement of October 12 sales less 5%.
21 Received notice that Foran note has been honored by the maker.
23 Made sales of $4,500 on Mudger credit cards.
25 Received notice that the Drexler note has been dishonored. Paid bank maturity value plus a $10 protest fee. (Assume that Drexler is expected to pay in future. Use Accounts Receivable—Other.)
27 Made sales of $900 on American Express credit cards.
30 Discounted the MGH Corp. note at 10%.

INSTRUCTIONS

(a) Journalize the October transactions and the October 31 adjusting entry for accrued interest receivable. (Round to two decimals.)

(b) Enter the balances at October 1 in the receivable accounts and post the entries to all of the receivable accounts.

(c) Show the balance sheet presentation of the receivable accounts at October 31.

P8-5A On January 1, 1987, Lundquist Company had Accounts Receivable $146,000, Notes Receivable $12,000, and Allowance for Doubtful Accounts $13,200. The note receivable is from the Annabelle Company. It is a 4-month 12% note dated December 31, 1986. Lundquist Company prepares financial statements annually. During the year the following selected transactions occurred.

Jan. 10 Sold $10,000 of merchandise to Earney Company, terms n/15.
20 Accepted Earney Company's $10,000 3-month 13% note for balance due.
31 Discounted the Annabelle Company note at the Central Bank at a discount rate of 12%.
Feb. 18 Sold $7,000 of merchandise to Swaim Company and accepted Swaim's $7,000 6-month 10% note for the amount due.
Mar. 10 Collected $72,000 in cash from customers on account and granted $12,400 of sales discounts for prompt payments.
Apr. 20 Earney Company pays $4,000 cash plus accrued interest and signs a new 3-month 14% note for the balance due on the January 20 note.
Apr. 30 Received notice that the Annabelle Company note had been honored.
May 25 Accepted Langley Inc.'s $6,000 3-month 12% note in settlement of a past-due balance on account.
June 25 Discounted the Langley note at Merchant National Bank at a discount rate of 12%.
July 20 Earney Company dishonors its note. The company is not bankrupt and future settlement is expected.
Aug. 18 Received payment in full from Swaim Company on note due.
Aug. 25 Received notice that the Langley Inc. note had been dishonored. Paid bank the maturity value of the rate plus a protest fee of $25. Langley Inc. is not bankrupt and future payment is anticipated.

Sept.	1	Sold $9,000 of merchandise to Louise Company and accepted a $9,000 6-month 10% note for the amount due.
Nov.	1	Discounted the Louise Company note at the Marine Bank at a discount rate of 10%.

INSTRUCTIONS

Journalize the transactions above.

DECISION CASE

Doris and Doug Dunham own Casual Fashions. From its inception Casual Fashions has sold merchandise on either a cash or credit basis but no credit cards have been accepted. During the past several months, the Dunhams have begun to question their sales policies. First, they have lost some sales because of refusing to accept credit cards. Second, representatives of two metropolitan banks have been persuasive in convincing them to accept their national credit cards. One bank, City National Bank, has stated that (1) its credit card fee is 4%, and (2) it pays the retailer 96 cents on each $1 of sales within three days of receiving the credit card billings.

The Dunhams decide that they should determine the cost of carrying their own credit sales. From the accounting records of the past three years they accumulate the following data:

	1986	1985	1984
Net credit sales	$500,000	$600,000	$400,000
Collection agency fees for slow paying customers	2,650	2,700	2,200
Salary of part-time accounts receivable clerk	3,600	3,600	3,600

Credit and collection expenses as a percentage of net credit sales: uncollectible accounts, 1.6%, billing and mailing costs, 0.5%, and credit investigation fee on new customers, 0.15%.

Doris and Doug also determine that the average accounts receivable balance outstanding during the year is 5% of net credit sales. The Dunhams estimate that they could earn an average of 10% annually on cash invested in other business opportunities.

INSTRUCTIONS

(a) Prepare a tabulation showing for each year total credit and collection expenses in dollars and as a percentage of net credit sales.

(b) Determine the net credit and collection expense in dollars and as a percentage of sales after the revenue earned from other investment opportunities. (Note: The income lost on the cash held by the bank for three days is considered to be immaterial.)

(c) Discuss both the financial and nonfinancial factors that are relevant to the decision.

CHAPTER 9

Columbia University

CHAPTER 9

INVENTORIES

STUDY OBJECTIVES

After studying this chapter, you should be able to:

1. Describe the steps in determining inventory quantities.
2. Explain the basis of accounting for inventories and the components of inventoriable costs.
3. Explain the effects of each of the inventory costing methods.
4. Identify the factors to consider in selecting an inventory costing method.
5. Discuss the circumstances that justify a departure from the cost basis of accounting for inventories.
6. Describe the two methods of estimating inventories.
7. List the essential accounting features of a perpetual inventory system.
8. Indicate the effects of inventory errors on the financial statements.

Merchandise inventory is an important factor in determining the cost of goods sold for retailers and wholesalers. In this chapter we will explain the procedures for determining inventory amounts and the costing methods that may be used in determining the cost of inventory on hand at the balance sheet date. In addition, the use of estimates in determining inventory amounts, perpetual inventory systems, and the effects of inventory errors on a company's financial statements will be discussed.

IMPORTANCE OF INVENTORIES

Inventories affect both the balance sheet and the income statement. In the **balance sheet** of merchandising and manufacturing companies, inventory is frequently the most significant current asset, although its amount and relative

significance can vary even for enterprises in the same industry. For example, J. P. Stevens & Co. recently reported inventory of $321 million, representing 45% of total current assets, whereas for the same period, J. C. Penney Company reported $1.7 billion of inventory, representing 65% of total current assets. These percentages are evidence of the importance of buying and selling of inventory in the operating cycle of these companies. In the **income statement,** inventory plays a vital role in determining the results of operations for a particular period. Moreover, gross profit (net sales − cost of goods sold) is closely watched by management, owners, and other interested parties.

Effective inventory management is frequently the key to successful business operations. Management attempts to maintain sufficient quantities and types of goods to meet expected customer demand, but it also seeks to avoid the cost of carrying inventories that are clearly in excess of anticipated sales. A delicate balance must be maintained between too little inventory and too much. A merchandiser or manufacturer with too little inventory to meet demand will have dissatisfied customers, whereas one with too much inventory will be burdened with unnecessary costs.

In our economy, inventories are an important barometer of business activity. The U.S. Commerce Department, for example, publishes monthly combined inventory data for retailers, wholesalers, and manufacturers. The amount of inventories and the time required to sell the goods on hand are two indicators that are closely watched. During downturns in the economy, there is an initial build-up of inventories, as the length of time needed to sell existing quantities increases. The reverse effects are generally associated with an upturn in business activity.

INVENTORY CLASSIFICATIONS

In a **merchandising enterprise** inventory consists of many different items. For example, in a grocery store, canned goods, dairy products, meats, and produce are just a few of the inventory items that might be on hand. These inventory items have two common characteristics: (1) they are owned by the company, and (2) they are in a form ready for sale to customers in the ordinary course of business. As a consequence, only one inventory classification, **merchandise inventory,** is needed to describe the many different items that make up the total inventory.

In a **manufacturing enterprise,** inventories are also owned by the company. In many cases, however, some goods are not yet ready for sale. As a result, inventory is usually classified into three categories: finished goods, work in process, and raw materials. General Motors classifies automobiles completed and ready for sale as **finished goods.** The automobiles on the assembly line in various stages of production are classified as **work in process.** The steel, glass, upholstery, and other automotive components that are on hand waiting to be used in the production of automobiles are referred to as **raw materials.**

The accounting principles and concepts discussed in this chapter are applicable to each of the above-mentioned inventory classifications. In this chapter, however, we will focus on merchandise inventory. In later chapters we

will discuss the accounting for the three inventory classifications used by manufacturers.

DETERMINING INVENTORY QUANTITIES

The objective in determining inventory quantities is to ascertain the number of units of inventory owned by the company at the statement date. For most companies, this task consists of two steps: (1) taking a physical inventory of goods on hand, and (2) determining the ownership of goods in transit.

TAKING A PHYSICAL INVENTORY

Taking a physical inventory involves actually counting, weighing, or measuring each kind of inventory on hand. In many companies, taking an inventory is a formidable task. Retailers, such as K mart, True Value Hardware, or your favorite stereo store, have thousands of different items of inventory. An inventory count is generally more accurate when goods are not being sold or received during the counting. Consequently, companies often take the inventory when the business is closed (weekends and holidays) or when business is slow. In other cases, companies suspend operations until the physical inventory is completed.

To minimize errors in taking the inventory, a company should adopt the following internal control procedures:

1. The counting should be done by employees who do not have custodial responsibility for the inventory. (Segregation of duties)
2. Each counter is expected to establish the authenticity of each inventory item, e.g., each box does contain a 25-inch television set, and each storage tank does contain gasoline. (Establishment of responsibility)
3. There should be a second count by another employee. (Independent internal verification)
4. Prenumbered inventory tags should be used, and all inventory tags should be accounted for. (Other controls)
5. A designated supervisor should ascertain at the conclusion of the count that all inventory items are tagged and that no items have more than one tag. (Independent internal verification)

Failure to observe the foregoing internal control procedures contributed to the Great Salad Oil Swindle. In this case, management intentionally overstated its salad oil inventory, which was stored in large holding tanks. The management used three procedures to overstate the oil inventory: (1) Water added to the bottom of the holding tanks caused the oil to float to the top. Inventory-taking crews who viewed the holding tanks from the top observed only salad oil, when, in fact, as much as 37 out of 40 feet of many of the holding tanks contained water. (2) The company's inventory records listed more holding tanks than it actually had. The company repainted numbers on the tanks after inventory crews examined them, so the crews counted the same tanks twice. (3) Underground pipes pumped oil from one holding tank to

another as the tanks were being inventoried; therefore, the same salad oil was counted more than once. Although the salad oil swindle was unusual, it demonstrates the complexities that may be involved in assuring that inventory is properly counted.

GOODS IN TRANSIT

Goods are considered to be in transit when they are in the hands of a public carrier, such as a railroad, trucking, or airline company at the statement date. Goods in transit should be included in the inventory of the party that has legal title to the goods. Legal title is determined by the terms of sale. When the terms are **FOB (Free on Board) shipping point,** ownership of the goods passes to the buyer when the public carrier accepts the goods from the seller. Conversely, when the shipping terms are **FOB destination,** legal title to the goods remains with the seller until the goods are delivered to the buyer by the transportation company. Significant errors may occur in determining inventory quantities if goods in transit at the statement date are ignored. Assume, for example, that Hargrove Company has 20,000 units of inventory on hand on December 31 and, the following goods in transit: (1) sales of 1,500 units shipped December 31 FOB destination, and (2) purchases of 2,500 units shipped FOB shipping point by the seller on December 31. Hargrove has legal title to both the units sold and the units purchased. Consequently, inventory quantities are understated by 4,000 units (1,500 + 2,500) if units in transit are ignored.

After the physical inventory is taken and the title to goods in transit is determined, the quantity of each kind of inventory is listed on **inventory summary sheets** in a manual accounting system. To assure the accuracy of the summary sheets, the listing should be verified by a second employee or supervisor. Subsequently, unit costs are applied to the quantities and a total inventory valuation is determined. Factors that affect the determination of unit costs are explained in the following sections.

In computerized systems, inventory quantities and accompanying inventory part numbers are entered into a computer. The data are then processed by a software program that applies unit cost data to the quantities, determines the total value of the inventory, and prints out the completed inventory summary sheets.

INVENTORIABLE COSTS

The primary basis of accounting for inventories is cost as required by the cost principle. Cost includes all expenditures necessary to acquire the goods and to place them in a condition ready for sale. The items included in inventoriable costs, their account titles, and their effects on inventoriable costs are shown in the following schedule.

Inventoriable costs

Item	Account Title	Effect on Inventoriable Costs
Invoice price	Purchases	Increase
Freight charges paid by purchaser	Freight-In	Increase
Purchase discounts taken by purchaser	Purchase Discounts	Decrease
Purchase returns and allowances granted by the seller	Purchase Returns and Allowances	Decrease

Conceptually, the costs of the purchasing, receiving, and warehousing departments should also be included in inventoriable costs. However, because of the practical difficulties in allocating these costs to individual units of inventories, they are generally accounted for as operating expenses in the period in which they are incurred.

Inventoriable costs may be regarded as a **pool of costs** that consist of two elements: (1) the cost of the beginning inventory, and (2) the cost of goods purchased during the period. The sum of these elements equals the cost of goods available for sale. It is then necessary to allocate the cost of goods available for sale to the ending inventory and to the cost of goods sold. In determining net income under a periodic inventory system, which was illustrated in Chapter 5, the allocation is made at the end of the accounting period. In the allocation, **the costs assignable to the ending inventory are determined first.** Then this total is subtracted from cost of goods available for sale to determine the cost of goods sold.

To illustrate, assume that General Suppliers Inc. has a cost of goods available for sale of $120,000, based on a beginning inventory of $20,000 and cost of goods purchased of $100,000. From the physical inventory it is determined that 5,000 units are on hand. The costs applicable to the units are $3.00 per unit. Thus, the allocation of the pool of costs is as follows:

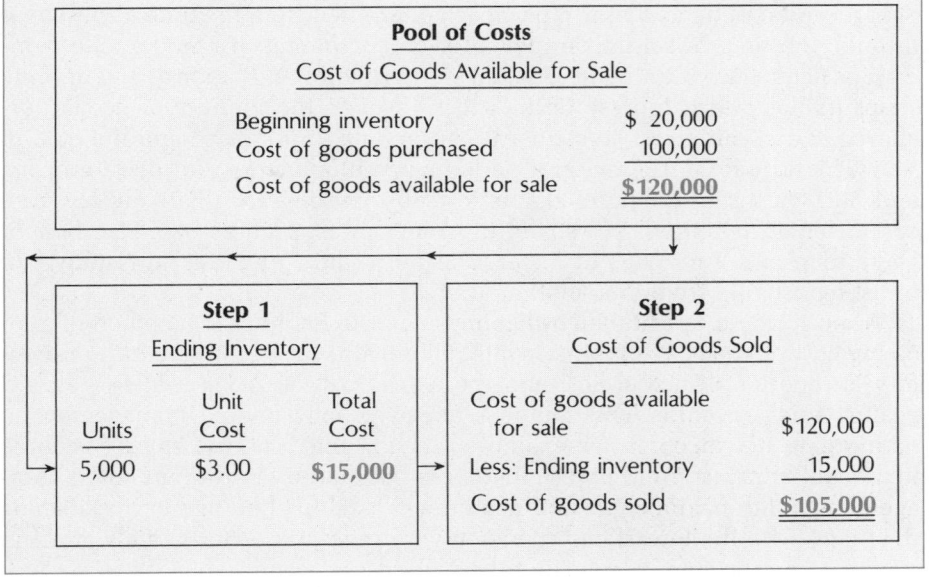

Allocation of pool of costs

Pool of Costs

Cost of Goods Available for Sale

Beginning inventory	$ 20,000
Cost of goods purchased	100,000
Cost of goods available for sale	$120,000

Step 1

Ending Inventory

Units	Unit Cost	Total Cost
5,000	$3.00	$15,000

Step 2

Cost of Goods Sold

Cost of goods available for sale	$120,000
Less: Ending inventory	15,000
Cost of goods sold	$105,000

As shown, the $120,000 of goods available for sale are allocated $15,000 to ending inventory and $105,000 to cost of goods sold.

The allocation of costs affects both the balance sheet (ending inventory) and the income statement (cost of goods sold). While both statements are important, **it is generally recognized that a major objective of accounting for inventory is the proper determination of net income.** Thus, the objective is the proper matching of appropriate costs with sales revenue in accordance with the matching principle.

ACTUAL PHYSICAL FLOW COSTING METHOD

Costing of the inventory is complicated because the units on hand for a specific item of inventory may have been purchased at different costs. For example, in a period of rising prices, a company may experience several significant increases in the cost of identical goods within a given year. Alternatively, unit costs may decline during the year, as in the case of the dramatic drop in the cost of gasoline in 1986. Under such circumstances, how should the different unit costs in the cost of goods available for sale be allocated between the ending inventory and cost of goods sold?

One answer is to use **specific identification** of the units purchased at each of the different unit costs. This method tracks the **actual physical flow** of the goods available for sale. Under this method, each item of inventory is marked, tagged, or coded with its unit cost. Items still in inventory at the end of the year are then specifically costed to arrive at the total cost of the ending inventory. Assume, for example, that Southland Music Company purchases three 27″ Zenith television sets at costs of $700, $750, and $800, respectively. During the year, two sets are sold at $1,200 each. At December 31, it is determined that the $750 set is still on hand. Accordingly, the ending inventory is $750 and the cost of goods sold is $1,500 ($700 + $800).

Specific identification is possible where a company sells a limited variety of high-unit cost items that can be clearly identified from the time of purchase through the time of sale. Examples of such companies are automobile dealerships (cars, trucks, and vans), music stores (pianos and organs), and antique shops (tables and cabinets). Ordinarily, however, the identity of goods purchased at a specific cost is lost between the date of purchase and the date of sale. This would be true under a periodic inventory system for drug, grocery, and hardware stores. These companies sell thousands of relatively low unit cost items of inventory. Moreover, inventory units, such as bath-size bars of Dove soap and 9-oz. cans of Faberge's super-hold Aqua Net hair spray, are indistinguishable from one another.

When feasible, specific identification seems to be the ideal method of allocating cost of goods available for sale. Under this method, the ending inventory is reported at actual cost and the actual cost of goods sold is matched against sales revenue. This method, however, may enable management to manipulate net income. For example, assume that a music store has three identical Steinway grand pianos that were purchased at different costs. Management could maximize its net income when selling one piano, by selecting the piano with the lowest cost to match with revenues. Alternatively, it could minimize net income by selecting the highest-cost piano.

ASSUMED FLOW COSTING METHODS

Because of the limitations of actual physical flow, it is recognized in accounting that the allocation of inventoriable costs may be made under any of the following assumptions as to the flow of costs:

1. First-in, first-out (FIFO)
2. Last-in, first-out (LIFO)
3. Average cost

There is no accounting requirement that the cost flow assumption be consistent with the physical movement of the goods. The selection of the appropriate cost flow assumption, commonly referred to as the appropriate **method** of inventory costing, is made by management. Companies in the same industry may reach different conclusions as to the most appropriate method.[1] For example, in the computer industry, Burroughs uses FIFO and IBM uses average cost. Once a method is selected, it should be used consistently to enhance the comparability of financial statements.

To illustrate these three inventory costing methods, we will assume that Bow Valley Electronics uses a periodic inventory system and has the following information for its Z202 Astro condensers:

Inventory, purchases, and sale information

BOW VALLEY ELECTRONICS
Z202 Astro Condensers

		Units	Unit Cost	Total Cost
1/1	Beginning inventory	100	$10	$ 1,000
4/15	Purchase	200	11	2,200
8/24	Purchase	300	12	3,600
11/27	Purchase	400	13	5,200
		1,000		$12,000

During the year, 550 units were sold, and 450 units are on hand at December 31.

FIRST-IN, FIRST-OUT (FIFO)

The FIFO method assumes that the costs of the earliest goods acquired are the first to be recognized as cost of goods sold. FIFO often parallels the actual physical flow of merchandise because it generally is good business management to sell the oldest units first. Under the FIFO method, **the ending inventory is obtained by taking the unit cost of the most recent purchases and working back until all units of inventory are accounted for.** The allocation of the cost of goods available for sale at Bow Valley Electronics is as follows:

[1] A company may use more than one costing method concurrently. Del Monte Corporation, for example, uses LIFO for domestic inventories and FIFO for foreign inventories. In a recent survey of the 600 largest companies in the United States, the frequency of use for the three costing methods was FIFO 41%, LIFO 36%, and Average 23%.

Allocation of costs—FIFO method

Pool of Costs

Cost of Goods Available for Sale

Date	Explanation	Units	Unit Cost	Total Cost
1/1	Beginning inventory	100	$10	$ 1,000
4/15	Purchase	200	11	2,200
8/24	Purchase	300	12	3,600
11/27	Purchase	400	13	5,200
	Total	1,000		$12,000

Step 1

Ending Inventory

Date	Units	Unit Cost	Total Cost
11/27	400	$13	$5,200
8/24	50	12	600
Total	450		$5,800

Step 2

Cost of Goods Sold

Cost of goods available for sale	$12,000
Less: Ending inventory	5,800
Cost of goods sold	$ 6,200

Note that the ending inventory is based on the latest units purchased. It is possible to verify the accuracy of the cost of goods sold by recognizing that the first units purchased are the first units sold. The computations for the 550 units sold are as follows:

Proof of cost of goods sold

Date	Units		Unit Cost		Total Cost
1/1	100	×	$10	=	$1,000
4/15	200	×	11	=	2,200
8/24	250	×	12	=	3,000
Total	550				$6,200

LAST-IN, FIRST-OUT (LIFO)

The **LIFO method** assumes that the costs of the latest units purchased are the first to be allocated to cost of goods sold. Under a periodic inventory system, which we are using here, **all goods purchased during the period are assumed to be available for the first sale, regardless of the date of purchase.** This means that unit costs of goods purchased in November can be included in the cost of goods sold in the preceding January. The LIFO method seldom coincides with the actual physical flow of goods. Under this method, **the ending inventory is obtained by taking the costs of earliest purchase and working forward until all units of inventory are accounted for.** The allocation of the cost of goods available for sale at Bow Valley Electronics is as follows:

Pool of Costs

Cost of Goods Available for Sale

Date	Explanation	Units	Unit Cost	Total Cost
1/1	Beginning inventory	100	$10	$ 1,000
4/15	Purchase	200	11	2,200
8/24	Purchase	300	12	3,600
11/27	Purchase	400	13	5,200
	Total	1,000		$12,000

Allocation of costs—LIFO method

Step 1

Ending Inventory

Date	Units	Unit Cost	Total Cost
1/1	100	$10	$1,000
4/15	200	11	2,200
8/24	150	12	1,800
Total	450		$5,000

Step 2

Cost of Goods Sold

Cost of goods available for sale	$12,000
Less: Ending inventory	5,000
Cost of goods sold	$ 7,000

As under FIFO, it is possible to prove the cost of goods sold amount obtained from the foregoing steps. The proof in this case is as follows:

Date	**Units**		**Unit Cost**		**Total Cost**
11/27	400	×	$13	=	$5,200
8/24	150	×	12	=	1,800
Total	550				$7,000

Proof of cost of goods sold

AVERAGE COST

The average cost method assumes that the goods available for sale are homogeneous. Under this method, the allocation of the cost of goods available for sale is made on the basis of the **weighted average unit cost** incurred. The formula and computation of the weighted average unit cost are:

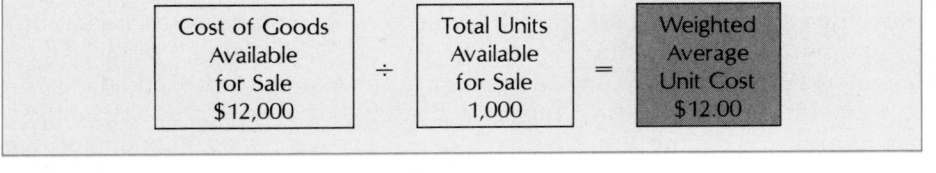

Cost of Goods Available for Sale	÷	Total Units Available for Sale	=	Weighted Average Unit Cost
$12,000		1,000		$12.00

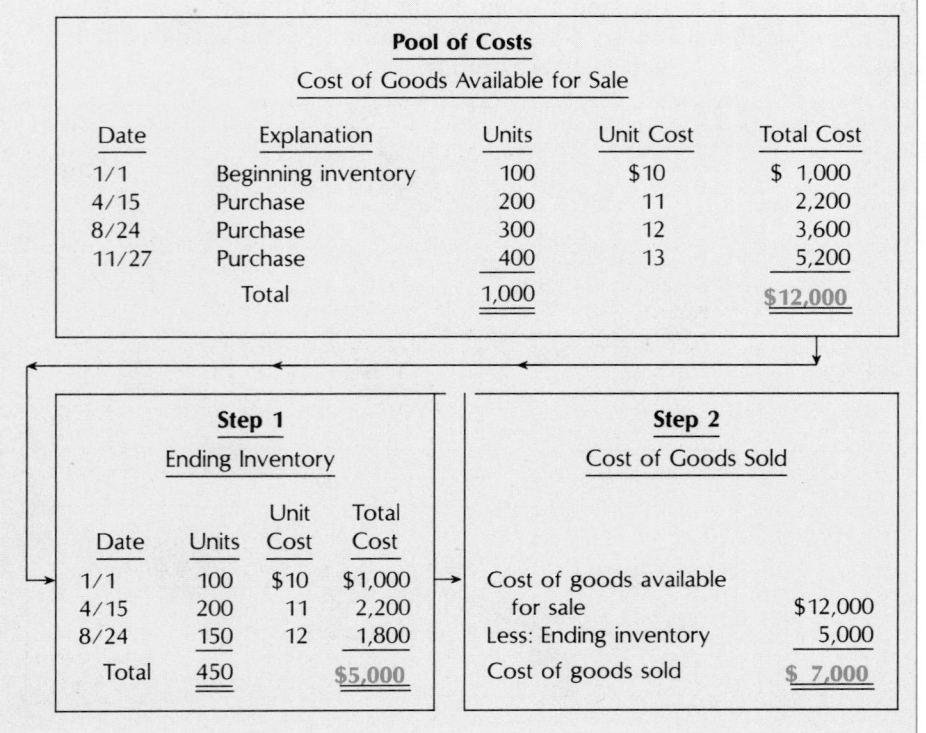

Formula for weighted average unit cost

The average unit cost is then applied to the units on hand to determine the cost of the ending inventory. The allocation of the cost of goods available for sale at Bow Valley Electronics is as follows:

Allocation of costs—average cost method

Pool of Costs

Cost of Goods Available for Sale

Date	Explanation	Units	Unit Cost	Total Cost
1/1	Beginning inventory	100	$10	$ 1,000
4/15	Purchase	200	11	2,200
8/24	Purchase	300	12	3,600
11/27	Purchase	400	13	5,200
	Total	1,000		$12,000

Step 1

Ending Inventory

$12,000 ÷ 1,000 = $12.00

Units	Unit Cost	Total Cost
450	$12.00	$5,400

Step 2

Cost of Goods Sold

Cost of goods available for sale	$12,000
Less: Ending inventory	5,400
Cost of goods sold	$ 6,600

Note that the average of the unit costs is not used in this method. This average is $11.50 ($46 ÷ 4). The correct average is the average weighted by the quantities purchased at each unit cost. The cost of goods sold can be verified easily under the average cost method by multiplying the units sold by the weighted average unit cost ($550 \times \$12 = \$6,600$).

FINANCIAL STATEMENT EFFECTS OF COSTING METHODS

Each of the methods discussed above is acceptable, because each is based on cost. For example, Black and Decker Manufacturing Company and Northwest Industries, Inc. currently use the FIFO method of inventory costing. Campbell Soup Company, Krogers, and Walgreen Drugs use LIFO for part or all of their inventory. Bristol-Meyers and Motorola use the average cost method.

To understand why these companies might use a particular costing method, it is useful to examine the effects of the different flow assumptions on the financial statements of Bow Valley Electronics, Inc. The following condensed income statements assume that Bow Valley sold its 550 units for $11,500; its operating expenses were $2,000; and its income tax rate is 30%.

Comparative effects of costing methods

BOW VALLEY ELECTRONICS, INC.
Condensed Income Statements

	FIFO	LIFO	Average Cost
Sales	$11,500	$11,500	$11,500
Beginning inventory	1,000	1,000	1,000
Purchases	11,000	11,000	11,000
Cost of goods available for sale	12,000	12,000	12,000
Ending inventory	**5,800**	**5,000**	**5,400**
Cost of goods sold	6,200	7,000	6,600
Gross profit	5,300	4,500	4,900
Operating expenses	2,000	2,000	2,000
Income before income taxes[2]	3,300	2,500	2,900
Income tax expense (30%)	990	750	870
Net income	**$ 2,310**	**$ 1,750**	**$ 2,030**

Although the cost of goods available for sale ($12,000) is the same under each of the three inventory costing methods presented, the ending inventories are different. This difference is related to the unit costs that are allocated to cost of goods sold and to ending inventory. In a period of rising prices (as is the case here) FIFO reports the highest net income ($2,310), and LIFO the lowest ($1,750); average cost falls in the middle ($2,030). If prices are falling, the results from the use of FIFO and LIFO are reversed; that is, FIFO will report the lowest net income and LIFO the highest.

SELECTION OF COSTING METHOD

The reasons why companies adopt different inventory costing methods are varied, but they usually involve one of the following:

1. Balance sheet effects.
2. Income statement effects.
3. Tax effects.

BALANCE SHEET EFFECTS

A major advantage of the FIFO method is that in a period of inflation, use of the FIFO method results in a more realistic inventory value. Under FIFO the costs of the most recent purchases are allocated to inventory; therefore, inventory costs stated on the balance sheet are closer to their current cost. Conversely, a major result of LIFO is that the inventory cost on the balance sheet represents the unit cost of goods purchased early in the period or, in some cases, inventory purchased in prior periods. As a result, the inventory

[2]Corporations are required to pay income taxes. As shown, the income statements for corporations show both income before income taxes and income tax expense.

costs may be out of date, and current assets and total assets may be significantly understated in terms of current value.

INCOME STATEMENT EFFECTS

Each dollar of difference in ending inventory results in a corresponding dollar difference in income before income taxes. For example, there is an $800 difference between FIFO and LIFO. In a period of inflation, FIFO produced a higher net income because the lower unit costs of the first units purchased are matched against revenues. To management, higher net income is an advantage that causes external users to view the company more favorably. In addition, if management bonuses are based on net income, FIFO will provide the basis for higher bonuses.

Some argue that the use of LIFO in a period of inflation enables the company to avoid reporting **paper or phantom profit** in terms of economic gain. To illustrate, assume that Bow Valley buys 200 XR492's at $20 per unit on January 10 and 200 more on December 31 at $24 each. During the year, 200 units are sold at $30 each. The results under FIFO and LIFO are as follows:

FIFO and LIFO compared

	FIFO		LIFO	
Sales (200 × $30)	$6,000		$6,000	
Cost of goods sold	4,000	(200 × $20)	4,800	(200 × $24)
Gross profit	$2,000		$1,200	

Under LIFO, the company has recovered the current replacement cost ($4,800) of the units sold. Thus, the gross profit in economic terms is real. However, under FIFO, the company has recovered only the January 10 cost ($4,000). To replace the units sold, it must reinvest $800 (200 × $4) of the gross profit. Thus, $800 of the gross profit is said to be phantom or illusory. As a result, reported net income is also overstated in real terms.

TAX EFFECTS

Even though the inventory amount on the balance sheet and net income on the income statement are both higher when FIFO rather than LIFO is used in a period of inflation, many companies have recently switched to LIFO. The reason is that LIFO results in lower income taxes (because of lower net income) than either FIFO or average cost.[3] For example, at Bow Valley Electronics, income taxes are $750 under LIFO, in comparison with $990 under FIFO. The tax saving of $240 makes more cash available for use in the business.

[3]Note that if LIFO is used for tax purposes, it must be used for financial reporting purposes as well.

DEPARTURES FROM COST BASIS OF ACCOUNTING

During the time goods purchased for resale remain in the company's inventory, the value of the goods may decline. For example, a diet soft drink inventory may become unsalable because the government bans certain ingredients (the use of cyclamates), and an inventory of calculators may cost more than the present selling price of the units because of substantial technological change. Alternatively, if the supply of goods far outweighs the demand for them, the selling price, and often the replacement cost, of the goods will be significantly below its original cost. **Accountants take the position in these cases that a departure from the cost basis is justified because the utility (revenue-producing ability) of the goods is no longer as great as its cost.** The inability to fully recover the cost of the goods represents a loss that should be recognized and reported in the period in which the decline in value occurs, rather than in the period when the goods are disposed of or sold. The measurement of the loss will depend on whether the loss is due to (1) damage or obsolescence or (2) price declines.

DAMAGE OR OBSOLESCENCE

A loss due to damage or obsolescence is measured by the difference between the cost of the unit and its expected net realizable value. **Net realizable value** is expected selling price less the expected costs to be incurred to dispose of the unit. To illustrate, assume Len's TV has ten television sets that are scratched and worn from being used as floor models. Each set cost $250 and originally retailed for $400. At the statement date, each set is expected to be sold for $230; disposal costs are expected to be $20 for repairs plus a 10% commission to the sales clerk. The net realizable value of each TV is $187, computed as follows:

Computation of net realizable value

Expected selling price		$230
Less: Disposal costs:		
Repairs	$20	
Commissions (10%)	23	43
Net realizable value		$187

Accordingly, a loss of $63 (cost, $250 − net realizable value, $187) per set should be recognized, and the total amount of the loss ($630) should be reported in the income statement of the current period. This result is justified because the loss (decline in value) was suffered during the period in which the goods were held. The entry to record the loss is:

Loss on Writedown of Inventories	630	
Inventory		630
(To write TV sets down to net realizable value)		

The loss is reported under other expenses and losses in the income statement. In the following period, assuming the expected net realizable value is received when the TV sets are sold, no gain or loss is reported.

PRICE DECLINES

The utility value of goods on hand may be impaired when there is a decline in the selling price of the goods. For example, if a grocery store has a quantity of apples on hand that were purchased at a cost of 30 cents a pound, and the replacement cost is currently 20 cents a pound because of a bumper apple crop, the store may not be able to realize its anticipated gross profit when the apples on hand are sold. In such case the company may use the **lower of cost or market basis (LCM)** of accounting for inventories rather than the cost basis. Under LCM, the inventory is recorded at cost or market value, whichever is lower. Market, in such cases, is measured by the **current replacement cost** of the goods which is the cost to replace the inventory item by purchase or reproduction.[4]

To illustrate, assume that Len's TV typically sells video cassette recorders (VCRs) costing $300 for $500. At the balance sheet date, the current replacement cost of the VCRs has dropped 20% to $240 [$300 − (20% × $300)]. Under LCM, Len's TV should recognize a decline in utility of $60 ($300 − $240) on each VCR in the current year. If Len has 10 VCRs in inventory at the end of the year, the following entry is made.

Dec. 31	Loss on Writedown of Inventories	600	
	Inventory		600
	(To write VCRs down to market under LCM basis)		

As soon as the inventory is written down to market, this new basis becomes the cost basis for future periods. An increase in the market price of the inventory after it has been written down is not recognized. Many believe that the lower of cost or market method is inconsistent because assets can be written down but cannot be written up.

METHODS OF APPLYING LOWER OF COST OR MARKET

The lower of cost or market basis may be applied to individual items of inventory, major categories of inventory, or total inventory. For example, assume that Len's TV has the following lines of merchandise with costs and market values as indicated. The LCM basis may produce the following three results:

[4]The reason for using replacement cost to represent market is that a decline in the replacement cost of an item usually reflects or predicts a decline in selling price. Using replacement cost therefore allows the company to maintain a consistent rate of gross profit on sales. Also, changes in replacement cost are easy to identify.

			Lower of Cost or Market by:		
	Cost	Market	Individual Items	Major Categories	Total Inventory
Television sets					
Consoles	$ 60,000	$ 55,000	$ 55,000		
Portables	45,000	52,000	45,000		
Total	105,000	107,000		$105,000	
Video equipment					
Recorders	48,000	45,000	45,000		
Movies	15,000	14,000	14,000		
Total	63,000	59,000		59,000	
Total inventory	$168,000	$166,000	$159,000	$164,000	$166,000

Alternative lower of cost or market results

The most common practice is to use individual items in determining the LCM valuation. As illustrated above, this approach gives the most conservative valuation for balance sheet purposes.

ESTIMATING INVENTORIES

Two circumstances explain the reasons for estimating inventories. First, management may want monthly or quarterly financial statements but a physical inventory is only taken annually. Second, a fire or other type of casualty may make it impossible to take a physical inventory. The need for estimating inventories is associated primarily with a periodic inventory system because of the absence of detailed inventory records. There are two widely used methods of estimating inventories: (1) the gross profit method and (2) the retail inventory method.

GROSS PROFIT METHOD

The **gross profit method** is widely used in the preparation of monthly financial statements when physical inventories are not taken. This method is a relatively simple but effective technique of estimation. To use the gross profit method, a company needs to know its sales revenue, cost of goods available for sale and gross profit rate. The formulas for using the gross profit method are as follows:

Use of estimated gross profit method

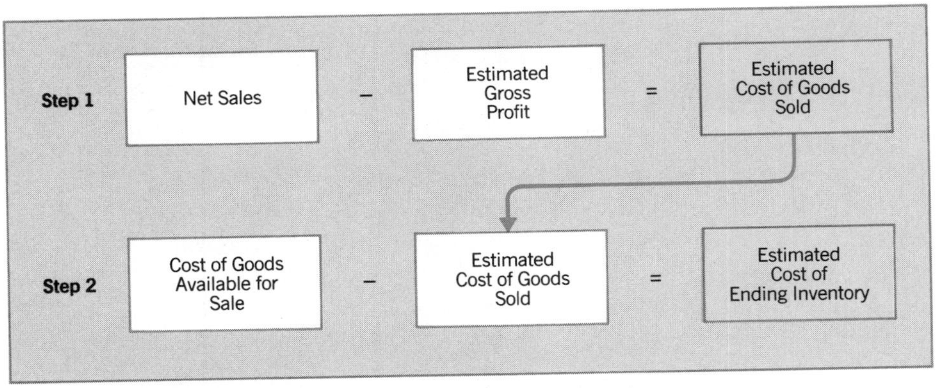

To illustrate, assume that Williams Company wishes to prepare an income statement for the month of January, when its records show net sales, $200,000; beginning inventory, $40,000; and cost of goods purchased, $120,000. In the preceding year, the company realized a 30% gross profit rate, and it expected to earn the same rate this year. Given these facts and assumptions, the estimated cost of the ending inventory at January 31 under the gross profit method is $20,000, computed as follows:

Illustration of gross profit method

	Net sales	$200,000
(1)	Less: Estimated gross profit (30% × $200,000)	60,000
	Estimated cost of goods sold	$140,000
	Beginning inventory	$ 40,000
	Cost of goods purchased	120,000
(2)	Cost of goods available for sale	160,000
	Less: Estimated cost of goods sold	140,000
	Estimated cost of ending inventory	$ 20,000

The gross profit method is based on the assumption that the rate of gross profit will remain constant from one year to the next. When it does not remain constant, either because of a change in merchandising policies or in market conditions, the rate of the prior period should be adjusted to reflect current operating conditions. In some cases, a more accurate estimate may be obtained by applying this method on a department or product-line basis.

The gross profit method should not be used in preparing a company's financial statements at the end of the year. These statements should be based on a physical inventory count.

RETAIL INVENTORY METHOD

A retail store such as K Mart, Ace Hardware, or Wal Mart has thousands of different types of merchandise at low unit costs. In such cases the application of either an actual physical flow or assumed cost flow to the goods would be extremely difficult. As a result, these methods are unsatisfactory when a large volume of goods is involved. An alternative is to compile the inventory at

retail prices and to use the **retail inventory method** to estimate the cost of the inventory. In most retail concerns, an observable pattern between cost and sales price can be established. This cost to retail percentage is then applied to the ending inventory at retail to determine inventory at cost.

To use the retail inventory method, a company must maintain records that show both the cost and retail value of the goods available for sale. The retail data are supplementary; thus they are not journalized and posted. Under the retail inventory method, the estimated cost of the ending inventory is derived from the following:

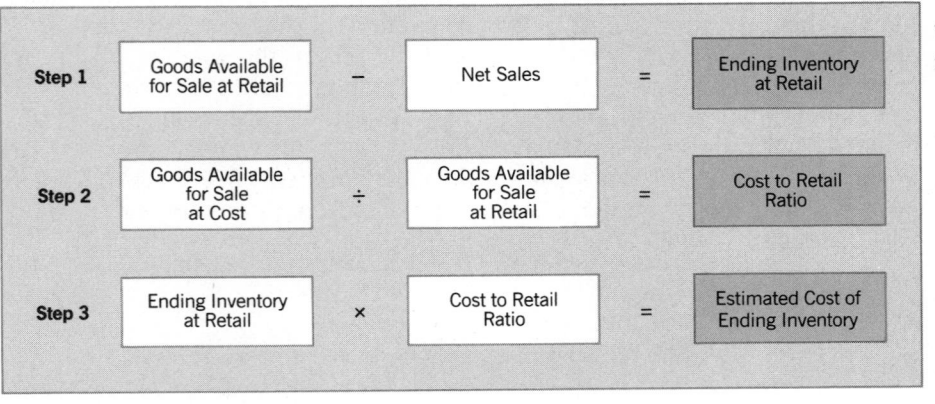

Use of retail inventory method

Step 1	Goods Available for Sale at Retail	−	Net Sales	=	Ending Inventory at Retail
Step 2	Goods Available for Sale at Cost	÷	Goods Available for Sale at Retail	=	Cost to Retail Ratio
Step 3	Ending Inventory at Retail	×	Cost to Retail Ratio	=	Estimated Cost of Ending Inventory

The logic of the retail method can be demonstrated by using unit cost data. Assume that 10 units purchased at $7.00 each are marked to sell for $10 per unit. Thus, the cost to retail ratio is 70% ($70 ÷ $100). If 4 units remain unsold, their retail value is $40 and their cost is $28 ($40 × 70%), which agrees with the total cost of goods on a per unit basis (4 × $7).

The applications of the retail method based on the accounting records and supplementary data for Lacy Inc. is illustrated below.

Illustration of retail inventory method

	At Cost	**At Retail**
Beginning inventory	$14,000	$ 21,500
Goods purchased	61,000	78,500
Goods available for sale	$75,000	100,000
Net sales		70,000
(1) Ending inventory at retail		$ 30,000
(2) Cost to retail ratio = ($75,000 ÷ $100,000) = 75%		
(3) Ending inventory at cost = ($30,000 × 75%)	$22,500	

Note that it is not necessary to take a physical inventory to determine the estimated cost of goods on hand at any given time.

The retail inventory method also facilitates taking a physical inventory at the end of year because the goods on hand can be valued at the prices marked on the merchandise. The cost to retail ratio is then applied to the goods actually on hand at retail to determine the ending inventory at cost. At

this time, a comparison of the actual inventory at retail and the ending inventory at retail computed under the retail method will reveal the goods lost through shrinkage, shoplifting, and other causes. To illustrate, assume that Lacy Company has actual inventory at retail of $28,000. Thus, a $2,000 loss at retail has occurred. The ending inventory at cost becomes $21,000 ($28,000 × 75%), and the cost of the inventory lost is $1,500 ($2,000 × 75%). If the loss is determined to be normal, it is included in cost of goods sold in the income statement. Alternatively, if the loss is abnormal, it is reported under other expenses and losses in the income statement.

The major disadvantage of the retail method is that it is an averaging technique. This may produce an incorrect inventory valuation if the mix of the ending inventory is not representative of the mix in the goods available for sale. Assume, for example, that the cost to retail ratio of 75% in the Lacy Co. consists of equal proportions of inventory items that have cost to retail ratios of 70%, 75%, and 80%, respectively. If the ending inventory contains only items with a 70% ratio, an incorrect inventory cost will result. This problem can be minimized by applying the retail method on a departmental or product-line basis.

PERPETUAL INVENTORY SYSTEMS

Companies that sell merchandise with high unit values, such as automobiles, furniture, and major home appliances, usually use a perpetual inventory system. The **perpetual inventory system** is so named because the accounting

A characteristic of automated accounting systems is the processing of transactions as close to their actual occurrence as possible. You, no doubt, have noticed, in Sears and many other large department stores, the uses of electronic point-of-sales systems. In these systems true real time processing happens when the sale takes place. The cash registers are, in effect, computer terminals. Here is a partial list of the information that can be gathered and processed at the time of an ordinary sale of merchandise on account with such systems.

Verify accuracy of selling price

Check credit standing, alert checker to halt transaction if customer is over credit limit or delinquent.

Identify time and date of sale and type of merchandise being sold for inclusion in sales analysis reports and to update perpetual inventory records.

The use of optical scanning devices permits the gathering of this information faster, more accurately, and less costly than in manual systems that only create paper trails of sales and accounts receivable.

records continuously (perpetually) show the inventory that should be on hand at any time. The accounting features of this type of system are:

1. Purchases of merchandise for resale are debited to Inventory rather than to Purchases.[5]
2. The cost of goods sold is recognized for each sale by debiting Cost of Goods Sold and crediting Inventory.
3. Inventory is a control account that is supported by a subsidiary ledger of individual inventory records. The subsidiary records show the quantity and cost of each item of inventory on hand.

OPERATION OF THE SYSTEM

To illustrate the operation of a perpetual inventory system, we will assume the following purchases and sales of model A2776 solar panels by Astro Energy Inc. during the month of June.

Illustrative data

Cash Purchases at $3,000 each		Cash Sales at $5,000 each	
June 5	10 panels	June 12	3 panels
June 20	2 panels	June 23	4 panels

The entries in general journal form are:

June	5	Inventory	30,000	
		Cash		30,000
		(To record purchase of 10 model A2776 solar panels)		
	12	Cash	15,000	
		Cost of Goods Sold	9,000	
		Sales		15,000
		Inventory		9,000
		(To record sale and cost of goods sold of 3 model A2776 solar panels)		
	20	Inventory	6,000	
		Cash		6,000
		(To record purchase of 2 model A2776 solar panels)		
	23	Cash	20,000	
		Cost of Goods Sold	12,000	
		Sales		20,000
		Inventory		12,000
		(To record sale of 4 model A2776 solar panels)		

These entries are posted to Inventory and Cost of Goods Sold in the general ledger and to the inventory record in the subsidiary ledger.

[5]Other transactions that affect the cost of goods purchased, such as freight and purchase returns and allowances, are also recorded in Inventory.

The general ledger accounts below are presented in columnar form to facilitate the tie in with the subsidiary ledger.

General ledger accounts and postings

Inventory				Cost of Goods Sold			
Date	Debit	Credit	Balance	Date	Debit	Credit	Balance
6/5	30,000		30,000	6/12	9,000		9,000
12		9,000	21,000	23	12,000		21,000
20	6,000		27,000				
23		12,000	15,000				

The posting of the subsidiary ledger record is illustrated below.

Posting of subsidiary ledger inventory record

Item: Solar Panels — Maximum Units: 30

Model No.: A2776 — Minimum Units: 6

	Purchases			Sales			Balance		
Date	Units	Cost	Total	Units	Cost	Total	Units	Cost	Total
6/5	10	$ 3,000	$30,000				10	$ 3,000	$30,000
12				3	$ 3,000	$ 9,000	7	3,000	21,000
20	2	3,000	6,000				9	3,000	27,000
23				4	3,000	12,000	5	3,000	15,000

Note that the subsidiary record is updated after each transaction and that the amounts shown in the Total Balance column equal the balances in the inventory control account. In addition, the units shown in the Balance column should be on hand. The account Cost of Goods Sold is a temporary account that is closed to Income Summary at the end of the year.

A perpetual inventory system contributes to better control over inventories. Since the inventory records show the quantities that should be on hand, the goods can be counted at any time to see whether they actually exist, and any shortages uncovered can be investigated immediately. Further, the maximum quantity shown on the inventory record helps prevent overinvestment in inventory, and the minimum quantity protects the company from losing sales on "out-of-stock" items. A major disadvantage of a perpetual inventory system is the additional clerical work that is involved in maintaining the subsidiary ledger. This difficulty is minimized when a computerized system is used.

INVENTORY COSTING METHODS

The inventory costing methods described earlier for periodic inventory systems also apply to perpetual systems. There is no change in using the specific identification method. However, there are several significant differences in using any of the cost flow assumption (FIFO, LIFO, or Average costing) methods.

1. The pool of costs is the cost of goods available for sale at **the time the sale is made.** This means that the dates of purchases and sales are important.
2. The cost allocation is made each time a sale occurs by determining the costs applicable to the goods sold.
3. Under the average cost method, a new average cost is determined **after each purchase.** Because the average may change with each purchase, the method is called the **moving average method.**

The three cost flow methods are illustrated in Appendix 9–A.

Automated inventory systems are capable of handling any cost flow assumption using either periodic or perpetual procedures. Until recently such systems were found only on mini and mainframe computers. With the increased power of microcomputers, however, these systems are now available for small businesses.

For instance, the IBM model 360 computer led in the business computing market from the mid 1960s through the early 1970s. The 360 cost around $500,000 and had to be installed in climate controlled rooms. Today's IBM PC well exceeds the processing speed and storage capacity of the 360s and costs less than 1% of the original 360 price tag!

INVENTORY ERRORS

Unfortunately, errors occasionally occur in taking or costing inventory. In some cases, errors are caused by failure to count or price the inventory correctly. In other cases, errors occur because proper recognition is not given to the transfer of legal title to goods that are in transit. When errors occur, they affect both the income statement and the balance sheet.

INCOME STATEMENT EFFECTS

As you know, both the beginning and ending inventories appear in the income statement, and the ending inventory of one period automatically becomes the beginning inventory of the next period. Inventory errors may affect the determination of cost of goods sold and net income. The effects of inventory errors on the current year's income statement are tabulated below:

Inventory error—effects on income statement

Inventory Error	Cost of Goods Sold	Net Income
Understate beginning inventory	Understated	Overstated
Overstate beginning inventory	Overstated	Understated
Understate ending inventory	Overstated	Understated
Overstate ending inventory	Understated	Overstated

An analysis of these results indicates that the effect of an error in beginning inventory is exactly the reverse of the same error in ending inventory. It should also be recognized that if an error in ending inventory is not corrected before the end of the next accounting period, it will have a reverse effect on net income of that accounting period. However, the total net income for the two years, and the balance sheet at the end of the second period, will be correct because the errors will counterbalance one another. These effects are tabulated below assuming a $3,000 understatement in the ending inventory of 1987 is not corrected in 1988.

Effects of inventory errors

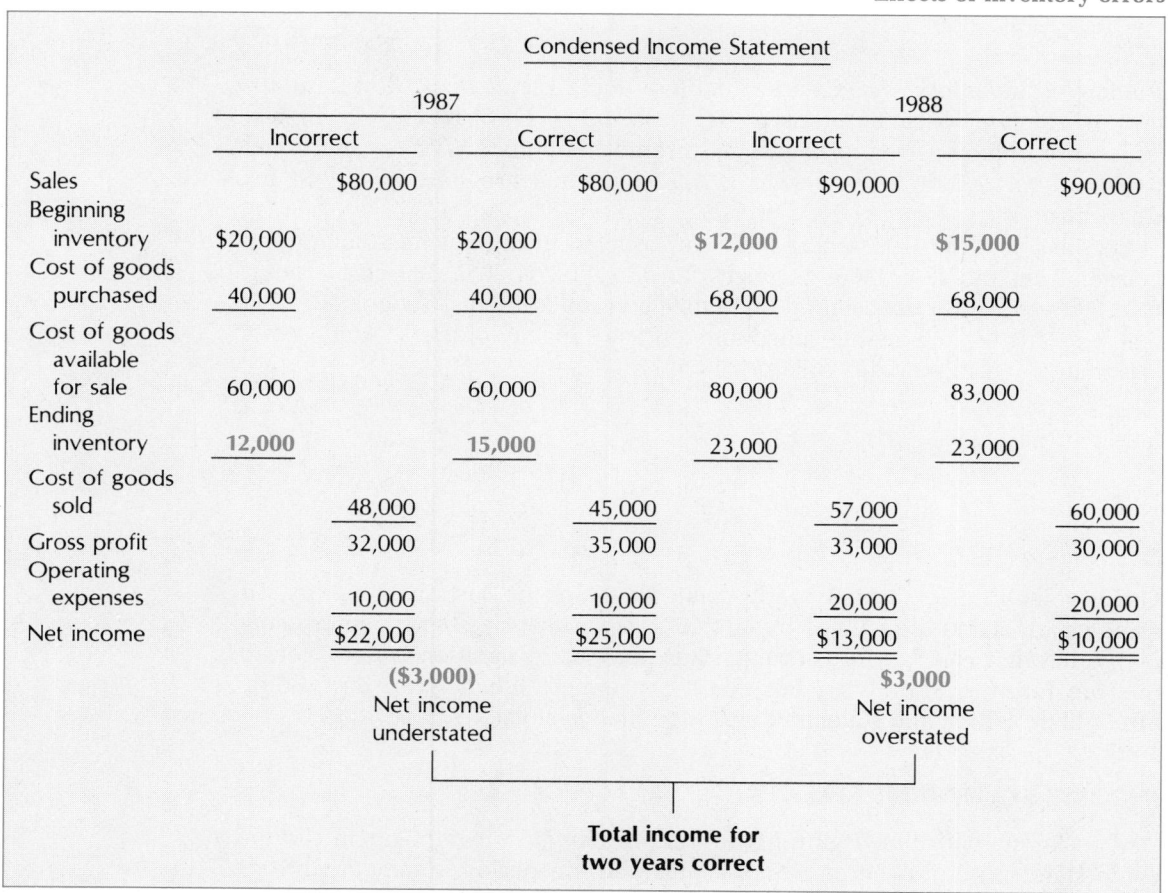

Condensed Income Statement

	1987				1988			
	Incorrect		Correct		Incorrect		Correct	
Sales		$80,000		$80,000		$90,000		$90,000
Beginning inventory	$20,000		$20,000		$12,000		$15,000	
Cost of goods purchased	40,000		40,000		68,000		68,000	
Cost of goods available for sale	60,000		60,000		80,000		83,000	
Ending inventory	12,000		15,000		23,000		23,000	
Cost of goods sold		48,000		45,000		57,000		60,000
Gross profit		32,000		35,000		33,000		30,000
Operating expenses		10,000		10,000		20,000		20,000
Net income		$22,000		$25,000		$13,000		$10,000
		($3,000) Net income understated				$3,000 Net income overstated		

Total income for two years correct

In the illustration above, net income is understated by $3,000 in 1987 and overstated by $3,000 in 1988. Over the two years, total income using the incorrect inventory balance is $35,000 ($22,000 + $13,000), which is the same as the total income using the correct inventory balances, $35,000 ($25,000 + $10,000). Thus, owner's equity at the end of 1988 is correct.

Note also that the error in beginning inventory for 1988 did not result in a corresponding error in the ending inventory for that period. The reason is that a physical inventory is taken at the end of each year and the inventory at December 31, 1988 is correct.

BALANCE SHEET EFFECTS

The effect of ending inventory errors on the balance sheet can be determined by using the basic accounting equation: assets equal liabilities plus owners' equity. Errors in the ending inventory have the following effects on these components:

Ending Inventory Error	Assets	Liabilities	Owners' Equity
Overstated	Overstated	None	Overstated
Understated	Understated	None	Understated

Ending inventory error—balance sheet effects

FINANCIAL STATEMENT PRESENTATION

As indicated in an earlier chapter, inventory is usually classified as a current asset after receivables in the balance sheet, and cost of goods sold is subtracted from sales in the income statement. In addition, there should be disclosure either in the balance sheet or in accompanying notes of (1) the major inventory classifications, (2) the basis of accounting (cost or lower of cost or market), and (3) the costing method (FIFO, LIFO, or average). Colgate-Palmolive Company, for example, reports inventory of $616,067,000 under current assets in a recent balance sheet. The accompanying notes to the financial statements disclose the following information:

Note 1. Inventories
Inventories are valued at the lower of cost or market. The last-in, first-out (LIFO) method is used to value substantially all inventories in the U.S. as well as in certain overseas locations. The remaining inventories are valued using the first-in, first-out (FIFO) method.

Inventory disclosures

SUMMARY OF STUDY OBJECTIVES

1. The steps in determining inventory quantities are: (1) taking a physical inventory of goods on hand and (2) determining the ownership of goods in transit.

2. The primary basis of accounting for inventories is cost. Cost includes all expenditures necessary to acquire goods and place them in condition ready for sale. Inventoriable costs include the invoice price plus freight-in less purchase discounts and purchase returns and allowances.

3. The cost of goods available for sale may be allocated to cost of goods sold and ending inventory by specific identification or by a method based on an assumed cost flow. The first-in, first-out method (FIFO) allocates the cost of the earliest purchases to cost of goods sold and the cost of the most recent purchases to inventory. The reverse is true under the last-in, first-out (LIFO) method. The average method uses a weighted average cost. This method assumes that the goods available for sale are homogeneous.

4. The selection of an inventory costing method is a management decision that usually involves one of the following: (a) balance sheet effects, (b) income statement effects, or (c) tax effects.

5. A departure from the cost basis of accounting is justified when the utility (revenue-producing ability) of the goods is no longer as great as its cost. This may occur when (a) goods are either damaged or obsolete, or (b) price declines.

6. The two methods of estimating inventories are the gross profit method and the retail inventory method. Under the gross profit method, a gross profit rate is applied to sales. Under the retail inventory method, a cost to retail ratio is applied to the ending inventory at retail.

7. Under a perpetual inventory system, (a) purchases of merchandise for resale are debited to Inventory; (b) the cost of goods sold is recognized each time a sale occurs by a debit to Cost of Goods Sold and a credit to Inventory; and (c) inventory is a control account that is supported by a subsidiary ledger of individual inventory records.

8. The effects of inventory errors on net income of the current year are: (a) an error in beginning inventory will have a reverse effect on net income (overstatement of inventory results in understatement of net income); (b) an error in ending inventory will have a similar effect on net income (overstatement of inventory results in overstatement of net income). If ending inventory errors are not corrected in the following period, their effect on net income for that period is reversed, and total net income for the two years will be correct. Ending inventory errors will have the same effect on total assets and total owner's equity and no effect on liabilities.

APPENDIX 9–A

INVENTORY COSTING IN PERPETUAL INVENTORY SYSTEMS

Each of the inventory costing methods described in the chapter for a periodic inventory system may be used in a perpetual inventory system. To illustrate the application of the three assumed cost flow methods (FIFO, LIFO, and Average Cost), we will use the following data for model X268L4 Econo microwaves in the Home Appliance Mart.

Illustrative data

Date	Purchases	Sales	Balance in Units
April 3	4,000 @ $8.00		4,000
April 10	12,000 @ $8.80		16,000
April 26		8,000 units	8,000
April 29	4,000 @ $8.30		12,000

FIRST-IN, FIRST-OUT (FIFO)

Under FIFO, the cost of the earliest goods on hand prior to each sale is charged to cost of goods sold. Therefore the cost of goods sold on April 26 would be made up on the items purchased on April 3 and April 10. The inventory on a FIFO method perpetual system would be as follows:

Perpetual system—FIFO

Date	Purchases		Sales	Balance	
April 3	(4,000 @ $8.00)	$ 32,000		(4,000 @ $8.00)	$ 32,000
April 10	(12,000 @ $8.80)	$105,600		(4,000 @ $8.00) (12,000 @ $8.80)	$137,600
April 26			(4,000 @ $8.00) (4,000 @ $8.80) **($67,200)**	(8,000 @ $8.80)	$ 70,400
April 29	(4,000 @ $8.30)	$ 33,200		(8,000 @ $8.80) (4,000 @ $8.30)	**$103,600**

The ending inventory in this situation is $103,600 and the cost of goods sold is $67,200 ([4,000 @ $8.00] + [4,000 @ $8.80]).

AVERAGE COST

As indicated in the chapter, this method is called the **moving average method** in a perpetual inventory system. Under this method a new average is computed **after each purchase.** The average cost is computed by dividing the cost of goods available for sale by the units on hand. The average cost is then applied to: (1) the units sold to determine the cost of goods sold, and (2) the remaining units on hand, to determine the ending inventory amount.

The application of the average cost method for Home Appliance Mart is shown below.

Perpetual system—average cost

Date	Purchases		Sales	Balance	
April 3	(4,000 @ $8.00)	$ 32,000		(4,000 @ $8.00)	$ 32,000
April 10	(12,000 @ $8.80)	$105,600		(16,000 @ $8.60)	$137,600
April 26			8,000 @ $8.60 (**$68,800**)	(8,000 @ $8.60)	$ 68,800
April 29	(4,000 @ $8.30)	$ 33,200		(12,000 @ $8.50)	**$102,000**

As indicated above, a new average is computed each time a purchase is made. On April 10, after 12,000 units are purchased for $105,600, 16,000 units costing $137,600 ($32,000 + $105,600) are on hand. The average unit cost is $137,600 divided by 16,000, or $8.60. This unit cost is used in costing withdrawals until another purchase is made, when a new unit cost is computed. Accordingly, the cost of the 8,000 units withdrawn on April 26 is shown at $8.60, a total cost of goods sold of $68,800. On April 29, following the purchase of 4,000 units for $33,200, a new unit cost of $8.50 is determined for an ending inventory of $102,000.

LAST-IN, FIRST-OUT (LIFO)

Under the LIFO method using a perpetual system, the most recent purchase prior to sale is allocated to the units sold. Therefore, the cost of the goods sold on April 26 is made up entirely from the April 10 purchase. The perpetual inventory on a LIFO method is computed as follows:

Perpetual system—LIFO

Date	Purchases		Sales	Balance	
April 3	(4,000 @ $8.00)	$ 32,000		(4,000 @ $8.00)	$ 32,000
April 10	(12,000 @ $8.80)	$105,600		(4,000 @ $8.00) (12,000 @ $8.80)	$137,600
April 26			8,000 @ $8.80 (**$70,400**)	(4,000 @ $8.00) (4,000 @ $8.80)	$ 67,200
April 29	(4,000 @ $8.30)	$ 33,200		(4,000 @ $8.00) (4,000 @ $8.80) (4,000 @ $8.30)	**$100,400**

The ending inventory in this situation is $100,400 and the cost of goods sold is $70,400. The LIFO periodic will usually differ from the LIFO perpetual because in a periodic system the latest costs incurred during a period are the first allocated to the cost of goods sold. Thus, when a purchase is made after the last sale for the period, the periodic method will apply this purchase to the previous sale.

GLOSSARY

Average cost method, p. 353
Current replacement cost, p. 358
First-in, first-out method (FIFO), p. 351
Gross profit method, p. 359
Inventoriable costs, p. 349
Inventory summary sheets, p. 348
Last-in, first-out method (LIFO), p. 352
Lower of cost or market basis (LCM), p. 358
Net realizable value, p. 357
Perpetual inventory system, p. 362
Retail inventory method, p. 361
Specific identification method, p. 350

DEMONSTRATION PROBLEM

The Helmers Company has the following inventory, purchases, and sales data for the month of March:

Inventory, March 1		200 units @ $4.00	$ 800
Purchases:			
	March 10	500 units @ $4.50	2,250
	March 20	400 units @ $4.75	1,900
	March 30	300 units @ $5.00	1,500
Sales:			
	March 15	500 units	
	March 25	400 units	

Helmers Company uses a periodic inventory system. The physical inventory count on March 31 shows 500 units on hand.

INSTRUCTIONS

Determine the cost of inventory on hand at March 31 and the cost of goods sold for March under the (a) First-in first-out (FIFO) method, (b) Last-in first out (LIFO) method, and (c) Average Cost Method.

SOLUTION TO DEMONSTRATION PROBLEM

The cost of goods available for sale is $6,450:

Inventory		200 units @ $4.00	$ 800
Purchases:			
	March 10	500 units @ $4.50	2,250
	March 20	400 units @ $4.75	1,900
	March 30	300 units @ $5.00	1,500
Total cost of goods available for sale			$6,450

The allocation of the pool of costs is as follows:

FIFO Method

Ending Inventory:

Date	Units	Unit Cost	Total Cost	
March 30	300	$5.00	1,500	
March 20	200	4.75	950	$2,450

Cost of goods sold: $6,450 − $2,450 = $4,000

LIFO Method

Ending Inventory:

Date	Units	Unit Cost	Total Cost	
March 1	200	$4.00	800	
March 10	300	4.50	$1,350	$2,150

Cost of goods sold: $6,450 − $2,150 = $4,300

Average Cost Method

Weighted average unit cost: $6,450 ÷ 1,400 = $4.607

Inventory: 500 × $4.607 = $2,303.50

Cost of goods sold: $6,450.00 − $2,303.50 = $4,146.50

***Note:** All **asterisked** Questions, Exercises, and Problems relate to material contained in the appendix to each chapter.

QUESTIONS

1. The key to successful business operations is effective inventory management. Do you agree? Explain.

2. An item must possess two characteristics to be classified as inventory. What are these two characteristics?

3. Your friend, Terry, has been hired to help take the physical inventory in Lavey's True-Value Hardware Store. Explain to Terry what this job will entail.

4. The Kay Company ships merchandise to Mark Corporation on December 30. The merchandise reaches the buyer on January 5. Indicate the terms of sale that will result in the goods being included in (a) Kay's December 31 inventory, and (b) Mark's December 31 inventory.

5. Phillip's Hat Shop received a shipment of hats for which it paid the wholesaler $2,940. The price of the hats was $3,000, but Phillip's was given a $60 purchase discount and required to pay freight charges of $50. In addition, Phillip's paid $100 to cover the travel expenses of an employee who negotiated the purchase of the hats. What amount should Phillip's include in inventory? Why?

6. What is the primary basis of accounting for inventories? What is the major objective in accounting for inventories? What accounting principles are involved here?

7. Joe Jenson believes that the allocation of inventoriable costs should be based on the actual physical flow of the goods. Explain to Joe why this may be both impractical and inappropriate.

8. The selection of an inventory cost method is an accounting decision. Do you agree? Explain. Once a method has been selected, what accounting requirement applies?

9. Which assumed cost flow inventory costing method:

(a) Usually parallels the actual physical flow of merchandise?

(b) Assumes that goods available for sale during an accounting period are homogeneous?

(c) Assumes that the latest units purchased are the first to be sold?

10. In a period of rising prices, the inventory reported in Senco Company's balance sheet is close to the current cost of the inventory, whereas Madison Company's inventory is considerably below its current cost. Identify the inventory costing method being used by each company. Which company has probably been reporting the higher gross profit?

11. Jewitt Corporation has been using the FIFO costing method during a prolonged period of inflation. During the same time period, Jewitt has been paying out all of its net income as dividends. What adverse effects may result from this policy?

12. Sandy Steib is studying for the next accounting midterm examination. What should Sandy know about (a) departing from the cost basis of accounting for inventories, and (b) the meaning and applicability of the terms "net realizable value" and "current replacement cost"?

13. At December 31, Fineline Furniture has two sofas costing $400 each. The sofas, which originally retailed for $700 each, will be marked to sell for $370 each because they are damaged. If a 5% sales commission is paid upon sale, at what amount should the two sofas be reported on the December 31 balance sheet?

14. At the balance sheet date, Jeff's Music Store has a stereo costing $600 that normally sells for $900. Jeff's cost to replace the stereo has decreased 25%, and the selling price is expected also to decline 25%. At what amount should the stereo be reported on the balance sheet under the lower of cost or market basis?

15. Why is it necessary to estimate inventories?

16. Both the gross profit method and the retail inventory method are based on aver-

ages. For each method, indicate the average used, how it is determined, and how it is applied.

17. Endluck Company has net sales of $360,000 and cost of goods available for sale of $300,000. If the gross profit rate is 25%, what is the estimated cost of the ending inventory? Show computations.

18. The London Shoe Shop had goods available for sale in 1987 with a retail price of $120,000. The cost of these goods was $90,000. If sales during the period were $100,000, what is the ending inventory at cost using the retail inventory method?

19. Mark Mitchell is uncertain about the accounting features of a perpetual inventory system. Explain these features to Mark.

20. Brenda Baron believes a perpetual inventory system requires a great deal of work for only marginal benefit. Explain to Brenda the advantages of a perpetual inventory system.

21. Huber Company discovers in 1987 that its ending inventory at December 31, 1986, was $5,000 understated. What effect will this error have on (a) 1986 net income, (b) 1987 net income, and (c) the combined net income for the two years?

22. The Peron Company's balance sheet shows Inventories $162,800. What additional disclosures should be made?

***23.** When perpetual inventory records are kept, the results under the FIFO and LIFO methods are the same as they would be in a periodic inventory system. Do you agree? Explain.

***24.** How does the average method of inventory costing differ between a perpetual inventory system and a periodic inventory system?

EXERCISES

E9-1 State Bank and Trust is considering giving the Burns Company a loan. Before doing so, they decide that further discussions with Burns's accountant may be desirable. One area of particular concern is the inventory account, which has a year-end balance of $295,000. Discussions with the accountant reveal the following:

1. The physical count of the inventory did not include goods costing $95,000 that were shipped to Burns FOB destination on December 27, and were still in transit at year-end.
2. Burns sold goods costing $35,000 to Peking Company FOB shipping point on December 28. The goods are not expected to arrive in China until January 12. The goods were not included in the physical inventory because they were not in the warehouse.
3. Burns received goods costing $20,000 on January 2. The goods were shipped FOB shipping point on December 26 by Cellar Co. The goods were not included in the physical count.

4. Burns sold goods costing $42,000 to Sterling of Canada FOB destination on December 30. The goods were received in Canada on January 8. They were not included in Burns's physical inventory.
5. Burns received goods costing $32,000 on January 4. The goods were shipped January 2, terms FOB shipping point.
6. Burns received goods costing $36,000 on January 2 that were shipped FOB destination on December 29. The shipment was a rush order that was supposed to arrive December 31. This purchase was included in the ending inventory of $295,000.

INSTRUCTIONS

Determine the correct inventory amount on December 31.

E9-2 Ashland Inc., which uses the periodic inventory system, records the following information for May 1987.

		Units	Unit Cost
May 1	Beginning Inventory	30	$ 8
May 5	Sale	20	
May 7	Sale	7	
May 8	Purchase	25	$10
May 10	Purchase	35	$13
May 20	Sale	50	

INSTRUCTIONS

Compute the ending inventory at May 31, using (a) FIFO, (b), LIFO, (c) weighted average cost. Prove the amount reported for cost of goods sold under each costing method.

E9-3 Chan Sales Company reported the following information for the month of May:

		Units	Cost	Total
5/1	Beginning inventory	300	$5	$1,500
5/12	Purchases	200	6	1,200
5/18	Purchases	300	7	2,100
	Total	800		$4,800

During the month, 600 units were sold.

INSTRUCTIONS

(a) Which inventory costing method gives the highest ending inventory? Why?

(b) Which inventory costing method results in the highest cost of goods sold? Why?

(c) Compute the ending inventory and cost of goods sold under the weighted average method.

E9-4 Wright Toon, the owner of the Melody Music Store, wants to know whether the following inventory items should be reported at cost in preparing financial statements at December 31, 1987.

1. Two pianos costing $2,500 each are scratched and worn from being used as floor models. The pianos originally retailed at $5,000 each. They are expected to sell for $3,000 each less sales commissions of 20% of sales.
2. One organ costing $4,000 has been used as a floor model since December 1. The original selling price of the organ was $7,500. At December 31, the organ is marked to sell for $6,000; sales commissions will be 15% of sales.

3. Six guitars costing $500 each are on hand. They have not been used as floor models. The guitars were expected to sell for $800 each. At December 31, the current replacement cost of each guitar is $400.

INSTRUCTIONS

(a) Indicate the circumstances in which there may be a departure from the cost basis in reporting inventories.

(b) Indicate the amount of the loss, if any, on writedown of inventories in each situation described above.

(c) Give the entry to record the loss on the writedown of the pianos.

E9–5 Copps Cameras uses the lower of cost or market basis for its inventory. The following data are available at December 31, 1987.

Item	Units	Unit Cost	Market
Cameras			
Minolta	5	$175	$160
Canon	7	150	155
Pentax	9	200	170
Light Meters			
Vivitar	12	125	110
Kodak	10	110	135

INSTRUCTIONS

Determine the amount of the ending inventory by applying the lower of cost or market basis to (a) individual items, (b) inventory categories, and (c) the total inventory.

E9–6 The inventory of the Sparma Company was destroyed by fire on March 1. From an examination of the accounting records, the following data for the first two months of the year are obtained: Sales $51,000, Sales Returns and Allowances $1,000, Purchases $28,000, Freight-in $1,200, and Purchases Returns and Allowances $1,400.

INSTRUCTIONS

Determine the merchandise lost by fire, assuming

(a) A beginning inventory of $20,000 and a gross profit rate of 25% on net sales;

(b) A beginning inventory of $25,000 and a gross profit rate of 30% on net sales.

E9–7 The Arbor Shoe Store uses the retail inventory method for its two departments: Women's Shoes and Men's Shoes. The following information for each department is obtained:

Item	Women's Department	Men's Department
Beginning inventory at cost	$32,000	$46,600
Cost of goods purchased at cost	48,000	52,000
Net sales	84,000	90,000
Beginning inventory at retail	45,000	60,000
Cost of goods purchased at retail	80,000	85,000

INSTRUCTIONS

Compute the estimated cost of the ending inventory for each department under the retail inventory method.

E9–8 On September 1, Sharp Office Supply had an inventory of 10 high-speed deluxe pocket calculators at a cost of $15 each. The company uses a perpetual inventory system. During September, the following transactions and events occurred.

Sept.	2	Purchased 90 calculators at $15 each from Digital Inc., terms n/30.
	5	Received credit of $60 for the return of four calculators purchased on September 2 that were defective.
	8	Sold 50 calculators for $25 each to University Bookstore, terms 2/10, n/30.
	12	Sold 30 calculators for $25 each to Hilltop Card Shop, terms n/30.
	20	Purchased 20 calculators at $14 each from Sterling Electronics, terms n/30.
	22	Paid freight of $20 on September 20 purchase.
	30	Determined that there were 36 calculators on hand.

INSTRUCTIONS

(a) Journalize the September transactions and events.

(b) Post the transactions to the inventory and cost of goods sold accounts.

E9–9 Carson Clothiers made the following cost of goods sold determinations during the past 4 years:

	1984	1985	1986	1987
Beginning inventory	$20,000	$ 25,000	$ 30,000	$ 30,000
Cost of goods purchased	50,000	90,000	75,000	80,000
Cost of goods available for sale	70,000	115,000	105,000	110,000
Ending inventory	25,000	30,000	30,000	12,000
Cost of goods sold	$45,000	$ 85,000	$ 75,000	$ 98,000

The following additional information is available:

1. Carson failed to record purchases of $25,000 in 1984.
2. The 1984 ending inventory was overstated $8,000 because of an error in taking the physical inventory.
3. The 1985 ending inventory did not include inventory costing $12,000 that was purchased FOB destination and in transit at year-end.
4. The 1986 ending inventory included goods costing $10,000 that were shipped on December 30 to Fever Fanatics FOB shipping point and were still in transit at year-end.

INSTRUCTIONS

Compute the revised cost of goods sold for each period.

E9–10 The Benson Company reported the following information over a four-year period.

	1984	1985	1986	1987
Sales	$210,000	$250,000	$300,000	$320,000
Cost of goods sold				
Beginning inventory	32,000	40,000	52,000	63,000
Cost of goods purchased	173,000	202,000	235,000	250,000
Cost of goods available for sale	205,000	242,000	287,000	313,000
Ending inventory	40,000	52,000	63,000	67,000
Cost of goods sold	165,000	190,000	224,000	246,000
Gross profit	$ 45,000	$ 60,000	$ 76,000	$ 74,000

The company uses a periodic inventory system. The inventories on January 1, 1984, and December 31, 1987, were correct. However, in reporting the results above, the accountant made the following errors in determining other ending inventories. These errors have not been corrected in a subsequent period.

Year	Error in Ending Inventory
1984	$4,000 understatement
1985	5,000 understatement
1986	3,000 overstatement

INSTRUCTIONS

(a) Prepare revised income statement data for each of the four years.

(b) What is the cumulative effect of the errors on total gross profit for the four-year period? Provide quantitative proof for your answer.

***E9-11** The Tanona Appliance Company uses a perpetual inventory system. For its model B4765 25″ television sets, the January 1 inventory was 4 sets at $600 each. During January, the following purchases and sales were made.

Purchases			Sales	
Date	Units	Unit Cost	Date	Units
Jan. 10	5	$642	Jan. 8	2
20	2	660	15	3
			27	2

Management sets the maximum units at 15 and the minimum units at 2.

INSTRUCTIONS

Compute the ending inventory under (1) FIFO, (2) LIFO, and (3) Average Cost.

PROBLEMS

P9-1 Foy Sales Company had a beginning inventory on January 1 of 100 units of Product SXL at a cost of $20 per unit. During the year, the following purchases and sales were made.

Purchases		Sales	
Mar. 15	300 units at $24	Apr. 10	200
July 20	300 units at 25	Aug. 20	300
Sept. 4	200 units at 28	Nov. 18	150
Dec. 2	100 units at 30	Dec. 12	200

The selling price was $40 per unit. Foy Company uses a periodic inventory system.

INSTRUCTIONS

(a) Determine the cost of goods available for sale.

(b) Determine (1) the ending inventory, and (2) the cost of goods sold under each of the assumed cost flow methods (FIFO, LIFO, and average). Prove the accuracy of the cost of goods sold under the FIFO and LIFO methods.

(c) Compute the gross profit under each costing method.

(d) Which costing method results in (1) the highest inventory amount for the balance sheet, and (2) the lowest gross profit for the income statement?

P9-2 The management of Musicland Inc. asks your help in determining the comparative effects of the three assumed cost flow inventory costing methods. For 1987, the accounting records show the following data:

Inventory, January 1 (10,000 units)	$ 35,000
Cost of 110,000 units purchased	463,000
Selling price of 95,000 units sold	665,000
Operating expenses	110,000

Units purchased consisted of 40,000 units at $4.00 on May 10; 50,000 units at $4.20 on August 15; and 20,000 units at $4.65 on November 20. Income taxes are 30%.

INSTRUCTIONS

(a) Compute the ending inventory and cost of goods sold under FIFO, LIFO, and average cost.

(b) Prepare comparative condensed income statements for 1987 under FIFO, LIFO, and average cost.

(c) Answer the following questions for management:

(1) Which inventory costing method produces the most meaningful inventory amount for the balance sheet? Why?

(2) Which inventory costing method produces the most meaningful net income? Why?

(3) Which inventory costing method is most likely to approximate actual physical flow of the goods? Why?

(4) How much additional cash will be available for management under LIFO than under FIFO? Why?

(5) How much of the gross profit under FIFO is illusionary in comparison with the gross profit under LIFO?

P9-3 The president and owner of Superior Appliance Company wants more information about the lower of cost or market basis for inventories. Selected inventory records show the following data at December 31 for inventory items expected to be sold in the ordinary course of business. All replacement cost declines are expected to result in corresponding selling price declines.

		Unit Cost in Dollars		
Item	Quantity	FIFO	Average	Market
Home Freezers				
Y296	5	$375	$360	$380
X437	4	400	405	420
Refrigerators				
T417	6	325	320	300
R208	4	350	360	375
Portable TV Sets				
A919	10	250	245	240
H738	6	200	205	190

INSTRUCTIONS

(a) Prepare a schedule showing the inventory valuation under the lower of cost or

market basis, applied to (a) individual items, (b) inventory categories, and (c) the total inventory, assuming that cost is determined by the FIFO method.

(b) Repeat (a) using the average cost method in determining cost.

P9-4 The Amal Company lost all of its inventory in a fire on December 27, 1987. The accounting records showed the following gross profit data for October, November, and December.

	October	November	December (to 12/27)
Sales	$396,710	$432,075	$315,000
Sales returns and allowances	17,100	21,000	12,000
Sales discounts	5,610	6,075	3,000
Beginning inventory	19,500	22,100	29,100
Purchases	297,710	322,675	226,000
Purchase returns and allowances	9,000	11,800	4,000
Purchase discounts	4,520	8,577	6,000
Freight-in	2,650	4,402	1,700
Ending inventory	22,100	29,100	?

Amal is fully insured for fire losses but must prepare a report for the insurance company.

INSTRUCTIONS

(a) Compute the gross profit rates for the months of October and November.

(b) Using the average of the two gross profit rates for the months of October and November, determine the estimated cost of the inventory lost in the fire.

P9-5 The Campus Book Store uses the retail inventory method to estimate its monthly ending inventories. The following information is available for two of its departments at October 31, 1987.

	Novels		Paperbacks	
	Cost	Retail	Cost	Retail
Beginning inventory	$ 260,000	$ 400,000	$ 63,000	$ 90,000
Purchases	1,158,000	1,800,000	273,800	375,000
Freight-in	5,000		2,000	
Purchase discounts	15,000		4,000	
Net sales		1,810,000		363,000

At December 31, Campus Book Store takes a physical inventory at retail. The actual retail values of the inventories in each department are: Novels $375,000, and Paperbacks $94,000.

INSTRUCTIONS

(a) If the beginning inventories at cost were computed by the retail inventory method, what were the cost to retail ratios for each department when the cost of the beginning inventory was determined?

(b) Determine the estimated cost of the ending inventory for each department at October 31, 1987, using the retail inventory method.

(c) Determine the cost of inventory lost through shoplifting and other causes in each department for the year, assuming (1) the retail inventory method shows ending

inventories at retail on December 31 of $380,000 for Novels and $100,000 for Paperbacks; and (2) the cost to retail ratios for the year are 65% for Novels and 70% for Paperbacks.

(d) How should the cost of inventory lost be reported in the financial statements, assuming that the loss is considered normal?

P9-6 Income statements of Horne Retailers for a two-year period ending December 31 are as follows:

	1986	1987
Net sales	$900,000	$800,000
Cost of goods sold		
Beginning inventory	265,000	270,000
Cost of goods purchased	565,000	480,000
Cost of goods available for sale	830,000	750,000
Ending inventory	270,000	265,000
Cost of goods sold	560,000	485,000
Gross profit	340,000	315,000
Operating expenses	234,000	210,000
Net income	$106,000	$105,000

The company uses a periodic inventory system. During the two years, the company has had difficulties with goods in transit and the physical inventory at the balance sheet date. Management asks you to review the statements above. Your review revealed the following items:

1. Merchandise costing $11,000 was shipped to a customer on December 31, 1986, FOB shipping point. Before being shipped, the merchandise was included in the December 31, 1986, inventory. The sales invoice for $18,000 was not prepared until January 4, 1987, and it was recorded at that time.
2. On December 31, 1986, goods costing $5,000 were shipped to a customer FOB destination. The goods were not included in the physical inventory. The sale for $8,000 was recorded when the goods were shipped.
3. Merchandise costing $9,000 shipped FOB destination by a vendor on December 12, 1986 was received December 31, 1986, after the physical inventory had been completed. The goods were reported as a purchase on January 3, 1987, when the invoice arrived.
4. Merchandising costing $7,500 was received on January 3, 1988. The goods were shipped by the vendor, FOB shipping point on December 31, 1987. The purchase was not recorded until 1988, and the goods were not included in the December 31, 1987 physical inventory.
5. On December 31, 1987, goods purchased on account for $6,500 were recorded as a purchase because the vendor's invoice had been received. The goods were shipped FOB destination on December 31 and arrived January 4, 1988. The goods were not included in the physical count on December 31, 1987.
6. One of the inventory counts sheets was overlooked on December 31, 1987, which caused the ending inventory to be $4,000 understated.

INSTRUCTIONS

(a) Determine the effects of the items above by completing the following schedule. Itemize each correction to arrive at total corrections.

	Effect On					
	1986			1987		
Item	Net Sales	Ending Inventory	Cost of Goods Purchased	Net Sales	Ending Inventory	Cost of Goods Purchased
Corrections (No. 1-6)	___	___	___	___	___	___
Total corrections	___	___	___	___	___	___
Amount reported	___	___	___	___	___	___
Correct amount	___	___	___	___	___	___

(b) Prepare correct income statements for each year in columnar form.

***P9-7** Hills Auto Sales uses a perpetual inventory system. On March 1, the new car inventory records show total inventory of $147,500 consisting of the following:

Model	Units	Unit Cost
Custom sedans	5	$ 9,500
Station wagons	4	$12,000
Convertibles	3	$10,000
Sports coupes	2	$11,000

During March the following purchases and sales were made. All purchases were on account, and all sales were for cash.

Mar.	5	Purchased three custom sedans for $9,800 each.
	7	Sold two custom sedans for $13,400 each.
	10	Sold two station wagons for $18,500 each.
	13	Purchased two sports coupes for $11,300 each.
	17	Sold two custom sedans for $13,600 each.
	20	Purchased one convertible for $10,500.
	24	Sold three sports coupes for $17,000 each.
	28	Sold two convertibles for $16,000 each.

INSTRUCTIONS

(a) Journalize the transactions, assuming Hills Auto Sales uses the last-in, first-out (LIFO) method of inventory cost.

(b) Post the transactions to the merchandising accounts in the general ledger (Inventory, Cost of Goods Sold, and Sales) and to the four perpetual inventory cards.

(c) Prepare a schedule showing the gross profit and gross profit rate realized on each model and in total. (Round to one decimal point.)

ALTERNATE PROBLEMS

P9-1A The Morton Company had a beginning inventory of 400 units of Product MLN at a cost of $8.00 per unit. During the year, the following purchases and sales were:

Date	Explanation	Date	Explanation
Feb. 20	Purchased 700 units at $9.00	Aug. 12	Purchased 200 units at $11.00
Mar. 10	Sold 600 units at $14.00	Nov. 25	Sold 500 units at $16.00
May 5	Purchased 500 units at $10.00	Dec. 8	Purchased 200 units at $12.00
July 16	Sold 400 units at $15.00		

Morton Company uses a periodic inventory system.

INSTRUCTIONS

(a) Determine the cost of goods available for sale.

(b) Determine (1) the ending inventory, and (2) the cost of goods sold under each of the assumed cost flow methods (FIFO, LIFO, and average). Prove the accuracy of the cost of goods sold under the FIFO and LIFO methods.

(c) Compute the gross profit under each costing method.

(d) Which costing method results in (1) the highest inventory amount for the balance sheet, and (2) the lowest gross profit for the income statement?

P9-2A The management of Raleigh Novelty Inc. is reevaluating the appropriateness of using its present inventory costing method, which is average cost. They request your help in determining the results of operations for 1987 if either the FIFO method or the LIFO method had been used. For 1987, the accounting records show the following data:

Inventories		Purchases and Sales	
Beginning (15,000) units	$34,000	Total net sales (220,000 units)	$845,000
Ending (25,000 units)	62,500	Total cost of goods purchased (230,000 units)	578,500

Purchases were made quarterly as follows:

Quarter	Units	Unit Cost	Total Cost
1	60,000	$2.30	$138,000
2	50,000	2.50	125,000
3	50,000	2.60	130,000
4	70,000	2.65	185,500
	230,000		$578,500

Operating expenses were $142,000, and the company's income tax rate is 30%. In 1986, prices were stable for novelties.

INSTRUCTIONS

(a) Compute the ending inventory and cost of goods sold under the FIFO, LIFO, and average cost methods.

(b) Prepare comparative condensed income statements for 1987 under FIFO, LIFO, and average cost.

(c) Answer the following questions for management:
   (1) Which inventory costing method produces the most meaningful inventory amount for the balance sheet? Why?
   (2) Which inventory costing method produces the most meaningful net income? Why?
   (3) Which inventory costing method is most likely to approximate actual physical flow of the goods? Why?
   (4) How much additional cash will be available for management under LIFO than under FIFO? Why?
   (5) How much of the gross profit under FIFO is illusionary in comparison with the gross profit under LIFO?

P9-3A Selected inventory records of the Easy Appliance Company show the following data at December 31 for inventory items expected to be sold in the ordinary course

of business. All replacement cost declines are expected to result in corresponding selling price declines.

		Unit Cost in Dollars		
Item	Quantity	FIFO	Average	Market
Washers				
W290	5	$395	$360	$390
W430	4	400	410	420
Dryers				
D410	6	335	320	300
D218	4	350	390	375
Microwaves				
M940	10	350	335	340
M730	6	300	305	290

INSTRUCTIONS

(a) Prepare a schedule showing the inventory valuation under the lower of cost or market basis, applied to (a) individual items, (b) inventory categories, and (c) the total inventory, assuming that cost is determined by the FIFO method.

(b) Repeat (a) using the average cost method to determine cost.

P9-4A The Bagozi Company lost 80% of its inventory in a fire on March 25, 1987. The accounting records showed the following gross profit data for January, February, and March.

	January	February	March (to 3/25)
Net sales	$298,000	$275,000	$260,000
Net purchases	212,000	186,000	191,000
Freight-in	4,500	2,900	2,500
Beginning inventory	25,000	17,340	20,440
Ending inventory	17,340	20,440	?

Your review of the records reveals the following errors: (1) $5,000 of January net sales were recorded in February, (2) $8,000 of February net purchases were recorded in March, and (3) the ending inventory at January 31 was understated $6,000.

The Bagozi Company is fully insured for fire losses but must prepare a report for the insurance company.

INSTRUCTIONS

(a) Compute the gross profit rates for the months of January and February.

(b) Using the average of the two gross profit rates for the months of January and February, determine both the estimated total inventory and inventory lost in the fire.

P9-5A Jenkins Department Store uses the retail inventory method to estimate its monthly ending inventories. The following information is available for two of its departments at August 31, 1987.

	Sporting Goods		Jewelry and Cosmetics	
	Cost	Retail	Cost	Retail
Sales		$1,040,000		$1,185,000
Sales returns		(20,000)		(25,000)
Purchases	$675,500	1,066,000	$725,000	1,208,000
Purchase returns	(26,000)	(40,000)	(12,000)	(20,000)
Purchase discounts	(15,360)	—	(9,440)	—
Freight-in	6,000	—	8,000	—
Beginning inventory	47,360	74,000	38,440	62,000

At December 31, Jenkins Department Store takes a physical inventory at retail. The actual retail values of the inventories in each department are: Sporting Goods $75,000, and Jewelry and Cosmetics $64,000.

INSTRUCTIONS

(a) If the beginning inventories at cost were computed by the retail inventory method, what were the cost to retail ratios for each department when the cost of the beginning inventories was determined?

(b) Determine the estimated cost of the ending inventory for each department on August 31, 1987 using the retail inventory method.

(c) Determine the cost of inventory lost as a result of shoplifting and other causes in each department for the year, assuming (1) the retail inventory method shows ending inventories at retail on December 31 of $77,000 for Sporting Goods and $68,000 for Jewelry and Cosmetics, and (2) the cost to retail ratios for the year are 63% in Sporting Goods and 61% in Jewelry and Cosmetics.

(d) How should the cost of inventory lost be reported, assuming that the loss is considered to be normal.

DECISION CASE

On April 10, 1987, fire damaged the office and warehouse of the Trudeau Company. Most of the accounting records were destroyed but the following account balances were determined as of March 31, 1987: Merchandise Inventory, January 1, 1987, $80,000; Sales (January 1–March 31, 1987), $150,000; Purchases (January 1–March 31, 1987), $84,000.

The company's fiscal year ends on December 31, and it uses a periodic inventory system.

From an analysis of the April bank statement you discover cancelled checks of $4,200 during the period April 1–10 for cash purchases. Deposits during the same period totaled $18,500 of which 60% were collections on accounts receivable and the balance was cash sales.

Correspondence with the company's principal suppliers revealed $12,400 of purchases on account from April 1 to April 10 of which $1,800 was for merchandise in transit on April 10 that was shipped FOB Destination.

Correspondence with the company's principal customers produced acknowledgments of credit sales totaling $28,000 from April 1 to April 10. It was estimated that customers owing $4,600 will never be acknowledged or recovered.

The Trudeau Company reached an agreement with the insurance company that its fire-loss claim should be based on the average of the gross profit rates for the preceding two years. The financial statements for 1985 and 1986 showed the following data:

	1986	1985
Net sales	$600,000	$480,000
Cost of goods purchased	428,000	356,000
Beginning inventory	60,000	40,000
Ending inventory	80,000	60,000

Inventory with a cost of $15,000 was salvaged from the fire.

INSTRUCTIONS

(a) Determine the balances in (1) Sales, and (2) Purchases at April 10.

(b) Determine the average gross profit rate for the years 1985 and 1986. (Hint: Find the gross profit rate for 1986 and 1985 and divide by 2.)

(c) Determine the inventory loss as a result of the fire, using the gross profit method.

CHAPTER 10

Austin Community College, Texas

CHAPTER 10

PLANT ASSETS: ACQUISITION AND DEPRECIATION

STUDY OBJECTIVES

After studying this chapter, you should be able to:

1. **Explain the application of the cost principle to plant assets.**
2. **Indicate how the effect of the method of acquiring a plant asset affects its cost.**
3. **Compute depreciation using different methods.**
4. **Describe the procedure for revising periodic depreciation.**
5. **Distinguish between revenue and capital expenditures and prepare the entries for these expenditures.**
6. **State the procedure for computing periodic depreciation after a capital expenditure.**

Plant assets, also called property, plant, and equipment, **plant and equipment** or **fixed assets,** are tangible resources that are used in the operations of the business and are not intended for sale to customers. These assets are generally long-lived and are expected to provide services to the company for a number of years. Except for land, plant assets experience a decline in service potential over their useful lives.

In this chapter, we first explain the application of the cost principle of accounting to plant assets. We then describe and compare the depreciation methods that may be used to allocate this cost over the useful life of the asset. The accounting for expenditures incurred during the useful life of an asset is also discussed. The disposal of plant assets and the financial statement presentation of plant assets are considered in Chapter 11.

IMPORTANCE OF PLANT ASSETS

Many companies have substantial investments in plant assets. In public utility companies, net plant assets (plant assets less accumulated depreciation) often represent more than 75% of total assets. Recently, for example, net plant assets were 79% of Consolidated Edison's total assets and 92% of Pennsylvania Power & Light Company's. In other types of companies the percentages of plant assets to total assets are:

Percentages of plant assets to total assets

McDonald's	86%	Delta Airlines	82%
Marriott Corporation	63%	General Motors Corporation	37%
Dow Chemical Company	43%	Revlon Inc.	26%

In the income statement, the relationship of depreciation expense and maintenance expense to total operating expenses is 10.4% for Consolidated Edison, 9.6% for Delta Airlines, and 6.2% for General Motors.

CLASSES OF PLANT ASSETS

Plant assets are often subdivided into four classes:

1. **Land,** such as a building site.
2. **Land improvements,** such as driveways, parking lots, fencing, and underground sprinkler systems.
3. **Buildings,** such as stores, offices, factories, and warehouses.
4. **Equipment,** such as store counters, shelves and coolers, office furniture, factory machinery, and delivery equipment.

Like the purchase of a home by an individual, the acquisition of plant assets is an important decision for a business enterprise. It is also important for a business enterprise to (1) keep the asset in good operating condition, (2) replace worn-out or outdated facilities, and (3) expand its productive resources as needed. The decline of rail travel in the United States can be traced in part to the failure of railroad companies to meet the first two conditions. Conversely, the growth of air travel in this country can be attributed in part to the willingness of airline companies to observe these essential conditions.

DETERMINING THE COST OF PLANT ASSETS

Plant assets are recorded at cost in accordance with the **cost principle** of accounting. Cost consists of all expenditures necessary to acquire the asset, and make it ready for its intended use. For example, the purchase price,

freight costs paid by the purchaser, and installation costs are considered part of the cost of factory machinery. Expenditures that are unnecessary should be recorded as expenses or losses, as will be illustrated below.

Cost is measured by the cash paid in a cash transaction or by the **cash equivalent price** paid when noncash assets are used in payment. **The cash equivalent price is equal to the fair market value of the asset given up or the fair market value of the asset received, whichever is more clearly determinable.** Once cost is established, it becomes the basis of accounting for the plant asset over its useful life. No attempt is made in accounting to recognize current market or replacement values during ownership of the asset. The application of the cost principle to each of the major classes of plant assets is explained below.

LAND

The cost of land includes (1) the cash purchase price, (2) closing costs such as title and attorneys' fees, (3) real estate brokers' commissions, and (4) accrued property taxes and other liens on the land assumed by the purchaser. For example, if the cash price is $50,000 and the purchaser agrees to pay accrued taxes of $5,000, the cost of the land is $55,000.

All necessary costs incurred in making land ready for its intended use that result in permanent improvements are debited to the Land account. When vacant land is acquired, these costs include expenditures for clearing, draining, filling, and grading. Sometimes the land has a building on it that must be removed to make the site suitable for construction of a new building. In this case, all demolition and removal costs less any proceeds from salvaged materials are chargeable to the Land account. To illustrate, assume that Hayes Manufacturing Company acquires real estate at a cash cost of $100,000. The property contains an old warehouse that is razed at a net cost of $6,000 ($7,500 in costs less $1,500 proceeds from salvaged materials). Additional expenditures consist of the attorney's fee, $1,000, and the real estate broker's commission, $8,000. Given these factors, the cost of the land is $115,000, computed as follows:

Computation of cost of land

Land	
Cash price of property	$100,000
Net removal cost of warehouse	6,000
Attorney's fee	1,000
Real estate broker's commission	8,000
Cost of land	**$115,000**

In recording the acquisition, Land is debited for $115,000 and Cash is credited for $115,000.

LAND IMPROVEMENTS

The cost of land improvements includes all expenditures necessary to make the improvements ready for their intended use. For example, the cost of a new company parking lot will include the amount paid for paving, fencing,

and lighting. These improvements have limited useful lives and their maintenance and replacement are the responsibility of the company. Thus, these costs are debited to Land Improvements and are depreciated over the useful lives of the improvements.

BUILDINGS

All necessary expenditures relating to the purchase or construction of a building should be charged to the building account. When a building is purchased, such costs include the purchase price, closing costs, and real estate broker's commission. Costs to make the building ready for its intended use consist of expenditures for remodeling rooms and offices and replacing or repairing the roof, floors, electric wiring, and plumbing.

When a company constructs a plant, such as the General Motors Saturn automobile facility, cost consists of the contract price plus payments made by the owner for architects' fees, building permits, and excavation costs. In addition, interest costs incurred to finance the project are included in the cost of the asset when (1) a significant period of time is required to get the asset ready for use, and (2) the effects are material in comparison with expensing interest.[1] In these circumstances, interest costs are considered as necessary a cost as the costs of materials and labor. The inclusion of interest costs in the cost of a constructed building is limited to the construction period. When construction has been completed, subsequent interest payments on funds borrowed to finance the construction are debited to Interest Expense.

EQUIPMENT

The cost of equipment consists of the cash purchase price, freight charges, and insurance during transit paid by the purchaser. It also includes expenditures required in assembling, installing, and testing the unit. Sales taxes are a proper addition to cost, but motor vehicle licenses and accident insurance on company trucks and cars are expensed as incurred, because they represent annual recurring expenditures and do not benefit future periods. Payments for damages suffered during transit, assembly, and installation represent unnecessary expenditures and are debited to a loss account. To illustrate, assume that the Lenard Company purchases a delivery truck at a cash price of $12,000. Related expenditures consist of sales taxes $720, painting and lettering $500, motor vehicle license $80, and a three-year accident insurance policy $800. The cost of the delivery truck is $13,220 computed as follows:

Computation of cost of delivery truck

Delivery Truck

Cash price	$12,000
Sales taxes	720
Painting and lettering	500
Cost of delivery truck	$13,220

[1] "Capitalization of Interest Costs," *Statement of Financial Accounting Standards No. 34* (Stamford, Conn.: FASB, 1979).

The motor vehicle license is expensed when incurred and the insurance policy is a prepaid asset. Thus, the summary entry to record the purchase of the truck and related expenditures is:

Delivery Truck	13,220	
License Expense	80	
Prepaid Insurance	800	
Cash		14,100
(To record delivery truck and related expenditures)		

For another example, assume the Merten Company purchases factory machinery at a cash price of $50,000. Related expenditures consist of sales taxes $3,000, insurance during shipping $500, installation and testing $1,000, and repairs of $400 for damages from an installation accident. The cost of the factory machinery is $54,500 computed as follows:

Computation of cost of factory machinery

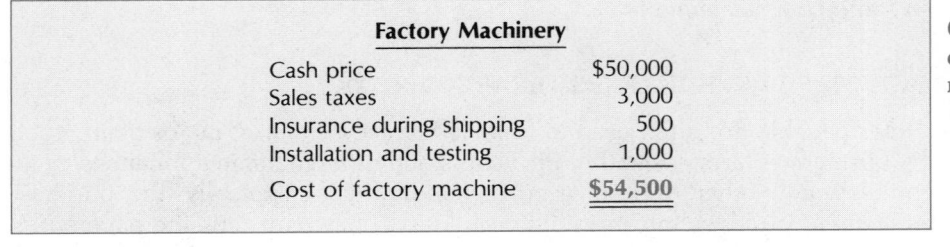

Factory Machinery	
Cash price	$50,000
Sales taxes	3,000
Insurance during shipping	500
Installation and testing	1,000
Cost of factory machine	**$54,500**

The repairs for damages is an unnecessary expenditure that should be debited to a loss account. The summary entry to record the purchase and related expenditures is:

Factory Machinery	54,500	
Accident Loss	400	
Cash		54,900
(To record purchase of factory machine and accident loss)		

The accident loss is reported under other expenses and losses in the income statement.

DETERMINING COST—ADDITIONAL CONSIDERATIONS

The method of acquiring a plant asset sometimes presents problems in measuring the cost of the asset. To highlight the issues, we will consider four different methods of acquisition as follows:

1. Purchase on account.
2. Purchase with interest-bearing note.
3. Lump-sum purchase.
4. Self-construction.

PURCHASE ON ACCOUNT

In a purchase on account, cost is the net invoice price. Thus, if the invoice price of equipment is $10,000 and credit terms are 2/10 n/30, the cash cost is $9,800 ($10,000 − $200 discount), regardless of whether the invoice is paid within the discount period. The purchase should be recorded as a debit to Equipment $9,800 and a credit to Accounts Payable $9,800. If the discount is lost, an unnecessary cost has been incurred, which should be debited to Discounts Lost when it is paid. To illustrate, if payment of the equipment is not made within the discount period, the entry is:

Accounts Payable	9,800	
Discounts Lost	200	
Cash		10,000
(To record payment after discount period)		

Like other losses, Discounts Lost is reported under other expenses and losses in the income statement.

PURCHASE WITH INTEREST-BEARING NOTE

Notes payable are often used to finance the acquisition of major plant assets by business enterprises and in the acquisition of large home appliances, automobiles, and other durable goods by individuals. Typically, the purchase agreement provides for an initial cash (down) payment plus the payment of the face value of the note plus interest at the maturity date of the note. In such cases, the cost of the asset is equal to the initial cash payment plus the face value of the note. The interest expense incurred on the note is considered a financing cost that should be debited to Interest Expense.

To illustrate, assume that the Herns Company purchases equipment for $10,000 by making a $2,000 down payment and signing a 1-year, $8,000 note with interest at 10%. The entry to record the purchase is:

Equipment	10,000	
Cash		2,000
Notes Payable		8,000
(To record down payment and issuance of 1-year, 10% note payable)		

At the maturity date of the note, Notes Payable is debited for $8,000, and the interest of $800 ($8,000 × 10%) is debited to Interest Expense.

LUMP-SUM PURCHASE

A **lump-sum purchase** (often referred to as a basket purchase) occurs when more than one type of asset is acquired in a single transaction. The purchase of a furnished condominium and the purchase of a baseball club are examples of lump-sum purchases. In the former, the purchaser acquires an apartment (building), furniture, fixtures, and drapes; in the latter, the purchaser may obtain a ball park, concession stands, baseball players, uniforms, and equipment. In a lump-sum purchase, the single lump-sum purchase price must be allocated equitably to the individual components. **The most common**

method of allocation is based on the relative fair market values of the individual assets. Assume, for example, that a national hotel chain, such as Hilton or Sheraton, buys a family-owned local motel at a cash cost of $1,200,000 on April 15, 1987. The allocation of the purchase price, using the fair market values of the individual classes of assets, is as follows:

Allocation of purchase price

Asset Class	Fair Market Value	Percent of Total Fair Market Value	Computation (% × Purchase Price)	Cost Allocation
Land	$ 300,000	20%	20% × $1,200,000	$ 240,000
Building	1,050,000	70	70% × 1,200,000	840,000
Equipment	150,000	10	10% × 1,200,000	120,000
	$1,500,000	100%		$1,200,000

The entry to record the lump-sum purchase is

Apr. 15	Land	240,000	
	Building	840,000	
	Equipment	120,000	
	Cash		1,200,000
	(To record purchase of motel)		

Normally, in a lump-sum purchase, the book values of the individual assets on the seller's books are not used, since they are rarely indicative of fair market values at the date of purchase.

SELF-CONSTRUCTION

Some companies construct their own plant assets. For example, a company's maintenance employees may build a garage, enlarge a receiving dock, or construct shelves, storage bins, and similar items. The cost of **self-constructed assets** consists of (1) materials and labor costs incurred, plus (2) other costs such as heat, light, power, and depreciation on company assets used in the construction. In addition, as indicated earlier, a company also includes interest costs on debt used to finance the construction project.

It is not proper, however, for a company to record a profit on its own construction. For example, suppose that the lowest price from an outside contractor on a garage is $50,000 and the self-constructed costs total only $47,000. The amount that should be recorded as the cost of the garage is $47,000. To record the garage at $50,000 and to recognize a gain on construction of $3,000 would be a violation of the cost principle.

CONCEPT OF DEPRECIATION

As explained in Chapter 3, **depreciation is the process of allocating the cost of a plant asset to expense over its service (useful) life in a rational and systematic manner.** The allocation of cost is designed to provide for the

proper matching of expenses with revenues in accordance with the matching principle. Depreciation is not a process of valuation. Accountants make no attempt to measure the change in an asset's market value during ownership because plant assets are not held for resale. Thus, the **book value** (cost less accumulated depreciation) of a plant asset may differ significantly from its market value.

During an asset's life, its usefulness in terms of service and revenue-producing ability will decline because of physical or functional causes. **Physical factors** consist of actual wear and tear. Thus, a delivery truck that has been driven 100,000 miles will be less useful to a company than a truck that has been driven only 800 miles. Similarly, trucks exposed to snow and salt will deteriorate faster than trucks that are not exposed to these elements.

Functional causes of depreciation are inadequacy and obsolescence. **Inadequacy** occurs when the capacity of a facility becomes insufficient to meet the present and future needs of the owner. The rerouting of major airlines from Chicago's Midway Airport to Chicago-O'Hare International Airport because Midway's runways were too short for jumbo jets is an example. **Obsolescence,** on the other hand, occurs when there is no future demand for the asset or facility. For example, diesel train engines made coal-burning locomotives obsolete, and municipal buses sent streetcars to the scrap heap. Functional depreciation need not be accompanied by physical deterioration.

Recognition of depreciation does not result in the accumulation of cash for the replacement of the asset. The balance in Accumulated Depreciation represents the total cost that has been charged to expense; it is not a cash fund.

DEPRECIATION METHODS

Depreciation may be recognized in the accounts and statements through one or more of the following methods: (1) straight-line, (2) units of activity, (3) declining-balance, and (4) sum-of-the-years' digits. Like inventory costing methods, each of these depreciation methods is acceptable under generally accepted accounting principles, and management selects the method(s) it believes to be appropriate in the circumstances. Once a method is chosen, it should be applied consistently over the useful life of the asset to enhance the comparability of financial statements. Depreciation affects the balance sheet through accumulated depreciation and the income statement through depreciation expense.

Periodic depreciation expense is based on three factors: (1) cost, (2) salvage value, and (3) useful life. **Salvage value,** also called residual value, is the expected cash value of the asset at the end of its useful life. **Useful life,** also called service life, is the length of time the company expects to use the asset. Alternatively, this factor may be expressed in terms of total units of activity expected from the asset. Salvage value and useful life are estimated on the basis of a company's prior experience with similar assets. To facilitate comparison of the depreciation methods, all computations will be based on the following data applicable to the purchase of a delivery truck by Barb's Florists on January 1, 1987.

Delivery truck data

Cost	$ 13,000
Expected salvage value	$ 1,000
Estimated useful life in years	5
Estimated useful life in miles	100,000

STRAIGHT-LINE

You may recall that the straight-line method of depreciation was used in Chapter 3. Under the **straight-line method,** periodic depreciation is the same throughout the service life of the asset. The formula for computing annual depreciation expense and the computation for the delivery truck of Barb's Florists are as follows:

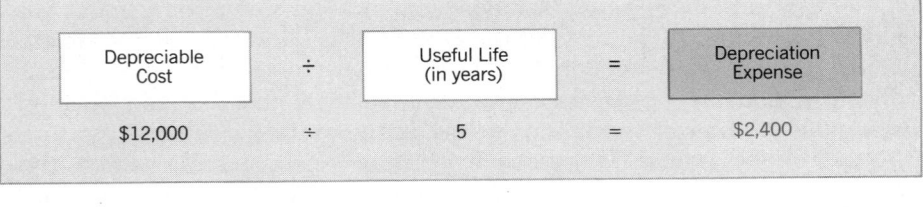

Formula for straight-line method

Depreciable Cost	÷	Useful Life (in years)	=	Depreciation Expense
$12,000	÷	5	=	$2,400

Recall that depreciable cost is cost less salvage value ($13,000 − $1,000). It is also possible to state that the delivery truck is being depreciated at an annual rate. In this case, the rate is 20% (100% ÷ 5). When this depreciation rate is used under the straight-line method, it is applied to the depreciable cost of the asset. For the five-year service life, the depreciation schedule is as follows:

Straight-line depreciation schedule

BARB'S FLORISTS

	Computation				End of Year	
Year	Depreciable Cost	× Depreciation Rate	=	Annual Depreciation Expense	Accumulated Depreciation	Book Value
1987	$12,000	20%		**$2,400**	$ 2,400	$10,600*
1988	12,000	20		**2,400**	4,800	8,200
1989	12,000	20		**2,400**	7,200	5,800
1990	12,000	20		**2,400**	9,600	3,400
1991	12,000	20		**2,400**	12,000	**1,000**

*($13,000 − $2,400).

Note that the depreciation expense of $2,400 is the same each year, and that the book value at the end of the useful life is equal to the estimated $1,000 salvage value.

When the asset is purchased during the year, it is necessary to prorate the annual depreciation for the proportion of time used. If Barb's Florists had purchased the delivery truck on April 1, 1987, the depreciation for 1984 would be $1,800 ($12,000 × 20% × 9/12).

The straight-line method predominates in practice.[2] For example, such large companies as Campbell Soup, Marriott Corporation, and General Foods

[2]A recent survey of 600 corporate financial statements showed that 559 companies use this method for some or all of their depreciable assets.

use this method. The straight-line method is simple to apply, and it matches expenses with revenues appropriately when the utilization of the asset is reasonably uniform throughout service life.

UNITS OF ACTIVITY

Under the **units of activity method,** service life is expressed in terms of the total units of production or use expected from the asset, rather than time. The units of activity method is ideally suited to factory machinery, where the production can be measured in terms of units of output or, alternatively, in terms of direct labor hours or machine hours used in operating the machinery. It is also possible to use this method for such items as delivery equipment (miles driven) and selected types of office and store equipment (hours in use). The units of activity method is generally not suitable for such assets as buildings or furniture, because depreciation is more a function of time than of use. Once the total units of activity for the entire service life have been estimated, the amount is divided into depreciable cost to determine the depreciation cost per unit. The depreciation cost per unit is then applied to the units of activity during the year to determine the annual depreciation.

To illustrate, assume that the delivery truck in Barb's Florists is driven 15,000 miles in the first year. The formulas and computations of depreciation expense in the first year are as follows:

Formula for units of activity method

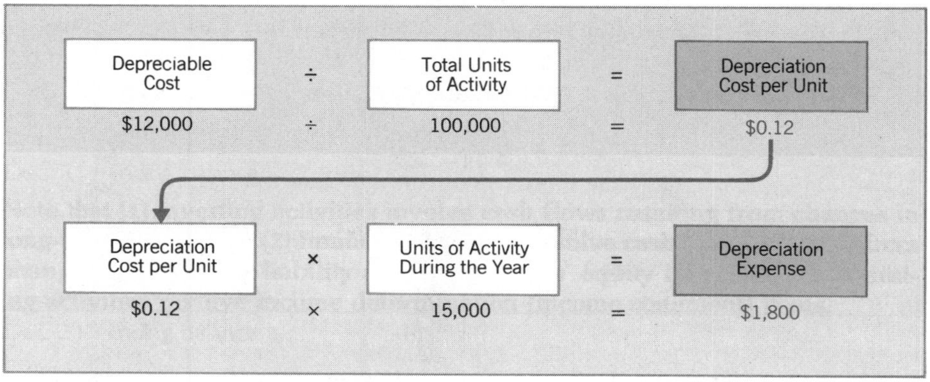

The depreciation schedule, using assumed mileage data, is as follows:

Units of activity depreciation schedule

BARB'S FLORISTS

	Computation				End of Year	
Year	Units of Activity	× Depreciation Cost/Unit	=	Annual Depreciation Expense	Accumulated Depreciation	Book Value
1987	15,000	$.12		**$1,800**	$ 1,800	$11,200*
1988	30,000	.12		**3,600**	5,400	7,600
1989	20,000	.12		**2,400**	7,800	5,200
1990	25,000	.12		**3,000**	10,800	2,200
1991	10,000	.12		**1,200**	12,000	**1,000**

*($13,000 − $1,800)

The units of activity method is not nearly as popular as the straight-line method, primarily because of the difficulty of making a reasonable estimate

of total activity. However, this method is used by some very large companies, such as Standard Oil Company of California and Boise Cascade Corporation. When the productivity of the asset varies significantly from one period to another, the units of activity method results in the best matching of expenses with revenues.

DECLINING-BALANCE

The **declining-balance method** produces a decreasing annual depreciation expense over the useful life of the asset. The method is so named because the computation of periodic depreciation is based on the book value of the asset, which declines each year. Annual depreciation expense is computed by multiplying the book value at the beginning of the year by the constant declining-balance depreciation rate. **The depreciation rate remains constant from year to year, but the book value to which the rate is applied declines each year.** Book value for the first year is the cost of the asset; in subsequent years, book value is the difference between cost and accumulated depreciation at the beginning of the year. Unlike the other depreciation methods, salvage value is ignored in determining the amount to which the declining balance rate is applied. Salvage value, however, does limit the total depreciation that can be taken. Depreciation stops when the asset's book value equals expected salvage value.

A common declining-balance rate is double the straight-line rate, and as a result, the method is often referred to as the double declining-balance method. Assuming that Barb's Florists uses this method, the depreciation rate is 40% (2 × 20%). The formula and computation of depreciation for the first year on the delivery truck are as follows:

Formula for declining-balance method

Book Value at Beginning of Year	×	Declining-Balance Rate	=	Depreciation Expense
$13,000	×	40%	=	$5,200

The depreciation schedule under this method is as follows:

Double-declining-balance depreciation schedule

BARB'S FLORISTS

	Computation				End of Year	
Year	Book Value Beginning of Year	×	Depreciation Rate	= Annual Depreciation Expense	Accumulated Depreciation	Book Value
1987	$13,000		40%	**$5,200**	$ 5,200	$7,800
1988	7,800		40	**3,120**	8,320	4,680
1989	4,680		40	**1,872**	10,192	2,808
1990	2,808		40	**1,123**	11,315	1,685
1991	1,685		40	**685***	12,000	**1,000**

*Adjusted to $685 because ending book value should not be greater than expected salvage value.

From an analysis of the schedule, you can see that the delivery equipment is 69% depreciated ($8,320 ÷ $12,000) at the end of the second year, whereas it

would be depreciated 40% ($4,800 ÷ $12,000) under the straight-line method. Because the declining-balance method produces higher depreciation expenses in the early years than in the later years, it is considered an **accelerated depreciation method.**

The declining-balance method is compatible with the matching principle. The higher depreciation expense in early years parallels the asset's greater earning power. Conversely, lower depreciation expense is recognized in later years when the asset's contribution to revenue is less.

When an asset is purchased during the year, it is necessary to prorate the declining balance depreciation in the first year on a time basis. For example, if Barb's Florists had purchased the delivery equipment on April 1, 1987, depreciation for 1987 would become $3,900 ($13,000 × 40% × 9/12). The book value for computing depreciation in 1988 then becomes $9,100 ($13,000 − $3,900), and the 1988 depreciation is $3,640 ($9,100 × 40%).

SUM-OF-THE-YEARS'-DIGITS

The sum-of-the-years'-digits method (SYD) also results in higher depreciation in the early years and lower depreciation in the later years. Thus, it too is considered an accelerated depreciation method. The **sum-of-the-years'-digits method** is so named because the depreciation rate is based on a fraction in which:

1. The numerator is the years of remaining service life from the beginning of the current year.
2. The denominator is the sum of the individual years that comprise total service life.

For a useful life of 5 years, the sum-of-the-years'-digits is 15 (1 + 2 + 3 + 4 + 5).[3] Annual depreciation is computed by multiplying depreciable cost by the appropriate SYD fraction. The formula and depreciation in the first year for the delivery truck of Barb's Florists are:

Formula for sum-of-the-years'-digits method

Depreciable Cost	×	SYD Fraction	=	Depreciation Expense
$12,000	×	5/15	=	$4,000

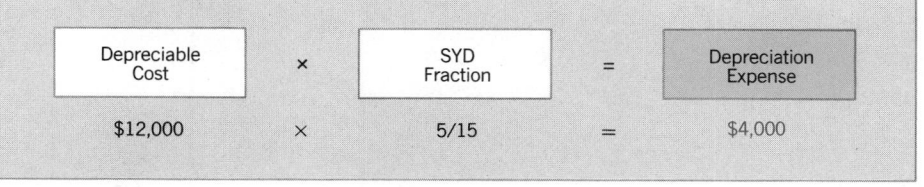

[3]A mathematical formula for this computation is **S** = **N**(**N** + 1)/2, where **N** is the number of years of service life, i.e., **S** = 5 (5 + 1)/2 = 15.

For Barb's Florists the depreciation schedule is as follows:

Sum-of-the-years'-digits depreciation schedule

BARB'S FLORISTS

	Computation				End of Year	
Year	Depreciable Cost	× SYD Fraction	=	Annual Depreciation Expense	Accumulated Depreciation	Book Value
1987	$12,000	5/15		**$4,000**	$ 4,000	$9,000*
1988	12,000	4/15		**3,200**	7,200	5,800
1989	12,000	3/15		**2,400**	9,600	3,400
1990	12,000	2/15		**1,600**	11,200	1,800
1991	12,000	1/15		**800**	12,000	**1,000**

*($13,000 – $4,000)

Note that under the sum-of-the-years'-digits method, the denominator (which for Barb's Florists is 15) remains constant, whereas the numerator decreases each year.

Two well-known companies that depreciate their assets using this method are General Electric and Du Pont. The rationale for using this method is the same as for the declining-balance method.

When an asset is acquired during the year, it is necessary to use the full year SYD fraction and then prorate the amount for the time the asset was used during the year and succeeding year. If Barb's Florists had purchased the delivery truck on April 1, the depreciation for 1987 and 1988 would be $3,000 and $3,400, respectively, computed as follows:

Fractional year's depreciation

1987	1988
$12,000 × 5/15 × 9/12 = $3,000	$12,000 × 5/15 × 3/12 = $1,000
	$12,000 × 4/15 × 9/12 = 2,400
	$3,400

COMPARISON OF METHODS

A comparison of annual and total depreciation expense under each of the four methods is shown below for Barb's Florists:

Comparison of depreciation methods

Year	Straight-Line	Units of Activity	Declining-Balance	Sum-of-the-Years'-Digits
1987	$ 2,400	$ 1,800	$ 5,200	$ 4,000
1988	2,400	3,600	3,120	3,200
1989	2,400	2,400	1,872	2,400
1990	2,400	3,000	1,123	1,600
1991	2,400	1,200	685	800
	$12,000	**$12,000**	**$12,000**	**$12,000**

Observe that periodic depreciation varies considerably among the methods, but total depreciation is the same for the five-year period. Each method is acceptable in accounting, because each recognizes the decline in service po-

tential of the asset in a rational and systematic manner. The depreciation expense pattern under each method is presented graphically below.

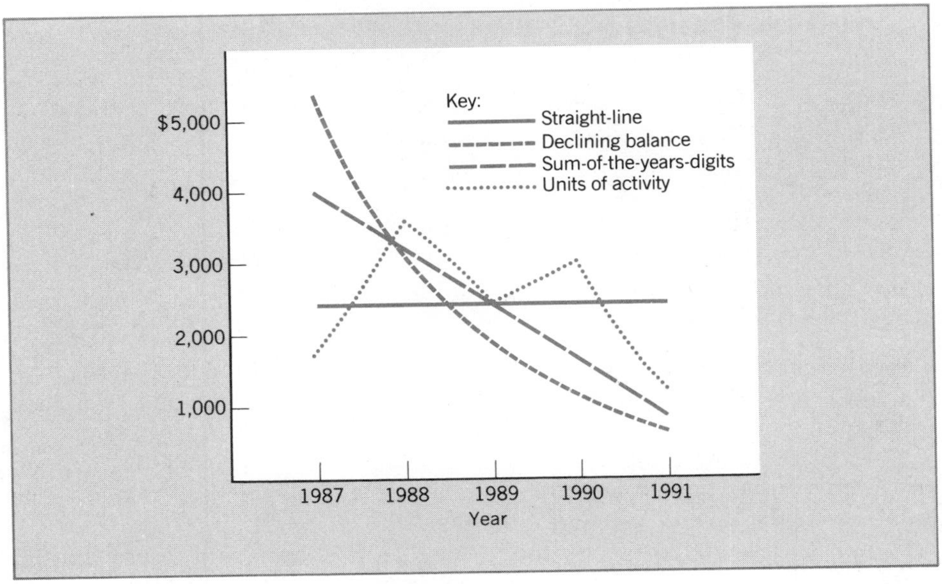

DEPRECIATION AND INCOME TAXES

The tax regulations of the Internal Revenue Service (IRS) do not require the taxpayer to use the same depreciation method on the tax return that is used in preparing financial statements. Consequently, many large corporations use straight-line depreciation in their financial statements to maximize net income, and an accelerated depreciation method on their tax returns to minimize their income taxes.

For tax purposes, taxpayers must use either the straight-line method or a special accelerated depreciation method called **Accelerated Cost Recovery** System (ACRS) on their tax returns. ACRS, as modified by the Tax Reform Act of 1986, is covered in Chapter 29.

REVISION OF PERIODIC DEPRECIATION

Depreciation is one example of the estimation procedures that are inherent in the accounting process. The adequacy of annual depreciation expense should be reviewed periodically by management. If physical or functional factors indicate that annual depreciation is inadequate or excessive, a change in the periodic amount should be made. When a change in an estimate is required,

Computer software programs can compute depreciation using straight-line, declining balance, sum-of-the-years'-digits, and ACRS methods. The programs can also automatically generate the required entries to record depreciation expense.

the change should be made in **current and future years but not retroactively.**[4] This means that at the time of change in depreciation, (1) there is no correction of previously recorded depreciation expense, and (2) depreciation expense for current and future years is revised. The rationale for this treatment is that continual restatement of prior periods would adversely affect the reader's confidence in financial statements.

To determine the new annual depreciable expense, the depreciable cost at the time of the revision is divided by the remaining useful life. To illustrate, assume that Barb's Florists decides on January 1, 1990 to extend the useful life of the truck one year because of the excellent condition of the vehicle. The company has used the straight-line method to depreciate the asset to date and book value is $5,800 ($13,000 − $7,200). The new annual depreciation is $1,600, computed as follows:

Revised depreciation computation

Book value, 1/1/90	$5,800	
Less: Salvage value	1,000	
Depreciable cost	$4,800	
Remaining useful life	3 years	(1990–1992)
Revised annual depreciation ($4,800 ÷ 3)	$1,600	

On January 1, 1990, or at any other time, Barb's Florists makes no entry for the change in estimate. On December 31, 1990, during the preparation of adjusting entries, it would record depreciation expense of $1,600.

EXPENDITURES DURING USEFUL LIFE

During the useful life of a plant asset a company may incur costs for ordinary repairs, additions, and improvements. **Ordinary repairs** are expenditures to maintain the operating efficiency and expected productive life of the unit. They usually are fairly small amounts that occur frequently throughout service life. Motor tune-ups and tire replacements on delivery trucks, the painting of buildings, and the replacing of worn-out gears on factory machinery are examples. These expenditures primarily benefit the current accounting period. Accordingly, they are debited to Repair (or Maintenance) Expense as

[4] "Accounting Changes," *Opinions of the Accounting Principles Board No. 20* (New York: AICPA, 1971) (adapted).

incurred. Because they are immediately charged against revenues as an expense, these costs are often referred to as **revenue expenditures.**

Additions and improvements are costs incurred to increase the operating efficiency, productive capacity, or expected useful life of the asset. These expenditures are usually material in amount and occur infrequently during the period of ownership. Expenditures for additions and improvements increase the company's investment in productive facilities; accordingly, they are often referred to as **capital expenditures.** Most of the major U.S. corporations disclose the amount of their annual capital expenditures. In a recent year, both IBM and General Motors reported capital expenditures slightly in excess of $6 billion. The accounting for capital expenditures varies depending on the nature of the expenditure.

ADDITIONS

An addition generally results in a larger physical unit and increased productive capacity. Additions are debited to the asset account to which the expenditure pertains. Thus, the construction of a new wing to a building is debited to Buildings, and the paneling of the body of an open pickup truck is debited to Delivery Equipment.

IMPROVEMENTS

Improvements, sometimes referred to as betterments, take a variety of forms. In some cases, an improvement results in the replacement of a subunit of a productive asset with a new unit. For example, a factory machine with 10 h.p. electric motor may be improved by replacing the motor with a 15 h.p. motor. Similarly, a complete overhaul of a truck motor and the sandblasting of a brick building to restore its original appearance are improvements.

The cost of improvements should be debited to a plant asset account or to accumulated depreciation. To illustrate, assume that on January 1, 1991, Barb's Florists incurs a $2,000 major repair of the motor on its delivery truck. The improvement will increase the useful life of the truck by one year. Thus, the expenditure has restored (or made good) a portion of the depreciation that has been recorded on the truck. In this sense, accumulated depreciation is overstated by the cost of the capital expenditure. The entry to record the improvement is:

Jan.	1	Accumulated Depreciation – Delivery Equipment	2,000	
		Cash		2,000
		(To record major overhaul of truck motor)		

When an improvement does not increase useful life, the capital expenditure is accounted for as an addition. Assume, for example, that Hawkins Company spends $50,000 to sandblast the exterior of its factory building on March 1. If no increase in useful life is expected, the entry to record the improvement is:

Mar.	1	Factory Building	50,000	
		Cash		50,000
		(To record improvement to building)		

The accounting for improvements that involve major replacements depend on whether the book value of the replaced unit can be readily determined. When the book value cannot be determined, the cost of the improvement is debited to either the plant asset account or to accumulated depreciation as illustrated above. If the book value of the replaced unit can be determined, it is necessary to eliminate the book value and then debit the plant asset account for the cost of the replacement. The entries for this situation are explained and illustrated in the next chapter.

MISCLASSIFICATION OF EXPENDITURES

The failure to distinguish between revenue and capital expenditures will result in incorrect annual financial statements for the remaining useful life of the asset. To illustrate, assume that at the beginning of the second year of useful life, Neal Construction Company makes a $4,000 addition to machinery. The expenditure does not extend the expected total five-year life of the machinery. If the addition is debited to Repair Expense, the following misstatements will result, assuming no salvage value on the addition and straight-line depreciation of $1,000 per year.

Misclassification effects

Year	Repair Expense Overstated	Depreciation Expense Understated	Net Income	
2	$4,000	$1,000	$3,000	(Understated)
3	-0-	1,000	1,000	(Overstated)
4	-0-	1,000	1,000	(Overstated)
5	-0-	1,000	1,000	(Overstated)
Total	$4,000	$4,000	$-0-	

Note that although annual net income is incorrect each year, the four-year cumulative effect on total operating expenses and net income is zero.

CAPITAL EXPENDITURES AND SUBSEQUENT DEPRECIATION

Every capital expenditure should result in additional depreciation over the asset's remaining useful life. The computation is similar to the procedures described earlier for a revision of periodic depreciation. In this instance, however, it is necessary to determine the revised depreciable cost of the asset **after** recording the capital expenditure.

To illustrate, we will use the $2,000 major repair of the truck motor in Barb's Florists. As indicated, this expenditure increased useful life by one year, and we will assume that salvage value is increased by $200. Under the straight-line method, the new annual depreciation for the remaining two years of useful life is $2,100, computed as shown on top of the next page.

At December 31, 1991, Barb's Florists will prepare the following entry for depreciation:

Dec. 31	Depreciation Expense	2,100	
	Accumulated Depreciation – Delivery Equipment		2,100
	(To record annual depreciation)		

Depreciation after capital expenditure

Book value prior to capital expenditure, 1/1/91	$3,400
Add: Cost of capital expenditure	2,000
Book value after capital expenditure	5,400
Less: New estimated salvage value	1,200
Revised depreciable cost	$4,200
Remaining useful life	2 years (1991-1992)
Revised annual depreciation ($4,200 ÷ 2)	$2,100

SUMMARY OF STUDY OBJECTIVES

1. The cost of plant assets includes all expenditures necessary to acquire the asset and make it ready for its intended use. Cost is measured by the cash or cash equivalent price paid.

2. When plant assets are purchased on account, cost equals the net invoice cost (invoice cost less available purchase discount). In a purchase with an interest-bearing note, the cash equivalent cost is the cash down payment, if any, plus the face value of the note. In a lump-sum purchase, cost is allocated on the basis of the relative fair market values of the components. When a company constructs its own plant assets, cost consists of materials and labor costs incurred plus other costs such as heat, light, power, and depreciation on company assets used in construction.

There are four depreciation methods:

Method	*Effect on Annual Depreciation*	*Formula*
Straight-line	Constant amount	Depreciable cost ÷ useful life (in years)
Units of activity	Varying amount	Depreciation cost per unit × units of activity during the year
Declining-balance	Decreasing amount	Book value at beginning of year × declining balance rate
Sum-of-the-years'-digits	Decreasing amount	Depreciable cost × SYD fraction

4. Revisions of periodic depreciation are made in present and future periods, not retroactively. The new annual depreciation is determined by dividing the depreciable cost at the time of the revision by the remaining useful life.

5. Revenue expenditures are incurred to maintain the operating efficiency and expected productive life of the asset. These expenditures are

debited to Repair Expense as incurred. Capital expenditures increase the operating efficiency, productive capacity, or expected useful life of the asset. Additions are debited to the asset account to which the expenditure pertains. Improvements are debited to accumulated depreciation when useful life is extended and to the principal asset account when useful life remains the same.

6. After a capital expenditure, it is necessary to compute both the revised depreciable cost and useful life. The new annual depreciation is determined by dividing the revised depreciable cost by remaining useful life.

GLOSSARY

Additions and improvements, p. 402
Capital expenditure, p. 402
Cash equivalent price, p. 389
Declining-balance method, p. 397
Lump-sum purchase, p. 392
Ordinary repairs, p. 401
Revenue expenditure, p. 402
Straight-line method, p. 395
Sum-of-the-years'-digits method, p. 398
Units of activity method, p. 396

DEMONSTRATION PROBLEM

The Dan Ryan Company purchases a factory machine at a cost of $18,000 on January 1, 1987. The machine is expected to have a salvage value of $2,000 at the end of its four-year useful life.

INSTRUCTIONS

Prepare depreciation schedules for (a) the straight-line method, (b) declining-balance method using double the straight-line rate, and (c) the sum-of-the-years'-digits method.

SOLUTION TO DEMONSTRATION PROBLEM

(a)

Straight-line Method

Year	Depreciable Cost	×	Depreciation Rate	=	Annual Depreciation Expense	End of Year Accumulated Depreciation	End of Year Book Value
1987	$16,000		25%		$4,000	$ 4,000	$14,000*
1988	16,000		25%		4,000	8,000	10,000

Year	Depreciable Cost	×	Depreciation Rate	=	Annual Depreciation Expense	End of Year Accumulated Depreciation	End of Year Book Value
1989	16,000		25%		4,000	12,000	6,000
1990	16,000		25%		4,000	16,000	2,000

*$18,000 − $4,000

(b)

Declining-Balance Method

Year	Book Value Beginning of Year	×	Depreciation Rate	=	Annual Depreciation Expense	End of Year Accumulated Depreciation	End of Year Book Value
1987	$18,000		50%		$9,000	$ 9,000	$9,000
1988	9,000		50%		4,500	13,500	4,500
1989	4,500		50%		2,250	15,750	2,250
1990	2,250		50%		250*	16,000	2,000

*Adjusted to $250 because ending book value should not be less than expected salvage value.

(c)

Sum-of-the-Years'-Digits Method

Year	Depreciable Cost	SYD Fraction	Annual Depreciation Expense	End of Year Accumulated Depreciation	End of Year Book Value
1987	$16,000	4/10	$6,400	$ 6,400	$11,600*
1988	16,000	3/10	4,800	11,200	6,800
1989	16,000	2/10	3,200	14,400	3,600
1990	16,000	1/10	1,600	16,000	2,000

*$18,000 − $6,400

QUESTIONS

1. Bill Bonds claims that there are two classes of plant assets: (a) nondepreciable, and (b) depreciable. Is Bill correct? What are the principal classes of plant assets?

2. Sherry Sims is uncertain about the applicability of the cost principle to plant assets. Explain the principle to Sherry.

3. How is cost measured in (a) a cash transaction, and (b) a noncash transaction?

4. Urban Company acquires the land and building owned by the Rural Company. What types of costs may be incurred to make the asset ready for its intended use if Urban Company wants to use (a) only the land, and (b) both the land and the building?

5. Your roommate does not understand the difference in accounting for sales taxes and motor vehicle licenses in purchasing a delivery truck. Explain the difference and the reasons for it to your roomie.

6. When can interest costs be added to the construction costs of a building? What limits are imposed on the inclusion of interest costs?

7. In a lump sum purchase it is possible to determine the purchase price and both the book values and fair market values of the acquired assets. Explain the relevance of each amount in allocating cost to the individual assets acquired.

8. In a recent newspaper release, the president of the Marshall Company asserted that something has to be done about depreciation. The president said, "Depreciation does not come close to accumulating the cash needed to replace the asset at the end of its useful life." What is your response to the president?

9. The decline in usefulness of a plant asset may be due to two principal causes. Identify and explain the two causes.

10. The selection of a depreciation method is a management decision that may be changed periodically. Do you agree? Explain.

11. Cleo Carr is studying for the next accounting examination. She asks your help on two questions: (a) What is salvage value? (b) Is salvage value used in determining depreciable cost under each depreciation method? Answer Cleo's questions.

12. Contrast the straight-line method and the units of activity method as to (a) useful life, and (b) the pattern of periodic depreciation over useful life.

13. Ron Reed is having a difficult time with the two accelerated depreciation methods. Explain to Ron the formulas for computing periodic depreciation in (a) the declining-balance method, and (b) the sum-of-the-years'-digits method.

14. Ron says the formulas help. However, he is not sure which of the factors in the two formulas change and which remain constant each year. Clarify these points for Ron.

15. Contrast the effects of the four depreciation methods on annual depreciation expense.

16. In the fourth year of an asset's five-year useful life, the company decides that the asset will have a six-year service life. How should the revision of depreciation be reported? Why?

17. On January 1, 1987, Fahr Company concludes that the useful life of equipment purchased for $15,000 on January 1, 1981 will be 12 years, rather than 10 years as originally anticipated. Assuming no salvage value, compute (a) the book value at January 1, 1987, and (b) 1987 depreciation expense.

18. Distinguish between revenue expenditures and capital expenditures during useful life.

19. Julie Jarvis believes that since all additions and improvements are capital expenditures, they should be debited to a plant asset account. Is Julie correct? Explain.

20. How is annual depreciation computed following a capital expenditure?

EXERCISES

E10-1 The following expenditures relating to plant assets were made by the Pullen Company during the first two months of 1987.

1. Paid $150 to have company name and advertising slogan painted on new delivery truck.
2. Paid $75 motor vehicle license fee on the new truck.
3. Paid $500 for attorney's fee on title search on land purchased as a plant site.
4. Paid $450 of sales taxes on new delivery truck.
5. Paid $100 to replace windows broken by vandals on building under construction.
6. Paid $7,500 for parking lots and driveways on new plant site.
7. Paid $5,000 of accrued taxes at time plant site was acquired.
8. Paid $800 for installation of new factory machinery.
9. Paid $900 for one year accident insurance policy on new delivery truck.
10. Paid $200 insurance to cover possible accident loss on new factory machinery while the machinery was in transit.

INSTRUCTIONS

(a) Explain the application of the cost principle in determining the acquisition cost of plant assets.

(b) List the numbers of the foregoing transactions, and opposite each indicate the account title to which each expenditure should be debited.

E10–2 On March 1, 1987, Dessi Corporation acquired real estate, on which they planned to construct an office building, by paying $40,000 cash and signing a 12%, 3-year, $50,000 note payable. An old warehouse on the property was razed at a cost of $6,600; the salvaged materials were sold for $1,700. Additional expenditures before construction began included $1,100 attorney's fee for work concerning the land purchase, $4,000 real estate broker's fee, $7,800 architect's fee, and $14,000 to put in driveways and a parking lot.

INSTRUCTIONS

(a) Determine the amount to be reported as the cost of the land.

(b) For each cost not used in part (a), indicate the account to be debited.

E10–3 Plant asset acquisitions for selected companies are as follows:

1. Cress Lithographics purchased a printing press for $50,000 cash. In addition, they paid $2,500 shipping charges, $500 insurance during transit, $3,000 installation costs, and $1,000 for repairs from an installation accident. Cress made the following entry for the printing press.

Printing press	54,000	
Freight-in	2,500	
Insurance expense	500	
Cash		57,000

2. Gooden Company purchased a delivery truck for $18,500 cash. In addition, it paid $1,110 sales taxes, $900 for the first year's insurance, $250 motor vehicle license, and $400 for painting the company name and logo on the truck. The truck was recorded as follows:

Delivery Truck	19,400	
Licenses and Taxes Expense	1,360	
Miscellaneous Expense	400	
Cash		21,160

3. Hosler Company purchased office equipment for $24,000, terms 2/10, n/60. Because they intended to take the discount, the company made no entry until they paid for the equipment. The entry was:

Office Equipment	24,000	
Cash		23,520
Purchase Discounts		480

4. Kemmer Company purchased store equipment for $12,000 by making a $2,000 cash down payment and signing a one-year $10,000 12% note payable. The purchase was recorded as follows:

Store Equipment	13,200	
Cash		2,000
Notes Payable		10,000
Interest Payable		1,200

5. The Sanfil Company built a warehouse for $520,000. They could have purchased a similar building for $570,000. Thus, the controller made the following entry:

Warehouse	570,000	
Cash		520,000
Gain on Construction		50,000

INSTRUCTIONS

Prepare the correct entry for each acquisition.

E10–4 The Ryan Company is considering the acquisition of equipment that has an invoice price of $40,000 under the following alternative purchase plans:

1. Purchase on account with terms of 3/10 EOM, N/60.
2. Purchase by paying $10,000 in cash and signing a $30,000 10% interest bearing note due in two years.
3. Lump sum purchase of plant assets at a total cost of $1,000,000. Appraised values are land $240,000, building $912,000, and equipment $48,000.

INSTRUCTIONS

(a) Journalize the purchase of the asset and payment of the balance due within the discount period under plan 1.

(b) Repeat (a) assuming payment was not made until after the discount period lapsed.

(c) Journalize the entry to record the acquisition under plan 2.

(d) Journalize the entry to record the acquisition under plan 3 assuming an immediate cash payment of $1,000,000.

E10–5 The Mills Company purchased a factory machine for $50,000 cash on January 1, 1987. The machine is expected to have a salvage value of $5,000 at the end of its four-year useful life. R. A. Mills, the owner, wishes to know the annual depreciation expense over the four-year period under each of the following depreciation methods: (1) straight-line, (2) units of activity based on 90,000 total estimated units of output with actual unit output of 20,000, 35,000, 25,000 and 10,000 in years 1–4 respectively, (3) declining balance using double the straight-line rate, and (4) sum-of-the-years'-digits.

INSTRUCTIONS

(a) Prepare separate depreciation schedules for each of the depreciation methods.

(b) Compare the accumulated depreciation at the end of the second year under each method in dollars and as a percentage of cost.

E10–6 Werner Company purchased a new machine on October 1, 1987 at a cost of $96,000. The company estimated that the machine will have a salvage value of $12,000. The machine is expected to be used for 42,000 working hours during its six-year life.

INSTRUCTIONS

Compute the depreciation expense under the following methods for the year indicated: (1) straight-line for 1987, (2) units of activity for 1987, assuming machine usage was 1,700 hours, (3) sum-of-the-years'-digits for 1988, and (4) declining-balance using double the straight-line rate for 1987 and 1988.

E10-7 The Ricky Company acquired two delivery trucks for cash at a cost of $9,000 each on January 1, 1987. It expects each truck to last four years and have a salvage value of $1,000. The straight-line method of depreciation is used and depreciation has been correctly taken during the first three years of useful life. In 1990, the following events and transactions occurred.

Jan. 1 Because truck A is in such good condition, the company decides to extend the useful life of the truck by one year to 12/31/91 with no change in salvage value.

Jan. 1 Incurred a major motor overhaul on truck B at a cost of $1,800. It is expected that this improvement will increase the truck's useful life one year to 12/31/91 with no change in salvage value.

INSTRUCTIONS

(a) Indicate what entry (ies), if any, should be made on January 1, 1990.

(b) Compute the amount of depreciation expense for 1991 on the trucks.

E10-8 Bill Potts and Evelyn Duesbury, presidents of small businesses were discussing the accounting issue of revenue and capital expenditures. The following is part of their conversation:

Bill: Two good examples of revenue expenditures are the cost of cleaning the exterior of our office building, and the cost of replacing broken windows. All costs of this nature should always be expensed.

Evelyn: Those are good examples, but on the other hand my company recently had some special situations where the cost of cleaning a building exterior and the cost of replacing windows were capitalized.

Bill: That is definitely incorrect. These costs are revenue expenditures, not capital expenditures.

INSTRUCTIONS

(a) Discuss what kind of special situations Evelyn might be referring to.

(b) Evaluate Bill's remarks.

E10-9 On January 1, 1986, the Mavis Company purchased and installed a word processor at a cost of $18,000. The equipment was expected to last five years and have an estimated salvage value of $2,000. On January 1, 1987, the company purchased a laser printer to be used with the word processor at a cost of $9,000. The printer was expected to have a useful life of four years. Through an error, the cost of the laser printer was debited to Repair Expense. Mavis Company uses the straight-line method of depreciation.

INSTRUCTIONS

(a) Prepare schedules showing the effects of the error on Repair Expense, Depreciation Expense, and net income in each year and in total during the useful life of the laser printer, assuming the printer

(1) is expected to have a salvage value of $1,000.

(2) is not expected to have any salvage value.

(b) Why do the cumulative effects on net income differ in the two situations?

E10-10 Betty Barton, the new controller of the Quinn Company, has reviewed the expected useful lives and salvage values of selected depreciable assets. Her findings are as follows:

Type of Asset	Date Acquired	Cost	Accumulated Depreciation 1/1/87	Useful Life in Years Old	Useful Life in Years Proposed	Salvage Value Old	Salvage Value Proposed
Building	1/1/81	$800,000	$114,000	40	45	$40,000	$62,000
Warehouse	1/1/84	100,000	11,400	25	20	5,000	3,600
Delivery truck	1/1/85	20,000	9,500	4	5	1,000	1,500

All assets are depreciated by the straight-line method. Quinn Company uses a calendar year in preparing annual financial statements. After discussion, management has agreed to accept Betty's proposed changes.

INSTRUCTIONS

(a) Compute the revised annual depreciation on each asset. (Show computations.)

(b) Prepare the entry (or entries) to record depreciation on the building in 1987.

E10-11 On January 1, 1987, the Doyle Company had two delivery trucks in its Delivery Equipment account as follows:

	Truck 1	Truck 2
Cost	$15,000	$18,000
Accumulated depreciation	8,100	8,100
Book value	$ 6,900	$ 9,900
Purchase date	1/1/84	7/1/84

Each truck has a useful life of 5 years. Salvage value is 10% of cost. The straight-line method of depreciation is used. During 1987, the following capital expenditures were made:

Jan. 1 Paneled truck No. 1 at a cost of $2,500. This addition will not increase useful life. However, total salvage value is now estimated to be $2,000.

July 1 Incurred a major overhaul of the motor of truck No. 2 at a cost of $2,520. This improvement will increase useful life one year with no change in salvage value.

INSTRUCTIONS

(a) Journalize the capital expenditures.

(b) Compute the revised annual depreciation for each truck following the capital expenditure.

(c) Determine the 1987 depreciation expense for each truck.

PROBLEMS

P10-1 The Dobson Company was organized on January 1. During the first year of operations, the following expenditures and receipts were recorded in random order in the account, Real Estate.

Debits	
1. Cost of real estate purchased as a plant site (land $100,000 and building $25,000)	$125,000
2. Installation cost of fences around property	4,000
3. Cost of demolishing building to make land suitable for construction of new building	13,000
4. Interest paid during construction on money borrowed for construction	15,000
5. Cost of repairs to building under construction caused by flooding	5,000
6. Excavation costs for new building	20,000
7. Accrued real estate taxes paid at time of purchase of real estate	2,000
8. Cost of parking lots and driveways	12,000
9. Insurance and taxes on building during construction	6,000
10. Architect's fees on building plans	10,000
11. Real estate taxes paid for the current year on land	3,000
12. Full payment to building contractor	600,000
	$815,000

Credits	
13. Proceeds from salvage of demolished building	$ 2,500
14. Insurance proceeds for flood damage	1,900
	$ 4,400

INSTRUCTIONS

(a) Analyze the foregoing transactions using the following tabular arrangement. Insert the number of each transaction in the Item space and insert the amounts in the appropriate columns. For amounts entered in the Other Accounts column also indicate the account title.

Item	Land	Building	Other Accounts

(b) Prepare a compound correcting entry at December 31. (Hint: Make one credit to Real Estate).

P10–2 In recent years, Rob Bell Corporation has purchased four machines. Because of heavy turnover in the accounting department, a different accountant was in charge of selecting depreciation methods for each machine, and various methods have been selected. Information concerning the four machines is summarized below:

Machine	Acquired	Cost	Salvage Value	Useful Life in Years	Depreciation Method
1	1/1/84	$ 76,000	$ 6,000	10	Straight-line
2	1/1/85	100,000	10,000	8	Declining balance
3	1/1/86	68,000	5,000	9	Sum-of-the-years'-digits.
4	1/1/87	90,000	8,000	10	Declining balance

INSTRUCTIONS

(a) Compute the amount of accumulated depreciation on each machine at December 31, 1987. Bell Corporation uses double the straight-line rate for the declining-balance method. (Round to two decimals.)

(b) Compute total 1988 depreciation expense.

(c) Assume that on January 1, 1989, Rob Bell changes its estimates on machine No. 1 to

a total useful life of 8 years with a $6,200 salvage value. Compute 1989 depreciation expense for machine No. 1.

(d) Assume, instead of the change in estimates in (c) above, that a major overhaul of the motor for machine No. 1 was made at a cost of $8,400 on January 1, 1989. The capital expenditure is expected to increase overall useful life to 12 years with no change in salvage value. Compute the 1989 depreciation for machine No. 1.

P10-3 Sagers Corporation purchased machinery on January 1, 1987 at a cost of $100,000. The estimated useful life of the machinery is five years, with an estimated residual value at the end of that period of $10,000. The company is considering different depreciation methods which could be used for financial reporting purposes.

INSTRUCTIONS

(a) Prepare separate depreciation schedules for the machinery using the following methods: straight-line, declining-balance using double the straight-line rate, and sum-of-the-years'-digits. Round to the nearest dollar.

(b) Which method would result in the highest reported 1987 income? In the highest total reported income over the five-year period?

(c) Which method would result in the lowest reported 1987 income? In the lowest total reported income over the five-year period?

(d) Assume Sagers decides to use the straight-line method. In 1989, the company decides that the useful life of the machinery will only be 4 years, with a salvage value of $10,000. Prepare the journal entry to record 1989 depreciation.

P10-4 Marks Company owns two delivery trucks and uses the straight-line method of depreciation with no salvage value. The company closes its books annually on December 31. The following events and transactions occurred during the first four years.

1987

Jan. 2 Purchased panel truck No. X7654 from Edson Motors for $11,700 cash plus sales taxes $300, and motor vehicle license $75.

Dec. 1 Installed new spark plugs in truck for cash at cost of $25.

Dec. 31 Recorded annual depreciation on basis of a 4 year life.

1988

July 1 Purchased panel truck No. Y8379 from Hirt Motor Company for cash, $7,800, plus sales taxes of $200. This was a used 1987 truck which is expected to last 3 years from date of purchase.

July 1 Installed 4 new tires on used truck for cash, $400.

Dec. 1 Paid $175 repair costs on truck No. X7654.

Dec. 31 Recorded depreciation on both trucks. (Round to nearest dollar.)

1989

Jan. 2 Paid $900 for major overhaul of motor on truck No. X7654. This expenditure is expected to extend useful life one year.

July 1 Installed 2-way CB radio in truck No. Y8379 at a cash cost of $600 to improve efficiency. This expenditure will not increase useful life or salvage value.

Dec. 31 Recorded depreciation on both trucks.

1990

Dec. 31 Recorded depreciation on both trucks.

INSTRUCTIONS

Journalize the transactions and events.

P10–5 On July 1, 1986, Graham Company purchased a new machine for $80,000, terms 2/10, n/30. On this date, Machinery was debited and Accounts Payable was credited for $80,000. When payment was made on July 9, Graham prepared the following entry:

Accounts Payable	80,000	
Cash		78,400
Interest revenue		1,600

Graham also paid 5% sales tax of $3,920 on July 9, which was debited to Sales Tax Expense. Additional costs incurred by Graham included freight charges for the delivery of the machine on July 10 of $1,750 (debited to Freight-in) and labor costs for installing the machine of $4,800 (debited to Salary Expense). While the new machine was being installed, carelessness by a worker caused damage to the machine, which was repaired at a cash cost of $980 (debited to Repair Expense) on July 11.

The useful life of the machine is 10 years with a salvage value of $4,000. Graham uses straight-line depreciation, and their depreciation policy would indicate that six months' depreciation (rounded to the nearest dollar) should be recorded in 1986. An inexperienced bookkeeper recorded $7,600 depreciation expense in both 1986 and 1987. Net income of $180,000 was recorded in 1987.

The following are selected amounts from Graham's records for 1986 and 1987:

	12/31/87	12/31/86
Machinery	$ 80,000	$ 80,000
Accumulated Depreciation – Machinery	15,200	7,600
Bill Graham, Capital	880,000	700,000

INSTRUCTIONS

(a) Prepare correct journal entries for the transactions described above, including the year-end entries for depreciation.

(b) Compute the correct amounts for the Machinery, Accumulated Depreciation—Machinery, and Bill Graham, Capital at December 31, 1986 and December 31, 1987.

ALTERNATE PROBLEMS

P10–1A The Murph Company was organized on January 1. During the first year of operations, the following expenditures and receipts were recorded in random order in the account, Land.

	Debits
1. Cost of real estate purchased as a plant site (land $100,000, and building $35,000)	$ 135,000
2. Accrued real estate taxes paid at time of purchase of real estate	2,000
3. Cost of demolishing building to make land suitable for construction of new building	12,000
4. Cost of filling and grading the land	4,000
5. Excavation costs for new building	20,000
6. Architect's fees on building plans	10,000
7. Insurance and taxes during construction	7,000
8. Cost of repairs to building under construction caused by flooding	6,000
9. Interest paid during the year, of which $60,000 pertains to the construction period	90,000

10. Full payment to building contractor	700,000
11. Cost of parking lots and driveways	14,000
12. Real estate taxes paid for the current year on land	5,000
	$1,005,000

Credits	
13. Insurance proceeds for flood damage	$ 2,900
14. Proceeds for salvage of demolished building	3,500
	$ 6,400

INSTRUCTIONS

(a) Analyze the foregoing transactions using the following tabular arrangement. Insert the number of each transaction in the Item space and insert the amounts in the appropriate columns. For amounts entered in the Other Accounts column, also indicate the account titles.

Item	Land	Building	Other Accounts

(b) Prepare a compound correcting entry at December 31. (Hint: Make a credit to Land to leave the correct balance in the account.)

P10-2A In recent years, Booster Transportation Corporation purchased four used buses. Because of frequent turnover in the accounting department, a different accountant selected depreciation methods for each bus, and various methods have been selected. Information concerning the four buses is summarized below:

Bus	Acquired	Cost	Salvage Value	Useful Life in Years	Depreciation Method
1	1/1/86	$ 86,000	$ 6,000	5	Straight-line
2	1/1/86	120,000	10,000	4	Declining balance
3	1/1/87	71,360	5,000	6	Sum-of-the-years'-digits
4	1/1/88	96,000	8,000	5	Declining balance

INSTRUCTIONS

(a) Compute the amount of accumulated depreciation on each bus at December 31, 1988. Booster uses double the straight-line rate for the declining balance method.

(b) Compute total 1989 depreciation expense.

(c) Assume that on January 1, 1990, Booster changes its estimates on bus No. 1 to a total useful life of 6 years with a $10,000 salvage value. Compute 1990 depreciation expense for bus No. 1.

(d) Assume, instead of the change in estimates in (c) above, that the company renovated the interior of bus No. 1 at a cost of $5,000 on January 1, 1990. The capital expenditure is not expected to increase useful life, but it will increase salvage value by $1,000. Compute the 1990 depreciation for bus No. 1.

P10-3A Ebert Corporation purchased machinery on January 1, 1987 at a cost of $243,000. The estimated useful life of the machinery is six years, with an estimated residual value at the end of that period of $12,000. The company is considering different depreciation methods which could be used for financial reporting purposes.

INSTRUCTIONS

(a) Prepare separate depreciation schedules for the machinery using the following methods: straight-line, declining balance using double the straight-line rate, and sum-of-the-years'-digits. Round to the nearest dollar.

(b) Which method would result in the highest reported 1987 income? In the highest total reported income over the six-year period?

(c) Which method would result in the lowest reported 1987 income? In the lowest total reported income over the six-year period?

(d) Assume that Ebert decides to use the straight-line method. In 1990, the company decided that the useful life should total 8 years, with a salvage value of $20,000. Prepare the journal entry to record 1990 depreciation.

P10–4A Moran Company owns two delivery trucks and uses the straight-line method of depreciation. Salvage value is estimated to be 10% of cost. The company closes its books annually on December 31. The following events and transactions took place during the first four years.

1987

Jan. 2 Purchased new panel truck No. N4521 from Barr Motors for $17,200 cash plus sales taxes $800, motor vehicle licenses $115, and paid $900 for a one-year accident insurance policy.

Dec. 1 Paid $90 for motor tune-up on truck.

Dec. 31 Recorded annual depreciation on basis of a 4-year life.

1988

Apr. 1 Purchased panel truck No. U2475 from Danny Motor Company for cash $11,000, plus sales taxes of $500. This was a used 1987 truck, which is expected to last 3 years from date of purchase.

Apr. 1 Installed 3 new tires on used truck for cash $500.

Dec. 1 Paid $310 repair costs on truck No. N4521.

Dec. 31 Recorded depreciation on both trucks.

1989

Jan. 1 Paid $1,500 for major overhaul of motor on truck No. N4521. This expenditure is expected to extend useful life one year.

Apr. 1 Installed 2-way CB radio in truck No. U2475 at a cash cost of $800 to improve efficiency. This expenditure will not increase useful life or salvage value.

Dec. 31 Recorded depreciation on both trucks.

1990

Dec. 31 Recorded depreciation on both trucks.

INSTRUCTIONS

Journalize the transactions and events.

P10–5A On September 1, 1987, Noel Company purchased a new machine for $90,000, terms 2/10, n/30. On this date, Machinery was debited and Accounts Payable credited for $90,000. When payment was made on September 9, Noel prepared the following entry:

Accounts Payable	90,000	
Cash		88,200
Purchase Discounts		1,800

Noel also paid a 5% sales tax of $4,410 on September 9, which was debited to Sales Tax Expense. Additional costs incurred by Noel included freight charges for the delivery of the machine on September 10 of $2,000 (debited to Freight-In) and labor costs

for installing the machine of $5,300 (debited to Salary Expense) September 11. While the new machine was being installed, carelessness by a worker damaged the machine, which was repaired at a cash cost of $1,200 (debited to Repair Expense). The machine was ready for service on September 11.

The useful life of the machine is 8 years with a salvage value of $4,000. Noel uses straight-line depreciation, and its depreciation policy would indicate that four months' depreciation should be recorded in 1987. An inexperienced bookkeeper recorded $5,375 depreciation expense in 1987 and a full year's depreciation of $10,750 in 1988. The company reported net income of $150,000 in 1988.

The following are selected amounts from Noel's records for 1988 and 1987:

	12/31/88	12/31/87
Machinery	$ 90,000	$ 90,000
Accumulated Depreciation—Machinery	16,125	5,375
Sara Noel, Capital	750,000	600,000

INSTRUCTIONS

(a) Prepare correct journal entries for the transactions described above, including the year-end entries for depreciation.

(b) Compute the corrected amounts for the Factory Machinery, Accumulated Depreciation—Machinery, and Sara Noel, Capital at December 31, 1987 and December 31, 1988.

DECISION CASE

Lake Company and River Company are two proprietorships that are similar in many respects except that Lake Company uses the straight-line method and River Company uses the declining-balance method at double the straight-line rate. On January 2, 1985, both companies acquired the following depreciable assets.

Asset	Cost	Salvage Value	Useful Life
Building	$320,000	$20,000	40 years
Equipment	110,000	10,000	10 years

Including the appropriate depreciation charges, annual net income for the companies in the years 1985, 1986, and 1987 and total income for the three years were as follows:

	1985	1986	1987	Total
Lake Company	$84,000	$88,400	$90,000	$262,400
River Company	68,000	76,000	82,000	226,000

At December 31, 1987, the balance sheets of the two companies are similar except that River Company has more cash and a significantly higher current ratio than Lake Company.

Dawna Remmers is interested in buying one of the companies and she comes to you for advice.

INSTRUCTIONS

(a) Determine the annual and total depreciation recorded by each company during the three years.

(b) Assuming that River Company also uses the straight-line method of depreciation instead of the declining balance method as in (a), prepare comparative income data for the three years.

(c) Which company should Ms. Remmers buy? Why?

CHAPTER 11

Miami University, Ohio

CHAPTER 11

PLANT ASSET DISPOSALS, NATURAL RESOURCES, AND INTANGIBLE ASSETS

STUDY OBJECTIVES

After studying this chapter, you should be able to:

1. Explain how to account for the disposal of a plant asset through retirement, sale, or exchange.
2. Explain the role of subsidiary plant ledgers.
3. Identify the basic accounting issues related to natural resources.
4. Contrast the accounting for intangible assets with the accounting for plant assets.
5. Indicate how plant assets, natural resources, and intangible assets are reported on the balance sheet.

The financial press recently reported on the following business developments:

"Armco writes off its idle facilities in the depressed oil field business."

"Times Mirror Co. to sell two television stations."

"Federal government acquires land from lumber companies for national park system in exchange for other Federal land."

As indicated from the headlines, plant assets are disposed of through retirement, sale, or exchange. In this chapter, we examine the issues related to the accounting for disposal of plant assets. In addition, we discuss the accounting for two other major long-term assets—natural resources and intangi-

ble assets. Although the accounting issues associated with these two topics are similar to those associated with plant assets, the differences are significant enough to merit separate discussion and illustration.

SECTION ONE—PLANT ASSET DISPOSALS

Plant assets may be disposed of in the following manner:

1. Retirement—the plant asset is scrapped or discarded.
2. Sale—the plant asset is sold to another party.
3. Exchange—an existing plant asset is traded in on a new plant asset.

At the time of disposal, it is necessary to determine the book value of the plant asset. The book value is the difference between the cost of the plant asset and the accumulated depreciation to date. If the disposal occurs at any time during the year, depreciation for the fraction of the year to the date of disposal must be recorded. The book value is then eliminated by debiting the Accumulated Depreciation account for the total depreciation to the date of disposal and crediting the asset account for the cost of the asset.

DISPOSAL BY RETIREMENT

To illustrate the accounting for a retirement, assume that Hobart Enterprises retires its computer printers, which cost $32,000. The accumulated depreciation on these computers is also $32,000; the equipment, therefore, is fully depreciated. The entry to record this retirement is as follows:

Accumulated Depreciation – Printing Equipment	32,000	
Printing Equipment		32,000
(To record retirement of fully depreciated equipment)		

What happens if a fully depreciated plant asset is still useful to the company? In this case, the plant asset and the related accumulated depreciation should continue to be reported on the balance sheet without further depreciation or adjustment until the asset is retired. Reporting the asset and related accumulated depreciation on the balance sheet informs the reader of the financial statements that the asset is still being used by the company. However, once an asset is fully depreciated, even if it is still being used, no additional depreciation should be taken. In no situation can the accumulated depreciation on the plant asset exceed its cost.

If a plant asset is retired before it is fully depreciated, and no scrap or salvage value is received, a loss on disposal occurs. For example, assume that Sunset Company discards delivery equipment that cost $18,000 and has accu-

mulated depreciation to the date of retirement of $14,000. The entry to record this retirement is as follows:

Accumulated Depreciation — Delivery Equipment	14,000	
Loss on Disposal	4,000	
Delivery Equipment		18,000
(To record retirement of delivery equipment at a loss)		

The loss on disposal is reported in the other expenses and losses section of the income statement.

DISPOSAL BY SALE

In a sale, the book value of the asset is compared with the proceeds received from the sale. If the proceeds of the sale exceed the book value of the plant asset, a gain on disposal occurs. If the proceeds of the sale are less than the book value of the plant asset sold, a loss on disposal occurs.

Only by coincidence will the book value and the fair market value of the asset be the same at the time the asset is sold. Gains and losses on sales of plant assets are, therefore, quite common. As an example, Delta Airlines, Inc. recently reported a $94,343,000 gain on the sale of five Boeing B-727-200 aircraft and five Lockheed L-1011-1 aircraft.

GAIN ON DISPOSAL

To illustrate a gain, assume that on July 1, 1987, Wright Company sells office furniture for $16,000 cash. The office furniture originally cost $60,000 and as of January 1, 1987, had accumulated depreciation of $41,000. Depreciation for the first six months of 1987 is $8,000. The entry to record depreciation expense and update accumulated depreciation to July 1 is as follows:

July	1	Depreciation Expense	8,000	
		Accumulated Depreciation — Office Furniture		8,000
		(To record depreciation expense for the first six months of 1987)		

After the accumulated depreciation balance is updated, a gain on disposal of $5,000 is computed in the following manner:

Cost of office furniture	$60,000
Less accumulated depreciation ($41,000 + $8,000)	49,000
Book value at date of disposal	11,000
Proceeds from sale	16,000
Gain on disposal	$ 5,000

Computation of gain on disposal

The entry to record the sale and the gain on disposal is as follows:

July	1	Cash	16,000	
		Accumulated Depreciation—Office Furniture	49,000	
		Office Furniture		60,000
		Gain on Disposal		5,000
		(To record sale of office furniture at a gain)		

The gain on disposal is reported in the other revenues and gains section of the income statement.

LOSS ON DISPOSAL

Assume that instead of selling the office furniture for $16,000, Wright sells it for $9,000. In this case, a loss of $2,000 is computed in the following manner:

Computation of loss on disposal

Cost of office furniture	$60,000
Less: Accumulated depreciation	49,000
Book value at date of disposal	11,000
Proceeds from sale	9,000
Loss on disposal	$ 2,000

The entry to record the sale and the loss on disposal is as follows:

July	1	Cash	9,000	
		Accumulated Depreciation—Office Furniture	49,000	
		Loss on Disposal	2,000	
		Office Furniture		60,000
		(To record sale of office furniture at a loss)		

The loss on disposal is reported in the other expenses and losses section of the income statement.

DISPOSAL BY EXCHANGE

Exchanges of assets occur frequently in practice because companies continue to upgrade their plant assets to meet competitive pressures. To account for an exchange, it is necessary to:

1. Eliminate the book value of the old asset at the date of exchange.
2. Record the acquisition cost of the new asset.
3. Account for the gain or loss, if any, on the old asset.

The first step is similar to accounting for a disposal by retirement or sale. The final two steps depend on whether the exchange involves dissimilar or similar assets.

DISSIMILAR ASSETS

An exchange of dissimilar assets involves different types of assets. This occurs when delivery equipment is exchanged for land, or when office furniture is traded for factory machinery. In an exchange of dissimilar assets, the new asset performs a different function than the old asset. In an exchange of dissimilar assets:

1. The acquisition cost of the new asset is equal to the **fair market value** of the asset given up plus any cash paid by the purchaser.
2. Gain or loss on the old asset is the difference between its fair market value and its book value.

In the exchange of dissimilar assets, all gains and losses are recognized in the accounts.

To illustrate the accounting for exchanges of dissimilar assets, assume that Mark's Express Delivery decides to exchange its old delivery equipment plus cash of $31,000 for land to be used as a new building site. At this time the book value of the old delivery equipment is $12,000 (cost $40,000 less accumulated depreciation $28,000). In addition, it is determined that the fair market value of the old delivery equipment is $19,000. Thus, the cost of the land is $50,000, computed as follows:

Cost of land

Fair market value of old delivery equipment	$19,000
Cash	31,000
Cost of land	$50,000

The gain on the disposal of $7,000 is determined in the following manner:

Computation of gain on disposal

Fair market value of old delivery equipment	$19,000
Book value of old delivery equipment ($40,000 – $28,000)	12,000
Gain on disposal	$ 7,000

The entry to record this transaction is as follows:

Land	50,000	
Accumulated Depreciation – Delivery Equipment	28,000	
Cash		31,000
Delivery Equipment		40,000
Gain on Disposal		7,000
(To record exchange of old delivery equipment and cash for land at a gain)		

If the fair market value of the old delivery equipment is only $3,000, the cost of land would be $34,000, computed as follows:

Cost of land

Fair market value of old delivery equipment	$ 3,000
Cash	31,000
Cost of land	$34,000

A loss on disposal of $9,000 would, therefore, be determined in the following manner:

Computation of loss on disposal

Book value of old delivery equipment	$12,000
Fair market value of old delivery equipment	3,000
Loss on disposal	$ 9,000

The entry to record the exchange is as follows:

Land	34,000	
Accumulated Depreciation—Delivery Equipment	28,000	
Loss on Disposal	9,000	
Delivery Equipment		40,000
Cash		31,000
(To record exchange of the old delivery equipment and cash for land at a loss)		

SIMILAR ASSETS

An exchange of similar assets involves assets of the same type. This occurs when old delivery equipment is exchanged for new delivery equipment or when old office furniture is exchanged for new office furniture. In an exchange of similar assets, the new asset performs the same function as the old asset.

The accounting for the exchange of similar assets depends on whether there is gain or a loss on the old asset. When there is a gain on the old asset, the accounting is as follows:

1. The acquisition cost of the new asset is equal to the **book value** of the asset given up plus any cash paid by the purchaser.
2. The gain on the old asset is the difference between its fair market value and its book value.
3. The gain is treated as a reduction of the cost of the new asset (instead of being credited to Gain on Disposal).

Gains are not recognized because the new asset performs the same function as the old asset. Thus, the earnings process of the old asset is not completed. Accordingly, a gain on the old asset is deferred by treating it as a downward adjustment of the cost basis of the new asset acquired.

To illustrate the accounting for a gain, assume that Mark's Express Delivery exchanged old delivery equipment for similar new delivery equipment with a fair market value of $50,000. The book value of the old delivery equipment is $12,000 (cost $40,000 less accumulated depreciation $28,000), its fair

market value is $19,000, and cash of $31,000 is paid. The cost of the new delivery equipment of $43,000 is computed as follows:

Cost of new equipment

Book value of old delivery equipment ($40,000 − $28,000)	$12,000
Cash	31,000
Cost of new delivery equipment	$43,000

Alternatively, the $43,000 cost can be determined by deducting the gain of $7,000 (the fair market value $19,000 less book value $12,000) from the $50,000 fair market value of the new delivery equipment, as shown below:

Cost of new equipment—alternative computation

Fair market value of new equipment	$50,000
Less: Gain deferred	7,000
Cost of new delivery equipment	$43,000

The entry to record the exchange is as follows:

Delivery Equipment (new)	43,000	
Accumulated Depreciation – Delivery Equipment (old)	28,000	
Delivery Equipment (old)		40,000
Cash		31,000
(To record exchange of old delivery equipment for similar new delivery equipment)		

This entry does not eliminate the gain; it just postpones or defers it to future periods. As a result, net income in future periods increases because depreciation expense on the newly acquired asset is less. It is less because the acquisition cost of the new asset is $7,000 less than the fair market value of the new asset acquired.

When a loss occurs on the exchange of similar assets, it is recorded in the same manner as a loss on the exchange of dissimilar assets. That is, it is not deferred but is recognized immediately. The profession does not allow the deferral of the loss, because it would increase the basis of the new asset above its fair market value, which is considered inappropriate.[1]

SUBSIDIARY PLANT LEDGERS

An executive recently remarked that "as much as 15% of an industry's plant assets have disappeared from companies, but they are still listed on the balance sheet." Even large buildings can disappear. For example, when one firm

[1]Special rules apply for federal income tax purposes. The regulations of the Internal Revenue Service provide that no gains or losses are to be reported from the exchange of similar plant assets. Thus, for tax purposes the basis of the new asset is adjusted upward by the amount of any loss just as it is adjusted downward by the amount of any gain.

started a new building program, it demolished an old building on the site. However, owing to a mix-up in the orders, the contractor demolished an adjacent structure as well. The accounting records were so snarled that the accounting department, in figuring the loss on demolition, failed to consider the smaller adjacent building that was demolished by mistake. Only after a period of time was it discovered that this $1.2 million asset was still being reported on the company's balance sheet![2]

This example illustrates the need for good internal control of plant assets. **One means of accomplishing this objective is to keep adequate records of each individual asset.** However, to keep such a record in the general ledger is impractical. As a result, most companies have a subsidiary plant ledger for each general ledger account that includes numerous individual assets. For example, a company may have separate subsidiary plant ledgers for office equipment, delivery equipment, and factory machinery. The **subsidiary plant ledger** is a set of records that contains for each plant asset: a description of the individual asset, explanation of transactions, cost, accumulated depreciation, and book value. An example of a subsidiary plant record for a delivery truck is illustrated below:

Subsidiary plant record

Subsidiary Plant Record

Acct. No. 136-103		General Ledger Accounts	Accumulated Depreciation/ Delivery Equipment
Item	1 ton Panel Truck	Description	1984 Ford (new)
Serial No.	X245y102	Estimated Life	5 years
Purchased From	Elroy Motor Company	Annual Depreciation	$2,400
Estimated Salvage	$1,000	Depreciation Method	Straight-line

		Cost			Accumulated Depreciation			Book
Date	Explanation	Debit	Credit	Bal.	Debit	Credit	Bal.	Value
1/1/84	Cash purchase	13,000		13,000				13,000
12/31/84	Annual depreciation					2,400	2,400	10,600
12/31/85	Annual depreciation					2,400	4,800	8,200
12/31/86	Annual depreciation					2,400	7,200	5,800
12/31/87	Annual depreciation					2,400	9,600	3,400
12/31/87	Sold		13,000		9,600			-0-

Note that at the top of each subsidiary plant record an account number is provided. The first three digits of the number indicate the asset account in the general ledger; the latter three digits refer to the account in the subsidiary ledger. This number is often stamped, etched, or affixed to an asset for identification and control purposes.

[2]This paragraph condensed and adapted from "Industry's Wasted Billions," *Dun's Review*, December 1977.

As indicated above, the subsidiary plant ledger is controlled by two general ledger accounts in this case. The control accounts are Delivery Equipment and Accumulated Depreciation—Delivery Equipment. The total of the subsidiary ledger balances should equal the total in the control accounts.

Subsidiary plant ledgers are useful in helping to keep track of periodic depreciation charges and in making entries upon the retirement of individual items. The subsidiary data are also helpful in determining the adequacy of insurance coverage, submitting insurance claims in the event of accidents, and filing income tax returns. The information concerning the plant asset can be expanded to include such items as the cost of repairs, the number of breakdowns on the equipment, and days out of service.

A typical software program for a computerized system would provide that each asset be on a master file that would include information such as date of acquisition, accumulated depreciation, and depreciation methods and lives for both book and tax purposes. The program would automatically compute depreciation for both book and tax purposes and related accumulated depreciation. Upon disposal of an asset, the program would figure gain or loss for both book and tax purposes.

SECTION TWO—NATURAL RESOURCES

Natural resources consist of standing timber and underground deposits of oil, gas, and minerals. Such resources include the much-publicized off-shore oil deposits of major petroleum companies and the oil deposits for which the Alaskan pipeline was built. These long-lived productive assets have two distinguishing characteristics: (1) they are physically extracted in operations, and (2) they are not replaceable. Because of these characteristics, natural resources are frequently called **wasting assets.**

ACQUISITION COST

The acquisition cost of a natural resource is the cash or cash equivalent price necessary to acquire the resource and prepare it for its intended use. For an already discovered resource, such as an existing coal mine, cost is the price paid for the property.

Determining the cost to capitalize becomes a problem when exploration is involved. For example, some argue that the costs of unsuccessful exploration as well as successful exploration should be capitalized. They believe that the cost of drilling the dry holes (using an oil well as an example) is a cost that is needed to find the commercially profitable wells. As a result, both successful

and unsuccessful explorations are capitalized and the costs are written off to expense over the useful life of the successful wells. This method is often referred to as the **full cost approach.**

Others disagree, arguing that only the costs of successful projects should be capitalized. They maintain that if only one of 50 exploratory wells becomes commercially viable, it is inappropriate to assign the costs of the forty-nine unsuccessful wells to the cost of the successful well. This method is referred to as the **successful efforts approach.** At present, both approaches are used in accounting for natural resources. For example, such companies as Texaco, Mobil, and Gulf use full costing, whereas American Petrofina, DuPont, Callahan Mining, and Copperweld use successful efforts.

WRITE-OFF OF ACQUISITION COST (DEPLETION)

The systematic write-off of the cost of natural resources is called **depletion. The units of activity method is generally used to compute depletion, because periodic depletion generally is a function of the units extracted during the year.** Under this method, the total cost of the natural resource is divided by the number of units estimated to be in the resource to obtain a cost per unit of product. The depletion cost per unit is then multiplied by the number of units extracted and sold to compute the depletion expense. These formulas are as follows:

Formula to compute depletion expense

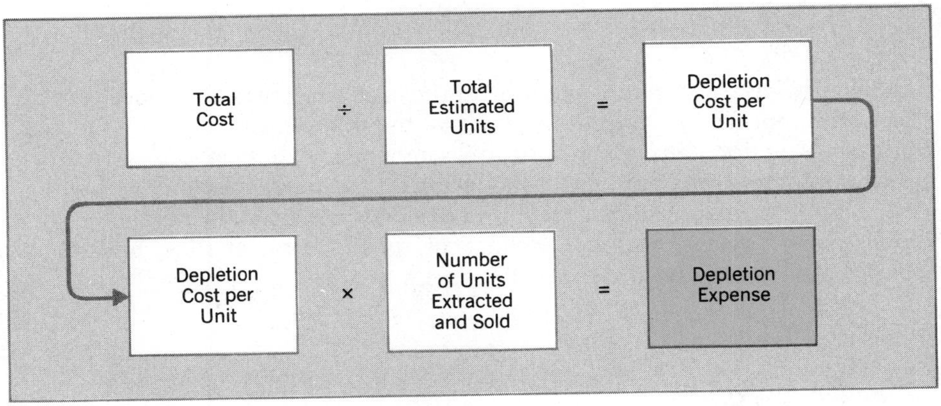

To illustrate, assume that the Lane Coal Company invests $5 million in a mine estimated to have 10 million tons of coal. In the first year, 800,000 tons of coal are extracted and sold. Using the formulas above, the computations are as follows:

$$\$5{,}000{,}000 \div 10{,}000{,}000 = \$.50 \text{ depletion cost per ton}$$

$$\$.50 \times 800{,}000 = \$400{,}000 \text{ depletion expense}$$

The entry to record depletion expense for the first year of operation is as follows:

Dec. 31	Depletion Expense	400,000	
	Accumulated Depletion		400,000
	(To record depletion expense on coal deposits)		

The account Depletion Expense is reported as a part of the cost of producing the product. Accumulated Depletion, a contra asset account similar to accumulated depreciation, is deducted from the cost of the natural resource in the balance sheet as follows:

Statement presentation of accumulated depletion

Coal mine	$5,000,000	
Less: Accumulated depletion	400,000	$4,600,000

In many companies an Accumulated Depletion account is not used, and the amount of depletion is credited directly to the natural resource account.

Firms in the oil industry maintain extensive computerized data bases on their oil deposits. Depletion costs (along with all other costs) are constantly monitored by these systems. Revisions in cost projections are automatically updated as new deposits are located or as estimates on existing deposits potential are changed. We all see the end result of this at the gas pump.

SECTION THREE—INTANGIBLE ASSETS

Intangible assets are rights, privileges, and competitive advantages that result from the ownership of long-lived assets that do not possess physical substance. Evidence of intangibles may exist in the form of contracts, licenses, and other documents. Intangibles may arise from:

1. Government grants such as patents, copyrights, franchises, trademarks, and trade names.
2. Acquisition of another business where the purchase price includes a payment for goodwill.
3. Private monopolistic arrangements arising from contractual agreements such as franchises and leases.

Among the most widely known intangibles are the patents of Polaroid, the franchises of McDonald's, the trade name of Col. Sander's Kentucky Fried Chicken, and the trademark 3M of Minnesota Mining and Manufacturing Company.

ACCOUNTING FOR INTANGIBLE ASSETS

In general, accounting for intangible assets parallels the accounting for plant assets. That is, intangible assets are recorded at cost, and this cost is written off over the useful life of the intangible asset in a rational and systematic manner. At disposal, the book value of the intangible asset is eliminated, and a gain or loss, if any, is computed.

There are, however, a few differences between accounting for intangible assets and accounting for plant assets. First, the term used to describe the write-off of an intangible asset is **amortization**, rather than depreciation. To record amortization of an intangible, an amortization expense is debited and the specific intangible asset is credited. An alternative is to credit an accumulated amortization account similar to accumulated depreciation. Most companies, however, choose simply to reduce the cost of the intangible. A second difference is that **the amortization period of an intangible asset cannot be longer than 40 years.** For example, if the useful life of an intangible asset is 60 years, it must be written off over 40 years. Conversely, if the useful life is less than 40 years, the useful life is used. This rule ensures that all intangibles, especially those with indeterminable lives, will be written off in a reasonable period of time.

Unlike plant assets, intangible assets are typically amortized on a straight-line basis. The universal use of this method adds comparability in accounting for intangible assets.

PATENTS

A **patent** is an exclusive right issued by the United States Patent Office that enables the recipient to manufacture, sell, or otherwise control his or her invention for a period of seventeen years from the date of the grant. A patent is nonrenewable, but the legal life of a patent may be extended beyond its original term by obtaining new patents for improvements and other changes in the basic design.

The initial cost of a patent is the cash or cash equivalent price paid when the patent is acquired. It should be noted that the saying, "A patent is only as good as the money you're prepared to spend defending it," is very true. Most patents are subject to some type of litigation by competitors. A well-known example is the patent infringement suit won by Polaroid against Eastman Kodak in protecting its patent on instant cameras. If the owner incurs legal costs in successfully defending the patent in an infringement suit, such costs are considered necessary to establish the validity of the patent. Thus, they are added to the Patent account and amortized over the **remaining life** of the patent.

The cost of a patent should be amortized over its legal life or useful life, whichever is shorter. In determining useful life, due consideration should be given to obsolescence, inadequacy, and other factors that may cause a patent to become economically ineffective before the end of its legal life. To illustrate the computation of patent expense, assume that National Labs purchases a patent at a cost of $60,000. If the useful life of the patent is eight years, the annual amortization expense is $7,500 ($60,000 ÷ 8). The entry to record the annual amortization is:

Dec. 31	Patent Expense	7,500	
	Patents		7,500
	(To record patent amortization)		

Patent expense is classified as an operating expense in the income statement.

COPYRIGHTS

Copyrights are granted by the federal government, giving the owner the exclusive right to reproduce and sell an artistic or published work. Copyrights extend for the life of the creator plus 50 years. The cost of the copyright consists of the cost of acquiring and defending it.

The useful life of a copyright generally is significantly shorter than its legal life. Similar to other intangible assets, the maximum write-off is 40 years. Because of the difficulties of determining the period over which benefits are to be received, copyrights usually are amortized over a relatively short period of time.

TRADEMARKS AND TRADE NAMES

A **trademark** or **trade name** is a word, phrase, jingle, or symbol that distinguishes or identifies a particular enterprise or product. Trade names like Wheaties, Trivial Pursuit, Sunkist, Kleenex, Coca-Cola, Big Mac, and Cadillac create immediate product identification in our minds and generally enhance the sale of the product. The creator or original user may obtain exclusive legal right to the trademark or trade name by registering it with the U.S. Patent Office. Such registration provides 20 years' protection and may be renewed indefinitely as long as the trademark or trade name is in use.

If the trademark or trade name is purchased, the cost is the purchase price. If it is developed by the enterprise itself, the cost includes attorney's fees, registration fees, design costs, successful legal defense costs, and other expenditures directly related to securing it.

As with other intangibles, the cost of trademarks and trade names must be amortized over the shorter of its useful life or 40 years. Because of the uncertainty involved in estimating the useful life, the cost is frequently amortized over a much shorter period.

FRANCHISES AND LICENSES

When you drive down the street in your Trans-Am purchased from a General Motors dealer, fill up your tank at the corner Standard Oil station, eat lunch at Wendy's, rent an apartment through Coldwell-Banker realty, or vacation at a Club Med resort, you are dealing with franchises. A **franchise** is a contractual arrangement under which the franchisor grants the franchisee the right to sell certain products or to render specific services, or to use certain trademarks or trade names, usually within a designated geographical area.

Another type of franchise is that entered into between a governmental body (commonly municipalities) and a business enterprise that permits the enterprise to use public property in performing its services. Examples are the use of city streets for a bus line or taxi service, use of public land for telephone or electric lines, public waterways for a ferry service, or the use of

airwaves for radio or TV broadcasting. Such operating rights are referred to as licenses or permits.

Franchises and licenses may be for a definite period of time, an indefinite period, or perpetual. When costs are identified with the acquisition of the franchise or license, an intangible asset should be recognized. In the case of a limited life, the cost of a franchise (or license) should be amortized as operating expense over the expected life. If the life is indefinite or perpetual, the cost may be amortized over a reasonable period not to exceed 40 years. Annual payments made under a franchise agreement should be entered as operating expenses in the period in which they are incurred.

ORGANIZATION COSTS

Costs incurred in the formation of a corporation are called **organization costs.** These costs include fees to underwriters for handling stock and bond issues, legal fees, state incorporation fees, and promotional expenditures involved in the organization of the business. These organization costs are capitalized as an intangible asset entitled Organization Costs. It may be argued that organization costs have an asset life equal to the life of the corporation. Many companies, however, amortize these costs over an arbitrary period of time, up to a maximum of 40 years. Because income tax regulations require the amortization of organization costs over a period of at least five years, some companies prefer to use the same period of amortization for accounting purposes.

GOODWILL

The largest intangible asset that usually appears on a company's balance sheet is goodwill. **Goodwill** is the value of all favorable attributes that relate to a business enterprise. These include exceptional management, desirable location, good customer relations, skilled employees, high-quality products, fair pricing policies, and harmonious relations with labor unions. Some view goodwill as expected earnings in excess of normal earnings. **Goodwill is, therefore, unusual because, unlike other assets such as investments, plant assets, and other intangibles that can be sold individually in the marketplace, goodwill can be identified only with the business as a whole.**

If goodwill can be identified only with the business as a whole, how can it be determined? Certainly, many of the factors above (exceptional management, desirable location, and so on) are present in many business enterprises. However, to determine the amount of goodwill in these types of situations would be too difficult and very subjective. In other words, the recognition of goodwill without any exchange transaction leads to subjective valuations that do not contribute to the reliability of financial statements. **As a result, goodwill is recorded only when there is an exchange transaction that involves the purchase of an entire business.**

Determining the Fair Market Value of Assets Acquired

When an entire business is purchased, goodwill is the excess of cost over the fair market value of the net assets (assets less liabilities) acquired. In making the determination, the purchase price (cost) is assigned first to the

fair market values of the identifiable assets and liabilities acquired. Any remainder of the purchase price is then assigned to goodwill. To illustrate, assume that Hatfield Company has decided to purchase Sausolito Company for $6,100,000 on December 31, 1987. A review of Sausolito's condensed balance sheet indicates the following:

Condensed balance sheet

Sausolito Company
Balance Sheet
December 31, 1987

Cash	$ 200,000	Notes payable	$ 950,000
Accounts receivable (net)	640,000	Accounts payable	150,000
Inventories	560,000	L. Sausolito, Capital	3,200,000
Plant assets (net)	2,900,000		
	$4,300,000		$4,300,000

The net assets of Sausolito Company are $2,900,000 as shown by the balance in the capital account and computed as follows:

Computation of net assets (historical cost)

Total assets	$4,300,000
Total liabilities	1,100,000
Net assets at historical cost	**$3,200,000**

If Hatfield is willing to pay $6,100,000 for these net assets, it appears that the amount of goodwill can be easily computed. However, we have to be careful because the assets and liabilities of Sausolito Company are reported at book value, not fair market value. Therefore, it is necessary to determine the fair market value of Sausolito's identifiable net assets.

The fair market value of the net assets of Sausolito are $5,250,000, computed as follows:

Computation of net assets (fair market value)

Assets		
Cash	$ 200,000	
Accounts receivable (net)	640,000	
Inventories	810,000	
Plant assets (net)	4,700,000	
Total assets		$6,350,000
Liabilities		
Notes payable	950,000	
Accounts payable	150,000	
Total liabilities		1,100,000
Net assets at fair market value		**$5,250,000**

A review of these fair market values indicates that substantial differences between cost and fair market value exist for inventories and plant assets. Inventories on a cost basis are $560,000, but on a fair market value basis they are $810,000. Plant assets are $2,900,000 on a cost basis, but $4,700,000 on a fair market value basis.

Finding differences between cost and fair market values in these two areas is not surprising. For example, Sausolito may have been using a LIFO method to report its inventory cost. If prices have been rising and the company growing, the inventory cost amount might include costs incurred in much earlier periods at lower price levels. Moreover, as previously explained, depreciation is a process of cost allocation. Consequently, the book value of plant assets may differ significantly from fair market value.

Computing Goodwill

Goodwill is computed as the difference between the purchase price and the fair market value of the net assets acquired. Goodwill, therefore, is $850,000, computed as follows:

Computation of goodwill

Purchase price (cost)	$6,100,000
Less: Fair market value of net assets	5,250,000
Goodwill	$ 850,000

In recording the purchase of a business, the net assets are shown at their fair market values, goodwill is recorded at its cost, and any cash is credited for the purchase price. Subsequently, goodwill is written off over its useful life not to exceed 40 years. The amortization entry generally results in a debit to Goodwill Expense and a credit to Goodwill. Goodwill is reported in the balance sheet under Intangible Assets.

In the final analysis, goodwill is an amount resulting from negotiations between buyer and seller. There are some rather complex mathematical models for estimating goodwill. The computer version of these calculations, sometimes called valuation models, allows even a small business to use these sophisticated techniques.

LEASES

A **lease** is a contractual understanding between a **lessor** (owner of the property) and a **lessee** (renter of the property) that grants the right to use specific property for a period of time in return for cash payments. Lease arrangements are extremely popular. Just as you would probably lease a campus apartment rather than buy one, companies also find many advantages to leasing rather than purchasing. One reason for leasing's increased popularity is that it can be a source of 100% financing, whereas with other types of financing arrangements only 60–80% can be financed. In addition, leasing may enable the company to protect itself against rapid changes in technology, thereby reducing the cost of obsolescence.

Most lease arrangements grant the lessee the right to use property of the lessor for stipulated periods. In such cases, the rent is included as an expense on the books of the lessee during the period of incurrence. However, special problems develop in the following cases.

Lease Prepayments

If a lump sum payment is made in advance in addition to periodic rental payments, it is necessary to allocate this prepaid rent to the proper periods. This prepayment, often referred to as a **leasehold,** gives the lessee the right to use the property for an extended period of time. Leaseholds are reported as an asset, which may be included under intangible assets.

Leasehold Improvements

Lease contracts generally indicate that any improvements made to the property by the lessee revert to the lessor at the end of the lease term. If the lessee, for example, constructs an additional wall in a leased facility, the lessee has the right to benefit from the improvement over the life of the lease, but the new improvement becomes the property of the lessor when the lease expires.

The lessee should charge the cost of any improvements to a Leasehold Improvements account. This account should be amortized over the life of the lease or the useful life of the improvement, whichever is shorter. Some accountants classify leasehold improvements as an intangible asset while other accountants classify them as property, plant, and equipment.

Capitalization of Leases

In some cases, the lease contract transfers substantially all of the benefits and the risk of ownership to the lessee, so that the leased asset is in effect a purchase of the property. In this case, a leased asset and related liability are reported. This subject is discussed more fully in Chapter 17.

RESEARCH AND DEVELOPMENT COSTS

Research and development costs are not intangible costs, but because their expenditure may lead to patents and copyrights, they are discussed in this section. Many companies spend considerable sums of money on research and development in an ongoing effort to develop new products or processes. For example, in a recent year IBM spent over $2.5 billion on research and development, an amount greater than the total expenditure level of many state governments.

Research and development costs present several accounting problems: (1) it is sometimes difficult to assign the costs to specific projects, and (2) there are uncertainties in identifying the extent and timing of future benefits. As a result, research and development costs are usually recorded as an expense when incurred.[3] The expensing of such costs is not contingent on whether the research and development is successful or unsuccessful.

To illustrate, assume that Laser Scanner Company has expended $3,000,000 in research and development costs. The research and development costs have led to the development of two patents that are highly successful.

[3]"Accounting for Research and Development Costs," Statement of Financial Accounting Standards No. 2 (Stamford, Conn.: FASB, 1974), par. 12.

The research and development cost, however, cannot be included in the cost of the patent; rather, the costs are recorded as an expense when incurred.

Many disagree with this accounting approach. They argue that to expense these costs leads to understated assets and net income. Others, however, argue that capitalizing these costs will lead only to highly speculative assets on the balance sheet. Who is right is difficult to determine. The controversy, however, illustrates how difficult it is to establish proper guidelines for financial reporting.

FINANCIAL STATEMENT PRESENTATION

Usually plant assets and natural resources are combined under Property, Plant, and Equipment, while intangibles are shown separately under Intangible Assets. Either within the balance sheet or in the notes, there should be disclosure of the balances of the major classes of assets, such as land, buildings, and equipment, and accumulated depreciation by major classes or in total. In addition, the depreciation and amortization methods used should be described and the amount of depreciation and amortization expense for the period disclosed. The following excerpts adapted from a recent balance sheet are illustrative.

Presentation of property, plant, and equipment and intangible assets

Owens-Illinois, Inc.
(In millions of dollars)

Property, plant, and equipment			
Timberlands, at cost, less accumulated depletion		$ 95.4	
Buildings and equipment, at cost	$2,207.1		
Less: Accumulated depreciation	1,229.0	978.1	
Total property, plant, and equipment			$1,073.5
Intangibles			
Patents			410.0
Total			$1,483.5

In the notes to its financial statements, Owens-Illinois identifies the major classes of property, plant, and equipment and indicates that depreciation is by the straight-line method, depletion is by the units of activity method, and amortization is by the straight-line method.

SUMMARY OF STUDY OBJECTIVES

1. The accounting for disposal of a plant asset through retirement or sale is as follows:

(a) Eliminate the book value of the plant asset at the date of disposal.

(b) Record cash proceeds, if any.
(c) Account for the difference between the book value and the cash proceeds as a gain or loss on disposal.

In accounting for exchanges

(a) Eliminate the book value of the old asset at the date of the exchange.
(b) Record the acquisition cost of the new asset.
(c) Account for the gain or loss, if any, on the old asset.
    1. If dissimilar assets are exchanged, record all gains and losses.
    2. If similar assets are exchanged, (a) record all losses but (b) recognize no gains.

2. Subsidiary plant ledgers are useful in helping to keep track of periodic depreciation charges and in making entries upon the retirement of individual items. The subsidiary data are also helpful in determining the adequacy of insurance coverage, submitting insurance claims in the event of accidents, and filing income tax returns.

3. The basic accounting issues related to natural resources are whether exploration costs on unsuccessful explorations should be capitalized or expensed. Under the full cost approach, both successful and unsuccessful explorations are capitalized and the costs amortized to expense over the useful life of the successful wells. This method is referred to as the full cost approach. The other approach is to capitalize only the costs of successful wells. This approach is referred to as the successful efforts approach.

4. The accounting for intangible assets and plant assets is much the same. One difference is that the term used to describe the write off of an intangible asset is amortization, rather than depreciation. In addition, the amortization of the intangible asset cannot be longer than 40 years. The straight-line method is normally used for amortizing intangible assets.

5. Usually plant assets and natural resources are combined under Property, Plant, and Equipment, while intangibles are shown separately under Intangible Assets. Either within the balance sheet or in the notes, there should be disclosure of the balances of the major classes of assets, such as land, buildings, and equipment, and accumulated depreciation by major classes or in total. In addition, the depreciation and amortization methods used should be described and the amount of depreciation and amortization expense for the period should be disclosed.

GLOSSARY

Amortization, p. 430

Copyrights, p. 431

Depletion, p. 428

Franchises (licenses), p. 431

Full cost approach, p. 428
Goodwill, p. 432
Intangible assets, p. 429
Lease, p. 434
Leasehold, p. 435
Lessee, p. 434
Lessor, p. 434
Natural resources, p. 427
Organization costs, p. 432
Patent, p. 430
Research and development costs, p. 435
Subsidiary plant ledger, p. 426
Successful efforts approach, p. 428
Trademarks (trade names), p. 431
Wasting assets, p. 427

DEMONSTRATION PROBLEM

On January 1, 1985, the Skyline Limousine Co. purchased a limousine at an acquisition cost of $28,000. The vehicle has been depreciated by the straight-line method using a four-year service life and a $4,000 salvage value. The company's fiscal year ends on December 31.

INSTRUCTIONS

Prepare the journal entry or entries to record the disposal of the limousine assuming that it was:

(1) Retired and scrapped with no salvage value on January 1, 1989.
(2) Sold for $5,000 on July 1, 1988.
(3) Traded in on new office equipment on January 1, 1988. The fair market value of the vehicle was $9,000 and $22,000 was paid in cash.
(4) Traded in on a new limousine on January 1, 1988. The fair market value of the old vehicle was $11,000 and $22,000 was paid in cash.

SOLUTION TO DEMONSTRATION PROBLEM

(1) 1/1/89	Accumulated Depreciation – Limousine	24,000	
	Loss on Disposal	4,000	
	Limousine		28,000
	(To record retirement of limousine)		
(2) 7/1/88	Depreciation Expense	3,000	
	Accumulated Depreciation – Limousine		3,000
	(To record depreciation to date of disposal)		
	Cash	5,000	
	Accumulated Depreciation – Limousine	21,000	
	Loss on Disposal	2,000	
	Limousine		28,000
	(To record sale of limousine)		

(3) 1/1/88	Office Equipment	31,000	
	Accumulated Depreciation – Limousine	18,000	
	Loss on Disposal	1,000	
	Limousine		28,000
	Cash		22,000
	(To record exchange of limousine for office equipment)		
(4) 1/1/88	Limousine (new)	32,000	
	Accumulated Depreciation – Limousine (old)	18,000	
	Limousine (old)		28,000
	Cash		22,000
	(To record exchange of limousines)		

QUESTIONS

1. In what ways may a company dispose of plant assets?

2. Bo Brady and Diedra Hall, two accounting students, are discussing the proper accounting for disposal of plant assets. Bo says, "All you have to do is eliminate the plant asset and related accumulated depreciation and record the gain or loss, where appropriate." How should Diedra respond?

3. Custer Corporation owns a machine which is fully depreciated but is still being used. How should Custer account for this asset and report it in the financial statements?

4. How is a gain or loss on the sale of a plant asset computed?

5. Jim McMahon is studying for an accounting test. He is having difficulty with the topic of exchanging plant assets. Explain to Jim what steps should be followed when accounting for such an exchange.

6. When dissimilar assets are exchanged, how is the gain or loss on disposal computed?

7. Perry Refrigeration Company trades in an old machine on a new model when the value of the old machine is greater than its book value. Should Perry recognize a gain on disposal? If the value of the old machine is less than its book value, should Perry recognize a loss on disposal?

8. The Dent Company experienced a gain on disposal when exchanging similar machines. In accordance with generally accepted accounting principles, the gain was not recognized. How will Dent's future financial statements be affected by not recognizing the gain?

9. Why are subsidiary plant ledgers useful?

10. What are natural resources and what are their distinguishing characteristics?

11. Otis Wilson and Wilbur Montgomery are arguing about the full cost approach and the successful efforts approach. Wilson says that the full cost approach will provide a greater reported asset value, while Montgomery says that the successful efforts approach would. Who is correct?

12. How are intangible assets different from plant assets? How are they the same?

13. What are the similarities and differences between the terms depreciation, depletion, and amortization?

14. The Hampton Company hires an accounting intern who says that intangible assets should always be amortized over their legal lives. Is the intern correct? Explain.

15. Define the terms: (a) patent, (b) franchise, and (c) organization costs.

16. What are the general requirements in accounting for intangible assets?

17. Goodwill has been defined as the value of all favorable attributes that relate to a business enterprise. What types of attributes could result in goodwill?

18. Jim Covert, a business major, is working on a case problem for one of his classes. In this case problem, the company needs to raise cash to market a new product they developed. Tom Thayer, an engineering major, takes one look at the company's balance sheet and says, "This company has an awful lot of goodwill. Why don't you recommend that they sell some of it to raise cash?" How should Jim respond to Tom?

19. Under what conditions is goodwill recorded?

20. When an entire business is purchased, how is the amount of goodwill measured?

21. Bortz Company leases a building for ten years and makes improvements to the building which have a useful life of 15 years. Over what period of years should these improvements be amortized?

22. Often research and development costs provide companies with benefits which last a number of years (for example, these costs can lead to the development of a patent which will increase the company's income for many years). However, generally accepted accounting principles require that such costs be recorded as an expense when incurred. Why?

EXERCISES

E11-1 Presented below are selected transactions of Haley Bible Company for 1987.

Jan. 1	Retired a piece of machinery which was purchased on January 1, 1977. The machine cost $48,000 on that date, and had a useful life of 10 years with no salvage value.
June 30	Sold a computer which was purchased on January 1, 1984. The computer cost $40,000, and had a useful life of 7 years with a salvage value of $12,000. The computer was sold for $23,000.
Dec. 31	Discarded a delivery truck which was purchased on January 1, 1981. The truck cost $17,000 and was depreciated based on an 8-year useful life with a $1,000 salvage value.

INSTRUCTIONS

Journalize all entries required on the above dates, including entries to update depreciation, where applicable, on assets disposed of. Haley Bible Company uses straight-line depreciation.

E11-2 Bilder Corporation sold the following two machines in 1987:

	Cost	Purchase Date	Useful Life	Salvage Value	Depr. Method	Date Sold	Sales Price
Machine A	$46,000	7/1/83	5 years	$6,000	S-L	7/1/87	$16,500
Machine B	$51,000	1/1/84	6 years	$9,000	S-Y-D	10/1/87	$13,000

INSTRUCTIONS

Journalize the entries required to update depreciation on, and record the sales of, the two assets in 1987. Assume that the company has taken depreciation to December 31, 1986 on both machines.

E11-3 On September 30, 1987, the Vanna White Company acquired a new machine that had a fair market value of $63,000, exchanging an old machine of similar type that had a fair market value of $13,000. The company paid cash of $15,000 and signed a one-year, 15% note payable for the balance. At December 31, 1986, the balances in the relevant accounts were:

Machine	$50,000
Accumulated Depreciation – Machine	$25,000

The old machine is being depreciated on a straight-line basis using a 9-year useful life, and a $5,000 salvage value.

INSTRUCTIONS

Journalize entries to record 1987 depreciation on the old machine and the acquisition of the new machine.

E11-4 Frank's Delivery Company and Kay's Express Delivery exchanged similar delivery trucks on January 1, 1987. Frank's truck cost $18,000, had acccumulated depreciation of $12,000, and has a fair market value of $5,000. Kay's truck cost $10,000, had accumulated depreciation of $8,000, and has a fair market value of $3,600. Kay paid Frank cash of $1,400 as part of the transaction.

INSTRUCTIONS

(a) Journalize the exchange for Frank's Delivery Company.
(b) Journalize the exchange for Kay's Express Delivery.
(c) If the assets exchanged were not similar, what amount of gain or loss would Frank recognize?
(d) If the assets exchanged were not similar, what amount of gain or loss would Kay recognize?

E11-5 The Republic Company exchanged equipment used in its manufacturing operations plus $2,000 in cash for similar equipment used in the operations of the Tyler Company. The following information pertains to the exchange:

	Republic Co.	Tyler Co.
Equipment (cost)	$24,000	$22,000
Accumulated depreciation	20,000	5,000
Fair market value of equipment	12,000	14,000
Cash paid	2,000	

INSTRUCTIONS

Prepare the journal entries to record the exchange on the books of both companies.

E11-6 On July 1, 1987, Klar Corporation purchased a patent for $135,000 and also invested $300,000 in a mine estimated to have 500,000 tons of ore of uniform grade.

The patent expires in 13 years, and is expected to be used by Klar for 9 years. During the last 6 months of 1987, 100,000 tons of ore were mined and sold.

INSTRUCTIONS

Prepare journal entries to record 1987 patent amortization and depletion expense.

E11-7 The following are selected 1987 transactions of Spikes Corporation.

Jan. 1	Purchased a small company and recorded goodwill of $50,000. The goodwill has a useful life of 50 years.
April 1	Timberland was purchased for $200,000. The amount of timber is estimated at 1,200,000 board feet. After all the timber is cleared, the land can be sold for $20,000. During 1987, 150,000 board feet of timber were cut and sold.
May 1	Purchased a patent with an estimated useful life of 7 years and a legal life of 17 years for $13,650.

INSTRUCTIONS

Prepare all adjusting entries at December 31 to record amortization and depletion required by the events above.

E11-8 Mike Corporation will purchase Pete Company for $9,300,000 cash on December 31, 1987. Presented below is Pete Company's balance sheet at that date.

PETE COMPANY
Balance Sheet
December 31, 1987

Cash	$ 110,000	Notes payable	$1,450,000
Temporary investments	250,000	Accounts payable	230,000
Accounts receivable (net)	900,000	Clare Pete, Capital	6,430,000
Inventories	850,000		
Plant assets (net)	6,000,000		
Total assets	$8,110,000	Total liabilities and owner's equity	$8,110,000

The fair market values of certain assets exceed their book values, as indicated below.

Assets	Fair market value
Temporary investments	$ 280,000
Inventories	1,010,000
Plant assets (net)	7,100,000

INSTRUCTIONS

(a) What amount should Mike Corporation record as goodwill on December 31, 1987?

(b) Mike chooses to amortize the goodwill over 25 years. What amount should be reported as goodwill on Mike Corporation's balance sheet at December 31, 1988?

E11-9 Randall Company, organized in 1987, has set up a single account for all intangible assets. The following summary discloses the debit entries that have been recorded during 1987.

1/2/87	Purchased patent (9-year life)	$ 270,000
4/1/87	Goodwill purchased (indefinite life)	320,000
7/1/87	10-year franchise; expiration date 7/1/97	450,000

8/1/87	Advance payment on leasehold (4-year lease)	120,000
9/1/87	Research and development costs	185,000
		$1,345,000

INSTRUCTIONS

Prepare the necessary entries to clear the Intangible Asset account and to set up separate accounts for distinct types of intangibles. Make the entries as of December 31, 1987, recording any necessary amortization and reflecting all balances accurately as of that date.

PROBLEMS

P11-1 At December 31, 1986, Benedict Corporation reported the following as plant assets:

Land		$ 2,000,000
Timberlands	$14,000,000	
Less: Accumulated depletion	3,700,000	10,300,000
Buildings	26,500,000	
Less: Accumulated depreciation—buildings	12,100,000	14,400,000
Equipment	30,000,000	
Less: Accumulated depreciation—equipment	5,000,000	25,000,000
Total plant assets		$51,700,000

During 1987, the following selected cash transactions occurred:

April 1	Purchased land and a building for $2,300,000. Appraised value of the land is $250,000 and the building $2,250,000.
April 30	Spent $400,000 remodeling the building purchased on April 1. The building was put into use on May 1. (Hint: Depreciation starts on building at this point.)
May 1	Sold equipment which cost $500,000 when purchased on January 2, 1983. The equipment was sold for $230,000.
June 1	Sold land and building purchased on June 1, 1977 for $1,800,000. The land cost $100,000 and the building cost $1,400,000 when purchased.
July 1	Sold equipment which cost $450,000 when purchased on January 3, 1982. The equipment was sold for $250,000.
July 1	Purchased equipment for $1,000,000. Spent an additional $50,000 for freight and installation.
Dec. 31	Retired equipment which cost $600,000 when purchased on December 31, 1977. No salvage value was received.

INSTRUCTIONS

(a) Journalize the above transactions. Benedict uses straight-line depreciation for buildings and equipment. The buildings are estimated to have a 40-year useful life and 10% salvage value, while the equipment is estimated to have a 10-year useful life and 10% salvage value. Update depreciation on assets disposed of at the time of sale or retirement. The timberlands will produce 32,500,000 board feet of timber and have a salvage value of $1,000,000 after the timber is removed. 3,000,000 board feet of timber were removed and sold in 1987.

(b) Record adjusting entries for depreciation and depletion for 1987.

(c) Prepare the plant asset section of Benedict's balance sheet at December 31, 1987.

P11-2 Hodges Company owns the following machinery at January 1, 1987. It uses straight-line (S-L) depreciation for some machines, and sum-of-the-years'-digits (S-Y-D) depreciation for others.

Machine No.	Cost	Date Purchased	Useful Life	Salvage	Depreciation Method	Accumulated Depreciation 1/1/87
1	$20,000	1/3/81	8 years	$3,000	S-L	?
2	24,000	1/4/82	8 years	3,600	S-L	?
3	26,000	7/1/82	8 years	3,900	S-L	?
4	27,000	9/1/82	8 years	4,050	S-L	?
5	28,000	1/3/83	10 years	2,800	S-L	?
6	30,500	1/2/84	10 years	3,050	S-L	?
7	48,000	1/2/84	6 years	6,000	S-Y-D	?
8	53,000	1/3/85	6 years	6,800	S-Y-D	?

The following transactions involving machinery occurred during 1987.

Jan. 2 Traded machine No. 1 for a similar machine (No. 9) that had a fair market value of $31,000 and paid a $22,000 cash difference.

July 1 Sold machine No. 2 for $7,325.

July 1 Traded machine No. 3 for a similar machine (No. 10) that had a fair market value of $32,000 and paid a cash difference of $21,000.

Oct. 1 Sold machine No. 7 for $16,000.

INSTRUCTIONS

(Round all computations to the nearest dollar.)

(a) Complete the last column in the table above.

(b) Prepare journal entries for the four transactions. Where necessary, first prepare a journal entry to update depreciation on the machine.

(c) Prepare an adjusting entry at December 31, 1987 to record depreciation expense on machines 4, 5, 6, 8, 9, and 10. Machines 9 and 10 will be depreciated on a straight-line basis over 10 years with a salvage value equal to 10% of cost.

P11-3 On January 2, 1987, the Rainey Corporation purchased a developed mine for $7,000,000. The expected capacity of the mine was 1,200,000 tons. The land can be sold at the end of the life of the mine for $1,000,000. On April 1, the corporation purchased equipment for $500,000. The equipment can be used on this and other mines, has a useful life of 10 years and an estimated salvage value of $80,000. Straight-line depreciation is used. In 1987, Rainey incurred labor costs of $800,000 to mine 200,000 tons, which sold at $16 per ton. The company incurred other operating expenses of $620,000.

In January 1988, Rainey spent an additional $600,000 to expand the capacity of the mine to 250,000 tons greater than originally expected. In 1988, the company incurred labor costs of $1,300,000 to mine 300,000 tons, which sold at $18 per ton. The company incurred other operating expenses of $810,000.

INSTRUCTIONS

(a) Compute depletion expense per ton in 1987.

(b) Compute depletion expense per ton in 1988. (Hint: Compute the book value of the mine at January 1, 1988.)

(c) Determine net income for 1987 and 1988. Ignore income taxes.

(d) Indicate how the mine will be presented in the balance sheets at December 31, 1987 and December 31, 1988.

P11-4 The intangible asset section of Conine Corporation at December 31, 1986 is presented below:

Patent ($40,000 cost less $4,000 amortization)	$36,000
Copyright ($35,000 cost less $14,000 amortization)	21,000
Total	$57,000

The patent was acquired in January of 1986 and has a useful life of 10 years. The copyright was acquired in January of 1983 and also has a useful life of 10 years. The following cash transactions may have affected intangible assets during 1987:

Jan. 2	Paid $9,000 legal costs to successfully defend the patent against infringement by another company.
Jan.-June	Developed a new product incurring $102,000 in research and development costs. A patent was granted for the product on July 1, and its useful life is equal to its legal life.
July 1	Acquired Farrey Company for $160,000. The balance sheet of Farrey showed assets of $112,500 and liabilities of $37,500. The fair market value of the recorded assets is $144,000. Farrey also owns a patent, not shown on its balance sheet, which has a fair market value of $6,000. The patent was transferred to Conine as a part of the $160,000 purchase. The patent will be amortized over 6 years, and any goodwill over 25 years. (Hint: Except for the unrecorded intangible assets, simply debit assets and credit liabilities.)
Sept. 1	Paid $50,000 to a "punky" quarterback to appear in commercials advertising the company's products. The commercials will air in September and October.
Oct. 1	Acquired a copyright for $60,000. The copyright has a useful life of 50 years.

INSTRUCTIONS

(a) Prepare journal entries to record the transactions above.

(b) Prepare journal entries to record the 1987 amortization expense for intangible assets.

(c) Prepare the intangible asset section of the balance sheet at December 31, 1987.

P11-5 Due to rapid turnover in the accounting department, a number of transactions involving intangible assets and natural resources were improperly recorded by Eirich Corporation in 1987.

1. Eirich developed a new manufacturing process at a cost of $85,000. The company also purchased a patent for $34,000. In early January, Eirich capitalized $119,000 as the cost of the patents. Patent amortization expense of $7,000 was recorded based on a 17-year useful life.
2. Also, in early January, Eirich paid $21,000 of legal costs to successfully defend a patent from infringement by a competitor. This amount was charged to legal expense. The patent had originally been purchased on January 1, 1984 at a cost of $150,000. The patent was being amortized over 10 years, and $15,000 was recorded as 1987 amortization expense.
3. On July 1, 1987, Eirich purchased a small company and as a result acquired goodwill of $44,000. Eirich recorded a half-year's amortization in 1987, based on a 50-year life ($440 amortization).

4. On September 1, 1987 Eirich permanently installed wall partitions, shelving, and counters in a store leased from another company. The cost of $18,000 was debited to Leasehold Improvements. Eirich recorded four months' amortization based on the 20-year physical life of the improvements ($300 amortization). The lease extends until December 31, 1995 and is not expected to be renewed.
5. On October 1, 1987, Eirich purchased a mine for $100,000. Eirich expects to extract all of the minerals over a 5-year period, so they recorded 1987 depletion expense of $5,000 ($20,000 × ¼). In 1987 the company extracted and sold 32,000 tons. The mine is expected to produce 400,000 tons.

INSTRUCTIONS

Prepare all journal entries necessary to correct any errors made during 1987. Assume the books have not yet been closed for 1987.

P11–6 During 1987, the Singletary Company completed the following transactions pertaining to the specific types of long-lived assets identified below:

Patents. On January 1 it purchased a patent for $50,000 cash. On September 1 it paid $5,600 in successfully defending the patent in an infringement suit. It is the company's practice to amortize patents by the straight-line method over 10 years.

Oil Properties. On October 31, it determined that $1,000,000 of exploration costs were successful in locating oil and $200,000 resulted in "dry holes." The Singletary Company expects to pump 5 million barrels of oil from the successful wells with no salvage value. In 1987, 100,000 barrels of oil were extracted and sold. The company uses the units-of-activity method for depletion and follows the successful efforts approach for recording exploration expenditures. (Hint: The $200,000 of unsuccessful exploration costs should be debited to Exploration Expense. The $1,000,000 of successful exploration costs should be capitalized.)

Office Equipment. On January 1, it purchased for cash 100 new RXC electromatic typewriters at a cost of $600 each. The typewriters are expected to have a useful life of four years with no salvage value. On September 1, two typewriters were damaged and sold for $100 each. The company uses straight-line depreciation.

Research and Development. The company's on-going research program resulted in the incurrence of $425,000 of research and development expenses during the year which were paid in cash. By year end, patent rights were granted on $125,000 of these expenditures.

INSTRUCTIONS

For each type of asset:

(a) Journalize the 1987 transactions.
(b) Journalize the December 31, 1987 entries for amortization, depletion, and depreciation.
(c) Give the balance sheet and income statement presentation at December 31, 1987.

ALTERNATE PROBLEMS

P11–1A At December 31, 1986, Lawrence Corporation reported the following as plant assets:

Land		$ 3,000,000
Timberlands	$14,000,000	
Less: Accumulated depletion	3,900,000	10,100,000
Buildings	28,500,000	
Less: Accumulated depreciation – building	12,100,000	16,400,000
Equipment	38,000,000	
Less: Accumulated depreciation – equipment	5,000,000	33,000,000
Total plant assets		$62,500,000

During 1987, the following selected cash transactions occurred:

April 1	Purchased land and a building, $2,530,000. Appraised value of the land is $280,000 and the building $2,520,000.
April 30	Spent $440,000 remodeling the building purchased on April 1. The building was put into use on May 1. (Hint: Depreciation starts on building at this point.)
May 1	Sold equipment which cost $500,000 when purchased on January 2, 1983. The equipment was sold for $220,000.
June 1	Sold land and building purchased on June 1, 1977 for $1,800,000. The land cost $100,000 and the building cost $1,680,000 when purchased.
July 1	Sold equipment which cost $480,000 when purchased on January 3, 1982. The equipment was sold for $250,000.
July 1	Purchased equipment for $1,000,000. Spent an additional $60,000 for freight and installation.
Dec. 31	Retired equipment which cost $600,000 when purchased on December 31, 1977. No salvage value was received.

INSTRUCTIONS

(a) Journalize the above transactions. Lawrence uses straight-line depreciation for buildings and equipment. The buildings are estimated to have a 40-year life and 10% salvage value, while the equipment is estimated to have a 10-year useful life and 10% salvage value. Update depreciation on assets disposed of at the time of sale or retirement. The timberlands will produce 32,500,000 board feet of timber and have a salvage value of $1,000,000 after the timber is removed. 3,800,000 board feet of timber were removed and sold in 1987.

(b) Record adjusting entries for depreciation and depletion for 1987.

(c) Prepare the plant asset section of Lawrence's balance sheet at December 31, 1987.

P11-2A Lei Ward Corporation owns the following machinery at January 1, 1987. It uses straight-line (S-L) depreciation for some machines and sum-of-the-years'-digits (S-Y-D) depreciation for others.

Machine No.	Cost	Date Purchased	Useful Life	Salvage	Depreciation Method	Accumulated Depreciation 1/1/87
1	$30,000	1/3/81	8 years	$4,500	S-L	?
2	36,480	1/4/82	8 years	5,472	S-L	?
3	38,400	7/1/82	8 years	5,760	S-L	?
4	41,600	9/1/82	8 years	6,240	S-L	?
5	42,000	1/3/83	10 years	4,200	S-L	?
6	46,000	1/2/84	10 years	4,600	S-L	?
7	72,000	1/2/84	6 years	9,000	S-Y-D	?
8	79,500	1/3/85	6 years	10,200	S-Y-D	?

The following transactions involving machinery occurred during 1987.

Jan. 2 Traded machine No. 1 for a similar machine (No. 9) that had a fair market value of $47,000 and paid a $33,000 cash difference.

July 1 Sold machine No. 2 for $10,950.

July 1 Traded machine No. 3 for a similar machine (No. 10) that had a fair market value of $48,000 and paid a cash difference of $32,000.

Oct. 1 Sold machine No. 7 for $24,300.

INSTRUCTIONS

(Round all computations to the nearest dollar.)

(a) Complete the last column in the table above on a separate sheet of paper.

(b) Prepare journal entries for the four transactions. Where necessary, first prepare a journal entry to update depreciation on the machine.

(c) Prepare an adjusting entry at December 31, 1987 to record depreciation expense on machines 4, 5, 6, 8, 9, and 10. Machines 9 and 10 will be depreciated on a straight-line basis over 10 years with a salvage value equal to 10% of cost.

P11-3A On January 2, 1987, the Theresa Corporation purchased a developed mine for $9,000,000. The expected capacity of the mine was 1,250,000 tons. The land can be sold at the end of the life of the mine for $1,000,000. On April 1, the corporation purchased equipment for $800,000. The equipment can be used on this and other mines, has a useful life of 10 years and an estimated salvage value of $80,000. Straight-line depreciation is used. In 1987, Theresa incurred labor costs of $900,000 to mine 200,000 tons, which sold at $18 per ton. The company incurred other operating expenses of $630,000.

In January 1988, Theresa spent an additional $800,000 to expand the capacity of the mine to 300,000 tons greater than originally expected. In 1988, the company incurred labor costs of $1,300,000 to mine 320,000 tons, which sold at $21 per ton. The company incurred other operating expenses of $840,000.

INSTRUCTIONS

(a) Compute depletion expense per ton in 1987.

(b) Compute depletion expense per ton in 1988. (Hint: Compute the book value of the mine at January 1, 1988.)

(c) Determine net income for 1987 and 1988. Ignore income taxes.

(d) Indicate how the mine will be presented in the balance sheets at December 31, 1987 and December 31, 1988.

P11-4A The intangible asset section of Boomer Company at December 31, 1986 is presented below:

Patent ($50,000 cost less $5,000 amortization)	$45,000
Copyright ($45,000 cost less $18,000 amortization)	27,000
Total	$72,000

The patent was acquired in January of 1986 and has a useful life of 10 years. The copyright was acquired in January of 1983 and also has a useful life of 10 years. The following cash transactions may have affected intangible assets during 1987:

Jan. 2 Paid $9,000 legal costs to successfully defend the patent against infringement by another company.

Jan.–June Developed a new product incurring $119,000 in research and development costs. A patent was granted for the product on July 1, and its useful life is equal to its legal life.

July 1	Acquired King Corporation for $208,000. The balance sheet of King showed assets of $146,250 and liabilities of $48,750. The fair market value of the recorded assets is $187,200. King also owns a patent, not shown on its balance sheet, which has a fair market value of $7,800. The patent was transferred to Boomer as a part of the $208,000 purchase. The patent will be amortized over 6 years, and any goodwill over 25 years. (Hint: Except for the unrecorded intangible assets, simply debit assets and credit liabilities.)
Sept. 1	Paid $77,000 to an extremely large defensive lineman to appear in commercials advertising the company's products. The commercials will air in September and October.
Oct. 1	Acquired a copyright for $62,400. The copyright has a useful life of 50 years.

INSTRUCTIONS

(a) Prepare journal entries to record the transactions above.

(b) Prepare journal entries to record the 1987 amortization expense.

(c) Prepare the intangible asset section of the balance sheet at December 31, 1987.

P11-5A Due to rapid turnover in the accounting department, a number of transactions involving intangible assets and natural resources were improperly recorded by the Anna Banana Company in 1987.

1. Anna developed a new manufacturing process at a cost of $102,000. The company also purchased a patent for $37,400. In early January, Anna capitalized $139,400 as the cost of the patents. Patent amortization expense of $8,200 was recorded based on a 17-year useful life.
2. Also in early January, Anna paid $24,000 of legal costs to defend a patent from infringement by a competitor. This amount was charged to legal expense. The patent had originally been purchased on January 1, 1984 at a cost of $150,000. The patent was being amortized over 15 years, and $10,000 was recorded as 1987 amortization expense.
3. On July 1, 1987, Anna purchased a small company and as a result acquired goodwill of $66,000. Anna recorded a half-year's amortization in 1987, based on a 50-year life ($660 amortization).
4. On September 1, 1987, Anna permanently installed wall partitions, shelving, and counters in a store leased from Schaeffer Realty. The cost of $21,600 was debited to Leasehold Improvements. Anna recorded four months' amortization based on the 20-year physical life of the improvements ($360 amortization). The lease extends until December 31, 1995 and is not expected to be renewed.
5. On October 1, 1987, Anna purchased a mine for $120,000. Anna expects to extract all of the minerals over a 5-year period, so 1987 depletion expense of $6,000 was recorded ($24,000 × ¼). In 1987, they extracted and sold 32,000 tons. The mine is expected to produce 400,000 tons.

INSTRUCTIONS

Prepare all journal entries necessary to correct any errors made during 1987. Assume the books have not yet been closed for 1987.

P11-6A During 1987, the Richardson Company completed the following transactions pertaining to the specific types of long-lived assets identified below:

Office Equipment. On January 1, it purchased for cash 100 new RXC electromatic typewriters at a cost of $650 each. The typewriters are expected to have a useful life of four years with no salvage value. On September 1, two typewriters were damaged and sold for $125 each. The company uses straight-line depreciation.

Research and Development. The company's on-going research program resulted in the incurrence of $450,000 of research and development expenses during the year which were paid in cash. By year end, patent rights were granted on $125,000 of these expenditures.

Patents. On January 1 it purchased a patent for $60,000 cash. On September 1 it paid $6,720 in successfully defending the patent in an infringement suit. It is the company's practice to amortize patents by the straight-line method over 10 years.

Oil Properties. On October 31, it determined that $1,100,000 of exploration costs were successful in locating oil and $200,000 resulted in "dry holes." The Richardson Company expects to pump 5 million barrels of oil from the successful wells with no salvage value. In 1987, 200,000 barrels of oil were extracted and sold. The company uses the units-of-activity method for depletion and follows the successful efforts approach for recording exploration expenditures. (Hint: The $200,000 of unsuccessful exploration costs should be debited to Exploration Expense. The $1,100,000 of successful exploration costs should be capitalized.)

INSTRUCTIONS

For each type of asset:

(a) Journalize the 1987 transactions.

(b) Journalize the December 31, 1987 entries for amortization, depletion, and depreciation.

(c) Give the balance sheet and income statement presentation at December 31, 1987.

DECISION CASE

Conglomerate Company is considering the acquisition of two companies whose balance sheets are as follows:

Assets	Allied Metals	Duke Systems
Cash	$ 60,000	$110,000
Receivables	90,000	80,000
Inventory	110,000	125,000
Plant assets (net)	360,000	420,000
Total assets	$620,000	$735,000
Liabilities and Owner's Equity		
Current liabilities	$120,000	$160,000
Long-term liabilities	100,000	125,000
Owner's capital	400,000	450,000
Total liabilities and owner's equity	$620,000	$735,000

The current fair market values of the inventories and plant assets are shown below:

	Allied Metals	Duke Systems
Inventories	$150,000	$195,000
Plant assets	460,000	500,000

The reported book value of the receivables approximate their current fair market value.

The owner of Allied Metals will sell at a price of 150% of the book value of the company's net assets. The owner of Duke Systems will sell at a price of 160% of the company's net assets.

The management of Conglomerate has concluded after carefully analyzing the financial position and earnings records of the two companies that it is willing to pay a purchase price of 105% of the fair market value of Allied Metal's net assets and 115% of the fair market value of Duke System's net assets.

INSTRUCTIONS

(a) Compute the selling price being asked for each company. Show computations.

(b) Compute the purchase price Conglomerate Company is willing to pay for each company. Show computations.

(c) On the basis of the selling prices being asked and the purchase prices offered, will either purchase occur? Why?

(d) After negotiation, an agreement is reached to purchase Allied Metals for $575,000 and Duke Systems for $700,000. How much goodwill, if any, should be recognized by Conglomerate Company in recording the acquisition of each company?

CHAPTER 12

University of California at Santa Cruz

CHAPTER 12

CURRENT LIABILITIES AND PAYROLL ACCOUNTING

STUDY OBJECTIVES

After studying this chapter, you should be able to:

1. Identify the major types of current liabilities.
2. Explain the accounting for interest-bearing and zero-interest-bearing notes payable.
3. Describe the accounting and disclosure requirements for contingent liabilities.
4. Discuss the objectives of internal control for payroll.
5. Record the payroll and related payroll taxes.
6. Identify additional fringe benefits associated with payroll.
7. Explain the two types of pension plans and indicate the basic accounting for them.

Whether it be a pizza parlor like Pizza Hut, a public accounting firm like Arthur Andersen & Co., or a large multinational company like IBM, all businesses have liabilities. Liabilities, in simplest terms, are debts owed by an enterprise. To elaborate further, a liability **is an obligation of an enterprise arising from a past transaction that involves a future payment of cash, goods, or services.** For example, the purchase of merchandise on account, the borrowing of money on a bank loan, and the obligation to pay wages for services performed clearly meet this definition. Liabilities are classified as current or long-term on the balance sheet. We will explain current liabilities in this chapter and long-term liabilities in Chapter 17. Payroll accounting and its impact on a company's current liabilities are also discussed in this chapter.

SECTION ONE—CURRENT LIABILITIES

WHAT IS A CURRENT LIABILITY?

A **current liability** is a debt that can reasonably be expected to be paid (1) within one year or the operating cycle, whichever is longer, and (2) out of existing current assets or result in the creation of other current liabilities. Current liabilities include notes payable, accounts payable, unearned revenues, and accrued liabilities such as taxes, wages, and interest payable.

As explained in Chapter 4, companies must be extremely careful about the level of current liabilities in relationship to current assets. A company that has more current liabilities than current assets is usually the subject of some concern, because it may be difficult for the company to meet its current obligations when they become due. **As a result, management, creditors, and investors pay particular attention to the amount of working capital (current assets minus current liabilities) and the ratio of current assets to current liabilities, often referred to as the current ratio.** For example, General Motors recently reported current assets of $21 billion and current liabilities of $15 billion, which means it has working capital of $6 billion and a current ratio of 1.4:1. These figures suggest that General Motors can pay off its current liabilities as they become due.

TYPES OF CURRENT LIABILITIES

A number of current liabilities have been discussed in previous chapters. For example, the entries for accounts payable and the adjustments for accrued liabilities have been explained. Other types of current liabilities that are frequently encountered in practice are discussed below.

NOTES PAYABLE

Obligations in the form of written promissory notes are recorded as notes payable. Notes payable are often used instead of accounts payable, because the lender wants written documentation related to the obligation in case legal remedies for collection become necessary. Notes payable usually require the borrower to pay interest and are frequently issued to meet short-term financing needs.

Notes are issued for varying periods; **those due for payment within one year of the balance sheet date are usually classified as current liabilities.** Notes may be interest bearing or zero-interest bearing. To illustrate these differing interest features, assume that Margo Sisters needs a four-month $100,000 loan to cover its short-term liquidity needs.

Interest-Bearing Note Issued

Assume that the First National Bank agrees to lend the $100,000 on June 1, 1987 if Margo Sisters signs a $100,000, 12%, four-month note. When a promissory note is interest bearing, the amount of assets received upon the issuance of the note is generally equal to the face value of the note. The entry to record the cash received by Margo Sisters on June 1 is as follows:

June 1	Cash	100,000	
	Notes Payable		100,000
	(To record receipt of cash and issuance of 12% four-month note)		

If Margo Sisters prepares financial statements on August 31, an adjusting entry is required to recognize interest expense and interest payable of $3,000 ($100,000 × 12% × 3/12) for the period June 1 to August 31. The entry on August 31 is recorded as follows:

Aug. 31	Interest Expense	3,000	
	Interest Payable		3,000
	(To record interest expense for three months on $100,000 interest-bearing note)		

The entry to record the payment of interest and face value of the note on October 1 is as follows:

Oct. 1	Notes Payable	100,000	
	Interest Expense	1,000	
	Interest Payable	3,000	
	Cash		104,000
	(To record interest expense for one month and payment of note)		

At the maturity date, Margo Sisters must pay the maturity value of the note $100,000 plus $4,000 interest (100,000 × 12% × 4/12). Only $1,000 is reported as interest expense, because interest expense for the period June 1 to August 31 was recognized earlier.

Zero-Interest-Bearing Note Issued

A zero-interest-bearing note may be issued instead of an interest-bearing note. A zero-interest-bearing note does not explicitly state an interest rate on the face of the note. Interest is still charged, however, because the borrower is required at maturity to pay back an amount greater than the cash received at the issuance date. In other words, the borrower receives in cash the discounted or present value of the note. The discounted value is equal to the face value of the note at maturity less the interest or discount rate charged by the lender for the term of the note. To illustrate, we will assume that Margo Sisters issues a $104,000 four-month zero-interest-bearing note to the First National Bank. The discounted value of the note is $100,000.[1] The entry to

[1]The bank discount rate in this example is slightly less than 12%.

record this transaction for Margo Sisters is as follows:

June 1	Cash	100,000	
	Discount on Notes Payable	4,000	
	Notes Payable		104,000
	(To record receipt of cash and issuance of four-month, zero-interest-bearing note)		

The Notes Payable account is credited for the face value of the note, which is $4,000 more than the actual cash received. The difference between the cash received and the face value of the note is debited to Discount on Notes Payable. **Discount on Notes Payable is a contra account to Notes Payable and therefore is subtracted from Notes Payable on the balance sheet.** The amount of the discount, $4,000 in this case, represents the cost of borrowing $100,000 for four months. Accordingly, the discount is charged to interest expense over the life of the note. That is, the Discount on Notes Payable balance **represents interest expense chargeable to future periods.**

The discount on notes payable may be reduced on a straight-line basis over the life of the loan. As the discount becomes lower, the net liability for Margo Sisters increases. If Margo Sisters prepares financial statements on August 31, an adjusting entry is required to recognize interest expense and to reduce the Discount on Notes Payable account by $3,000 ($4,000 × 3/4). The entry on August 31 is recorded as follows:

Aug. 31	Interest Expense	3,000	
	Discount on Notes Payable		3,000
	(To record interest expense for three months on $104,000 zero-interest-bearing note)		

The financial statement presentation of the above note payable on the balance sheet on August 31 is as follows:

Statement presentation of discount on notes payable

Notes payable	$104,000
Less: Discount on notes payable	1,000
	$103,000

At maturity, the Discount on Notes Payable account has a zero balance and the maturity (face) value is paid. At October 1, the entry to recognize the interest expense applicable to September and to pay off the note is as follows:

Oct. 1	Notes Payable	104,000	
	Interest Expense	1,000	
	Discount on Notes Payable		1,000
	Cash		104,000
	(To record interest expense for one month and payment of note)		

The final entry recognizes the $1,000 interest for September and the payment of the face value of $104,000 at maturity.

Interest Versus Zero-Interest-Bearing

The saying that "there is no such thing as a free lunch" is particularly appropriate for zero-interest-bearing notes. Zero-interest-bearing implies that no interest is charged, which is not true. For example, the net results are the same for Margo Sisters whether an interest-bearing or zero-interest-bearing note is employed. To illustrate, on August 31, 1987, the financial statements for Margo reported the following:

Interest-bearing versus zero-interest bearing notes

INTEREST-BEARING		ZERO-INTEREST-BEARING	
Income Statement		Income Statement	
Interest expense	3,000	Interest expense	3,000
Balance Sheet		Balance Sheet	
Notes payable	100,000	Notes payable	104,000
Interest payable	3,000	Discount on notes payable	1,000
	103,000		103,000

As indicated, interest expense and the liability for notes and interest are the same. Only the accounts employed to report the liability are different.

SALES TAX PAYABLE

As consumers, we are well aware that many of the products we purchase at retail stores are subject to sales taxes. The tax is expressed as a stated percentage of the sales price. The retailer (or selling company) collects the tax from the customer when the sale occurs, and periodically (usually monthly) remits the collections to the state's department of revenue.

Under most state sales tax laws, the amount of the sale and the amount of the sales tax collected must be rung up separately on the cash register (gasoline sales are a major exception). The cash register readings are then used to credit Sales and Sales Tax Payable. Assuming that the cash register readings for March 25 for Cool-Jewelry Company show sales of $10,000 and sales taxes of $600 (sales tax rate of 6%), the entry is:

Mar. 25	Cash	10,600	
	Sales		10,000
	Sales Tax Payable		600
	(To record daily sales and sales taxes)		

When the taxes are remitted to the taxing agency, Sales Tax Payable is debited and Cash is credited. Thus, Cool-Jewelry serves only as a collection agent for the taxing authority. The company does not report sales taxes as an expense; it simply forwards the amount paid by the customer to the government.

When sales taxes are not recorded separately, it is necessary to divide the total proceeds from sales received by 100% plus the sales tax percentage to determine the sales and the sales taxes. For example, assume that Madison Gasoline does not segregate sales from sales taxes. Its total receipts for a month are $21,000 and the sales tax is 5%. Sales are $20,000 ($21,000 ÷ 105%) and the sales tax payable is $1,000 ($21,000 − $20,000).

Similar entries are made when products are also subject to federal excise taxes. This tax is also a fixed percentage of the sales price. When a product is subject to both state sales and federal excise taxes, each tax is computed separately on the sales price. For example, if the $10,000 sales of Cool-Jewelry were also subject to a 10% excise tax, the total cash received would be $11,600 [$10,600 + ($10,000 × 10%)], and an additional credit to Excise Taxes Payable of $1,000 would be required.

ADVANCES FROM CUSTOMERS (UNEARNED REVENUES)

A mail order company such as L. L. Bean may receive a customer's check when goods are ordered, and an airline company, such as American Airlines, often sells tickets for future flights. How do these companies account for advances from customers (unearned revenues) that are received before goods are delivered or services are rendered?

1. When the advance is received, Cash is debited and a current liability account, Advances from Customers, is credited.
2. When the goods are delivered or the services rendered, Advances from Customers is debited and an appropriate earned revenue account, such as Sales, Ticket Revenues, etc., is credited.

To illustrate, assume that Superior University sells 10,000 season football tickets at $50 each for its five-game home schedule. The entry for the sales of season tickets is:

Cash	500,000	
Advances from Customers		500,000
(To record sale of 10,000 season tickets)		

As each game is completed, the following entry is made:

Advances from Customers	100,000	
Ticket Revenues		100,000
(To record earning of season ticket revenue)		

Advances from Customers are, therefore, unearned revenues. As the revenue is earned, a transfer from Unearned Revenue to Earned Revenue occurs. Although unearned revenues are usually not material for most enterprises, there are exceptions. For example, the airline industry reports tickets sold for future flights as a current liability, and these unearned revenues represent almost 50% of their total current liabilities.

CURRENT MATURITIES OF LONG-TERM DEBT

Companies often have a portion of long-term debt that comes due in the current year. For example, assume that Wendy Construction issues a 5-year interest-bearing $25,000 note on January 1, 1987. This note specifies that each January 1, starting January 1, 1988, $5,000 of the note should be paid. When

financial statements are prepared on December 31, 1987, $5,000 should be reported as a current liability and $20,000 as a long-term liability. Current maturities of long-term debt are often identified as **long-term debt due within one year** on the balance sheet.

CONTINGENT LIABILITIES

Whether it be notes payable, interest payable, accounts payable, sales taxes payable, and so on, we know that an obligation exists to make payment. But suppose that you are currently involved in a dispute with the Internal Revenue Service (IRS) over the amount of your income tax liability. Do you have to report the disputed amount on your balance sheet as a liability? Or, suppose that you sold your used car to a friend, guaranteeing that you would pay any major repair bill that occurred in the first year after the sale. Would you report an estimated liability on your balance sheet, even though no repair costs have yet been incurred? The answers to these questions are difficult, because these liabilities are dependent (contingent) upon some future event. In other words, a **contingent liability** is a potential liability that may become an actual liability in the future.

What then should be done with contingent liabilities? Fortunately, accountants have adopted guidelines that are helpful in resolving these problems. The guidelines require that if it is **probable** (likely to occur) the contingency will happen and the amount is **reasonably estimable,** the liability should be recorded in the accounts. However, if it is only **reasonably possible** (it could occur), then it need only be disclosed in the notes accompanying the financial statements. If the possibility that the contingency will happen is **remote** (unlikely to occur), it need not be recorded or disclosed.

Recording a Contingent Liability

Product warranties are a good example of a contingent liability that should be recorded in the accounts. Warranty contracts result in future costs that may be incurred in replacing defective units or repairing malfunctioning units without charge to the customer for a specified period after the product is sold. Generally, a manufacturer, such as Westinghouse Electric Corporation, knows that some warranty costs will be incurred on products sold under warranty. Moreover, on the basis of prior experience with the product (or similar products), the company usually can make a reasonable estimate of the anticipated cost of servicing (honoring) the contract.

The accounting for warranty costs is based on the matching principle. To comply with this principle, **the estimated cost of honoring product warranty contracts should be recognized as an expense in the period in which the sale occurs.** To illustrate, assume that in 1987 Atlas Manufacturing Company sells 10,000 washers and dryers at an average price of $600 each. The selling price includes a one-year warranty on parts. It is expected that 500 units (5%) will be defective and that warranty repair costs will average $80 per unit. In the year of sale, warranty contracts are honored on 300 units at a total cost of $23,400.

At December 31, it is necessary to accrue the remaining estimated warranty costs on the 1987 sales. The computation is as follows:

Computation of estimated product warranty liability

Number of units sold	10,000
Estimated rate of defective units	× 5%
Total estimated defective units	500
Less: Units failed to date	300
Estimated remaining defective units	200
Average warranty repair cost	× $80
Estimated product warranty liability	$16,000

The adjusting entry, therefore, is:

Dec. 31	Warranty Expense	16,000	
	Estimated Warranty Liability		16,000
	(To accrue estimated warranty costs)		

Total warranty expense for the year is $39,400 ($23,400 actual expenses incurred plus $16,000 estimated future costs.) Warranty expense is reported under selling expenses in the income statement, and estimated warranty liability is classified as a current liability on the balance sheet.

In the following year, all expenses incurred in honoring warranty contracts on 1987 sales should be debited to Estimated Warranty Liability. To illustrate, assume that 20 defective units are replaced in January, 1988, at an average cost of $82 in parts and labor. The summary entry is:

Jan. 31	Estimated Warranty Liability	1,640	
	Repair Parts/Wages Payable		1,640
	(To record honoring of 20 warranty contracts on 1987 sales)		

Disclosure of Contingent Liabilities

When a loss contingency meets one but not both conditions for recording the contingency described above, or the loss is only reasonably possible, only disclosure of the contingency is required. Examples of contingencies that may require disclosure are pending or threatened lawsuits and assessment of additional income taxes pending an IRS audit of the tax return.

The disclosure should identify the nature of the item, and if known, the amount of the contingency, and the expected outcome of the future event. Disclosure is usually accomplished through a note to the financial statements, as illustrated by the following from USAir:

Disclosure of contingent liability

> Legal Proceedings
>
> USAir has been named as a defendant in various suits and proceedings which allege, among other things, employment discrimination practices and environmental concerns about noise and air pollution. The suits and proceedings are in various stages of litigation and their outcome is difficult to predict. However, in the opinion of management, the ultimate disposition of these matters will not have a material adverse effect on USAir's financial condition.

STATEMENT PRESENTATION OF CURRENT LIABILITIES

As indicated in Chapter 4, current liabilities is the first category under liabilities on the balance sheet. Each of the principal types of current liabilities is listed separately within the category. In addition, the terms of notes payable and other pertinent information concerning the individual items are disclosed in the notes to the financial statements.

Current liabilities are seldom listed in the order of maturity because of the varying maturity dates that may exist for a specific type of obligation such as notes payable. A more common, and entirely satisfactory, method of presenting current liabilities is to list them by order of magnitude, with the largest obligations first. Many companies, as a matter of custom, show notes payable and accounts payable first regardless of amount. The following adapted excerpt from a recent balance sheet of USX Corp. (formerly U.S. Steel) illustrates this practice.

Illustration of current liability section

USX CORP.
Current Liabilities (in millions)

Notes payable	$ 362
Accounts payable	1,498
Payroll and related benefits payable	733
Accrued taxes	356
Long-term debt due within one year	278
Accrued interest	190
Other	65
Total current liabilities	$3,482

For homework problems, use the approach followed by USX Corp.

SECTION TWO—PAYROLL ACCOUNTING

As indicated in the current liability section for USX Corp., payroll and related benefits payable often constitutes a substantive percentage of current liabilities. In addition, employee compensation is often the most significant expense that a company incurs. For example, General Motors recently reported total employees of 691,000 and labor costs of $19.6 billion, or approximately 26% of net sales. Add to labor costs such fringe benefits as health insurance, life insurance, disability insurance, and so on, and you can see why proper accounting and control of payroll are so important.

It should be emphasized that payroll accounting involves more than paying employees' wages. Companies are required by law to maintain payroll records for each employee, file and pay payroll taxes, and comply with numerous state and federal tax laws applicable to employee compensation.[2]

[2]Accounting for payroll has become much more complex as a result of these regulations. As one business person commented, "When I started as a college student, there was withholding and there was Social Security. . . . Then all the state programs began, taxes, unemployment, workers' compensation. Payroll became a burden for the small business."

WHO IS AN EMPLOYEE?

The term "payroll" pertains to all salaries and wages paid to employees. Managerial, administrative, and sales personnel are generally paid **salaries,** which are often expressed in terms of a specified amount per month or per year. In contrast, store clerks, factory employees, and manual laborers are normally paid **wages,** which are based on a rate per hour, or on a piecework basis (such as per unit of product). Frequently, the terms "salaries" and "wages" are used interchangeably.

The term "payroll" does not extend to payments made for personal service to a company by professionals such as certified public accountants, attorneys, and architects. Such professionals are independent contractors, and payments to them are called **fees,** rather than salaries and wages. This distinction is important because regulations relating to the payment and reporting of payroll taxes apply only to employees.

IMPORTANCE OF INTERNAL CONTROL

Internal control was introduced in Chapter 7. As applied to payrolls, the objectives of internal accounting control are (1) to safeguard company assets against unauthorized payments of payrolls, and (2) to assure the accuracy and reliability of the accounting records pertaining to payrolls. The importance of these objectives should be obvious. Issuing payroll checks to fictitious employees or paying wages in excess of actual earnings will result in a loss of cash. Moreover, inaccurate records will result in incorrect paychecks, financial statements, and payroll tax returns.

Unfortunately, irregularities often result if internal control is lax. For example, one of the largest frauds ever perpetrated involved an accountant at a metal fabricating plant who padded the payroll in order to extract funds for his own use. Overstating hours, using unauthorized pay rates, adding fictitious employees to the payroll, continuing terminated employees on the payroll, and distributing duplicate payroll checks are all methods of stealing from a company.

In computerized payroll systems, separate programs are often used for internal control purposes. For example, one program generates the actual payroll checks while a second maintains files on personnel currently employed. A third program (perhaps controlled by the internal auditor) can then compare the checks issued by the first program against the active employee records in the second program to detect any fictitious employees.

Payroll activities involve four functions: hiring employees, timekeeping, preparing the payroll, and paying the payroll. For an internal control system

to work effectively, these four functions should be assigned to different departments or individuals. To illustrate these functions in more detail, we will examine the case of Academy Company and one of its employees, Michael Jackson.

HIRING EMPLOYEES

Posting job openings, screening and interviewing of applicants, and hiring employees are responsibilities of the personnel department. From a control standpoint, the personnel department provides significant documentation and authorization. When Michael Jackson is hired, the personnel department prepares an authorization form like the one used by Academy Company below:

Personnel authorization form

ACADEMY COMPANY

Employee Name: Jackson, (LAST) Michael (FIRST) (MI) — Effective Date: 9/01/84
Classification: Skilled-Level 10 — Social Security No.: 329-36-9547
Branch/Department: Music — Division: Entertainment

NEW HIRE	Classification: Clerk — Salary Grade: Level 10 — Trans. from Temp. ☐ Rate $ 9.00 per hour — Bonus N/A — Non-exempt ☒ Exempt ☐
RATE CHANGE	(Attach Performance Evaluation made within last three (3) months of effective date) New Rate $ 12.00 — Bonus ____ — Non-exempt ☒ Exempt ☐ Present Rate $ 9.00 — Bonus ____ — Non-exempt ☒ Exempt ☐ Merit ☒ Promotion ☐ Decrease ☐ Other ____ Previous Increase Date: None — Amount $ ____ per ____ Type ____
SEPARATION	Resignation ☐ Discharge ☐ Retirement ☐ Reason ____ Leave of Absence ☐ From ____ to ____ Type ____ Last Day Worked ____
APPROVALS	BEW (BRANCH OR DEPT. MANAGER) — 9/1/84 (DATE) — EMW (DIVISION V.P.) — 9-1-86 (DATE) James E. Speer (PERSONNEL DEPARTMENT)

Any changes to this information must be properly documented and approved by the personnel department. The hiring authorization form is sent to the payroll department, where it is used to place the new employee on the payroll. A chief concern of the personnel department is insuring the accuracy of this form. The reason is quite simple: one of the most common types of payroll frauds is adding fictitious employees to the payroll.

The personnel department is also responsible for authorizing (1) changes in pay rates during employment and (2) terminations of employment. In each instance, the authorization should be in writing, and a copy of the change in status should be sent to the payroll department.

TIMEKEEPING

Another area in which internal control is important is timekeeping. Hourly employees are usually required to record time worked by "punching" a time clock. The time of arrival and departure are automatically recorded by the employee when he or she inserts a time card into the clock. The time card for Michael Jackson is shown below:

Time card

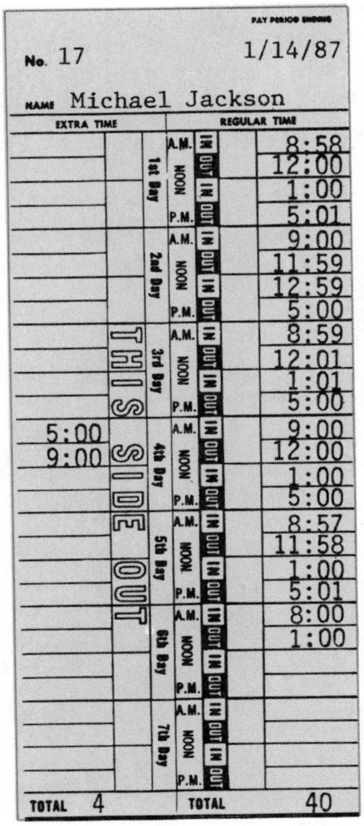
PAY PERIOD ENDING 1/14/87
No. 17
NAME Michael Jackson

EXTRA TIME	Day		REGULAR TIME
	1st Day	A.M. IN	8:58
		NOON OUT	12:00
		NOON IN	1:00
		P.M. OUT	5:01
	2nd Day	A.M. IN	9:00
		NOON OUT	11:59
		NOON IN	12:59
		P.M. OUT	5:00
	3rd Day	A.M. IN	8:59
		NOON OUT	12:01
		NOON IN	1:01
		P.M. OUT	5:00
5:00	4th Day	A.M. IN	9:00
9:00		NOON OUT	12:00
		NOON IN	1:00
		P.M. OUT	5:00
	5th Day	A.M. IN	8:57
		NOON OUT	11:58
		NOON IN	1:00
		P.M. OUT	5:01
	6th Day	A.M. IN	8:00
		NOON OUT	1:00
		NOON IN	
		P.M. OUT	
	7th Day	A.M. IN	
		NOON OUT	
		NOON IN	
		P.M. OUT	
TOTAL 4		TOTAL	40

THIS SIDE OUT

As indicated in Chapter 7, the use of mechanical and electronic equipment (such as a time clock) contributes to the accuracy of data and minimizes the likelihood that they can be altered. Time clock procedures are often monitored by a supervisor or security guard to make sure an employee punches only one card. At the end of the pay period, the employee's supervisor is generally required to approve the hours shown by signing the time card. When overtime hours are involved, approval by a supervisor should be mandatory to guard against unauthorized overtime. The approved time card is then sent to the payroll department. For salaried employees, a manually prepared weekly or monthly time report kept by a supervisor may be used to record time worked.

PREPARING THE PAYROLL

The payroll is prepared in the payroll department on the basis of two sources of input: (1) personnel department authorizations and (2) approved time cards.

Because of the numerous calculations involved in determining gross wages and payroll deductions, it is customary for a second payroll department employee, working independently, to verify all amounts and for a payroll department supervisor to approve the payroll. The payroll department is also responsible for preparing (but not signing) payroll checks, maintaining payroll records, and preparing payroll tax returns.

With the widespread use of microcomputers, the error-prone task of manually searching tax tables for the proper payroll deductions is becoming extinct even in small businesses. Now computers with entire tax tables stored internally perform this table lookup function errorlessly and calculate accurately all payroll information.

PAYING THE PAYROLL

The payroll is paid by the treasurer's department. **Payment by check minimizes the risk of loss from theft, and the endorsed check provides proof of payment.** For good internal control, payroll checks should be prenumbered, and all checks should be accounted for. All checks must be signed by the treasurer (or a designated agent), and their distribution to employees should be controlled by the treasurer's department. Checks may be distributed by the treasurer or paymaster.[3]

If the payroll is paid in currency, it is customary to have a second person count the cash in each pay envelope and for the paymaster to obtain a signed receipt from the employee upon payment. Thus, if alleged discrepancies arise, adequate safeguards have been established to protect each party involved.

GROSS EARNINGS

Three major sources of gross earnings are wages, salaries, and bonuses. Because the computation of bonuses is computed on a different basis, it is discussed separately.

WAGES AND SALARIES

Gross wages for an employee are determined by applying the hourly rate of pay to the number of hours worked. In addition to the hourly pay rate, most companies are required by law to pay a minimum of one and one-half times the regular hourly rate for overtime work in excess of 8 hours per day or 40 hours per week. For example, companies involved in interstate commerce

[3]When internal control is weak (such as when authorization forms are lacking), it is imperative that checks be distributed directly to individuals rather than through plant managers. An unscrupulous manager could submit fictitious names and when the checks for these names are received, deposit them to his or her account.

are required by the Fair Labor Standards Act to pay 1½ times the regular rate. In addition, many employers pay overtime rates for work done at night, on weekends, and on holidays. The computation of Michael Jackson's gross earnings for the 44 hours shown on his time card for the weekly pay period ending January 14 is as follows:

Computation of total wages

Type of Pay	Hours	Rate	Gross Earnings
Regular	40	$12.00	$480.00
Overtime	4	18.00	72.00
Total wages			**$552.00**

This computation assumes that Jackson receives one and one-half times his regular hourly rate ($12.00 × 1½) for his overtime hours. Union contracts often require that overtime rates be as much as twice the regular rates.[4]

The salary for an employee is often based on a monthly or a yearly rate. These rates are then applied ratably to the payroll periods used by the company.

BONUSES

Most companies have some type of bonus agreement with their key salaried employees. For example, a recent survey indicated that over 94% of the largest manufacturing companies in the United States provided annual bonuses to their key executives. Bonus arrangements can be based on many different factors, such as a given increase in sales or the amount of net income. To illustrate, assume that the Sanford Company states that a bonus is to be paid to employees on the basis of 10% of sales. If sales are $200,000, the bonus is $20,000 (10% × $200,000).

The entry for the bonus is:

Bonus Expense	20,000	
Bonus Payable		20,000
(To record bonus)		

When the bonuses are paid, the liability is debited and cash is credited.

PAYROLL DEDUCTIONS

As anyone who has received a paycheck knows, gross earnings and the amount received by an employee are usually very different. A number of payroll deductions are made from your gross wages to arrive at your **net pay.** As explained below, these deductions may be mandatory or voluntary.

[4]It should be noted that most executive and administrative positions are exempt from the Fair Labor Standards Act, and overtime pay is not required for such positions.

MANDATORY DEDUCTIONS

Mandatory deductions consist of FICA taxes and income taxes. These deductions do not result in payroll tax expense to the employer because the company only serves as a collection agency for the government.

FICA Taxes

In 1937, Congress enacted the Federal Insurance Contribution Act (FICA). **FICA taxes are designed to provide workers with supplemental retirement, employment disability, and medical benefits.** This program is financed by a tax levied on employees' earnings. A more common term for these taxes is **social security taxes.**

The tax rate and the tax base for FICA taxes are set by Congress. When FICA taxes were first imposed, the rate was 1% on the first $3,000 of gross earnings, or a maximum of $30 per year. The rate and base have changed dramatically since that time! In 1987, the rate is 7.15% on the first $43,800 of gross earnings, or a maximum of $3,132.[5] For purpose of illustration in this chapter, we will assume a rate of 8% on the first $42,000 of gross earnings, or a maximum of $3,360. Using the rate of 8%, the FICA withholding for Michael Jackson for the weekly pay period ending January 14 is $44.16 ($552 × 8%).

Income Taxes

Under the United States pay-as-you-go system of federal income taxes, employers are required to withhold income taxes from employees each pay period. The amount to be withheld is determined by three variables: (1) the employee's gross earnings; (2) the number of allowances claimed by the employee for herself or himself, his or her spouse, and other dependents; and (3) the length of the pay period. **To indicate to the Internal Revenue Service the number of allowances claimed, the employee must complete an Employee's Withholding Allowance Certificate (Form W-4).** As shown below, Michael Jackson claims three allowances on his W-4.

Form W-4

Form **W-4** (Rev. January 1984) — Department of the Treasury—Internal Revenue Service — **Employee's Withholding Allowance Certificate** — OMB No. 1545-0010

1 Type or print your full name: Michael Jackson
2 Your social security number: 329-36-9547
Home address (number and street or rural route): 3413 Mifflin Ave.
City or town, State, and ZIP code: Hampton, MI 48292
3 Marital Status: ☐ Single ☒ Married ☐ Married, but withhold at higher Single rate
Note: If married, but legally separated, or spouse is a nonresident alien, check the Single box.
4 Total number of allowances you are claiming (from line F of the worksheet on page 2) . . . 3
5 Additional amount, if any, you want deducted from each pay . . . $
6 I claim exemption from withholding because (see instructions and check boxes below that apply):
a ☐ Last year I did not owe any Federal income tax and had a right to a full refund of **ALL** income tax withheld, **AND**
b ☐ This year I do not expect to owe any Federal income tax and expect to have a right to a full refund of **ALL** income tax withheld. If both a and b apply, enter the year effective and "EXEMPT" here . . . ▶ Year
c If you entered "EXEMPT" on line 6b, are you a full-time student? . . . ☐ Yes ☐ No
Under penalties of perjury, I certify that I am entitled to the number of withholding allowances claimed on this certificate, or if claiming exemption from withholding, that I am entitled to claim the exempt status.
Employee's signature ▶ Michael Jackson Date ▶ September 1, 1984

[5] This tax is quite significant and is the subject of intense public scrutiny. The entire issue has become even more complex, because the social security program has been operating at a loss for many years.

The number of allowances claimed is used with the withholding tables furnished by the Internal Revenue Service to determine the amount of income tax to be withheld from gross wages. These tables indicate the amount of tax to be withheld from the employee. Separate tables are provided for weekly, biweekly, semimonthly, and monthly pay periods. The portion of the withholding tax table for Michael Jackson (assuming he earns $552 per week) is illustrated below.

Withholding tax table

MARRIED Persons–WEEKLY Payroll Period
(For Wages Paid After December 1985)

And the wages are–		And the number of withholding allowances claimed is–										
At least	But less than	0	1	2	3	4	5	6	7	8	9	10
		The amount of income tax to be withheld shall be–										
$500	$510	$76	$71	$66	$62	$57	$52	$49	$45	$41	$37	$34
510	520	78	73	68	64	59	55	50	47	43	39	35
520	530	81	76	71	66	61	57	52	48	45	41	37
530	540	83	78	73	68	64	59	54	50	46	43	39
540	550	86	81	75	70	66	61	57	52	48	45	41
550	560	88	83	78	73	68	63	59	54	50	46	43
560	570	91	86	80	75	70	66	61	56	52	48	44
570	580	93	88	83	78	72	68	63	59	54	50	46
580	590	96	91	85	80	75	70	65	61	56	52	48
590	600	98	93	88	83	77	72	68	63	59	54	50
600	610	101	96	90	85	80	75	70	65	61	56	52
610	620	104	98	93	88	82	77	72	67	63	58	54
620	630	106	101	95	90	85	80	75	70	65	61	56
630	640	109	103	98	93	87	82	77	72	67	63	58
640	650	112	106	100	95	90	85	80	74	70	65	60
650	660	115	109	103	98	92	87	82	77	72	67	63
660	670	118	112	106	100	95	90	85	79	74	69	65
670	680	120	115	109	103	97	92	87	82	77	72	67
680	690	123	117	112	106	100	95	90	84	79	74	69
690	700	126	120	114	109	103	97	92	87	82	76	71

As indicated in the table, for a weekly salary of $552 with 3 allowances, the income tax to be withheld is $73.00.

Most states and some cities also require employers to withhold income taxes from the earnings of employees. As a general rule, the amounts to be withheld are determined by applying a percentage specified in the state revenue code to the amount withheld for the federal income tax or to the employee's earnings. For the sake of simplicity, we have assumed that Jackson's wages are subject to state income taxes of 2% or $11.04 (2% × $552).

There is no limit on the amount of gross earnings subject to income tax withholdings. In fact, the higher the earnings, the higher the amount of taxes withheld.

VOLUNTARY DEDUCTIONS

Employees may voluntarily authorize withholdings for charitable, retirement, and other purposes. All voluntary deductions from gross earnings should be authorized in writing by the employee. The authorization(s) may be made individually or as part of a group plan. Deductions for charitable organizations, such as the United Fund, U.S. savings bonds, and repayment of loans from company credit unions are made individually. In contrast, deductions for union dues, health and life insurance, and pension plans are often made on a group basis. For purpose of illustration, we will assume that Jackson has voluntary deductions of $10 for the United Fund and $5 for union dues.

NET PAY

Net (or take-home) pay is determined by subtracting payroll deductions from gross earnings. For Michael Jackson, net pay is $408.80, computed as follows:

Computation of net pay

Gross earnings		$552.00
Payroll deductions:		
FICA taxes	$44.16	
Federal income taxes	73.00	
State income taxes	11.04	
United Fund	10.00	
Union dues	5.00	143.20
Net pay		$408.80

Assuming that Michael Jackson's wages for each week during the year are $552, total wages for the year are $28,704 (52 × $552), and all of Jackson's wages are subject to FICA tax during the year. However, if Jackson's wages are $1,000 per week, or $52,000 for the year, only the first $42,000 of these wages is subject to FICA taxes. In such case, the maximum FICA withholdings from Michael Jackson would be $3,360 ($42,000 × 8%).

PAYROLL DEPARTMENT RECORDS

To comply with state and federal laws, an employer must keep a cumulative record of each employee's gross earnings, deductions, and net pay during the year. The record that provides this information and other essential data is the **employee earnings record.** Michael Jackson's employee's earnings record is shown on the next page.

A separate earnings record is kept for each employee; it is updated after each pay period. The cumulative payroll data on the earnings record are used by the employer in (1) determining when an employee has earned the maximum earnings subject to FICA taxes, (2) filing state and federal payroll tax returns (as explained later in the chapter), and (3) providing each employee with a statement of gross earnings and tax withholdings for the year, as explained on page 475.

In addition to employee earnings records, many companies find it useful to prepare a **payroll register** to accumulate the gross earnings, deductions, and net pay for each employee for each pay period. The payroll register is illustrated on page 470 with the data for Michael Jackson shown in the wages section.

Note that this record is a listing of each employee's payroll data for the pay period. In some companies, a payroll register is a journal or book of original entry, and postings are made directly to ledger accounts from the register. In other companies, the payroll register is a memorandum record that provides the data for a general journal entry and subsequent posting to the ledger accounts. In the Academy Company situation, the latter procedure is followed.

Employee earnings record

ACADEMY COMPANY
Employee Earnings Record
For the Year 1987

Name	Michael Jackson	Address	3413 Mifflin Ave.
Social Security Number	329-36-9547		Hampton, Michigan 48292
Date of Birth	December 24, 1959	Telephone	238-9051
Date Employed	September 1, 1984	Date Employment Ended	
Sex	Male	Exemptions	3
Single		Married	X

1987 Period Ending	Total Hours	Gross Earnings: Regular	Over-time	Total	Cumulative	Deductions: FICA	Fed. Inc. Tax	State Inc. Tax	United Fund	Union Dues	Total	Payment: Net Amount	Check No.
1/7	42	480.00	36.00	516.00	516.00	41.28	64.00	10.32	10.00	5.00	130.60	385.40	974
1/14	44	480.00	72.00	552.00	1,068.00	44.16	73.00	11.04	10.00	5.00	143.20	408.80	1028
1/21	43	480.00	54.00	534.00	1,602.00	42.72	68.00	10.68	10.00	5.00	136.40	397.60	1077
1/28	42	480.00	36.00	516.00	2,118.00	41.28	64.00	10.32	10.00	5.00	130.60	385.40	1133
Jan. Total		1,920.00	198.00	2,118.00		169.44	269.00	42.36	40.00	20.00	540.80	1,577.20	
2/4	44	480.00	72.00	552.00	2,670.00	44.16	73.00	11.04	10.00	5.00	143.20	408.80	1191
2/11	44	480.00	72.00	552.00	3,222.00	44.16	73.00	11.04	10.00	5.00	143.20	408.80	1260

Payroll register

ACADEMY COMPANY
Payroll Register
For the Week Ending January 14, 1987

Employee	Total Hours	Earnings: Regular	Over-time	Gross Pay	Deductions: FICA	Federal Income Tax	State Income Tax	United Fund	Union Dues	Total Deduc-tions	Paid: Net Pay	Check No.	Accounts Debited: Office Salaries	Wages Expense
Office Salaries														
Arnold, Patricia	40	580.00		580.00	46.40	123.00	11.60	15.00		196.00	384.00	998	580.00	
Canton, Matthew	40	590.00		590.00	47.20	119.00	11.80	20.00		198.00	392.00	999	590.00	
Mueller, William	40	530.00		530.00	42.40	79.00	10.60	11.00		143.00	387.00	1000	530.00	
Subtotal		5,200.00		5,200.00	416.00	1,090.00	104.00	120.00		1,730.00	3,470.00		5,200.00	
Wages														
Bennett, Robin	42	480.00	36.00	516.00	41.28	94.00	10.32	18.00	5.00	168.60	347.40	1025		516.00
Dunlop, Robert	42	480.00	36.00	516.00	41.28	94.00	10.32	15.00	5.00	165.60	350.40	1026		516.00
Hemander, Paul	43	480.00	54.00	534.00	42.72	88.00	10.68	20.00	5.00	166.40	367.60	1027		534.00
Jackson, Michael	44	480.00	72.00	552.00	44.16	73.00	11.04	10.00	5.00	143.20	408.80	1028		552.00
Milroy, Lee	43	480.00	54.00	534.00	42.72	77.00	10.68	10.00	5.00	145.40	388.60	1029		534.00
Subtotal		11,000.00	1,010.00	12,010.00	960.80	2,400.00	240.20	301.50	115.00	4,017.50	7,992.50			12,010.00
Total		16,200.00	1,010.00	17,210.00	1,376.80	3,490.00	344.20	421.50	115.00	5,747.50	11,462.50		5,200.00	12,010.00

In addition to supplying the entry to record the payroll, the output for a computerized payroll system would include (1) payroll checks, (2) a payroll check register with sorts by check and department, and (3) updated employee earning records which become the source for monthly, quarterly, and annual reporting of wages to taxing agencies.

RECORDING THE PAYROLL

On the basis of the payroll register on page 470, the journal entry to record the payroll for the week ending January 14 is:

Jan.	14	Office Salaries	5,200.00	
		Wages Expense	12,010.00	
		FICA Taxes Payable		1,376.80
		Federal Income Taxes Payable		3,490.00
		State Income Taxes Payable		344.20
		United Fund Payable		421.50
		Union Dues Payable		115.00
		Salaries and Wages Payable		11,462.50
		(To record payroll for the week ending January 14)		

Specific liability accounts are credited for the mandatory and voluntary deductions made during the pay period. In the example, debits to Office Salaries and Wages Expense are used for gross earnings. In other cases, there may be additional debits such as Store Salaries and Sales Salaries.

PAYING EMPLOYEES

Payment by check is made either from the employer's regular bank account or a payroll bank account. Each check is usually accompanied by a detachable **statement of earnings** document that indicates the employee's gross earnings, payroll deductions, and net pay. The Academy Company uses its regular bank account for payroll checks. The check and statement of earnings for Michael Jackson are illustrated on the next page.

Following payment of the payroll, the check numbers are entered in the payroll register. The entry to record payment of the payroll for Academy Company is as follows:

Jan.	14	Salaries and Wages Payable	11,462.50	
		Cash		11,462.50
		(To record payment of payroll)		

Check and statement of earnings

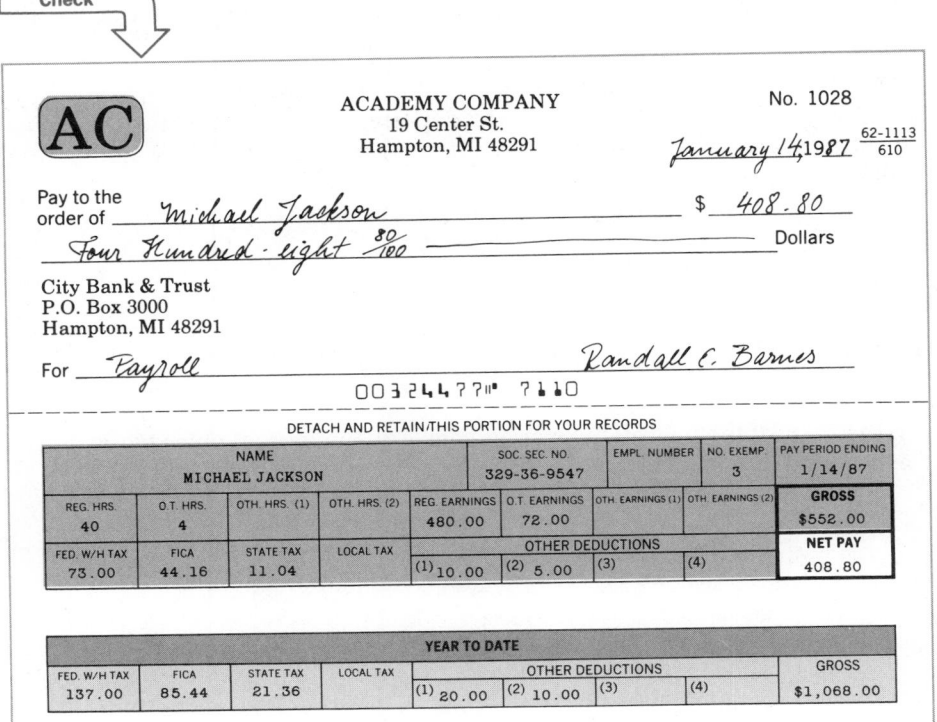

Check

AC

ACADEMY COMPANY
19 Center St.
Hampton, MI 48291

No. 1028

January 14, 1987 — 62-1113/610

Pay to the order of Michael Jackson $ 408.80

Four Hundred-eight 80/100 Dollars

City Bank & Trust
P.O. Box 3000
Hampton, MI 48291

For Payroll — Randall C. Barnes

003244772‴ 7110

DETACH AND RETAIN THIS PORTION FOR YOUR RECORDS

NAME	SOC. SEC. NO.	EMPL. NUMBER	NO. EXEMP.	PAY PERIOD ENDING
MICHAEL JACKSON	329-36-9547		3	1/14/87

REG. HRS.	O.T. HRS.	OTH. HRS. (1)	OTH. HRS. (2)	REG. EARNINGS	O.T. EARNINGS	OTH. EARNINGS (1)	OTH. EARNINGS (2)	GROSS
40	4			480.00	72.00			$552.00

FED. W/H TAX	FICA	STATE TAX	LOCAL TAX	OTHER DEDUCTIONS (1)	(2)	(3)	(4)	NET PAY
73.00	44.16	11.04		10.00	5.00			408.80

YEAR TO DATE

FED. W/H TAX	FICA	STATE TAX	LOCAL TAX	OTHER DEDUCTIONS (1)	(2)	(3)	(4)	GROSS
137.00	85.44	21.36		20.00	10.00			$1,068.00

When currency is used in payment, one check is prepared for the net pay. The check is then cashed, and the coins and currency are inserted in individual pay envelopes for disbursement to individual employees.

EMPLOYER PAYROLL TAXES

Payroll tax expense results from three taxes levied on employers by governmental agencies. These taxes are: FICA, federal unemployment tax (FUTA), and state unemployment tax (SUTA). Each of these taxes plus such items as paid vacations and pensions are collectively referred to as "fringe benefits." As indicated earlier, the cost of fringe benefits in many companies is substantial. For example, it was recently estimated that for every $100 of gross earnings paid to employees, the employer paid $35.00 in fringe benefit costs.[6]

FICA TAXES

The employer must match each employee's FICA contribution. Thus, the employer's tax is subject to the same rate and maximum earnings applicable to

[6]A U.S. Chamber of Commerce study, for example, included the following benefits: FICA taxes; insurance; pensions; paid vacations; paid rest periods, coffee breaks, and lunch periods; and paid holidays.

the employee. The account, FICA Taxes Payable, is used for both the employee's and the employer's FICA contributions. For the January 14 payroll, Academy Company's FICA tax is $1,376.80 ($17,210.00 × 8%).

FEDERAL UNEMPLOYMENT TAXES

The Federal Unemployment Tax Act (FUTA) is another feature of the federal social security program. **Federal unemployment taxes** provide benefits for a limited period of time to employees who lose their jobs through no fault of their own. Under provisions of the Act, the employer is required to pay a tax of 6.2% on the first $7,000 of gross wages paid to each employee during a calendar year. The law, however, allows the employer a maximum credit of 5.4% on the federal rate for contributions to state unemployment taxes. Because of this provision, state unemployment tax laws generally provide for a 5.4% rate, and the effective federal unemployment tax rate becomes .8% (6.2% − 5.4%). This tax is borne entirely by the employer; there is no deduction or withholding from employees. The account, Federal Unemployment Taxes Payable, is used to recognize this liability. The federal unemployment tax for Academy Company for the January 14 payroll is $137.68 ($17,210.00 × .8%).

STATE UNEMPLOYMENT TAXES

All states have unemployment compensation programs that are financed by state unemployment taxes. Like federal unemployment taxes, **state unemployment taxes** provide benefits to employees who lose their jobs. These taxes are levied on employers, and the basic rate is usually 5.4% on the first $7,000 of wages paid to an employee during the year.[7] The basic rate is adjusted according to the employer's experience rating. Companies with unstable employment may pay more than the basic rate. Regardless of the rate paid, the credit on the federal unemployment tax is still 5.4%. The account, State Unemployment Taxes Payable, is used for this liability. The state unemployment tax for Academy Company for the January 14 payroll is $929.34 ($17,210.00 × 5.4%).

RECORDING EMPLOYER'S PAYROLL TAXES

Employer payroll taxes are usually accrued at the same time the payroll is journalized. The entire amount of gross earnings ($17,210.00) shown in the payroll register for January 14 on page 470 is subject to each of the three taxes mentioned above. Accordingly, the entry to record the payroll tax expense associated with the January 14 payroll is:

[7] In a few states, the employee is also required to make a contribution.

Jan.	14	Payroll Tax Expense	2,443.82	
		FICA Taxes Payable		1,376.80
		Federal Unemployment Taxes Payable		137.68
		State Unemployment Taxes Payable		929.34
		(To record employer's payroll taxes on January 14 payroll)		

Separate liability accounts are used instead of a single credit to Payroll Taxes Payable, because these liabilities are payable to different taxing authorities at different dates. The liability accounts are classified as current liabilities since they will be paid within the next year. Payroll Tax Expense is classified on the income statement as an operating expense.

FILING AND REMITTING PAYROLL TAXES

A company's payroll procedures should provide for the filing of payroll tax returns and the paying of payroll taxes in accordance with applicable tax laws. Preparation of the tax returns is the responsibility of the payroll department; payment of the taxes is made by the treasurer's department. Much of the information for the returns is obtained from employee earnings records.

For purposes of reporting and remitting, FICA taxes and federal income taxes withheld are combined. The taxes must be reported quarterly on a prescribed form (Form 941) no later than one month following the close of each quarter. The remitting requirements depend on the amount of taxes withheld and the length of the pay period. Specific dates range from three banking days following the end of the week for weekly pay periods to the end of the following month for monthly pay periods. Remittances are made through deposits in either a Federal Reserve Bank or an authorized commercial bank.

Federal unemployment taxes are generally filed and remitted annually on a prescribed tax form (Form 940) on or before January 31 following the preceding year. Earlier payments are required, however, when the tax exceeds a specified amount. State unemployment taxes usually must be filed and paid by the end of the month following each quarter. For example, April 30 is the due date for the first quarter's tax.

The employer is also required to provide each employee with a **Wage and Tax Statement (Form W-2)** by January 31 following the end of a calendar year. This statement shows gross earnings, FICA taxes withheld, and income taxes withheld for the year. The required W-2 form for Michael Jackson, using assumed annual data, is illustrated on the next page.

The employer must send a copy of each employee's Wage and Tax Statement to the Social Security Administration. This agency subsequently furnishes the Internal Revenue Service with the data required in examining the employee's income tax return.

Form **W-2 Wage and Tax Statement**

1 Control number		OMB No. 1545-0008	
2 Employer's name, address and ZIP code Academy Company 19 Center St. Hampton, MI 48291		3 Employer's identification number 36-2167852	4 Employer's State number
		5 Stat. employee ☐ Deceased ☐ Legal rep. ☐	942 emp. ☐ Subtotal ☐ Void ☐
		6 Allocated tips	7 Advance EIC payment
8 Employee's social security number 329-36-9547	9 Federal income tax withheld $3240.00	10 Wages, tips, other compensation $26,300.00	11 Social security tax withheld $2,104.00
12 Employee's name, address, and ZIP code Michael Jackson 3413 Mifflin Ave. Hampton, MI 48292		13 Social security wages $26,300.00	14 Social security tips
		16	
		17 State income tax $526.00	18 State wages, tips, etc. / 19 Name of State Michigan
		20 Local income tax	21 Local wages, tips, etc. / 22 Name of locality

Large employers, like General Motors, transmit their W-2s on magnetic tape. The taxing agencies copy these tapes directly into their computer system for subsequent comparison against earnings and taxes withheld reported on employees' income tax returns.

ADDITIONAL FRINGE BENEFITS

In addition to the fringe benefits mentioned above, employers incur other substantial fringe benefit costs. Two of the most important are paid absences and pensions.

PAID ABSENCES

Employees often have rights to receive compensation for future absences when certain conditions of employment are met. The compensation may pertain to paid vacations, sick pay benefits, and paid holidays. When the payment of such compensation is **probable** and the amount can be **reasonably estimated,** a liability should be accrued for paid future absences; when the amount cannot be reasonably estimated, the potential liability should be disclosed. Ordinarily, vacation pay[8] is the only paid absence that is accrued, whereas the other types of paid absences are only disclosed.

To illustrate, assume that Academy Company employees are entitled to one day's vacation for each month worked. If thirty employees earn an average of $110 per day in a given month, the accrual for vacation benefits in one

[8] The typical U.S. company provides an average of 12 days of paid vacations for its employees at an average cost of 5% of gross earnings.

month is $3,300. The liability is recognized at the end of the month by the following adjusting entry:

Jan.	31	Vacation Benefits Expense
		  Liability for Vacation Benefits
		    (To accrue vacation benefits expense)
			3,300	3,300

This accrual is required by the matching principle. When vacation benefits are paid, Liability for Vacation Benefits is debited and Cash is credited.

In most companies, an employee's vacation benefits begin at the time of employment, but the employee must remain with the company for a specified period of time, such as six months, or the accumulated vacation time is forfeited. Where there is frequent employee turnover, as for example in a McDonald's fast-foods restaurant, the company must estimate the number of employees that will remain through the eligibility period. When all employees are expected to meet the minimum time requirement, the accrual of vacation benefits can be based entirely on gross earnings.

The magnitude of unpaid absences has recently gained employers' attention. Take the case of an assistant superintendent of schools who worked for around 20 years and rarely took a vacation or sick day. A month or so before she retired, the city discovered that she was due nearly $30,000 in accrued benefits. Yet that liability was never on the city's books. Or in the late 1970's, the city of Dallas had vacation liabilities of $8.6 million and a potential $33 million of sick pay liabilities; yet it had a mere $3.5 million in the general fund for that year.[9]

PENSION PLANS

A **pension plan** is an arrangement whereby an employer provides benefits (payments) to employees after they retire. Over 50 million workers currently participate in pension plans in the United States, and by 1995, assets of private pension plans are expected to reach $3 trillion. Most pension plans are subject to the provisions of ERISA (Employment Income Security Act), which was enacted to curb abuses in the administration and funding of such plans.

Three parties are generally involved in a pension plan. The employer (company) sponsors the pension plan. The plan administrator receives the contributions from the employer, invests the pension assets, and makes the benefit payments to the pension recipients (retired employees). The diagram below shows the three distinct parties involved in a pension plan and indicates the flow of cash among them.

Parties in a pension plan

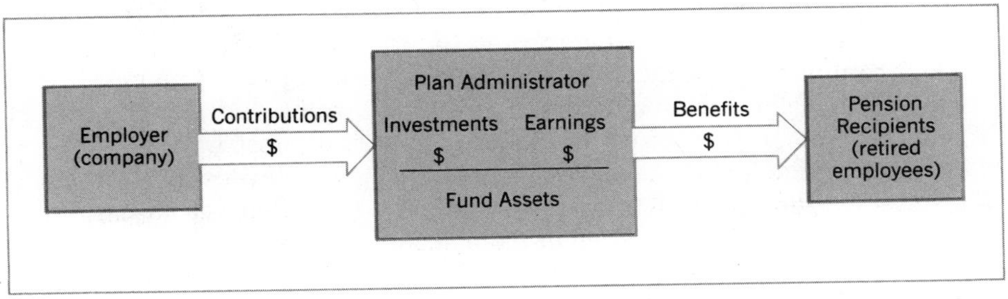

[9]Adapted from Alyssa Lappen "Off-the-Book Time Bombs" *Forbes*, May 11, 1981.

The two most common types of pension arrangements for providing benefits to employees after they retire are defined contribution plans and defined benefit plans.

Defined Contribution Plan. In a **defined contribution plan,** the employer's contribution to the plan is defined by the terms of the plan; that is, the employer agrees to contribute a certain sum each period based on a formula. This formula might consider such factors as age, length of service, employer's profits, and compensation level. It is important to note that only the employer's contribution is defined; no promise is made concerning the ultimate benefits to be paid out to the employees.

The accounting for a defined contribution plan is straightforward. In this type of plan, the benefit of gain or the risk of loss from the assets contributed to the pension plan is borne by the employee. The employer's responsibility is simply to make a contribution each year based on the formula established in the plan. As a result, the employer's obligation is easily determined. It follows that the amount of the contribution required each period is reported as pension expense.

To illustrate, assume that Alba Office Interiors has a defined contribuiton plan in which it contributes $200,000 each year to the pension fund for its employees. The entry to record this transaction is as follows:

Pension Expense	200,000	
Cash		200,000
(To record pension expense and contribution to pension fund)		

Pension payments to retired employees are made from the pension fund by the plan administrator.

Defined Benefit Plan. On the other hand, a **defined benefit plan** defines the benefits that the employee will receive at the time of retirement. The formula that is typically used provides for the benefits to be a function of an employee's compensation level when he or she nears retirement and the employee's years of service. In these plans it is necessary to determine what the contribution should be today to meet the pension benefit commitments that will arise at retirement. It is important to recognize that many different contribution approaches could be used to fund (pay for) the pension benefit at the time of retirement. Naturally, whatever funding method is employed, it should provide enough money at retirement to meet the benefits defined by the plan.

In a defined benefit plan, because the benefits are defined in terms of uncertain future variables, an appropriate funding pattern must be established to assure that enough funds will be available at retirement to meet the benefits promised. This funding level depends on a number of factors such as turnover, mortality, length of employee service, compensation levels, and investment earnings. Employers are at risk because they must be sure to make enough contributions to meet the cost of benefits that are defined in the pension plan. The expense recognized each period by actuarial methods and accounting standards is not necessarily equal to the cash contribution.

To illustrate, assume that Lopez Enterprises, Inc. has a defined benefit plan in which total pension expense for the year is $90,000. If Lopez decides

to fund $70,000 this year, the entry to record the expense and related funding is as follows:

Pension Expense	90,000	
Cash		70,000
Pension Liability		20,000
(To record pension expense and related liability)		

On the income statement, pension expense is reported as an operating expense. The pension liability is classified as a current or long-term liability, depending upon the time it will take to pay this obligation.

SUMMARY OF STUDY OBJECTIVES

1. The major types of current liabilities are notes payable, accounts payable, unearned revenues, and accrued liabilities such as taxes, wages, and interest payable.

2. When a promissory note is interest-bearing, the amount of assets received upon the issuance of the note is generally equal to the face value of the note and interest expense is accrued over the life of the note. When a note is zero-interest-bearing, the borrower receives the discounted or present value of the instrument. A Discount on Notes Payable account is debited for the discount and this amount is charged to interest expense over the life of the note.

3. If it is probable (likely to occur) the contingency will happen and the amount is reasonably estimable, the liability should be recorded in the accounts. However, if it is only reasonably possible (it could occur), then it need only be disclosed in the notes to the financial statements. If the possibility that the contingency will happen is remote (unlikely to occur), it need not be recorded or disclosed.

4. The objectives of internal control for payroll are (1) to safeguard company assets against unauthorized payments of payrolls, and (2) to assure the accuracy and reliability of the accounting records pertaining to payrolls.

5. In recording the payroll, salaries (or wages) expense is debited for gross earnings, individual tax and other liability are credited for payroll deductions, and salaries (wages) payable is credited for net pay. When payroll taxes are recorded, Payroll Tax Expense is debited and individual tax liability accounts are credited.

6. Additional fringe benefits associated with wages are paid absences (paid vacations, sick pay benefits, and paid holidays) and pensions.

7. The two most common types of pension arrangements are a defined contribution plan and a defined benefit plan. In a contribution plan, the amount of the employer's required contribution is reported as pension expense. In a benefit plan, pension expense is determined by actuarial methods and accounting standards.

GLOSSARY

Contingent liability, p. 459

Current liability, p. 454

Defined benefit plan, p. 477

Defined contribution plan, p. 477

Employee earnings record, p. 469

Employee's withholding allowance certificate (Form W-4), p. 467

Federal unemployment taxes, p. 473

FICA taxes, p. 467

Payroll register, p. 469

Pension plan, p. 476

Salaries, p. 462

Statement of earnings, p. 471

State unemployment taxes, p. 473

Wages, p. 462

Wage and Tax Statement (Form W-2), p. 474

DEMONSTRATION PROBLEM

The Payton Company had the following selected transactions in 1987.

Feb. 1 Signs a $53,000 six-month zero-interest-bearing note payable to Citi Bank receiving $50,000 in cash.

Feb. 10 Cash register sales total $43,200 which includes an 8% sales tax.

Feb. 28 The payroll for the month consists of Sales Salaries $32,000 and Office Salaries $18,000. All wages are subject to 8% FICA taxes. A total of $8,900 federal income taxes are withheld. The salaries are paid on March 1.

Feb. 28 The following adjustment data are developed:

1. Interest expense of $500 has been incurred on the note.
2. Employer payroll taxes include 8% FICA taxes, a 5.4% state unemployment tax, and a .8% federal unemployment tax.
3. Some sales were made under warranty. Of the units sold, 350 are expected to become defective. Repair costs are estimated to be $40 per unit. No warranties were honored in February.

INSTRUCTIONS

(a) Journalize the February transactions.

(b) Journalize the adjusting entries at February 28.

SOLUTION TO DEMONSTRATION PROBLEM

(a) Feb.	1	Cash	50,000	
		Discount on Notes Payable	3,000	
		Notes Payable		53,000
		(To record issue of six-month zero-interest-bearing note)		

Feb. 10	Cash	43,200	
	Sales		40,000
	Sales Taxes Payable		3,200
	(To record sales and sales taxes payable)		
Feb. 28	Sales Salaries Expense	32,000	
	Office Salaries Expense	18,000	
	FICA Taxes Payable		4,000
	Federal Income Taxes Payable		8,900
	Salaries Payable		37,100
	(To record February salaries)		
(b) Feb. 28	Interest Expense	500	
	Discount on Notes Payable		500
	(To record interest expense on zero-interest-bearing note)		
Feb. 28	Payroll Tax Expense	7,100	
	FICA Taxes Payable		4,000
	Federal Unemployment Taxes Payable		400
	State Unemployment Taxes Payable		2,700
	(To record employer's payroll taxes on February payroll)		
Feb. 28	Warranty Expense	14,000	
	Estimated Warranty Liability		14,000
	(To record estimated product warranty liability)		

QUESTIONS

1. What is a current liability?

2. Smith Co. has a liability which will be paid during the current year, but they do not classify it as a current liability. Under what circumstances is this acceptable?

3. What is the principal difference between an interest-bearing note and a zero-interest-bearing note?

4. What is a contingent liability? Give an example of a contingent liability that is usually recorded in the accounts.

5. Under what circumstances is a contingent liability only disclosed in the notes to the financial statements? Under what circumstances can a contingent liability be neither recorded in the accounts nor disclosed in the notes to the financial statements?

6. All-American University sold 5,000 season football tickets at $60 each for its five-game home schedule. What entries should be made (a) when the tickets were sold, and (b) after each game?

7. You are a newly hired accountant with the Flutie Company. On your first day, the controller asks you to identify the main internal control objectives related to payroll accounting. How would you respond?

8. What are the four functions associated with payroll activities?

9. What is the difference between gross pay and net pay? Which amount should a company record as wages or salaries expense?

10. Which payroll tax is levied on both employers and employees?

11. Are the federal and state income taxes withheld from employee paychecks a payroll tax expense for the employer? Explain your answer.

12. What do the following acronyms stand for: FICA, FUTA, and SUTA?

13. What information is shown on a W-4 statement? A W-2 statement?

14. Distinguish between the two types of payroll deduction and give examples of each.

15. What is the difference between an employee earnings record and a payroll register?

16. What are the primary uses of the employee earnings record?

17. Often during job interviews, the candidate asks the potential employer about the firm's paid absences policy. What are paid absences? How are they accounted for?

18. Identify the three parties in a pension plan. What role does each party have in the plan?

19. Cindy Krause and Marty Mayo are reviewing pension plans. They ask your help in distinguishing between a defined contribution plan and a defined benefit plan. Explain the principal differences to Cindy and Marty.

20. How is pension expense determined under (a) a defined contribution plan, and (b) a defined benefit plan?

EXERCISES

E12–1 The Buyer Company is considering two alternative loan arrangements on May 31.

1. Borrow $50,000 from Midcity Bank on a 6-month, $50,000, 15% note.
2. Borrow $50,000 from Suburban Bank on a 6-month, $53,750, zero-interest-bearing note.

INSTRUCTIONS

For each plan,

(a) Prepare the entry on June 1.

(b) Prepare the adjusting entry on June 30.

(c) Prepare the entry at maturity (November 30), assuming monthly adjusting entries have been made through October 31.

(d) What was the total financing cost (interest expense)?

E12–2 In providing accounting services to small businesses, you encounter the following situations pertaining to cash sales:

1. The Weir Company rings up sales and sales taxes separately on its cash register. On April 10, the register totals are sales, $12,200; and sales taxes, $732.

2. The Beth Company does not segregate sales and sales taxes. Its register total for April 15 is $14,840, which includes a 6% sales tax.
3. The Ted Company does not segregate sales, sales taxes (5%), and excise taxes (10%). Its register total for April 20 is $20,700, including taxes.

INSTRUCTIONS

Prepare the entry to record the sales transactions and related taxes for each client.

E12-3 The Keaton Company is preparing adjusting entries at December 31. Analysis reveals the following:

1. The company has been named as a defendant in a $100,000 damage suit. Legal counsel believes the company probably will have to pay the amount requested.
2. A product introduced on December 1 carries a 60-day warranty against defects. In December 1,000 units were sold for $15,000. The company expects 5% of the units to be defective and it believes the average repair (replacement) cost per unit will be $6.
3. Employees are entitled to two days' vacation for each month worked. Five employees worked the entire month of December at an average daily wage of $100 per employee.
4. The company is a defendant in a patent infringement involving $50,000 of damages. Legal counsel believes it is unlikely that the company will have to pay any damages.

INSTRUCTIONS

Prepare separate adjusting entries, if required, for each of the foregoing items.

E12-4 Haines Company sells automatic can openers under a 75-day warranty for defective merchandise. Based on past experience, Haines Company estimates that 3% of the units sold will become defective during the warranty period. Management estimates that the average cost of replacing or repairing a defective unit is $12. The following sales occurred during the last quarter of 1987.

Month	Units Sold	Units Defective Prior to December 31
October	24,000	700
November	30,000	650
December	32,000	400

INSTRUCTIONS

(a) Determine the estimated product warranty liability at December 31, assuming all October sales were made prior to October 15.

(b) Prepare the journal entry to record the estimated liability at December 31.

(c) Give the entry to record the honoring of 350 warranty contracts in January at an average cost of $12.

E12-5 Howard Publications publishes a monthly computer magazine entitled P. C. Preview which it sells to newsstands for $2.00 a copy. Yearly subscriptions to P. C. Preview cost $18.00 per year. During December 1987, Howard Publications sells 2,000 copies of P. C. Preview to newsstands and receives payment for 5,000 1988 subscriptions. Financial statements are prepared each month end.

INSTRUCTIONS

(a) Prepare all necessary December 1987 journal entries.

(b) Prepare all necessary December 31, 1987 adjusting entries.

(c) Prepare all necessary January 31, 1988 adjusting entries, assuming the January 1988 issue of P. C. Preview has been mailed to subscribers.

E12-6 Ellen Mear's regular hourly wage rate is $13.00, and she receives a wage of 1½ times the regular hourly rate for work in excess of 40 hours. During a September weekly pay period Ellen works 42 hours. Her gross earnings prior to the current week were $19,000. Ellen is married and claims two withholding allowances. Her only voluntary deduction is for group hospitalization insurance at $10.00 per week.

INSTRUCTIONS

(a) Compute the following amounts for Ellen's wages for the current week.
   1. Gross earnings
   2. FICA taxes (assume 8% rate)
   3. Federal income taxes withheld (use wage-bracket table in text)
   4. State income taxes withheld (assume 2.0% rate)
   5. Net pay

(b) Record Ellen's pay, assuming she is a store clerk.

E12-7 The Foster Company has the following salary data for warehouse employees for the week ending November 15.

Employee	Gross Earnings	Federal Income Tax Withholdings	United Fund Contributions	Prior Earnings
M. Didka	$900	$100	$15	$41,600
R. Cady	600	60	5	16,200
G. Long	550	72	0	21,000
S. Mira	500	48	10	18,000
L. Copa	800	120	25	38,600

The FICA tax rate is 8% on the first $42,000 of gross earnings.

INSTRUCTIONS

(a) Compute net pay for each employee for the November 15 payroll.

(b) Prepare the journal entry to record the November 15 payroll.

E12-8 The Adamle Company has the following data for the weekly payroll ending January 31.

	Hours							Federal	
Employee	M	T	W	T	F	S	Hourly Rate	Income Tax Withholding	Health Insurance
H. Ane	8	8	9	8	10	0	$10	$34	$10
W. Hart	8	8	8	8	8	2	12	42	15
C. Muno	9	10	8	8	9	0	12	38	15
N. Chow	7	8	8	8	8	0	10	32	10
R. Short	8	8	8	8	8	0	11	30	5

Employees are paid 1½ times the regular hourly rate for all hours worked in excess of 40 hours per week. FICA taxes are 8% on the first $42,000 of gross earnings. The

Adamle Company is subject to 5.4% state unemployment taxes and .8% federal unemployment taxes.

INSTRUCTIONS

(a) Prepare the payroll register for the weekly payroll.

(b) Prepare the journal entry to record the payroll and the Adamle Company's payroll tax expense.

E12-9 Selected data from a January payroll register for the Lance Company are presented below with some amounts intentionally omitted.

Gross earnings:			
Regular	$8,900	State income taxes	$ 190
Overtime	(1)	Union dues	100
Total	(2)	Total deductions	(4)
Deductions:		Net Pay	7,310
FICA taxes	(3)	Accounts debited:	
Federal income taxes	1,140	Warehouse wages	4,500
		Store wages	(5)

FICA taxes are 8% and state income taxes are 2% of gross earnings.

INSTRUCTIONS

(a) Fill in the missing amounts.

(b) Journalize the January payroll.

(c) Prepare the adjusting entry at January 31 to record the employer's payroll taxes using the standard rates specified in the chapter.

E12-10 According to a payroll register summary of Mallory Company, the amount of employee's gross pay in December was $700,000, of which $65,000 was not subject to FICA tax and $679,000 was not subject to state and federal unemployment taxes.

INSTRUCTIONS

(a) Determine the employer's payroll tax expense for the month, using the following rates: FICA, 8%; state unemployment, 5.4%; federal unemployment, 0.8%.

(b) Prepare the journal entry to record December payroll tax expense.

PROBLEMS

P12-1 On January 1, 1987, the ledger of the Gibson Company contains the following liability accounts.

Notes Payable	$20,000
Accounts Payable	42,500
Interest Payable	600
Sales Taxes Payable	5,400
Advances from Customers	15,000

The note payable was issued on September 30, 1986. It bears interest at 12% and matures on January 31, 1987. During January the following selected transactions occurred:

Jan. 5 Sold merchandise for cash totaling $7,800 which includes 4% sales taxes.
9 Paid $20,000 of accounts payable within a 2% discount period and $5,000 after the discount period had lapsed.
12 Provided services for customers who had made advance payments of $7,000.
14 Paid state treasurer's department for sales taxes collected in December 1986 ($5,400).
16 Borrowed $30,000 in cash from City Bank on a zero-interest-bearing, six-month note having a face value of $32,700.
20 Sold 500 units of a new product on credit at $40 per unit. This new product is subject to a 1-year warranty.
21 Borrowed $15,000 in cash from Midland Bank on a four-month, 12%, $15,000 note.
25 Sold merchandise for cash totaling $10,752 which includes 4% sales taxes and 8% federal excise taxes.
31 Paid the note due this date.

INSTRUCTIONS

(a) Journalize the January transactions.

(b) Journalize the adjusting entries at January 31 for (1) the outstanding notes payable, and (2) estimated warranty liability, assuming warranty costs are expected to equal 8% of sales of the new product. (Hint: Use one-half a month for the City Bank note and one-third of a month for the Midland Bank note.)

(c) Prepare the current liability section of the balance sheet at January 31, 1987.

P12–2 The T-Mart has seven employees who are paid on an hourly basis plus time-and-one-half for all hours worked in excess of 40 a week. Payroll data for the week ended February 15, 1987 are presented below:

Employees	Hours Worked	Hourly Rate	Withholding Allowances	United Fund
L. Albion	40	$12.50	0	$5.00
R. Boader	39	13.00	2	-0-
W. Chaney	42	12.00	4	5.00
T. Decker	40	13.00	1	-0-
M. Grant	44	13.00	3	7.50
P. Morris	40	12.75	2	2.50
D. Tolley	46	12.00	6	5.00

The following tax rates are applicable: FICA 8.0%, state income taxes 3%, state unemployment taxes 5.4%, and federal unemployment .8%. The first four employees are sales clerks (store wages expense) and the other employees perform administrative duties (office wages expense).

INSTRUCTIONS

(a) Prepare a payroll register for the weekly payroll. (Use the wage-bracket withholding table in the text for federal income tax withholdings.)

(b) Journalize the payroll on February 15, 1987 and the accrual of employer payroll taxes.

(c) Journalize the payment of the payroll on February 16, 1987.

(d) Journalize the deposit in a federal reserve bank on February 28, 1987 of the FICA and federal income taxes payable to the government.

P12–3 The payroll procedures used by three different companies are described below:

1. In the Paris Company each employee is required to mark the hours worked on a clock card. At the end of each pay period, the employee must have this clock card approved by the department manager. The approved card is then given to the payroll department by the employee. Subsequently, the treasurer's department pays the employee by check.
2. In the Rome Company employees are required to record hours worked on clock cards by "punching" a time clock. At the end of each pay period, the clock cards are collected by the department manager. The manager prepares a payroll register in duplicate and forwards the original to payroll. In payroll, the accuracy of the summaries are checked for mathematical accuracy and a payroll supervisor pays each employee by check.
3. In the Oslo Company clock cards and time clocks are used. At the end of each pay period, the department manager initials the cards, indicates the rates of pay, and sends them to payroll. A payroll register is prepared from the cards by the payroll department. Cash equal to the total net pay in each department is given to the department manager who pays the employees in cash.

INSTRUCTIONS

(a) Indicate the weakness(es) in internal control in each company.

(b) For each weakness, describe the control procedure(s) that will provide effective internal control. Use the following format for your answer.

(a) Weaknesses	(b) Recommended Procedures

P12–4 The following payroll liability accounts are included in the ledger of the Tatum Company on January 1, 1987:

FICA Taxes Payable	$ 662.20
Federal Income Taxes Payable	954.60
State Income Taxes Payable	102.15
Federal Unemployment Taxes Payable	2,400.00
State Unemployment Taxes Payable	1,954.40
Union Dues Payable	140.00
U.S. Savings Bonds Payable	350.00

In January, the following transactions occur:

Jan. 10 Sent check for $140.00 to union treasurer for union dues.
12 Deposited check for $1,616.80 in Federal Reserve Bank for FICA taxes and federal income taxes withheld.
15 Purchased U.S. Savings Bonds for employees by writing check for $350.00.
17 Paid state income taxes withheld from employees.
20 Paid federal and state unemployment taxes.
31 Completed monthly payroll register which shows office salaries $14,800, store wages $27,400, FICA taxes withheld $3,376, federal income taxes payable $1,654, state income taxes payable $360, union dues payable $400, United Fund contributions payable $1,688, and net pay $34,722.
31 Prepared payroll checks for the net pay and distributed checks to employees.

At January 31, the company also makes the following accrued adjustments pertaining to employee compensation:

1. Employer payroll taxes: FICA taxes (8%), state unemployment taxes (5.4%), and federal unemployment taxes (.8%).
2. Employer pension contribution: 6% of gross earnings.
3. Vacation pay: 3% of gross earnings.

INSTRUCTIONS

(a) Journalize the January transactions.

(b) Journalize the adjustments pertaining to employee compensation at January 31.

(c) Determine the adjusted balances at January 31 in the payroll expense and payroll liability accounts.

(d) What is the percentage of fringe benefit costs to gross earnings?

P12-5 For the year ended December 31, 1987, Dawson Electrical Repair Company reports the following summary payroll data:

Gross Earnings	
Administrative Salaries	$180,000
Electricians' Wages	370,000
Total	$550,000
Deductions	
FICA taxes	$ 38,000
Federal income taxes withheld	168,000
State income taxes withheld (2.6%)	14,300
United Fund contributions payable	27,500
Hospital insurance premiums	17,200
Total	$265,000

Dawson Company's payroll taxes are: FICA 8%, state unemployment 2.5% (due to a stable employment record), and .8% federal unemployment. Gross earnings subject to unemployment taxes total $370,000. Dawson's pension contribution is 7% of gross earnings.

INSTRUCTIONS

(a) Prepare a summary journal entry at December 31 for the full year's payroll.

(b) Journalize the adjusting entries at December 31 to record the employer's payroll taxes and pension liability.

(c) The W-2 Wage and Tax Statement requires the following dollar data:

Wages, tips, other compensation	Federal income tax withheld	State income tax withheld	FICA wages	FICA tax withheld

Complete the required data for the following employees:

Employee	Gross Earnings	Federal Taxes Withheld
J. Rudy	$60,000	$27,500
M. Cleo	26,000	10,200

(d) Calculate the total fringe benefit costs and the percentage relationship of this total to gross earnings.

P12-6 The following are selected transactions of Kirk Company:

Jan. 20 Purchased merchandise on account from Starship Enterprises, $6,000, terms 2/10, n/30.

29 Paid Starship for the merchandise purchased on January 20.

30 Purchased merchandise on account from McCoy Company, $15,000, terms 2/10, n/30.

Mar. 1 Issued a 12%, 2-month, $15,000 note to McCoy in payment of account.

May 1 Borrowed $40,000 from the Federation Bank by issuing a three-month zero-interest-bearing note with a face amount of $41,500.
1 Paid principal and interest on McCoy note.
June 1 Purchased merchandise on account from Starship Enterprises, $10,000, terms 2/10, n/30.
July 1 Issued a 13½%, 2-month, $10,000 note to Starship in payment of account.
Aug. 1 Paid the $41,500 note to the Federation Bank by paying $21,500 cash and issuing a three-month zero-interest-bearing note with a face amount of $20,750.
Sept. 1 Paid principal and interest on Starship note.
Oct. 30 Paid $20,750 cash to the Federation Bank to retire the note.
Dec. 1 Borrowed $10,000 from the Federation Bank by issuing a three-month zero-interest-bearing note with a face amount of $10,375.
1 Purchased equipment from Scottie Equipment for $35,000, paying $10,000 cash and signing a $25,000, 16% note payable which requires payment of $2,500 principal and interest accrued to date every 30 days (10 payments total).
31 Made the first payment to Scottie Equipment.
31 Recognized interest expense on the Federation note.

INSTRUCTIONS

(a) Prepare journal entries for the transactions and events above.
(b) Show the presentation of notes payable in the December 31 balance sheet.

ALTERNATE PROBLEMS

P12-1A On January 1, 1987, the ledger of the Alex Company contains the following liability accounts:

Notes Payable	$40,000	Sales Taxes Payable	$ 6,400
Accounts Payable	52,000	Advances from Customers	16,000
Interest Payable	1,200		

The note payable was issued on September 30, 1986. It bears interest at 12% and matures on January 31, 1987. During January the following selected transactions occurred:

Jan. 5 Sold merchandise for cash totaling $15,600 which includes 4% sales taxes.
9 Paid $25,000 of accounts payable within a 2% discount period and $5,000 after the discount period had lapsed.
12 Provided services for customers who had made advance payments of $9,000.
14 Paid state department for sales taxes collected in December 1986 ($6,400).
16 Borrowed $30,000 in cash from City Bank on zero-interest bearing, six-month note having a face value of $32,700.
20 Sold 500 units of a new product on credit at $50 per unit. This new product is subject to a 1-year warranty.
21 Borrowed $18,000 from Midland Bank on a three-month, 12%, $18,000 note.
25 Sold merchandise for cash totaling $10,976 which includes 4% sales taxes and 8% federal excise taxes.
31 Paid the note due this date.

INSTRUCTIONS

(a) Journalize the January transactions.
(b) Journalize the adjusting entries at January 31 for (1) the outstanding notes payable, and (2) estimated warranty liability, assuming warranty costs are expected to equal

8% of sales of the new product. (Hint: Use one-half a month for the City Bank note and one-third of a month for the Midland Bank note.)

(c) Prepare the current liability section of the balance sheet at January 31, 1987.

P12-2A The Z-Mart has seven employees who are paid on an hourly basis plus time-and-one-half for all hours worked in excess of 40 a week. Payroll data for the week ended February 15, 1987 are presented below:

Employee	Hours Worked	Hourly Rate	Withholding Allowances	United Fund
A. Babac	40	$13.00	0	$ 5.00
D. Feff	39	14.00	2	-0-
G. Higgin	42	13.00	4	5.00
J. Kolm	40	12.75	1	-0-
N. Quip	44	13.00	3	8.00
R. Satvey	40	12.75	2	10.00
W. Zex	46	13.00	6	5.00

The following tax rates are applicable: FICA 8.0%, state income taxes 3%, state unemployment taxes 5.4%, and federal unemployment .8%. The first four employees are sales clerks (store wages expense) and the other employees perform administrative duties (office wages expense).

INSTRUCTIONS

(a) Prepare a payroll register for the weekly payroll. (Use the wage-bracket withholding table in the text for federal income tax withholdings.)

(b) Journalize the payroll on February 15, 1987 and the accrual of employer payroll taxes.

(c) Journalize the payment of the payroll on February 16, 1987.

(d) Journalize the deposit in a federal reserve bank on February 28, 1987 of the FICA and federal income taxes payable to the government.

P12-3A Selected payroll procedures of the Colter Company are described below:

1. Department managers interview applicants and on the basis of the interview either hire or reject the applicants. When an applicant is hired, the applicant fills out a W-4 form (Employer's Withholding Exemption Certificate). One copy of the form is sent to the personnel department and one copy is sent to the payroll department as notice that the individual has been hired. On the copy of the W-4 sent to payroll, the managers manually indicate the hourly pay rate for the new hire.
2. There are two clerks in the payroll department. The payroll is divided alphabetically with one clerk having employees A to L and the other employees M to Z. Each clerk computes the gross earnings, deductions, and net pay for employees in the section and posts the data to the employee earning records.
3. The payroll checks are manually signed by the chief accountant and given to the department managers for distribution to employees in their department. The managers are responsible for seeing that any absent employees receive their checks.

INSTRUCTIONS

(a) Indicate the weaknesses in internal control.

(b) For each weakness, describe the control procedures that will provide effective internal control. Use the following format for your answer.

(a) Weaknesses	(b) Recommended Procedures

P12-4A The following payroll liability accounts are included in the ledger of the O'Neal Company on January 1, 1987:

FICA Taxes Payable	$ 760.00
Federal Income Taxes Payable	954.60
State Income Taxes Payable	108.95
Federal Unemployment Taxes Payable	288.95
State Unemployment Taxes Payable	1,954.40
Union Dues	840.00
U.S. Savings Bonds Payable	360.00

In January, the following transactions occur:

Jan. 10 Sent check for $840.00 to union treasurer for union dues.

12 Deposited check for $1,714.60 in federal reserve bank for FICA taxes and federal income taxes withheld.

15 Purchased U.S. Savings Bonds for employees by writing check for $360.00.

17 Paid state income taxes withheld from employees.

20 Paid federal and state unemployment taxes.

31 Completed monthly payroll register which shows office salaries $14,800, store wages $28,400, FICA taxes withheld $3,456, federal income taxes payable $1,684, state income taxes payable $360, union dues payable $400, United Fund contributions payable $1,888, and net pay $35,412.

31 Prepared payroll checks for the net pay and distributed checks to employees.

At January 31, the company also makes the following accrued adjustments pertaining to employee compensation:

1. Employer payroll taxes: FICA taxes (8%), federal unemployment taxes (0.8%), and state unemployment taxes (5.4%).
2. Employer pension liability: 7% of gross earnings.
3. Vacation pay: 3% of gross earnings.

INSTRUCTIONS

(a) Journalize the January transactions.

(b) Journalize the adjustments pertaining to employee compensation at January 31.

(c) Determine the adjusted balances at January 31 in the payroll expense and payroll liability accounts.

(d) Compute the percentage of fringe benefit costs to gross earnings.

P12-5A For the year ended December 31, 1987, Richard Electrical Repair Company reports the following summary payroll data:

Gross Earnings	
Administrative Salaries	$180,000
Electricians' Wages	470,000
Total	$650,000
Deductions	
FICA taxes	$ 44,900
Federal income taxes withheld	188,000
State income taxes withheld (2.6%)	16,900
United Fund contributions payable	32,500
Hospital insurance premiums	20,300
Total	$302,600

Dawson Company's payroll taxes are: FICA 8%, state unemployment 2.5% (due to a stable employment record), and .8% federal unemployment. Gross earnings subject to unemployment taxes total $400,000. Richard's pension contribution is 9% of gross earnings.

INSTRUCTIONS

(a) Prepare a summary journal entry at December 31 for the full year's payroll.

(b) Journalize the adjusting entries at December 31 to record the employer's payroll taxes and pension contribution.

(c) The W-2 Wage and Tax Statement requires the following dollar data:

Wages, tips, other compensation	Federal income tax withheld	State income tax withheld	FICA wages	FICA tax withheld

Complete the required data for the following employees:

Employee	Gross Earnings	Federal Taxes Withheld
R. Judy	$62,000	$28,500
O. Clem	28,000	10,800

(d) Calculate the total fringe benefit costs and the percentage relationship of this total to gross earnings.

P12–6A The following are selected transactions of Spock Company:

Jan.	20	Purchased merchandise on account from Vulcan Enterprises, $9,000, terms 2/10, n/30.
	29	Paid Vulcan for the merchandise purchased on January 20.
	30	Purchased merchandise on account from Benson Company, $18,000, terms 2/10, n/30.
Mar.	1	Issued a 12%, 2-month, $18,000 note to Benson in payment of account.
May	1	Borrowed $50,000 from the Federation Bank by issuing a three-month zero-interest-bearing note with a face amount of $51,875.
	1	Paid principal and interest on Benson note.
June	1	Purchased merchandise on account from Vulcan Enterprises, $20,000, terms 2/10, n/30.
July	1	Issued a 13½%, 2-month, $20,000 note to Vulcan in payment of account.
Aug.	1	Paid the $51,875 note to the Federation Bank by paying $21,875 cash and issuing a three-month zero-interest-bearing note with a face amount of $31,125.
Sept.	1	Paid principal and interest on Vulcan note.
Oct.	30	Paid $31,125 cash to the Federation Bank to retire the note.
Dec.	1	Borrowed $12,000 from the Federation Bank by issuing a three-month zero-interest-bearing note with a face amount of $12,450.
	1	Purchased equipment from Sulu Equipment for $37,000, paying $12,000 cash and signing a $25,000, 12% note payable which requires payment of $2,500 principal and interest accrued to date every 30 days (10 payments total).
	31	Made the first payment to Sulu Equipment.
	31	Recognized interest expense on the Federation note.

INSTRUCTIONS

(a) Prepare journal entries for the transactions and events above.

(b) Show the presentation of notes payable in the December 31 balance sheet.

DECISION CASE

Data Processing Company provides word-processing services for clients and students in a university community. The work for clients is fairly steady throughout the year but the work for students peaks significantly in December and May as a result of term papers, research project reports, and dissertations.

Two years ago, the company attempted to meet the peak demand by hiring part-time help. However, this led to numerous errors and considerable customer dissatisfaction. A year ago, the Company hired four experienced employees on a permanent basis instead of using part-time help. This proved to be much better in terms of productivity and customer satisfaction. However, it has caused an increase in annual payroll costs and a significant decline in annual net income.

Recently, Sue Stone, a sales representative of Manpower Services Inc., has made a proposal to the company. Under the plan, Manpower Services will provide up to four experienced workers at a daily rate of $100 per person for an 8-hour workday. Data Processing would only have to pay the daily rate for the workers used.

The owner of Data Processing, Denise Denby, asks you as the company's accountant, to prepare a report on the expenses that are pertinent to the decision. If the Manpower plan is adopted, Denise will terminate the employment of two permanent employees who are each earning an average annual salary of $25,000. Data Processing pays 8% FICA taxes, 0.8% Federal Unemployment Taxes, and 5.4% State Unemployment Taxes. The unemployment taxes only apply to the first $7,000 of gross earnings. In addition, Data Processing pays $40 per month for each employee for medical and dental insurance.

Denise indicates that if the Manpower Service plan is accepted, her needs for workers will be as follows:

Months	Number	Working Days per Month
January–March	1.5	20
April–May	3	25
June–October	1.5	18
November–December	3	24

INSTRUCTIONS

(a) Prepare a report showing the comparative payroll expense of continuing to employ permanent workers compared to adopting the Manpower Services Inc. plan.

(b) What other factors should Denise consider before finalizing her decision?

CHAPTER 13

Illinois State University

CHAPTER 13

ACCOUNTING PRINCIPLES AND INFLATION ACCOUNTING

STUDY OBJECTIVES

After studying this chapter, you should be able to:

1. Understand what are generally accepted accounting principles.
2. Identify the key items of the conceptual framework.
3. Describe the basic objectives of financial reporting.
4. Discuss the qualitative characteristics of accounting information and elements of financial statements.
5. Identify and illustrate the basic operating guidelines used by accountants.
6. Compare the two basic approaches used by accountants to adjust financial information for changing price levels.

Up to this point, we have emphasized that enterprises follow certain basic guidelines (such as the cost principle, the matching principle, the economic entity assumption) in reporting financial information. Without these basic guidelines, each enterprise would have to develop its own set of accounting rules and practices. If this happened, we would have to become familiar with every company's peculiar accounting and reporting rules in order to understand their financial statements. Thus, it would be difficult, if not impossible, to compare the financial statements of different companies.

This chapter is divided into two sections. In Section One we discuss in more depth the basic guidelines followed by accountants in developing specific accounting rules. Certain basic guidelines such as the revenue recognition principle and the matching principle are discussed in detail to indicate the difficult choices that accountants must make in attempting to present useful financial information. In Section Two the difficult problem of how to

account for changing prices during inflation (or deflation) is examined and illustrated.

SECTION ONE—GENERALLY ACCEPTED ACCOUNTING PRINCIPLES

The accounting profession has established a set of rules and practices that are recognized as a general guide for financial reporting purposes. This recognized set of practices is called **generally accepted accounting principles (GAAP).** "Generally accepted" means that these principles must have "substantial authoritative support." Substantial authoritative support usually comes from two standard-setting bodies: the Financial Accounting Standards Board (FASB) and the Securities and Exchange Commission (SEC).[1]

Accounting principles must be developed or decreed. Since the early 1970's the business and governmental communities has given the FASB the responsibility for developing accounting principles in this country. The development of a body of accounting principles is an on-going process because accounting principles must change to reflect changes in the business environment and changes in the needs of users of accounting information.

Prior to the establishment of the FASB, accounting principles were developed on a problem-by-problem basis. Thus, rule-making bodies developed and issued accounting rules and methods to solve specific problems. Critics charged that the problem-by-problem approach led to inconsistent rules and practices over time. Unfortunately, no clearly developed conceptual framework of accounting theory existed for the accounting rule makers to refer to in solving problems.

As a result of these criticisms, the FASB was directed to develop a **conceptual framework** that would serve as the basis for resolving accounting and reporting problems. The FASB has spent considerable time and effort on this project. The Board views its conceptual framework project as the drafting of "... a constitution, a coherent system of interrelated objectives and fundamentals that can lead to consistent standards that prescribes the nature, function, and limits of financial accounting and financial statements."[2]

The FASB's conceptual framework consists of the following:

1. Objectives of Financial Reporting.
2. Qualitative Characteristics of Accounting Information.
3. Elements of Financial Statements.
4. Operating Guidelines (Assumptions, Principles, and Constraints).

[1]The SEC is an agency of the U.S. government that was established to administer laws and regulations relating to the exchange of securities and the publication of financial information by U.S. businesses. The agency has the authority to mandate generally accepted accounting principles for companies under its jurisdiction. However, throughout its history, the SEC has been willing to accept the principles promulgated by the FASB and similar bodies.

[2]Conceptual Framework for Financial Accounting and Reporting: Elements of Financial Statements and Their Measurement," *FASB Discussion Memorandum* (Stamford, Conn.: 1976), p. 1.

If the accounting profession can agree on these four items, it should be better able to develop a coherent set of standards to help make accounting practice more consistent and uniform.

OBJECTIVES OF FINANCIAL REPORTING

Financial statements are the end product of the accounting process. In small companies, financial statements often are the only means by which financial information is communicated to creditors and other external users. In large companies, however, the communication of financial information is usually made through annual reports that include the financial statements plus other information such as financial highlights, five-year financial summaries, and management's discussion and analyses of results of operations and financial condition. Selected portions of the annual report of PepsiCo, Inc. are presented in the Appendix at the end of this textbook.

In developing the conceptual framework, the FASB concluded that the first level of study was to determine the objectives of financial reporting. Determining these objectives required answers to such basic questions as: Who uses financial statements? What do they use financial statements for? What information do they need? How knowledgeable about business and accounting are the users of financial statements? How should financial information be reported so that it is best understood?

Answers to these questions may appear obvious. But, only if they are answered correctly and completely will it be possible to measure and communicate the most useful information. The FASB's study concluded that the objectives (goals and purposes) of financial reporting are to provide information that:

1. Is useful to those making investment and credit decisions.
2. Is helpful in assessing future cash flows.
3. Identifies the economic resources (assets), the claims to those resources (liabilities), and the changes in those resources and claims.

The objectives of financial reporting, therefore, begin with a broad concern about providing information that is useful to investors and creditors. The objectives narrow that concern to the investor and creditor interests in the amounts, timing, and uncertainty of future cash flows to the enterprise. Finally, the objectives focus on the financial statements that provide information that help investors and creditors (1) identify the enterprise's financial strengths and weaknesses, (2) assess the enterprise's liquidity (ability to convert assets to cash) and solvency (ability to pay its debts), and (3) evaluate the enterprise's progress and performance over a period of time.

Before these objectives could be fully implemented in practice, the FASB found it necessary to provide certain fundamental concepts to explain the qualitative characteristics of accounting information and define the elements contained in financial statements.

QUALITATIVE CHARACTERISTICS OF ACCOUNTING INFORMATION

How does one decide on the amount of information to be disclosed, or the format in which information should be presented, or between alternative methods of measuring assets, liabilities, revenues, and expenses? **The FASB concluded that the overriding criterion by which such accounting choices can be judged is decision usefulness.** The accounting alternative selected or policy adopted should be the one that generates the most useful financial information for making a decision. To be useful, information should possess the following qualitative characteristics: relevance, reliability, comparability, and consistency.

RELEVANCE

To be **relevant,** accounting information must be capable of making a difference in a decision; that is, it must have a bearing on the decision. Relevant information helps users make predictions about the outcome of past, present, and future events (that is, it has **predictive value**), or it confirms or corrects prior expectations (that is, it has **feedback value**). For example, when Exxon issues an annual report, the information in the report is considered relevant because it provides a basis for forecasting future earnings and provides feedback on past performance. In addition, for accounting information to be relevant, it must be available to decision makers before it loses its capacity to influence their decisions (that is, it must be **timely**). Thus, if Exxon reported its financial information only every five years, the information would have limited usefulness for decision-making purposes. Thus, relevant information has predictive or feedback value and it is timely.

RELIABILITY

Reliability is the quality of information that gives assurance that it is free of error and bias; it can be depended on. To be reliable, accounting information must be **verifiable**; we must be able to prove that it is free of error and bias. To be reliable, the information must be a **faithful representation** of what it purports to be; it must be factual. And finally, to be reliable, accounting information must be **neutral**—it cannot be selected, prepared, or presented to favor one set of interested users over another. Thus, for the annual report of Exxon to be considered reliable, it must be verifiable by outside parties. Just as the Internal Revenue Service audits tax returns, certified public accountants audit financial statements to insure their reliability.

COMPARABILITY AND CONSISTENCY

Accounting information about an enterprise is more useful when it is comparable with accounting information about other enterprises. **Comparability** results when companies use the same accounting principles. For example, Sears Roebuck, Montgomery Ward, and J. C. Penney all use the cost principle in reporting plant assets on the balance sheet. Moreover, each company uses the revenue recognition and matching principles in determining its net income.

Conceptually, comparability should also extend to the methods used by companies in complying with an accounting principle. Accounting methods include the FIFO and LIFO methods of inventory costing, and the straight-line and sum-of-the-years digits methods for depreciation. At this point in the development of a conceptual framework, comparability of methods is not required, even for companies in the same industry. Thus, Ford, General Motors, and Chrysler may use different inventory costing and depreciation methods in their financial statements. The only accounting requirement is that each company must disclose the accounting methods used. From the disclosures, the external user can determine whether the financial information is comparable.

Consistency means using the same accounting principles and methods from year to year within a company. Thus, if FIFO is selected as the inventory costing method in the first year of operations, the company is expected to continue to use FIFO in succeeding years. When financial information has been reported on a consistent basis, the financial statements permit meaningful analysis of trend results within a company.

It is possible for a company to change to a new method of accounting if management can justify that the new method results in more meaningful financial information. In the year in which the change occurs, there must be disclosure of the change in the notes to the financial statements so that users of the financial statements are aware of the lack of consistency.

The qualitative characteristics of accounting are highlighted in the following chart:

Major qualitative characteristics

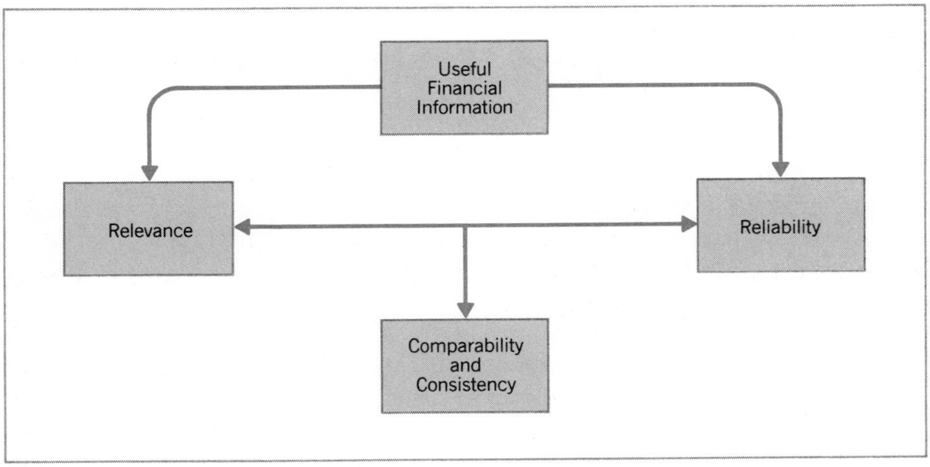

ELEMENTS OF FINANCIAL STATEMENTS

An important part of an accounting conceptual framework is a set of definitions that describe the basic terms used in accounting. The FASB has chosen to refer to this set of definitions as the **elements of financial statements.** Thus,

these definitions include such terms as assets, liabilities, equity, revenues, and expenses.

Because these elements are so important, it is imperative that they be precisely defined and universally understood and applied. Finding the appropriate definition for many of these elements is not easy. For example, how should an asset be defined? Should the value of a company's employees be reported as an asset on a balance sheet? Should the death of the president be reported as a loss? A good set of definitions should provide answers to these types of questions. Because you have already encountered most of these definitions in earlier chapters, they are not repeated here.

OPERATING GUIDELINES

The objectives of financial statements, the qualitative characteristics of accounting information, and the elements of financial statements are very broad. However, because practicing accountants and standard-setting bodies must solve practical problems, more detailed guidelines are needed. In its conceptual framework, the FASB recognizes the need for operating guidelines. We have chosen to classify these guidelines as assumptions, principles, and constraints. These guidelines are well-established and accepted in accounting.

ASSUMPTIONS

Assumptions provide a foundation for the accounting process. You have already studied the following major assumptions in preceding chapters:

Economic Entity Assumption—states that economic events can be identified with a particular unit of accountability. Thus, it is assumed that the activities of IBM can be distinguished from those of other computer companies such as Apple Computer and Burroughs Corporation.

Monetary Unit Assumption—states that only transaction data capable of being expressed in terms of money should be included in the accounting records of the economic entity. One reason why the death of a company president (discussed in the previous section on elements) is not reported as a loss is that it cannot be expressed easily in dollars. An important corollary to the monetary unit assumption is the added assumption that the unit of measure remains sufficiently constant over time. This point will be discussed in more detail later in this chapter.

Periodicity Assumption—states that the economic life of a business can be divided into artificial time periods. Thus, it is assumed that the activities of business enterprises such as General Electric, Exxon, or any enterprise can be subdivided into months, quarters, and years for meaningful financial reporting purposes.

Another assumption that accountants use is the going concern assumption. The **going concern assumption** assumes that the enterprise will continue in operation long enough to carry out its existing objectives and commitments.

Experience indicates that, in spite of numerous business failures, companies have a fairly high continuance rate, and it has proved useful to adopt a going concern or continuity assumption for accounting purposes.

The accounting implications of adopting this assumption are critical. Only if we assume some permanence to the enterprise are depreciation and amortization policies justifiable and appropriate. Without this assumption, the current-noncurrent classification of assets and liabilities would otherwise lose much of its significance. Labeling anything as fixed or long-term would be difficult to justify.

Acceptance of the going concern assumption gives credibility to the cost principle. If, instead, liquidation were assumed, assets would be better stated at net realizable value (sales price less costs of disposal) than at cost. Only when liquidation appears imminent is the going concern assumption inapplicable.

PRINCIPLES

On the basis of these fundamental assumptions of accounting, the accounting profession has developed principles that dictate how transactions and other economic events should be recorded and reported. In Chapter 1, for example, we discussed the cost principle. In Chapter 3, the revenue recognition and matching principles were illustrated. We now examine a number of reporting issues related to these principles. In addition, another principle, the full disclosure principle, is discussed.

Revenue Recognition Principle

As indicated in Chapter 3, the revenue recognition principle dictates that revenue should be recognized in the accounting period in which it is earned. Applying this general principle in practice, however, can create difficulties. For example, the financial press often publishes stories questioning the revenue recognition practices of a given company or industry. To illustrate, it was recently reported that Automatic Inc. was improperly recognizing revenue on goods that had not been shipped and improperly recording revenue at the time of shipment on equipment that was only ordered on approval. Similarly, many have recently questioned the revenue recognition practices in the savings and loan industry which records a large portion of its fees for granting a loan as revenue immediately rather than spreading them over the life of the loan.

When a sale is involved, revenue is recognized at the point of sale. The sales basis involves an exchange transaction between the seller and buyer and the sales price provides an objective measure of the amount of revenue realized. There are, however, two exceptions to the sales basis for revenue recognition that have become generally accepted.

Percentage-of-Completion Method. In long-term construction contracts, recognition of revenue is usually required before the contract is completed. For example, assume that Warrior Construction Co. had a contract to build a dam at Windswept Canyon for the U.S. Bureau of the Interior for $400 million, with construction estimated to take three years (starting in 1985) at a construc-

tion cost of $360 million. If Warrior applies the point-of-sale basis, it will report no revenues and no profit in the first two years. But, in 1987 when completion and sale take place, Warrior will report $400 million in revenues, costs of $360 million, and the entire profit of $40 million. Was Warrior really producing no revenues and earning no profit in 1985 and 1986? Obviously not. The dam will be as good as sold when Warrior completes the project according to specifications. Although technically an exchange transaction (transfer of ownership) has not occurred until completion of the dam, the earning process is considered substantially completed at various stages as construction progresses.

To overcome this deficiency, Warrior can apply the **percentage-of-completion method,** which recognizes revenue and income over three years on the basis of reasonable estimates of the project's progress toward completion. A project's progress toward completion is measured by comparing the costs incurred in a year to the total estimated costs for the entire project; this is referred to as the **cost-to-cost** approach. That percentage is multiplied by the total revenue for the project; the answer is then recognized as revenue for the period. The formulas for this method are as follows:

Formula to recognize revenue

Cost Incurred During the Period ÷ Total Estimated Cost × Total Revenue = Revenue Recognized for the Period

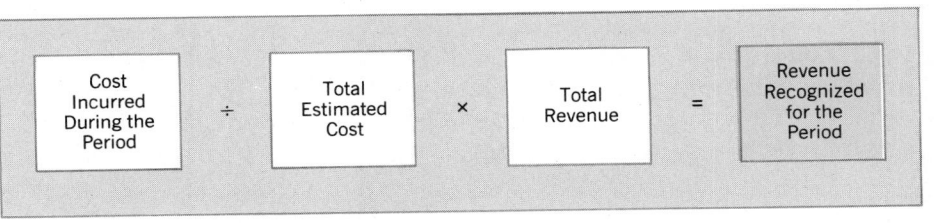

The costs incurred in the current period are then subtracted from the revenue recognized during the current period to arrive at the gross profit.

To illustrate the percentage-of-completion method using the cost-to-cost basis to determine percent complete, assume that Warrior Construction Co. incurs costs of $54 million in 1985, $180 million in 1986, and $126 million in 1987 on the Windswept Canyon Dam project. The portion of the $400 million of revenue recognized in each of the three years is as follows:

Revenue recognized—percentage-of-completion method

Year	Costs Incurred (Current Period)	Ratio of Costs Incurred (Current Period) to Total Estimated Cost	=	Percent Complete (Current Period)	×	Total Revenue	=	Revenue Recognized (Current Period)
1985	$ 54,000,000	$ 54,000,000/$360,000,000		15%		$400,000,000		$ 60,000,000
1986	180,000,000	$180,000,000/$360,000,000		50%		400,000,000		200,000,000
1987	126,000,000	Balance required to complete the contract						140,000,000
Totals	$360,000,000							$400,000,000

Note that no estimate is made of the percentage of work completed during the final period. In the final period, all remaining revenue is recognized. In this example, the company's cost estimates have been very accurate; the

costs incurred in the third year were 35% of the total estimated cost ($126,000 ÷ $360,000). The gross profit recognized each period is as follows:

Gross profit recognized—percentage-of-completion method

Year	Revenue Recognized (Current Period)	−	Actual Cost Incurred (Current Period)	=	Gross Profit Recognized (Current Period)
1985	$ 60,000,000		$ 54,000,000		$ 6,000,000
1986	200,000,000		180,000,000		20,000,000
1987	140,000,000		126,000,000		14,000,000
Totals	$400,000,000		$360,000,000		$40,000,000

Application of the percentage-of-completion method involves some subjectivity and hence, possible error in the determination of the amount of revenue recognized and net income reported. Yet recognition appears most appropriate here because to wait until completion seriously distorts each period's financial statements. Naturally, if it is not possible to obtain dependable estimates of costs and progress, then the revenue should be at the completion date and not on a percentage of completion basis.

Cash Basis. Another basis for revenue recognition is the receipt of cash. The cash basis is generally used only when it is difficult to determine the revenue amount at the time of a credit sale because collection is so uncertain. One popular approach to the recognition of revenue using the cash basis is the **installment method.** Under this method revenue and income are recorded over time only as the cash installments are received.

Under the installment method, each cash collection from a customer is considered to be revenue and to consist of (1) a partial recovery of the cost of the goods sold, and (2) partial gross profit from the sale. For example, if the gross profit rate at date of sale is 40%, each subsequent receipt consists of 60% recovery of cost of goods sold and 40% gross profit. The formula to recognize gross profit is as follows:

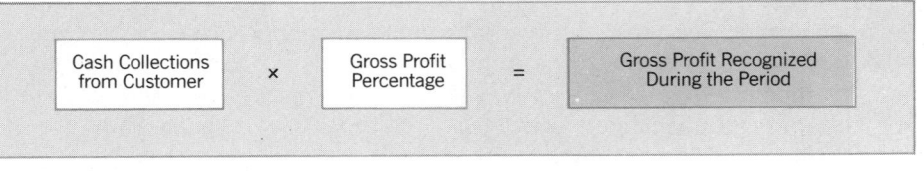

Gross profit formula—installment method

Cash Collections from Customer × Gross Profit Percentage = Gross Profit Recognized During the Period

To illustrate, assume that an Iowa farm machinery dealer in the first year of operations had installment sales of $600,000 and a cost of goods sold on installment of $420,000. Total gross profit is, therefore, $180,000 ($600,000 − $420,000), and the gross profit percentage is 30% ($180,000 ÷ $600,000). The collections on the installment sales were as follows: First year, $280,000 (down payments plus monthly payments); second year, $200,000; and, third year, $120,000. The collections of cash and recognition of the gross profit are summarized at the top of the next page (interest charges are ignored in this illustration):

Gross profit recognized—installment method

Year	Cash Collected	Gross Profit Percentage	Gross Profit Recognized
1985	$280,000	30%	$ 84,000
1986	200,000	30%	60,000
1987	120,000	30%	36,000
Total	$600,000		$180,000

Under the installment method of accounting, gross profit is therefore recognized in the period in which the cash is collected.

As indicated earlier, use of the installment method is justified when the risk of not collecting an account receivable may be so great that the sale is not sufficient evidence for revenue to be recognized. Companies selling goods on the installment plan also frequently use the installment method of accounting for income tax purposes because it postpones the payment of income taxes until cash is collected from the customers.

Matching Principle (Expense Recognition)

Expense recognition is traditionally tied to revenue recognition: "Let the expense follow the revenue." This practice is referred to as the **matching principle** because it dictates that expenses be matched with revenues whenever it is reasonable and practicable to do so. Expenses are not recognized when cash is paid, or when the work is performed, or when the product is produced; they are recognized when the labor (service) or the product actually makes its contribution to revenue.

The problem is that it is sometimes difficult to determine the accounting period in which the expense contributed to the generation of revenues. Accountants have therefore devised several approaches to expense recognition, that is, approaches for matching expenses and revenues on the income statement. To understand these approaches, it is necessary to examine the nature of expenses. All expenses begin as incurred costs. Incurred costs that will only generate revenues in the current accounting period are expensed immediately and are reported as operating expenses in the income statement. Examples include such costs as advertising, sales salaries, and repairs. These expenses are often called period costs (or expenses) because they are expensed in the period in which they are incurred.

Incurred costs that will generate revenues in current and future accounting periods are recognized as assets when incurred. Examples include merchandise inventory, prepaid expenses, and plant assets. These costs represent unexpired costs. Costs associated with merchandise inventory are often referred to as **product costs,** and those associated with long-lived assets are sometimes referred to as **capitalized costs.** Unexpired costs become expenses in two ways:

1. **Cost of goods sold.** Costs carried as merchandise inventory are expensed as cost of goods sold in the period when the sale occurs. Thus, there is a direct matching of expenses with revenues.

2. **Operating expenses.** Unexpired costs become operating expenses through use or consumption as in the case of store supplies or through the passage of time as in the case of prepaid insurance and prepaid rent. The cost of plant assets and other long-lived productive resources are expensed through rational and systematic allocation methods that result in periodic depreciation and amortization. Operating expenses contribute to the revenues of the period but their association with revenues is less direct than for cost of goods sold.

The points made above relative to expense recognition are illustrated below:

Expense recognition pattern

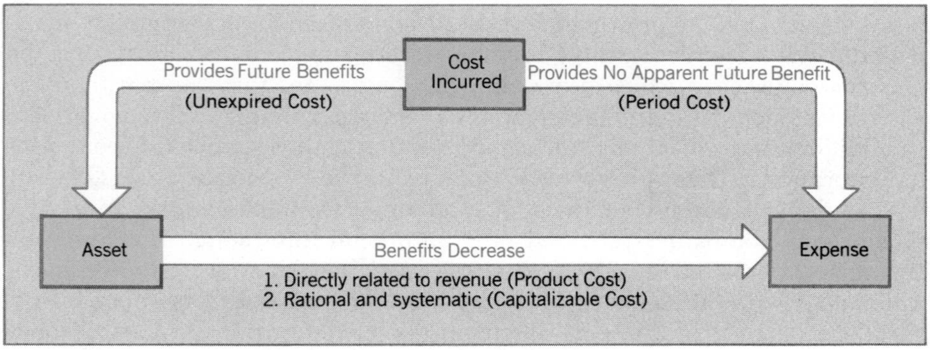

Implementing these guidelines can be difficult. Consider, for example, Harold's Club (a gambling casino) in Reno, Nevada. How should it report expenses related to the payoff of its progressive slot machines? Progressive slot machines, which generally have no ceiling on their jackpots, are capable of providing a lucky winner with all the money that many losers had previously poured into the machines. Payoffs tend to be huge, but infrequent; at Harold's, the progressive slots pay off on average every 4½ months. The basic accounting question is: Can Harold's deduct the millions of dollars sitting in its progressive slot machines from the revenue recognized at the end of its fiscal period? One might argue that no, you cannot deduct the money until the "winning handle pull." However, a winning handle pull might not occur for many months or even years.[3]

What would you do in this situation? Although admittedly an estimate would have to be used, the better answer is to match these costs with the revenue recognized, assuming that on average 4½ months' payout is well documented. This example demonstrates the difficulty of applying the matching principle in a practical situation.

Full Disclosure Principle

The **full disclosure principle** dictates that circumstances and events that make a difference to financial statement users be disclosed. Thus, most accountants would agree that Manville Corporation should have disclosed the

[3]Illustration adapted from *Fortune*, July 7, 1986, p. 100.

52,000 asbestos liability suits (totaling $2 billion) pending against it so that interested parties were made aware of this contingent loss. Similarly, it is generally agreed that companies should disclose the major provisions of employee pension plans and long-term lease contracts.

Compliance with the full disclosure principle occurs through the data contained in the financial statements and the information presented in the notes that accompany the financial statements. The first note in most cases is a **summary of significant accounting policies.** The summary includes the methods used by the company for inventory costing, depreciation of plant assets, and amortization of intangible assets.

Deciding how much disclosure is enough is difficult. Accountants could disclose every financial event that occurs and every contingency that exists. However, accounting information must be condensed and combined to make it understandable. Providing additional information entails a cost, and the benefits of providing this information in some cases may be less than the costs. Many companies, today, complain of an accounting standards overload. In addition, they object to requirements that force them to disclose confidential information. Determining where to draw the line on disclosure is not easy.

One thing is certain: financial statements were much simpler years ago, when many companies provided little additional information regarding the financial statements. In 1930, General Electric had no notes to the financial statements; today it has over 10 pages! Why this change? A major reason is that the objectives of financial statements have changed. In the past, accoun-

---

In his book FUTURE SHOCK, Alvin Toffler pointed out that some 90% of the scientists that ever lived are living today. A similar analogy could be made about the information explosion in the accounting profession. It would go something like this—Ninety percent of all the informative literature in accounting has been written in the current generation. Not all accountants would agree with this statement. Some would insist that the last ten or twenty years would be more like it. In any case, there is no doubt that the accountant's research needs are great, and that there are computerized data bases to aid in the research effort.

NAARS was one of the first such data bases and has been a mainstay of accounting research since the mid 1970s. NAARS contains the complete financial statements for over 4,200 companies. Today, there are several data bases like NAARS (such as LEXIS, NEXIS, DISCLOSURE, and COMPUSTAT) that service almost every business (and non business) need imaginable. Here are examples of just some of the uses of such data bases:

Determine preferred accounting procedure in a particular industry or situation.

Locate prior decisions in legal and accounting conflicts.

Identify industry and individual firm statistics.

Before computers, scholars and business researchers had to know what reference books were available. Today, the informed researcher must also know what data base to access. Indeed, much information is entered into data bases before it gets into print (if it ever does).

---

tants were interested only in presenting information on what the business had done. Today the objectives of financial reporting are more future-oriented; accounting is trying to provide information that makes it possible to predict the amount, timing, and uncertainty of future cash flows.

Cost Principle

One of the oldest and most basic principles of accounting is the cost principle. Cost is used because it is both relevant and reliable. Cost is relevant because it represents the price paid, the assets sacrificed, or the commitment made at date of acquisition. It is the amount for which someone or some entity should be accountable. Cost is reliable because it is objectively measurable, factual, and verifiable. It is the result of an arm's length exchange transaction. As a result, cost is the basis used in preparing financial statements.

The cost principle, however, has come under much criticism. While cost is relevant and reliable because it represents the actual exchange value at the date of acquisition, cost is criticized as irrelevant because subsequent to acquisition, cost is not equivalent to market value or current value.

CONSTRAINTS IN APPLYING GUIDELINES

The FASB recognizes two constraints in applying the operating guidelines within its conceptual framework:

1. **Cost-benefit relationship.** The cost-benefit constraint means that the cost of applying an accounting principle should not exceed its benefit. For example, a company could be required to report depreciation expense and accumulated depreciation for each plant asset rather than for each major class of plant assets. The cost of providing this additional information is likely to be much greater than its usefulness to an external user of the financial statements.
2. **Materiality.** An item is material when it is likely to influence the decision of a reasonably prudent investor or creditor. The materiality of an amount is usually determined by comparing it with other amounts in the financial statements such as total assets, total liabilities, and net income. When the amount is material, the operational guidelines should be followed. However, if the item is immaterial, application of a particular guideline may not be necessary.

These two constraints permit a modification of one or more of the accepted operating guidelines (assumptions and principles) without reducing the usefulness of the reported information.

SUMMARY OF CONCEPTUAL FRAMEWORK

The conceptual framework that is followed in developing sound reporting practices starts with a set of objectives for financial reporting and follows with the development of qualities that make information useful. In addition, a

set of definitions is developed. Operating guidelines in the form of assumptions and principles are then provided. The conceptual framework also recognizes that important constraints exist on the reporting environment. These points are illustrated graphically below:

Conceptual framework

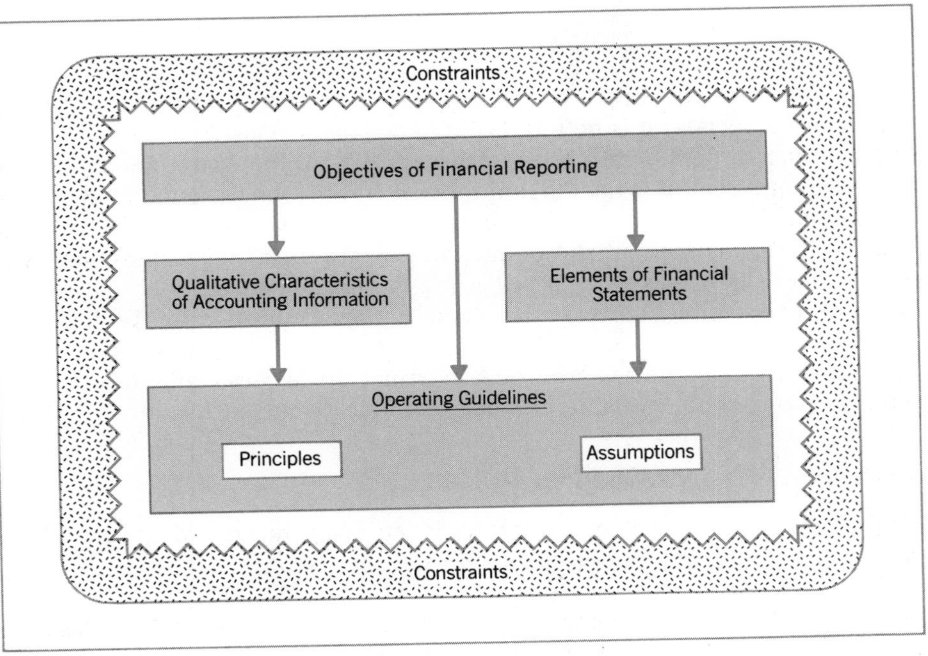

SECTION TWO—ACCOUNTING FOR CHANGING PRICES

One assumption made in accounting is that the monetary unit remains stable over a period of time. But is that assumption realistic? Consider the classic story about the individual who went to sleep and woke up ten years later. Hurrying to a telephone, he got through to his broker and asked what his formerly modest stock portfolio was worth. He was told that he was a multimillionaire—his General Motors stock was worth $5 million and his AT&T stock was up to $10 million. Elated, he was about to inquire about his other holdings, when the telephone operator cut in with "Your time is up. Please deposit $100,000 for the next three minutes."[4]

What this little story demonstrates is that prices can and do change over a period of time, and that one is not necessarily better off when they do. Although the example above is extreme, consider some more realistic data that compare prices in 1980 with what is expected in 1990, assuming prices increase either an average of 6% per year or 13% per year.

[4]Adapted from *Barron's*, January 28, 1980, p. 27.

Example of changing prices

	1980	1990	
Assumed Average Price Increase		6%	13%
Public college, yearly average cost	$3,350.00	$6,000.00	$11,400.00
Average taxi ride, New York City (before tip and abuse)	2.95	5.30	10.00
Slice of pizza	.65	1.20	2.25
First-class postage stamp	.15	.27	.50
Run-of-the-mill suburban $150,000 house, New York City	150,000.00	270,000.00	510,000.00
McDonald's milk shake	.75	1.35	2.55

Despite the inevitability of changing prices during a period of inflation, the accounting profession still follows the stable monetary unit assumption in the preparation of a company's primary financial statements. While admitting that some changes in prices do occur, the profession believes the unit of measure (e.g., the dollar) has remained sufficiently constant over time to provide meaningful financial information.

The profession, however, at one time required and now encourages the disclosure of certain price-level adjusted data in the form of supplemental information. The two most widely used approaches to show the effects of changing prices on a company's financial statement are (1) constant dollar accounting, and (2) current cost accounting.

CONSTANT DOLLAR ACCOUNTING

The real value of the dollar is determined by the goods or services for which it can be exchanged. This real value is commonly called **purchasing power.** As the economy experiences **inflation** (rising price-levels) or **deflation** (falling price-levels), the amount of goods or services for which a dollar can be exchanged changes; that is, the purchasing power of the dollar changes from one period to the next.

Constant dollar accounting restates financial statement items into dollars that have equal purchasing power. As one executive from Shell Oil Company explained, "Constant dollar accounting is a restatement of the traditional financial information into a common unit of measurement." In other words, constant dollar accounting changes the unit of measurement; it does not, however, change the underlying accounting principles used to report historical cost amounts. Constant dollar accounting is cost based.

Through constant dollar restatement, financial data are rendered comparable; thus, important trends can be detected. For example, a newspaper article recently lamented the fact that workers in the United States were losing ground economically. This article noted that a worker who earned $23,750 in 1973 earned in real terms only $17,520 in 1983, a 26.2% drop. The worker in 1983 is worse off because he/she has less purchasing power in 1983 than in 1973. This information suggests that the standard of living in the United States is declining.

PRICE-LEVEL INDEXES

To restate financial information into constant dollars, it is necessary to measure a change in the price of a "basket of goods" from one period to the next. Developing this basket of goods is a complex process and involves judgment in selecting the most appropriate items to be part of this market basket. Fortunately, the government puts together a number of different baskets of goods and computes indexes for them. One of the most popular, and the one that accountants use, is the Consumers Price Index for all Urban Consumers (CPI-U). The CPI-U reflects the average change in the retail prices of a fairly broad group of consumer goods.

The procedure for restating reported historical cost dollars, which vary in purchasing power, to dollars of constant purchasing power is relatively straightforward. The restatement is accomplished by multiplying the amount to be restated by a fraction, the numerator of which is the index for current prices and the denominator of which is the index for prices that prevailed at the date related to the amount being restated. The denominator is often referred to as the base year. The formula is as follows:

Formula to restate historical cost

$$\text{Amount to be Restated} \times \frac{\text{Index of Current Year}}{\text{Index of Base Year}} = \text{Restated Amount}$$

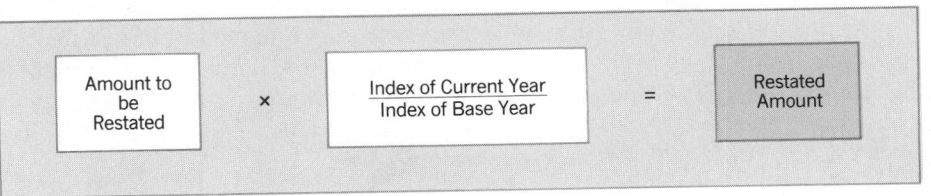

To illustrate how this restatement process works, assume that land was purchased in 1980 for $100,000 and another parcel of land was purchased in 1984 for $80,000. If the price-level index was 100 in 1980, 120 in 1984, and 180 in 1987, the land parcels would be restated to the 1987 price level as follows:

Land restated

1980 purchase	$\left(\$100{,}000 \times \frac{180}{100}\right)$ =	$180,000
1984 purchase	$\left(\$\ 80{,}000 \times \frac{180}{120}\right)$ =	120,000
Land as restated		$300,000

The land is restated to $300,000 in terms of 1987 dollars using the 1987 index of 180 as the numerator for both parcels and the base year indexes of 100 and 120 as the denominators. If historical cost dollars are not restated, dollars of different purchasing power are added together, and the total dollar amount is not meaningful.

MONETARY AND NONMONETARY ITEMS

In preparing constant dollar statements, it is essential to distinguish between monetary and nonmonetary items. **Monetary items** are contractual claims to receive or pay a fixed amount of cash. Monetary assets include cash, accounts and notes receivable, and investments that pay a fixed rate of interest and

will be repaid at a fixed amount in the future. Monetary liabilities include accounts and notes payable, accruals such as wages and interest payable, and long-term obligations payable in a fixed sum.

All assets and liabilities not classified as monetary items are classified as nonmonetary for constant dollar accounting purposes. **Nonmonetary items** are items whose prices in terms of the monetary unit change in proportion to changes in the general price level. Examples of nonmonetary assets are inventories, property, plant, and equipment, and intangible assets. Most liabilities are monetary items, while capital stock equity is usually nonmonetary.

The following chart indicates some major monetary and nonmonetary items.

Examples of monetary and nonmonetary items

Monetary Items	Nonmonetary Items
Cash	Inventories
Notes and accounts receivable	Investments in common stock
Investments that pay a fixed rate of interest	Property, plant, and equipment
Notes and accounts payable	Intangible assets
	Capital stock

EFFECTS OF HOLDING MONETARY AND NONMONETARY ITEMS

Holders of monetary assets lose during a period of inflation because a given amount of money buys progressively fewer goods and services. Conversely, liabilities such as accounts payable and notes payable held during a period of inflation become less burdensome because they are payable in dollars of reduced general purchasing power. The gains or losses that result from holding monetary items during periods of price changes are often referred to as **purchasing power gains and losses.** As Northwestern National Life Insurance explained in its annual report, "If a company's equity is invested in monetary assets, the purchasing power of its equity is gradually eroded at a rate equal to inflation."

To illustrate the effects of holding monetary and nonmonetary items in a period of inflation, assume that Helio Company has the following balance sheet at the beginning of the year:

Balance sheet (beginning of period)—historical cost

HELIO COMPANY
Balance Sheet
(Beginning of Period)
Price index = 100

Cash	$1,000	Capital stock	$4,000
Inventory	3,000		
Total assets	$4,000	Total stockholders' equity	$4,000

If the general price-level doubles during the year, and no transactions take place, then for the company to be in the same economic position at the end of the year as it was at the beginning, it should have the balance sheet shown at the top of the next page.

Balance sheet (end of period)—historical cost

HELIO COMPANY
Balance Sheet
(End of Period)
Price index = 200

Cash	$2,000	Capital stock	$8,000
Inventory	6,000		
Total assets	$8,000	Total stockholders' equity	$8,000

As illustrated, all items should have doubled if the company is to be in the same economic position. However, only the inventory and the capital stock can be doubled. Helio still has only $1,000 of cash; therefore, it has experienced a purchasing power loss in holding cash during a period of inflation. Helio's balance sheet presented on a constant dollar basis would appear as follows:

Balance sheet (end of period)—constant dollar

HELIO COMPANY
Balance Sheet
(End of Period)
Price index = 200

Cash	$1,000	Capital stock	$8,000
Inventory	6,000	Retained earnings	(1,000)
Total assets	$7,000	Total stockholders' equity	$7,000

As noted, Helio Company has experienced a purchasing power loss of $1,000, which is shown as a reduction of retained earnings.

In summary, because monetary assets and liabilities are already stated in terms of current purchasing power in the historical cost balance sheet, they appear at the same amounts in statements adjusted for general price-level changes. The fact that the end-of-the-current-year amounts are the same in historical dollar statements as in constant dollar statements does not obscure the fact that purchasing power gains or losses result from holding them during a period of general price-level change. Conversely, nonmonetary items are reported at different amounts in the constant dollar statements than they are in the historical cost statements, when there is a change in the general price level. As a result, both the inventory and the capital stock are adjusted to recognize changes in the purchasing power of the dollar.

CONSTANT DOLLAR ILLUSTRATION

To illustrate the preparation of financial statements on a constant dollar basis, assume that Hartley Company starts business on December 31, 1986, by selling $190,000 of capital stock for cash. Land costing $80,000 is purchased immediately. During 1987, the company reports $190,000 of sales, cost of goods sold of $100,000, and operating expenses of $20,000. The income statement for Hartley Company on a historical cost basis is as follows:

Income statement

HARTLEY COMPANY
Income Statement (Historical Cost)
For the Year Ended December 31, 1987

Sales	$190,000
Cost of goods sold	100,000
Gross profit	90,000
Operating expenses	20,000
Net income	$ 70,000

The comparative balance sheets on a historical cost basis are as follows:

Comparative balance sheets

HARTLEY COMPANY
Balance Sheet (Historical Cost)
December 31

Assets	1987	1986
Cash	$145,000	$110,000
Inventory	35,000	—
Land	80,000	80,000
Total assets	$260,000	$190,000
Liabilities and Stockholders' Equity		
Capital stock	$190,000	$190,000
Retained earnings	70,000	—
Total liabilities and stockholders' equity	$260,000	$190,000

The relevant price indexes for use in preparing constant dollar financial statements are presented below. These price indexes are magnified here to illustrate their effect.

Relevant price indexes

	Price Indexes
December 31, 1986	100
1987 average	160
December 31, 1987	200

Constant Dollar Income Statement

When a constant dollar income statement is prepared, revenues and expenses are restated to end-of-year dollars. The difference between restated revenues and expenses is reported as income (loss) before purchasing power gain (loss). The purchasing power gain (loss) is then added (deducted) to produce "constant dollar net income (loss)."

Revenues and expenses are usually assumed to occur evenly throughout the period. Therefore, the historical dollar amounts are multiplied by the restatement ratio, of which the numerator is the end-of-year index and the

denominator is the average index. The constant dollar income statement for Hartley Company is provided below (the explanations highlighted in color are not part of the formal statement; they are provided to help you understand how the statement is prepared).

Constant dollar income statement

HARTLEY COMPANY
Constant Dollar Income Statement
For the Year Ended December 31, 1987

Sales	$237,500	$\left(\$190{,}000 \times \frac{200}{160}\right)$
Cost of goods sold	125,000	$\left(\$100{,}000 \times \frac{200}{160}\right)$
Gross profit	112,500	
Operating expenses	25,000	$\left(\$\ 20{,}000 \times \frac{200}{160}\right)$
Income before purchasing power loss	87,500	
Purchasing power loss	(118,750)	(Per computation below)
Constant dollar net loss	$(31,250)	

Restatement of the items above is explained below:

Sales—Because sales were spread evenly over the year, the average index is used in the computation to restate sales to end-of-year dollars.

Cost of Goods Sold—The cost of goods sold of $100,000 consists of two amounts, purchases of $135,000 less ending inventory of $35,000. Because the costs of purchases and ending inventories were spread evenly over the year, the average index is used in the computation to restate cost of goods sold to end-of-year dollars.

Operating Expenses—Because operating expenses were spread evenly over the year, the average index is used in the computation to restate operating expenses to end-of-year dollars.

Purchasing Power Loss—Computation of the purchasing power gain (loss) on monetary items requires a reconciliation of the beginning and ending balances of each monetary item for the period. A restatement ratio is then applied to the beginning balance and each reconciling amount. Hartley Company has only one monetary item, cash. Because prices are rising, it will experience a purchasing power loss for 1987. The computation of the loss is shown at the top of the next page.

The first column of this schedule provides a reconciliation of the beginning and ending cash balances. Note that purchases is determined by adding ending inventory ($35,000) to cost of goods sold ($100,000) for Hartley Company. The restatement ratio for the beginning cash balance is based on the price index at the beginning of the year (100). The other ratios are based on the average price index during the year (160). The totaled restated dollars, $263,750, indicates how much cash the company should have to stay even with the price increases that have occurred. This amount is then compared with the historical cost ending balance to determine the amount of the purchasing power gain or loss. In this case, Hartley should have $263,750; it has

Computation of purchasing power loss

	1987 Historical ×	Restatement Ratio	= Restated to 12/31/87 Dollars
Cash:			
Beginning balance	$110,000	$\frac{200}{100}$	$ 220,000
Add: Sales	190,000	$\frac{200}{160}$	237,500
Deduct: Purchases	(135,000)	$\frac{200}{160}$	(168,750)
Operating expenses	(20,000)	$\frac{200}{160}$	(25,000)
Total restated dollars			263,750
Ending balance	$145,000		145,000
Purchasing power loss			**$(118,750)**

only $145,000. Therefore, it has experienced a purchasing power loss of $118,750.

Constant Dollar Balance Sheet

When a constant dollar balance sheet is prepared, all monetary items are stated in end-of-year dollars and therefore do not need adjustment. Nonmonetary items, however, must be restated to end-of-year dollars. The constant dollar balance sheet for Hartley Company is provided below (the explanations highlighted in color are not part of the formal statement; they are provided to help you understand how the statement is prepared).

Constant dollar balance sheet

HARTLEY COMPANY
Constant Dollar Balance Sheet
December 31, 1987

Assets		
Cash	$145,000	**(Same as historical cost)**
Inventory	43,750	**$\left(\$35{,}000 \times \frac{200}{160}\right)$**
Land	160,000	**$\left(\$80{,}000 \times \frac{200}{100}\right)$**
Total assets	$348,750	
Liabilities and Stockholders' Equity		
Capital stock	$380,000	**$\left(\$190{,}000 \times \frac{200}{100}\right)$**
Retained earnings	(31,250)	**(See constant dollar income statement)**
Total liabilities and stockholders' equity	$348,750	

Restatement of the items above is explained as follows:

Cash—Cash is a monetary item; therefore, no restatement is necessary.

Inventory—Inventory is a nonmonetary item and therefore it must be restated. Because inventory was purchased evenly throughout the year, the $35,000 must be multiplied by the ratio of the ending index, 200, to the index at the time the inventory was purchased, which was the average for the year of 160.

Land—Land is a nonmonetary item; therefore, it must be restated. Because land was purchased at the end of the preceding year, the $80,000 must be multiplied by the ratio of the ending index to the index at the time the land was purchased, which was 100.

Capital Stock—Capital stock is a nonmonetary item; therefore, restatement is necessary. Because capital stock was issued at the end of the preceding year, the $190,000 must be multiplied by the ratio of the ending index, 200, to the index at the time the capital stock was issued, which was 100.

Retained Earnings—Since no balance existed in retained earnings at the beginning of the year, the retained earnings in constant dollars includes only the constant dollar net loss for the current period of $31,250. Thus, Hartley Company on a constant dollar basis reports a negative retained earnings after its first year of operations.

CURRENT COST ACCOUNTING

The price of a specific item may be affected not only by general inflation, but also by individual market forces. For example, between 1980 and 1986, certain items changed more or less than the general price level. To illustrate, during this period of time, the cost of a local telephone call increased 150%, guaranteed overnight mail delivery increased 4,575%, a gallon of gasoline decreased over 30%, and a flawless one-carat diamond decreased over 70%. Thus, changes in the specific price of items may be very different from the change in the general price-level.

A popular means to measure the change in a specific price is current cost. **Current cost** is the cost of replacing the identical asset owned. Current cost may be approximated by reference to current catalog prices or by applying a specific index to the book value of the asset. Unlike the constant dollar approach, which is simply a restatement of historical dollars into constant purchasing power, the current cost approach changes the basis of measurement from historical cost to current value.

CURRENT COST ADJUSTMENTS

When current cost statements are prepared, it is also necessary to distinguish between monetary and nonmonetary items. Monetary items are stated at their current cost in the historical cost financial statements. As a result, no adjustment is necessary to items such as cash, accounts receivable, notes payable, or accounts payable when preparing a current cost balance sheet. A purchasing power gain or loss on the monetary items is not computed under current cost

accounting because the measuring unit, the dollar, is not considered to have changed from one period to the next.

Conversely, nonmonetary items as a rule must be adjusted at year-end. The current cost of nonmonetary items tends to change over time. For example, land held over a period of time will usually experience some type of price change. The same is true of other nonmonetary items such as inventory; property, plant, and equipment; and intangible assets.

When a nonmonetary item is restated, a holding gain or loss arises and must be reported on the financial statements. A **holding gain (loss)** is an increase or decrease in an item's value while it is held by the company. For example, if the current cost of land is $20,000 on January 1, 1987, and $32,000 on December 31, 1987, the company has a holding gain on this land of $12,000, computed as follows:

Computation of holding gain

Current cost of land, December 31, 1987	$32,000
Current cost of land, January 1, 1987	20,000
Holding gain on land	**$12,000**

Other revenues and expenses appearing on a current cost income statement are the same as the historical cost amounts, because at the time they are earned or incurred they represent current cost. A major exception is the cost of goods sold, which will be explained later.

To illustrate the preparation of financial statements on a current cost basis, assume that Sensor, Inc. starts business on December 31, 1986 by selling $90,000 of capital stock for cash. Land costing $40,000 is purchased immediately. During the next year, the company reports $160,000 of sales revenue, cost of goods sold of $75,000, and operating expenses of $25,000. The income statement for Sensor, Inc. on a historical cost basis is as follows:

Historical cost income statement

SENSOR, INC.
Income Statement (Historical Cost)
For the Year Ended December 31, 1987

Sales	$160,000
Cost of goods sold	75,000
Gross profit	85,000
Operating expenses	25,000
Net income	$ 60,000

The comparative balance sheets on a historical cost basis are as follows:

Historical cost balance sheet

SENSOR, INC.
Balance Sheet (Historical Cost)
December 31

Assets	1987	1986
Cash	$ 30,000	$50,000
Inventory	80,000	—
Land	40,000	40,000
Total assets	$150,000	$90,000
Liabilities and Stockholders' Equity		
Capital stock	$ 90,000	$90,000
Retained earnings	60,000	—
Total liabilities and stockholders' equity	$150,000	$90,000

The relevant current cost amounts for the income statement and balance sheet items for 1987 are as follows:

Relevant current costs

Income Statement		Balance Sheet	
Sales	$160,000	Cash	$ 30,000
Cost of goods sold	95,000	Inventory	105,000
Operating expenses	25,000	Land	48,000
		Capital stock	90,000

CURRENT COST INCOME STATEMENT

In a current cost income statement, two income numbers are reported. The first, **current cost income from operations,** is sales revenues less the current cost of goods sold plus operating expenses. This amount is the income a company has earned after providing for the replacement of assets used in operations.

Current cost income statement

SENSOR, INC.
Current Cost Income Statement
For the Year Ended December 31, 1987

Sales	$160,000	(Same as historical cost)
Cost of goods sold	95,000	(Restated to current cost)
Gross profit	65,000	
Operating expenses	25,000	(Same as historical cost)
Current cost income from operations	40,000	
Holding gain	53,000	(Increase in current cost)
Current cost net income	$ 93,000	

The second income number, **current cost net income,** measures the total income of a company from one period to the next. Thus, holding gains (losses)

are added (deducted) to current cost income from operations to arrive at this number. The current cost income statement for Sensor, Inc. is provided above (the explanations highlighted in color are not part of the formal statement; they are provided to help you understand how the statement is prepared).

The above items are explained below.

Sales and Operating Expenses—Sales and operating expenses are already stated at their current cost amounts on historical cost statements; therefore, no adjustment is needed for these items.

Cost of Goods Sold—Goods are sold at varying times of the year. At the time these goods are sold, the current cost of the inventory sold must be determined. The historical cost of goods sold and the current cost of goods sold are usually different.

Total Holding Gain—The holding gain for Sensor comprises three items as shown below.

Computation of total holding gain

Current cost of goods sold	$95,000	
Historical cost of goods sold	75,000	
		$20,000
Current cost of inventory	105,000	
Historical cost of inventory	80,000	
		25,000
Current cost of land	48,000	
Historical cost of land	40,000	
		8,000
Total holding gain		$53,000

Recall that a holding gain is an increase in an item's value from one period to the next. If the item is sold during the period, however, the holding gain (loss) is computed only to the point of sale. Thus, the inventory sold, as reported in the current cost of goods sold amount, had increased $20,000. Also, inventory on hand and land experienced holding gains of $25,000 and $8,000, respectively. Holding gains or losses indicate how effective management is in acquiring and holding assets.

CURRENT COST BALANCE SHEET

The preparation of a current cost balance sheet is relatively straightforward. Monetary items are not adjusted because they are already stated at current cost. Similarly, capital stock equity is not adjusted because its balance represents the current cost of capital stock. All other nonmonetary items must be adjusted to current costs. The current cost balance sheet for Sensor, Inc. is shown on the next page (the explanations highlighted in color are not part of the formal statement; they are provided to help you understand how the statement is prepared).

As indicated from the statement on the next page, Retained Earnings is determined by adding the current cost net income amount to the beginning balance of retained earnings.

Current cost balance sheet

SENSOR, INC.
Current Cost Balance Sheet
December 31, 1987

Assets		
Cash	$ 30,000	(Same as historical cost)
Inventory	105,000	(Restated to current cost)
Land	48,000	(Restated to current cost)
Total assets	$183,000	
Liabilities and Stockholders' Equity		
Capital stock	$ 90,000	(Same as historical cost)
Retained earnings	93,000	(From current cost income statement)
Total liabilities and stockholders' equity	$183,000	

PROFESSION'S POSITION ON CHANGING PRICE INFORMATION

In September 1979, the FASB, in response to a perceived need for information on the effects of changing prices on financial statements, required large publicly held companies to disclose certain price-level adjusted financial information. The required price-level adjusted information was provided on an experimental basis and consisted of restated information from the primary financial statements to reflect changes in (a) general price levels (constant dollar data) and (b) specific price levels (current cost data).

An FASB survey of financial statement users, preparers, and auditors revealed that both the number of users and the extent of use of the data were limited. Many respondents commented that the price-level adjusted data did not appear to have been used by the institutional investment community, bankers, or investors in general. Therefore, partly as a result of nonuse and partly as a result of prevailing low inflation rates, the accounting profession in 1987 was persuaded to cease requiring the disclosure of supplementary information on the effects of changing prices. Companies now are only encouraged to disclose price-level adjusted information and are not discouraged from experimenting with different forms of disclosure.

SUMMARY OF STUDY OBJECTIVES

1. Generally accepted accounting principles are a set of rules and practices that are recognized as a general guide for financial reporting purposes. Generally accepted means that these principles must have "substantial authoritative support."

2. The key items of the conceptual framework are: (1) Objectives of Financial Reporting; (2) Qualitative Characteristics of Accounting Information; (3) Elements of Financial Statements; and (4) Operating Guidelines (Assumptions, Principles, and Constraints).

3. The basic objectives of financial reporting are to provide information that is (1) useful to those making investment and credit decisions; (2) helpful in assessing future cash flows; and (3) about the economic resources (assets), the claims to those resources (liabilities), and the changes in those resources and claims.

4. To judge usefulness, information should possess the following qualitative characteristics: relevance, reliability, comparability, and consistency. The elements of financial statements are a set of definitions that can be used to describe the basic terms used in accounting.

5. The operating guidelines followed by accountants are assumptions, principles, and constraints. The major assumptions are: economic entity, monetary unit, periodicity, and going concern. The major principles are: revenue recognition, matching, full disclosure, and cost. The major constraints are: cost-benefit relationship and materiality.

6. Many criticize the cost principle and the monetary unit assumption in a period of changing prices. Two approaches to accounting for changing prices are constant dollar accounting and current cost accounting. Constant dollar accounting restates financial statement items into dollars that have equal purchasing power. Current cost measures the change in the specific price of an item from one period to the next.

GLOSSARY

DEMONSTRATION PROBLEM 1

Carver Construction Company is under contract to build a high-rise condominium at a cost of $2,000,000. The building will take eighteen months to complete at an estimated cost of $1,400,000. Construction began in November, 1986 and was finished in April, 1988. Actual construction costs incurred in each year were: 1986 $140,000; 1987 $910,000; and 1988 $350,000.

INSTRUCTIONS

Compute the gross profit to be recognized in each year.

SOLUTION TO DEMONSTRATION PROBLEM 1

Year	Costs Incurred (Current Period)	Ratio of Costs Incurred (Current Period) to Total Estimated Cost	=	Percent Complete (Current Period)	×	Total Revenue	=	Revenue Recognized (Current Period)
1986	$ 140,000	$140,000/$1,400,000		10%		$2,000,000		$ 200,000
1987	910,000	910,000/1,400,000		65%		2,000,000		1,300,000
1988	350,000	Balance to complete contract						500,000
	$1,400,000							$2,000,000

Year	Revenue Recognized (Current Period)	−	Actual Costs Incurred (Current Period)	=	Gross Profit Recognized (Current Period)
1986	$ 200,000		$ 140,000		$ 60,000
1987	1,300,000		910,000		390,000
1988	500,000		350,000		150,000
	$2,000,000		$1,400,000		$600,000

DEMONSTRATION PROBLEM 2

The Santana Company has one monetary item, cash. On January 1, 1987 when the price index was 125, the cash balance was $90,000. During the year, cash sales were $680,000, cash purchases were $595,000, and cash operating expenses were $102,000. These transactions occurred evenly during the year. The average price index in 1987 was 170, and the index was 200 at December 31, 1987.

INSTRUCTIONS

Compute the purchasing power gain or loss.

SOLUTION TO DEMONSTRATION PROBLEM 2

	1987 Historical	× Restatement Ratio	= Restated to 12/31/87 Dollars
Cash:			
Beginning balance	$ 90,000	$\frac{200}{125}$	$144,000
Add: Sales	680,000	$\frac{200}{170}$	800,000
Deduct: Purchases	(595,000)	$\frac{200}{170}$	(700,000)
Operating exp.	(102,000)	$\frac{200}{170}$	(120,000)
Total restated dollars			124,000
Ending balance	$ 73,000		73,000
Purchasing power loss			$ (51,000)

QUESTIONS

1. Prior to the establishment of the Financial Accounting Standards Board, accounting principles had been developed on a problem-by-problem basis. Has the Financial Accounting Standards Board attempted to change this approach to problem solving? How?

2. What are the major objectives of financial reporting?

3. Define relevance and reliability. What characteristics are needed for information to be relevant? Reliable?

4. Joe Broz, the president of Royal Gown Company, is pleased. Royal Gown substantially increased its net income in 1986 while keeping its unit inventory relatively the same. Tom Erhardt, Royal Gown's chief accountant, cautions Broz, however. Erhardt says that since Royal Gown changed from the LIFO to the FIFO method of inventory valuation, there is a consistency problem and it would be difficult to determine if Royal Gown is better off. Is Erhardt correct? Why?

5. What is the distinction between comparability and consistency?

6. Why is it necessary for accountants to assume that an economic entity will remain a going concern?

7. When should revenue be recognized? Why has the date of sale been chosen as the point at which to recognize the revenue resulting from the entire producing and selling process?

8. Hillcrest Construction Company has a $100 million contract to build a bridge. Its total estimated cost for the project is $85 million. Costs incurred in the first year of the project were $17 million. Hillcrest appropriately uses the percentage-of-completion method. How much revenue and gross profit should Hillcrest recognize in the first year of the project?

9. Merchandise with a cost of $90,000 was sold during the year for $120,000. Cash collected for the year amounted to $60,000. How much gross profit should be recognized during the year if the company uses the installment method?

10. Distinguish between product costs and period costs.

11. (a) Where does the accountant disclose information about an entity's financial position, operations, and cash flows? (b) The full disclosure principle recognizes that the nature and amount of information included in financial reports reflects a series of judgmental trade-offs. What are the objectives of these trade-offs?

12. Robert Parker is the president of Hawk Books. He has no accounting background. Parker cannot understand why current cost is not used as the basis for accounting measurement and reporting. Explain what basis is used and why.

13. Describe the two major constraints inherent in the presentation of accounting information.

14. (a) What is meant by constant dollar accounting? (b) What is purchasing power?

15. Distinguish between monetary items and nonmonetary items. Give two examples of each.

16. Joe LaBrava, the president of Educator Publications, is confused. He does not understand how a purchasing power gain or loss can exist when monetary assets and liabilities are unadjusted in constant dollar financial statements. Explain why this treatment is proper.

17. Flatware Co. purchased equipment in 1980 for $150,000. Flatware purchased another piece of equipment in 1986 for $70,000. If the price level index was 100 in 1980, and 125 in 1986, and 130 in 1987, what would be the restated amount of the equipment in 1987 dollars?

18. How are income statement items restated on a constant dollar income statement?

19. What is current cost accounting? How does it differ from constant dollar accounting?

20. Is both a purchasing power gain or loss and holding gain or loss to be recognized when using current cost accounting? Explain.

21. A company has land which cost $100,000. It has a current cost of $130,000 on December 31, 1987. The company also had a cash balance of $30,000 throughout the year. What is the holding gain on the land for 1987?

22. What information does current cost income from operations and current cost net income provide to the financial statement user?

23. What is the accounting profession's position on reporting changing price information?

EXERCISES

E13–1 A number of operational guidelines used by accountants are described below.

(a) Escanaba Company uses the direct write-off method of accounting for uncollectible accounts.

(b) Newberry Hospital Supply Corporation reports only current assets and current liabilities on its balance sheet. Property, plant, and equipment and bonds payable are reported as current assets and current liabilities, respectively. Liquidation of the company is unlikely.

(c) Roth, Inc. is carrying marketable equity securities at its current market value of $100,000. The securities had an original cost of $110,000.

(d) Americas Company is in its fifth year of operation and has yet to issue financial statements. (Do not use full disclosure principle.)

(e) Michelle Boivin, president of the New Music Company, bought a computer for her personal use. She paid for the computer by using company funds and debited the "computers" account.

(f) Milner Company has inventory on hand which cost $400,000. Milner reports inventory on its balance sheet at its current market value of $425,000.

(g) In preparing its financial statements, Schallmoser Company omitted information concerning its method of accounting for inventories.

(h) Smith Company recognizes revenue at the end of the production cycle, but before sale. The price of the product, as well as the amount that can be sold, is not certain.

INSTRUCTIONS

For each of the above, list the assumption, principle, or constraint that has been violated, if any. List only one term for each case.

E13-2 Presented below are some business transactions that occurred during 1987 for Cactus Co.

(a) The president of Cactus Co., Clay Wanfield, purchased a truck for personal use and charged it to his expense account. The following entry was made:

Travel Expense	7,000	
Cash		7,000

(b) A pencil sharpener costing $45 is being depreciated over 5 years. The following entry was made:

Depreciation Expense—Pencil Sharpener	9	
Accumulated Depreciation—Pencil Sharpener		9

(c) Equipment worth $70,000 was acquired at a cost of $49,000 from a company which had water damage in a flood. The following entry was made:

Equipment	70,000	
Cash		49,000
Gain		21,000

(d) Merchandise inventory with a cost of $195,000 is reported at its market value of $210,000. The following entry was made:

Merchandise Inventory	15,000	
Gain		15,000

(e) An account receivable has been deemed to be a bad debt. The following entry was made:

Allowance for Doubtful Accounts	4,000	
Accounts Receivable		4,000

INSTRUCTIONS

In each of the situations above, identify the assumption, principle, or constraint that has been violated, if any, and discuss the appropriateness of the journal entries. Give the correct journal entry, if necessary.

E13-3 Consider the following transactions of Gazvoda Company for 1987.

(a) Sold a 6-month insurance policy to Littleson Corporation for $3,000 on March 1.

(b) Leased office space to Bates Motel Supplies for a 1-year period beginning October 1. The rent of $15,000 was paid in advance.

(c) A sales order for merchandise costing $7,500 which had a sales price of $9,800 was received on December 28 from Depalma Company. The goods were shipped FOB shipping point on December 31 and Depalma received them on January 3.

(d) Signed a long-term contract to construct a building at a total price of $1,000,000. Total estimated cost of construction is $600,000. During 1987, the company incurred $150,000 of costs and collected $300,000 in cash. The percentage of completion method is used to recognize revenue.

(e) Merchandise inventory on hand at year end amounted to $145,000. Gazvoda expects to sell the inventory in 1988 for $180,000.

INSTRUCTIONS

For each item above, indicate the amount of revenue Gazvoda should recognize in 1987. Explain.

E13-4 Speedy Construction Company currently has two long-term construction projects. Project 1 has a contract price of $100,000,000 with total estimated costs of $80,000,000. Project 2 has a contract price of $130,000,000 and total estimated costs of $120,000,000. Speedy appropriately uses the percentage-of-completion method. After 2 years of construction, the following costs have been accumulated.

	Project 1	Project 2
Actual cost incurred, Year 1	$20,000,000	$30,000,000
Total estimated cost remaining after Year 1	60,000,000	90,000,000
Actual cost incurred, Year 2	30,000,000	60,000,000
Total estimated cost remaining after Year 2	30,000,000	30,000,000

INSTRUCTIONS

Determine the gross profit for each project for the first two years of the construction contracts.

E13-5 Club Company sold equipment for $180,000 in 1986. Collections on the sale were as follows: 1986, $40,000; 1987, $80,000; 1988, $60,000. Club's cost of goods sold are typically 75% of sales.

INSTRUCTIONS

(a) Determine Club's gross profit for 1986, 1987, and 1988, assuming that Club recognizes income under the installment method.

(b) Determine Club's gross profit for 1986, 1987, and 1988, assuming that Club recognizes income under the point-of-sale basis.

E13-6 Cockburn Co. has made the following purchases of property, plant, and equipment since its formation in 1980:

Year	Price level index	Item	Cost
1980	100	Land	$140,000
1980	100	Building	200,000
1980	100	Machinery	80,000
1982	120	Office Equipment	25,000
1984	125	Machinery	30,000
1986	150	Office Equipment	8,000

The price level index for 1987 is 160.

INSTRUCTIONS

Restate the above items in terms of 1987 dollars. (Round to two decimals.)

E13-7 Stipe, Inc. had the following income statement data for 1987:

Sales	$240,000
Cost of goods sold	168,000
Gross profit	72,000
Operating expenses	34,000
Net income	$ 38,000

The following price levels were observed during the year:

	Price Index
December 31, 1987	150
1987 average	125
December 31, 1986	100

INSTRUCTIONS

Determine Stipe's constant dollar income before purchasing power gain or loss for 1987.

E13-8 Presented below is comparative financial statement information for Steve Gilmour Corp. for the years 1987 and 1986:

	December 31, 1987	December 31, 1986
Cash	$ 88,000	$ 57,000
Inventory	40,000	25,000
Sales	230,000	200,000
Cost of goods sold	150,000	132,000
Operating expenses	34,000	30,000

The following price level indexes were observed during the year:

	Price Index
December 31, 1987	140
1987 average	125
December 31, 1986	100

INSTRUCTIONS

Determine Gilmour's purchasing power gain or loss for 1987. Assume all transactions involved cash.

E13-9 Berry Corp. in its first year of operations reported the following financial information for the year ended December 31, 1987 before closing:

Cash	$ 85,500	Retained earnings	$ 67,500
Inventory	42,000	Sales	215,000
Land	90,000	Cost of goods sold	122,500
Capital stock	150,000	Operating expenses	25,000

The following price level indexes were observed during the year:

	Price Index
December 31, 1987	121
1987 average	110
January 1, 1987	100

Berry experienced a purchasing power loss of $15,150 during 1987. Land was purchased and capital stock issued on January 1, 1987.

INSTRUCTIONS

Prepare the following financial statements for Berry Corp.

(a) Constant dollar income statement for the year ended December 31, 1987.

(b) Constant dollar balance sheet on December 31, 1987.

E13-10 Rockford Co. reported the following financial information for 1987, its first year of operations:

ROCKFORD CO.
Income Statement
For the Year Ended December 31, 1987

Sales	$290,000
Cost of goods sold	197,200
Gross profit	92,800
Operating expenses	41,300
Net income	$ 51,500

ROCKFORD CO.
Balance Sheet
December 31, 1987

Assets		Liabilities and Stockholders' Equity	
Cash	$ 40,000	Capital stock	$270,000
Inventory	95,000	Retained earnings	40,000
Land	175,000	Total liabilities and stockholders' equity	$310,000
Total assets	$310,000		

Current cost information for 1987 is as follows:

Sales	$290,000	Inventory	$107,000
Cost of goods sold	215,000	Land	190,000
Operating expenses	41,300	Capital stock	270,000
Cash	40,000		

INSTRUCTIONS

(a) Determine Rockford's holding gain for 1987.

(b) Prepare Rockford's current cost income statement for 1987.

E13-11 Sandley Chemical, Inc. is experimenting with the use of current costs. In 1987, the company purchased inventory that had a cost of $50,000, of which $30,000 was sold

by year end at a sales price of $45,000. It is estimated that the current cost of the inventory at the date of sale was $33,000, and the current cost of the ending inventory at December 31, 1987 is $26,000. Operating expenses are $10,000.

INSTRUCTIONS

(a) Determine current cost income from operations.

(b) Determine current cost net income.

E13-12 Assume that the Corrine Company has the following net monetary assets (monetary assets less monetary liabilities) at the beginning and the end of 1987.

	1/1/87	12/31/87
Net monetary assets	$300,000	$200,000

Transactions causing a change in net monetary assets during the period were incurrence and payments of accounts payable, collections of accounts receivable, and purchase and sales of merchandise during the period. All these transactions occurred evenly throughout the year.

Assume the following price-level indexes:

January 1, 1987	120
Average for the year	150
December 31, 1987	160

INSTRUCTIONS

(Round all computations to the nearest dollar.)

(a) What is the amount of purchasing power gain or loss from holding the January 1 balance of net monetary items throughout the year?

(b) What is the amount of purchasing power gain or loss from holding net monetary items?

(c) Explain why the company had a purchasing power gain or loss.

PROBLEMS

P13-1 Dunham and Jones are accountants for Americo Computers. They are having disagreements concerning the following transactions that occurred during the calendar year 1987.

(a) Americo purchased equipment for $25,000 at a going-out-of-business sale. The equipment was worth $30,000. Dunham believes that the following entry should be made:

Equipment	30,000	
Cash		25,000
Gain		5,000

(b) A 1-year insurance policy was purchased by Americo on September 1, 1987 for $6,000. Dunham believes that the following entry should be made on September 1:

Insurance Expense	6,000	
Cash		6,000

(c) Land costing $50,000 was appraised at $60,000. Dunham suggests the following journal entry:

Land	10,000	
Gain on Appreciation of Land		10,000

(d) Depreciation for the year was $15,000. Since net income is expected to be lower this year, Dunham suggests deferring depreciation to a year when there is more net income.

(e) Americo bought a custom made piece of equipment for $15,000. This equipment has a useful life of 5 years. Americo depreciates equipment using the straight-line method. "Since the equipment is custom made, it will have no resale value and, therefore, shouldn't be depreciated but instead expensed immediately," argues Dunham. "Besides, it provides for lower net income."

(f) Dunham suggests that Americo should carry equipment on the balance sheet at its liquidation value which is $10,000 less than its cost.

Jones disagrees with Dunham on each of the above situations.

INSTRUCTIONS

For each transaction, indicate why Jones disagrees. Identify the accounting principle or assumption that Dunham would be violating if his suggestions were used. Prepare the correct journal entry for each transaction, if any.

P13-2 Lange Construction Company is involved in a long-term construction contract to build an office building at a total estimated cost of $20 million. Additional information follows:

	Office Building	
	Cash Collections	Actual Costs Incurred
1986	$5,000,000	$3,000,000
1987	8,000,000	7,000,000
1988	6,500,000	6,000,000
1989	5,500,000	4,000,000

The project is completed in 1989 and all cash to be received from the contract has been received.

In a separate transaction, Lange sold apartments it had constructed to Centi Management Company for $2 million. Lange's cost to construct the apartments was $1.7 million. Lange appropriately uses the installment method. Additional information follows:

	Cash Collected
1986	$400,000
1987	900,000
1988	700,000

INSTRUCTIONS

(a) Prepare a schedule to determine the gross profit for 1986, 1987, 1988, and 1989 for the long-term contract using the percentage of completion method.

(b) Prepare a schedule to determine the gross profit for 1986, 1987, and 1988 from the installment sale.

P13-3 The income statement for 1987 and balance sheet on December 31, 1987 for Jackson Cage Co. appear on the next page.

JACKSON CAGE CO.
Income Statement
For the Year Ended December 31, 1987

Sales	$341,600
Cost of goods sold	246,000
Gross profit	95,600
Operating expenses	30,400
Net income	$ 65,200

JACKSON CAGE CO.
Balance Sheet
December 31, 1987

Assets		Liabilities and Stockholders' Equity	
Cash	$ 59,000	Notes payable	$ 40,400
Accounts receivable	47,100	Accounts payable	$ 61,000
Inventory	75,600	Capital stock	300,000
Land	316,500	Retained earnings	96,800
Total assets	$498,200	Total liabilities and stockholders' equity	$498,200

Additional information:

1. The relevant price indexes are as follows:

January 1, 1982	105
June 30, 1984	112
August 31, 1986	120
December 31, 1987	168
Average for 1987	140

2. The company was founded on January 1, 1982. All capital stock was issued at that time.
3. One-fifth of the land was acquired on August 31, 1986; the remainder of the land was acquired on January 1, 1982.
4. A purchasing power loss of $20,400 was computed for 1987.

INSTRUCTIONS

(a) Prepare a constant dollar income statement for Jackson Cage for the year ended December 31, 1987.

(b) Prepare a constant dollar balance sheet for Jackson Cage on December 31, 1987. (Hint: Retained earnings is a balancing item.)

P13-4 Bill's Fisheries Co. income statement for 1987 and balance sheet on December 31, 1987, its first year of operations, are presented below.

BILL'S FISHERIES
Income Statement
For the Year Ended December 31, 1987

Sales	$795,000
Cost of goods sold	550,000
Gross profit	245,000
Operating expenses	57,000
Net income	$188,000

BILL'S FISHERIES CO.
Balance Sheet
December 31, 1987

Assets		Liabilities and Stockholders' Equity	
Cash	$ 74,000	Notes payable	$ 42,000
Accounts receivable	91,000	Accounts payable	63,000
Inventory	187,000	Capital stock	559,000
Land	450,000	Retained earnings	188,000
Goodwill	50,000	Total liabilities and stockholders' equity	$852,000
Total assets	$852,000		

The current cost of the following items on December 31, 1987 is as follows:

Inventory	$200,000
Land	495,000
Goodwill	20,000
Cost of goods sold	585,000

INSTRUCTIONS

(a) Prepare a schedule to show the total holding gain (loss) for Bill's Fisheries for 1987.

(b) Prepare a current cost income statement for Bill's Fisheries for the year ended December 31, 1987.

(c) Prepare a current cost balance sheet for Bill's Fisheries on December 31, 1987.

P13-5 Hoyt Enterprises is considering the adoption of a current cost system. Presented below is Hoyt's balance sheet based on historical cost at the end of its first year of operations.

HOYT ENTERPRISES
Balance Sheet
December 31, 1987

Cash	$25,000	Accounts payable	$ 9,000
Inventory	42,000	Capital stock	50,000
Land	16,000	Retained earnings	24,000
	$83,000		$83,000

The following additional information is presented:

1. Cost of goods sold on a historical cost basis is $54,000; on a current cost basis $58,000.
2. No dividends were paid in the first year of operations.
3. Ending inventory on a current cost basis is $46,000; land on a current cost basis is $22,000 at the end of the year.
4. Operating expenses for the first year were $19,000.

INSTRUCTIONS

(a) Prepare an income statement for the current year on a (1) historical cost basis, (2) current cost basis.

(b) Prepare a balance sheet for the current year on a current cost basis.

(c) Assume that the general price level at the beginning of the year was 100; the average for the year was 160; and the ending 200. Also assume that revenues were earned and costs were incurred uniformly during the year. The land was purchased and the capital stock was issued at the beginning of the year. Determine the following:

1. Income before purchasing power gain or loss on a constant dollar income statement for 1987.
2. Amount reported for land on a constant dollar balance sheet at December 31, 1987.
3. Amount reported for cash on a constant dollar balance sheet at December 31, 1987.

ALTERNATE PROBLEMS

P13-1A Durston and Smith are accountants for Canam Printers. They are having disagreements concerning the following transactions that occurred during the year.

(a) Depreciation for the year was $21,000. Since net income is expected to be lower this year, Durston suggests deferring depreciation to a year when there is more net income.

(b) Canam bought equipment for $20,000, including installation costs. The equipment has a useful life of 5 years. Canam depreciates equipment using the straight-line method. "Since the equipment as installed into our system cannot be removed without considerable damage, it will have no resale value, and therefore should not be depreciated but instead expensed immediately," argues Durston. "Besides, it lowers net income."

(c) Durston suggests that Danam should carry equipment on the balance sheet at its liquidation value which is $15,000 less than its cost.

(d) Canam purchased equipment at a fire sale for $16,000. The equipment was worth $20,000. Durston believes that the following entry should be made:

Equipment	20,000	
Cash		16,000
Gain		4,000

(e) Canam rented office space for 1 year starting October 1, 1986. The total amount of $24,000 was paid in advance. Durston believes that the following entry should be made on October 1:

Rent Expense	24,000	
Cash		24,000

(f) Land costing $40,000 was appraised at $46,000. Durston suggests the following journal entry:

Land	6,000	
Gain on Appreciation of Land		6,000

Smith disagrees with Durston on each of the situations above.

INSTRUCTIONS

For each transaction, indicate why Smith disagrees. Identify the accounting principle or assumption that Durston would be violating if her suggestions were used. Prepare the correct journal entry for each transaction, if any.

P13-2A Tacks Construction Company is involved in a long-term construction contract. Tacks contracted to build a health club with a total estimated cost of $10 million. Additional information follows:

	Health Club	
	Cash Collections	Actual Costs Incurred
1986	$1,500,000	$1,000,000
1987	5,000,000	4,000,000
1988	4,000,000	3,000,000
1989	1,500,000	2,000,000

The project was completed in 1989 and all cash collections related to the contract have been received.

In a separate transaction, Tacks sold condominiums it had constructed to Pedal Management Company for $5 million. Tack's cost to construct the condominiums was $3.5 million. Tacks appropriately uses the installment method. Additional information follows:

	Cash Collected
1986	$ 800,000
1987	3,200,000
1988	1,000,000

INSTRUCTIONS

(a) Prepare a schedule to determine the gross profit for 1986, 1987, 1988, and 1989 for the long-term contract, using the percentage of completion method.

(b) Prepare a schedule to determine the gross profit for 1986, 1987, and 1988 from the installment sale.

P13-3A The income statement for 1987 and balance sheet on December 31, 1987 for Albatross Video Co. appears below:

ALBATROSS VIDEO CO.
Income Statement
For the Year Ended December 31, 1987

Sales	$614,880
Cost of goods sold	442,800
Gross profit	172,080
Operating expenses	51,680
Net income	$120,400

ALBATROSS VIDEO CO.
Balance Sheet
December 31, 1987

Assets		Liabilities and Stockholders' Equity	
Cash	$ 94,400	Notes payable	$ 64,600
Accounts receivable	75,300	Accounts payable	91,500
Inventory	113,400	Capital stock	500,000
Land	453,000	Retained earnings	80,000
Total assets	$736,100	Total liabilities and stockholders' equity	$736,100

Additional information:

1. The relevant price indexes are as follows:

January 1, 1983	104
July 31, 1985	120

September 30, 1986	130
December 31, 1987	156
Average for 1987	150

2. The company was founded on January 1, 1983. All capital stock was issued at that time.
3. One-fifth of the land was acquired on September 30, 1986; the remainder of the land was acquired on January 1, 1983.
4. A purchasing power loss of $39,700 was computed for 1987.

INSTRUCTIONS

(a) Prepare a constant dollar income statement for Albatross Video for the year ended December 31, 1987. (Round all numbers to the nearest dollar.)

(b) Prepare a constant dollar balance sheet for Albatross Video on December 31, 1987. (Round all numbers to the nearest dollar.) (Hint: Retained earnings is a balancing item.)

P13-4A Weaver Forestry Products' income statement for 1987 and balance sheet on December 31, 1987, its first year of operations, are presented below:

WEAVER FORESTRY PRODUCTS
Income Statement
For the Year Ended December 31, 1987

Sales	$993,750
Cost of goods sold	687,500
Gross profit	306,250
Operating expenses	71,250
Net income	$235,000

WEAVER FORESTRY PRODUCTS
Balance Sheet
December 31, 1987

Assets		Liabilities and Stockholders' Equity	
Cash	$ 81,400	Notes payable	$ 54,600
Accounts receivable	109,200	Accounts payable	75,600
Inventory	243,100	Capital stock	583,500
Patent	70,000	Retained earnings	235,000
Land	445,000	Total liabilities and stockholders' equity	$948,700
Total assets	$948,700		

The current cost of the following items on December 31, 1987 is as follows:

Inventory	$260,000
Patent	50,000
Cost of goods sold	700,000
Land	500,000

INSTRUCTIONS

(a) Prepare a schedule to show the total holding gain (loss) of Weaver Forestry Products for 1987.

(b) Prepare a current cost income statement for Weaver Forestry Products for the year ended December 31, 1987.

(c) Prepare a current cost balance sheet for Weaver Forestry Products on December 31, 1987.

P13-5A Lewis Enterprises is considering the adoption of a current cost system. Presented below is Lewis's balance sheet based on historical cost at the end of its first year of operations.

LEWIS ENTERPRISES
Balance Sheet
December 31, 1987

Cash	$30,000	Accounts payable	$10,000
Inventory	42,000	Capital stock	55,000
Land	16,000	Retained earnings	23,000
	$88,000		$88,000

The following additional information is presented:

1. Cost of goods sold on an historical cost basis is $54,000; on a current cost basis $58,000.
2. No dividends were paid in the first year of operation.
3. Ending inventory on a current cost basis is $46,000; land on a current cost basis is $21,000 at the end of the year.
4. Operating expenses for the first year were $20,000.

INSTRUCTIONS

(a) Prepare an income statement for the current year on an (1) historical cost basis, (2) current cost basis.

(b) Prepare a balance sheet for the current year on a current cost basis.

(c) Assume that the general price level at the beginning of the year was 100; the average for the year was 120; and the ending 150. Also assume that revenues were earned and costs were incurred uniformly during the year. The land was purchased and the capital stock was issued at the beginning of the year. Determine the following:
   1. Income before purchasing power gain or loss on a constant dollar income statement for 1987.
   2. Amount reported for land on a constant dollar balance sheet at December 31, 1987.
   3. Amount reported for accounts payable on a constant dollar balance sheet at December 31, 1987.

DECISION CASE

Beth Wainwright has successfully completed her first accounting course during the spring semester, and is now working as a management trainee for First Arizona Bank during the summer. One of her fellow management trainees, Bart Holmes, is taking the same accounting course this summer, and has been having a "lot of trouble." On the second examination, for example, Bart Holmes became confused about inventory valuation methods and completely missed all the points on a problem involving LIFO and FIFO.

Bart's instructor recently indicated that the third examination will probably have a number of essay questions dealing with accounting principle issues. Bart is quite concerned about the third examination for two reasons. First, he has never taken an accounting examination where essay answers were required. Second, Bart feels he has to do well on this examination to get an acceptable grade in the course.

Bart has therefore asked Beth to help him prepare for the next examination. Beth agrees, and suggests that Bart develop a set of possible questions on the accounting principles material that they might discuss.

INSTRUCTIONS

Answer the following questions that were developed by Bart.

1. What is a conceptual framework?
2. Why is there a need for a conceptual framework?
3. What are the objectives of financial reporting?
4. If you had to explain generally accepted accounting principles to a nonaccountant, what essential characteristics would you include in your explanation?
5. What are the qualitative characteristics of accounting? Explain each one.
6. Identify the basic assumptions used in accounting.
7. What are two major constraints involved in financial reporting? Explain both of them.

CHAPTER 14

Macomb Community College, Michigan

CHAPTER 14

ACCOUNTING FOR PARTNERSHIPS

STUDY OBJECTIVES

After studying this chapter, you should be able to:

1. Identify the characteristics of the partnership form of business organization.
2. Explain the accounting entries for the formation of a partnership.
3. Identify the bases for dividing net income or net loss.
4. Describe the form and content of partnership financial statements.
5. Explain the effects of the entries when a new partner is admitted.
6. Describe the effects of the entries when a partner withdraws from the firm.
7. State the entries to record the liquidation of a partnership.

At some time in your business career, you may become involved in a partnership. For example, you may find it advantageous in a business venture, such as a retail establishment or small manufacturing company, to be a co-owner with one or more other individuals. Similarly, if you enter a profession such as accounting, law, or medicine, you may find it desirable to form a partnership with other professionals in your field because of restrictions in state laws and professional codes of ethics. Professional partnerships vary in size from a medical partnership of 3 to 5 doctors to 30 to 40 partners in a large law firm and more than 1,000 partners in an international public accounting firm.

It is not surprising, therefore, that the partnership form of business organization is growing at a fast rate in the United States. In a recent 25 year period, partnerships increased 60% to more than 1.5 million.[1] In this chapter we will

[1]Internal Revenue Service Publication No. 1289, *Source Book: Partnership Returns* 1957–1983.

discuss the essential features of the partnership form of business organization and explain the major issues in accounting for partnerships.

CHARACTERISTICS OF A PARTNERSHIP

The Uniform Partnership Act provides the basic rules for the formation and operation of partnerships in more than 90% of the states. This act defines a **partnership** as "an association of two or more persons to carry on as co-owners of a business for profit." The partnership form of business organization is not restricted to any particular type of business, but it is most often used in relatively small companies and in professional fields, as mentioned above.

The principal characteristics of the partnership form of business organization are graphically illustrated below.

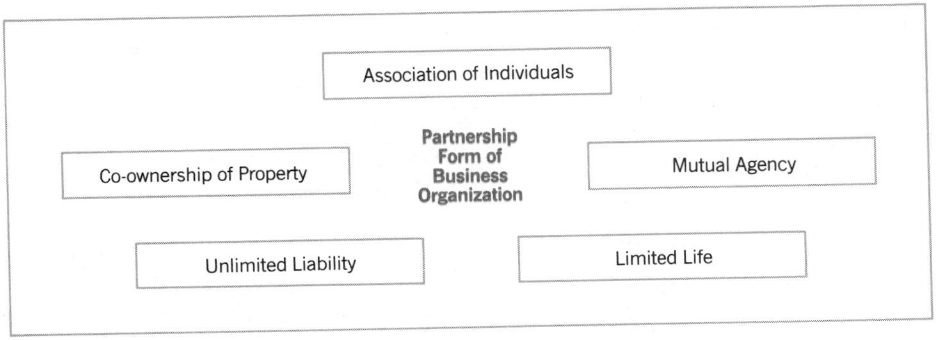

ASSOCIATION OF INDIVIDUALS

A partnership is a voluntary association of two or more individuals based on a legally binding contract, which may be written, oral, or implied. Under the Uniform Partnership Act, a partnership is considered a legal entity for certain purposes. For instance, property (land, buildings, equipment) can be owned in the name of the partnership, and the firm can sue or be sued. **A partnership also represents an accounting entity for financial reporting purposes.** Thus, the purely personal assets, liabilities, and personal transactions of the partners are excluded from the accounting records of the partnership, just as they are in a proprietorship. In addition, the net income of a partnership is not taxed as a separate entity. However, a partnership is required to file an information tax return showing partnership net income and each partner's share of the net income. Each partner's share is taxable, regardless of the amount of net income withdrawn from the business during the year.

MUTUAL AGENCY

Each partner acts on behalf of the partnership when engaging in partnership business. The act of any partner is binding on all other partners, even when partners act beyond the scope of their authority, so long as the act appears to

be appropriate for the partnership. For example, a partner of a grocery store who purchases a delivery truck creates a binding contract in the name of the partnership, even if the partnership agreement denies this authority. On the other hand, if a partner in a law firm purchased a snowmobile for the partnership, such an act would not be binding on the partnership, because it is clearly outside the scope of partnership business.

LIMITED LIFE

A partnership does not have unlimited life. Its continuance as a going concern rests in the partnership contract. As long as existing partners are willing to be bound by the contract, the maximum life of a partnership is equal to the life of any one of its partners. A partnership may be ended voluntarily at any time through the acceptance of a new partner into the firm or the withdrawal of a partner. A partnership may be ended involuntarily by the death or incapacity of a partner. In short, any change in the number of partners, regardless of the cause, effects the **dissolution** of the partnership. Thus, the life of a partnership is unpredictable.

UNLIMITED LIABILITY

Each partner is personally and individually liable for all partnership liabilities. Creditors' claims attach first to partnership assets and then to the personal resources of any partner, irrespective of that partner's capital equity in the company. To illustrate, assume that: (1) the Rowe-Sanchez partnership is terminated when the claims of company creditors exceed partnership assets by $30,000, and (2) L. Rowe's personal assets total $40,000 but B. Sanchez has no personal assets. Creditors can collect their total claims from Rowe regardless of Rowe's capital balance in the firm, even though Sanchez and Rowe may be equal partners. Rowe, in turn, has a legal claim on Sanchez, but this would be worthless under the conditions described. Some states allow **limited partnerships** in which the liability of a partner is limited to the partner's capital equity. However, there must always be at least one partner with unlimited liability, often referred to as the **general partner.**

CO-OWNERSHIP OF PROPERTY

Partnership assets are co-owned by the partners. Once assets have been invested in the partnership, they are owned jointly by all the partners. Moreover, if the partnership is terminated, the assets do not legally revert to the original contributor. Each partner has a claim on total assets equal to the balance in his or her respective capital account, but this claim does not attach to specific assets that an individual partner may have contributed to the firm.

Similarly, if a partner invests a building in the partnership valued at $100,000, and the building is sold later at a gain of $20,000, that partner does not personally receive the entire gain. Partnership net income (or net loss) is also co-owned; if the partnership agreement does not specify to the contrary, all net income or net loss is shared equally by the partners. As you will see later, however, the partnership agreement may provide for unequal sharing of net income or net loss.

ADVANTAGES AND DISADVANTAGES OF A PARTNERSHIP

What are the major advantages and disadvantages of a partnership? One major advantage is that the **skills and resources of two or more individuals can be combined.** For example, a large public accounting firm such as Price Waterhouse must have combined expertise in auditing, taxation, and management consulting, not to mention specialists within each of these areas. In addition, a partnership does not have to contend with the "red tape" that a corporation must face; that is, a partnership is **easily formed and is relatively free from governmental regulations and restrictions.** Decisions can be made quickly on substantive matters affecting the firm, whereas in a corporation, formal meetings with the board of directors are often needed.

On the other hand, the major disadvantages of a partnership are **mutual agency, limited life,** and **unlimited liability.** Unlimited liability is particularly troublesome to many individuals, because they may lose not only their initial investment but also their personal assets, if they are needed to pay partnership creditors. As a result, it is often difficult to obtain large amounts of investment capital in a partnership. That is one reason why the largest business enterprises in the United States are corporations, not partnerships.

The advantages and disadvantages of the partnership form of business organization are summarized below:

Advantages and disadvantages of a partnership

Advantages	Disadvantages
Combining skills and resources of two or more individuals	Mutual agency
Ease of formation	Limited life
Freedom from governmental regulations and restrictions	Unlimited liability
Ease of decision making	

THE PARTNERSHIP AGREEMENT

A partnership is created by a contract expressing the voluntary agreement of two or more individuals. The written partnership agreement, often referred to as the partnership agreement or **articles of co-partnership,** contains such basic information as the name and principal location of the firm, the purpose of the business, and date of inception. In addition, different relationships that will exist among the partners, such as the following, should be specified:

1. Names and capital contributions of partners.
2. Rights and duties of partners.
3. Basis for sharing net income or net loss.
4. Provision for withdrawals of income.
5. Procedures for submitting disputes to arbitration.
6. Procedures for the withdrawal or addition of a partner.
7. Rights and duties of surviving partners in the event of a partner's death.

The importance of a written contract cannot be overemphasized. The agreement should be drawn with care and should attempt to anticipate all possible situations, contingencies, and disagreements. The help of a lawyer is highly desirable in preparing the agreement. A poorly drawn contract may create friction among the partners and eventually cause the termination of the partnership.

FORMATION OF A PARTNERSHIP

Each partner's initial investment in a partnership should be recorded at the fair market value of the assets at the date of their transfer to the partnership. The values assigned must be agreed to by all of the partners.

To illustrate, assume that A. Rolfe and T. Shea combine their proprietorships to start a partnership named U.S. Software, which will specialize in developing financial modeling software packages. Rolfe and Shea invest in the partnership as follows:

Book and market value of assets invested

	Book Value		Market Value	
	A. Rolfe	T. Shea	A. Rolfe	T. Shea
Cash	$ 8,000	$ 9,000	$ 8,000	$ 9,000
Office equipment	5,000		4,000	
Accumulated depreciation	(2,000)			
Accounts receivable		4,000		4,000
Allowance for doubtful accounts		(700)		(1,000)
	$11,000	$12,300	$12,000	$12,000

The entries to record the investments are:

Investment of A. Rolfe

Cash	8,000	
Office Equipment	4,000	
A. Rolfe, Capital		12,000
(To record investment of Rolfe)		

Investment of T. Shea

Cash	9,000	
Accounts Receivable	4,000	
Allowance for Doubtful Accounts		1,000
T. Shea, Capital		12,000
(To record investment of Shea)		

Note that neither the original cost of the equipment ($5,000) nor its book value ($5,000 − $2,000) is recorded by the partnership. The equipment has not been used by the partnership, so there can be no accumulated depreciation. In contrast, the gross claims on customers ($4,000) are carried forward to the partnership, and the allowance for doubtful accounts is adjusted to $1,000 to arrive at a cash (net) realizable value of $3,000. A partnership may start with

an Allowance for Doubtful Accounts account, because this balance pertains to existing accounts receivable that are expected to be uncollectible in the future. In addition, this procedure maintains the control and subsidiary relationship between accounts receivable and the customers' ledger.

After the partnership has been formed, the accounting for its transactions is similar to accounting for transactions of any other type of business organization. For example, all transactions with outside parties, such as the purchase or sale of merchandise inventory and the payment or receipt of cash, should be recorded in the same manner for a partnership as for a proprietorship.

DIVISION OF NET INCOME OR NET LOSS

Partnership net income or net loss is shared equally unless the partnership contract specifically indicates the manner in which net income and net loss are to be divided. The same basis of division usually applies to both net income and net loss. As a result, it is customary to refer to the basis as the **income ratio,** the **income and loss ratio,** or the **profit and loss ratio.** Because of its wide acceptance, we will use the term **income ratio** to identify the basis for dividing both net income and net loss. A partner's share of net income or net loss is recognized in the accounts through closing entries.

CLOSING ENTRIES

You may recall from Chapter 4 that four closing entries are made for a partnership. The first two entries close revenues and expenses to Income Summary; the last two entries transfer the balance in Income Summary to the partners' capital accounts and close their drawing accounts to their capital accounts.

To refresh your memory concerning the closing entries for a partnership, assume that L. Arbor and D. Barnett share net income and net loss equally. After closing all revenue and expense accounts, there is a credit balance in Income Summary of $32,000, which is the net income for the period. The entry to close this balance to the respective capital accounts is as follows:

Income Summary	32,000	
L. Arbor, Capital		16,000
D. Barnett, Capital		16,000
(To close net income to partners' capitals)		

If Arbor and Barnett have balances in their drawing accounts of $8,000 and $6,000, respectively, the entry to close these accounts is:

L. Arbor, Capital	8,000	
D. Barnett, Capital	6,000	
L. Arbor, Drawing		8,000
D. Barnett, Drawing		6,000
(To close partners' drawings)		

Assuming the beginning capital balance is $47,000 for Arbor and $36,000 for Barnett, the following capital and drawing accounts will appear in the general ledger.

Ledger balances after closing

L. Arbor, Capital				D. Barnett, Capital			
Drawing	8,000	Beg. Bal.	47,000	Drawing	6,000	Beg. Bal.	36,000
		Net income	16,000			Net income	16,000
		End Bal.	55,000			End Bal.	46,000

L. Arbor, Drawing				D. Barnett, Drawing			
End Bal.	8,000	To Capital	8,000	End Bal.	6,000	To Capital	6,000

The capital accounts indicate each partner's "permanent" investment, while the partners' drawing accounts are temporary owners' equity accounts. Normally, the capital accounts will have credit balances, whereas the drawing accounts will have debit balances. The drawing account is commonly debited in situations where cash or other assets are withdrawn by the partner for personal use. For example, the partnership contract may permit each partner to withdraw cash monthly for personal living expenses.

INCOME RATIOS

As indicated earlier, the partnership agreement should specify the basis for sharing net income or net loss. The following are typical of the ratios that may be used.

1. A fixed ratio, expressed as a proportion (6:4), a percentage (70% and 30%), or a fraction (2/3 and 1/3).
2. A ratio based either on capital balances at the beginning of the year or on average capital balances during the year.
3. Salaries to partners and the remainder on a fixed ratio.
4. Interest on partners' capitals and the remainder on a fixed ratio.
5. Salaries to partners, interest on partners' capitals, and the remainder on a fixed ratio.

The objective is to reach agreement on a basis that will equitably reflect the differences among partners in terms of their capital investment and service to the partnership.

A fixed ratio is easy to apply, and it may be an equitable basis in some circumstances. Assume, for example, that Hughes and Lane are partners. Each contributes the same amount of capital, but Hughes expects to work full-time in the partnership and Lane expects to work only half-time. Accordingly, the partners agree to a fixed ratio of 2/3 to Hughes and 1/3 to Lane.

A ratio based on capital balances may be appropriate when the funds invested in the partnership are considered the critical factor. This might be true when the partners expect to give equal service to the partnership. Capital

balances may also be equitable when a manager is hired to run the business and the partners do not plan to take an active role in daily operations.

The three remaining ratios give specific recognition to differences that may exist among partners by providing salary allowances for time worked and interest allowances for capital invested. Then, any remaining net income or net loss is allocated on a fixed ratio. Some caution needs to be exercised in working with these types of income ratios. These ratios pertain exclusively to the computations that are required in dividing net income or net loss. **Salaries to partners and interest on partners' capitals are not expenses of the partnership.** Therefore, these items do not enter into the matching of expenses with revenues and the determination of net income or net loss. For a partnership, as well as for other entities, salaries expense pertains to the cost of services performed by employees, and interest expense relates to the cost of borrowing money from creditors. Partners in their ownership capacity are not considered either employees or creditors. When the income ratio includes a salary allowance for partners, some partnership agreements permit the partner to make monthly withdrawals of cash based on their "salary." In such cases, the withdrawals are debited to the partner's drawing account.

In large professional partnerships, like major law and CPA firms, with hundreds of partners, computerized accounting is almost essential to facilitate maintaining the partners' capital accounts. In such professional firms, computerized timekeeping systems are often used to track billable hours for both partners and staff. These systems are usually integrated into the automated general ledger. With this system, client billings can be prepared directly from the timekeeping system and automatically recorded into the general ledger and accounts receivable subsidiary ledgers.

SALARIES, INTEREST, AND REMAINDER ON A FIXED RATIO

Under this income ratio the provisions for salaries and interest must be applied **before** the remainder is allocated on the specified fixed ratio. This is true even if the provisions exceed net income or the partnership has suffered a net loss for the year. Detailed information concerning the division of net income or net loss should be shown at the bottom of the income statement.

To illustrate this income ratio, we will assume that Sara King and Ray Lee are co-partners in the Kingslee Company. The partnership agreement provides for (1) salary allowances of $8,400 to King and $6,000 to Lee, (2) interest allowances of 10% on capital balances at the beginning of the year, and (3) the remainder equally. Capital balances on January 1 were King, $28,000, and Lee, $24,000. In 1987, partnership net income was $22,000. The division of net income is as follows:

Income statement with division of net income

KINGSLEE COMPANY
Income Statement
For the Year Ended December 31, 1987

Sales			$200,000
Net income			$ 22,000

Division of Net Income

	Sara King	Ray Lee	Total
Salary allowance	$ 8,400	$6,000	$14,400
Interest allowance			
Sara King ($28,000 × 10%)	2,800		
Ray Lee ($24,000 × 10%)		2,400	
Total interest			5,200
Total salaries and interest	11,200	8,400	19,600
Remaining income, $2,400			
Sara King ($2,400 × 50%)	1,200		
Ray Lee ($2,400 × 50%)		1,200	
Total remainder			2,400
Total division	$12,400	$9,600	$22,000

The entry to record the division of net income is:

Dec. 31	Income Summary	22,000	
	Sara King, Capital		12,400
	Ray Lee, Capital		9,600
	(To close net income to partners' capitals)		

To illustrate a situation in which the salary and interest allowances exceed net income, we will assume that net income in the Kingslee Company was only $18,000. In this case, the allowances will create a deficiency of $1,600 ($19,600 − $18,000). Since the computations of the salary and interest allowances are the same as those above, we will begin the division of net income with total salaries and interest as follows:

Division of net income—income deficiency

	Sara King	Ray Lee	Total
Total salaries and interest	$11,200	$8,400	$19,600
Remaining deficiency ($1,600)			
Sara King ($1,600 × 50%)	(800)		
Ray Lee ($1,600 × 50%)		(800)	
Total remainder			(1,600)
Total division	$10,400	$7,600	$18,000

PARTNERSHIP FINANCIAL STATEMENTS

The financial statements of a partnership are similar to those of a proprietorship. The differences are generally related to the fact that a number of owners are involved in a partnership. In a balance sheet, for instance, each partner's capital balance is reported. The income statement for a partnership is identical to the income statement for a proprietorship except for the division of net income, as shown earlier.

The owners' equity statement for a partnership is called the **partners' capital statement.** Its function is to explain the changes in each partner's capital account and in total partnership capital during the year. As in a proprietorship, changes in capital may result from three causes: additional capital investment, drawings, and net income or net loss.

The partners' capital statement for the Kingslee Company shown below is based on the division of $22,000 of net income. The statement includes assumed data for the additional investment and for drawings.

Partners' capital statement

KINGSLEE COMPANY
Partners' Capital Statement
For the Year Ended December 31, 1987

	Sara King	Ray Lee	Total
Capital, January 1	$28,000	$24,000	$52,000
Add: Additional investment	2,000		2,000
Net income	12,400	9,600	22,000
	42,400	33,600	76,000
Less: Drawings	7,000	5,000	12,000
Capital, December 31	$35,400	$28,600	$64,000

The capital statement is prepared from the income statement and the partners' capital and drawing accounts.

ADMISSION OF A PARTNER

The admission of a new partner results in the legal dissolution of the existing partnership and the beginning of a new partnership. From an economic standpoint, however, the admission of a new partner (or partners) may be of minor significance in the continuity of the business. For example, in large public accounting firms, 50 or more partners may be admitted annually without any change in operating policies established by the continuing 750 to 1,000 plus partners. **To recognize the economic effects, it is necessary only to open a capital account for each new partner.** The entries described and illustrated below are based on the assumption that the accounting records of the predecessor firm will continue to be used by the new partnership.

A new partner may be admitted either by (1) purchasing the interest of one or more existing partners, or (2) investing assets in the partnership. The for-

mer affects only the capital accounts of the partners who are parties to the transaction, whereas the latter increases both net assets (total assets less total liabilities) and total capital of the partnership.

PURCHASE OF A PARTNER'S INTEREST

The admission of a partner by purchase of a partner's interest (often referred to simply as **purchase of an interest**) in the firm is a personal transaction between one or more existing partners and the new partner. Each party is acting as an individual separate from the partnership entity. The price paid is negotiated and determined by the individuals involved. It may be equal to or different from the capital equity acquired. The amount of the purchase price passes directly from the new partner to the partners who are giving up part or all of their ownership claims. Any money or other consideration exchanged is the personal property of the participants and not the property of the partnership. Upon purchase of an interest, the new partner acquires each selling partner's capital interest and income ratio. A partner does not have to obtain the approval of the other partners to sell his or her interest. However, the Uniform Partnership Act provides that the purchaser does not become a partner until he or she is accepted into the firm by the continuing partners.

Accounting for the purchase of an interest is very straightforward. As far as the partnership is concerned, only the realignment of partners' capital is recorded. **Each partner's capital account is debited for the ownership claims that have been relinquished, and the new partner's capital account is credited with the capital equity purchased.** Total assets, total liabilities, and total capital remain unchanged, as do all individual asset and liability accounts.

To illustrate, assume that L. Carson agrees to pay $10,000 each to C. Ames and D. Barker for one-third of their interest in the Ames-Barker partnership. At the time of the admission of Carson, each partner has a $30,000 capital balance. Both partners, therefore, give up $10,000 of their capital equity. The entry to record the admission of Carson is:

C. Ames, Capital	10,000	
D. Barker, Capital	10,000	
L. Carson, Capital		20,000
(To record admission of Carson by purchase)		

The effect of this entry on net assets and partners' capital is diagrammed below:

Ledger balances after purchase of partners' interest

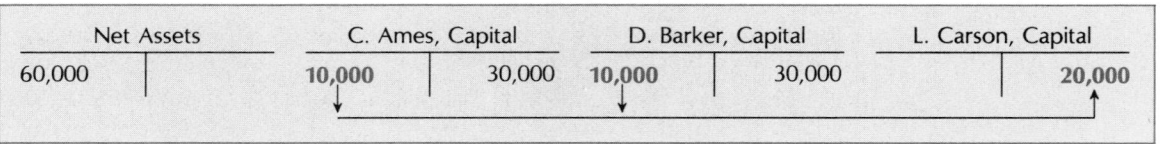

Net Assets		C. Ames, Capital		D. Barker, Capital		L. Carson, Capital	
60,000		**10,000**	30,000	**10,000**	30,000		**20,000**

Note that net assets remain unchanged at $60,000 and each partner has a $20,000 capital balance.

Regardless of the amount paid by Carson for the one-third interest, the entry above would be exactly the same. For example, if Carson pays $12,000

each to Ames and Barker for a one-third interest in the partnership the above entry is still made. The cash paid by Carson goes directly to the individual partners and not to the partnership.

INVESTMENT OF ASSETS IN PARTNERSHIP

A very different situation develops if an individual is admitted to a partnership by investing assets in the firm (sometimes referred to simply as **admission by investment**). In this situation, both the total net assets and the total capital of the partnership increase. To illustrate, instead of purchasing an interest, assume that Carson invests $30,000 in cash in the Ames-Barker partnership for a 1/3 capital interest. In such a case, the entry is:

Cash	30,000	
L. Carson, Capital		30,000
(To record admission of new partner)		

The effects of this transaction on the partnership accounts may be diagrammed as follows:

Ledger balances after investment of assets

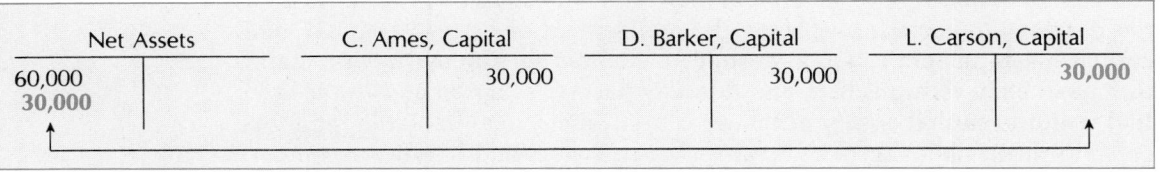

Net Assets		C. Ames, Capital		D. Barker, Capital		L. Carson, Capital	
60,000			30,000		30,000		**30,000**
30,000							

Note that both net assets and total capitals have increased by $30,000.

It should be emphasized that Carson's 1/3 capital interest might not result in a 1/3 income ratio. Carson's income ratio should be specified in the new partnership agreement, and it may or may not be equal to the 1/3 capital interest.

The different effects between the purchase of an interest and investing assets in a partnership will be evident when the net assets and capital balances shown below are examined:

Comparison of purchase of an interest and investment of assets

Purchase of a Partner's Interest		Investment of Assets in Partnership	
Net Assets	$60,000	Net Assets	$90,000
Capital		Capital	
C. Ames	$20,000	C. Ames	$30,000
D. Barker	20,000	D. Barker	30,000
L. Carson	20,000	L. Carson	30,000
Total capital	$60,000	Total capital	$90,000

When an interest is purchased, the total net assets and total capital of the partnership do not change. However, when a partner is admitted by investment, both the total net assets and the total capital change.

In the case of admission by investment of assets in the partnership, further complications occur when the new partner's investment differs from the capital equity acquired. When those amounts are not the same, the difference is considered a bonus either to (1) the existing (old) partners or (2) the new partner.

Bonus to Old Partners

The existing partners may be unwilling to admit a new partner without receiving a bonus for both personal and business reasons. In an established firm, existing partners may insist on a bonus as compensation for the personal sacrifices they have made for the company over the years. Two accounting-related factors underlie the business reason. First, total partners' capital equals the **book value** of the recorded net assets of the partnership. At the time the new partner is admitted, the fair market values of assets such as land and buildings may be higher than their book values. Second, when the partnership has been profitable, goodwill may exist. However, the goodwill will not be recorded or included in total partners' capital. In such cases the new partner is usually willing to pay the bonus to become a partner.

A bonus to old partners results when the new partner's capital credit on the date of admittance is less than his or her investment in the firm. The bonus results in an increase in the capital balances of the old partners and is allocated to them **on the basis of their income ratios before the admission of the new partner.**

To illustrate, assume that the Bart-Cohen partnership owned by Sam Bart and Tom Cohen has a total capital of $120,000 when Lea Eden is admitted to the partnership. Lea acquires a 25% ownership (capital) interest by making a cash investment of $80,000 in the partnership. The procedure for determining Eden's capital credit and the bonus to the old partners is as follows:

1. Determine the total capital of the new partnership by adding the new partner's investment to the total capital of the old partnership. In this case the total capital of the new firm is $200,000, computed as follows:

Total capital of existing partnership	$120,000
Investment by new partner, Eden	80,000
Total capital of new partnership	$200,000

2. Determine the new partner's capital credit by multiplying the total capital of the new partnership by the new partner's ownership interest. Eden's capital credit is $50,000 ($200,000 × 25%).
3. Determine the amount of bonus by subtracting the new partner's capital credit from the new partner's investment. The bonus in this case is $30,000 ($80,000 − $50,000).
4. Allocate the bonus to the old partners on the basis of their income ratios. Assuming the ratios are Bart, 60%, and Cohen, 40%, the allocation is: Bart, $18,000 ($30,000 × 60%) and Cohen, $12,000 ($30,000 × 40%).

The entry to record the admission of Eden is:

Cash	80,000	
Sam Bart, Capital		18,000
Tom Cohen, Capital		12,000
Lea Eden, Capital		50,000
(To record admission of Eden and bonus to old partners)		

Bonus to New Partner

A bonus to a new partner results when the new partner's capital credit is greater than his or her investment of assets in the firm. This may occur when recorded book values on the partnership books are higher than their market values. It may also result when the new partner possesses resources or special attributes that are desired by the partnership. For example, when bank interest rates are high, the new partner may be able to supply cash that is urgently needed for expansion or to meet maturing debts. Alternatively, the new partner may be a recognized expert or authority in a relevant field. Thus, an engineering firm may be willing to give a world-renowned engineer a bonus to join the firm. Similarly, the partners of a sporting goods store may offer a bonus to a sports celebrity in order to add the athlete's name to the partnership name.

A bonus to a new partner results in a decrease in the capital balances of the old partners **based on their income ratios before the admission of the new partner.** To illustrate, assume that Lea Eden invests $20,000 in cash for a one-fourth ownership interest in the Bart-Cohen partnership. Using the procedures described in the preceding section, the computations for Eden's capital credit and the bonus are as follows:

Computation of capital credit and bonus

1. Total capital of Bart-Cohen partnership		$120,000
Investment by new partner, Eden		20,000
Total capital of new partnership		$140,000
2. Eden's capital credit (25% × $140,000)		$ 35,000
3. Bonus to Eden ($35,000 − $20,000)		$ 15,000
4. Allocation of bonus:		
Bart ($15,000 × 60%)	$9,000	
Cohen ($15,000 × 40%)	6,000	$ 15,000

The entry to record the admission of Eden is as follows:

Cash	20,000	
Sam Bart, Capital	9,000	
Tom Cohen, Capital	6,000	
Lea Eden, Capital		35,000
(To record Eden's admission and bonus)		

WITHDRAWAL OF A PARTNER

A partner may withdraw from a partnership **voluntarily** by selling his or her equity in the firm or **involuntarily** by reaching mandatory retirement age or dying. The withdrawal of a partner, like the admission of a partner, legally dissolves the partnership. Although the legal effects may be recognized in accounting for a withdrawal, it is customary to record only the economic effects. As indicated earlier, the partnership agreement should specify the terms of withdrawal. The withdrawal of a partner may be accomplished by (1) payment from partners' personal assets, or (2) payment from partnership assets. The former affects only the partners' capital accounts, whereas the latter decreases total net assets and total capital of the partnership.

PAYMENT FROM PARTNERS' PERSONAL ASSETS

The withdrawal of a partner when payment is made from partners' personal assets is the direct opposite of admitting a new partner who purchases a partner's interest. The event is a personal transaction between the partners, and payment to the retiring partner is made directly from the remaining partners' personal assets. Partnership assets are not involved in any way and total capital does not change. Thus, the effect on the partnership is limited to a realignment of the partners' capital balances.

To illustrate, assume that Anne Morz, Mary Nead, and Jill Odom have capital balances of $25,000, $15,000, and $10,000, respectively, when Morz and Nead agree to buy out Odom's interest. Each of them agrees to pay Odom $8,000 in exchange for one-half of Odom's total interest of $10,000. The entry to record the withdrawal is:

Jill Odom, Capital	10,000	
Anne Morz, Capital		5,000
Mary Nead, Capital		5,000
(To record purchase of Odom's interest)		

The effect of this entry on the partnership accounts is diagrammed below:

Ledger balances after payment from partners' personal assets

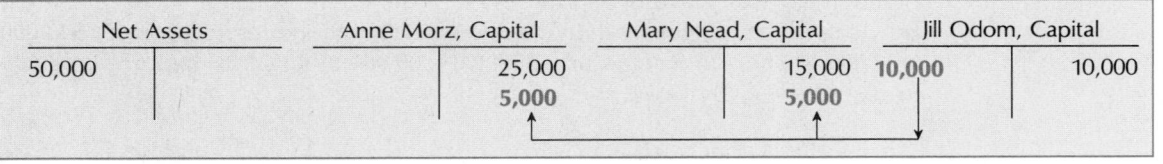

Net Assets		Anne Morz, Capital		Mary Nead, Capital		Jill Odom, Capital	
50,000			25,000		15,000	**10,000**	10,000
			5,000		**5,000**		

Note that net assets and total capital remain the same and that the $16,000 paid to Odom is not recorded. Morz's capital equity becomes $30,000, and Nead's interest $20,000. Morz and Nead both pay Odom $8,000 in cash directly. Odom's capital is debited only for $10,000, not for the $16,000 that she received. Similarly, both Morz and Nead credit their capital accounts for only $5,000, not the $8,000 they each paid. Morz and Nead will share income or loss equally unless they specifically provide another income ratio in the partnership agreement.

PAYMENT FROM PARTNERSHIP ASSETS

Using partnership assets to pay for a withdrawing partner's interest is the reverse of admitting a partner through the investment of assets in the partnership. This event is a transaction that involves the partnership. Both partnership net assets and total capitals are decreased.

Many partnership agreements provide that the amount paid should be based on the fair market value of the assets at the time of the partner's withdrawal. When this basis is required, some accountants maintain that any differences between recorded asset balances and their fair market values should be (1) recorded by an adjusting entry and (2) allocated to all partners on the basis of their income ratios. There are serious flaws in this position. Recording the revaluations violates the cost principle, which requires that assets be stated at original cost. It also is a departure from the going-concern assumption, which assumes the entity will continue indefinitely. The terms of the partnership contract should not dictate the accounting for the event. In accounting for a withdrawal by payment from partnership assets:

1. Asset revaluations should not be recorded.
2. Any difference between the amount paid and the withdrawing partner's capital balance should be considered a bonus to the retiring partner or a bonus to the remaining partners.

Bonus to Retiring Partner

A bonus may be paid to a retiring partner when (1) the fair market value of partnership assets is more than their book value; (2) there is unrecorded goodwill resulting from the partnership's superior earnings record; or (3) the remaining partners are anxious to remove the partner from the firm. **The bonus is deducted from the remaining partners' capital balances on the basis of their income ratios at the time of the withdrawal.**

To illustrate, assume that the following capital balances exist in the RST partnership: Fred Roman, $500,000; Dee Sando, $300,000; and Betty Terk, $200,000. The partners share income in the ratio of 3:2:1, respectively. Terk retires from the partnership and receives a cash payment of $280,000 from the partnership. The bonus is $80,000 ($280,000 − $200,000), which is allocated (debited) to Roman and Sando on the basis of the income ratios that exist between them. Because their ratios are 3:2, the bonus is divided $48,000 ($80,000 × 60%) to Roman and $32,000 ($80,000 × 40%) to Sando. The entry to record the withdrawal of Terk is:

Betty Terk, Capital	200,000	
Fred Roman, Capital	48,000	
Dee Sando, Capital	32,000	
Cash		280,000
(To record withdrawal of and bonus to Terk)		

The remaining partners, Roman and Sando, will recover the bonus given to Terk as the undervalued assets are sold or used in the partnership.

Bonus to Remaining Partners

The retiring partner may pay a bonus to the remaining partners when (1) recorded assets are overvalued; (2) the partnership has a poor earnings record; or (3) the partner is anxious to leave the partnership. In such cases, the cash paid to the retiring partner will be less than the retiring partner's capital balance, and the bonus will be allocated (credited) to the capital accounts of the remaining partners on the basis of their income ratios. If, instead of the example above, Terk is only paid $160,000 for her $200,000 equity upon withdrawing from the RST partnership, the bonus is $40,000 ($200,000 − $160,000). The bonus is divided $24,000 ($40,000 × 60%) to Roman and $16,000 ($40,000 × 40%) to Sando. The entry to record the withdrawal is:

Betty Terk, Capital	200,000	
Fred Roman, Capital		24,000
Dee Sando, Capital		16,000
Cash		160,000
(To record withdrawal of Terk and bonus to remaining partners)		

It is important to note that if Sando had withdrawn from the partnership, any bonus would be divided between Roman and Terk on the basis of their income ratios which are 3:1 or 75% and 25%.

DEATH OF A PARTNER

The death of a partner dissolves the partnership, but provision generally is made for the surviving partners to continue operations. When a partner dies, it usually is necessary to determine the partner's equity at the date of death by (1) determining the net income or loss for the year to date, (2) closing the books, and (3) preparing financial statements. The partnership agreement may also require an audit of the financial statements by independent auditors and a revaluation of assets by an independent appraisal firm.

The surviving partners may agree to (1) purchase the deceased partner's equity or (2) use partnership assets to settle with the deceased partner's estate. In both instances, the entries to record the withdrawal of the partner are similar to those presented in previous illustrations.

To facilitate the payment from partnership assets, some companies obtain life insurance policies on each partner with the partnership as the beneficiary. The proceeds from the insurance policy on the deceased partner are then used to settle with the estate.

LIQUIDATION OF A PARTNERSHIP

The liquidation of a partnership terminates the business. Liquidation may result from the sale of the business by mutual agreement of the partners, from the death of a partner, or from bankruptcy.

The liquidation process may occur at a specific time, or it may occur over a period of time. To liquidate a partnership it is necessary to (1) convert noncash assets into cash and allocate any gains or losses on the basis of the partners' income ratios, (2) pay partnership creditors, and (3) distribute the remaining cash to the partners on the basis of their remaining capital balances. **Each of the steps must be performed in sequence** because creditors must be paid before partners receive any cash distributions. Each step also must be recorded by an accounting entry.

When a partnership is liquidated, all partners may have credit balances in their capital accounts (no capital deficiency) or at least one partner's capital account may have a debit balance (a capital deficiency). To illustrate each of these conditions, assume that the Ace Company is liquidated when its ledger shows the following assets, liabilities, and owners' equity accounts.

Account balances prior to liquidation

Assets		Liabilities and Owners' Equity	
Cash	$ 5,000	Notes payable	$15,000
Accounts receivable	15,000	Accounts payable	16,000
Inventory	18,000	R. Arnet, Capital	15,000
Equipment	35,000	P. Carey, Capital	17,800
Accumulated depreciation – equipment	(8,000)	W. Eaton, Capital	1,200
	$65,000		$65,000

NO CAPITAL DEFICIENCY

By mutual agreement of the partners, the company is sold. The sales agreement provides for (1) a payment of $75,000 in cash by Jackson Enterprises for the noncash assets of the partnership, and (2) payment of partnership liabilities by the partnership. The income ratios of the partners are 3:2:1, respectively. The steps in the liquidation process are as follows:

1. The noncash assets (receivables, inventory, and equipment) are sold for $75,000. Since the book value of these assets is $60,000 ($15,000 + $18,000 + $35,000 − $8,000), a gain of $15,000 is realized on the sale. The entry to record the sale and the allocation of the gain to the partners on the basis of their income ratios is as follows:

Cash	75,000	
Accumulated Depreciation – Equipment	8,000	
Accounts Receivable		15,000
Inventory		18,000
Equipment		35,000
R. Arnet, Capital ($15,000 × 3/6)		7,500
P. Carey, Capital ($15,000 × 2/6)		5,000
W. Eaton, Capital ($15,000 × 1/6)		2,500
(To record sale of noncash assets and allocation of gain to partners)		

2. The creditors are paid in full by a cash payment of $31,000. The entry for the payment is:

	Debit	Credit
Notes Payable	15,000	
Accounts Payable	16,000	
Cash		31,000
(To record payment to creditors)		

3. The remaining cash is distributed to the partners on the **basis of their capital balances.** After the entries above have been posted, the following four accounts will have balances as follows: Cash, $49,000; R. Arnet, Capital, $22,500; P. Carey, Capital, $22,800; and W. Eaton, Capital, $3,700. These accounts are presented below:

Ledger accounts before distribution of cash

Cash (Dr.)	Cash (Cr.)	R. Arnet, Capital (Dr.)	R. Arnet, Capital (Cr.)	P. Carey, Capital (Dr.)	P. Carey, Capital (Cr.)	W. Eaton, Capital (Dr.)	W. Eaton, Capital (Cr.)
Bal. 5,000	(2) 31,000		Bal. 15,000		Bal. 17,800		Bal. 1,200
(1) 75,000			(1) 7,500		(1) 5,000		(1) 2,500

The entry to record the distribution of cash to the partners is as follows:

	Debit	Credit
R. Arnet, Capital	22,500	
P. Carey, Capital	22,800	
W. Eaton, Capital	3,700	
Cash		49,000
(To record final cash distribution to partners)		

After this entry is posted, all partnership accounts will have zero balances.

A word of caution: **Cash should not be distributed to partners on the basis of their income-sharing ratios.** On this basis, for example, Arnet would receive 50%, or $24,500, which would produce an erroneous debit balance of $2,000. The income ratio is a proper basis for allocating net income or loss, but it is not a proper basis for making the final distribution of cash to the partners.

CAPITAL DEFICIENCY

A capital deficiency may be caused by net losses or excessive drawings before liquidation or by losses suffered during liquidation. To illustrate, assume that Ace Company is on the brink of bankruptcy. The partners decide to liquidate and proceed to have a "going-out-of-business" sale in which merchandise is sold at substantial discounts, and the equipment is sold at auction. Cash proceeds from these sales and collections from customers total only $42,000. Accordingly, the loss from liquidation is $18,000 ($60,000 − $42,000). The entry for the conversion of noncash assets into cash and the allocation of the loss to the partners is:

(1)

	Debit	Credit
Cash	42,000	
Accumulated Depreciation—Equipment	8,000	
R. Arnet, Capital ($18,000 × 3/6)	9,000	
P. Carey, Capital ($18,000 × 2/6)	6,000	
W. Eaton, Capital ($18,000 × 1/6)	3,000	

	Debit	Credit
Accounts Receivable		15,000
Inventory		18,000
Equipment		35,000
(To record sale of noncash assets and allocation of loss to partners)		

The entry to record the payment of cash to the creditors is:

(2)

	Debit	Credit
Notes Payable	15,000	
Accounts Payable	16,000	
Cash		31,000
(To record payment to creditors)		

After posting these two entries, the partnership books will have two accounts with debit balances—Cash, $16,000, and W. Eaton, Capital, $1,800, and two with credit balances—R. Arnet, Capital, $6,000, and P. Carey, Capital, $11,800, as shown below:

Ledger accounts before distribution of cash

Cash (Dr.)	Cash (Cr.)	R. Arnet, Capital (Dr.)	R. Arnet, Capital (Cr.)	P. Carey, Capital (Dr.)	P. Carey, Capital (Cr.)	W. Eaton, Capital (Dr.)	W. Eaton, Capital (Cr.)
Bal. 5,000	(2) 31,000	(1) 9,000	Bal. 15,000	(1) 6,000	Bal. 17,800	(1) 3,000	Bal. 1,200
(1) 42,000							

Eaton has a capital deficiency of $1,800. Eaton, therefore, owes the partnership $1,800, and Arnet and Carey have a legally enforceable claim against Eaton's personal assets. Pending settlement of Eaton's deficiency, distribution of partnership cash can be made safely only on the assumption that Eaton will not make good on this deficiency. As a result, the **cash distributed to each partner is the difference between the partner's present capital balance and the loss that the partner may have to absorb if the capital deficiency is not paid.** The capital deficiency is allocated on the basis of the income ratios that exist between the partners with credit balances. The partners with credit balances are Arnet and Carey and their income ratios are 3:2 or 3/5 and 2/5. Thus, the allocation of Eaton's capital deficiency is as follows:

Allocation of capital deficiency

Capital deficiency (loss)		$1,800
Allocated to:		
R. Arnet $1,800 × 3/5	= $1,080	
W. Carey 1,800 × 2/5	= 720	$1,800

Note that the income ratios are not the same as those used to allocate the loss from realization of partnership assets. Three partners were involved in that allocation, whereas only two partners are involved in this allocation. **You should also realize that this allocation is not journalized and posted.** The cash distribution is:

Computation of cash distributions

	Present capital balance	−	Capital deficiency	=	Cash distribution
R. Arnet	$ 6,000		$1,080		**$ 4,920**
W. Carey	11,800		720		**11,080**

The entry to record the cash distribution is:

(3)

R. Arnet, Capital	4,920	
P. Carey, Capital	11,080	
Cash		16,000
(To record cash distribution to partners)		

After this entry is posted, the four partnership accounts will have the following balances.

Account balances after distribution of cash

Cash (Dr.)	Cash (Cr.)	R. Arnet, Capital (Dr.)	R. Arnet, Capital (Cr.)	P. Carey, Capital (Dr.)	P. Carey, Capital (Cr.)	W. Eaton, Capital (Dr.)	W. Eaton, Capital (Cr.)
Bal. 5,000	(2) 31,000	(1) 9,000	Bal. 15,000	(1) 6,000	Bal. 17,800	(1) 3,000	Bal. 1,200
(1) 42,000	(3) 16,000	(3) 4,920		(3) 11,080			
Bal. -0-			Bal. 1,080		Bal. 720	Bal. 1,800	

These balances show that Arnet and Carey have a legal claim on Eaton's personal assets of $1,800.

Schedule of Cash Payments

Some accountants prepare a cash payments schedule to determine the distribution of cash to the partners. The **schedule of cash payments,** sometimes

ACE COMPANY
Schedule of Cash Payments

Item		Cash	+	Noncash Assets	=	Liabilities	+	R. Arnet Capital	+	P. Carey Capital	+	W. Eaton Capital
Balances before liquidation		5,000	+	60,000	=	31,000	+	15,000	+	17,800	+	1,200
Sale of noncash assets	(1)	42,000	+	(60,000)	=			(9,000)	+	(6,000)	+	(3,000)
New balances		47,000	+	-0-	=	31,000	+	6,000	+	11,800	+	(1,800)
Pay liabilities	(2)	(31,000)			=	(31,000)						
New balances		16,000	+	-0-	=	-0-	+	6,000	+	11,800	+	(1,800)
Allocate capital deficiency					=			(1,080)	+	(720)	+	1,800
New balances		16,000	+	-0-	=	-0-	+	4,920	+	11,080	+	-0-
Cash distribution	(3)	(16,000)			=			(4,920)	+	(11,080)		

called a **safe cash payments schedule,** is organized around the basic accounting equation, as shown at the bottom of page 559. All data in the schedule are based on the liquidation of the Ace Company that resulted in a capital deficiency. The numbers in parentheses refer to the three required steps in the liquidation of a partnership. These numbers also identify the accounting entries that must be made. The cash payments schedule is especially useful when the liquidation process extends over a period of time and the noncash assets are sold at different times.

Removal of Capital Deficiency

When a capital deficiency exists, an additional step is required in liquidating the partnership. **This step is removing the capital deficiency.** If the deficient partner honors the debt, it is necessary to record both the receipt of the cash and the distribution of cash to the partners with credit balances. Assuming Eaton pays the deficiency, the entries are:

Cash	1,800	
W. Eaton, Capital		1,800
(To record receipt of capital deficiency)		
R. Arnet, Capital	1,080	
P. Carey, Capital	720	
Cash		1,800
(To record distribution of cash and termination of partnership)		

After these entries have been posted, all the partnership accounts will have zero balances.

If Eaton refuses to pay the capital deficiency, Arnet and Carey may take legal action to obtain payment. If this effort is unsuccessful, the partnership books will be closed by writing off Eaton's deficiency against the partners' credit balances. The entry is:

R. Arnet, Capital	1,080	
P. Carey, Capital	720	
W. Eaton, Capital		1,800
(To record write-off of Eaton's capital deficiency and termination of partnership)		

After this entry is posted, all the capital accounts will have zero balances.

SUMMARY OF STUDY OBJECTIVES

1. The principal characteristics of a partnership are: (a) association of individuals, (b) mutual agency, (c) limited life, (d) unlimited liability and (e) co-ownership of property.

2. When a partnership is formed, each partner's initial investment should be recorded at the fair market value of the assets at the date of their transfer to the partnership.

3. Net income or net loss is divided on the basis of the income ratio which may be (a) a fixed ratio, (b) a ratio based on beginning or average capital balances, (c) salaries to partners and the remainder on a fixed ratio, (d) interest on partners' capitals and the remainder on a fixed ratio, and (e) salaries to partners, interest on partners' capitals, and the remainder on a fixed ratio.

4. The financial statements of a partnership are similar to those of a proprietorship. The principal differences are: (a) each partner's capital is reported on the balance sheet, (b) the division of net income is shown on the income statement, and (c) the owner's equity statement is called a partners' capital statement.

5. The entry to record the admittance of a new partner by purchase of a partner's interest affects only partners' capital accounts. The entries to record the admittance by investment of assets in the partnership (a) increases both net assets and total capital and (b) may result in recognition of a bonus to either the old partners or the new partner.

6. The entry to record a withdrawal from the firm when payment is made from partners' personal asset only affects partners' capital accounts. The entry to record a withdrawal when payment is made from partnership assets (a) decreases net assets and total capitals and (b) may result in recognizing a bonus either to the retiring partner or the remaining partners.

7. When a partnership is liquidated, it is necessary to record the (a) sale of noncash assets, (b) payment to creditors, and (c) distribution of cash to the partners.

GLOSSARY

Income ratio,p. 544

Partners' capital statement,p. 548

Partnership,p. 540

Partnership agreement,p. 542

Schedule of cash payments,p. 559

DEMONSTRATION PROBLEM

On January 1, 1987, the capital balances in the Hollingsworth Company are Lois Holly $26,000, and Jim Worth $24,000. In 1987, the company reports net income of $30,000. The income ratio provides for salary allowances of $12,000 for Holly and $10,000 to Worth and the remainder equally. Neither partner had any drawings in 1987.

In 1988, assume that the following independent transactions occur on January 1:

1. Donna Reichenbacher purchases one-half of Holly's capital interest for $25,000.
2. Marsha Mears is admitted with a 25% capital interest by a cash investment of $40,000.
3. Stan Wells is admitted with a 35% capital interest by a cash investment of $40,000.

INSTRUCTIONS

(a) Journalize the division of 1987 net income to the partners.

(b) Journalize the 1988 transactions.

SOLUTION TO DEMONSTRATION PROBLEM

(a)	12/31/87	Income Summary	30,000	
		Lois Holly, Capital ($12,000 + $4,000)		16,000
		Jim Worth, Capital ($10,000 + $4,000)		14,000
		(To close net income to partners' capitals)		
		1.		
(b)	1/1/88	Lois Holly, Capital ($42,000 × ½)	21,000	
		Donna Reichenbacher, Capital		21,000
		(To record purchase of one-half of Holly's interest)		
		2.		
	1/1/88	Cash	40,000	
		Lois Holly, Capital		5,000
		Jim Worth, Capital		5,000
		Marsha Mears, Capital		30,000
		(To record admission of Mears and bonus to old partners)		
		Mears' capital credit (25% × $120,000)		$30,000
		Bonus to old partners ($40,000 − $30,000)		$10,000
		Allocation of bonus:		
		Holly ($10,000 × 50%)	$ 5,000	
		Worth ($10,000 × 50%)	5,000	$10,000

3.

1/1/88	Cash	40,000	
	Lois Holly, Capital	1,000	
	Jim Worth, Capital	1,000	
	Stan Wells', Capital		42,000
	(To record Wells' admission and bonus)		
	Wells' capital credit (35% × $120,000)		$42,000
	Bonus to Wells ($42,000 − $40,000)		$ 2,000
	Allocation of bonus:		
	Holly ($2,000 × 50%)	$1,000	
	Worth ($2,000 × 50%)	1,000	$ 2,000

QUESTIONS

1. Sue Gilgen and Enid Stottrup are considering opening a fashion agency called Personna, but they cannot decide the form of organization to use. Explain to them the possible advantages and disadvantages of the partnership form of organization.

2. In discussing with his tax attorney the possibility of forming a partnership, Mike Kantile becomes confused about two terms, "mutual agency" and "unlimited liability," used by his attorney. Explain the meaning of these two terms as they apply to a partnership.

3. Ron Darling has been listening to a discussion about President Reagan's new tax reform proposals in which the speaker indicated that limited partnerships in real estate will be hit hard by the new proposal. Explain the terms (a) "limited partnership" and (b) "general partner."

4. S. Brown and D. Clarke form a partnership. Brown contributes land with a book value of $40,000 and a fair market value of $65,000. Brown also contributes equipment with a book value of $52,000 and a fair market value of $46,000. The partnership assumes a $20,000 mortgage on the land. What should be the balance in Brown's capital account upon formation of the partnership?

5. R. Hay, S. Ing, and L. Joyner have a partnership called Express Wings. A dispute has arisen among the partners because R. Hay has invested twice as many assets as the other two partners and believes net income and net losses should be shared in accordance with the capital ratios. The partnership agreement is silent as to the division of profits and losses. How will net income and net loss be divided?

6. S. Hark and R. Jones are discussing how income and losses should be divided in a partnership they plan to form. What factors should be considered in determining the division of net income or net loss?

7. R. Lowry and S. Monroe have capital balances of $42,000 and $84,000, respectively, in a partnership. The partnership agreement indicates that net income or net loss should be shared equally. If the net income for the partnership is $21,000, how should the net income be divided?

8. H. Astor and S. Sunder share net income and net loss equally. (a) Which accounts are debited and which are credited to record the division of net income between the partners? (b) If H. Astor withdraws $30,000 in cash for personal use in lieu of salary, which accounts are debited and which are credited?

9. R. Rowe and B. Sands receive salaries of $27,000 and $24,000, respectively. They divide the remainder of the partnership income in a ratio of 45:55. If partnership net income were $48,000, how much would Rowe and Sands receive?

10. Are the financial statements of a partnership similar to those of a proprietorship? Discuss.

11. Sally Carter decides to pay Mark Haller $20,000 for a one-third interest in the partnership of Haller and Rose. How much do the partnership's net assets increase?

12. R. Jones decides to invest $13,000 in the Centro-David partnership for a 1/6 capital interest. How much do the partnership's net assets increase? Does Jones also acquire a 1/6 income ratio through this investment?

13. Sarto purchases Ramos' interest in Morgan-Ramos partnership for $70,000. Assuming that Ramos has a $65,000 capital balance in the partnership, what journal entry is made by the partnership to record this transaction?

14. Jan Jackson has a $30,000 capital balance in a partnership. She sells her interest to Karen Kress for $40,000. What entry is made by the partnership for this transaction?

15. Randy Rolfe retires from the partnership of Rolfe, Sanko, and Tankin. He receives $90,000 of partnership assets in settlement of his capital balance of $75,000. Assuming that the income-sharing ratios are 5:3:2, respectively, how much of Rolfe's bonus is debited to Tankin?

16. Your roommate argues that partnership assets should be revalued in situations like those in question 15. Why is this generally not done?

17. How is a deceased partner's equity determined?

18. Rick Riley claims that the steps in liquidating a partnership may be performed in any order. Do you agree? Explain.

19. Joe and Joanne are discussing the liquidation of a partnership. Joe maintains that all cash should be distributed to partners on the basis of their income ratios. Is Joe correct? Explain.

20. In continuing their discussion, Joanne says that even in the case of a capital deficiency, all cash should still be distributed on the basis of capital balances. Is Joanne correct? Explain.

21. Mike, Larry, and Jean have income ratios of 4:3:2 and capital balances of $34,000, $29,000, and $28,000, respectively. Noncash assets are sold at a gain. After creditors are paid, $118,000 of cash is available for distribution to the partners. How much cash should be paid to Mike?

22. Before the final distribution of cash, account balances are: Cash $24,000; R. Kahn, Capital $18,000 (cr); M. Mott, Capital $10,000 (cr); and T. Zaret, Capital $4,000 (dr). If the income-sharing ratios are 5:3:2, respectively, how much cash should be paid to R. Kahn?

EXERCISES

E14–1 Thad Carr has owned and operated a proprietorship for several years. On January 1, he decides to terminate this business and become a partner in the firm of Payne and Carr. Carr's investment in the partnership consists of $15,000 in cash, and the following assets of the proprietorship: accounts receivable $12,000 less allowance for doubtful accounts of $2,000, and equipment $20,000 less accumulated depreciation of $4,000. It is agreed that the expected cash realizable value of the receivables to the partnership is $11,000 and the fair market value of the equipment is $14,000.

INSTRUCTIONS

(a) Journalize Carr's admission to the firm of Payne and Carr.

(b) Repeat (a) above, assuming that the expected cash realizable value of the receivables is $9,000 and the fair market value of the equipment is $18,000.

E14–2 R. Hume and W. Kahler have capital balances on January 1 of $50,000 and $40,000, respectively. The partnership income sharing agreement provides for (1) annual salaries of $12,000 for Hume and $8,000 for Kahler, (2) interest at 10% on beginning capital balances, and (3) remaining income or loss to be shared 70% by Hume and 30% by Kahler.

INSTRUCTIONS

(a) Prepare a schedule showing the distribution of net income, assuming net income is (1) $45,000 and (2) $25,000.

(b) Journalize the allocation of net income in each of the situations above.

E14–3 T. Knox, K. Rose, and J. Lamb share income on a 5:3:2 basis. They have capital balances of $30,000, $20,000, and $15,000, respectively, when R. Hahn is admitted to the partnership.

INSTRUCTIONS

Prepare the journal entry to record the admission of Hahn under each of the following assumptions:

(1) Purchase of one-half of Knox's equity for $20,000.

(2) Purchase of one-half of Rose's equity for $8,000.

(3) Purchase of one-third of Lamb's equity for $7,000.

E14–4 Joe Kehoe and Mike McClory share income on a 3:2 basis. They have capital balances of $80,000 and $70,000, respectively, when Ed Oehler is admitted to the partnership.

INSTRUCTIONS

Prepare the journal entry to record the admission of Ed Oehler under each of the following assumptions:

(1) Investment of $50,000 cash for a one-fourth ownership interest.

(2) Investment of $80,000 cash for a one-fourth ownership interest with bonuses to the existing partners.

(3) Investment of $60,000 cash for a one-third ownership interest with a bonus to the new partner.

E14–5 Theresa Adams and Bart Bowers have capital accounts of $36,000 and $40,000, respectively. Two individuals, Sean Conners and Erin Dunn, wish to join the partner-

ship. Sean Conners invests $39,000 in the partnership for which he receives a capital credit of $39,000. Erin Dunn purchases a one-third interest from Adams for $14,000 and a one-fourth interest from Bowers for $18,000.

INSTRUCTIONS

(a) Prepare the journal entries to record the admission of Conners and Dunn to the partnership.

(b) Determine the capital balances of the partners after the admission of Conners and Dunn.

E14-6 Mary Lohr, Vera Mills, and Debra Noll have capital balances of $50,000, $30,000, and $20,000, respectively, and their income ratios are 6:3:1. Noll withdraws from the partnership under each of the following independent conditions:

1. Lohr and Mills agree to purchase Noll's equity by paying $15,000 each from their personal assets.
2. Mills agrees to purchase all of Noll's equity by paying $16,000 cash from her personal assets.
3. Lohr and Mills agree to purchase Noll's equity by paying $13,000 each from their personal assets. Lohr receives 60% of the equity and Mills receives 40%.

INSTRUCTIONS

Journalize the withdrawal of Noll under each of the assumptions above.

E14-7 Dale Phillips, Keith Whitman, and Dan Marana have capital balances of $95,000, $75,000, and $60,000, respectively. They share income or loss on a 6:3:2 basis. Whitman withdraws from the partnership under the following conditions:

1. Whitman is paid $75,000 in cash from partnership assets.
2. Whitman is paid $85,000 in cash from partnership assets, and a bonus is granted to the retiring partner.
3. Whitman is paid $68,000 in cash from partnership assets, and bonuses are granted to the remaining partners.

INSTRUCTIONS

Journalize the withdrawal of Whitman under each of the assumptions above.

E14-8 Rob Ingram and Sally Joiner have formed I & J partnership, and have capital balances of $38,000 and $41,000, respectively, on January 1, 1987, the beginning of the fiscal year. On June 10, 1987, Ingram invested an additional $14,000. Also during the year, Ingram withdrew $18,000 and Joiner $20,000. Net income for the year of $62,000 was divided 60% to Ingram and 40% to Joiner.

INSTRUCTIONS

(a) Present the journal entries to close (1) income summary, and (2) drawing accounts for the year.

(b) Prepare a partners' capital statement for 1987.

E14-9 The Nagy, McEllen, and Relias partnership is liquidated when its ledger shows the following assets, liabilities, and owners' equity accounts.

Assets		Liabilities and Owners' Equity	
Cash	$ 20,000	Notes payable	$ 18,000
Marketable securities	10,000	Accounts payable	12,000
Accounts receivable	30,000	Mortgage payable	25,000
Inventory	45,000	Nagy, Capital	25,000
Equipment	35,000	McEllen, Capital	30,000
Accumulated depreciation – equipment	(11,000)	Relias, Capital	19,000
	$129,000		$129,000

Additional information:

(1) Noncash assets are sold for $140,000.

(2) Partnership liabilities are paid by the partnership.

(3) The income ratios of the partners are 5:3:2, respectively.

INSTRUCTIONS

Prepare journal entries to record:

(a) The sale of the noncash assets and allocation of the gain or loss.

(b) The payment of partnership liabilities.

(c) The distribution of cash to the partners.

E14-10 The DEL partnership is liquidated when the ledger shows: Cash $12,000, Noncash Assets $90,000, Liabilities $18,000, Dale Capital $42,000, Ely Capital $36,000, and Loken Capital $6,000. The partners' income ratios are 5:3:2, respectively.

INSTRUCTIONS

(a) Prepare separate entries to record the liquidation of the partnership assuming that the noncash assets are sold for $80,000 in cash. Use an account titled Noncash Assets to record the decrease.

(b) Prepare a schedule of cash payments, assuming that noncash assets are sold for $50,000. Assume that any capital deficiencies will not be paid.

E14-11 Prior to liquidation, R. Stallings and B. Tidrick have cash $20,000; noncash assets $60,000; liabilities $14,000 and R. Stallings, Capital $30,000 and B. Tidrick, Capital $36,000. They share profits and losses equally.

INSTRUCTIONS

(a) Assume that the noncash assets are sold for $70,000. How much cash would R. Stallings and B. Tidrick receive?

(b) Assume that the noncash assets are sold for $45,000. How much cash would R. Stallings and B. Tidrick receive?

(c) Assume that R. Stallings and B. Tidrick receive total cash upon final liquidation of $11,000 and $17,000, respectively. At what amount did the noncash assets sell for?

PROBLEMS

P14-1 The post-closing trial balances of two proprietorships on January 1, 1987 are presented below.

	Creal Company		Donald Company	
	Dr.	Cr.	Dr.	Cr.
Cash	$ 7,000		$ 9,000	
Accounts receivable	14,500		22,000	
Allowance for doubtful accounts		$ 2,500		$ 4,000
Merchandise inventory	28,000		17,000	
Equipment	52,000		30,000	
Accumulated depreciation—equipment		24,000		13,000
Notes payable		20,000		
Accounts payable		25,000		37,000
R. T. Creal, Capital		30,000		
A. C. Donald, Capital				24,000
	$101,500	$101,500	$78,000	$78,000

Creal and Donald decide to form the Donald Creal Company with the following agreed upon valuations for noncash assets:

	Creal Company	Donald Company
Accounts receivable, net	$13,000	$19,500
Merchandise inventory	30,000	20,000
Equipment	29,000	15,000

All cash will be transferred to the partnership, and the partnership will assume all the liabilities of the two proprietorships. Further, it is agreed that Creal and Donald will each invest additional cash to produce a beginning capital equity of 60% for Creal and 40% for Donald resulting in total capital of $80,000.

INSTRUCTIONS

(a) Prepare separate journal entries to record the transfer of each proprietorship's assets and liabilities to the partnership.

(b) Journalize the additional cash investment by each partner.

(c) Prepare a balance sheet for the partnership on January 1, 1987.

(d) Prepare a partner's capital statement for the year 1987, assuming partnership net income of $32,000 and drawings of $10,000 by Creal and $12,000 by Donald.

P14-2 At the end of its first year of operations on December 31, 1987, the LMN Company's accounts show the following:

Partner	Drawings	Capital
Lois Long	$12,000	$30,000
Mary Moore	9,000	20,000
Sue Norton	6,000	10,000

The capital balance represents each partner's initial capital investment. Therefore, net income or net loss for 1987 has not been closed to the partners' capital accounts.

INSTRUCTIONS

(a) Journalize the entry to record the division of net income for the year 1987 under each of the following assumptions:

1. Net income is $24,000, and income is shared 6:3:1.
2. Net income is $30,000; each partner is allowed interest of 10% on beginning capital balances; and the remainder is shared equally.
3. Net income is $27,000; Long and Moore are given salary allowances of $10,000 and $8,000, respectively, and the remainder is shared equally.
4. Net income is $19,500; each partner is allowed interest of 10% on beginning capital balances; Long is given a $15,000 salary allowance; and the remainder is shared equally.

(b) Prepare a schedule showing the division of net income under assumption (4) above.

(c) Prepare a partner's capital statement for the year under assumption (3) above.

P14-3 At April 30, partners' capital balances in the ELM Company are: A. Ellis $50,000, C. Leone $30,000, and W. Matte $10,000. The income sharing ratios are 5:4:1, respectively. On May 1, the ELMO Company is formed by admitting N. Ortiz to the firm as a partner.

INSTRUCTIONS

(a) Journalize the admission of Ortiz under each of the following assumptions:

1. Ortiz purchases one-half of Matte's ownership interest by paying Matte $8,000 in cash.
2. Ortiz purchases one-half of Leone's ownership interest by paying Leone $12,000 in cash.
3. Ortiz invests $30,000 cash in the partnership for a one-fourth ownership interest.
4. Ortiz invests $35,000 cash in the partnership for a 30% ownership interest that includes a bonus to the new partner.
5. Ortiz invests $30,000 in the partnership for a one-sixth ownership interest and bonuses are given to the old partners.

(b) Answer the following questions:

1. Matte's capital balance is $12,000 after admitting Ortiz to the partnership by investment. If Matte's ownership interest is 10% of total partnership capital, what was Ortiz's cash investment and the total bonus paid to the old partners?
2. Leone's capital balance is $28,000 after admitting Ortiz to the partnership by investment. If Leone's ownership interest is 20% of total partnership capital, what were Ortiz's cash investment and the bonus given to the new partner?
3. If Ellis's capital balance is $44,000 after admitting Ortiz by investment, and Ortiz's initial capital balance of $52,000 is 40% of the new partnership's total capital, what were Ortiz's cash investment and the bonus given to the new partner?

P14-4 On December 31, 1987, the capital balances and income ratios in the ART Company are as follows:

Partner	Capital Balance	Income Ratio
E. Attle	$70,000	50%
P. Rosen	30,000	30
L. Tower	20,000	20

INSTRUCTIONS

(a) Journalize the withdrawal of Tower under each of the following assumptions:

1. Each of the remaining partners agrees to pay $12,500 in cash from personal funds to purchase Tower's ownership equity. Each receives 50% of Tower's equity.
2. Rosen agrees to purchase Tower's ownership interest for $18,000 in cash.
3. From partnership assets, Tower is paid $28,000, which includes a bonus to the retiring partner.
4. Tower is paid $16,000 from partnership assets, and bonuses to the remaining partners are recognized.

(b) Answer the following questions pertaining to the withdrawal of one of the partners through the use of partnership assets.

1. If Rosen's capital balance after Tower's withdrawal is $33,000, what was the total bonus paid to the remaining partners and the cash paid to Tower?
2. If Tower's capital balance after the withdrawal of Rosen is $18,000, what was the bonus and the total amount of cash paid to Rosen?

P14-5 The partners in the Great Lakes Company decide to liquidate the firm when the balance sheet shows the following:

GREAT LAKES COMPANY
Balance Sheet
April 30, 1987

Assets		Liabilities and Owners' Equity	
Cash	$24,000	Notes payable	$12,000
Accounts receivable	18,000	Accounts payable	26,000
Allowance for doubtful accounts	(1,000)	Wages payable	2,000
Merchandise inventory	30,000	T. E. Huron, Capital	26,000
Equipment	17,000	P. A. Erie, Capital	12,800
Accumulated depreciation—equip.	(8,000)	C. R. Lake, Capital	1,200
Total	$80,000	Total	$80,000

The partners share income and loss 6:3:1. During the process of liquidation, the transactions below were completed in the following sequence:

1. A total of $38,000 was received from converting noncash assets into cash.
2. Creditors were paid in full.
3. The available cash was distributed to the partners with credit balances.
4. Lake paid his capital deficiency.
5. Cash was paid to the partners with credit balances.

INSTRUCTIONS

(a) Prepare general journal entries to record the transactions.

(b) Post to the cash and capital accounts.

(c) Prepare a schedule of cash payments showing the final distribution of cash in the partnership before Lake paid his deficiency (Note: Use one column for noncash assets and one column for all liabilities.)

P14-6 Hanley and Frank formed a partnership on January 1, 1984 and agreed to the following income ratios for the three years as follows:

	Hanley	Frank
1984	60%	40%
1985	50%	50%
1986	60%	40%

The net income or net loss for the three years was as follows:

1984	$30,000 net income
1985	10,000 net loss
1986	20,000 net income

On January 1, 1987, it was discovered that

1. The ending inventory on December 31, 1984, should have been $10,000, instead of $1,000.
2. Excessive depreciation of $2,000 a year has been charged on equipment purchased January 1, 1985.

INSTRUCTIONS

Prepare the journal entry to correct the books on January 1, 1987, assuming that the books have been closed for 1986. (Hint: Prepare an analysis showing for each year, the amount allocated and the amount that should have been allocated to each partner.)

ALTERNATE PROBLEMS

P14-1A The post-closing trial balances of two proprietorships on January 1, 1987 are presented below.

	Gampfer Company		Miller Company	
	Dr.	Cr.	Dr.	Cr.
Cash	$13,000		$16,000	
Accounts receivable	17,500		26,000	
Allowance for doubtful accounts		$ 3,000		$ 4,200
Merchandise inventory	26,500		18,400	
Equipment	45,000		28,000	
Accumulated depreciation		24,000		12,000
Notes payable		20,000		15,200
Accounts payable		20,000		31,000
L. Gampfer, Capital		35,000		
P. Miller, Capital				26,000
	$102,000	$102,000	$88,400	$88,400

Gampfer and Miller decide to form the Gampfer Miller Company with the following agreed upon valuations for noncash assets:

	Gampfer Company	Miller Company
Accounts receivable, net	$15,500	$23,000
Merchandise inventory	28,000	20,000
Equipment	24,000	18,000

All cash will be transferred to the partnership, and the partnership will assume all the liabilities of the two proprietorships. Further, it is agreed that Gampfer and Miller will

each invest additional cash to produce a beginning capital equity of 60% for Gampfer and 40% for Miller resulting in total capital of $100,000.

INSTRUCTIONS

(a) Prepare separate journal entries to record the transfer of each proprietorship's assets and liabilities to the partnership.

(b) Journalize the additional cash investment by each partner.

(c) Prepare a balance sheet for the partnership on January 1, 1987.

(d) Prepare a partner's capital statement for the year 1987, assuming partnership net income of $42,000 and drawings of $15,000 by Miller and $18,000 by Gampfer.

P14-2A At the end of its first year of operations on December 31, 1987, HRT Company's accounts show the following:

Partner	Drawings	Capital
Susie Horton	$23,000	$45,000
Tracey Ruger	14,000	30,000
Eileen Thorsen	10,000	25,000

The capital balance represents each partner's initial capital investment; therefore, net income or net loss for 1987 has not been closed to the partners' capital accounts.

INSTRUCTIONS

(a) Journalize the entry to record the division of net income for the year 1987 under each of the following assumptions:
   1. Net income is $36,000, and income is shared 5:3:2.
   2. Net income is $40,000; each partner is allowed interest of 10% on beginning capital balances; and the remainder is shared equally.
   3. Net income is $31,000; Horton and Ruger are given salary allowances of $12,000 and $10,000, respectively; and the remainder is shared equally.
   4. Net income is $25,000; each partner is allowed interest of 10% on beginning capital balances; Horton is given an $18,000 salary allowance; and the remainder is shared equally.

(b) Prepare a schedule showing the division of net income under assumption (4) above.

(c) Prepare a partners' capital statement for the year under assumption (3) above.

P14-3A At March 31, partners' capital balances in NSZ Company are: A. Nolan $60,000, D. Swoboda $35,000, and T. Zalewski $20,000. The income sharing ratios are 6:3:1, respectively. On May 1, the NSZO Company is formed by admitting M. Ottoson to the firm as a partner.

INSTRUCTIONS

(a) Journalize the admission of Ottoson under each of the following assumptions.
   1. Ottoson purchases one-half Zalewski's ownership interest by paying Zalewski $12,000 in cash.
   2. Ottoson purchases one-half of Swoboda's ownership interest by paying Swoboda $15,000 in cash.
   3. Ottoson invests $28,750 in the partnership for a one-fifth ownership interest.
   4. Ottoson invests $60,000 for a 30% ownership interest, and bonuses are paid to the old partners.
   5. Ottoson invests $25,000 for a one-fourth ownership interest which includes a bonus to the new partner.

(b) Answer the following questions:

1. Zalewski's capital balance is $23,000 after admitting Ottoson to the partnership by investment. If Zalewski's ownership interest is 10% of total partnership capital, what was Ottoson's cash investment and the total bonus paid to the old partners?
2. Swoboda's capital balance is $32,000 after admitting Ottoson to the partnership by investment. If Swoboda's ownership interest is 20% of total partnership capital, what was Ottoson's cash investment and the bonus given to the new partner?
3. If Nolan's capital balance is $45,000 after admitting Ottoson, and Ottoson's initial capital balance of $60,000 is 40% of the new partnership's total capital, what was Ottoson's cash investment and the bonus given to the new partner?

P14-4A On December 31, 1987, the capital balances and income ratios in the BAG Company are as follows:

Partner	Capital Balance	Income Ratio
R. Baird	$60,000	40%
D. Abrahamson	40,000	30%
P. Gabriel	30,000	30%

INSTRUCTIONS

(a) Journalize the withdrawal of Gabriel under each of the following assumptions:

1. Each of the continuing partners agrees to pay $17,800 in cash from personal funds to purchase Gabriel's ownership equity. Each receives 50% of Gabriel's equity.
2. Abrahamson agrees to purchase Gabriel's ownership interest for $27,500 cash.
3. Gabriel is paid $37,000 from partnership assets, which includes a bonus to the retiring partner.
4. Gabriel is paid $25,800 from partnership assets and bonuses to the remaining partners are recognized.

(b) Answer the following questions pertaining to the withdrawal of one of the partners through the use of partnership assets. (Round to the nearest dollar.)

1. If Abrahamson's capital balance after Gabriel's withdrawal is $42,800, what was the total bonus to the remaining partners and the cash paid to Gabriel?
2. If Gabriel's capital balance after the withdrawal of Abrahamson is $26,500, what was the bonus and the total amount of cash paid to Abrahamson?

P14-5A The partners in the Michiana Company decide to liquidate the firm when the balance sheet shows the following:

Assets		Liabilities and Owner's Equity	
Cash	$ 27,400	Notes payable	$ 13,500
Accounts receivable	24,870	Accounts payable	28,000
Allowance for doubtful accounts	(1,000)	Wages payable	2,870
Merchandise inventory	34,500	M. Jagger, Capital	34,200
Equipment	21,000	K. Richards, Capital	20,000
Accumulated depreciation – equip.	(6,200)	R. Wood, Capital	2,000
Total	$100,570	Total	$100,570

The partners share income and loss 7:5:3. During the process of liquidation, the following transactions were completed in the following sequence:

1. A total of $48,000 was received from converting noncash assets into cash.
2. Creditors were paid in full.
3. The available cash was distributed to the partners with credit balances.
4. Wood paid his capital deficiency.
5. Cash was paid to the partners with credit balances.

INSTRUCTIONS

(a) Prepare general journal entries to record the transactions. (Round all computations to the nearest dollar.)
(b) Post to the cash and capital accounts.
(c) Prepare a schedule of cash payments showing the final distribution of cash in the partnership before Wood paid his deficiency. (Note: Use one column for noncash assets and one column for all liabilities.)

P14-6A Edwards and Dantley formed a partnership on January 1, 1984 and agreed to share net income and net loss as follows:

	Edwards	Dantley
1984	50%	50%
1985	70%	30%
1986	40%	60%

The net income or net loss for the three years was as follows:

1984	$12,000 net loss
1985	40,000 net income
1986	10,000 net income

On January 1, 1987, it was discovered that
1. The ending inventory on December 31, 1984 should have been $11,000, instead of $17,000.
2. Excessive depreciation of $4,000 a year has been charged on equipment purchased January 1, 1985.

INSTRUCTIONS

Prepare the journal entry to correct the books on January 1, 1987, assuming that the books have been closed for 1986. (Hint: Prepare an analysis showing for each year, the amount allocated and the amount that should have been allocated to each partner.)

DECISION CASE

Bart Holmes and Sally Ing are two professionals in the finance area who have worked for Advanced Leasing for a number of years. Advanced Leasing is a company that leases high-tech medical equipment to hospitals. Bart and Sally have decided that, with their financial expertise, they might start their own company to provide consulting services to individuals interested in leasing equipment. One form of organization they are considering is a partnership.

If they start a partnership, each individual plans to contribute $15,000 in cash. In addition, Bart Holmes has used IBM microcomputer that originally cost $3,800, which he intends to invest in the partnership. The computer has a present market value of $1,800.

Although both Bart and Sally are financial wizards, they do not know a great deal about how a partnership operates. As a result, they have come to you for advice.

INSTRUCTIONS

Answer the following questions:

1. What are the major disadvantages of starting a partnership?
2. What type of document is needed for a partnership and what should this document contain?
3. Both Bart and Sally plan to work full-time in the new partnership. Therefore they believe that net income or net loss should be shared equally. However, they are wondering how they can provide compensation to Bart Holmes for his additional investment of the microcomputer. What would you tell them?
4. Bart is not sure how the computer equipment should be reported on his tax return. What would you tell him?
5. As indicated above, Bart and Sally have worked together for a number of years. Bart's skills complement Sally's and vice versa. If one of them dies, it will be very difficult for the other to maintain the business, not to mention the difficulty of paying the deceased partner's estate for his or her partnership interest. What would you tell them to do?

CHAPTER 15

Southwest Texas State University

CHAPTER 15

CORPORATIONS: ORGANIZATION AND CAPITAL STOCK TRANSACTIONS

STUDY OBJECTIVES

After studying this chapter, you should be able to:

1. **Identify and discuss the major characteristics of a corporation.**
2. **Differentiate between paid-in capital and retained earnings.**
3. **Record the issuance of common stock.**
4. **Explain the accounting for treasury stock.**
5. **Differentiate preferred stock from common stock.**
6. **Compute book value per share.**

The dominant form of business organization in the United States in terms of dollar volume of sales, earnings, and employees is the corporation. All of the 500 largest industrial companies in the U.S. are corporations. One of the biggest, Exxon, recently reported sales of $108 billion, net income of $5.5 billion, and total employees of 180,000. Exxon's sales figure is larger than the gross national product of such countries as Sweden ($65 billion), Hungary ($32 billion), the Netherlands ($60 billion), and Norway ($32 billion). It is important, therefore, that you have a basic understanding of the corporate form of business organization and the accounting for a corporation. In this chapter we will explain the essential features of a corporation and the accounting for a corporation's capital stock transactions.

WHAT IS A CORPORATION?

In 1819, Chief Justice John Marshall defined a corporation as "an artificial being, invisible, intangible, and existing only in contemplation of law." This definition has become the foundation for the prevailing legal interpretation that a corporation is an **entity separate and distinct from its owners.**

A corporation is created by law, and its continued existence is dependent upon the corporate statutes of the state in which it is incorporated. As a legal entity, a corporation possesses most of the privileges of a natural person. The major exceptions relate to privileges that can be exercised only by a living person, such as the right to vote or to hold public office. At the same time, a corporation is subject to the same duties and responsibilities as a person.

Corporations may be classified in a variety of ways. Two of the more common bases are by purpose and by ownership. A corporation may be organized for the purpose of making a **profit** or it may be **nonprofit.** Corporations for profit include such well-known companies as McDonald's, General Motors, and Apple Computer. Nonprofit corporations are organized for charitable, medical, and educational purposes and include the Salvation Army, American Cancer Society, and the Ford Foundation.

Classification by **ownership** results in distinguishing between publicly held and privately held corporations. A **publicly held corporation** has thousands of stockholders, and its stock is regularly traded on a national securities market such as the New York Stock Exchange. Most of the largest U.S. corporations are publicly held. Examples of publicly held corporations are International Business Machines, Caterpillar Company, and General Electric. In contrast, a **privately held corporation,** often referred to as a closely held corporation, has only a few stockholders, and the stock is not available for sale to the general public. Privately held companies are generally much smaller than publicly held companies. However, there are exceptions as was the case of Howard Hughes with TWA.

CHARACTERISTICS OF A CORPORATION

A number of characteristics distinguish a corporation from proprietorships and partnerships. The most important of these characteristics are explained below.

SEPARATE LEGAL EXISTENCE

As an entity separate and distinct from its owners, the corporation acts under its own name rather than in the name of its stockholders. A corporation may buy, own, and sell property, borrow money, and enter into legally binding contracts in its own name. It may also sue or be sued, and it pays its own taxes.

In contrast to a partnership, in which the acts of the owners (partners) bind the partnership, the acts of the owners (stockholders) do not bind the corporation unless such owners are duly appointed agents of the corporation. For

example, if you owned shares of Ford Motor Company stock, you would not have the right to purchase automobile parts for the company unless you were appointed as an agent of the corporation.

LIMITED LIABILITY OF STOCKHOLDERS

Since a corporation is a separate legal entity, creditors ordinarily have recourse only to corporate assets to satisfy their claims. The liability of stockholders is normally limited to their investment in the corporation, and creditors have no legal claim on the personal assets of the owners unless fraud has occurred. Thus, even in the event of bankruptcy of the corporation, stockholders' losses are generally limited to their capital investment in the corporation.

TRANSFERABLE OWNERSHIP RIGHTS

Ownership of a corporation is evidenced by transferable units known as shares of capital stock. Stockholders may dispose of part or all of their interest in a corporation by selling their shares. In contrast to the transfer of an ownership interest in a partnership, which requires the consent of each owner, the transfer of stock is entirely at the discretion of the stockholder and does not require the approval of either the corporation or other stockholders. The transfer of ownership rights between stockholders has no effect on the operating activities of the corporation or on a corporation's assets, liabilities, and total ownership equity. That is, the enterprise does not participate in the transfer of these ownership rights after it issues the capital stock.

CONTINUOUS LIFE

The life of a corporation is stipulated in its charter; it may be perpetual or it may be limited to a specific number of years. In the case of limited life, the period of existence can be extended through renewal of the charter. Since a corporation is a separate legal entity, the life of a corporation and its continuance as a going concern are not affected by the withdrawal, death, or incapacity of a stockholder, employee, or officer. As a result, a successful enterprise can have a continuous and perpetual life.

ORGANIZATIONAL STRUCTURE (DELEGATION OF RESPONSIBILITY)

Although stockholders legally own the corporation, they manage the corporation indirectly through a board of directors they elect. The board, in turn, formulates the operating policies for the company and selects officers, such as a president and one or more vice-presidents, to execute policy and to perform the daily management functions.

A typical organization chart showing the delegation of responsibility is shown on the next page. The **president** is the chief executive officer with direct responsibility for managing the business. As illustrated in the organization chart, the president delegates responsibility to other officers. The chief accounting officer is the **controller.** The controller's responsibilities include (1) maintaining the accounting records, (2) maintaining an adequate system of

Corporation organization chart

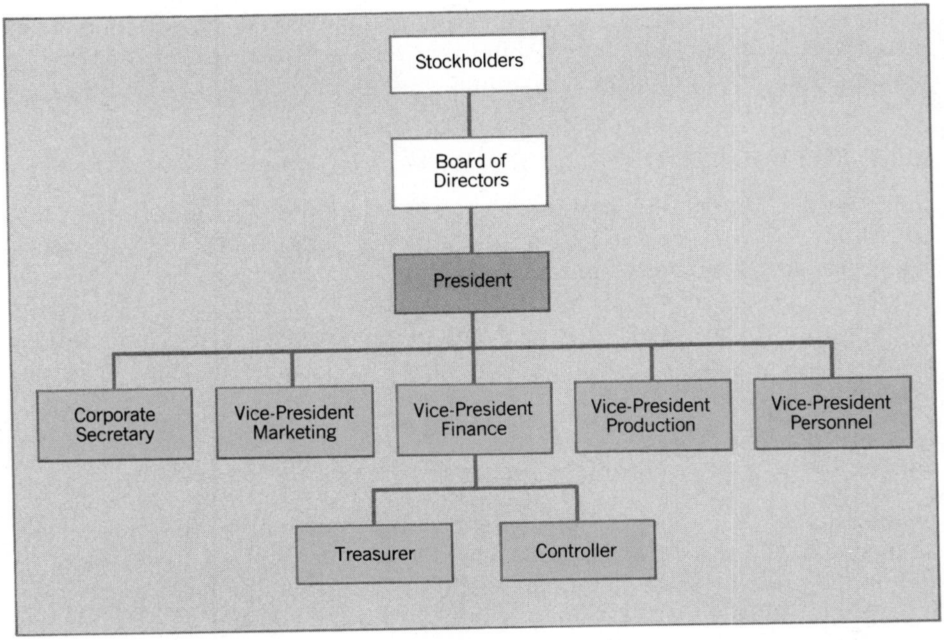

internal control, and (3) preparing financial statements, tax returns, and internal reports. The **treasurer** has custody of the corporation's funds and is responsible for maintaining the company's cash position.

The organizational structure of a corporation enables a company to hire professional managers to run the business. On the other hand, the separation of ownership and management prevents owners from having an active role in managing the company.

GOVERNMENT REGULATIONS

A corporation is subject to numerous state and federal regulations that add considerably to the cost of doing business. For example, state laws usually prescribe the requirements for issuing stock, the treatment of proceeds of issued stock, the distributions permitted to stockholders, and the effects of retiring stock, as well as other procedures and restrictions. Similarly, federal securities laws govern the sale of capital stock to the general public, and most publicly held corporations are required to make extensive disclosure of their financial affairs to the Securities and Exchange Commission through quarterly and annual reports. In addition, when a corporate stock is listed and traded on organized securities markets, the corporation must comply with the reporting requirements of these exchanges.

ADDITIONAL TAXES

Neither proprietorships nor partnerships pay income taxes. The owner's share of these organizations' earnings is reported on his or her personal income tax return. Taxes are then paid on this amount. Corporations, on the other hand, must pay federal and state income taxes. These taxes are substan-

tial; they can amount to as much as 40% of taxable income. In addition, when the corporation distributes cash to stockholders in the form of dividends, the stockholders are required to pay taxes on these dividends. Thus, many argue that corporate income is **taxed twice (double taxation),** once at the corporate level, and again at the individual level.

From the foregoing, we can identify the following advantages and disadvantages of a corporation compared to a proprietorship and partnership:

Advantages and disadvantages of a corporation

Advantages	Disadvantages
Separate legal existence	Organizational structure – separation of ownership and management
Limited liability of owners	Government regulations
Transferable ownership rights	Additional taxes
Continuous life	
Organizational structure – professional management	

FORMATION OF A CORPORATION

The initial step in the formation of a corporation is to file an application with the Secretary of State in the state in which incorporation is desired. The application contains the following types of information: (1) the name, purpose, and duration of the proposed corporation; (2) amounts, kinds, and number of shares of capital stock to be authorized; and (3) the address of the corporation's principal office, the names and addresses of the incorporators, and the shares of stock to which each has subscribed.

After the incorporation fee is paid and the application approved, a **charter** is granted. The charter may be an approved copy of the application form or it may be a separate document containing the same basic data. The issuance of the charter, often referred to as the **articles of incorporation,** creates the corporation. Upon receipt of the charter, by-laws are developed. The **by-laws**[1] establish the internal rules and procedures for conducting the affairs of the corporation and indicate the relationships and powers of the stockholders, directors, and officers of the enterprise.

Regardless of the number of states in which a corporation has operating divisions, it is incorporated in only one state. It is to the company's advantage to incorporate in the state whose laws are most favorable to the corporate form of business organization. General Motors, for example, is incorporated in Delaware, whereas USX Corp. is a New Jersey corporation. In fact, some corporations have increasingly been incorporating in states with rules favorable to existing management. For example, Gulf Oil changed its state of incorporation to thwart possible unfriendly takeovers (sometimes referred to as

[1]Following approval by two-thirds of the stockholders, the by-laws become binding upon all stockholders, directors, and officers. Legally, a corporation is regulated first by the laws of the state, second by its charter, and third by its by-laws. Care must be exercised to ensure that the provisions of the by-laws are not in conflict with either state laws or the charter.

shark attacks). In Delaware, certain defensive tactics can be approved by the board of directors alone without a vote by shareholders.

Corporations engaged in interstate commerce must obtain a license from each state in which they do business. The license subjects the corporation's operating activities to the general corporation laws of the state.

CORPORATE CAPITAL

Owners' equity in a corporation is identified as **stockholders' equity, shareholders' equity,** or **corporate capital.** The stockholders' equity section of a corporation's balance sheet consists of: (1) paid-in (contributed) capital, and (2) retained earnings (earned capital).

PAID-IN CAPITAL

The principal source of **paid-in capital** is the investment of cash and other assets in the corporation by stockholders in exchange for capital stock. When a corporation has only one class of capital stock, the stock is identified as **common stock.** To record the issuance of the stock, the assets received by the corporation are debited, and the account, Common Stock, is credited. The balance in Common Stock represents paid-in capital that is not subject to withdrawal by stockholders.

RETAINED EARNINGS

Retained earnings is net income retained in a corporation. Net income is recorded in Retained Earnings by a closing entry in which Income Summary is debited and Retained Earnings is credited. For example, assuming that net income for Delta Robotics in its first year of operations is $130,000, the closing entry is:

Income Summary	130,000	
Retained Earnings		130,000
(To close income summary and transfer net income to retained earnings)		

Assuming that Delta Robotics has a balance of $800,000 in Common Stock at the end of its first year, its stockholders' equity section is as follows:

Stockholders' equity section

Stockholders' equity	
Common stock	**$800,000**
Retained earnings	**130,000**
Total stockholders' equity	$930,000

Retained earnings is part of the stockholders' claim on the total assets of the corporation. However, it does not indicate the form of these assets at the statement date. That is, the cash resulting from the excess of revenues over

expenses may have been used to purchase additional buildings, equipment, and other assets. Therefore, the balance in retained earnings is not likely to equal the balance in the cash account. In a recent balance sheet, for example, General Motors Corporation reported $280 million in cash and $15.5 billion in retained earnings. Similarly, McDonald's Corporation reported a cash balance of $155 million and a retained earnings balance of $2.5 billion.

When expenses exceed revenues, a **net loss** results. A net loss is recorded in Retained Earnings by crediting Income Summary and debiting Retained Earnings. Net losses are not debited to paid-in capital accounts, because this action would destroy the distinction between paid-in and earned capital. If a corporation experiences net losses, the retained earnings account at the end of a reporting period may have a **debit** balance. A debit balance in retained earnings is identified as a **deficit** and reported as a deduction in the stockholders' equity section. Thus, if Delta Robotics suffered a $50,000 net loss in its first year, the stockholders' equity section would report the following:

Stockholders' equity—deficit illustrated

Stockholders' equity	
Common stock	$800,000
Deficit	(50,000)
Total stockholders' equity	$750,000

OWNERSHIP RIGHTS

Each share of common stock gives the stockholder the following ownership rights.

1. **To vote.** Each share of stock entitles the owner to one vote in the election of the board of directors and in corporate actions that require stockholder approval.
2. **To share in corporate earnings.** Through the receipt of dividends, a stockholder participates in corporate earnings.
3. **To maintain the same percentage ownership when additional shares of common stock are issued.** In most states, common stockholders are granted the right to purchase any additional shares of stock issued in proportion to their present holdings. Because this right applies before the additional shares can be sold to the general public, it is referred to as the **preemptive right.**[2]
4. **To share in assets upon liquidation.** Common stockholders have a claim on corporate assets in proportion to their holdings if the corporation is terminated. This claim is often referred to as a **residual claim,** because the claims of creditors must first be paid in full.

The ownership rights of a share of stock are stated in the articles of incorporation or in the by-laws.

[2]A number of companies have eliminated the preemptive right, because they believe it makes an unnecessary and cumbersome demand on management. For example, IBM, by stockholder approval, has dropped its preemptive right for stockholders.

The ownership of stock is evidenced by a printed or engraved form known as a stock certificate. As illustrated below, the face of the certificate shows the name of the corporation, the stockholder's name, the class and special features of the stock, the number of shares owned, and the signatures of duly authorized corporate officials. Certificates are prenumbered to facilitate their accountability; they may be issued for any quantity of shares.

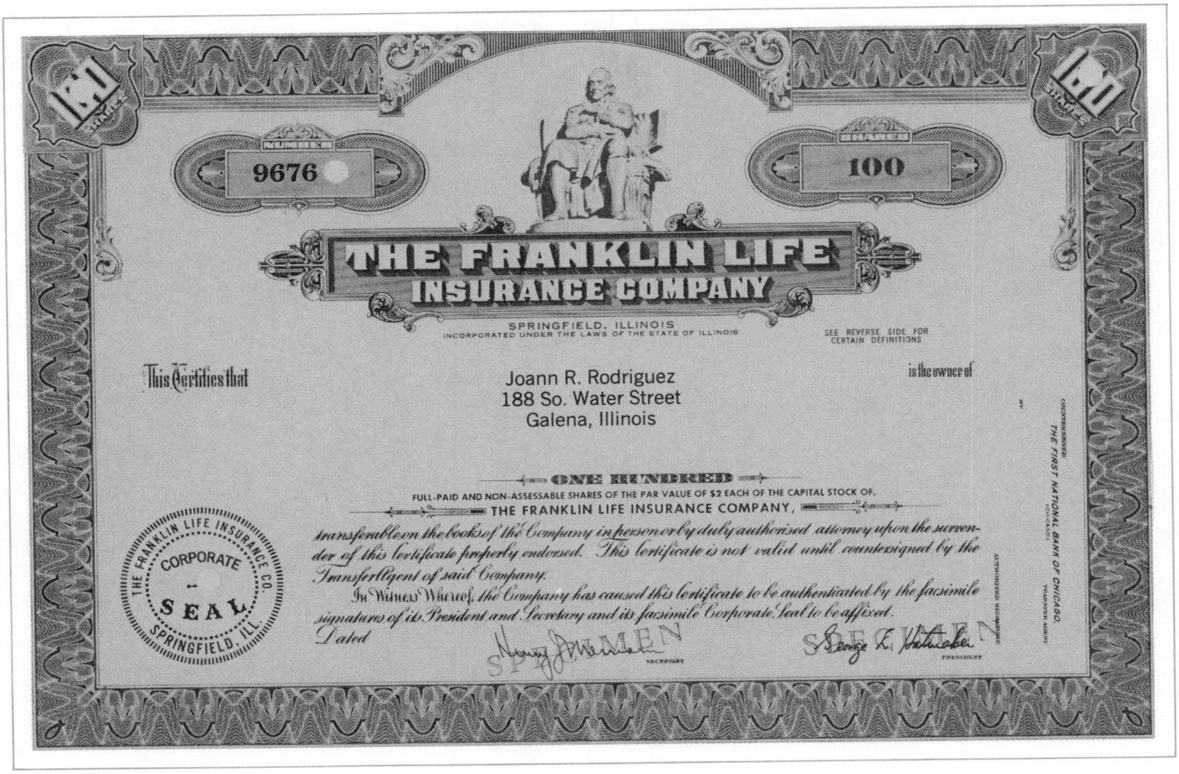

CHARACTERISTICS OF STOCK ISSUANCE

In considering the issuance of stock, a number of basic questions need to be resolved. For example, how many shares should the corporation be authorized to sell? How should the stock be issued? At what price should the shares be issued? Should a par value or no par value be assigned the stock? For purposes of discussion, these questions are considered under the following headings:

1. Authorized stock.
2. Issuance of stock.
3. Market value of stock.
4. Par and no par value stocks.

AUTHORIZED STOCK

The amount of stock that a corporation is **authorized** to sell is indicated in its charter. The total amount of **authorized stock** at the time of incorporation normally anticipates both initial and subsequent capital needs of a company. As a result, the number of total shares authorized generally exceeds the number of shares initially sold. In the event that full authorization is reached, a corporation must obtain consent of the state to amend its charter before it can issue additional shares.

The authorization of capital stock does not result in a formal accounting entry, since the event has no immediate effect on either corporate assets or stockholders' equity. However, disclosure of the number of shares of authorized stock is required in the stockholders' equity section. By subtracting the total shares issued from the total authorized, it is possible to determine the number of unissued shares that can be issued without amending the charter. For example, if Advanced Micro was authorized to sell 100,000 shares of common stock and issued 80,000 shares, unissued shares would be 20,000 shares.

ISSUANCE OF STOCK

A corporation may issue common stock directly to investors or indirectly through an investment banking firm (brokerage house) that specializes in bringing securities to the attention of prospective investors. Direct issue is typical in closely held companies, whereas indirect issue is customary for a publicly held corporation. In an indirect issue, the investment banking firm may agree to **underwrite** the entire stock issue. Under this arrangement, the investment banker buys the stock from the corporation at a stipulated price and resells the shares to investors. The corporation avoids any risk of being unable to sell the shares, and it obtains immediate use of the cash received from the underwriter. The investment banking firm, in turn, assumes the risk of reselling the shares in return for the profits expected to be realized from a sales price to the public higher than the price paid to the corporation.[3] For example, Kolff Medical, maker of the Jarvik artificial heart, which kept Barney Clark (first artificial heart transplant patient) alive for 112 days, used an underwriter to help it issue common stock to the public. The underwriter charged a 6.6% underwriting fee on Kolff Medical's approximately $20 million public offering.

MARKET VALUE OF STOCK

How does a corporation set the market price for a new issue of stock? Among the factors to be considered are (1) the company's anticipated future earnings, (2) its expected dividend rate per share, (3) its current financial position, (4) the current state of the economy, and (5) the current state of the securities markets.

Following its issuance, the stock of publicly held companies is traded on a national securities market at dollar prices per share established by the inter-

[3]Alternatively, the investment banking firm may agree only to enter into a **best efforts** contract with the corporation. In such cases, the banker agrees to sell as many shares as possible at a specified price, and the corporation bears the risk of unsold stock. Under a best efforts arrangement, the banking firm is paid a fee or commission for its services.

action between buyers and sellers. In general, the prices set by the marketplace tend to follow the trend of a company's earnings and dividends. However, factors beyond a company's control, such as the imposition of an oil embargo, new estimates on the size of the national debt, changes in interest rates, and the outcome of a presidential election, may cause day-to-day fluctuations in market prices.

The volume of trading is heavy. Shares in excess of 150 million are often traded daily on the New York Stock Exchange alone. For each listed security the financial press reports the highs and lows of the stock during the year, the total volume of stock traded for a given day, the high and low price for the day, and the closing market price, with the net change for the day. The listing for Boeing Aircraft is shown below:

Stock market price information

	52 Weeks		Sales				Net
Stock	High	Low	10/5	High	Low	Close	Change
Boeing	48 1/4	20 5/8	3942	42	41 1/4	41 3/8	+ 3/8

These numbers indicate that the high and low market price for the year have been 48 1/4 and 20 5/8; the trading volume for October 5 was 394,200 shares; the high and low and the close for October 5 were 42, 41 1/4, and 41 3/8, respectively; and the net change for the day is a positive 3/8 or 37½ cents per share.

The giant, publicly held corporation could not exist without the organized stock markets, and the stock markets could not exist without massive computerization. Not too many years ago, the NYSE "ticker" would run behind, or trading would even be halted, when sales exceeded 30 million shares or so. Now, with sales sometimes in excess of 150 million shares, the NYSE and its companion exchanges throughout the country operate efficiently with computer technology.

Par value is the amount assigned to each share of stock in the corporate charter. Par value may be any amount selected by the corporation. Generally, the amount of par value is quite low, because states often levy a tax on the corporation based on par value. For example, International Business Machines has a par of $5, Ford Motor Company, $2.50, General Motors Corporation, $1.67, and Pan American World Airways, Inc., $.50.

Par value is not indicative of the worth or market value of the stock. As indicated above, IBM has a par value of $5, but its recent market price was $120 per share. **The significance of par value is a legal matter.** Par value represents the **legal capital** per share that must be retained in the business for the protection of corporate creditors. Thus, most states require the corporation to sell its shares at par or above.

No-par value stock is capital stock that has not been assigned a value in the corporate charter. No-par value stock is quite common today. For exam-

ple, Procter & Gamble and North American Van Lines both have no-par stock.

In many states the board of directors is permitted to assign a **stated value** to the shares, which becomes the legal capital per share. The stated value of no-par stock may be changed at any time by action of the directors. Stated value, like par value, is not indicative of the market value of the stock. When there is no assigned stated value, the entire proceeds received upon issuance of the shares is considered to be legal capital.

The relationship of par and no-par value to legal capital is graphically shown below.

Relationship of par and no-par value stock to legal capital

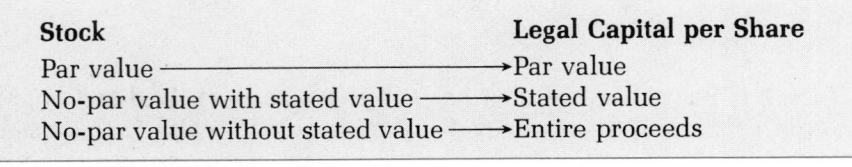

Stock		**Legal Capital per Share**
Par value	→	Par value
No-par value with stated value	→	Stated value
No-par value without stated value	→	Entire proceeds

As will be explained, a common stock account is credited for the legal capital per share each time stock is issued.

ACCOUNTING FOR COMMON STOCK ISSUES

The primary objectives in accounting for the issuance of common stock are to (1) identify the specific sources of paid-in capital and (2) maintain the distinction between paid-in capital and retained earnings. As shown below, the sale and issue of common stock only affects paid-in capital accounts.

ISSUING PAR VALUE COMMON STOCK FOR CASH

The cash proceeds from issuing par value stock may be equal to, greater than, or less than par value. When the issuance of common stock for cash is recorded, the par value of the shares is credited to Common Stock, and the portion of the proceeds that is above or below par value is recorded in a separate paid-in capital account.

To illustrate, assume that Hydro-Slide, Inc. issues 1,000 shares of $1 par value common stock at par. The entry to record this transaction is:

Cash	1,000	
Common Stock		1,000
(To record issuance of common stock at par)		

If Hydro-Slide, Inc. issues an additional 1,000 shares of the $1 par value common stock at $5 per share, the entry is:

Cash	5,000	
Common Stock		1,000
Paid-in Capital in Excess of Par		4,000
(To record issuance of common stock in excess of par)		

The total paid-in capital from these two transactions is $6,000, and the legal capital is $2,000. If Hydro-Slide, Inc. has retained earnings of $27,000, the stockholders' equity section is as follows:

Stockholders' equity—paid-in capital in excess of par illustrated

Stockholders' equity	
Paid-in capital	
Common stock	**$ 2,000**
Paid-in capital in excess of par	**4,000**
Total paid-in capital	6,000
Retained earnings (assumed)	27,000
Total stockho'ders' equity	$33,000

If stock is issued for less than par value, the account, Paid-in Capital in Excess of Par, is debited, assuming that a credit balance exists in this account. If a credit balance does not exist, then the amount less than par is debited to Retained Earnings. The sale of common stock below par value is not permitted in most states, because stockholders may be held personally liable for the difference between the price paid upon original sale and par value.

ISSUING NO-PAR COMMON STOCK FOR CASH

When no-par common stock has a stated value, the entries are similar to those illustrated above for par value stock. The stated value represents legal capital and therefore is credited to Common Stock. In addition, when the selling price exceeds stated value, the excess is credited to Paid-in Capital in Excess of Stated Value. As an example, assume that instead of $1 par value stock, Hydro-Slide, Inc. has $5 stated value no-par stock and that it issues 5,000 shares at $8 per share. The entry is:

Cash	40,000	
Common Stock		25,000
Paid-in Capital in Excess of Stated Value		15,000
(To record issue of 5,000 shares of $5 stated value no-par stock)		

Paid-in Capital in Excess of Stated Value is reported as part of additional paid-in capital in the stockholders' equity section.

When no-par stock does not have a stated value, the entire proceeds from the issue become legal capital and are credited to Common Stock. Thus, if Hydro-Slide does not assign a stated value to its no-par stock, the issuance of the 5,000 shares at $8 per share is recorded as follows:

Cash	40,000	
Common Stock		40,000
(To record issue of 5,000 shares of no-par stock)		

The amount of legal capital for Hydro-Slide with a $5 stated value is $25,000; without a stated value, it is $40,000.

ISSUING COMMON STOCK FOR SERVICES OR NONCASH ASSETS

Stock may be issued for services (compensation to attorneys, consultants, and others) or for noncash assets (land, buildings, and equipment). In such cases, a question arises as to the cost that should be recognized in the exchange transaction. **To comply with the cost principle, cost should be either the fair market value of the consideration given up or the fair market value of the consideration received, whichever is more clearly evident.**

To illustrate, assume that the attorneys for Advanced Design Inc., agree to accept 4,000 shares of $1 par value common stock in payment of their bill of $5,000 for services performed in helping the company to incorporate. At the time of the exchange, there is no established market price for the stock. In this case, the market value of the consideration received, $5,000, is more clearly evident. Accordingly, the entry is:

Organization Costs	5,000	
Common Stock		4,000
Paid-in Capital in Excess of Par		1,000
(To record issuance of stock to attorneys)		

In contrast, assume that Athletic Research Inc., is a publicly held corporation whose $5 par value stock is actively traded at $8 per share. The company issues 10,000 shares of stock to acquire land recently advertised for sale at $90,000. On the basis of these facts the most clearly evident value is the market price of the consideration given, $80,000. Thus, the transaction is recorded as follows:

Land	80,000	
Common Stock		50,000
Paid-in Capital in Excess of Par		30,000
(To record issuance of stock for land)		

As illustrated in these examples, the par value of the stock is never a factor in determining the cost of the assets received. This is also true of the stated value of no-par stock.

SALE OF COMMON STOCK ON A SUBSCRIPTION BASIS

Instead of selling stock for cash, a corporation may sell stock on a subscription basis. The **subscription agreement** usually requires the investor to pay the contract price over a series of installment payments, and the corporation does not issue the shares until the contract price is paid in full. Stock may be sold on a subscription basis when a corporation offers stock to its employees to encourage them to acquire an ownership interest in the company. In addition, small businesses often use stock subscriptions, because they cannot afford the cost of underwriting. In accounting for stock sold on a subscription basis, it is necessary to record (1) the receipt of the subscription contract, (2) the collection of the installment payments, and (3) the issuance of the shares. When

subscriptions are received, Stock Subscriptions Receivable is debited for the contract price; Common Stock Subscribed is credited for the par or stated value of the shares; and Paid-in Capital in Excess of Par (or Stated) Value is credited for any excess over legal capital. As an example, assume that Lakeland Estates receives subscriptions for 5,000 shares of $10 par value common stock at a contract price of $12 per share. The entry for the subscriptions is:

Stock Subscriptions Receivable	60,000	
Common Stock Subscribed		50,000
Paid-in Capital in Excess of Par		10,000
(To record receipt of stock subscriptions)		

The classification of Stock Subscriptions Receivable is controversial. For homework problems, assume that it should be classified as a current asset. Common Stock Subscribed is considered to be legal capital and is reported as an addition to common stock within the stockholders' equity section.

Collections from subscribers are recorded in the same manner as collections from customers; that is, Cash is debited and Subscriptions Receivable is credited. Assuming that the Lakeland Estates' subscription agreement requires three equal installment payments, the receipt of the first installment is recorded as follows:

Cash	20,000	
Stock Subscriptions Receivable		20,000
(To record collection of first installment)		

In most states, the corporation is not required to issue shares sold on a subscription basis until all installment payments have been made. Therefore even though the collection above fully pays for the equivalent of 1,667 ($20,000 ÷ $12) shares, Lakeland Estates would not issue any shares until the total amount subscribed is received. In addition, a subscriber is precluded from paying in full for fewer shares than the number specified in the contract.

Upon receipt of the final installment payment on a subscription contract, the corporation is required to issue the shares. The issuance of the shares results in a debit to Common Stock Subscribed and a credit to Common Stock. Assuming that the subscribers make their two remaining installments, the entry to record the issuance of the 5,000 shares by Lakeland Estates is:

Common Stock Subscribed	50,000	
Common Stock		50,000
(To record issuance of 5,000 shares)		

DONATED CAPITAL

Donated capital results when a corporation receives assets as a result of a gift or donation from municipalities, charitable foundations, or other sources. If the donation is received in cash, Cash is debited and Donated Capital is credited for the amount received.

A problem of valuation arises when the donation involves a noncash asset. Assume, for example, that Southern Corporation receives land having a fair market value of $195,000 from a municipality as a donation. Should the plant site be valued at cost to Southern, which is zero, or should it be recorded at fair market value? The use of cost in this case is inappropriate, because no basis of accountability for the asset received would exist. Fair market value should be used, because it provides a more realistic basis of accountability for the resources received through the donation. Thus, the entry is:

Land	195,000	
Donated Capital		195,000
(Donation of land from city)		

Donated Capital is classified as part of paid-in capital in the stockholders' equity section of the balance sheet.

TREASURY STOCK

Treasury stock is a corporation's own stock that has been issued, fully paid for, and reacquired by the corporation but not canceled. A corporation may acquire treasury stock to:

1. Reissue the shares to officers and employees under bonus and stock compensation plans.
2. Increase trading of the company's stock in the securities market in the hopes of enhancing its price.
3. Have additional shares available for use in the acquisition of other companies.
4. Reduce the number of shares outstanding and thereby increase earnings per share.

Many corporations have treasury stock. For example, one survey of the largest 600 companies in the United States indicated that 68% have treasury stock.[4] Specifically, in a recent year, Texaco, Inc. reported 16 million treasury shares, Pepsico 1.5 million, and Revlon 2 million.

TREASURY STOCK ENTRIES

The cost method is generally used in accounting for treasury stock. This method derives its name from the fact that the Treasury Stock account is maintained at the cost of shares purchased. Under the cost method, Treasury Stock is debited at the price paid to reacquire the shares, and the same amount is credited to Treasury Stock when the shares are reissued. To illustrate, assume that on January 1, 1987, the stockholders' equity section of

[4] *Accounting Trends & Techniques 1985* (New York: American Institute of Certified Public Accountants).

Mead, Inc. has 100,000 shares of $5 par value common stock outstanding (all issued at par value) and Retained Earnings of $200,000. On February 1, 1987, Mead acquires 4,000 shares of its stock at $8 per share. The entry is:

Feb. 1	Treasury Stock	32,000	
	Cash		32,000
	(To record purchase of 4,000 shares of treasury stock at cost)		

Note that Treasury Stock is debited for the cost of the shares purchased and that the original paid-in capital account, Common Stock, is not affected. Treasury Stock is a contra stockholders' equity account. **Thus, the acquisition of treasury stock reduces both total assets and total stockholders' equity.**

Treasury stock may be sold and reissued. If the selling price of the treasury shares is equal to cost, the reissuance of the shares is recorded by a debit to Cash and a credit to Treasury Stock. When the selling price of the shares is greater than cost, the difference is credited to Paid-in Capital from Treasury Stock. To illustrate, assume that 1,000 shares of treasury stock of Mead, Inc. previously acquired at $8 per share, are sold at $10 per share on July 1. The entry is as follows:

July 1	Cash	10,000	
	Treasury Stock		8,000
	Paid-in Capital from Treasury Stock		2,000
	(To record sale of 1,000 shares of treasury stock above cost)		

When treasury stock is sold below its cost, the excess of cost over selling price is usually debited to Paid-in Capital from Treasury Stock. Thus, if Mead, Inc. sells an additional 800 shares of treasury stock on October 1 at $7 per share, the entry is as follows:

Oct. 1	Cash	5,600	
	Paid-in Capital from Treasury Stock	800	
	Treasury Stock		6,400
	(To record sale of 800 shares of treasury stock below cost)		

When the balance in this paid-in capital account has been absorbed, Retained Earnings is debited.

Observe from the two entries that (1) Treasury Stock is credited at cost in each entry, (2) Paid-in Capital from Treasury Stock is used for the difference between the cost and resale price of the shares, and (3) the original paid-in capital account, Common Stock, again is not affected. The sale of treasury stock increases both total assets and total stockholders' equity.

FINANCIAL STATEMENT PRESENTATION

At a statement date, there may be two accounts in the ledger pertaining to treasury stock: Treasury Stock and Paid-in Capital from Treasury Stock. Treasury Stock is deducted from total paid-in capital and retained earnings; Paid-in Capital from Treasury Stock is listed separately as part of paid-in capital. In addition, the number of treasury shares should be disclosed, so that the

total number of shares of common stock issued and outstanding can be determined. Given the information in the previous section, the stockholders' equity section for Mead, Inc. is as follows:

Stockholders' equity—treasury stock illustrated

Stockholders' equity	
Paid-in capital	
Common stock, $5 par value, 100,000 shares issued and 97,800 outstanding	$500,000
Paid-in capital from treasury stock	1,200
Total paid-in capital	501,200
Retained earnings	200,000
Total paid-in capital and retained earnings	701,200
Less: Treasury stock (2,200 shares)	17,600
Total stockholders' equity	$683,600

As shown above, both the number of shares issued (100,000) and in the treasury (2,200) are disclosed. The difference is the number of shares of stock that are outstanding (97,800). The term **outstanding stock** means the number of shares of issued stock that are being held by stockholders.

Some maintain that treasury stock should be reported as an asset because it can be reissued for cash. Under this reasoning, unissued stock should also be shown as an asset, clearly an erroneous conclusion. Rather than being an asset, treasury stock reduces stockholder claims on corporate assets. This effect is correctly shown by reporting treasury stock as a deduction from total paid-in capital and retained earnings.

A corporation does not realize a gain or suffer a loss from stock transactions with its own stockholders. Thus, paid-in capital arising from the sale of treasury stock should not be included in the measurement of net income.

PREFERRED STOCK

To appeal to a larger segment of potential investors, a corporation may issue both common and preferred stock. **Preferred stock** has contractual provisions that give it a preference or priority over common stock in certain areas. Typically, preferred stockholders have a preference as to (1) dividends and (2) assets in the event of liquidation. However, they do not have voting rights.

Like common stock, preferred stock may be issued for cash, issued for noncash assets, or sold on a subscription basis. The entries for these transactions are similar to the entries for common stock. However, when a corporation has more than one class of stock, each paid-in capital account title should identify the stock to which it relates (e.g., Preferred Stock, Preferred Stock Subscribed, and Paid-in Capital in Excess of Par Value—Preferred Stock).

Preferred stock may have either a par value or no par value. For example, Nabisco has $1 par value preferred and General Motors has three classes of no-par preferred stock, each with a stated value of $100. In the stockholders' equity section, preferred stock is shown first because of its dividend and liquidation preferences over common stock.

DIVIDEND PREFERENCES

As indicated above, preferred stockholders have the right to share in the distribution of corporate income before common stockholders. For example, if the dividend rate on preferred stock is $5 per share, common shareholders will not receive any dividends in the current year until preferred stockholders have received $5 per share. The first claim to dividends does not, however, guarantee dividends. Dividends depend on many factors, such as adequate retained earnings and availability of cash.

The per share dividend amount is stated as a percentage of the par value of preferred stock or as a specified amount. For example, the Crane Company specifies a 3 3/4% dividend on its $100 par value preferred, while duPont indicates that it has both a $4.50 and a $3.50 series of no-par preferred stock.

Cumulative

Preferred stock contracts often contain a **cumulative dividend** feature. This right means that preferred stockholders must be paid both current-year dividends and unpaid prior-year dividends before common stockholders receive any dividends. When preferred stock is cumulative, preferred dividends not declared in a given period are called **dividends in arrears.** To illustrate, assume that Scientific-Leasing has 5,000 shares of 7%, $100 par value cumulative preferred stock outstanding. The annual dividend is $35,000 (5,000 × $7). If dividends are two years in arrears, preferred stockholders are entitled to receive the following dividends in the current year before any distribution is made to common stockholders.

Computation of total dividends to preferred

Dividends in arrears ($35,000 × 2)	$ 70,000
Current year dividends	35,000
Total preferred dividend	$105,000

Dividends in arrears are not considered a liability, because no obligation exists until the dividend is declared by the board of directors. However, the amount of the arrearage should be disclosed in the notes to the financial statements, so that investors can assess the potential impact of this commitment on the corporation's financial position.

No dividends may be paid on common stock while any dividend on preferred stock is in arrears. The cumulative feature is often critical in investor acceptance of a preferred stock issue. When preferred stock is noncumulative, a dividend passed in any year is lost forever. It should be noted that companies that are unable to meet their dividend obligations are not looked upon favorably by the investment community. As one financial officer noted in discussing one company's failure to pay its cumulative preferred dividend for a period of time, "Not meeting your obligations on something like that is a major black mark on your record." The accounting entries for preferred stock dividends are explained in Chapter 16.

Participating

Preferred stock may also have a **participating dividend** feature. This right enables the preferred stockholder to share ratably (proportionately) with common stockholders in any dividends beyond the rate specified on the preferred stock. Examples of corporations issuing participating preferred stock are Hertz Corp., ITT, Litton Industries, and Southern California Edison.

The participating feature does not apply until common stockholders receive a percentage rate of return on their shares equal to the prescribed dividend rate on preferred stock. Assume, for example, that Lifemark Inc. has outstanding $100,000 of 8% $100 par value preferred stock and $500,000 of par value common stock. It must pay $8,000 in dividends to preferred stock (8% × $100,000) and $40,000 in dividends to common stock (8% × $500,000) before the participating right takes effect. If additional dividends are paid in the year, the amount is distributed between the preferred and common stock on the basis of their respective total par values. For Lifemark, the total par values are $600,000 ($100,000 + $500,000). Thus, the additional dividends are paid 1/6 to preferred stock and 5/6 to common stock. If $60,000 of additional dividends are paid, preferred stockholders will receive $10,000 (1/6 of $60,000) and common stockholders will receive $50,000 (5/6 × $60,000). These computations are summarized as follows:

Computation of participating dividends

	Preferred Stock	Common Stock
Regular dividend		
Preferred – 8% × $100,000	$ 8,000	
Common – 8% × $500,000		$40,000
Total regular dividend	8,000	40,000
Participating dividend		
Preferred – 1/6 × $60,000	10,000	
Common – 5/6 × $60,000		50,000
Total participating dividend	10,000	50,000
Total dividend	$18,000	$90,000

As illustrated, each class of stock receives the same percentage dividend, 18%. The preferred stock is 18% ($18,000 ÷ $100,000), and the common stock is 18% ($90,000 ÷ $500,000).

LIQUIDATION PREFERENCE

Most preferred stocks have a preference on corporate assets in the event of insolvency. This feature provides security for the preferred stockholder in the event that the corporation suffers ongoing operating losses. The preference to assets may be for the par value of the shares or a specified liquidating value. For example, Commonwealth Edison issued preferred stock that entitles the holders to receive $31.80 per share, plus accrued and unpaid dividends, in the event of involuntary liquidation. The liquidating preference is used in computing the book value per share of stock, as explained later in this chapter.

PREFERRED STOCK—OTHER RIGHTS

In addition to the privileges described above, preferred stock may be convertible or callable. These two features are explained below.

CONVERTIBLE PREFERRED STOCK

The attractiveness of preferred stock as an investment is enhanced by adding a conversion privilege. **Convertible preferred stock** provides for the exchange of preferred stock into common stock at a specified ratio.

Convertible preferreds are purchased by investors who want the greater security of a preferred stock, but who also desire the added option of conversion if the market value of the common stock appreciates significantly. To illustrate, assume that Ross Industries issues at par value 1,000 shares of $100 par value convertible preferred stock. One share of preferred is convertible into 10 shares of $5 par value common (current price $9 per share). At this point, it would not be advantageous for the holders of the preferred to convert, because they would exchange preferred stock worth $100,000 (1,000 × $100) for common stock worth $90,000 (10,000 × $9). However, if the price of the common stock were to increase above $10 per share, it often would be advantageous for the preferred holders to convert.

In recording the conversion, it is customary to transfer the amount paid in on the preferred stock to appropriate common stock accounts. To illustrate, assume that the 1,000 shares of Ross Industries preferred issued at par value are converted into 10,000 shares of common stock ($5 par) when the market value per share of the two classes of stock are $101 and $12 respectively. The entry to record the conversion is:

Preferred Stock	100,000	
Common Stock		50,000
Paid-in Capital in Excess of Par Value		50,000
(To record conversion of 1,000 shares of preferred stock)		

If the preferred stock was issued for more than its par value, the paid-in capital in excess of the par value on the preferred stock should be eliminated. Note that the market values of the shares at the time of transaction are not considered in recording the transaction. The reason is that the exchange of shares is made directly through the corporation and the corporation has not received any assets equal to fair market value.

CALLABLE PREFERRED STOCK

Many preferred stocks are callable. A **callable preferred stock** grants the issuing corporation the right to purchase the stock from stockholders at specified future dates and prices. The **call (or redemption) price** is frequently slightly above the par or stated value of the shares. The callable feature offers some flexibility to a corporation by enabling it to eliminate this type of equity security when it is advantageous to do so. When preferred stock is callable, the call price tends to set a ceiling on the market price of the shares.

Normally, preferred stock is retired (or canceled) when the call option is exercised. At this time, the amount paid in on the shares should be eliminated from the accounts.

STATEMENT PRESENTATION OF STOCKHOLDERS' EQUITY

In the stockholders' equity section, paid-in capital and retained earnings are reported and the specific sources of paid-in capital are identified.

Within paid-in capital, two classifications are recognized:

1. **Capital stock,** which consists of issued and subscribed stock. Preferred stock is shown before common stock because of its preferential rights. Information as to the par value, shares authorized, shares issued, and shares outstanding is also reported for each class of stock.
2. **Additional paid-in capital,** which includes the excess of amounts paid in over par or stated value, paid-in capital from sale of treasury stock, and donated capital.

The stockholders' equity section of Connally Inc. shown below includes most of the accounts discussed in this chapter.

Stockholders' equity section

CONNALLY INC.

Stockholders' equity		
Paid-in capital		
Capital stock		
9% Preferred stock $100 par value, cumulative, 10,000 shares authorized, 6,000 shares issued and outstanding		$ 600,000
Common stock, no par, $5 stated value, 500,000 shares authorized, 400,000 shares issued, and 390,000 outstanding	$2,000,000	
Common stock subscribed (20,000 shares)	100,000	2,100,000
Total capital stock		2,700,000
Additional paid-in capital		
In excess of par value—preferred stock	30,000	
In excess of stated value—common stock	800,000	
Donated capital	100,000	
Total additional paid-in capital		930,000
Total paid-in capital		3,630,000
Retained earnings		1,058,000
Total paid-in capital and retained earnings		4,688,000
Less: Treasury stock (10,000 common shares)		(80,000)
Total stockholders' equity		$4,608,000

In Connally Inc., Retained Earnings is reported as one amount. As explained earlier, the cost of treasury stock is then subtracted from total paid-in

capital and retained earnings to complete the presentation. From the disclosures pertaining to common stock, it can be determined that 400,000 shares are issued, 100,000 shares are unissued (500,000 authorized less 400,000 issued), and 390,000 shares are issued and outstanding (400,000 less 10,000 shares in treasury).

In financial statements prepared for stockholders, the individual sources of additional paid-in capital are often combined and condensed into a single amount as shown below.

Zenith Electronics stockholders' equity section

Zenith Electronics

Stockholders' equity	
Common stock, $1 par value, 50,000,000 shares authorized, 22,000,000 issued	$ 22,000,000
Additional paid-in capital	**60,900,000**
Retained earnings	292,300,000
Total stockholders' equity	$375,200,000

In practice, the term "capital surplus" is sometimes used in place of additional paid-in capital and "earned surplus" in place of retained earnings. The use of the term "surplus" suggests that an excess amount of funds is available. Such is not necessarily the case, and that is why **the term surplus should not be employed in accounting.** Unfortunately, a number of financial statements still include these terms.

BOOK VALUE—ANOTHER PER SHARE AMOUNT

You have learned about a number of per share amounts in this chapter. Another per share amount of some importance is **book value per share.** This per share amount represents the equity a common stockholder has in the net assets of the corporation from owning one share of stock. Since the net assets of a corporation must be equal to total stockholders' equity the formula for computing book value per share when a company has only one class of stock outstanding is:

Book value per share formula

Total Stockholders' Equity ÷ Number of Shares of Common Stock Outstanding = Book Value per Share

Thus, if the Marlo Corporation has total stockholders' equity of $1,500,000 and 50,000 shares of common stock outstanding, book value per share is $30 ($1,500,000 ÷ 50,000).

Book value per share is not synonymous with liquidation value per share. If the corporation is liquidated, it is unlikely that noncash assets will be converted into cash without gain or loss to the company. Moreover, book

value per share, like the book value of a plant asset, may not equal fair market value. Book value is based on recorded costs; market value reflects the subjective judgment of thousands of stockholders and prospective investors about a company's potential for future earnings and dividends. The fact that market value per share exceeds book value per share does not necessarily mean that the stock is overpriced. The correlation between book value and the annual range of a company's market value per share is often remote, as indicated by the following recent data:

Book values and market values compared

Company	Book Value	Market Range
Texaco Inc.	$55	$26–35
UAL (United Airlines)	$44	$40–59
Black and Decker	$12	$14–24

Book value per share is useful in determining the trend of a stockholder's per share equity in a corporation. Book value is also significant in many contracts and in court cases where the rights of individual parties are based on historical cost information.

When a company has both preferred stock and common stock, the computation of book value is more complex. Since preferred stockholders have a prior claim on net assets over common stockholders, their equity must be deducted from total stockholders' equity to determine the stockholders' equity applicable to the common stock. To illustrate the computation, we will use the stockholders' equity section of Connally Inc. In this case, the preferred stock equity is equal to the par value of the issued shares, or $600,000. Thus, the book value per share of common stock is $10.28 computed as follows:

Computation of book value per share with preferred stock

Total stockholders' equity	$4,608,000
Less: Preferred stock equity	600,000
Common stock equity	$4,008,000
Shares of common stock outstanding	390,000
Book value per share ($4,008,000/390,000)	**$10.28**

When the preferred stock has a liquidation value, this value is used instead of par value in determining the preferred stock equity.

SUPPORTING STOCK RECORDS AND PROCEDURES

To maintain a complete record of its stock transactions with individual stockholders, a corporation must maintain a variety of detailed records. Typically, a corporation uses the following control and subsidiary arrangements on the next page.

A corporation also keeps a stock transfer book, which is a log of transfers of stock among investors. The stock transfer book facilitates the updating of the stockholders' ledger.

Stock ledger accounts

General Ledger Control Account	Subsidiary Ledger
Preferred or Common Stock	Stockholders
Subscriptions Receivable	Subscriptions Receivable
Preferred or Common Stock Subscribed	Subscribed Stock

Today's giant corporations with their large number of shareholders must use computer technology. Think of the record-keeping chores involved in maintaining current name and address information on the 2 million shareholders of General Motors Corporation. Each of these shareholders must receive corporate financial data and other information each year, and, of course, they like to receive dividend checks on a fairly regular basis as well.

Instead of maintaining its own supporting stock records and transfer book, a corporation may engage a bank or trust company to serve as a transfer agent and registrar. Periodically, this outside agency provides the corporation with a current list of registered stockholders.

An important source of accounting information in a corporation is the **minutes book,** which contains a record of decisions made at the annual stockholders' meeting and at meetings of the board of directors. For example, the minutes book will reveal the board of directors' authorizations for dividends, compensation of officers, and commitments to purchase major plant assets. The minutes book is usually kept by the corporate secretary.

SUMMARY OF STUDY OBJECTIVES

1. The major characteristics of a corporation are separate legal existence, limited liability of stockholders, transferable ownership rights, continuous life, organizational structure (delegation of responsibility), government regulations, and additional taxes.

2. Paid-in capital is the investment of cash and other assets in the corporation by stockholders in exchange for capital stock. It is often referred to as contributed capital. Retained earnings is net income retained in a corporation. It is often referred to as earned capital.

3. When the issuance of capital stock for cash is recorded, the par value of the shares is credited to the appropriate capital stock account and the portion of the proceeds that is above or below par value is recorded in a separate paid-in capital account. When no-par common stock has a stated value, the entries are similar to those for par value stock. When no-par does not have a stated value, the entire proceeds from the issue become legal capital and are credited to Common Stock.

4. Treasury stock is a corporation's own stock that has been issued, fully paid for, and reacquired by the corporation but not canceled. The cost method is generally used in accounting for treasury stock. Under this approach, Treasury Stock is debited at the price paid to reacquire the shares, and the same amount is credited to Treasury Stock when the shares are reissued.

5. Preferred stock has contractual provisions that give it priority over common stock in certain areas. Typically, preferred stockholders have a preference as to (1) dividends and (2) assets in the event of liquidation. However, they usually do not have voting rights. In addition, preferred stock may be convertible and/or callable. A convertible preferred stock entitles the holder of the preferred stock to convert those shares to common stock in a specified ratio. The callable feature grants the issuing corporation the right to purchase the stock from stockholders at specified future dates and prices.

6. Book value per share represents the equity a common stockholder has in the net assets of a corporation from owning one share of stock. When there is only common stock outstanding, the formula for computing book value is: Total Stockholders Equity ÷ Number of Shares of Common Stock Outstanding = Book Value per Share.

GLOSSARY

Authorized stock, p. 585
Book value per share, p. 598
By-laws, p. 581
Callable preferred stock, p. 596
Charter, p. 581
Convertible preferred stock, p. 596
Cumulative dividend, p. 594
Deficit, p. 583
Donated capital, p. 590
Legal capital, p. 586
Minutes book, p. 600
No-par value stock, p. 586
Outstanding stock, p. 593
Paid-in capital, p. 582
Par value stock, p. 586
Participating dividend, p. 595
Preferred stock, p. 593
Privately held corporation, p. 578
Publicly held corporation, p. 578
Retained earnings, p. 582
Treasury stock, p. 591

DEMONSTRATION PROBLEM

The Rolman Corporation is authorized to issue 1,000,000 shares of $5 par value common stock. During 1987, its first year, the company has the following stock transactions.

Jan.	10	Issued 400,000 shares of stock at $8 per share.
July	1	Issued 100,000 shares of stock for land. The land had an asking price of $900,000. The stock is currently selling on a national exchange at $8.25 per share.
Sept.	1	Purchased 10,000 shares of common stock for the treasury at $9.00 per share.
Dec.	1	Sold 4,000 shares of the treasury stock at $10 per share.

INSTRUCTIONS

(a) Journalize the transactions.

(b) Prepare the stockholders' equity section assuming the company had retained earnings of $200,000 at December 31, 1987.

SOLUTION TO DEMONSTRATION PROBLEM

(a)	Jan.	10	Cash	3,200,000	
			Common Stock		2,000,000
			Paid-in Capital in Excess of Par		1,200,000
			(Issued 400,000 shares at $8 per share)		
	July	1	Land	825,000	
			Common Stock		500,000
			Paid-in Capital in Excess of Par		325,000
			(Issued 100,000 shares for land)		
	Sept.	1	Treasury Stock	90,000	
			Cash		90,000
			(Purchased 10,000 shares for the treasury)		
	Dec.	1	Cash	40,000	
			Treasury Stock		36,000
			Paid-in Capital from Treasury Stock		4,000
			(Sold 4,000 shares of treasury stock)		

(b)

Stockholders' Equity	
Paid-in capital	
Common Stock, $5 par, 1,000,000 shares authorized, 500,000 shares issued, 494,000 shares outstanding	$2,500,000
Paid-in capital in excess of par value	1,525,000
Paid-in capital from treasury stock	4,000
Total paid-in capital	4,029,000
Retained earnings	200,000
Total paid-in capital and retained earnings	4,229,000
Less: Treasury stock, 6000 shares	54,000
Total stockholders' equity	$4,175,000

QUESTIONS

1. What is the difference between public and private corporations?

2. Mike Jones and Sally Harper are discussing the advantages and disadvantages of a corporation. Mike indicates one major advantage is that a stockholder's liability to the creditors of a corporation is less than a partner's liability to the creditors of a partnership. Do you agree? Why?

3. A corporation has been defined as an entity separate and distinct from its owners. In what ways is a corporation a separate legal entity?

4. On the Senate floor recently, one senator stated that taxes should be eliminated on dividends of common and preferred stock. He said that to tax these dividends amounts to "double taxation." What is "double taxation"?

5. What are the two principal components of stockholders' equity?

6. Mark Hassler is reviewing the retained earnings balance of Largo Enterprises. Mark does not understand why the balance in retained earnings is not equal to the cash balance. Explain.

7. In examining the financial statements of Henley Enterprises, Sue Holt finds that the stockholders' equity section has a negative retained earnings balance. (a) What might be the cause of a negative retained earnings balance? (b) What term is used to describe this balance?

8. What are the basic ownership rights of common stockholders in the absence of restrictive provisions?

9. The corporate charter of Letterman Corporation allows the issuance of a maximum of 100,000 shares of common stock. During its first two years of operations, Letterman sold 65,000 shares to shareholders and reacquired 7,000 of these shares. After these transactions, how many shares are authorized, issued, and outstanding?

10. Which is the better investment, common stock with a par value of $1 per share or common stock with a par value of $20 per share?

11. What factors help determine the market value of stock?

12. What effect does the issuance of stock at a price above par value have on the issuer's net income? Explain.

13. Why is common stock usually not issued at a price that is less than par value?

14. Land appraised at $70,000 is purchased by issuing 1,000 shares of $10 par value common stock. The market price of the shares at the time of the exchange, based on active trading in the securities market, is $65 per share. Should the land be recorded at $10,000, $65,000, or $70,000? Explain.

15. Sea Craft, Inc. has received subscriptions to 1,000 shares of $5 par value common stock at $15 per share. The subscriber has paid 40% of the subscription price. List the balances in the following accounts at this time as related to these transactions: (a) Subscriptions Receivable, (b) Common Stock, (c) Common Stock Subscribed, and (d) Paid-in Capital in Excess of Par.

16. How should the receipt of land as a donation be recorded by the corporation that received the donation?

17. For what reasons might IBM repurchase some of its stock (treasury stock)?

18. Patty Gilmour, Inc. purchases 1,000 shares of its own previously issued $5 par common stock for $12,000. Assuming the shares are held in the treasury, what effect does this transaction have on (a) net income, (b) total assets, (c) total paid-in capital, and (d) total stockholders' equity?

19. The treasury stock purchased in question 18 above is resold by Sharp, Inc. for $13,500. What effect does this transaction have on (a) net income, (b) total assets, (c) total paid-in capital, and (d) total stockholders' equity?

20. (a) What are the principal differences between common stock and preferred stock? (b) Preferred stock may be cumulative or participating or both. Discuss these features.

21. A preferred stockholder exercises her right to convert her convertible preferred stock into common stock. What effect does this have on (a) the corporation's total assets, (b) its total liabilities, and (c) total stockholders' equity?

22. Should the terms "capital surplus" and "earned surplus" be used in a corporation's financial statements?

23. SAS, Inc.'s common stock has a par value of $1, a book value of $27, and a current market value of $10. Explain why these amounts are all different.

24. Indicate how each of the following accounts should be classified in the stockholders' equity section.

(a) Common Stock
(b) Retained Earnings
(c) Paid-in Capital in Excess of Par
(d) Treasury Stock
(e) Paid-in Capital from Treasury Stock
(f) Common Stock Subscribed
(g) Donated Capital
(h) Preferred Stock

EXERCISES

E15–1 During its first year of operations, the Beamer Corporation had the following transactions pertaining to its common stock.

Jan.	10	Issued 100,000 shares for cash at $5 per share.
Mar.	1	Issued 5,000 shares to attorneys in payment of a bill for $26,000 for services rendered in helping the company to incorporate.
July	1	Issued 40,000 shares for cash at $6 per share.
Sept.	1	Issued 60,000 shares for cash at $7 per share.

INSTRUCTIONS

(a) Journalize the transactions, assuming that the common stock has a par value of $5 per share.

(b) Journalize the transactions, assuming that the common stock is no par with a stated value of $1 per share.

E15–2 The Valley View Corporation sells its $10 par value common stock on a subscription basis. During its first year of operations, the company had the following stock transactions.

Feb. 1 Sold subscriptions for 50,000 shares at $12 per share.
Apr. 1 Received one-third of contract price from all subscribers.
Oct. 1 Received remaining amount due from subscribers and issued stock.

INSTRUCTIONS

(a) Journalize the stock transactions.

(b) Prepare the paid-in capital section of stockholders' equity.

(c) Indicate the statement presentation of Stock Subscriptions Receivable and Common Stock Subscribed.

E15-3 On January 1, 1987, the stockholders' equity section of the Marlo Corporation shows: Common Stock ($5 par value, 500,000 shares authorized, 300,000 shares issued) $1,500,000; Paid-in Capital in Excess of Par Value $1,000,000; and Retained Earnings $1,200,000.

During the year, the following treasury stock transactions occurred:

Mar. 1 Purchased 50,000 shares for cash at $15 per share.
July 1 Sold 10,000 shares for cash at $16 per share.
Sept. 1 Sold 8,000 shares for cash at $14 per share.
Dec. 1 Sold 5,000 shares for cash at $17 per share.

INSTRUCTIONS

(a) Journalize the treasury stock transactions.

(b) Restate the entry for December 1, assuming the treasury shares were sold at $12 per share.

E15-4 The Foster Corporation has 10,000 shares of $100 par value, 8%, preferred stock and 50,000 shares of $10 par value common stock outstanding at December 31, 1987.

INSTRUCTIONS

Answers the questions in each of the following independent situations.

1. If the preferred stock is cumulative and dividends were last paid on the preferred stock on December 31, 1985, what are the dividends in arrears that should be reported on the December 31, 1987, balance sheet?
2. If the preferred stock is fully participating (but not cumulative) and a cash dividend of $600,000 is declared at December 31, 1987, how is the total dividend distributed between the preferred and common stock?
3. If the preferred stock is convertible into eight shares of $10 par value common stock and 5,000 shares are converted, what entry is required for the conversion?
4. If the preferred stock was issued at $104 per share, how should the preferred stock be reported in the stockholders' equity section?

E15-5 As an auditor for the CPA firm of Burr and Cody, you encounter the following situations in auditing different clients.

(1) The Ruther Corporation is a closely held corporation whose stock is not publicly traded. On December 5, the corporation acquired land by issuing 5,000 shares of its $20 par value common stock. The owner's asking price for the land was $125,000, and the fair market value of the land was $110,000.

(2) The Handover Corporation is a publicly held corporation whose stock is traded on the securities markets. On June 1, it acquired land by issuing 20,000 shares of its $10 par value stock. At the time of the exchange, the land was advertised for sale at $250,000, and the stock was selling at $11 per share.

(3) The Berea Corporation had outstanding 10,000 shares of $100 par value preferred stock. Each share of stock was convertible into five shares of $15 par value common stock. When the market values of the two classes of stock were $101 and $21, respectively, 2,000 shares of preferred stock issued at par value were converted into common stock.

(4) The Vitale Corporation received land having a fair market value of $250,000 as a donation from the city of Greenview. The gift was made when Vitale Corporation agreed to build its new plant on the land.

INSTRUCTIONS

Prepare the journal entries for each of the situations above.

E15–6 The Teel Corporation recently hired a new accountant with extensive experience in accounting for partnerships. Because of the pressure of the new job, the accountant was unable to review what he had learned earlier about corporation accounting. During the first month, he made the following entries for the corporation's $10 par value common stock.

May	2	Cash	156,000	
		Capital Stock		156,000
		(Issued 12,000 shares at $13 per share)		
	10	Accounts Receivable	120,000	
		Capital Stock		120,000
		(Sold 8,000 shares on a subscription basis at $15 per share)		
	15	Capital Stock	14,000	
		Cash		14,000
		(Reacquired 1,000 shares for the treasury at $14 per share)		
	25	Cash	30,000	
		Accounts Receivable		30,000
		(Received 50% of subscription price on 4,000 shares sold on May 10)		
	31	Cash	8,000	
		Capital Stock		7,000
		Gain on Sale of Stock		1,000
		(Sold 500 shares of treasury stock at $16 per share)		

INSTRUCTIONS

On the basis of the explanation for each entry, prepare the entry that should have been made for the capital stock transactions.

E15–7 The Colt Corporation has the following classes of stock outstanding at December 31, 1987:

Common stock, $20 par value, 35,000 shares.

Preferred stock, 8%, $50 par, 2,000 shares.

At December 31, 1987, the board of directors declares a $120,000 cash dividend.

INSTRUCTIONS

Calculate the amount of dividend payable to preferred stockholders and to common stockholders under the following assumptions.

1. The preferred stock is cumulative and nonparticipating, and no dividends have been declared since December 31, 1984.

2. The preferred stock is cumulative and fully participating, and no dividends have been declared since December 31, 1985.
3. The preferred stock is noncumulative and fully participating.

E15-8 In a recent year, the stockholders' equity accounts of Martin Marietta Corporation were as follows: Additional Paid-in Capital $570,233,000; Common Stock $69,488,000; Preferred Stock $115,000,000; Retained Earnings $1,132,226,000; and Treasury Stock—Common $1,041,591,000.

The preferred stock is without par value and is noncumulative. Ten million shares of preferred are authorized, and 2.3 million shares are issued and outstanding. The common stock is $1 par, and 100 million shares are authorized. Treasury stock is at cost, and 35,115,942 shares are in the treasury.

INSTRUCTIONS

(a) Prepare the stockholders' equity section, including disclosure of all relevant data.
(b) Compute the book value per share of common stock. (Round to two decimals.)

E15-9 For a recent two-year period, the balance sheet of Hilton Hotels Corporation showed the following stockholders' equity:

	(in thousands) 1985	1984
Common stock	$ 67,369	$ 67,155
Additional paid-in capital	13,152	10,358
Retained earnings	682,416	626,804
	762,937	704,317
Treasury stock, at cost	111,491	111,491
Total stockholders' equity	$651,446	$592,826

Common shares issued were 26,861,947 at December 31, 1984, and 26,947,483 at December 31, 1985. In each year there were 2,163,934 shares of stock in the treasury. Ninety million and sixty million shares of common stock with a par value of $2.50 were authorized in 1985 and 1984, respectively.

INSTRUCTIONS

(a) Compute the book value per share of common stock in each year. (Round to two decimals.)
(b) Prepare the stockholders' equity section at December 31, 1985.

E15-10 The stockholders' equity section of the Scharff Corporation is as follows:

Stockholders' Equity

Paid-in capital		
Preferred stock, cumulative, 10,000 shares authorized, 6,000 shares issued and outstanding		$ 600,000
Common stock, no par, 500,000 shares authorized, 400,000 shares issued	$2,000,000	
Common stock subscribed (20,000)	100,000	2,100,000
Total paid-in capital		2,700,000
Retained earnings		1,058,000
Total paid-in capital and retained earnings		3,758,000
Less treasury stock (10,000 common shares)		(80,000)
Total stockholders' equity		$3,678,000

INSTRUCTIONS

From a review of the stockholders' equity section, answer the following questions.

1. How many shares of common stock are outstanding?
2. What is the stated value of the common stock?
3. What is the par value of the preferred stock?
4. If the annual dividend on preferred stock is $54,000, what is the dividend rate on preferred stock?
5. If dividends of $96,000 were in arrears on preferred stock, what would be the balance reported for Retained Earnings?
6. If total dividends declared were $200,000 and this amount was 40% of net income, what was the beginning retained earnings balance?

PROBLEMS

P15-1 The Kozar Corporation was organized on January 1, 1987. It is authorized to issue 10,000 shares of 6%, $100 par value preferred stock, and 500,000 shares of no par common stock with a stated value of $2 per share. The following stock transactions were completed during the first year.

Jan.	10	Issued 100,000 shares of common stock for cash at $3 per share.
Mar.	1	Issued 5,000 shares of preferred stock for cash at $102 per share.
Apr.	1	Issued 25,000 shares of common stock for land. The asking price of the land was $90,000; the fair market value of the land was $80,000.
May	1	Received subscriptions for 75,000 shares of common stock at $4 per share.
July	1	Received one-half of the subscription price on common stock from all subscribers.
Aug.	1	Issued 10,000 shares of common stock to attorneys in payment of their bill for $50,000 pertaining to services rendered in helping the company organize.
Sept.	1	Received $40,000 cash in partial payment of remaining balance due on subscription contracts.
Nov.	1	Issued 1,000 shares of preferred stock for cash at $104 per share.

INSTRUCTIONS

(a) Journalize the transactions.
(b) Post to the stockholders' equity accounts and to Stock Subscriptions Receivable.
(c) Prepare the paid-in capital section of stockholders' equity at December 31, 1987.

P15-2 The Muir Corporation and the Pryor Corporation have the following stockholders' equity accounts on January 1, 1987.

Muir Corporation		Pryor Corporation	
Common Stock, no par stated value $1	$ 400,000	Common Stock, $5 par	$500,000
Paid-in Capital in Excess of Stated Value	500,000	Paid-in Capital in Excess of Par Value	100,000
Retained Earnings	100,000	Retained Earnings	200,000
Total	$1,000,000	Total	$800,000

Both companies use the cost method of accounting for treasury stock. During 1987, the companies had the following treasury stock transactions.

Muir Corporation

Mar.	1	Purchased 5,000 shares at $10 per share.
June	1	Sold 1,000 shares at $11 per share.
Sept.	30	Sold 2,000 shares at $12 per share.
Dec.	10	Sold 1,000 shares at $9 per share.

Pryor Corporation

Feb.	1	Purchased 5,000 shares at $7 per share.
July	1	Sold 2,000 shares at $8 per share.
Sept.	1	Sold 2,000 shares at $5 per share.
Dec.	1	Sold 1,000 shares at $6 per share.

INSTRUCTIONS

(a) Journalize the treasury stock transactions for both companies.

(b) Prepare a stockholders' equity section for Muir Corporation at December 31, 1987, assuming the company earned $50,000 of net income in 1987.

P15-3 The following stockholders' equity accounts arranged alphabetically are in the ledger of Rohr Corporation at December 31, 1987.

Common Stock ($10 stated value)	$1,500,000
Common Stock Subscribed	300,000
Donated Capital	50,000
Paid-in Capital from Treasury Stock	6,000
Paid-in Capital in Excess of Stated Value of Common Stock	900,000
Paid-in Capital in Excess of Par Value of Preferred Stock	120,000
Preferred Stock (8%, $100 par, noncumulative)	500,000
Retained Earnings	1,000,000
Treasury Stock – Common (6,000 shares)	72,000

INSTRUCTIONS

(a) Prepare a stockholders' equity section at December 31, 1987.

(b) Compute the book value per share of the common stock, assuming the preferred stock has a liquidating value of $110 per share.

(c) Answer the following questions:

1. What is the total number of shares of common stock outstanding at December 31, 1987?
2. If 30% of the balance of Paid-in Capital in Excess of Stated Value of Common Stock is applicable to subscribed stock, and subscriptions are 40% collected, what is the balance in Stock Subscriptions Receivable—Common?
3. The number of shares of treasury stock represents 75% of the shares reacquired at one price. What was the selling price per share of the treasury stock that was sold?
4. If Retained Earnings is debited in 1988 for $12,000 when all of the remaining treasury stock is sold, what was the selling price per share of the treasury stock?

P15-4 Since January 1, 1982, the Poller Company has had two classes of capital stock outstanding: 1,000 shares of cumulative 9%, $100 par preferred stock and 4,000 shares of $50 par value common stock. The annual dividends declared by Poller during the period 1982–1987 were:

1982	$ 5,000	1984	$50,000	1986	$12,000
1983	10,000	1985	75,000	1987	80,000

There were no dividends in arrears at January 1, 1982.

INSTRUCTIONS (Round all computations to two decimals.)

(a) Assuming the preferred stock does not have a participating feature:

1. Compute the total dividend and the per-share dividend for each class of stock for each of the six years. Present your answer in the following format:

		Preferred Dividends		Common Dividends	
Year	Total Dividends	Total	Per Share	Total	Per Share

2. Compute the average annual dividend per share for the six-year period for each class of stock.

(b) Assuming that the preferred stock is fully participating as well as cumulative, repeat (a) 1 and (a) 2.

P15–5 Legend Corporation has been authorized to issue 20,000 shares of $100 par value, 10%, noncumulative preferred stock and 1,000,000 shares of no par common stock. The corporation assigned a $2.50 stated value to the common stock. At December 31, 1987, the ledger contained the following balances pertaining to stockholders' equity:

Stock Subscription Receivable – Common	405,000
Land	124,000
Preferred Stock	120,000
Paid-in Capital in Excess of Par Value – Preferred	4,000
Common Stock	1,000,000
Paid-in Capital in Excess of Stated Value – Common	2,990,000
Common Stock Subscribed	150,000
Treasury Stock – Common (1,000 shares)	11,000
Paid-in Capital from Treasury Stock	1,000
Retained Earnings	52,000

The preferred stock was issued for the land. All shares of common stock were sold or subscribed at the same per-share amount. A 25% down payment was received on the subscribed stock. In November, 1,500 shares of common stock were purchased for the treasury at the same per-share price. In December, some of the treasury shares were sold for cash. No dividends were declared or paid in 1987.

INSTRUCTIONS

(a) Compute the price per share at which (1) the common stock was issued and subscribed, and (2) the treasury stock was sold.

(b) Prepare journal entries for the
  (1) Issuance of the preferred stock.
  (2) Issuance of the common stock for cash.
  (3) Subscription and down payment for common stock sold on a subscription basis.
  (4) Purchase and sale of the treasury stock.

(c) Prepare the stockholders' equity section at December 31, 1987.

(d) Compute the book value per share of common stock, assuming the preferred stock has no liquidating value. (Round to two decimals.)

P15–6 The stockholders' equity accounts of the Borke Corporation on January 1, 1987, were as follows:

Preferred Stock (10%, $100 par cumulative, 5,000 shares authorized)	$ 300,000
Common Stock ($5 stated value, 300,000 shares authorized)	1,000,000
Common Stock Subscribed	50,000
Paid-in Capital in Excess of Par Value – Preferred Stock	15,000

Paid-in Capital in Excess of Stated Value—Common Stock	400,000
Retained Earnings	529,000
Treasury Stock—Common (5,000 shares)	40,000

During 1987, the corporation had the following transactions and events pertaining to its stockholders' equity.

Jan. 15	Collected the balance due of $20,000 on common stock subscriptions receivable and issued the fully paid shares.
Mar. 20	Purchased 200 shares of the preferred stock for the treasury at a cost of $21,200.
Apr. 14	Sold 4,000 shares of treasury stock—common for $34,000.
June 20	Sold the remaining shares of treasury stock—common for $7,500.
Sept. 3	Issued 1,500 shares of common stock for a patent valued at $13,000.
Dec. 31	Determined that net income for the year was $113,000.

INSTRUCTIONS

(a) Journalize the transactions and the closing entry for net income.

(b) Determine the total amount to be reported in the stockholders' equity section at December 31, 1987 for (1) capital stock, (2) additional paid-in capital, (3) paid-in capital and retained earnings, and (4) stockholders' equity.

ALTERNATE PROBLEMS

P15-1A The Midtown Corporation was organized on January 1, 1987. It is authorized to issue 10,000 shares of 8%, $100 par value preferred stock, and 500,000 shares of no par common stock with a stated value of $1 per share. The following stock transactions were completed during the first year.

Jan. 10	Issued 80,000 shares of common stock for cash at $3 per share.
Mar. 1	Issued 5,000 shares of preferred stock for cash at $103 per share.
Apr. 1	Issued 24,000 shares of common stock for land. The asking price of the land was $90,000; the fair market value of the land was $80,000.
May 1	Received subscriptions for 80,000 shares of common stock at $4 per share.
July 1	Received one-half of subscription price on common stock from all subscribers.
Aug. 1	Issued 10,000 shares of common stock to attorneys in payment of their bill of $50,000 for services rendered in helping the company organize.
Sept. 1	Received $40,000 in partial payments of remaining balance due on subscription contracts.
Nov. 1	Issued 1,000 shares of preferred stock for cash at $106 per share.

INSTRUCTIONS

(a) Journalize the transactions.

(b) Post to the stockholders' equity accounts and to Stock Subscriptions Receivable.

(c) Prepare the paid-in capital section of stockholders' equity at December 31, 1987.

P15-2A The Buckner Corporation and the Reynolds Corporation have the following stockholders' equity accounts on January 1, 1987.

Buckner Corporation		Reynolds Corporation	
Common Stock, no par stated value $1	$ 400,000	Common Stock, $5 par	$500,000
Paid-in Capital in Excess of Stated Value	500,000	Paid-in Capital in Excess of Par Value	100,000
Retained Earnings	100,000	Retained Earnings	200,000
Total	$1,000,000	Total	$800,000

Both companies use the cost method of accounting for treasury stock. During 1987, the companies had the following treasury stock transactions:

Buckner Corporation

Mar.	1	Purchased 5,000 shares at $8.00 per share.
June	15	Sold 1,000 shares at $8.75 per share.
Sept.	30	Sold 2,000 shares at $9.50 per share.
Dec.	10	Sold 1,000 shares at $7.00 per share.

Reynolds Corporation

Feb.	1	Purchased 5,000 shares at $5.00 per share.
July	1	Sold 2,000 shares at $5.80 per share.
Sept.	1	Sold 2,000 shares at $3.25 per share.
Dec.	1	Sold 1,000 shares at $4.25 per share.

INSTRUCTIONS

(a) Journalize the treasury stock transactions for both companies.

(b) Prepare a stockholders' equity section for Buckner Corporation at December 31, 1987, assuming the company earned $50,000 of net income in 1987.

P15-3A The following stockholders' equity accounts arranged alphabetically are in the ledger of Dwyer Corporation at December 31, 1987.

Common Stock ($10 stated value)	$2,500,000
Common Stock Subscribed	500,000
Donated Capital	85,000
Paid-in Capital from Treasury Stock	10,000
Paid-in Capital in Excess of Stated Value of Common Stock	1,500,000
Paid-in Capital in Excess of Par Value of Preferred Stock	200,000
Preferred Stock (8%, $100 par, noncumulative)	830,000
Retained Earnings	1,700,000
Treasury Stock—Common (10,000 shares)	120,000

INSTRUCTIONS

(a) Prepare a stockholders' equity section at December 31, 1987.

(b) Compute the book value per share of the common stock, assuming the preferred stock has a liquidating value of $110 per share and that the current year's cash dividend in preferred stock has not been paid.

(c) Answer the following questions:

1. What is the total number of shares of common stock outstanding at December 31, 1987?
2. If 30% of the balance of Paid-in Capital in Excess of Stated Value of Common Stock is applicable to subscribed stock, and subscriptions are 40% collected, what is the balance in Stock Subscriptions Receivable—Common?
3. The number of shares of treasury stock represented 80% of the shares reacquired at one price. What was the selling price per share of the treasury stock that was sold?
4. If Retained Earnings is debited in 1988 for $10,000 when all of the remaining treasury stock is sold, what was the selling price per share of the treasury stock?

P15-4A Since January 1, 1982, the Burt Company has had two classes of capital stock outstanding: 1,000 shares of cumulative 8% preferred stock ($100 par), and 4,000 shares of common stock ($50 par). The annual dividends declared by Burt during the period 1982–1987 are as follows:

1982	$ 5,000	1985	$67,000
1983	$ 9,000	1986	$11,000
1984	$44,000	1987	$71,000

There were no dividends in arrears at January 1, 1982.

INSTRUCTIONS (Round all computations to two decimals.)

(a) Assuming the preferred stock does not have a participating feature,

1. Compute the total dividend and the per-share dividend for each class of stock for each of the six years. Present your answer in the following format:

	Total	Preferred Dividends		Common Dividends	
Year	Dividends	Total	Per Share	Total	Per Share

2. Compute the average annual dividend per share for the six-year period for each class of stock.

(b) Assuming that the preferred stock is fully participating as well as cumulative, repeat (a) 1 and (a) 2.

P15-5A The Mystick Corporation was organized on July 1, 1987, with authorized stock consisting of 10,000 shares of $50 par value, 9%, cumulative preferred stock and 500,000 shares of no par common stock. The corporation assigned a $5 stated value to the common stock. At December 31, 1987, the ledger included the following balances pertaining to stockholders' equity:

Stock Subscriptions Receivable—Common	336,000
Land	250,000
Preferred Stock	500,000
Paid-in Capital in Excess of Par Value—Preferred	50,000
Donated Capital	250,000
Common Stock	1,500,000
Paid-in Capital in Excess of Stated Value—Common	2,380,000
Common Stock Subscribed	200,000
Treasury Stock—Common	45,000
Paid-in Capital from Treasury Stock	6,000
Retained Earnings	94,000

Ten thousand shares of preferred stock were issued at $55 per share. All shares of common stock were sold or subscribed at the same per-share amount. A 30% down payment was received on the subscribed stock. The land was donated to the corporation. In November, 5,000 shares of common stock were purchased for the treasury at the same per-share price. In December, 40% of the treasury shares were sold for cash. Dividends on preferred stock were paid in 1986, but no dividends were declared in 1987.

INSTRUCTIONS

(a) Compute the price per share at which (1) the common stock was issued and subscribed, and (2) the treasury stock was sold.

(b) Prepare journal entries for the

1. Issuance of the preferred stock.
2. Issuance of the common stock for cash.
3. Subscription and down payment for common stock sold on a subscription basis.
4. Donation of the land.
5. Purchase and sale of the treasury stock.

(c) Prepare the stockholders' equity section at December 31, 1987.
(d) Compute the book value per share of common stock, assuming the preferred stock has no liquidating value.

DECISION CASE

The stockholders' meeting for Randle Corporation has been in progress for some time. The chief financial officer for Randle is presently reviewing the company's financial statements and is explaining the items that comprise the stockholders' equity section of the balance sheet for the current year. The stockholders' equity section of Randle Corporation at December 31, 1987 is as follows:

Stockholders' equity		
Paid-in capital		
Capital stock		
Preferred stock, authorized 1,000,000 shares cumulative, $100 par value, $8 per share, 6,000 shares issued and outstanding		$ 600,000
Common stock, authorized 5,000,000 shares, $1 par value, 3,000,000 shares issued, and 2,700,000 outstanding		3,000,000
Common stock subscribed		220,000
Total capital stock		3,820,000
Additional paid-in capital		
In excess of par value-preferred stock	$ 50,000	
In excess of par value-common stock	25,000,000	
Total additional paid-in capital		25,050,000
Total paid-in capital		28,870,000
Retained earnings		900,000
Total paid-in capital and retained earnings		29,770,000
Less: Common treasury stock (300,000 shares)		9,300,000
Total stockholders' equity		$20,470,000

A number of questions regarding the stockholders' equity section of the Randle Corporation's balance sheet have been raised at the meeting.

INSTRUCTIONS

Answer the following questions as if you were the chief financial officer for Randle Corporation.

1. What does the cumulative provision related to the preferred stock mean?
2. I thought the common stock was presently selling at $29.75, and yet the company has the stock stated at $1 per share. How can that be?
3. What is meant by common stock subscribed? When I took my finance course in college, I do not remember any financial statements that used this term.
4. Why is the company buying back its common stock? Furthermore, the treasury stock has a debit balance because it is subtracted from stockholders' equity. Why is treasury stock not reported as an asset if it has a debit balance?
5. Why is it necessary to show additional paid-in capital? Why not just show common stock at the total amount paid in?
6. Retained earnings is $900,000 but cash is only $370,000. What happened to the difference?

CHAPTER 16

Pace University, New York

CHAPTER 16

CORPORATIONS: INCOME REPORTING, DIVIDENDS, AND RETAINED EARNINGS

STUDY OBJECTIVES

After studying this chapter, you should be able to:

1. Understand where income taxes are reported on a corporation's income statement.
2. Explain the concept of intraperiod tax allocation.
3. Identify and account for material items not typical of regular operations.
4. Compute earnings per share.
5. Differentiate a cash dividend from a stock dividend.
6. Understand how to report a prior period adjustment.
7. Explain how to account for appropriations of retained earnings.

Net income and its components reported in the income statement measure a company's performance. The amount and trend of income are, therefore, of vital importance to management, creditors, and stockholders. Many factors affect the market price of a stock at a given time; reported income is one of the most significant. For example, when IBM recently announced that its net income would be 7.7% lower, the price of its stock dropped $3.875 per share in one day. Conversely, when St. Regis Paper noted that its net income was 20% greater than expected, its price increased $3 per share in one day.

Net income also provides an indication of the amount of dividends that a company can distribute. The higher the income level, the more likely it be-

comes that dividends can be maintained or raised. In addition, net income leads to a growth in retained earnings.

In this chapter we will discuss the issues pertaining to the reporting of net income for a corporation. In addition, we will explain the accounting for dividends and retained earnings.

CORPORATION INCOME STATEMENT AND INCOME TAXES

The income statement for a corporation includes essentially the same sections as an income statement for a proprietorship or a partnership. **The major difference is that an additional section is required before net income for income taxes.** The following condensed income statement for Leads Inc. illustrates a typical presentation.

Income statement with income taxes

LEADS INC.
Income Statement
For the Year Ended December 31, 1987

Sales	$800,000
Cost of goods sold	600,000
Gross profit	200,000
Operating expenses	50,000
Income from operations	150,000
Other revenues and gains	10,000
Other expenses and losses	4,000
Income before income taxes	156,000
Income tax expense	**46,800**
Net income	$109,200

Unlike a proprietorship or a partnership, a corporation is considered a separate entity for taxation purposes. As a result, income taxes or income tax expense must be reported on Leads Inc.'s income statement.

EXPANSION OF THE INCOME STATEMENT

The income statements that you studied in earlier chapters provide considerable insight into a company's income-related activities. In studying an income statement, the user may ask: (1) Are the results typical for this company? (2) Are the results a reasonable indicator of the company's future earnings?

To provide answers to these questions, accountants have concluded that additional sections should be added to the income statement to report material items not typical of regular operations. These items are reported in the

income statement immediately before net income. The nontypical items include (1) discontinued operations, (2) extraordinary items, and (3) changes in accounting principle. Each item reported in the income statement should be carefully explained in the notes to the financial statements. The income statement should also report the income tax expense or savings applicable to each item, as explained in the following section.

INTRAPERIOD TAX ALLOCATION

Intraperiod tax allocation refers to the procedure of associating income taxes with the specific item that directly affects the income taxes for the period. Under intraperiod tax allocation, the applicable income tax expense or tax saving is shown for income before income taxes and each of the three nontypical items identified above. Intraperiod tax allocation provides statement users with informative disclosure as to the income tax effects on these components of net income (loss). The general concept is "let the tax follow the income or loss."

To illustrate the importance of intraperiod tax allocation, we will first show the misleading results that may occur when intraperiod tax allocation is not followed. Assume that Dale Realty Corporation has income before income tax of $250,000, an extraordinary loss from a flood of $80,000, and, therefore, taxable income of $170,000. Both the extraordinary loss and taxable income are subject to a 30% tax rate. Without intraperiod tax allocation, the income statement will show:

Without tax allocation

(Partial Income Statement)

	Without tax allocation
Income before income taxes	$250,000
Income tax expense ($170,000 × 30%)	51,000
Income before extraordinary item	199,000
Extraordinary loss from flood	80,000
Net income	$119,000

This presentation is misleading because the income taxes do not follow the income or loss. The tax effects of income before income taxes and the extraordinary loss have been combined in reporting income tax expense of $51,000. Thus, income tax expense is understated $24,000 (30% × $80,000), and the effect of the extraordinary loss on net income is overstated by the same amount.

Under intraperiod tax allocation, the tax rate of 30% is applied to income before income taxes of $250,000 to show income taxes of $75,000, and the extraordinary item of $80,000 is reported net of the $24,000 tax saving, as shown on the next page.

Note that net income remains unchanged at $119,000 when intraperiod tax allocation is applied. However, intraperiod tax allocation matches the tax to the items that affect the tax, correcting the deficiencies of the first presentation.

(Partial Income Statement)

	With tax allocation
Income before income taxes	$250,000
Income tax expense ($250,000 × 30%)	75,000
Income before extraordinary item	175,000
Extraordinary loss from flood, net of $24,000 income tax saving	56,000
Net income	$119,000

DISCONTINUED OPERATIONS

During its financial crisis in the early 1980s, Chrysler Corporation sold its profitable defense division (Chrysler Defense Inc.) to General Dynamics Corporation for $348.5 million in cash to obtain needed working capital for its automobile business. In its income statement, Chrysler was required to report the effects of terminating this segment of its business as "discontinued operations," separately from the results of its continuing operations.

Discontinued operations refers to the disposal of a significant segment of a business, such as the cessation of an entire activity or the elimination of a major class of customers. Thus, the decision by the Singer Co. to end its manufacture and sale of computers and the decision to close all overseas offices and terminate all foreign sales were both reported as discontinued operations. On the other hand, the phasing out of a model or part of a line of business is not considered to be a disposal of a segment. For example, Ford Motor Company's termination of the Edsel automobile because of poor sales and Boeing's decision to stop production of its 727 planes because of the introduction of its 767 jumbo jets did not qualify as discontinued operations, because the two companies continued to sell automobiles and airplanes, respectively.

When the disposal of a significant segment occurs, the income statement should report both income from continuing operations and income (loss) from discontinued operations. **The income (loss) from discontinued operations consists of the income (loss) from operations and the gain (loss) on disposal of the segment.** To illustrate, assume that Acro Energy Inc. has revenues of $2.5 million and expenses of $1.7 million from continuing operations in 1987, and therefore, has income before income taxes of $800,000. During 1987 the company discontinued and sold its unprofitable chemical division. The loss in 1987 from chemical operations (net of $60,000 taxes) was $140,000 and the loss on disposal of the chemical division (net of $30,000 taxes) was $70,000. Assuming a 30% tax rate on income before income taxes, the income statement presentation is shown on the top of the next page.

Note that the caption "Income from continuing operations" is used and that a section "Discontinued operations" is added. **Within the new section, both the operating loss and the gain on disposal are reported net of applicable taxes.** This presentation clearly indicates the separate effects of continuing operations and discontinued operations on net income.

Statement presentation of discontinued operations

ACRO ENERGY INC.
Partial Income Statement
For the Year Ended December 31, 1987

Income before income taxes		$800,000
Income tax expense		240,000
Income from continuing operations		560,000
Discontinued operations		
Loss from operations of chemical division, net of $60,000 income tax saving	$140,000	
Loss from disposal of chemical division, net of $30,000 income tax saving	70,000	210,000
Net income		$350,000

EXTRAORDINARY ITEMS

Extraordinary items are events and transactions that are: (1) **unusual in nature,** and (2) **infrequent in occurrence.** To be considered unusual, the item should be abnormal and be only incidentally related to the customary activities of the entity. To be regarded as infrequent, the event or transaction should not be reasonably expected to recur in the foreseeable future. Both criteria must be evaluated in terms of the environment in which the entity operates. Thus, Weyerhaeuser Co. reported the $36 million in damages to its timberland caused by the eruption of Mount St. Helens as an extraordinary item because the event was both unusual and infrequent. In contrast, Florida Citrus Company does not report frost damage to its citrus crop as an extraordinary item because such frost damage is not viewed as infrequent. The following illustrate the appropriate classification of extraordinary and ordinary items.

Examples of extraordinary and ordinary items

Extraordinary	Ordinary
1. Effects of major casualties (acts of God), if rare in the area.	1. Effects of major casualties (acts of God), frequent in the area.
2. Expropriation of property by a foreign government.	2. Write-down of inventories or write-off of receivables.
3. Effects of a newly enacted law or regulation such as a condemnation action on company property by a governmental agency.	3. Losses attributable to labor strikes.
	4. Gains or losses from sales of property, plant, or equipment.

Extraordinary items are reported net of taxes in a separate section of the income statement immediately below discontinued operations. To illustrate, assume that in 1987 a revolutionary foreign government expropriated property held as an investment by Acro Energy Inc. If the loss is $70,000 and the applicable income tax rate is 30%, the income statement presentation is as follows:

Statement presentation of extraordinary item

ACRO ENERGY INC.
Partial Income Statement
For the Year Ended December 31, 1987

Income before income taxes		$800,000
Income tax expense		240,000
Income from continuing operations		560,000
Discontinued operations		
Loss from operations of chemical division, net of $60,000 income tax saving	$140,000	
Loss from disposal of chemical division, net of $30,000 income tax saving	70,000	210,000
Income before extraordinary item		350,000
Extraordinary item		
Expropriation of investment, net of $21,000 income tax saving		**49,000**
Net income		$301,000

As illustrated, the caption, Income before extraordinary item is added immediately before the section for the extraordinary item. This presentation clearly indicates the effect of the extraordinary item on net income.

If a transaction or event meets one (but not both) of the criteria for an extraordinary item, it is reported under either other revenues and gains or other expenses and losses at its gross amount (not net of tax). This is true, for example, of gains (losses) resulting from the sale of property, plant, and equipment, as explained in Chapter 11.

CHANGE IN ACCOUNTING PRINCIPLE

To enhance their comparability, financial statements are expected to be prepared on a basis **consistent** with that used for the preceding period. That is, where a choice of accounting principles is available, the principle initially chosen should be consistently applied from period to period. A **change in an accounting principle** occurs when the principle used in the current year is different from the one used in the preceding year. A change is permitted, when (1) management can show that the new principle is preferable to the old principle, and (2) the effects of the change are clearly disclosed in the income statement. Examples of a change in accounting principle include a change in depreciation methods (e.g., declining-balance to straight-line) and a change in inventory costing methods (e.g., FIFO to average cost). The effect of a change in an accounting principle on net income may be significant. Bethlehem Steel Corporation recently changed its method of accounting for depreciation. As a result, the company reported a $127.2 million increase in prior years' earnings in its current year's income statement.

When a change in an accounting principle has occurred,

1. The new principle should be used in reporting the results of operations of the current year.

2. The cumulative effect of the change on all prior year income statements should be disclosed net of applicable taxes in a special section immediately preceding net income.

To illustrate, assume that at the beginning of 1987, Acro Energy Inc. changes from the straight-line method to the sum-of-the-years'-digits method for depreciation on equipment that was purchased on January 1, 1984 for $120,000 and was expected to last 5 years with no salvage value. Annual depreciation charges under the two methods to the date of the change are as follows:

Computation of cumulative effect

Year	New Depreciation Method Sum-of-the-Years'-Digits	Old Depreciation Method Straight-Line	Cumulative Effect (Difference)
1984	$40,000*	$24,000**	**$16,000**
1985	32,000	24,000	**8,000**
1986	24,000	24,000	—
	$96,000	$72,000	**$24,000**

* $120,000 × 5/15
** $120,000 ÷ 5

In the 1987 income statement, depreciation is reported under the new method at $16,000 ($120,000 × 2/15). The cumulative effect of the change in accounting principle is $24,000 and, assuming a 30% tax rate, the net of tax effect is $16,800 ($24,000 × 70%). The income statement presentation is as follows:

Statement presentation of cumulative effect of change in accounting principle

ACRO ENERGY INC.
Partial Income Statement
For the Year Ended December 31, 1987

Income before income taxes		$800,000
Income tax expense		240,000
Income from continuing operations		560,000
Discontinued operations		
Loss from operations of chemical division, net of $60,000 income tax saving	$140,000	
Loss from disposal of chemical division, net of $30,000 income tax saving	70,000	210,000
Income before extraordinary item and cumulative effect of change in accounting principle		350,000
Extraordinary item		
Expropriation of investment, net of $21,000 income tax saving		49,000
Cumulative effect of change in accounting principle		
Effect on prior years of change in depreciation method, net of $7,200 income tax saving		**16,800**
Net income		$284,200

In this case the caption, Income before extraordinary item and cumulative effect of change in accounting principle, is inserted immediately following

the effects of discontinued operations. This presentation clearly indicates the cumulative effect of the change on prior years' income.

EARNINGS PER SHARE

Earnings per share data are frequently reported in the financial press and are widely used by stockholders and potential investors in evaluating the profitability of a company. Investors especially attempt to link earnings per share to the market price per share.[1] **Earnings per share (EPS)** indicates the net income earned by each share of outstanding common stock. Thus, **earnings per share is reported only for common stock.** The formula for computing earnings per share is as follows:

Earnings per share formula

Net Income ÷ Weighted Average Common Shares Outstanding = Earnings per Share

For example, if Modem Inc. has net income of $200,000 and a weighted average of 50,000 shares of common stock outstanding for the year, earnings per share is $4 ($200,000 ÷ 50,000).

Because of the importance of earnings per share (EPS), most companies are required to report it on the face of the income statement. Generally this amount is simply reported below net income on the statement. For Modem Inc. the presentation would be:

Basic earnings per share disclosure

Net income	$200,000
Earnings per share	$ 4.00

When the income statement contains any of the three additional sections described earlier in the chapter, EPS should be disclosed for each component. Assuming that Acro Energy Inc. had a weighted average of 100 thousand shares of common stock outstanding during the year, the additional EPS disclosures for the income statement shown on page 623 would be as shown at the top of the next page.

These disclosures enable the decision maker to recognize the effects on EPS of income from continuing operations, as distinguished from income or loss from material items not typical of regular operations. Earnings per share from continuing operations is generally the most useful per share amount, because it represents the results of continuing and ordinary business activity. Thus, it provides the best basis for predicting future operating results.

[1]The ratio of the earnings per share to the market price per share is referred to as the *price-earnings ratio*. This ratio is reported daily in the *Wall Street Journal* and other newspapers for common stocks listed on major stock exchanges.

Net income	$284,200
Earnings per share	
Income from continuing operations	$5.60
Loss from discontinued operations	(2.10)
Income before extraordinary item and cumulative effect of change in accounting principle	3.50
Extraordinary loss	(.49)
Cumulative effect of change in accounting principle	(.17)
Net income	$2.84

Additional earnings per share disclosures

EARNINGS PER SHARE—ADDITIONAL COMPLICATIONS

The computation of earnings per share may involve one or all of the following: (1) weighted average shares outstanding, (2) preferred stock dividends, and (3) complex capital structures.

WEIGHTED AVERAGE SHARES OUTSTANDING

If there has been any change in the number of shares of common stock outstanding during the year, the weighted average shares outstanding should be used in computing EPS. The weighted average shares are computed by determining the time a given number of shares is outstanding during the period. To illustrate, assume that Rally Inc. had 100,000 shares of common stock outstanding on January 1 and issued an additional 10,000 shares of stock on October 1. The weighted average number of shares of stock for the year is computed as follows:[2]

100,000 shares × 9/12 of a year	75,000
110,000 shares × 3/12 of a year	27,500
Weighted average shares outstanding	102,500

Computation of weighted average shares outstanding

The weighted average is used because the issuance or purchase of stock changes the amount of net assets that is available during the period on which to earn revenues.

PREFERRED STOCK DIVIDENDS

Earnings per share relates to earnings per share of **common stock.** When a corporation has both preferred and common stock outstanding, the current

[2]An alternative acceptable computation of weighted average shares outstanding is:

100,000 × 12/12 =	100,000	shares outstanding for a full year.
10,000 × 3/12 =	2,500	shares outstanding for three months annualized.
	102,500	Total weighted average shares outstanding.

year's dividend declared on preferred stock is subtracted from net income to arrive at income available to common stockholders.[3] The formula for computing EPS then becomes:

Expanded earnings per share formula

Net Income Minus Preferred Dividends	÷	Weighted Average of Common Shares Outstanding	=	Earnings Per Share

To illustrate, assume that Rally Inc. reports net income of $211,000 on its 102,500 weighted average common shares. During the year it also declares a $6,000 dividend on its preferred stock. Earnings per share is $2 [($211,000 − $6,000) ÷ 102,500]. If the preferred stock is cumulative, the dividend for the current year is deducted whether or not it is declared.

COMPLEX CAPITAL STRUCTURE

When a corporation has securities that may be converted into common stock, which, if converted, would reduce or dilute earnings per share, the corporation is said to have a **complex capital structure.** Two examples of such securities are convertible bonds and convertible preferred stock. The adverse effect that these securities can have on EPS is significant and, more importantly, unexpected unless financial statements in some manner call attention to the potential dilutive effect.

Two earnings per share figures are computed and reported when convertible securities have a material dilutive effect on EPS.[4] The first EPS figure, referred to as **primary earnings per share** is based on the weighted average common shares outstanding plus shares referred to as common stock equivalents. Common stock equivalents are securities that will probably be converted into common shares. For example, convertible preferred stock might be classified as a common stock equivalent if it is likely to be converted into common stock. Special tests are used to determine whether the convertible security is in substance equivalent to common stock.

The second EPS figure, referred to as **fully diluted earnings per share,** assumes the maximum dilution possible. It reflects the dilution in earnings per share that would occur if all dilutive securities were converted into common shares. Potentially dilutive securities that are not considered a common stock equivalent for purposes of computing primary earnings per share are included for purposes of computing fully diluted earnings per share. Thus, fully diluted earnings per share is lower than or equal to primary earnings per share. The following excerpt from the income statement of the Hartmarx Corporation illustrates the statement presentation of primary and fully diluted earnings per share.

[3] If cumulative preferred stock exists and a net loss occurs, the current dividend requirement is added to the loss.

[4] The profession in *APB Opinion No. 15,* "Earnings Per Share" (New York: AICPA, 1969), considers material dilutive effect to exist when the potential dilution to earnings per share is 3% or more.

Hartmarx Corporation	
Net income (in thousands)	$41,735
Earnings per share	
Primary	$3.36
Fully diluted	$3.14

Primary and fully diluted earnings per share disclosure

The computations for computing primary and fully diluted earnings per share are complex; they are discussed extensively in advanced accounting courses.

DIVIDENDS

A dividend is a distribution by a corporation to its stockholders on a pro rata (equal) basis. Potential buyers and sellers of a corporation's stock are very interested in a company's dividend policies and practices. Dividends may take four forms: cash, property, scrip (promissory note to pay cash), or (capital) stock. Cash dividends, which predominate in practice, and stock dividends, which are declared with some frequency, will be the focus of discussion in this chapter.

One measure of a company's dividend policy is its **payout ratio,** which is calculated by dividing cash dividends by net income. Thus, if dividends are $20,000 and net income is $50,000, the payout ratio is 40% ($20,000 ÷ $50,000). Payout ratios vary considerably among different types of companies, depending upon the stability of income and the need for additional funds to finance expansion or research and development. For a public utility, such as Pacific Gas and Electric, a payout ratio of 60% is typical, whereas for high-technology companies such as Apple Computer or Cerberonics (advanced weapons design), the ratio is often less than 10% and in many cases, zero. These latter companies are often referred to as **growth stock companies** because their management uses all available funds to meet expanding business opportunities.

Dividends may be expressed as a percentage of the par or stated value of the stock or as a dollar amount per share. In the financial press, dividends are generally reported quarterly as a dollar amount per share. For example, Chrysler Corporation at one time raised its quarterly dividend 33% to 20 cents a share from the 15 cents set three months earlier.

CASH DIVIDENDS

A **cash dividend** is a pro rata distribution of cash to stockholders. For a cash dividend to be paid, a corporation must have

1. **Unrestricted retained earnings.** The legality of a cash dividend depends on state corporation laws. In general, cash dividends based on

retained earnings are legal, and distributions based on common stock (legal capital) are illegal. Statutory provisions vary considerably with respect to cash dividends based on paid-in capital in excess of par or stated value, but surprisingly, many states permit such dividends. A dividend based on paid-in capital is termed a **liquidating dividend,** because the amount originally paid in by stockholders is being reduced or "paid back."

2. **Adequate cash.** The legality of a dividend does not indicate a company's ability to pay a dividend. For example, a company such as UAL, with a cash balance of $51.6 million and retained earnings of $814.4 million, could legally declare a dividend of $814.4 million. However, if it attempted to pay the dividend, it would need to raise additional cash through the sale of other assets or through additional financing. It follows that before declaring a cash dividend, the board of directors must carefully consider both current and future demands on the company's cash resources. In some cases, maturing obligations may make a cash dividend inappropriate; in other cases, a major plant expansion program may warrant only a relatively small dividend.
3. **Declared dividends.** The board of directors has full authority to determine the amount of income to be distributed in the form of a dividend and the amount to be retained in the business. Dividends do not accrue like interest on a note payable and they are not a liability until declared.

The amount and timing of a dividend are important issues for management that should be considered carefully. The payment of a large cash dividend could lead to liquidity problems for the enterprise. Conversely, a small dividend may cause unhappiness among stockholders who expect to receive a reasonable cash payment from the company on a periodic basis.

ENTRIES FOR CASH DIVIDENDS

Three dates are important in connection with dividends: (1) the declaration date, (2) the record date, and (3) the payment date. Normally, there is a time span of two to four weeks between each date. As explained below, accounting entries are required on two of the dates—the declaration date and the payment date.

On the **declaration date,** the board of directors formally declares (authorizes) the cash dividend and announces it to stockholders. The declaration of a cash dividend commits the corporation to a binding legal obligation that cannot be rescinded. Thus, an entry is required to recognize the decrease in Retained Earnings and the increase in the liability, Dividends Payable, that has occurred. To illustrate, assume that on December 1, 1987, the directors of Media General declare a 50¢ per share cash dividend on 100,000 shares of $10 par value common stock. The dividend is $50,000 (100,000 × 50¢), and the entry to record the declaration is:

Dec.	1	Retained Earnings	50,000	
		Dividends Payable		50,000
		(To record declaration of cash dividend)		

Dividends Payable is a current liability because it will normally be paid within the next several months. Instead of debiting Retained Earnings, the account **Dividends** may be debited. This account provides additional information in the ledger. For example, a company may have separate dividend accounts for each class of stock. When a dividend account is used, its balance is transferred to Retained Earnings at the end of the year by a closing entry. Consequently, the effect of the declaration is the same; retained earnings is decreased and a current liability is increased. For homework problems, you should use the Retained Earnings account for recording declarations.

The **record date** marks the time when ownership of the outstanding shares is determined for dividend purposes from the stockholders' records maintained by the corporation. The time interval between the declaration date and the record date enables the corporation to update its stock ownership records. Between the declaration date and record date, the number of shares outstanding should remain the same. Thus, the purpose of the record date is to identify the persons or entities that will receive the dividend, not to determine the amount of the dividend liability. For Media General, the record date is December 22. No entry is required on this date because the corporation's liability recognized on the declaration date is unchanged.

On the **payment date,** dividend checks are mailed to the stockholders and the payment of the dividend is recorded. Assuming that the payment date is January 20 for Media General, the entry on that date is:

Jan.	20	Dividends Payable	50,000	
		Cash		50,000
		(To record payment of cash dividend)		

Note that payment of the dividend reduces both current assets and current liabilities but has no effect on stockholders' equity. The cumulative effect of the declaration and payment of a cash dividend on a company's financial statements is to decrease both stockholders' equity and total assets.

STOCK DIVIDENDS

A **stock dividend** is a pro rata distribution of the corporation's own stock to stockholders. While a cash dividend is paid in cash, a stock dividend is paid in stock. **A stock dividend results in a decrease in retained earnings and an increase in paid-in capital.** Unlike a cash dividend, a stock dividend does not decrease total stockholders' equity or total assets.

To illustrate a stock dividend, assume that you have a 2% ownership interest in Cetus Inc. by virtue of owning 20 of its 1,000 shares of common stock. In a 10% stock dividend (100 shares), you would receive two shares (10% of 20 shares) but your ownership interest would remain at 2% (22 ÷ 1100). You now own more shares of stock but your ownership interest has not changed. Moreover, no cash is disbursed and no liabilities have been assumed by the corporation. What then are the purposes and benefits of a stock dividend?

Corporations issue stock dividends generally for one or more of the following reasons:

1. To satisfy stockholders' dividend expectations without distributing cash.
2. To increase the marketability of its stock by increasing the number of shares outstanding and thereby decreasing the market price per share. Decreasing the market price of the stock makes it easier for smaller investors to purchase the shares.
3. To emphasize that a portion of stockholders' equity has been permanently reinvested in the business and therefore is unavailable for cash dividends.

The size of the stock dividend and the value to be assigned to each dividend share for accounting purposes are determined by the board of directors when the dividend is declared. The per share amount to be recorded must be at least equal to the par or stated value of the shares in order to meet statutory requirements. In most cases, however, the directors use the current **fair market value** of the stock, as required by the accounting profession.[5]

ENTRIES FOR STOCK DIVIDENDS

To illustrate the accounting for stock dividends, assume that Medland Corporation has a balance of $300,000 in retained earnings and declares a 10% stock dividend on its 50,000 shares of $10 par value common stock. The current fair market value of its stock is $15 per share. The number of shares to be issued is 5,000 (10% × 50,000) and the total amount to be debited to Retained Earnings is $75,000 (5,000 × $15). The entry to record this transaction at the declaration date is as follows:

Retained Earnings	75,000	
Common Stock Dividends Distributable		50,000
Paid-in Capital in Excess of Par		25,000
(To record declaration of 10% stock dividend)		

Retained Earnings is debited for the fair market value of the stock issued; Common Stock Dividends Distributable is credited for the par value of the dividend shares (5,000 × $10); and the excess over par ($5 × 5,000) is credited to an additional paid-in capital account. Common Stock Dividends Distributable is a stockholders' equity account; it is not a liability because assets will not be used to pay the dividend. If a balance sheet is prepared before the dividend shares are issued, the distributable account is reported in paid-in capital as an addition to common stock issued as shown below:

Statement presentation of common stock dividends distributable

Paid-in capital		
Common stock	$500,000	
Common stock dividends distributable	**50,000**	$550,000

When the dividend shares are issued, Common Stock Dividends Distributable is debited and Common Stock is credited as follows:

[5]American Institute of Certified Public Accountants, Accounting Research and Terminology Bulletins, No. 43 (New York: AICPA, 1961), Ch. 7, par. 10.

Common Stock Dividends Distributable	50,000	
Common Stock		50,000
(To record issuance of 5,000 shares in a stock dividend)		

EFFECTS OF STOCK DIVIDENDS

Stock dividends change the composition of stockholders' equity because a portion of retained earnings is transferred to paid-in capital. However, total stockholders' equity remains the same. Stock dividends also have no effect on the par or stated value per share, but the number of shares outstanding increases and the book value per share decreases. These effects are shown below for the Medland Corporation.

Stock dividend effects

Stockholders' equity	Before Dividend	After Dividend
Paid-in capital		
Common stock, $10 par	$500,000	$550,000
Paid-in capital in excess of par	—	25,000
Total paid-in capital	500,000	575,000
Retained earnings	300,000	225,000
Total stockholders' equity	**$800,000**	**$800,000**
Outstanding shares	**50,000**	**55,000**
Book value per share	**$ 16.00**	**$ 14.55**

Occasionally a stock dividend may be quite large. If the fair market value of the stock were used in such cases, retained earnings could be quickly eliminated. Consequently, when a stock dividend is equal to or greater than 20–25% of the stock outstanding, par value instead of market value is assigned to the dividend shares. As a result, no increase in paid-in capital in excess of par value occurs.

STOCK SPLITS

A **stock split**, like a stock dividend, involves the issuance of additional shares of stock to stockholders according to their percentage ownership. However, a stock split results in a reduction in the par or stated value per share. The purpose of a stock split is to increase the marketability of the stock by lowering its market value per share. This, in turn, makes it easier for the corporation to issue additional stock. The effect of a split on market value is generally inversely proportional to the size of the split. For example, after a 4 for 1 stock split, the market value of IBM stock fell from $284 to approximately $71. In announcing the split, the chief executive of IBM said, "We want to make our stock more attractive to the small investor."

In a stock split, the number of shares is increased in the same proportion that par or stated value is decreased. For example, in a 2 for 1 split, one share

of $10 par value stock is exchanged for two shares of $5 par value stock. Such a split does not have any effect on total paid-in capital, retained earnings, or total stockholders' equity. The effect of the split on the stockholders' equity accounts is limited entirely to disclosure of the new par or stated value and the new number of shares now outstanding. **Thus, it is not necessary to formally journalize a stock split, since adequate disclosure can be made by a memorandum notation in the capital stock account.**

Some confusion exists as to the distinction between a stock split and a stock dividend. This is especially true when a 2 for 1 split of par value stock is compared with a 100% stock dividend on par value stock. There are many similarities. Both events will cause an identical increase in the number of shares outstanding and a corresponding decrease in market value. In addition, neither event affects total stockholders' equity, the relative equity of each stockholder, or total assets.

There are, however, significant differences between stock splits and stock dividends. A stock split may occur in the absence of retained earnings, whereas a stock dividend usually can be declared only when retained earnings are present. The two events also have different effects on the following items:

Effects of stock splits and stock dividends differentiated

Item	Stock Split	Stock Dividend
Total paid-in capital	No change	Increase
Total retained earnings	No change	Decrease
Total par value (common stock)	No change	Increase
Par value per share	Decrease	No change

PRIOR PERIOD ADJUSTMENTS

Suppose that after the books have been closed and the financial statements have been issued, a corporation discovers that a material error has been made in reporting net income. How should this situation be recorded in the accounts and reported in the financial statements? The correction of this error is known as a **prior period adjustment.** As such, the correction is made directly to Retained Earnings and not to any current income statement account. The correction is then reported in the current year's retained earnings statement as an **adjustment of the beginning balance of Retained Earnings.**

To illustrate, assume that General Microwave in 1987 discovers that it understated depreciation expense in 1985 by $300,000 as a result of a computational error. The entry to correct for this error, assuming all tax effects are ignored, is as follows:

Retained Earnings	300,000	
Accumulated Depreciation		300,000
(To adjust for depreciation error in a prior period)		

A debit to an income statement account in 1987 would be incorrect because the adjustment pertains to a prior year.

The presentation of the prior period adjustment in the 1987 retained earnings statement of General Microwave, assuming a beginning balance of $800,000, is as follows:

Retained earnings, January 1, as reported	$800,000
Correction for understatement of depreciation in prior period	300,000
Retained earnings, January 1, as adjusted	$500,000

Statement presentation of prior period adjustment

Normally, any errors made in a given year are discovered and corrected before the financial statements for that year are issued. Thus, prior period adjustments occur infrequently. Nevertheless, they are required at times. For example, Saxon Industries, Inc., upon discovering that the inventory it reported in an earlier period was overstated by $24 million, recorded a prior period adjustment to its retained earnings balance in the current year.

RETAINED EARNINGS APPROPRIATIONS

Corporations sometimes segregate retained earnings into two categories—appropriated and unappropriated. **Appropriated retained earnings** indicates that a portion of retained earnings is currently unavailable for dividend declarations. In contrast, **unappropriated retained earnings** is the portion of retained earnings that is available for dividend declarations. Appropriations are sometimes required by state law or contractual provisions. In addition, they may be made voluntarily by management.

ACCOUNTING ENTRIES

The accounting effects of an appropriation are limited entirely to the retained earnings section of stockholders' equity. The authorization of the appropriation results in a debit to Retained Earnings and a credit to a specified appropriation account. After the appropriation has served its purpose, the board of directors should authorize its return to an unappropriated status. At this time, the specified appropriation account is debited and Retained Earnings is credited.

To illustrate, assume that when Hendricks Inc. has a balance of $900,000 in Retained Earnings, the directors authorize a $100,000 appropriation for contingencies because the company is a defendant in a lawsuit whose outcome is uncertain. The entry to record the authorization is:

Retained Earnings	100,000	
Appropriation for Contingencies		100,000
(To record authorization of appropriation)		

The appropriation cannot be used to pay any damages that might be sustained when the suit is settled. However, the appropriation may cause the directors to lower its dividend declarations by $100,000, and as a result, more cash may be available. Upon settlement of the lawsuit, the directors should

authorize the return of the appropriation to an unrestricted status. Assuming this action is taken, the entry is:

Appropriation for Contingencies	100,000	
Retained Earnings		100,000
(To record return of appropriation to unappropriated retained earnings)		

Appropriation accounts always have credit balances. Accordingly, appropriations do not represent cash or any other asset.

STATEMENT PRESENTATION

Appropriations are reported as part of retained earnings in the stockholders' equity section. The statement presentation for Hendricks Inc. immediately following the appropriation for contingencies explained above is:

Appropriation reported in financial statements

Retained earnings		
Appropriated for contingencies	$100,000	
Unappropriated	800,000	
Total retained earnings		$900,000

Note that appropriations are listed first and are considered part of total retained earnings. The amount designated as **unappropriated** is the balance in the retained earnings account.

Instead of the formalized presentation shown above, an appropriation may be disclosed entirely by a note to the balance sheet, as follows:

Appropriation disclosed in notes

Retained Earnings (see note 1)	$900,000
Note 1: Retained earnings are appropriated in the amount of $100,000 for contingencies.	

An insight into the real significance of appropriation accounts may be drawn from this method of presentation. An appropriation account is nothing more than a formalized note to the financial statements.

RETAINED EARNINGS STATEMENT

Many corporations prepare a retained earnings statement in order to explain the changes in **unappropriated retained earnings** during the year. The statement for Conally Inc. based on assumed data is as follows:

Retained earnings statement

CONALLY INC.		
Retained Earnings Statement		
For the Year Ended December 31, 1987		
Balance, January 1, as reported		$1,050,000
Correction for understatement of net income in prior period (inventory error)		50,000
Balance, January 1, as adjusted		1,100,000
Add: Net income		360,000
		1,460,000
Less: Cash dividends	$100,000	
Appropriation for bond redemption	200,000	300,000
Balance, December 31		$1,160,000

STOCKHOLDERS' EQUITY SECTION

The stockholders' equity section of Conally Inc. is presented below. The presentation is identical to the stockholders' equity section illustrated in Chapter

Comprehensive stockholders' equity section

CONALLY INC.		
Stockholders' equity		
Paid-in capital		
Capital stock		
9% Preferred stock, $100 par value, cumulative 10,000 shares authorized, 6,000 shares issued		$ 600,000
Common stock, no par, $5 stated value, 500,000 shares authorized, 400,000 shares issued and 390,000 outstanding	$2,000,000	
Common stock subscribed (20,000 shares)	100,000	
Common stock dividends distributable	50,000	2,150,000
Total capital stock		2,750,000
Additional paid-in capital		
In excess of par value—preferred stock	30,000	
In excess of stated value—common stock	800,000	
Donated capital	100,000	
Total additional paid-in capital		930,000
Total paid-in capital		3,680,000
Retained earnings		
Appropriated		
For bond redemption	200,000	
Unappropriated	1,160,000	
Total retained earnings		1,360,000
Total paid-in capital and retained earnings		5,040,000
Less: Treasury stock (10,000 common shares)		80,000
Total stockholders' equity		$4,960,000

15 except that (1) Common Stock Dividends Distributable is shown under paid-in capital, and (2) additional data are shown for retained earnings. The amount reported for unappropriated retained earnings is the December 31 balance shown in the retained earnings statement at the top of page 635.

SUMMARY OF STUDY OBJECTIVES

1. Income taxes are reported on the income statement after income before income taxes.

2. Intraperiod tax allocation refers to the procedure of associating income taxes with the specific item that directly affects the income taxes for the period.

3. Material items not typical of regular operations are reported in sections on the income statement immediately before net income. They include (1) discontinued operations, (2) extraordinary items, and (3) changes in accounting principle.

4. Earnings per share is computed by dividing net income by the weighted average number of common shares outstanding during the period.

5. A dividend is a distribution by a corporation to its stockholders on a pro rata (equal) basis. A cash dividend is a distribution paid in cash, whereas a stock dividend is one paid in stock. Cash dividends decrease total assets and stockholders' equity whereas stock dividends have no affect on these totals.

6. A prior period adjustment arises from an error in the financial statements of a prior period. A correction is reported in the current year's retained earnings statement as an adjustment of the beginning balance of retained earnings.

7. The accounting effects of an appropriation are limited entirely to the retained earnings section of stockholders' equity. The authorization of the appropriation results in a debit to Retained Earnings and a credit to a specified appropriation account.

GLOSSARY

Appropriated retained earnings, p. 633

Cash dividend, p. 627

Change in accounting principle, p. 622

Complex capital structure, p. 626

Discontinued operations, p. 620
Earnings per share, p. 624
Extraordinary items, p. 621
Fully diluted earnings per share, p. 626
Intraperiod tax allocation, p. 619
Liquidating dividend, p. 628
Primary earnings per share, p. 626
Prior period adjustment, p. 632
Stock dividend, p. 629
Stock split, p. 631
Unappropriated retained earnings, p. 633

DEMONSTRATION PROBLEM

At December 31, the ledger of the Dever Corporation shows the following stockholders' equity accounts:

Appropriation for Contingencies	$ 100,000
Common Stock, no par, $5 stated value, 1,000,000 shares authorized, 500,000 shares issued	2,500,000
Common Stock Dividends Distributable	250,000
Common Stock Subscribed, 30,000 shares	150,000
Donated Capital	200,000
Paid-in Capital from Treasury Stock	15,000
Paid-in Capital in Excess of Par Value—Preferred	300,000
Paid-in Capital in Excess of Stated Value—Common	500,000
Preferred Stock, $10 par, Noncumulative, 200,000 shares authorized, 60,000 shares issued	600,000
Retained Earnings (Unappropriated)	800,000
Treasury Stock—Common, 10,000 shares	90,000

INSTRUCTIONS

Prepare a stockholders' equity section.

SOLUTION TO DEMONSTRATION PROBLEM

DEVER CORPORATION

Stockholders' equity	
Paid-in capital	
Capital stock	
Prefered stock, $10 par, noncumulative 200,000 shares authorized, 60,000 shares issued	$ 600,000
Common stock, no par, $5 stated value, 1,000,000 shares authorized, 500,000 shares issued, 490,000 shares outstanding	2,500,000
Common stock subscribed	150,000
Common stock dividends distributable	250,000
Total capital stock	3,500,000

Additional paid-in capital		
In excess of par value – preferred stock	$300,000	
In excess of stated value – common stock	500,000	
From treasury stock	15,000	
Donated capital	200,000	
Total additional paid-in capital		1,015,000
Total paid-in capital		4,515,000
Retained earnings		
Appropriation for contingencies	100,000	
Unappropriated	800,000	
Total retained earnings		900,000
Total paid-in capital and retained earnings		5,415,000
Less: Treasury stock – common, 10,000 shares		90,000
Total stockholders' equity		$5,325,000

QUESTIONS

1. Doreen Nelson, who owns many investments in common stock, says, "I don't care what a company's net income is. The balance sheet tells me everything I need to know!" How would you respond to Doreen?

2. Define the term "intraperiod tax allocation." Why is this type of allocation important?

3. Why is it important to report discontinued operations separately from income from continuing operations?

4. You are considering investing in Perry Refrigeration, which reports 1987 earnings per share of $6.50 on income before extraordinary items, and $4.75 on net income. Which EPS figure would you consider most relevant to your investment decision? Why?

5. Iron Microphones, Inc. reported 1986 earnings per share of $3.26, and had no extraordinary items. In 1987, EPS on income before extraordinary items was $2.99, and EPS on net income was $3.49. Is this a favorable trend?

6. Indicate which of the following items would be reported as an extraordinary item in Larussa Corporation's income statement.
(a) Loss from damages caused by volcano eruption (Mount St. Helens).
(b) Loss from sale of temporary investments.
(c) Loss attributable to a labor strike.
(d) Loss caused when manufacture of a product was prohibited by the Food and Drug Administration.
(e) Loss from flood damage (the Black River floods every two to three years).
(f) Write-down of obsolete inventory.
(g) Expropriation of a factory by a foreign government.

7. When studying for an accounting test, a fellow student says, "Changes in accounting principle are reported in the retained earnings statement." Is your friend correct, or should he study harder?

8. Why must preferred stock dividends be subtracted from net income in computing earnings per share?

9. Jean Marie owns 100 shares of Yellow Bird Corporation. She tells you, "The corporation earned a net income of $1,000,000 and had 200,000 shares of common stock outstanding. That should be earnings per share of $5.00. But they reported primary earnings per share of $4.10 and fully diluted earnings per share of $3.69. What do these figures mean?" Explain the meaning of these EPS figures to Jean Marie.

10. What are the three conditions that must exist before a cash dividend is paid?

11. Three dates associated with Galena Company's cash dividend are May 1, May 15, and May 31. Discuss the significance of each date.

12. Contrast the effects of a cash dividend and a stock dividend on a corporation's balance sheet.

13. Jack Sims asks, "Since stock dividends don't change anything, why declare them?" What is your answer to Jack?

14. The Beil Corporation has 10,000 shares of $15 par value common stock outstanding when they announce a 3 for 1 stock split. Before the split, the stock had a market price of $150 per share. After the split, how many shares of stock will be outstanding, and what will be the approximate market price per share?

15. The board of directors is considering a stock split or a stock dividend. They understand that total stockholders' equity will remain the same under either action. However, they are not sure of the different effects of the two types of actions on other aspects of stockholders' equity. Explain the differences to the directors.

16. What is a prior period adjustment and how is it reported in the financial statements?

17. Kevin Sagers says, "Just because Timbers Corporation has Retained Earnings Appropriated for Plant Expansion of $200,000 does not mean they have $200,000 of cash set aside in a special fund." Do you agree? Explain.

18. If retained earnings of $150,000 is appropriated for contingencies, and the corporation suffers a loss of $140,000 on a lawsuit, what effect will the loss have on net income?

19. Amad Radha indicates that both the beginning and ending balances of retained earnings accounts are shown in the stockholders' equity section. Is he correct? Discuss.

EXERCISES

E16-1 For its fiscal year ending October 31, 1987, the Rachel Corporation reports the following partial data:

Income before income taxes	$640,000
Income tax expense (30% × $500,000)	150,000
Income before extraordinary items	490,000

Extraordinary losses		
From fire	$130,000	
From loss on sale of equipment	10,000	140,000
Net income		$350,000

The fire loss is considered an extraordinary item. The loss on sale of equipment is not an extraordinary item. The income tax rate is 30% on all items.

INSTRUCTIONS

(a) Prepare a correct income statement, beginning with income before income taxes.

(b) Why is the company prepared income statement misleading?

E16-2 The Davis Company has income from continuing operations of $210,000 for the year ended December 31, 1987. It also has the following items (before considering income taxes): (1) an extraordinary fire loss of $50,000, (2) a gain of $30,000 on the discontinuance of a division, (3) a cumulative change in an accounting principle that resulted in an increase in prior year's depreciation of $20,000, and (4) a correction of an error in last year's financial statements that resulted in a $15,000 understatement of 1986 net income. Assume all items are subject to income taxes at a 30% tax rate.

INSTRUCTIONS

(a) Prepare an income statement, beginning with income from continuing operations.

(b) Indicate the statement presentation of any item not included in (a) above.

E16-3 The Murray Corporation has a simple capital structure. At December 31, 1987, the company has outstanding $200,000 of $100 par value, 8%, preferred stock and $1,000,000 of $10 par value common stock. Murray's net income for the year is $300,000.

INSTRUCTIONS

Compute the earnings per share of common stock under the following independent situations. (Round to two decimals.)

(1) The dividend to preferred stockholders was declared, and there has been no change in the number of shares of common stock outstanding during the year.

(2) The dividend to preferred stockholders was declared, and 20,000 shares of common stock were issued on April 1, 1987.

(3) The dividend to preferred stockholders was not declared, and 30,000 shares of common stock were issued on July 1, 1987. The preferred stock is not cumulative.

(4) The dividend to preferred stockholders was not declared, and 10,000 shares of common treasury stock were held throughout the year. The preferred stock is cumulative.

E16-4 On January 1, Yarow Corporation had 73,000 shares of no par common stock issued and outstanding. The stock has a stated value of $5 per share. During the year, the following occurred:

Apr. 1	Issued 3,000 additional shares of common stock.
June 15	Declared a cash dividend of $1 per share to stockholders of record on June 30.
July 10	Paid the $1 cash dividend.
Dec. 1	Purchased 1,000 shares of common stock for the treasury.
Dec. 15	Declared a cash dividend on outstanding shares of $1.20 per share to stockholders of record on December 31.

INSTRUCTIONS

(a) Journalize the declaration and payment of dividends.

(b) Indicate the presentation of dividends in the financial statements prepared at December 31.

E16-5 On January 1, 1987, the Knight Corporation had $1,500,000 of common stock outstanding that was issued at par and retained earnings of $750,000. The company issued 50,000 shares of common stock at par on July 1 and earned net income of $400,000 for the year.

INSTRUCTIONS

(a) Journalize the declaration of a 10% stock dividend on December 10, 1987, for the following independent assumptions:

(1) Par value is $10 and market value is $15.

(2) Par value is $5 and market value is $20.

(b) What is total capital stock for assumption (1) above, assuming the dividend shares are not to be issued until 1988?

E16-6 On October 1, 1987, Valente Corporation's stockholders' equity is as follows:

Common stock $5 par value	$100,000
Paid-in capital in excess of par value	25,000
Retained earnings	75,000
Total stockholders' equity	$200,000

On October 1, Valente declares and distributes a 10% stock dividend when the market value of the stock is $12 per share.

INSTRUCTIONS

(a) Compute the book value per share (1) before the stock dividend, and (2) after the stock dividend. (Round to two decimals.)

(b) Indicate the balances in the three stockholders' equity accounts after the stock dividend has been completed.

E16-7 On January 1, 1987, the Wilson Corporation had the following retained earnings accounts: Retained Earnings (Unappropriated) $1,920,000; Appropriated for Plant Expansion $1,200,000; and Appropriated for Contingencies $500,000. In 1987, the following transactions and events occurred.

Feb. 15	A contractor is paid $800,000 for completing an addition to a building.
Apr. 15	The board of directors authorizes an $800,000 reduction in the appropriation for plant expansion.
June 1	Damages of $300,000 are paid on a legal suit for which an appropriation of $250,000 had been established.
July 15	The board of directors authorizes an increase of $200,000 in the appropriation for contingencies because of recent litigation against the company.
Oct. 15	The board of directors approve the construction of a $1,500,000 plant addition. They decide to increase the appropriation for plant expansion by $1,500,000.
Dec. 31	Net income for the year is $2,100,000. (Prepare the closing entry.)

INSTRUCTIONS

(a) Journalize the transactions and events.

(b) Post to the retained earnings accounts.

(c) Prepare the retained earnings subdivision of the stockholders' equity section of the balance sheet.

E16–8 During 1987, the Kittle Corporation had the following transactions and events:

1. Issued par value common stock for cash at par value.
2. Declared a cash dividend.
3. Established an appropriation for contingencies.
4. Completed a 3 for 1 stock split in which $15 par value stock was changed to $5 par value stock.
5. Declared a stock dividend when the market value was higher than par value.
6. Reduced the appropriation for plant expansion.
7. Issued the shares of common stock required by the stock dividend declaration in no. 5 above.
8. Paid the cash dividend declared in no. 2 above.
9. Issued par value common stock for cash above par value.

INSTRUCTIONS

Indicate the effect(s) of each of the foregoing items on the subdivisions of stockholders' equity. Present your answer in tabular form with the following columns. Use (I) for increase, (D) for decrease, and (NE) for no effect. Item 1 is given as an example.

	Paid-in Capital		Retained Earnings	
Item	Capital Stock	Additional	Unappropriated	Appropriated
1.	(I)	NE	NE	NE

E16–9 Before preparing financial statements for the current year, the chief accountant for the Daugherty Company discovered the following errors in the accounts:

1. The declaration and payment of a $25,000 cash dividend was recorded as a debit to Interest Expense $25,000 and a credit to Cash $25,000.
2. A 10% stock dividend (1,000 shares) was declared on the $10 par value stock when the market value per share was $15. The only entry made was: Retained Earnings (Dr.) $10,000 and Dividends Payable (Cr.) $10,000. The shares have not been issued.
3. The payment of damages in a lawsuit was recorded by debiting Appropriation for Contingencies $50,000 and crediting Cash $50,000.
4. A 4 for 1 stock split involving the issue of 400,000 shares of $5 par value common stock for 100,000 shares of $20 par value common stock was recorded as a debit to Retained Earnings $2,000,000 and a credit to Common Stock $2,000,000.

INSTRUCTIONS

Prepare the correcting entries at December 31.

E16–10 On January 1, 1987, Valex Corporation had two retained earnings accounts in its ledger: Retained Earnings $540,000, and Appropriation for Contingencies $100,000. During the year, Valex had the following selected transactions:

1. Declared cash dividends $120,000.
2. Corrected overstatement of 1986 net income because of depreciation error (net of taxes) $30,000.
3. Earned net income $310,000.
4. Transferred $25,000 from Appropriation for Contingencies to Unappropriated Retained Earnings because of a favorable outcome of a lawsuit against the company.

INSTRUCTIONS

Prepare a retained earnings statement for the year.

E16-11 The following accounts appear in the ledger of Omar Inc. after the books are closed at December 31, 1987:

Appropriation for Plant Expansion	$ 100,000
Common Stock, no par, $1 stated value, 400,000 shares authorized; 300,000 shares issued	300,000
Common Stock Subscribed, 50,000 shares	50,000
Common Stock Dividends Distributable	25,000
Donated Capital	120,000
Paid-in Capital in Excess of Stated Value of Common Stock	1,200,000
Preferred Stock, $5 par value, 8%, 40,000 shares authorized; 30,000 shares issued	150,000
Unappropriated Retained Earnings	650,000
Treasury Stock (10,000 common shares)	60,000
Paid-in Capital in Excess of Par—Preferred Stock	124,000

INSTRUCTIONS

Prepare a stockholders' equity section at December 31.

PROBLEMS

P16-1 The Trailblazer Corporation owns a number of travel agencies and a chain of motels in the Northwest. Its condensed operating results for 1987 show the following:

Operating revenues	$14,580,000
Operating expenses	10,600,000
Income from operations	$ 3,980,000

An additional analysis of the data indicate that the travel agencies are very profitable but the motel chain has been unprofitable. Through September 30, the motels lost $600,000 from operating revenues of $4,200,000 and operating expenses of $4,800,000. On October 1, the motel operation was discontinued and sold at a loss of $1,000,000 before taxes. The loss is not included in the operating results shown above. During the year, the corporation had interest expense of $80,000, which is not included in the operating results. In November, a condemnation action was taken against the company to obtain property for a new national park. As a result, the corporation suffered an extraordinary loss of $700,000 before taxes. The corporation is in a 30% tax bracket.

At December 31, Trailblazer has 400,000 shares of $1 par value common stock outstanding, of which 120,000 were issued on October 1.

INSTRUCTIONS

(a) Prepare a condensed income statement for the year.

(b) Compute all of the earnings per share amounts that should appear on the income statement. (Round to two decimals.)

P16-2 The income statement for the Decker Corporation, which was prepared by an inexperienced accountant, is as follows:

DECKER CORPORATION
Income Statement
For the Year Ended December 31, 1987

Net sales		$1,500,000
Cost of goods sold		800,000
Gross profit		700,000
Selling and administrative expenses	$250,000	
Loss from operation of discontinued division	100,000	350,000
Income from operations		350,000
Other revenues and gains		
Gain on sale of marketable securities	15,000	
Gain on sale of discontinued division	60,000	75,000
		425,000
Other expenses and losses		
Interest expense	10,000	
Fire loss	70,000	
Correction of overstatement of 1986 net income	40,000	120,000
Income before income taxes		305,000
Income tax expense (30%)		91,500
Net income		$ 213,500

Your analysis reveals the following:

1. All items are reported before income taxes except for income tax expense.
2. The income tax rate on all items and prior period adjustments is 30%.
3. In 1987, Decker changed its depreciation method from the straight-line method to the declining-balance method. The cumulative effect of the change on prior years was to decrease reported income before income taxes by $50,000. The cumulative effect was reported in the 1987 retained earnings statement as a prior period adjustment. Assume proper depreciation was reported in 1987.
4. The correction of 1986 net income resulted from a computational error that caused bad debt expense to be understated by $40,000.
5. The fire loss is considered extraordinary.
6. Selling and administrative expenses are understated $15,000 because of an error in computing bad debts expense at December 31, 1987.

INSTRUCTIONS

(a) Prepare a correct 1987 income statement for Decker Corporation.
(b) Present the earnings per share data that should appear on the income statement, assuming there are 100,000 shares of common stock outstanding throughout the year.

P16-3 On January 1, 1987, the Acquino Corporation had the following stockholders' equity accounts:

Common Stock ($10 par value, 500,000 shares authorized; 100,000 shares issued and outstanding)	$1,000,000
Paid-in Capital in Excess of Par Value	200,000
Appropriation for Plant Expansion	300,000
Retained Earnings	740,000

During the year, the following transactions occurred:

Jan. 15	Declared a $1 cash dividend to stockholders of record on January 31, payable February 15.
Feb. 15	Paid the dividend declared in January.
Apr. 15	Declared a 10% stock dividend to stockholders of record on April 30, distributable May 15. On April 15, the market price of the stock was $13 per share.
May 15	Issued the shares for the stock dividend.
July 1	Announced a 3 for 1 stock split. The market price per share prior to the announcement was $15. (Round the new par to $3.33.)
Oct. 1	Reacquired for cash 10,000 shares of stock for the treasury at $6 per share.
Nov. 1	Authorized a reduction of $50,000 in the appropriation for plant expansion.
Dec. 1	Declared a $.50 per share cash dividend to stockholders of record on December 15, payable January 10, 1988.
Dec. 31	Closed the credit balance of $350,000 in Income Summary to Retained Earnings.

INSTRUCTIONS

(a) Journalize the transactions.

(b) Prepare a stockholders' equity section at December 31.

P16-4 The stockholders' equity accounts of the Osburn Company at January 1, 1987, are as follows:

Common Stock, $5 par	$800,000
Preferred Stock, $100 par, 8%	300,000
Paid-in Capital in Excess of Par Value of Common Stock	200,000
Paid-in Capital in Excess of Par Value of Preferred Stock	200,000
Appropriation for Contingencies	100,000
Retained Earnings (Unappropriated)	500,000

During 1987, the company had the following transactions and events:

Mar. 1	Paid $25,000 in settlement of a lawsuit for which a $40,000 appropriation for contingencies had been established in 1986.
July 1	Declared an 8% cash dividend on preferred stock.
Aug. 1	Discovered a $12,000 overstatement of 1986 depreciation. Ignore income taxes.
Sept. 1	Paid the cash dividend declared on July 1 to preferred stockholders.
Dec. 1	Declared 10% stock dividend on common stock when the market value of the stock was $12 per share.
Dec. 31	Authorized reduction in Appropriation for Contingencies $40,000 and establishment of Appropriation for Plant Expansion of $50,000.
Dec. 31	Determined that net income for the year was $350,000. (Prepare the closing entry.)

INSTRUCTIONS

(a) Journalize the transactions and events.

(b) Prepare a retained earnings statement for the year.

(c) Prepare a stockholders' equity section at December 31, 1987.

P16-5 The Herdon Corporation was organized on January 1, 1987. It is authorized to issue 1,000,000 shares of $5 par value common stock and 100,000 shares of $20 par value 9% cumulative preferred stock. In 1987, the following events and transactions occurred.

Four hundred thousand shares of common stock were issued for cash at an average price of $8 per share. In September, a major stockholder died and the company purchased her 40,000 shares for the treasury at $9 per share. In December, one-half of the treasury shares were sold at $11 per share.

Fifty thousand shares of preferred stock were sold on a subscription basis at $25 per share. Prior to December 31, subscriptions to 30,000 shares were paid in full by subscribers and the shares were issued.

During the year, the board of directors took the following actions:

1. Accepted land as a donation from a municipality. The land had a fair market value of $200,000 at the time of the gift.
2. Authorized a $.50 per share cash dividend on common stock outstanding on December 31.
3. Established a $50,000 appropriation for contingencies because of pending legal suits.
4. Authorized the payment of a 9% cash dividend to preferred stockholders.

The income statement for the year shows income from continuing operations $451,000 and an extraordinary loss (net of 30% taxes) $51,000.

INSTRUCTIONS

(a) Prepare a retained earnings statement for the year ended December 31, 1987.

(b) Prepare a stockholders' equity section at December 31, 1987. (Hint: Preferred dividends are not paid on preferred stock subscribed.)

ALTERNATE PROBLEMS

P16-1A The Seabreeze Corporation owns a number of cruise ships and a chain of hotels. The hotels, which have not been profitable, were discontinued on September 1, 1987. The 1987 operating results for the company were as follows:

Operating revenues	$12,800,000
Operating expenses	8,600,000
Operating income	$ 4,200,000

Analysis discloses that these data include the operating results of the hotel chain, which were: operating revenues $3,200,000, and operating expenses $3,900,000. The hotels were sold at a gain of $300,000 before taxes. During the year, Seabreeze suffered an extraordinary fire loss of $800,000, before taxes. In 1987, the company incurred $100,000 of interest expense, which is not included in the operating results. The corporation is in the 30% income tax bracket.

Seabreeze Corporation had 450,000 shares of common stock outstanding on January 1, 1987, and issued an additional 150,000 shares on May 1, 1987.

INSTRUCTIONS

(a) Prepare a condensed income statement.

(b) Compute the earnings per share data that should appear in the income statement.

P16-2A The income statement for the Jeanne Corporation, which was prepared by an inexperienced accountant, is as follows:

JEANNE CORPORATION
Income Statement
For the Year Ended December 31, 1987

Net sales		$1,800,000
Cost of goods sold		1,000,000
Gross profit		800,000
Selling and administrative expenses		250,000
Operating income		550,000
Gain from operations of discontinued division		40,000
Income from operations		590,000
Other revenues and gains		
Gain on sale of equipment	$10,000	
Correction of overstatement of 1986 net income	20,000	
Other expenses and losses		
Interest expense	18,000	
Hurricane loss	80,000	
Loss on sale of discontinued division	50,000	118,000
Income before income taxes		472,000
Income tax expense (30%)		141,600
Net income		$ 330,400

Your analysis reveals the following:

1. All items are reported before income taxes except for income taxes expense.
2. The income tax rate on all items and prior period adjustments is 30%.
3. In 1987, Jeanne changed its depreciation method from the sum-of-the-years'-digits method to the straight-line method. The cumulative effect of the change on prior years was to increase reported net income by $30,000 before taxes. The cumulative effect of this change was reported in the 1987 retained earnings statement as a prior period adjustment. Assume proper depreciation was reported for 1987.
4. Selling and administrative expenses for 1987 are understated $20,000 because of an error in computing sales commissions expense at December 31, 1987.
5. The correction of 1986 net income resulted from a computational error that caused goodwill expense to be overstated by $20,000.
6. The hurricane loss is considered extraordinary.

INSTRUCTIONS

(a) Prepare a correct 1987 income statement for Jeanne Corporation.
(b) Present the earnings per share data that should appear on the income statement, assuming there are 100,000 shares of common stock outstanding throughout the year.

P16-3A On January 1, 1987, the Fernano Corporation had the following stockholders' equity accounts:

Common Stock ($5 par value, 1,000,000 shares authorized; 300,000 shares issued and outstanding)	1,500,000
Paid-in capital in excess of par value	300,000
Appropriation for contingencies	200,000
Retained earnings	800,000

During the year, the following transactions occurred:

Feb. 1 Declared a $.50 cash dividend to stockholders of record on February 15, payable March 1.

Mar. 1 Paid the dividend declared in February.

Apr. 1 Announced a 2 for 1 stock split. Prior to the split, the market price per share was $6.

July 1 Declared a 5% stock dividend to stockholders of record on July 15, distributable July 31. On July 1, the market price of the stock was $3 per share.

July 15 Issued the shares for the stock dividend.

Sept. 1 Reacquired for cash 20,000 shares of stock for the treasury at $3.20 per share.

Dec. 1 Declared a $.25 per share dividend to stockholders of record on December 15, payable January 5, 1988.

Dec. 10 Authorized a $100,000 increase in the appropriation for contingencies.

Dec. 31 Closed the credit balance of $300,000 in Income Summary to Retained Earnings.

INSTRUCTIONS

(a) Journalize the transactions.

(b) Prepare a stockholders' equity section at December 31.

P16–4A The stockholders' equity accounts of the Benjamin Company at January 1, 1987 are as follows:

Common Stock, $5 par	$700,000
Preferred Stock, 9%, $100 par	300,000
Paid-in Capital in Excess of Par Value of Common Stock	300,000
Paid-in Capital in Excess of Par Value of Preferred Stock	200,000
Appropriation for Contingencies	100,000
Retained Earnings (Unappropriated)	600,000

During 1987, the company had the following transactions and events:

Mar. 1 Paid $30,000 in settlement of a lawsuit for which a $45,000 appropriation for contingencies was established in 1986.

July 1 Declared a 9% cash dividend on preferred stock.

Aug. 1 Discovered $15,000 overstatement of 1986 depreciation. Ignore income taxes.

Sept. 1 Paid the cash dividend declared on July 1 to preferred stockholders.

Dec. 1 Declared 10% stock dividend on common stock when the market value of the stock was $12 per share.

Dec. 31 Authorized reduction in Appropriation for Contingencies of $45,000 and establishment of an appropriation for plant expansion of $40,000.

Dec. 31 Determined that net income for the year was $380,000. (Prepare the closing entry).

INSTRUCTIONS

(a) Journalize the transactions and events.

(b) Prepare a retained earnings statement for the year.

(c) Prepare a stockholders' equity section at December 31, 1987.

P16–5A The Bunker Corporation was organized on January 1, 1987. It is authorized to issue 1,000,000 shares of $5 par value common stock and 100,000 shares of $20 par value, 8%, cumulative preferred stock. In 1987, the following events and transactions occurred.

Four hundred thousand shares of common stock were issued for cash at an average price of $9 per share. In September, a major stockholder died and the company pur-

chased his 40,000 shares for the treasury at $10 per share. In December one-half of the treasury shares were sold at $13 per share.

Fifty thousand shares of preferred stock were sold on a subscription basis at $28 per share. Prior to December 31, subscriptions to 30,000 shares were paid in full by subscribers and the shares were issued.

During the year the board of directors took the following actions:

1. Accepted land as a donation from a municipality. The land had a fair market value of $100,000 at the time of the gift.
2. Authorized a $.50 share cash dividend on common stock outstanding on December 31.
3. Established a $60,000 appropriation for contingencies because of pending legal suits.
4. Authorized the payment of an 8% cash dividend to preferred stockholders.

The income statement for the year shows income from continuing operations $379,000, and an extraordinary gain (net of 30% taxes) $51,000. (Hint: Preferred dividends are not paid on preferred stock subscribed.)

INSTRUCTIONS

(a) Prepare a retained earnings statement for the year ended December 31, 1987.

(b) Prepare a stockholders' equity section at December 31, 1987.

DECISION CASE

General Dynamics develops, produces, and supports innovative, reliable, and highly sophisticated military and commercial products. In July of a recent year, the Corporation announced that its Quincy Shipbuilding Division (Quincy) will be closed following the completion of the Maritime Prepositioning Ship construction program.

Prior to discontinuance, the operating results of Quincy were: net sales $246.8 million, income from operations before income taxes $28.3 million, and income taxes $12.5 million. The Corporation's loss on disposition of Quincy was $5.0 million, net of $4.3 million income tax benefits.

From its other operating activities, General Dynamics' financial results were: net sales $8,163.8 million, cost of goods sold $6,958.8 million, and selling and administrative expenses $537.0 million. In addition, the Corporation had interest expense of $17.2 million and interest revenue of $3.6 million. Income taxes were $282.9 million.

General Dynamics had an average of 42.3 million shares of common stock outstanding during the year.

INSTRUCTIONS

(a) Prepare the income statement for the year, assuming that the year ended on December 31, 1987. Show earnings per share data on the income statement. All dollars should be stated in millions, except for per share amounts. For example, $8 million would be shown as $8.0.

(b) In the preceding year, Quincy's earnings were $51.6 million before income taxes of $22.8 million. For comparative purposes, General Dynamics reported earnings per share of $.61 from discontinued operations for Quincy in the preceding year.

1. What was the average number of common shares outstanding during the preceding year?
2. If earnings per share from continuing operations was $7.47, what was income from continuing operations during the preceding year? (Round to two decimals.)

CHAPTER 17

North Carolina State University

CHAPTER 17

LONG-TERM LIABILITIES

STUDY OBJECTIVES

After studying this chapter, you should be able to:

1. Explain why bonds are issued.
2. Prepare the entries when bonds are issued.
3. Contrast the effects of the straight-line and effective interest methods of amortizing bond discount and bond premium.
4. Describe the entries when bonds are redeemed or converted prior to maturity.
5. Indicate the entries required for a bond sinking fund.
6. Contrast the accounting for operating and capital leases.
7. Describe the accounting for deferred income taxes.
8. Identify the requirements for the financial statement presentation of long-term liabilities.

Imagine that you had to finance construction of Seabrook III, a nuclear power plant servicing much of New England, which in today's dollars could cost in excess of $4 billion. Long-term financing is desirable because refinancing the project on a year-by-year basis would be time consuming, if not risky, if financing suddenly became difficult to obtain. For long-term financing, enterprises may use either equity financing (usually common stock) or debt financing. Equity financing is available but common stockholders might not favor this source because of the decrease in earnings per share that would result. As an alternative, long-term debt, with its accompanying interest cost, is used by many large corporations. For example, United Air Lines has more than one and a half dollars of long-term debt ($2.9 billion) to every dollar of stockholders' equity ($1.8 billion) and Potomac Electric Power Company has a one to one ratio of long-term debt to equity.

Long-term liabilities (debt) are obligations that are expected to be paid beyond one year (or the operating cycle, whichever is longer) from the balance sheet date. In this chapter we will explain the accounting for the principal types of obligations reported in the long-term liability section of the balance sheet. These obligations may be in the form of bonds, long-term notes, lease liabilities, and deferred income taxes.

WHY ISSUE BONDS?

Bonds are a widely used type of long-term debt financing. Because bonds, like common stock, can be sold in small denominations (usually a thousand dollars), they can attract many investors. In contrast, the two other principal types of long-term debt financing, notes payable and leasing, usually involve one individual, a company, or a financial institution. Notes payable and leasing are therefore seldom sufficient to furnish the funds needed for plant expansion and major projects like Seabrook III. To obtain large amounts of long-term capital, corporate management usually must decide whether to issue bonds or to use equity financing.

From the standpoint of the corporation seeking long-term financing, bonds offer the following advantages over common stock.

1. **Stockholder control is not affected.** Bondholders do not have voting rights, so current stockholders retain full control of the company.
2. **Tax savings result.** Bond interest is deductible for tax purposes; dividends on stock are not. For example, if a bond pays 10% interest and the corporation is in the 30% tax bracket, the net cash cost to the corporation is only 7%. If a corporation pays a 10% cash dividend, the cash resources of the company are reduced by the full 10%.
3. **Income to common stockholders may increase.** If a company can earn more on borrowed funds than the interest cost on these funds, the income to common stockholders will increase. For example, if a company can earn 15% on money obtained from issuing $1,000,000 bonds at 12%, income before taxes will increase $30,000 (3% × $1,000,000). This phenomenon, known as leveraging or trading on the equity, is discussed further in Chapter 20.
4. **Earnings per share of common stock may be higher.** Although bond interest expense will reduce net income, earnings per share of common stock will often be higher under bond financing because no additional shares of common stock are issued.

To illustrate the potential effect on earnings per share, assume that Microsystems, Inc. is considering two plans for financing the construction of a new $5 million plant: (1) issuance of 200,000 shares of common stock at the current market price of $25 per share, or (2) issuance of $5 million, 12% bonds at face value. Income before interest and taxes on the new plant will be $1.5 million; income taxes are expected to be 30%. Microsystems currently has 100,000 shares of common stock outstanding. The alternative effects on earnings per share are as follows:

Effects on earnings per share—stocks vs. bonds

	Issue stock	Issue bonds
Income before interest and taxes	$1,500,000	$1,500,000
Interest (12% × $5,000,000)	—	600,000
Income before income taxes	1,500,000	900,000
Income tax expense (30%)	450,000	270,000
Net income	$1,050,000	$ 630,000
Outstanding shares	300,000	100,000
Earnings per share	$ 3.50	$ 6.30

Note that net income is $420,000 ($1,050,000 − $630,000) less with long-term debt financing. However, earnings per share is higher than it would be if equity financing were used, because there are 200,000 fewer shares of common stock outstanding.

The major disadvantages resulting from the use of bonds are that interest must be paid on a periodic basis and the principal (face value) of the bonds must be paid at maturity. A company with fluctuating earnings and a relatively weak cash position may experience great difficulty in meeting interest requirements in periods of low earnings. In addition, if the rate of return on assets falls below the cost of debt during the term of the bonds, trading on the equity will result in a net loss to stockholders. During the recession in the late 1970s and early 1980s, many corporations found that trading on the equity magnified their losses and contributed significantly to their financial problems.

CHARACTERISTICS OF BOND ISSUANCE

As in the case of issuing capital stock, a number of basic questions need to be resolved in issuing bonds. For example, what type of bond should be sold? How should the bond be sold? At what price should the bonds be issued? For purposes of discussion these questions are considered under the following headings:

1. Types of Bonds
2. Issuing Procedures
3. Trading of Bonds
4. Determining the Market Value of Bonds

TYPES OF BONDS

Bonds may have many different features. Some types of bonds commonly issued are:

Secured and Unsecured Bonds. **Secured bonds** have specific assets of the issuer pledged as collateral for the bonds. A bond secured by real estate, for example, is called a **mortgage bond.** **Unsecured bonds** are issued against the

general credit of the borrower. These bonds, called **debenture bonds,** are used extensively by large corporations with good credit ratings. For example, in a recent annual report, DuPont reported over $2 billion of debenture bonds outstanding.

Term and Serial Bonds. Bonds that mature at a single specified future date are called **term bonds.** In contrast, bonds that mature in installments are called **serial bonds.** For example, Caterpillar Inc. debentures due in 2007 are term bonds, and their debentures due between 1993 and 2007 are serial bonds.

Registered and Bearer Bonds. Bonds issued in the name of the owner are called **registered bonds**; interest payments are made by check to bondholders of record. Bonds not registered are called **bearer (or coupon) bonds**; bondholders are required to send in coupons to receive interest payments. Coupon bonds may be transferred to another party by delivery, whereas the transfer of registered bonds requires cancellation of the bonds and the issuance of new bonds.

Convertible and Callable Bonds. Bonds that permit bondholders to convert them into common stock at their option are called **convertible bonds.** Bonds subject to call and retirement at a stated dollar amount prior to maturity at the option of the issuer are known as **callable bonds.**

ISSUING PROCEDURES

State corporation laws grant corporations the power to issue bonds. Within the corporation, formal approval of both the board of directors and stockholders is usually required before bonds can be issued. **In authorizing the bond issue, the board of directors must stipulate the total number of bonds to be authorized and the contractual interest rate.**

The total authorization will often exceed the number of bonds originally issued. This is done intentionally to help ensure that the corporation will have the flexibility it needs to meet future cash requirements. Only a memorandum entry is made for the authorization of bonds.

The contractual interest rate is usually set as close as possible to the current market rate for comparable investment opportunities so that the bonds will sell at face value. Factors influencing this decision include the type of bonds being issued, the anticipated bond rating of the issue (AAA is the highest), the state of the economy, and current industry conditions. Usually the contractual interest rate is stated as an annual rate, and interest is generally paid semiannually.

The terms of the bond issue are set forth in a formal legal document called a **bond indenture.** In addition to the terms, the indenture summarizes the respective rights and privileges of the bondholders and their trustees, as well as the obligations and commitments of the issuing company. The trustee keeps records of each bondholder, maintains custody of unissued bonds, and holds conditional title to pledged property.

After the bond indenture is prepared, bond certificates are printed. The indenture and the certificate are separate documents. A bond certificate is

illustrated below. Bonds are generally sold through an investment company that specializes in selling securities. In most cases, the issue is underwritten by the investment company. Under an underwriting arrangement, the company sells the bonds to the investment company, which, in turn, sells the bonds to individual investors.

Bond certificate

TRADING OF BONDS

Corporate bonds, like capital stock, are traded on national securities markets. Thus, bondholders have the opportunity to convert their holdings into cash at any time by selling the bonds at the current market price. Bond prices are quoted as a percentage of the face value of the bond, which is usually $1,000. Thus, a $1,000 bond with a quoted price of 97 means that the selling price of the bond is 97% of face value, or $970 in this case. Bond prices and trading activity are published daily in newspapers and the financial press, as illustrated by the following:

Market information for bonds

Bonds	Current Yield	Volume	High	Low	Close	Net Change
IBM 10 1/2 15	9.7	35	110	108	108	−2½

The information above indicates that IBM Corporation has outstanding 10½%, $1,000 bonds maturing in 2015 and currently yielding a 9.7% return. In addition, 35 bonds were traded today; the high selling price for the day was

110; the low was 108; and at the close of trading, the price was also 108. The net change column indicates the difference between today's closing price and the previous day's closing price.

Transactions between a bondholder and other investors are not journalized by the issuing corporation. A corporation only makes journal entries when it issues or repurchases bonds.

DETERMINING THE MARKET VALUE OF BONDS

If you were an investor interested in purchasing bonds, how would you determine how much to pay for a bond? To be more specific, assume that Coronet, Inc. issues a zero-interest bond with a face value of $1,000,000 due in twenty years. For these bonds, the only cash you receive is a million dollars at the end of twenty years. Would you pay a million dollars for this bond? We doubt it, because a million dollars received twenty years from now is not the same as a million dollars received today. The reason you would not pay a million dollars relates to the time value of money. If you had a million dollars today, you would invest it and earn interest such that at the end of twenty years, your investment would be worth much more than a million dollars. Thus, if someone is going to pay you a million dollars twenty years from now, you would want to find its equivalent today, or **present value**. In other words, you would want to determine how much must be invested today at current interest rates to have a million dollars in twenty years.

The present value (market price) of a bond is, therefore, a function of three factors: (1) the expected dollar amounts to be received, (2) the length of time until the amount is received, and (3) the investor's required rate of return. The process of finding the present value is referred to as **discounting** the future amounts. To illustrate, assume that Laughlin Steel issues $10,000,000 of 12% bonds, due in ten years with interest payable semiannually. The purchaser of the bonds would receive the following in cash payments: (1) principal $10,000,000 to be paid at maturity, and (2) twenty $600,000 interest payments ($10,000,000 × 12% × ½) over the term of the bonds. The present values of these amounts are approximately as follows:

Computing the market price of bonds

Present value of $10,000,000 received in twenty periods	$ 3,118,000
Present value of $600,000 received semiannually for twenty periods	6,882,000
Market price of bonds	$10,000,000

Tables are available to provide the present value numbers to be used, or they can be determined mathematically[1]. Further discussion of the concepts and the mechanics of these computations is provided in the appendix to this chapter.

[1] For those knowledgeable in the use of present value tables, the computations in this example are: $10,000,000 × .31180 = $3,118,000 and $600,000 × 11.46992 = $6,882,000 (rounded).

ISSUING BONDS AT FACE VALUE

To illustrate the accounting for bonds, assume that Devor Corporation issues 1,000, 10-year, 9%, $1,000 bonds dated January 1, 1987 at 100. The entry to record the sale is:

Jan. 1	Cash	1,000,000	
	Bonds Payable		1,000,000
	(To record sale of bonds at face value)		

Bonds payable are reported in the long-term liability section of the balance sheet because the maturity date is January 1, 1997.

Over the term (life) of the bonds, entries are required for bond interest. Interest on bonds payable is computed in the same manner as interest on notes payable. Assuming that interest is payable semiannually on January 1 and July 1 on the bonds described above, interest of $45,000 ($\$1{,}000{,}000 \times 9\% \times 6/12$) must be paid on July 1, 1987. The entry for the payment, assuming no accrual of interest, is:

July 1	Bond Interest Expense	45,000	
	Cash		45,000
	(To record payment of bond interest)		

At December 31, an adjusting entry is required to recognize the $45,000 of interest expense incurred since July 1. The entry is:

Dec. 31	Bond Interest Expense	45,000	
	Bond Interest Payable		45,000
	(To accrue bond interest)		

Bond interest payable is classified as a current liability, because it is scheduled for payment within the next year. When the interest is paid on January 1, 1988, Bond Interest Payable is debited and Cash is credited for $45,000

At the maturity date (January 1, 1997), Devor Corporation is required to make the final payment of interest and to pay the face value of the bonds. The entry is:

Jan. 1	Bonds Payable	1,000,000	
	Bond Interest Payable	45,000	
	Cash		1,045,000
	(To record final payment of bond interest and payment of bonds at maturity)		

ISSUING BONDS AT FACE VALUE PLUS ACCRUED INTEREST

Bonds are often issued between interest payment dates. When this occurs, the issuer requires the investor to pay the market price for the bonds plus accrued

interest since the last interest date. Subsequently, the corporation will return the accrued interest to the investor by paying the full amount of interest due on outstanding bonds at the next interest date.

To illustrate, assume that instead of being sold on January 1, the Devor bonds are sold on March 1 at face value plus accrued interest. The accrued interest is $15,000 ($1,000,000 × 9% × 2/12). The total proceeds on the sale of the bonds, therefore, are $1,015,000 and the entry to record the sale is:

Mar. 1	Cash	1,015,000	
	Bonds Payable		1,000,000
	Bond Interest Payable		15,000
	(To record sale of bonds at face value plus accrued interest)		

At the first interest date, it is necessary to eliminate the bond interest payable balance and to recognize interest expense for the four months (March 1–June 30) the bonds have been outstanding. Interest expense in this example is, therefore, $30,000 ($1,000,000 × 9% × 4/12). The entry on July 1 for the $45,000 interest payment is:

July 1	Bond Interest Payable	15,000	
	Bond Interest Expense	30,000	
	Cash		45,000
	(To record payment of bond interest)		

ISSUING BONDS BELOW OR ABOVE FACE VALUE

In the previous illustrations, it was assumed that the interest rate paid on the bonds, often referred to as the **stated** rate or **contractual** rate, and the **market rate** or **effective rate** were the same. As a result, the bonds were issued at face value (or par). Suppose, however, that the investor could find alternative investments of the same type that would pay a higher rate of interest. In this case, the investor has one of two options: either purchase the other investment or pay less for the existing bonds. By paying less for the existing bonds, investors increase the effective interest rate they receive on the bonds and thus make the investment comparable. **In other words, if the market rate is higher than the stated rate, the bonds will sell at less than face value, or at a discount. Conversely, if the market rate of interest is less than the stated rate on the bonds, the bonds will sell at a premium.** These relationships are shown graphically on the next page.

Issuance of bonds at an amount different than face value is quite common because the market rate changes daily. By the time a company prints the bond certificate and markets the bonds, it will be a coincidence if the market rate and the stated rate are the same. Thus, the issuance of bonds at a discount does not mean that the financial strength of the issuer is suspect. Conversely, the sale of bonds at a premium does not indicate that the financial strength of the issuer is exceptional.

Interest rates and bond prices

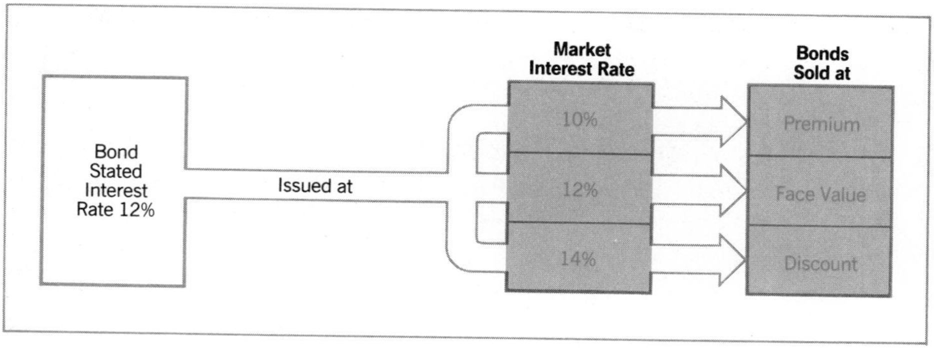

BONDS ISSUED AT A DISCOUNT

To illustrate the issuance of bonds at a discount, assume that on January 1, 1987, Candlestick, Inc. sells $1 million, 5-year, 13% bonds at 98 with interest payable on July 1 and January 1. The entry to record the issuance is:

Jan. 1	Cash	980,000	
	Discount on Bonds Payable	20,000	
	Bonds Payable		1,000,000
	(To record sale of bonds at a discount)		

Although Discount on Bonds Payable has a debit balance, it is not an asset. **Rather it is a contra account, which is deducted from bonds payable,** as illustrated below.

Statement presentation of discount on bonds payable

Long-term liabilities		
Bonds payable	$1,000,000	
Less: Discount on bonds payable	20,000	$980,000

The $980,000 represents the **carrying (or book) value** of the bonds. On the date of issue this amount equals the market price.

The issuance of bonds below face value causes the total cost of borrowing to differ from the bond interest paid. That is, the issuing corporation must pay not only the stated rate of interest over the term of the bonds, but also the face value (rather than the issuance price) at maturity. Therefore, the difference between the issuance price and face value of the bonds—the discount—is an additional cost of borrowing that should be recorded as bond interest expense over the life of the bonds. The total cost of borrowing $980,000 for Candlestick, Inc. is $670,000, computed as follows:

Total cost of borrowing

Bonds Issued at a Discount	
Semiannual interest payments	
(1,000,000 × 13% × ½) = $65,000; $65,000 × 10	$650,000
Add: Bond discount ($1,000,000 − $980,000)	20,000
Total cost of borrowing	$670,000

Alternatively, the total cost of borrowing can be determined as follows:

Alternative computation of total cost of borrowing

Bonds Issued at a Discount	
Principal at maturity	$1,000,000
Semiannual interest payments ($65,000 × 10)	650,000
Cash to be paid to bondholders	1,650,000
Cash received from bondholders	980,000
Total cost of borrowing	$ 670,000

To comply with the matching principle, it follows that bond discount should be allocated systematically to each accounting period benefiting from the use of the cash proceeds.

One method, the **straight-line method,** allocates the same amount each interest period. The amount is determined as follows:

Formula for bond discount amortization

Bond Discount ÷ Number of Interest Periods = Bond Discount Amortization

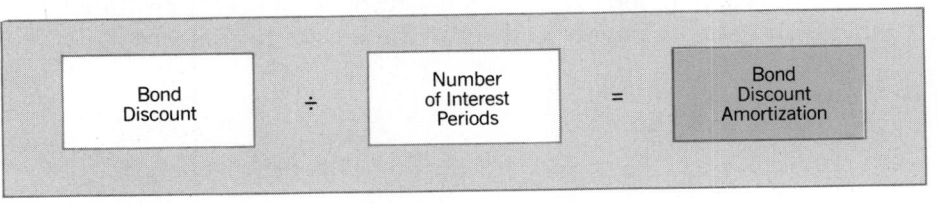

In this example, the bond discount amortization is $2,000 ($20,000 ÷ 10). The entry to record the payment of bond interest and the amortization of bond discount on the first interest date (July 1, 1987) is:

July	1	Bond Interest Expense	67,000	
		Discount on Bonds Payable		2,000
		Cash		65,000
		(To record payment of bond interest and amortization of bond discount)		

At December 31, the adjusting entry is:

Dec.	31	Bond Interest Expense	67,000	
		Discount on Bonds Payable		2,000
		Bond Interest Payable		65,000
		(To record accrued bond interest and amortization of bond discount)		

Over the term of the bonds, the balance in Discount on Bonds Payable will decrease annually by the same amount until it has a zero balance at the maturity date of the bonds. Thus, the carrying value of the bonds at maturity will be equal to the face value of the bonds.

When bonds are sold at a discount during an interest period, it is necessary to compute a monthly amortization amount. To illustrate, assume that $200,000 of the bonds above are sold at a discount of $11,400 on April 1, 1987. From the date of sale, the bonds will be outstanding 57 months (60 − 3) and the monthly amortization of the bond discount is $200 ($11,400 ÷ 57). Thus, on July 1, 1987, $600 ($200 × 3) of bond discount will be amortized. For each subsequent interest period, the amortization will be $1,200 ($200 × 6).

BONDS ISSUED AT A PREMIUM

The issuance of bonds at a premium can be illustrated by assuming the Candlestick, Inc. bonds described above are sold at 102 rather than at 98. The entry to record the sale is:

Jan. 1	Cash	1,020,000	
	Bonds Payable		1,000,000
	Premium on Bonds Payable		20,000
	(To record sale of bonds at a premium)		

Premium on Bonds Payable is an **adjunct account.** Therefore, it is added to bonds payable as shown below:

Statement presentation of bond premium

Long-term liabilities		
Bonds payable	$1,000,000	
Add: Premium on bonds payable	20,000	$1,020,000

The sale of bonds above face value causes the total cost of borrowing to be less than the bond interest paid, because the borrower is not required to pay the bond premium at the maturity date of the bonds. Thus, the premium is considered to be a reduction in the cost of borrowing that should be credited to Bond Interest Expense over the life of the bonds. The total cost of borrowing $1,020,000 for Candlestick, Inc. is $630,000, computed as follows:

Total cost of borrowing

Bonds Issued at a Premium	
Semiannual interest payments ($1,000,000 × 13% × ½) = $65,000; $65,000 × 10	$650,000
Less: Bond premium ($1,020,000 − $1,000,000)	20,000
Total cost of borrowing	$630,000

Alternatively, the cost of borrowing can be computed as follows:

Alternative computation of total cost of borrowing

Bonds Issued at a Premium	
Principal at maturity	$1,000,000
Semiannual interest payments ($65,000 × 10)	650,000
Cash to be paid to bondholders	1,650,000
Cash received from bondholders	1,020,000
Total cost of borrowing	$ 630,000

The premium amortization for each interest period is $2,000 ($20,000 ÷ 10). The entry to record the first payment of interest on July 1 is:

July 1	Bond Interest Expense	63,000	
	Premium on Bonds Payable	2,000	
	Cash		65,000
	(To record payment of bond interest and amortization of bond premium)		

At December 31, the adjusting entry is:

Dec. 31	Bond Interest Expense	63,000	
	Premium on Bonds Payable	2,000	
	Bond Interest Payable		65,000
	(To record accrued bond interest and amortization of bond premium)		

Over the term of the bonds, the balance in Premium on Bonds Payable will decrease annually by the same amount until it has a zero balance at maturity.

EFFECTIVE INTEREST AMORTIZATION

The **effective interest method of amortization** is an alternative to straight-line amortization. Under the effective interest method

1. Bond interest expense is computed first by multiplying the carrying value of the bonds at the beginning of the period by the effective interest rate.
2. The bond discount or premium amortization is then determined by comparing the bond interest expense with the interest to be paid.

The computation of the amortization is depicted graphically as follows:

Computation of amortization—effective interest method

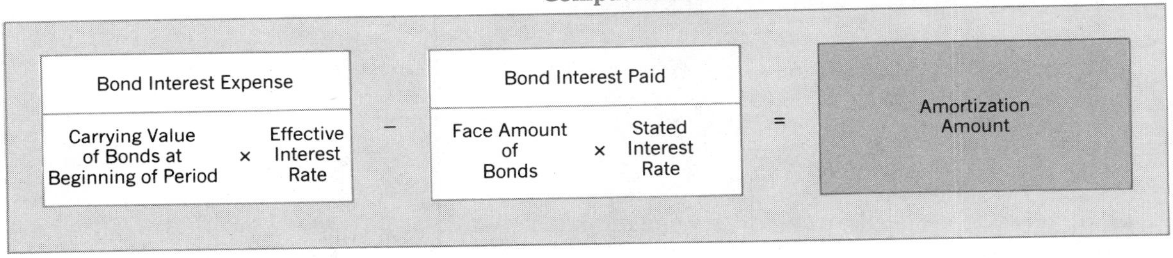

The effective interest method produces a periodic interest expense equal to a **constant percentage of the carrying value of the bonds.** Since the percentage is the effective rate of interest incurred by the borrower at the time of issuance, the effective interest method results in a better matching of expenses with revenues than the straight-line method.

Both amortization methods result in the same total amount of interest expense over the term of the bonds, and the annual amounts of interest expense are generally quite similar. However, **when the annual amounts are materially different, the effective interest method is required under generally accepted accounting principles.**

BONDS ISSUED AT A DISCOUNT

To illustrate the effective interest method of bond discount amortization, assume that Wrightway Inc. issues $100,000 of 10%, 5-year bonds on January 1, 1987, with interest payable each July 1 and January 1. The bonds sell at 92.639

which results in bond discount of $7,361 and an effective interest rate of 12%. The preparation of the bond discount amortization schedule shown below facilitates the recording of interest expense and the discount amortization.

Bond discount amortization schedule

WRIGHTWAY INC.
Bond Discount Amortization
Effective Interest Method—Semiannual Interest Payments
10% Bonds Issued at 12%

Semiannual Interest Periods	(A) Interest to be Paid	(B) Interest Expense	(C) Discount Amortization (B) − (A)	(D) Unamortized Discount (D) − (C)	(E) Carrying Value of Bonds ($100,000 − D)
1/1/87 (Issue date)				$7,361[4]	$ 92,639[5]
1	5,000[1]	$ 5,558[2]	$ 558[3]	6,803	93,197
2	5,000	5,592	592	6,211	93,789
3	5,000	5,627	627	5,584	94,416
4	5,000	5,665	665	4,919	95,081
5	5,000	5,705	705	4,214	95,786
6	5,000	5,747	747	3,467	96,533
7	5,000	5,792	792	2,675	97,325
8	5,000	5,840	840	1,835	98,165
9	5,000	5,890	890	945	99,055
10	5,000	5,945	945	-0-	100,000
	$50,000	$57,361	$7,361		

[1]Column (A) remains constant because the face value of the bonds ($100,000) is multiplied by the semiannual stated interest rate (5%).
[2]Column (B) is computed as the carrying value of the bonds times the semiannual effective interest rate (6%).
[3]Column (C) indicates the discount amortization each period.
[4]Column (D) decreases each period until it reaches zero at maturity.
[5]Column (E) increases each period until it equals face value at maturity.

100000
92600
7400

For the first interest period, the computations of bond interest expense and the bond discount amortization are as follows:

Computation of bond discount amortization

Bond interest expense ($92,639 × 6%)	$5,558
Stated interest ($100,000 × 5%)	5,000
Bond discount amortization	**$ 558**

As a result, the entry to record the payment of interest and amortization of bond discount by Wrightway Inc. on July 1, 1987 is:

July	1	Bond Interest Expense	5,558	
		Discount on Bonds Payable		558
		Cash		5,000
		(To record payment of bond interest and amortization of bond discount)		

For the second interest period, interest expense will be $5,592 ($93,197 × 6%), and the discount amortization will be $592. At December 31, the following adjusting entry is therefore made:

Dec. 31	Bond Interest Expense	5,592	
	Discount on Bonds Payable		592
	Bond Interest Payable		5,000
	(To record accrued interest and amortization of bond discount)		

On January 1, payment of the interest is recorded by a debit to Bond Interest Payable and a credit to Cash.

The amortization schedule is an excellent example of an operation that can be done using an electronic spreadsheet. Once the initial amounts are entered into the computer in columns D and E, all of the other computations are performed by the computer.

BONDS ISSUED AT A PREMIUM

The amortization of bond premium by the effective interest method is similar to the procedures described above for bond discount. As an example, assume that Lombard Corporation issues $100,000, 12%, 5-year bonds on January 1, 1987, with interest payable on July 1 and January 1. The bonds sell for $107,721, which results in bond premium of $7,721 and an effective interest rate of 10%. The bond premium amortization schedule is shown on page 665.

For the first interest period, the computations of bond interest expense and the bond premium amortization are:

Computation of bond premium amortization

Bond interest expense ($107,721 × 5%)	$5,386
Stated interest ($100,000 × 6%)	6,000
Bond premium amortization	**$ 614**

The entry on the first interest date is:

July 1	Bond Interest Expense	5,386	
	Premium on Bonds Payable	614	
	Cash		6,000
	(To record payment of bond interest and amortization of bond premium)		

For the second interest period, interest expense will be $5,355 and the premium amortization will be $645.

Bond premium amortization schedule

LOMBARD CORPORATION
Bond Premium Amortization
Effective Interest Method—Semiannual Interest Payments
12% Bonds Issued at 10%

Semiannual Interest Periods	(A) Interest to be Paid	(B) Interest Expense	(C) Premium Amortization (A) − (B)	(D) Unamortized Premium (D) − (C)	(E) Carrying Value of Bonds ($100,000 + D)
1/1/87 (Issue date)				$7,721[4]	$107,721[5]
1	6,000[1]	$ 5,386[2]	$ 614[3]	7,107	107,107
2	6,000	5,355	645	6,462	106,462
3	6,000	5,323	677	5,785	105,785
4	6,000	5,289	711	5,074	105,074
5	6,000	5,254	746	4,328	104,328
6	6,000	5,216	784	3,544	103,544
7	6,000	5,177	823	2,721	102,721
8	6,000	5,136	864	1,857	101,857
9	6,000	5,093	907	950	100,950
10	6,000	5,050	950	-0-	100,000
	$60,000	$52,279	$7,721		

[1]Column (A) remains constant because the face value of the bonds ($100,000) is multiplied by the semiannual stated interest rate (6%).
[2]Column (B) is computed as the carrying value of the bonds times the semiannual effective interest rate (5%).
[3]Column (C) indicates the premium amortized each period.
[4]Column (D) decreases each period until it reaches zero at maturity.
[5]Column (E) decreases each period until it equals face value at maturity.

REDEMPTION OF BONDS BEFORE MATURITY

Bonds may be redeemed before maturity under terms of the bond contract, as in the case of callable bonds, or through purchase in the securities markets. The decision to retire bonds before maturity is made by financial management in light of a corporation's present and anticipated cash resources and the saving in interest that may be realized. When bonds are retired before maturity, it is necessary to (1) eliminate the carrying value of the bonds at the redemption date, (2) record the cash paid, and (3) recognize the gain or loss on redemption. The carrying value of the bonds is the face value of the bonds less unamortized bond discount or plus unamortized bond premium at the redemption date.

To illustrate, assume at the end of the eighth interest period Lombard Corporation retires its bonds at 103 after paying the semiannual interest. The carrying value of the bonds at the redemption date, as shown in the bond premium amortization schedule, is $101,857. The entry to record the redemption on January 1, 1991 is:

Jan.	1	Bonds Payable	100,000	
		Premium on Bonds Payable	1,857	
		Loss on Bond Redemption	1,143	
		Cash		103,000
		(To record redemption of bonds at 103)		

Losses (gains) on bond redemption are reported in the income statement as extraordinary items as required by the accounting profession.

If the Lombard Corporation had used the straight-line method of amortization, the premium amortization each period would have been \$772 (\$7,721 ÷ 10), and the premium for the two remaining interest periods (\$1,544) would have been unamortized at the redemption date. Thus, the carrying value of the bonds on January 1, 1991 would have been \$101,544, and the loss on redemption would have been \$1,456 (\$103,000 − \$101,544).

CONVERSION OF BONDS

Convertible bonds have features that are attractive both to bondholders and to the issuer. The conversion often gives bondholders an opportunity to benefit if the market price of the common stock increases substantially. Furthermore, until conversion, the bondholder receives interest on the bond. For the issuer, the bonds sell at a higher price and pay a lower rate of interest than other comparable debt securities that do not have a conversion option. Many corporations, such as USAir, USX Corp., and Chrysler Corporation have convertible bonds outstanding.

When the conversion of bonds into common stock is recorded, the current market price of the bonds and the stock are usually ignored. Instead the carrying value of the bonds is transferred to paid-in capital accounts, and no gain or loss is recognized. To illustrate, assume that on July 1 Saunders Associates converts \$100,000 bonds sold at face value into 2,000 shares of \$10 par value common stock. Both the bonds and the common stock have a market value of \$130,000. The entry to record the conversion is:

July	1	Bonds Payable	100,000	
		Common Stock		20,000
		Paid-in Capital in Excess of Par		80,000
		(To record bond conversion)		

Note that the current market price of the bonds and stocks (\$130,000) is not considered in making the entry. This method of recording the bond conversion is often referred to as the book (or carrying) value method.

BOND SINKING FUNDS

Many bond issues require the borrower to make periodic cash contributions to a sinking (redemption) fund over the life of the bonds. A **sinking fund** is

cash or other assets segregated to retire debt. **A sinking fund makes the bonds more attractive to investors, because the fund enhances the likelihood that the bonds will be redeemed at maturity.** For example, Nabisco Brands, Texaco, and Alcoa have sinking funds for their debenture bonds. Sinking funds are usually under the control of a trustee, such as a bank or a trust company. The trustee may be permitted to invest the periodic deposits in high-quality income-producing securities. It is expected that the deposits plus the earnings from the investments will equal the face value of the bonds at maturity. Shortly before the maturity date, the trustee sells the securities and uses the total cash in the fund to redeem the bonds. Any excess cash in the fund is returned to the issuer.

DETERMINING THE PERIODIC CONTRIBUTION

The amount of the periodic contributions is determined from interest tables using an assumed average annual rate of investment income. For example, if Lombard Corporation establishes a sinking fund for its $100,000, 5-year bonds, and the trustee estimates an 8% annual earning rate on fund assets, the annual periodic contribution is $17,046. As shown in the following schedule, the deposits plus interest earned equal the maturity value of the bonds.

Schedule of sinking fund balances

End of Year	(A) Annual Deposit	(B) Interest Earned (C) × 8%	(C) Balance End of Year
1987	$17,046	—	$ 17,046
1988	17,046	1,364	35,456
1989	17,046	2,836	55,338
1990	17,046	4,427	76,811
1991	17,046	6,143	100,000

SINKING FUND ENTRIES

Entries for the sinking fund are required to record (1) periodic contributions, (2) annual income, and (3) redemption of the bonds.

The entry to record the first deposit by Lombard Corporation is:

Dec. 31	Bond Sinking Fund	17,046	
	Cash		17,046
	(To record annual sinking fund deposit)		

At the end of the second year the Lombard Corp. records actual earnings of $1,364. The entry to record the revenue is:

Dec. 31	Bond Sinking Fund	1,364	
	Bond Sinking Fund Revenue		1,364
	(To record revenue earned on fund assets)		

At the maturity date, fund assets are used to redeem the bonds. The entry to record the redemption is:

Dec. 31	Bonds Payable	100,000	
	Bond Sinking Fund		100,000
	(To redeem bonds at maturity)		

The bond sinking fund is reported as a single amount in the investment section of the balance sheet. Bond sinking fund revenue is classified as other revenues and gains in the income statement.

The bond contract may also require the corporation to establish an appropriation for bond redemption. As explained in Chapter 16, the appropriation is reported as part of retained earnings.

ACCOUNTING FOR LONG-TERM NOTES PAYABLE

The use of notes payable in long-term debt financing is quite common. Long-term notes payable may be similar in substance to short-term interest bearing notes payable except that the term of the note exceeds one year. In periods of unstable interest rates, long-term notes may contain special features that tie the interest rate to changes in the market rate for comparable loans. Examples are the 8.03% adjustable rate notes issued by General Motors and the floating rate notes issued by American Express Company.

A long-term note may be secured by a document called a **mortgage** that pledges title to specific units of property as security for a loan. Mortgage notes payable are widely used in the purchase of homes by individuals and in the acquisition of plant assets by many small and some large companies. For example, approximately 18% of McDonald's (the fast-food restaurant) long-term debt relates to mortgage notes on land, buildings, and improvements. Like the notes described above, the mortgage loan terms may stipulate either a fixed or an adjustable interest rate. Typically, the terms require the borrower to make installment payments over the term of the loan. Each payment consists of (1) interest on the unpaid balance of the loan, and (2) a reduction of loan principal. The interest decreases each period, while the portion applied to the loan principal increases each period.

Mortgage notes payable are recorded initially at face value, and entries are required subsequently for each installment payment. To illustrate, assume that Karey Technology Inc. issues a $500,000, 12%, 20-year mortgage note on January 1, 1987 to obtain needed financing for the construction of a new research laboratory. The terms provide for semiannual installment payments, exclusive of real estate, taxes, and insurance, of $33,231. The installment payment schedule for the first two years is as follows:

Mortgage installment payment schedule

Semiannual Interest Period	(A) Cash Payment	(B) Interest Expense (D) × 6%	(C) Reduction of Principal (A) − (B)	(D) Principal Balance (D) − (C)
1/1/87				$500,000
6/30/87	$33,231	$30,000	$3,231	496,769
12/31/87	33,231	29,806	3,425	493,344
6/30/88	33,231	29,601	3,630	489,714
12/31/88	33,231	29,383	3,848	485,866

The entries to record the mortgage loan and first installment payment are as follows:

Jan. 1	Cash	500,000	
	Mortgage Note Payable		500,000
	(To record mortgage loan)		
June 30	Interest Expense	30,000	
	Mortgage Note Payable	3,231	
	Cash		33,231
	(To record semiannual payment on mortgage)		

In the balance sheet, the reduction in principal for the next year is reported as a current liability, and the remaining unpaid principal balance is classified as a long-term liability. At December 31, 1987, the total liability is $493,344 of which $7,478 ($3,630 + $3,848) is current, and $485,866 ($493,344 − $7,478) is long-term.

Many electronic spreadsheet programs can create a schedule of installment loan payments. One reason that this is so practical is that you can put in the data for your own mortgage loan and get an illustration that really hits home.

LEASE LIABILITY

As indicated in Chapter 11, a lease is a contractual understanding between the lessor (owner of the property) and a lessee (renter of the property) that grants the right to use specific property for a period of time in return for cash payments. Leasing is big business. For example, an estimated $61 billion of capital equipment was leased in a recent year—more than was financed by bank loans, corporate bonds, preferred and common stock, and mortgages. The two most common types of leases are operating leases and capital leases.

OPERATING LEASES

The renting of an apartment on campus and the rental of a car at an airport are examples of operating leases. **In an operating lease the intent is temporary use of the property by the lessee with continued ownership of the property by the lessor.** The lease (or rental) payments are recorded as an expense by the lessee and as revenue by the lessor. For example, assuming that a sales representative for Western Inc. leases a car from Hertz Car Rental at the Los Angeles airport and that Hertz charges a total of $275, the entry by the lessee, Western Inc., is:

Car Rental Expense	275	
Cash		275
(To record payment of lease rental charge)		

In addition, the lessee may incur other costs during the lease period. For example, in the case above, the lessee may be required to pay for gas and oil. These costs are also reported as an expense.

CAPITAL LEASES

In most lease contracts, a periodic payment is made by the lessee and is recorded as rent expense in the income statement. However, in some cases, the lease contract transfers substantially all of the benefits and risks of ownership to the lessee, so that the lease is in effect a purchase of the property. This type of lease is called a **capital lease** because the present value of the cash payments for the lease are capitalized and recorded as an asset. The lessee must record the lease as an asset if one of the following conditions exist:

1. **The lease transfers ownership of the property to the lessee. Rationale**—If during the lease term, the lessee receives ownership of the asset, the leased asset should be reported as an asset on the lessee's books.
2. **The lease contains a bargain purchase option. Rationale**—If during the term of the lease, the lessee can purchase the asset at a price substantially below its fair market value, the lessee will obviously exercise this option. Thus, the lease should be reported as a leased asset on the lessee's books.
3. **The lease term is equal to 75% or more of the economic life of the leased property. Rationale**—If the lease term is for much of the asset's useful life, the asset should be recorded by the lessee.
4. **The present value of the lease payments equals or exceeds 90% of the fair market value of the leased property. Rationale**—If the present value of the lease payments is equal to or almost equal to the fair market value of the asset, the lessee has essentially purchased the asset. As a result, the leased asset should be recorded on the books of the lessee.

To illustrate, assume the Gonzalez Company decides to lease a new Corniche Rolls Royce for use as a promotional device for its firm. Gonzalez leases the Rolls for four years; its economic life is estimated to be five years. The present value of the lease payments is $190,000 which is equal to the fair market value of the Rolls. There is no transfer of ownership during the lease term nor is there any bargain purchase option.

In this example, Gonzalez has essentially purchased the Rolls Royce. First, the lease term is 75% or more of the economic life of the asset and secondly the present value of cash payments is equal to the fair market value of the Rolls. The entry to record the transaction is as follows:

Leased Asset – Rolls Royce	190,000	
Lease Liability		190,000
(To record leased asset and lease liability)		

The leased asset is reported on the balance sheet under plant assets. The lease liability is reported as a liability on the balance sheet. The portion of the lease liability expected to be paid in the next year is reported as a current

liability. The remainder is classified as a long-term liability. For example, in a recent year, Uniroyal, Inc. reported $5.3 million as the current portion of a lease liability and $86.5 million as a long-term liability.

Most lessees do not like to report leases on their balance sheets. The reason is that the lease liability increases the company's total liabilities. This, in turn, may make it more difficult for the company to obtain needed funds from lenders. As a result, companies attempt to keep leased assets and lease liabilities off the balance sheet by not meeting any one of the four conditions mentioned above. This procedure of keeping liabilities off the balance sheet is often referred to as **off-balance sheet financing.**

DEFERRED INCOME TAXES

A company's **taxable income** is computed in accordance with prescribed tax regulations, whereas a company's **accounting income** (i.e., income before income taxes) is measured in accordance with generally accepted accounting principles (GAAP). Differences between tax regulations and GAAP often exist because the former are designed to raise revenue and the latter are designed to provide useful financial statements. Therefore, taxable income and accounting income often differ.

To illustrate, assume that at the beginning of 1987, you purchase a new Xerox machine for your business at a total cost of $4,000. **For tax purposes,** you may expense the equipment in the period of purchase. However, **for accounting purposes,** the Xerox equipment is depreciated over two years. Assuming that your company had income before depreciation and taxes in these two years of $50,000, your taxable and accounting income (using a 30% tax rate) are as follows for the two years.

Computation of taxable and accounting income

	Taxable Income		Accounting Income	
	1987	1988	1987	1988
Income before depreciation	$50,000	$50,000	$50,000	$50,000
Depreciation expense				
Tax	(4,000)	-0-		
Book ($4,000 ÷ 2)			(2,000)	(2,000)
Income before income taxes	46,000	50,000	48,000	48,000
Income tax expense (30%)	(13,800)	(15,000)	(14,400)	(14,400)
Total income	$32,200	$35,000	$33,600	$33,600
	$67,200		$67,200	

Total same for two years

The illustration shows that accounting income and taxable income differ each year but are the same in total for the two years. These results are attributable in part to the amounts shown for income taxes in the two years. For

example, in 1987, income taxes for accounting purposes were $600 higher than the income taxes for tax purposes ($14,400 − $13,800) and the reverse was true in 1988 ($15,000 − $14,400).

Differences between income taxes based on taxable income and accounting income result in **deferred income taxes** for two reasons. First, Income Tax Expense is debited for the taxes based on accounting income in accordance with the matching of revenues and expenses. Thus, for 1987, Income Tax Expense is debited for 30% of accounting income before income taxes or $14,400 (30% × $48,000). Second, Income Taxes Payable is credited for the taxes based on taxable income to show the correct tax liability. For 1987, the tax liability is $13,800 (30% × $46,000). Therefore, the deferred income taxes are $600 ($14,400 − $13,800). The entry for 1987 is as follows:

Dec. 31	Income Tax Expense	14,400	
	Income Taxes Payable		13,800
	Deferred Income Taxes		600
	(To record 1987 income taxes)		

For 1988, Income Tax Expense is again $14,400 (30% × $48,000) and Income Taxes Payable is $15,000 (30% × $50,000). The entry, therefore, is as follows:

Dec. 31	Income Tax Expense	14,400	
	Deferred Income Taxes	600	
	Income Taxes Payable		15,000
	(To record 1988 income taxes)		

Note that in 1987 Deferred Income Taxes is credited and that the account has a zero balance at the end of 1988. Normally, Deferred Income Taxes has a credit balance and is reported under long-term liabilities.

In practice, many corporations experience extended time periods when the credits to deferred income taxes exceed the debits to deferred income taxes. This is true because most companies attempt to defer the payment of their income taxes as long as possible. Therefore, accounting income is usually higher than taxable income. Consequently, the cumulative balance in deferred income taxes may be substantial as shown by the $150 million recently reported by American Express Company and the $488 million reported by Delta Air Lines. For a growth company, deferred income taxes are often considered to be a tax saving of infinite duration.

STATEMENT PRESENTATION OF LONG-TERM LIABILITIES

Long-term liabilities are reported in a separate section of the balance sheet immediately following current liabilities. The section might appear as shown on page 673.

Alternatively, summary data may be presented in the balance sheet with detailed data being shown in a supporting schedule. The current maturities of long-term debt should be reported under current liabilities if they are to be paid from current assets.

Long-term liabilities		
Bonds payable 12% due in 2006	$1,000,000	
Less: Unamortized bond discount	80,000	$ 920,000
Mortgage notes payable 14% due 2010 and secured by plant assets		500,000
Lease liability		390,000
Deferred income taxes		150,000
Total long-term liabilities		$1,960,000

Statement presentation of long-term liabilities

SUMMARY OF STUDY OBJECTIVES

1. Bonds may be sold to many investors, and they offer the following advantages over common stock: (a) stockholder control is not affected, (b) tax savings result, (c) income to common stockholders may increase, and (d) earnings per share of common stock may be higher.

2. When bonds are issued, Cash is debited for the cash proceeds and Bonds Payable is credited for the face value of the bonds. In addition, Bond Interest Payable is credited if there is accrued interest, and the accounts Premium on Bonds Payable and Discount on Bonds Payable are used to show the bond premium and bond discount.

3. The straight-line method of amortization results in a constant amount of amortization and interest expense per period but a varying rate of interest. In contrast, the effective interest method results in varying amounts of amortization and interest expense per period but a constant rate of interest. When the difference between the straight-line and effective interest method is material, the use of the effective interest method is required under GAAP.

4. When bonds are redeemed before maturity, it is necessary to (a) eliminate the carrying value of the bonds at the redemption date, (b) record the cash paid, and (c) recognize the gain or loss on redemption. When bonds are converted to common stock, the book (or carrying) value of the bonds is transferred to appropriate paid-in capital accounts, and no gain or loss is recognized.

5. Entries are required for a bond sinking fund to record (a) periodic contributions, (b) annual income, and (c) redemption of the bonds.

6. For an operating lease, lease (or rental) payments are recorded as an expense by the lessee (renter). For a capital lease, the lessee records the asset and related obligation at the present value of the future lease payments.

7. Deferred income taxes arise because of differences between accounting income computed under GAAP and taxable income deter-

mined in accordance with tax regulations. When deferred income taxes are recorded, Income Tax Expense is debited for the tax on accounting income; Income Taxes Payable is credited for the tax on taxable income; and the difference is recognized as deferred income taxes.

8. The nature and amount of each long-term debt should be reported in the balance sheet or in schedules in the notes accompanying the statements.

APPENDIX 17–A

PRESENT VALUE CONCEPTS

In this chapter, a number of long-term liabilities were presented that involved the use of a **present value computation.** For example, to determine the market price of a bond, the present value of the principal and interest payments was computed. In addition, the determination of the amount to be reported for notes payable and lease liability involved present value computations.

The present value computation is based on the premise that money has a time value. For example, $1,000 received today is more valuable than $1,000 received one year from now. An individual would prefer to have the $1,000 today because a return could be earned on this amount over the year. The present value, therefore, is based on three factors: (1) the expected dollar amount to be received, (2) the length of time until the amount is received, and (3) the individual's required rate of return. **The process of determining the present value is referred to as discounting the future amount.**

PRESENT VALUE OF A SINGLE FUTURE AMOUNT

To illustrate these concepts, assume that you are willing to invest a sum of money that will yield $1,000 at the end of one year. In other words, what amount would you need to invest today to have $1,000 one year from now? If you want a 10% rate of return, the present value is $909.09 ($1,000 ÷ 1.10). This amount can be verified as follows:

Present value computation

Present Value × (1 + interest rate)	=	Future Value
Present Value × (1 + 10%)	=	$1,000
Present Value	=	$1,000 ÷ 1.10
Present Value	=	**$909.09**

Thus, \$909.09 invested today at 10% will give you \$90.91 in interest which when added to \$909.09 will equal \$1,000 in a year. If you are willing to wait 2 years for the \$1,000, the present value at a 10% rate of return is \$826.45 ([\$1,000 ÷ 1.10] ÷ 1.10). A higher rate of return will produce a smaller present value. For example, using a 12% return, the present value of \$1,000 due in one year is \$892.86.

The present value of a single future amount may also be determined through tables that show the present value of the amount of 1 for n periods. In Table 1 below, n is the number of interest compounding periods involved. The percentages are the periodic required rate of return, and the decimal numbers in the respective columns are the discount rates.

Illustration of present value table for a single future amount

TABLE 1
PRESENT VALUE OF A SINGLE FUTURE AMOUNT

(n) Periods	5%	6%	8%	9%	10%	11%	12%	15%
1	.95238	.94340	.92593	.91743	.90909	.90090	.89286	.86957
2	.90703	.89000	.85734	.84168	.82645	.81162	.79719	.75614
3	.86384	.83962	.79383	.77218	.75132	.73119	.71178	.65752
4	.82270	.79209	.73503	.70843	.68301	.65873	.63552	.57175
5	.78353	.74726	.68058	.64993	.62092	.59345	.56743	.49718
6	.74622	.70496	.63017	.59627	.56447	.53464	.50663	.43233
7	.71068	.66506	.58349	.54703	.51316	.48166	.45235	.37594
8	.67684	.62741	.54027	.50187	.46651	.43393	.40388	.32690
9	.64461	.59190	.50025	.46043	.42410	.39092	.36061	.28426
10	.61391	.55839	.46319	.42241	.38554	.35218	.32197	.24719
11	.58468	.52679	.42888	.38753	.35049	.31728	.28748	.21494
12	.55684	.49697	.39711	.35554	.31863	.28584	.25668	.18691
13	.53032	.46884	.36770	.32618	.28966	.25751	.22917	.16253
14	.50507	.44230	.34046	.29925	.26333	.23199	.20462	.14133
15	.48102	.41727	.31524	.27454	.23939	.20900	.18270	.12289
16	.45811	.39365	.29189	.25187	.21763	.18829	.16312	.10687
17	.43630	.37136	.27027	.23107	.19785	.16963	.14564	.09293
18	.41552	.35034	.25025	.21199	.17986	.15282	.13004	.08081
19	.39573	.33051	.23171	.19449	.16351	.13768	.11611	.07027
20	.37689	.31180	.21455	.17843	.14864	.12403	.10367	.06110

When the tables are used, the future value amount is multiplied by the discount rate specified at the intersection of the number of periods and the required rate of return. Note, for example, that the discount for 1 period (years) at a required rate of 10% is .90909. For 2 periods at a required rate of 10%, the discount is .82645.

PRESENT VALUE OF A SERIES OF FUTURE PAYMENTS

Instead of a single future amount, assume that you will receive $1,000 cash annually for three years. In this case, you are receiving an **annuity,** which is a series of equal payments at equal time intervals. Based on a 10% rate of return, the present value is $2,486.86, computed as follows:

Present value of a series of future payments computation

Future Amount	×	Present Value of 1	=	Present Value
$1,000		.90909		$ 909.09
1,000		.82645		826.45
1,000		.75132		751.32
				$2,486.86

This method of calculation is required when the periodic cash flows are not uniform in each period. However, when the future receipts are the same in each period, there are two other ways to compute present value. First, the annual cash flow can be multiplied by the sum of the three present values. In the example above, $1,000 × 2.48686 equals $2,486.86. Second, annuity tables may be used. As illustrated in Table 2 below, these tables show the present value of 1 to be received periodically for a given number of periods.

Illustration of present value tables for a series of future payments

TABLE 2
PRESENT VALUE OF A SERIES OF FUTURE PAYMENTS

(n) Periods	5%	6%	8%	9%	10%	11%	12%	15%
1	.95238	.94340	.92593	.91743	.90909	.90090	.89286	.86957
2	1.85941	1.83339	1.78326	1.75911	1.73554	1.71252	1.69005	1.62571
3	2.72325	2.67301	2.57710	2.53130	2.48685	2.44371	2.40183	2.28323
4	3.54595	3.46511	3.31213	3.23972	3.16986	3.10245	3.03735	2.85498
5	4.32948	4.21236	3.99271	3.88965	3.79079	3.69590	3.60478	3.35216
6	5.07569	4.91732	4.62288	4.48592	4.35526	4.23054	4.11141	3.78448
7	5.78637	5.58238	5.20637	5.03295	4.86842	4.71220	4.56376	4.16042
8	6.46321	6.20979	5.74664	5.53482	5.33493	5.14612	4.96764	4.48732
9	7.10782	6.80169	6.24689	5.99525	5.75902	5.53705	5.32825	4.77158
10	7.72173	7.36009	6.71008	6.41766	6.14457	5.88923	5.65022	5.01877
11	8.30641	7.88687	7.13896	6.80519	6.49506	6.20652	5.93770	5.23371
12	8.86325	8.38384	7.53608	7.16073	6.81369	6.49236	6.19437	5.42062
13	9.39357	8.85268	7.90378	7.48690	7.10336	6.74987	6.42355	5.58315
14	9.89864	9.29498	8.24424	7.78615	7.36669	6.98187	6.62817	5.72448
15	10.37966	9.71225	8.55948	8.06069	7.60608	7.19087	6.81086	5.84737
16	10.83777	10.10590	8.85137	8.31256	7.82371	7.37916	6.97399	5.95424
17	11.27407	10.47726	9.12164	8.54363	8.02155	7.54879	7.11963	6.04716
18	11.68959	10.82760	9.37189	8.75563	8.20141	7.70162	7.24967	6.12797
19	12.08532	11.15812	9.60360	8.95012	8.36492	7.83929	7.36578	6.19823
20	12.46221	11.46992	9.81815	9.12855	8.51356	7.96333	7.46944	6.25933

From Table 2 it can be seen that the discount rate for three periods at 10% is 2.48685. Applying this amount to the annual cash flow of $1,000 produces a present value of $2,486.85.[2]

Tables 1 & 2 are further examples of templates that can be created on electronic spreadsheets. With one template, present values can be computed for any amount at any interest rate for any reasonable number of periods in seconds.

TIME PERIODS AND DISCOUNTING

In the preceding calculations, the discounting has been done on an annual basis using an annual interest rate. Discounting may also be done over shorter periods of time such as monthly, quarterly, or semiannually. When the time frame is less than one year, it is necessary to convert the annual interest rate to the applicable time frame. Assume, for example, that the investor in the preceding example received $500 **semiannually** for three years instead of $1,000 annually. In such case, the number of periods becomes 6(3x2), the rate of return is 5% (10% ÷ 2), the discount rate is 5.07569, and the present value of the future cash flows is $2,537.85 (5.07569 × $500). This amount is slightly higher than the $2,486.85 computed above because of compounding (interest is earned on interest).

COMPUTING THE PRESENT VALUE OF A BOND

The present value (or market price) of a bond is a function of three factors: (1) the expected dollar amounts to be received, (2) the length of time until the amounts are received, and (3) the investor's required rate of return. Because the first two factors are determined by the terms of the bond issue, they are fixed. By contrast, the third factor is variable.

When the investor's required rate of return is equal to the bond interest rate, the present value of the bonds will equal the face value of the bonds. To illustrate, assume that Southmark Corporation issues $1,000,000 par value 5-year bonds with interest of 10% payable semiannually when the investor's required rate of return is also 10%. In this case, the investor will receive (1) $1,000,000 at maturity and (2) a series of ten $50,000 interest payments [($1,000,000 × 10%) ÷ 2] over the term of the bonds. The length of time is expressed in terms of interest periods, in this case, 10, and the required rate of return per interest period, 5%. The computation of present value is shown below:

[2]The difference between 2.48686 and 2.48685 is due to rounding.

Present value of principal and interest (face value)

Present value of principal to be received at maturity	
$1,000,000 × PV of 1 due in 10 periods at 5%	
$1,000,000 × .61391 (Table 1)	$ 613,910
Present value of interest to be received periodically over the term of the bonds	
$50,000 × PV of 1 due periodically for 10 periods at 5%	
$50,000 × 7.72173 (Table 2)	386,090*
Present value of bonds	**$1,000,000**

*(Rounded).

Assume instead of the foregoing, that the investor's required rate of return is 12%. The future amounts are again $1,000,000 and $50,000, respectively, but now an interest rate of 6% (12% ÷ 2) must be used. The present value of the bonds is $926,395, as computed below:

Present value of principal and interest (discount)

10% Stated Interest Rate—12% Effective Rate	
Present value of principal to be received at maturity	
$1,000,000 × .55839 (Table 1)	$558,390
Present value of interest to be received periodically over the term of the bonds	
$50,000 × 7.36009 (Table 2)	368,005
Present value of bonds	**$926,395**

Conversely, if the stated interest rate is 12% and the effective interest rate is 10%, the present value of the bonds is $1,077,214 computed as follows:

Present value of principal and interest (premium)

12% Stated Interest Rate—10% Effective Rate	
Present value of principal to be received at maturity	
$1,000,000 × .61391 (Table 1)	$ 613,910
Present value of interest to be received periodically over the term of the bonds	
$60,000 × 7.72173 (Table 2)	463,304
Present value of bonds	**$1,077,214**

GLOSSARY

Bearer (coupon) bonds, p. 654
Bond indenture, p. 654
Callable bonds, p. 654
Capital lease, p. 670
Convertible bonds, p. 654
Debenture bonds, p. 654
Deferred income taxes, p. 672
Effective interest method of amortization, p. 662
Long-term liabilities, p. 652
Market (effective) interest rate, p. 658
Mortgage bonds, p. 653

Operating lease, p. 669
Present value, p. 656
Registered bonds, p. 654
Secured bonds, p. 653
Serial bonds, p. 654
Sinking fund, p. 666
Stated (contractual) interest rate, p. 658
Term bonds, p. 654
Unsecured bonds, p. 653

DEMONSTRATION PROBLEM

The Bando Corporation issues $1,000,000 five-year 12% A bonds on January 1, 1987 at 103. On July 1, 1987, the corporation issues $500,000 five-year 10% B bonds for $463,000. Both bonds pay interest on January 1 and July 1.

INSTRUCTIONS

(a) Journalize the issuance of the bonds.

(b) Journalize the accrual of interest and amortization of bond premium on December 31, 1987 assuming the straight-line method of amortization is used.

(c) Journalize the accrual of interest and amortization of bond discount at December 31, 1987 assuming the effective interest method of amortization is used and the effective interest rate is 12%.

SOLUTION TO DEMONSTRATION PROBLEM

(a)	Jan. 1	Cash	1,030,000	
		Premium on Bonds Payable		30,000
		Bonds Payable		1,000,000
		(To record sale of A bonds at a premium)		
	July 1	Cash	463,000	
		Discount on Bonds Payable	37,000	
		Bonds Payable		500,000
		(To record sale of B bonds at a discount)		
(b)	Dec. 31	Bond Interest Expense	57,000	
		Premium on Bonds Payable	3,000	
		Bond Interest Payable		60,000
		(To accrue bond interest and amortization of premium on A bonds from July 1 to Dec. 31)		
(c)	Dec. 31	Bond Interest Expense	27,780(a)	
		Discount on Bonds Payable		2,780
		Bond Interest Payable		25,000(b)
		(To accrue bond interest and amortization of discount on B bonds from July 1 to Dec. 31)		

(a) $463,000 × .12 × ½
(b) $500,000 × .10 × ½

*Note: All **asterisked** Questions, Exercises, and Problems relate to material contained in the Appendix to each chapter.

QUESTIONS

1. What is a long-term liability? Give some examples.

2. Fischer Company is considering financing the purchase of a new office building through bond financing. What are the possible advantages of bond financing over common stock financing? Explain.

3. Explain each of the following terms as they relate to a bond issue: (a) debenture; (b) secured; (c) serial; (d) registered; and (e) callable.

4. Describe the two major obligations incurred by a company when bonds are issued.

5. Assume that Mattco Inc. sold bonds with a par value of $100,000 for $95,000. Was the market rate of interest equal to, less than, or greater than the bonds' stated rate of interest? Explain.

6. Susan Shapiro and Mark Lane are discussing how the market price of a bond is determined. Susan believes that the market price of a bond is solely a function of the amount of the principal payment at the end of the term of a bond. Is she right? Discuss.

7. If a 12%, 10-year, $500,000 bond is issued at par and interest is paid semiannually, what is the amount of the interest payment at the end of the first semiannual period?

8. If the Bonds Payable account has a balance of $800,000 and the Premium on Bonds Payable account has a balance of $26,000, what is the carrying value of the bonds?

9. What are the two methods of amortizing discount and premium on bonds payable? Explain each.

10. Elan Corporation issues $200,000 of 8%, 5-year bonds on January 1, 1987, at 103. Assuming that the straight-line method is used to amortize the premium, what is the total amount of interest expense for 1987?

11. From question 10, if Elan Corporation used the effective interest method in amortizing the premium, will the annual interest expense increase or decrease over the life of the bonds? Explain.

12. Bob Hall is discussing the advantages of the effective interest method of amortization of bond discount with his accounting staff. What do you think Bob is saying?

13. Which accounts are debited and which are credited if a bond issue originally sold at a premium is redeemed at 98 immediately following the payment of interest?

14. Wayne Corporation is considering issuing a convertible bond. What is a convertible bond? Discuss the advantages of a convertible bond from the standpoint of (a) the bondholders and (b) the issuing corporation.

15. The financial statements of Afro-Arts Inc. discloses that it has a Bond Sinking Fund. What is a bond sinking fund? What is its purpose?

16. Garth Jones, a friend of yours, has recently purchased a home for $125,000, paying $25,000 down and the remainder financed by a 10½% mortgage, payable at $483.18 per month. At the end of the first year, Garth receives a statement from the bank indicating that only $350 of principal was paid during the year. At this rate, he calculates that it will take over 285 years to pay off the mortgage. Is he right? Discuss.

17. (a) What is a lease agreement? (b) What are the two most common types of leases? (c) Distinguish between the two types of leases.

18. Rodriquez Company rents a warehouse on a month-to-month basis for the storage of its excess inventory. The company periodically must rent space when its production greatly exceeds actual sales. For several years the company officials have discussed building their own storage facility, but their enthusiasm wavers when sales increase sufficiently to absorb the excess inventory. What is the nature of this type of lease agreement, and what accounting treatment should be accorded it?

19. Pickert Company entered into an agreement to lease 12 computers from Melissa Electronics Inc. The present value of the lease payments is $96,400. Assuming that this is a capital lease, what entry would Pickert Company make on the date of the lease agreement?

20. How is a company's taxable income measured? How is book income computed? Is there a difference between taxable and book income for a company in any given year?

21. In general, what are the requirements for the financial statement presentation of long-term liabilities?

***22.** On what factors is the present value of a future amount based?

***23.** From the tables in the chapter, find the appropriate present value discount factor for each of the following.

(a) A future amount to be received in 3 years with 12% annual interest.

(b) A future amount to be received in 5 years with 10% semiannual interest.

(c) A future amount to be received each of the next 4 years with 10% annual interest.

(d) A future amount to be received each of the next 3 years with 12% semiannual interest.

EXERCISES

E17-1 Hargrove Airlines is considering two alternatives for the financing of a purchase of a fleet of airplanes. These two alternatives are:

1. Issue 50,000 shares of common stock at $40 per share. (Cash dividends have not been paid nor is the payment of any contemplated.)
2. Issue 13%, 10-year bonds at par for $2,000,000.

It is estimated that the company will earn $800,000 before interest and taxes as a result of this purchase. The company has an estimated tax rate of 30% and has 90,000 shares of common stock outstanding prior to the new financing.

INSTRUCTIONS

Determine the effect on net income and earnings per share for these two methods of financing.

E17-2 Presented below are two independent situations.

(1) On January 1, the Freeman Company issued $80,000 of 12%, 10-year bonds at par. Interest is payable semiannually on July 1 and January 1.

(2) On March 1, the Hansen Company issued $60,000 of 10%, 10-year bonds dated January 1 at par plus accrued interest. Interest is payable semiannually on July 1 and January 1.

INSTRUCTIONS

For each of these two independent situations, present journal entries to record:

(a) The issuance of the bonds.
(b) The payment of interest on July 1.
(c) The accrual of interest on December 31.

E17–3 Duvick Company issued $200,000 of 8%, 20-year bonds on January 1, 1987, at 101. Interest is payable semiannually on July 1 and January 1. Duvick uses straight-line amortization for bond premium or discount.

INSTRUCTIONS

Prepare the journal entries to record:

(a) The issuance of the bonds.
(b) The payment of interest and the premium amortization on July 1, 1987.
(c) The accrual of interest and the premium amortization on December 31, 1987.

E17–4 Navarro Company issued $160,000 of 11%, 20-year bonds on December 31, 1986 for $173,720. This price provided a yield of 10% on the bonds. Interest is payable semiannually on June 30 and December 31. Navarro uses the effective interest method to amortize bond premium or discount.

INSTRUCTIONS

Prepare the journal entries to record (round to the nearest dollar):

(a) The issuance of the bonds.
(b) The payment of interest and the premium amortization on June 30, 1987.
(c) The payment of interest and the premium amortization on December 31, 1987.

E17–5 Vicki Prince Corporation issued $240,000 of 9%, 10-year bonds on June 30, 1987, for $225,045. This price provided a yield of 10% on the bonds. Interest is payable semiannually on December 31 and June 30. Prince uses the effective interest method to amortize bond premium or discount.

INSTRUCTIONS

Prepare the journal entries to record (round to the nearest dollar):

(a) The issuance of the bonds.
(b) The payment of interest and the discount amortization on December 31, 1987.
(c) The payment of interest and the discount amortization on June 30, 1988.

E17–6 Presented below are three independent situations:

(a) Mouis Corporation retired $110,000 par value of 12% bonds on June 30, 1987, at 103. The carrying value of the bonds at the redemption date was $106,350. The bonds pay semiannual interest and the interest payment due on June 30, 1987 has been made and recorded.
(b) Dougherty, Inc. retired $130,000 par value of 12.5% bonds on June 30, 1987, at 98. The carrying value of the bonds at the redemption date was $128,875. The bonds pay semiannual interest and the interest payment due on June 30, 1987, has been made and recorded.
(c) Struthers Company has $80,000 of 10%, 12-year convertible bonds outstanding. These bonds were sold at par and pay semiannual interest on June 30 and December 31 of each year. The bonds are convertible into 25 shares of Struthers $2 par common stock for each $1,000 worth of bonds. On December 31, 1987, after the

bond interest has been paid, $20,000 par value of bonds was converted. The market value of Struthers' common stock was $46 per share on December 31, 1987.

INSTRUCTIONS

For each independent situation above, prepare the appropriate journal entry for the redemption or conversion of the bonds on June 30, 1987.

E17-7 Dave Kukura Co. decides to establish a sinking fund for its $5,000,000 20-year bonds which are outstanding. The trustee indicates that an annual periodic contribution of $435,923 made at the end of the year is needed, assuming that an earnings rate of 6% is appropriate.

INSTRUCTIONS

Prepare the journal entries to record:

(a) The first deposit by Dave Kukura Co.

(b) The actual earnings in the second year. (Round to nearest dollar.)

(c) The redemption of the bonds at maturity.

E17-8 The Nair Co. purchases land costing $150,000 on January 1, 1987. Nair pays $30,000 in cash and issues a $120,000, 10%, mortgage note payable to finance the remainder. The terms provide for semiannual installment payments of $7,000.

INSTRUCTIONS

Prepare the journal entries to record the purchase of the land and the first two installment payments.

E17-9 Presented below are two independent situations.

1. American Car Rental leased a car to Jolitz Energy Company for one year. Terms of the operating lease agreement call for monthly payments of $400.
2. On January 1, 1987, Durham Digitronics, Inc. entered into an agreement to lease 20 computers from Guz Electronics. The terms of the lease agreement require an initial payment of $40,000 and then three annual rental payments of $100,000 (including 10% interest) beginning December 31, 1987. The present value of the three rental payments is $248,680. Durham considers this a capital lease.

INSTRUCTIONS

(a) Prepare the appropriate journal entry to be made by Jolitz Energy Company for the first lease payment.

(b) Prepare the journal entry to record the lease agreement on the books of Durham Digitronics on January 1, 1987. (Note that the down payment is made on this date.)

E17-10 Due to the difference in treatment of an expense item for taxable and accounting income, Lapeska Company reported the following taxable and accounting income figure for the three years given below:

	1985	1986	1987
Taxable income	$150,000	$130,000	$300,000
Accounting income	190,000	120,000	280,000

The company's income is taxed at 30%.

INSTRUCTIONS

Prepare the journal entry to record income tax expense, income tax liability, and deferred income taxes at the end of each of the three years.

E17-11 The adjusted trial balance for Barbara Corporation at the end of the current year contained the following accounts:

Lease liability	$ 58,500
Deferred income taxes (credit)	75,200
12% bonds payable	100,000
9% bonds payable	300,000
Premium on 12% bonds payable	32,000
Discount on 9% bonds payable	84,000
Bond sinking fund	243,750
Bond interest payable	6,000

INSTRUCTIONS

(a) Prepare the long-term liabilities section of the balance sheet.

(b) Indicate the proper balance sheet classification for the accounts listed above that do not belong in the long-term liabilities section.

***E17-12** Sally Weber Company intends to issue $50,000 of bonds paying 8% annual interest and due in 10 years.

INSTRUCTIONS

What would be the selling price if the bonds are sold to yield: (a) 6%, (b) 8%, and (c) 10%?

PROBLEMS

P17-1 Kish Gravel Company sold $3,600,000 of 6%, 18-year bonds on July 31, 1987. The bonds were dated July 31, 1987, and pay interest on January 31 and July 31. Kish Gravel Company uses the straight-line method to amortize bond premium or discount. The bonds were sold at 94.

INSTRUCTIONS

(a) Prepare the journal entry to record the issuance of the bonds on July 31, 1987.

(b) Prepare the journal entries to record the interest accrual and the amortization of the discount on December 31, 1987.

(c) Prepare the journal entries to record the payment of interest and the amortization of the discount on January 31, 1988.

(d) Prepare the journal entries to record the payment of interest and the amortization of the discount on July 31, 1988.

P17-2 McGhee Corporation sold $1,000,000 of 8%, 10-year bonds on April 1, 1987. The bonds were dated January 1, 1987 and pay interest on July 1 and January 1. McGhee Corporation uses the straight-line method to amortize bond premium or discount.

INSTRUCTIONS (Round all computations to nearest dollar.)

(a) Prepare all the necessary journal entries to record the issuance of the bonds and bond interest expense for 1987, assuming that the bonds sold at 104 plus accrued interest. (Note that the bonds will be outstanding for only nine years and nine months.)

(b) Prepare journal entries as in part (a) assuming that the bonds sold at 97 plus accrued interest.

P17–3 The following is taken from the Jeffrey Babcock Corp. balance sheet at December 31, 1987:

Current liabilities		
Bond interest payable (for two months from November 1 to December 31)		$36,667
Long-term liabilities		
Bonds payable, 11%, due November 1, 1998	$2,000,000	
Less: Discount on bonds payable	65,000	$1,935,000

The bonds are callable on any semiannual interest date. Babcock uses straight-line amortization for any bond premium or discount.

INSTRUCTIONS (Round all computations to the nearest dollar.)

(a) Prepare the necessary journal entries to record the semiannual interest payments and the discount amortization on both May 1 and November 1, 1988. (Note that as of December 31, 1987, the bonds will be outstanding for an additional 130 months.)

(b) Prepare the journal entry to record the redemption of $1,000,000 face value bonds on November 1, 1988. The bonds were called at 101 following payment of the interest in part (a).

(c) Prepare the journal entry to record the accrual of the bond interest at December 31, 1988 on the remaining bonds. Include the amortization of the remaining bond discount.

P17–4 On June 30, 1987, Soffner Satellites issued $1,000,000 face value of 9%, 10-year bonds at $937,689 to yield 10%. Soffner uses the effective interest method to amortize bond premium or discount. The bonds pay semiannual interest June 30 and December 31.

INSTRUCTIONS (Round all computations to the nearest dollar.)

(a) Prepare the journal entry to record the issuance of the bonds on June 30, 1987.

(b) Prepare the journal entry to record the payment of interest and the amortization of the discount on December 31, 1987.

(c) Prepare the journal entry to record the payment of interest and the amortization of the discount on June 30, 1988.

(d) Prepare the journal entry to record the payment of interest and the amortization of the discount on December 31, 1988.

(e) Prepare an amortization table through December 31, 1988 (three interest periods) for this bond issue.

P17–5 On June 30, 1987, Akers Chemical Company issued $2,000,000 face value of 13%, 20-year bonds at $2,150,460, a yield of 12%. Akers uses the effective interest methods to amortize bond premium or discount. The bonds pay semiannual interest on each June 30 and December 31.

INSTRUCTIONS

(a) Prepare the journal entries to record the following transactions.

1. The issuance of the bonds on June 30, 1987.

2. The payment of interest and the amortization of the premium on December 31, 1987.
3. The payment of interest and the amortization of the premium on June 30, 1988.
4. The payment of interest and the amortization of the premium on December 31, 1988.

(b) Show the proper balance sheet presentation for the liability for bonds payable on the December 31, 1988 balance sheet.

(c) Provide the answers to the following questions.
1. What amount of interest expense is reported for 1988?
2. Will the bond interest expense reported in 1988 be the same as, greater than, or less than the amount that would be reported if the straight-line method of amortization were used.
3. Determine the total cost of borrowing over the life of the bond.
4. Will the total bond interest expense be greater than, the same as, or less than the total interest expense if the straight-line method of amortization were used.

P17-6 Miller Corporation issued $200,000 face value of 10%, 5-year bonds on June 30, 1987, with interest payable June 30 and December 31. The bonds sold for $216,220, a yield of 8%. The company uses the effective interest method to amortize bond premium.

INSTRUCTIONS

(a) Prepare an amortization table through December 31, 1989 (five interest periods) for this bond issue. (Round all computations to the nearest dollar.)

(b) Show the proper balance sheet presentation of Bonds Payable and Premium on Bonds Payable at December 31, 1989.

P17-7 On January 1, 1987, Rubok Co. sold $500,000 (face value) of bonds. The bonds are dated January 1, 1987, and will mature on January 1, 1992. Interest is paid annually. The following amortization schedule was prepared by the accountant for the first year of the life of the bonds.

AMORTIZATION SCHEDULE

Yearly Interest Period	Interest to be Paid	Interest Expense	Amortization	Unamortized Amount	Carrying Value of Bonds
1/1/87 (Issue date)				$39,926	$539,926
1	$50,000	$43,194	$6,806	33,120	533,120

INSTRUCTIONS

On the basis of the information above, answer the following questions. (Round your answer to the nearest dollar or percent.)

(a) What is the stated (coupon) rate of interest for the bond issue?

(b) What is the market (effective) rate of interest for this bond issue?

(c) Prepare the journal entry to record the sale of the bond issue.

(d) Prepare the journal entry to record the accrual of interest on December 31, 1987.

(e) Indicate how the bonds are reported in the balance sheet at December 31, 1988.

(f) On January 1, 1989, the bonds were redeemed at a price of 103. Assume that all entries have been made to record bond interest and amortization to this date. Record the redemption.

P17-8 Presented below are three different lease transactions that occurred for Bicknell Inc. in 1987. Assume that all lease contracts start on January 1, 1987. In no case does Bicknell receive title to the properties leased during or at the end of the lease term.

	Lessor		
	Aetna Delivery	Matco Co.	Warren Auto
Type of property	Delivery equipment	Computer	Automobile
Yearly rental	$ 7,000	$ 3,000	$ 3,700
Lease term	5 years	3 years	1 year
Estimated economic life	6 years	7 years	5 years
Fair market value of lease asset	$31,000	$17,000	$11,000
Present value of the lease rental payments	$31,000	$ 6,800	$ 3,300
Bargain purchase option	None	None	None

INSTRUCTIONS

(a) Which of the leases above are operating leases and which are capital leases? Explain.

(b) How should the lease transaction for Matco Co. be recorded in 1987?

(c) How should the lease transaction for Aetna Delivery be recorded on January 1, 1987?

P17-9 The financial information for Reynolds Industries Inc. includes the following:

1.

Year	Income Taxes Payable
1986	$140,000
1987	75,000

2. On January 1, 1986, equipment costing $300,000 was purchased. For accounting purposes, the company uses straight-line depreciation over a 10-year life. For tax purposes, the company uses an accelerated method that results in depreciation of $45,000 in 1986 and $66,000 in 1987, respectively.
3. In January 1987, $225,000 was collected in advance rentals on a building for a three-year period. The entire $225,000 was reported as taxable income in 1987, but $150,000 of the $225,000 was reported as unearned revenue in 1987 for accounting purposes.
4. The tax rate is 30% in both 1986 and 1987.

INSTRUCTIONS

(a) Determine the amount entered in the Deferred Income tax account for 1986 and whether the amount is a debit or credit.

(b) Determine the amount entered in the Deferred Income tax account for 1987 and whether the amount is a debit or credit.

(c) Determine the balance in the Deferred Income tax account at December 31, 1987 and whether it is a debit or a credit balance.

(d) Prepare the entries for income taxes for both 1986 and 1987.

ALTERNATE PROBLEMS

P17-1A Kurt Bay Electric sold $2,400,000 of 8%, 12-year bonds on September 30, 1987. The bonds were dated September 30 and pay interest March 31 and September 30. Kurt Bay Electric uses the straight-line method to amortize bond premium or discount. The bonds were sold at 102.

INSTRUCTIONS

(a) Prepare the journal entry to record the issuance of the bonds on September 30, 1987.

(b) Prepare the journal entries to record the interest accrual and the amortization of the premium on December 31, 1987.

(c) Prepare the journal entries to record the payment of interest and the amortization of the premium on March 31, 1988.

(d) Prepare the journal entries to record the payment of interest and the amortization of the premium on September 30, 1988.

P17-2A Meyers Company sold $1,200,000 of 10%, 10-year bonds on April 1, 1987. The bonds were dated January 1, 1987 and pay interest July 1 and January 1. Meyers Company uses the straight-line method to amortize bond premium or discount.

INSTRUCTIONS (Round all computations to the nearest dollar.)

(a) Prepare all the necessary journal entries to record the issuance of the bonds and bond interest expense for 1987, assuming that the bonds sold at 102 plus accrued interest. (Note that the bonds will be outstanding for only nine years and nine months.)

(b) Prepare journal entries as in part (a) assuming that the bonds sold at 96 plus accrued interest.

P17-3A The following is taken from the Hamsmith Oil Company balance sheet at December 31, 1987:

Current liabilities		
Bond interest payable (for three months from October 1 to December 31)		$ 90,000
Long-term liabilities		
Bonds payable, 12%, due October 1, 1998	$3,000,000	
Add: Premium on Bonds Payable	258,000	$3,258,000

The bonds are callable on any semiannual interest date. Hamsmith uses straight-line amortization for any bond premium or discount.

INSTRUCTIONS

(a) Prepare the necessary journal entries to record the semiannual interest payments and the premium amortization on both April 1 and October 1, 1988. (Note that as of December 31, 1987, the bonds will be outstanding for an additional 129 months.)

(b) Prepare the journal entry to record the redemption of $1,000,000 face value bonds on October 1, 1988. The bonds were called at 102.

(c) Prepare the journal entry to record the accrual of the bond interest at December 31, 1988 on the remaining bonds. Include the amortization of the remaining bond premium.

P17-4A On June 30, 1987, Springborn Corporation issued $1,000,000 face value of 10%, 10-year bonds at $1,135,807, a yield of 8%. Springborn uses the effective interest method to amortize bond premium or discount. The bonds pay semiannual interest June 30 and December 31.

INSTRUCTIONS (Round all computations to the nearest dollar.)

(a) Prepare the journal entry to record the issuance of the bonds on June 30, 1987.
(b) Prepare the journal entry to record the payment of interest and the amortization of the premium on December 31, 1987.
(c) Prepare the journal entry to record the payment of interest and the amortization of the premium on June 30, 1988.
(d) Prepare the journal entry to record the payment of interest and the amortization of the premium on December 31, 1988.
(e) Prepare an amortization table through December 31, 1988 (three interest periods) for this bond issue.

P17-5A On June 30, 1987, the Albright Light Company issued $2,000,000 face value of 14%, 20-year bonds at $1,761,500, a yield of 16%. Albright uses the effective interest method to amortize bond premium or discount. The bonds pay semiannual interest June 30 and December 31.

INSTRUCTIONS

(a) Prepare the journal entries to record the following transactions.
   1. The issuance of the bonds on June 30, 1987.
   2. The payment of interest and the amortization of the discount on December 31, 1987.
   3. The payment of interest and the amortization of the discount on June 30, 1988.
   4. The payment of interest and the amortization of the discount on December 31, 1988.
(b) Show the proper balance sheet presentation for the liability for bonds payable on the December 31, 1988 balance sheet.
(c) Provide the answers to the following questions.
   1. What amount of interest expense is reported for 1988?
   2. Will the bond interest expense reported in 1988 be the same as, greater than, or less than the amount that would be reported if the straight-line method of amortization were used?
   3. Determine the total cost of borrowing over the life of the bond.
   4. Will the total bond interest expense be greater than, the same as, or less than the total interest expense that would be reported if the straight-line method of amortization were used?

P17-6A Martner Corporation issued $300,000 face value of 8%, 5-year bonds on June 30, 1987, with interest payable June 30 and December 31. The bonds sold for $276,830, a yield of 10%.

INSTRUCTIONS

(a) Prepare an amortization table for the first three years (five interest periods) of this bond issue. (Round all computations to the nearest dollar.)
(b) Show the proper balance sheet presentation of Bonds Payable and Discount on Bonds Payable at December 31, 1989.

P17-7A On June 30, 1987, Sanchez Inc. sold $1,000,000 (face value) of bonds. The bonds are dated June 30, 1987, and will mature on June 30, 1990. Interest is paid semiannually. The following schedule was prepared by the accountant for 1987.

AMORTIZATION SCHEDULE

Semi Annual Interest Period	Interest to be Paid	Interest Expense	Amortization	Unamortized Amount	Carrying Value of Bonds
6/30/87 (Issue date)				$50,752	$949,248
1	$40,000	$47,462	$7,462	43,290	956,710

INSTRUCTIONS

On the basis of the information above, answer the following questions. (Round your answer to the nearest dollar or percent.)

(a) What is the stated (coupon) rate of interest for this bond issue?

(b) What is the market (effective) rate of interest for this bond issue?

(c) Prepare the journal entry to record the sale of the bond issue.

(d) Prepare the journal entry to record the payment of interest and amortization on December 31, 1987.

(e) Indicate how the bonds would be reported on the balance sheet at June 30, 1988, if financial statements are prepared on this date.

(f) On January 1, 1989, the bonds were redeemed at a price of 104. Assume that all entries have been made to record the bond interest and amortization to date. Record the redemption.

P17-8A Presented below are three different lease transactions in which Smith Enterprises engaged in 1987. Assume that all lease transactions start on January 1, 1987. In no case does Smith receive title to the properties leased during or at the end of the lease term.

	Lessor		
	Caden Inc.	Nankin Co.	Madison Associates
Type of property	Furniture	Truck	Bulldozer
Bargain purchase option	None	None	None
Lease term	1 year	6 years	3 years
Estimated economic life	5 years	6 years	8 years
Yearly rental	$ 7,000	$ 6,000	$12,000
Fair market value of leased asset	$27,500	$24,000	$79,000
Present value of the lease rental payments	$ 6,500	$24,000	$28,000

INSTRUCTIONS

(a) Identify the leases above as operating or capital leases. Explain.

(b) How should the lease transaction for Nankin Co. be recorded on January 1, 1987?

(c) How should the lease transactions for Caden Inc. be recorded in 1987?

P17-9A The financial information for Garvey Company includes the following:

1.

Year	Income Taxes Payable
1986	$170,000
1987	120,000

2. On January 1, 1986, equipment costing $400,000 was purchased. For accounting purposes, the company uses straight-line depreciation over an eight-year period. For tax purposes, the company uses an accelerated method that results in depreciation of $60,000 in 1986 and $88,000 in 1987, respectively.
3. In January 1987, $300,000 was collected in advance rentals on a building for a four-year period. The entire $300,000 was reported as taxable income in 1987, but $180,000 of the $300,000 was reported as unearned revenue in 1987 for accounting purposes.
4. The tax rate is 30% in both 1986 and 1987.

INSTRUCTIONS

(a) Determine the amount entered in the Deferred Income tax account for 1986 and whether the amount is a debit or credit.

(b) Determine the amount entered in the Deferred Income tax account for 1987 and whether the amount is a debit or credit.

(c) Determine the balance in the Deferred Income tax account at December 31, 1987, and whether it is a debit or a credit balance.

(d) Prepare the entries for income taxes for both 1986 and 1987.

DECISION CASE

Presented below is the condensed balance sheet for Heartland, Inc. as of December 31, 1987:

HEARTLAND, INC.
Balance Sheet
December 31, 1987

Current assets	$ 700,000	Current liabilities	$1,100,000
Plant assets	1,400,000	Long-term liabilities	600,000
		Common stock	300,000
		Retained earnings	100,000
Total assets	$2,100,000		$2,100,000

Heartland has decided that it needs to purchase a new crane for its operations. The new crane costs $750,000 and has a useful life of 15 years. However, Heartland's bank has refused to provide any help in financing the purchase of the new equipment, even though Heartland is willing to pay an above market interest rate for the financing.

The chief financial officer for Heartland, Sue Atkins, has discussed with the manufacturer of the crane the possibility of a lease arrangement. After some negotiation, the manufacturer of the equipment agrees to lease the crane to Heartland under the following terms: length of the lease, 7 years; payments, $100,000 per year. The present value of the lease payments is $516,042.

The board of directors at Heartland is delighted with this new lease. They reason they have the use of the crane for the next seven years. In addition, Sue Atkins notes that this type of financing is a good deal because it will keep debt off the balance sheet.

INSTRUCTIONS

(a) Why do you think the bank decided not to loan money to Heartland, Inc.?

(b) How should this lease transaction be reported in the financial statements?

(c) What did Sue Atkins mean when she said "leasing will keep debt off the balance sheet"?

CHAPTER 18

University of Colorado

CHAPTER 18

LONG-TERM INVESTMENTS AND CONSOLIDATED FINANCIAL STATEMENTS

STUDY OBJECTIVES

After studying this chapter, you should be able to:

1. Explain the entries for long-term investments in bonds.
2. Identify the guidelines for determining the accounting treatment of long-term investments in stocks.
3. Describe the nature and purpose of consolidated financial statements.
4. Indicate the content of a work sheet for a consolidated balance sheet.
5. Enumerate the steps to recognize the minority stockholders' interest in subsidiary companies.
6. Explain the content and form of a consolidated income statement.
7. Distinguish between the methods of accounting for a business combination.

Many corporations have a separate section entitled long-term investments (or simply investments) in their balance sheets. This section, which is generally listed immediately below current assets, may include (1) investments in bonds, (2) investments in common and preferred stocks, (3) bond sinking funds, and (4) miscellaneous items such as long-term receivables and advances to other companies. A company's long-term investments may represent a significant portion of its total assets. As examples, American Can Company's investments were 43% of its total assets and General Electric Company's investments were 20% of its total assets.

This chapter is divided into two sections. First, accounting for long-term investments in bonds and stocks is discussed. Then the preparation of consolidated financial statements is explained. Large companies, such as General Motors Corporation (owns Hughes Aircraft Company and Electronic Data Systems) control other companies, and it is often useful to combine (consolidate) these companies for financial reporting purposes. In such cases, consolidated financial statements are prepared for reporting purposes.

SECTION ONE—INVESTMENTS IN BONDS AND STOCKS

For accounting purposes, investments in bonds and stocks are classified as either short term or long term. An investment is considered to be short term when it is readily marketable and it is expected that the securities will be converted into cash within the next year or the operating cycle, whichever is longer. In contrast, an investment is considered to be long term when it is expected that the securities will be held for a longer period.

LONG-TERM INVESTMENTS IN BONDS

Long-term investments in bonds consist of a wide variety of city, state, and federal bonds and bonds issued by corporations. Recall that in Chapter 17, bonds are rated on the basis of their quality. Thus, an investor can minimize risk by buying only highly rated bonds. An investment in high-quality U.S. government bonds, for example, is virtually risk free. Long-term investments in bonds are generally made for the purpose of earning periodic interest rather than for market appreciation.

ACCOUNTING ENTRIES

Accounting for long-term investments in bonds is similar to the accounting for marketable debt securities. For example, **the investment is recorded at cost, which consists of the market price of the bonds plus brokerage fees but excludes any accrued interest.** Entries are made periodically for the receipt and accrual of bond interest. Additional entries, however, are required when the cost of the bonds differs from the face value of the bonds. A bond sells at a discount (below face value) when the prevailing market (effective) rate of interest for the security is higher than the stated (contractual) interest rate. Conversely, a bond sells at a premium (above face value) when the foregoing relationship between the market and stated interest rate is reversed. **For a long-term investment in bonds, any bond discount or premium is amortized to interest revenue over the remaining term of the bonds.** Like the issuer of the bonds, the investor uses either the straight-line or effective interest method of amortization.

Entries at Acquisition

To illustrate the accounting for long-term bond investments, assume that on January 1, 1987, Steeb Company pays $92,000 plus brokerage fees of $600 for 100 Fox Corporation 10% bonds due in 5 years with interest payable semiannually on July 1 and January 1. The bonds are purchased at a discount of $7,400, since cost ($92,600) is below face value ($100,000). Steeb's investment is recorded as follows:

Jan.	1	Investment in Fox Bonds	92,600	
		Cash		92,600
		(To record purchase of 100 bonds)		

Note that the discount ($7,400) is not recorded in a separate discount account. This procedure reflects current practice, and enables the investment account to be carried directly at cost.[1]

If bonds are purchased with accrued interest, the accrued interest is usually debited to Interest Receivable. On the next interest date, the receipt of interest must be allocated between Interest Receivable and Interest Revenue.

Entries for Bond Interest

During the time the bonds are held, it is necessary to record the receipt of bond interest revenue and the amortization of any bond discount or premium. For bonds purchased at a discount, the Investment account is written up to face value through amortization. Conversely, for bonds purchased at a premium, the Investment account is written down to face value through amortization. If the straight-line method of amortization is used, the semiannual amortization of bond discount for Steeb Company is $740 ($7,400 ÷ 10). The entry on July 1 to record the receipt of $5,000 of interest ($100,000 × 10% × ½) and the amortization of bond discount is:

July	1	Cash	5,000	
		Investment in Fox Bonds	740	
		Interest Revenue		5,740
		(To record receipt of interest and amortization of bond discount)		

Note that the discount amortization is debited directly to the Investment account.

If the effective interest method of amortization is used by Steeb Company, the credit to Interest Revenue and the debit to Investment in Fox Bonds are different. Under this method, (1) interest revenue is determined by multiplying the carrying (book) value of the bonds at the beginning of the period by the effective rate of interest, and (2) the amortization amount for bond discount or premium is the difference between bond interest expense and the

[1]An acceptable alternative entry, which will not be used in this textbook, would be to debit the investment account for $100,000 and credit a contra asset account, Discount on Investment in Bonds, for $7,400.

interest to be received. For example, assume that the purchase of the Fox Corporation bonds for $92,600 results in a market rate of interest of 12% annually. Given that interest is paid semiannually, the credit to Interest Revenue is the carrying value of the bonds on January 1 ($92,600), times 6% or $5,556, and the debit to the Investment in Fox Bonds is $556 ($5,556 − $5,000). Thus, the entry under the effective interest method on July 1 is:

July	1	Cash	5,000	
		Investment in Fox Bonds	556	
		Interest Revenue		5,556
		(To record receipt of interest and amortization of bond discount)		

Entries For Sale of Bonds

If the bonds are sold before maturity, the Investment account is credited for its carrying value as of the date of disposal. For example, if the Fox Corporation bonds are sold on January 1, 1989, the carrying value (using the straight-line method) is $95,560 ($92,600 + $2,960 [4 × $740]). Assuming that cash proceeds are $98,000, the entry is:

Jan.	1	Cash	98,000	
		Investment in Fox Bonds		95,560
		Gain on Sale of Bonds		2,440
		(To record sale of Fox Corporation bonds)		

STATEMENT PRESENTATION

Long-term investments in bonds are separately reported in the investment section of the balance sheet immediately below current assets at their carrying value, which is cost plus or minus amortization to date. In the income statement, interest revenue and any gains from the sale of the bonds are reported under other revenues and gains whereas any losses are reported under other expenses and losses.

LONG-TERM INVESTMENTS IN STOCKS

Generally, the primary reason for the investment in stock is to increase the investor's net income. This may be achieved (1) through dividends received, (2) by selling the shares at a market price that is higher than cost, or (3) by using the investments for leverage in developing new markets and in diversifying operations. For example, at one time Gulf & Western Industries, Inc. had the following investments in common stock as illustrated at the top of page 699 that affected its operations.

The accounting for long-term investments in common stock is based on the extent of the investor's influence on the operating and financial affairs of the issuing corporation (commonly called the investee). For accounting purposes, the extent of an investor's influence is classified as either (1) insignificant, (2)

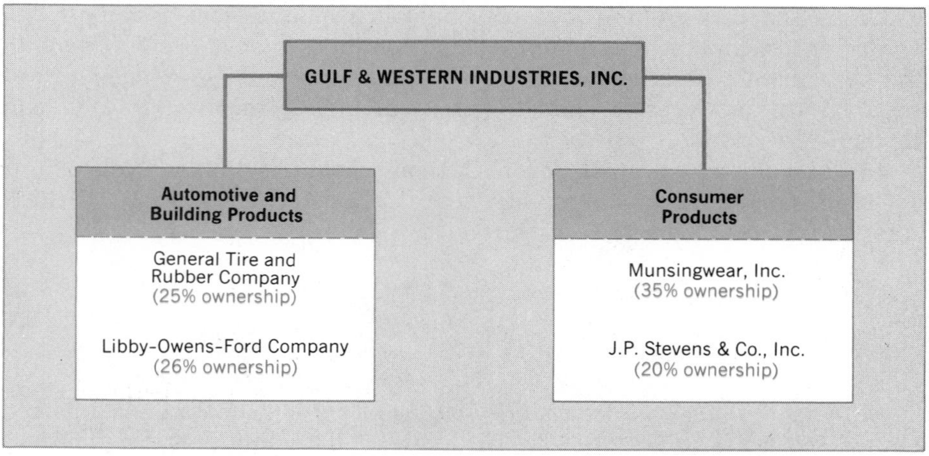

Diversified investments of Gulf & Western Industries, Inc.

significant, or (3) controlling based on the investor's ownership interest in the investee. For each level of influence, a specific method should be used in accounting for the investment as indicated by the following:

Guidelines for accounting for investor's ownership interest

Investor's Ownership Interest in Investee	Presumed Influence on Investee	Accounting Guidelines
Less than 20%	Insignificant	Cost method or lower of cost or market method
Between 20 and 50%	Significant	Equity method
More than 50%	Controlling	Consolidated financial statements

The presumed influence may be negated by extenuating circumstances. For example, a company that acquires a 25% interest in another company in a "hostile" takeover may not have any significant influence over the investee.[2] In other words, companies are required to use judgment instead of blindly following the guidelines above.

COST METHOD

As indicated above, when an investor owns less than 20% of the common stock of another corporation, it is presumed that the investor has relatively little influence on the investee. **As a result, the earning of net income by the investee is not considered a proper basis for recognition of income from the investment by the investor.** The reason is that increased net assets resulting from the investee's profitable operation may be permanently retained in the business by the investee. Therefore, net income is not considered earned by the investor until dividends are received from the investee.

[2]Among the factors that should be considered in determining an investor's influence are whether (1) the investor has representation on the investee's board of directors, (2) the investor participates in the investee's policy-making process, (3) there are material transactions between the investor and investee, and (4) the common stock held by other stockholders is concentrated or dispersed.

Under the **cost method** the investment in common stock is initially recorded at cost, and the investment account continues to be carried at cost until the shares are sold. The investor (1) makes no entry for net income (loss) reported by the investee and (2) credits dividends received to Dividend Revenue.

To illustrate, assume that Saxon Company acquires 10% of Nolex Inc.'s 100,000 shares of common stock at a cost of $15 per share on March 4, 1987. The entry is as follows:

Mar. 4	Investment in Nolex Common Stock	150,000	
	Cash		150,000
	(To record purchase of 10,000 shares)		

At the end of 1987, Nolex reports $80,000 of net income and declares and pays a $50,000 ($.50 per share) cash dividend. The only entry required by Saxon is for the dividends received of $5,000 (10,000 shares × $.50) as shown below:

Dec. 31	Cash	5,000	
	Dividend Revenue		5,000
	(To record receipt of $.50 per share dividend)		

Note that no entry is made to record Saxon Company's 10% share of Nolex Inc.'s net income.

When the stock is sold, the Investment account is credited for the cost of the shares sold. Thus, if 5,000 shares of Nolex common stock are sold on February 3, 1988 at $18 per share, a gain of $3 per share is realized, and the following entry results:

Feb. 3	Cash	90,000	
	Investment in Nolex Common Stock		75,000
	Gain on Sale of Nolex Common Stock		15,000
	(To record sale of 5,000 shares of Nolex Stock)		

The gain is reported in the other revenue and gains section of the income statement.

The cost method is also applicable to long-term investments in preferred stocks. Because preferred stock is usually nonvoting, ownership of preferred stock gives the investor no opportunity to exert significant influence over the affairs of the investee.

LOWER OF COST OR MARKET METHOD

The lower of cost or market method should be used when the investor's influence is insignificant and the stocks held are marketable equity securities. Marketable equity securities include ownership shares (e.g., common stock and preferred stock) that are publicly traded. These types of securities should be reported at the lower of cost or market value on a total portfolio basis, rather than item-by-item.

The application of the **lower of cost or market method** to long-term marketable equity securities is similar to the procedures followed for short-term

marketable equity securities. **The major difference is that the unrealized loss account that results when market is less than cost is reported as a deduction from total stockholders' equity.**

To illustrate, assume that on December 31, 1987, the aggregate cost of long-term marketable equity securities held by Dawson, Inc. exceeds their aggregate market value by $100,000. The entry to recognize the unrealized loss is:

Dec. 31	Unrealized Loss on Long-Term Marketable Equity Securities	100,000	
	Allowance for Excess of Cost of Long-Term Marketable Equity Securities over Market Value		100,000
	(To value long-term investment at lower of cost or market)		

The allowance account is a contra asset account which is deducted from the investment account in the balance sheet. The unrealized loss account is reported under stockholders' equity. Assuming that Dawson, Inc. has common stock of $3,000,000 and retained earnings of $1,500,000, the statement presentation of the unrealized loss is as follows:

Statement presentation of unrealized loss

Stockholders' equity	
Common stock	$3,000,000
Retained earnings	1,500,000
Total paid-in capital and retained earnings	4,500,000
Less: Unrealized loss on long-term marketable equity securities	(100,000)
Total stockholders' equity	$4,400,000

Note that the presentation of the unrealized loss is similar to the statement presentation of treasury stock within the stockholders' equity section. This presentation informs the statement user of the potential loss that may be suffered from its investment in long-term marketable equity securities.

If, at the end of 1988, the aggregate cost of the securities exceeds their market value by $80,000, the allowance account is debited for $20,000 and the unrealized loss account is credited for $20,000. The entry is as follows:

Dec. 31	Allowance for Excess of Cost of Long-Term Marketable Equity Securities over Market Value	20,000	
	Unrealized Loss on Long-Term Marketable Equity Securities		20,000

Thus, the allowance balance and the unrealized loss account are adjusted each period as required. The allowance account can never have a debit balance, however, because the carrying value of the investment would be reported at higher than its original cost.

EQUITY METHOD

When an investor owns between 20% and 50% of the common stock of a corporation, it is generally presumed that the investor has significant influence over the financial and operating activities of the investee. As a result,

the investor should record its share of the net income (net loss) of the investee in the year when it is earned. In this case, the investor can insure that any net asset increases resulting from net income will be paid in dividends if desired. To wait until a dividend is received ignores the fact that the investor is better off if the investee has earned income.

In addition, using dividends as a basis for recognizing income poses additional problems. For example, assume that the investee reports a net loss, but the investor exerts influence to force a dividend payment from the investee. In this case, the investor reports income, even though the investee is experiencing a loss. **In other words, if dividends are used as a basis for recognizing income, the economics of the situation are not properly reported.**

Under the **equity method,** the investment in common stock is initially recorded at cost, and the investment account is adjusted annually. Each year, the investor (1) debits the investment account and credits income for its share of the investee's net income[3] and (2) credits dividends received to the investment account. The investment account is reduced for dividends received, because the investor's interest in the net assets of the investee is decreased when a dividend is paid.

To illustrate, assume that Milar Corporation acquires a 30% equity in the common stock of Beck Company for $120,000 on January 1, 1987. The entry to record this transaction is:

Jan. 1	Investment in Beck Company Stock	120,000	
	Cash		120,000
	(To record purchase of Beck common stock)		

For 1987, Beck reports net income of $100,000 and declares and pays a $40,000 cash dividend. Milar is required to record (1) its share of Beck's income, $30,000 (30% × $100,000) and (2) the reduction in the investment account for the dividends received, $12,000 ($40,000 × 30%). The entries are:

(1)

Dec. 31	Investment in Beck Common Stock	30,000	
	Income from Investment in Beck Company		30,000
	(To record 30% equity in Beck's 1987 net income)		

(2)

Dec. 31	Cash	12,000	
	Investment in Beck Common Stock		12,000
	(To record dividends received)		

During the year, the investment account has increased by $18,000 ($30,000 − $12,000), which is 30% of Milar's equity in the $60,000 increase in Beck's retained earnings ($100,000 − $40,000). In addition, Milar will report $30,000 of income from its investment, which is 30% of Beck's net income of $100,000. Note that the difference between reported income under the cost method and reported income under the equity method can be significant. For

[3]Conversely, the investor debits a loss account and credits the investment account for its share of the investee's net loss.

example, Milar would report only $12,000 of income (30% × $40,000) under the cost method with no change in the investment account balance.

RECEIPT OF STOCK DIVIDENDS OR STOCK SPLITS

While holding stock as an investment, the investor may receive additional shares of stock as a result of a stock dividend or a stock split. Both events result in an increase in the number of shares held. However, neither event results in revenue to the investor, because (1) no assets are received, and (2) the investor's percentage ownership interest in the issuing corporation remains the same.

The investor, therefore, does not make a formal accounting entry for a stock dividend or a stock split under either the cost or equity method. Instead, a notation is made in the investment account indicating the additional shares that have been received. The carrying value of the investment at the time of the event is then divided by the total shares currently being held to determine a new cost per share basis for the stock. To illustrate, assume that the Landon Corporation holds 10,000 shares (15%) of the common stock of Jones Inc. acquired at a cost of $132,000 ($13.20 per share). The issuer effects a 2 for 1 stock split on May 1 and a 10% stock dividend on December 1. The revised cost after each event is $6.60 and $6.00 per share, as shown below.

Stock split and stock dividend effects on cost per share

Transaction	Shares Acquired	Total Cost	Cost per Share
Purchase	10,000	$132,000	$13.20
Stock split (2 for 1)	10,000	-0-	-0-
Total shares	20,000	132,000	**6.60**
Stock dividend (10%)	2,000	-0-	-0-
Total shares	22,000	$132,000	**$ 6.00**

If Landon Company sells 1,000 shares of Jones Inc. on December 20 (after the stock split and stock dividend) at $8.00 per share, the following entry is made:

Dec. 20	Cash	8,000	
	Investment in Jones Inc. Stock		6,000
	Gain on Sale of Investment		2,000
	(To record sale of 1,000 shares of common stock)		

Note that the investment account is credited for the adjusted cost per share ($6.00) rather than the original cost per share ($13.20).

STATEMENT PRESENTATION

Long-term investments in stock are reported in the investment section of the balance sheet. Based on the method of accounting used, the investment in stocks may be reported at cost, lower of cost or market, or at equity. When the lower of cost or market method is used, unrealized losses are reported as a deduction in the stockholders' equity section.

In the income statement, dividend revenue is reported under other revenues and gains. Income recognized under the equity method is also shown in this section as are all gains on the sale of long-term investments in stock. Losses from sales and losses recognized under the equity method are reported under other expenses and losses.

SECTION TWO—CONSOLIDATED FINANCIAL STATEMENTS

When a company owns more than 50% of the common stock of another company, consolidated financial statements are usually prepared; that is, the investor and the investee report their assets, liabilities, revenues, and expenses as one company. Provided below are examples of two companies and some of the companies they own:

Examples of investor and investee relationships

Beatrice Foods	**American Brands, Inc.**
Tropicana Frozen Juices	American Tobacco Company
Switzer Candy Company	Master Lock Company
Samsonite Corporation	Pinkerton's Security Service
Dannon Yogurt Company	Titleist Golf Company

Companies under common control are referred to as **affiliated companies.**

PARENT AND SUBSIDIARY COMPANY RELATIONSHIPS

A company that owns more than 50% of the common stock of another entity is known as the **parent** company. The entity whose stock is owned by the parent company is called the **subsidiary** company. Because of its stock ownership, the parent company has a **controlling interest** in the subsidiary company.

Mobil Corporation, for example, owns 100% of the common stock of Montgomery Ward. The common stockholders of Mobil will elect the board of directors of Mobil Corporation, who, in turn, will select the officers and managers of the company. The board of directors will control the property owned by the corporation, which includes the common stock of Montgomery Ward. Thus, they are in a position to elect the board of directors of Montgomery Ward and, in effect, control its operations. These relationships are graphically illustrated at the top of page 705.

If the parent company acquires 100% of the stock of the subsidiary, that subsidiary is said to be **wholly owned.** When the parent company's controlling interest in a subsidiary is less than 100%, the subsidiary is only **partially owned.** Under this arrangement, the ownership of the subsidiary is divided into two classes: (1) the **majority interest** represented by the stockholders who own the controlling interest, and (2) the **minority interest** represented by the stockholders who are not part of the controlling group.

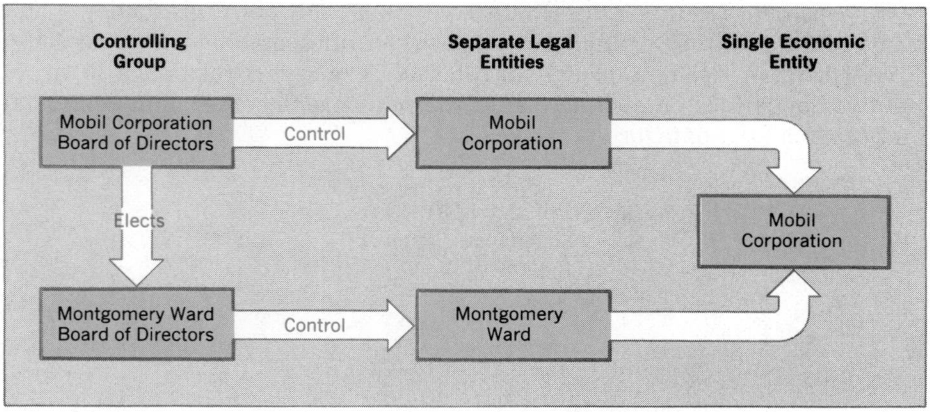

Mobil Corporation's control of Montgomery Ward

PURPOSE OF CONSOLIDATED FINANCIAL STATEMENTS

Consolidated financial statements present the details of the assets and liabilities controlled by the parent company and the aggregate profitability of the affiliated companies. **These statements are especially useful to the stockholders, board of directors, and management of the parent company.** Moreover, consolidated statements inform creditors, prospective investors, and regulatory agencies as to the magnitude and scope of operations of the companies operating under common control. For example, regulators and the courts undoubtedly used the consolidated statements of American Telephone & Telegraph (AT&T) to determine whether a breakup of AT&T was in the public interest.

Conversely, consolidated financial statements are of limited value to minority stockholders and creditors of the subsidiary companies, because they do not report separate financial position or earning power of any of the individual entities. For this information, interested parties should use the financial statements of the separate subsidiary companies.

PREPARATION OF CONSOLIDATED BALANCE SHEET

Consolidated balance sheets are prepared from the individual balance sheets of the affiliated companies. They are not prepared from ledger accounts kept by the consolidated entity because only the separate legal entities maintain accounting records.

All items in the individual balance sheets are included in the consolidated balance sheet except amounts that pertain to transactions between the affiliated companies. Such transactions are identified as **intercompany transactions.** The process of excluding these transactions in preparing consolidated statements is referred to as **intercompany eliminations.** These eliminations are necessary to avoid overstating assets, liabilities, and stockholders' equity in the consolidated balance sheet.

To illustrate, assume that on January 2, 1987, Powers Construction Company acquires through purchases on the securities markets 100% of Serto Brick Company's common stock for $150,000. The separate balance sheets of the two companies immediately after the purchase, together with combined and consolidated data, are presented below.[4]

Combined and consolidated information

POWERS COMPANY AND SERTO COMPANY
Balance Sheets
January 2, 1987

Assets	Powers Company	Serto Company	Combined Data	Consolidated Data
Current assets	$ 50,000	$ 80,000	$130,000	$130,000
Investment in Serto Company common stock	150,000		150,000	-0-
Plant and equipment (net)	325,000	145,000	470,000	470,000
Total assets	$525,000	$225,000	$750,000	$600,000
Liabilities and stockholders' equity				
Current liabilities	$ 50,000	$ 75,000	$125,000	$125,000
Common stock	300,000	100,000	400,000	300,000
Retained earnings	175,000	50,000	225,000	175,000
Total liabilities and stockholders' equity	$525,000	$225,000	$750,000	$600,000

The balances in the "combined" column are obtained by adding the items in the separate balance sheets of the affiliated companies. The combined totals do not represent a consolidated balance sheet, because there has been a double counting of assets and owners' equity in the amount of $150,000.

The Investment in Serto Company common stock that appears on the balance sheet of Powers Company represents an interest in the net assets of Serto. As a result, there has been a double counting of assets. Similarly, there has been a double counting in stockholders' equity, because the common stock of Serto Company is completely owned by the stockholders of Powers Company.

The balances in the consolidated columns above are the amounts that should appear in the consolidated balance sheet. The double counting has been eliminated by showing Investment in Serto Company at zero and by reporting only the common stock and retained earnings of Powers Company as stockholders' equity.

USE OF A WORK SHEET

The preparation of consolidated balance sheets is usually facilitated by the use of a work sheet. As illustrated on page 707, the work sheet for a consolidated balance sheet contains columns for (1) the balance sheet data for the separate legal entities, (2) intercompany eliminations, and (3) consolidated

[4]Condensed data will be used throughout this material to keep details at a minimum.

data. All data in the work sheet relate to the preceding example in which Powers Company acquires 100% ownership of Serto Company for $150,000. The intercompany elimination results in a credit to the Investment account maintained by Powers Company for its balance, $150,000, and debits to the Common Stock and Retained Earnings accounts of Serto Company for their respective balances, $100,000 and $50,000. The credit amount equals the sum of the debits in this example, because (1) the elimination is made at the date of acquisition, (2) the parent company acquired 100% ownership, and (3) the cost of the investment ($150,000) is equal to the book value ($150,000) of the subsidiary's net assets.

Work sheet—Cost equals book value

POWERS COMPANY AND SUBSIDIARY
Work Sheet—Consolidated Balance Sheet
January 2, 1987 (Acquisition Date)

Assets	Powers Company	Serto Company	Eliminations Dr.	Eliminations Cr.	Consolidated Data
Current assets	50,000	80,000			130,000
Investment in Serto Company common stock	150,000			150,000	-0-
Plant and equipment, net	325,000	145,000			470,000
Totals	525,000	225,000			600,000
Liabilities and stockholders' equity					
Current liabilities	50,000	75,000			125,000
Common stock – Powers Company	300,000				300,000
Common stock – Serto Company		100,000	100,000		-0-
Retained earnings – Powers Company	175,000				175,000
Retained earnings – Serto Company		50,000	50,000		-0-
Totals	525,000	225,000	150,000	150,000	600,000

It is important to recognize that intercompany eliminations are made solely on the work sheet to present correct consolidated statements. They are not journalized or posted by either of the affiliated companies and therefore do not affect the ledger accounts. Powers Company's investment account and Serto Company's common stock and retained earnings accounts are reported by the separate entities in preparing their own financial statements.

ACQUISITION COST ABOVE OR BELOW BOOK VALUE OF NET ASSETS

The cost of acquiring the common stock of another company may be above or below its book value. The management of the parent company may pay more than book value because it believes (1) the fair market values of identifiable assets such as land, buildings, and equipment are higher than their recorded book values or (2) the subsidiary's future earnings prospects warrant a payment for goodwill.

The consolidated work sheet is another good spreadsheet application. At this stage in the course you, hopefully, have familiarized yourself enough with electronic spreadsheets to be able to create your own templates. If not, this is a good work sheet to attempt since the required instructions are very straightforward.

However, computer programs are available that can merge multiple general ledgers for consolidated entities. All you need to do is supply the eliminating information, enter a few command keystrokes, and the consolidated financial statements will come off the printer, ready for distribution.

To illustrate, assume the same data used above, except that Powers Company pays $165,000 in cash for 100% of Serto's common stock. The excess of cost over book value is $15,000 ($165,000 − $150,000). This amount is separately recognized in eliminating the parent company's investment account, as shown below:

Work sheet—Cost above book value

POWERS COMPANY AND SUBSIDIARY
Work Sheet—Consolidated Balance Sheet
January 2, 1987 (Acquisition Date)

Assets	Powers Company	Serto Company	Eliminations Dr.	Eliminations Cr.	Consolidated Data
Current assets	35,000	80,000			115,000
Investment in Serto Company common stock	165,000			**165,000**	-0-
Plant and equipment (net)	325,000	145,000			470,000
EXCESS OF COST OVER BOOK VALUE OF SUBSIDIARY			**15,000**		**15,000**
Totals	525,000	225,000			600,000
Liabilities and stockholders' equity					
Current liabilities	50,000	75,000			125,000
Common stock – Powers Company	300,000				300,000
Common stock – Serto Company		100,000	**100,000**		-0-
Retained earnings – Powers Company	175,000				175,000
Retained earnings – Serto Company		50,000	**50,000**		-0-
Totals	525,000	225,000	165,000	165,000	600,000

Note that a separate line is added to the work sheet for the excess of cost over book value of subsidiary.

Total assets and total liabilities and stockholders' equity are the same as in the preceding example ($600,000). However, in this case, total assets include $15,000 of Excess of Cost Over Book Value of Subsidiary. In the consolidated balance sheet, this amount is first allocated to specific assets, such as inventory and plant and equipment, if their fair market values exceed their book value. Any remainder is considered goodwill. For example, assume that the $15,000 excess of cost over book value is allocated $10,000 to plant and equip-

ment (net) and the remaining $5,000 to goodwill. The condensed consolidated balance sheet of Powers Company would be reported as follows:

Consolidated balance sheet with goodwill

POWERS COMPANY
Consolidated Balance Sheet
January 2, 1987

Current assets	$115,000	Current liabilities	$125,000
Plant and equipment (net)	480,000	Common stock	300,000
Goodwill	5,000	Retained earnings	175,000
	$600,000		$600,000

The goodwill portion of the excess of cost over book value should be amortized by the straight-line method over the period benefited but not in excess of 40 years.

A parent company may pay an acquisition cost below book value if the subsidiary company has an unsatisfactory earnings record or the book values of identifiable assets are higher than current market values. As expected, such companies do not attract many purchasers, and instances where the book value is in excess of cost are much less common. Accounting recognition of this excess is complicated and is beyond the scope of this textbook.

ACQUISITION OF LESS THAN 100% OWNERSHIP

When less than 100% ownership is acquired in a subsidiary company, it is necessary to recognize the minority stockholders' interest. This interest is recognized when the parent company's investment is eliminated against the subsidiary company's stockholders' equity. The steps in making the elimination are:

1. Credit the parent company's Investment in Subsidiary Stock for its balance.
2. Debit the subsidiary company's Common Stock, Retained Earnings, and additional paid-in capital (if any), for their balances.
3. Credit Minority Interest for the minority's percentage ownership of the subsidiary's stockholders' equity.
4. Recognize any difference between cost and book value at acquisition.

The eliminations when cost (1) equals the book value of the net assets and (2) is greater than book value are explained below.

Cost Equal to Book Value of Net Assets

When cost equals book value, the only change from the preceding eliminations is to recognize the minority interest in the subsidiary company. To illustrate, assume that Powers Company acquires 80% of the common stock of Serto Company on January 2, 1987 at book value. Cost is $120,000 (80% × $150,000), and the minority interest is $30,000 (20% × $150,000). When the first three steps above are applied, the intercompany elimination is as follows:

Work sheet—Minority interest

POWERS COMPANY AND SUBSIDIARY
Work Sheet—Consolidated Balance Sheet
January 2, 1987 (Acquisition Date)

Assets	Powers Company	Serto Company	Eliminations Dr.	Eliminations Cr.	Consolidated Data
Current assets	80,000	80,000			160,000
Investment in Serto Company common stock	120,000			**120,000**	-0-
Plant and equipment, (net)	325,000	145,000			470,000
Totals	525,000	225,000			630,000
Liabilities and stockholders' equity					
Current liabilities	50,000	75,000			125,000
Common stock – Powers Company	300,000				300,000
Common stock – Serto Company		100,000	**100,000**		-0-
Retained earnings – Powers Company	175,000				175,000
Retained earnings – Serto Company		50,000	**50,000**		-0-
MINORITY INTEREST—SERTO COMPANY				**30,000**	**30,000**
Totals	525,000	225,000	150,000	150,000	630,000

Note that a separate line is added to the work sheet for the minority interest.

Minority interest is reported separately within the stockholders' equity section of the consolidated balance sheet, as illustrated by the condensed consolidated balance sheet of Powers Company.

Consolidated balance sheet with minority interest

POWERS COMPANY
Consolidated Balance Sheet
January 2, 1987

Current assets	$160,000	Current liabilities	$125,000
Plant and equipment, net	470,000	Common stock	300,000
		Minority interest	**30,000**
		Retained earnings	175,000
	$630,000		$630,000

Classification within stockholders' equity is justified because the minority group has an ownership interest in the subsidiary. Separate disclosure is warranted, because these stockholders do not have a controlling interest in the subsidiary and have no role in electing the board of directors of the parent company.

Cost in Excess of Book Value of Net Assets

All of the steps indicated on pages 709 are required in eliminating the parent company's investment account when cost exceeds the book value of

the net assets. To illustrate, assume that instead of paying $120,000 for an 80% interest in Serto Company, Powers Company pays $130,000. Thus, cost exceeds book value by $10,000 ($130,000 − $120,000). Note that the minority interest is again $30,000 (20% × $150,000), because the minority interest is not affected by the price paid for a specific ownership interest in a company. The elimination, therefore, is as follows:

Work sheet—Cost above book value and minority interest

POWERS COMPANY AND SUBSIDIARY
Work Sheet—Consolidated Balance Sheet
January 2, 1987 (Acquisition Date)

Assets	Powers Company	Serto Company	Eliminations Dr.	Eliminations Cr.	Consolidated Data
Current assets	70,000	80,000			150,000
Investment in Serto Company common stock	130,000			130,000	-0-
Plant and equipment (net)	325,000	145,000			470,000
EXCESS OF COST OVER BOOK VALUE OF SUBSIDIARY			10,000		10,000
Totals	525,000	225,000			630,000
Liabilities and stockholders' equity					
Current liabilities	50,000	75,000			125,000
Common stock—Powers Company	300,000				300,000
Common stock—Serto Company		100,000	100,000		-0-
Retained earnings—Powers Company	175,000				175,000
Retained earnings—Serto Company		50,000	50,000		-0-
MINORITY INTEREST—SERTO COMPANY				30,000	30,000
Totals	525,000	225,000	160,000	160,000	630,000

OTHER INTERCOMPANY ELIMINATIONS

To report correctly the assets and liabilities of companies under common control, all intercompany receivables and payables should be eliminated. Assume, for example, that on December 31, 1987, Serto Company owes Powers Company $10,000 on an intercompany credit purchase. Thus, Serto's current liabilities include a $10,000 account payable to Powers Company, and Powers' current assets include a $10,000 account receivable from Serto Company. On the basis of the condensed balance sheet data used in previous examples, the elimination of the intercompany balances on the work sheet is as follows:

Dec. 31	Current Liabilities—Serto Company	10,000	
	Current Assets—Powers Company		10,000
	(Elimination of intercompany account receivable and payable)		

Unless this elimination is made, both assets and liabilities will be overstated on the consolidated balance sheet. Similar eliminations are necessary for receivables and payables resulting from intercompany notes, interest, bonds, and dividends.

CONSOLIDATED INCOME STATEMENT

A consolidated income statement shows the results of operations of affiliated companies as though they were one economic unit. This means that the statement should show only revenue and expense transactions between the consolidated entities and companies and individuals who are outside the affiliated group. Consequently, all revenue and expense transactions between parent and subsidiary companies must be eliminated.

USE OF A WORK SHEET

A work sheet also facilitates the preparation of a consolidated income statement. The income statement data for each of the separate companies in the group provide the starting point for the preparation of a consolidated income statement. Eliminations are then made for transactions between the parent and subsidiary. To illustrate, assume that Parker Company and its wholly owned subsidiary, Slade Company, had two intercompany revenue and expense transactions: (1) Slade Company paid $10,000 in interest to the parent on an intercompany loan, and (2) Slade sold merchandise costing $42,000 to Parker for $50,000. The consolidated information is provided on the work sheet as follows:

Work sheet—Consolidated income statement

PARKER COMPANY AND SUBSIDIARY
Work Sheet—Consolidated Income Statement
For the Year Ended December 31, 1987

	Parker Company	Slade Company	Eliminations Dr.	Eliminations Cr.	Consolidated Data
Sales	900,000	400,000	(2)50,000		1,250,000
Cost of goods sold	600,000	280,000		(2)50,000	830,000
Operating expenses	150,000	70,000			220,000
Interest revenue	10,000		(1)10,000		-0-
Interest expense		10,000		(1)10,000	-0-
Income tax expense	70,000	20,000			90,000
Net income	90,000	20,000	60,000	60,000	110,000

Key to eliminations: (1) Intercompany interest.
(2) Intercompany sales.

The elimination of intercompany interest is straightforward. As shown in the work sheet, Interest Expense of $10,000 reported by Slade is credited and

Interest Revenue of $10,000 shown by Parker is debited. To determine the elimination for the intercompany sale, it is necessary to know the status or disposition of the inventory acquired in the transaction. In this case, it is assumed that Parker has sold all of the goods to customers (outsiders) for $60,000. Thus, no intercompany profit remains in inventory. The effects of the sales transactions on the individual companies and the consolidated income statement are tabulated below.

Effects of intercompany sales

	Slade	Parker	Consolidated
Sales	$50,000	$60,000	$60,000
Cost of Goods Sold	42,000	50,000	42,000

From the viewpoint of the single economic entity, goods purchased by Slade Company from suppliers for $42,000 were sold by Parker Company to customers for $60,000. To achieve the desired consolidated result, Slade's sales of $50,000 should be eliminated against Parker's cost of goods sold of $50,000 as shown on the work sheet.

STATEMENT PRESENTATION

The consolidated income statement is prepared directly from the work sheet. When a subsidiary company is wholly owned, the consolidated income statement may be identical in form and content to the income statement for an individual company. However, **when a subsidiary is only partially owned, the minority interest in the earnings of the subsidiary must be shown on the consolidated income statement.** Minority interest in subsidiary earnings may be reported as a deduction in the other expense and losses section or as a deduction immediately following income taxes at the bottom of the statement. The latter presentation is illustrated below using data adapted from a financial statement issued by General Electric Company:

Partial consolidated income statement—presentation of minority interest

GENERAL ELECTRIC COMPANY

Income before income taxes and minority interest (in millions)	$2,753,000,000
Income taxes	(900,000,000)
Minority interest in earnings of consolidated affiliates	(36,000,000)
Net income	$1,817,000,000

When there is a minority interest, consolidated net income represents the majority stockholders' interest in the total net income of the affiliated companies.

NONCONSOLIDATED SUBSIDIARIES

The Goodyear Tire & Rubber Company shows "Investment in nonconsolidated subsidiaries" in its consolidated balance sheet. This presentation indicates that the accounts of the subsidiaries have not been included in the

consolidated balance sheet. A majority or wholly owned subsidiary may be nonconsolidated because (1) its operations are so dissimilar to those of the parent that the consolidated results would not be useful to interested parties, or (2) the parent is unable to exercise control because of extenuating circumstances.

For merchandising and manufacturing companies, dissimilar operations include finance-related subsidiaries such as credit, insurance, and leasing companies, and real estate subsidiaries. For example, Ford Motor Company includes its wholly owned finance company, Ford Motor Credit Company, as a nonconsolidated subsidiary. Similarly, Xerox Corporation includes its ownership of Crum and Forster, an insurance company, as an investment in a nonconsolidated subsidiary. In these circumstances, the investments in the subsidiary should be accounted for under the equity method of accounting for long-term investments in common stock.

Significant restrictions on the parent company's ability to control a subsidiary may exist, particularly when the subsidiary is located in a foreign country. For example, International Telephone and Telegraph excludes its telecommunications subsidiaries in France because of that government's nationalization of such companies. ITT uses the cost method in accounting for these investments, which is in accordance with generally accepted accounting principles, since the investor (ITT) is unable to exert significant influence, much less control, over the investee (the French subsidiaries).

When a company reports an investment in unconsolidated subsidiaries on its balance sheet, the income statement should show income (loss) from the investment under the cost or equity method, as appropriate. Generally, the amount is reported in the nonoperating section of the income statement. USX Corp., for example, shows "Income from affiliates—equity method" in the other revenue and gains section.

BUSINESS COMBINATIONS—PURCHASE vs. POOLING OF INTERESTS

A **business combination** occurs when one entity acquires part or all of another entity for the purpose of combining resources. In a business combination, (1) one or more of the acquired enterprises may become a subsidiary of the acquiring company, (2) the acquired enterprise may transfer its net assets to the acquiring company, or (3) each of the entities may transfer its net assets to a newly formed enterprise. The purchase method and the pooling-of-interests method are both acceptable in accounting for business combinations but not as alternatives for the same business combination. Both methods are used in practice, as illustrated at the top of the following page.

From an accounting standpoint, the critical difference between these business combinations (acquisitions) is the manner of payment. Du Pont used cash and common stock, whereas American Express used only common stock. When the acquiring company obtains 90% or more of another company's common stock by issuing its own common stock, the acquisition is usually

Example of purchase and pooling of interests

Du Pont

The company acquired 95% of the outstanding common stock of CONOCO for cash and Du Pont common stock. This acquisition was accounted for as a **purchase.**

American Express Company

The company exchanged 21.3 million of its common stock for all of the outstanding stock of Shearson Loeb Rhoades Inc. This acquisition was accounted for as a **pooling of interests.**

deemed a pooling of interests.[5] When this condition is not met, the business combination is considered a purchase.

BALANCE SHEET EFFECTS

Under the **purchase method** the assets of the acquired company are recorded by the acquiring company at their fair market values, and the excess of cost (i.e., the purchase price) over the sum of the fair market values of the assets less liabilities assumed is recognized as goodwill. In addition, no part of the stockholders' equity section of the acquired company is recorded on the books of the purchaser. **The rationale underlying the purchase method is that when cash (or other assets) is the primary means of payment, the ownership interests in the acquired company are eliminated and a purchase has taken place.** As a result, the assets of the acquired company should be recorded at cost. Recall that cost and fair market value are the same at the date of acquisition. The purchase method has been assumed in preparing consolidated financial statements in this chapter.

In contrast, under the **pooling-of-interests method,** the assets of the acquired company are recorded by the acquiring company at their book values, and no goodwill is recognized. The retained earnings of the acquired company are added to the retained earnings of the purchaser. **The rationale underlying the pooling-of-interests method is that when the business combination is accomplished primarily by the issuance of the common stock of the acquiring company, the ownership interests in the acquired company are continued.** As a result, no revaluation of assets is necessary, since the ownership interest of the acquired company is not eliminated. In a pooling of interests, it is assumed that two companies have combined their stockholders, resources, and operations. As one writer has noted, "It is like two rivers flowing into one, each now unidentifiable."

INCOME STATEMENT EFFECTS

There are also significant differences between the two methods in reporting net income in the year of acquisition. **Under the purchase method, only the acquired company's net income after the date of acquisition is included in the purchaser's net income.** This treatment is based on the view that the benefits (net income) from any purchase do not begin until after the date of acquisition.

[5] "Business Combinations," *Opinions of the Accounting Principles Board No. 16* (New York: AICPA, 1970) par. 47.

In contrast, under the pooling-of-interests method, the acquired company's entire net income in the year of acquisition is included in the purchaser's net income. This treatment is based on the view that since the companies have combined their operations, the income statement should report the net income earned from the beginning of the year. For example, American Express Company acquired Shearson Loebs Rhoades on June 29, and Shearson's net income of $56 million for the first six months of the year was added to American Express's net income of $185 million for the same period in reporting the net income of the combined companies. However, under the purchase method, American Express could report only $185 million of net income. As a result, in the year of acquisition, net income will be higher under a pooling of interests than under a purchase. In addition, the prospects for future earnings are generally higher under the pooling-of-interests method than under the purchase method, because of the following factors:

Effects on future earnings

Pooling-of-Interests Method	Purchase Method
• Depreciation on book values of acquired depreciable assets is continued.	• Depreciation is applied to the fair market values of acquired depreciable assets.
• Goodwill amortization cannot occur.	• Goodwill amortization occurs.

The notes to the financial statements should indicate that a business combination occurred and the method of accounting used.

SUMMARY OF STUDY OBJECTIVES

1. Long-term investments in bonds are recorded at cost. Subsequently, it is necessary to record (a) the receipt of bond interest and the amortization of any bond discount or premium, and (b) the sale of the bonds, which will include the recognition of any gain or loss.

2. The guidelines for the accounting treatment of long-term investments in stocks are based on the investor's ownership interest and presumed influence on the investee. When ownership is less than 20%, the cost method or lower of cost or market method should be used. When ownership is between 20% and 50%, the equity method should be used. When ownership is more than 50%, consolidated financial statements should be prepared.

3. Consolidated financial statements present the details of the assets and liabilities controlled by the parent company and the aggregate profitability of the affiliated companies. The purpose of the statements is to inform interested parties as to the magnitude and scope of operations of the companies operating under common control.

4. The work sheet for a consolidated balance sheet contains columns for (a) the balance sheet data for the separate legal entities, (b) intercompany eliminations, and (c) consolidated data.

5. When less than 100% ownership is acquired in a subsidiary company, it is necessary to recognize the minority stockholders' interest when eliminating the parent company's investment and the subsidiary company's stockholders' equity. Minority interest is reported separately within the stockholders' equity section of the consolidated balance sheet.

6. A consolidated income statement shows the results of operations of affiliated companies as though they were one economic unit. When a subsidiary company is wholly owned, the form and content of the statement may be identical to those of the statement of an individual company. However, when the subsidiary company is only partially owned, the minority interest in the earnings of the subsidiary is reported as a deduction in the consolidated income statement.

7. Under the purchase method, (a) the assets of the acquired company are recorded at their fair market values and goodwill may be recognized, (b) no part of the stockholders' equity of the acquired company is recorded by the purchaser, and (c) only the acquired company's net income after the date of acquisition is included in the purchaser's net income. Under the pooling-of-interests method, the assets of the acquired company are recorded by the acquiring company at their book values, and no goodwill is recognized. The retained earnings of the acquired company are added to the retained earnings of the purchaser. In a pooling, the acquired company's entire net income in the year of acquisition is included in the purchaser's net income.

APPENDIX 18–A

INTERNATIONAL ACCOUNTING

Foreign goods are almost as common to us today as are domestic, "made in the U.S.A." goods. We drive Japanese cars, wear Italian shoes and Scottish woolens, drink Brazilian coffee and Indian tea, eat Swiss chocolate bars, sit on Danish furniture, and use Arabian oil. Likewise, foreigners use American computers, eat American breakfast cereals, read American magazines, listen to American rock music, watch American movies and TV shows, and drink American soda pop. The tremendous variety and volume of both exported and imported goods indicates the extensive involvement of U.S. business in international trade. For many U.S. companies, the world is their market.

The following schedule lists the 10 U.S. corporations having the largest foreign sales.

Foreign sales— U.S. corporations

U.S. Corporation	Foreign Sales In Millions	Foreign Sales As a % of Total Sales
Exxon	$59,086	68%
Mobil	32,678	57
Texaco	21,864	47
IBM	21,545	43
General Motors	16,167	17
Ford Motor	15,995	30
Philbro-Salomon	15,100	54
Chevron	12,722	30
Citicorp	10,600	47
Du Pont	10,551	36

Source: Forbes, July 28, 1986.

Firms that conduct their operations in more than one country through subsidiaries, divisions, or branches in foreign countries are referred to as **multinational corporations.** The accounting for multinational corporations is complicated because foreign currencies are involved in international transactions and operations. As a result, these international transactions and operations must be translated into U.S. dollars. One type of translation involves the **translation of foreign currency transactions** and another type involves the **translation of foreign currency financial statements.** Both of these situations are explained in the following pages. But, first you need to understand the importance and meaning of exchange rates.

FOREIGN EXCHANGE RATES

An **exchange rate** is the value of one currency expressed in terms of another currency. Exchange rates are used to convert one currency into a different currency. For example, as shown in the schedule below, the British pound was quoted recently as equivalent to $1.50, while the French franc was quoted as equivalent to $0.1502. These rates mean that it would take $1.50 to buy 1 British pound and 15.02 cents to buy 1 French franc. This form of exchange rate (in terms of the number of domestic units—U.S. dollars) is referred to as a **direct exchange quotation.** It is also possible for the exchange rate to be quoted in terms of the number of foreign units that are equal to one U.S. dollar. This form is referred to as an **indirect exchange quotation.** For example, recently the Japanese yen was quoted at a rate of 155 yen to the U.S. dollar. This means that it would take 155 yen to buy 1 dollar. To avoid confusion, we will quote exchange rates only in terms of the number of U.S. dollars it takes to buy 1 unit of the foreign currency. Thus, for the yen we will use an exchange rate of $0.00645. The following schedule illustrates some selected direct exchange rates.

Selected foreign exchange rates

Country	Currency	Price in U.S. dollars
Brazil	Cruzado	$0.07262
Britain	Pound	1.50
Canada	Dollar	0.7207
France	Franc	0.1502
Italy	Lira	0.00071
Japan	Yen	0.00645
Mexico	Peso	0.00143
Saudi Arabia	Riyal	0.2668
Spain	Peseta	0.0075
West Germany	Mark	0.4921

Source: The Wall Street Journal, September 5, 1986.

Exchange rates change continually to reflect changes in the demand for and supply of different currencies.

TRANSLATING FOREIGN CURRENCY TRANSACTIONS

Many U.S. companies conduct transactions with customers, suppliers, and banks in foreign countries. Some transactions, such as the purchase and sale of crude oil, are expressed and settled in terms of the U.S. dollar. These transactions present no special accounting problem for the U.S. firm because it has no need to use an exchange rate. When transactions are expressed in U.S. dollars, the foreign company accepts, and the U.S. company avoids, the risks and rewards related to changes in currency exchange rates. However, when a U.S. company agrees to transact business expressed in terms of foreign currencies, it accepts the risks and rewards related to changes in currency exchange rates.

When transactions are expressed in terms of the foreign currency, the accounting entries must be recorded by the U.S. company in U.S. dollars. That requires translating the foreign currency into U.S. dollars at the exchange rates in effect on the days foreign exchange transactions occur. The following paragraphs illustrate the accounting for both foreign purchase and foreign sale transactions.

FOREIGN PURCHASES

When a U.S. company purchases from a foreign firm, it may be billed either in U.S. currency or in foreign currency. For example, assume that American Fruit Company purchases a boatload of bananas from Brazilian Plantation Co. for $300,000, which is **billed and payable in U.S. currency.** The entries to record the purchase on December 10 and the subsequent payment on January 27 are similar to any transaction expressed in terms of U.S. dollars, as shown below.

Dec.	10	Purchases	300,000	
		Accounts Payable — Brazilian Plantation Co.		300,000
		(To record the purchase of merchandise on account)		
Jan.	27	Accounts Payable — Brazilian Plantation Co.	300,000	
		Cash		300,000
		(To record payment on account)		

However, if Brazilian Plantation Co. **bills American Fruit Company in Brazilian cruzados and requires payment in cruzados, an exchange gain or loss may be incurred by American Fruit.** An exchange gain or loss occurs if the exchange rate of dollars to cruzados changes between the date of purchase and the date of payment. For example, assume that the purchase of bananas for $300,000 above was billed and payable in 4,000,000 cruzados, reflecting an exchange rate of $.075 on December 10. And, assume that the exchange rate on January 27, the date of payment, had risen to $.079. On December 10, $300,000 was equivalent to 4,000,000 cruzados, but on January 27, $316,000 was equivalent to 4,000,000 cruzados. The entries to record the purchase and the payment are as follows:

Dec.	10	Purchases (4,000,000 cruzados @ $.075)	300,000	
		Accounts Payable — Brazilian Plantation Co.		300,000
		(To record purchase of merchandise on account)		
Jan.	27	Accounts Payable — Brazilian Plantation Co.	300,000	
		Foreign Exchange Loss	16,000	
		Cash (4,000,000 cruzados @ $.079)		316,000
		(To record payment on account and exchange loss)		

American Fruit Co. incurred a foreign exchange loss of $16,000 because it agreed to pay a fixed number of Brazilian cruzados, and by the time payment

was made the cruzado increased in value relative to the U.S. dollar. If the exchange rate of the cruzado decreased, say to \$.065, American Fruit would have realized a foreign exchange gain of \$40,000 [4,000,000 cruzados × (\$.075 − \$.065)].

REALIZED VS. UNREALIZED FOREIGN EXCHANGE GAIN OR LOSS

The illustration above showed the purchase and the payment as a complete, settled transaction that resulted in a realized foreign exchange loss of \$16,000. However, if financial statements are prepared between the purchase and the payment, unrealized gains or losses arise from changes in the exchange rate. The accounting profession requires that such unrealized gains or losses from currency translations "be included in determining net income for the period in which the exchange rate changes."[1]

To illustrate, assume that in the foregoing purchase transaction between American Fruit Co. and Brazilian Plantation Co. financial statements are prepared on December 31 when the exchange rate for Brazilian cruzados is .085. A summary of the exchange rates is as follows:

Exchange rates: Dollars per cruzado

	Date	Exchange Rate ($ per cruzado)
Date of purchase	Dec. 10	.075
Balance sheet date	Dec. 31	.085
Date of settlement	Jan. 27	.079

The computation of the unrealized foreign exchange loss of \$40,000 from December 10 to December 31 is shown below:

Computation of unrealized exchange loss

	Dec. 10	Dec. 31	Exchange Gain (Loss)
Exchange rate	$ .075	$ .085	$(.010)
Account payable (dollars equivalent to 4,000,000 cruzados)	$300,000	$340,000*	$(40,000) Loss
*4,000,000 × $.085			

The \$40,000 loss is recognition of an unrealized loss due to the strengthening of the cruzado relative to the dollar. The foreign currency adjusting entry to recognize the unrealized foreign exchange loss of \$40,000 at December 31 is recorded as follows:

Dec. 31	Foreign Exchange Loss	40,000	
	Accounts Payable—Brazilian Plantation Co.		40,000
	(To record exchange loss and increase in accounts payable)		

[1] "Foreign Currency Translation," *Statement of Financial Accounting Standards No. 52* (Stamford, Conn.: FASB, 1981), par. 15.

Any additional foreign currency exchange gain or loss recognized at the date of payment, then, relates only to exchange rate changes subsequent to the balance sheet date of December 31. The effect of the change in exchange rates from $.085 on December 31 to $.079 on January 27 is shown below:

Computation of exchange gain

	Dec. 31	Jan. 27	Exchange Gain (Loss)
Exchange rate	$ .085	$ .079	$ .006
Account payable (dollars equivalent to 4,000,000 cruzados)	$340,000	$316,000*	$24,000 Gain

*4,000,000 × $.079

Thus, the entry to record the payment on January 27 and to recognize the change in the exchange rate from $.085 on December 31 to $.079 on January 27 is as follows:

Jan. 27	Accounts Payable—Brazilian Plantation Co.	340,000	
	Foreign Exchange Gain		24,000
	Cash		316,000
	(To record payment on account and exchange gain)		

To summarize, on December 31 a $40,000 foreign exchange loss is recorded to reflect the strengthening of the cruzado from an exchange rate of $.075 to $.085 between December 10 and December 31. Because the accounts payable is not settled at December 31, the loss of $40,000 is unrealized. However, it is recognized in the income statement ending December 31. Between December 31 and the payment on January 27 the Brazilian cruzado weakened from $.085 to $.079. Therefore, a $24,000 foreign exchange gain is recognized on January 27 and included in that year's income statement. The transaction in its entirety resulted in a net loss of $16,000 ($40,000 loss minus the $24,000 gain) which is measured by the change in the cruzado exchange rate from $.075 (December 10) to $.079 (January 27).

FOREIGN SALES

Foreign sales are the opposite of purchases. To illustrate a foreign sale, assume that Cincinnati Machinery Co. sells robotic equipment to the West German company Volkswagenwerk AG on account at a price of 900,000 deutsche marks (DM). The exchange rates are summarized below:

Exchange rate: Dollars per Deutsche mark

	Date	Exchange Rate ($ per Deutsche Mark)
Date of sale	Dec. 4	.50
Balance sheet date	Dec. 31	.44
Date of settlement	Jan. 29	.53

At the date of sale, when the exchange rate is $.50, $450,000 is equivalent to 900,000 DM. The entry for the sale on December 4 is as follows:

Dec. 4	Accounts Receivable – Volkswagenwerk AG	450,000	
	Sales		450,000
	(To record sale of merchandise)		

The computation of the unrealized foreign exchange loss of $54,000 from December 4 to December 31 is shown below:

Computation of unrealized exchange loss

	Dec. 4	Dec. 31	Exchange Gain (Loss)
Exchange rate	$ .50	$ .44	$(.06)
Account receivable (dollars equivalent to 900,000 DM)	$450,000	$396,000*	$(54,000) Loss

*900,000 × $.44

Thus, the foreign currency adjusting entry to recognize the unrealized loss of $54,000 at December 31 is recorded by Cincinnati Machinery Co. as follows:

Dec. 31	Foreign Exchange Loss	54,000	
	Accounts Receivable – Volkswagenwerk AG		54,000
	(To record exchange loss and decrease in accounts receivable)		

The computation of the foreign exchange gain of $81,000 from December 31 to January 29 is shown below:

Computation of exchange gain

	Dec. 31	Jan. 29	Exchange Gain (Loss)
Exchange rate	$ .44	$ .53	$ .09
Account receivable (dollars equivalent to 900,000 DM)	$396,000	$477,000*	$81,000 Gain

*900,000 × $.53

Thus, the entry to record the collection on January 29 and to recognize the change in the exchange rate from $.44 on December 31 to $.53 on January 29 is as follows:

Jan. 29	Cash	477,000	
	Foreign Exchange Gain		81,000
	Accounts Receivable – Volkswagenwerk AG		396,000
	(To record collection of cash on account and exchange gain)		

Volkswagenwerk has an obligation to pay 900,000 DM as settlement no matter what the exchange rate at the date of payment. Because Cincinnati Machinery Co. can convert these 900,000 marks into a greater number of U.S. dollars at the date of settlement ($477,000) than at the date of sale ($450,000), it realizes a net foreign exchange gain of $27,000 ($477,000 − $450,000). The net gain of $27,000 is recognized in the form of a $54,000 unrealized foreign exchange loss on December 31 and exchange gain of $81,000 on January 29.

FINANCIAL STATEMENT PRESENTATION

For financial reporting purposes, the balances in the Foreign Exchange Loss and the Foreign Exchange Gain accounts are combined into one amount, as either a net gain or a net loss. The net gain or loss is reported under other revenues and gains or other expenses and losses in the income statement. For example, Cincinnati Machinery Co. would report the exchange loss of $54,000 on its income statement for the period ending December 31 as follows:

Presentation of exchange loss on income statement

CINCINNATI MACHINERY CO.
Income Statement (Partial)
For the Period Ending December 31

Income from operations	xxxxxx
Other expenses and losses	
Foreign exchange loss	54,000
Income before income taxes	xxxxxx

TRANSLATION OF FOREIGN CURRENCY FINANCIAL STATEMENTS

Multinational corporations often use foreign subsidiary companies to conduct business in foreign countries. For instance, the Quaker Oats Company has the following subsidiaries operating in some foreign countries: Fabrica de Chocolates, Mexico; Quaker Lutz G.m.b.H., Germany; Elboradora de Cereales S.A., Argentina; Benelux, Holland; Chiari & Forti S.p.A., Italy; and Ota A/S, Denmark. If the foreign subsidiary is more than 50% owned and if the U.S. parent company exercises control, then the foreign subsidiary is generally included in the consolidated statements. And, if the foreign subsidiary's accounting records and financial statements are expressed in a foreign currency, then its financial statements must be translated into U.S. dollars for purposes of consolidation.

In the following illustration, we assume that the foreign subsidiary (Su-Yung Company) is fully integrated into the foreign economy; that is, it buys, manufactures, sells, and finances in the foreign country. The foreign subsidiary also conducts its business in the foreign currency and maintains its accounting records and financial statements in the foreign currency. Under these circumstances, the foreign currency expressed financial statements are translated into U.S. dollars by applying the following rates to the account balances presented in the statements:[2]

[2]The degree to which the foreign subsidiary is (1) integrated into the foreign economy, (2) autonomous of the parent company, and (3) independent of the U.S. dollar, determines the accounting method of translation. Therefore, different methods of translation are available, including the current rate method (illustrated here) and the remeasurement method. In-depth coverage of various translation methods is reserved for more advanced courses.

Translation rates

Accounts	Translation Rate
Assets	Current
Liabilities	Current
Common stock and paid-in capital	Historical
Retained earnings	No adjustment
Revenues	Average
Expenses	Average

As indicated above, all assets and liabilities are translated into U.S. dollars using the current exchange rate at the balance sheet date. Common stock and other paid-in capital are translated using the historical exchange rate—the rate in existence on the day the assets were received in exchange for the stock. Retained earnings is the beginning retained earnings plus net income from the translated income statement minus any paid dividends translated at the exchange rate existing on the payment date.

It is impractical to translate all of the individual revenue and expense transactions at the exchange rate in effect when they occurred during the period. Therefore, an average rate for the period is typically used to translate the revenues and expenses.

To illustrate the translation of foreign financial statements into U.S. dollars, assume that Osaka Company is a Japanese company that was 100% acquired on January 1, 1987 by Campbell Soup Company, a U.S. corporation. Osaka's year-end financial statements are expressed in yen, the Japanese currency. Exchange rates for the Japanese yen during the year 1987 are as follows:

Exchange rates: Dollars per yen

Date	Exchange Rate ($ per yen)
January 1, date of acquisition	$0.0062
Average for 1987	0.0071
December 31, 1987, balance sheet date	0.0080

These translation rates are applied to Osaka's balance sheet and income statement account balances at December 31, 1987 using the rules presented above. The objective of these procedures is to translate the yen amounts into dollar amounts. Through this process, the financial relationships among assets and liabilities and the financial results that were affected by the subsidiary's operations in its foreign environment are maintained.

INCOME STATEMENT TRANSLATION

Osaka Company's income statement for the year ended December 31, 1987 is shown in both Japanese yen and U.S. dollars on the next page.

Because this is the first year of operations for the 100% owned subsidiary Osaka Company, the amount in retained earnings is equal to the net income. In succeeding years retained earnings is computed by adding net income from the income statement to the beginning balance in Retained Earnings.

Translated income statement

OSAKA COMPANY
Income Statement
For the Year Ended December 31, 1987

	Japanese Yen	Exchange Rate	U.S. Dollars
Sales	Y990,000,000	$0.0071	$7,029,000
Cost of goods sold	450,000,000	0.0071	3,195,000
Gross profit	540,000,000		3,834,000
Expenses	380,000,000	0.0071	2,698,000
Income from operations	160,000,000		1,136,000
Income tax expense	70,000,000	0.0071	497,000
Net income	Y 90,000,000		$ 639,000

BALANCE SHEET TRANSLATION

Osaka Company's December 31, 1987 balance sheet for the year 1987 is shown in both Japanese yen and U.S. dollars as follows:

Translated balance sheet

OSAKA COMPANY
Balance Sheet
December 31, 1987

	Japanese Yen	Exchange Rate	U.S. Dollars
Cash	Y 80,000,000	$0.0080	$ 640,000
Accounts receivable (net)	140,000,000	0.0080	1,120,000
Inventory	200,000,000	0.0080	1,600,000
Property, plant, and equipment (net)	530,000,000	0.0080	4,240,000
Total assets	Y950,000,000		$7,600,000
Accounts payable	Y 60,000,000	0.0080	$ 480,000
Bonds payable	340,000,000	0.0080	2,720,000
Common stock	460,000,000	0.0062	2,852,000
Retained earnings	90,000,000	See net income	639,000
Translation adjustment			**909,000**
Total liabilities and stockholders' equity	Y950,000,000		$7,600,000

Note the **translation adjustment** shown as an addition to stockholders' equity is in U.S. dollars. It is the amount needed to balance the total debits and credits in the balance sheet after all the individual items have been translated. The translation adjustment arises because some accounts are translated at current exchange rates and other accounts are translated at historical exchange rates. Depending on the direction of the changes in the exchange rate, this adjustment may reduce stockholders' equity or increase stockholders' equity (as in this illustration).

UNIFORM INTERNATIONAL ACCOUNTING STANDARDS

Many investment and credit decisions require the analysis and interpretation of foreign financial statements. Unfortunately, there is little uniformity in accounting standards from country to country, and there are few recognized worldwide accounting standards. This lack of uniformity is the result of different legal systems, different processes for developing accounting standards, differences in governmental requirements, and differences in economic environments.

Some efforts have been made to obtain uniformity in international accounting practices. In 1973 the International Accounting Standards Committee (IASC) was formed by agreement of accounting organizations in the United States, United Kingdom, Canada, Australia, France, Germany, Japan, Mexico, and the Netherlands. The IASC now has 88 accounting organizations representing 62 countries participating in the development of international accounting standards. To date, 24 International Accounting Standards have been issued for IASC members to introduce to their respective countries. But, because the IASC has no enforcement powers, these standards are by no means universally applied. These standards are, however, generally followed by the large multinational companies that are audited by international public accounting firms. Thus, the foundation has been laid for considerable progress toward greater uniformity in international accounting.

GLOSSARY

Affiliated companies, p. 704
Business combination, p. 714
Consolidated financial statements, p. 705
Controlling interest, p. 704
Cost method, p. 700
Direct exchange quotation, p. 719
Equity method, p. 702
Exchange rate, p. 719
Indirect exchange quotation, p. 719
Intercompany eliminations, p. 705
Intercompany transactions, p. 705
Lower of cost or market method, p. 700
Majority interest, p. 704
Minority interest, p. 704
Parent company, p. 704
Partially owned, p. 704
Pooling-of-interests method, p. 715
Purchase method, p. 715
Subsidiary company, p. 704
Wholly owned, p. 704

DEMONSTRATION PROBLEM

On July 1, 1987, Giant Inc. acquires the controlling interest in Small Corporation. At the date of acquisition, Small Corporation has $200,000 of common stock and $150,000 of retained earnings.

INSTRUCTIONS

Prepare the work sheet elimination entry for a consolidated balance sheet as of the date of acquisition for each of the following independent situations:

1. Giant Inc. pays $350,000 for all of the common stock of Small Corporation.
2. Giant Inc. pays $315,000 for 90% of the common stock of Small Corporation.
3. Giant Inc. pays $260,000 for 70% of the common stock of Small Corporation.
4. Giant Inc. pays $300,000 for 80% of the common stock of Small Corporation.

SOLUTION TO DEMONSTRATION PROBLEM

1. Common Stock – Small Corporation	200,000	
Retained Earnings – Small Corporation	150,000	
Investment in Small Corporation Common Stock		350,000
2. Common Stock – Small Corporation	200,000	
Retained Earnings – Small Corporation	150,000	
Investment in Small Corporation Common Stock		315,000
Minority Interest – Small Corporation		35,000
3. Common Stock – Small Corporation	200,000	
Retained Earnings – Small Corporation	150,000	
Excess of Cost over Book Value of Subsidiary	15,000	
Investment in Small Corporation Common Stock		260,000
Minority Interest – Small Corporation		105,000
4. Common Stock – Small Corporation	200,000	
Retained Earnings – Small Corporation	150,000	
Excess of Cost over Book Value of Subsidiary	20,000	
Investment in Small Corporation Common Stock		300,000
Minority Interest – Small Corporation		70,000

***Note:** All **asterisked** Questions, Exercises, and Problems relate to material contained in the Appendix to each chapter.

QUESTIONS

1. Differentiate between short-term and long-term investments in stocks.

2. A company buys 50 bonds at 102, which includes broker's commission. The bonds have a stated interest rate of 11%, a 10-year remaining life, and a $1,000 par value each. The purchase is made on a semiannual interest payment date immediately after interest has been paid. Assuming straight-line amortization, what is the total interest revenue for the first interest period the bonds are held?

3. Lynn Company pays $96,000 plus brokerage fees of $400 for 100 Madden Corporation 10% bonds due in 6 years. Each bond has a face value of $1,000 and pays interest annually. Answer the following for Lynn Company.

(a) What account is debited for the purchase of these bonds?

(b) What amount of interest will be received on each interest payment date?

(c) If the bonds are held to maturity, what gain or loss will be recognized on the redemption of the bonds?

4. John Staffin, an accounting major, bought a bond between interest dates and paid, as a part of the purchase price, the accrued interest since the last interest date. John's brother, Jim, purchased common stock on the same day but no "accrued dividend" was added to the market price. Jim asked John why this difference exists. Help John answer Jim's question.

5. Where are the interest revenue from bond investments and the gains or losses from the sale of bond investments reported?

6. When should an investment in common stock be accounted for by the equity method?

7. If less than 20% interest is held by an investor company in an investee's common stock, when is income recognized on the investment?

8. On December 31, 1987 the aggregate cost of long-term marketable equity securities held by Lockwood, Inc. exceeds their aggregate market value by $80,000. On December 31, 1986 the aggregate cost exceeded aggregate market by $50,000. What entry would Lockwood, Inc. need to make on December 31, 1987 for the long-term securities?

9. What is the proper statement presentation of the account Unrealized Loss on Long-term Marketable Equity Securities?

10. Culhane Corporation uses the equity method to account for its ownership of 25% of the common stock of Flynn Packing. During 1987 Flynn reported a net income of $80,000 and declared and paid cash dividends of $10,000. What recognition should Culhane Corporation give to these events?

11. Jan Myers, a business major, received notice that she was to receive a 10% stock dividend on her 100-share Old Second Bank common stock investment. She has come to you to ask advice about what to do with her windfall. Explain to Jan what a stock dividend is and is not.

12. What are consolidated financial statements?

13. What is: (a) A parent company? (b) A subsidiary company?

14. (a) What account balances are eliminated in order to prepare a consolidated balance sheet for a parent and a wholly owned subsidiary? (b) Why are they eliminated?

15. Why would a parent company pay more than the book value for a common stock investment in a subisidiary?

16. Webber Company pays $325,000 to purchase all the outstanding common stock of Woodall Corporation. At the date of purchase the net assets of Woodall have a book value of $290,000. Webber's management allocates $20,000 of the excess cost to undervalued land on the books of Woodall. What should be done with the rest of the excess?

17. (a) What is meant by minority interest? (b) Where is this item disclosed on a consolidated balance sheet?

18. At the end of the current year, Samson Co. (a subsidiary of Padre Inc.) owes Padre $30,000 on an intercompany credit purchase. The following is reported on the respective balance sheets of Padre and Samson regarding all receivables and payables.

	Padre Inc.	Samson Co.
Accounts Receivable	$300,000	$210,000
Accounts Payable	170,000	120,000

Determine the amount that is reported on the consolidated balance sheet for accounts receivable and accounts payable.

19. Chrysler Corporation, in a recent consolidated balance sheet, reported an amount under investments that pertained to a 100% interest in Chrysler Credit Corp. Why was this amount not eliminated in preparing the consolidated balance sheet of Chrysler Corporation?

20. Byzalot Corporation acquired all of Frienda Mine common stock by issuing its own common shares in a one-for-one stock exchange. Is this business combination accounted for as a purchase or a pooling of interests? Why?

21. Paley Corporation purchased 100% of Sundstrom Company on August 10, 1987 by issuing common stock worth $900,000. The book value of the net assets of Sundstrom Company were $800,000 at that time. Explain why the consolidated earnings of the two companies will probably be higher if the pooling-of-interests method is required to record the business combination as opposed to the purchase method.

***22.** What is the difference between a direct exchange quotation and an indirect exchange quotation?

***23.** If an American firm does business with a Japanese firm and all their transactions take place in Japanese yen, which firm may incur an exchange gain or loss and why?

***24.** Melman Imports owes a West German firm 100,000 marks from a December 10 purchase. Payment is due January 10, and Melman's year-end is December 31. The direct exchange rates are $.48, $.52, and $.51 on December 10, December 31, and January 10. What amount of exchange gain or loss should Melman recognize each year?

***25.** What effect does a translation adjustment have on net income?

EXERCISES

E18-1 Frank Corporation had $800,000 of 10%, 15-year bonds outstanding on December 31, 1986. The bonds were issued at par on December 31, 1981 and pay semiannual interest on December 31 and June 30 of each year. Beth Company acquired $200,000 par value of these bonds on December 31, 1986 at 101 as a long-term investment. Beth sold $100,000 face value of the bonds on December 31, 1987 for $104,000.

INSTRUCTIONS

Prepare the necessary journal entries for Beth Company to:

(a) Record the acquisition of the bonds on December 31, 1986.

(b) Record the receipt of interest and amortization of the premium on June 30, 1987. (Use straight-line amortization.)

(c) Record the sale of the bonds on December 31, 1987, assuming that the receipt of interest and amortization of premium has been recorded at December 31.

E18–2 On April 1, 1987, Dan Corporation purchased, on the open market, 30 of the $1,000, 11%, bonds of Jeannie Company at 97 plus accrued interest as a long-term investment. Jeannie Company had issued the 10-year bonds at 101 on June 30, 1983. The bonds pay annual interest each June 30.

INSTRUCTIONS

(a) Prepare the necessary journal entries for Dan Corporation to:
  (1) Record the acquisition of the bonds.
  (2) Record the receipt of interest and amortization of discount on June 30, 1987. (Use straight-line amortization.)

(b) Determine how much interest revenue should be recognized in 1987.

E18–3 Presented below are two independent situations.

1. Karen Marie Cosmetics acquired 10% of the 200,000 shares of common stock of Bill's Clothiers at a total cost of $12 per share on March 18, 1987. On June 30, Bill's declared and paid a $70,000 dividend. On Decemer 31, Bill's reported net income of $122,000 for the year.
2. Barb BQ, Inc. acquired control of Jerry's Diner Corporation by buying 30% of Jerry's 30,000 outstanding shares of common stock at a total cost of $9 per share on January 1, 1987. On June 15, Jerry's declared and paid a cash dividend of $36,000. On December 31, Jerry's reported a net income of $60,000 for the year. Assume that the book value of the net assets of Jerry's on January 1, 1987 was $9 per share.

INSTRUCTIONS

Prepare all the necessary journal entries for 1987 for (a) Karen Marie Cosmetics in 1. above, and (b) Barb BQ, Inc. in 2. above.

E18–4 Rico Manufacturing, Inc. carries its portfolio of long-term investments in common stock at the lower of cost or market. The aggregate cost and market values of the portfolio at the end of 1986 and 1987 are shown below.

	Cost	Market Value
December 31, 1986	$326,500	$311,000
December 31, 1987	280,000	252,500

INSTRUCTIONS

Prepare journal entries for the following:

(a) On December 31, 1986, Rico adjusted the accounts to show the lower of aggregate cost or market value.

(b) On July 15, 1987 Rico sold a long-term investment in Atlas Corp. common stock that originally cost $46,500 for $40,000 cash.

(c) On December 31, 1987 Rico adjusted the allowance account for the portfolio.

E18–5 Heather Worrell Corporation purchased all the outstanding shares of John Patton Company common stock for $900,000. At the date of acquisition, John Patton Company's balance sheet included the following stockholders' equity:

Common stock, $1 par; authorized 350,000 shares; issued 180,000 shares	$180,000
Additional paid-in capital	350,000
Total paid-in capital	530,000
Retained earnings	300,000
Total stockholders' equity	$830,000

The excess of the purchase price over the book value of John Patton Company is considered goodwill.

INSTRUCTIONS

(a) Prepare the necessary journal entry on the books of the Heather Worrell Corporation at the date of acquisition.

(b) Prepare, in journal entry form, the eliminating entry necessary on the work sheet to consolidate the balance sheets of these two companies at the date of acquisition.

E18-6 Selected account balances from the separate balance sheets of Chally Company and its wholly owned subsidiary, Doss Corporation, as of the date of acquisition are shown below:

	Chally Company	Doss Corporation	Consolidated Balance
Cash	$120,000	$ 57,000	$
Accounts Receivable	159,000	48,000	
Notes Receivable—Chally Co.		35,000	
Investment in Doss Corp.	730,000		
Accounts Payable	82,000	46,500	
Notes Payable—Doss Corp.	35,000		
Bonds Payable	20,000	50,000	
Common Stock	900,000	650,000	
Retained Earnings	113,500	80,000	

Chally Company owes Doss Corporation $35,000 on a short-term note (ignore interest) and Doss Corporation owes Chally Company $16,500 on account for consulting services.

INSTRUCTIONS

Provide the amount that should appear in the Consolidated Balance column for each of the selected accounts. If the account would not appear in a consolidated balance sheet, indicate "None". Assume that all accounts have normal balances and that Doss Corporation stock was acquired for cash at a price equal to its book value.

E18-7 On December 31, 1987, Swisher Corporation purchased 80% of the outstanding common stock of Lake Air Freight for $210,000 in the open market. Condensed balance sheets of the two companies immediately after the acquisition were as follows:

	Swisher Corporation	Lake Air Freight
Current Assets	$ 50,000	$ 40,000
Investment in Lake Air Freight	210,000	
Plant and Equipment (net)	300,000	200,000
	$560,000	$240,000

	Swisher Corporation	Lake Air Freight
Liabilities	$180,000	$ 40,000
Common Stock	50,000	75,000
Retained Earnings	330,000	125,000
	$560,000	$240,000

Swisher Corporation management allocated the excess of the cost over the book value of the net assets acquired: $35,000 to Plant and Equipment and $15,000 to Goodwill.

INSTRUCTIONS

Prepare, in journal entry form, the eliminating entry necessary on the work sheet to consolidate the balance sheets of these two companies on the date of acquisition.

E18–8 Atwell Aviation owns 80% of the outstanding common stock of Daw Company. The income statement for each company for the year ended December 31, 1987, is shown below:

	Atwell Aviation	Daw Company
Sales	$960,000	$580,000
Cost of goods sold	640,000	420,000
Gross profit	$320,000	$160,000
Operating expenses	120,000	80,000
Income from operations	$200,000	$ 80,000
Interest revenue	40,000	
Interest expense		40,000
Income before taxes	$240,000	$ 40,000
Income tax expense	72,000	12,000
Net income	$168,000	$ 28,000

During the past year, Daw sold Atwell merchandise for $80,000. These goods had cost Daw $55,000. Atwell resold all of this merchandise to outsiders. Daw Company paid $40,000 of interest during the year to Atwell on an intercompany loan.

Atwell Aviation has not yet recorded its share of Daw Company's net income for this past year.

INSTRUCTIONS

Prepare a consolidated work sheet for the current year.

E18–9 On December 31, 1987, the Pillar Company purchases 90% of the common stock of the Sand Company for $1,300,000. On that date, the Sand Company's net assets amount to $1,200,000 (common stock is $1,000,000, and retained earnings is $200,000). The book value of Sand Company's net assets are equal to the fair market value of these net assets. Also, the Sand Company owes the Pillar Company $80,000 which is shown on the books of the two companies as an account payable and an account receivable, respectively.

INSTRUCTIONS

(a) When preparing balance sheets on December 31, 1987, for the two companies separately, where and at what amount will the Pillar Company report the shares of Sand Company stock and the amount due from the Sand Company.

(b) When preparing a consolidated balance sheet on December 31, 1987, where and at what amounts will the following items be reported.

1. Goodwill
2. Minority interest
3. Consolidated retained earnings (assume that the Pillar Company's retained earnings amounted to $300,000 on December 31, 1987.

E18-10 Pullman has been negotiating several months to purchase Salisbury, Inc. The book value of the net assets of Salisbury, Inc. is $9,000,000. At current market prices, the Pullman Co. would issue about $12,000,000 in common stock in exchange for all the common stock of Salisbury, Inc. The difference of $3,000,000 between cost and book value is attributable one-half to undervalued assets (inventory and property, plant and equipment) and the other half represents a favorable earning capacity for Salisbury. Pullman and Salisbury reported $600,000 and $350,000, respectively, of net income for calendar year 1987.

INSTRUCTIONS

Compute (1) the amount of goodwill to be recognized, and (2) net income to be reported under each of the following assumptions:

(a) Assume that Pullman Co. accounts for the combination as a pooling-of-interests and that it occurs on December 31, 1987.

(b) Assume that Pullman Co. accounts for the combination as a purchase and that it occurs on December 31, 1987.

***E18-11** Liberty Corporation, a U.S. company, purchased machinery from a German corporation on credit for 50,000 marks. At the date of purchase, the exchange rate was $.45 per mark. On the date of payment, which was made in marks, the exchange rate was $.43 per mark.

INSTRUCTIONS

Prepare journal entries for Liberty Corporation to record the purchase and payment.

***E18-12** Presented below are selected transactions of RWB, Inc., a U.S. company.

Dec. 18 Purchased merchandise on account from Trois Company, a French firm, for 70,000 francs. The exchange rate is $.14 per franc.

Dec. 18 Purchased merchandise on account from Genevieve Corporation, a French firm. $20,000 U.S. dollars are due in one month.

Dec. 31 The exchange rate is $.15 per franc at year-end.

Jan. 10 Paid 70,000 francs to Trois. The exchange rate is $.12 per franc.

Jan. 15 Paid $20,000 to Genevieve. The exchange rate is $.13 per franc.

INSTRUCTIONS

Prepare journal entries for RWB for the above transactions.

***E18-13** Presented below are selected transactions of Chicago Corporation, a U.S. company which has dealings with Canadian companies.

Dec. 20 Sold merchandise, on account, to Yukon Company for 20,000 Canadian dollars. The exchange rate is $.70 per Canadian dollar.

Dec. 26 Purchased merchandise on account from Quebec Enterprises for 30,000 Canadian dollars. The exchange rate is $.715.

Dec. 31 The exchange rate is $.72 at year-end.

Jan. 4 Received from Yukon Company 20,000 Canadian dollars when the exchange rate is $.71.

Jan. 12 Paid 30,000 Canadian dollars to Quebec Enterprises when the exchange rate is $.69.

INSTRUCTIONS

Prepare journal entries for Chicago Corporation for the above transactions.

PROBLEMS

P18-1 On March 1, 1987, Marcus Machinery purchased $80,000 par value of Troy Foundry, Inc. bonds at 95 plus accrued interest. The bonds carry a face rate of 12% and pay interest semiannually each June 30 and December 31. The bonds will mature on June 30, 1992 and Marcus plans on holding the bonds to maturity.

INSTRUCTIONS

Prepare the necessary journal entries to record the purchase of the bonds and the receipt of interest and discount amortization on both June 30 and December 31, 1987, assuming (round to the nearest whole dollar):

(a) Marcus uses the straight-line method to amortize the discount.

(b) Marcus uses the effective interest method to amortize the discount. (Assume the yield on the bonds is 13% annually at this selling price.)

P18-2 On December 31, 1987 F. Harris and Associates owned a portfolio of long-term stock investments acquired as shown below:

Description	Date Acquired	Cost
A Company common stock, 1,000 shares	January 10, 1987	$20,000
B Company common stock, 500 shares	March 20, 1987	36,600
C Company preferred stock, 300 shares	August 15, 1987	20,800

On March 1, 1988, B Company declared and distributed a stock dividend of 2 additional shares for every share held. F. Harris and Associates sold its holdings in A Company on September 15, 1988 for $26,000 including broker's fees. C Company declared and paid a cash dividend of $2 per share on December 1, 1988.

The per share market values of each of the securities at December 31, 1987 and 1988 was as follows:

	12/31/87	12/31/88
A Company	$25	$27
B Company	52	20 (adjusted for stock dividend)
C Company	80	78

INSTRUCTIONS

(a) Prepare the necessary year-end adjusting entry to value the investment portfolio at the aggregate lower of cost or market at December 31, 1987.

(b) Prepare the necessary journal entries to record the activity in the portfolio during 1988.

(c) Prepare the necessary year-end adjusting entry to value the long-term portfolio at the aggregate lower of cost or market at December 31, 1988.

P18–3 Cardinal Concrete acquired 20% of the outstanding common stock of Edra, Inc. on January 4, 1987. Cardinal paid a total of $1,200,000 for the 60,000 shares acquired. Edra declared and paid an $.80 per share cash dividend on June 30 and again on December 31, 1987. Edra reported net income of $700,000 for the year.

INSTRUCTIONS

(a) Prepare the necessary journal entries for the above for Cardinal Concrete under the cost method for 1987.

(b) Prepare the necessary journal entries for the above for Cardinal Concrete under the equity method for 1987.

(c) Assuming that the equity method is used, prepare the journal entry for the sale of the Edra, Inc. stock investment on January 2, 1988 for $1,300,000.

P18–4 Neal Company purchased all the outstanding common stock of Wheaton Company on December 31, 1987. Just before the purchase, the condensed balance sheets of the two companies appeared as follows:

	Neal Company	Wheaton Company
Current assets	$1,476,000	$379,000
Plant and equipment (net)	1,882,000	353,000
	$3,358,000	$732,000
Current liabilities	$ 868,000	$ 92,000
Common stock	1,947,000	360,000
Retained earnings	543,000	280,000
	$3,358,000	$732,000

Neal used current assets of $720,000 to acquire the stock of Wheaton. The excess of this purchase price over the book value of Wheaton's net assets is determined to be attributable: $36,000 to Wheaton's plant and equipment, and the remainder to goodwill.

INSTRUCTIONS

(a) Prepare the necessary journal entry for Neal to record the acquisition of Wheaton Company stock.

(b) Prepare a consolidated work sheet at December 31, 1987.

(c) Prepare a consolidated balance sheet at December 31, 1987.

P18–5 On June 30, 1987, Perkins, Inc. purchases 80% of SIU, Co. for $2,500,000 in cash. The balance sheets for Perkins and SIU immediately following the acquisition are:

	Perkins, Inc.	SIU, Co.
Cash	$ 200,000	$ 100,000
Accounts receivable (net)	1,300,000	300,000
Notes receivable		200,000
Inventories	2,000,000	600,000
Investment in SIU, Co.	2,500,000	
Plant and equipment (net)	6,600,000	2,000,000
	$12,600,000	$3,200,000

	Perkins, Inc.	SIU, Co.
Notes payable	$ 1,200,000	
Accounts payable	800,000	$ 200,000
Common stock	7,500,000	2,000,000
Retained earnings	3,100,000	1,000,000
	$12,600,000	$3,200,000

At the date of acquisition SIU, Co. owes Perkins, Inc. $100,000 on open account while SIU holds Perkins' note for $200,000. The plant and equipment of SIU has a fair market value of $30,000 more than its book value. Any additional amount paid for SIU, Co. should be reported as goodwill.

INSTRUCTIONS

(a) Prepare a consolidated work sheet at the date of acquisition.

(b) Prepare a consolidated balance sheet for Perkins, Inc. at the date of acquisition.

P18-6 The Patrick Company has acquired a portion of Sibling Company by paying cash for Sibling Company common stock. The data below shows the balance sheets for Patrick and Sibling just after the acquisition.

Assets	Patrick Company	Sibling Company	Consolidated
Cash	$ 220,000	$ 67,000	$ 287,000
Notes receivable	600,000	210,000	600,000
Accounts receivable	415,000	251,000	466,000
Merchandise inventory	405,000	140,000	545,000
Investment in Sibling Co. common stock	800,000		
Property, plant, and equipment (net)	1,039,000	710,000	1,800,000
Goodwill			26,500
Totals	$3,479,000	$1,378,000	$3,724,500
Liabilities and Stockholders' Equity			
Notes payable	$ 500,000	$ 300,000	$ 590,000
Accrued liabilities	99,000	28,000	127,000
Account payable	580,000	200,000	580,000
Common stock	1,500,000	550,000	1,500,000
Paid-in capital in excess of par	200,000	50,000	200,000
Retained earnings	600,000	250,000	600,000
Minority interest			127,500
Totals	$3,479,000	$1,378,000	$3,724,500

INSTRUCTIONS

(a) Explain whether the acquisition of Sibling Company is recorded as a purchase or a pooling-of-interests. Explain.

(b) How much did Patrick Company spend to acquire Sibling Company's common stock? What percentage of Sibling Co. does Patrick Co. own?

(c) Explain why the following consolidated amounts are not the sum of Patrick and Sibling's separate accounts: (1) notes receivable; (2) accounts receivable; (3) notes payable; and (4) accounts payable.

(d) What is the excess of the cost over book value of purchasing Sibling Company? How much of the excess was due to undervalued property, plant, and equipment?

P18-7 The following two investments are in Shogun Company's investment portfolio as of December 31, 1986.

	Cost
700 shares of HAL Corporation common stock.	$42,000
400 shares of Rendahl Rental Corporation cumulative preferred stock.	16,800

Shogun had the following transactions related to investment in bonds and stocks during 1987.

January	10	Purchased 200 shares, $70 par value common stock of Mintor Corporation at $78 per share, plus brokerage commission of $240.
	26	Received a quarterly dividend of $1.15 per share on HAL Corporation common stock.
February	2	Received dividends of $.40 per share on Rendahl Rental Corporation preferred stock.
	10	Sold all 400 shares of Rendahl Rental Corporation preferred stock at $28.00 per share less a brokerage commission of $180.
April	30	Received 700 shares of HAL Corporation common stock as a result of a 2 for 1 stock split.
June	1	Purchased $100,000 face value (100 bonds) 9% Hesselburg Steel Co. bonds for $95,400 plus accrued interest. The bonds are dated January 1, 1987. Interest is payable July 1 and January 1. Maturity date is January 1, 1997.
July	1	Received semiannual interest on Hesselburg Steel Co. bonds.
August	3	Received 20 shares of Mintor Corporation common stock as the result of a 10% stock dividend.
September	1	Purchased an additional 400 shares of the $70 par value common stock of Mintor Corporation at $81.50 per share, plus brokerage commissions of $400.

At December 31, 1987, the prevailing market prices for the investments held by Shogun were:

Hesselburg Steel Co. bonds	$970 per bond
HAL Corporation common stock	32 per share
Mintor Corporation common stock	71 per share

INSTRUCTIONS

(a) Prepare journal entries to record the transactions listed above. (Bond investments should be amortized on a straight-line basis.)

(b) Prepare the journal entries to recognize accrued interest on bond investments, amortization of bond premium or discount, and the unrealized loss (if any) on the marketable equity securities at December 31, 1987. (At the end of 1986, the market value of investments in marketable equity securities exceeded cost.)

***P18-8** Oyle Company was organized in Saudi Arabia on January 1, 1987 as a wholly owned subsidiary of Mayberry, Inc., a U.S. company. Oyle's opening balance sheet, in Riyal (R) consisted of the following assets and stockholders' equity:

Assets		Stockholders' Equity	
Cash	R 20,000	Common stock	R1,010,000
Inventory	190,000		
Plant assets	800,000		
	R1,010,000		

Oyle's 1987 income statement and December 31, 1987 balance sheet, in Riyal, follow:

OYLE COMPANY
Income Statement
For the Year Ended December 31, 1987

Sales	R1,700,000
Cost of goods sold	1,000,000
Gross profit	700,000
Operating expenses	190,000
Net income	R 510,000

OYLE COMPANY
Balance Sheet
December 31, 1987

Assets		
Cash		R 140,000
Accounts receivable (net)		400,000
Inventory		380,000
Plant assets (net)		700,000
Total assets		R1,620,000
Liabilities and Stockholders' Equity		
Accounts payable		R 100,000
Common stock	R1,010,000	
Retained earnings	510,000	1,520,000
Total liabilities and stockholders' equity		R1,620,000

Exchange rates for the Riyal are:

January 1, 1987	$0.27
Average for 1987	$0.29
December 31, 1987	$0.30

INSTRUCTIONS

Translate Oyle's 1987 income statement and 12/31/87 balance sheet into U.S. dollars.

ALTERNATE PROBLEMS

P18-1A On June 1, 1987, Universal Electronics purchased $160,000 par value of Gremlins, Inc. bonds at 103 plus accrued interest. The bonds carry a face rate of 10% and pay interest semiannually each June 30 and December 31. The bonds will mature on June 30, 1989 and Universal plans on holding the bonds to maturity.

INSTRUCTIONS

Prepare the necessary journal entries to record the purchase of the bonds and the receipt of interest and premium amortization on both June 30 and December 31, 1987, assuming (round to the nearest whole dollar):

(a) Universal uses the straight-line method to amortize the premium.

(b) Universal uses the effective interest method to amortize the premium. (Assume the yield on the bonds is 8.6% annually at this selling price.)

P18-2A On December 31, 1987 W. Payton and Company owned a portfolio of long-term stock investments acquired as shown below:

Description	Date Acquired	Cost
X Company common stock, 800 shares	February 24, 1987	$23,600
Y Company common stock, 600 shares	March 3, 1987	18,000
Z Company preferred stock, 200 shares	December 27, 1987	42,000

On June 30, 1988, Y Company declared and distributed a 100% stock dividend. W. Payton and Company sold one-half of its holdings in X Company on August 12, 1988 for $12,000. Z Company declared and paid a cash dividend of $3 per share on December 1, 1988.

The per share market values of each of the securities at December 31, 1987 and 1988 was as follows:

	12/31/87	12/31/88
X Company	$ 30	$ 32
Y Company	28	15 (adjusted for stock dividend)
Z Company	170	190

INSTRUCTIONS

(a) Prepare the necessary year-end adjusting entry to value the investment portfolio at the aggregate lower of cost or market at December 31, 1987.

(b) Prepare the necessary journal entries to record the activity in the portfolio during 1988.

(c) Prepare the necessary year-end adjusting entry to value the investment portfolio at the aggregate lower of cost or market at December 31, 1988.

P18-3A DFM Services acquired 20% of the outstanding common stock of BNA Company on January 5, 1987. DFM paid a total of $800,000 for the 50,000 shares acquired. BNA declared and paid $.20 per share cash dividends on March 15, June 15, September 15, and December 15, 1987. BNA reported net income of $250,000 for the year.

INSTRUCTIONS

(a) Prepare the necessary journal entries for the above for DFM Services under the cost method for 1987.

(b) Prepare the necessary journal entries for the above for DFM Services under the equity method for 1987.

(c) Assuming that the equity method is used, prepare the journal entry for the sale of the BNA Company stock investment on January 2, 1988 for $820,000.

P18-4A Linger Corporation purchased all the outstanding common stock of Chrissy Foods, Inc. on December 31, 1987. Just before the purchase, the condensed balance sheets of the two companies appeared as follows:

	Linger Corporation	Chrissy Foods, Inc.
Current Assets	$1,480,000	$ 439,500
Plant and Equipment (net)	2,100,000	672,000
	$3,580,000	$1,111,500
Current Liabilities	$ 578,000	$ 92,500
Common Stock	1,950,000	525,000
Retained Earnings	1,052,000	494,000
	$3,580,000	$1,111,500

Linger used current assets of $1,250,000 to acquire the stock of Chrissy Foods. The excess of this purchase price over the book value of Chrissy Foods' net assets is determined to be attributable, $61,000 to Chrissy Foods' plant and equipment, and the remainder to goodwill.

INSTRUCTIONS

(a) Prepare the journal entry for Linger to record the acquisition of Chrissy Foods, Inc. stock.

(b) Prepare a consolidated work sheet at December 31, 1987.

(c) Prepare a consolidated balance sheet at December 31, 1987.

P18-5A On November 31, 1987, Sunco, Inc. purchases 90% HAL, Co. for $3,200,000, in cash. The balance sheets for Sunco and HAL immediately following the acquisition are:

	Sunco, Inc.	HAL, Co.
Cash	$ 200,000	$ 75,000
Accounts receivable (net)	1,000,000	425,000
Notes receivable	200,000	100,000
Inventories	2,000,000	1,000,000
Investment in HAL, Co.	3,200,000	
Plant and equipment (net)	10,000,000	2,300,000
	$16,600,000	$3,900,000
Notes payable	2,050,000	100,000
Accounts payable	400,000	400,000
Common stock	10,000,000	1,200,000
Retained earnings	4,150,000	2,200,000
	$16,600,000	$3,900,000

At the date of acquisition, HAL, Co. owes Sunco, Inc. $250,000 on open account while HAL holds Sunco's note for $100,000. The plant and equipment of HAL has a fair market value of $50,000 more than its book value. Any additional amount paid for HAL, Co. should be reported as goodwill.

INSTRUCTIONS

(a) Prepare a consolidated work sheet at the date of acquisition.

(b) Prepare a consolidated balance sheet for Sunco, Inc. Do not classify the balance sheet into current assets, current liabilities, and so on.

P18-6A The following information related to the separate balance sheets of Burnell, Inc. and Burgstahler Company.

Assets	Burnell, Inc.	Burgstahler Company
Cash	$170,000	$ 60,000
Notes receivable	50,000	25,000
Accounts receivable	25,000	7,500
Merchandise inventory	93,000	75,000
Marketable equity securities (current)	0	10,000
Investment in Burgstahler common stock	70,000	0
Total assets	$408,000	$177,500

Liabilities and Stockholders' Equity		
Notes payable (short term)	50,000	50,000
Accounts payable	110,000	22,500
Accrued liabilities	25,000	5,000
Common stock	90,000	40,000
Preferred stock	20,000	0
Retained earnings	113,000	60,000
	$408,000	$177,500

These balance sheets were compiled immediately after Burnell acquired a significant interest in Burgstahler common stock.

INSTRUCTIONS

(a) Burnell's investment in Burgstahler common stock represents a purchase of common stock by using a combination of cash, notes, and preferred stock. If Burnell has purchased 65% of Burgstahler's common stock, what is the minority interest in consolidation?

(b) How much goodwill if any would be shown on the consolidated balance sheet? Assume that book value and market value are the same for the net assets of Burgstahler Company.

(c) If half of Burnell's notes payable were owed to Burgstahler, what would be the balance of notes payable on the consolidated balance sheet?

(d) The trade accounts of Burnell include $10,000 of accounts receivable due from Burgstahler and $5,000 of accounts payable due to Burgstahler. What would be the balance of accounts receivable and accounts payable on the consolidated balance sheet?

(e) What is consolidated retained earnings?

(f) What amount is reported for total assets on the consolidated balance sheet?

P18-7A K. McCord Co. has the following two investments as of December 31, 1986.

	Cost
600 shares of Miller, Inc. common stock	$72,000
300 shares of Anderson Corp. common stock	24,000

McCord had the following transactions related to investments in bonds and stocks during 1987.

January	15	Received a quarterly dividend of $1.50 per share on Anderson Corp. common stock.
February	2	Purchased 500 shares, $1 par value common stock of McSherry common stock at $22 per share plus brokerage commission of $209.
	6	Received dividends of $.60 per share on Miller, Inc. common stock.
	13	Sold all 300 shares of Anderson Corp. common stock for $28,000 less a brokerage commission of $230.
April	29	Received 600 shares of Miller, Inc. common stock as a result of a 2 for 1 stock split.
June	1	Purchased $200,000 face value (200 bonds) 10% Berger Co. bonds at $196,000 plus accrued interest. The bonds are dated March 1, 1987. Interest is payable March 1 and September 1. Maturity date is March 1, 1997.
July	10	Received 25 shares of McSherry common stock as a result of a 5% stock dividend.
September	1	Received semiannual interest on Berger Co. bonds.

At December 31, 1987, the prevailing market prices for the investments held by McCord were:

Berger Co. bonds	$975 per bond
Miller, Inc. common stock	$55 per share
McSherry common stock	$25 per share

INSTRUCTIONS

(Round to the nearest whole dollar.)

(a) Prepare the journal entries to record the transactions listed above. (Bond investments should be amortized on a straight-line basis.)

(b) Prepare the journal entries to recognize accrued interest on bond investments, amortization of bond premium or discount, and the unrealized loss (if any) on the marketable equity securities at December 31, 1987. (At the end of 1986, the market value of investments in marketable equity securities exceeded cost.)

DECISION PROBLEM

At the beginning of the question and answer portion of the annual stockholders' meeting of Revell Corporation, stockholder Carol Finstrom asks, "Why did management sell the holdings in AHM Company at a loss when this company has been very profitable during the period its stock was held by Revell?"

Since president Larry Wisdom has just concluded his speech on the recent success and bright future of Revell, he is taken aback by this question and responds, "I remember we paid $1,100,000 for that stock some years ago and I am sure we sold that stock at a much higher price; you must be mistaken."

Finstrom retorts, "Well, right here in footnote number 7 to the annual report it shows that 240,000 shares, a 30% interest in AHM, was sold on the last day of the year. Also, it states that AHM earned $550,000 this year and paid out $150,000 in cash dividends. Further, a summary statement indicates that in past years, while Revell held AHM stock, AHM earned $1,240,000 and paid out $440,000 in dividends. Finally, the income statement for this year shows a loss on the sale of AHM stock of $180,000. So, I doubt that I am mistaken."

Red-faced, president Wisdom turns to you.

INSTRUCTIONS

What dollar amount did Revell receive upon the sale of the AHM stock? Explain why both stockholder Finstrom and president Wisdom are correct.

CHAPTER 19

University of New Mexico

CHAPTER 19

STATEMENT OF CASH FLOWS

STUDY OBJECTIVES

After studying this chapter, you should be able to:

1. **Indicate the primary purpose of the statement of cash flows.**
2. **Identify the major sources and uses of cash reported in a statement of cash flows.**
3. **Explain the difference between the direct and indirect approaches.**
4. **Prepare a statement of cash flows.**
5. **Explain the usefulness of the statement of cash flows.**

Explanatory Note

This chapter explains and illustrates only the statement of cash flows. As indicated in a recent survey,[1] over 75% of the Fortune 500 largest U.S. corporations are now (1986) reporting cash flow information. By mid-1987, all companies complying with GAAP will be required to present a statement of cash flows as one of the primary financial statements in lieu of the previously required statement of changes in financial position. Therefore, to learn any other approach, such as the formerly popular working capital basis, has little value or applicability.

How was Delta Airlines able to purchase 20 new jet planes costing $900 million in a year in which it reported a net loss of $86 million? How much of Marriott's recent hotel expansion program was financed through cash provided by operations? How much through borrowing? How much through issu-

[1]"Statement of Cash Flows," *Financial Reporting Developments* (Cleveland, Ohio: Ernst & Whinney, October, 1986), page 3.

ance of stock? How was General Electric Corporation able to finance the $6.5 billion purchase of RCA? Answers to these questions often cannot be found in the balance sheet, income statement, and retained earnings statement. As a result, companies are required to prepare a fourth basic financial statement, the **statement of cash flows.** The purpose of this chapter is to explain and illustrate this basic financial statement.

PURPOSE OF THE STATEMENT OF CASH FLOWS

The primary purpose of the **statement of cash flows** is to provide information about the cash receipts and cash payments of an entity during a period. A secondary objective is to provide information about the investing and financing activities of the entity during the period.[2] This statement, therefore, summarizes the operating, financing, and investing activities of the business; it provides a detailed summary of the sources of cash during the period and the uses to which cash was put. It thus helps to provide the answers to the questions raised in the previous section. For example, the statement indicates how it is possible to report a net loss and still make large capital expenditures or pay dividends. Or, it will tell you whether the company issued or retired debt or common stock or both during the period.

The balance sheet, income statement, and retained earnings statement do present to a limited extent and in a fragmented manner information about the financing and investing activities of an enterprise during a period. For example, comparative balance sheets help to show what new assets have been acquired or disposed of and what liabilities have been incurred or liquidated. The income statement gives some hint as to the amount of cash and noncash resources generated by operations. And the statement of retained earnings discloses the resources used to pay dividends. But none of these statements presents a detailed summary of all the cash and significant noncash operating, investing, and financing activities of an entity during the period.

Reporting the net increase or decrease in cash[3] is considered useful because investors, creditors, and other interested parties want to know and can generally comprehend what is happening to a company's most liquid resource—its cash. As one writer noted:

Though my bottom line is black, I am flat upon my back,
My cash flows out and customers pay slow.
The growth of my receivables is almost unbelievable,
The result is certain—unremitting woe!
And I hear the banker utter an ominous low mutter, "Watch cash flow."[4]

[2]"Statement of Cash Flows," *Proposed Statement of FInancial Accounting Standards* (Stanford, Conn.: October 31, 1986), par. 4.

[3]The basis recommended by the FASB for the statement of cash flows is actually "cash and cash equivalents." **Cash equivalents** are short-term, highly liquid investments, such as treasury bills, commercial paper, and money market funds, purchased with cash that is in excess of immediate needs.

[4]Anonymous.

A statement of cash flows helps us "watch cash flow" because it provides answers to the following simple, but important, questions about the enterprise:

1. Where did the cash come from during the period?
2. What was the cash used for during the period?
3. What was the change in the cash balance during the period?

CLASSIFICATION OF CASH FLOWS

The statement of cash flows classifies cash receipts and cash payments by investing, financing, and operating activities. Transactions and other events characteristic of each kind of activity are presented below:

1. **Investing activities** include (a) lending money and collecting on those loans, and (b) acquiring and disposing of investments and productive long-lived assets.
2. **Financing activities** involve liability and owners' equity items and include (a) obtaining cash from creditors and repaying the amounts borrowed, and (b) obtaining capital from owners and providing them with a return on their investment.
3. **Operating activities** include all transactions and events that are not investing and financing activities. Operating activities involve the cash effects of transactions that enter into the determination of net income, such as cash receipts from sales of goods and services and cash payments to suppliers and employees for acquisitions of inventory and expenses.

The schedule on page 748 lists the typical receipts and payments of a business enterprise that are classified according to investing, financing, and operating activity classifications.

Some cash flows relating to investing or financing activities must be classified as operating activities. For example, receipts of investment income (interest and dividends) and payments of interest to lenders are classified as operating activities. Conversely, some cash flows relating to operating activities must be classified as investing or financing activities. For example, the cash received from the sale of property, plant, and equipment at a gain is classified as an investing activity, and the effects of the related gain would not be included in cash provided by operations. Likewise, a gain or loss on the payment (extinguishment) of debt would generally be part of the cash outflow related to the repayment of the amount borrowed and therefore is a financing activity.

Investing
- Cash inflows
  - From sale of property, plant, and equipment.
  - From sale of debt or equity securities of other entities.
  - From collection of principal on loans to other entities.
- Cash outflows
  - To purchase property, plant, and equipment.
  - To purchase debt or equity securities of other entities.
  - To make loans to another entity.

Financing
- Cash inflows
  - From sale of equity securities.
  - From issuance of debt (bonds and notes).
- Cash outflows
  - To shareholders as dividends.
  - To redeem long-term debt or reacquire capital stock.

Operating
- Cash inflows
  - From sale of goods or services.
  - From returns on loans (interest) and on equity securities (dividends).
- Cash outflows
  - To suppliers for inventory.
  - To employees for services.
  - To government for taxes.
  - To lenders for interest.
  - To others for expenses.

Note that (1) investing activities involve cash flows resulting from changes in long-term asset items, (2) financing activities involve cash flows resulting from changes in long-term liability and stockholders' equity items, and (3) operating activities involve income determination (income statement) items.

FORMAT OF STATEMENT OF CASH FLOWS

The three activities discussed above constitute the general format of the statement of cash flows, as illustrated on the next page. The cash flows from the operating activities section always appears first, followed by the investing activities and the financing activities sections. Also, the individual inflows and outflows from investing and financing activities are reported separately. Thus, cash outflow from the purchase of property, plant, and equipment is reported separately from the cash inflow from the sale of property, plant, and equipment. Similarly, the cash inflow from the issuance of debt securities is reported separately from the cash outflow from the retirement of debt. Not reporting them separately obscures the investing and financing activities of the enterprise and thus makes it more difficult to assess future cash flows.

Format of statement of cash flows

COMPANY NAME
Statement of Cash Flows
Period Covered

Cash flows from operating activities		
Net income		xxx
Add (or deduct) items not affecting cash		
(List of individual items)	xx	xx
Cash provided (used) by operations		xxx
Cash flows from investing activities		
(List of individual inflows and outflows)	xx	
Cash provided (used) by investing activities		xxx
Cash flows from financing activities		
(List of individual inflows and outflows)	xx	
Cash provided (used) by financing activities		xxx
Net increase (decrease) in cash		xxx

PREPARATION OF THE STATEMENT

Unlike the other major financial statements, the statement of cash flows is not prepared from the adjusted trial balance. The information to prepare this statement usually comes from three sources:

Comparative balance sheets. Information in these statements indicate the amount of the changes in assets, liabilities, and equities from the beginning to the end of the period.

Current income statement. Information in this statement helps the reader determine the amount of cash provided by or used by operations during the period.

Selected transaction data. These data from the general ledger provide additional detailed information needed to determine how cash was provided or used during the period.

Preparing the statement of cash flows from the data sources above involves three major steps:

1. **Determine the change in cash.** This procedure is straightforward because the difference between the beginning and ending cash balance can be easily computed from an examination of the comparative balance sheets.
2. **Determine cash provided by operations.** This procedure is complex; it involves analyzing not only the current year's income statement, but also comparative balance sheets as well as selected transaction data.

3. **Determine cash from investing and financing activities.** All other changes in the balance sheet accounts must be analyzed to determine their effect on cash.

FIRST ILLUSTRATION—1987

To illustrate a statement of cash flows, we will use **the first year of operations** for Computer Services Company. Computer Services started on January 1, 1987, when it issued 50,000 shares of $1.00 par value common stock for $50,000 cash. The company rented its office space and furniture and performed consulting services throughout the first year. The comparative balance sheets at the beginning and end of the year 1987 appear as follows.

Comparative balance sheet—1987

COMPUTER SERVICES COMPANY
Balance Sheets

Assets	Dec. 31, 1987	Jan. 1, 1987	Change Increase/Decrease
Cash	$44,000	$ -0-	$44,000 Increase
Accounts receivable (net)	30,000	-0-	30,000 Increase
Total	$74,000	$ -0-	
Liabilities and Stockholders' Equity			
Accounts payable	$ 4,000	$ -0-	4,000 Increase
Common stock	50,000	-0-	50,000 Increase
Retained earnings	20,000	-0-	20,000 Increase
Total	$74,000	$ -0-	

The income statement and additional information for Computer Services Company are as follows:

Income statement and additional information—1987

COMPUTER SERVICES COMPANY
Income Statement
For the Year Ended December 31, 1987

Revenues	$85,000
Operating expenses	40,000
Income before income taxes	45,000
Income tax expense	10,000
Net income	$35,000

Additional information:
Examination of selected data indicates that a dividend of $15,000 was paid during the year.

To prepare a statement of cash flows, the first step, **determining the change in cash,** is a simple computation. For example, Computer Services Company had no cash on hand at the beginning of the year 1987, but $44,000

was on hand at the end of 1987; thus, the change in cash for 1987 was an increase of $44,000. The other two steps are more complex and involve additional analysis.

Determine Cash Provided by Operations

A useful starting point in **determining cash provided by operations** is to understand why net income must be converted. Under generally accepted accounting principles, most companies use the accrual basis of accounting. This basis requires that revenue be recorded when earned and that expenses be recorded when incurred. Earned revenues may include credit sales that have not been collected in cash and expenses incurred that may not have been paid in cash. Thus, under the accrual basis of accounting, net income will not indicate the cash provided by operations. In order to arrive at cash provided by operations, it is necessary to report revenues and expenses on a **cash basis.** This is done by eliminating the effects of income statement transactions that did not result in a corresponding increase or decrease in cash. The relationship between net income and cash provided by operations is graphically depicted as follows:

Net income versus cash provided by operations

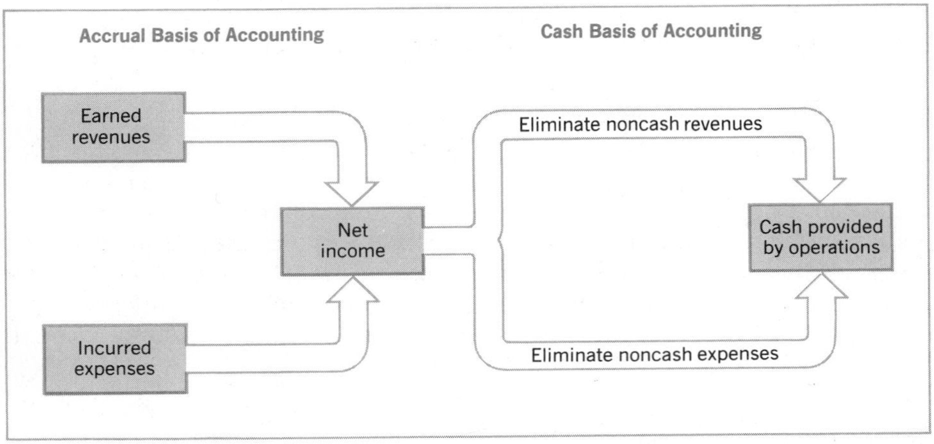

In this chapter, we will use the term net income to refer to accrual based net income. The conversion of net income to cash provided by operations may be done through either a direct approach or an indirect approach as explained below.

Direct Approach. Under the **direct approach,** cash revenues and cash expenses are determined. The difference between these two amounts is the cash provided by operations. In other words, the direct approach deducts from cash revenues only those expenses that used cash.

As indicated from the accrual-based income statement, Computer Services Company reported revenues of $85,000. However, because the company's accounts receivable (net) increased during 1987 by $30,000, only $55,000 ($85,000 − $30,000) in cash was collected on these revenues. Similarly, Computer Services Company reported operating expenses of $40,000, but accounts payable increased during the period by $4,000. Assuming that these pay-

ables related to operating expenses, cash operating expenses were $36,000 ($40,000 – $4,000). Because no taxes payable exist at the end of the year, the $10,000 income tax expense for 1987 must have been paid in cash during the year. Then the computation of cash provided by operations is as follows:

Direct approach—computation of cash provided by operations

Cash collected from revenues	$55,000
Cash payments for operating expenses	36,000
Income before income taxes	19,000
Cash payments for income taxes	10,000
Cash provided by operations	$ 9,000

"Cash provided by operations" is the equivalent of cash basis net income.

Indirect Approach. Another approach, referred to as the **indirect approach** (or reconciliation approach), is simply to start with net income and convert it to cash provided by operations. In other words, **the indirect approach adjusts net income for items that affected reported net income but did not affect cash.** That is, noncash charges in the income statement are added back to net income and noncash credits are deducted to compute cash provided by operations. Explanations for the two adjustments to net income in this example, namely, the increases in accounts receivable (net) and accounts payable, are as follows.

Increase in Accounts Receivable (Net). When accounts receivable (net) increase during the year, revenues on an accrual basis are higher than revenues on a cash basis because goods sold on account are reported as revenues. In other words, operations of the period led to increased revenues, but not all of these revenues resulted in an increase in cash. Some of the increase in revenues resulted in an increase in accounts receivable. To convert net income to cash provided by operations, the increase of $30,000 in accounts receivable must be deducted from net income.

Increase in Accounts Payable. When accounts payable increase during the year, expenses on an accrual basis are higher than they are on a cash basis because expenses are incurred for which payment has not taken place. To convert net income to cash provided by operations, the increase of $4,000 in accounts payable must be added to net income.

As a result of the accounts receivable and accounts payable adjustments, the cash provided by operations is determined to be $9,000 for the year 1987. This computation is shown as follows:

Indirect approach—computation of cash provided by operations

Net income		$35,000
Add (or deduct) items not affecting cash		
Increase in accounts receivable (net)	$(30,000)	
Increase in accounts payable	4,000	(26,000)
Cash provided by operations		$ 9,000

Note that cash provided by operations is the same whether the direct or the indirect method is used.

Determine Cash from Investing and Financing Activities

Once the cash provided by operations is computed, the next step is to determine whether any other changes in balance sheet accounts caused an increase or decrease in cash. For example, an examination of the remaining balance sheet accounts shows that both common stock and retained earnings have increased. The common stock increase of $50,000 resulted from the issuance of common stock for cash. The issuance of common stock is a receipt of cash from a financing activity and is reported as such in the statement of cash flows. The retained earnings increase is caused by two items:

1. Net income of $35,000 increased retained earnings.
2. Dividends declared of $15,000 decreased retained earnings.

Net income has been converted into cash provided by operations as explained on page 752. The additional data indicates that the dividend was paid. Thus, the dividend payment on common stock is reported as a cash outflow classified as a financing activity.

Statement of Cash Flows—1987

Having performed the analysis above, we are ready to prepare the statement of cash flows. The statement starts with the operations section. Either the direct or indirect method may be used to report cash provided by operations. The indirect method, which is used extensively in practice, is used throughout this chapter. You should use the indirect method in doing homework assignments unless instructed otherwise.

The statement of cash flows for Computer Services Company is as follows:

Statement of cash flows—1987

COMPUTER SERVICES COMPANY
Statement of Cash Flows
For the Year Ended December 31, 1987

Cash flows from operating activities		
Net income		$35,000
Add (or deduct) items not affecting cash		
Increase in accounts receivable (net)	$(30,000)	
Increase in accounts payable	4,000	(26,000)
Cash provided by operations		9,000
Cash flows from financing activities		
Issuance of common stock	$ 50,000	
Payment of cash dividends	(15,000)	
Cash provided by financing activities		35,000
Net increase in cash		$44,000

As indicated, the increase of $50,000 in common stock results in a cash inflow from a financing activity. The payment of $15,000 in cash dividends is classified as a use of cash from a financing activity. The increase in cash of $44,000 reported in the statement of cash flows agrees with the increase of $44,000 shown as the change in the cash account in the comparative balance sheets.

SECOND ILLUSTRATION—1988

Presented below is information related to the second year of operations for Computer Services Company.

Comparative balance sheet

COMPUTER SERVICES COMPANY
Comparative Balance Sheet
December 31

Assets	1988	1987	Change Increase/Decrease
Cash	$ 32,000	$44,000	$ 12,000 Decrease
Accounts receivable (net)	20,000	30,000	10,000 Decrease
Prepaid expenses	6,000	-0-	6,000 Increase
Land	110,000	-0-	110,000 Increase
Building	200,000	-0-	200,000 Increase
Accumulated depreciation – building	(11,000)	-0-	11,000 Increase
Equipment	28,000	-0-	28,000 Increase
Accumulated depreciation – equipment	(2,000)	-0-	2,000 Increase
Total	$383,000	$74,000	
Liabilities and Stockholders' Equity			
Accounts payable	$ 39,000	$ 4,000	35,000 Increase
Bonds payable	150,000	-0-	150,000 Increase
Common stock	50,000	50,000	-0-
Retained earnings	144,000	20,000	124,000 Increase
Total	$383,000	$74,000	

Income statement and additional information—1988

COMPUTER SERVICES COMPANY
Income Statement
For the Year Ended December 31, 1988

Revenues		$505,000
Operating expenses (excluding depreciation)	$264,000	
Depreciation expense	13,000	277,000
Income from operations		228,000
Income tax expense		89,000
Net income		$139,000

Additional information:

(a) In 1988, the company paid a $15,000 cash dividend.

(b) The company obtained $150,000 cash through the issuance of long-term bonds.

(c) Land, building, and equipment were acquired for cash.

To prepare a statement of cash flows from this information, the first step is to **determine the change in cash.** As indicated from the information presented, cash decreased $12,000 ($44,000 – $32,000). The second and third steps are discussed below.

Determine Cash Provided by Operations

Net income on an accrual basis must be adjusted to arrive at cash provided by operations. Explanations for the adjustments to net income are as follows.

Decrease in Accounts Receivable (Net). When accounts receivable (net of the allowance for doubtful accounts) decrease during the period, revenues on a cash basis are higher than revenues on an accrual basis, because cash collections are higher than revenues reported on an accrual basis. To convert net income to cash provided by operations, the decrease of $10,000 in accounts receivable (net) must be added to net income.

Increase in Prepaid Expenses. When prepaid expenses increase during a period, expenses on an accrual basis income statement are lower than they are on a cash basis income statement. Expenditures (cash payments) have been made in the current period, but expenses (as charges to the income statement) have been deferred to future periods. To convert net income to cash provided by operations, the increase of $6,000 in prepaid expenses must be deducted from net income. An increase in prepaid expenses results in a decrease in cash during the period.

Increase in Accounts Payable. Like the increase in 1987, the 1988 increase of $35,000 in accounts payable must be added to net income to convert to cash provided by operations.

Depreciation Expense (Increase in Accumulated Depreciation). The purchase of depreciable assets is shown as a use of cash in the investing section in the year of acquisition. The depreciation expense of $13,000 (also represented by the increase in accumulated depreciation) is a noncash charge that is added back to net income in order to arrive at cash provided by operations. The $13,000 is the sum of the depreciation on the building of $11,000 and depreciation on the equipment of $2,000.

Other charges to expense for a period that do not require the use of cash, such as the amortization of intangible assets and depletion expense, are treated in the same manner as depreciation. Depreciation and similar noncash charges are frequently listed in the statement as the first adjustments to net income.

As a result of the foregoing, cash provided by operations is $191,000 as computed below:

Computation of cash provided by operations

Net income		$139,000
Add (or deduct) items not affecting cash		
Depreciation expense	$13,000	
Decrease in accounts receivable (net)	10,000	
Increase in prepaid expense	(6,000)	
Increase in accounts payable	35,000	52,000
Cash provided by operations		$191,000

Determine Cash from Investing and Financing Activities

After the items affecting the cash provided by operations are determined, the next step involves analyzing the remaining changes in balance sheet accounts.

Increase in Land. As indicated from the change in the land account, land of $110,000 was purchased during the period. This transaction is an investing activity that should be reported as a use of cash.

Increase in Building and Related Accumulated Depreciation. As indicated in the additional data, an office building was acquired using cash of $200,000. This transaction is a cash outflow reported in the investing section. The accumulated depreciation account increase of $11,000 is fully explained by the recording of depreciation expense for the period. As indicated earlier, the reported depreciation expense has no effect on cash.

Increase in Equipment and Related Accumulated Depreciation. An increase in equipment of $28,000 resulted because equipment was purchased for cash. This transaction should be reported as an outflow of cash from an investing activity. The increase in Accumulated Depreciation—Equipment was explained by the recording of depreciation expense for the period.

Increase in Bonds Payable. The bonds payable account increased $150,000. As indicated from the additional information, cash received from the issuance of these bonds represents an inflow of cash from a financing activity.

Increase in Retained Earnings. Retained earnings increased $124,000 during the year. This increase can be explained by two factors: (1) net income of $139,000 increased retained earnings; (2) dividends of $15,000 decreased retained earnings. The net income is adjusted to cash provided by operations in the operations section. Payment of the dividends is a financing activity that involves a cash outflow.

Statement of Cash Flows—1988

Combining the foregoing items, a statement of cash flows for 1988 for Computer Services Company is presented below.

Statement of cash flows—1988

COMPUTER SERVICES COMPANY
Statement of Cash Flows
For the Year Ended December 31, 1988

Cash flows from operating activities		
Net income		$139,000
Add (or deduct) items not affecting cash		
Depreciation expense	$ 13,000	
Decrease in accounts receivable (net)	10,000	
Increase in prepaid expense	(6,000)	
Increase in accounts payable	35,000	52,000
Cash provided by operations		191,000
Cash flows from investing activities		
Purchase of land	(110,000)	
Purchase of building	(200,000)	
Purchase of equipment	(28,000)	
Cash used by investing activities		(338,000)

Cash flows from financing activities		
Issuance of bonds	150,000	
Payment of cash dividends	(15,000)	
Cash provided by financing activities		135,000
Net decrease in cash		$ (12,000)

SUMMARY OF CONVERSION TO CASH PROVIDED BY OPERATIONS

As shown in the previous illustrations, the statement of cash flows starts with net income and adds (or deducts) items not affecting cash to arrive at cash provided by operations. The additions and deductions consist of (1) changes in specific current assets and current liabilities, and (2) noncash charges and credits reported in the income statement. A summary of the current assets and current liabilities is provided first.

Adjustment for current assets and current liabilities

	Adjustments to Convert Net Income to Cash Provided by Operations	
Current assets and current liabilities	Add to Net Income	Deduct from Net Income
Accounts receivable (net)	Decrease	Increase
Inventory	Decrease	Increase
Prepaid expenses	Decrease	Increase
Accounts payable	Increase	Decrease
Accrued liabilities	Increase	Decrease

The noncash charges and credits reported in the income statement are reported as follows:

Adjustment for noncash charges and credits

Noncash charges and credits	Adjustments to Convert Net Income to Cash Provided by Operations: Add to (Deduct from) Net Income
Depreciation expense	Add
Patent amortization expense	Add
Depletion expense	Add
Loss on sale of equipment	Add
Gain on sale of equipment	Deduct

These noncash charges and credits will be discussed more fully later in the chapter.

ADDITIONAL PROBLEMS

A number of additional items that can affect the statement of cash flows merit discussion. These are:

1. Retirement of debt and retirement or reacquisition of capital stock.
2. Gross receipts and payments.
3. Significant noncash transactions.

REDEMPTION OF DEBT AND RETIREMENT OR REACQUISITION OF CAPITAL STOCK

When debt or capital stock of a company is retired or redeemed, a cash outflow from a financing activity must be reported. For example, assume that R. J. Stoddard Co. retired bonds at their face value of $200,000. In this case, the transaction results in a cash outflow and is reported in the statement of cash flows as follows:

Presentation of retirement of bonds payable

Cash flows from financing activities	
Retirement of bonds payable	$(200,000)

If capital stock was purchased, the transaction would be described as the retirement of capital stock or the purchase of treasury stock.

GROSS RECEIPTS AND PAYMENTS

The change in an account balance during the year may be the result of numerous transactions that produce a net increase or decrease in cash. For example, a $200,000 increase in Bonds Payable may have resulted from the issuance of $500,000 of bonds at face value and the redemption of $300,000 of bonds at face value. In order to fully disclose the effects of the company's financing activities, the gross receipts of $500,000 should be reported as a cash inflow and the gross payment of $300,000 should be reported as a cash outflow. Similarly, the cash receipts from the sale of plant assets should be reported separately from the cash paid for plant assets acquired.

To avoid reporting the net cash receipts or cash payments, additional analysis of the change in an account balance is required. To illustrate, assume that R. J. Stoddard has the following ending and beginning balances for equipment and related accumulated depreciation.

Ledger balances

	Dec. 31 1988	Dec. 31 1987	Change Increase/Decrease
Equipment	$153,000	$28,000	$125,000 Increase
Accumulated depreciation	10,000	2,000	8,000 Increase

Absent additional information, one conclusion that might be drawn from these data is that the equipment was purchased for $125,000. However, an

analysis of the Equipment account indicates that both a purchase and a sale of equipment occurred during the year as shown below:

Analysis of equipment account

Beginning balance (Dec. 31, 1987)	$ 28,000
Purchase equipment	**165,000**
	193,000
Sale of equipment	**(40,000)**
Ending balance (Dec. 31, 1988)	$153,000

In order to fully disclose the company's investing activities, the effects of the purchase and sale should be reported separately in the statement of cash flows. First, equipment in the amount of $165,000 was purchased for cash. This transaction is reported as a cash outflow and is entered on the statement of cash flows in the following manner:

Presentation of purchase of equipment

Cash flows from investing activities	
Purchase of equipment	$(165,000)

Second, equipment having a cost of $40,000 and a book value of $35,000 was sold for $33,000 cash. The proceeds from the sale are a cash inflow and are reported as follows:

Presentation of sale of equipment

Cash flows from investing activities	
Sale of equipment	$33,000

Loss on Sale

In the sale of equipment, the company suffered a $2,000 loss (book value $35,000 − cash proceeds $33,000). The loss was reported in the income statement and was deducted in determining net income. Since the loss is a noncash charge, it must be added to net income in reporting cash provided by operations. To illustrate, assuming that R. J. Stoddard's net income for the year was $210,000, the operating section of the statement of cash flows is as follows:

Operating section and loss on sale

Cash flows from operating activities		
Net income		$210,000
Add (or deduct) items not affecting cash		
Loss on sale of equipment	**$2,000**	

A similar analysis is followed to explain the change in the Accumulated Depreciation—Equipment account. As indicated above, equipment with a book value of $35,000 (cost $40,000 less accumulated depreciation $5,000) was sold. It follows that if Accumulated Depreciation—Equipment decreased $5,000 as a result of the sale, and the net change for the year was an increase of $8,000, then depreciation expense for the year is $13,000. An analysis of the Accumulated Depreciation—Equipment account verifies this conclusion.

Analysis of accumulated depreciation account

Beginning balance (Dec. 31, 1987)	$ 2,000
Depreciation for the year	13,000
	15,000
Sale of equipment	5,000
Ending balance (Dec. 31, 1988)	$10,000

The depreciation expense along with the loss on sale of equipment is reported in the operating activities section of Stoddard's statement of cash flows as follows:

Operating section and depreciation

Cash flows from operating activities		
Net income		$210,000
Add (or deduct) items not affecting cash		
Depreciation expense	$13,000	
Loss on sale of equipment	2,000	

Gain on Sale

A different situation results when plant assets are sold at a gain. The gain is reported in the income statement and it is added in determining net income. To prevent both the proceeds from the sale and the gain on sale from being reported as a cash inflow, the gain must be deducted from net income in reporting cash provided by operations. To illustrate, assume that Stoddard sold land costing $10,000 for $14,000, and therefore reported a gain of $4,000 in the income statement. The cash proceeds of $14,000 from the sale is reported in the statement of cash flows as follows:

Presentation of sale of land

Cash flows from investing activities	
Sale of land	$14,000

It follows that allowing the $4,000 gain in net income to flow through to cash provided by operations would be double counting the gain—once in net income and secondly in the sales proceeds. Therefore, the gain is deducted from net income in the operating activities section as illustrated below:

Operating section and gain on sale

Cash flows from operating activities		
Net income		$210,000
Add (or deduct) items not affecting cash		
Depreciation expense	$13,000	
Loss on sale of equipment	2,000	
Gain on sale of land	(4,000)	

SIGNIFICANT NONCASH TRANSACTIONS

When the statement of cash flows only reports the effects of transactions on cash, some major transactions may be omitted. For example, although issuance of common stock for land has no effect on cash, it is a significant transaction that merits disclosure. Examples of other significant noncash transac-

tions are conversions of bonds into common stock, the acquisition of assets by issuing bonds, and exchanges of plant assets. As a result, significant financing and investing activities not affecting cash are required to be reported in the statement of cash flows. These transactions are individually reported immediately below the increase (or decrease) in cash in a section entitled **noncash investing and financing activities.** To illustrate, assume that Stoddard purchased a building for $90,000 by issuing a 5-year note payable. If Stoddard had a decrease in cash for the period of $97,000, the presentation of this significant noncash transaction is as follows:

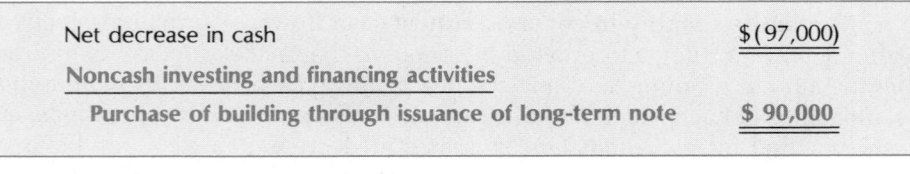

Partial statement—illustration of noncash transaction

Net decrease in cash	$(97,000)
Noncash investing and financing activities	
Purchase of building through issuance of long-term note	$ 90,000

The reporting of the transaction in this manner satisfies the full disclosure principle because it identifies significant noncash investing and financing activities of the enterprise. At the same time, the effects are segregated from the cash transactions, so that the users of the financial statements can identify both the cash and noncash transactions.

ADDITIONAL PROBLEMS—A RECAP

A number of transactions were presented for R. J. Stoddard Co. to highlight some additional reporting issues related to the preparation of a statement of cash flows. Presented below is a statement of cash flows for Stoddard given the transactions in the previous section:

Statement of cash flows—1988

R. J. STODDARD CO.
Statement of Cash Flows
For the Year Ended December 31, 1988

Cash flows from operating activities		
Net income		$210,000
Add (or deduct) items not affecting cash		
Depreciation expense	$ 13,000	
Loss on sale of equipment	2,000	
Gain on sale of land	(4,000)	11,000
Cash provided by operations		221,000
Cash flows from investing activities		
Sale of equipment	33,000	
Sale of land	14,000	
Purchase of equipment	(165,000)	
Cash used by investing activities		(118,000)
Cash flows from financing activities		
Retirement of bonds payable		(200,000)
Net decrease in cash		$ (97,000)
Noncash investing and financing activities		
Purchase of building through issuance of long-term note		$ 90,000

Noncash investing and financing activities are disclosed only if they are material in amount.

USEFULNESS OF THE STATEMENT OF CASH FLOWS

The information in a statement of cash flows should help investors, creditors, and others to assess:

1. **The entity's ability to generate future cash flows.** A primary objective of financial reporting is to provide information that makes it possible to predict the amounts, timing, and uncertainty of future cash flows. By examining relationships between such items as sales and cash provided by operations, or cash provided by operations and increases or decreases in cash, predictions of the amount, timing, and uncertainty of future cash flows can be made better than from accrual basis data.

2. **The entity's ability to pay dividends and meet obligations.** Simply put, if a company does not have adequate cash, employees cannot be paid, debts settled, dividends paid, or equipment acquired. A statement of cash flows indicates how cash is used and its sources. Employers, creditors, stockholders, and customers should be particularly interested in this statement, because it alone shows the flows of cash in a business.

3. **The reasons for the difference between net income and cash flow from operations.** The net income number is important, because it provides information on the success or failure of a business enterprise from one period to another. But some are critical of accrual basis net income because estimates must be made to arrive at it. As a result, the reliability of the number is often challenged. Such is not the case with cash. Thus, many readers of the financial statement want to know the reasons for the difference between net income and cash provided by operations. Then they can assess for themselves the reliability of the income number.

4. **The cash and noncash investing and financing transactions during the period.** By examining a company's investing activities (purchase and sales of assets other than its products) and its financing transactions (borrowings and repayments of borrowings, investments by owners and distribution to owners), a financial statement reader can better understand why assets and liabilities increased or decreased during the period. For example, the following questions might be answered:

   How did cash increase when there was a net loss for the period?
   How were the proceeds of the bond issue used?
   How was the expansion in the plant and equipment financed?
   Why were dividends not increased?
   How was the retirement of debt accomplished?
   How much money was borrowed during the year?
   Is cash flow greater or less than net income?

SUMMARY OF STUDY OBJECTIVES

1. The primary purpose of the statement of cash flows is to provide information about the cash receipts and cash payments of an entity during a period. A secondary objective is to provide information about the investing and financing activities of the entity during the period.

2. The major sources and uses of cash reported in the statement of cash flows are operating activities (transactions that relate to the income statement), investing activities (transactions that involve noncash asset items), and financing activities (transactions that involve liability and owners' equity items).

3. The direct approach reports cash revenues less cash expenses to arrive at cash provided by operations. The indirect approach adjusts accrual basis net income to cash provided by operations.

4. The preparation of a statement of cash flows involves three major steps (1) determine the change in cash; (2) determine cash provided by operations; and (3) determine cash flows from investing and financing activities. Significant noncash investing and financing activities must also be reported in a separate section.

5. The statement of cash flows helps in assessing (1) the entity's ability to generate future cash flows, (2) the entity's ability to pay dividends and meet obligations, (3) the reasons for the difference between net income and cash flow from operations, and (4) the cash and noncash financing and investing transactions during the period.

APPENDIX 19–A

USING A WORK SHEET FOR PREPARING THE STATEMENT OF CASH FLOWS

When numerous adjustments are necessary, or other complicating factors are present, **many accountants prefer to use a work sheet to assemble and classify the data that will appear on the statement of cash flows.** The work sheet is merely a device that aids in the preparation of the statement; its use is optional. The skeleton format of the work sheet for preparation of the statement of cash flows is shown on the next page.

Format of work sheet

XYZ COMPANY
Work Sheet
Statement of Cash Flows
For the Year Ended . . .

Balance Sheet Accounts	End of Last Year Balances	Reconciling Items Debits	Reconciling Items Credits	End of Current Year Balances
Debit balance accounts	XX	XX	XX	XX
	XX	XX	XX	XX
Totals	XXX			XXX
Credit balance accounts	XX	XX	XX	XX
	XX	XX	XX	XX
Totals	XXX			XXX
Statement of Cash Flows Effects		Debits	Credits	
Operating activities				
Net income		XX		
Adjustments		XX	XX	
Investing activities				
Receipts and payments		XX	XX	
Financing activities				
Receipts and payments		XX	XX	
Totals		XXX	XXX	
Increase (decrease) in cash		(XX)	XX	
Totals		XXX	XXX	

The following guidelines are important in using a work sheet:

1. In the balance sheet accounts section, accounts with debit balances are listed separately from those with credit balances. This means, for example, that Accumulated Depreciation is listed under credit balances and not as a contra account under debit balances. The beginning and ending balances of each account are entered in the appropriate columns. The transactions that caused the change in the account balance during the year are entered as reconciling items in the two middle columns. After all reconciling items have been entered, each line pertaining to a balance sheet account should foot across. That is, the beginning balance plus or minus the reconciling item(s) must equal the ending balance. When this agreement exists for all balance sheet accounts, all changes in account balances have been reconciled.
2. The bottom portion of the work sheet consists of the operating, investing, and financing activities sections. Accordingly, it provides the information necessary to prepare the formal statement of cash flows. Inflows of cash are entered as debits in the reconciling columns and outflows

of cash are entered as credits in the reconciling columns. Thus, in this section, the sale of equipment for cash at book value is entered as a debit under inflows of cash from investing activities. Similarly, the purchase of land for cash is entered as a credit under outflows of cash from investing activities.

3. The reconciling items shown in the work sheet are not entered in any journal or posted to any account. They do not represent either adjustments or corrections of the balance sheet accounts. They are used only to facilitate the preparation of the statement of cash flows.

This work sheet can be easily turned into a spreadsheet template. The template should be made to ensure balancing and can be expanded to automatically generate the formal statement itself.

All major public accounting firms insist that their staff members become proficient in the use of spreadsheets. Even many nonaccounting employers consider a working knowledge of microcomputer applications to be an "entry level" skill. Versions of the spreadsheet applications, that are provided in this textbook, are all found in use by practicing accountants and other business professionals.

PREPARATION OF THE WORK SHEET

As in the case of work sheets illustrated in earlier chapters, the preparation of a work sheet involves a series of prescribed steps. The steps in this case are:

1. Enter the balance sheet accounts and their beginning and ending balances in the balance sheet accounts section.
2. Enter the data that explains the changes in the balance sheet accounts (other than cash) and their effects on the statement of cash flows in the reconciling columns of the work sheet.
3. Enter the increase or decrease in cash on the cash line and at the bottom of the work sheet. This entry should enable the totals of the reconciling columns to be in agreement.

To illustrate the preparation of a work sheet, we will use the 1988 data for Computer Services Company. Your familiarity with these data should facilitate your understanding of the use of a work sheet. For ease of reference, the comparative balance sheets, income statement, and selected data for 1988 are as follows:

Comparative balance sheet

COMPUTER SERVICES COMPANY
Comparative Balance Sheet
December 31

Assets	1988	1987	Change Increase/Decrease
Cash	$ 32,000	$44,000	$ 12,000 Decrease
Accounts receivable (net)	20,000	30,000	10,000 Decrease
Prepaid expenses	6,000	-0-	6,000 Increase
Land	110,000	-0-	110,000 Increase
Building	200,000	-0-	200,000 Increase
Accumulated depreciation – building	(11,000)	-0-	11,000 Increase
Equipment	28,000	-0-	28,000 Increase
Accumulated depreciation – equipment	(2,000)	-0-	2,000 Increase
Totals	$383,000	$74,000	
Liabilities and Stockholders' Equity			
Accounts payable	$ 39,000	$ 4,000	35,000 Increase
Bonds payable	150,000	-0-	150,000 Increase
Common stock	50,000	50,000	-0-
Retained earnings	144,000	20,000	124,000 Increase
	$383,000	$74,000	

Income statement and additional information—1988

COMPUTER SERVICES COMPANY
Income Statement
For the Year Ended December 31, 1988

Revenues		$505,000
Operating expenses (excluding depreciation)	$264,000	
Depreciation expense	13,000	277,000
Income from operations		228,000
Income tax expense		89,000
Net income		$139,000

Additional information:
(a) In 1988, the company paid a $15,000 cash dividend.
(b) The company obtained $150,000 cash through the issuance of long-term bonds.
(c) Land, building, and equipment were purchased for cash.

DETERMINING THE RECONCILING ITEMS

Several approaches may be used to determine the reconciling items. For example, the changes affecting cash provided by operations could be completed first and then the effects of financing and investing transactions could be determined. Alternatively, the balance sheet accounts can be analyzed in the order in which they are listed on the work sheet. We will follow this approach for Computer Services except for cash. As indicated above, cash is handled last.

Accounts Receivable (net). The decrease of $10,000 in accounts receivable means that cash collections from revenues are higher than the revenues reported in the income statement. To convert net income to cash provided by operations, the decrease of $10,000 must be added to net income. The entry in the reconciling columns of the work sheet is:

(a)	Operating — Increase in Accounts Receivable	10,000	
	Accounts Receivable		10,000

Prepaid Expenses. An increase of $6,000 in prepaid expenses means that expenses deducted in determining net income are less than expenses that were paid in cash. Thus, the increase of $6,000 must be deducted from net income in determining cash provided by operations. The work sheet entry is:

(b)	Prepaid Expenses	6,000	
	Operating — Decrease in Prepaid Expenses		6,000

Land. The increase in land of $110,000 resulted from a cash purchase. This change is an investing activity cash outflow. Therefore, the work sheet entry is:

(c)	Land	110,000	
	Investing — Purchase of Land		110,000

Building. As in the case of land, the cash purchase of a building for $200,000 is an investing activity cash ouflow. The entry in the reconciling columns of the work sheet is:

(d)	Buildings	200,000	
	Investing — Purchase of Building		200,000

Equipment. The increase in equipment of $28,000 also resulted from a cash purchase. Thus, the work sheet entry is:

(e)	Equipment	28,000	
	Investing — Purchase of Equipment		28,000

Accounts Payable. The increase of $35,000 in accounts payable must be added to net income to obtain cash provided by operations. The following work sheet entry is made:

(f)	Operating — Increase in Accounts Payable	35,000	
	Accounts Payable		35,000

Bonds Payable. The increase of $150,000 in this account resulted from the issuance of bonds for cash. This is a financing transaction that should be reported as a financing activity cash inflow. The work sheet entry is:

(g)	Financing — Issuance of Bonds	150,000	
	Bonds Payable		150,000

Accumulated Depreciation—Building and Accumulated Depreciation—Equipment. The increases in these accounts of $11,000 and $2,000, respectively, resulted from depreciation expense. Depreciation expense is a noncash charge that must be added to net income in determining cash provided by operations. The work sheet entries are:

(h)	Operating – Depreciation Expense – Building	11,000	
	Accumulated Depreciation – Building		11,000
(i)	Operating – Depreciation Expense – Equipment	2,000	
	Accumulated Depreciation – Equipment		2,000

Retained Earnings. The $124,000 increase in retained earnings resulted from net income of $139,000 and the declaration of a $15,000 cash dividend that was paid in 1988. Net income is included in cash provided by operations and the dividends are a financing activity cash outflow. The entries in the reconciling columns of the work sheet are:

(j)	Operating – Net Income	139,000	
	Retained Earnings		139,000
(k)	Retained Earnings	15,000	
	Financing – Payment of Dividends		15,000

Disposition of Change in Cash. In Computer Services, Cash decreased $12,000 in 1988. The final entry on the work sheet, therefore, is:

(l)	Decrease in Cash	12,000	
	Cash		12,000

As shown in the work sheet, the decrease in cash is entered in the reconciling debit column as a **balancing** amount. It is not a cash inflow. This entry should complete the reconciliation of the changes in the balance sheet accounts. In addition, it should permit the totals of the reconciling columns to be in agreement. When all changes have been explained and the reconciling columns are in agreement, the reconciling columns are ruled to complete the work sheet. The completed work sheet for Computer Services Company is shown on page 769.

PREPARATION OF THE STATEMENT

The statement of cash flows is prepared entirely from the data that appears in the work sheet under Statement of Cash Flows Effects. The formal statement is shown on pages 756 and 757.

Completed work sheet

COMPUTER SERVICES COMPANY
Work Sheet
Statement of Cash Flows
For the Year Ended December 31, 1988

Balance Sheet Accounts	Balance 12/31/87	Reconciling Items: Debit	Reconciling Items: Credit	Balance 12/31/88
Debits				
Cash	44,000		(l) 12,000	32,000
Accounts receivable (net)	30,000		(a) 10,000	20,000
Prepaid expenses	-0-	(b) 6,000		6,000
Land	-0-	(c) 110,000		110,000
Buildings	-0-	(d) 200,000		200,000
Equipment	-0-	(e) 28,000		28,000
Total	74,000			396,000
Credits				
Accounts payable	4,000		(f) 35,000	39,000
Bonds payable	-0-		(g) 150,000	150,000
Accumulated depreciation-building	-0-		(h) 11,000	11,000
Accumulated depreciation-equipment	-0-		(i) 2,000	2,000
Common stock	50,000			50,000
Retained earnings	20,000	(k) 15,000	(j) 139,000	144,000
Total	74,000			396,000
Statement of Cash Flows Effects				
Operating activities				
Net income		(j) 139,000		
Decrease in accounts receivable (net)		(a) 10,000		
Increase in prepaid expenses			(b) 6,000	
Increase in accounts payable		(f) 35,000		
Depreciation expense – buildings		(h) 11,000		
Depreciation expense – equipment		(i) 2,000		
Investing activities				
Purchase of land			(c) 110,000	
Purchase of building			(d) 200,000	
Purchase of equipment			(e) 28,000	
Financing activities				
Issuance of bonds		(g) 150,000		
Payment of dividend			(k) 15,000	
Totals		706,000	718,000	
Decrease in cash		(l) 12,000		
Totals		718,000	718,000	

GLOSSARY

Direct approach, p. 751

Indirect approach, p. 752

Statement of cash flows, p. 746

DEMONSTRATION PROBLEM

The income statement for the year ended December 31, 1987, for J. Milbourn Manufacturing Company contains the following condensed information:

Revenues		$6,583,000
Operating expenses (excluding depreciation)	$4,920,000	
Depreciation expense	880,000	5,800,000
Income before income taxes		783,000
Income tax expense		353,000
Net income		$ 430,000

Included in operating expenses is a $24,000 loss resulting from the sale of machinery.

The following balances are reported on Milbourn's comparative balance sheet at December 31:

	1987	1986
Accounts receivable	$775,000	$610,000
Inventories	834,000	867,000
Accounts payable	521,000	501,000

Income tax expense of $353,000 represents the amount paid and due for 1987.

INSTRUCTIONS

(a) Prepare the cash flows from operating activities section of the statement of cash flows using the indirect method.

(b) Prepare the cash flows from operating activities section of the statement of cash flows using the direct method.

SOLUTION TO DEMONSTRATION PROBLEM

J. MILBOURN MANUFACTURING COMPANY
Partial Statement of Cash Flows
For the Year Ended December 31, 1986

(Indirect Method)

Cash flows from operating activities		
Net income		$ 430,000
Add (or deduct) items not affecting cash		
Depreciation expense	$880,000	
Loss on sale of machinery	24,000	
Increase in accounts receivable	(165,000)	
Decrease in inventories	33,000	
Increase in accounts payable	20,000	792,000
Cash provided by operations		$1,222,000

(Direct Method)

Cash flows from operating activities	
Cash collections from customers	$6,418,000(a)
Cash payments for operating expenses	4,843,000(b)
Income before income taxes	1,575,000
Cash payment for income taxes	353,000
Cash provided by operations	$1,222,000

(a) Computation of cash collection from customers:	
Revenues per the income statement	$6,583,000
Less increase in accounts receivable	165,000
Cash collections from customers	$6,418,000
(b) Computation of cash payments for operating expenses:	
Operating expenses per the income statement	$4,920,000
Deduct loss from sale of machinery	(24,000)
Deduct decrease in inventories	(33,000)
Deduct increase in accounts payable	(20,000)
Cash payments for operating expenses	$4,843,000

***Note:** All **asterisked** Questions, Exercises, and Problems relate to material contained in the Appendix to each chapter.

QUESTIONS

1. What is the purpose of the statement of cash flows? What information does it provide?

2. Why are businesses now using the statement of cash flows?

3. Differentiate between investing activities and financing activities.

4. What are the major sources of cash (inflows) in a statement of cash flows? What are the major uses (outflows) of cash?

5. Why is it necessary to use comparative balance sheets, a current income statement, and certain transaction data in preparing a statement of cash flows?

6. Why is it necessary to convert accrual based net income to cash basis income when preparing a statement of cash flows?

7. Describe the direct approach for determining cash provided from operations.

8. Describe the indirect approach for determining cash provided from operations.

9. Bill Rugen, Inc., reported net income of $2.5 million in 1987. Depreciation for the year was $260,000, accounts receivable increased $350,000, and accounts payable increased $200,000. Compute cash provided from operations using the indirect approach.

10. When the total cash inflows exceed the total cash outflows in the statement of cash flows, how and where is this excess identified?

11. The president of Sandle Company is puzzled. During the last year, the company experienced a net loss of $900,000, yet its cash increased $300,000 during the same period of time. Explain to the president how this situation could occur.

12. The board of directors of Nunnery Corp. declared cash dividends of $130,000 during the current year. If dividends payable was $41,000 at the beginning of the year and $36,000 at the end of the year, how much cash was paid in dividends during the year?

13. Mark Fedenia, Inc. reported sales of $2 million for 1987. Accounts receivable decreased $300,000 and accounts payable increased $200,000. Compute cash sales, assuming that the receivable and payable transactions related to operations.

14. The net income for Topco Engineering Co. for 1987 was $280,000. For 1987, depreciation on plant assets was $60,000, amortization of goodwill was $35,000, and the company incurred a loss on sale of plant assets of $8,000. Compute cash provided from operations.

15. Each of the following items must be considered in preparing a statement of cash flows for Erica Shin Co. for the year ended December 31, 1987. For each item, state where it is to be shown in the statement, if at all.

(a) During the year, bonds with a face value of $200,000 were issued for $195,000.

(b) Plant assets with a book value of $60,000 were sold for $53,000.

(c) During the year, goodwill of $100,000 was written off to expense.

16. Classify the following items as operating, investing, financing, or significant noncash investing and financing activities.

(a) Purchase of equipment.
(b) Redemption of bonds.
(c) Sale of building.
(d) Depreciation.
(e) Exchange of equipment for furniture.
(f) Issuance of capital stock.
(g) Amortization of intangible asset.
(h) Purchase of treasury stock.
(i) Issuance of bonds for land.
(j) Payment of dividends.
(k) Receipt of interest on notes receivable.

17. Duke Shin and Heather Remmers were discussing the presentation format of the statement of cash flows of Hinz Lithographing Co. At the bottom of Hinz's statement of cash flows was a separate section entitled "Noncash investing and financing activities." Give three examples of significant noncash transactions that would be reported in this section.

18. During 1987, Edward A. Messman Company converted $1,500,000 of its total $2,000,000 of bonds payable into common stock. Indicate how the transaction would be reported on a statement of cash flows, if at all.

19. Why is the statement of cash flows useful?

***20.** Why is it advantageous to use a work sheet when preparing a statement of cash flows? Is a work sheet required to prepare a statement of cash flows?

EXERCISES

E19-1 Mary Ann Benson Company had the following transactions during 1987:

1. Issued $50,000 par value common stock for cash.
2. Purchased a machine for $10,000, giving a short-term note in exchange.
3. Collected $16,000 of accounts receivable.
4. Declared and paid a cash dividend of $25,000.
5. Sold a long-term investment with a cost of $15,000 for $18,000.
6. Purchased treasury stock for $50,000.
7. Issued $200,000 par value common stock to retire at face value $200,000 of the company's long-term bonds.
8. Paid $12,000 in settling accounts payable.

INSTRUCTIONS

Analyze the transactions above and indicate whether each transaction resulted in a cash flow from (a) operating activities, (b) investing activities, (c) financing activities, or (d) noncash investing and financing activities.

E19-2 Marian Corcoran Company has just completed its first year of operations on December 31, 1987. Its initial income statement showed that Corcoran had revenues of $157,000 and operating expenses of $78,000. Accounts receivable and accounts payable at year end were $45,000 and $26,000, respectively. Assume that accounts payable related to operating expenses. Ignore income taxes.

INSTRUCTIONS

Compute cash provided by operations using the direct method.

E19-3 Vicki Worrell Company reported net income of $167,000 for 1987. Worrell also reported depreciation expense of $35,000, had an increase in accounts receivable of $15,000 for the year, and experienced a $7,000 increase in accounts payable.

INSTRUCTIONS

Determine the amount of cash provided by operations for 1987 (indirect method).

E19-4 The current sections of Mary Burgin Company's balance sheets at December 31, 1986 and 1987 are presented below.

	1987	1986
Current Assets		
Cash	$105,000	$ 99,000
Accounts receivable	110,000	97,000
Inventory	174,000	186,000
Prepaid expenses	27,000	32,000
Total current assets	$416,000	$414,000
Current liabilities		
Notes payable	$ 45,000	$ 35,000
Accounts payable	55,000	62,000
Total current liabilities	$100,000	$ 97,000

The note was issued for merchandise. Burgin's net income for 1987 was $132,000. Depreciation expense was $25,000.

INSTRUCTIONS

Prepare the cash provided by operations section of Mary Burgin Company's statement of cash flows for the year ended December 31, 1987 (indirect method).

E19-5 Presented below are three accounts that appear in the general ledger of Mary George Corp.

Equipment

Date		Debit	Credit	Balance
Jan. 1, 1987	Balance			160,000
July 31	Purchase of equipment	70,000		230,000
Sept. 2	Cost of equipment constructed	53,000		283,000
Nov. 10	Cost of equipment sold		45,000	238,000

Accumulated Depreciation—Equipment

Date		Debit	Credit	Balance
Jan. 1, 1987	Balance			71,000
Nov. 10	Accumulated depreciation on equipment sold	30,000		41,000
Dec. 31	Depreciation for 1987		24,000	65,000

Retained Earnings

Date		Debit	Credit	Balance
Jan. 1, 1987	Balance			105,000
Aug. 23	Dividends (cash)	11,000		94,000
Dec. 31	Net income		41,000	135,000

INSTRUCTIONS

From the entries in the accounts above, indicate how the information is reported on a statement of cash flows by preparing a partial statement of cash flows (indirect method). The loss on sale of equipment was $6,000.

E19-6 Presented below are a number of transactions related to Hartland Company for 1987.

1. Hartland purchased 200 shares of treasury stock at a cost of $30 per share. These shares were subsequently resold at $38 per share.
2. Hartland issued 1,000 shares of its $10 par common stock for a patent. The market value of shares on the date of the transaction was $36 per share.
3. During the year, Hartland wrote down by $11,000 its inventory to market from original cost.
4. Depreciation expense for the year was $110,000.
5. Hartland received $17,000 for interest earned on Marcille Voss' notes receivable of $200,000.
6. During the year, equipment was sold to Kenneth R. Olson for $8,500. The equipment cost $18,000 originally and had a book value of $12,000 at time of sale.
7. Issued a long-term note to Michael Willging in the amount of $22,000 to purchase equipment.

INSTRUCTIONS

Indicate by classification and description how each of these transactions should be reported on a statement of cash flows.

E19-7 A comparative balance sheet for Roger Tuttle Company is presented below.

	December 31	
Assets	1987	1986
Cash	$ 69,000	$ 22,000
Accounts receivable (net)	82,000	66,000
Inventories	180,000	189,000
Land	75,000	110,000
Equipment	260,000	200,000
Accumulated depreciation – equipment	(69,000)	(42,000)
Total	$597,000	$545,000
Liabilities and Stockholders' Equity		
Accounts payable	$ 34,000	$ 47,000
Bonds payable	150,000	200,000
Common stock ($1 par)	214,000	164,000
Retained earnings	199,000	134,000
Total	$597,000	$545,000

Additional information:

1. Net income for 1987 was $115,000.
2. Cash dividends of $50,000 were declared and paid.
3. Bonds payable amounting to $50,000 were retired through issuance of common stock.

INSTRUCTIONS

Prepare a statement of cash flows for 1987 (indirect method). Do not use a work sheet.

E19-8 An analysis of comparative balance sheets, the current year's income statement and the general ledger accounts of Nadine Barnas Corp. uncovered the following items.

(a) Payment of dividends.
(b) Purchase of land.
(c) Sale of building for cash at book value.
(d) Exchange of land for patent.
(e) Depreciation.
(f) Redemption of bonds.
(g) Receipt of interest on receivable.
(h) Issuance of capital stock.
(i) Purchase of treasury stock.
(j) Amortization of patent.
(k) Issuance of bonds for land.
(l) Payment of interest on notes payable.
(m) Conversion of bonds into common stock.
(n) Receipt of dividends on investment in stock.
(o) Loss on sale of land for cash.

INSTRUCTIONS

Indicate how the above items should be classified in the statement of cash flows using the following four major classifications: operating activity (indirect method), investing activity, financing activity, and significant noncash investing and financing activity.

E19-9 The following balances and transactions are determined from an analysis of the statements and accounts of F. Vincent Steidl and Company, Incorporated. The balance in equipment was $200,000 on January 1, and $260,000 on December 31, 1987. The balance in Accumulated Depreciation—Equipment was $120,000 on January 1 and $140,000 on December 31, 1987. During 1987, equipment costing $25,000, with accumulated depreciation of $15,000 was sold for $10,000 cash. There were no divi-

dends paid during the year 1987 nor were there any changes in long-term debt or in common stock. Net income (including depreciation expense) per the income statement was $45,000. All current account balances remained unchanged from the beginning to the end of the year except for cash which increased $5,000.

INSTRUCTIONS

Prepare a statement of cash flows for the year 1987 using the indirect method. (Hint: Work backwards from changes in plant asset accounts.)

***E19-10**

INSTRUCTIONS

Refer to Exercise E19-7 (Roger Tuttle Company) and use these data to prepare a work sheet for a statement of cash flows for 1987. Enter the reconciling items directly on the work sheet identifying the entries alphabetically.

PROBLEMS

P19-1 The income statement of Donna Smith Company is shown below:

DONNA SMITH COMPANY
Income Statement
For the Year Ended November 30, 1987

Sales		$6,900,000
Cost of goods sold		
Beginning inventory	$1,900,000	
Purchases	4,400,000	
Goods available for sale	6,300,000	
Ending inventory	1,600,000	
Cost of goods sold		4,700,000
Gross profit		2,200,000
Operating expenses		
Selling expenses	450,000	
Administrative expense	700,000	1,150,000
Net income		$1,050,000

Additional information:

1. Accounts receivable increased $450,000 during the year.
2. Prepaid expenses decreased $150,000 during the year.
3. Accounts payable increased $300,000 during the year.
4. Accrued liabilities decreased $100,000 during the year.
5. Administrative expense includes depreciation expense of $50,000.

INSTRUCTIONS

Prepare the cash provided by operations section of the statement of cash flows for the year ended November 30, 1987, for Donna Smith Company, using the indirect method.

P19-2 Laura Marquette Company's income statement for the year ended December 31, 1987, contained the following condensed information:

Revenue from fees		$840,000
Operating expenses (excluding depreciation)	$650,000	
Depreciation expense	60,000	710,000
Income before income taxes		130,000
Income tax expense		39,000
Net income		$ 91,000

Included in operating expenses is a $6,000 loss from sale of equipment. Marquette's balance sheet contained the following comparative data at December 31:

	1987	1986
Accounts receivable	$35,000	$55,000
Accounts payable	41,000	33,000
Income taxes payable	4,000	9,000

INSTRUCTIONS

(a) Prepare the cash flows from operating activities section of the statement of cash flows using the direct method.

(b) Prepare the cash flows from operating activities section of the statement of cash flows using the indirect method.

P19-3 The financial statements of Jewel Kadlec Company appear below.

JEWEL KADLEC COMPANY
Balance Sheet
December 31

		1987		1986
Assets				
Cash		$ 25,000		$ 13,000
Accounts receivable		29,000		14,000
Merchandise inventory		26,000		35,000
Property, plant, and equipment	$60,000		$78,000	
Less accumulated depreciation	(20,000)	40,000	(24,000)	54,000
		$120,000		$116,000
Liabilities and Stockholders' Equity				
Accounts payable		$ 34,000		$ 23,000
Federal income taxes payable		25,000		30,000
Bonds payable		37,000		33,000
Common stock		6,000		14,000
Retained earnings		18,000		16,000
		$120,000		$116,000

JEWEL KADLEC COMPANY
Income Statement
For the Year Ended December 31, 1987

Sales		$220,000
Cost of goods sold		180,000
Gross profit		40,000
Selling expenses	$18,000	
Administrative expenses	6,000	24,000

Income from operations	16,000
Interest expense	5,000
Income before income taxes	11,000
Income tax expense	2,000
Net income	$ 9,000

The following additional data were provided:

1. Dividends for the year 1987 were $3,500.
2. During the year equipment was sold for $8,500 cash. This equipment cost $18,000 originally and had a book value of $12,000 at the time of sale. The loss on sale was incorrectly charged to retained earnings. The accounting for this loss did not affect the amount of income taxes.
3. All depreciation expense is in the selling expense category.
4. All sales and purchases are on account.

INSTRUCTIONS

(a) Prepare a statement of cash flows using the indirect approach.

(b) Prepare the operating section of the statement of cash flows using the direct method.

P19-4 Condensed financial data of LeGault Company for 1986 and 1987 appear below.

LEGAULT COMPANY
Comparative Balance Sheet
December 31

	1987	1986
Assets		
Cash	$109,800	$ 38,400
Accounts receivable (net)	97,200	49,000
Inventories	112,500	102,850
Investments	86,000	94,000
Plant assets	270,000	242,500
Accumulated depreciation—plant assets	(50,000)	(52,000)
	$625,500	$474,750
Liabilities and Stockholders' Equity		
Accounts payable	$100,000	$ 67,300
Accrued expenses payable	16,500	17,000
Bonds payable	75,000	110,000
Common stock	200,000	175,000
Retained earnings	234,000	105,450
	$625,500	$474,750

LEGAULT COMPANY
Income Statement Data
For the Year Ended December 31, 1987

Sales		$342,780
Less:		
Cost of goods sold	$115,460	
Selling and administrative expenses (excluding depreciation)	12,410	
Depreciation expense	42,000	

Income taxes	7,275	
Interest expense	2,730	
Loss on sale of plant assets	12,000	191,875
Net income		150,905
Dividends		22,355
Income retained in business		$128,550

Additional information:

1. New plant assets costing $85,000 were purchased during the year.
2. Old plant assets having an original cost of $57,500 were sold for $1,500.
3. Investments were sold at book value.
4. Bonds were redeemed at face and book value.

INSTRUCTIONS

Prepare a statement of cash flows using the indirect method without using a work sheet.

P19-5 Presented below is the comparative balance sheet for Linda Sander Toy Company as of December 31:

LINDA SANDER TOY COMPANY
Comparative Balance Sheet
December 31

	1987	1986
Assets		
Cash	$ 39,000	$ 45,000
Accounts receivable (net)	47,500	52,000
Inventory	151,450	142,000
Prepaid expenses	16,780	21,000
Land	100,000	130,000
Equipment	180,000	155,000
Accumulated depreciation—equipment	(45,000)	(35,000)
Building	200,000	200,000
Accumulated depreciation—building	(60,000)	(40,000)
	$629,730	$670,000
Liabilities and Stockholders' Equity		
Accounts payable	$ 43,670	$ 40,000
Bonds payable	250,000	300,000
Common stock, $1 par	200,000	100,000
Retained earnings	136,060	230,000
	$629,730	$670,000

Additional information:

1. Operating expenses include depreciation expense of $42,000 and charges from prepaid expenses of $4,220.
2. Land was sold at book value.
3. Cash dividends of $107,990 were paid.
4. Net income for 1987 was $14,050.
5. Equipment was purchased for $47,000. In addition, equipment costing $22,000 with a book value of $10,000 was sold for $8,100.

6. Bonds were redeemed at face value by issuing 50,000 shares of $1 par value common stock.

INSTRUCTIONS

Prepare a statement of cash flows for the year ended December 31, 1987, using the indirect method.

***P19-6**

INSTRUCTIONS

Refer to Problem 19-4 (LeGault Company) and use this data to prepare a work sheet for a statement of cash flows for 1987. Enter the reconciling entries directly on the work sheet identifying the entries alphabetically.

ALTERNATE PROBLEMS

P19-1A The income statement of Clarence Avery Company is shown below.

CLARENCE AVERY COMPANY
Income Statement
For the Year Ended December 31, 1987

Sales		$7,100,000
Cost of goods sold		
Beginning inventory	$1,700,000	
Purchases	5,430,000	
Goods available for sale	7,130,000	
Ending inventory	1,920,000	
Cost of goods sold		5,210,000
Gross profit		1,890,000
Operating expenses		
Selling expense	400,000	
Administrative expense	525,000	
Depreciation expense	75,000	
Amortization expense	30,000	1,030,000
Net income		$ 860,000

Additional information:

1. Accounts receivable increased $490,000 during the year.
2. Prepaid expenses increased $170,000 during the year.
3. Accounts payable decreased by $75,000 during the year.
4. Accrued liabilities decreased by $150,000 during the year.

INSTRUCTIONS

Prepare the cash provided by operations section of the statement of cash flows for the year ended December 31, 1987, for Clarence Avery Company, using the indirect method.

P19-2A The income statement of Dukes International Inc. for the year ended December 31, 1987, reported the following condensed information:

Revenues from sales	$390,000
Operating expenses	280,000
Income from operations	110,000
Income tax expense	33,000
Net income	$ 77,000

Dukes' balance sheet contained the following comparative data at December 31:

	1987	1986
Accounts receivable	$50,000	$40,000
Accounts payable	32,000	41,000
Income taxes payable	6,000	4,000

INSTRUCTIONS

(a) Prepare the cash flows from operating activities section of the statement of cash flows using the direct method.

(b) Prepare the cash flows from operating activities section of the statement of cash flows using the indirect method.

P19-3A Radha Inc. had the following condensed balance sheet at the end of 1987.

RADHA INC.
Balance Sheet
December 31, 1987

Cash	$ 7,500	Current liabilities	$ 15,000
Accounts receivable	30,000	Long-term notes payable	25,500
Investments	20,000	Bonds payable	25,000
Plant assets (net)	67,500	Capital stock	75,000
Land	40,000	Retained earnings	24,500
	$165,000		$165,000

During 1988 the following occurred:

1. A tract of land was purchased for $7,750.
2. Bonds payable in the amount of $6,000 were retired at face and book value.
3. An additional $12,500 in capital stock was issued at par.
4. Dividends totaling $9,375 were paid to stockholders.
5. Net income for 1988 was $26,250 after allowing for depreciation of $11,250.
6. Land was purchased through the issuance of $22,500 in bonds.
7. Radha Inc. sold part of its investment portfolio for $12,875. This transaction resulted in a gain of $1,375 for the firm.
8. Current liabilities increased to $18,000 at 12/31/88.
9. Accounts receivable at December 31, 1988, total $24,000.
10. The cash balance at December 31, 1988, is $54,875.

INSTRUCTIONS

Prepare a statement of cash flows for 1988 using the indirect method. Assume that all transactions involved cash, except for transaction (6).

P19-4A Condensed financial data of Fistler Company for 1987 and 1986 appear below.

FISTLER COMPANY
Comparative Balance Sheet
December 31

	1987	1986
Assets		
Cash	$ 95,810	$ 47,250
Accounts receivable (net)	87,200	57,000
Inventories	114,000	107,650
Investments	77,500	82,000
Plant assets	250,000	205,000
Accumulated depreciation	(49,500)	(40,000)
	$575,010	$458,900
Liabilities and Stockholders' Equity		
Accounts payable	$ 60,210	$ 48,280
Accrued expenses payable	17,090	18,830
Bonds payable	110,000	70,000
Common stock	250,000	200,000
Retained earnings	137,710	121,790
	$575,010	$458,900

FISTLER COMPANY
Income Statement Data
For the Year Ended December 31, 1987

Sales		$297,500
Gain on sale of plant assets		8,750
		306,250
Less:		
Cost of goods sold	$99,460	
Selling and administrative expenses (excluding depreciation expense)	14,670	
Depreciation expense	49,700	
Income taxes	7,275	
Interest expense	2,940	174,045
Net income		132,205
Dividends		116,285
Income retained in business		$ 15,920

Additional information:

1. New plant assets costing $92,000 were purchased during the year.
2. Investments were sold at book value.

INSTRUCTIONS

Prepare a statement of cash flows using the indirect method without using a work sheet.

P19-5A Presented below is the comparative balance sheet for Peter W. Messman Company at December 31:

PETER W. MESSMAN COMPANY
Comparative Balance Sheet
December 31

	1987	1986
Cash	$ 45,000	$ 57,000
Accounts receivable, net	67,000	64,000
Inventory	132,000	140,000
Prepaid expenses	12,140	16,540
Land	125,000	150,000
Equipment	200,000	175,000
Accumulated depreciation—equipment	(55,000)	(42,000)
Building	250,000	250,000
Accumulated depreciation—building	(75,000)	(50,000)
	$701,140	$760,540
Accounts payable	$ 39,000	$ 45,000
Bonds payable	240,000	265,000
Common stock, $1 par	275,000	250,000
Retained earnings	147,140	200,540
	$701,140	$760,540

Additional information:

1. Operating expenses include depreciation expense of $65,000 and amortization of prepaid expenses of $4,400.
2. Land was sold at book value.
3. Cash dividends of $81,290 were paid.
4. Net income for 1987 was $27,890.
5. Equipment was purchased for $65,000. In addition, equipment costing $40,000 with a book value of $13,000 was sold for $15,000.
6. Bonds were redeemed at face value by issuing 25,000 shares of $1 par value common stock.

INSTRUCTIONS

Prepare a statement of cash flows for 1987 using the indirect method.

***P19–6A**

INSTRUCTIONS

Refer to Problem 19–4A (Fistler Company) and use this data to prepare a work sheet for a statement of cash flows. Enter the reconciling items directly in the work sheet columns identifying the debit and credit amounts alphabetically.

DECISION CASE

Steve Maier and Christy Worrell are examining the following statement of cash flows for Olsen Discount Center's first year of operations.

Olsen Discount Center
Statement of Cash Flows
For the Year Ended January 31, 1988

Sources of cash	
From sales of merchandise	$350,000
From sale of capital stock	440,000
From sale of investment	80,000
From depreciation	70,000
From issuance of note for truck	20,000
From interest on investments	8,000
Total sources of cash	968,000
Uses of cash	
For purchase of fixtures and equipment	340,000
For merchandise purchased for resale	250,000
For operating expenses (including depreciation)	160,000
For purchase of investment	85,000
For purchase of truck by issuance of note	20,000
For purchase of treasury stock	10,000
For interest on note	3,000
Total uses of cash	868,000
Net increase in cash	$100,000

Steve claims that Olsen's statement of cash flows is an excellent portrayal of a superb first year with cash increasing $100,000. Christy replies that it was not a superb first year, that the year was an operating failure, that the statement was incorrectly presented, and that $100,000 is not the actual increase in cash.

INSTRUCTIONS

(a) With whom do you agree, Steve or Christy? Explain your position.

(b) Using the data provided, prepare a statement of cash flows in proper form. The only noncash items in the income statement are depreciation and the loss from the sale of the investment.

CHAPTER 20

Bates College, Maine

CHAPTER 20

FINANCIAL STATEMENT ANALYSIS

STUDY OBJECTIVES

After studying this chapter, you should be able to:

1. Discuss the need for comparative analysis.
2. Identify the tools of financial statement analysis.
3. Explain horizontal (trend) analysis.
4. Describe vertical analysis.
5. Identify and compute ratios and describe their purpose and use in analyzing a firm's short-term liquidity, profitability, and long-term solvency.
6. Recognize the limitations of financial statement analysis.

Should you invest excess cash in stocks or bonds, apartment buildings, land, or some other form of business investment? If stocks are your choice, should your investment be in more conservative utility stocks such as Pacific Gas & Electric Company or in more speculative research or high-tech stocks such as Genetic Inc. or Satellite Communications Corp.? If you buy bonds, should you invest in General Electric's quality bonds which generally have greater stability, less risk (AAA rated), and lower yields, or in Sunshine Mining bonds, which are less stable, and of greater risk (BCC rated), but offer higher rates of return? To answer these types of questions, it is helpful for you to understand how to analyze and interpret financial statement information.

In analyzing and interpreting financial statement information, three major characteristics are generally evaluated: **liquidity, profitability,** and **solvency.** For example, a **short-term creditor** (such as a bank) is primarily interested in the ability of the borrower to pay obligations when they come due. The liquidity of the borrower in such a case is extremely important in evaluating

the safety of a loan. A **long-term creditor** (such as a bondholder), however, looks to more long-term indicators such as profitability and solvency (ability to survive over a long period of time). Earnings per share, the relationship of income to total assets invested, the amount of debt in the company's existing capital structure, and the ability to meet interest payments when due are analyzed to determine whether money should be lent and at what interest rate. Similarly, **stockholders** are interested in the profitability and solvency of the enterprise in assessing the likelihood of dividends and the growth potential of the stock.

NEED FOR COMPARATIVE ANALYSIS

Any item reported in a financial statement has significance because it indicates that at a given time it exists and that it exists in a certain quantity. For example, when Xerox Corporation reports $326,200,000 on its balance sheet as cash, we know that Xerox Corporation did have cash and that the quantity it had was $326,200,000. But whether it represents an increase over prior years, much less whether it is adequate in relation to the company's needs, cannot be determined from the amount alone. This amount must be compared with other financial data to obtain this information.

Comparisons can be made on a number of different bases. The following three are illustrated in this chapter.

1. **Intracompany basis**—Comparisons within a company are often useful to detect changes in financial relationships and significant trends. For example, a comparison of Xerox's current year's cash amount with the prior year's cash amount shows either an increase or a decrease. Or, a comparison of Xerox's year-end cash amount with the amount of its total assets at year end shows the proportion of total assets in the form of cash.
2. **Intercompany basis**—Comparisons with other companies provide insight into a company's competitive position. For example, Xerox's total sales for the year can be compared with the total sales of its competitors in the copying equipment area such as Canon or Savin.
3. **Industry averages**—Comparisons with industry averages provide information as to a company's relative position within the industry. For example, Xerox's financial data can be compared with the averages for the copying equipment industry compiled by such organizations as Dun & Bradstreet, Moody's, Standard & Poors, *Forbes*, or *Business Week*.

TOOLS OF FINANCIAL STATEMENT ANALYSIS

Various tools are used in financial statement analysis to highlight the significance of financial statement data. Three basic tools are:

(a) Horizontal analysis.
(b) Vertical analysis.
(c) Ratio analysis.

HORIZONTAL ANALYSIS

Horizontal analysis, also called **trend analysis,** is a technique for evaluating a series of financial statement data over a period of time to determine the amount and/or percentage increase or decrease that has taken place. For example, the recent net sales figures of General Motors Corporation are as follows:

GM's net sales

GENERAL MOTORS CORPORATION
(Net Sales Stated in Millions)

1985	1984	1983	1982	1981
$96,372	$83,890	$74,582	$60,026	$62,698

If we assume that 1981 is the base year, we can measure all percentage increases or decreases from this base period amount. For example, we can determine that net sales for General Motors decreased approximately 4% [($62,698 − $60,026) ÷ $62,698] from 1981 to 1982. Similarly, we can determine that net sales increased almost 54% [($96,372 − $62,698) ÷ $62,698] from 1981 to 1985. The percentage increases or decreases for each of the five years, assuming 1981 as the base period, are as follows:[1]

Horizontal analysis of GM's net sales

GENERAL MOTORS CORPORATION
(Net Sales Stated in Millions)
Base Period 1981

1985	1984	1983	1982	1981
$96,372	$83,890	$74,582	$60,026	$62,698
154%	134%	119%	96%	100%

To further illustrate horizontal analysis, we will use the financial statements of Quality Department Store Inc. Quality Department Store Inc. is a downtown full-line department store in a southeastern city of 55,000. Its two-year condensed balance sheets for 1987 and 1986 showing dollar and percentage changes are presented on the next page.

The comparative balance sheet on page 790 above shows that a number of changes have occurred in Quality Department Store's financial structure from 1986 to 1987. In the asset section, current assets increased $75,000, or 7.9%, while plant assets (net) increased $167,500, or 26.5%. In the liabilities section, current liabilities increased $41,500, or 13.7%, while long-term liabilities decreased $9,500, or 1.9%. In the stockholders' equity section, we find that

[1]While comparative balance sheets are generally prepared for two consecutive years and comparative income statements are prepared for three consecutive years, many companies publish selected comparative financial data for a 5- or 10-year period to facilitate further trend analysis.

Horizontal analysis of a balance sheet

QUALITY DEPARTMENT STORE INC.
Condensed Balance Sheet
December 31

	1987	1986	Increase or (Decrease) Amount	Increase or (Decrease) Percentage
Assets				
Current assets	$1,020,000	$ 945,000	$ 75,000	7.9%
Plant assets (net)	800,000	632,500	167,500	26.5%
Intangible assets	15,000	17,500	(2,500)	(14.3%)
Total assets	$1,835,000	$1,595,000	$240,000	15.0%
Liabilities				
Current liabilities	$ 344,500	$ 303,000	$ 41,500	13.7%
Long-term liabilities	487,500	497,000	(9,500)	(1.9%)
Total liabilities	832,000	800,000	32,000	4.0%
Stockholders' Equity				
Common stock, $1 par	275,400	270,000	5,400	2.0%
Retained earnings	727,600	525,000	202,600	38.6%
Total stockholders' equity	1,003,000	795,000	208,000	26.2%
Total liabilities and stockholders' equity	$1,835,000	$1,595,000	$240,000	15.0%

retained earnings increased $202,600, or 38.6%. This suggests that the company expanded its asset base during 1987 and financed this expansion primarily by retaining income in the business rather than assuming additional long-term debt.

Presented below is a two-year comparative income statement of Quality Department Store inc. for the years 1987 and 1986 in a condensed format.

Horizontal analysis of an income statement

QUALITY DEPARTMENT STORE INC.
Condensed Income Statement
For the Years Ended December 31

	1987	1986	Increase or (Decrease) Amount	Increase or (Decrease) Percentage
Sales	$2,195,000	$1,960,000	$235,000	12.0%
Sales returns and allowances	98,000	123,000	(25,000)	(20.3%)
Net sales	2,097,000	1,837,000	260,000	14.2%
Cost of goods sold	1,281,000	1,140,000	141,000	12.4%
Gross profit	816,000	697,000	119,000	17.1%
Selling expenses	253,000	211,500	41,500	19.6%
Administrative expenses	104,000	108,500	(4,500)	(4.1%)
Total operating expenses	357,000	320,000	37,000	11.6%
Income from operations	459,000	377,000	82,000	21.8%

Other revenues and gains				
Interest and dividends	9,000	11,000	(2,000)	(18.2%)
Other expenses and losses				
Interest expense	36,000	40,500	(4,500)	(11.1%)
Income before income taxes	432,000	347,500	84,500	24.3%
Income tax expense	168,200	139,000	29,200	21.0%
Net income	$ 263,800	$ 208,500	$ 55,300	26.5%

Horizontal analysis of the comparative income statement shows the following changes: net sales increased $260,000, or 14.2%, from 1986 to 1987; cost of goods sold increased $141,000, or 12.4%; total operating expenses increased $37,000, or 11.6%. Overall, gross profit and net income were up substantially. Gross profit, for example, increased 17.1% and net income 26.5%. It appears, therefore, that Quality's profit trend is favorable.

Presented below is Quality Department Store's comparative retained earnings statement for the years 1987 and 1986 analyzed horizontally.

Horizontal analysis of retained earnings statement

QUALITY DEPARTMENT STORE INC.
Retained Earnings Statement
For the Years Ended December 31

			Increase or (Decrease)	
	1987	1986	Amount	Percentage
Retained earnings, Jan. 1	$525,000	$376,500	$148,500	39.4%
Add: Net income	263,800	208,500	55,300	26.5%
Total	788,800	585,000	203,800	
Deduct: Dividends	61,200	60,000	1,200	2.0%
Retained earnings, Dec. 31	$727,600	$525,000	$202,600	38.6%

Net income increased $55,300, or 26.5%, whereas dividends on the common stock increased only $1,200, or 2%. Ending retained earnings, as indicated in the horizontal analysis of the balance sheet increased 38.6%. As indicated earlier, Quality Department Store Inc. retained a significant portion of its net income to finance expenditures for additional plant facilities.

The measurement of changes from period to period in terms of percentages is relatively straightforward and is quite useful. However, complications can result in making the computations. If an item has no value in a base year or preceding year and a value in the next year, no percentage change can be computed. And, if a negative amount appears in the base or preceding period and a positive amount exists the following year, or vice versa, no percentage change can be computed.

VERTICAL ANALYSIS

Vertical analysis, sometimes referred to as **common size analysis,** expresses each item within a financial statement in terms of a percent of a base amount. For example, with reference to a balance sheet we might say that current assets are 22% of total assets (total assets being the base amount). Or, on an

income statement, we might say that selling expenses are 16% of net sales (net sales being the base amount).

Presented below is the comparative balance sheet of Quality Department Store Inc. for 1987 and 1986 analyzed vertically. The base for the asset items is total assets, and the base for the liability and stockholders' equity items is total liabilities and stockholders' equity.

Vertical analysis of a balance sheet

QUALITY DEPARTMENT STORE INC.
Condensed Balance Sheet
December 31

	1987		1986	
	Amount	Percent	Amount	Percent
Assets				
Current assets	$1,020,000	55.6%	$ 945,000	59.2%
Plant assets (net)	800,000	43.6%	632,500	39.7%
Intangible assets	15,000	.8%	17,500	1.1%
Total assets	$1,835,000	100.0%	$1,595,000	100.0%
Liabilities				
Current liabilities	$ 344,500	18.8%	$ 303,000	19.0%
Long-term liabilities	487,500	26.5%	497,000	31.2%
Total liabilities	832,000	45.3%	800,000	50.2%
Stockholders' Equity				
Common stock, $1 par	275,400	15.0%	270,000	16.9%
Retained earnings	727,600	39.7%	525,000	32.9%
Total stockholders' equity	1,003,000	54.7%	795,000	49.8%
Total liabilities & stockholders' equity	$1,835,000	100.0%	$1,595,000	100.0%

In addition to showing the relative size of each category on the balance sheet, vertical analysis may show the percentage change in the individual asset, liability, and stockholders' equity items. In this case, even though current assets increased $75,000 from 1986 to 1987, they decreased from 59.2% to 55.6% of total assets. Plant assets (net) have increased from 39.7% to 43.6% of total assets, while retained earnings have increased from 32.9% to 39.7% of total liabilities and stockholders' equity. These results reinforce the earlier observations that Quality is choosing to finance its growth through retention of earnings rather than through the issuance of additional debt.

Vertical analysis of the comparative income statements of Quality, shown on the next page, reveals the following.

Cost of goods sold as a percentage of net sales declined 1% (62.1% vs. 61.1%); total operating expenses declined .4% (17.4% vs. 17.0%). As a result, it is not surprising to see net income as a percent of sales increase from 11.4% to 12.6%. As indicated from the horizontal analysis presented earlier, Quality appears to be a profitable enterprise that is becoming even more successful.

An associated benefit of vertical analysis is that it enables you to compare companies of different sizes. For example, Quality's main competitor is a J. C.

Vertical analysis of an income statement

QUALITY DEPARTMENT STORE INC.
Condensed Income Statement
For the Years Ended December 31

	1987		1986	
	Amount	Percent	Amount	Percent
Sales	$2,195,000	104.7%	$1,960,000	106.7%
Sales returns and allowances	98,000	4.7%	123,000	6.7%
Net sales	2,097,000	100.0%	1,837,000	100.0%
Cost of goods sold	1,281,000	61.1%	1,140,000	62.1%
Gross profit	816,000	38.9%	697,000	37.9%
Selling expenses	253,000	12.0%	211,500	11.5%
Administrative expenses	104,000	5.0%	108,500	5.9%
Total operating expenses	357,000	17.0%	320,000	17.4%
Income from operations	459,000	21.9%	377,000	20.5%
Other revenues and gains				
Interest and dividends	9,000	0.4%	11,000	0.6%
Other expenses and losses				
Interest expense	36,000	1.7%	40,500	2.2%
Income before income taxes	432,000	20.6%	347,500	18.9%
Income tax expense	168,200	8.0%	139,000	7.5%
Net income	$ 263,800	12.6%	$ 208,500	11.4%

Penney store in a nearby town. Using vertical analysis, the condensed income statements of the small local retail enterprise, Quality Department Store Inc., can be more meaningfully compared with the income statement of a giant international retailer, J. C. Penney Company, as shown below:

Intercompany income statement comparison

CONDENSED INCOME STATEMENTS

	Quality Department Store Inc.		J. C. Penney Company	
(In thousands)	Dollars	Percent	Dollars	Percent
Net sales	$2,097	100.0%	$13,747,000	100.0%
Cost of goods sold	1,281	61.1%	9,240,000	67.2%
Gross profit	816	38.9%	4,507,000	32.8%
Selling and administrative expenses	357	17.0%	3,454,000	25.1%
Income from operations	459	21.9%	1,053,000	7.7%
Other expenses and revenues (including income taxes)	195	9.3%	656,000	4.8%
Net income	$ 264	12.6%	$ 397,000	2.9%

Although J. C. Penney's net sales are 6,556 times greater than the net sales of relatively tiny Quality Department Store, vertical analysis eliminates this difference in size. The percentages show that Quality's and Penney's gross

profit rates were somewhat comparable at 38.9% and 32.8%, while the percentages related to income from operations were significantly different at 21.9% and 7.7%. This disparity can be attributed to Quality's selling and administrative expense percentage, 17%, which is much lower than Penney's 25.1%. Although Penney earned net income that is more than 1,500 times larger than Quality's, Penney's net income as a percent of each sales dollar 2.9% is less than one quarter of Quality's 12.6%.

RATIO ANALYSIS

A **ratio** expresses the mathematical relationship between one quantity and another. The relationship is expressed in terms of either a percentage, a rate, or a simple proportion. To illustrate, recently General Motors Corporation had current assets of $23,713,300,000 and current liabilities of $17,436,600,000. Because the cash to pay current liabilities is included within the current assets or will flow from other current assets such as receivables and inventories, a ratio of current assets to current liabilities is computed. This relationship could be expressed as a **percentage** by stating that current assets are 136% of current liabilities, as a **rate** by stating that current assets are 1.36 times as great as current liabilities, or as a **proportion** by stating that the relationship of current assets to current liabilities is 1.36:1. The latter method is more commonly used for this particular ratio.

For analysis of the primary financial statements, ratios can be classified as follows:

1. **Liquidity ratios**—measures of the short-term ability of the enterprise to pay its maturing obligations and to meet unexpected needs for cash.
2. **Profitability ratios**—measures of the income or operating success of an enterprise for a given period of time.
3. **Solvency ratios**—measures of the ability of the enterprise to survive over a long period of time.

As a tool of analysis, ratios can provide clues to underlying conditions that may not be apparent from an inspection of the individual components of a particular ratio. But, a single ratio by itself is not very meaningful. Accordingly, in the following discussion we will use:

1. **Intracompany comparisons** covering two years for the Quality Department Store.
2. **Industry average comparisons** based on Dun & Bradstreet's median ratios for department stores and *Forbes* and *Business Week*'s nonfood retailing industry averages.
3. **Intercompany comparisons** based on the J. C. Penney Company as Quality Department Store's principal competitor.

LIQUIDITY RATIOS

The ability of an enterprise to meet its current obligations is important in evaluating financial position. Short-term creditors such as bankers and sup-

Many general ledger accounting programs include the generation of financial ratios as routine output. All of the ratio computations presented in this chapter can be done with electronic spreadsheets as well. There are also many programs available written specifically for financial statement analysis. These packages are written for both general purpose use and use in specific industries. For example, financial institutions routinely use over 60 ratios geared specifically to the banking industry.

pliers are particularly interested in assessing **liquidity.** The ratios that can be used to determine the enterprise's short-term debt paying ability are the current ratio, the acid-test ratio, receivables turnover, and inventory turnover.

1. **Current Ratio.** The **current ratio** expresses the relationship of current assets to current liabilities. It is a widely used measure for evaluating a company's liquidity and short-term debt paying ability. It is sometimes referred to as the working capital ratio because working capital is the excess of current assets over current liabilities. The 1987 and 1986 current ratios for Quality Department Store and comparative data are as follows:

Current ratio

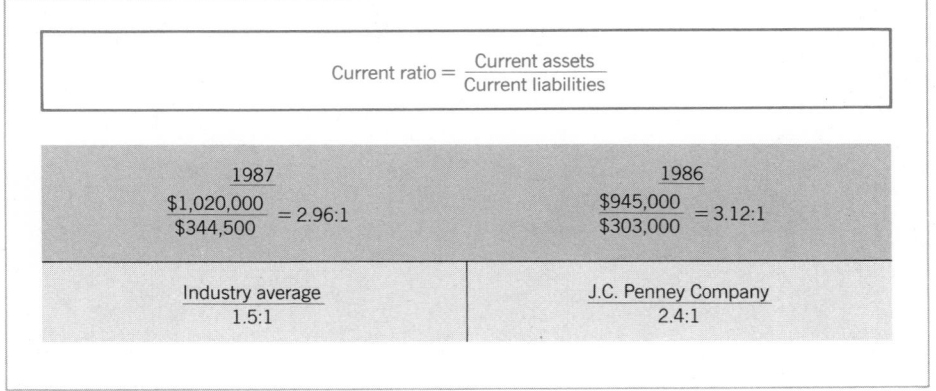

$$\text{Current ratio} = \frac{\text{Current assets}}{\text{Current liabilities}}$$

1987	1986
$\frac{\$1,020,000}{\$344,500} = 2.96:1$	$\frac{\$945,000}{\$303,000} = 3.12:1$
Industry average	J.C. Penney Company
1.5:1	2.4:1

The 1987 proportion of 2.96:1, for example, means that for every dollar of current liabilities Quality has 2.96 dollars of current assets. Quality's current ratio has decreased in the current year. However, compared to the industry average of 1.5:1, and J. C. Penney Company's 2.4:1 current ratio, Quality appears to be reasonably liquid.[2]

The current ratio is only one measure of determining liquidity. It does not take into account the composition of the current assets. For example, a satisfactory current ratio does not disclose the fact that a portion of the current assets may be tied up in slow moving inventory. A dollar of cash is more readily available to pay the bills than is a dollar of slow-moving inventory.

[2]As explained in Chapter 4, the current ratio is a more dependable indicator of liquidity than working capital (current assets — current liabilities). Two companies with the same amount of working capital may have significantly different current ratios.

2. **Acid-test Ratio.** The acid-test or quick ratio relates cash, marketable securities, and net receivables to current liabilities. This ratio indicates a company's immediate ability to pay its short-term debt. Thus, it is an important complement to the current ratio. For example, assume that the current assets of Quality Department Store for 1987 and 1986 comprise the following items:

Current assets of Quality Department Store

	1987	1986
Current assets		
Cash	$ 100,000	$155,000
Marketable securities	20,000	70,000
Receivables (net)	230,000	180,000
Inventory	620,000	500,000
Prepaid expenses	50,000	40,000
Total current assets	$1,020,000	$945,000

Cash, marketable securities, and receivables (net) are highly liquid as compared with the inventory and prepaid expenses. The inventory may not be readily saleable and the prepaid expenses may not be transferable to others. The 1987 and 1986 acid-test ratios for Quality Department Store and comparative data are as follows:

Acid-test ratio

$$\text{Acid-test ratio} = \frac{\text{Cash} + \text{marketable securities} + \text{receivables (net)}}{\text{Current liabilities}}$$

1987

$$\frac{\$100{,}000 + \$20{,}000 + \$230{,}000}{\$344{,}500} = 1.02{:}1$$

1986

$$\frac{\$155{,}000 + \$70{,}000 + \$180{,}000}{\$303{,}000} = 1.34{:}1$$

Industry average	J.C. Penney Company
1:1	1.03:1

Is an acid-test ratio of 1.02:1 adequate? The ratio has declined in 1987. However, when compared with the industry median of 1:1 and J. C. Penney's 1.03:1, Quality's acid-test ratio seems to be adequate.

3. **Receivables Turnover.** Liquidity may be measured by how quickly certain assets can be converted to cash. How liquid, for example, are the receivables? The ratio used to assess the liquidity of the receivables is the receivables turnover ratio. This ratio measures the number of times, on average, receivables are collected during the period. The receivables turnover ratio is computed by dividing net credit sales by the average net receivables during the year. Unless seasonal factors are significant, average net receivables outstanding can be computed from the beginning and ending balance of the net receivables.[3]

[3] If seasonal factors are significant, the average receivables balance might be determined by using monthly amounts.

Assuming that all sales are credit sales and the balance of accounts receivable (net) at the beginning of 1986 is $200,000, the receivables turnover ratio for Quality Department Store and comparative data are as follows:

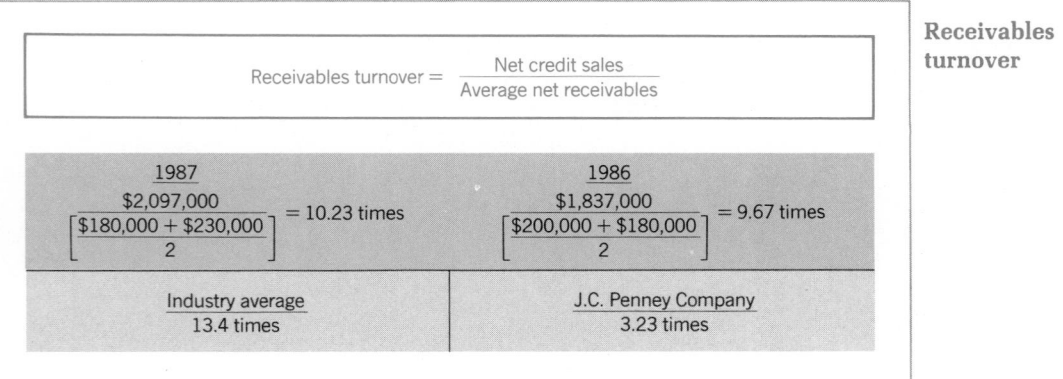

Receivables turnover

$$\text{Receivables turnover} = \frac{\text{Net credit sales}}{\text{Average net receivables}}$$

1987	1986
$\dfrac{\$2{,}097{,}000}{\left[\dfrac{\$180{,}000 + \$230{,}000}{2}\right]} = 10.23 \text{ times}$	$\dfrac{\$1{,}837{,}000}{\left[\dfrac{\$200{,}000 + \$180{,}000}{2}\right]} = 9.67 \text{ times}$
Industry average 13.4 times	J.C. Penney Company 3.23 times

Quality's receivables turnover has improved in 1987. The turnover of 10.23 times compares quite favorably with J. C. Penney's 3.23 times, but it is slightly below the department store industry's median of 13.4 times.

In some cases, receivable turnover may be misleading. Some companies, especially large retail chains, encourage credit and revolving charge sales and slow collections in order to earn a healthy return on the outstanding receivables in the form of interest at rates of 18% to 22%. This may explain why J. C. Penney's turnover is only 3.23 times. In general, however, the faster the turnover, the greater the reliance that can be placed on the current and acid-test ratios for assessing liquidity.

A popular variant of the receivables turnover ratio is to convert it into an **average collection period** in terms of days. This is done by dividing the turnover ratio into 365 days. For example, the receivable turnover in 1987 of 10.23 times is divided into 365 days to obtain approximately 35.7 days. This means that the average collection period for receivables is 36 days, or approximately every five weeks. The average collection period is frequently used to assess the effectiveness of a company's credit and collection policies. The general rule is that the collection period should not exceed the credit term period (i.e., the time allowed for payment) by more than 10 to 15 days.

4. **Inventory Turnover.** The **inventory turnover ratio** measures the number of times on average the inventory was sold during the period. It measures the liquidity of the inventory. The inventory turnover is computed by dividing cost of goods sold by the average inventory during the year. Unless seasonal factors are significant, average inventory can be computed from the beginning and ending inventory balances. Assuming that the inventory balance for Quality Department Store at the beginning of 1986 was $450,000, its inventory turnover and comparative data are on the next page. Quality's inventory turnover has declined slightly in 1987. The turnover ratio of 2.29 times is relatively low compared with the industry average of 3.2 and J. C. Penney's 3.63. Generally, the faster the inventory turnover, the less cash that is tied up in inventory and the less the chance of inventory obsolescence.

A variant of the inventory turnover ratio is to compute the **average days to**

Inventory turnover

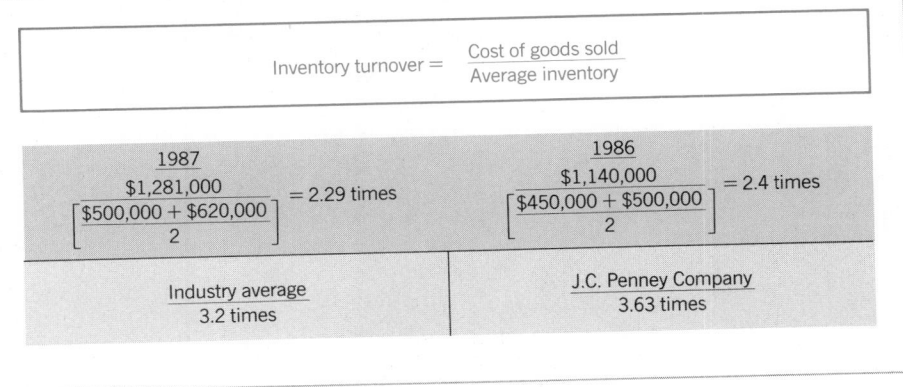

$$\text{Inventory turnover} = \frac{\text{Cost of goods sold}}{\text{Average inventory}}$$

1987	1986
$\dfrac{\$1{,}281{,}000}{\left[\dfrac{\$500{,}000 + \$620{,}000}{2}\right]} = 2.29 \text{ times}$	$\dfrac{\$1{,}140{,}000}{\left[\dfrac{\$450{,}000 + \$500{,}000}{2}\right]} = 2.4 \text{ times}$
Industry average: 3.2 times	J.C. Penney Company: 3.63 times

sell the inventory. For example, the inventory turnover in 1987 of 2.29 times divided into 365 is approximately 159 days. An average selling time of 159 days is also relatively high compared with the industry average of 114 days (365 ÷ 3.2) and J. C. Penney Company's 101 days (365 ÷ 3.63).

Inventory turnover ratios vary considerably between industries. For example, grocery store chains have a turnover of 10 times and an average selling period of 37 days. In contrast, jewelry stores have an average turnover of 1.3 times and an average selling period of 281 days. Within a company there may be significant differences in inventory turnover among different types of products. Thus, in a grocery store the turnover of perishable items such as produce, meats, and dairy products will be faster than the turnover of soaps and detergents.

PROFITABILITY RATIOS

Income, or the lack of it, affects the company's ability to obtain debt and equity financing, the company's liquidity position, and the company's ability to grow. As a consequence, creditors and investors alike are interested in evaluating enterprise earning power (profitability). Profitability is frequently used as the ultimate test of management's operating effectiveness.

5. **Profit Margin.** The **profit margin ratio** is a measure of the percentage of each revenue dollar that results in net income. It is computed by dividing net income by net sales for the period. Quality Department Store's profit margin ratios and comparative data are shown at the top of the next page.

Quality experienced an increase in its profit margin from 1986 to 1987. Its profit margin is unusually high in comparison with the industry average of 4.1% and J. C. Penney Company's 3.9%.

High-volume (high inventory turnover) enterprises such as grocery stores (A & P) and discount stores (K mart) generally experience low profit margins, whereas low-volume enterprises such as jewelry stores (Tiffany & Co.) or airplane manufacturers (Boeing Aircraft) have high profit margins.

6. **Asset Turnover.** The **asset turnover ratio** measures how efficiently a company uses its assets to generate sales. It is determined by dividing net sales by average assets for the period and shows the dollars of sales produced by each

Profit margin ratio

$$\text{Profit margin on sales} = \frac{\text{Net income}}{\text{Net sales}}$$

1987	1986
$\frac{\$263{,}800}{\$2{,}097{,}000} = 12.6\%$	$\frac{\$208{,}500}{\$1{,}837{,}000} = 11.4\%$
Industry average 4.1%	J.C. Penney Company 3.9%

dollar invested in assets. Unless seasonal factors are significant, average total assets can be computed from the beginning and ending balance of total assets. Assuming that the total assets at the beginning of 1986 were $1,446,000, the 1987 and 1986 asset turnover ratios for Quality Department Store and comparative data are as follows:

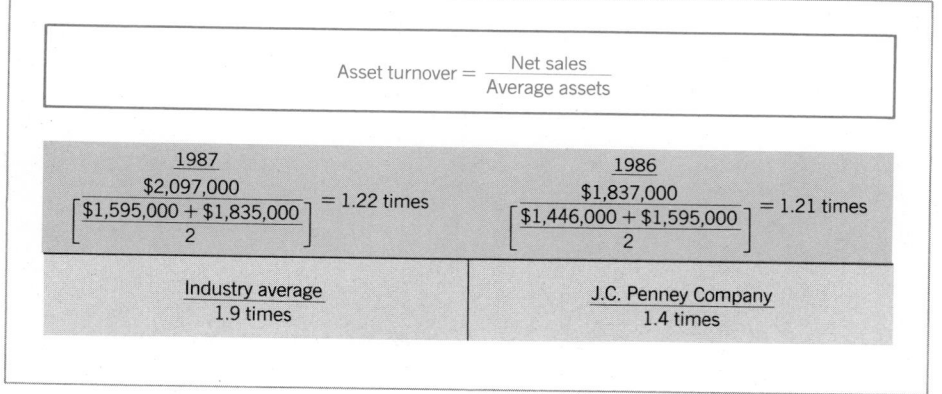

Asset turnover

$$\text{Asset turnover} = \frac{\text{Net sales}}{\text{Average assets}}$$

1987	1986
$\frac{\$2{,}097{,}000}{\left[\frac{\$1{,}595{,}000 + \$1{,}835{,}000}{2}\right]} = 1.22 \text{ times}$	$\frac{\$1{,}837{,}000}{\left[\frac{\$1{,}446{,}000 + \$1{,}595{,}000}{2}\right]} = 1.21 \text{ times}$
Industry average 1.9 times	J.C. Penney Company 1.4 times

The asset turnover ratio shows that Quality generates sales of $1.22 in 1987 for each dollar it has invested in assets. The ratio changed little from 1986 to 1987. Quality's asset turnover ratio is below the industry median of 1.9 times and J. C. Penney's ratio of 1.4 times.

Asset turnover ratios vary considerably between industries. For example, a large utility company like Pacific Gas and Electric has a ratio of 0.30 times and the grocery chain Safeway Stores has a ratio of 4.3 times.

7. **Return on Assets.** An overall measure of profitability is the **rate of return on assets ratio.** This ratio measures the rate earned on each dollar invested in assets. It is computed by dividing net income by average assets. The 1987 and 1986 return on assets for Quality Department Store and comparative data are shown at the top of the next page.

Quality's return on assets improved from 1986 to 1987. Its return of 15.38% is very high as compared with the department store industry median of 3.8% and J. C. Penney Company's 5.46%.

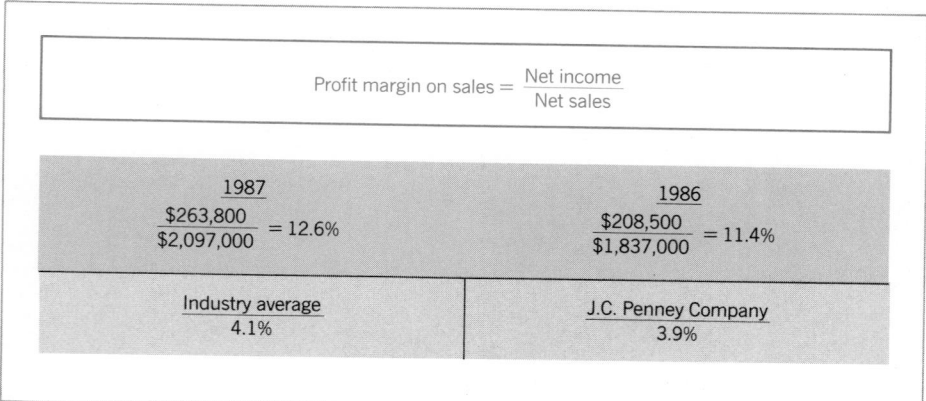

Return on assets

$$\text{Rate of return on assets} = \frac{\text{Net income}}{\text{Average assets}}$$

1987	1986
$\dfrac{\$263,800}{\left[\dfrac{\$1,595,000 + \$1,835,000}{2}\right]} = 15.38\%$	$\dfrac{\$208,500}{\left[\dfrac{\$1,446,000 + \$1,595,000}{2}\right]} = 13.71\%$
Industry average 3.8%	J.C. Penney Company 5.46%

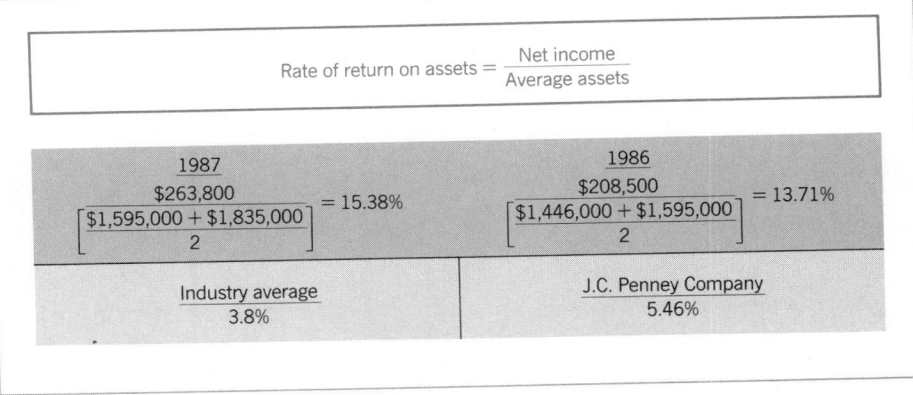

8. **Return on Common Stockholders' Equity.** Another widely used ratio that measures profitability from the common stockholder's viewpoint is the **rate of return on common stockholders' equity.** This ratio shows how many dollars of net income were earned for each dollar invested by the owners. It is computed by dividing net income by average common stockholders' equity. Assuming that common stockholders' equity at the beginning of the year was $667,000, the 1987 and 1986 ratios for Quality Department Store and comparative data are as follows:

Return on common stockholders' equity

$$\text{Rate of return on common stockholders' equity} = \frac{\text{Net income}}{\text{Average common stockholders' equity}}$$

1987	1986
$\dfrac{\$263,800}{\left[\dfrac{\$795,000 + \$1,003,000}{2}\right]} = 29.3\%$	$\dfrac{\$208,500}{\left[\dfrac{\$667,000 + \$795,000}{2}\right]} = 28.5\%$
Industry average 15.3%	J.C. Penney Company 13.1%

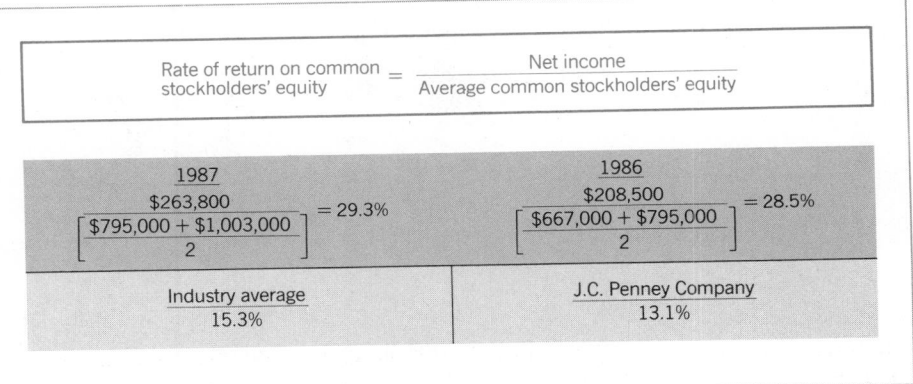

Quality's rate of return on common stockholders' equity is unusually high at 29.3% considering an industry average of 15.3% and a rate of 13.1% for J. C. Penney Company. Quality's return on equity compares favorably with industry leaders, such as Wal-Mart Stores (33.3%), Ames Department Store (23.8%), and SCOA Industries (20.5%).

When preferred stock is present, **preferred dividend** requirements are deducted from net income to compute income available to common stockholders. Similarly, the par value of preferred stock accounts must be deducted from total stockholders' equity to arrive at the amount of common stock equity used in this ratio.

Note that Quality's rate of return on stockholders' equity (29.3%) is substantially higher than its rate of return on assets (15.38%). The reason is that Quality has made effective use of **leverage** or **trading on the equity** at a gain.

Leveraging or trading on the equity at a gain means that the company has borrowed money through the issuance of bonds or notes at a lower rate of interest than it is able to earn by using the borrowed money. A comparison of the rate of return on total assets with the rate of interest paid for borrowed money indicates the profitability of leveraging or trading on the equity. Leverage is simply trying to use money supplied by nonowners to increase the return to the owners. Note that trading on the equity is a two-way street; for example, if you borrow money at 11% and earn only 8% on it, you are trading on the equity at a loss.

9. **Earnings Per Share (EPS).** **Earnings per share** of stock is a measure of the net income earned on each share of common stock. As explained in Chapter 16, it is computed by dividing net income by the number of weighted average common shares outstanding during the year. Stockholders usually think in terms of the number of shares they own or plan to buy or sell. Reducing net income earned to a per share basis provides a useful perspective for determining profitability. Assuming that there is no change in the number of outstanding shares during 1986 and that the 1987 increase occurred midyear, the net income per share for Quality Department Store for 1987 and 1986 is computed as follows:

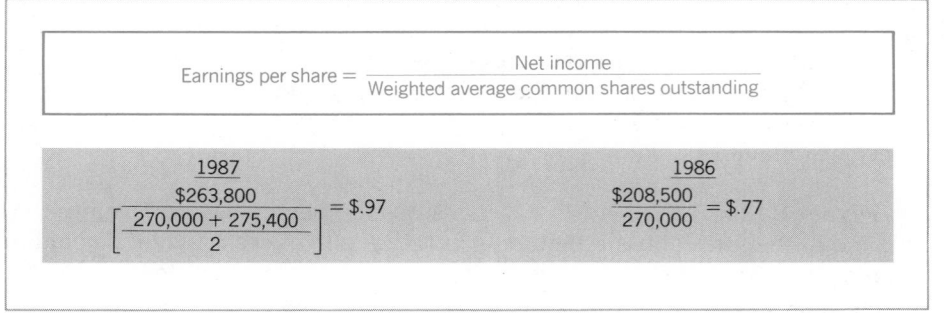

Earnings per share

$$\text{Earnings per share} = \frac{\text{Net income}}{\text{Weighted average common shares outstanding}}$$

1987	1986
$\dfrac{\$263{,}800}{\left[\dfrac{270{,}000 + 275{,}400}{2}\right]} = \$.97$	$\dfrac{\$208{,}500}{270{,}000} = \$.77$

Note that no industry or J. C. Penney data are presented. The reason is that such comparisons are not meaningful because of the wide variations in the number of shares of outstanding stock between companies.

Quality's earnings per share increased 20 cents per share in 1987. This represents a 26% increase over the 1986 earnings per share of 77 cents.

When the term 'net income per share' or 'earnings per share' is used, it refers to the amount of net income applicable to each share of **common stock.** Therefore, in computing net income per share, if there are preferred dividends declared for the period, they must be deducted from net income to arrive at income available to the common stockholders.

10. **Price-Earnings Ratio.** The **price-earnings ratio** is an oft-quoted statistic that measures the ratio of the market price of each share of common stock to the earnings per share. The price-earnings (PE) ratio is a reflection of investor's assessments of a company's future earnings. It is computed by dividing the market price of the stock by earnings per share. Assuming that the market price of Quality Department Store Inc. stock is $8 in 1986 and $12 in 1987, the price-earnings ratio is computed as follows:

Price-earnings ratio

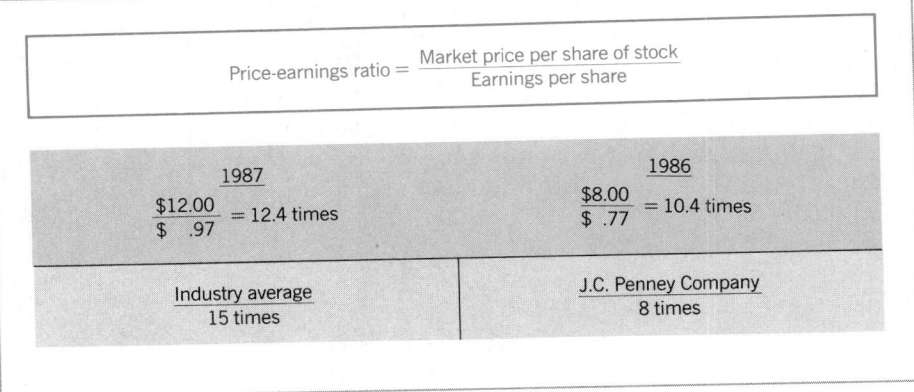

$$\text{Price-earnings ratio} = \frac{\text{Market price per share of stock}}{\text{Earnings per share}}$$

1987	1986
$\frac{\$12.00}{\$\ .97} = 12.4$ times	$\frac{\$8.00}{\$\ .77} = 10.4$ times
Industry average: 15 times	J.C. Penney Company: 8 times

This means that in 1987 each share of Quality's stock is selling for 12.4 times the amount that was earned on each share. Quality's price-earnings ratio is less than the industry average of 15 times but is significantly higher than the ratio of 8 for J. C. Penney Company. The average price-earnings ratio for the stocks that constitute the Dow-Jones industrial average on the New York Stock Exchange in mid-1986 was 14 times.

For the stock of some companies investors are willing to pay over 20 times the current per-share earnings because they feel the future growth in earnings will provide an adequate return on the investment. Examples of companies with price-earnings ratios over twenty are Club-Med (27), Federal Express (23), and PepsiCo (22). Examples of companies with low price-earnings ratios are General Motors Corporation (6), Chrysler Corporation (4), and Chase Manhattan Bank (6).

11. **Payout Ratio.** The **payout ratio** measures the percentage of earnings distributed in the form of cash dividends. It is the ratio of cash dividends paid to net income. Companies that have high growth rates are characterized by low payout ratios because they reinvest most of their net income into the business. The 1987 and 1986 payout ratios for Quality Department Store are computed as follows:

Payout ratio

$$\text{Payout ratio} = \frac{\text{Cash dividends}}{\text{Net income}}$$

1987	1986
$\frac{\$61,200}{\$263,800} = 23.2\%$	$\frac{\$60,000}{\$208,500} = 28.8\%$
Industry average: N/A	J.C. Penney Company: 44.4%

Quality's payout ratio is comparatively low when compared with J. C. Penney's payout ratio of 44.4%. As indicated earlier, the company has ap-

parently decided to fund its purchase of plant assets through retention of earnings.

Generally, companies with stable earnings have high payout ratios. For example, a utility such as Philadelphia Electric Company has had an 88% payout ratio over the last five years, and Kroger Co. has had a 50% payout over the same period. Conversely, companies that are expanding rapidly, such as Apple Computer and Quest Medical, have never paid a cash dividend.

LONG-TERM SOLVENCY RATIOS

Long-term creditors and stockholders are interested in a company's long-run solvency, particularly its ability to pay interest as it comes due and to repay the face value of the debt at maturity. Debt to total assets and times interest earned are two ratios that provide information about this debt paying ability.

12. **Debt to Total Assets.** The **debt to total assets ratio** measures the percentage of the total assets provided by creditors. It is computed by dividing total debt (both current and long-term liabilities) by total assets. This ratio provides some indication of the company's ability to withstand losses without impairing the interests of creditors. The higher the percentage of debt to total assets, the greater the risk that the company may be unable to meet its maturing obligations. The 1987 and 1986 ratios for Quality Department Store and comparative data are as follows:

Debt to total assets

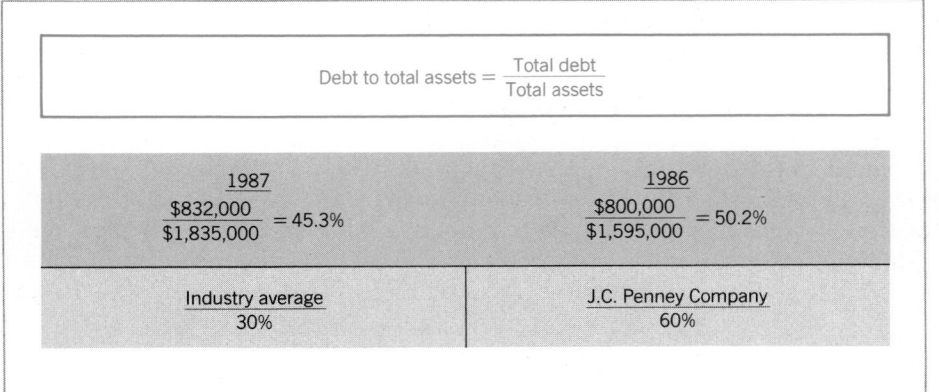

$$\text{Debt to total assets} = \frac{\text{Total debt}}{\text{Total assets}}$$

1987	1986
$\frac{\$832,000}{\$1,835,000} = 45.3\%$	$\frac{\$800,000}{\$1,595,000} = 50.2\%$
Industry average	J.C. Penney Company
30%	60%

A ratio of 45.3% means that creditors have provided 45.3% of Quality Department Store's total assets. Quality's 45.3% is above the industry average of 30%, but it is considerably below the 60% ratio of J. C. Penney Company. The lower the ratio, the more equity "buffer" there is available to the creditors if the company becomes insolvent. Thus, from the creditors' point of view a low ratio of debt to total assets is usually desirable.

The adequacy of this ratio is often judged in the light of the company's earnings. Companies with relatively stable earnings, such as public utilities, have higher debt to total assets ratios than cyclical companies with widely fluctuating earnings, such as many high-tech companies.

13. **Times Interest Earned.** The **times interest earned ratio** (also called interest coverage) provides an indication of the company's ability to meet inter-

est payments as they become due. It is computed by dividing income before interest expense and income taxes by interest expense. The 1987 and 1986 ratios for Quality Department Store and comparative data are as follows:

Times interest earned

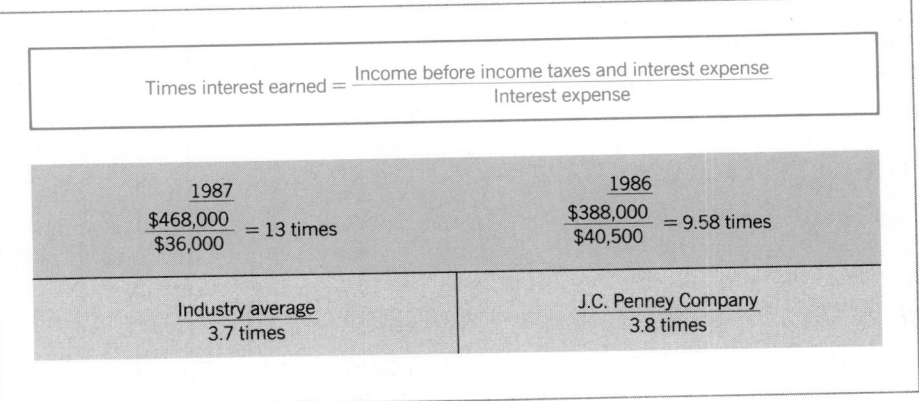

$$\text{Times interest earned} = \frac{\text{Income before income taxes and interest expense}}{\text{Interest expense}}$$

1987	1986
$\frac{\$468{,}000}{\$36{,}000} = 13$ times	$\frac{\$388{,}000}{\$40{,}500} = 9.58$ times
Industry average: 3.7 times	J.C. Penney Company: 3.8 times

Note that the times interest earned ratio uses income before interest and income taxes, because this amount represents the amount available to cover interest. For Quality Department Store the 1987 amount of $468,000 is computed by taking the income before income taxes of $432,000 and adding back the $36,000 of interest expense. The interest expense of Quality is well covered at 13 times relative to the industry average of 3.7 times and J. C. Penney Company's 3.8 times.

In terms of the types of financial information that is available and the ratios used by various industries, you should be aware that what can be practically covered in this textbook only gives you the "Titanic approach." That is, you are only seeing the tip of the iceberg compared to the vast data bases and different types of ratio analysis that are available on computers. The availability of information is not a problem. The real trick is to be discriminating enough to perform relevant analysis and to select pertinent comparative data.

LIMITATIONS OF FINANCIAL ANALYSIS

Significant business decisions are frequently made using one or more of the three analytical tools illustrated in this chapter. You should be aware of some of the limitations of these tools and of the financial statements on which they are based.

ESTIMATES

Financial statements contain numerous estimates. Estimates, for example, are used in measuring the allowance for uncollectible receivables, the useful

lives of depreciable assets, the costs of warranties and guarantees, and contingent losses. To the extent that these estimates are inaccurate, the financial ratios and percentages are inaccurate.

HISTORICAL COST

Traditional financial statements are based on historical cost and are not adjusted for price-level changes. Comparisons of unadjusted financial data from different periods may be rendered invalid by significant inflation or deflation. For example, a five-year comparison of J. C. Penney's revenues shows a growth of 21% over the period 1981–1985. But this growth trend is invalidated to the extent that the general price-level increased more than 30% during that same five-year period.

ALTERNATIVE ACCOUNTING METHODS

Variations among companies in the application of generally accepted accounting principles may hamper comparability. For example, one company may use the FIFO method of inventory costing, while another company in the same industry may use LIFO. If inventory is a significant asset to both companies, it is unlikely that their current ratios are comparable. For example, if General Motors had used FIFO instead of LIFO in valuing its inventories at December 31, 1985, its inventories would have been 26% higher, significantly affecting the current ratio (and other ratios as well). In addition to differences in inventory costing methods, differences also exist in reporting such items as depreciation, depletion, and amortization. While these differences in accounting methods might be detectable from reading the notes to the financial statements, adjusting the financial data to compensate for the different methods is difficult, if not impossible in some cases.

ATYPICAL DATA

Fiscal year-end data may not be typical of the financial condition during the year. Firms frequently establish a fiscal year-end that coincides with the low point in operating activity or in inventory levels. Therefore, certain account balances (cash, receivables, payables, and inventories) may not be representative of the balances in the accounts during the year.

DIVERSIFICATION OF FIRMS

Care must be taken in making comparisons because of the diversification in American industry. Many firms today are so diversified that they cannot be classified by industry. Others appear to be comparable but are not. You might think that PepsiCo, Inc. and Coca Cola Company would permit valid comparisons as soft drink industry competitors. But are they comparable in all respects when PepsiCo, in addition to producing Pepsi-Cola, owns Pizza Hut, Kentucky Fried Chicken, Taco Bell, and Frito-Lay; and Coca-Cola, in addition to producing Coke, owns Hi-C (fruit drinks), Minute Maid (frozen concentrate), and Columbia Pictures (motion pictures, TV shows, and commercials)?

SUMMARY OF STUDY OBJECTIVES

1. Comparative analysis is performed to evaluate a firm's short-term liquidity, profitability, and long-term solvency. Comparisons are necessary to detect change in financial relationships and significant trends and to provide insight into a company's competitive position and relative position in its industry.

2. Financial statements may be analyzed horizontally, vertically, and with ratios.

3. Horizontal analysis is a technique for evaluating a series of data over a period of time to determine the amount and/or percentage of increase or decrease that has taken place.

4. Vertical analysis expresses each item within a financial statement in terms of a percent of a relevant total or a base amount.

5. A summary of financial ratios is as follows:

Ratio	Formula	Purpose or Use
Short-Term Liquidity Ratios		
1. Current ratio	$\frac{\text{Current assets}}{\text{Current liabilities}}$	Measures short-term debt paying ability.
2. Acid-test or quick ratio	$\frac{\text{Cash + marketable securities + receivables (net)}}{\text{Current liabilities}}$	Measures immediate short-term liquidity.
3. Receivables turnover	$\frac{\text{Net credit sales}}{\text{Average net receivables}}$	Measures liquidity of receivables.
4. Inventory turnover	$\frac{\text{Cost of goods sold}}{\text{Average inventory}}$	Measures liquidity of inventory.
Profitability Ratios		
5. Profit margin	$\frac{\text{Net income}}{\text{Net sales}}$	Measures net income generated by each dollar of sales.
6. Asset turnover	$\frac{\text{Net sales}}{\text{Average assets}}$	Measures how efficiently assets are used to generate sales.
7. Return on assets	$\frac{\text{Net income}}{\text{Average assets}}$	Measures overall profitability of assets used.
8. Return on common stockholders' equity	$\frac{\text{Net income}}{\text{Average common stockholders' equity}}$	Measures profitability of owner's investment.

Ratio	Formula	Purpose
9. Earnings per share	Net income / Weighted average common shares outstanding	Measures net income earned on each share of common stock.
10. Price-earnings ratio	Market price of stock / Earnings per share	Measures the ratio of the market price per share to earnings per share.
11. Payout ratio	Cash dividends / Net income	Measures percentage of earnings distributed in the form of cash dividends.
Long-Term Solvency Ratios		
12. Debt to total assets	Total debt / Total assets	Measures the percentage of total assets provided by creditors.
13. Times interest earned	Income before income taxes and interest expense / Interest expense	Measures ability to cover interest expense.

6. The usefulness of analytical tools is limited by the use of estimates, the historical cost basis, the application of alternative accounting methods, atypical data at year-end, and the diversification of firms.

GLOSSARY

DEMONSTRATION PROBLEM

The condensed financial statements of Wendy's International Inc. for the years 1985 and 1984 are presented below:

WENDY'S INTERNATIONAL, INC.
Balance Sheet
December 31

Assets

	1985 (In thousands)	1984 (In thousands)
Current assets		
Cash and short-term investments	$ 15,963	$ 33,065
Accounts and notes receivable	17,192	11,794
Inventories	17,633	13,783
Total current assets	50,788	58,642
Property, plant and equipment (net)	680,310	498,593
Intangibles and other assets	80,281	56,401
Total assets	$811,379	$613,636

Liabilities and Stockholders' Equity

	1985	1984
Current liabilities	$119,392	$111,682
Long-term liabilities	248,458	137,488
Stockholders' equity	443,529	364,466
Total liabilities and stockholders' equity	$811,379	$613,636

WENDY'S INTERNATIONAL, INC.
Income Statement
For the Year Ended December 31

	1985 (In thousands)	1984 (In thousands)
Revenues	$1,125,617	$944,768
Cost and expenses		
Cost of goods sold	588,710	491,772
General, administrative, and operating expenses	388,612	319,778
Interest expense	14,884	6,336
Total costs and expenses	992,206	817,886
Income before income taxes	133,411	126,882
Income tax expense	57,220	58,175
Net income	$ 76,191	$ 68,707

INSTRUCTIONS

Compute the following ratios for Wendy's for 1985 and 1984.

(a) Current ratio

(b) Inventory turnover (Inventory 12/31/83, $12,400)

(c) Profit margin ratio

(d) Rate of return on assets (Assets 12/31/83, $510,200)

(e) Return on stockholders' equity (Equity 12/31/83, $308,282)
(f) Debt to total assets
(g) Times interest earned

SOLUTION TO DEMONSTRATION PROBLEM

	1985	1984
(a) Current ratio:		
$50,788 ÷ $119,392 =	.43:1	
$58,642 ÷ $111,682 =		.53:1
(b) Inventory turnover:		
$588,710 ÷ [($17,633 + $13,783) ÷ 2] =	37.5 times	
$491,772 ÷ [($13,783 + $12,400) ÷ 2] =		37.6 times
(c) Profit margin ratio:		
$76,191 ÷ $1,125,617 =	6.8%	
$68,707 ÷ $944,768 =		7.3%
(d) Rate of return on assets:		
$76,191 ÷ [($811,379 + $613,636) ÷ 2] =	10.7%	
$68,707 ÷ [($613,636 + $510,200) ÷ 2] =		12.2%
(e) Return on stockholders' equity:		
$76,191 ÷ [($443,529 + $364,466) ÷ 2] =	18.9%	
$68,707 ÷ [($364,466 + $308,282) ÷ 2] =		20.4%
(f) Debt to total assets:		
$367,850 ÷ $811,379 =	45.3%	
$249,170 ÷ $613,636 =		40.6%
(g) Times interest earned:		
($133,411 + $14,884) ÷ $14,884 =	9.96 times	
($126,882 + $6,336) ÷ $6,336 =		21 times

QUESTIONS

1. What are the characteristics of a business enterprise that can be evaluated when analyzing and interpreting financial statement data? Who is interested in these characteristics?

2. By comparing reported financial data, valuable insights can be provided. Name and describe three different bases of comparing financial information.

3. Two popular methods of financial statement analysis are horizontal analysis and vertical analysis. Explain the difference between these two methods.

4. Using the following data from the comparative balance sheet of Eskimo Company, illustrate (a) horizontal analysis, and (b) vertical analysis:

	December 31, 1988	December 31, 1987
Inventory	$ 600,000	$ 400,000
Total assets	1,800,000	1,600,000

5. (a) If Boniface Company had net income of $480,000 in 1987 and it experienced a 24.5% increase in net income for 1988, what is its net income for 1988? (b) If six cents of every dollar of Boniface's revenue is net income in 1987, what is the dollar amount of 1987 revenue?

6. What is a ratio? What are the different ways of expressing the relationship of two amounts? What information does a ratio provide?

7. Name the major ratios useful in assessing (a) liquidity, and (b) solvency.

8. Eric Davis is puzzled. His company had a profit margin of 10% in 1987. He feels that this is an indication that the company is doing well. Nadine E. Barnas, his accountant, says that more information is needed to determine Davis' financial well-being. Who is correct? Why?

9. What do the following classes of ratios measure? (a) Short-term liquidity ratios. (b) Profitability ratios. (c) Long-term solvency ratios.

10. What is the difference between the current ratio and the acid-test ratio?

11. Benton Company, a retail store, has a receivable turnover ratio of 4.5 times. The industry average is 12.5 times. Does Benton have a collection problem with its receivables?

12. Which ratios should be used to help answer the following questions?

(a) How near to sale is the inventory on hand?

(b) How efficient is a company in using its assets to produce sales?

(c) How many dollars of net income were earned for each dollar invested by the owners?

(d) How able is a company to meet interest charges as they fall due?

13. Barb Little Corporation has net income of $150,000 and net sales of $1,000,000 for 1987. Its assets were $1,150,000 at the beginning of the year and $1,300,000 at the end of the year. Compute Little's asset turnover and profit margin on sales ratios. (Round to two decimals.)

14. Which two ratios do you think should be of greatest interest to:

(a) A bank contemplating a short-term loan?

(b) A pension fund considering the purchase of 20-year bonds?

(c) A common stockholder?

15. (a) What is meant by leveraging? (b) How would you determine the profitability of leveraging?

16. Nel Bruggemann Company has owners' equity of $400,000 and net income of $50,000. It has a payout ratio of 30% and a rate of return on assets of 16%. How much did Bruggemann pay in cash dividends and what were its average assets?

17. Wayne, Inc. has net income of $200,000, weighted average shares of common stock outstanding of 50,000, and preferred dividends for the period of $40,000. What is Wayne's earnings per share of common stock? Linda Kielar, the president of Wayne Inc., believes the computed EPS of the company is high. Comment.

18. Identify and briefly explain four limitations of financial analysis.

19. Explain how the choice of one of the following accounting methods over the other raises or lowers a company's net income during a period of continuing inflation.

(a) Use of a six-year life for machinery instead of a nine-year life.

(b) Use of FIFO instead of LIFO for inventory costing.
(c) Use of straight-line depreciation instead of accelerated declining-balance depreciation.

EXERCISES

E20-1 Financial information for John Clyde Smith Company is presented below.

	December 31, 1987	December 31, 1986
Current assets	$120,000	$100,000
Plant assets (net)	380,000	330,000
Current liabilities	90,000	70,000
Long-term liabilities	125,000	95,000
Common stock, $1 par	150,000	115,000
Retained earnings	135,000	150,000

INSTRUCTIONS

Prepare a schedule showing a horizontal analysis for 1987 using 1986 as the base year.

E20-2 Operating data for Garvey Corporation are presented below.

	1988	1987
Sales	$800,000	$600,000
Cost of goods sold	496,000	390,000
Selling expenses	104,000	72,000
Administrative expenses	80,000	54,000
Income tax expense	80,000	45,000
Net income	40,000	39,000

INSTRUCTIONS

Prepare a schedule showing a vertical analysis for 1987 and 1988.

E20-3 Kenneth P. Rittenhouse, Jr. Incorporated had the following transactions occur involving current assets and current liabilities during February 1987.

Feb. 3 Accounts receivable of $15,000 are collected.
7 Equipment is purchased for $25,000 cash.
11 Paid $3,000 for a 3-year insurance policy.
14 Accounts payable of $8,000 are paid.
18 Dividends are declared, $6,000.
25 Inventory purchases are made for $10,000 cash.
28 Additional stock is sold, $20,000.

Additional information:

1. As of February 1, 1987, current assets were $140,000 and current liabilities were $50,000.
2. As of February 1, 1987, current assets included $15,000 of inventory and $5,000 of prepaid expenses.

INSTRUCTIONS

(Follow the rounding procedures used in the chapter.)

(a) Compute the current ratio as of the beginning of the month and after each transaction.

(b) Compute the acid test ratio as of the beginning of the month and after each transaction.

E20-4 The Crystal Company has the following comparative balance sheet data:

	December 31, 1987	December 31, 1986
Cash	$ 40,000	$ 30,000
Receivables (net)	65,000	60,000
Inventories	60,000	50,000
Plant assets (net)	200,000	180,000
	$365,000	$320,000
Accounts payable	$ 50,000	$ 60,000
Mortgage payable (15%)	100,000	100,000
Common stock, $10 par	150,000	120,000
Retained earnings	65,000	40,000
	$365,000	$320,000

Additional information for 1987:

1. The net income was $25,000.
2. Sales on account were $420,000. Sales returns and allowances amounted to $20,000.
3. Cost of goods sold was $180,000.

INSTRUCTIONS

(Follow the rounding procedures used in the chapter.) Compute the following ratios at December 31, 1987:

(a) Current.

(b) Acid-test.

(c) Receivables turnover.

(d) Inventory turnover.

E20-5 Selected comparative statement data for the Bothwell Company are presented below. All balance sheet data are as of December 31.

	1987	1986	1985
Net sales	$800,000	$720,000	$600,000
Cost of goods sold	480,000	420,000	350,000
Interest expense	7,000	5,000	8,000
Net income	63,000	50,000	40,000
Accounts receivable	120,000	100,000	80,000
Inventory	85,000	75,000	61,000
Total assets	600,000	500,000	400,000
Total stockholders' equity	450,000	325,000	245,000

INSTRUCTIONS

(Follow the rounding procedures used in the chapter.) Compute the following ratios for 1986 and 1987:

(a) Profit margin.

(b) Asset turnover.

(c) Return on assets.
(d) Return on stockholders' equity.

E20-6 Condensed balance sheet and income statement data for Hiroshi Corporation appear below.

HIROSHI CORPORATION
Balance Sheet
December 31

	1987	1986	1985
Cash	$ 25,000	$ 20,000	$ 18,000
Receivables (net)	50,000	45,000	48,000
Other current assets	90,000	85,000	64,000
Investments	75,000	70,000	45,000
Plant and equipment (net)	400,000	370,000	358,000
	$640,000	$590,000	$533,000
Current liabilities	$ 75,000	$ 80,000	$ 70,000
Long-term debt	85,000	90,000	50,000
Common stock, $10 par	350,000	300,000	300,000
Retained earnings	130,000	120,000	113,000
	$640,000	$590,000	$533,000

HIROSHI CORPORATION
Income Statement
For the Years Ending December 31

	1987	1986
Sales	$740,000	$700,000
Less: Sales returns and allowances	40,000	50,000
Net sales	700,000	650,000
Cost of goods sold	420,000	400,000
Gross profit	280,000	250,000
Operating expenses (including income taxes)	250,000	228,000
Net income	$ 30,000	$ 22,000

Additional information:

1. The market price of Hiroshi's common stock was $4.00, $5.00, and $6.50 for 1985, 1986, and 1987, respectively.
2. All dividends were paid in cash.
3. On July 1, 1987, 5,000 shares of common stock were issued.

INSTRUCTIONS

(Follow the rounding procedures used in the chapter.)

(a) Compute the following ratios for 1986 and 1987:
   1. Profit margin.
   2. Asset turnover.
   3. Earnings per share.
   4. Price-earnings.
   5. Payout.
   6. Debt to total assets.

(b) Based on the ratios calculated, discuss briefly the improvement or lack thereof in financial position and operating results from 1986 to 1987 of the Hiroshi Corporation.

E20-7 The income statement for the year ended December 31, 1987 of Riverside, Inc. appears below.

Sales	$400,000
Cost of goods sold	230,000
Gross profit	170,000
Operating expenses (including $20,000 interest and $24,000 income taxes)	100,000
Net income	$ 70,000

Additional information:

1. Common stock outstanding on January 1, 1987 was 40,000 shares. On July 1, 1987, 20,000 more shares were issued.
2. The market price of Riverside, Inc. stock was $15 in 1987.
3. Cash dividends of $25,000 were paid, $5,000 of which were to preferred stockholders.

INSTRUCTIONS

(Follow the rounding procedures used in the chapter.) Compute the following ratios for 1987:

(a) Earnings per share.
(b) Price-earnings.
(c) Payout.
(d) Times interest earned.

E20-8 Joel Corporation experienced a fire on December 31, 1987 in which its financial records were partially destroyed. It has been able to salvage some of the records and has ascertained the following balances:

	December 31, 1987	December 31, 1986
Cash	$ 30,000	$ 10,000
Receivables (net)	72,500	126,000
Inventory	200,000	180,000
Accounts payable	50,000	90,000
Notes payable	30,000	60,000
Common stock, $100 par	400,000	400,000
Retained earnings	113,500	101,000

Additional information:

1. The inventory turnover is 3.2 times.
2. The return on stockholders' equity is 26.7%. The company had no additional paid-in capital.
3. The receivables turnover is 9.4 times.
4. The return on assets is 20%.
5. Total assets at December 31, 1986 were $700,000.

INSTRUCTIONS

(Follow the rounding procedures used in the chapter.) Compute the following for Joel Corporation:

(a) Cost of goods sold for 1987.
(b) Net sales for 1987.
(c) Net income for 1987.
(d) Total assets at December 31, 1987.

PROBLEMS

P20-1 Comparative statement data for Jay Company and Taylor Company, two competitors, appear below. All balance sheet data are as of December 31, 1987 and December 31, 1986.

	Jay Company		Taylor Company	
	1987	1986	1987	1986
Net sales	$250,000		$1,200,000	
Cost of goods sold	160,000		720,000	
Operating expenses	52,500		252,000	
Interest expense	3,000		10,000	
Income tax expense	14,000		90,000	
Current assets	130,000	$120,000	700,000	$650,000
Plant assets (net)	170,000	155,000	800,000	750,000
Current liabilities	60,000	52,000	250,000	275,000
Long-term liabilities	50,000	68,000	200,000	150,000
Common stock, $10 par	130,000	105,000	750,000	700,000
Retained earnings	60,000	50,000	300,000	275,000

INSTRUCTIONS

(a) Prepare a horizontal analysis of the balance sheet data for Jay Company using 1986 as a base.
(b) Prepare a vertical analysis of the 1987 income statement data for Jay Company and Taylor Company in columnar form.
(c) Comment on the relative profitability of the companies.

P20-2 The comparative statements of the Data Control Company are presented below.

DATA CONTROL COMPANY
Income Statement
For the Year Ended December 31

	1987	1986
Net sales	$660,000	$624,000
Cost of goods sold	440,000	405,600
Gross profit	220,000	218,400
Selling and administrative expense	143,880	149,760
Income from operations	76,120	68,640
Other expenses and losses		
Interest expense	7,920	7,200
Income before income taxes	68,200	61,440
Income tax expense	25,300	24,000
Net income	$ 42,900	$ 37,440

DATA CONTROL COMPANY
Balance Sheet
December 31

	1987	1986
Assets		
Current assets		
Cash	$ 23,100	$ 21,600
Marketable securities	19,800	18,000
Accounts receivable (net)	101,200	88,800
Inventory	92,400	84,000
Total current assets	236,500	212,400
Plant assets (net)	465,300	459,600
Total assets	$701,800	$672,000
Liabilities and stockholders' equity		
Current liabilities		
Accounts payable	$134,200	$132,000
Income taxes payable	25,300	24,000
Total current liabilities	159,500	156,000
Bonds payable	132,000	120,000
Total liabilities	291,500	276,000
Stockholders' equity		
Common stock ($5 par)	137,500	150,000
Retained earnings	272,800	246,000
Total stockholders' equity	410,300	396,000
Total liabilities and stockholders' equity	$701,800	$672,000

On July 1, 1987, 2,500 shares were repurchased and cancelled. All sales were on account.

INSTRUCTIONS

(Follow the rounding procedures used in the chapter.) Compute the following ratios for 1987:

(a) Earnings per share.
(b) Return on stockholders' equity.
(c) Return on assets.
(d) Current.
(e) Acid-test.
(f) Receivables turnover.
(g) Inventory turnover.
(h) Times interest earned.
(i) Asset turnover.
(j) Debt to total assets.

P20–3 Presented below is an incomplete income statement and an incomplete comparative balance sheet of Program, Inc.

PROGRAM, INC.
Income Statement
For the Year Ended December 31, 1987

Sales	$9,000,000
Cost of goods sold	?
Gross profit	?
Operating expenses	1,920,000
Income from operations	?

Other expenses and losses:	
Interest expense	?
Income before income taxes	?
Income tax expense	552,000
Net income	$?

PROGRAM, INC.
Balance Sheet
December 31, 1987 and 1986

	1987	1986
Assets		
Current assets		
Cash	$ 218,000	$ 375,000
Accounts receivable (net)	?	925,000
Inventory	?	1,100,000
Total current assets	?	2,400,000
Plant assets (net)	4,500,000	4,600,000
Total assets	$?	$7,000,000
Liabilities and stockholders' equity		
Current liabilities	$?	$1,100,000
Long-term notes payable	?	$2,300,000
Total liabilities	?	3,400,000
Common stock, $1 par	3,000,000	3,000,000
Retained earnings	740,000	600,000
Total stockholders' equity	3,740,000	3,600,000
Total liabilities and stockholders' equity	$?	$7,000,000

Additional information:

1. The current ratio on December 31, 1987 is 2:1.
2. The receivables turnover for 1987 is 9.6 times.
3. The inventory turnover for 1987 is 5 times.
4. Return on assets is 12% for 1987.
5. The profit margin for 1987 is 9.2%.
6. All sales were on account.

INSTRUCTIONS

Compute the missing information, given the ratios above. Show computations. (Note: Start with one ratio and derive as much information from it before trying another ratio. List all missing amounts under the ratio used to find the information.)

P20-4 Financial information for the Russell Company is presented below.

RUSSELL COMPANY
Balance Sheet
December 31

	1987	1986
Assets		
Cash	$ 50,000	$ 42,000
Receivables (net)	100,000	87,000

	1987	1986
Short-term investments	80,000	100,000
Inventories	440,000	400,000
Prepaid expenses	25,000	31,000
Land	75,000	75,000
Building and equipment (net)	570,000	500,000
	$1,340,000	$1,235,000
Liabilities and stockholders' equity		
Accounts payable	$ 160,000	$ 140,000
Notes payable	125,000	125,000
Accrued liabilities	50,000	50,000
Bonds payable, due 1995	200,000	200,000
Common stock, $1 par	500,000	500,000
Retained earnings	305,000	220,000
	$1,340,000	$1,235,000

RUSSELL COMPANY
Income Statement
For the Years Ended December 31

	1987	1986
Sales	$1,000,000	$940,000
Cost of goods sold	550,000	535,000
Gross profit	450,000	405,000
Operating expenses	335,000	315,000
Net income	$ 115,000	$ 90,000

Additional information:

1. Inventory at the beginning of 1986 was $350,000.
2. Receivables at the beginning of 1986 were $80,000.
3. Total assets at the beginning of 1986 were $1,175,000.
4. No common stock transactions occurred during 1986 or 1987.
5. All sales were on account.

INSTRUCTIONS

(Follow the rounding procedures used in the chapter.)

(a) Indicate by using ratios, the change in liquidity and profitability of the Russell Company from 1986 to 1987.

(b) Given below are three independent situations and a ratio that may be affected. For each situation, compute the affected ratio (1) as of December 31, 1987, and (2) as of December 31, 1988 after giving effect to the situation. Net income for 1988 was $125,000. Total assets on December 31, 1988 were $1,400,000.

Situation	Ratio
(1) 300,000 shares of common stock were sold at par on July 1, 1988.	Return on stockholders' equity
(2) All of the notes payable were paid.	Debt to total assets
(3) Market price of common stock on December 31, 1988 was $5. Market price on December 31, 1987 was $4.	Price-earnings ratio

P20–5 Comparative data for three competing record companies for the year 1987 appears below.

	New Wave Company	Rock Company	Pop Company
Net sales (all on account)	$340,787	$203,423	$201,858
Cost of goods sold	237,708	142,804	130,835
Operating expenses	66,500	47,400	52,499
Interest expense	1,537	751	1,084
Income tax expense	18,416	6,360	9,459
Net income	$ 16,626	$ 6,108	$ 7,981
Current assets	$ 78,234	$ 54,168	$106,459
Plant assets (net)	125,114	71,323	112,800
Other assets	26,795	18,325	12,011
Total assets	$230,143	$143,816	$231,270
Current liabilities	$ 16,878	$ 50,002	$ 33,100
Long-term liabilities	25,080	19,253	104,744
Stockholders' equity	188,185	74,561	93,426
Total liabilities and stockholders' equity	$230,143	$143,816	$231,270

Additional information:			
Average receivables	$ 15,000	$ 9,200	$ 12,400
Average inventory	30,000	20,000	28,500
Average assets	220,400	128,600	225,000
Stockholders' equity (January 1)	150,015	70,039	87,324
Par value of common stock	10	5	2
Weighted average shares outstanding	5,000	8,000	20,000
Market price of stock	15	8	4
Cash dividends paid	6,000	2,400	2,800

INSTRUCTIONS

(Follow the rounding procedures used in the chapter.)

(a) Compute the following ratios for the three companies above.

1. Current.
2. Receivables turnover.
3. Inventory turnover.
4. Profit margin.
5. Asset turnover.
6. Return on assets.
7. Return on stockholders' equity.
8. Earnings per share.
9. Price-earnings.
10. Payout.
11. Debt to total assets.
12. Times interest earned.

Rank the companies numerically (1 is the best) using the following format:

	New Wave	Rock	Pop
Ratio Name	Ratio Rank	Ratio Rank	Ratio Rank

(b) Comment on the relative liquidity, profitability, and solvency of each company.

(c) What limitations are there in the analysis above?

P20–6 The comparative statements of the Daytum Company are presented below.

DAYTUM COMPANY
Income Statement
For Year Ended December 31

	1987	1986
Net sales (all on account)	$600,000	$520,000
Expenses		
Cost of goods sold	400,000	338,000
Selling and administrative	130,800	124,800
Interest expense	7,200	6,000
Income tax expense	23,000	20,000
Total expenses	561,000	488,800
Net income	$ 39,000	$ 31,200

DAYTUM COMPANY
Balance Sheet
December 31

	1987	1986
Assets		
Current assets		
Cash	$ 21,000	$ 18,000
Marketable securities	18,000	15,000
Accounts receivable (net)	92,000	74,000
Inventory	84,000	70,000
Total current assets	215,000	177,000
Plant assets (net)	423,000	383,000
Total assets	$638,000	$560,000
Liabilities and stockholders' equity		
Current liabilities		
Accounts payable	$122,000	$110,000
Income taxes payable	23,000	20,000
Total current liabilities	145,000	130,000
Long-term liabilities		
Bonds payable	120,000	80,000
Total liabilities	265,000	210,000
Stockholders' equity		
Common stock ($5 par)	125,000	125,000
Retained earnings	248,000	225,000
Total stockholders' equity	373,000	350,000
Total liabilities and stockholders' equity	$638,000	$560,000

Additional data:
The common stock recently sold at $22.50 per share.

INSTRUCTIONS

(Follow the rounding procedures used in the chapter.) Compute the following ratios for 1987:

(a) Current ratio.
(b) Acid-test ratio.
(c) Receivables turnover.
(d) Inventory turnover.
(e) Profit margin ratio.
(f) Asset turnover.
(g) Return on assets.
(h) Return on common stockholders' equity.
(i) Earnings per share.
(j) Price-earnings ratio.
(k) Payout ratio.
(l) Debt to total assets.
(m) Times interest earned.

ALTERNATE PROBLEMS

P20-1A Comparative statement data for Terry Company and Kaster Company, two competitors, appear below. All balance sheet data are as of December 31, 1987 and December 31, 1986.

	Terry Company		Kaster Company	
	1987	1986	1987	1986
Net sales	$1,549,035		$339,038	
Cost of goods sold	1,080,490		238,006	
Operating expenses	302,275		79,000	
Interest expense	6,800		1,252	
Income tax expense	83,710		10,600	
Current assets	325,975	$312,410	83,336	$79,467
Plant assets (net)	521,310	500,000	109,728	99,812
Current liabilities	70,325	75,815	35,348	30,281
Long-term liabilities	104,500	90,000	29,620	25,000
Common stock, $10 par	500,000	500,000	90,000	90,000
Retained earnings	172,460	146,595	38,096	33,998

INSTRUCTIONS

(a) Prepare a horizontal analysis of the balance sheet data for Terry Company using 1986 as a base.

(b) Prepare a vertical analysis of the 1987 income statement data for Terry Company and Kaster Company in columnar form.

(c) Comment on the relative profitability of the companies.

P20-2A The comparative statements of the Durham Company are presented below.

DURHAM COMPANY
Income Statement
For the Year Ended December 31

	1987	1986
Net sales	$1,818,500	$1,750,500
Cost of goods sold	1,005,500	996,000
Gross profit	813,000	754,500
Selling and administrative expense	506,000	479,000
Income from operations	307,000	275,500

	1987	1986
Other expenses and losses		
Interest expense	18,000	19,000
Income before income taxes	289,000	256,500
Income tax expense	115,600	102,600
Net income	$ 173,400	$ 153,900

DURHAM COMPANY
Balance Sheet
December 31

	1987	1986
Assets		
Current assets		
Cash	$ 60,100	$ 64,200
Marketable securities	54,000	50,000
Accounts receivable (net)	107,800	102,800
Inventory	123,000	115,500
Total current assets	344,900	332,500
Plant assets (net)	625,300	604,300
Total assets	$970,200	$936,800
Liabilities and stockholders' equity		
Current liabilities		
Accounts payable	$150,000	$145,400
Income taxes payable	43,500	42,000
Total current liabilities	193,500	187,400
Bonds payable	210,000	200,000
Total liabilities	403,500	387,400
Stockholders' equity		
Common stock ($5 par)	280,000	300,000
Retained earnings	286,700	249,400
Total stockholders' equity	566,700	549,400
Total liabilities and stockholders' equity	$970,200	$936,800

On July 1, 1987, 4,000 shares were repurchased and cancelled. All sales were on account.

INSTRUCTIONS

(Follow the rounding procedures used in the chapter.) Compute the following ratios for 1987:

(a) Earnings per share.
(b) Return on stockholders' equity.
(c) Return on assets.
(d) Current.
(e) Acid-test.
(f) Receivables turnover.
(g) Inventory turnover.
(h) Times interest earned.
(i) Asset turnover.
(j) Debt to total assets.

P20-3A Presented below is an incomplete income statement and an incomplete comparative balance sheet of Quinn Corporation.

QUINN CORPORATION
Income Statement
For the Year Ended December 31, 1987

Sales (all on account)	$11,000,000
Cost of goods sold	?
Gross profit	?
Operating expenses	1,760,000
Income from operations	?
Other expenses and losses	
Interest expense	?
Income before income taxes	?
Income tax expense	425,000
Net income	$?

QUINN CORPORATION
Balance Sheet
December 31

	1987	1986
Assets		
Current assets		
Cash	$ 450,000	$ 375,000
Accounts receivable (net)	?	950,000
Inventory	?	1,720,000
Total current assets	?	3,045,000
Plant assets (net)	4,200,000	3,955,000
Total assets	$?	$7,000,000
Liabilities and stockholders' equity		
Current liabilities	$?	$ 925,000
Long-term notes payable	?	$2,700,000
Total liabilities	?	3,625,000
Common stock, $1 par	3,000,000	3,000,000
Retained earnings	400,000	375,000
Total stockholders' equity	3,400,000	3,375,000
Total liabilities and stockholders' equity	$?	$7,000,000

Additional information:

1. The current ratio on December 31, 1987 is 3:1.
2. The receivables turnover for 1987 is 11 times.
3. The inventory turnover for 1987 is 4 times.
4. Return on assets is 22% for 1987.
5. The profit margin for 1987 is 14.5%.

INSTRUCTIONS

Compute the missing information given the ratios above. Show computations. (Note: Start with one ratio and derive as much information from it before trying another ratio. List all missing amounts under the ratio used to find the information.)

P20-4A Financial information for the Yates Company is presented below.

YATES COMPANY
Balance Sheet
December 31

	1987	1986
Assets		
Cash	$ 70,000	$ 65,000
Receivables (net)	94,000	90,000
Short-term investments	45,000	40,000
Inventories	130,000	125,000
Prepaid expenses	25,000	23,000
Land	130,000	130,000
Building and equipment (net)	190,000	175,000
	$684,000	$648,000
Liabilities and stockholders' equity		
Accounts payable	$ 45,000	$ 42,000
Notes payable	100,000	100,000
Accrued liabilities	40,000	40,000
Bonds payable, due 1995	150,000	150,000
Common stock, $1 par	200,000	200,000
Retained earnings	149,000	116,000
	$684,000	$648,000

YATES COMPANY
Income Statement
For the Years Ended December 31

	1987	1986
Sales	$525,000	$490,000
Cost of goods sold	295,000	275,000
Gross profit	230,000	215,000
Operating expenses	194,000	180,000
Net income	$ 36,000	$ 35,000

Additional information:

1. Inventory at the beginning of 1986 was $115,000.
2. Receivables at the beginning of 1986 were $88,000.
3. Total assets at the beginning of 1986 were $630,000.
4. No common stock transactions occurred during 1986 or 1987.
5. All sales were on account.

INSTRUCTIONS

(Follow the rounding procedures used in the chapter.)

(a) Indicate by using ratios, the change in liquidity and profitability of the Yates Company from 1986 to 1987.

(b) Given below are three independent situations and a ratio that may be affected. For each situation, compute the affected ratio (1) as of December 31, 1987, and (2) as of December 31, 1988 after giving effect to the situation. Net income for 1988 was $40,000. Total assets on December 31, 1988 were $700,000.

Situation	Ratio
1. 200,000 shares of common stock were sold at par on July 1, 1988.	Return on stockholders' equity
2. All of the notes payable were paid.	Debt to total assets
3. Market price of common stock was $2 and $2.75 on December 31, 1987 and 1988, respectively.	Price-earnings ratio

P20-5A Comparative data for three competing record companies for the year 1987 appears below.

	Classical Company	Jazz Company	Country Company
Net sales (all on account)	$1,147,510	$ 894,340	$510,400
Cost of goods sold	624,000	497,710	302,250
Operating expenses	149,140	130,050	72,140
Interest expense	27,830	19,100	12,810
Income tax expense	110,080	67,390	49,030
Net income	$ 236,460	$ 180,090	$ 74,170
Current assets	$ 315,800	$ 294,100	$257,500
Plant assets (net)	800,000	718,000	640,900
Other assets	90,100	77,400	87,400
Total assets	$1,205,900	$1,089,500	$985,800
Current liabilities	$ 194,600	$ 187,700	$147,900
Long-term liabilities	479,000	500,000	275,000
Stockholders' equity	532,300	401,800	562,900
Total liabilities and stockholders' equity	$1,205,900	$1,089,500	$985,800
Additional information:			
Average receivables	$ 105,700	$ 92,700	$ 74,300
Average inventory	192,300	175,600	151,000
Average assets	1,160,200	1,070,200	980,000
Stockholders' equity (January 1)	500,100	498,200	500,000
Par value of common stock	4	5	10
Weighted average shares outstanding	70,000	50,000	28,000
Market price of stock	21	23	16
Cash dividends paid	70,000	42,000	12,000

INSTRUCTIONS

(Follow the rounding procedures used in the chapter.)

(a) Compute the following ratios for the three companies above:

1. Current.
2. Receivables turnover.
3. Inventory turnover.
4. Profit margin.
5. Asset turnover.
6. Return on assets.
7. Return on stockholders' equity.
8. Earnings per share.
9. Price-earnings share.
10. Payout.
11. Debt to total assets.
12. Times interest earned.

Rank the companies numerically (1 is the best) using the following format:

	Classical	Jazz	Country
Ratio Name	Ratio Rank	Ratio Rank	Ratio Rank

(b) Comment on the relative liquidity, profitability, and solvency of each company.

(c) What limitations are there in the analysis above?

P20-6A The comparative condensed statements of General Foods Corporation from its 1985 Annual Report are presented below.

GENERAL FOODS CORPORATION
Income Statements
For the Year Ended December 31
(in thousands of dollars)

	1985	1984
Net sales	$9,090,910	$8,686,086
Costs and expenses		
Cost of sales	5,508,195	5,263,151
Marketing, general, and administrative expenses	2,888,843	2,704,491
Interest expense	150,056	145,139
Total costs and expenses	8,547,094	8,112,781
Income before income taxes	543,816	573,305
Income tax expense	218,909	256,200
Net income	$ 324,907	$ 317,105

GENERAL FOODS CORPORATION
Balance Sheet
March 31
(in thousands of dollars)

	1985	1984
Assets		
Current assets		
Cash	$ 131,606	$ 51,145
Temporary investments	156,830	225,641
Receivables (net)	948,598	906,401
Inventories	1,074,538	1,097,119
Prepaid expenses	66,394	65,977
Total current assets	$2,377,966	$2,346,283
Land, buildings, and equip. (net)	1,751,461	1,614,620
Investments	125,288	175,181
Goodwill and intangibles	299,010	295,698
Total	$4,553,725	$4,431,782
Liabilities and stockholders' equity		
Current liabilities	$1,402,597	$1,244,500
Long-term debt	725,061	749,969
Other noncurrent liabilities	485,823	397,133
Total liabilities	2,613,481	2,391,602
Stockholders' equity		
Common Stock	$ 145,604	$ 176,848
Retained earnings	2,121,593	1,919,703
Treasury stock at cost	(326,953)	(56,371)
Total stockholders' equity	1,940,244	2,040,180
Total	$4,553,725	$4,431,782

Additional data:

1. Weighted average number of shares outstanding; 49,166,000 in fiscal 1985.
2. Dividends paid in fiscal 1985; $123,017,000.
3. Market value per share at year end 1985; $52.
4. Average interest rate for fiscal 1985; 12%.
5. Assume all sales on account.

INSTRUCTIONS

Compute the following ratios for General Foods Corporation for the fiscal year ended March 31, 1985.

(a) Current ratio.
(b) Acid-test ratio.
(c) Receivables turnover.
(d) Inventory turnover.
(e) Profit margin ratio.
(f) Asset turnover.
(g) Return on assets.
(h) Return on common stockholders' equity.
(i) Earnings per share.
(j) Price-earnings ratio.
(k) Payout ratio.
(l) Debt to total assets.
(m) Times interest earned.

DECISION CASE

Your parents are considering investing in PepsiCo, Inc. common stock. They ask you, as an accounting expert, to make an analysis of the company for them. Fortunately, excerpts from a current annual report of the PepsiCo are presented in Appendix A of this textbook and note that all amounts omit 000's.

INSTRUCTIONS

(Follow the approach in the chapter for rounding numbers.)

(a) Make a five-year trend analysis, using 1981 as the base year, of (1) net sales, and (2) income from operations. Comment on the significance of the trend results.

(b) Compute for 1985 and 1984 the (1) current ratio, (2) acid test ratio, (3) receivables turnover (assuming that notes and accounts receivable less allowance for doubtful accounts was $647,329 at December 31, 1983), and (4) inventory turnover. Assume that inventory as of December 31, 1983 was $360,500 and that all sales are credit sales. (Hint: Do not include net assets held for disposal in the acid-test ratio.) What conclusions can you reach about PepsiCo's short-term solvency from these data?

(c) Compute for 1985 and 1984, the (1) profit margin, (2) asset turnover, (3) return on assets, and (4) return on common stockholders' equity. How would you evaluate PepsiCo's profitability? Assume that total assets at December 31, 1983 was $4,100,000 and the total stockholders' equity at December 31, 1983 was $1,800,000.

(d) Compute for 1985 and 1984, the (1) debt to total assets, and (2) times interest earned. How would you evaluate PepsiCo's long-term solvency?

(e) What information outside the annual report may also be useful to your parents in making a decision about PepsiCo., Inc.?

CHAPTER 21

University of California at Berkeley

CHAPTER 21

MANAGERIAL ACCOUNTING AND ANALYSIS OF SEGMENTS

STUDY OBJECTIVES

After studying this chapter, you should be able to:

1. **Explain the distinguishing features of managerial accounting.**
2. **Define a segment and explain the three types of segments.**
3. **Identify the three approaches to evaluating profit centers.**
4. **Distinguish between direct and indirect operating expenses and indicate the guidelines for allocating indirect expenses.**
5. **Assess the usefulness of departmentalized income statements.**
6. **Contrast the approaches to evaluating the profitability of investment centers.**

A primary purpose of accounting is to provide information that is useful to a wide variety of decision makers. The preceding chapters have described the preparation of annual financial statements primarily for external users such as stockholders, creditors, and regulatory agencies. These financial statements represent the principal end product of financial accounting. The remaining chapters of this textbook focus on managerial accounting, which includes the preparation of reports for **internal users** within an enterprise.

In this chapter, we will first highlight the major differences between managerial accounting and financial accounting, and then, we will explain the accounting for the components of a business, such as a department or a division.

MANAGERIAL ACCOUNTING

Managerial accounting, also called management accounting, is a field of accounting that provides economic and financial information for managers and other internal users. The activities that are part of managerial accounting and the chapter(s) in which they are discussed are as follows:

1. Accounting for and evaluating the profitability of segments of an entity. (Chapter 21)
2. Computing the cost to an entity of rendering a service or manufacturing a product. (Chapters 22 and 23)
3. Determining the behavior of costs and expenses as activity levels change and analyzing cost-volume-profit relationships within a company. (Chapter 24)
4. Assisting management in profit planning and formalizing the plans in the form of budgets. (Chapter 25)
5. Providing a basis for controlling costs and expenses by comparing actual results with planned objectives and standard costs. (Chapters 26 and 27)
6. Accumulating and presenting relevant data for management decision making. (Chapter 28)
7. Indicating the impact of income taxes on management's decisions. (Chapter 29)

Managerial accounting is applicable to all types of businesses—service, merchandising, and manufacturing—and all forms of business organizations—proprietorships, partnerships, and corporations. Moreover, managerial accounting is needed in not-for-profit entities as well as in profit-oriented enterprises.

MANAGERIAL ACCOUNTING AND FINANCIAL ACCOUNTING

There are both similarities and differences between managerial and financial accounting. An important similarity is that each field of accounting deals with the economic events of an enterprise. Thus, there is overlap between managerial and financial accounting. For example, determining the unit cost of manufacturing a product is part of managerial accounting. In contrast, reporting the total cost of goods manufactured and sold is part of financial accounting. In addition, both managerial and financial accounting require the quantification of the results of an entity's economic events and communication of the results to interested parties. The diverse needs for economic data among parties interested in an enterprise are responsible for many of the differences between the two fields of accounting. The principal differences are as follows:

PRIMARY USERS

Financial accounting is primarily concerned with external users, such as stockholders, creditors, and regulatory agencies. In contrast, managerial accounting relates primarily to internal users who are officers (top management), department heads, managers, and supervisors in the company.

TYPE AND FREQUENCY OF REPORTS

Classified financial statements are the end product of financial accounting. They are prepared quarterly and annually. In managerial accounting, data are communicated through internal reports. These reports may be prepared daily, weekly, monthly, quarterly, or annually. Internal reports satisfy management's need for timely information.

PURPOSE OF REPORTS

The financial statements produced by financial accounting are considered to be **general-purpose reports** for all users. These reports must be adapted by the user to the decision that is to be made. Conversely, in managerial accounting, reports can be designed for use by a particular user for a specific decision. To a large degree, internal reports are **special-purpose** reports.

CONTENT OF REPORTS

Information in financial statements generally pertains to the enterprise as a whole and usually is highly aggregated. The data are normally limited to information developed within the double-entry accounting system. Therefore, the reports are based on completed transactions and include only historical cost data. The reporting standard is generally accepted accounting principles.

Information in internal reports usually pertains to subunits of the entity such as divisions, departments, and branches. Accordingly, the data are often very detailed. The content of internal reports often extend beyond the double-entry accounting system. Thus, the reports may show all amounts at market values or the effects of prospective events. Moreover, the data do not have to be reported in accordance with generally accepted accounting principles. **The reporting standard for internal reports is relevance to the decision to be made.**

The principal differences between financial accounting and managerial accounting are summarized below.

Differences between financial and managerial accounting

Financial Accounting	Managerial Accounting
Primary Users of Reports	
• External users who are stockholders, creditors, and regulatory agencies	• Internal users who are officers, department heads, managers, and supervisors in the company
Types and Frequency of Reports	
• Classified financial statements	• Internal reports
• Issued quarterly and annually	• Issued as frequently as the need arises

Purpose of Reports	
• To provide general-purpose information for all users	• To provide special-purpose information for a particular user for a specific decision
Content of Reports	
• Pertains to entity as a whole and is highly aggregated	• Pertains to subunits of the entity and may be very detailed
• Limited to double-entry accounting system and historical cost data	• May extend beyond double-entry accounting system to any type of relevant data
• Reporting standard is generally accepted accounting principles	• Reporting standard is relevance to the decision to be made

MANAGEMENT FUNCTIONS

The management of an organization performs four broad functions. They are:

1. Planning.
2. Organizing.
3. Directing.
4. Controlling.

In performing these functions, management must make decisions that have a significant impact on the organization.

Planning requires management to look ahead and to establish objectives. A primary objective of a business enterprise is to earn a profit. In addition, a company may want to be the leader in research and technology and have an excellent reputation for dependability. A company may also wish to maximize its commitment to environmental protection and its contribution to social programs for the benefit of society.

Organizing involves coordinating the diverse activities and human resources of a company to produce a smooth-running operation. This function relates to the implementation of planned objectives. For example, in a national retail department store such as Lord & Taylor, purchasing, warehousing, and selling must be coordinated. Similarly, it is necessary to select executives, appoint managers and supervisors, and hire and train employees. Most companies prepare **organization charts** to show the interrelationship of activities and the delegation of authority and responsibility within the company.

Directing requires active, on-going surveillance of day-to-day operations by management. The objective of this function is to keep all activities running smoothly. To achieve this goal, management must be available to deal with problems as they arise, to answer questions, and to make recommendations.

Controlling is the process of keeping the activities of the enterprise on track. In controlling operations, management determines whether planned goals are being met and what changes are necessary when there are deviations from targeted objectives. The control function involves performance evaluation by management. The evaluation may relate to the ability of a

salesperson to meet sales quotas or to the effectiveness of a department head to reduce costs within the department. Performance evaluation is generally based on internal reports prepared for various levels of management.

As illustrated in the graphic below, the four functions may be depicted as the spokes of a wheel that move around the axle or hub of decision making.

Four functions of management

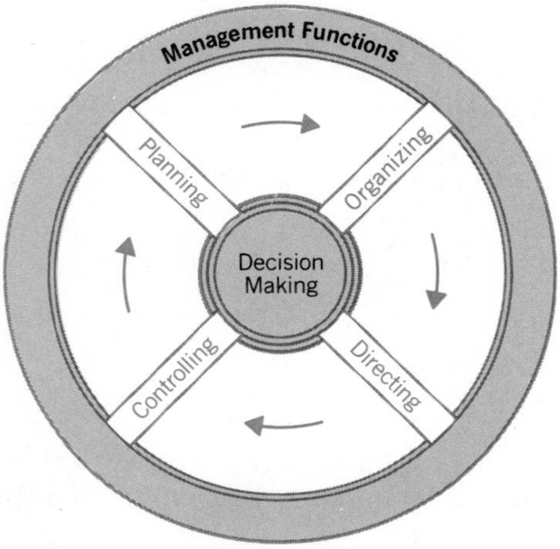

Decision making is not a separate management function. Rather, it involves the exercise of good judgment in planning, organizing, directing, and controlling. In many cases, decision making requires management to choose among alternatives. For example, management may have to decide between buying or leasing equipment and whether to work existing markets more intensively or enter new markets.

You are now ready to study specific applications of managerial accounting. As you study the managerial chapters, you will encounter many new terms, concepts, and reports. At the same time, you will find some new uses and interpretations of a number of familiar financial accounting terms. Your study of managerial accounting begins with the accounting for segments of a business enterprise.

WHAT IS A SEGMENT?

A **segment** is any subunit or activity of an organization for which management information is desired. **Divisions in a decentralized company, sales territories, product lines, and departments are all examples of segments of an organization.** Decentralization often results in more effective management. As one corporate executive at 3M remarked: "Although we are a multimillion dollar corporation, we are accustomed to thinking small. We are virtually organized into over 40 divisions and departments, and many more subsidiaries, each of which is run like a small company of its own."[1]

[1]Donald E. Garreston, "Business Planning at 3M," *Management Accounting,* November 1974,

As indicated, the diversity and number of segments in any organization can be substantial. For example, Sears, Roebuck and Co. is generally considered to be a retail operation; however, it is comprised of four companies: retailing (Sears, Roebuck), insurance (Allstate), investments (Dean Witter), and real estate (Coldwell Banker). Each segment acts fairly independently of the others, although they are under single ownership. Within Sears, the retailing segment, Sears, Roebuck, can be further subdivided into geographical regions of the country, individual stores, and individual departments within the store. As a consequence, it is not surprising that accountants spend much time preparing information on individual segments to help management evaluate whether the overall goals and objectives of the enterprise are being met.

BASIS FOR SEGMENTING

The number of segments in an enterprise is influenced by many factors. They include the philosophy of top management, the type of product sold, and the location of physical facilities. Different organizations adopt different approaches for segmenting their operations, and the basis for segmentation may change over time as the enterprise grows.

The reasons for segmenting business operations are varied. First, to plan, organize, direct, and control an organization such as Sears, Roebuck and Co., it is necessary to evaluate separately **the major components of the business.** Second, **it is generally considered useful to have a number of individuals involved in the decision-making process.** As one writer noted: "A great deal of improvement is believed to result in any firm where the creative talents of responsible individuals are encouraged to develop in a climate of individual responsibility, authority, and dignity—a climate that is made possible by the decentralization of decision-making.[2] Finally, **segmenting operations provides management with an effective means of training its younger executives.** Managing a segment may be similar to running the entire organization. Accordingly, the segment manager's skills of leadership and decision making are often enhanced.

The costs as well as the benefits of segmenting business operations must be considered. Often, a heavy cost is involved in the use of management talent. As a business becomes more decentralized, more managers are needed to manage the individual segments, and substantial duplication of effort may result. In addition, segmentation can lead to intersegment competition that in the long run may reduce the company's overall net income. For example, a manufacturer such as General Motors may have four automobile reporting segments, full-size, mid-size, compacts, and subcompacts. Each segment is evaluated separately, but General Motors must make sure that sales from one division do not erode sales of another division to such an extent that an overall reduction in net income occurs.

[2]John F. Burlingame, "Information Technology and Decentralization," *Harvard Business Review*, November-December 1961, p. 122.

TYPES OF SEGMENTS

Segments may be classified into one of three types of centers: cost centers, profit centers, and investment centers. These centers, sometimes called **responsibility centers,** indicate the degree of responsibility the segment manager has for the performance of the segment.

A **cost center** incurs costs (and expenses) but does not directly generate revenues. Managers of cost centers have the authority to incur costs. They are evaluated on their ability to control costs. Cost centers are usually classified as being either production departments or service departments. The former participate directly in making the product whereas the latter provide only support services. In an automobile plant, the welding, painting, and assembling departments are production departments, and the maintenance, cafeteria, and personnel departments are service departments. Much more will be said about cost centers in later chapters.

A **profit center** incurs costs (and expenses) but also generates revenues. Managers of profit centers are judged on the profitability of their centers. Examples of profit centers include the individual departments of a retail store, such as clothing, furniture, and automotive products in Montgomery Ward, and branch offices of banks. Internal reports for evaluating profit centers are discussed later in this chapter.

Like a profit center, an **investment center** incurs costs (and expenses) and generates revenues. In addition, an investment center has control over the investment funds available for use. Managers of investment centers are evaluated on the profitability of the center and on the rate of return earned on the funds invested. Investment centers are often associated with subsidiary companies. For example, PepsiCo owns Frito-Lay (potato chips) and Pizza Hut and Kentucky Fried Chicken (restaurants), whereas General Mills owns Parker Brothers (games) and Izod Lacoste (fashions). In each of these instances, the manager of the segment is able to control or significantly influence investment decisions pertaining to such matters as plant expansion and entry into new market areas. In practice, the term "profit center" is often used to refer either to a profit center or to an investment center. However, we will consider them separate and distinct types of segments in this textbook.

MANAGEMENT USES OF SEGMENT DATA

Segment data are useful to top management in discharging each of the management functions described earlier. For example, segment information is useful in:

1. **Planning.** Knowledge of a segment's past performance is helpful in establishing future goals for the segment. In addition, the profitability of a segment may influence top management's decisions concerning the allocation of resources among the various segments of the business.
2. **Organizing.** The reporting of segment data should follow the assignment of responsibility within the firm. From the reports, top management should be able to identify both strong managers and weak managers.

3. **Directing.** Frequent reporting of segment data informs top management about problems that require their attention. For critical areas of activity, reports may be prepared daily or weekly. For example, daily reports on spoilage in the meat department and the produce department of a grocery store may indicate the need for more effective purchasing and storage procedures.
4. **Controlling.** Internal reports on segments should identify those segments that are not meeting planned objectives. When a problem area is identified, top management should be able to determine the cause(s) and initiate corrective action.

EVALUATING PROFIT CENTERS

We will use sales departments of a retail store to illustrate the evaluation of profit centers. However, the general approach also applies to profit centers in service and manufacturing companies. Internal reports in the form of segment income statements are used in evaluating the profitability of the profit center. Views vary as to the level of detail that should be presented in departmental income statements. Generally, one of the following approaches is adopted for reporting the profitability of a department to top management.

1. Departmental gross profit.
2. Departmental income from operations.
3. Departmental margin.

DEPARTMENTAL GROSS PROFIT

As explained in earlier chapters, gross profit is a significant financial relationship in external analysis. It is also important in internal analysis. **Departmental gross profit** is the difference between a department's net sales and its cost of goods sold. To determine departmental gross profit, it is necessary to identify the sales, purchases, and inventories for each department. In most companies this is done through a **coding system** in which a department code number must appear on each business document, such as purchase and sales invoices, debit and credit memos, and so on. The coded transaction data are then recorded in multicolumn sales and purchase journals that contain separate columns for each department. Subsequently, the data are posted to individual departmental sales and purchases accounts.

Many large department stores and supermarkets use **electronic point-of-sales systems** to collect departmental sales data and to update inventory records. These systems require the operators of electronic cash registers to include departmental code data when they ring up each sale. The cash registers are also computer terminals that transmit the data directly into the central computer.

An income statement for the Borg Company that has two sales departments, Appliances and Clothing, is shown below. The statement presents departmental gross profit and data for the store as a whole. Note that separate columns are provided for each department's net sales, cost of goods sold, and gross profit. As shown in this statement, the amount of gross profit may vary significantly between departments. The remainder of the income statement is not departmentalized. In the interest of brevity, condensed data are shown for net sales and cost of goods purchased (net purchases plus freight-in). In practice, detailed data are ordinarily presented. Similarly, operating expenses have not been classified.

Income statement showing departmental gross profit

BORG COMPANY
Income Statement
For the Year Ended December 31, 1987

	Appliance Department	Clothing Department	Total
Net sales	$540,000	$360,000	$900,000
Cost of goods sold			
Inventory, January 1	110,000	90,000	200,000
Cost of goods purchased	295,000	216,000	511,000
Cost of goods available for sale	405,000	306,000	711,000
Inventory, December 31	81,000	64,000	145,000
Cost of goods sold	324,000	242,000	566,000
Gross profit	**$216,000**	**$118,000**	334,000
Operating expenses			
Sales salaries expense			120,000
Advertising expense			15,000
Rent expense			40,000
Depreciation expense – Store equipment			10,000
Bad debts expense			9,000
Utilities expense			22,000
Insurance expense			15,000
General office expense			32,000
Total operating expenses			263,000
Income from operations			71,000
Interest revenue			10,000
Income before income taxes			81,000
Income tax expense			21,500
Net income			$ 59,500

This income statement is prepared for management use only. In all likelihood, the top management of the Borg Company would also want monthly or quarterly statements during the year on the profitability of the two departments and the company as a whole.

From an analysis of departmental gross profit it is possible to determine the gross profit rate. The gross profit rate is 40% for the Appliance Department ($216,000 ÷ $540,000) and 32.8% for the Clothing Department ($118,000 ÷

$360,000). Like the amount of gross profit, the gross profit rate may vary considerably between departments.

DEPARTMENTAL INCOME FROM OPERATIONS

In addition to showing departmental gross profit, income statements may show departmental income from operations. **Departmental income from operations is the difference between a department's net sales and the sum of its cost of goods sold and operating expenses.** It is more difficult to develop reliable data for determining departmental income from operations because subjective judgments are usually required in departmentalizing operating expenses.

In accounting for segments, operating expenses are classified into two categories:

Direct expenses, which relate specifically to one segment and are incurred for the sole benefit of that segment. Examples include salaries of employees who work only in one department and advertising expenses incurred by a department for its benefit.

Indirect expenses, which relate to the company as a whole and are incurred for the benefit of two or more segments. Examples include the salary of the store manager and advertising expenses incurred for the benefit of the entire store.

In distinguishing between these categories, it is helpful to recognize that direct expenses will be eliminated if the segment is discontinued. In contrast, indirect expenses will continue if only one of several segments is eliminated.

Direct expenses are assigned (charged) to the segment to which they pertain on the basis of the expenses incurred. Assignment of expenses is facilitated by maintaining separate ledger accounts for each segment's direct expenses. When a direct expense is incurred, the appropriate segment expense account is debited. If the Borg Company used this approach, two sales salary expense accounts would be required—one for each department. Alternatively, the departmentalizing of direct expenses could be deferred to the end of an accounting period. Under this approach, the Borg Company would charge both Appliance Department and Clothing Department sales salaries to Sales Salaries Expense when incurred. The balance in each direct expense account would then be assigned to the appropriate department at the end of the period on the basis of the expense incurred by that department.

In contrast, **indirect expenses are allocated to the segments on some type of equitable basis.** Typically, only one account is maintained for each indirect expense, such as Rent Expense, and this account is debited each time the expense is incurred. At the end of an accounting period, the balances in the expense accounts are allocated to the appropriate segments.

Allocation Guidelines

When indirect expenses are allocated, two basic principles should be kept in mind. **First, the allocation should approximate as closely as possible the benefit received by each segment.** This principle relates to the fairness or

equity of the allocation. For example, allocating the expense of the company cafeteria to each sales department on the basis of number of employees is generally considered a better basis than square feet of floor space in a department. **Second, the cost of allocating the expenses should not be greater than the usefulness of the segmented data.** This principle relates to a cost-benefit trade-off. To illustrate, the president's salary could be allocated among a company's departments on the basis of time spent with each department. However, it would be both costly and impractical to collect actual time data. Under the cost-benefit principle, simple allocation schemes based on readily available data may be preferable to complex schemes based on data that are costly to prepare.

The selection of the appropriate basis for allocating each indirect expense is an important top management policy decision. The decision will have a direct impact on the profitability of each segment. Consequently, the opinions of the segment managers should be obtained during the decision-making process. To enhance the comparability of the financial statements, the bases of allocation should be applied consistently from period to period.

Some companies use allocation groupings in allocating expenses. Instead of determining the appropriate allocation base for each expense, the expense is identified with an allocation group. Then the allocation base for the group is used in allocating the individual expenses within the group. The following schedule illustrates the types of allocation groupings and bases that may be used.

Allocation groupings and bases

Allocation Grouping	Allocation Base	Specific Expenses
Building occupancy expenses	Space (square footage) occupied by each department	Rent, depreciation, insurance, utilities, property taxes, and repairs
Central organization	Number of employees in department	Administrative and clerical salaries, telephone, office supplies, personnel department salaries, payroll department salaries
Selling expenses	Departmental sales or net sales	Freight-out, shipping department salaries, sales manager's salary
Buying expenses	Departmental purchases, net purchases, or cost of goods purchased	Freight-in, purchasing department salaries, receiving department salaries

Allocation groupings facilitate the allocation of indirect expenses to segments.

Assigning and Allocating Illustrated

To illustrate this task, we will continue to use the Borg Company. We will assume that no departmental expense accounts are maintained in the ledger; this means that each of the operating expenses shown in the income statement on page 837 must be assigned or allocated to the Appliance and Clothing departments at the end of the year. The expenses are discussed in the order in which they are listed in the income statement.

Sales Salaries Expense ($120,000). Sales salaries are considered a direct expense. Thus, the balance in Sales Salaries Expense is assigned to the two sales departments on the basis of the salaries incurred by each department. An analysis of payroll records shows that Appliance Department salaries were $70,000 and Clothing Department salaries were $50,000. The assignment of Sales Salaries Expense, therefore, is as follows:

Assigning sales salaries expense

Department	Assigned Direct Expense	Total Sales Salaries Expense
Appliance	$ 70,000	$ 70,000
Clothing	50,000	50,000
	$120,000	$120,000

Advertising Expense ($15,000). Newspaper advertising is done directly by each department, and radio and television commercials are made for the company as a whole. Thus, the balance in Advertising Expense of $15,000 consists of both direct and indirect expenses. An analysis of the newspaper advertising bills shows that $4,000 was spent by the Appliance Department and $2,000 by the Clothing Department. The cost of the radio and television commercials, $9,000, is allocated on the basis of departmental net sales. Since net sales are $540,000 and $360,000, respectively, total net sales are $900,000; the ratio is 60% for the Appliance Department ($540,000 ÷ $900,000) and 40% for the Clothing Department ($360,000 ÷ $900,000). The assignment and allocation of total advertising expense of $15,000 therefore are as follows:

Assigning and allocating advertising expense

Department	Assigned Direct Expense	Allocated Indirect Expense	Total Advertising Expense
Appliance	$4,000	60% × $9,000 = $5,400	$ 9,400
Clothing	2,000	40% × $9,000 = 3,600	5,600
	$6,000	$9,000	$15,000

Alternatively, indirect advertising expense could be allocated on the basis of the direct advertising expense incurred by each department.

Rent Expense ($40,000). Rent is an indirect expense that is grouped under building occupancy expense. The principal basis for allocating these expenses is the floor space occupied by each department. In the Borg Company, the square footage of space occupied by the Appliance and Clothing departments are 55,000 and 45,000, respectively. Since the total square footage is 100,000 (55,000 + 45,000), the ratio is 55% for the Appliance Department and 45% for the Clothing Department. Thus, the allocation of the $40,000 of rent expense is shown on the top of the next page.

When the square footage is not considered of equal value, adjustments should be made in the allocation base. For example, in retail stores, footage near the main entrance to the store usually is more valuable than footage at the rear of the store. Similarly, footage on the main floor may be more valuable than footage on other floors.

Department	Allocated Indirect Expense	Total Rent Expense
Appliance	55% × $40,000 = $22,000	$22,000
Clothing	45% × $40,000 = 18,000	18,000
	$40,000	$40,000

Allocating rent expense

Depreciation Expense—Store Equipment ($10,000). Depreciation on store equipment is a direct expense of the department that uses the equipment. Plant asset records show that the cost of store equipment is $30,000 in the Appliance Department and $70,000 in the Clothing Department. Equipment is depreciated at an annual rate of 10%. The assignment of depreciation expense is as follows:

Department	Assigned Direct Expense	Total Depreciation Expense
Appliance	10% × $30,000 = $ 3,000	$ 3,000
Clothing	10% × $70,000 = 7,000	7,000
	$10,000	$10,000

Assigning depreciation expense

Bad Debts Expense ($9,000). Borg Company uses the percentage of sales method for estimating bad debts expense. Thus, this expense is a direct expense that is assigned to each department on the basis of net sales. Since Bad Debts Expense is $9,000 and total net sales are $900,000, the bad debt percentage is 1% ($9,000 ÷ $900,000). Accordingly, the assignment of bad debts expense is as follows:

Department	Assigned Direct Expense	Total Bad Debts Expense
Appliance	1% × $540,000 = $5,400	$5,400
Clothing	1% × $360,000 = 3,600	3,600
	$9,000	$9,000

Assigning bad debts expense

Utilities Expense ($22,000). Expenses for heat, light, water, and power are indirect expenses within the building occupancy group. Thus, the balance of $22,000 is allocated on the basis used of floor space, or 55% to the Appliance Department and 45% to the Clothing Department. The allocation is:

Department	Allocated Indirect Expense	Total Utilities Expense
Appliance	55% × $22,000 = $12,100	$12,100
Clothing	45% × 22,000 = 9,900	9,900
	$22,000	$22,000

Allocating utilities expense

The use of square footage as the basis of allocation is based on the assumption that the benefit from energy costs is relatively uniform throughout the store. Adjustments in the base should be made when the benefit is not uniform.

Insurance Expense ($15,000). The Borg Company carries insurance on store equipment and merchandise inventory. Since these assets can be specifically identified with each department, insurance expense is a direct expense. These assets are insured for $300,000. Thus, the rate is 5 cents per dollar of insurance coverage ($15,000 ÷ $300,000). An analysis of the insurance policies shows that the insurable value of the store equipment and inventory in the two departments is Appliance, $180,000, and Clothing, $120,000. Thus, the assignment of insurance expense is as follows:

Assigning insurance expense

Department	Assigned Direct Expense	Total Insurance Expense
Appliance	5% × $180,000 = $ 9,000	$ 9,000
Clothing	5% × 120,000 = 6,000	6,000
	$15,000	$15,000

Insurance on a building is an indirect expense that should be allocated to departments on the basis of square footage of space occupied.

General Office Expense ($32,000). This group of indirect expenses consists of administrative expenses that are incurred for the benefit of all departments. Accordingly, the balance in this account must be allocated to the departments. The allocation is made on the basis of the number of employees in each department, which total 6 in Appliances and 4 in Clothing. Thus, the allocation is:

Allocating general office expense

Department	Allocated Indirect Expense	Total General Office Expense
Appliance	6/10 × $32,000 = $19,200	$19,200
Clothing	4/10 × 32,000 = 12,800	12,800
	$32,000	$32,000

Allocation on the basis of employees is appropriate when there is a correlation between the number of employees and the general office expenses incurred. This is often the case when the expenses relate to personnel and payroll department costs. Alternatively, allocation may be made on the basis of sales. This basis is justified on the premise that the higher the sales in a department, the greater the expense pertaining to that department. This is often the case when the expenses relate to recording sales invoices and handling collections from customers.

When the assignment and allocation of operating expenses have been completed, the results may be tabulated in a departmental operating expense summary, as shown on the top of the next page.

Departmental operating expense summary

BORG COMPANY
Departmental Expense Summary
For the Year Ended December 31, 1987

Type of Expense	Total Expense	Direct Expense Appliance	Direct Expense Clothing	Indirect Expense Appliance	Indirect Expense Clothing	Total Department Expense Appliance	Total Department Expense Clothing
Sales salaries	$120,000	$70,000	$50,000	$ -0-	$ -0-	$ 70,000	$ 50,000
Advertising	15,000	4,000	2,000	5,400	3,600	9,400	5,600
Rent	40,000	-0-	-0-	22,000	18,000	22,000	18,000
Depreciation	10,000	3,000	7,000	-0-	-0-	3,000	7,000
Bad debts	9,000	5,400	3,600	-0-	-0-	5,400	3,600
Utilities	22,000	-0-	-0-	12,100	9,900	12,100	9,900
Insurance	15,000	9,000	6,000	-0-	-0-	9,000	6,000
General office	32,000	-0-	-0-	19,200	12,800	19,200	12,800
Total	$263,000	$91,400	$68,600	$58,700	$44,300	$150,100	$112,900

Income Statement Illustrated

After all operating expenses have been assigned and allocated to departments, an income statement is prepared showing departmentalized income from operations. The statement for the Borg Company is shown below.

Income statement showing departmental income from operations

BORG COMPANY
Income Statement
For the Year Ended December 31, 1987

	Appliance Department	Clothing Department	Total
Sales	$540,000	$360,000	$900,000
Cost of goods sold	324,000	242,000	566,000
Gross profit	216,000	118,000	334,000
Operating expenses			
Sales salaries expense	70,000	50,000	120,000
Advertising expense	9,400	5,600	15,000
Rent expense	22,000	18,000	40,000
Depreciation expense — Store equipment	3,000	7,000	10,000
Bad debts expense	5,400	3,600	9,000
Utilities expense	12,100	9,900	22,000
Insurance expense	9,000	6,000	15,000
General office expense	19,200	12,800	32,000
Total operating expenses	150,100	112,900	263,000
Income from operations	**$ 65,900**	**$ 5,100**	71,000
Interest revenue			10,000
Income before income taxes			81,000
Income tax expense			21,500
Net income			$ 59,500

Note that departmental data are reported through income from operations, but the remaining items (interest revenue and income tax expense in this case) are not allocated to departments. In this statement, departmental costs of goods sold are reported on one line. If desired, the details of these amounts may be included in the statement.

Analysis of the statement shows that the return on sales based on income from operations is 12.2% ($65,900 ÷ $540,000) in the Appliance Department but only 1.4% ($5,100 ÷ $360,000) in the Clothing Department. As shown, the return on sales may vary considerably between departments.

DEPARTMENTAL MARGIN

The third approach to evaluating the profitability of a profit center is departmental margin. **Departmental margin is the excess of a department's net sales over the sum of its cost of goods sold and direct operating expenses.** Under this approach, indirect operating expenses are not allocated to departments.

Income statement showing departmental margin

BORG COMPANY
Income Statement
For the Year Ended December 31, 1987

	Appliance Department	Clothing Department	Total
Net sales	$540,000	$360,000	$900,000
Cost of goods sold	324,000	242,000	566,000
Gross profit	216,000	118,000	334,000
Direct operating expenses			
Sales salaries expense	70,000	50,000	120,000
Advertising expense	4,000	2,000	6,000
Depreciation expense—Store equipment	3,000	7,000	10,000
Bad debts expense	5,400	3,600	9,000
Insurance expense	9,000	6,000	15,000
Total direct operating expenses	91,400	68,600	160,000
Departmental margin	$124,600	$ 49,400	174,000
Indirect operating expenses			
Advertising expense			9,000
Rent expense			40,000
Utilities expense			22,000
General office expense			32,000
Total indirect operating expenses			103,000
Income from operations			71,000
Interest revenue			10,000
Income before income taxes			81,000
Income tax expense			21,500
Net income			$ 59,500

In our previous discussion, we determined that the Borg Company had the following direct expenses: sales salaries, advertising ($6,000 only), depreciation, bad debts, and insurance. From the assignment of these expenses to the Appliance and Clothing departments, the income statement on page 844 can be prepared. Note in the statement that the direct expenses are deducted from the gross profit in each department to arrive at departmental margin. Indirect expenses are charged to the company as a whole. Thus, they are subtracted from total departmental margin.

As shown, departmental margin may vary significantly among departments. From an analysis of the statement, it is also possible to compute a departmental margin rate by dividing departmental margin by net sales. In the Borg Company, the rates are 23.1% ($124,600 ÷ $540,000) in the Appliance Department and 13.7% ($49,400 ÷ $360,000) in the Clothing Department.

ASSESSMENT OF DEPARTMENTALIZED INCOME STATEMENTS

Three approaches for measuring the profitability of the Borg Company's departments have been explained and illustrated. The profit measures are summarized as follows:

Alternative profit measures

Profit Measures	Appliance Department	Clothing Department	From Income Statement
Departmental gross profit	$216,000	$118,000	page 837
Departmental income from operations	65,900	5,100	page 843
Departmental margin	124,600	49,400	page 844

Which of these profit measures is most appropriate for evaluating the profitability of departments?

Departmental gross profit is, at best, a partial or piecemeal measure because the department's operating expenses are excluded. Gross profit measures only the relationship between a department's net sales and cost of goods sold. Thus, it is an incomplete measure of a department's profitability. However, we should recognize that gross profit is an objective measure of a company's merchandising activities. A comparison of a department's gross profit with that of prior years may reveal a significant trend in the department's performance. Top management can also rank departments on the basis of their gross profit performance.

Departmental income from operations is the most complete measure because it includes all of the department's operating expenses. It also makes the department manager more aware of the total expenses involved in running the department. However, a major disadvantage of this approach is that allocation bases for indirect expenses are subjective and inequitable allocations may result.

For example, inequities may result when net sales are used as the basis for allocating indirect expenses. Assume that through your skill and hard work,

sales in your department increase by 20%. Because of your efforts, your department now must accept a higher proportion of any indirect expenses that are allocated on the basis of net sales. Furthermore, because the other departments' share of indirect expenses will decrease, the income from operations of other departments will increase because of your increase in sales! A further weakness of income from operations as a measure of profitability is that a department manager generally has no control over the incurrence of an indirect expense. **Department managers normally prefer a profit measure that is based on expenses they are in a position to control.**

Departmental margin has two major advantages as a measure of profitability: (1) it includes only operating expenses that the department manager has incurred directly, and (2) it excludes the effects of allocated indirect expenses. For these reasons, **departmental margin is generally considered the most useful measure for evaluating the profitability of a department.**

EVALUATION OF INVESTMENT CENTERS

Each of the profitability measures described above for a profit center can also be used to evaluate the profitability of investment centers. However, these measures may not provide a sufficient basis to determine which of several segments is most profitable. For example, assume the following operating data for three K mart stores in your area.

Assumed operating data

Operating Data	East Store	North Store	South Store
Sales	$800,000	$700,000	$600,000
Gross profit	240,000	245,000	230,000
Income from operations	130,000	125,000	120,000
Departmental margin	140,000	138,000	144,000

The profitability rankings of the stores are as follows:

Profitability rankings

Profitability Measure	East Store	North Store	South Store
Gross profit	2	**1**	3
Income from operations	**1**	2	3
Departmental margin	2	3	**1**

From these rankings, there may be some uncertainty as to which store is the most profitable. If gross profit is used, the North Store is the most profitable; if income from operations is used, the East Store is the most profitable; and if departmental margin is used, the South Store is the most profitable.

What is missing from this analysis is a determination of how efficiently each store is utilizing its operating assets to accomplish its results. For example, if the East Store used the most assets to generate its income from operations, is it the most profitable? To answer this question, it is necessary to relate profitability to the asset (or investment) base of the store. This is accomplished by computing the store's return on investment.

RETURN ON INVESTMENT (ROI)

As indicated earlier, an important characteristic of an investment center is that it has control over the investment funds available for use. Thus, the evaluation of the profitability of an investment center is oriented toward its **return on investment.** This basis of analysis is very similar to the return on assets formula used in Chapter 20 in evaluating the profitability of different companies. The formula for computing return on investment in segment analysis is:

$$\text{Income from Operations} \div \text{Average Operating Assets} = \text{Return on Investment}$$

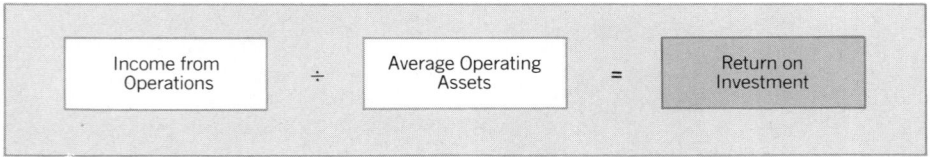

Operating assets consist of current assets and plant assets used in operations by the segment. Nonoperating assets such as idle plant assets and land held for future use of the segment are excluded. Average operating assets is usually based on the beginning and ending **recorded book values** of the assets.

To illustrate the computation of ROI, assume that the three K mart stores have the following average operating assets: East $1,000,000, North $500,000, and South $800,000. The computations are:

ROI computations

Store	Computation		Return on Investment
East	$\frac{\$\ 130{,}000}{\$1{,}000{,}000}$	=	13%
North	$\frac{\$\ 125{,}000}{\$\ 500{,}000}$	=	25%
South	$\frac{\$\ 120{,}000}{\$\ 800{,}000}$	=	15%

These results indicate that the North Store was the most efficient in using operating assets under its control. After considering its other profit performance rankings, many would now conclude that the North Store is the most profitable.

ROI—Expanded Formula

In using ROI, managers quickly realized that ROI can also be derived by considering two separate but interrelated financial relationships: (1) the profit margin earned on sales, and (2) the number of times operating assets are turned over during the period.[3] The formula for computing ROI under this approach is:

[3]This approach, pioneered by the DuPont Company, is widely used in evaluating investment centers.

$$\text{Profit Margin} \times \text{Asset Turnover} = \text{Return on Investment}$$

where:

$$\text{(1) Profit margin} = \frac{\text{Income from Operations}}{\text{Sales}}$$

$$\text{(2) Asset turnover} = \frac{\text{Sales}}{\text{Average Operating Assets}}.$$

Thus, the expanded formula for ROI is:

$$\frac{\text{Income from Operations}}{\text{Sales}} \times \frac{\text{Sales}}{\text{Average Operating Assets}} = \text{Return on Investment}$$

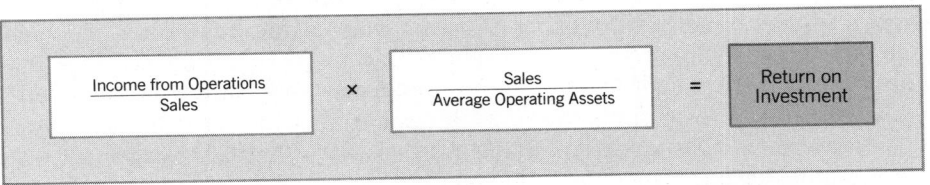

From the expanded formula, you can see that a high profit margin and a high asset turnover will, of course, produce a high ROI. It is also possible to achieve a satisfactory ROI when a low profit margin occurs with a high turnover rate and vice versa. For example, a grocery chain such as Safeway normally has a low profit margin but a high turnover rate. In contrast, a jewelry store such as Cartier normally has a high profit margin but a low turnover rate.

Controlling ROI

The manager of a segment can improve ROI by (1) increasing sales, (2) reducing operating expenses, or (3) reducing operating assets. To illustrate, we will use the data for K mart's East Store, which has an ROI of 13% (income from operations, $130,000, and average net operating assets $1,000,000).

(1) **Sales are increased by $100,000.** An increase in sales can increase ROI by increasing income from operations and by increasing asset turnover. In the East Store, we will assume that the $100,000 increase in sales results in a $30,000 increase in income from operations. Thus, sales become $900,000 ($800,000 + $100,000) and income from operations is $160,000 ($130,000 + $30,000). ROI increases to 16%, computed as follows:

ROI computation—sales increase

$$\frac{\$160{,}000}{\$900{,}000} \times \frac{\$\ 900{,}000}{\$1{,}000{,}000} = 16\%.$$

An increase in sales is beneficial both to the segment and to the company if it results from new business. It would not be beneficial to the company as a whole if the increase in the East Store was achieved at the expense of the North Store and South Store.

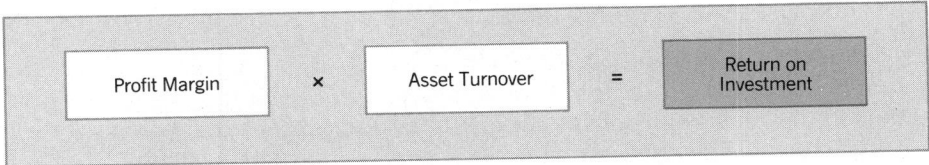

(2) **Operating expenses are decreased $100,000.** A $100,000 reduction in operating expenses results in a corresponding increase in income from operations. Thus, income from operations is $230,000 ($130,000 + $100,000), and ROI becomes 23%, as shown by the following:

$$\frac{\$230{,}000}{\$800{,}000} \times \frac{\$\ 800{,}000}{\$1{,}000{,}000} = 23\%.$$

ROI computation—operating expense decrease

This course of action is clearly beneficial when "fat," waste, and inefficiencies are eliminated. However, a reduction in needed maintenance or other vital expenses for the sake of an immediate increase in ROI is not likely to be acceptable to top management.

(3) **Average operating assets are decreased $100,000.** This change causes operating assets to be $900,000 ($1,000,000 − 100,000). Thus, ROI becomes 14.4%, as computed below:

$$\frac{\$130{,}000}{\$800{,}000} \times \frac{\$800{,}000}{\$900{,}000} = 14.4\%.$$

ROI computation—average operating assets decrease

Like decreases in operating expenses, reductions in operating assets may or may not be prudent. It is beneficial to eliminate overinvestment in inventories and to dispose of excessive plant assets. However, it is unwise to reduce inventory below current market needs or to dispose of essential plant assets.

Judgmental Factors in ROI

The return on investment approach includes a number of judgemental factors. Some of these are:

1. **Operating asset allocation.** Operating assets include joint warehouse and computer facilities and buildings that house more than one segment. Thus, questions arise as to the proper allocation of assets to segments.
2. **Income measure selection.** Some believe that departmental margin, and not departmental income from operations, should be used.
3. **Investment base selection.** Some believe that average total assets or average net assets, and not average operating assets, should be used.

It follows that care should be taken in interpreting the return on investment. For example, the ratio can be improved by simply decreasing the investment base. To illustrate, assume that a department generates $60,000 operating income on an asset base of $300,000 for a return on investment of 20% ($60,000 ÷ $300,000). If the department manager disposes of $50,000 of assets, the return on investment increases to 24% ($60,000/$250,000). In the short run, it may be possible to maintain the $60,000 level of income, but in the long run, the department's ability to generate income may be impaired by the disposal of critical assets.

RESIDUAL INCOME

Another approach to measuring the profitability of an investment center is to use residual income. **Residual income** is income from operations that is above a center's minimum required rate of return on average operating assets. Under this approach, the objective is to maximize the amount of residual income rather than to maximize ROI.

To illustrate the residual income approach, consider the following data for the Aero Division of the Whitney Company: (1) average operating assets, $200,000, (2) income from operations, $40,000, and (3) minimum required ROI is 15%. Residual income is $10,000, as shown below:

Computations of residual income

Aero Division	
Average operating assets	$200,000
Income from operations	40,000
Minimum required rate of return ($200,000 × 15%)	30,000
Residual income	**$ 10,000**

Many managers believe residual income is a better measure of profitability than return on investment, because it is more compatible with the overall profit objectives of a company. To illustrate, assume that the manager of the Aero Division has an opportunity to make an investment that will increase average operating assets by $50,000. It is expected that the assets will earn $8,750. Thus, a 17.5% ROI ($8,750 ÷ $50,000) will be achieved. Under the ROI approach, the manager will be reluctant to accept any new project that offers an ROI less than the rate currently being earned in the division. In this case, the new project's 17.5% ROI is less than the current ROI of 20% ($40,000 ÷ $200,000). If the project is accepted, the Aero Division's ROI will be reduced to 19.5%, as shown below.

Effects on ROI

ROI Approach

	Current	New Investment	Total
Average operating assets (a)	$200,000	$50,000	$250,000
Income from operations (b)	$ 40,000	$ 8,750	$ 48,750
ROI, (b) ÷ (a)	20.0%	17.5%	**19.5%**

By contrast, under the residual income approach, the division manager will accept the investment opportunity. The project's ROI of 17.5% is higher than the Aero Division's minimum required ROI of 15%. Thus, the division's residual income will be increased by $1,250, as shown on the next page. The acceptance of the investment opportunity under the residual income approach will be beneficial for both the division and the Whitney Company.

Residual Income Approach

	Current	New Investment	Total
Average operating assets	$200,000	$50,000	$250,000
Income from operations	$ 40,000	$ 8,750	$ 48,750
Minimum required ROI:			
$200,000 × 15%	30,000		30,000
$50,000 × 15%		7,500	7,500
Residual income	$ 10,000	**$ 1,250**	$ 11,250

Effects on residual income

SUMMARY OF STUDY OBJECTIVES

1. The distinguishing features of managerial accounting are:
Primary users of reports—internal users who are officers, department heads, managers, and supervisors in the company.
Type and frequency of reports—internal reports that are issued as frequently as the need arises.
Purpose of reports—to provide special-purpose information for a particular user for a specific decision.
Content of reports—pertains to subunits of the entity and may be very detailed; may extend beyond double-entry accounting systems; the reporting standard is relevance to the decision being made.

2. A segment is any subunit or activity of an organization for which management information is desired. The principal types of segments are cost centers, profit centers, and investment centers.

3. The profitability of profit centers may be evaluated on the basis of (a) departmental gross profit, which is the difference between a department's net sales and cost of goods sold, (b) departmental income from operations, which is the difference between a department's net sales and the sum of its cost of goods sold and operating expenses, and (c) departmental margin, which is the difference between a department's net sales and the sum of its cost of goods sold and direct operating expenses.

4. Direct expenses relate specifically to one segment and are incurred for the sole benefit of that segment. Indirect expenses relate to the company as a whole and are incurred for the benefit of two or more segments. The two guidelines for allocating indirect expenses are that (a) the allocation should approximate the benefit received by the segment, and (b) the cost of allocating should not be greater than the usefulness of the segmented data.

5. Departmental gross profit is only a partial measure of a department's profitability. Departmental income from operations is the most

complete measure of profitability. The major disadvantage of this method is that allocation bases for indirect expenses are subjective and inequitable allocations may result. Departmental margin is generally considered the most useful measure of profitability because only operating expenses directly incurred are included and the effects of allocated indirect expenses are excluded.

6. The profitability of investment centers may be evaluated through either a return on investment (ROI) or residual income approach. Under ROI, the objective is to maximize the rate of return on average operating assets. Under residual income, the objective is to maximize the income from operations above the segment's minimum required rate of return on average operating assets.

GLOSSARY

Asset turnover, p. 848
Cost center, p. 835
Departmental gross profit, p. 836
Departmental income from operations, p. 838
Departmental margin, p. 844
Direct expenses, p. 838
Indirect expenses, p. 838
Investment center, p. 835
Managerial accounting, p. 830
Operating assets, p. 847
Profit center, p. 835
Profit margin, p. 848
Residual income, p. 850
Return on investment, p. 847
Segment, p. 833

DEMONSTRATION PROBLEM

Fellers Furniture Company has three stores in Ingham county: Longbrook, Riverside, and Lakeshore. During the month of May, the stores report the following operating data:

	Longbrook	Riverside	Lakeshore
Sales	$900,000	$820,000	$700,000
Gross profit rate	32%	30%	33%
Direct operating expenses	145,000	114,000	86,000
Allocated indirect operating expenses	68,000	55,000	75,000
Average operating assets	600,000	580,000	500,000

INSTRUCTIONS

For each store determine its gross profit, departmental margin, income from operations, and return on investment.

SOLUTION TO DEMONSTRATION PROBLEM

	Longbrook	Riverside	Lakeshore
Sales	$900,000	$820,000	$700,000
Cost of goods sold	612,000	574,000	469,000
Gross profit	288,000 (32%)	246,000 (30%)	231,000 (33%)
Direct operating expenses	145,000	114,000	86,000
Departmental margin	143,000	132,000	145,000
Indirect operating expenses	68,000	55,000	75,000
Income from operations	$ 75,000	$ 77,000	$ 70,000
Return on investment	12.5%	13.3%	14%
	($75,000 ÷ $600,000)	($77,000 ÷ $580,000)	($70,000 ÷ $500,000)

QUESTIONS

1. Managerial accounting provides accounting information for managers of manufacturing corporations. Is this an accurate description of managerial accounting? Explain.

2. Carl Carson believes that the only similarity between managerial accounting and financial accounting is that they both deal with economic events of an enterprise. Is Carl correct? Discuss.

3. Contrast the type and frequency of reports prepared by managerial accountants and financial accountants.

4. How do reports prepared in managerial accounting differ as to purpose and content from reports prepared in financial accounting?

5. Dawn Davis is studying for the next accounting midterm examination. Summarize for Dawn what she should know about management functions.

6. Decision making is management's most important function. Do you agree? Why or why not?

7. A segment is the same as a department. Is this true? Explain.

8. What are the primary reasons for segmenting business operations?

9. Identify and distinguish the responsibility centers that can be used in classifying segments.

10. Pat Putnam understands how segment data may be helpful to top management in its directing and controlling functions. Explain to Pat how segment data are also useful in the management planning and organizing functions.

11. What approaches may be used in evaluating the profitability of a profit center?

12. Mike Mead is uncertain about the difference between direct and indirect expenses in accounting for segments. Explain the difference to Mike.

13. What criteria should be used in allocating indirect expenses?

14. How is an indirect expense allocated when allocation groupings are used?

15. In the Metro Tire and Muffler Company, total advertising expense is $22,000. Of this sum, $9,000 is incurred directly by the Tire Department and $7,000 by the Muffler Department. The remainder is allocated on the basis of net sales which are $600,000 for tires and $300,000 for mufflers. What is the total advertising expense for each department in determining (a) departmental margin, and (b) departmental income from operations?

16. Wendy Weller believes that the most complete measure of profitability for a segment is the best method for reporting segment results. Do you agree? Explain.

17. The profitability of an investment center should not be based entirely on income statement data. Is this correct? Why?

18. State the formula for computing return on investment.

19. If profit margin, sales, and investment are considered, what is the expanded formula for computing return on investment?

20. What changes may improve the return on investment of a segment?

21. Define the term, residual income. Why may this measure of profitability be better than return on investment?

22. In the Rene Company the average operating assets of a division are $500,000 and the minimum required rate of return is 18%. If income from operations is $96,000, what is the amount of residual income?

EXERCISES

E21-1 The Faulk Grocery is organized into three departments: Grocery, Produce, and Dairy. During the first quarter of 1987, total sales were $260,000. An analysis of cash register tapes reveals the following departmental sales data: grocery 60%, produce 15% and dairy 25%. The gross profit rates for the departments are: grocery 15%, produce 20%, and dairy 25%.

INSTRUCTIONS

Prepare a departmental income statement through gross profit for the first quarter.

E21-2 The Birch Lumber Company is organized into three departments: lumber, supplies, and equipment. Condensed operating data for the year ending September 30, 1987 are as follows:

	Lumber	Supplies	Equipment
Net sales	$700,000	$500,000	$300,000
Gross profit rate	30%	25%	40%
Direct expenses (as a percentage of sales)	15%	20%	17%
Indirect expenses (as a percentage of sales)	8%	10%	12%

INSTRUCTIONS

(a) Prepare an income statement for the year showing departmental data through gross profit.

(b) Prepare an income statement for the year showing departmental data through departmental margin.

(c) Prepare an income statement for the year showing departmental data through income from operations.

E21-3 Big Jim's Appliance Center has three departments: Major Appliances (such as washers, dryers, refrigerators and freezers), Minor Appliances (such as toasters, blenders, kitchen-aids, and can openers), and Television. During the year ended December 31, 1987, the company incurred the following indirect department expenses:

1. Rent	$36,000	5. Delivery	$15,000
2. Utilities	24,000	6. Warehouse	30,000
3. Office supplies	8,000	7. Freight-in	12,000
4. Administrative salaries	30,000	8. Purchasing	20,000

The allocation bases for the expenses are as follows:

Expenses	Allocation Base	Major Appliances	Minor Appliances	Television
(1) & (2)	Square footage	1,500	1,000	1,500
(3) & (4)	Number of employees	9	6	5
(5) & (6)	Net sales	$800,000	$200,000	$500,000
(7) & (8)	Cost of goods purchased	$600,000	$100,000	$300,000

INSTRUCTIONS

Prepare a schedule showing the allocation of the indirect expenses to the three departments.

E21-4 The Vanity Fair Department Store has five departments. Comparative data for the departments are as follows:

	Departments				
Departmental Item	1	2	3	4	5
Sales	$600,000	$450,000	$500,000	$400,000	$425,000
Gross profit	(a)	153,000	(e)	140,000	145,000
Direct expenses	71,000	(c)	68,000	66,000	(i)
Margin	109,000	98,000	(f)	(g)	75,000
Indirect expenses	48,000	(d)	45,000	30,000	(j)
Income from operations	(b)	65,000	47,000	(h)	41,000

INSTRUCTIONS

Compute the missing amounts. Show computations.

E21-5 The shoe department of the Helene Company reported the following results for the current year.

Sales	$ 800,000
Cost of goods sold	600,000
Operating expenses	100,000
Average department operating assets	1,000,000

The management of the Helene Company is unhappy with the department's return on investment (ROI). Management is considering the following independent actions to improve ROI:

1. Increase selling prices by 10% with no change in volume, costs, and operating expenses.
2. Reduce operating expenses by 10% with no change in sales or cost of goods sold.
3. Reduce operating assets by 10% with no change in income from operations.

INSTRUCTIONS (Round to one decimal.)

(a) Compute the return on investment (ROI) for the current year.

(b) Compute the ROI under each of the proposed independent courses of actions.

E21-6 The Quicko Company operates three fast-food restaurants in the city. Operating results and other data for the restaurants are as follows.

	Central	Eastgate	Westgate
Sales	$900,000	$600,000	$750,000
Gross profit	252,000	186,000	240,000
Income from operations	120,000	102,000	117,000
Average operating assets	800,000	850,000	900,000

INSTRUCTIONS

(a) Compute the return on investment (ROI) for each restaurant.

(b) Compute the gross profit rate for each restaurant.

E21-7 Comparative data for the following divisions of the Lisa Bonder Company are given below.

	North	South	East	West
Sales	$1,200,000	(d)	(g)	$600,000
Income from operations	(a)	(e)	76,500	54,000
Average operating assets	(b)	900,000	750,000	(j)
Profit margin on sales	12%	10%	(h)	(k)
Asset turnover	1.5	(f)	1.2	(l)
Return on investment (ROI)	(c)	8%	(i)	18%

INSTRUCTIONS

Compute the missing amounts. (Round to one decimal.)

E21-8 Revlon Inc. reports financial data for two industry segments. Data for a recent three-year period are as follows. (All data are in millions of dollars.)

	1987	1986	1985
Sales:			
Beauty products	$1,116	$1,160	$1,253
Health products and services	1,263	1,191	1,113
Income from operations			
Beauty products	112	125	208
Health products and services	188	161	152
Operating assets			
Beauty products	844	951	975
Health products and services	1,053	1,054	998

INSTRUCTIONS

(a) Compute for each segment the following ratios for 1987 and 1986: (1) margin on sales, (2) asset turnover, and (3) return on investment. (Round to one decimal.)

(b) Comment on the profitability of the segments.

E21-9 The McNair Company has two divisions: Retail and Wholesale. Selected data for the departments are as follows:

	Retail	Wholesale
Sales	$4,000,000	$3,200,000
Income from operations	280,000	256,000
Average operating assets	2,000,000	1,280,000
Minimum required rate of return	16%	16%

McNair has an opportunity for an additional investment that will require average operating assets of $750,000. The additional investment is expected to produce sales of $1,200,000 and income from operations of $127,500.

INSTRUCTIONS

(a) Compute the return on investment for (1) the two divisions, and (2) the additional investment.

(b) If return on investment is used by each division manager in deciding whether to accept the new investment, what are the likely decisions?

(c) If residual income is used for the decision, what is the likely decision of each manager? Why?

PROBLEMS

P21-1 Betty Blair, a retired tennis professional, owns and operates the B&B Sports Shop as a corporation. The store is organized into two departments: Clothing and Equipment. Through the use of electronic point-of-sale cash registers, the following departmental data are obtained for the year 1987.

	Clothing	Equipment
Sales	$450,000	$320,000
Cost of goods sold	350,000	200,000

The adjusted trial balance at December 31, 1987 shows the following expenses.

Store salaries	$80,000	Utilities	$18,000
Advertising	12,000	Insurance	6,000
Rent	24,000	Administrative	9,000
Depreciation — store equipment	12,000		

Store salaries, depreciation, and insurance are considered direct expenses of the departments. Analysis shows that 60% of each expense was incurred by the Clothing Department and 40% by the Equipment Department.

Indirect expenses are to be allocated on the following bases:

Indirect Expense	Basis
Advertising	Newspaper space: 35% Clothing; 65% Equipment
Rent and utilities	Floor space: 2,400 square feet, Clothing; 1,600 square feet, Equipment
Administrative	Full-time employees: 4 Clothing; 2 Equipment

During the year, B&B Sports Shop earned interest revenue of $2,000. Income taxes are expected to be 25%. Income taxes are not allocated to departments.

INSTRUCTIONS

(a) Prepare a departmental expense summary for the year.

(b) Prepare an income statement for the year showing departmental margin.

(c) Prepare an income statement for the year showing departmental income from operations.

(d) Contrast the results of the two profitability measures.

P21-2 The Campus Bookstore is organized into four departments: Textbooks, Other Books, Supplies, and Souvenirs. For the year ending June 30, 1987, the company accountant has accumulated the following departmental data:

Departmental Item	Textbooks	Other Books	Supplies	Souvenirs
Net sales	$900,000	$300,000	$200,000	$80,000
Gross profit	315,000	120,000	50,000	20,000
Margin	135,000	54,000	24,000	8,000
Income from operations	72,000	30,000	14,000	4,000

Direct expenses consist of salaries, advertising, and depreciation. The percentage of each expense to total direct expenses for the department are as follows:

Departmental Item	Textbooks	Other Books	Supplies	Souvenirs
Salaries	50%	60%	50%	60%
Advertising	30	25	20	20
Depreciation	20	15	30	20
	100%	100%	100%	100%

Indirect expenses and their percentage relationships to total department indirect expenses are: advertising 10%, utilities 20%, rent 30%, janitorial 10%, supervision 20%, and administrative 10%.

During the year, Campus Bookstore earned $2,000 of interest revenue. Corporation income taxes are expected to be 30% of income before income taxes. Income taxes are not allocated to departments.

INSTRUCTIONS

(a) Prepare the income statement for the year showing departmental margin.

(b) Prepare the income statement for the year showing departmental income from operations.

(c) Which department is earning the highest and the lowest (1) gross profit rate, (2) departmental margin rate, and (3) income from operations rate?

P21-3 Milan Hardware has three stores in the city of Troy. Data for the stores are as follows:

	Midtown	Suburbia	Plaza
Sales	$1,200,000	$1,400,000	$ 900,000
Gross profit	300,000	280,000	288,000
Departmental margin	180,000	185,000	176,000
Income from operations	140,000	154,000	138,000
Average operating assets	1,200,000	1,100,000	1,000,000

INSTRUCTIONS

(Round all computations to one decimal.)

(a) Rank the profitability of the stores in three categories: gross profit, departmental margin, and income from operations. Use dollar amounts, not percentages.

(b) Compute the return on investment (ROI) for each store. (Round to one decimal.)

(c) Using the data in (a) and (b), comment on the profitability of the stores.

(d) Compute the new ROI for each store, assuming the following changes:

1. Midtown increases selling prices by 10% with no change in volume, cost of goods sold, and operating expenses.
2. Suburbia reduces its direct operating expenses 10% with no effect on sales or cost of goods sold.
3. Plaza reduces its average operating assets by 10% with no effect on net income.

P21-4 Jennifer Kidon, the controller for the Hoffman Furniture Store, returned from her vacation on January 15, 1988 and found the following income statement on her desk. The company's bookkeeper prepared the income statement by distributing all operating expenses on the basis of net sales.

HOFFMAN FURNITURE STORE
Income Statement
For the Year Ended December 31, 1987

	Accessories	Furniture	Total
Sales (net)	$240,000	$480,000	$720,000
Cost of goods sold	170,000	310,000	480,000
Gross profit	70,000	170,000	240,000
Operating expenses			
Rent	4,000	8,000	12,000
Administrative salaries	13,500	27,000	40,500
Sales salaries and commissions	30,000	60,000	90,000
Bad debts expense	2,400	4,800	7,200
Advertising	6,600	13,200	19,800
Insurance	600	1,200	1,800
Property taxes	800	1,600	2,400
Utilities	8,000	16,000	24,000
General office	6,000	12,000	18,000
Total expenses	71,900	143,800	215,700
Income from operations	$ (1,900)	$ 26,200	24,300
Interest revenue			5,700
Income before income taxes			30,000
Income tax expense (30%)			9,000
Net income			$ 21,000

The president is very unhappy with the performance of the Accessories Department and has called a meeting for tomorrow morning. Jennifer must prepare a corrected

income statement before the meeting and has requested your help. The following data are available for use in completing this task.

1. The Accessories Department occupies 30% of the 10,000 square feet of floor space available to the Hoffman Furniture Store. The Furniture Department occupies the remainder.
2. The manager of the Accessories Department receives a $14,000 salary, and the manager of the Furniture Department receives a $26,500 salary.
3. There are two salespersons in the Accessories Department and five in the Furniture Department. Each receives a monthly salary of $780 and commissions of 3.4% on sales.
4. Advertising space consists of $1,000 incurred directly by the Furniture Department and $680 incurred directly by the Accessories Department. The remainder is allocated on the basis of net sales.
5. Insurance and property taxes are based on the physical inventory on April 1, which was $30,000 in Accessories and $120,000 in Furniture.
6. Utilities are allocated on the basis of floor space. General office expenses are allocated on the basis of the number of salespersons in each department.

INSTRUCTIONS

(a) Prepare a departmental expense summary for the year.
(b) Prepare an income statement showing departmental income from operations, assuming income tax expense is not allocated to the departments.
(c) Prepare an income statement showing departmental margin.
(d) Comment on the profitability of the two departments.

P21–5 General Foods operates through the following segments:

Packaged grocery products which includes cereals, Jell-O products, Kool-Aid soft drinks, and Entenmann's bakery products.

Grocery coffee which includes Maxwell House brand, Yuban, and Brim.

Processed meats which includes Oscar Mayer meats and Louis Rich turkey luncheon meats.

Food service and other which includes the Food Service Products Oscar Mayer Food Service Divisions, Maxpax beverage vending service, and Oroweat.

Selected segment data for General Foods Corporation for a recent three-year period are as follows. (All data are in millions of dollars):

	1985	1984	1983
Net sales			
Packaged grocery products	$3,798	$3,788	$3,376
Grocery coffee	2,536	2,300	2,287
Processed meats	1,608	1,533	1,564
Food service and other	1,081	979	1,030
Income from operations			
Packaged grocery products	419	471	427
Grocery coffee	127	108	131
Processed meats	104	97	90
Food service and other	51	40	38

	1985	1984	1983
Operating assets			
Packaged grocery products	2,023	1,984	1,929
Grocery coffee	919	876	854
Processed meats	583	577	581
Food service and other	458	443	436

In 1982, operating assets were: Packaged grocery products $1,469, Grocery coffee $962, Processed meats $616, and Food services and other $443.

INSTRUCTIONS

(a) Rank the segments in each year as to (1) net sales and (2) income from operations.

(b) Determine for each year each segments (1) profit margin on sales, (2) assets turnover, and (3) return on investment. (Round to one decimal.)

(c) Rank the segments in each of the categories in (b) above for each year.

(d) Comment on the relative profitability of the segments.

ALTERNATE PROBLEMS

P21-1A Debbie Donley, a retired golf professional, owns and operates the D&D Sports Shop as a corporation. The store is organized into two departments: Clothing and Equipment. Through the use of electronic point-of-sale cash registers, the following departmental data are obtained for the year 1987.

	Clothing	Equipment
Sales	$480,000	$520,000
Cost of goods sold	360,000	300,000

The adjusted trial balance at December 31, 1987 shows the following operating expenses.

Store salaries	$90,000	Utilities	$21,000
Advertising	15,000	Insurance	5,000
Rent	30,000	General office	8,000
Depreciation—store equipment	18,000		

Store salaries, depreciation, and insurance are considered direct expenses of the departments. Analysis shows that 40% of each expense was incurred by the Clothing Department and 60% by the Equipment Department.

Indirect expenses are to be allocated on the following bases:

Indirect Expense	Basis
Advertising	Newspaper space: 30% Clothing; 70% Equipment
Rent and utilities	Floor space: 2,400 square feet, Clothing; 2,600 square feet, Equipment
General office	Full-time employees: 3 Clothing; 5 Equipment

D&D Sports Shop incurred $3,000 of interest expense in 1987. The income tax rate is expected to be 25%. Income taxes are not allocated to departments.

INSTRUCTIONS

(a) Prepare a departmental expense summary for the year.

(b) Prepare an income statement for the year showing departmental margin.

(c) Prepare an income statement for the year showing departmental income from operations.

(d) Contrast the results of the two profitability measures.

P21-2A The University Bookstore is organized into four departments: Textbooks, Other Books, Supplies, and Souvenirs. For the year ending June 30, 1987, the company accountant has accumulated the following departmental data:

Departmental Item	Textbooks	Other Books	Supplies	Souvenirs
Net sales	$800,000	$200,000	$150,000	$50,000
Gross profit	280,000	80,000	32,000	12,000
Margin	120,000	38,000	18,000	5,000
Income from Operations	64,000	18,000	9,000	3,000

Direct expenses consist of salaries, advertising, and depreciation. The percentage of each expense to total direct expenses for the department are as follows:

Departmental Item	Textbooks	Other Books	Supplies	Souvenirs
Salaries	60%	60%	50%	80%
Advertising	30	20	25	10
Depreciation	10	20	25	10
	100%	100%	100%	100%

Indirect expenses and their percentage relationships to total department indirect expenses are: advertising 10%, utilities 20%, rent 30%, janitorial 10%, supervision 20%, and general administrative 10%.

During the year, University Bookstore incurred $2,000 of interest expense. Corporation income taxes are expected to be 30% of income before income taxes. Income taxes are not allocated to departments.

INSTRUCTIONS

(a) Prepare the income statement for the year showing departmental margin.

(b) Prepare the income statement for the year showing departmental income from operations.

(c) Which department is earning the highest and the lowest (1) gross profit rate, (2) departmental margin rate, and (3) income from operations rate?

P21-3A Maine Hardware has three stores in the city of York. Data for the stores are as follows:

	Midtown	Suburbia	Plaza
Sales	$1,400,000	$1,600,000	$1,000,000
Gross profit	350,000	320,000	300,000
Departmental margin	260,000	270,000	265,000
Income from operations	180,000	176,000	140,000
Average operating assets	1,500,000	1,200,000	1,000,000

INSTRUCTIONS

(Round all computations to nearest dollar.)

(a) Rank the profitability of the stores in three categories: gross profit, departmental margin, and income from operations. Use dollar amounts, not percentages.

(b) Compute the return on investment (ROI) for each store. (Round to one decimal.)

(c) Using the data in (a) and (b), comment on the profitability of the stores.

(d) Compute the new ROI for each store, assuming the following changes:

1. Midtown increases selling prices by 15% with no change in volume, cost of goods sold, and operating expenses.
2. Suburbia reduces its direct operating expenses 12% with no effect on sales or cost of goods sold.
3. Plaza reduces its average operating assets by 11% with no effect on net income.

P21-4A Jackie Karcher, the controller for the Faber Fashion Store, returned from a skiing holiday on January 15, 1988 and found the following income statement on her desk. The company's bookkeeper prepared the income statement by distributing all expenses on the basis of net sales.

FABER FASHION STORE
Income Statement
For the Year Ended December 31, 1987

	Accessories	Clothes	Total
Sales (net)	$160,000	$640,000	$800,000
Cost of goods sold	120,000	400,000	520,000
Gross profit	40,000	240,000	280,000
Operating expenses			
Rent	3,000	12,000	15,000
Administrative salaries	9,600	38,400	48,000
Sales salaries and commissions	20,160	80,640	100,800
Bad debts expense	1,600	6,400	8,000
Advertising	4,200	16,800	21,000
Insurance	600	2,400	3,000
Property taxes	640	2,560	3,200
Other expenses	8,800	35,200	44,000
Total expenses	48,600	194,400	243,000
Income from operations	$ (8,600)	$ 45,600	37,000
Interest revenue			5,000
Income before income taxes			42,000
Income tax expense (30%)			12,600
Net income			$ 29,400

Because the president is dissatisfied with the performance of the Accessories Department, she has called a meeting for tomorrow morning. Jackie must prepare a corrected income statement before the meeting and has requested your help. The following data are available for use in completing this task.

1. The Accessories Department occupies 30% of the 10,000 square feet of floor space available to the store. The Clothes Department occupies the remainder.
2. The manager of the Accessories Department receives a $12,000 salary; the manager of the Clothes Department receives a $36,000 salary.
3. There is one salesperson in the Accessories Department and seven in the Clothes Department. Each receives a monthly salary of $800 and commissions of 3% on sales.
4. Advertising space in the local newspaper is 10% for Accessories and 90% for Clothes.

5. Insurance and property taxes are based on the physical inventory on April 1, which was $20,000 in Accessories and $180,000 in Clothes.
6. Other expenses include a variety of general office expenses. It has been agreed to allocate these expenses on the basis of the number of salespersons in each department.

INSTRUCTIONS

(a) Prepare a departmental expense summary for the year.
(b) Prepare an income statement showing departmental income from operations, assuming income tax expense is not allocated to the departments.
(c) Prepare an income statement showing departmental margin.
(d) Comment on the profitability of the two departments.

P21-5A General Mills operates through the following segments:

Consumer foods which include Big G cereals, Betty Crocker products, snack foods, seafood, and yogurt.

Restaurants which include Red Lobster, Olive Gardens, York Steakhouses, and Leeinn Chins.

Specialty retailing which includes Talbots, Eddie Bauer, and Pennsylvania House.

Selected segment data for a recent four year period are as follows: (All data are in millions of dollars)

	1986	1985	1984	1983
Net sales				
Consumer foods	$3,061	$2,771	$2,713	$2,793
Restaurants	1,051	1,140	1,080	985
Specialty retailing	474	374	325	305
Income from operations				
Consumer foods	308	266	275	269
Restaurants	88	92	70	80
Specialty retailing	27	(2)	20	10
Operating assets				
Consumer foods	1,092	1,000	929	979
Restaurants	468	425	585	573
Specialty retailing	196	205	153	177

In 1982, operating assets were consumer foods $918, restaurants $496, and specialty retailing $260.

INSTRUCTIONS

(a) Rank the segments in each year as to (1) net sales and (2) income from operations.
(b) Determine for each year each segments (1) profit margin on sales, (2) assets turnover, and (3) return on investment. (Round to one decimal.)
(c) Rank the segments in each of the categories in (b) above for each year.
(d) Comment on the relative profitability of the segments.

DECISION CASE

The Better Appliance Center has a store in three suburban shopping malls: Pinehurst, Maplewood, and Oakmont. Condensed income statements for the year for the stores are as follows:

	Pinehurst	Maplewood	Oakmont
Sales	$1,200,000	$1,500,000	$1,000,000
Cost of goods sold	840,000	1,080,000	680,000
Gross profit	360,000	420,000	320,000
Direct expenses	192,000	216,000	200,000
Departmental margin	168,000	204,000	120,000
Indirect expenses	36,000	45,000	30,000
Income from operations	$ 132,000	$ 159,000	$ 90,000

As president and chief executive officer of the Better Appliance Center, you wish to rank the stores on the basis of their profitability. During your analysis, you determine that the average operating assets for each store during the year were: Pinehurst $1,000,000; Maplewood $1,200,000; and Oakmont $750,000.

INSTRUCTIONS

(Round all computations to one decimal.)

(a) Rank the stores on the basis of each of the following profitability rates: gross profit, departmental margin, and income from operations.

(b) How were indirect expenses allocated, assuming the expenses pertain exclusively to overall administrative services? What effect does this basis of allocation have on the relative profitability of the stores? What other bases might have been used in the allocation?

(c) Compute the return on investment for each store and rank the stores by this profitability measure.

(d) What evaluations can you make concerning the relative profitability of the stores? What suggestions would you make to the store managers to increase the profitability of their stores?

CHAPTER 22

Hofstra University, New York

CHAPTER 22

MANUFACTURING OPERATIONS: JOB ORDER COST ACCOUNTING

STUDY OBJECTIVES

After studying this chapter, you should be able to:

1. Identify the distinctive features of manufacturing company financial statements.
2. Define the three classes of manufacturing costs.
3. State how the cost of goods manufactured is determined
4. Explain the characteristics and purposes of cost accounting.
5. Describe the flow of costs in a job order cost accounting system.
6. Explain the nature and importance of a job cost sheet.
7. Indicate how the predetermined overhead rate is determined and used.
8. Distinguish between under- and overapplied manufacturing overhead.

Assume that you, as the owner of Warren Printing Shop, have decided to bid for the job of printing university calendars for next year. To determine your bid price, you must estimate the amount of materials, labor, and other costs necessary to perform this job. To this amount, a profit margin should be added. Your business would be classified as a **manufacturing operation,** because it consists of activities and processes that convert raw materials (paper) into finished goods (university calendars). Contrast this type of enterprise with a merchandising enterprise, which sells merchandise in the form in which it is purchased. For example, University Bookstores (a merchandising enterprise) purchases the finished goods (university calendars) and then sells them to the general public.

In this chapter we will focus our attention on manufacturing enterprises. Large manufacturing companies include airplane manufacturers (Boeing

Aircraft), automobile manufacturers (General Motors), and computer manufacturers (International Business Machines). Smaller manufacturers include a soft drink bottling company, cement plant, dairy, bakery, meat processing plant, or furniture maker. Initially, we will draw comparisons between accounting for merchandising companies and accounting for manufacturing companies. Then we will explain and illustrate accounting for manufacturing costs in job order cost accounting.

Computerized systems are used extensively in manufacturing operations. As in manual vs. computerized general ledger systems, the frameworks for manual and computerized manufacturing systems parallel one another. The manufacturing model, with its emphasis on cost accumulation and control, is also applicable to construction contractors and firms in service industries, such as hospitals and financial institutions.

ACCOUNTING FOR MANUFACTURING OPERATIONS

Accounting for manufacturing operations ranges from the simple to the complex. In its simplest form, the accounting is basically an extension of the accounting for merchandising operations when periodic inventory procedures are used. Under this type of accounting, manufacturing costs are recorded as incurred. At the end of an accounting period, physical inventories are taken for finished goods, work in process, and raw materials. As in a merchandising company, closing entries are made to record the ending inventories and the cost of goods manufactured.

In its more complex form, the accounting for manufacturing operations involves perpetual inventory procedures and an extensive network of documents and accounting records. We will explain both types of operations in the remainder of this chapter, beginning with the simple form.

MANUFACTURING COMPANY FINANCIAL STATEMENTS

The financial statements of a manufacturing company are very similar to those of a merchandising company. The principal differences pertain to the current asset section of the balance sheet and the cost of goods sold section of the income statement.

BALANCE SHEET

A manufacturing company may have three inventory accounts. They are:

Finished Goods Inventory which shows the cost of completed goods on hand.

Work in Process Inventory which shows the cost applicable to units that have been started into production but are only partially completed.

Raw Materials Inventory which shows the cost of raw materials on hand.

Finished Goods Inventory is to a manufacturing enterprise what Merchandise Inventory is to a merchandising firm because it represents the goods available for sale.

The current asset sections presented below contrast the presentation of inventories of a merchandising company and those of a manufacturing company.

Current asset sections

Merchandising Company
Current Asset Section
December 31, 1987

Current assets	
Cash	$100,000
Receivables (net)	210,000
MERCHANDISE INVENTORY	400,000
Prepaid expenses	22,000
Total	$732,000

Manufacturing Company
Current Asset Section
December 31, 1987

Current assets		
Cash		$180,000
Receivables (net)		210,000
INVENTORIES:		
FINISHED GOODS	$ 80,000	
WORK IN PROCESS	95,000	
RAW MATERIALS	160,000	335,000
Prepaid expenses		18,000
Total		$743,000

The remainder of the balance sheet is similar for the two types of companies.

INCOME STATEMENT

The income statements of a merchandising company and a manufacturing company differ in the cost of goods sold section. The different components are shown graphically below:

Cost of goods sold components

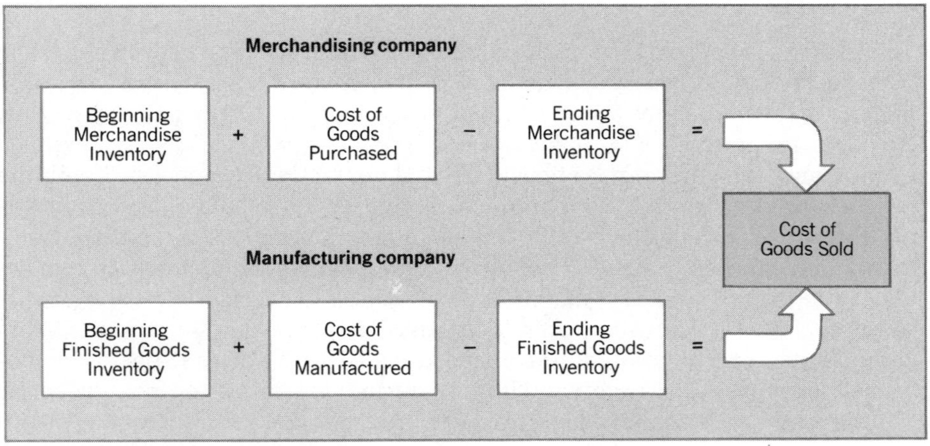

A number of accounts are involved in determining the cost of goods manufactured. To eliminate excessive detail in the income statement, it is customary to show only the total amount in the income statement and to present the details in a Cost of Goods Manufactured Schedule. This schedule is illustrated later in the chapter.

The cost of goods sold sections for merchandising and manufacturing enterprises presented below illustrate the different presentations:

Cost of goods sold sections

Merchandising Company
Income Statement
For the Year Ended December 31, 1987

Cost of goods sold		
MERCHANDISE INVENTORY, January 1	$ 70,000	
COST OF GOODS PURCHASED	650,000	
Cost of Goods Available for Sale	720,000	
MERCHANDISE INVENTORY, December 31	400,000	
Cost of goods sold	$320,000	

Manufacturing Company
Income Statement
For the Year Ended December 31, 1987

Cost of goods sold	
FINISHED GOODS INVENTORY, January 1	$ 90,000
COST OF GOODS MANUFACTURED (see schedule)	870,000
Cost of Goods Available for Sale	960,000
FINISHED GOODS INVENTORY, December 31	80,000
Cost of goods sold	$880,000

The other sections of an income statement are similar for both a merchandising and a manufacturing company.

MANUFACTURING COSTS

A variety of manufacturing costs may be included in the cost of goods manufactured. Manufacturing costs are typically classified as either: (1) direct materials, (2) direct labor, or (3) manufacturing overhead.

DIRECT MATERIALS

To obtain the materials that will be converted into the finished product, the manufacturer purchases raw materials. Raw materials represent the basic materials and parts that are to be used in the manufacturing process such as steel, plastics, and tires in making automobiles.

Raw materials that can be physically and conveniently associated with the finished product during the manufacturing process are called **direct materials.** Examples include flour in the baking of bread, syrup in the bottling of soft drinks, and steel in the making of automobiles. Conversely, some raw materials are considered indirect materials. **Indirect materials** (1) do not physically become part of the finished product, such as lubricants, rosin, and polishing compounds used in the manufacturing process, or (2) cannot be traced because their physical association with the finished product is too small in terms of cost, such as cotter pins, lock washers, and the like. Indirect materials are part of manufacturing overhead, as explained on the next page.

DIRECT LABOR

The work of factory employees that can be physically and conveniently associated with converting raw materials into finished goods is considered **direct labor.** Bottlers in a soft drink plant, bakers in a bakery, and typesetters in a print shop, are examples of employees whose activities are usually classified as direct labor. In contrast, the wages of maintenance people, timekeepers, and supervisors are usually identified as **indirect labor,** because their efforts have no physical association with the finished product, or it is impractical to trace the costs to the goods produced. Like indirect materials, indirect labor is classified as manufacturing overhead.

MANUFACTURING OVERHEAD

Manufacturing overhead consists of costs that are indirectly associated with the manufacture of the finished product. These costs may also be defined as manufacturing costs that cannot be classified as either direct materials or direct labor. Manufacturing overhead includes indirect materials, indirect labor, depreciation on factory buildings and machinery, and insurance, taxes, and maintenance on factory facilities. Terms such as **factory overhead, indirect manufacturing costs** and **burden,** are sometimes used instead of manufacturing overhead.

Manufacturing overhead sometimes represent the major portion of total manufacturing costs, and they often are the most difficult costs for management to control. For example, General Dynamics, one of the nation's biggest defense contractors, recently billed the government for $170 million in overhead expenses on government contracts over a three-year period. After the Defense Audit Agency challenged $63.6 million of this amount, General Dynamics withdrew $23 million of the charges.

PRODUCT AND PERIOD COSTS

Each of the manufacturing cost elements (direct materials, direct labor, and manufacturing overhead) are product costs. As the term suggests, **product costs** are costs that are a necessary and integral part of producing the finished product. Product costs are also called **inventoriable costs.** These costs do not become expenses under the matching principle until the inventory to which they attach is sold. The expense is cost of goods sold. Direct materials and direct labor are often referred to as **prime costs** because of their direct association with the manufacturing of the finished product. In addition, because direct labor and manufacturing overhead are incurred in converting raw materials into finished goods, these two cost elements are often referred to as **conversion costs.**

Period costs are costs that are identified with a specific time period rather than with a salable product. These costs relate to nonmanufacturing costs and therefore are not inventoriable costs. Period costs include selling and administrative expenses that are deducted from revenues in the period in which they are incurred.

The foregoing relationships and cost terms are summarized on the next page.

Cost of goods manufactured formulas

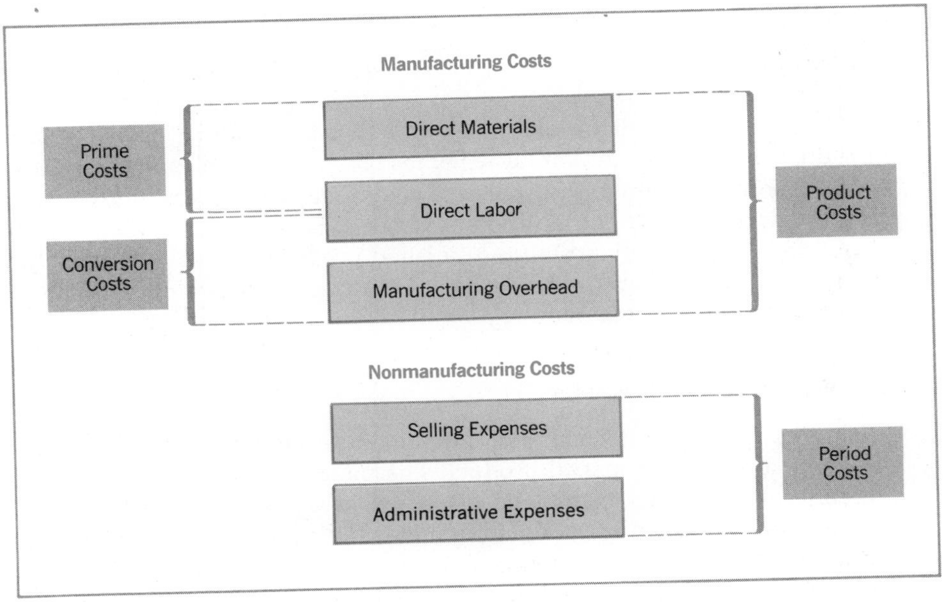

Our main concern in this chapter is with product costs.

DETERMINING THE COST OF GOODS MANUFACTURED

An example may be helpful in showing how the cost of goods manufactured for a period is determined. Assume that the Ford Motor Company has a number of automobiles in various stages of production on January 1. These vehicles represent **beginning work in process inventory.** The costs assigned to beginning work in process inventory are based on the manufacturing costs incurred in the prior period. In the current year, Ford Motor continues the production of automobiles. The manufacturing costs incurred in the current year are used first to complete the work in process on January 1 and then to start the production of other vehicles. The sum of the direct materials costs, direct labor costs, and manufacturing overhead incurred is the **total manufacturing costs for the current year.**

We now have two cost amounts: (1) the cost of the beginning work in process and (2) the total manufacturing costs for the current period. The sum of these costs is the total cost of work in process for the year.

At the end of the year, some vehicles may only be partially completed. The costs of these units become the cost of the **ending work in process inventory.** We then subtract this cost from the total cost of work in process to find the cost of goods manufactured.

The determination of the cost of goods manufactured can be shown graphically as follows on the top of the next page.

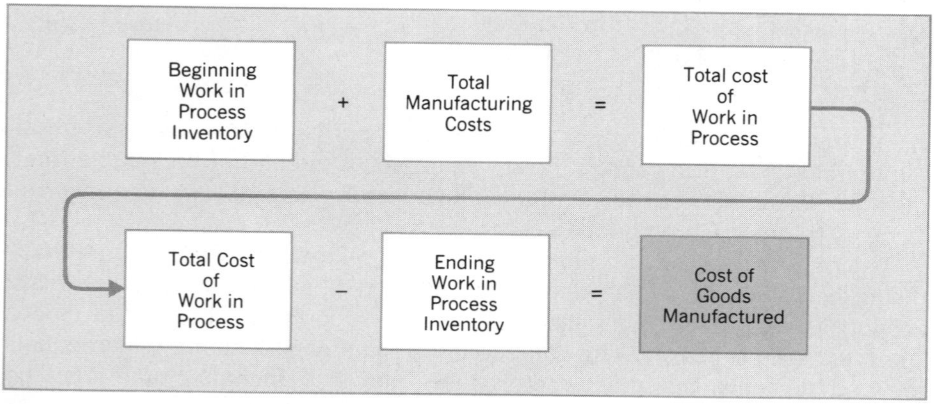

Product versus period costs

COST OF GOODS MANUFACTURED SCHEDULE

The cost of goods manufactured schedule shows each of the cost factors explained above. The schedule for Olsen Manufacturing Company using assumed data is shown below.

Cost of goods manufactured schedule

OLSEN MANUFACTURING COMPANY
Cost of Goods Manufactured Schedule
For the Year Ended December 31, 1987

Work in process, January 1			$ 18,400
Direct materials			
Raw materials inventory, January 1	$ 16,700		
Raw materials purchases	152,500		
Total raw materials available for use	169,200		
Less: Raw materials inventory, December 31	22,800		
Direct materials used		$146,400	
Direct labor		175,600	
Manufacturing overhead			
Indirect labor	14,300		
Factory repairs	12,600		
Factory utilities	10,100		
Factory depreciation	9,440		
Factory insurance	8,360		
Total manufacturing overhead		54,800	
Total manufacturing costs			376,800
Total cost of work in process			395,200
Less: Work in process, December 31			25,200
Cost of goods manufactured			$370,000

Note that detailed data are presented for direct materials and manufacturing overhead.

ACCOUNTING CYCLE FOR A MANUFACTURING COMPANY

Each step in the accounting cycle for a merchandising company is applicable to a manufacturing company. For example, at the end of the year, adjusting and closing entries are required. The adjusting entries are essentially the same as those of a merchandising company.

The closing process in a manufacturing company differs from a merchandising company. In a manufacturing company a Manufacturing Summary account is used to close all accounts that are reported in the Cost of Goods Manufactured schedule. The balance in this summary account, which equals the cost of goods manufactured, is then closed to Income Summary. The Manufacturing Summary account for Olsen Manufacturing Company is as follows:

Manufacturing summary account

Manufacturing Summary

Dec. 31	Work in process inventory 1/1	18,400	Dec. 31	Work in process inventory, 12/31	25,200
31	Raw materials inventory, 1/1	16,700	31	Raw materials inventory, 12/31	22,800
31	Raw materials purchases	152,500	31	To income summary	370,000
31	Direct labor	175,600			
31	Manufacturing overhead	54,800			
		418,000			418,000

The remainder of the closing entries for a manufacturing company are the same as for a merchandising company. The use of a work sheet and the journalizing of closing entries for Olsen Manufacturing are illustrated in Appendix 22-A.

NEED FOR UNIT MANUFACTURING COSTS

Until this point, we have emphasized the total cost of goods manufactured. However, in most companies, information about unit costs is needed in making management decisions. To illustrate, consider the competitive automobile market. If Chrysler can manufacture a Plymouth Voyager van for less than Ford can make an Aerostar van, Chrysler may have a competitive advantage. A knowledge of unit costs may influence the market strategies and future production goals of each company. Knowledge of unit costs may also be useful in controlling costs and in deciding to implement cost reduction programs. To provide unit cost data it is necessary to use a more complex form of accounting for manufacturing operations. This accounting is called cost accounting.

Cost accounting involves the measuring, recording, and reporting of product costs. From the data accumulated, the unit cost of each product is determined. In addition, cost accounting provides data that can be used by management to measure performance and control costs.

A **cost accounting system** consists of manufacturing cost accounts that are fully integrated into the general ledger of a company. An important feature of a cost accounting system is the use of a perpetual inventory system. Unlike the simple manufacturing accounting system discussed in earlier sections of this chapter, a cost accounting system provides information immediately on the cost of a product or process. For example, no longer do we have to wait until the end of an accounting period to determine the cost of goods sold because the accounting records are updated continuously.

One would think that all companies would have good cost accounting systems but surprisingly many systems are found to be deficient. For example, the chairman of Sherwin-Williams Co. recently acknowledged that "we lacked a good cost accounting system."

There are two basic types of cost accounting systems: (1) a job order system and (2) a process cost system. Under a **job order system,** costs are assigned to each **job,** such as the manufacture of a high-speed drilling machine, or each **batch** of goods, such as 300 wedding invitations. Jobs or batches may be completed to fill a specific customer order or to replenish inventory. An important feature of job order costing is the fact that each job (or batch) has its own distinguishing characteristics. For example, each house is custom built, each motion picture is unique, and each printing job is different. The important thing to remember is that a cost per job must be computed. At each point in the manufacturing process, the job can be identified.

A **process cost system** is applicable when a series of connected manufacturing processes or departments produce a large volume of uniform or relatively homogeneous products. Production is continuous to ensure that adequate inventories of the finished product(s) are always on hand. A process cost system is used in the manufacture of cereal, the refining of petroleum, and the production of automobiles.

A company may use both types of cost systems. For example, General Motors uses process cost accounting for its standard model cars, such as Chevrolets and Buicks, and job order cost accounting for a custom-made limousine for the President of the United States. The job order cost system will be explained in this chapter; the process cost system will be discussed in the next chapter.

JOB ORDER COST FLOW

Direct materials, direct labor, and manufacturing overhead in a job order system are identical to those in a simple manufacturing system. The flow of costs in job order cost accounting parallels the physical flow of the materials as they are converted into finished goods. There are two major steps in the flow of costs: (1) **accumulating** the manufacturing costs incurred and (2) **assigning** the accumulated costs to the work done. As shown below, manufac-

turing costs incurred are accumulated in entries 1–3 by debits to Raw Materials Inventory, Factory Labor, and Manufacturing Overhead.

Job order cost system

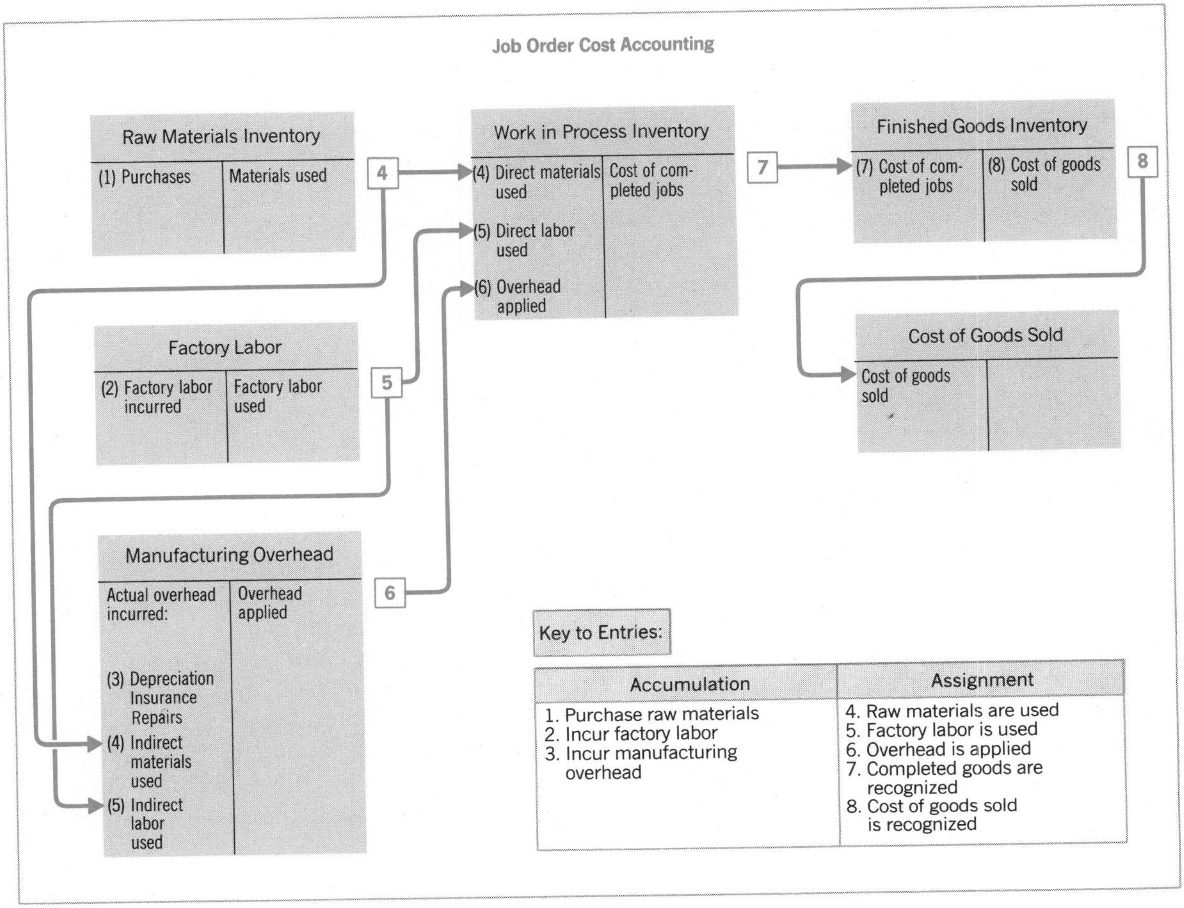

The remaining entries (entries 4–8) pertain to the assignment of manufacturing costs incurred. First, as illustrated, costs are assigned to the work in process inventory account. All debits to this account must also be assigned to specific jobs. When a job is finished, its cost is transferred to finished goods. Later, when the goods are sold, their cost is transferred to cost of goods sold.

ACCUMULATION OF MANUFACTURING COSTS

In a job order cost system, manufacturing costs are recorded in the period in which they are incurred. To illustrate, we will use the January transactions of Wallace Manufacturing Company, which makes tools and dies for automobile companies.

Raw Materials Costs

The costs of raw materials purchased are debited to Raw Materials Inventory when materials are received. This account is debited for the invoice cost

and freight costs chargeable to the purchaser. It is credited for purchase discounts taken and purchase returns and allowances. The procedures for ordering, receiving, recording, and paying for raw materials are similar to the purchasing procedures of a merchandising company.

Computerized job cost systems follow the same pattern of entries illustrated in the next few pages. The paperwork and reports generated by such systems are basically the same as shown for Wallace Manufacturing Company. The major difference between manual and computerized systems is the time involved in converting data into information and in getting feedback (reports) to management.

To illustrate the purchase of raw materials, assume that Wallace Manufacturing Company purchases 2,000 handles (Stock No. AA2746) at $5 per unit and 800 modules (Stock No. AA2850) at $40 per unit from the Hurdle Company on account on January 4. The entry is as follows:

Jan. 4	Raw Materials Inventory	42,000	
	Accounts Payable		42,000
	(Purchase of raw materials on account)		

Raw Materials Inventory is a **control account.** The subsidiary ledger consists of individual records for each item of raw materials. The records may take the form of accounts (or cards) that are manually or mechanically prepared, or data files maintained electronically on disks or magnetic tape. The records, sometimes referred to as **materials inventory records** (also referred to as stores ledger cards), are similar to the perpetual inventory records illustrated in Chapter 9 for a merchandising company. After all postings have been completed, the sum of the balances in the raw materials subsidiary ledger should equal the balance in the raw materials inventory control account.

Factory Labor Costs

The procedures for accumulation of factory labor costs are similar to those used in computing the payroll for a merchandising company. For example, time clocks and time cards are used to determine total hours worked; gross and net earnings for each employee are listed in a payroll register; and individual employee earnings records are maintained. To help ensure the accuracy of payroll data, a company should follow the principles of internal control for payrolls described in Chapter 12.

In a manufacturing company, the cost of factory labor consists of (1) gross earnings of factory workers, (2) employer payroll taxes on such earnings, and (3) fringe benefits (such as sick pay, pensions, and vacation pay) incurred by the employer. These costs are debited to Factory Labor. To illustrate, assume that Wallace Manufacturing incurs $32,000 of factory labor costs, of which $27,000 relates to wages payable, and $5,000 relates to payroll taxes payable in January. The entry is:

Jan.	31	Factory Labor	32,000	
		Factory Wages Payable		27,000
		Employer Payroll Taxes Payable		5,000
		(To record factory labor costs)		

Factory Labor is **not** a control account. Labor costs do not accumulate in advance of utilization. The balance in this account is then assigned to work in process and manufacturing overhead as explained on page 881.

Manufacturing Overhead Costs

A company may have many types of overhead costs. The accumulation of these costs may be recognized daily, as in the case of machinery repairs and the use of indirect materials and indirect labor. Alternatively, overhead costs may be recorded periodically through adjusting entries, as in the case of property taxes, depreciation, and insurance. Using assumed data, a summary entry for manufacturing overhead in Wallace Manufacturing Company is as follows:

3

Jan.	31	Manufacturing Overhead	13,800	
		Utilities Payable		4,800
		Prepaid Insurance		2,000
		Accounts Payable (for repairs)		2,600
		Accumulated Depreciation		3,000
		Property Taxes Payable		1,400
		(To record overhead costs)		

Manufacturing Overhead is a **control** account. The subsidiary ledger consists of individual accounts for each type of cost. The subsidiary accounts are similar to those illustrated earlier in Chapter 6 for customer accounts in the accounts receivable ledger.

ASSIGNMENT OF MANUFACTURING COSTS TO WORK IN PROCESS

As shown in the flow chart, the assignment of manufacturing costs to work in process results in debits to Work in Process Inventory and credits to Raw Materials Inventory, Factory Labor, and Manufacturing Overhead. An indispensable accounting record in assigning costs to jobs is the job cost sheet, illustrated at the top of page 879. A **job cost sheet** is a form used to record the costs chargeable to a specific job and to determine the total and unit cost of the completed job.

A separate job cost sheet is kept for each job. Job cost sheets constitute the subsidiary ledger for the work in process inventory account. **Each entry to Work in Process must be accompanied by a corresponding posting to one or more job cost sheets.**

Raw Materials Costs

Raw materials costs are assigned when the materials are issued by the storeroom. To achieve effective internal control over the issuance of materials, the

Job cost sheet

Job Cost Sheet

Job No. ______ Quantity ______

Item ______ Date Requested ______

For ______ Date Completed ______

Date	Direct Materials	Direct Labor	Manufacturing Overhead

Cost of completed job

Direct materials $______

Direct labor ______

Manufacturing overhead ______

Total cost $______

Unit cost (total dollars ÷ quantity) $______

storekeeper should obtain a written authorization each time materials are released to production. The authorization for issuing materials is made on a prenumbered **materials requisition slip** signed by an authorized employee such as a department supervisor. Materials may be used directly on a job or indirectly. As illustrated below, the requisition should indicate the quantity and type of materials withdrawn and the account to be charged. The account is Work in Process for direct materials and Manufacturing Overhead for indirect materials. In the example, the account is Work in Process—Job No. 101.

Materials requisition slip

Wallace Manufacturing Company
Materials Requisition Slip

Deliver to: Assembly Department Req. No. R247

Charge to: Work in Process–Job No. 101 Date: 1/6/87

Quantity	Description	Stock No.	Cost Per Unit	Total
200	Handles	AA2746	$5.00	$1,000

Requested by Bruce Howart Received by Herb Crowley

Approved by Kap Shin Costed by Heather Remmers

The requisition is prepared in duplicate. A copy is retained in the storeroom as evidence of the materials released; the original is sent to accounting,

where the cost per unit and total cost of the materials used are determined. Any of the inventory costing methods (FIFO, LIFO, or average cost) may be used in costing the requisitions. The method selected by management should be followed consistently. After the requisition slips have been costed, they are posted daily to the materials inventory records. In addition, requisitions for direct materials are posted daily to the individual job cost sheets.

Periodically, the requisitions are sorted, totaled and journalized. For example, if $24,000 of direct materials and $6,000 of indirect materials are used in Wallace Manufacturing in January, the entry is:

4

Jan.	31	Work in Process Inventory	24,000	
		Manufacturing Overhead	6,000	
		Raw Materials Inventory		30,000
		(To record materials used)		

The requisition slips show total direct materials costs of $12,000 for Job No. 101, $7,000 for Job No. 102, and $5,000 for Job No. 103. The posting of requisition slip R247 (above) and other assumed postings to the job cost sheets are illustrated below.

Job cost sheets—materials

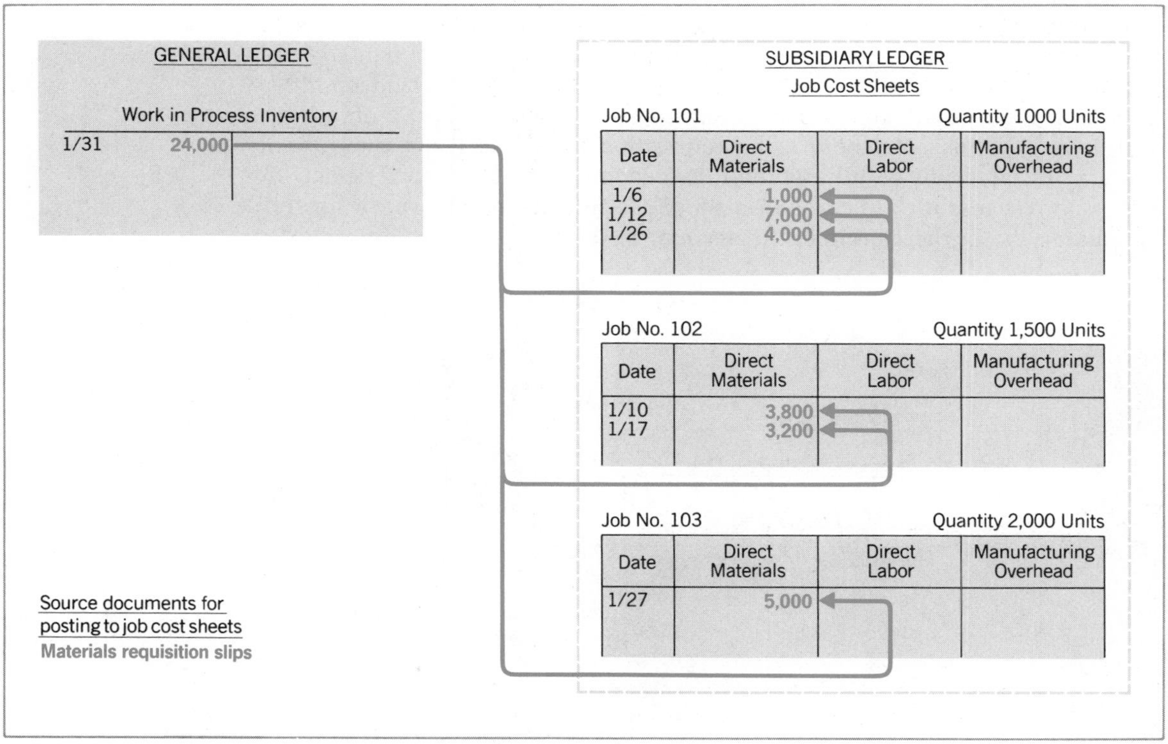

After all postings have been completed, the sum of the totals of the direct materials columns of the job cost sheets should equal the direct materials debited to work in process inventory.

Factory Labor Costs

Factory labor costs are assigned to jobs on the basis of time tickets prepared when the work is performed. The **time ticket** should indicate the employee, the hours worked, and the account to be charged, which is Work in Process Inventory for direct labor and Manufacturing Overhead for indirect labor. When direct labor is involved, the job number must be indicated as shown below.

Time ticket

Wallace Manufacturing Company
Time Ticket

Date: 1/6/87

Employee: John Nash — Employee No. 124

Charge to: Work in Process — Job No. 101

Time			Hourly Rate	Total Cost
Start	Stop	Total Hours		
0800	1200	4	10.00	40.00

Approved by *Bob Kadler* — Costed by *S. Bono*

In some companies, different colored time tickets are used for direct and indirect labor. All time tickets should be approved by the employee's supervisor.

The time tickets are later sent to the payroll department where the total time reported for an employee for a pay period is reconciled with total hours shown on the employee's time (clock) card. Then the employee's hourly wage rate is applied and the total labor cost is computed. The time tickets are then sorted, totaled, and journalized. For example, if the total factory labor cost incurred of $32,000 consists of $28,000 of direct labor and $4,000 of indirect labor, the entry is:

5

Jan.	31	Work in Process Inventory	28,000	
		Manufacturing Overhead	4,000	
		Factory Labor		32,000
		(To assign factory labor to production)		

As a result of this entry, Factory Labor is left with a zero balance, and gross earnings are assigned to the appropriate manufacturing accounts. In some companies the accumulation and assignment of factory labor are combined into an entry in which Work in Process and Manufacturing Overhead are debited and Factory Wages Payable and the tax liability accounts are credited.

We will assume that the labor costs chargeable to the three jobs are $15,000, $9,000, and $4,000. Thus, the work in process inventory and job cost sheets after posting will be as follows:

Job cost sheets—direct labor

GENERAL LEDGER

Work in Process Inventory

1/31	24,000-
1/31	28,000-

SUBSIDIARY LEDGER

Job Cost Sheets

Job No. 101 — Quantity 1,000 units

Date	Direct Materials	Direct Labor	Manufacturing Overhead
1/6	1,000		
1/10		9,000	
1/12	7,000		
1/26	4,000		
1/31		6,000	

Job No. 102 — Quantity 1,500 units

Date	Direct Materials	Direct Labor	Manufacturing Overhead
1/10	3,800		
1/15		4,000	
1/17	3,200		
1/22		5,000	

Job No. 103 — Quantity 2,000 units

Date	Direct Materials	Direct Labor	Manufacturing Overhead
1/27	5,000		
1/29		4,000	

Source documents for posting to Job cost sheets:
Time tickets

As in the case of direct materials, the postings to the direct labor columns of the job cost sheets should equal the posting of direct labor to Work in Process.

A job cost computer program provides summaries of material and labor expenses by job. The program enables the company to accumulate costs by jobs, provide data to accounts receivable for billings, assign overhead costs, and provide up-to-date management reports.

Manufacturing Overhead Costs

Unlike direct materials and direct labor that apply to specific jobs, manufacturing overhead relates to production operations as a whole. Consequently, these costs cannot be assigned to specific jobs on the basis of actual costs incurred. Instead, manufacturing overhead is assigned to work in process and to specific jobs on an estimated basis through the use of a predetermined overhead rate.

The **predetermined overhead rate** is based on the relationship between estimated annual overhead costs and expected annual operating capacity expressed in terms of a common activity base. The common activity base may be stated in terms of direct labor costs, direct labor hours, machine hours, or any other measure that will provide an equitable basis for applying overhead costs to jobs. The predetermined overhead rate is established at (or prior to) the beginning of the year. The formula for a predetermined overhead rate is:

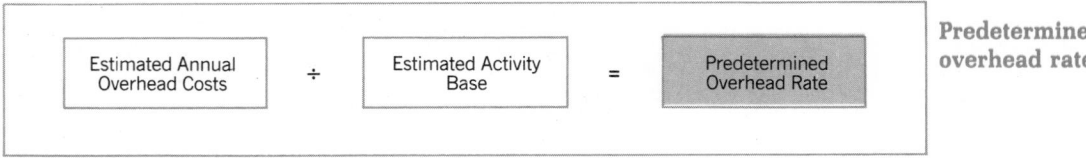

Predetermined overhead rate

Estimated Annual Overhead Costs	÷	Estimated Activity Base	=	Predetermined Overhead Rate

At Wallace Manufacturing, direct labor cost is the activity base. Assuming that annual overhead costs are expected to be \$280,000 and that \$350,000 of direct labor cost are anticipated, the overhead rate is 80%, computed as follows:

$$\$280{,}000 \div \$350{,}000 = 80\%$$

This means that for every dollar of direct labor, 80 cents of manufacturing overhead will be assigned to a job.

Historically, direct labor cost or direct labor hours have often been used as the activity base because of the relatively high correlation between direct labor and manufacturing overhead. In recent years, however, there has been a significant trend toward use of machine hours as the activity base because of increased reliance on automation in manufacturing operations. The use of a predetermined overhead rate enables the company to determine the approximate total cost of each job when the job is **completed.**

Manufacturing overhead is usually recognized in the accounts and charged to jobs when direct labor costs are assigned. For Wallace Manufacturing, overhead applied for January is \$22,400 (\$28,000 × 80%), and the application is recorded through the following entry.

6

Jan.	31	Work in Process Inventory	22,400	
		Manufacturing Overhead		22,400
		(To assign overhead to jobs)		

After posting, the work in process inventory account and the job cost sheets will appear as shown at the top of the next page.

At any point in time, the balance in Work in Process Inventory should equal the sum of the costs shown on the job cost sheets of unfinished jobs. Assuming that all jobs are unfinished, proof of the agreement of the control and subsidiary accounts in Wallace Manufacturing is shown in the middle of the next page.

Job cost sheets—manufacturing overhead

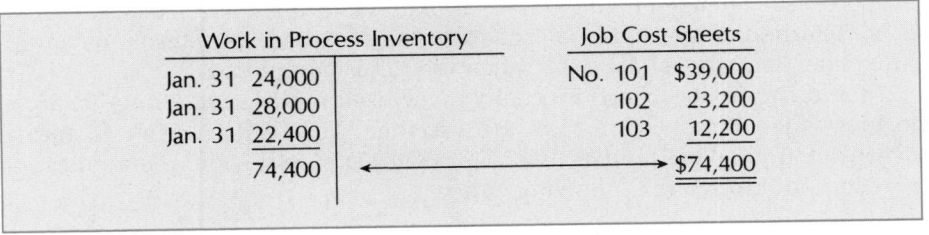

GENERAL LEDGER

Work in Process Inventory

1/31	24,000	
1/31	28,000	
1/31	22,400	

SUBSIDIARY LEDGER

Job cost sheets

Job No. 101 — Quantity 1,000 units

Date	Direct Materials	Direct Labor	Manufacturing Overhead
1/6	1,000		
1/10		9,000	7,200
1/12	7,000		
1/26	4,000		
1/31		6,000	4,800

Job No. 102 — Quantity 1,500 units

Date	Direct Materials	Direct Labor	Manufacturing Overhead
1/10	3,800		
1/15		4,000	3,200
1/17	3,200		
1/22		5,000	4,000

Job No. 103 — Quantity 2,000 units

Date	Direct Materials	Direct Labor	Manufacturing Overhead
1/27	5,000		
1/29		4,000	3,200

Source documents for posting to Job cost sheets:
Predetermined overhead rate (80% of direct labor cost)

Proof of job cost sheets to work in process inventory

Work in Process Inventory			Job Cost Sheets	
Jan. 31	24,000		No. 101	$39,000
Jan. 31	28,000		102	23,200
Jan. 31	22,400		103	12,200
	74,400	←→		$74,400

It is also possible to prove the agreement of the control and subsidiary data by comparing the postings to Work in Process with the sum of the postings to the job cost sheets for each of the manufacturing cost elements as shown below.

Alternative proof

Item	Direct Materials	Direct Labor	Manufacturing Overhead
Work in Process Inventory	$24,000	$28,000	$22,400
Job No. 101	$12,000	$15,000	$12,000
102	7,000	9,000	7,200
103	5,000	4,000	3,200
	$24,000	$28,000	$22,400

RECORDING THE COST OF COMPLETED JOBS

When a job is completed, the assigned costs are summarized and the lower portion of the applicable job cost sheet is completed. For example, if we assume that Job No. 101 is completed on January 31, the job cost sheet will show the following:

Completed job cost sheet

Job Cost Sheet

Job No.	101	Quantity	1,000
Item	Magnetic Sensors	Date Requested	February 5
For	Tanner Company	Date Completed	January 31

Date	Direct Materials	Direct Labor	Manufacturing Overhead
1/6	$ 1,000		
1/10		$ 9,000	$ 7,200
1/12	7,000		
1/26	4,000		
1/31		6,000	4,800
	$12,000	$15,000	$12,000

Cost of completed job:	
Direct materials	$ 12,000
Direct labor	15,000
Manufacturing overhead	12,000
Total cost	$ 39,000
Unit cost ($39,000 ÷ 1,000)	$ 39.00

When a job is finished, an entry is made to transfer its total cost to finished goods inventory. The entry for Wallace Manufacturing is:

7

Jan. 31	Finished Goods Inventory	39,000	
	Work in Process Inventory		39,000
	(To record completion of Job No. 101)		

Finished Goods Inventory is a control account that controls individual **finished goods records** in a finished goods subsidiary ledger. The records are similar to the perpetual inventory records illustrated in Chapter 9. Postings to the receipts columns are made directly from completed job cost sheets. The finished goods inventory record for Job No. 101 is illustrated on page 886.

RECORDING THE COST OF GOODS SOLD

Recognition of the cost of goods sold is made when each sale occurs. The cost of goods sold is obtained from the individual finished goods inventory records. For example, if Wallace Manufacturing sells Job No. 101 for $50,000, on account on February 2, the entries are:

8

Feb.	2	Accounts Receivable	50,000	
		Sales		50,000
		(To record sale of Job No. 101)		
	2	Cost of Goods Sold	39,000	
		Finished Goods Inventory		39,000
		(To record cost of Job No. 101)		

The units sold, the cost per unit, and the total cost of goods sold for each job sold is recorded in the issues section of the finished goods record as shown below.

Finished goods record

Item: Magnetic Sensors — Job No: 101

	Receipts			Issues			Balance		
Date	Units	Cost	Total	Units	Cost	Total	Units	Cost	Total
1/31	1,000	$39	$39,000				1,000	$39	$39,000
2/2				1,000	$39	$39,000			-0-

SUMMARY OF JOB ORDER COST FLOWS

A completed flow chart for a job order cost accounting system is shown on page 887. All postings are keyed to entries (1)–(8) in Wallace Manufacturing. The chart includes only the accounts presented in the cost flow graphic shown on page 876. The graphic also provides a summary of the inventory control accounts, subsidiary ledgers, and source documents for assigning costs to jobs.

UNDER- OR OVERAPPLIED MANUFACTURING OVERHEAD

In the flow chart on page 887, Manufacturing Overhead has a debit balance of $1,400 as follows:

Manufacturing Overhead account

Manufacturing Overhead

(3)	13,800	(6)	22,400
(4)	6,000		
(5)	4,000		
Bal.	1,400		

Job order cost system

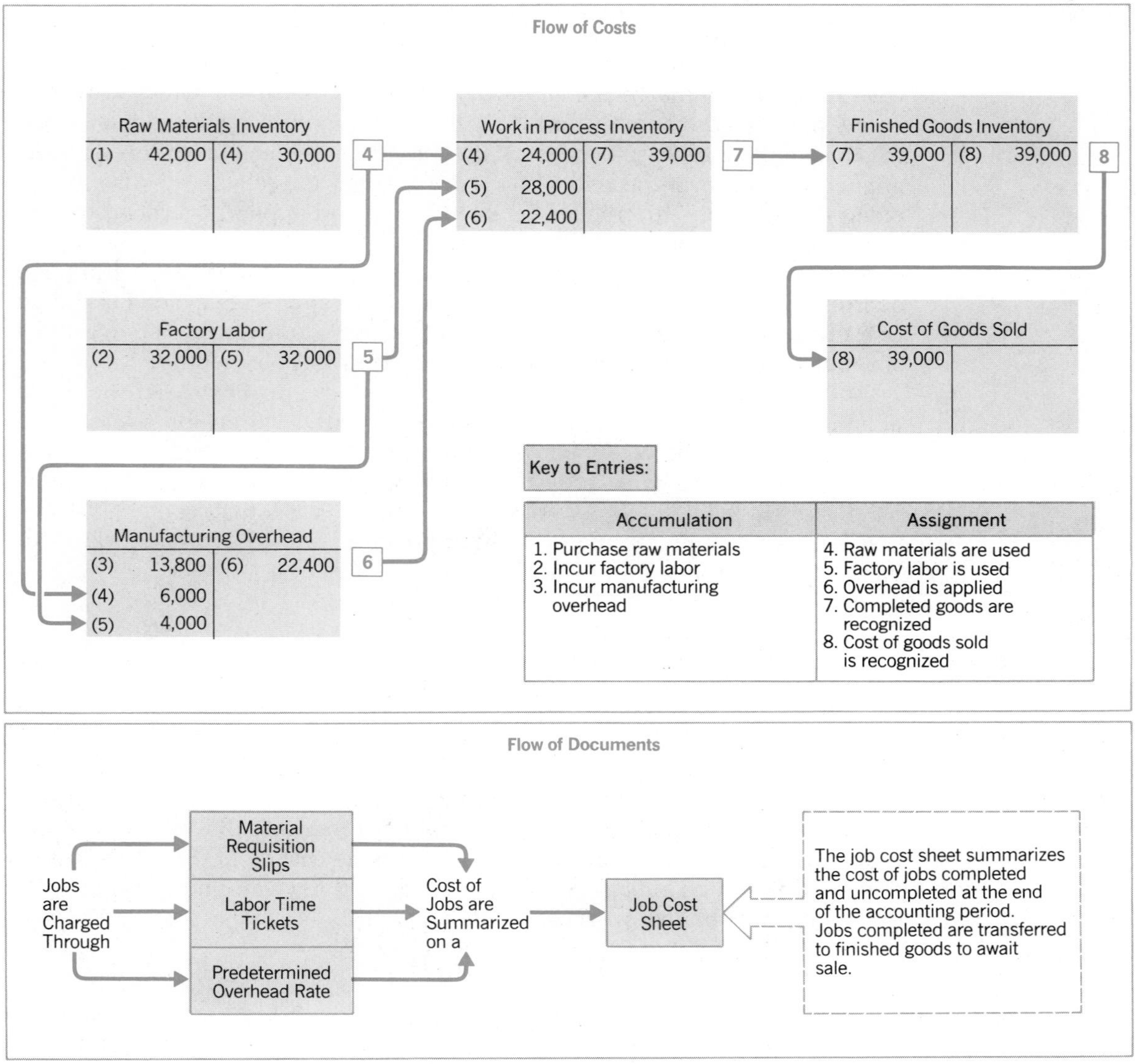

When Manufacturing Overhead has a debit balance at the end of the month, overhead is said to be underapplied. **Underapplied overhead** means that the overhead assigned to work in process is less than the overhead incurred. Conversely, when manufacturing overhead has a credit balance at the end of the month, overhead is overapplied. **Overapplied overhead** means that the overhead assigned to work in process is greater than the overhead incurred.

The existence of under- or overapplied overhead at the end of a month usually does not require corrective action by management. If the result is attributable to normal fluctuations in costs and production, no corrective action may even be possible. In Wallace Manufacturing, the predetermined overhead rate was based on expected annual overhead costs of $280,000 and annual direct labor costs of $350,000. This does not mean that each month will

have one-twelfth of both factors. For example, $48,000 of utility costs may be anticipated for the year, but variations in heating costs are expected to produce higher utility costs in the winter months and smaller utility costs in the summer months. Thus, the January costs of $4,800 may be offset by July costs of $3,200. Similarly, January direct labor cost of $28,000, which is slightly below the average monthly cost ($29,167), may be offset by direct labor costs in other months of $30,000 or more. In sum, the existence of under- or overapplied overhead at the end of a month is often expected. It is also anticipated that monthly differences between actual and applied overhead will be offsetting over the course of the year.

When monthly financial statements are prepared, under- or overapplied overhead is reported on the balance sheet. **Underapplied overhead is shown as a prepaid expense in the current asset section and overapplied overhead is reported as unearned revenue in the current liability section.**

At the end of the year, any balance in Manufacturing Overhead should be eliminated through an adjusting entry. Generally, under- or overapplied overhead is considered to be an adjustment of cost of goods sold. Thus, underapplied overhead is debited to cost of goods sold, and overapplied overhead is credited to cost of goods sold. To illustrate the adjusting entry, assume that Wallace Manufacturing has underapplied overhead of $900 on December 31. The adjusting entry is:

Dec. 31	Cost of Goods Sold	900	
	Manufacturing Overhead		900
	(To transfer underapplied overhead to cost of goods sold)		

Conceptually, it can be argued that under- or overapplied overhead at the end of the year should be allocated among ending work in process, finished goods, and cost of goods sold. Most companies feel that the increased accuracy resulting from this allocation is not worth the cost and effort. The bulk of this amount will be allocated to cost of goods sold anyway, and the amount of under- or overapplied overhead is often small.

SUMMARY OF STUDY OBJECTIVES

1. The distinctive features of manufacturing company financial statements are:
   a. The balance sheet shows three inventory accounts in current assets: finished goods, work in process, and raw materials.
   b. The cost of goods sold section of the income statement shows the beginning finished goods inventory, the cost of goods manufactured, and the ending finished goods inventory.

2. The three classes of manufacturing costs are:
   a. Direct materials, which are raw materials that can be physically and conveniently associated with the finished product.
   b. Direct labor, which is the work of factory workers that can be physically and conveniently associated with converting raw materials into finished goods.
   c. Manufacturing overhead, which consists of costs that are indirectly associated with the manufacture of the finished product.

3. The cost of goods manufactured is determined by adding the total manufacturing costs for the current period to the beginning work in process inventory. This sum equals the total cost of work in process. Ending work in process inventory is then subtracted from the total cost of work in process to obtain the cost of goods manufactured.

4. Cost accounting involves the procedures for measuring, recording, and reporting the actual costs to produce individual products. From the data accumulated, the unit cost of each product is determined. Another purpose of cost accounting is to provide data that allows management to measure performance and control costs.

5. In job order cost accounting, manufacturing costs are first accumulated in three accounts: Raw Materials Inventory, Factory Labor, and Manufacturing Overhead. The accumulated costs are then assigned to Work in Process Inventory and eventually to Finished Goods Inventory and Cost of Goods Sold.

6. A job cost sheet is a form used to record the costs chargeable to a specific job and to determine the total and unit cost of the completed job. Job cost sheets constitute the subsidiary ledger for the work in process control account.

7. The predetermined overhead rate is based on the relationship between estimated annual overhead costs and expected annual operating capacity expressed in terms of a common activity base, such as direct labor cost. The rate is used in assigning overhead costs to work in process and to specific jobs.

8. Underapplied manufacturing overhead means that the overhead assigned to work in process is less than the overhead incurred. Conversely, overapplied overhead means that the overhead assigned to work in process is greater than the overhead incurred.

APPENDIX 22–A

ACCOUNTING CYCLE FOR A MANUFACTURING COMPANY

As explained in the chapter, the accounting cycle for a manufacturing company is the same as for a merchandising company when a periodic inventory system is used. Except for the additional manufacturing inventories and manufacturing cost accounts, the journalizing and posting of transactions is the same. Similarly, the preparation of a trial balance and the journalizing and posting of adjusting entries are the same. Some changes, however, occur in the use of a work sheet and in preparing closing entries.

To illustrate the changes in the work sheet, we will use the cost of goods manufactured schedule for Olsen Manufacturing presented on page 873 of the chapter and other assumed data. For convenience, the cost of goods manufactured schedule is reproduced below:

Cost of goods manufactured schedule

OLSEN MANUFACTURING COMPANY
Cost of Goods Manufactured Schedule
For the Year Ended December 31, 1987

Work in process, January 1			$ 18,400
Direct materials			
Raw materials inventory, January 1	$ 16,700		
Raw materials purchases	152,500		
Total raw materials available for use	169,200		
Less: Raw materials inventory, December 31	22,800		
Direct materials used		$146,400	
Direct labor		175,600	
Manufacturing overhead			
Indirect labor	14,300		
Factory repairs	12,600		
Factory utilities	10,100		
Factory depreciation	9,440		
Factory insurance	8,360		
Total manufacturing overhead		54,800	
Total manufacturing costs			376,800
Total cost of work in process			395,200
Less: Work in process, December 31			25,200
Cost of goods manufactured			$370,000

WORK SHEET

When a work sheet is used in the preparation of financial statements, two additional columns are needed for the cost of goods manufactured schedule. As illustrated in the work sheet below debit and credit columns for this schedule have been inserted before the income statement columns.

Partial work sheet

OLSEN MANUFACTURING COMPANY
(Partial) Work Sheet
For the Year Ended December 31, 1987

	Adjusted Trial Balance		Cost of Goods Manufactured		Income Statement		Balance Sheet	
	Dr.	Cr.	Dr.	Cr.	Dr.	Cr.	Dr.	Cr.
Cash	42,500						42,500	
Accounts Receivable (Net)	71,900						71,900	
Finished Goods Inv.	24,600				24,600	19,500	19,500	
Work in Process Inv.	18,400		18,400	25,200			25,200	
Raw Materials Inv.	16,700		16,700	22,800			22,800	
Plant Assets	724,000						724,000	
Accumulated Depr.		278,400						278,400
Notes Payable		100,000						100,000
Accounts Payable		40,000						40,000
Income Taxes Payable		5,000						5,000
Common Stock		200,000						200,000
Retained Earnings		205,100						205,100
Sales		680,000				680,000		
Raw Materials Purchases	152,500		152,500					
Direct Labor	175,600		175,600					
Indirect Labor	14,300		14,300					
Factory Repairs	12,600		12,600					
Factory Utilities	10,100		10,100					
Factory Depreciation	9,440		9,440					
Factory Insurance	8,360		8,360					
Selling Expenses	114,900				114,900			
Administrative Exp.	92,600				92,600			
Income Tax Exp.	20,000				20,000			
Totals	1,508,500	1,508,500	418,000	48,000				
Cost of Goods Manufactured				370,000	**370,000**			
Totals			418,000	418,000	622,100	699,500	905,900	828,500
Net Income					77,400			77,400
Totals					699,500	699,500	905,900	905,900

In the cost of goods manufactured columns, the beginning inventories of direct materials and work in process are entered as debits and the ending inventories are entered as credits. In addition, all of the manufacturing costs are

entered as debits. The balancing amount for these columns is the cost of goods manufactured. Note that the amount, $370,000, agrees with the amount reported for cost of goods manufactured in the schedule. This amount is also entered in the income statement debit column.

The income statement and balance sheet columns for a manufacturing company are basically the same as for a merchandising company. For example, the treatment of the finished goods inventories is identical with the treatment of merchandise inventory. That is, the beginning inventory is entered in the debit column, and the ending finished goods inventory is entered in the income statement credit column and the balance sheet debit column.

As in the case of a merchandising company, financial statements can be prepared from the statement columns of the work sheet. In addition, the cost of goods manufactured schedule can also be prepared directly from the work sheet.

CLOSING ENTRIES

The closing entries for a manufacturing company are different than for a merchandising company. As indicated in the chapter, a Manufacturing Summary account is used to close all accounts that appear in the cost of goods manufactured schedule. The closing entries can be prepared from the cost of goods manufactured and income statement columns of the work sheet. As illustrated below, the closing entries for the manufacturing accounts are prepared first. The closing entries for Olsen Manufacturing are as follows:

Dec. 31	Work in Process Inventory (Dec. 31)	25,200	
	Raw Materials Inventory (Dec. 31)	22,800	
	Manufacturing Summary		48,000
	(To record ending raw materials and work-in process inventories)		
31	Manufacturing Summary	418,000	
	Work in Process Inventory (Jan. 1)		18,400
	Raw Materials Inventory (Jan. 1)		16,700
	Raw Materials Purchases		152,500
	Direct Labor		175,600
	Indirect Labor		14,300
	Factory Repairs		12,600
	Factory Utilities		10,100
	Factory Depreciation		9,440
	Factory Insurance		8,360
	(To close beginning raw materials and work in process inventories and manufacturing cost accounts)		
31	Finished Goods Inventory (Dec. 31)	19,500	
	Sales	680,000	
	Income Summary		699,500
	(To record ending finished goods inventory and close sales account)		

31	Income Summary	622,100	
	Finished Goods Inventory (Jan. 1)		24,600
	Manufacturing Summary		370,000
	Selling Expenses		114,900
	Administrative Expenses		92,600
	Income Tax Expense		20,000
	(To close beginning finished goods inventory, manufacturing summary, and expense accounts)		
31	Income Summary	77,400	
	Retained Earnings		77,400
	(To close net income to retained earnings)		

After posting, the summary accounts will show the following:

Manufacturing Summary			
Dec. 31	418,000	Dec. 31	48,000
		Dec. 31	370,000
	418,000		418,000

Income Summary			
Dec. 31	622,100	Dec. 31	699,500
31	77,400		
	699,500		699,500

These data precisely track the closing entries. It also would be possible to post each account balance to the Manufacturing Summary account.

GLOSSARY

Conversion costs, p. 871
Cost accounting, p. 875
Cost accounting system, p. 875
Direct labor, p. 871
Direct materials, p. 870
Indirect labor, p. 871
Indirect materials, p. 870
Job cost sheet, p. 878
Job order system, p. 875
Manufacturing overhead, p. 871
Materials requisition slip, p. 879
Overapplied overhead, p. 887
Period costs, p. 871
Prime costs, p. 871
Predetermined overhead rate, p. 883
Product costs, p. 871
Time ticket, p. 881
Underapplied overhead, p. 887

DEMONSTRATION PROBLEM

During February, Cardel Manufacturing works on two jobs: Numbers A16 and B17. Summary data concerning these jobs are as follows:

<u>Manufacturing Costs Incurred:</u>

Purchased $54,000 of raw materials on account.
Factory labor $76,000 plus $4,000 employer payroll taxes.
Manufacturing overhead exclusive of indirect materials and indirect labor $59,800.

<u>Assignment of Costs:</u>

Direct materials:	Job A16 $27,000, Job B17 $21,000
Indirect materials:	$3,000
Direct labor:	Job A16 $52,000, Job B17 $26,000
Indirect labor:	$2,000

Manufacturing overhead rate 80% of direct labor costs.

Job A16 was completed and sold on account for $150,000. Job B17 was only partially completed.

INSTRUCTIONS

(a) Journalize the February transactions in the sequence followed in the chapter.
(b) What was the amount of under-or overapplied manufacturing overhead?

SOLUTION TO DEMONSTRATION PROBLEM

(a)

Date	Account	Debit	Credit
	1.		
Feb. 28	Raw Materials Inventory	54,000	
	Accounts Payable		54,000
	(Purchase of raw materials on account)		
	2.		
28	Factory Labor	80,000	
	Factory Wages Payable		76,000
	Payroll Taxes Payable		4,000
	(To record factory labor costs)		
	3.		
28	Manufacturing Overhead	59,800	
	Accounts Payable, Accumulated Depreciation, and Prepaid Insurance		59,800
	(To record overhead costs)		
	4.		
28	Work in Process Inventory	48,000	
	Manufacturing Overhead	3,000	
	Raw Materials Inventory		51,000
	(To assign raw materials to production)		

		Debit	Credit
	5.		
28	Work in Process Inventory	78,000	
	Manufacturing Overhead	2,000	
	Factory Labor		80,000
	(To assign factory labor to production)		
	6.		
28	Work in Process Inventory	62,400	
	Manufacturing Overhead		62,400
	(To assign overhead to jobs)		
	7.		
28	Finished Goods Inventory	120,600	
	Work in Process Inventory		120,600
	(To record completion of Job A16: direct materials, $27,000, direct labor $52,000, and manufacturing overhead $41,600)		
	8.		
28	Accounts Receivable	150,000	
	Cost of Goods Sold	120,600	
	Sales		150,000
	Finished Goods Inventory		120,600
	(To record sale of Job A16)		

(b) Manufacturing Overhead has a debit balance of $2,400 as shown below:

Manufacturing Overhead

(3)	59,800	(6)	62,400
(4)	3,000		
(5)	2,000		
Bal.	2,400		

Thus, manufacturing overhead is underapplied during the month.

***Note:** All **asterisked** Questions, Exercises, and Problems relate to material contained in the Appendix to each chapter.

QUESTIONS

1. Lynn Lang is studying for her next accounting examination. Explain to Lynn what she should know about the differences between the income statements for a manufacturing company and a merchandising company.

2. Holly Holm is unclear as to the difference between the balance sheets of a merchandising company and a manufacturing company. Explain the difference to Holly.

3. How are manufacturing costs classified?

4. Joe Jenson claims that the distinction between direct and indirect materials is based entirely on physical association with the product. Is Joe correct? Why?

5. Tim Pearson is confused about the differences between a product cost and a period cost. Explain the differences to Tim.

6. Ray Rolfe also asks your help with the terms (a) "prime costs" and (b) "conversion costs." Distinguish between the terms.

7. In the Chem Company, direct materials are $12,000, direct labor is $18,000, and manufacturing overhead is $9,000. What is the amount of (a) prime costs and (b) conversion costs?

8. The determination of the cost of goods manufactured involves the following factors: (a) beginning work in process inventory, (b) total manufacturing costs, and (c) ending work in process inventory. Identify the meaning of x in the following formulas:

(a) $A + B = x$

(b) $A + B - C = x$

9. Why is the unit cost of a manufactured product important to management?

10. Distinguish between cost accounting and a cost accounting system.

11. Describe the major steps in the flow of costs in a job order cost accounting system.

12. There are three inventory control accounts in a job order system. Identify the control accounts and their subsidiary ledgers.

13. Jean Jorden is confused about the source documents used in assigning materials and labor costs. Identify the documents and give the entry for each document.

14. What is the purpose of a job cost sheet?

15. Indicate the source documents that are used in charging costs to specific jobs.

16. Amy Adare believes actual manufacturing overhead should be charged to jobs. Do you agree? Why or why not?

17. What relationships are involved in computing a predetermined overhead rate?

18. Marty Malloy is confused about under- and overapplied manufacturing overhead. Define the terms for Marty and indicate the balance in the manufacturing overhead account applicable to each term.

19. Under- or overapplied overhead is reported in the income statement when monthly financial statements are prepared. Do you agree? If not, indicate the proper presentation.

20. At the end of the year, under- or overapplied overhead is closed to Income Summary. Is this correct? If not, indicate the customary treatment of this account.

***21.** Indicate how the manufacturing inventory accounts are entered in the last six columns of the work sheet.

EXERCISES

E22-1 Incomplete manufacturing cost data for the Anton Company are presented on the top of the next page.

	Direct Materials Used	Direct Labor Used	Manufacturing Overhead	Total Manufacturing Costs	Work in Process 1/1	Work in Process 12/31	Cost of Goods Manufacturing
(1)	$110,000	$140,000	$ 70,000	(a)	$30,000	(b)	$330,000
(2)	(c)	200,000	120,000	$450,000	(d)	$40,000	420,000
(3)	80,000	100,000	(e)	260,000	50,000	60,000	(f)
(4)	70,000	(g)	75,000	280,000	45,000	(h)	290,000
(5)	(i)	120,000	80,000	(j)	60,000	70,000	310,000

INSTRUCTIONS

(a) Indicate the missing amount for each letter.

(b) Prepare a condensed cost of goods manufactured schedule for situation (1) for the year ended December 31, 1987.

E22-2 An analysis of the accounts of Saxon Manufacturing, Inc. reveals the following manufacturing cost data for the month ended June 30, 1988.

Inventories:	Beginning	Ending
Raw Materials	$8,000	$11,000
Work in process	6,000	8,000
Finished goods	7,000	6,000

Costs incurred:

Raw materials purchases $62,000, direct labor $50,000, Manufacturing overhead $18,200. The specific overhead costs were: indirect labor $5,000, factory insurance $4,000, machinery depreciation $4,000, machinery repairs $1,800, factory utilities $2,400, miscellaneous factory costs $1,000.

INSTRUCTIONS

(a) Prepare the cost of goods manufactured schedule for the month ended June 30, 1988.

(b) Show the presentation of the ending inventories on the June 30, 1988 balance sheet.

E22-3 The Corrado Company reports the following costs and expenses in April.

Factory utilities	$ 7,500	Direct labor	$79,100
Depreciation on factory equipment	12,650	Sales salaries	39,400
Depreciation on delivery trucks	3,500	Property taxes on factory building	1,500
Indirect factory labor	46,900	Repairs to office equipment	1,300
Indirect materials	86,200	Factory repairs	2,000
Direct materials used	127,800	Advertising	15,000
President's salary	10,000	Office supplies used	2,000
Factory manager's salary	8,000		

INSTRUCTIONS

From the information, determine the total amount of

(a) prime costs.

(b) manufacturing overhead.

(c) conversion costs.

(d) product costs.

(e) period costs.

E22-4 The All-Purpose Manufacturing Company does not have a cost accounting system. From its accounting records it prepares the following schedule and financial statements on a yearly basis:

(a) Schedule of Cost of Goods Manufactured
(b) Income Statement
(c) Balance Sheet

The following items are found in its ledger and accompanying data:

1. Direct labor
2. Raw materials inventory, 1/1
3. Work in process inventory, 12/31
4. Finished goods inventory, 1/1
5. Indirect labor
6. Cost of operating the billing department
7. Depreciation on office building
8. Depreciation on factory machinery
9. Finished goods inventory, 12/31
10. Work in process, 1/1
11. Cost of goods manufactured
12. Factory maintenance salaries
13. Depreciation on delivery equipment
14. Cost of goods available for sale
15. Direct materials used
16. Office supplies used
17. Heat and electricity for factory
18. Office supplies inventory, 12/31
19. Repairs to roof of factory building
20. Cost of raw materials purchases

INSTRUCTIONS

List the items (1)-(20). For each item, indicate by using the appropriate letter or letters, the schedule and/or financial statements in which the item will appear.

E22-5 The gross earnings of the factory workers for the Kozlowski Company during the month of January is $88,000. The employer's payroll taxes for the factory payroll is $9,000 and the fringe benefits to be paid by the employer on this payroll is $4,500. Of the total accumulated cost of factory labor, 90% is related to direct labor and 10% is attributable to indirect labor.

INSTRUCTIONS

(a) Prepare the entry to record the factory labor costs for the month of January.
(b) Prepare the entry to assign factory labor to production.
(c) Prepare the entry to assign manufacturing overhead to production, assuming the predetermined overhead rate is 120% of direct labor cost.

E22-6 Kline Manufacturing uses a job order cost accounting system. On May 1, the company has a balance in Work in Process Inventory of $3,200 and two jobs in process: Job No. 429, $2,000, and Job No. 430, $1,200. During May, a summary of source documents reveals the following:

For	Materials Requisition Slips	Labor Time Tickets
Job No. 429	$1,500	$ 2,500
Job No. 430	2,000	3,000
Job No. 431	2,500	3,500
General Use	800	1,200
Job No. 432	3,000	4,000
	$9,800	$14,200

Kline Manufacturing applies manufacturing overhead to jobs at an overhead rate of 70% of direct labor cost. Job No. 429 is completed during the month.

INSTRUCTIONS

(a) Prepare summary journal entries to record the requisition slips, time tickets, the assignment of manufacturing overhead to jobs, and the completion of Job No. 429.

(b) Post the entries to Work in Process Inventory and prove the agreement of the control account with the job cost sheets.

E22-7 A job order cost sheet for the Heath Company is shown below.

Job No. 92			For 2,000 Units
Date	Direct Materials	Direct Labor	Manufacturing Overhead
1/1	4,000	6,000	4,500
8	6,000		
12		8,000	6,400
25	2,000		
27		4,000	3,200
	12,000	18,000	14,100
Cost of completed job:			
Direct materials			$12,000
Direct labor			18,000
Manufacturing overhead			14,100
Total cost			$44,100
Unit cost ($44,100 ÷ 2,000)			$22.05

INSTRUCTIONS

(a) On the basis of the foregoing data answer the following questions:

1. What was the balance in Work in Process Inventory on January 1 if this was the only unfinished job?
2. If manufacturing overhead is applied on the basis of direct labor cost, what overhead rate was used in each year?

(b) Prepare summary entries at January 31 to record the current year's transactions pertaining to Job No. 92.

E22-8 Manufacturing cost data for Garrow Company, which uses a job order cost system, are presented below:

	Case A	Case B	Case C	Case D
Direct Materials Used	A	$75,000	H	$ 65,000
Direct Labor	$ 50,000	96,000	I	L
Manufacturing Overhead Applied	42,500	D	$102,000	M
Total Manufacturing Costs	180,650	E	260,000	250,000
Work in Process 1/1/86	B	15,500	J	60,000
Total Cost of Work in Process	201,500	F	307,000	N
Work in Process 12/31/86	C	9,000	60,000	O
Cost of Goods Manufactured	189,275	G	K	310,000

INSTRUCTIONS

Indicate the missing amount for each letter. Assume that in all cases manufacturing overhead is applied on the basis of direct labor cost and the rate is the same. (Hint: In Case C, Item I must be computed before Item H.)

E22-9 The Canton Company applies manufacturing overhead to jobs on the basis of machine hours used. Overhead costs are expected to total $300,000 for the year, and machine usage is estimated at 200,000 hours.

In January, $26,000 of overhead costs are incurred and 16,000 machine hours are used. For the remainder of the year, $284,000 of overhead costs are incurred and 194,000 machine hours are worked.

INSTRUCTIONS

(a) Compute the manufacturing overhead rate for the year.

(b) What is the amount of under- or overapplied overhead at January 31? How should this amount be reported in the financial statements prepared on January 31?

(c) What is the amount of under- or overapplied overhead at December 31?

(d) Assuming the under- or overapplied overhead for the year is not allocated to inventory accounts, give the journal entry to assign the amount to cost of goods sold.

E22-10 A job cost sheet of the Tabler Company is given below.

Job Cost Sheet

JOB NO. 469 — Quantity 3,500
ITEM Widgets — Date Requested 7/31
FOR J&R Company — Date Completed 7/31

Date	Direct Materials	Direct Labor	Manufacturing Overhead
7/10	700		
12	952		
15		440	528
22		360	432
24	1,600		
27	1,500		
31		540	648

Cost of completed job	
Direct materials	____
Direct labor	____
Manufacturing overhead	____
Total cost	____
Unit cost	____

INSTRUCTIONS

(a) Answer the following questions:

1. What are the source documents for direct materials, direct labor, and manufacturing overhead costs assigned to this job?
2. What is the predetermined manufacturing overhead rate?
3. What is the total cost and unit cost of the completed job?

(b) Prepare (1) summary journal entries on July 31 for the costs assigned to this job, and (2) the entry to record the completion of the job.

E22-11 The McCarthy Corporation incurred the following transactions.

1. Purchased raw materials on account, $45,900.

2. Raw Materials of $36,000 were requisitioned to the factory. An analysis of the materials requisition slips indicated that $8,500 was classified as indirect materials.
3. Factory labor costs totaled to $59,000. In addition the employer's payroll taxes were 10% of the labor costs.
4. Time tickets indicated that $60,000 was direct labor and $4,900 was indirect labor.
5. Overhead costs incurred on account were $10,500.
6. Manufacturing overhead was applied at the rate of 90% of direct labor cost.
7. Goods costing $87,000 were completed and transferred to finished goods.
8. Finished goods costing $51,000 to manufacture were sold on account for $103,000.

INSTRUCTIONS

Journalize the transactions. (Omit explanations.)

***E22-12**

INSTRUCTIONS

Using the data in Exercise 22-2, prepare a partial work sheet for Saxon Manufacturing, Inc.

PROBLEMS

P22-1 The following data were taken from the records of the Lucette Manufacturing Company for the year ended December 31, 1987.

Raw Materials Inventory 1/1/87	$ 39,500	Factory Insurance	$ 3,400
Raw Materials Inventory 12/31/87	43,200	Factory Machinery Depreciation	7,700
Finished Goods Inventory 1/1/87	85,000	Freight-in on Raw Materials Purchased	3,900
Finished Goods Inventory 12/31/87	77,800	Factory Utilities	14,900
Work in Process Inventory 1/1/87	10,200	Office Utilities Expense	8,600
Work in Process Inventory 12/31/87	6,600	Sales	425,000
Direct Labor	125,100	Sales Discounts	1,200
Indirect Labor	19,100	Plant Manager's Salary	30,000
Accounts Receivable	26,000	Factory Property Taxes	6,100
		Factory Repairs	800
		Raw Materials Purchases	62,600
		Cash	28,000

INSTRUCTIONS

(a) Prepare a cost of goods manufactured schedule.
(b) Prepare an income statement through gross profit.
(c) Prepare the current asset section of the balance sheet at December 31.
(d) Prepare the manufacturing summary account at December 31. Show manufacturing overhead as one amount.

P22-2 Franklin Manufacturing uses a job order cost accounting system. On January 1, 1987, the company had Raw Materials Inventory $25,000 and Finished Goods Inventory, represented by Job No. 12, $124,000. During the month, the following summary transactions and events occurred.

1. Purchased raw materials on account $225,000.
2. Incurred factory labor $300,000. (Credit Factory Wages Payable.)
3. Incurred manufacturing overhead on account $200,000.
4. Recognized $5,000 of depreciation on factory machinery.
5. Charged direct materials to jobs: No. 13 $80,000; No. 14 $60,000; and No. 15 $40,000; and charged indirect materials of $30,000 to manufacturing overhead. The jobs call for the production of 10,000, 5,000, and 8,000 units, respectively.
6. Charged factory labor to jobs on basis of time tickets: No. 13 $120,000; No. 14 $100,000; and No. 15 $60,000. The remaining labor was indirect.
7. Charged overhead to jobs at the rate of 90% of direct labor cost.
8. Completed Job. No. 13 and Job No. 14.
9. Sold Job Nos. 12 and 14 on account for $460,000.

INSTRUCTIONS

(a) Journalize the transactions and events.
(b) Open accounts for the beginning inventories and post the entries to the job order cost accounts and to the job cost sheets.
(c) Reconcile the balance in Work in Process Inventory with the costs of unfinished jobs.
(d) Show the balance sheet presentation of the January 31 inventories.
(e) Indicate how the balance in the Manufacturing Overhead account should be reported on January 31, assuming the company's fiscal year ends on December 31.

P22-3 For the year ended December 31, 1987, the job cost sheets of the Gleason Company contained the following data.

Job Number	Explanation	Direct Materials	Direct Labor	Manufacturing Overhead	Total Costs
7650	Balance 1/1	$18,000	$20,000	$25,000	$ 63,000
	Current year's costs	22,000	30,000	37,500	89,500
7651	Balance 1/1	12,000	18,000	22,500	52,500
	Current year's costs	28,000	40,000	50,000	118,000
7652	Current year's costs	40,000	60,000	75,000	175,000
7653	Current year's costs	50,000	70,000	87,500	207,500

Other data:

1. Raw materials inventory totaled $20,000 on January 1. During the year, $150,000 of raw materials were purchased on account.
2. Finished goods on January 1 consisted of Job. No. 7648 for $98,000 and Job No. 7649 for $62,000.
3. Job No. 7650 for 20,000 units and Job No. 7651 for 40,000 units were completed during the year.
4. Job Nos. 7648, 7649, and 7650 were sold on account for $380,000.
5. Manufacturing overhead incurred on account totaled $210,000.
6. Other manufacturing overhead consisted of indirect materials $12,000, indirect labor $18,000, and depreciation on factory machinery $6,000.

INSTRUCTIONS

(a) Journalize the transactions in the sequence followed in the chapter. Credit Factory Wages Payable when recording factory labor.
(b) Prove the agreement of Work in Process Inventory with job cost sheets pertaining to unfinished work.

(c) Prepare the adjusting entry for manufacturing overhead, assuming the balance is allocated entirely to cost of goods sold.

(d) Prepare an income statement for the year through gross profit. (Hint: Show cost of goods sold as one line.)

(e) Show the balance sheet presentation of the inventory accounts at December 31.

P22-4 Stanley Gruber is a contractor specializing in custom-built garages. On May 1, 1987, his ledger contains the following data:

Raw Materials Inventory	$30,000
Work in Process Inventory	9,800
Manufacturing Overhead	2,500 (dr.)

The Manufacturing Overhead account has debit totals of $12,500 and credit totals of $10,000. Subsidiary data on May 1 include:

Job Cost Sheets

Job By Customer	Direct Materials	Direct Labor	Manufacturing Overhead
Fox	$1,500	$2,000	$1,300
Cox	1,200	1,200	780
Lox	500	800	520
	$3,200	$4,000	$2,600

A summary of materials requisition slips and time tickets for the month of May reveals the following:

Job by Customer	Materials Requisition Slips	Time Tickets
Fox	$ 200	$ 400
Cox	600	1,000
Lox	1,500	1,300
Box	1,400	1,900
Pox	1,300	1,800
	5,000	6,400
General Use	1,200	1,800
	$6,200	$8,200

During May the following costs were incurred: (a) raw materials purchased on account, $5,000, (b) labor paid, $8,200, (c) manufacturing overhead paid, $3,400. Overhead was charged to jobs on the basis of direct labor cost at the same rate as in the previous month.

The garages for customers Fox, Cox, and Lox were completed during May. Each garage was sold for $9,000 cash.

INSTRUCTIONS

(a) Prepare journal entries for the May transactions. (Credit Factory Wages Payable for factory labor.)

(b) Post the entries to Work in Process Inventory and Manufacturing Overhead.

(c) Reconcile the balance in Work in Process Inventory with the costs of unfinished jobs.

(d) Is manufacturing overhead under- or overapplied? How should this amount be reported in the May 31 financial statements if the company's fiscal year ends December 31?

P22-5 Lujack Company's fiscal year ends on June 30. The following accounts are found in its job order cost accounting system for the first month of the new fiscal year.

Raw Materials Inventory

July 1	Beginning balance	19,000	July 31	Requisitions	(B)
31	Purchases	(A)			
July 31	Ending balance	26,500			

Work in Process Inventory

July 1	Beginning balance	(C)	July 31	Jobs completed	(F)
31	Direct materials	72,000			
31	Direct labor	(D)			
31	Overhead	(E)			
July 31	Ending balance	(G)			

Finished Goods Inventory

July 1	Beginning balance	(H)	July 31	Cost of goods sold	(J)
31	Completed jobs	(I)			
July 31	Ending balance	(K)			

Factory Labor

July 31	Factory wages	(L)	July 31	Wages assigned	(M)

Manufacturing Overhead

July 31	Indirect materials	6,400	July 31	Overhead applied	91,000
31	Indirect labor	12,000			
31	Other overhead	(N)			

Other data:

1. On July 1, two jobs were in process: Job No. 4085 and Job No. 4086 with costs of $17,000 and $8,200, respectively.
2. During July, Job Nos. 4087, 4088, and 4089, were started. On July 31, Job. No. 4089 was unfinished. This job had charges for direct materials $2,000, direct labor $1,500 plus manufacturing overhead.
3. On July 1, Job No. 4084, costing $135,000, was in the finished goods warehouse. On July 31, Job No. 4088, costing $143,000, was in finished goods.
4. Manufacturing overhead was applied at the rate of 130% of direct labor cost. Overhead was $2,000 underapplied in July.

INSTRUCTIONS

(a) List the letters A through N and indicate the amount pertaining to each letter. Show computations.

(b) Indicate the statement presentation of underapplied manufacturing overhead on July 31.

***P22-6** The Pickford Manufacturing Company uses a simple manufacturing accounting system. At the end of its fiscal year on August 31, 1987, the adjusted trial balance contains the following accounts.

Debits		Credits	
Cash	$ 14,700	Accumulated Depreciation	$ 350,000
Accounts Receivable (net)	63,900	Notes Payable	55,000
Finished Goods Inventory	55,000	Accounts Payable	36,200
Work in Process Inventory	27,800	Income Taxes Payable	9,000
Raw Materials Inventory	36,200	Common Stock	350,000
Plant Assets	890,000	Retained Earnings	205,300
Raw Materials Purchases	238,500	Sales	990,000
Direct Labor	280,900		
Indirect Labor	27,400		
Factory Repairs	17,200		
Factory Depreciation	19,000		
Factory Manager's Salary	40,000		
Factory Insurance	12,000		
Factory Property Taxes	11,900		
Factory Utilities	14,300		
Selling Expenses	98,500		
Administrative Expenses	112,200		
Income Taxes Expense	36,000		
	$1,995,500		$1,995,500

Physical inventory counts on August 31, 1987 show the following inventory amounts: Finished goods $48,600, Work in process $32,400, and Raw materials $44,500.

INSTRUCTIONS

(a) Enter the adjusted trial balance data on a work sheet in financial statement order and complete the work sheet.
(b) Prepare a cost of goods manufactured schedule for the year.
(c) Prepare an income statement for the year and a balance sheet at August 31, 1987.
(d) Journalize the closing entries.
(e) Post the closing entries to Manufacturing Summary and to Income Summary.

ALTERNATE PROBLEMS

P22-1A The following data were taken from the records of the Hackney Manufacturing Company for the year ended June 30, 1988.

Raw Materials Inventory 7/1/87	$ 45,500	Factory Insurance	$ 4,600
Raw Materials Inventory 6/30/88	38,600	Factory Machinery Depreciation	10,000
Finished Goods Inventory 7/1/87	96,000	Freight-in on Raw Materials Purchased	8,600
Finished Goods Inventory 6/30/88	99,900	Factory Utilities	24,600
Work in Process Inventory 7/1/87	24,000	Office Utilities Expense	8,650
Work in Process Inventory 6/30/88	18,700	Sales	537,000
Direct Labor	147,250	Sales Discounts	3,300
Indirect Labor	24,460	Plant Manager's Salary	28,000
Accounts Receivable	17,000	Factory Property Taxes	9,600
		Factory Repairs	1,400
		Raw Materials Purchases	88,800
		Cash	32,000

INSTRUCTIONS

(a) Prepare a cost of goods manufactured schedule.

(b) Prepare an income statement through gross profit.

(c) Prepare the current asset section of the balance sheet at June 30, 1988.

(d) Prepare the manufacturing summary account at June 30, 1988. Show manufacturing overhead as one amount.

P22-2A Frances Manufacturing uses a job order cost accounting system. On January 1, 1987, the company had Raw Materials Inventory $10,000 and Finished Goods Inventory, represented by Job No. 18, $135,000. During the month, the following summary transactions and events occurred.

1. Purchased raw materials on account $270,000.
2. Incurred factory labor $340,000. (Credit Factory Wages Payable.)
3. Incurred manufacturing overhead on account $350,000.
4. Recognized $10,000 of depreciation on factory machinery.
5. Charged direct materials to jobs: No. 19 $90,000; No. 20 $70,000; and No. 21 $60,000. The jobs call for the production of 12,000, 9,000, and 11,000 units, respectively.
6. Charged factory labor to jobs on basis of time tickets: No. 19 $150,000; No. 20 $130,000; and No. 21 $50,000. The remaining labor was indirect.
7. Charged overhead to jobs at the rate of 110% of direct labor cost.
8. Completed Job No. 19 and Job No. 20.
9. Sold Job Nos. 18 and 20 on account for $600,000.

INSTRUCTIONS

(a) Journalize the transactions and events.

(b) Open accounts for the beginning inventories and post the entries in (a) to the job order cost accounts and to the job cost sheets.

(c) Reconcile the balance in Work in Process Inventory with the costs of unfinished jobs.

(d) Indicate the balance sheet presentation of the January 31 inventories.

(e) Indicate how the balance in the Manufacturing Overhead account should be reported on January 31, assuming the company's fiscal year ends December 31.

P22-3A For the year ended December 31, 1987, the job cost sheets of the Gleason Company contained the following data.

Job Number	Explanation	Direct Materials	Direct Labor	Manufacturing Overhead	Total Costs
7640	Balance 1/1	$20,000	$24,000	$28,800	$ 72,800
	Current year's costs	26,000	36,000	43,200	105,200
7641	Balance 1/1	10,000	18,000	21,600	49,600
	Current year's costs	32,000	48,000	57,600	137,600
7642	Current year's costs	42,000	60,000	72,000	174,000
7643	Current year's costs	38,000	56,000	67,200	161,200

Other data:

1. Raw materials inventory totaled $15,000 on January 1. During the year, $145,000 of raw materials were purchased on account.
2. Finished goods on January 1 consisted of Job No. 7638 for $87,000 and Job No. 7639 for $92,000.

3. Job No. 7640 for 25,000 units and Job No. 7641 for 32,000 units were completed during the year.
4. Job Nos. 7638, 7639, and 7641 were sold on account for $440,000.
5. Manufacturing overhead incurred on account totaled $195,000.
6. Other manufacturing overhead consisted of indirect materials $14,000, indirect labor $20,000, and depreciation on factory machinery $8,000.

INSTRUCTIONS

(a) Journalize the transactions in the sequence followed in the chapter. (Credit Factory Wages Payable when recording factory labor.)
(b) Prove the agreement of Work in Process Inventory with job cost sheets pertaining to unfinished work.
(c) Prepare the adjusting entry for manufacturing overhead, assuming the balance is allocated entirely to Cost of Goods Sold.
(d) Prepare an income statement for the year through gross profit. (Hint: Show cost of goods sold as one line.)
(e) Show the balance sheet presentation of the inventory accounts at December 31.

P22-4A Summer Living, Inc. is a construction company specializing in custom patios. The patios are constructed of concrete, brick, fiber glass, and lumber, depending upon customer preference. On June 1, 1987, the general ledger for Summer Living contains the following data:

Raw Material Inventory	$4,200	Manufacturing overhead applied	$6,700
Work in Process Inventory	$4,928	Manufacturing overhead incurred	$5,900

Subsidiary data for work in process on June 1 are as follows:

Job Cost Sheets

	Customer Job		
Cost Element	Lex	Mex	Tex
Direct materials	$ 600	$ 800	$ 900
Direct Labor	330	540	590
Manufacturing overhead	264	432	472
	$1,194	$1,772	$1,962

A summary of materials requisition slips and time tickets for June shows the following:

Customer Job	Materials Requisition Slips	Time Tickets
Lex	$ 800	$ 450
Rex	1,600	700
Mex	500	375
Tex	1,300	800
Wex	400	300
Lex	300	250
	4,900	2,875
General use	400	1,200
	$5,300	$4,075

During June, raw materials purchased on account were $3,900 and all wages were paid. Additional overhead costs consisted of depreciation on equipment $500 and miscellaneous costs of $300 incurred on account. Overhead was charged to jobs at the same rate that was used in May. The patios for customers Lex, Mex, and Tex were completed during June and sold for a total $18,700. Each customer paid in full.

INSTRUCTIONS

(a) Journalize the June transactions.
(b) Post the entries to Work in Process and Manufacturing Overhead.
(c) Reconcile the balance in Work in Process with the costs of unfinished jobs.
(d) Is manufacturing overhead under- or overapplied? How should this amount be reported in the June 30 financial statements if the company's fiscal year ends on September 30?

P22-5A The Rancom Corporation's fiscal year ends on November 30. The following accounts are found in its job order cost accounting system for the first month of the new fiscal year.

Raw Materials Inventory

Dec. 1	Beginning balance	(A)	Dec. 31	Requisitions	15,850
31	Purchases	13,025			
Dec. 31	Ending balance	6,775			

Work in Process Inventory

Dec. 1	Beginning balance	(B)	Dec. 31	Jobs completed	(E)
31	Direct materials	(C)			
31	Direct labor	7,200			
31	Overhead	(D)			
Dec. 31	Ending balance	(F)			

Finished Goods Inventory

Dec. 1	Beginning balance	(G)	Dec. 31	Cost of goods sold	(I)
31	Completed jobs	(H)			
Dec. 31	Ending balance	(J)			

Factory Labor

Dec. 31	Factory wages	9,700	Dec. 31	Wages assigned	(K)

Manufacturing Overhead

Dec. 31	Indirect materials	1,900	Dec. 31	Overhead applied	(M)
31	Indirect labor	(L)			
31	Other overhead	1,130			

Other data:

1. On December 1, two jobs were in process: Job No. 154 and Job No. 155. These jobs had combined direct materials costs of $9,750 and direct labor costs of $12,000. Overhead was applied at a rate that was 80% of direct labor cost.
2. During December, Job Nos. 156, 157, and 158 were started. On December 31, Job No. 158 was unfinished. This job had charges for direct materials $3,800, direct labor $4,400 plus manufacturing overhead. All jobs, except for Job No. 158, were completed in December.

3. On December 1, Job No. 153 was in the finished goods warehouse. It had a total cost of $5,000. On December 31, Job No. 157 was the only job finished that was not sold. It had a cost of $4,000.
4. Manufacturing overhead was $230 overapplied in December.

INSTRUCTIONS

(a) List the letters A through M and indicate the amount pertaining to each letter.

(b) Indicate the statement presentation of overapplied manufacturing overhead on December 31.

DECISION CASE

The Van Tyle Products Company uses a job order cost system. For a number of months there has been an on-going rift between the sales department and the production department concerning a special order product, Super X. Super X is a seasonal product that is manufactured in batches of 1,000 units. Super X is sold at cost plus a mark-up of 40% of cost.

The sales department is unhappy because fluctuating unit production costs significantly affect selling prices. Sales personnel complain that this has caused excessive customer complaints and the loss of considerable orders for Super X.

The production department maintains that each job order must be fully costed on the basis of the costs incurred during the period in which the goods are produced. Production personnel maintain that the only real solution to the problem is for the sales department to increase sales in the slack periods.

W. E. Van Tyle, president of the company, asks you as the company accountant to collect quarterly data for the past year on Super X. From the cost accounting system, you accumulate the following production quantity and cost data:

	Quarter			
Costs	1	2	3	4
Direct materials	$ 25,000	$ 55,000	$ 20,000	$ 50,000
Direct labor	60,000	132,000	48,000	120,000
Manufacturing overhead	105,000	123,000	97,000	125,000
Total	$190,000	$310,000	$165,000	$295,000
Production in batches	5	11	4	10
Unit cost (per batch)	$ 38,000	$ 28,182	$ 41,250	$ 29,500

INSTRUCTIONS

(a) What manufacturing cost element is responsible for the fluctuating unit costs? Why?

(b) What is your recommended solution to the problem of fluctuating unit cost?

(c) Restate the quarterly data on the basis of your recommended solution.

CHAPTER 23

St. Petersburg Junior College, Florida

CHAPTER 23

PROCESS COST ACCOUNTING

STUDY OBJECTIVES

After studying this chapter, you should be able to:

1. Identify the features of process cost accounting.
2. Contrast the flow of costs between process cost accounting and job order cost accounting.
3. State the end-of-period procedures in process cost accounting.
4. Compute the physical units of production.
5. Compute equivalent units of production for each process or department.
6. Indicate how unit costs are computed.
7. Explain the method and objective of assigning costs in process cost accounting.
8. Prepare and explain the content of the production cost report.
9. Identify the special problems that may occur in process cost accounting.

Process cost accounting is the system of accounting used by companies that manufacture products through a series of continuous processes or operations. In contrast to job order cost accounting, in which the focus is on the individual job, process cost accounting focuses on the processes involved in producing homogeneous products.

The major accounting differences between job order and process cost systems are highlighted first in this chapter. Then we explain and illustrate the entries, accounts, and reports associated with process cost accounting. At the end of the chapter, special problems associated with process cost accounting are considered.

CHARACTERISTICS OF CONTINUOUS PROCESS MANUFACTURING

Continuous process manufacturing, sometimes referred to as mass production operations, occurs in producing such items as steel (USX Corp.), cereals (Kellogg's), petroleum products (Exxon), and paint (Sherwin-Williams). One characteristic of this type of manufacturing is that **once the production begins, it continues without interruption until the finished product emerges.** For example, in a beverage company such as Coca-Cola, the process begins with the blending of the beverage. Next, the beverage is dispensed into bottles that are moved into position by automated machinery. The bottles are then capped, packaged, and forwarded to the finished goods warehouse. A second characteristic is that **when the finished product emerges, all units will have been processed in the same manner with precisely the same amount of materials, labor, and overhead.** Each finished unit, such as a bottle of Coke, will therefore be indistinguishable one from another.

Continuous processing manufacturing companies generally produce for stock (inventory) rather than for specific orders. In recent years, manufacturing operations in these companies have become highly automated and there has been a marked increase in the use of robotic equipment.

FEATURES OF PROCESS COST ACCOUNTING

In process cost accounting, as in a job order system, it is necessary to record both the accumulation and assignment of manufacturing costs. A distinctive feature of process cost accounting, however, is that **individual work in process accounts are maintained for each production department or manufacturing process.** For example, in our beverage company there would be a work in process account for each of the manufacturing processes as illustrated below:

Manufacturing processes and work in process accounts

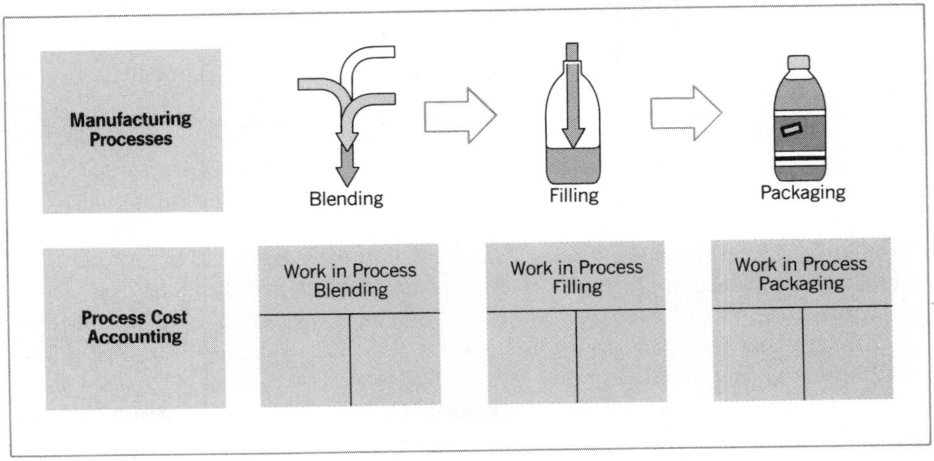

A second feature of process costing is that **costs charged to work in process are summarized in production cost reports rather than in job cost sheets.**

There are also significant differences between process and job order cost accounting in determining total manufacturing costs and unit costs. In process cost accounting, total costs are determined at the end of a period of time, such as a month, rather than when a job is finished. Unit costs in process costing are computed by dividing total manufacturing costs by the units produced during the period.

The major differences between job order cost accounting and process cost accounting are summarized below.

Differences between job order and process cost accounting

Feature	Job Order Cost Accounting	Process Cost Accounting
Work in process accounts	One	One for each process
Summarizing of manufacturing costs	Job cost sheets	Production cost reports
Determining total manufacturing costs	Each job	Each accounting period
Unit cost computation	Cost of each job ÷ Units produced for the job	Total manufacturing costs ÷ Units of output for the period

PROCESS COST FLOW

The flow of costs in a process cost accounting system is illustrated on the next page. Note that separate work in process accounts are provided for each producing department. The other accounts and the flow of costs are the same as in job order cost accounting. For example, manufacturing costs are accumulated by debits to Raw Materials Inventory, Factory Labor, and Manufacturing Overhead. These costs are then assigned to work in process, finished goods, and cost of goods sold. The method of assigning costs, however, differs significantly. These differences are explained and illustrated later in the chapter.

The entries pertaining to the accumulation and assignment of costs are explained in the following pages, using the June transactions of the Tyler Manufacturing Company. The entries are keyed to the numbers in the flow chart on page 914. Tyler Company manufactures automatic can openers that are sold to retail outlets for $19.95. Manufacturing consists of two processes: Machining and Assembly. In the Machining Department, the raw materials are shaped, honed, and drilled. In the Assembly Department, the parts are assembled and packaged. On June 1, the ledger includes the following balances:

Beginning ledger balances

Raw Materials Inventory		Work in Process — Assembly		Finished Goods Inventory	
June 1 $24,000		June 1 $3,600		June 1 $6,000	

At June 1, there is no work in process in the Machining Department.

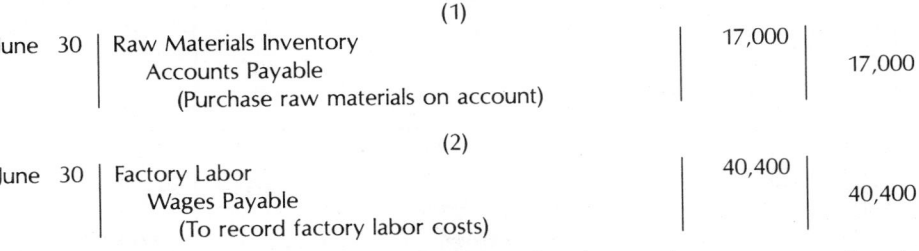

Flow of costs in process cost accounting

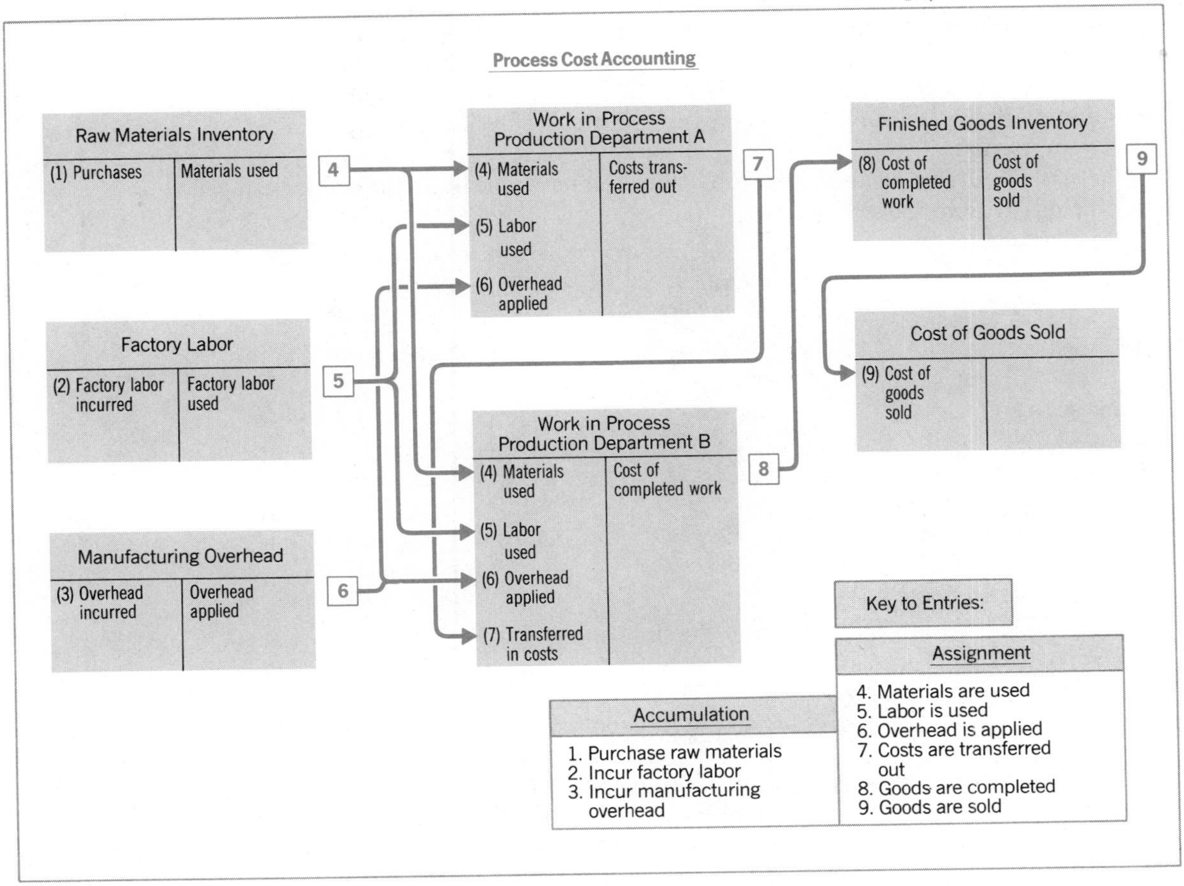

ACCUMULATION OF MANUFACTURING COSTS

Each of the three manufacturing cost elements—direct materials, direct labor, and overhead—occur in a process cost system. The accumulation of the costs of materials and labor is the same in process costing as in job order costing. All raw materials are debited to Raw Materials when the materials are purchased. Similarly, all factory labor is debited to Factory Labor when the labor costs are incurred. In the month of June, Tyler Manufacturing purchases $17,000 of raw materials and incurs $40,400 of factory labor. The summary entries for these costs are as follows:

(1)

June 30	Raw Materials Inventory	17,000	
	Accounts Payable		17,000
	(Purchase raw materials on account)		

(2)

June 30	Factory Labor	40,400	
	Wages Payable		40,400
	(To record factory labor costs)		

The accumulation of manufacturing overhead costs in process costing is also the same as in job order costing. During June, overhead costs incurred

totaled $21,000. The summary entry to recognize these costs is:

(3)

June 30	Manufacturing Overhead	21,000	
	Cash, Accounts Payable, Accumulated Depreciation		21,000
	(To record overhead incurred)		

ASSIGNMENT OF MANUFACTURING COSTS

The assignment of the three manufacturing cost elements in process cost accounting is as follows:

Materials Costs

All raw materials issued for production are a materials cost to the producing department. Material requisition slips may be used in a process cost system, but **fewer requisitions are generally required, because the materials are used for processes rather than jobs.** This means that requisitions may be made in large quantities, and they are issued less frequently than in a job order system. When a raw material is used by only one department, it is possible to determine the quantity used by a physical inventory count.

Materials are usually added to production at the beginning of the first process. However, in subsequent processes, materials may be added at various points. For example, in the manufacture of Hershey candy bars, the chocolate and other ingredients are added at the beginning of the first process, and the wrappers and cartons are added at the end of the packaging process. At Tyler Manufacturing, materials are entered at the beginning of each process. During June, materials used are: Machining, $15,000, and Assembly, $4,000. The entry to record the materials used is:

(4)

June 30	Work in Process—Machining	15,000	
	Work in Process—Assembly	4,000	
	Raw Materials Inventory		19,000
	(To record materials used)		

Factory Labor Costs

In process costing, as in job order costing, time tickets may be used in determining the cost of labor assignable to the production departments. Factory employees in a process manufacturing company, however, usually work in only one department. As a result, the labor cost chargeable to a process can be obtained from the payroll register or **departmental payroll summaries,** which provide the necessary data with a minimum of clerical effort and expense.

All labor costs incurred within a producing department are a cost of processing the raw materials. Thus, labor costs for the Machining Department will include the wages of employees who shape, hone, and drill the raw materials, as well as those who work as timekeepers and supervisors. At the Tyler Company, labor costs occur uniformly within each process. During June, the labor costs are: Machining, $24,000, and Assembly, $16,400. The entry to assign these costs is:

(5)

Date	Account	Debit	Credit
June 30	Work in Process – Machining	24,000	
	Work in Process – Assembly	16,400	
	Factory Labor		40,400
	(To assign factory labor to production)		

Manufacturing Overhead Costs

The assignment of manufacturing overhead to Work in Process is similar to the procedure used in job order costing. Tyler Manufacturing's predetermined overhead rate is 50% of the labor costs assigned to each production department.[1] The entry to apply manufacturing overhead to the two processes, therefore, is as follows:

(6)

Date	Account	Debit	Credit
June 30	Work in Process – Machining	12,000	
	Work in Process – Assembly	8,200	
	Manufacturing Overhead		20,200
	(To assign overhead to processes)		

After the foregoing entries are posted, the work in process accounts of Tyler Manufacturing Company show the following data. The question marks indicate that the amount is yet to be determined.

Work in process accounts

Work in Process—Machining

June 1	Balance	—0—	June 30	Transferred to assembly	?
30	Materials	15,000			
30	Labor	24,000			
30	Overhead applied	12,000			
30	Balance	?			

Work in Process—Assembly

June 1	Balance	3,600	June 30	Transferred to finished goods	?
30	Materials	4,000			
30	Labor	16,400			
30	Overhead applied	8,200			
30	Transferred from Machining	?			
30	Balance	?			

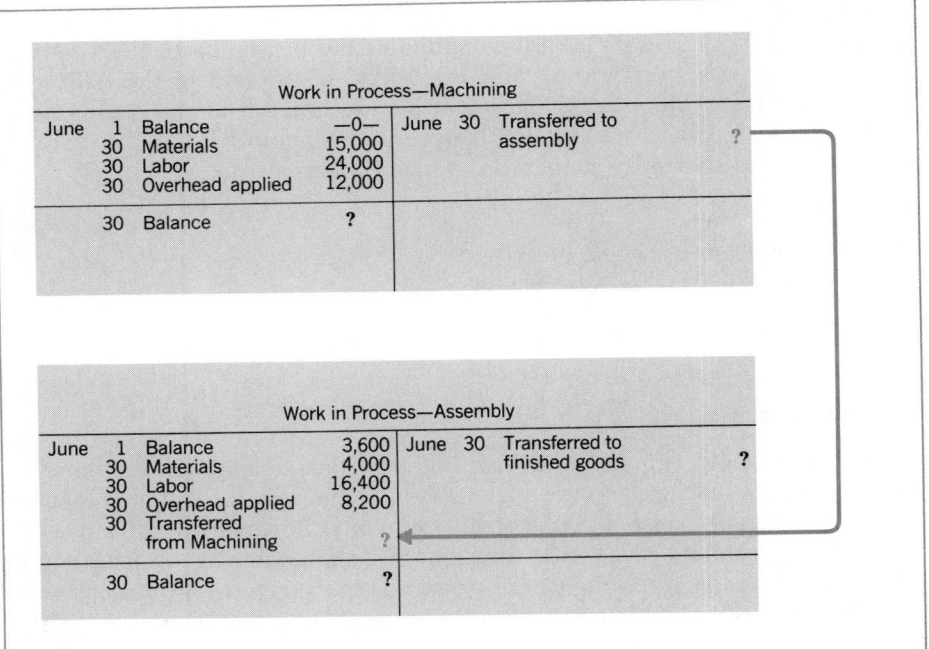

The answers to the question marks are obtained through special end-of-period procedures.

[1]When manufacturing overhead is incurred uniformly throughout the year and production is relatively stable during the year, it is permissible to assign overhead to production on an **actual cost basis.** This basis is explained and illustrated in cost accounting textbooks.

END-OF-PERIOD PROCEDURES

By the end of the period, Tyler Manufacturing has accumulated the materials, labor, and overhead costs in each production department's work in process account. Now we must assign these accumulated costs to (1) the units transferred out of each department and (2) the units in the ending work in process in each department. The procedures used in computing and assigning the costs present the most difficult challenge to your understanding of process cost accounting. For each process, it is necessary at the end of the period to:

1. Compute the physical units.
2. Compute equivalent units of production.
3. Compute unit costs of production.
4. Assign costs to the units transferred and in process.
5. Prepare the production cost report.

First, we will make all of the required computations for the Machining Department of Tyler Manufacturing. Then we will explain the computations for the Assembly Department.

SECTION ONE—MACHINING DEPARTMENT

COMPUTING PHYSICAL UNITS

In a process cost system it is important to keep track of the physical units of product in each process. This involves adding the units started (or transferred) into production during the period to the units in process at the beginning of the period to determine the total units to be accounted for. These units then must be accounted for by the output of the period which consists of units transferred out during the period and any units in process at the end of the period. Production records for Tyler Manufacturing in June show the following data in units on page 918. The records indicate that 10,000 units must be accounted for in the Machining Department. Of this sum, 8,000 units were transferred to the Assembly Department and 2,000 units are still in process. A similar analysis occurs in the Assembly Department where the units to be accounted for include the units transferred in from the Machining Department.

The percentages pertaining to the units in work in process above refer to the percentage of completion of the units. The percentages are not relevant in accounting for physical units, but they are needed in the other end-of-period procedures, as explained on the following pages.

Product data in units

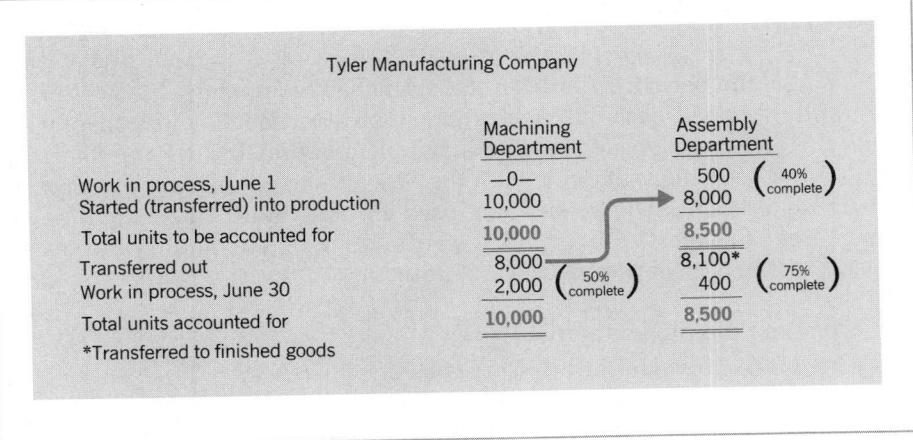

Tyler Manufacturing Company

	Machining Department		Assembly Department	
Work in process, June 1	—0—		500	(40% complete)
Started (transferred) into production	10,000		8,000	
Total units to be accounted for	10,000		8,500	
Transferred out	8,000		8,100*	
Work in process, June 30	2,000	(50% complete)	400	(75% complete)
Total units accounted for	10,000		8,500	

*Transferred to finished goods

COMPUTING EQUIVALENT UNITS OF PRODUCTION

Once the physical flow of the units is established, it is necessary to measure each department's productivity in terms of **equivalent units of production. Equivalent units of production are the work done during the period on the physical units of output expressed in terms of fully completed units.** For example, if a department's output consists entirely of 4,000 units of work in process that is 60% complete, equivalent units of production are 2,400 (4,000 × 60%). The concept of equivalent units is not unique to cost accounting. For example, your university probably expresses enrollment statistics in terms of equivalent full-time students in addition to the total number of students. If you are taking 9 hours of course work when 15 hours is considered full-time, you would be counted as a 60% equivalent full-time student; two half-time students would be counted as one equivalent full-time student.

Equivalent units of production are determined by applying the percentage of work done to the physical units of output. When there is no beginning work in process, as in Tyler's Machining Department, equivalent units are the sum of the work performed to:

1. Complete the units started into production during the period.
2. Start, but only partially complete, the units in ending work in process inventory.

EQUIVALENT UNITS FOR MATERIALS

At Tyler Manufacturing, materials are entered at the beginning of each process, and conversion costs (labor and overhead) are incurred uniformly during the process. Thus, two computations of equivalent units are required: one for materials and the other for conversion costs. From the production data

given earlier, we know that the 2,000 units in ending work in process are 50% complete. This percentage pertains only to conversion costs. The percentage of completion for materials is not stated, because in this case it is 100%. The computation of equivalent units for materials is as follows:

Computation of equivalents units—materials

Machining Department

Production Data	Physical Units	Materials Added This Period	Equivalent Units
Started and finished	8,000	100%	**8,000**
Work in process, June 30	2,000	100%	**2,000**
	10,000		**10,000**

In the Machining Department, the equivalent units for materials, 10,000, equal the physical units to be accounted for, 10,000.

The term "started and finished" may be confusing to you. **It means the number of units that were both started and completed during the period.** As a consequence, the units in work in process at the beginning and at the end of the period are not included in units "started and finished." The easiest way to compute the units started and finished is to determine the units of completed work transferred out of the department and subtract the units in work in process at the beginning of the period. The computation for the Machining Department is as follows:

Computation of units started and finished

Units transferred out	8,000
Less: Units of work in process, June 1	-0-
Units started and finished	8,000

Note that the units in ending work in process are ignored in determining the units started and finished.

EQUIVALENT UNITS FOR CONVERSION COSTS

The computation of equivalent units for conversion costs is basically the same as for material costs as illustrated below.

Computation of equivalent units—conversion costs

Machining Department

Production Data	Physical Units	Work Added This Period	Equivalent Units
Started and finished	8,000	100%	**8,000**
Work in process, June 30	2,000	50%	**1,000**
	10,000		**9,000**

Alternatively, the following graphic may be used in computing the equivalent units of conversion costs:

Equivalent units for conversion costs—graphic illustration

Machining Department

Production Data	Physical Units	Work Added This Period	%	Equivalent Units
Started and finished	8,000		100	8,000
Work in process, June 30	2,000		50	1,000
	10,000	0 20 40 60 80 100		9,000

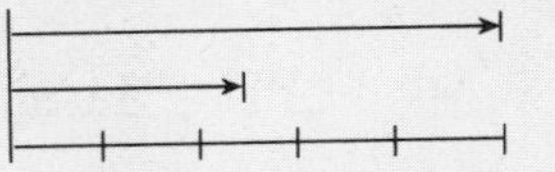

Note in this case, that equivalent units, 9,000, do not equal the physical units to be accounted for, 10,000.

COMPUTING UNIT COSTS OF PRODUCTION

Armed with knowledge of the equivalent units of production, we can now compute the unit production costs. The computation of total manufacturing cost per unit is simply total manufacturing costs divided by equivalent units. When materials and conversion costs do not occur in the process at the same time, unit costs are also determined for (1) materials and (2) conversion costs.

As indicated by the Machining Department work in process account shown on page 916, materials costs for June are $15,000, and conversion costs are $36,000 (labor, $24,000 plus overhead, $12,000). The formulas for determining the unit costs and the computations are as follows:

Unit cost formulas and computations—Machining Department

(1)	Total Materials Costs	÷	Equivalent Units of Materials	=	Unit Materials Cost
	$15,000	÷	10,000	=	$1.50
(2)	Total Conversion Costs	÷	Equivalent Units of Conversion Costs	=	Unit Conversion Cost
	$36,000	÷	9,000	=	$4.00
(3)	Unit Materials Cost	+	Unit Conversion Cost	=	Total Manufacturing Cost per Unit
	$1.50	+	$4.00	=	$5.50

As shown, the unit costs are $1.50 for materials, $4.00 for conversion costs, and $5.50 for total production costs.

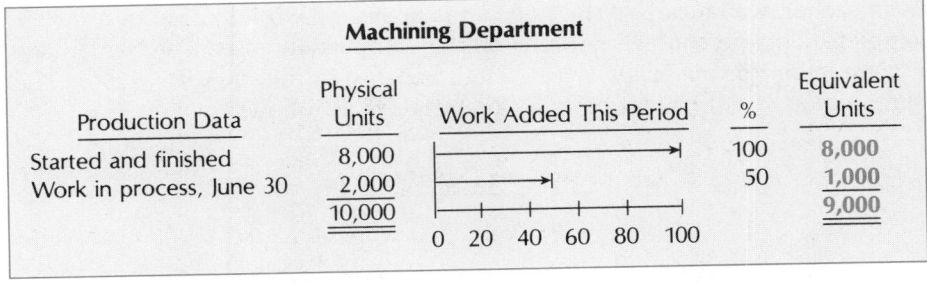

ASSIGNING COSTS TO UNITS TRANSFERRED AND IN PROCESS

Our next task is to determine the total cost of the units transferred out and the total cost of the units in ending work in process. To obtain these amounts, unit costs are assigned to the equivalent units of production for the period. The computations for the Machining Department are as follows:

Assignment of costs—Machining Department

Machining Department

Costs to be Assigned	Assignment of Costs	Equivalent Units	Unit Cost		Total Costs Assigned
Total manufacturing costs	Transferred out				
	Started and finished	8,000	$5.50		$44,000
$51,000	Ending work in process				
	Materials	2,000	$1.50	$3,000	
	Conversion costs	1,000	$4.00	4,000	7,000
					$51,000

Note that total manufacturing cost per unit, $5.50, is used in costing the units started and finished. In contrast, the unit cost of materials and the unit cost of conversion are needed in costing the units in process. As indicated in the above schedule, the total costs to be assigned must equal the total costs assigned. Alternatively, the following chart can be used in assigning costs to the work performed.

Assignment of costs—alternative illustration

Machining Department

	Costs to be Assigned	Unit Cost	Equivalent Units × Unit Cost		Costs Assigned To Units: Transferred Out		Costs Assigned To Units: In Ending Work in Process
Materials	$15,000	$1.50	Started and finished: 8,000 × $1.50	=	$12,000		
			Ending work in process: 2,000 × $1.50	=			$3,000
Conversion costs	36,000	$4.00	Started and finished: 8,000 × $4.00	=	32,000		
			Ending work in process: 1,000 × $4.00	=			4,000
	$51,000			=	$44,000	+	$7,000

When the costs have been assigned, an entry is needed to record the cost of goods transferred out of the department. In this case, the transfer is to the Assembly Department, and the following entry is made:

(7)

June 30	Work in Process—Assembly Department	44,000	
	Work in Process—Machining Department		44,000
	(To record transfer of 8,000 units to the Assembly Department)		

PREPARING THE PRODUCTION COST REPORT

The final end-of-period procedure is the preparation of the production cost report. This is an internal report for management that shows both production

Production cost report

TYLER MANUFACTURING COMPANY
Machining Department
Production Cost Report
For the Month Ended June 30, 1987

	Physical Units (Step 1)	Equivalent Units: Materials (Step 2)	Equivalent Units: Conversion Costs (Step 2)	
QUANTITIES				
Units charged to department				
In process, June 1	-0-			
Started into production	10,000			
Total units charged	10,000			
Units accounted for				
Transferred out	8,000	8,000	8,000	
In process, June 30	2,000	2,000	1,000	
Total units accounted for	10,000	10,000	9,000	
COSTS				
Unit costs (Step 3)		Materials	Conversion Costs	Total
Costs in June	(a)	$15,000	$36,000	$51,000
Equivalent units	(b)	10,000	9,000	
Unit costs (a) ÷ (b)		$1.50	$4.00	$5.50
Costs charged to department				
In process, June 1				$ -0-
Costs in June				51,000
Total costs charged				$51,000
Costs accounted for (Step 4)				
Transferred out				
Started and finished (8,000 × $5.50)				$44,000
In process, June 30				
Materials (2,000 × $1.50)			$ 3,000	
Conversion costs (1,000 × $4.00)			4,000	7,000
Total costs accounted for				$51,000

quantity and production cost data. There are five sections in the report: (1) Units charged to the department, (2) Units accounted for, (3) Unit costs, (4) Costs charged to the department, and (5) Costs accounted for. The production cost report for the Machining Department of Tyler Manufacturing is shown on page 922. Each of the preceding end-of-period procedures are identified in the report. As shown, the total physical units accounted for must equal the total units charged to the department. Similarly, the total costs accounted for must equal the total costs charged.

Production cost reports provide a basis for evaluating the productivity of a department. In addition, the cost data can be used to assess whether unit costs and total costs are reasonable. When the quantity and cost data are compared with predetermined goals, top management can also ascertain whether current performance is meeting planned objectives.

SECTION TWO—ASSEMBLY DEPARTMENT

COMPUTING PHYSICAL UNITS

The physical units to be accounted for in the Assembly Department are determined in the same manner as in the Machining Department. From the Tyler Manufacturing production data presented earlier, the physical units for the Assembly Department are:

Production data in physical units

Assembly Department

	Units
Work in process, June 1 (40% complete)	500
Transferred in	8,000
Total units to be accounted for	8,500
Transferred out	8,100
Work in process, June 30 (75% complete)	400
Units accounted for	8,500

In this case the units transferred out, 8,100, plus the units in ending work in process, 400, equal the total units to be accounted for, 8,500.

COMPUTING EQUIVALENT UNITS OF PRODUCTION

The equivalent units of production for the Assembly Department are computed in the same way as for the Machining Department. However, the pres-

ence of a beginning work in process adds a new dimension to process cost accounting.

When there are units in process at the beginning of the period, it is necessary to identify the cost flow assumption (FIFO, LIFO, average) used by the company. We will assume that the Tyler Manufacturing uses the **FIFO method,** though other methods are equally acceptable. For homework problems, the FIFO method should be used.

The FIFO cost flow assumption affects the determination of equivalent units in two ways. First, it means that the initial units finished during the period were the units in beginning work in process. Since there were 500 units in beginning inventory and 8,100 units were transferred out, 7,600 units were started and finished in the period (8,100 − 500). Second, only the work required to finish the units of beginning inventory is included in the equivalent units of production for the current period. In other words, under the FIFO method, work performed in the preceding period is not included in the equivalent units of the current period.

When there is both a beginning and an ending work in process, equivalent units of production consist of the sum of the work performed to:

1. Finish the units of beginning work in process inventory.
2. Complete the units started into production during the period.
3. Start, but only partially complete, the units in ending work in process inventory.

EQUIVALENT UNITS FOR MATERIALS

Since materials are added at the beginning of the process, no additional materials costs are required to complete the beginning work in process. In addition, 100% of the materials cost has been incurred on the ending work in process. Thus, the computation of equivalent units for materials is as follows:

Computation of equivalent units—materials

Assembly Department

Production Data	Physical Units	Materials Added This Period	Equivalent Units
Work in process, June 1	500	-0-	0
Started and finished	7,600	100%	7,600
Work in process, June 30	400	100%	400
	8,500		8,000

Note that the equivalent units of materials are different from physical units when there is beginning work in process.

EQUIVALENT UNITS FOR CONVERSION COSTS

As indicated above, 500 units of beginning work in process were 40% complete in terms of conversion costs. Thus, 300 equivalent units (60% × 500 units) of conversion costs were required to complete the beginning inventory. In addition, the 400 units of ending work in process were 75% complete in

terms of conversion costs. Thus the computation of equivalent units for conversion costs is as follows:

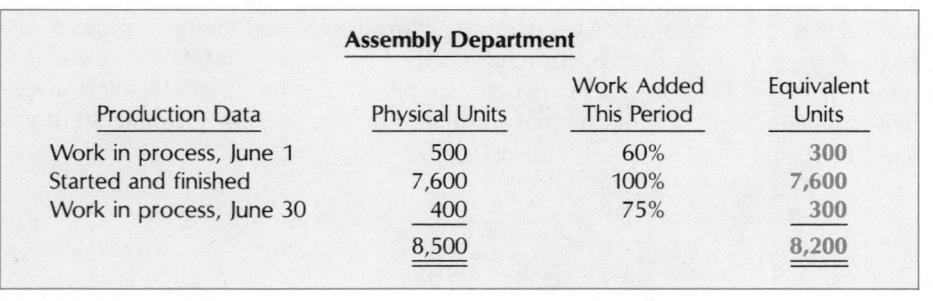

Computation of equivalent units—conversion costs

Assembly Department

Production Data	Physical Units	Work Added This Period	Equivalent Units
Work in process, June 1	500	60%	300
Started and finished	7,600	100%	7,600
Work in process, June 30	400	75%	300
	8,500		8,200

Alternatively, the 8,200 equivalent units can be determined from the following graphic:

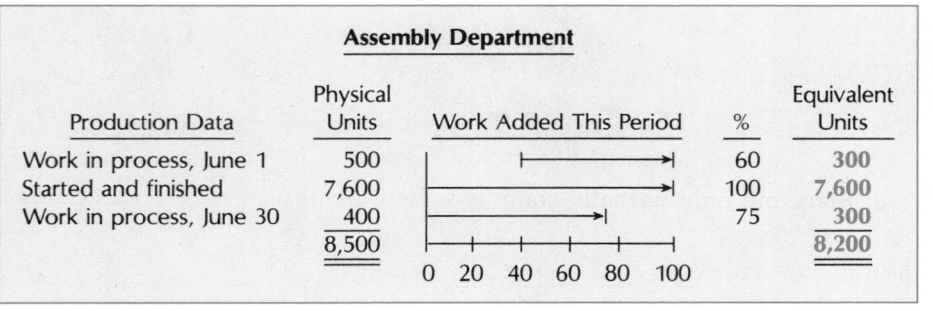

Equivalent units for conversion costs—graphic illustration

Assembly Department

Production Data	Physical Units	Work Added This Period	%	Equivalent Units
Work in process, June 1	500		60	300
Started and finished	7,600		100	7,600
Work in process, June 30	400		75	300
	8,500	0 20 40 60 80 100		8,200

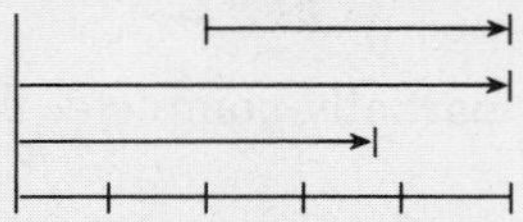

COMPUTING UNIT COSTS OF PRODUCTION

The production costs chargeable to the Assembly Department in June consist of the following debits to work in process.

Costs charged to assembly department

Work in Process – Assembly Department

June 1	Balance	3,600	
30	Materials	4,000	
30	Labor	16,400	
30	Overhead	8,200	
30	Transferred from Machining Dept.	44,000	
	Total	76,200	

Our objective is to determine the unit costs of production for the month of June. Under the FIFO method, this determination is based entirely on the **production costs incurred on work done during the month.** Thus, the costs in the beginning work in process are not relevant, because they were incurred on work done in the preceding month.

To determine unit costs, we need to classify the June costs as either materials costs or conversion costs. How should transferred-in costs be classified?

Transferred-in costs **are recognized as materials cost to the receiving department** when materials are added at the beginning of the process. At Tyler Manufacturing, these costs represent the cost of making the materials ready for use by the Assembly Department. Therefore, total materials costs are $48,000 (materials added by the Assembly Department, $4,000 + the transferred-in costs, $44,000). Conversion costs total $24,600 (labor $16,400 + overhead $8,200). The computations of unit costs in the Assembly Department are as follows:

Unit cost computations—Assembly Department

(1)	Total Materials Costs	÷	Equivalent Units of Materials	=	Unit Materials Cost
	$48,000	÷	8,000	=	$6.00
(2)	Total Conversion Costs	÷	Equivalent Units of Conversion Costs	=	Unit Conversion Cost
	$24,600	÷	8,200	=	$3.00
(3)	Unit Materials Cost	+	Unit Conversion Cost	=	Total Manufacturing Cost per Unit
	$6.00	+	$3.00		$9.00

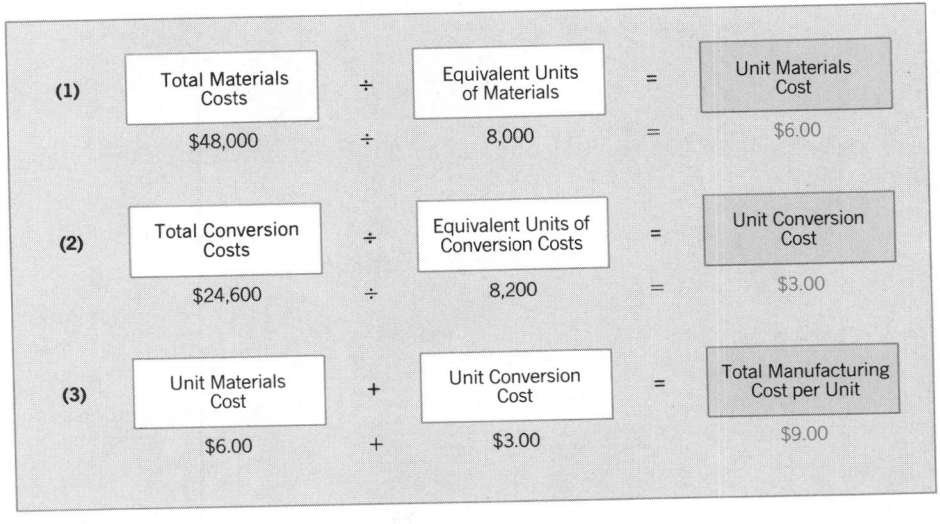

As shown, the unit costs are $6.00 for materials, $3.00 for conversion costs, and $9.00 for total production costs.

ASSIGNING COSTS TO UNITS TRANSFERRED AND IN PROCESS

Under the FIFO assumption, the first goods to be completed during the accounting period are the units in beginning work in process. Thus, the cost of the beginning work in process is always assigned to the goods transferred to finished goods (or to the next department). The FIFO assumption also means that ending work in process will be assigned only production costs that are incurred in the current period. The assignment of the manufacturing costs in the Assembly Department is as follows:

Assignment of costs—Assembly Department

Assembly Department

Costs to be Assigned	Assignment of Costs	Equivalent Units	Unit Cost		Total Costs Assigned
Total manufacturing costs	Transferred out				
	Work in process, June 1	-0-	$-0-	$3,600	
$76,200	Conversion costs	300	$3.00	900	$ 4,500
	Started and finished	7,600	$9.00		68,400
					72,900
	Ending work in process				
	Materials	400	$6.00	2,400	
	Conversion costs	300	$3.00	900	3,300
					$76,200

Again, you can see that the costs assigned equal the costs to be assigned. Alternatively, the assignment of costs may be made through a chart as shown below.

Assignment of costs—alternative illustration

Assembly Department

Costs to be Assigned		Unit Cost	Equivalent Units × Unit Cost		Costs Assigned To Units: Transferred Out		Costs Assigned To Units: In Ending Work in Process
In process, June 1	$ 3,600			=	$ 3,600		
Materials	48,000	$6.00	Started and finished 7,600 × $6.00	=	45,600		
			Ending work in process 400 × $6.00	=			$2,400
Conversion costs	24,600	$3.00	Beginning work in process 300 × $3.00	=	900		
			Started and finished 7,600 × $3.00	=	22,800		
			Ending work in process 300 × $3.00	=			900
	$76,200			=	$72,900	+	$3,300

The units completed in the Assembly Department are transferred to the finished goods warehouse. The entry for this transfer is:

(8)

June 30	Finished Goods Inventory	72,900	
	Work in Process—Assembly Department		72,900
	(To record transfer of 8,100 units to finished goods)		

PREPARING THE PRODUCTION COST REPORT

As previously explained, a production cost report is prepared for the month's activity. The report for the Assembly Department of the Tyler Company is presented below.

TYLER MANUFACTURING COMPANY
Assembly Department
Production Cost Report
For the Month Ended June 30, 1987

	Physical Units (Step 1)	Equivalent Units: Materials	Equivalent Units: Conversion Costs	
		(Step 2)		
QUANTITIES				
Units charged to department				
In process, June 1	500			
Transferred in	8,000			
Total units charged	8,500			
Units accounted for				
Transferred out	8,100	7,600	7,900*	
In process, June 30	400	400	300	
Total units accounted for	8,500	8,000	8,200	
COSTS				
Unit costs (Step 3)		Materials	Conversion Costs	Total
Costs in June	(a)	$48,000	$24,600	$72,600
Equivalent units	(b)	8,000	8,200	
Unit costs (a) ÷ (b)		$6.00	$3.00	$9.00
Costs charged to department				
In process, June 1				$ 3,600
Costs in June				72,600
Total costs charged				$76,200
Costs accounted for (Step 4)				
Transferred out				
In process, June 1		$ 3,600		
Conversion costs (300 × $3.00)		900	$ 4,500	
Started and finished (7,600 × $9.00)			68,400	$72,900
In process, June 30				
Materials (400 × $6.00)			2,400	
Conversion costs (300 × $3.00)			900	3,300
Total costs accounted for				$76,200

*300 units to complete beginning work in process plus 7,600 units started and finished.

As in the report for the Machining Department, the total physical units accounted for equals the units charged to the department. Similarly, the total costs accounted for equals the total costs charged to the department.

Manufacturing accounting is an application that requires a great deal of internal (RAM) and external (hard disc) memory. Until recently, microcomputers with really large memories of both kinds were not available. Now manufacturing accounting programs are available for microcomputers, having up to a megabyte of RAM and 20 magabytes of hard disc external storage capacity. For those students not familiar with magabytes, let's just say that that's a lot of memory!

PROCESS COST FLOW SUMMARY

The flow of costs in process cost accounting was graphically presented earlier in this chapter. The ledger accounts after posting the June transactions of Tyler Manufacturing Company and the flow of documents are shown below.

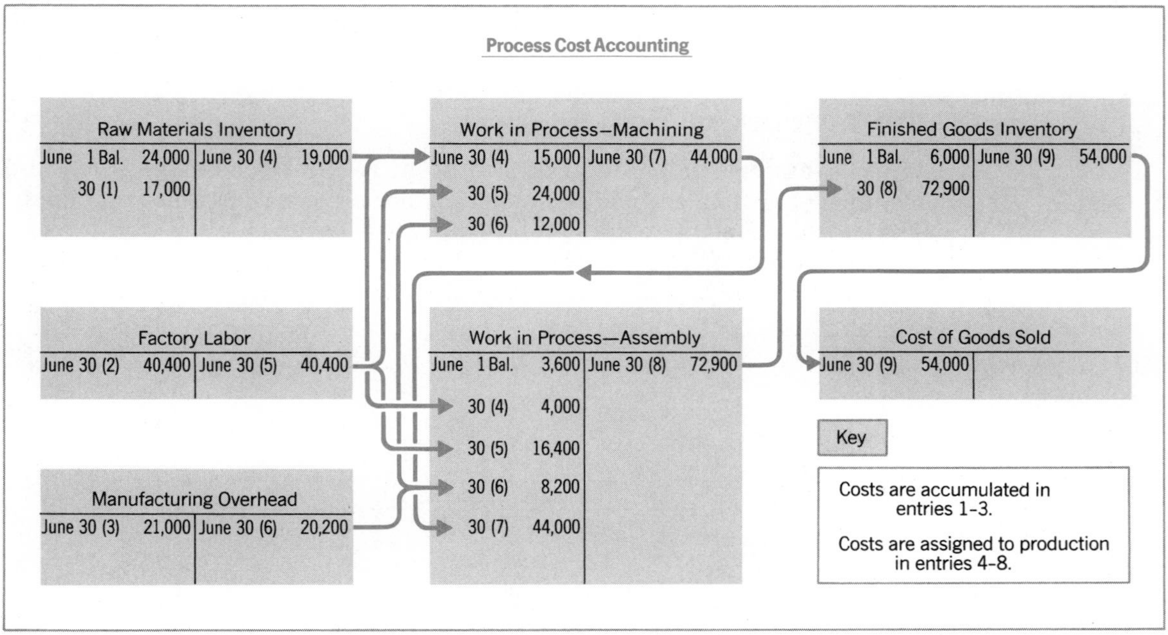

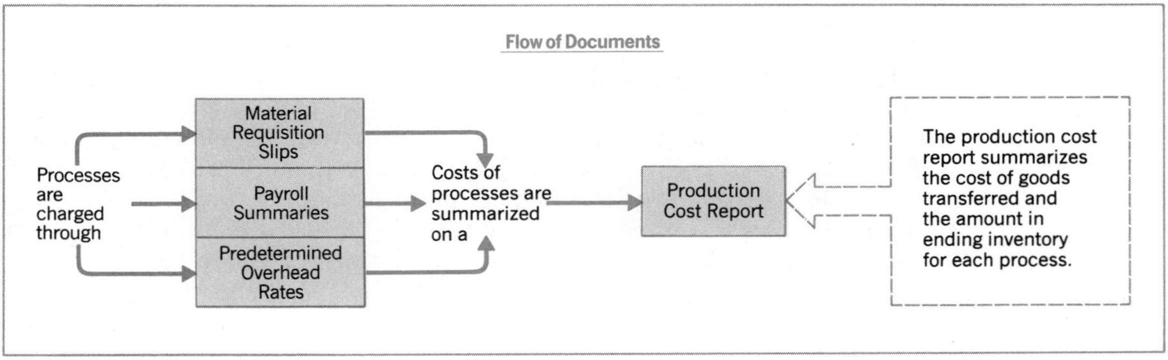

Each posting is based on journal entries illustrated earlier except for the postings pertaining to the cost of goods sold. Data for this entry are obtained from finished goods perpetual inventory records. Assuming 6,000 of the can openers costing $9.00 each are sold in June, the entry to record the cost of goods sold is as follows:

(9)

June 30	Cost of Goods Sold	54,000	
	Finished Goods Inventory		54,000
	(To record cost of 6,000 units sold)		

In addition, an entry would be made to record the sale of the units for $119,700 (6,000 × the selling price of $19.95).

SPECIAL PROBLEMS

Special problems related to process cost accounting involve the proper accounting for: (1) Joint products and (2) By-products. Each of these problem areas is discussed below.

JOINT PRODUCTS

When a number of products of significant revenue-generating ability are manufactured from a single raw material, they are considered **joint products.** The costs incurred up to the **split-off point** are referred to as the **joint product costs.** The split-off point is where the individual products can be identified. These relationships can be illustrated graphically as follows:

Joint product cost relationships

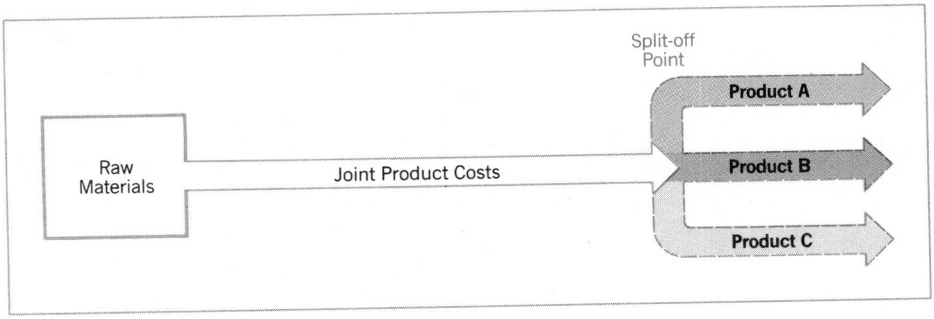

The question that arises is how should the joint product costs prior to the split-off point be allocated to the joint products? To illustrate, assume that the Hargrove Meat Packing Company incurs $120 of joint product costs in processing a 200-pound hog. Hargrove accumulates the data shown at the top of the next page concerning the four joint products that are produced.

One approach to allocating joint product cost is on the basis of pounds produced. Such a procedure results in an allocation of $1.00 per lb. ($120 ÷ 120 lbs.) to each joint product. For example, the side portion of a hog would be allocated a total cost of $30 (30 lbs. × $1), and the ham portion would be allocated $40 (40 lbs. × $1).

Joint product data

Joint Products	Number of Pounds	Sales Price per Pound	Total Sales Value
Shoulder	20	$1.45	$ 29
Loin	30	2.10	63
Side	30	1.20	36
Ham	40	1.80	72
	120		$200

Unfortunately, this approach does not take into consideration the relative sales value of each of the joint products. For example, loin has a higher sales value than the ham, which has a higher sales value than the shoulder. As a result, a more appropriate basis of allocation is **relative sales value.** Under this approach, costs are allocated on the basis of the relative sales value of each individual product as shown below:

Relative sales basis of allocation

Allocating Joint Product Costs

Joint Products	Total Sales Value	Relative Sale Value	×	Total Cost	=	Cost Allocated to Product
Shoulder	$ 29	29/200		$120		$ 17.40
Loin	63	63/200		120		37.80
Side	36	36/200		120		21.60
Ham	72	72/200		120		43.20
	$200					$120.00

In this case, the side portion of the hog would be allocated a total cost of $21.60, and the ham portion would be allocated $43.20.

BY-PRODUCTS

By-products are products that have a relatively small value in relation to the main product. For example, a steer's hide and beef fat have value, but their value is small in relationship to the value of the whole steer.

A number of approaches are used to account for by-products. **A common approach is to assign to them their estimated sales value less cost of disposal.** This amount is then transferred from work in process to a by-product inventory account. To illustrate, assume that a steer's hide has a sales value less cost of disposal of $34. The entry to record this transaction is as follows:

	Debit	Credit
By-Product Inventory—Hides	34	
Work in Process		34

The effect of this transaction is to reduce the cost of the main product by the net amount transferred to the by-product inventory. When the by-product is sold, little, if any, income will be reported.

It should be noted that a by-product may be used in the processing of another product. For example, in the steel industry, by-products are often

used as fuel to produce new steel. In such a case, the estimated sales value less cost of disposal of the by-product should be charged as a cost of producing the new steel.

SUMMARY OF STUDY OBJECTIVES

1. The features of process cost accounting are: (a) work in process accounts are kept for each process; (b) manufacturing costs are summarized in a production report; (c) total manufacturing costs are determined at the end of a period of time; and (d) unit costs are obtained by dividing total manufacturing costs by the units of output for the period.

2. The cost flow in process cost accounting is basically the same as in job order cost accounting. The accumulation of costs is identical. In process costing, costs are assigned to more than one work in process account, and the method of assigning cost is significantly different.

3. End-of-period procedures are used to:
   (a) Compute the physical units.
   (b) Compute equivalent units of production.
   (c) Compute unit costs of production.
   (d) Assign costs to units transferred and in process.
   (e) Prepare the production cost report.

4. The physical units of product consist of adding the units started into production during the period to the units in process at the beginning of the period to determine the total units to be accounted for. These units then are accounted for by the output of the period which consists of units transferred out during the period and any units in process at the end of the period.

5. There are two steps in determining unit costs: (a) determine the equivalent units of production, and (b) divide the appropriate costs by the equivalent units. Unit costs are computed for total manufacturing costs and generally it is also necessary to compute unit costs for materials and conversion costs.

6. Costs are assigned to work done by applying unit costs to the equivalent units of work done. The objective of assigning costs is to determine the costs to be assigned to units transferred out and the units in ending work in process.

7. The production cost report contains both quantity and cost data. There are five sections in the report: (a) Units charged to the department, (b) Units accounted for, (c) Unit costs, (d) Costs charged to the department, and (e) Costs accounted for.

8. Special problems occur in process cost accounting with (a) joint products, and (b) by-products.

GLOSSARY

By-products, p. 931

Departmental payroll summaries, p. 915

Equivalent units of production, p. 918

Joint products, p. 930

Joint product costs, p. 930

Process cost accounting, p. 911

DEMONSTRATION PROBLEM

Karlene Industries produces plastic ice cube trays in two processes: heating and stamping. All materials are added at the beginning of the Heating Department.

On November 1, 1,000 trays were in process in the Heating Department that were 70% complete. During November, 12,000 trays were started into production. On November 30, 2,000 trays were in process that were 60% complete.

The following cost information for the Heating Department was also available:

Work in process, November 1	$1,000	Labor	$2,300
Materials	3,000	Overhead	4,600

INSTRUCTIONS

(a) Prepare a production cost report for the Heating Department for the month of November.

(b) Journalize the transfer of costs to the Stamping Department.

SOLUTION TO DEMONSTRATION PROBLEM

(a)

KARLENE INDUSTRIES
Heating Department
Production Cost Report
For the Month Ended November 30, 1987

		Equivalent Units	
Quantities	Physical Units (Step 1)	Materials (Step 2)	Conversion Costs (Step 2)
Units charged to department			
In process, November 1	1,000		
Started into production	12,000		
Total units charged	13,000		
Units accounted for			
Transferred out	11,000	10,000 (1)	10,300 (2)
In process, November 30	2,000	2,000	1,200 (2,000 × 60%)
Total units accounted for	13,000	12,000	11,500

	Materials	Conversion Costs	Total
Unit costs (Step 3)			
Costs in November	(a) $ 3,000	$ 6,900 (3)	$ 9,900
Equivalent units	(b) 12,000	11,500	
Unit costs (a) ÷ (b)	$ .25	$ .60	$ .85
Costs charged to department			
In process, November 1			$ 1,000
Costs in November			9,900
Total costs charged			$10,900
Costs accounted for (Step 4)			
Transferred out			
In process, November 1	$ 1,000		
Conversion costs (300 × $.60)	180	$ 1,180	
Started and finished (10,000 × $.85)		8,500	$ 9,680
In process, November 30			
Materials (2,000 × $.25)		500	
Conversion costs (1,200 × $.60)		720	1,220
Total costs accounted for			$10,900

(1) 11,000 units transferred out less 1,000 units in beginning work in process.
(2) 300 units to complete beginning work in process plus 10,000 units started and finished.
(3) Labor $2,300 plus overhead of $4,600.

(b) Nov. 30	Work in Process – Stamping	9,680	
	Work in Process – Heating		9,680
	(To record transfer of 11,000 units to Stamping Department)		

QUESTIONS

1. What are the distinguishing characteristics of continuous process manufacturing?

2. Identify the features of process cost accounting.

3. Joan Jones believes there are significant differences in the flow of costs between job order cost accounting and process cost accounting. Do you agree? Explain.

4. What source documents are used in assigning (a) materials and (b) labor to production?

5. The Terrell Company has three processing departments: Cutting, Sanding, and Assembly. Using XX's for amounts, journalize the assignment of material costs and labor costs to each department.

6. Ken Kruse is confused about computing physical units. Explain to Ken how physical units to be accounted for and physical units accounted for are determined.

7. What is meant by the term "equivalent units of production"?

8. How are equivalent units computed when there is no beginning work in process?

9. The Mario Company had 600 units of beginning work in process. During the period, 8,000 units were completed, and there were 400 units of ending work in process. What are the units started and finished?

10. Sandwich Co. has 300 units of beginning work in process one-third complete. During the period 9,000 units were completed, and there were 500 units of ending working in process two-fifths complete. What are the equivalent units of production?

11. Cessna Co. has units started and completed of 1,000 units for the period. Its beginning inventory is 700 units one-half complete and its ending inventory is 500 units one-fifth complete. How many units were transferred out this period?

12. The Herr Company transfers out 12,000 units and has 4,000 units of ending work in process that are 25% complete. Materials are entered at the beginning of the process and there is no beginning work in process. Assuming unit materials costs of $3 and unit conversion costs of $9, what are the costs to be assigned to units (a) transferred out and (b) in ending work in process?

13. Jason Jelk believes the production cost report is an external report for stockholders. Is Jason correct? Explain.

14. What purposes are served by a production cost report?

15. Pam Palmer is studying for the next accounting examination. What should Pam know about computing equivalent units of production when there is both a beginning and an ending work in process?

16. When units are transferred from one department to another, how should the receiving department handle the costs transferred in?

17. In the Grubb Company, there are 800 units of ending work in process that are 100% complete as to materials and 25% complete as to conversion costs. If the unit cost of materials is $4 and the costs assigned to the 800 units is $5,200, what is the per unit conversion cost?

18. Distinguish between the following terms: joint products, split-off point, and joint product cost.

19. Contrast the two approaches for allocating the joint product cost to the joint products.

20. What alternative approaches may be used in accounting for by-products?

EXERCISES

E23-1 In the McKay Company, materials are entered at the beginning of each process. Work in process inventories, with the percentage of work done on conversion

costs, and production data for its Sterilizing Department in selected months during 1987 are as follows:

	Beginning Work in Process			Ending Work in Process	
Month	Units	Conversion Cost %	Units Started and Finished	Units	Conversion Cost %
January	-0-	—	8,000	1,000	60
March	4,000	30	10,000	3,000	25
May	5,000	20	14,000	2,500	80
July	3,500	70	9,000	1,500	90
October	1,000	25	11,000	-0-	—

INSTRUCTIONS

(a) Compute the physical units for January and May.

(b) Compute the equivalent units of production for (1) materials and (2) conversion costs for each month.

E23-2 The Smelting Department of the Leeds Manufacturing Company has the following production and cost data for November 1987.

Production: Beginning work in process 2,000 units that are 100% complete as to materials and 30% complete as to conversion costs; units started and finished 9,000 units; and ending work in process 1,500 units, 100% complete as to materials and 40% complete as to conversion costs.

Manufacturing costs: Work in process, November 1, $15,800; materials added $42,000; labor and overhead $143,000.

INSTRUCTIONS

(a) Compute the equivalent units of production for (1) materials, and (2) conversion costs for the month of November.

(b) Compute the unit costs for the month.

(c) Determine the costs to be assigned to the units transferred out and in process.

E23-3 The Finishing Department of Moran Manufacturing has the following production and cost data for July 1987.

Production

1. Completed 250 units of work in process that were 20% complete on July 1.
2. Started and finished 8,000 units.
3. Started 1,000 units that are 30% completed at July 31.

Costs

Beginning work in process	$ 950
Materials	27,000
Labor	24,000
Manufacturing overhead	10,000

Materials are entered at the beginning of the process. Conversion costs are incurred uniformly during the process.

INSTRUCTIONS

(a) Determine the equivalent units of production for (1) materials and (2) conversion costs. Use the graphic approach shown on page 920 for conversion costs.

(b) Show the assignment of costs, using the chart illustrated on the bottom of page 921.

E23-4 The Plating Department of the Keenan Manufacturing Company has the following production and manufacturing cost data for September 1987. Materials are entered at the beginning of the process.

Production: Beginning inventory 2,600 units that are 100% complete as to materials and 30% complete as to conversion costs; units started that came from a prior department 12,000; ending inventory of 3,000 units 10% complete as to conversion costs.

Manufacturing costs: Beginning inventory costs of $63,180; costs transferred into Plating during the month, $120,000; materials costs added in Plating during the month, $42,000; labor and overhead applied in Plating during the month, $133,440 and $266,880, respectively.

INSTRUCTIONS

(a) Compute the equivalent units of production for materials and conversion costs for the month of September.

(b) Compute the unit costs for materials and conversion costs for the month.

(c) Determine the costs to be assigned to the units transferred out and in process.

(d) Reconcile the total costs charged to the department with the total costs assigned.

E23-5 The Sanding Department of the Copay Furniture Company has the following production and manufacturing cost data for March 1987.

Production: 12,000 units started and finished; 4,000 units started that are 100% completed as to materials and 25% completed as to conversion costs.

Manufacturing costs: Materials $48,000; labor $52,000; overhead $26,000.

INSTRUCTIONS

Prepare a production cost report.

E23-6 The Maria Company manufactures pizza sauce through two production departments: Cooking and Canning. In each process, materials and conversion costs are incurred evenly throughout the process. For the month of April, the work in process accounts show the following debits.

	Cooking	Canning
Beginning Inventory	-0-	$ 4,000
Materials	$19,000	6,000
Labor	28,500	15,000
Overhead	9,500	11,800
Costs transferred in		54,000

INSTRUCTIONS

(a) Journalize the April transactions.

(b) If 110,000 units were started into production in Cooking and 90,000 units were transferred to Canning, what is the percentage of completion of the units in process in Cooking at April 30? (Hint: Only one equivalent unit determination is needed, as material is added evenly throughout the process.)

(c) If the percentage of completion of the units in process in Cooking at April 30 is 33⅓%, and 90,000 units were transferred out, how many units were started into production in April?

E23-7 The Grinding Department of the Tomlyn Manufacturing Company has the following production and manufacturing cost data for February 1987. All materials are added at the beginning of the process.

Manufacturing Costs		Production Data	
Beginning inventory	$32,175	Beginning inventory	15,000 units 1/20 complete
Costs transferred in	75,000		
Materials	48,000	Units transferred out	49,000
Labor and overhead	101,555	Units transferred in	60,000
		Ending inventory	26,000 units 1/5 complete

INSTRUCTIONS

Prepare a production cost report for the Grinding Department for the month of February.

E23-8 The ledger of the Toberg Company has the following work in process account:

Work in Process — Painting

5/1	Balance	4,000	5/31	Transferred out	?
5/31	Materials	880			
5/31	Labor	1,200			
5/31	Overhead	1,200			
5/31	Costs transferred in	3,300			
5/31	Balance	?			

Production records show that there were 800 units in the beginning inventory, 50% complete 1,100 units transferred in and 1,300 units transferred out. The units in ending inventory were $16\frac{2}{3}\%$ complete. Materials are entered at the beginning of the painting process. The FIFO method is used.

INSTRUCTIONS

Answer the following questions:

(a) How many units are in process at May 31?
(b) What is the unit materials cost for May?
(c) What is the unit conversion cost for May?
(d) What is the total cost of units started in April and completed in May?
(e) What is the total cost of units started and finished in May?
(f) What is the cost of the May 31 inventory?

E23-9 The Zajac Manufacturing Company has two production departments: Cutting and Assembly. July 1 inventories are Work in Process—Cutting $2,900, Work in Process—Assembly $10,600, and Finished Goods $31,000. During July, the following transactions occurred.

1. Purchased $35,600 of raw materials on account.
2. Incurred $56,000 of factory labor. (Credit Wages Payable.)
3. Incurred $70,000 of manufacturing overhead; $42,000 was paid and the remainder is unpaid.
4. Requisitioned materials for Cutting $15,700 and Assembly $8,900.
5. Used factory labor for Cutting $29,000 and Assembly $27,000.
6. Applied overhead at the rate of 120% of labor costs.
7. Transferred goods costing $77,700 from the Cutting Department to the Assembly Department.
8. Transferred goods costing $134,900 from Assembly to Finished Goods.
9. Sold goods costing $125,000 for $200,000 on account.

INSTRUCTIONS

(a) Journalize the transactions. (Omit explanations.)

(b) Determine the ending balances in the two work in process accounts and the finished goods account.

E23-10 Klem's Meat Packing Company incurs $450 of joint product costs in processing a 1,000-pound steer. The following data concerning the four joint products are:

Product	Number of Pounds	Sales Price/lb.
Hamburger	250	$1.50
T-bone steak	90	$3.00
Porterhouse steak	50	$3.50
Roast	180	$1.00

INSTRUCTIONS

(a) Prepare a schedule using the relative sales value method to indicate the allocation of the joint cost of $450 to each of the four products.

(b) Assume that 200 pounds of beef fat (by-product) also result from the processing. The fat can be sold for $.35 a pound, but it will cost $.05 a pound to make the sale. Prepare the entry to record the by-product inventory.

PROBLEMS

P23-1 Aqua-Marine Corporation manufactures water skis through two processes: Molding and Packaging. In the Molding Department fiber glass is heated and shaped into the form of a ski. In the Packaging Department, the skis are placed in cartons and sent to the finished goods warehouse. Materials are entered at the beginning of both processes. Labor and manufacturing overhead are incurred uniformly throughout each process. Production and cost data for the Molding Department during the first two months of 1987 are presented below.

	January	February
Production Data		
Beginning work in process units	-0-	2,500
Units started into production	42,500	52,000
Ending work in process units	2,500	5,000
Percent complete—ending inventory	80%	20%
Cost Data		
Materials	$595,000	$832,000
Labor	176,400	218,250
Overhead	117,600	145,500

INSTRUCTIONS

(a) For each month:

(1) Compute the physical units transferred and in process.

(2) Determine the equivalent units of production for materials and conversion costs.

(3) Compute the unit costs of production.

(4) Determine the costs to be assigned to the units transferred and in process.

(b) Prepare a production cost report for the Molding Department for the month of January only.

P23-2 The Basile Company manufactures a nutrient, Everlife, through two manufacturing processes: (1) Blending and (2) Packaging. All materials are entered at the beginning of each process. On August 1, 1987, inventories consisted of Raw Materials $5,000, Work in Process—Blending -0-, Work in Process—Packaging $3,945, and Finished Goods $7,500. The beginning inventory for Packaging consisted of 500 units, 2/5 complete as to conversion costs. During August, 9,000 units were started into production and the following transactions were completed:

1. Purchased $25,000 of raw materials on account.
2. Issued raw materials for production: Blending $16,200 and Packaging $6,150.
3. Incurred labor costs of $35,125.
4. Used factory labor: Blending $26,700 and Packaging $8,425.
5. Incurred $18,000 of manufacturing overhead on account.
6. Applied manufacturing overhead at the rate of 50% of labor costs.
7. Transferred 8,200 units from Blending to Packaging. Unfinished units in Blending are 7/8 complete as to conversion costs.
8. Transferred 8,600 units from Packaging to Finished Goods. Unfinished units in the Packaging Department are 1/4 complete as to conversion costs.
9. Sold goods costing $62,000 for $90,000 on account.

INSTRUCTIONS

(a) Journalize the August transactions.

(b) Post the entries to the work in process accounts.

(c) Prepare a production cost report for the Blending Department.

(d) Prepare a production cost report for the Packaging Department.

P23-3 The work in process accounts of the Tastie Cereal Co. that pertain to the making of "Fast Pops," a new breakfast cereal, during the month of July are presented below.

Work in Process—Mixing

July 31	Materials	63,000	July 31	Transferred out	100,000
31	Labor	27,000			
31	Overhead	13,800			

Work in Process—Baking

July 1	Inventory	2,200	July 31	Transferred out	122,400
31	Labor	14,000			
31	Overhead	6,200			
31	Transferred in	100,000			

Work in Process—Packaging

July 1	Inventory	6,720	July 31	To Finished Goods	206,000
31	Materials	40,800			
31	Labor	24,000			
31	Overhead	17,600			
31	Transferred in	122,400			

Production and inventory data are as follows:

	Inventory, July 1		Inventory, July 31		
Department	Units	% Complete	Units	% Complete	Units Transferred Out
Mixing	-0-	—	10,000	40	200,000
Baking	4,000	50	-0-	—	204,000
Packaging	8,000	20	6,000	60	206,000

All materials are entered at the beginning of a process.

INSTRUCTIONS

(a) Determine the equivalent units of production for materials and conversion costs in each process.

(b) Determine the unit cost of materials, the unit conversion costs, and the total manufacturing cost per equivalent unit for each process.

(c) Show the assignment of costs to units transferred out and in process in each department.

P23-4 The Hope Manufacturing Co. has three processing departments. Manufacturing cost data for the departments in October 1987 were as follows:

Costs charged to department	Stamping	Enameling	Assembly
Inventory, October 1	$ -0-	$ 28,200	$ 67,500
Materials	210,000	120,000	124,500
Labor	280,000	114,000	140,000
Overhead	128,000	50,800	61,000
Transferred in	-0-	?	?
Total costs to be accounted for	$618,000	?	?

Production Data			
Inventory, October 1			
Units	-0-	15,000	25,000
Percentage completed	—	20	40
Inventory, October 31			
Units	20,000	-0-	35,000
Percentage completed	40	—	20
Transferred In (units)	—	400,000	415,000

Raw materials are entered at the beginning of each process.

INSTRUCTIONS

(a) Determine the equivalent units of production and the unit costs in each process.

(b) Journalize the October transactions that affect work in process inventory accounts.

(c) Prepare a production cost report for the Assembly Department.

P23-5 The Zephyr Furniture Company manufactures living room furniture through two departments: Framing and Upholstering. Materials are entered at the beginning of each process. For May 1987, the following cost data are obtained from the two work in process accounts.

	Framing	Upholstering
Work in process, May 1	$ -0-	$?
Materials	360,000	?
Conversion costs	270,000	345,000
Costs transferred in	-0-	550,000
Costs transferred out	550,000	?

INSTRUCTIONS

Answer the following questions:

(a) If 3,000 sofas were started into production on May 1, and 2,500 units were transferred to Upholstering, what is the percentage of completion of the units in process at May 31 in the Framing Department?

(b) If the materials cost per unit in Upholstering is $350, what was the cost of materials added in Upholstering in May?

(c) If the conversion cost per unit in Upholstering is $150, what is the percentage of completion of the 800 units in work in process at May 31 if there were 1,000 units 60% complete in work in process at May 1?

(d) Disregard your answers above. Assume in Upholstering that unit costs in May were: materials added $100, conversion costs $125, and transferred in costs $200. If 1,500 units were 40% complete on May 1 and unit costs were the same in April as in May, what is the cost of the beginning work in process inventory?

(e) Assuming the data given in (d) above, what is the cost of the May 1 work in process in Upholstering if there are 1,200 units 25% complete at May 1?

ALTERNATE PROBLEMS

P23-1A Bowlmor Company manufactures bowling balls through two processes: Molding and Packaging. In the Molding Department, the urethane, rubber, plastics, and other materials are molded into bowling balls. In the Packaging Department, the balls are placed in cartons and sent to the finished goods warehouse. All materials are entered at the beginning of each process. Labor and manufacturing overhead are incurred uniformly throughout each process. Production and cost data for the Molding Department during June and July 1987 are presented below.

	June	July
Production Data		
Beginning work in process units	-0-	2,000
Units started into production	22,000	26,500
Ending work in process units	2,000	3,000
Percent complete—ending inventory	45%	80%
Cost Data		
Materials	$198,000	$259,700
Labor	125,400	175,725
Overhead	41,800	53,775

INSTRUCTIONS

(a) For each month:

(1) Compute the physical units transferred and in process.

(2) Determine the equivalent units of production for materials and conversion costs.

(3) Compute the unit costs of production.

(4) Determine the costs to be assigned to the units transferred and in process.

(b) Prepare a production cost report for the Molding Department for the month of June only.

P23-2A The Anderson Company manufactures a finished product, Vitadrink, through two manufacturing processes: (1) Mixing and (2) Packaging. All materials are entered at the beginning of each process. On October 1, 1988, inventories consisted of Raw Materials $26,000, Work in Process—Mixing $0, Work in Process—Packaging $252,500, and Finished Goods $89,000. The beginning inventory for Packaging consisted of 10,000 units that were 50% complete as to conversion costs. During October, 50,000 units were started into production in the Mixing Department and the following transactions were completed:

1. Purchased $300,000 of raw materials on account.
2. Issued raw materials for production: Mixing $200,000 and Packaging $45,000.
3. Incurred labor costs of $351,300.
4. Used factory labor: Mixing $277,500 and Packaging $73,800.
5. Incurred $700,000 of manufacturing overhead on account.
6. Applied manufacturing overhead at the rate of 200% of labor costs.
7. Transferred 45,000 units from Mixing to Packaging. Unfinished units in Mixing are 25% complete as to conversion costs.
8. Transferred 53,000 units from Packaging to Finished Goods. Units unfinished in the Packaging Department are 60% complete as to conversion costs.
9. Sold goods costing $1,460,000 for $2,100,000 on account.

INSTRUCTIONS

(a) Journalize the October transactions.

(b) Post the entries to the work in process accounts.

(c) Prepare a production cost report for the Mixing Department.

(d) Prepare a production cost report for the Packaging Department.

P23-3A The work in process accounts of the Yummy Candy Co. that pertain to the making of "Tastee Snacks," a new candy bar, during the month of July are presented below.

Work in Process — Mixing

July 31	Materials	50,000	July 31	Transferred out	120,000
31	Labor	48,800			
31	Overhead	24,400			

Work in Process — Baking

July 1	Inventory	2,700	July 31	Transferred out	183,600
31	Labor	40,600			
31	Overhead	20,300			
31	Transferred in	120,000			

Work in Process — Packaging

July 1	Inventory	5,370	July 31	To Finished Goods	242,800
31	Materials	24,480			
31	Labor	24,620			
31	Overhead	12,310			
31	Transferred in	183,600			

Production and inventory data are as follows:

	Inventory, July 1		Inventory, July 31		
Department	Units	% Complete	Units	% Complete	Units Transferred Out
Mixing	-0-	—	50,000	40	1,200,000
Baking	24,000	25	-0-	—	1,224,000
Packaging	30,000	30	40,000	65	1,214,000

All materials are entered at the beginning of a process.

INSTRUCTIONS

(a) Determine the equivalent units of production for (1) materials and (2) conversion costs in each process.

(b) Determine (1) the unit cost of materials, (2) the unit conversion costs, and (3) the total manufacturing cost per equivalent unit for each process.

(c) Show the assignment of costs to units transferred out and in process in each department.

P23-4A The Weber Manufacturing Co. has three processing departments. Manufacturing cost data for the departments in November 1987 were as follows:

Costs charged to department	Machining	Enameling	Assembly
Inventory, November 1	$ -0-	$ 97,000	$ 96,300
Materials	508,000	180,000	128,000
Labor	436,800	189,000	271,320
Overhead	291,600	126,000	180,880
Transferred in	-0-	?	?
Total costs to be accounted for	$1,236,400	?	?

Production Data			
Inventory, November 1			
Units	-0-	40,000	30,000
Percentage completed	—	25	30
Inventory, November 30			
Units	35,000	-0-	25,000
Percentage completed	20	—	40
Transferred In (units)	—	600,000	640,000

Raw materials are entered at the beginning of each process.

INSTRUCTIONS

(a) Determine the equivalent units of production and the unit costs in each process.

(b) Journalize the November transactions that affect work in process inventory accounts.

(c) Prepare a production cost report for the Assembly department.

P23-5A The Vaughan Furniture Company manufactures patio chairs through two departments: Framing and Upholstering. Materials are entered at the beginning of each process. For June 1987, the following cost data are obtained from the two work in process accounts.

	Framing	Upholstering
Work in process, June 1	$ -0-	$?
Materials	320,000	?
Conversion costs	224,000	160,000
Costs transferred in	-0-	450,000
Costs transferred out	450,000	?

INSTRUCTIONS

Answer the following questions:

(a) If 4,000 patio chairs were started into production on June 1, and 3,000 units were transferred to Upholstering, what is the percentage of completion of the units in process at June 30 in the Framing department?

(b) If the materials cost per unit in Upholstering is $210, what was the cost of materials added in Upholstering in May?

(c) If the conversion cost per unit in Upholstering is $50, what is the percentage of completion of the 500 units in work in process at June 30 if there were 800 units 25% complete in work in process at June 1?

(d) Disregard your answers above. Assume in Upholstering that unit costs in June were: materials added $75, conversion costs $100, and transferred-in costs $175. If 1,200 units were 30% complete on June 1 and unit costs were the same in May as in June, what is the cost of the beginning work in process inventory?

(e) Assuming the data given in (d) above, what is the cost of the June 1 work in process in Upholstering if there are 1,500 units 40% complete at June 1?

DECISION CASE

The Key West Company manufactures suntan lotion called Surtan in 11-ounce plastic bottles. Surtan is sold in a very competitive market. As a result, management is very cost-conscious. Surtan is manufactured through two processes: mixing and filling. Materials are entered at the beginning of each process and labor and manufacturing overhead occur uniformly throughout each process. Unit costs are based on the cost per gallon of Surtan.

On June 30, 1987, Sara Simmons, the chief accountant for the past 20 years, opted to take early retirement. Her replacement, Joe Jacobs, had extensive accounting experience with motels in the area but only limited contact with manufacturing accounting.

During July, Joe correctly accumulates the following production quantity and cost data for the Mixing Department.

Production Quantities: Work in process, July 1, 8,000 gallons 75% complete; started into production 100,000 gallons; work in process, July 31, 5,000 gallons 20% complete.

Production costs: Beginning work in process $82,000; incurred in July: materials $500,000, conversion costs $686,000.

Joe proceeded to prepare a production cost report on the basis of physical units involved. His report showed a production cost of $13.78 per gallon of Surtan. The management of Key West was shocked at the high unit cost. The president comes to you, as Sara's top assistant, to review Joe's report and prepare a correct report if necessary.

INSTRUCTIONS

(a) Show how Joe arrived at the unit cost of $13.78 per gallon of Surtan.

(b) What error(s) did Joe make in preparing his production cost report?

(c) Prepare a correct production cost report for July.

CHAPTER 24

Bentley College, Massachusetts

CHAPTER 24

COST-VOLUME-PROFIT RELATIONSHIPS

STUDY OBJECTIVES

After studying this chapter, you should be able to:

1. Distinguish between variable, fixed, and mixed costs.
2. Explain the meaning and importance of the relevant range.
3. State the four components of cost-volume-profit analysis.
4. Indicate the meaning of contribution margin and the ways it may be expressed.
5. Identify the three ways that the break-even point may be determined.
6. Define the term "margin of safety" and the formulas for computing it.
7. Give the formula for determining sales required to earn target net income.
8. Explain the term "sales mix" and its effects in determining break-even sales.
9. Describe the essential features of a cost-volume-profit income statement.

Business is dynamic, not static. Conditions are constantly changing. Management, therefore, is frequently faced with decisions that relate to the effects of change on its costs, revenues, and net income. Some typical decisions are:

1. If United Airlines is to make a profit when it reduces its fares from $149 to $99 on its flights from Chicago to Miami, what reduction in costs or increase in passengers will be required?
2. What increase in sales revenue will be needed to maintain current profit levels if Ford Motor Company meets the United Auto Workers' demands for higher wages?
3. What level of sales will General Motors need to cover its costs exactly in the first year it markets the Saturn automobile?

4. What will the effect be on the cost of producing one ton of steel at USX Corp. if its program to modernize plant facilities reduces the work force by 50%?
5. If McDonald's doubles its annual advertising expenditures for its restaurants, what increase in sales volume will be required to increase net income by 10%?

In making these decisions, management must understand the manner in which costs respond to changes in sales volume and the effect of this interaction of costs and revenues on profits. Cost-volume-profit (CVP) relationships are applicable to a company as a whole, but they are more frequently applied to segments, such as profit or investment centers. Management looks to accounting for quantitative data that are relevant for these types of business decisions. A prerequisite to understanding CVP relationships is knowledge of the behavior of costs.

In this chapter, we first explain the considerations involved in cost behavior analysis. Then we discuss and illustrate CVP analysis.

SECTION ONE—

Cost behavior analysis is the study of how specific costs respond to changes in the level of activity within a company. As expected, some costs change, and others remain the same. A knowledge of cost behavior is important to management in planning business operations and in deciding between alternative courses of action. Cost behavior analysis applies to all types of entities. The essential starting point in this analysis is a consideration of the activity index.

ACTIVITY INDEX

There are many ways to measure business activity within a company. Activity levels may be expressed in terms of sales dollars in a retail company, miles driven in a trucking company, room occupancy in a hotel, and number of customers called on by a salesperson. Many companies use more than one measurement base. A manufacturing company, for example, may use direct labor hours or units of output for manufacturing costs and sales revenue or units sold for selling expenses.

For an activity level to be useful in cost behavior analysis, there should be correlation between changes in the level or volume of activity and changes in costs. The activity level selected is referred to as the activity (or volume) index. The **activity index** identifies the activity that causes changes in the behavior of costs. Once an appropriate activity index is selected, it is possible to classify the behavior of costs in response to changes in activity levels into three categories: variable, fixed, or mixed.

VARIABLE COSTS

Variable costs are costs that vary **in total** directly and proportionately with changes in the activity level. If the level increases 25%, total variable costs will increase 25%; if the level of activity decreases by 30%, variable costs will be reduced 30%. Examples of variable costs include direct materials and direct labor in a manufacturing company; cost of goods sold, sales commissions, and freight-out in a merchandising company; and gasoline in airline and trucking companies. A variable cost may also be defined as a cost that remains the same **per unit** at every level of activity.

To illustrate the behavior of a variable cost, assume that the Damon Company manufactures radios that contain a $10 digital clock. The activity index is the number of radios produced. For each radio manufactured, the total cost of the clocks increases by $10. As illustrated in the left diagram below, total cost of the clocks will be $20,000 if 2,000 radios are manufactured, and $100,000 when 10,000 radios are produced. The digital clocks can also be used to show that a variable cost remains the same per unit as the level of activity changes. As shown in the right diagram below, the unit cost of $10 for the clocks is the same whether 2,000 or 10,000 radios are produced.

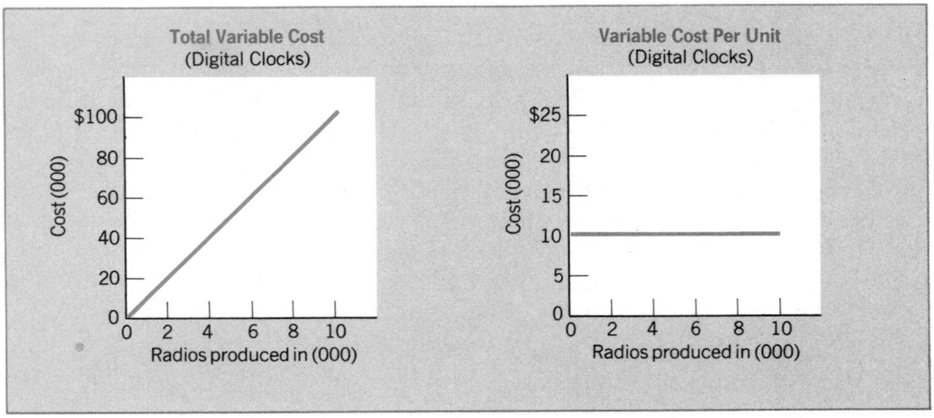

Behavior of total and unit variable costs

Companies that rely heavily on labor to manufacture a product or to render a service are likely to have many variable costs. In contrast, companies that use a high proportion of machinery and equipment in producing revenue, such as public utilities, may have few variable costs.

FIXED COSTS

Fixed costs are costs that remain the same **in total** regardless of changes in the activity level. Examples include property taxes, insurance, rent, supervisory salaries, and depreciation on buildings and equipment. Because fixed costs remain constant in total as activity changes, it follows that **fixed costs per unit** vary inversely with activity. As volume increases, unit cost declines and vice versa.

To illustrate the behavior of fixed costs, assume that the Damon Company leases all of its productive facilities at a cost of $10,000 per month. Total fixed costs will remain constant at every level of activity. However, on a per unit basis, the cost of rent will decline as activity increases. At 2,000 units, the unit cost is $5 ($10,000 ÷ 2,000), whereas when 10,000 radios are produced, the unit cost is only $1 ($10,000 ÷ 10,000). The cost behavior patterns are graphically shown below.

Behavior of total and unit fixed costs

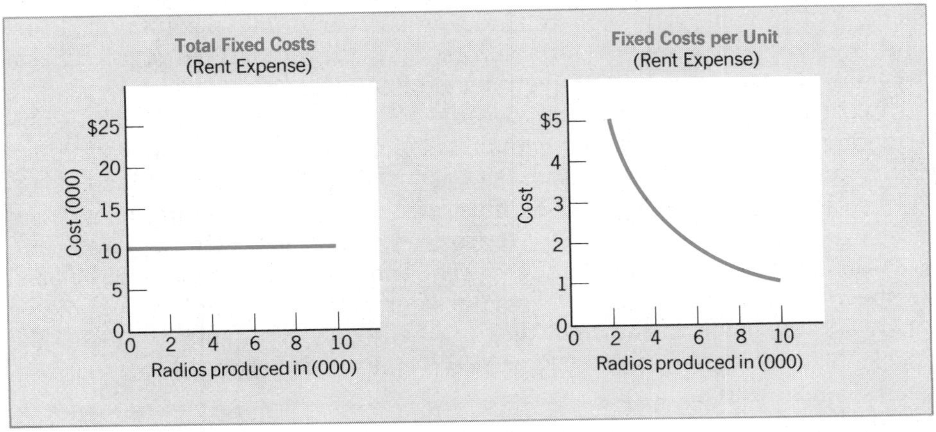

In planning, fixed costs are classified as either committed or discretionary. **Committed fixed costs** are long-term in nature and remain unchanged over extremely wide fluctuations in activity levels. These costs pertain to a company's investment in plant facilities. They include depreciation, property taxes, and insurance on buildings and equipment. Committed fixed costs cannot be eliminated without adversely affecting a company's ability to meet long-term goals. **Discretionary fixed costs** are costs that are avoidable within a relatively short time period such as a month or a year. These costs pertain to advertising, new product development, and management training programs. Discretionary costs often can be reduced to zero for short periods of time without jeopardizing a company's ability to meet long-term goals. Once incurred, however, discretionary costs are fixed.

The trend in many companies is to have more fixed costs and fewer variable costs. This development results from increased use of automation and less use of the work force. As a result, depreciation and lease charges, which are fixed costs, increase whereas direct labor costs, which are variable costs, decrease.

RELEVANT RANGE

In the preceding graphs, straight lines were drawn throughout the entire activity index for total variable costs and total fixed costs. In essence, the assumption was made that the costs were **linear.** It is now necessary to ask: Is the straight-line relationship realistic? Can the linear assumption produce useful data for CVP analysis?

In most business situations, a straight-line relationship does not exist for variable costs throughout the entire range of activity. At abnormally low levels of activity, it may be impossible to be cost efficient, since the scale of operations may not allow the company to obtain quantity discounts in the purchase of raw materials or use specialization of labor. In contrast, at abnormally high levels of activity, labor costs may increase sharply because of overtime pay, and materials costs may jump significantly because of excess spoilage caused by worker fatigue. Consequently, in the real world, the relationship between the behavior of a variable cost and changes in the activity level is often **curvilinear,** as shown in the left diagram below.

Total fixed costs also do not have a straight-line relationship over the entire range of activity. While committed fixed costs will not change, it is possible for management to change discretionary fixed costs. The behavior of total fixed costs through all levels of activity is shown in the right diagram below.

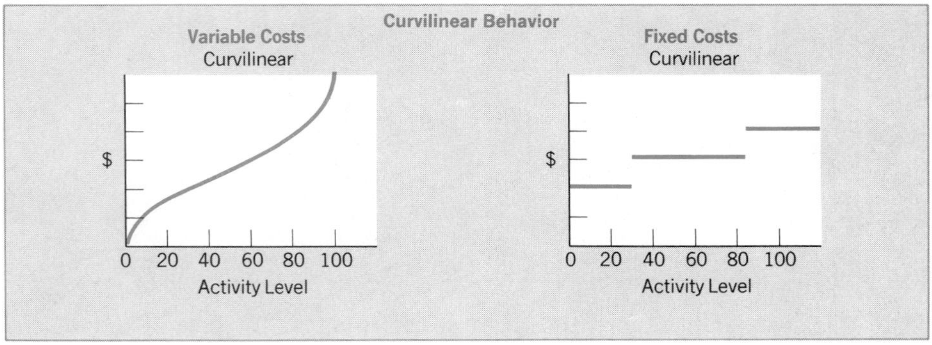

Curvilinear behavior

For most companies, operating at almost zero or 100% capacity is the exception rather than the rule. Instead, companies often operate over a somewhat narrower range, such as 40–80% of capacity. The range over which a company expects to operate during a year is called the **relevant range** of the activity index. Within this range, as illustrated in both diagrams below, a straight-line relationship generally exists for both variable and fixed costs.

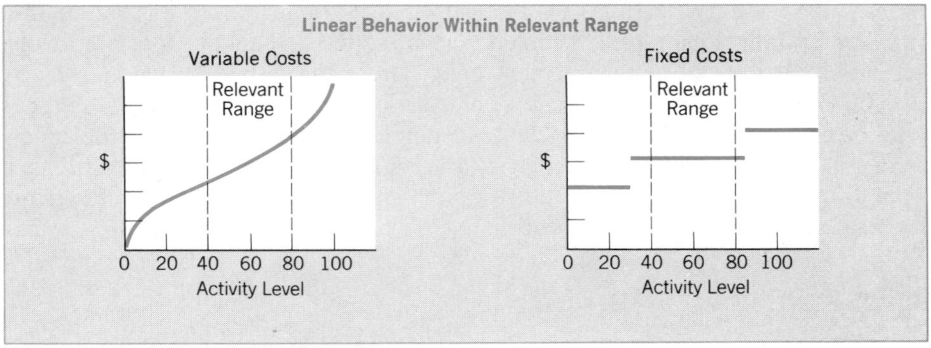

Linear behavior within relevant range

Thus, as you can see, although the straight-line relationship may not be completely realistic, the linear assumption produces useful data for CVP analysis as long as the level of activity remains within the relevant range.

MIXED COSTS

Mixed costs contain both a variable cost element and a fixed cost element. Sometimes called **semivariable costs,** mixed costs increase in total but not proportionately with changes in the activity level. The rental of a car from Hertz or Avis is a good example of a mixed cost. To illustrate, assume that the rental (or lease) terms are $30 per day plus 10 cents per mile. The per diem charge is a fixed cost with respect to miles driven, whereas the mileage charge is variable. The graphic presentation of this cost for a one-day rental is as follows:

Behavior of a mixed cost

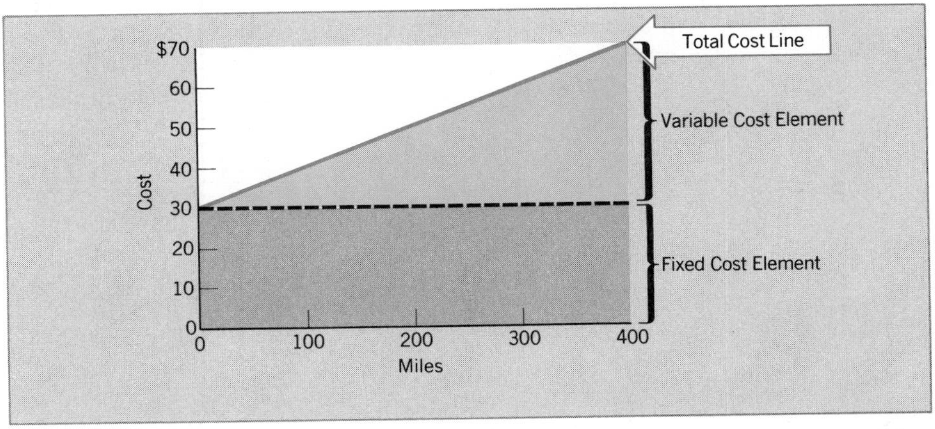

In this case, as in others, the fixed cost element is the cost of having the service available, whereas the variable cost element is the cost of actually using the service. Other examples of mixed costs include utility costs (electric, telephone, and so on), where there is a flat service fee plus a usage charge, and maintenance costs, where some costs are incurred regardless of the activity level and additional maintenance and repair work results as activity levels increase.

For purposes of CVP analysis, **mixed costs must be classified into their fixed and variable elements.** Accordingly, we must ask: How does management make the classification? One possibility is to determine the variable and fixed components each time a mixed cost is incurred. This approach is rarely followed because of time and cost constraints. Instead, the customary approach is to make the determination of variable and fixed costs on an **aggregate basis** at the end of a period of time, using the company's past experience with the behavior of the mixed cost at various levels of activity. With this approach, two of the methods management may use are the **scatter diagram method** and the **high-low method.**

SCATTER DIAGRAM METHOD

In the **scatter diagram method,** costs incurred at various levels of activity over the relevant range during a representative period of time are entered as single points on a diagram. A straight line is then **visually** fitted through the plotted points. The objective in fitting the line is to determine the **average** relationship between total costs and the activity levels. Typically, the line is

located so that approximately equal numbers of points fall above and below the line.

The fitted line is a line of averages.[1] Its slope indicates the average variable cost per unit of activity. In addition, average total fixed costs are indicated where the line intersects the vertical (or cost) axis. To illustrate, assume that the Metro Transit Company has the following monthly maintenance costs for its fleet of buses.

Assumed maintenance costs and mileage data

Month	Miles Driven	Total Cost	Month	Miles Driven	Total Cost
January	20,000	$30,000	May	50,000	$63,000
February	30,000	40,000	June	45,000	50,000
March	35,000	49,000	July	40,000	47,000
April	43,000	55,000	August	30,000	45,000

The scatter diagram is as follows:

Scatter diagram

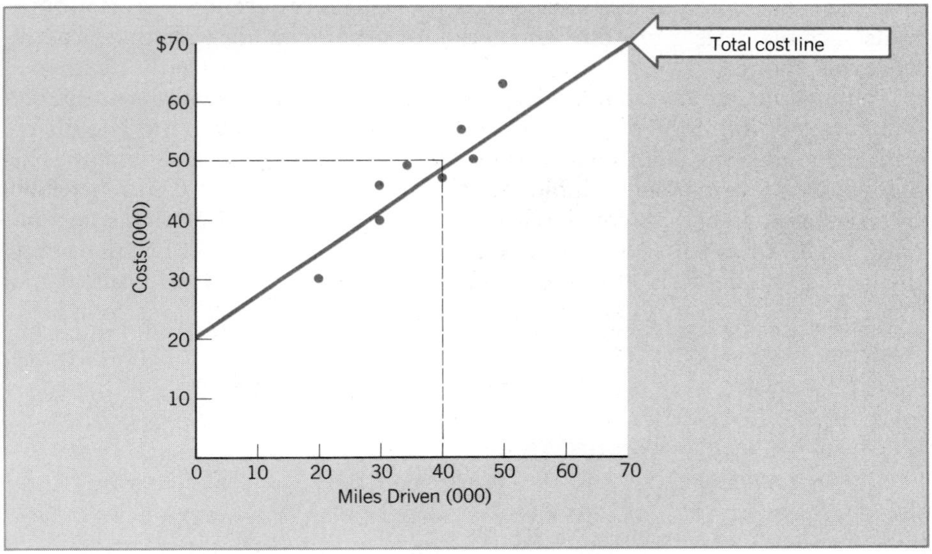

The intersection of the fitted line and the vertical axis indicates that the fixed cost element is $20,000. The variable cost element can be computed for any level of activity. Using the data shown where the dashed lines intersect with the fitted line and the horizontal and vertical axes, the computation is as follows:

[1]Statistical techniques, such as least squares regression analysis, can be used to compute a more exact straight line called a **regression line.**

Scatter diagram computation

Total cost at 40,000 miles	$50,000
Less: Fixed cost element	20,000
Variable cost element	$30,000
Variable cost per mile ($30,000 ÷ 40,000)	$.75

Thus, maintenance costs may be expressed as $20,000 per month plus $.75 per mile.

The accuracy of the fixed and variable cost components depends on the judgment exercised by the cost analyst in visually drawing the fitted line. When carefully done, the scatter diagram method of classifying mixed costs produces satisfactory results for CVP analysis.

HIGH-LOW METHOD

The **high-low method** is a mathematical method that uses the total costs incurred at the high and low levels of activity. The difference in costs represents variable costs, since only the variable cost element can change as activity levels change.

To illustrate, assume that a salesperson incurs $50 of expenses in calling on one customer and $110 of expenses in calling on three customers. The difference in total costs ($60) clearly represents the variable cost element. This amount is converted to a variable cost per unit by dividing the difference ($60) by the change in activity level, which is 2 customers (3 − 1). Variable cost per unit, therefore, is $30 ($60 ÷ 2). Fixed costs are then obtained by subtracting the total variable costs at either level of activity from the total costs at that level of activity. In this example, fixed costs are $20, computed as follows:

Example of high-low method

	(3 customers)	(1 customer)
Total costs	$110	$50
Less: Variable costs		
$30 × 3	90	
$30 × 1		30
Total fixed costs	$ 20	$20

As indicated, the cost of calling customers involves $20 of fixed costs plus variable costs of $30 per call.

To illustrate the high-low method in more detail, we will again use the data from Metro Transit Company shown on page 953. For the Metro Transit Company the high and low levels are 50,000 miles in May and 20,000 miles in January. The maintenance costs at these two levels are $63,000 and $30,000, respectively. The steps in computing fixed and variable costs using the high-low method are as follows:

(1) Determine variable cost per unit from the following formula:

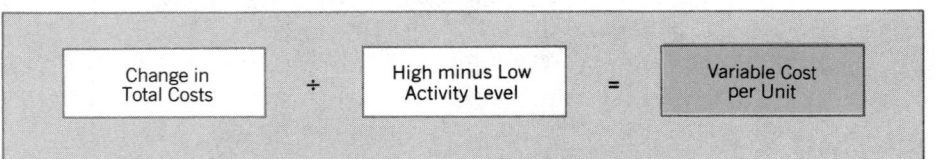

Variable cost per unit

Change in Total Costs	÷	High minus Low Activity Level	=	Variable Cost per Unit

The difference in maintenance costs is $33,000 ($63,000 − $30,000) and the difference in miles is 30,000 (50,000 − 20,000). Therefore, for Metro Transit, variable cost per unit is $1.10, computed as follows:

$$\$33{,}000 \quad \div \quad 30{,}000 \quad = \quad \$1.10$$

(2) Determine the fixed cost by subtracting the total variable cost at either activity level from the total cost at that activity level. For Metro Transit, the computations are:

High-low method computations

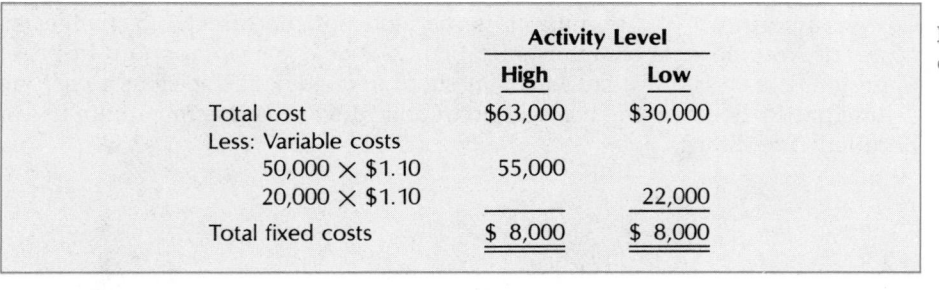

	Activity Level	
	High	**Low**
Total cost	$63,000	$30,000
Less: Variable costs		
50,000 × $1.10	55,000	
20,000 × $1.10		22,000
Total fixed costs	$ 8,000	$ 8,000

On the basis of these findings, it is possible to say that maintenance costs are $8,000 per month plus $1.10 per mile. The high-low method generally is not as accurate as the scatter diagram method, because it ignores costs incurred between the high and low levels of activity.

IMPORTANCE OF IDENTIFYING VARIABLE AND FIXED COSTS

Why is it important to segregate costs into variable and fixed elements? The answer may become apparent if we return to the five questions raised on the first page of this chapter.

1. To make a profit when Chicago to Miami fares are reduced from $149 to $99, United Airlines will have to increase the number of passengers or cut its variable costs for those flights. Its fixed costs will not change.
2. Higher wages to UAW members at Ford Motor Company will increase the variable costs of manufacturing automobiles. To maintain present profit levels, Ford will have to cut other variable costs or increase the price of its automobiles.

3. To cover its costs exactly on the Saturn automobile, General Motors must determine the sales volume at which sales revenue will equal total costs, both fixed and variable.
4. The modernizing of plant facilities at USX Corp. changes the proportion of fixed and variable costs of producing one ton of steel. Fixed costs increase because of higher depreciation charges whereas variable costs decrease due to the reduction in the number of steelworkers.
5. Doubling its advertising expense increases McDonald's discretionary fixed costs. Sales volume must be increased to cover three items: (1) the increase in advertising, (2) the variable costs of the increased sales volume, and (3) the desired additional net income.

SECTION TWO—COST-VOLUME-PROFIT ANALYSIS

Cost-volume-profit (CVP) analysis is the study of the effects of changes in costs and volume on a company's profits. CVP analysis is important in profit planning. It also is a critical factor in such management decisions as setting selling prices, determining the best product mix, and making maximum use of production facilities.

BASIC COMPONENTS

CVP analysis involves a consideration of the interrelationships among the following components.

1. Volume or level of activity.
2. Unit selling prices.
3. Variable cost per unit.
4. Total fixed costs.

The following assumptions underlie each CVP application:

1. The behavior of both costs and revenues is linear throughout the entire range of the activity index.
2. All costs can be classified as either variable or fixed with reasonable accuracy.
3. Changes in activity are the only factors that affect costs.
4. All units produced are sold.
5. When more than one type of product is sold, total sales will be in a constant sales mix.

When these assumptions are not valid, the results of CVP analysis may be inaccurate.

In the applications of CVP analysis that follow, we will assume that the term "cost" includes **all** direct and indirect costs and expenses pertaining to production and sale of the product. That is, cost includes manufacturing costs plus selling and administrative expenses. We will use the Vargo Video Company as an example. Relevant data for the video-cassette recorders (VCRs) made by this company are as follows:

Assumed selling price and cost data

Unit selling price	$500
Unit variable costs	$300
Total monthly fixed costs	$200,000

CONTRIBUTION MARGIN

One of the key relationships in CVP analysis is **contribution margin (CM).** **Contribution margin is the amount of revenue remaining after deducting variable costs.** This revenue is then available to cover fixed costs and to produce income for the company.

Views differ as to the best way to express contribution margin (CM). Some individuals favor a per unit basis. The formula for contribution margin per unit is:

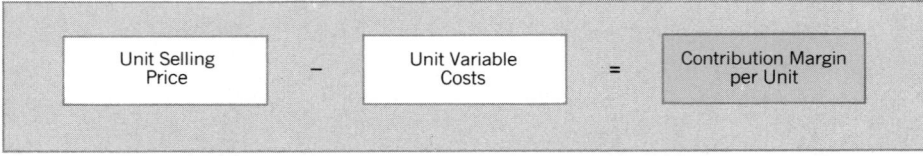

Contribution margin per unit

Unit Selling Price − Unit Variable Costs = Contribution Margin per Unit

At Vargo Video, the contribution margin per unit is $200, computed as follows:

$$\$500 \quad - \quad \$300 \quad = \quad \$200$$

Contribution margin per unit indicates that for every VCR sold, Vargo will have $200 to apply to its fixed costs and contribute to income. Since fixed costs are $200,000, Vargo Video must sell 1,000 VCRs ($200,000 ÷ 200) before there is any income. Above that sales volume, every sale will contribute $200 to income. Thus, if 1,500 units are sold, income will be $100,000 (500 × $200).

Others prefer to use a contribution margin ratio. The formula for this ratio is:

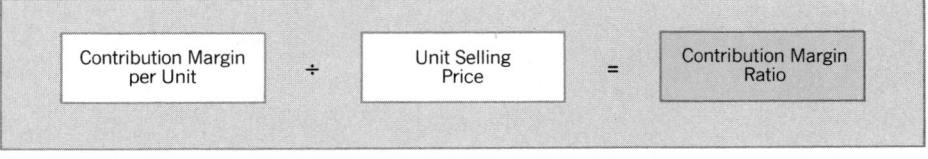

Contribution margin ratio

Contribution Margin per Unit ÷ Unit Selling Price = Contribution Margin Ratio

At Vargo Video, the ratio is 40%, as shown below.

$$\$200 \quad \div \quad \$500 \quad = \quad 40\%$$

The CM ratio of 40% means that 40 cents of each sales dollar ($1 × 40%) is available to cover fixed costs and to produce income. This expression of contribution margin is very helpful in determining the effect of changes in sales on income. To illustrate, if the management of Vargo Video wants to know the effect of a $50,000 increase in sales, they simply multiply $50,000 by the CM ratio (40%) to determine that income will increase $20,000.

BREAK-EVEN ANALYSIS

A second key relationship in CVP analysis is the level of activity at which total revenues equals total costs, both fixed and variable. This level of activity is called the **break-even point,** because at this volume of sales, the company will realize no income and suffer no loss. Since income is not involved when the break-even point is the objective, the analysis is often referred to simply as **break-even analysis.** Knowledge of the break-even point is useful to management in deciding whether to introduce new product lines, change sales prices on established products, and enter new market areas.

The break-even point can be

1. Computed from a mathematical equation.
2. Computed by using contribution margin.
3. Derived from a cost-volume-profit (CVP) graph.

The break-even point can be expressed either in sales dollars or sales units.

MATHEMATICAL EQUATION

In its simplest form, the equation for break-even sales is:

Break-even equation

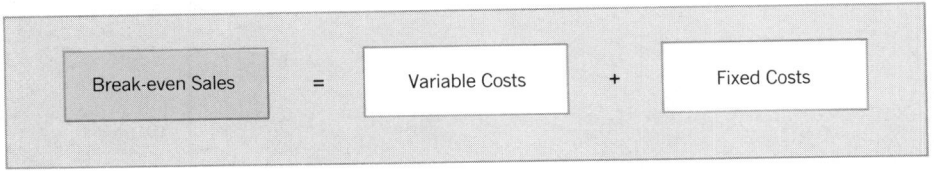

Break-even Sales	=	Variable Costs	+	Fixed Costs

The break-even point in dollars is found by expressing variable costs as a percentage of unit selling price. For Vargo Video, the percentage is 60% ($300 ÷ $500). The computation is:

$$X = .60X + \$200{,}000$$

$$.40X = \$200{,}000$$

$$X = \$500{,}000$$

where:

$$X = \text{sales dollars at the break-even point}$$
$$.60X = \text{variable costs as a percentage of unit selling price}$$
$$\$200{,}000 = \text{total fixed costs.}$$

Sales, therefore, must be $500,000 for Vargo Video to break-even.

The break-even point in units can be determined by dividing break-even sales dollars by unit selling price. Thus, break-even units are 1,000 ($500,000 ÷ $500). The break-even point in units can be computed directly from the mathematical equation by using unit selling prices and unit variable costs. The computation is:

$$\$500X = \$300X + \$200{,}000$$
$$\$200X = \$200{,}000$$
$$X = 1{,}000 \text{ units}$$

where:

$$\$500X = \text{unit selling price} \times \text{sales volume}$$
$$\$300X = \text{variable cost per unit} \times \text{sales volume}$$
$$\$200{,}000 = \text{total fixed costs.}$$

The accuracy of the computations above can be proved as follows:

Break-even proof

Sales (1,000 × $500)		$500,000
Total costs:		
Variable (1,000 × $300)	$300,000	
Fixed	200,000	500,000
Net income		$ -0-

CONTRIBUTION MARGIN TECHNIQUE

Since we know that contribution margin equals total revenues less variable costs, it follows that at the break-even point, **contribution margin must equal total fixed costs.** On the basis of this relationship, the break-even point can be computed by using either the contribution margin per unit or the contribution margin ratio.

When the contribution margin per unit is used, the formula to compute break-even sales in units is as follows:

Break-even point—contribution margin per unit

Fixed Costs	÷	Contribution Margin per Unit	=	Break-even Point in Units

For Vargo Video, the contribution margin per unit is $200, as explained above. Thus, the computation is:

$200,000 ÷ $200 = 1,000 units

When the contribution margin ratio is used, the formula to compute break-even sales in dollars is:

Break-even point—contribution margin ratio

Fixed Costs	÷	Contribution Margin Ratio	=	Break-even Point in Dollars

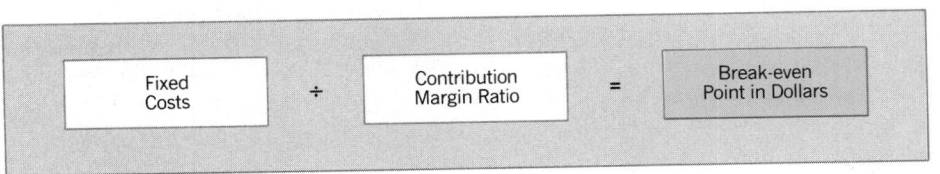

We know that the contribution margin ratio for Vargo Video is 40%. Thus, the computation is:

$200,000 ÷ 40% = $500,000

GRAPHIC PRESENTATION

An effective way to derive the break-even point is to prepare a break-even chart (or graph). Since the graphic provides much more information than the break-even point, we shall refer to it as the **cost-volume profit (CVP) graph.**

In the graph on page 961, volume is measured along the horizontal axis. This axis should extend to the maximum level of expected sales. Both total revenues (sales) and total costs (fixed plus variable) are measured on the vertical axis. The construction of the graph, using the data for Vargo Video, is as follows:

1. Plot the total revenue line starting at the zero activity level. For every VCR sold, total revenue increases by $500. For example, at 200 units, sales are $100,000, and at the upper level of activity (1,800 units), sales are $900,000. Note that the revenue line is assumed to be linear throughout the full range of activity.
2. Plot the total fixed cost by a horizontal line. For the VCRs, this line is plotted at $200,000, and it is the same at every level of activity.
3. Plot the total cost line starting at the fixed cost line at zero activity and increasing the amount by the variable cost at each level of activity. For each VCR, variable costs are $300. Thus, at 200 units, total variable cost is $60,000 and the total cost is $260,000; at 1,800 units total variable cost is $540,000, and total cost is $740,000. On the graph, the amount of the variable cost can be derived from the difference between the total cost and fixed cost lines at each level of activity.
4. Determine the break-even point from the intersection of the total cost line and the total revenue line. The break-even point in dollars is found by drawing a horizontal line from the break-even point to the vertical axis. The break-even point in units is obtained by drawing a vertical line from the break-even point to the horizontal axis. For the VCRs, the break-even point is $500,000 of sales, or 1,000 units.

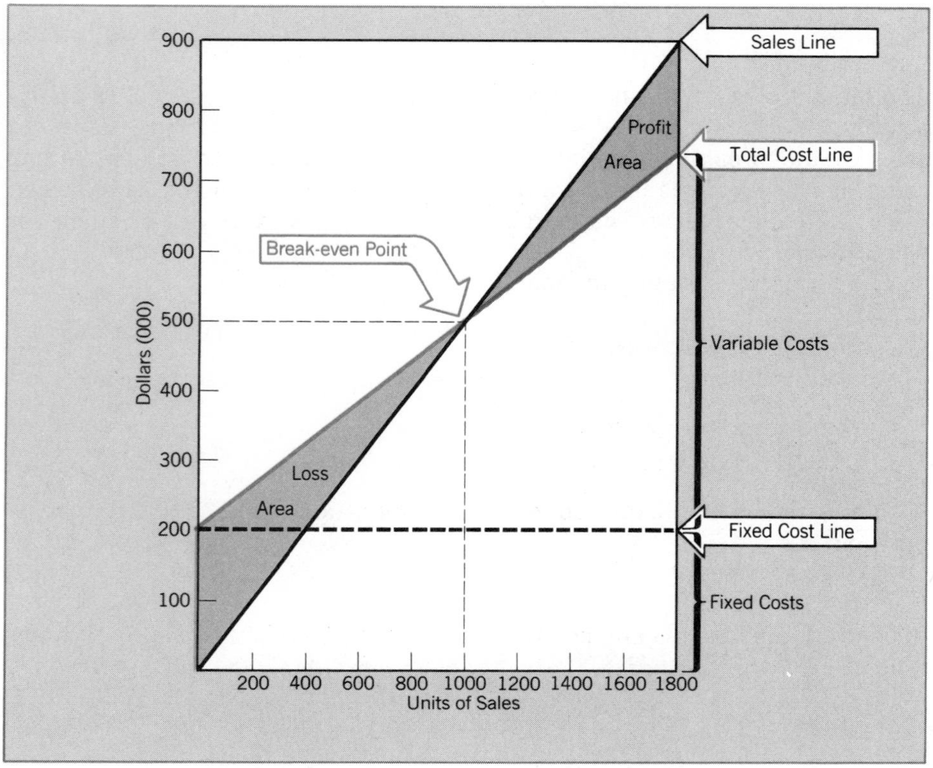

CVP graph

In addition to identifying the break-even point, the CVP graph shows both the net income and net loss areas. Thus, the amount of income or loss at each level of sales can be derived from the total sales and total cost line.

A CVP graph is especially useful in management meetings because the effects of a change in any element in the CVP analysis can be promptly portrayed on a screen. For example, a 10% increase in selling price will change the location of the total revenue line. In addition, the effects on total costs of wage increases to both office employees and factory workers can be quickly observed.

The use of computer graphics is a valuable companion to spreadsheets and data bases. (These are the three components in the LOTUS 1-2-3 program.) In the meeting setting noted above, all sorts of graphic displays can be turned into video output. The graphs, of course, can be changed instantly to provide visual what-if analysis. This can all be done in color for either video or hard copy output. You should familiarize yourself with different forms of graphs (pie charts, bar, stacked bar, etc.). Computerized graphics is a modern example of the old adage that one picture is worth a thousand words.

MARGIN OF SAFETY

The margin of safety is another relationship that may be used in CVP analysis. **Margin of safety** is the difference between actual or expected sales and sales at the break-even point. This relationship measures the "breathing room" or "cushion" management has to break even should actual or expected sales fail to materialize. The margin of safety may be expressed in dollars or as a ratio.

The formula for stating the margin of safety in dollars is:

Margin of safety in dollars

Actual (Expected) Sales	−	Break-even Sales	=	Margin of Safety in Dollars

Assuming that actual (expected) sales for Vargo Video are $750,000, the computation is:

$750,000 − $500,000 = $250,000

In contrast, the formula and computation for determining the margin of safety ratio are:

Margin of safety ratio

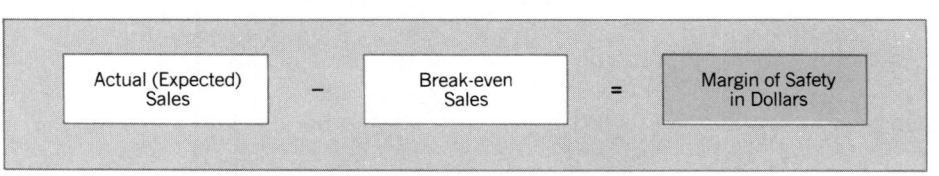

Margin of Safety in Dollars	÷	Actual (Expected) Sales	=	Margin of Safety Ratio
$250,000	÷	$750,000	=	33 1/3%

The higher the dollars or the percentage, the greater is the margin of safety. The adequacy of the margin of safety should be evaluated by management in terms of such factors as the vulnerability of the product to competitive pressures and to downturns in the economy.

TARGET NET INCOME

Management usually sets an income objective for individual product lines. **Target net income** is extremely useful to management because it indicates the sales necessary to achieve a specified level of income. Target net income sales can be determined from each of the approaches used in determining break-even sales.

MATHEMATICAL EQUATION

From our consideration of the break-even point, we know that the break-even equation results in no profit or loss for the company. By adding a factor for

target net income, we obtain the following equation to determine the required sales:

Required sales—target net income

$$\text{Required Sales} = \text{Variable Costs} + \text{Fixed Costs} + \text{Target Net Income}$$

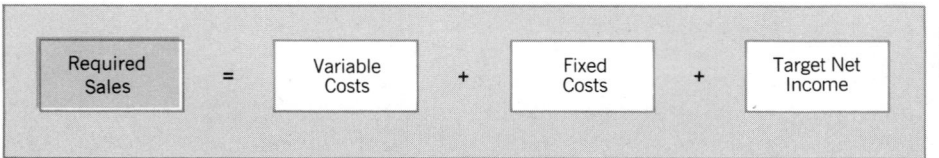

Required sales may be expressed in either sales dollars or sales units. Assuming that target net income is $120,000 for Vargo Video, the computation of required sales in dollars is as follows:

$$X = .60X + \$200{,}000 + \$120{,}000$$

$$.40X = \$320{,}000$$

$$X = \$800{,}000$$

where:

X = required sales

$.60X$ = variable costs as a percentage of unit selling price

$200,000 = total fixed costs

$120,000 = target net income

The sales volume at the targeted income level is found by dividing the sales dollars by the unit selling price ($800,000 ÷ $500) = 1,600 units.[2]

CONTRIBUTION MARGIN TECHNIQUE

As in the case of break-even sales, the sales required to meet a target net income can be explained in either dollars or in units. The formula using the contribution margin ratio is as follows:

Required sales—contribution margin ratio

$$\text{Fixed Costs} + \text{Target Net Income} \div \text{Contribution Margin Ratio} = \text{Required Sales}$$

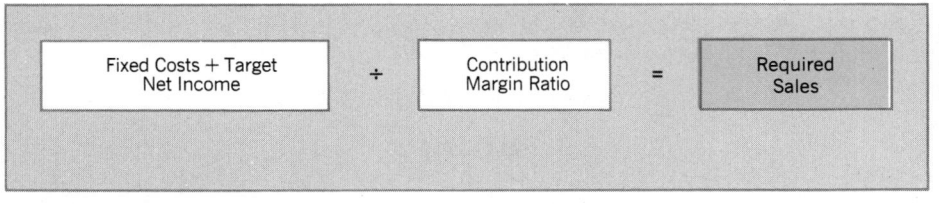

The computation for Vargo Video is as follows:

$$\$320{,}000 \div 40\% = \$800{,}000$$

[2]The units can be derived directly by using unit prices in the equation: $\$500X = \$300X + \$200{,}000 + \$120{,}000$; $\$200X = \$320{,}000$ or 1,600 units.

Proof of the accuracy of this amount is shown in the income statement presented on page 968.

GRAPHIC PRESENTATION

The CVP graphs presented earlier can also be used to derive the sales required to meet target net income. In the profit area of the graph, the distance between the total sales line and the total cost line at any point equals net income. Required sales are found by analyzing the differences between the two lines until the desired net income is found.

SALES MIX

In the preceding discussion, we have focused on one product, video-cassette recorders. One of the assumptions of CVP analysis is that if more than one product is involved, the sales mix of the products remains constant. **Sales mix** is the ratio of the number of units of each type of product sold to the total units of product sold. For example, if 2 units of Product A are sold for every 1 unit of Product B, the ratio between the two products is 2:1. Break-even sales can be computed for a mix of two or more products by determining the **weighted average unit contribution margin** of all the products.

To illustrate, we will assume that Vargo Video sells both VCRs and television sets (TVs) at the following per unit data:

Per unit data—sales mix

Unit Data	VCRs	TVs
Selling price	$500	$800
Variable costs	300	400
Contribution margin	$200	$400
Sales mix	3	1

The total contribution margin of the 4 units sold is $1,000 ($200 × 3 + $400 × 1), and the weighted average unit contribution margin is $250 ($1,000 ÷ 4). The break-even formula is as follows:

Break-even formula—sales mix

Fixed Costs ÷ Weighted Average Unit Contribution Margin = Break-even Sales in Units

The computation for Vargo Video, assuming $200,000 of fixed costs, is as follows:

$200,000 ÷ $250 = 800 units

Thus, to break even at this sales mix, Vargo Video must sell 600 VCRs (¾ × 800) and 200 TVs (¼ × 800). This can be verified by the following:

Break-even proof—sales mix

Product	Unit Sales	×	Unit CM	=	Total CM
VCRs	600	×	$200	=	$120,000
TVs	200	×	400	=	80,000
	800				$200,000

Management should continually review its sales mix. At any specified volume of sales, net income will be greater if more sales are made of products with high contribution margins than of those with low contribution margins. For Vargo Video, the television sets produce the higher contribution margin. Consequently, if 300 TVs and 50 VCRs are sold, net income would be higher at the same total volume of sales than in the current sales mix. An analysis of these relationships shows that (1) a shift from low margin sales to high margin sales may increase net income, even though there is a decline in total sales volume, and (2) a shift from high to low margin sales may result in a decrease in net income, even though there is an increase in total sales volume.

CVP AND CHANGES IN THE BUSINESS ENVIRONMENT

When the IBM PC was introduced, it sold for $2,500; today the same type of computer sells for $1,100. When high oil prices collapsed, the break-even point for airline and trucking companies dropped dramatically. Because of lower prices for imported steel, the demand for domestic steel dropped significantly. The point should be clear: business conditions change rapidly and management must respond intelligently to these changes. CVP analysis has been helpful in the past, and it will be helpful in the future. To illustrate how CVP analysis can be used in responding to change, we will use the following independent situations that might occur at Vargo Video. Each case is based on the original VCR sales and cost data which were:

Original VCR sales and cost data

Unit selling price	$500
Unit variable cost	$300
Total fixed costs	$200,000
Break-even sales	$500,000 or 1,000 units

Case I

Question: A competitor is offering a 10% discount on the selling price of its VCRs. Management must decide whether to offer a similar discount. What effect will a 10% discount on selling price have on the break-even point for VCRs?

Answer: A 10% discount on selling price reduces the selling price per unit to $450 [$500 − ($500 × 10%)]. Variable costs per unit remain unchanged at $300. Thus, the contribution margin per unit is $150. Assuming no change in fixed costs, break-even sales are 1,333 units, computed as follows:

Break-even sales in units

Fixed Costs	÷	Contribution Margin per Unit	=	Break-even Sales
$200,000	÷	$150	=	1,333 units (rounded)

For Vargo Video, this change would require monthly sales to increase by 333 units or 33⅓% in order to break even. In reaching a conclusion about offering a 10% discount to customers, management must determine the likelihood of achieving the increased sales. Also, management should estimate the possible loss of sales if the competitor's discount price is not matched.

Case II

Question: To meet the continuing threat of foreign competition, management invests in new robotic equipment that will significantly lower the amount of direct labor required to make the VCRs. It is estimated that total fixed costs will increase 30% and that variable cost per unit will decrease 30%. What effect will the new equipment have on the sales volume required to break even?

Answer: Total fixed costs become $260,000 [$200,000 + (30% × $200,000)], and variable cost per unit is now $210 [$300 − (30% × $300)]. The new break-even point is 900 units, computed as follows:

Break-even in units

Fixed Costs	÷	Contribution Margin per Unit	=	Break-even Sales
$260,000	÷	($500 − $210)	=	900 units (rounded)

These changes appear to be advantageous for Vargo Video because the break-even point is reduced by 10%, or 100 units.

Case III

Question: The principal supplier of raw materials has just announced a price increase. It is estimated that the higher cost will increase the variable cost of VCRs by $25 per unit. Management would like to hold the line on the selling price of VCRs. It plans a cost-cutting program that will save $17,500 in fixed costs per month. Vargo is currently realizing monthly net income of $80,000 on sales of 1,400 VCRs. What increase in sales will be needed to maintain the same level of net income?

Answer: The variable cost per unit increases to $325 ($300 + $25), and fixed costs are reduced to $182,500 ($200,000 − $17,500). Because of the change in variable cost, the variable cost becomes 65% of sales ($325 ÷ $500). Using the equation for target net income, we find that required sales are $750,000, computed as follows on the next page.

To achieve the required sales, 1,500 VCRs will have to be sold ($750,000 ÷ $500), an increase of 100 units. If this does not seem to be a reasonable expectation, management will either have to effect further reductions in costs or accept less net income if the selling price remains unchanged.

Computation of required sales

$$\text{Required sales} = \text{Variable Costs} + \text{Fixed Costs} + \text{Target Net Income}$$
$$X = .65X + \$182{,}500 + \$80{,}000$$
$$.35X = \$262{,}500$$
$$X = \$750{,}000$$

CVP INCOME STATEMENT

As you have learned, cost behavior and contribution margin are key factors in CVP analysis. Because management makes its decisions on these factors, it often wants the results of these decisions reported in a similar format. This has led to the development for **internal use only** of a **CVP** or **contribution margin format** for the income statement. The **CVP income statement** classifies costs and expenses as variable or fixed and specifically reports contribution margin in the body of the statement. This is in contrast to the income statement traditionally prepared for external use, in which no disclosure is made of the behavior of costs and expenses. In the traditional statement, costs and expenses are classified only by function, such as cost of goods sold, selling expenses, and general expenses.

To illustrate the CVP income statement, we will assume that Vargo Video is successful in reaching its target net income of $120,000 (see page 963). From an analysis of the transactions, the following information is obtained on the $680,000 of costs that were incurred in June:

Assumed cost and expense data

	Variable	Fixed	Total
Cost of goods sold	$400,000	$120,000	$520,000
Selling expenses	60,000	40,000	100,000
Administrative expenses	20,000	40,000	60,000
	$480,000	$200,000	$680,000

The CVP income statement and the conventional income statement based on these data are as follows on the next page.

Note that net income is the same ($120,000) in both of the statements. The major difference is the format for the expenses. As illustrated, the CVP statement classifies costs and expenses as either variable or fixed. Another difference is that the traditional statement shows gross profit, whereas the CVP statement shows contribution margin.

The CVP income statement facilitates the evaluation of results pertaining to prior management decisions based on CVP analysis. This type of income statement may also be prepared at the time the decision is made to show the expected results.

Traditional versus CVP income statement

VARGO VIDEO COMPANY
Income Statement
For the Month Ended June 30, 1987

Traditional Format

Sales		$800,000
Cost of goods sold		520,000
Gross profit		280,000
Operating expenses		
Selling expenses	$100,000	
Administrative expenses	60,000	
Total operating expenses		160,000
Net income		$120,000

CVP Format

Sales		$800,000
Variable expenses		
Cost of goods sold	$400,000	
Selling expenses	60,000	
Administrative expenses	20,000	
Total variable expenses		480,000
CONTRIBUTION MARGIN		320,000
Fixed expenses		
Cost of goods sold	$120,000	
Selling expenses	40,000	
Administrative expenses	40,000	
Total fixed expenses		200,000
Net income		$120,000

SUMMARY OF STUDY OBJECTIVES

1. Costs may be variable, fixed, or mixed. Variable costs are costs that vary in total directly and proportionately with changes in the activity index. Fixed costs are costs that remain the same in total regardless of changes in the activity index. Mixed costs are costs that remain fixed at some levels of activity but are variable at other levels.

2. The relevant range is the range of activity in which a company expects to operate during a year. It is important in CVP analysis because the behavior of costs is linear throughout the relevant range.

3. The four components of CVP analysis are (a) volume or level of activity, (b) unit selling prices, (c) the variable cost per unit, and (d) total fixed costs.

4. Contribution margin is the amount of revenue remaining after deducting variable costs. It can be expressed as a per unit amount or as a ratio.

5. The break-even point can be (a) computed from a mathematical equation, (b) computed by using a contribution margin technique, and (c) derived from a CVP graph.

6. Margin of safety is the difference between actual or expected sales and sales at the break-even point. The formulas for margin of safety are Actual (Expected) Sales − Break-even Sales = Margin of Safety in

Dollars; Margin of Safety in Dollars ÷ Actual (Expected Sales) = Margin of Safety Ratio.

7. The formula for computing sales required to earn target net income is: Required Sales = Variable Costs + Fixed Costs + Target Net Income.

8. Sales mix is the ratio of the number of units of each type of product sold to the total units of product sold. Break-even sales are determined by using the weighted average unit contribution margin of all the products.

9. The CVP income statement classifies costs and expenses as variable or fixed and reports contribution margin in the body of the statement.

GLOSSARY

Activity index, p. 948

Break-even point, p. 958

Committed fixed costs, p. 950

Contribution margin, p. 957

Cost behavior analysis, p. 948

Cost-volume-profit analysis, p. 956

Cost-volume-profit graph, p. 960

Cost-volume-profit income statement, p. 967

Discretionary fixed costs, p. 950

Fixed costs, p. 949

High-low method, p. 954

Margin of safety, p. 962

Mixed costs, p. 952

Relevant range, p. 951

Sales mix, p. 964

Scatter diagram method, p. 952

Target net income, p. 962

Variable costs, p. 949

DEMONSTRATION PROBLEM

The Mabo Company makes pocket calculators that sell for $20 each. For the coming year, management expects fixed costs to total $220,000 and variable costs to be $9.00 per unit.

INSTRUCTIONS

(a) Compute break-even sales in dollars using the mathematical equation.
(b) Compute break-even sales using the contribution margin (CM) ratio.
(c) Compute the margin of safety percentage assuming actual sales are $500,000.
(d) Compute the sales required to earn net income of $165,000.

SOLUTION TO DEMONSTRATION PROBLEM

(a) Break-even Sales = Variable Costs + Fixed Costs

$$X = .45X + \$220{,}000$$
$$.55X = \$220{,}000$$
$$X = \$400{,}000$$

(b) Contribution Margin = Selling Price less Variable Costs.

Contribution Margin = \$11 (\$20 − \$9).

Contribution Margin Ratio = Contribution Margin ÷ Selling Price.

Contribution Margin Ratio = 55% (\$11 ÷ \$20).

Break-even Sales = Fixed Cost ÷ Contribution Margin Ratio

$$X = \$220{,}000 \div 55\%$$
$$X = \$400{,}000$$

(c) Margin of Safety $= \dfrac{\text{Actual Sales} - \text{Break-Even Sales}}{\text{Actual Sales}}$

$$= \frac{\$500{,}000 - \$400{,}000}{\$500{,}000}$$
$$= 20\%$$

(d) Required Sales = Variable Costs + Fixed Costs + Net Income

$$X = .45X + \$220{,}000 + \$165{,}000$$
$$.55X = \$385{,}000$$
$$X = \$700{,}000$$

QUESTIONS

1. Lee Stern argues that cost behavior analysis is a study of how specific costs (and expenses) vary between companies. Do you agree? Explain.

2. Variable costs are costs that vary in total directly and proportionately with changes in net income. Is this a true statement? Why?

3. Contrast the behavior of a variable cost and a fixed cost, both in total and on a per unit basis, in response to changes in the level of activity.

4. Mary Miles claims that the relevant range concept is not important for fixed costs. Do you agree? Explain.

5. The relevant range is indispensable in cost behavior analysis. Is this true? Why?

6. Stan Speers is confused. He does not understand why rent on his apartment is a fixed cost and rent on an Avis rental car is a semivariable cost. Explain the difference to Stan.

7. How should mixed costs be classified in CVP analysis? What approaches are used to effect the appropriate classification?

8. In a scatter diagram, the total cost line intersects the vertical axis at \$10,000. At 30,000 miles the total cost on the vertical axis is \$34,000. What is the variable cost per mile?

9. At the high and low levels of activity during the month, direct labor hours are 80,000 and 40,000, respectively, and the related costs are $120,000 and $70,000. What are the fixed and variable costs at any level of activity?

10. Cost-volume-profit (CVP) analysis is based entirely on unit costs. Do you agree? Explain.

11. Chuck Caros defines contribution margin as the amount of profit available to cover operating expenses. Is there any truth in this definition? Discuss.

12. In the Margo Company, the Speedo pocket calculator sells for $40 and variable costs per unit are estimated to be $28. What is the contribution margin per unit and the contribution margin ratio?

13. Break-even analysis is of limited use to management because a company cannot survive by just breaking even. Do you agree? Explain.

14. Assume that total fixed costs are $12,000 for Hartwig Inc., and it has a contribution margin per unit of $12 and a contribution margin ratio of 20%. Compute the break-even sales in dollars.

15. Janice Jaret asks your help in constructing a CVP graph. Explain to Janice how (a) the break-even point is plotted and (b) the level of activity and dollar sales at the break-even point are determined.

16. Define the term "margin of safety." If Largo Company expects to sell 1,250 units of its product at $10 per unit, and break-even sales for the product is $10,000, what is the margin of safety ratio?

17. The Elmo Company's break-even sales are $600,000. Assuming fixed costs are $180,000, what sales volume is needed to achieve a target net income of $45,000?

18. The sales mix of the Harmon Company's two products is 5:2. What does 5:2 mean? What effect, if any, does a company's sales mix have on CVP analysis?

19. The Meyer Company sells two products: X and Y. Their unit contribution margins are $55 and $70, respectively, and their sales mix is 2:1. What is the weighted average unit contribution margin if 600 units are sold?

20. What are the similarities and differences between a CVP income statement and a traditional income statement?

21. The traditional income statement for the Bryant Company shows Sales $950,000, Cost of Goods Sold $500,000, and Operating Expenses $300,000. Assuming all costs and expenses are 70% variable and 30% fixed, prepare a CVP income statement through contribution margin.

EXERCISES

E24-1 The Deller Company manufactures a single product. Annual production costs incurred in the manufacturing process are shown below for two levels of production.

	Costs Incurred			
Production in Units	5,000		10,000	
Production Costs	Total Cost	Cost/ Unit	Total Cost	Cost/ Unit
Direct materials	$6,250	$1.25	$12,500	$1.25
Direct labor	7,500	1.50	15,000	1.50
Utilities	1,200	.24	1,400	.14
Rent	3,000	.60	3,000	.30
Indirect labor	750	.15	1,500	.15
Supervisory salaries	1,000	.20	1,000	.10
Maintenance	600	.12	700	.07
Depreciation	1,500	.30	1,500	.15

INSTRUCTIONS

(a) Define the terms "variable costs," "fixed costs," and "mixed costs."

(b) Classify each cost above as either variable, fixed, or mixed.

E24-2 The Garbay Company observes the following monthly behavior of two costs.

Volume (units)	Rent	Volume (units)	Maintenance
2,000	$2,000	5,000	$10,000
4,000	3,200	10,000	14,000
6,000	4,400	15,000	20,000
8,000	5,600	20,000	30,000
10,000	6,800	25,000	42,000

INSTRUCTIONS

(a) Identify the fixed and variable cost elements in each cost, using the high-low method.

(b) Use the scatter-diagram method, plot the behavior of rent cost, and fit the total cost line. Use 2,000 unit increments and $2,000 increments

(c) Prepare a graph showing the behavior of maintenance cost and identify the fixed and variable cost elements. Use 5,000 unit increments and $10,000 increments.

E24-3 The controller of Wilson Industries has collected the following monthly expense data for use in analyzing the cost behavior of maintenance costs.

Month	Total Maintenance Costs	Total Machine Hours
January	$ 2,800	3,000
February	2,900	4,000
March	3,600	6,000
April	3,000	5,000
May	4,000	8,000
June	3,700	7,500
July	3,500	5,500
August	3,225	4,000
September	3,100	4,000
October	4,200	7,000
November	3,600	6,500
December	4,300	8,000
	$41,925	68,500

INSTRUCTIONS

(a) Prepare a scattergraph to assist the controller in analyzing the maintenance costs. Find the total fixed maintenance cost and, using 6,000 machine hours, compute the variable maintenance cost per unit. Use 1,000 hour increments and $500 increments.

(b) Use the high-low method to separate the maintenance costs into fixed and variable components. Find the total fixed maintenance costs and compute the variable maintenance cost per unit.

E24-4 In the month of June, Betty's Beauty Salon gave 1,000 haircuts, shampoos, and permanents at an average price of $20. During the month, fixed costs were $5,000 and variable costs were 60% of sales.

INSTRUCTIONS

(a) Determine the contribution margin in dollars, per unit, and as a ratio.

(b) Using the contribution margin technique, compute the break-even point in dollars and in units.

(c) Compute the margin of safety in dollars and as a ratio.

E24-5 The Millard Company estimates that variable costs will be 50% of sales and fixed costs will total $400,000. The selling price of the product is $2, and management believes the relevant range for sales is 200,000–700,000 units.

INSTRUCTIONS

(a) Prepare a CVP graph, assuming maximum sales of $800,000. (Note: Use $200,000 increments for sales and costs and 100,000 increments for units.)

(b) Compute the break-even point in (1) units and (2) dollars.

(c) Compute (1) the margin of safety in dollars and as a ratio and (2) the net income, assuming actual sales are $1.0 million.

E24-6 In 1987, the Krueger Company had a break-even point of $250,000 based upon a selling price of $5 per unit and fixed costs of $50,000. In 1988, the selling price and the variable cost per unit did not change, but the break-even point increased to $300,000.

INSTRUCTIONS

(a) Compute the variable cost per unit and the contribution margin ratio for 1987.

(b) Compute the increase in fixed costs for 1988.

E24-7 The Bass Company had $50,000 of net income in 1987 when the selling price per unit was $125, the variable costs per unit were $75, and the fixed costs were $375,000. Management expects per unit data and total fixed costs to remain the same in 1988. The president of the Bass Company is under pressure by the stockholders to double profits in 1988.

INSTRUCTIONS

(a) Compute the number of units sold in 1987.

(b) Compute the number of units that would have to be sold in 1988 to reach the stockholders' desired profit level.

(c) Assume that the Bass Company sells the same number of units in 1988 as they did in 1987. What would the selling price have to be in order to reach the stockholders' desired profit level?

(d) Again assume that the number of units sold in 1988 will be the same as the number of units sold in 1987. If the selling price cannot be changed, by how much must the variable costs per unit be decreased to reach the stockholders' desired profit level?

(e) Again assume that the number of units sold in 1988 will be the same as the number of units sold in 1987. If the selling price and variable costs per unit do not change, how much would fixed costs have to be reduced to reach the stockholders' desired profit level?

E24-8 The following information is selected from the records of the Century Company, which produces and sells two products.

	Product A	Product B
Selling price per unit	$ 7.50	$15.00
Units sold	75,000	25,000
Variable manufacturing cost per unit	$ 3.50	$ 7.00

Fixed manufacturing overhead costs are $175,000, and fixed administrative expenses are $75,000.

INSTRUCTIONS

(a) Compute the sales mix for the Century Company.

(b) Calculate the weighted average unit contribution margin.

(c) Compute the break-even point in units, assuming the sales mix computed in part (a).

(d) Compute the break-even point in units, if the product mix of Product A is 50,000 units and Product B is 50,000 units. (All other data remain the same.)

E24-9 The Home Appliance Center sells three models of Sure Freeze refrigerators. Selling price and variable cost data for the models are as follows:

	Economy	Standard	Deluxe
Unit selling price	$450	$600	$750
Unit variable costs	$300	$400	$500
Expected sales volume (units)	500	300	200

INSTRUCTIONS

(a) Compute the break-even point in units, assuming total fixed costs are $111,000.

(b) Prove the correctness of your answer.

E24-10 The Owens Company reports the following operating results for the month of August: Sales $200,000 (units 4,000); variable costs $140,000; and fixed costs $50,000. Management is considering the following independent courses of action to increase net income.

1. Increase selling price by 10% with no change in total variable costs.
2. Reduce variable costs to 50% of sales.
3. Reduce fixed costs by $10,000.

INSTRUCTIONS

Compute the net income to be earned under each alternative. Which course of action will produce the highest net income?

E24-11 Bower Manufacturing Inc. has sales of $1.2 million for the first quarter of 1987. In making the sales, the company incurred the following costs and expenses:

	Variable	Fixed
Cost of goods sold	$480,000	$240,000
Selling expenses	130,000	70,000
Administrative expenses	40,000	60,000

INSTRUCTIONS

Prepare a CVP income statement for management for the quarter ended March 31, 1987.

E24-12 The Poppa Company had sales in 1987 of $1,200,000 on 48,000 units. Variable costs totaled $624,000, and fixed costs totaled $450,000.

A new raw material is available that will decrease the variable costs per unit by 20% or $2.60. However, to process the new raw material, fixed operating costs will increase by $50,000. Management feels that one-half of the decline in the variable costs per unit should be passed on to the company's customers in the form of a sales price reduction. The marketing department expects that this sales price reduction will result in a 5% increase in the number of units sold.

INSTRUCTIONS

(a) Prepare a CVP income statement for 1987 before any of the proposed changes are made.

(b) Prepare a CVP income statement, assuming the changes are made as described.

E24-13 Jennifer Petersen is the advertising manager for the Grand Avenue Shoe Store. She is currently working on a major promotional campaign. Her ideas include the installation of a new lighting system and increased display space that will add $20,000 in fixed costs to the $180,000 currently spent. In addition, Jennifer is proposing that a 10% price decrease ($25.00 to $22.50) will produce a 30% increase in sales volume (15,000 to 19,500). Variable costs will remain at $10.00 per pair of shoes. Management is impressed with Jennifer's ideas but concerned about the effects that these changes will have on the break-even point and the margin of safety.

INSTRUCTIONS

(a) Compute the current break-even point in units and compare it to the break-even point in units if Jennifer's ideas are used.

(b) Compute the margin of safety ratio for current operations and after Jennifer's changes are introduced. (Round to nearest full percent.)

(c) Prepare a CVP income statement for current operations and after Jennifer's changes are introduced. Would you make the changes suggested?

PROBLEMS

P24-1 The Stevens Company is reviewing its monthly automobile expenses. Current policy provides each salesperson with a company car. To evaluate this policy, Stevens Company gathered the following information at various levels of activity.

Month	Automobile Expense	Miles Driven
January	$ 5,600	14,500
March	9,800	31,000
May	10,400	32,500
July	12,600	42,500
September	6,300	17,500
November	7,500	19,200

A closer examination of the automobile expenses indicated that they consisted of depreciation, gasoline, and regularly scheduled maintenance. A cost behavior analysis showed that depreciation is a fixed cost, maintenance is a mixed cost, and gasoline is a variable cost. In January, these costs were:

Depreciation	$1,500
Maintenance	1,925
Gasoline	2,175
	$5,600

The company believes the relevant range is 10,000–50,000 miles per month.

INSTRUCTIONS

(a) Compute how much of the July automobile expense is (1) depreciation, (2) maintenance, and (3) gasoline. (Hint: Use the January expense data and the cost behavior analysis.)

(b) Compute the variable maintenance costs per mile driven and the total fixed maintenance costs per month, using the high-low method.

(c) On the basis of the high-low method used in question (b), express the formula for determining the total automobile expense.

(d) If the salespersons drive 12,000 miles in December, how much should the Stevens Company plan to spend on automobile expense for the month?

(e) Prepare a scatter diagram using increments of 5,000 miles on the horizontal axis and $2,000 on the vertical axis. If 35,000 miles are driven, what is the estimated automobile expense that will be incurred?

P24–2 The Campus Barber Shop employs four barbers. One barber, who also serves as the manager, is paid a salary of $1,200 per month. The other barbers are paid $1,000 per month. In addition, each barber is paid a commission of $2 per haircut. Other monthly costs are: store rent $900 plus 30 cents per haircut, depreciation on equipment $200, barber supplies 20 cents per haircut, utilities $400, and advertising $300. The price of a haircut is $10.

INSTRUCTIONS

(a) Determine the variable cost per haircut and the total monthly fixed costs.

(b) Compute the break-even point in units and dollars.

(c) Prepare a CVP graph, assuming a maximum of 1,200 haircuts in a month. Use increments of 200 haircuts on the horizontal axis and $2,000 increments on the vertical axis.

(d) Determine the net income and margin of safety ratio, assuming 1,000 haircuts are given in a month.

P24–3 The Luis Company bottles and distributes LOKAL, a diet soft drink. The beverage is sold for 30 cents per 16 oz.-bottle to retailers who charge customers 50 cents per bottle. At full (100%) plant capacity, management estimates the following revenues and costs.

Net sales	$1,500,000	Selling expenses – variable	$70,000
Direct materials	300,000	Selling expenses – fixed	50,000
Direct labor	400,000	Administrative expenses – variable	30,000
Manufacturing overhead – variable	250,000	Administrative expenses – fixed	40,000
Manufacturing overhead – fixed	180,000		

INSTRUCTIONS

(a) Prepare a CVP income statement for the year 1987 based on management's estimates.

(b) Compute the break-even point in (1) units and (2) dollars.

(c) Compute the contribution margin ratio and the margin of safety ratio.

(d) Determine net income at 80% of capacity.

(e) Determine the sales required to earn net income of $210,000.

P24-4 P&G Manufacturing had a bad year in 1987. For the first time in its history it operated at a loss. The company's income statement showed the following results from selling 50,000 units of product: Net sales $1,000,000; total costs and expenses $1,160,000; and net loss $160,000. Costs and expenses consisted of the following:

	Total	Variable	Fixed
Cost of goods sold	$ 800,000	$520,000	$280,000
Selling expenses	280,000	50,000	230,000
Administrative expenses	80,000	30,000	50,000
	$1,160,000	$600,000	$560,000

Management is considering the following independent alternatives for 1988.

1. Increase unit selling price 20% with no change in costs, expenses, and sales volume.
2. Change the compensation of salespersons from fixed annual salaries totaling $150,000 to total salaries of $30,000 plus an 8% commission on net sales.
3. Purchase new high-tech factory machinery that will reduce total cost of goods sold by 12.5% and change the proportion between variable and fixed cost of goods sold to 50:50.

INSTRUCTIONS

(a) Compute the break-even point in dollars for the year 1987.

(b) Compute the break-even point in dollars under each of the alternative courses of action. Which course of action do you recommend?

P24-5 Banff Camera manufactures two models of camera: Sureshot and Ultrashot. Unit data for each model are as follows:

	Sureshot	Ultrashot
Selling price	$200	$300
Variable costs and expenses:		
Direct materials	50	60
Direct labor	40	60
Manufacturing overhead	24	36
Selling	20	25
Administrative	16	19
Total variable	$150	$200

Monthly fixed costs are: manufacturing overhead $40,000; selling expenses $30,000; and administrative expenses $20,000.

INSTRUCTIONS

(a) Compute the contribution margin ratio for each model.

(b) Compute the break-even point in dollars for each model, assuming fixed costs are divided equally between the products.

(c) Compute the sales necessary to make net income of $25,000 on Sureshot and $45,000 on Ultrashot. Each model incurs 50% of the fixed costs.

(d) Assuming unit sales are 1,500 for Sureshot and 1,100 for Ultrashot, prepare a CVP income statement showing the net income on each product line and for the company as a whole. Each model incurs 50% of the fixed costs.

ALTERNATE PROBLEMS

P24-1A The Sherwood Company is considering a new method of handling its automobile expenses. Current policy provides each salesperson with a company car. To evaluate this policy, Sherwood Company gathered the following information at various levels of activity.

Month	Automobile Expense	Miles Driven
February	$11,200	22,000
April	18,200	46,000
June	26,680	65,000
August	21,100	54,000
October	15,600	32,000
December	12,000	25,000

An analysis of the automobile expenses indicates that they consisted of depreciation, gasoline, and regularly scheduled maintenance. A cost behavior analysis showed that depreciation is a fixed cost, maintenance is a mixed cost, and gasoline is a variable cost. In February, these costs were:

Depreciation	$ 2,000
Maintenance	4,800
Gasoline	4,400
	$11,200

The company believes the relevant range is 10,000–80,000 miles per month.

INSTRUCTIONS

(a) Compute how much of the June automobile expense is (1) depreciation, (2) maintenance, and (3) gasoline. (Hint: Use the February expense data and the cost behavior analysis.)

(b) Compute the variable maintenance costs per mile driven and the total fixed maintenance costs per month, using the high-low method.

(c) On the basis of the high-low method, express the formula for determining the total automobile expense.

(d) If the salespersons drive 15,000 miles in a month, how much should the Sherwood Company plan to spend on automobile expense for the month?

(e) Prepare a scatter diagram using increments of 10,000 miles on the horizontal axis

and $4,000 on the vertical axis. If 50,000 miles are driven, what is the estimated automobile expense that will be incurred?

P24-2A Stanley Clipper owns the Clipper Barber Shop. He employs five barbers and pays each a base rate of $500 per month. One of the barbers serves as the manager and receives an extra $300 per month. In addition to the base rate, each barber also receives a commission of $2.80 per haircut.

Other costs are as follows:

Advertising	$200 per month
Rent	$400 per month
Barber supplies	$.30 per haircut
Utilities	$175 per month plus $.10 per haircut
Magazines	$25 per month

Stanley currently charges $8 per haircut.

INSTRUCTIONS

(a) Determine the variable cost per haircut and the total monthly fixed costs.

(b) Compute the break-even point in units and dollars.

(c) Prepare a CVP graph, assuming a maximum of 1,600 haircuts in a month. Use increments of 200 haircuts on the horizontal axis, and $2,000 on the vertical axis.

(d) Determine the net income and margin of safety ratio, assuming 1,400 haircuts are given in a month.

P24-3A The Felipe Company bottles and distributes NOKAL, a diet soft drink. The beverage is sold for 40 cents per 16 oz.-bottle to retailers who charge customers 60 cents per bottle. At full (100%) plant capacity, management estimates the following revenues and costs.

Net sales	$1,560,000
Direct materials	360,000
Direct labor	440,000
Manufacturing overhead — variable	259,000
Manufacturing overhead — fixed	153,000
Selling expenses — variable	77,000
Selling expenses — fixed	55,000
Administrative expenses — variable	34,000
Administrative expenses — fixed	42,000

INSTRUCTIONS

(a) Prepare a CVP income statement for the year 1987 based on management's estimates.

(b) Compute the break-even point in (1) units and (2) dollars.

(c) Compute the contribution margin ratio and the margin of safety ratio. (Round to full percents.)

(d) Determine net income at 75% of capacity.

(e) Determine the sales required to earn net income of $180,000.

P24-4A L&H Manufacturing's sales slumped badly in 1987. For the first time in its history, it operated at a loss. The company's income statement showed the following results from selling 500,000 units of product: Net sales $2,000,000; total costs and expenses $2,140,000; and net loss $140,000. Costs and expenses consisted of the following:

	Total	Variable	Fixed
Cost of goods sold	$1,700,000	$1,200,000	$500,000
Selling expenses	280,000	60,000	220,000
Administrative expenses	160,000	40,000	120,000
	$2,140,000	$1,300,000	$840,000

Management is considering the following independent alternatives for 1988.

1. Increase unit selling price 25% with no change in costs, expenses, and sales volume.
2. Change the compensation of salespersons from fixed annual salaries totaling $200,000 to total salaries of $50,000 plus a 5% commission on net sales.
3. Purchase new automated equipment that will reduce total cost of goods sold by 15% and change the proportion between variable and fixed cost of goods sold to 60% variable and 40% fixed.

INSTRUCTIONS

(a) Compute the break-even point in dollars for the year 1987.

(b) Compute the break-even point in dollars under each of the alternative courses of action. (Round to full percents.) Which course of action do you recommend?

P24-5A Arbor Implement Company manufactures two models of lawn mowers: Surecut and Ultracut. Unit data for each model are as follows:

	Surecut	Ultracut
Selling price	$300	$400
Variable costs and expenses:		
Direct materials	80	85
Direct labor	50	60
Manufacturing overhead	40	48
Selling	22	26
Administrative	18	21
Total variable	$210	$240

Monthly fixed costs are: manufacturing overhead $60,000; selling expenses $40,000; and administrative expenses $20,000.

INSTRUCTIONS

(a) Compute the contribution margin ratio for each model.

(b) Compute the break-even point in dollars for each model, assuming fixed costs and expenses are divided equally between the products.

(c) Compute the sales necessary to make net income of $30,000 on Surecut and $48,000 on Ultracut. Each model incurs 50% of all fixed costs.

(d) Assuming unit sales are 1,200 for Surecut and 1,000 for Ultracut, prepare a CVP income statement showing the net income on each product line and for the company as a whole. Each model incurs 50% of all fixed costs.

DECISION CASE

The condensed income statement for the Hill and Dale partnership for 1987 is presented on the top of the next page.

HILL AND DALE COMPANY
Income Statement
For the Year Ended December 31, 1987

Sales (200,000 units)		$900,000
Cost of goods sold		600,000
Gross profit		300,000
Operating expenses		
Selling	$200,000	
Administrative	120,000	320,000
Net loss		($20,000)

A cost behavior analysis indicates that 65% of the cost of goods sold are variable; 60% of the selling expenses are variable; and 25% of the administrative expenses are variable.

INSTRUCTIONS

(Round to nearest unit, dollar, and percentage, where necessary.)

(a) Prepare a CVP income statement for 1987.

(b) Compute the break-even point in total sales dollars and in units.

(c) Hill has proposed a plan to get the partnership "out of the red" and improve its profitability. She feels that the quality of the product could be substantially improved by spending $.55 more per unit on better raw materials. The selling price per unit could be increased to only $4.80 because of competitive pressures. Hill estimates that sales volume will increase by 30%. What effect will Hill's plan have on the profits and the break-even point in dollars of the partnership?

(d) Dale was a marketing major in college. He believes that sales volume could be increased only by intensive advertising and promotional campaigns. He, therefore, proposed the following plan as an alternative to Hill's: (1) increase variable selling expenses to $.85 per unit; (2) lower the selling price per unit by $.20; and (3) increase fixed selling expenses by 25%. Dale quoted an old marketing research report that said that sales volume would increase by 50% if these changes were made. What effect will Dale's plan have on the profits and the break-even point in dollars of the partnership?

(e) Which plan should be accepted? Explain your answer.

CHAPTER 25

Iowa State University

CHAPTER 25

BUDGETARY PLANNING

STUDY OBJECTIVES

After studying this chapter, you should be able to:

1. State the essentials of effective budgeting.
2. Indicate the advantages of budgeting.
3. Identify the budgets that comprise the master budget.
4. Describe the sources for preparing a budgeted income statement.
5. Explain the principal sections of a cash budget.
6. Explain the features of long-range planning.
7. Describe innovative budgeting techniques.

Budgeting is an integral part of our society. As students, you budget your study time and your money. Families budget their income, governmental agencies budget revenues and expenditures, and business enterprises use budgets in planning and controlling their operations.

Our primary focus in this chapter is budgeting by business enterprises. Through budgeting it should be possible for management to "run a tighter ship" and to eliminate the following situations:

From day-to-day, management never knows whether enough cash will be available to pay creditors.

Some product lines have excessive inventories, whereas others have inadequate inventories.

Substantial operating losses occur because management does not consider the impact of foreign competition on its product lines.

In this chapter, we will consider the role of budgeting as a **planning tool** of management. We also will describe the budgeting process and the types of budgets that may be developed.

BUDGETING AND MANAGEMENT

One of management's major responsibilities is planning. As explained in Chapter 21, **planning** is the process of establishing enterprise objectives. The term "goal congruence" is sometimes used in planning to indicate that there is agreement among all levels of management as to the objectives of the company and the proposed means of accomplishing them.

A **budget** is a formal written summary (or statement) of management's plans for a specified future time period expressed in financial terms. It normally represents the primary means of communicating agreed-upon objectives throughout the business organization. Once adopted, a budget becomes an important basis for evaluating performance. Thus, it promotes efficiency and serves as a deterrent to waste and inefficiency.

A budget is an aid to management; it is not a substitute for management. A budget cannot operate or enforce itself. The benefits of budgeting will be realized only when budgets are carefully prepared and properly administered by management.

BUDGETING AND ACCOUNTING

Accounting information makes major contributions to the budgeting process. Past performance is often the starting point in budgeting. From the accounting records, historical data on revenues, costs, and expenses that may be helpful in formulating goals.

Normally, accounting has the responsibility for expressing management's budgeting goals in financial terms. In this role, it becomes the translator of management's plans, and it provides the means of communicating the budget to all areas of responsibility. Accounting also prepares periodic budget reports that provide the basis for measuring performance and comparing actual results with planned objectives. The budget itself, and the administration of the budget, however, are entirely management responsibilities.

ESSENTIALS OF EFFECTIVE BUDGETING

If budgets are to be effective, there must be a sound organizational structure, research and analysis, and management acceptance of the budget program.

In large firms, the computer is an essential tool in the budgeting process. Entire computer programs are designed to aid in budget preparation. These systems can also be integrated into the general ledger and provide a complete reporting package for monitoring budgeted vs. actual results. Packages with similar features are available for microcomputers so even small companies can adopt the budgeting practices found in major companies.

SOUND ORGANIZATIONAL STRUCTURE

Effective budgeting is dependent on an organizational structure in which authority and responsibility over all phases of operations are clearly defined. The establishment of responsibility is a prerequisite for budgeting. The budget is constructed along lines of responsibility, and subsequent comparisons of actual results and budget expectations are made to determine how well individuals have discharged their responsibility.

RESEARCH AND ANALYSIS

A budget based entirely on past performance is ineffective. In our highly competitive economic and business environment, management must look ahead. Through research and analysis it is possible to determine the feasibility of new products, services, and operating techniques, as well as the market potential of new territories and branches. Research and analysis lead to careful investigation and informed judgments. **Budgets based on research and analysis should represent realistic goals that will contribute to the growth and profitability of a company.**

MANAGEMENT ACCEPTANCE

The effectiveness of the budget program is directly related to its acceptance by all levels of management. Acceptance of budgets by division managers, department heads, and supervisors is enhanced when these individuals participate fully in the preparation of the budgets. As illustrated on page 986, the flow of input data for budgeting should be from the lowest level of responsibility to the highest.

A powerful feature of many spreadsheet packages is the ability to merge and consolidate budget data as it flows up the organizational chain of command.

The input is reviewed and then consolidated as it moves to each higher level of management.

Flow of budget data

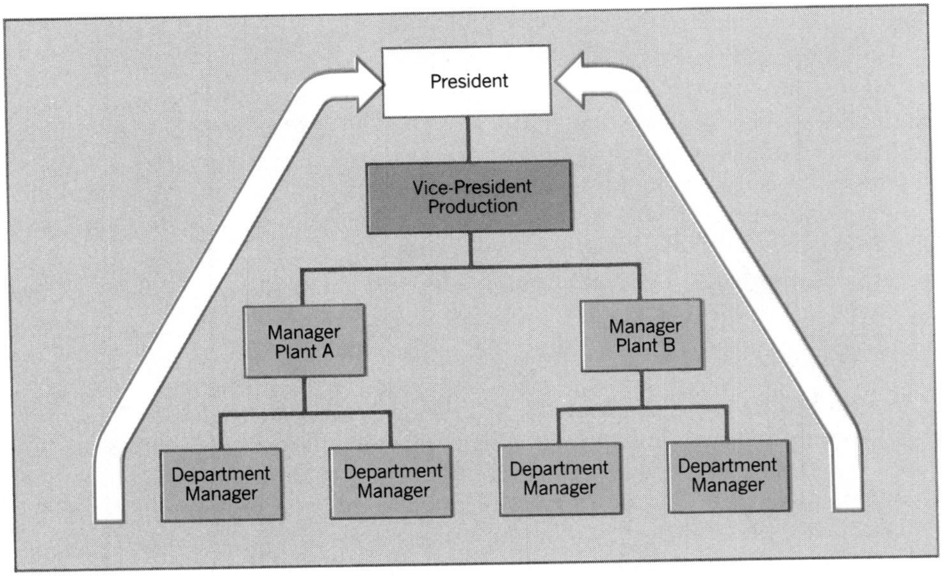

The budget must have the support of top management. Once the budget has been adopted, it should be an important basis for evaluating performance. Variations between actual and expected results should be systematically reviewed to determine their cause(s), and care should be exercised to see that individuals are not held responsible for variations that are beyond their control.

BUDGETING AND HUMAN BEHAVIOR

A budget can have a significant effect on human behavior. On the one hand, a budget may have a strong positive effect that inspires a manager to higher levels of performance. On the other hand, a budget may discourage additional effort and have a negative effect on the morale of a manager. Why do these diverse effects occur? The answer is found in the manner in which the budget is developed and administered.

In developing the budget, each level of management should be invited and encouraged to participate. The overall objective is to reach agreement on a budget that the manager considers to be fair and achievable. When this objective is met, the budget will have a positive effect on the manager. In contrast, if the manager views the budget as being unfair and unrealistic, he or she may become discouraged and uncommitted to the budget goals. The risk of having unrealistic budgets is generally greater when the budget is developed from top management down to lower management than vice versa.

Administering the budget relates to the manner in which the budget is used by top management. As explained earlier, the budget should have the complete support of top management. In addition, the budget should be an important basis for evaluating performance. The effect of an evaluation on a manager will be positive when top management tempers criticism with advice and assistance. In contrast, the response of a manager is likely to be negative

when the budget is used exclusively to assess blame. Top management should also be sensitive to the behavioral implications of its actions. An understanding and flexible attitude has a positive effect on human behavior. Conversely, a rigid and inflexible attitude has a negative effect on the manager who is being evaluated.

A budget may be used as a pressure device to force improved performance. Alternatively, it can be used as a positive aid in the achievement of projected goals. In sum, a budget can become a friend or a foe to the manager.

The human factor is an important aspect of budgeting. When properly used, budgets can be a positive motivating force within a company.

ADVANTAGES OF BUDGETING

Budgeting offers many advantages to a company. The primary benefits are:

1. It requires all levels of management to **plan ahead** and to formalize their future goals on a recurring basis.
2. It provides **definite objectives** for evaluating performance at each level of responsibility.
3. It creates an **early warning system** of potential problems, which gives management additional time to solve the problem. For example, the cash budget may reveal the need for outside financing several months before an actual cash shortage occurs.
4. It facilitates the **coordination of activities** within the business by correlating the goals of each segment with overall company objectives. Thus, production and sales promotion can be integrated with expected sales.
5. It results in greater **management awareness** of the entity's overall operations and the impact of external factors, such as economic trends, on the company's operations.
6. It contributes to **positive behavior patterns** throughout the organization by motivating personnel to meet planned objectives.

LENGTH OF BUDGET PERIOD

A budget may be prepared for any period of time. Such factors as the type of budget, the nature of the company, the need for periodic appraisal, and prevailing business conditions will influence the length of the budget period. For example, cash may be budgeted monthly, whereas a plant expansion program budget may cover a ten-year period.

The budget period should be long enough to provide an attainable goal under normal business conditions. Ideally, the time period should minimize the impact of seasonal and cyclical business fluctuations. On the other hand, the budget period should not be so long that reliable estimates are impossible.

The **most common budget period is one year.** The annual budget, in turn, is often supplemented by monthly and quarterly budgets. Many companies

today use **continuous twelve-month budgets** by dropping the month just ended and adding a future month. One advantage of continuous budgeting is that it keeps management planning a full year ahead.

BUDGETING PROCESS

The development of the budget for the coming year generally starts several months before the end of the current year. It is put in final form and adopted before the start of the new year.

In many companies, responsibility for coordinating the preparation of the budget is assigned to a **budget committee.** The committee is often headed by a budget director. It ordinarily includes the president, treasurer, chief accountant (controller), and management personnel from each of the major areas of the company, such as sales, production, and research.

The budgeting process usually begins with the collection of data from each of the organizational units of the company. These data are then reviewed, modified if necessary, and integrated. During this part of the budgeting process, the budget committee serves as a review board where managers and supervisors can defend their budget goals and requests. After differences are reconciled, the budget is prepared by the budget committee and approved. Copies of the budget are subsequently distributed to the various levels of management responsibility.

THE MASTER BUDGET

The **master budget** is a set of interrelated budgets that constitutes a plan of action for a specified time period. The individual budgets included in a master budget for a manufacturing company are illustrated on page 989. The master budget is developed within the framework of a **sales forecast** that includes potential sales for the industry and the company's expected share of such sales. Sales forecasting involves a consideration of such factors as (1) general economic conditions, (2) industry trends, (3) market research studies, (4) anticipated advertising and promotion, (5) previous market share, (6) changes in prices, and (7) technological developments.

The inputs of sales personnel and top management are essential in preparing the sales forecast. Because a forecast involves many uncertainties, various approaches are taken in an effort to increase the reliability of the forecast. These include a variety of sophisticated statistical and mathematical techniques. Today, many companies use **financial planning models** to forecast sales. A model can express the effects of both internal and external factors on sales.

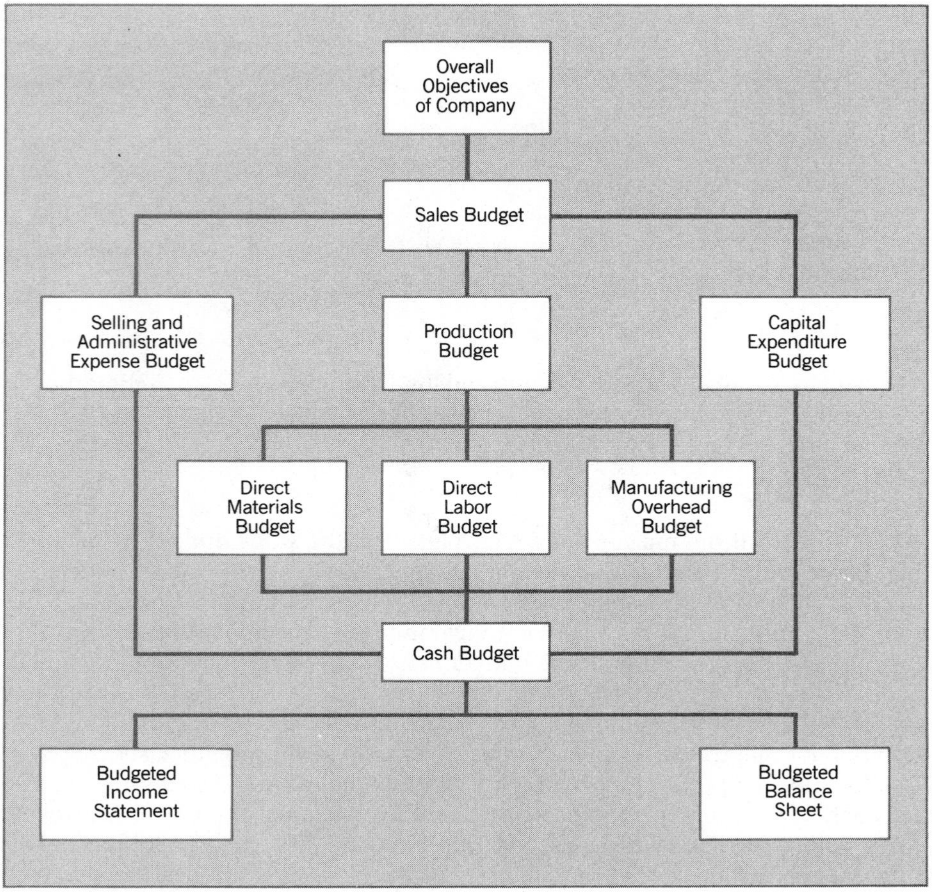

Master budget interrelationships

In computerized budgeting models, once the basic budget data are entered, the output is budgeted financial statements. Since input data can be easily revised, sensitivity, or what if, analysis can easily be performed at any level of the budgeting process. Budgeting is one of the top uses of electronic spreadsheets. Template versions of every one of the Hayes Company budgets shown in this chapter could easily be prepared. This would be an outstanding learning project for anyone wanting to gain hands-on experience with spreadsheets.

PREPARATION OF MASTER BUDGET

The Hayes Company, a manufacturer that makes a single product called Kitchen-mate, will be used to illustrate the preparation of the master budget. The master budget will be prepared for the year 1987, by quarters. All of the

budgets illustrated in the master budget will be prepared except the capital expenditure budget.[1] The following data from the December 31, 1986 budgeted balance sheet are needed in preparing selected budgets:

Selected 1986 budgeted balance sheet data

Cash	$30,000
Accounts receivable	60,000
Finished goods inventory (600 units)	26,400
Raw materials inventory (620 pounds)	2,480
Accounts payable	10,600

The Hayes Company begins its annual budgeting process on September 1, 1986 and it completes the budget for 1987 by December 1, 1986.

SALES BUDGET

As illustrated in the master budget on page 989, **the sales budget is the starting point in preparing the master budget.** Each of the other budgets is dependent on the sales budget. The **sales budget** is derived from the sales forecast, and it should represent management's best estimate of sales revenue for the year. An inaccurate sales budget may adversely affect net income. For example, an overly optimistic sales budget may result in excessive inventories that may have to be sold at reduced prices. In contrast, an unduly conservative budget may result in loss of sales revenue due to inventory shortages.

The sales budget is prepared by multiplying the expected unit sales volume for each product by its anticipated unit selling price. For the Hayes Company, sales volume is expected to be 3,000 units in the first quarter with 500-unit increments in each succeeding quarter. Based on a sales price of $60 per unit, the sales budget for the year, by quarters, is shown in Schedule 1 below.

Schedule 1.

Sales budget

HAYES COMPANY
Sales Budget
For the Year Ending December 31, 1987

	Quarter 1	2	3	4	YEAR
Expected unit sales	3,000	3,500	4,000	4,500	15,000
Unit selling price	× $60	× $60	× $60	× $60	× $60
Total sales	$180,000	$210,000	$240,000	$270,000	$900,000

The anticipated sales revenue may be classified as cash or credit sales and by geographical regions or salespersons. In the Hayes Company, all sales are for credit, and it is expected that 60% of the sales will be collected in cash in the period of sale and the remaining 40% will be collected in the following quar-

[1]Capital budgeting is explained in Chapter 28.

ter. This information will be needed later in preparing the cash budget. For example, cash collections in the first and second quarters will be as follows:

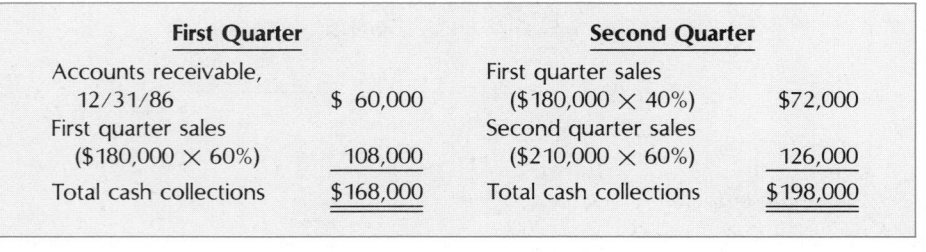

Computation of cash collections

First Quarter		Second Quarter	
Accounts receivable, 12/31/86	$ 60,000	First quarter sales ($180,000 × 40%)	$72,000
First quarter sales ($180,000 × 60%)	108,000	Second quarter sales ($210,000 × 60%)	126,000
Total cash collections	$168,000	Total cash collections	$198,000

PRODUCTION BUDGET

The **production budget** shows the units that must be produced to meet anticipated sales. Production requirements are determined from the following formula:[2]

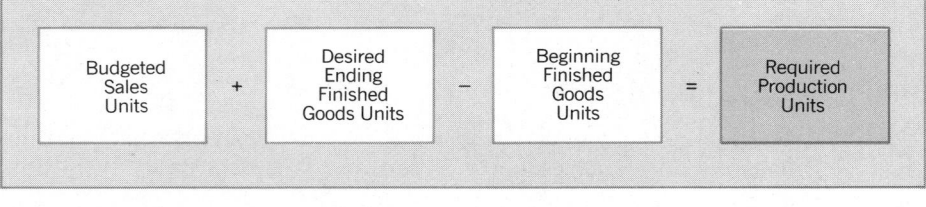

Production requirements formula

Budgeted Sales Units + Desired Ending Finished Goods Units − Beginning Finished Goods Units = Required Production Units

A realistic estimate of ending inventory is essential in scheduling production requirements. Excessive inventories in one quarter may lead to cutbacks in production and layoffs of employees in a subsequent quarter. Conversely, inadequate inventories may result either in overtime work or in lost sales in a later period. On the basis of past experience, the Hayes Company believes it can meet future sales requirements by maintaining an ending inventory equal to 20% of the next quarter's budgeted sales volume. For example, the ending finished goods inventory for the first quarter is 700 units (20% × anticipated second-quarter sales of 3,500 units). The production budget is illustrated in Schedule 2 on the next page.

Note in the Year column that expected quarterly unit sales are totaled; this is not true of the inventory units. These units pertain to the beginning and end of the year. Thus, (1) the ending inventory at December 31 is the desired inventory at the end of the fourth quarter (1,000 units), and (2) the beginning inventory on January 1 is the inventory at the beginning of the first quarter (600 units).

The production budget provides the basis for determining the budgeted costs for each manufacturing cost element, as explained on the following page.

[2]This formula ignores any work in process inventories, which are assumed to be nonexistent in the Hayes Company.

Production budget

Schedule 2.

HAYES COMPANY
Production Budget
For the Year Ending December 31, 1987

	Quarter 1	Quarter 2	Quarter 3	Quarter 4	YEAR
Expected unit sales (Schedule 1)	3,000	3,500	4,000	4,500	15,000
Add: Desired ending finished goods units[a]	700	800	900	1,000[b]	1,000[b]
Total required units	3,700	4,300	4,900	5,500	16,000
Less: Beginning finished goods units	600[c]	700	800	900	600[c]
Required production units	3,100	3,600	4,100	4,600	15,400

[a]20% of next quarter's sales
[b]Expected 1988 first quarter sales, 5,000 units × 20%
[c]Budgeted 12/31/86 balance sheet amount

DIRECT MATERIALS BUDGET

The **direct materials budget** contains both the quantity and cost of direct materials to be purchased. The quantities of direct materials are derived from the following formula:

Formula for direct materials quantities

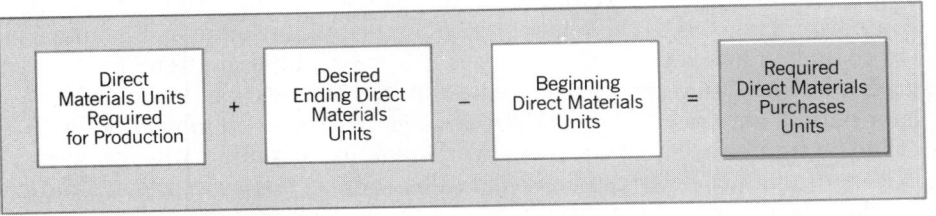

Direct Materials Units Required for Production + Desired Ending Direct Materials Units − Beginning Direct Materials Units = Required Direct Materials Purchases Units

The budgeted cost of direct materials to be purchased is then computed by multiplying the required units of direct materials by the anticipated cost per unit.

The desired ending inventory is again a critical component in the budgeting process. For example, inadequate inventories could result in temporary shutdowns of production. Because of its close proximity to suppliers, Hayes Company has found that an ending inventory of raw materials equal to 10% of the next quarter's production is sufficient. The manufacture of each Kitch-en-mate requires two pounds of raw materials and the expected cost per pound is $4. The direct materials budget is shown in Schedule 3 on the next page.

Note that the desired ending inventory for the year (1,020 pounds) is the pounds desired at the end of the fourth quarter, and the pounds of beginning inventory (620) are the pounds on hand at the beginning of the first quarter.

The direct materials budget is used subsequently in computing the cost of direct materials used in determining the budgeted cost of goods manufactured. In addition, the raw materials purchases are used in preparing the cash

Schedule 3.

Direct materials budget

HAYES COMPANY
Direct Materials Budget
For the Year Ending December 31, 1987

	Quarter 1	Quarter 2	Quarter 3	Quarter 4	YEAR
Units to be produced (Schedule 2)	3,100	3,600	4,100	4,600	15,400
Direct materials per unit	× 2	× 2	× 2	× 2	× 2
Total pounds needed for production	6,200	7,200	8,200	9,200	30,800
Add: Desired ending direct materials (pounds)[a]	720	820	920	1,020[b]	1,020[b]
Total materials required	6,920	8,020	9,120	10,220	31,820
Less: Beginning direct materials (pounds)	620[c]	720	820	920	620[c]
Direct materials purchases	6,300	7,300	8,300	9,300	31,200
Cost per pound	× $4	× $4	× $4	× $4	× $4
Total cost of direct materials purchases	$25,200	$29,200	$33,200	$37,200	$124,800

[a]10% of next quarter's production
[b]Estimated 1988 first quarter production, 10,200 units × 10%
[c]Budgeted 12/31/86 balance sheet amount

budget. The Hayes Company normally pays for 50% of the purchases in the current quarter and the remainder in the following quarter. For example, cash payments for direct materials in the second quarter are $27,200 computed as follows:

Computation of cash payments

First quarter purchases ($25,200 × 50%)	$12,600
Second quarter purchases ($29,200 × 50%)	14,600
Total second quarter payments	$27,200

DIRECT LABOR BUDGET

Like the direct materials budget, the **direct labor budget** contains both quantity (hours) and cost data necessary to meet production requirements. Direct labor hours are determined from the production budget. At the Hayes Company, two hours of direct labor are required to produce each unit of finished goods, and the anticipated hourly wage rate is $10. These data are shown in Schedule 4 on the next page.

The direct labor budget is critical in maintaining a labor force that can meet the expected levels of production. This budget is also used in preparing the budgeted cost of goods manufactured and the cash budget. At the Hayes Company, all direct labor costs are paid in the quarter in which they are incurred.

Schedule 4.

Direct labor budget

HAYES COMPANY
Direct Labor Budget
For the Year Ending December 31, 1987

	Quarter 1	Quarter 2	Quarter 3	Quarter 4	YEAR
Units to be produced (Schedule 2)	3,100	3,600	4,100	4,600	15,400
Direct labor time (hours) per unit	× 2	× 2	× 2	× 2	× 2
Total required direct labor hours	6,200	7,200	8,200	9,200	30,800
Direct labor cost per hour	× $10	× $10	× $10	× $10	× $10
Total direct labor cost	$62,000	$72,000	$82,000	$92,000	$308,000

MANUFACTURING OVERHEAD BUDGET

The **manufacturing overhead budget** shows the expected indirect manufacturing costs for the year. As illustrated in Schedule 5 below, this budget distin-

Schedule 5.

Manufacturing overhead budget

HAYES COMPANY
Manufacturing Overhead Budget
For the Year Ending December 31, 1987

	Quarter 1	Quarter 2	Quarter 3	Quarter 4	YEAR
Variable costs					
Indirect materials	$ 6,200	$ 7,200	$ 8,200	$ 9,200	$ 30,800
Indirect labor	8,680	10,080	11,480	12,880	43,120
Utilities	2,480	2,880	3,280	3,680	12,320
Maintenance	1,240	1,440	1,640	1,840	6,160
Total variable	18,600	21,600	24,600	27,600	92,400
Fixed costs					
Supervisory salaries	20,000	20,000	20,000	20,000	80,000
Depreciation	3,800	3,800	3,800	3,800	15,200
Property taxes and insurance	9,000	9,000	9,000	9,000	36,000
Maintenance	5,700	5,700	5,700	5,700	22,800
Total fixed	38,500	38,500	38,500	38,500	154,000
Total manufacturing overhead	$57,100	$60,100	$63,100	$66,100	$246,400
Direct labor hours	6,200	7,200	8,200	9,200	30,800
Manufacturing overhead rate per direct labor hour ($246,400 ÷ 30,800)					$8.00

guishes between variable and fixed overhead costs. From previous experience, the Hayes Company expects variable costs to fluctuate with production volume on the basis of the following rates per direct labor hour: indirect materials, $1.00, indirect labor, $1.40, utilities, $.40, and maintenance, $.20. Thus, for 6,200 direct labor hours, budgeted indirect materials are $6,200 (6,200 × $1) and budgeted indirect labor is $8,680 (6,200 × $1.40). The Hayes Company also recognizes that some maintenance is fixed. The amounts reported for fixed costs are assumed.

In the Hayes Company, overhead is applied to production on the basis of direct labor hours. Thus, as shown in Schedule 5, the annual rate is $8 per hour ($246,400 ÷ 30,800). Like the two preceding budgets, this budget is used later in computing the cash budget. For the cash budget, it is necessary to recognize that depreciation is a noncash expense that must be subtracted from total manufacturing overhead to determine cash disbursements. The Hayes Company pays all of its cash overhead costs in the quarter in which they are incurred. Thus, first-quarter cash disbursements are $53,300 ($57,100 less depreciation, $3,800).

SELLING AND ADMINISTRATIVE EXPENSE BUDGET

The Hayes Company combines its operating expenses into one budget, the **selling and administration expense budget.** In this budget, as in the preceding budget, expenses are classified as to whether they are variable or fixed. In this case, the variable expense rates per unit of sales are sales commissions, $3.00, and freight-out, $1.00. Variable expenses per quarter are based on the unit sales projected in the sales budget (Schedule 1). For example, sales in the first quarter are expected to be 3,000 units. Thus, Sales Commissions Expense is $9,000 (3,000 × $3), and Freight-out is $3,000 (3,000 × $1). Fixed expenses are based on assumed data. The selling and administrative expense budget is shown in Schedule 6 on the next page.

This budget is also used in preparing the budgeted income statement and the cash budget. The Hayes Company pays these expenses in the quarter in which they are incurred. Cash disbursements in the first quarter, therefore, are $41,000 (total expenses, $42,000, less depreciation, $1,000).

CASH BUDGET

The **cash budget** shows anticipated cash flows. Because cash is so vital in a company's operating cycle, this budget is often considered to be the single most important output of the budgeting process. As illustrated in Schedule 7, page 997, the cash budget contains three sections (cash receipts, cash disbursements, and financing) and the beginning and ending cash balances. The financing section is needed when the ending cash balance shows a cash deficiency or is below management's minimum required balance. The cash budget for the Hayes Company is prepared on a quarterly basis for the year. In practice, cash budgets are often prepared on a monthly basis.

Data for preparing the cash budget are obtained from other budgets, as indicated in the Schedule column. The cash budget for the Hayes Company is based on the following assumptions that have been described previously.

Schedule 6.

Selling and administrative expense budget

HAYES COMPANY
Selling and Administrative Expense Budget
For the Year Ending December 31, 1987

	Quarter 1	2	3	4	YEAR
Variable expenses					
Sales commissions	$ 9,000	$10,500	$12,000	$13,500	$ 45,000
Freight-out	3,000	3,500	4,000	4,500	15,000
Total variable	12,000	14,000	16,000	18,000	60,000
Fixed expenses					
Advertising	5,000	5,000	5,000	5,000	20,000
Sales salaries	15,000	15,000	15,000	15,000	60,000
Office salaries	7,500	7,500	7,500	7,500	30,000
Depreciation	1,000	1,000	1,000	1,000	4,000
Property taxes and insurance	1,500	1,500	1,500	1,500	6,000
Total fixed	30,000	30,000	30,000	30,000	120,000
Total selling and administrative expenses	$42,000	$44,000	$46,000	$48,000	$180,000

1. Sales—60% are collected in the quarter sold; 40% are collected in the following quarter.
2. Direct materials—50% are paid in the quarter purchased; 50% are paid in the following quarter.
3. Direct labor—100% paid in the quarter.
4. Manufacturing overhead and selling and administrative expenses—all items except depreciation are paid in the quarter in which they are incurred.

In addition, it is assumed that the Hayes Company makes equal quarterly payments of its estimated annual income taxes of $12,000 and wishes to maintain a minimum cash balance of $15,000. The cash budget is shown in Schedule 7 on page 997.

A major use of computers in budgeting is "what if" analyses. For example, suppose that the collection period for accounts receivable changed from 60% in the quarter sold to 45% in the quarter sold because of a recession in the economy. What impact would the change have on the rest of the budgeting process and the financing needs of the business? The computer can provide this information as well as data on other collection rates in a matter of minutes.

The cash budget indicates that $3,000 of financing will be needed in the second quarter to maintain a minimum cash balance of $15,000. Since there is

Schedule 7.

Cash budget

HAYES COMPANY
Cash Budget
For the Year Ending December 31, 1987

	Schedule	Quarter 1	Quarter 2	Quarter 3	Quarter 4	YEAR
Beginning cash balance		$ 30,000	$ 15,500	$ 15,000	$ 19,400	$ 30,000
Add: Receipts						
Collections from customers						
Previous quarter	1	60,000[a]	72,000	84,000	96,000	312,000
Current quarter	1	108,000	126,000	144,000	162,000	540,000
Total receipts		168,000	198,000	228,000	258,000	852,000
Total available cash		198,000	213,500	243,000	277,400	882,000
Less: Disbursements						
Direct materials						
Previous quarter	3	10,600[b]	12,600	14,600	16,600	54,400
Current quarter	3	12,600	14,600	16,600	18,600	62,400
Total direct materials		23,200	27,200	31,200	35,200	116,800
Direct labor	4	62,000	72,000	82,000	92,000	308,000
Manufacturing overhead	5	53,300	56,300	59,300	62,300	231,200
Selling and administrative expenses	6	41,000	43,000	45,000	47,000	176,000
Income tax expense		3,000	3,000	3,000	3,000	12,000
Total disbursements		182,500	201,500	220,500	239,500	844,000
Excess (deficiency) of available cash over disbursements		15,500	12,000	22,500	37,900	38,000
Financing						
Borrowings		-0-	3,000	-0-	-0-	3,000
Repayments ($3,000 principal, $100 interest)		-0-	-0-	3,100	-0-	3,100
Ending cash balance		$ 15,500	$ 15,000	$ 19,400	$ 37,900	$ 37,900

[a]Budgeted 12/31/86 accounts receivable
[b]Budgeted 12/31/86 accounts payable

an expected excess of available cash over disbursements of $22,500 at the end of the third quarter, it is assumed that the additional financing will be repaid in this quarter plus interest expense of $100.

In the Year column, the beginning cash balance is the balance on January 1, 1987. It should also be noted that both the borrowings and repayments are extended to the Year column.

A cash budget contributes to more effective cash management. For example, it can show when additional financing will be necessary well before the actual need arises. Conversely, it can indicate when excess cash will be available for investments or other purposes.

BUDGETED INCOME STATEMENT

The **budgeted income statement** is one of the important end products of the budgeting process. This budget indicates the expected profitability of oper-

ations in the next year. Once established, the budgeted income statement provides the basis for evaluating company performance. As you would expect, this budget is prepared from the previous budgets. For example, to find the cost of goods sold, it is first necessary to determine the total unit cost of producing one Kitchen-mate as follows:

Computation of total unit cost

Cost of One Kitchen-mate

Cost Element	Schedule	Quantity	Unit Cost	Total
Direct materials	3	2 pounds	$ 4.00	$ 8.00
Direct labor	4	2 hours	$10.00	20.00
Manufacturing overhead	5	2 hours	$ 8.00	16.00
Total unit cost				$44.00

Cost of goods sold can then be determined by multiplying the units sold by the unit cost. For the Hayes Company, budgeted cost of goods sold is $660,000 (15,000 × $44). The budgeted income statement is shown in Schedule 8.

Schedule 8.

Budgeted income statement

HAYES COMPANY
Budgeted Income Statement
For the Year Ending December 31, 1987

Sales (Schedule 1)	$900,000
Cost of goods sold (15,000 × $44)	660,000
Gross profit	240,000
Selling and administrative expenses (Schedule 6)	180,000
Income from operations	60,000
Interest expense (Schedule 7)	100
Income before income taxes	59,900
Income tax expense (Schedule 7)	12,000
Net income	$ 47,900

BUDGETED BALANCE SHEET

The **budgeted balance sheet** is developed from the budgeted balance sheet for the preceding year and the budgets for the current year. Pertinent data from the budgeted balance sheet at December 31, 1986 are as follows:

Building and equipment	$192,000	Common stock	$225,000
Accumulated depreciation	$ 28,800	Retained earnings	$ 46,480

The budgeted balance sheet at December 31, 1987 is shown in Schedule 9 with the sources of the data shown in parenthesis.

Schedule 9.

Budgeted balance sheet

HAYES COMPANY
Budgeted Balance Sheet
December 31, 1987

Assets		
Cash (Schedule 7)		$37,900
Accounts receivable (Schedule 1)		108,000[a]
Raw materials inventory (Schedule 3)		4,080[b]
Finished goods inventory (Schedule 2)		44,000[c]
Buildings and equipment (12/31/86 balance sheet)	$192,000	
Less: Accumulated depreciation	48,000[d]	144,000
Total assets		$337,980
Liabilities and Stockholders' Equity		
Accounts payable (Schedule 3)		$ 18,600[e]
Common stock (12/31/86 balance sheet)		225,000
Retained earnings		94,380[f]
Total liabilities and stockholders' equity		$337,980

[a] 40% × fourth-quarter sales, $270,000
[b] 1,020 × $4
[c] 1,000 units × $44
[d] 12/31/86 balance, $28,800 + depreciation expense, $15,200 (Schedule 5) and $4,000 (Schedule 6)
[e] 50% × fourth-quarter purchases $37,200
[f] 12/31/86 balance, $46,480 + net income, $47,900 (Schedule 8)

As explained earlier, a capital expenditure budget can also be prepared.

BUDGETING AND LONG-RANGE PLANNING

Budgeting and long-range planning are not the same. One important difference is the **time period involved.** The maximum length of a budget is usually one year, and budgets are often prepared for shorter periods of time, such as a month or a quarter. In contrast, long-range planning usually encompasses a period of at least five years. A second significant difference is **in emphasis.** Budgeting is concerned with the achievement of specific short-term goals, such as meeting annual profit objectives. **Long-range planning,** on the other hand, involves the selection of strategies to achieve long-term goals and the development of policies and plans to implement the strategies. In long-range planning, consideration is also given to anticipated trends in the economic and political environment and policies the company should follow to cope with them. The final difference between budgeting and long-range planning pertains to the **amount of detail presented.** Budgets, as you have seen earlier in this chapter, can be very detailed. The detail is needed to provide a basis for control. Long-range plans contain considerably less detail, because the data are intended more for a review of progress toward long-term goals than for an evaluation of specific results to be achieved.

Long-range planning should be a systematic and formalized process. The primary objective of long-range planning is to develop the best strategy to maximize the company's performance over an extended future period. Neither budgeting nor long-range planning can solve all the problems of a manager. Moreover, they cannot guarantee the success of the company. However, the two activities should contribute to better planning, control, and decision making by management.

BUDGETING IN NONMANUFACTURING COMPANIES

Budgeting is not limited to manufacturing companies. Budgets may also be used in profit planning by merchandising companies, service enterprises, and not-for-profit organizations.

MERCHANDISING COMPANIES

As in manufacturing operations, the sales budget is both the starting point and the key factor in the development of the master budget for a merchandising company. The major differences between the master budget of a merchandising company and a manufacturing budget are that, (1) a purchases budget is used instead of a production budget, and (2) the manufacturing budgets (direct materials, direct labor, and manufacturing overhead) are not applicable. The **purchases budget** is similar to the direct materials budget illustrated in this chapter. The purchases budget for the Lima Company for the first quarter of 1987 is shown below:

Purchases budget

LIMA COMPANY
Purchases Budget
For the Quarter Ending March 31, 1987

Estimated sales in units	15,000
Desired ending inventory units	1,200
Total required units	16,200
Less: Beginning inventory units	1,400
Required unit purchases	14,800
Average delivered cost of purchases	× $5
Total cost of purchases	$74,000

When the merchandising company is departmentalized, separate budgets are prepared for each department. For example, a grocery store may start by preparing sales budgets and purchases budgets for each of its major departments, such as meats, dairy, and produce. These budgets are then combined into a master budget for the store.

When a retailer has branch stores, separate master budgets are prepared for each store. Then these objectives are incorporated into master budgets for the company as a whole.

SERVICE ENTERPRISES

In service enterprises, such as a public accounting firm, a law office, or a medical practice, the critical factor in budgeting is coordinating professional staff needs with anticipated services. If a firm is overstaffed, (1) labor costs will be disproportionately high, (2) profits will be lower, and (3) staff turnover may increase because of lack of challenging work. In contrast, if an enterprise is understaffed, revenue may be lost because existing and prospective client needs for service cannot be met, and professional staff may seek other positions because of excessive work loads.

Budget data for service revenue may be obtained from expected output or expected input. When output is used, it is necessary to determine the expected billings of clients for services rendered. For a public accounting firm, output would be the sum of its billings in auditing, tax, and consulting services. When service revenue is derived from input data, each professional staff member is required to project his or her billable time. Billing rates are then applied to billable time to produce expected service revenue.

NOT-FOR-PROFIT ORGANIZATIONS

Budgeting is just as important for not-for-profit organizations as for profit-oriented enterprises. The budget process, however, is significantly different. In most cases not-for-profit entities budget on the basis of cash flows (expenditures and receipts), rather than on a revenue and expense basis. Further, the starting point in the process is usually expenditures, not receipts. For the not-for-profit entity, management's task generally is to find the receipts needed to support the planned expenditures. The activity index is also likely to be significantly different. For example, in a not-for-profit entity, such as a university, budgeted faculty positions may be based on full-time equivalent students or credit hours expected to be taught in a department.

For some governmental units, the budget must be approved by voters. In other cases, such as state governments and the federal government, legislative approval is required. After the budget is adopted, it must be strictly followed, and overspending is often illegal. In governmental budgets, authorizations tend to be on a line-by-line basis. That is, the budget for a municipality may have a specified authorization for police and fire protection, garbage collection, street paving, and so on. The line item authorization of governmental budgets significantly limits the amount of discretion management can exercise. The city manager often cannot use savings in one line item, such as street paving, to cover increased spending in snow removal.

INNOVATIVE BUDGETING TECHNIQUES

From time to time, new techniques of budgeting are introduced. Two fairly recent innovations that have received considerable attention are (1) zero-base budgeting and (2) program budgeting.

ZERO-BASE BUDGETING

This technique of budgeting was popularized by Jimmy Carter when he was Governor of Georgia and President of the United States as a means of cutting government expenditures and reducing government deficits. **Zero-base budgeting** is so named because each manager is required to start at a zero budget level each year and to justify all expenditures as though the area of activity were being started for the first time. This type of budgeting is an alternative to the conventional incremental basis of budgeting in which each manager is only required to justify only the changes from the preceding year's budget.

In zero-base budgeting, the department manager must rank all of the department's activities according to relative importance in a series of "decision packages" that range from full support to complete elimination of the activity. Top management then evaluates each decision package and selects those that are compatible with overall company objectives and available resources.

It is generally recognized that zero-base budgeting results in a more comprehensive analysis than incremental budgeting. However, zero-base budgeting is also far more costly in terms of the time and effort required in its preparation. Many argue that this type of budgeting is not feasible for **indispensable activities,** such as sales and production in a business enterprise. In contrast, many believe that zero-base budgeting is appropriate for **discretionary activities** in which service and support are the primary output. This is particularly true in government, where many expenditures are considered discretionary in nature. In government, a major concern is the frequency of applying zero-base budgeting. Many believe that the in-depth analysis required by this type of budgeting should be made only every five years (or so), rather than annually.

PROGRAM BUDGETING

Program budgeting differs from traditional budgeting by requiring managers to request funds for specific programs. In a city government that uses program budgeting, the head of the police department would be required to request the funds needed for crime prevention, juvenile work, crime detection, and police training. In a business enterprise that uses program budgeting, the manager of research and development would be required to identify the research projects that are to be funded. In their request for funds, managers are often required to state the effects on planned programs if they are not fully funded.

In program budgeting, emphasis is placed on the department's overall results. Accordingly, the manager has the authority to move funds from one program to another, as long as the transfers serve the overall objective of the department. For example, the manager of street maintenance in a city could move funds from street repairs to snow removal.

Program budgeting has contributed to better accountability by governmental agencies. By specifying goals, taxpayers can see where their tax dollars are going, and, eventually, they can determine whether the money was used effectively.

SUMMARY OF STUDY OBJECTIVES

1. The essentials of effective budgeting are (a) sound organizational structure, (b) research and analysis, and (c) management acceptance.

2. The primary advantages of budgeting are that it (a) requires management to plan ahead, (b) provides definite objectives for evaluating performance, (c) creates an early warning system of potential problems, (d) facilitates coordination of activities, (e) results in greater management awareness, and (f) contributes to positive behavior patterns.

3. The master budget consists of the following budgets: (a) sales, (b) production, (c) direct materials, (d) direct labor, (e) manufacturing overhead, (f) selling and administrative expense, (g) capital expenditures budget, (h) cash budget, (i) budgeted income statement, and (j) budgeted balance sheet.

4. The budgeted income statement is prepared from (a) the sales budget, (b) the budgets for direct materials, direct labor, and manufacturing overhead, and (d) the selling and administrative expense budget.

5. The cash budget has three sections (receipts, disbursements, and financing) and the beginning and ending cash balances.

6. Long-range planning usually encompasses a period of at least five years. It involves the selection of strategies to achieve long-term goals and the development of policies and plans to implement the strategies. Long-range plans contain considerably less detail than a budget.

7. Innovative budgeting techniques consist of zero-base budgeting and program budgeting. In zero-base budgeting, the manager is required to start at zero and to justify all expenditures as though the activity were being started for the first time. Program budgeting differs from traditional budgeting by requiring managers to request funds for specific programs.

GLOSSARY

Budget, p. 984

Budget committee, p. 988

Budgeted balance sheet, p. 998

Budgeted income statement, p. 997

Cash budget, p. 995

Direct labor budget, p. 993

Direct materials budget, p. 992

Long-range planning, p. 999

Manufacturing overhead budget, p. 994

Master budget, p. 988

Production budget, p. 991

Program budget, p. 1002

Purchases budget, p. 1000

Sales budget, p. 990

Sales forecast, p. 988

Selling and administrative expense budget, p. 995

Zero-base budgeting, p. 1002

DEMONSTRATION PROBLEM

The Soroco Company is preparing its master budgets for 1987. Relevant data pertaining to its sales and production budgets are as follows:

Sales. Sales for the year are expected to total 1,200,000 units. Quarterly sales are 20%, 25%, 30%, and 25% respectively. The sales price is expected to be $50 per unit for the first three quarters and $55 per unit beginning in the fourth quarter. Sales in the first quarter of 1988 are expected to be 10% higher than the budgeted sales volume for the first quarter of 1987.

Production. Management desires to maintain ending finished goods inventories at 25% of the next quarter's budgeted sales volume.

INSTRUCTIONS

Prepare the sales budget and production budget by quarters for 1987.

SOLUTION TO DEMONSTRATION PROBLEM

SOROCO COMPANY
Sales Budget
For the Year Ending December 31, 1987

	Quarter 1	Quarter 2	Quarter 3	Quarter 4	Year
Expected unit sales	240,000	300,000	360,000	300,000	1,200,000
Unit selling price	$50	$50	$50	$55	–
	$12,000,000	$15,000,000	$18,000,000	$16,500,000	$61,500,000

SOROCO COMPANY
Production Budget
For the Year Ending December 31, 1987

	Quarter 1	Quarter 2	Quarter 3	Quarter 4	Year
Expected unit sales	240,000	300,000	360,000	300,000	1,200,000
Add: Desired ending finished goods units	75,000	90,000	75,000	66,000[1]	66,000
Total required units	315,000	390,000	435,000	366,000	1,266,000
Less: Beginning finished goods units	60,000[2]	75,000	90,000	75,000	60,000
Units to be produced	255,000	315,000	345,000	291,000	1,206,000

[1]Estimated first quarter 1988 sales volume 240,000 + (240,000 × 10%) = 264,000; 264,000 × 25%.

[2]25% of estimated first quarter 1987 sales units.

QUESTIONS

1. How does a budget aid management in planning?

2. Accounting's role in budgeting is limited to expressing management's goals in financial terms. Do you agree? Explain.

3. Cora Corely asks your help in understanding the essentials of effective budgeting. Identify the essentials for Cora.

4. Bert and Diane are discussing the advantages of budgeting. They ask you to identify the primary benefits for them. Comply with their request.

5. What criteria are helpful in determining the length of the budget period? What is the most common budget period?

6. Distinguish between a master budget and a sales forecast.

7. What budget is the starting point in preparing the master budget? What may result if this budget is inaccurate?

8. The production budget shows both unit production data and unit cost data. Is this true? Explain.

9. The Scio Company has 8,000 beginning finished goods units. Budget sales units are 120,000. If management desires 10,000 ending finished goods units, what are the required units of production?

10. In preparing the direct materials budget for the Shula Company, management concludes that required purchases are 50,000 units. If 45,000 direct materials units are required in production and there are 6,000 units of beginning direct materials, what is the desired units of ending direct materials?

11. The production budget of the Shelly Company calls for 62,000 units to be produced. If it takes 30 minutes to make one unit and the direct labor rate is $12 per hour, what is the total budgeted direct labor cost?

12. The Gilmore Company's manufacturing overhead budget shows total variable costs of $186,000 and total fixed costs of $125,250. Total production in units is expected to be 100,000 units, and it takes 15 minutes to make one unit and the direct labor rate is $15 per hour. Express the manufacturing overhead rate as (a) a percentage of direct labor cost, and (b) an amount per direct labor hour.

13. McCoy Company's variable selling and administrative expenses are 10% of net sales and fixed expenses are $75,000 per quarter. The sales budget shows expected sales of $200,000 and $250,000 in the first and second quarters, respectively. What are the total budgeted selling and administrative expenses for each quarter?

14. For the Elaine Company, the budgeted cost for one unit of product is direct materials $12, direct labor $20, and manufacturing overhead is 75% of direct labor cost. If 50,000 units are expected to be sold at $60 each, what is the budgeted gross profit?

15. Identify the three sections of a cash budget. What balances are also shown in this budget?

16. Fry Company has credit sales of $250,000 in January. Past experience suggests that 40% is collected in the month of sale, 50% in the month following the sale, and 5% in the second month following the sale. Indicate the cash collections from customers in January, February, and March.

17. Cal Cokley maintains that the only difference between budgeting and long-range planning is time. Do you agree? Why or why not?

18. How may expected revenues in a service enterprise be computed?

19. What are the essential features of zero-base budgeting?

20. How has program budgeting contributed to better accountability by governmental agencies?

EXERCISES

E25–1 Electro Electronics, Inc. produces and sells three models of pocket calculators: XQ-103, XQ-104, and XQ-105. The calculators sell for $10, $15, and $25, respectively. Because of the intense competition Electro faces, management budgets sales semi-annually. Its projections for the first two quarters of 1987 are as follows:

	Unit Sales	
Product	Quarter 1	Quarter 2
XQ-103	20,000	22,000
XQ-104	12,000	13,000
XQ-105	6,000	6,000

No changes in selling prices are anticipated.

INSTRUCTIONS

Prepare a sales budget for the two quarters ending June 30, 1987. List the products and show for each quarter and for the six months, units, selling price, and total sales by product and in total.

25–2 The Fregosi Company produces and sells two types of automobile batteries: the heavy-duty HD-240 and the long-life LL-250. The 1987 sales budget for the two products is as follows:

	HD-240	LL-250
1st quarter	5,000	10,000
2nd quarter	7,000	15,000
3rd quarter	9,000	20,000
4th quarter	10,000	30,000

The January 1, 1987 inventory of HD-240 and LL-250 units are 4,000 and 8,000, respectively. Management desires an ending inventory each quarter equal to 80% of the next quarter's sales. Sales in the first quarter of 1988 are expected to be 20% higher than sales in the same quarter in 1987.

INSTRUCTIONS

Prepare separate quarterly production budgets for each product by quarters for 1987.

E25–3 Schultz Industries has adopted the following production budget for the first seven months of 1987.

Month	Units	Month	Units
January	12,000	May	9,000
February	8,000	June	10,000
March	6,000	July	12,500
April	4,000		

Each unit requires six pounds of raw materials costing $1.25 per pound. A 20% price increase is expected in May. On December 31, 1986, the ending raw materials inventory was 43,200 pounds. Schultz's management wants to have a raw materials inventory at the end of the month equal to 60% of next month's production.

INSTRUCTIONS

Prepare a direct material purchases budget by months for the first six months of 1987.

E25-4 The Travis Company budget committee has reached agreement on the following data for the year ending December 31, 1987:

Sales units (by quarters):	(1) 5,000, (2) 6,000, (3) 7,000, (4) 8,000
Ending raw materials inventory:	40% of the next quarter's production requirements
Ending finished goods inventory:	25% of the next quarter's expected sales units

The ending raw materials and finished goods inventories at December 31, 1986 follow the same percentage relationships to production and sales that occur in 1987. Three pounds of raw materials are required to make each unit of finished goods. Raw materials purchased are expected to cost $5 per pound. Sales of 9,000 units and required production of 9,250 units are expected in the first quarter of 1988.

INSTRUCTIONS

(a) Prepare a production budget by quarters for the year.

(b) Prepare a direct materials budget by quarters for the year.

E25-5 Xavier, Inc. is preparing its direct labor budget for 1987 from the following production budget based on a calendar year basis:

Quarter	Units	Quarter	Units
1	20,000	3	40,000
2	25,000	4	30,000

Each unit requires 1.2 hours of direct labor. The union contract provides for a 10% increase in the wage rate to $11 per hour on July 1. Payroll taxes and company paid health and life insurance are estimated to be 40% of the hourly rate.

INSTRUCTIONS

Prepare a direct labor cost budget for 1987. (Note: Combine the hourly rate and other payroll costs into one total hourly rate for purposes of preparing the budget.)

E25-6 The Marygrove Company is preparing its direct labor and manufacturing overhead budgets for 1987. Relevant data consist of the following:

Units to be produced (by quarters): 10,000; 12,000; 14,000; 16,000.

Direct labor: time—1.5 hours per unit; hourly rate $10.

Variable overhead costs per direct labor hour: indirect materials $.70; indirect labor $1.20; and maintenance $.10.

Fixed overhead costs per quarter: supervisory salaries $25,000; depreciation $9,000; and maintenance $5,000.

INSTRUCTIONS

(a) Prepare the direct labor budget for the year, showing quarterly data.

(b) Prepare the manufacturing overhead budget for the year, showing quarterly data.

E25-7 The Elena Company combines its operating expenses for budget purposes in a selling and administrative expense budget. For the first six months of 1987, the following data are developed:

1. Sales: 10,000 units quarter 1; 12,000 units quarter 2.
2. Variable costs per dollar of sales: sales commissions 5%; delivery expense 2%; and advertising 3%.
3. Fixed costs per quarter: sales salaries $10,000; office salaries $6,000; depreciation $2,000; insurance $1,000; utilities $800, and repairs expense $500.
4. Unit selling price $20.

INSTRUCTIONS

Prepare a selling and administrative expense budget for the first six months of 1987 by quarters.

E25-8 The Ewing Company has accumulated the following budget data for the year 1987:

1. Sales: 25,000 units; unit selling price $80.
2. Cost of one unit of finished goods: direct materials, 2 pounds at $5 per pound; direct labor, 3 hours at $12 per hour; and manufacturing overhead $6 per direct labor hour.
3. Inventories: raw materials only: beginning, 10,000 pounds; ending, 15,000 pounds.
4. Raw materials cost: $5 per pound.
5. Selling and administrative expenses: $240,000.
6. Income taxes: 25% of income before income taxes.

INSTRUCTIONS

Prepare a budgeted income statement for 1987. Show the computation of cost of goods sold.

E25-9 Lopez Enterprises offers its customers the following credit terms: (1) a 4% cash discount if paid in full at time of sale, (2) a 2% discount if paid in full within one month following the sale, and (3) balance due two months following the sale.

Management estimates that gross sales for August, September, October, and November will be $90,000, $125,000, $150,000, and $175,000, respectively. Experience has shown that collections are made as follows:

At time of sale	20%
Within 2% discount period	60%
After 2% discount period but within two-month credit period	18%

INSTRUCTIONS

Determine the collections from customers for October and November. Show computations.

E25-10 The ROK Company begins operations with a cash balance of $50,000 on January 1, 1987. Relevant quarterly budgeted data pertaining to a cash budget for the first two quarters of the year are as follows:

Sales: (1) $120,000, (2) $200,000. All sales are on account; 50% of the sales are expected to be collected in cash in the period of sale, and the balance in the following quarter.

Direct materials purchases: (1) $50,000, (2) $150,000. 40% of each purchase is paid in cash at the time of purchase, and the balance is paid in the following quarter.

Direct labor: (1) $30,000, (2) $40,000. Wages are paid at the time they are incurred.

Manufacturing overhead: (1) $23,000, (2) $33,000. These costs include depreciation of $3,000 per quarter. All cash overhead costs are paid as incurred.

Selling and administrative expenses: (1) $15,000, (2) $20,000. These expenses include $1,000 of depreciation per quarter. All cash selling and administrative costs are paid when incurred.

The company has a line of credit at a local bank that enables it to borrow up to $25,000 per quarter. Interest on any loans and income taxes may be ignored.

The ROK Company wants to maintain a minimum quarterly cash balance of $20,000.

INSTRUCTIONS

Prepare a cash budget by quarters for the six months ending June 30, 1987.

PROBLEMS

P25-1 Westly Inc. is preparing its annual budgets for the year ending December 31, 1987. Accounting assistants furnish the following data:

	Product ST 35	Product ST 40
Sales:		
Unit selling price	$ 15.00	$ 28.00
Anticipated volume (in units)	400,000	150,000
Unit production costs:		
Direct materials	$ 4.00	$ 9.00
Direct labor	$ 4.00	$ 6.00
Manufacturing overhead	$ 2.00	$ 3.00
Selling expenses:		
Variable, as percentage of sales	6%	7%
Fixed	$100,000	$ 80,000
Administrative expenses:		
Variable, as percentage of sales	3%	4%
Fixed	$220,000	$200,000
Raw materials inventories:		
Beginning:		
Pounds	40,000	10,000
Cost	$ 80,000	$ 30,000
Desired ending pounds	50,000	20,000
Finished goods inventories:		
Beginning:		
Units	20,000	5,000
Cost	$200,000	$ 90,000
Desired ending units	30,000	15,000

	Product ST 35	Product ST 40
Unit production data:		
Direct materials (in pounds)	2	3
Direct labor hours	.5	.75

The cost per pound of raw materials is expected to remain the same throughout the year. Income taxes are expected to be 30%.

INSTRUCTIONS

Prepare the following budgets for the year. Show data for each product. Quarterly budgets should not be prepared.

1. Sales
2. Production
3. Direct materials
4. Direct labor
5. Selling and administrative (Note: Use variable and fixed in place of individual expenses.)
6. Income statement (Note: Income taxes are not allocated to the products.)

P25–2 Agrow Farm Supply Company manufactures and sells a fertilizer called Suregro. The following data are developed for preparing budgets for Suregro for the first two quarters of 1987.

1. Sales: Quarter 1, 40,000 bags: Quarter 2, 60,000 bags. Selling price is $45 per bag.
2. Direct materials: Each bag of Suregro requires 5 pounds of Kemo at a cost of $2 per pound and 10 pounds of Ozo at $1.50 per pound.
3. Desired inventory levels:

Type of inventory	January 1	April 1	July 1
Suregro (bags)	10,000	15,000	20,000
Kemo (pounds)	8,000	12,000	14,000
Ozo (pounds)	16,000	24,000	28,000

4. Direct labor: direct labor time is 15 minutes per bag at an hourly rate of $9 per hour.
5. Manufacturing overhead: Overhead costs are expected to total 80% of direct labor cost. Variable costs per direct labor hour are: indirect labor $2.00; indirect materials $1.40. Fixed costs per quarter are supervision $30,000, depreciation $8,000, utilities $9,000, and maintenance $5,250.
6. Selling and administrative expenses are expected to be 10% of sales plus $100,000 per quarter.

INSTRUCTIONS

Prepare the budgeted income statement for the first six months of 1987 and all required supporting budgets by quarters. (Note: Prepare separate direct materials budgets for each material.)

P25–3 Spring Industries had sales in 1986 of $5,250,000 and gross profit of $1,387,500. Management is considering two alternative budget plans to increase its gross profit in 1987.

Plan A would increase the selling price per unit from $6.00 to $6.60. Sales volume would decrease by 10% from its 1986 level. Plan B would decrease the selling price per unit by 5%. The marketing department expects that the sales volume would increase by 100,000 units.

At the end of 1986, Spring has 75,000 units on hand. If Plan A is accepted, the 1987 ending inventory should be equal to 87,500 units. If Plan B is accepted, the ending inventory should be equal to 85,000 units. Each unit produced will cost $2.00 in direct materials, $1.00 in direct labor, and $.50 in variable overhead. The fixed overhead for 1987 should be $800,000.

INSTRUCTIONS

(a) Prepare a sales budget for 1987 under (1) Plan A, and (2) Plan B.
(b) Prepare a production budget for 1987 under (1) Plan A, and (2) Plan B.
(c) Compute the cost per unit under (1) Plan A, and (2) Plan B. Explain why the cost per unit is different for each of the two plans. (Round to two decimals.)
(d) Which plan should be accepted? (Hint: Compute the gross profit under each plan.)

P25–4 Jagger Industries' balance sheet at December 31, 1986 is presented below.

JAGGER INDUSTRIES
Balance Sheet
December 31, 1986

Assets		
Current assets		
Cash		$ 7,500
Accounts receivable		82,500
Finished goods inventory (2,000 units)		30,000
Total current assets		120,000
Property, plant, and equipment		
Equipment	$40,000	
Less: Accumulated depreciation	10,000	30,000
Total assets		$150,000
Liabilities and Stockholders' Equity		
Liabilities		
Notes payable		$ 25,000
Accounts payable		45,000
Total liabilities		70,000
Stockholders' equity		
Common stock	$50,000	
Retained earnings	30,000	
Total stockholders' equity		80,000
Total liabilities and stockholders' equity		$150,000

During 1987, 8,000 units should be sold for $30 each. Sales commissions will be 10% of gross sales. Gross sales less commissions are then multiplied by 5% to determine advertising expense. Rent, utilities, and other occupancy expenses should be $36,000 per year.

Production should be enough to have 2,400 units in the December 31, 1987 inventory. During the year, $75,600 in materials, $50,400 in labor, and $25,200 in manufacturing overhead will be spent. The Jagger Company uses the FIFO method for costing finished goods inventory.

All sales are on account. Experience shows that 70% of all customers pay in the discount period in order to get 2% off the gross sales amount. The discount period has expired on all December 31, 1986 accounts receivable. Improved collection policies should reduce the Accounts Receivable balance to $62,000 by December 31, 1987. As a result, the Accounts Payable balance will be cut in half by December 31, 1987. Five thousand dollars of the current Notes Payable will be paid, plus interest of $3,000. An additional $10,000 will be borrowed from the bank to purchase equipment, and the 1987 depreciation expense will be $4,000. Cash dividends of $2,000 will be declared

and paid in 1987. The company's cash budget shows an expected cash balance of $10,140 at December 31, 1987. The income tax rate is 25% and the entire amount will be unpaid at December 31, 1987.

INSTRUCTIONS

Prepare a budgeted income statement and budgeted balance sheet for 1987.

P25-5 The Boyce Company prepares monthly cash budgets. Relevant budget data include the following:

	January	February	March
Sales	$200,000	$220,000	$250,000
Purchases	130,000	140,000	180,000
Operating expenses	70,000	80,000	90,000

Fifty percent of the sales are expected to be for cash. It is believed that 70% of the charge sales will be collected in the month following the sale and the remainder in the second month after the sale. Forty percent of the purchases are for cash. All charge purchases are paid in the following month.

Depreciation and other prepayments have been excluded in determining the relevant budget data for operating expenses. Seventy percent of the operating expenses are paid within the current month, and the balance is paid the following month.

Other expenditures consist of an anticipated purchase of land in February for $5,000 and a March payment of $4,120 for a note payable plus interest. Other receipts will include collection of a $2,000 note plus $20 of interest in February, and $1,000 from the sale of marketable securities in March.

On December 31, the ledger included Cash $68,000; Marketable Securities $5,000; Accounts Receivable $100,000, of which $20,000 pertain to November charge sales; Notes Receivable $2,000; Accounts Payable (to suppliers) $67,000; Notes Payable $4,000; and Accrued Expenses Payable (for operating expenses) $12,000.

The Boyce Company wishes to maintain a minimum cash balance of $50,000.

INSTRUCTIONS

Prepare a cash budget for the first quarter by months.

ALTERNATE PROBLEMS

P25-1A Wimbly Inc. is preparing its annual budgets for the year ending December 31, 1987. Accounting assistants furnish the following data:

	Product RH 50	Product RH 60
Sales:		
Unit selling price	$ 20.00	$ 30.00
Anticipated volume (in units)	450,000	160,000
Unit production costs:		
Direct materials	$ 6.00	$ 12.00
Direct labor	$ 4.00	$ 6.00
Manufacturing overhead	$ 2.00	$ 3.00
Selling expenses:		
Variable, as percentage of sales	6%	8%
Fixed	$120,000	$100,000

	Product RH 50	Product RH 60
Administrative expenses:		
Variable, as percentage of sales	2%	3%
Fixed	$240,000	$220,000
Raw materials inventories:		
Beginning:		
Pounds	40,000	10,000
Cost	$120,000	$ 40,000
Desired ending pounds	60,000	15,000
Finished goods inventories:		
Beginning:		
Units	20,000	10,000
Cost	$240,000	$180,000
Desired ending units	25,000	15,000
Unit production data:		
Direct materials (in pounds)	2	3
Direct labor hours	.5	.75

The cost per pound of raw materials is expected to remain the same throughout the year. Income taxes are expected to be 30%.

INSTRUCTIONS

Prepare the following budgets for the year. Show data for each product. Quarterly budgets should not be prepared.

1. Sales
2. Production
3. Direct materials
4. Direct labor
5. Selling and administrative (Note: Use variable and fixed in place of individual expenses.)
6. Income statement (Note: Income taxes are not allocated to the products.)

P25-2A Acro Farm Supply Company manufactures and sells a pesticide called Getum. The following data are developed for preparing budgets for Getum for the first two quarters of 1987.

1. Sales: Quarter 1, 32,000 bags; Quarter 2, 48,000 bags. Selling price is $50 per bag.
2. Direct materials: Each bag of Getum requires 6 pounds of Liko at a cost of $2 per pound and 8 pounds of Moro at $1.50 per pound.
3. Desired inventory levels:

Type of inventory	January 1	April 1	July 1
Getum (bags)	8,000	12,000	18,000
Liko (pounds)	9,000	10,000	13,000
Moro (pounds)	14,000	20,000	25,000

4. Direct labor: direct labor time is 20 minutes per bag at an hourly rate of $12 per hour.
5. Manufacturing overhead: Overhead costs are expected to total 60% of direct labor cost. Variable costs per direct labor hour are: indirect labor $2.00 and indirect materials $1.50. Fixed costs per quarter are supervision $30,000, depreciation $11,000, utilities $9,000, and maintenance $5,500.
6. Selling and administrative expenses are expected to be 8% of sales plus $120,000 per quarter.

INSTRUCTIONS

Prepare the budgeted income statement for the first six months and all required sup-

porting budgets by quarters. (Note: Prepare separate direct materials budgets for each raw material.)

P25-3A Grace Industries had sales in 1987 of $6,000,000, and gross profit of $1,600,000. Management is considering two alternative budget plans to increase its gross profit in 1988.

Plan A would increase the selling price per unit from $8.00 to $8.40. Sales volume would decrease by 5% from this 1987 level. Plan B would decrease the selling price per unit by $.50. The marketing department expects that the sales volume would increase by 150,000 units.

At the end of 1987, Grace has 60,000 units of inventory on hand. If Plan A is accepted, the 1988 ending inventory should be equal to 8% of the 1988 sales. If Plan B is accepted, the ending inventory should be equal to 90,000 units. Each unit produced will cost $1.50 in direct labor, $2.00 in direct materials, and $.90 in variable overhead. The fixed overhead for 1988 should be $900,000.

INSTRUCTIONS

(a) Prepare a sales budget for 1988 under each plan.

(b) Prepare a production budget for 1988 under each plan.

(c) Compute the production cost per unit under each plan. Why is the cost per unit different for each of the two plans? (Round to two decimals.)

(d) Which plan should be accepted? (Hint: Compute the gross profit under each plan.)

P25-4A The Valdez Industries' December 31, 1986 balance sheet is presented below.

VALDEZ INDUSTRIES
Balance Sheet
December 31, 1986

Assets		
Current assets		
Cash		$ 8,000
Accounts receivable		72,500
Inventory (1,500 units)		45,000
Total current assets		$125,500
Property, plant, and equipment		
Equipment	$59,500	
Less: Accumulated depreciation	12,000	47,500
Total assets		$173,000
Liabilities and Owners' Equity		
Liabilities		
Notes Payable		$ 30,000
Accounts Payable		52,000
Total liabilities		82,000
Stockholders' equity		
Common stock	$75,000	
Retained earnings	16,000	
Total stockholders' equity		91,000
Total liabilities and owners' equity		$173,000

During 1987, 10,000 units are expected to be sold for $32.00 each. Sales commissions will be 8% of gross sales. Gross sales less commissions are then multiplied by 10% to determine advertising expense. Rent, utilities, and other occupancy expenses should be $42,000 per year.

Production should be geared to having 3,000 units in the December 31, 1987 inventory. During the year, $82,400 in materials, $52,600 in labor, and $26,000 in manufacturing overhead will be spent. Valdez uses FIFO inventory costing.

All sales are on account. Experience shows that 75% of all customers pay in the discount period in order to get 2% of the gross sales amount. The discount period has expired on all December 31, 1986 accounts receivable. Improved collection policies should reduce the Accounts Receivable balance to $60,000 by December 31, 1987. As a result, the 1986 Accounts Payable balance will be cut by 40% by December 31, 1987. $8,000 of the current Notes Payable will be paid, plus interest of $3,000. An additional $12,000 will be borrowed to purchase equipment and the 1987 depreciation expense will be $6,000.

Cash dividends of $2,000 will be declared and paid in 1987. The company's cash budget shows an expected cash balance of $43,860 at December 31, 1987. The income tax rate is 25% and the entire amount will be unpaid at December 31, 1987.

INSTRUCTIONS

Prepare a budgeted income statement and budgeted balance sheet for 1987.

P25-5A The O'Brien Company prepares monthly cash budgets. Relevant budget data include the following:

	January	February	March
Sales	$240,000	$280,000	$300,000
Purchases	140,000	160,000	200,000
Operating Expenses	90,000	100,000	110,000

Sixty percent of the sales are expected to be for cash. It is believed that 80% of the charge sales will be collected in the month following the sale and the remainder in the second month after the sale. Fifty percent of the purchases are for cash. All charge purchases are paid in the following month.

Depreciation and other prepayments have been excluded in determining the relevant budget data for operating expenses. Seventy-five percent of the operating expenses are paid within the current month and the balance in the following month.

Other expenditures consist of an anticipated purchase of land in February for $9,000 and a March payment of $6,120 for a note payable plus interest. Other receipts will include collection of a $4,000 note plus $60 of interest in February and $2,000 from the sale of marketable securities in March.

On December 31, the ledger included Cash $55,000; Marketable Securities $5,000; Accounts Receivable $120,000, of which $30,000 pertains to November charge sales; Notes Receivable $4,000; Accounts Payable (to suppliers) $65,000; Notes Payable $6,000, and Accrued Expenses Payable (for operating expenses) $15,000.

The O'Brien Company wishes to maintain a minimum cash balance of $60,000.

INSTRUCTIONS

Prepare a cash budget for the first quarter by months.

DECISION CASE

Springfield Corporation operates on a calendar-year basis. It begins the annual budgeting process in late August when the president establishes targets for the total dollar sales and net income before taxes for the next year.

The sales target is given to the marketing department where the marketing manager formulates a sales budget by product line in both units and dollars. From this budget, sales quotas by product line in units and dollars are established for each of the corporation's sales districts. The marketing manager also estimates the cost of the marketing activities required to support the target sales volume and prepares a tentative marketing expense budget.

The executive vice president uses the sales and profit targets, the sales budget by product line, and the tentative marketing expense budget to determine the dollar amounts which can be devoted to manufacturing and corporate office expense. The executive vice president prepares the budget for corporate expenses, and then forwards to the production department the product-line sales budget in units and the total dollar amount which can be devoted to manufacturing.

The production manager meets with the factory managers to develop a manufacturing plan which will produce the required units when needed within the cost constraints set by the executive vice president. The budgeting process usually comes to a halt at this point because the production department does not consider the financial resources allocated to be adequate.

When this standstill occurs, the vice president of finance, the executive vice president, the marketing manager, and the production manager meet together to determine the final budgets for each of the areas. This normally results in a modest increase in the total amount available for manufacturing costs while the marketing expense and corporate office expense budgets are cut. The total sales and net income figures proposed by the president are seldom changed. Although the participants are seldom pleased with the compromise, these budgets are final. Each executive then develops a new detailed budget for the operations in his or her area.

None of the areas has achieved its budget in recent years. Sales often run below the target. When budgeted sales are not achieved, each area is expected to cut costs so that the president's profit target can still be met. However, the profit target is seldom met because costs are not cut enough. In fact, costs often run above the original budget in all functional areas (marketing, production, and corporate office). The president is disturbed that Springfield has not been able to meet the sales and profit targets. He hired a consultant with considerable experience with companies in Springfield's industry. The consultant reviewed the budgets for the past four years. He concluded that the product-line sales budgets were reasonable and that the cost and expense budgets were adequate for the budgeted sales and production levels.

INSTRUCTIONS

(a) Discuss how the budgeting process as employed by Springfield Corporation contributes to the failure to achieve the president's sales and profit targets.

(b) Suggest how Springfield Corporation's budgeting process could be revised to correct the problems.

(c) Should the functional areas be expected to cut their costs when sales volume falls below budget? Explain your answer. (CMA adapted.)

CHAPTER 26

Duke University

CHAPTER 26

BUDGETARY CONTROL

STUDY OBJECTIVES

After completing the study of this chapter, you should be able to:

1. Describe the concept of budgetary control.
2. Evaluate the usefulness of static budget reports.
3. Explain how the flexible budget is developed.
4. Indicate the content and purposes of flexible budget reports.
5. Describe the concept of responsibility accounting.
6. Distinguish between controllable and noncontrollable costs.
7. Explain the features of a responsibility reporting system.
8. Explain the concept and usefulness of variable costing.

Now that you know how management formulates future plans through budgeting, it is time to consider the way management exercises its control function. Such questions as the following will be answered:

How close is the company to meeting its profit target for the year?
What are the causes of the cost overruns in production?
Which department is doing the best job of controlling costs?

This chapter focuses on three aspects of management control: (1) budgetary control, (2) responsibility accounting, and (3) variable costing.

CONCEPT OF BUDGETARY CONTROL

As stated at the beginning of the managerial accounting chapters, one of management's major functions is controlling the operations of the company. Control was defined as the steps taken by management to see that planned objectives are met. We now need to ask: How do budgets assist management in controlling operations?

The use of budgets in controlling operations is known as **budgetary control.** The centerpiece of budgetary control is the use of budget reports that compare actual results with planned objectives. The preparation and use of budget reports is based on the belief that planned objectives lose much of their potential value without some monitoring of progress along the way. Just as your professors give mid-term examinations to evaluate your progress, so top management requires monthly and quarterly reports on the progress that department managers are making toward planned annual objectives. Budget reports provide the feedback needed by management to see whether actual operations are on course. The feedback for a crucial objective, such as having enough cash on hand to pay bills, may be made daily. For other objectives, such as meeting budgeted annual sales and operating expenses, monthly budget reports may suffice. Because of the flexibility of managerial accounting, budget reports can be prepared as frequently as needed. On the basis of the budget reports, management first analyzes any differences between actual and planned results to determine their causes. From this analysis, management may take corrective action, or it could decide to modify the future plans.

Budgetary control involves the following:

Budgetary control

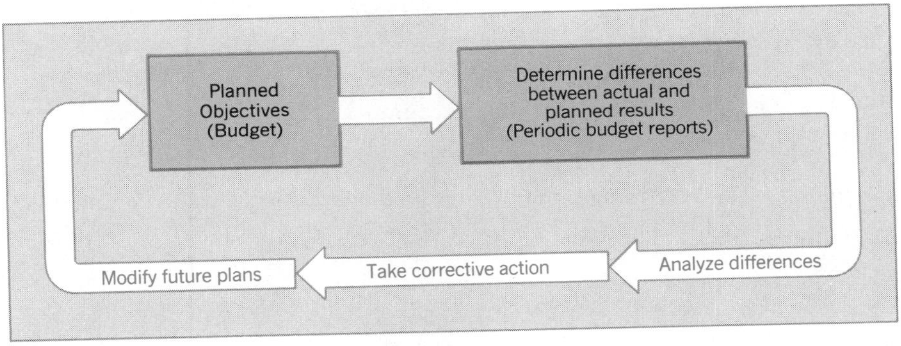

Budgetary control is facilitated when a company has a formalized reporting system. The system should (1) identify the name of the budget report, such as the sales budget, the manufacturing overhead budget, and so on; (2) state the frequency of the report, such as weekly, or monthly; (3) specify the purpose of the report; and (4) indicate the primary recipient(s) of the report. The following schedule illustrates a partial budgetary control system for a manufacturing company. Note the emphasis on control in the reports and the frequency of the reports. For example, there is a daily report on scrap, and a weekly report on labor.

Budgetary control reporting system

Name of Report	Frequency	Purpose	Primary Recipient(s)
Sales	Weekly	Determine whether sales goals are being met	Top management and sales manager
Labor	Weekly	Control direct and indirect labor cost	Vice president of production and production department managers
Scrap	Daily	Determine efficient use of materials	Production manager
Departmental overhead costs	Monthly	Control overhead costs	Department manager
Selling expenses	Monthly	Control selling expenses	Sales manager
Income statement	Monthly and quarterly	Determine whether income objectives are being met	Top management

MASTER BUDGET PERFORMANCE REPORTS

You learned in Chapter 25 that the master budget formalizes management's planned objectives for the coming year. To produce the financial statements desired at the end of the year, the budgetary process also sets forth the means of achieving planned goals. Thus, to achieve its planned net income, the company also budgets sales, cost of goods sold, and operating expenses. To illustrate the role of the master budget in budgetary control, we will use the budget developed for the Hayes Company in Chapter 25. Budget and actual sales data for the Kitchen-mate product in the first and second quarters of 1987 are as follows:

Budget and actual sales data

Sales	First Quarter	Second Quarter	Total
Budgeted	$180,000	$210,000	$390,000
Actual	179,000	199,500	378,500
Difference	$ 1,000	$ 10,500	$ 11,500

The sales budget report for the first quarter is shown below.

Sales budget report—first quarter

HAYES COMPANY
Sales Budget Report
For the Quarter Ended March 31, 1987

Product Line	Budget	Actual	Difference Favorable F Unfavorable U
Kitchen-mate[a]	$180,000	$179,000	$1,000 U

[a]In practice, each product line would be included in the report.

The report shows that sales are $1,000 under budget—an unfavorable result. This difference is less than 1% of budgeted sales ($1,000 ÷ $180,000 = .0056). Top management's analysis of unfavorable differences is often influenced by the materiality (significance) of the difference. Since the difference of $1,000 is immaterial in this case, we will assume that the management of the Hayes Company makes no analysis and takes no specific action.

The budget report for the second quarter presented below contains one new feature: cumulative year-to-date information.

Sales budget report—second quarter

HAYES COMPANY
Sales Budget Report
For the Quarter Ended June 30, 1987

	Second Quarter			Year-to-Date		
Product Line	Budget	Actual	Difference Favorable F Unfavorable U	Budget	Actual	Difference Favorable F Unfavorable U
Kitchen-mate	$210,000	$199,500	$10,500 U	$390,000	$378,500	$11,500 U

This report indicates that sales for the second quarter were $10,500 below budget, which is 5% of budgeted sales ($10,500 ÷ $210,000). Top management may conclude that the difference between budgeted and actual sales in the second quarter merits analysis.

The analysis should involve a discussion with the sales manager to determine the cause(s) of the shortfall. If corrective action is needed, it also should be discussed. For example, management may decide to spur sales by offering sales incentives to customers or by increasing the advertising of Kitchen-mates. On the other hand, if management concludes that a downturn in the economy is responsbile for the lower sales, it may decide to modify planned sales and profit goals.

From the examples above, you can see that a master sales budget is useful in evaluating the performance of a sales manager. It is now necessary to ask: How appropriate is the master budget for evaluating a manager's performance in controlling costs? The master budget for the Hayes Company was geared to one level of activity—expected annual sales of $900,000. In this case, the master budget is a static budget. In a **static budget,** the data are not modified or adjusted regardless of changes in activity during the year. This means that **actual results are always compared with budget data at the original budgeted activity level.** Thus, we can say that the static budget is appropriate in evaluating a manager's effectiveness in controlling costs when:

1. The actual level of activity closely approximates the master budget activity level, and/or
2. The behavior of the costs in response to changes in activity is fixed.

A static budget report is, therefore, appropriate for fixed manufacturing costs and fixed selling and administrative expenses. However, as will be explained shortly, static budget reports may not be a proper basis for evaluating a manager's performance in controlling variable costs.

THE FLEXIBLE BUDGET

In contrast to a static budget, which is based on one level of activity, a **flexible budget** projects budget data for various levels of activity. In essence, the flexible budget is a series of static budgets at different levels of activity. The flexible budget recognizes that the budgetary process has greater usefulness if it is adaptable to changed operating conditions.

Flexible budgets can be prepared for each of the types of budgets included in the master budget. For example, Marriott Hotels can budget revenues and net income on the basis of 60%, 80%, and 100% of room occupancy. Similarly, American Van Lines can budget its operating expenses on the basis of various levels of truck miles driven. In addition, the bottling department of Coca-Cola can budget manufacturing costs on the basis of 70%, 80%, and 100% of direct labor costs.

WHY FLEXIBLE BUDGETS?

Assume that you are the manager in charge of manufacturing overhead in the Forging Department of Barton Steel. In preparing the manufacturing overhead budget for 1987, you prepare the following budget based on a production volume of 10,000 units of steel ingots.

Static overhead budget

BARTON STEEL
Manufacturing Overhead Budget (Static)
Forging Department
For the Year Ended December 31, 1987

Budgeted production in units (steel ingots)	10,000
Budgeted costs:	
Indirect materials	$ 250,000
Indirect labor	260,000
Utilities	190,000
Depreciation	280,000
Property taxes	70,000
Supervision	50,000
	$1,100,000

Fortunately for the company, the demand for steel ingots has increased, and 12,000 units are produced during the year, rather than 10,000. You are elated because increased sales means increased profitability, which should mean a large raise for you and the employees in your department. Unfortunately, a comparison of the actual costs incurred with the budgeted costs for the year in the Forging Department has put you on the spot. The budget report is shown on the next page.

Note that this comparison is based on budget data based on the original activity level (10,000 steel ingots). The comparison indicates that the Forging Department is significantly over budget for three of the six overhead costs. Moreover, there is a total unfavorable difference of $132,000, which is 12% over budget ($132,000 ÷ $1,100,000). Your supervisor is very unhappy! Instead

Static overhead budget report

BARTON STEEL
Manufacturing Overhead Budget Report (Static)
Forging Department
For the Year Ended December 31, 1987

	Budget	Actual	Difference Favorable F Unfavorable U
Production in units	10,000	12,000	
Costs			
Indirect materials	$ 250,000	$ 295,000	$45,000 U
Indirect labor	260,000	312,000	52,000 U
Utilities	190,000	225,000	35,000 U
Depreciation	280,000	280,000	-0-
Property taxes	70,000	70,000	-0-
Supervision	50,000	50,000	-0-
	$1,100,000	$1,232,000	$132,000 U

of sharing in the company's success, you may find yourself looking for another job. What would you do in this situation?

A careful examination of the manufacturing overhead budget identifies the problem. The budget data are not relevant! At the time the budget was developed, it was anticipated that only 10,000 units of steel ingots would be produced, but 12,000 ingots were manufactured. As a result, the comparison of actual costs with budgeted costs is meaningless. The reason is that as production increases, the budget allowances for variable costs should increase both directly and proportionately. The variable costs in this example are indirect materials, indirect labor, and utilities.

An analysis of the budget data for these costs at 10,000 units produces the following per unit results:

Variable costs per unit

Item	Total Cost	Per Unit
Indirect materials	$250,000	$25
Indirect labor	260,000	26
Utilities	190,000	19
	$700,000	$70

The budgeted variable costs at 12,000 units, therefore are as follows:

Budgeted variable costs (12,000 units)

Item	Computation	Total
Indirect materials	$25 × 12,000	$300,000
Indirect labor	26 × 12,000	312,000
Utilities	19 × 12,000	228,000
		$840,000

The budget cost data at 12,000 units are referred to as flexible budget data. Since fixed costs do not change in total as activity changes, the budget

allowance for these costs remains the same within a company's relevant range of activity. Thus, the budget report based on the flexible budget shows the following:

Flexible overhead budget report

BARTON STEEL
Manufacturing Overhead Budget Report (Flexible)
Forging Department
For the Year Ended December 31, 1987

	Budget	Actual	Difference Favorable F Unfavorable U
Production in units	12,000	12,000	
Variable Costs			
Indirect materials	$ 300,000	$ 295,000	$5,000 F
Indirect labor	312,000	312,000	-0-
Utilities	228,000	225,000	3,000 F
Total variable	840,000	832,000	8,000 F
Fixed Costs			
Depreciation	280,000	280,000	-0-
Property taxes	70,000	70,000	-0-
Supervision	50,000	50,000	-0-
Total fixed	400,000	400,000	-0-
Total costs	$1,240,000	$1,232,000	$8,000 F

This report indicates that the Forging Department is below budget—a favorable difference. Instead of worrying about being fired, you may be in line for a raise or a promotion! As indicated from the foregoing analysis, the only appropriate comparison is between actual costs at 12,000 units of production and budgeted costs at 12,000 units of production. Flexible budget data provide this comparison.

DEVELOPING THE FLEXIBLE BUDGET

To develop the flexible budget, the following steps are taken:

1. Select an activity index and the relevant range of activity.
2. Classify the individual items that comprise total costs as either variable or fixed.
3. Prepare a budget for selected increments of activity within the relevant range.

The activity index should significantly influence the costs that are being budgeted. For manufacturing overhead costs, the activity index is usually the same as the index used in developing the predetermined overhead rate, that is, direct labor hours or direct labor costs. For selling and administrative expenses, the activity index usually is sales or net sales. As explained in Chapter 24, the behavior of variable costs and fixed costs is assumed to be linear within the relevant range.

The choice of selected increments of activity is largely a matter of expediency. For example, if the relevant range is 8,000 to 12,000 direct labor hours, increments of 1,000 hours may be selected. The flexible budget is prepared in columnar form for each increment within the relevant range, as illustrated on page 1027

FLEXIBLE BUDGET ILLUSTRATED

To illustrate the preparation of the flexible budget, we will use the Fox Manufacturing Company. The management of Fox Manufacturing wants to use the flexible budget for monthly comparisons of actual and budgeted manufacturing overhead costs of the Finishing Department. The flexible budget is prepared from the master overhead budget for the year, which shows the following:

Master overhead budget data

Expected annual operating capacity	120,000 direct labor hours
Variable overhead costs	
Indirect materials	$180,000
Indirect labor	240,000
Utilities	60,000
Total variable	480,000
Fixed overhead costs	
Depreciation	180,000
Supervision	120,000
Property taxes	60,000
Total fixed	360,000
Total costs	$840,000

Management concludes that the relevant range of monthly activity is 8,000–12,000 direct labor hours. They ask that the flexible budget be prepared in 1,000 direct labor hour increments.

The first step in preparing the flexible budget is to determine the variable cost data per direct labor hour from the master budget. For Fox Manufacturing, the computations are:

Variable cost per direct labor hour

Variable Cost	Computation	Variable Cost Per Direct Labor Hour
Indirect materials	$180,000 ÷ 120,000	$1.50
Indirect labor	240,000 ÷ 120,000	2.00
Utilities	60,000 ÷ 120,000	.50
Total		$4.00

Next, it is necessary to determine the monthly budget amounts for each of the fixed costs. This is done by dividing the annual budgeted amounts by 12. The amounts are: Depreciation, $15,000; Supervision, $10,000; and Property taxes, $5,000.

The flexible budget, therefore, is as follows:

Flexible overhead budget

FOX MANUFACTURING COMPANY
Flexible Manufacturing Overhead Budget
Finishing Department

Activity level					
Direct labor hours	8,000	9,000	10,000	11,000	12,000
Variable costs					
Indirect materials	$12,000	$13,500	$15,000	$16,500	$18,000
Indirect labor	16,000	18,000	20,000	22,000	24,000
Utilities	4,000	4,500	5,000	5,500	6,000
Total variable	32,000	36,000	40,000	44,000	48,000
Fixed costs					
Depreciation	15,000	15,000	15,000	15,000	15,000
Supervision	10,000	10,000	10,000	10,000	10,000
Property taxes	5,000	5,000	5,000	5,000	5,000
Total fixed	30,000	30,000	30,000	30,000	30,000
Total costs	$62,000	$66,000	$70,000	$74,000	$78,000

Note that at each level of activity, total budgeted costs equal the fixed costs plus variable costs of $4.00 per direct labor hour times the direct labor hours worked. At 10,000 direct labor hours, the total budgeted costs of $70,000 consist of fixed costs of $30,000 and variable costs of $40,000 (10,000 × $4). Similarly, at 8,622 direct labor hours, the total budgeted costs are $64,488 [(8,622 × $4.00) + $30,000].

Total budgeted costs can also be shown graphically. In a graph, the activity index is shown on the horizontal axis and costs are indicated on the vertical axis. To minimize detail, we limit the graphic to two of the 1,000 increments (10,000 and 12,000). As shown, the total budgeted overhead costs at these two levels of activity are $70,000 [(10,000 × $4) + $30,000] and $78,000 [(12,000 × $4) + $30,000], respectively.

Graphic flexible budget data

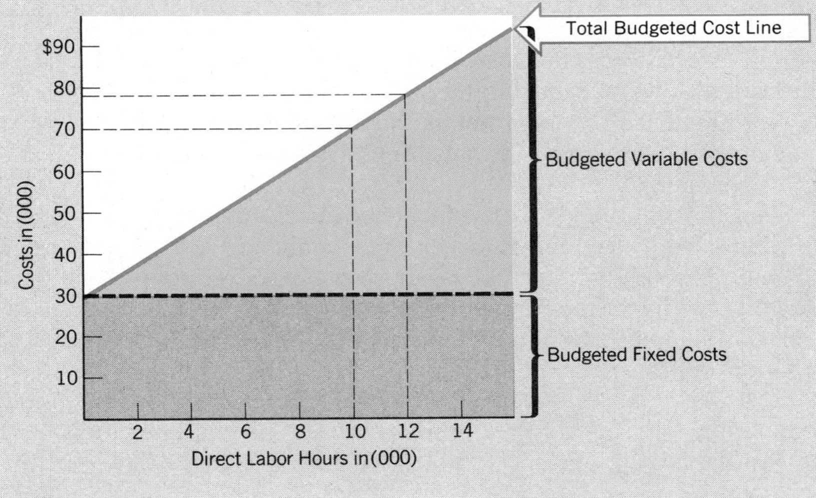

FLEXIBLE BUDGET REPORTS

Flexible budget reports represent another type of internal report produced by managerial accounting. The flexible budget report consists of two sections: (1) production data and (2) cost data. Consequently, the report provides a basis for evaluating a manager's performance in two areas: production control and cost control. Flexible budgets are widely used in cost centers. A budget report for the Finishing Department of Fox Company for the month of January is presented below. In this month, 8,800 direct labor hours were expected but 9,000 hours were worked. The budget data are based on the flexible budget for 9,000 hours on page 1027. The actual cost data are assumed.

Flexible overhead budget report

FOX MANUFACTURING COMPANY
Manufacturing Overhead Budget Report (Flexible)
Finishing Department
For the Month Ended January 31, 1987

Direct labor hours (DLH)		Budget at 9,000 DLH	Actual Costs 9,000 DLH	Difference Favorable F Unfavorable U	
Expected	8,800				
Actual	9,000				
Variable costs					
Indirect materials		$13,500	$14,000	$500	U
Indirect labor		18,000	17,000	1,000	F
Utilities		4,500	4,600	100	U
Total variable		36,000	35,600	400	F
Fixed costs					
Depreciation		15,000	15,000	–	
Supervision		10,000	10,000	–	
Property taxes		5,000	5,000	–	
Total fixed		30,000	30,000		
Total costs		$66,000	$65,600	$400	F

How appropriate is this report in evaluating the Finishing Department manager's performance in controlling costs? The report clearly provides a reliable basis for this purpose. Both actual and budget costs are based on the activity level worked during January. Since variable costs generally are incurred directly by the department, the differences between the budget allowance for those hours and the actual costs are the responsibility of the department manager.

From the standpoint of production control, the report shows a 200-hour difference betweeen actual direct labor hours and expected hours. This difference is favorable if actual production orders required 9,000 direct labor hours. The difference is unfavorable if actual production orders required only 8,800 direct labor hours. In either case, the budget for purposes of cost control is based on 9,000 direct labor hours.

In subsequent months, other flexible budget reports will be prepared. For each month, the budget data are based on the actual activity level attained. In February that level may be 11,000 direct labor hours, in July, 10,000, and so on.

FLEXIBLE BUDGETS AND PRODUCT COSTING

You have now seen two types of manufacturing overhead budgets: (1) the master (static) budget for the year, and (2) the flexible budget for an interim period. The master manufacturing overhead budget provides the basis for computing the predetermined overhead rate for the year. This rate is then used to apply overhead to work in process in both job order and process cost accounting. The **master manufacturing overhead budget is used in costing work in process and finished goods inventories** because management wants consistency in the costing of work done throughout the year.

By contrast, it is possible for a different flexible budget to be used for each month in a year. If these budgets were used for the predetermined overhead rate, the rate could vary each month. Thus, there would be inconsistencies in costing identical work done in different months. In addition, if these costs were used in determining selling prices, there would also be inconsistencies in selling prices. In sum, the **flexible budget is not used in costing work in process and finished goods.**

The Fox Manufacturing Company gives us an opportunity to show the differences that might result if the flexible budget were used in costing inventories. As indicated on page 1026, the master budget shows total manufacturing overhead costs of $840,000 for the year (variable $480,000 + fixed $360,000) at expected annual activity of 120,000 direct labor hours. Thus, the predetermined overhead rate is $7 ($840,000 ÷ 120,000). If the flexible budget is used, different overhead rates would result. For example, in January, as shown in the flexible budget report on page 1028, the department worked at an activity level of 9,000 direct labor hours. The total budget for this activity is $66,000. Therefore, the overhead rate would be $7.33 ($66,000 ÷ 9,000). Fixed costs account for the difference. They remain the same in total at every level of activity but the fixed cost per unit changes with the activity level.

CONCEPT OF RESPONSIBILITY ACCOUNTING

Like budgeting, responsibility accounting is an important part of management accounting. **Responsibility accounting** involves the accumulation and reporting of costs (and revenues, where relevant) on the basis of the individual manager who has the authority to make the day-to-day decisions about the items. Under responsibility accounting, the evaluation of a manager's performance is based on the costs directly under that manager's control. Responsibility accounting can be used at every level of management in which the following conditions exist:

1. Costs can be directly associated with the specific level of management responsibility.
2. The costs are controllable at the level of responsibility with which they are associated.
3. Budget data can be developed for evaluating the manager's effectiveness in controlling the costs.

Responsibility accounting rests on the premise that an organization is essentially a group of individuals striving toward common goals. In effect, responsibility accounting personalizes the managerial accounting system. Under responsibility accounting, any individual who has any control over costs can be recognized as a separate responsibility center. Thus, responsibility accounting may extend to the lowest level of control within a company. Once responsibility has been established, the effectiveness of the individual's performance in controlling costs is then measured and reported upward in the organization.

Responsibility accounting is essential to any effective system of budgetary control. The accumulation of data and reporting of information under responsibility accounting differ from budgeting in two respects: (1) a distinction is made between controllable and noncontrollable costs, and (2) performance reports include only data that are controllable by the individual manager.

CONTROLLABLE VERSUS NONCONTROLLABLE COSTS

All costs are controllable at some level of responsibility by someone within a company. This truth underscores the adage by the chief executive officer of any organization that "the buck stops here." Under responsibility accounting, the critical issue is whether a cost is controllable at the level of responsibility with which it is associated. If the cost is controllable, it is accumulated and reported in evaluating the relevant manager's performance. However, if a cost associated with a particular level of responsibility is not controllable at that level, it is not considered in evaluating the manager's performance.

A cost is considered **controllable** at a given level of managerial responsibility if that manager has the power to authorize the incurrence of the cost within a given period of time. From this criterion, it follows that (1) all costs are controllable by top management because of the broad range of its activity, and (2) fewer costs are controllable as one moves down to each lower level of managerial responsibility because of the manager's decreasing authority. In general, costs incurred directly by the level of responsibility are controllable, whereas costs allocated to the responsibility level are **noncontrollable.** Allocated costs are often referred to as **indirect or common costs.** It should be emphasized that the terms "controllable costs" and "noncontrollable" costs are not synonymous with variable costs and fixed costs, respectively. However, variable costs usually are controllable at the level where they are incurred.

In practice, it is often difficult to distinguish between controllable and uncontrollable costs. One might presume that direct materials and direct labor costs incurred by a production department would be controllable by the manager. However, both the price paid for the material and the labor pay rate are frequently controlled outside the department. Only direct material and direct labor usage are controllable within the department. Repairs on department machinery made by a maintenance department also present a problem. Here, the charge for the service will depend on the efficiency of the maintenance personnel, which is clearly beyond the control of the production department manager.

In some cases, time is a significant factor in determining the controllability of a cost. If the time span is long enough, all costs are probably controllable, whereas, in a short time period, few costs may be controllable.

For example, if the maintenance department has months to repair stand-by equipment, the maintenance manager can schedule the repairs during regular working hours, whereas if a machine must be repaired by early the following morning, the manager may be forced to incur overtime work.

RESPONSIBILITY PERFORMANCE REPORT

Responsibility performance reports usually compare actual costs with flexible budget data. A responsibility performance report is illustrated below. The report is adapted from the budget report for the Fox Company on page 1028. It assumes that the Finishing Department manager is able to control all manufacturing overhead costs except depreciation and property taxes.

Responsibility report

FOX MANUFACTURING COMPANY
Manufacturing Overhead Responsibility Report
Finishing Department
For the Month Ended January 31, 1987

Controllable Costs	Budget	Actual	Difference Favorable F Unfavorable U	
Indirect materials	$13,500	$14,000	$ 500	U
Indirect labor	18,000	17,000	1,000	F
Utilities	4,500	4,600	100	U
Supervision	10,000	10,000	-0-	
	$46,000	$45,600	$ 400	F

Note that only controllable costs are included in the report, and that no distinction is made between variable and fixed costs. Like budget performance reports, the responsibility report continues the concept of management by exception. By focusing on the difference column, management can quickly identify amounts that should be analyzed to determine the reasons why planned objectives have not been met.

Electronic data-processing can play a major role in increasing the timeliness of performance reports. The computer's speed in processing data has enabled management to receive feedback performance reports of exceptions much sooner after they have occurred than would be possible with a manual system. Quicker after-the-fact performance reports should lead to increased operating efficiency, because management's attention is directed to significant deviations requiring corrective action before these deviations get too far "out of hand."

RESPONSIBILITY REPORTING SYSTEM

A **responsibility reporting system** involves the preparation of a report for each level of responsibility shown in the company's organization chart. Each

report shows the controllable costs for the level of responsibility, as well as summary data for departments responsible to it. For example, the report for Manufacturing Plant A will include the costs of Plant A plus data on subdepartments, such as fabricating, enameling, and so on. To illustrate a responsibility reporting system, we will use the following partial organization chart of the Francis Company.

Partial organization chart

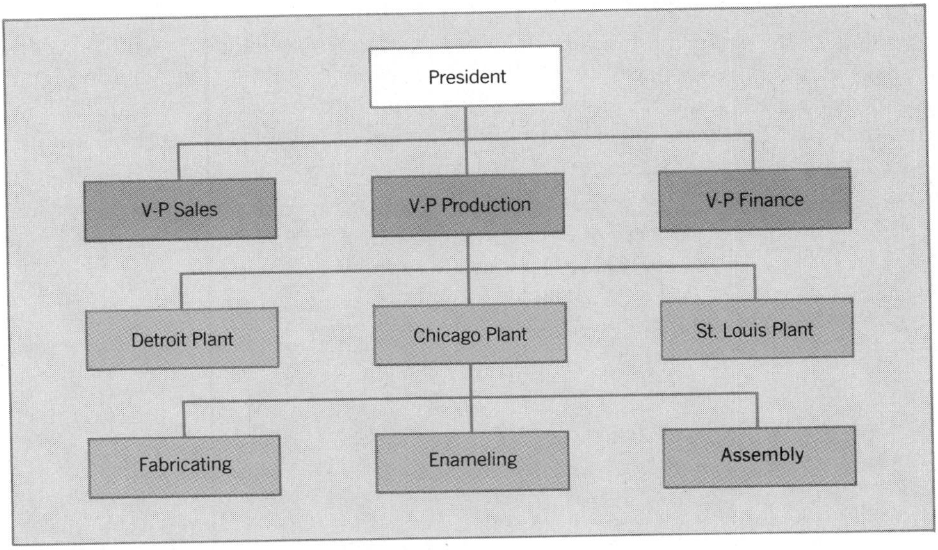

The responsibility reporting system begins with the lowest level of responsibility and moves upward to each higher level, as illustrated on the next page.

Report D is the report for the lowest level of responsibility. In this report additional detail may be presented for each cost element. Similar reports are prepared for the managers of the Enameling and Assembly Departments. The plant manager's report (Report C) shows the costs of the Chicago plant that are controllable at the second level of responsibility. In addition, Report C shows summary data for each department that is accountable to the plant manager. Similar reports are prepared for the Detroit and St. Louis plant managers. Report B shows the controllable costs of the vice-president of production and summary data on the three assembly plants for which this officer is responsible. At the top level of responsibility, the president receives a report (Report A) that shows the controllable costs and expenses of this office and summary data on the vice-presidents that are accountable to the president.

A responsibility reporting system permits management by exception at each level of responsibility within the organization. In addition to the information illustrated on page 1033, each higher level of responsibility can obtain the detailed report for each lower level of responsibility. For example, the vice-president of production in the Francis Company may request the Chicago plant manager's report because this plant is $5,300 over budget.

This type of reporting system also permits comparative evaluations. In the illustration above, the Chicago plant manager can easily rank the department manager's effectiveness in controlling manufacturing costs. Comparative rankings provide further incentive for a manager to control costs. For exam-

ple, the Detroit plant manager will want to continue to be No. 1 in the report to the vice-president of production, and the Chicago plant manager will not want to remain No. 3 in future reporting periods.

Responsibility reporting system

A

To President		Month:	January
Controllable Costs:	Budget	Actual	Fav/Unfav
President	$ 150,000	$ 151,500	$ 1,500 U
Vice-Presidents:			
Sales	185,000	187,000	2,000 U
Production	**1,179,000**	**1,186,300**	**7,300 U**
Finance	100,000	101,000	1,000 U
Total	$1,614,000	$1,625,800	$11,800 U

B

To Vice-President Production		Month:	January
Controllable Costs:	Budget	Actual	Fav/Unfav
V-P Production	$ 125,000	$ 126,000	$ 1,000 U
Assembly Plants:			
Detroit	420,000	418,000	2,000 F
Chicago	**304,000**	**309,300**	**5,300 U**
St. Louis	330,000	333,000	3,000 U
Total	**$1,179,000**	**$1,186,300**	**$ 7,300 U**

C

To Plant Manager-Chicago		Month:	January
Controllable Costs:	Budget	Actual	Fav/Unfav
Chicago Plant	$110,000	$113,000	$ 3,000 U
Departments:			
Fabricating	**84,000**	**85,300**	**1,300 U**
Enameling	62,000	64,000	2,000 U
Assembly	48,000	47,000	1,000 F
Total	**$304,000**	**$309,300**	**$ 5,300 U**

D

To Fabricating Department Manager		Month:	January
Controllable Costs:	Budget	Actual	Fav/Unfav
Direct Materials	$ 20,000	$ 20,500	$ 500 U
Direct Labor	40,000	41,000	1,000 U
Overhead	24,000	23,800	200 F
Total	**$ 84,000**	**$ 85,300**	**$ 1,300 U**

VARIABLE COSTING

In addition to budgetary control and responsibility accounting, the ability of management to control costs is often influenced by the manner in which costs are reported to management. For example, the conventional income statement does not differentiate between variable and fixed costs or between controllable and noncontrollable costs. One approach to better internal reports for controlling costs is to use variable costing. Under variable costing a distinction is made between variable and fixed costs. In addition, income statements prepared for management use the cost-volume-profit format that was illustrated in Chapter 24. As explained below, variable costing may be used by management in product costing and in controlling costs.

PRODUCT COSTING

In earlier chapters, all manufacturing costs, both variable and fixed, have been classified as product costs. In job order costing, for example, a job is assigned the costs of direct materials, direct labor, and both variable and fixed manufacturing overhead. This costing approach is referred to as **full or absorption costing** because all manufacturing costs are charged to, or absorbed by, the product. An alternative approach is to use variable costing. Under **variable costing** only direct materials, direct labor, and variable manufacturing costs are considered product costs; fixed manufacturing costs are recognized as period costs (expenses) when incurred. The difference between absorption costing and variable costing is graphically shown as follows:

Difference between absorption costing and variable costing

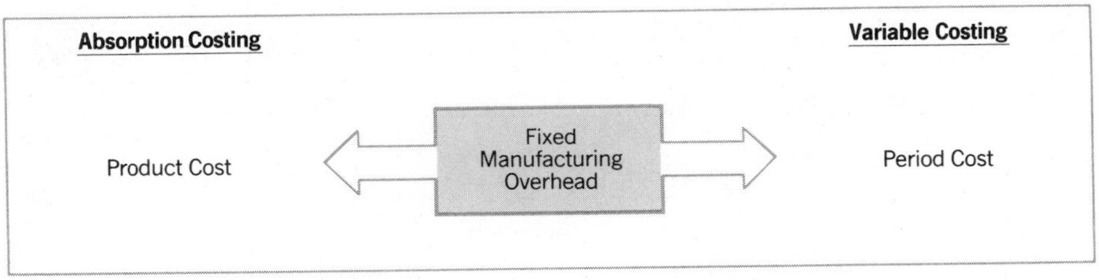

Selling and administrative expenses are period costs under both absorption and variable costing.

To illustrate the computation of unit production cost under absorption and variable costing, assume that Premium Product Corporation manufactures a polyurethane sealant called Fix-it for car windshields. Relevant data for Fix-it in January 1987, the first month of production, is as follows:

Selling price: $20 per unit.
Units: Produced 30,000; sold 20,000; beginning inventory -0-.
Variable unit costs: Manufacturing $9 (direct materials $5, direct labor $3, and variable overhead $1), and selling and administrative expenses $2.
Fixed costs: Manufacturing overhead $120,000 and selling and administrative expenses $15,000.

The per unit production cost under each costing approach is:

Computation of per unit production cost

Type of Cost	Absorption Costing	Variable Costing
Direct materials	$ 5	$5
Direct labor	3	3
Variable manufacturing overhead	1	1
Fixed manufacturing overhead ($120,000 ÷ 30,000 units produced)	4	0
Total unit cost	$13	$9

The difference in total unit cost of $4 ($13 − $9) occurs because fixed manufacturing costs are a product cost under absorption costing and a period cost under variable costing. Based on these data, each unit sold and each unit remaining in inventory are costed at $13 under absorption costing and at $9 under variable costing.

Effects on Income

The income statements under the two costing approaches are illustrated below and on the top of the next page. The conventional income statement format is used with absorption costing and the cost-volume-profit format is used with variable costing. Computations are inserted parenthetically in the statements to facilitate your understanding of the amounts.

Absorption costing income statement

PREMIUM PRODUCTS COMPANY
Income Statement
For the Month Ended January 31, 1987
(Absorption Costing)

Sales (20,000 units × $20)		$400,000
Cost of goods sold		
Inventory, January 1	$ -0-	
Cost of goods manufactured (30,000 units × $13)	390,000	
Cost of goods available for sale	390,000	
Inventory, January 31 (10,000 units × $13)	130,000	
Cost of goods sold (20,000 units × $13)		260,000
Gross profit		140,000
Selling and administrative expenses (Variable, 20,000 units × $2 + fixed, $15,000)		55,000
Income from operations		$ 85,000

Income from operations under absorption costing shown above is $40,000 higher than under variable costing ($85,000 − $45,000) shown on page 1036. As highlighted in the two income statements, there is a $40,000 difference in the ending inventories ($130,000 under absorption costing and $90,000 under variable costing). Under absorption costing, $40,000 of the fixed overhead costs (10,000 units × $4) have been deferred to a future period as a product cost. In contrast, the entire fixed manufacturing costs are expensed when incurred under variable costing.

As shown above, when units produced exceed units sold, income under absorption costing is higher than under variable costing. Conversely, when units produced are less than units sold, income under absorption costing is

Variable costing income statement

PREMIUM PRODUCTS COMPANY
Income Statement
For the Month Ended January 31, 1987
(Variable Costing)

Sales (20,000 units × $20)		$400,000
Variable expenses		
Variable cost of goods sold		
Inventory, January 1	$ -0-	
Variable manufacturing costs (30,000 units × $9)	270,000	
Cost of goods available for sale	270,000	
Inventory, January 31 (10,000 units × $9)	**90,000**	
Variable cost of goods sold	180,000	
Variable selling and administrative expenses (20,000 units × $2)	40,000	
Total variable expenses		220,000
Contribution margin		180,000
Fixed expenses		
Manufacturing overhead	120,000	
Selling and administrative expenses	15,000	
Total fixed expenses		135,000
Income from operations		**$ 45,000**

lower than under variable costing. The reason is that the cost of the beginning inventory will be higher under absorption costing than under variable costing. For example, if 30,000 units of Fix-it are sold in February and only 20,000 units are produced, income from operations will be $40,000 less under absorption costing than under variable costing because of the $40,000 difference ($130,000 vs. $90,000) in the beginning inventories.

When units produced and sold are the same, income from operations will be equal under the two costing approaches. Since there is no ending inventory, there is no deferral of any fixed overhead costs of the current period to future periods through the ending inventory. The foregoing effects of the two costing approaches on income from operations may be summarized as follows:

Summary of income effects

Circumstance	Effects on Income From Operations
Units produced exceed units sold	Income higher under absorption costing than under variable costing
Units produced less than units sold	Income lower under absorption costing than under variable costing
Units produced equal units sold	Income same under either approach

Rationale for Variable Costing

The rationale for variable costing centers on the purpose of fixed manufacturing costs which is to have productive facilities available for use. Conceptually, these costs are incurred whether a company operates at zero or 100% of capacity. Thus, proponents of variable costing argue that these costs should be expensed in the period in which they are incurred.

Supporters of absorption costing defend the assignment of fixed manufacturing overhead costs to inventory on the basis that these costs are as much a cost of getting a product such as Fix-it ready for sale as direct materials or direct labor. Accordingly, these costs should not be matched with revenues until the product is sold.

The use of variable costing in product costing is only acceptable for internal use by management. It cannot be used in determining product costs in financial statements prepared in accordance with generally accepted accounting principles because it understates inventory costs. To comply with the matching principle, a company must use absorption costing for its work in process and finished goods inventories. Similarly, absorption costing must be used for income tax purposes.

Is is also maintained that variable costing is more compatible with responsibility accounting than absorption costing. The costing of products at variable manufacturing costs results in a product cost that is controllable by the manager of the production department. In contrast fixing manufacturing costs often are not controllable at the department level.

SUMMARY OF STUDY OBJECTIVES

1. Budgetary control consists of (a) preparing periodic budget reports that compare actual results with planned objectives, (b) analyzing the differences to determine their causes, (c) taking appropriate corrective action, and (d) modifying future plans, if necessary.

2. Static budget reports are useful in evaluating the progress toward meeting planned sales and profit goals. They are also appropriate in assessing a manager's effectiveness in controlling fixed costs and expenses when (a) actual activity closely approximates the master budget activity level and/or (b) the behavior of the costs in response to changes in activity is fixed.

3. To develop the flexible budget it is necessary to
   a. Select an activity index and the relevant range of activity.
   b. Classify the individual items that comprise total costs as either variable or fixed.
   c. Prepare a budget for selected increments of activity within the relevant range.

4. Flexible budget reports present actual and budget data for both production activity and manufacturing costs. The reports permit an eval-

uation of a manager's performance in controlling production and in controlling costs.

5. Responsibility accounting involves the accumulation and reporting of costs on the basis of the individual manager who has the authority to make the day-to-day decisions about the items. Under responsibility accounting, the evaluation of a manager's performance is based on the costs directly under the manager's control.

6. Costs are controllable at a given level of management if that management has the authority to authorize the incurrence of the cost within a given period of time. Noncontrollable costs are common costs that are allocated to a responsibility level.

7. A responsibility reporting system involves the preparation of a report for each level of responsibility shown in a company's organization chart. The system begins with the lowest level of responsibility and moves upward to each higher level of responsibility.

8. Variable costing is an approach in which only variable manufacturing costs are charged to the product and fixed manufacturing overhead is recognized as a period cost when incurred. Variable costing is useful for internal use by management in costing work in process and finished goods and in controlling manufacturing costs.

GLOSSARY

Absorption costing, p. 1034

Budgetary control, p. 1020

Controllable costs, p. 1030

Flexible budget, p. 1023

Noncontrollable costs, p. 1030

Responsibility accounting, p. 1029

Responsibility reporting system, p. 1031

Static budget, p. 1022

Variable costing, p. 1034

DEMONSTRATION PROBLEM

The Glenda Company uses a flexible budget for manufacturing overhead based on direct labor hours. For 1987 the master overhead budget for the Packaging Department at normal capacity of 300,000 direct labor was as follows:

Variable Costs		Fixed Costs	
Indirect labor	$360,000	Supervision	$ 60,000
Supplies and lubricants	150,000	Depreciation	24,000
Maintenance	210,000	Property taxes	18,000
Utilities	120,000	Insurance	12,000
	$840,000		$114,000

During July, 24,000 direct labor hours were worked when 25,000 hours were expected to be worked. The company incurred the following variable costs in July: Indirect labor $30,200, Supplies and lubricants $11,600, Maintenance $17,500, and Utilities $9,200. Actual fixed overhead costs were the same as monthly budgeted fixed costs.

INSTRUCTIONS

Prepare a flexible budget report for the Packaging Department for July.

SOLUTION TO DEMONSTRATION PROBLEM

GLENDA COMPANY
Manufacturing Overhead Budget Report (Flexible)
Packaging Department
For the Month Ended July 31, 1987

Direct labor hours (DLH) Expected 25,000 Actual 24,000	Budget 24,000 DLH	Actual Costs 24,000 DLH	Difference Favorable F Unfavorable U
Variable costs			
Indirect labor	$28,800	$30,200	$1,400 U
Supplies and lubricants	12,000	11,600	400 F
Maintenance	16,800	17,500	700 U
Utilities	9,600	9,200	400 F
Total variable	67,200	68,500	1,300 U
Fixed costs			
Supervision	5,000	5,000	-0-
Depreciation	2,000	2,000	-0-
Property taxes	1,500	1,500	-0-
Insurance	1,000	1,000	-0-
Total fixed	9,500	9,500	-0-
Total costs	$76,700	$78,000	$1,300 U

QUESTIONS

1. The centerpiece of budgetary control is taking corrective action. Do you agree? Explain.

2. Lee Lane is critiquing budgetary control. What essential steps should she include in her critique?

3. Budgetary control is facilitated when a company has a formalized reporting system. List the features of such a system.

4. How may a budget report for the second quarter differ from a budget report for the first quarter?

5. Dan Drake questions the usefulness of a master sales budget in evaluating sales performance. Is there justification for Dan's concern? Explain.

6. Under what circumstances may a static budget be an appropriate basis for evaluating a manager's effectiveness in controlling costs?

7. A flexible budget is really a series of static budgets. Is this true? Why?

8. The static manufacturing overhead budget based on 40,000 direct labor hours shows budgeted indirect labor costs of $56,000. During March, the department incurs $67,000 of indirect labor while working 50,000 direct labor hours. Is this a favorable or unfavorable performance? Why?

9. A static overhead budget based on 40,000 direct labor hours shows Factory Insurance $6,400 as a fixed cost. At the 50,000 direct labor hours worked in March, factory insurance costs were $6,800. Is this a favorable or unfavorable performance? Why?

10. Andrea Andrews is confused about how a flexible budget is prepared. Identify the steps for Andrea.

11. The Marr Company has prepared a graph of flexible budget data. At zero direct labor hours, the total budgeted cost line intersects the vertical axis at $25,000. At 12,000 direct labor hours, the line drawn from the total budgeted cost line intersects the vertical axis at $85,000. How may the fixed and variable costs be expressed?

12. The flexible budget formula is fixed costs $40,000 plus variable costs of $3 per direct labor hour. What is the total budgeted cost at (a) 9,200 hours and (b) 12,345 hours?

13. Are flexible budgets useful in assessing a manager's performance in production control? Explain.

14. Jack Jelk argues that if flexible budgets are used in controlling costs, they should also be used in product costing. Do you agree? Why?

15. What is responsibility accounting? Explain the purpose of responsibility accounting.

16. Alice Alcot is studying for an accounting examination. Describe for Alice what conditions are necessary for responsibility accounting to be used effectively.

17. Distinguish between controllable and noncontrollable costs.

18. How do responsibility reports differ from budget reports?

19. What is the relationship, if any, between a responsibility reporting system and a company's organization chart?

20. Distinguish between absorption costing and variable costing.

21. Galt Company's fixed overhead costs are $5 per unit, and its variable overhead costs are $8 per unit. In the first month of operations, 50,000 units are produced and 45,000 units are sold. What will be the difference in income under absorption costing and variable costing? Which costing approach will produce the higher income? Why?

22. (a) What is the major rationale for the use of variable costing? (b) Discuss why variable costing may not be used for financial reporting purposes.

EXERCISES

E26-1 The Diane Company uses a flexible budget for manufacturing overhead based on direct labor hours. Variable manufacturing overhead costs per direct labor hour are as follows:

Indirect labor	$1.00
Indirect materials	.50
Maintenance	.25
Utilities	.10

Fixed overhead costs per month are: Supervision $3,000, Depreciation $1,500, Insurance $400, and Property Taxes $300.

The company believes it will normally operate in a range of 6,000–10,000 direct labor hours per month.

INSTRUCTIONS

Prepare a flexible manufacturing overhead budget for the expected range of activity, using 1,000 increments of direct labor hours.

E26-2 Given the information in Exercise 26-1, assume that in July 1987, the Diane Company incurs the following manufacturing overhead costs:

Variable		Fixed	
Indirect labor	$8,700	Supervision	$3,000
Indirect materials	4,300	Depreciation	1,500
Maintenance	2,480	Insurance	400
Utilities	900	Property Taxes	300

INSTRUCTIONS

(a) Prepare a flexible budget performance report, assuming that the company worked 9,000 direct labor hours during the month. The company expected to work 9,000 direct labor hours.

(b) Prepare a flexible budget performance report, assuming that the company worked 8,500 direct labor hours during the month. The company expected to work 8,500 direct labor hours.

(c) Comment on your findings.

E26-3 The Lloyd Company uses flexible budgets to control its selling expenses. Monthly sales are expected to range from $160,000 to $200,000. Variable costs and their percentage relationship to sales are: Sales Commissions (5%), Advertising (4%), Traveling (3%), and Delivery (2%). Fixed selling expenses will consist of Sales Salaries $30,000, Depreciation on Delivery Equipment $5,000, and Insurance on Delivery Equipment $1,000.

INSTRUCTIONS

Prepare a flexible budget for each $10,000 increment of sales within the relevant range.

E26-4 The actual selling expenses incurred in March, 1987 by the Lloyd Company are as follows:

Variable Expenses		Fixed Expenses	
Sales Commission	$8,700	Sales Salaries	$30,000
Advertising	7,200	Depreciation	5,000
Travel	5,100	Insurance	900
Delivery	3,550		

INSTRUCTIONS

(a) Prepare a flexible budget performance report for March using the budget data in Exercise 26-3, assuming that March sales were $170,000. Expected and actual sales are the same.

(b) Prepare a flexible budget performance report, assuming that March sales were $180,000. Expected sales and actual sales are the same.

(c) Comment on the importance of using flexible budgets in evaluating the performance of the sales manager.

E26-5 The Higgins Company's manufacturing overhead budget for the first quarter of 1987 contained the following data:

Variable Costs		Fixed Costs	
Indirect materials	$12,000	Supervisory salaries	$30,000
Indirect labor	10,000	Depreciation	7,000
Utilities	8,000	Property taxes and insurance	8,000
Maintenance	6,000	Maintenance	5,000

Actual variable costs were: indirect materials $13,200, indirect labor $9,600, utilities $9,000, and maintenance $4,000. Actual fixed costs equaled budgeted costs except for property taxes and insurance, which were $8,100.

All costs are considered controllable by the production department manager except for depreciation, property taxes, and insurance.

INSTRUCTIONS

(a) Prepare a flexible overhead budget report for the first quarter.

(b) Prepare a responsibility performance report for the first quarter.

E26-6 Glen Pentel was given the following static budget report for the Clothing Department of the Glenco Company for the month of October.

CLOTHING DEPARTMENT
Budget Report
For the Month Ended October 31, 1987

	Budget	Actual	Difference Favorable F Unfavorable U
Sales in units	8,000	9,000	1,000 F
Variable Costs:			
Sales commissions	$ 2,000	$ 2,250	$ 250 U
Advertising expense	800	850	50 U
Travel expense	4,000	4,900	900 U
Free samples given out	1,000	1,300	300 U
Total variable costs	7,800	9,300	1,500 U

	Budget	Actual	Difference Favorable F Unfavorable U
Fixed costs:			
Rent	1,500	1,500	-0-
Sales salaries	1,200	1,200	-0-
Office salaries	800	800	-0-
Depreciation – autos (sales staff)	300	300	-0-
Advertising expense	200	200	-0-
Total fixed costs	4,000	4,000	-0-
Total costs	$11,800	$13,300	$1,500 U

As a result of this budget report, Glen was called into the president's office and congratulated on his fine sales performance. He was reprimanded, however, for allowing his costs to get out of control. The president pointed out that the 1,000 extra units sold brought in $1,200 dollars in additional gross profit, but at an apparent cost of $1,500 extra dollars.

Glen knew something was wrong with the performance report that he had been given. However, he was not sure what to do, and comes to you for advice.

INSTRUCTIONS

(a) Prepare a budget report based on flexible budget data to help Glen.

(b) Was the president right when he said, "The 1,000 extra units sold actually cost us more than what we got?"

(c) Was Glen right about being evaluated using the wrong performance report?

(d) If the president was right, what can we say about Glen's performance? If the president was wrong, explain why.

E26–7 The Sandra Company has three production departments: Fabricating, Enameling, and Assembling. At a department managers' meeting, the controller uses flexible budget graphs to explain total budgeted costs. Separate graphs based on direct labor hours are used for each department. The graphs show the following:

1. At zero direct labor hours, the total budgeted cost line and the fixed cost line intersect the vertical axis at $40,000 in the Fabricating Department, $50,000 in the Enameling Department, and $28,000 in the Assembling Department.
2. At normal capacity of 60,000 direct labor hours, the line drawn from the total budgeted cost line intersects the vertical axis at $160,000 in the Fabricating Department, $140,000 in the Enameling Department, and $103,000 in the Assembling Department.

INSTRUCTIONS

(a) State the total budgeted cost formula (fixed cost plus variable cost per direct labor hour) for each department.

(b) Compute the total budgeted cost for each department, assuming actual direct labor hours worked were 62,000, 58,000, and 59,000, in the Fabricating, Enameling, and Assembling Departments, respectively.

(c) Prepare the flexible budget graph for the Fabricating Department, assuming the maximum direct labor hours in the relevant range is 100,000. Use increments of 20,000 direct labor hours on the horizontal axis and increments of $50,000 on the vertical axis.

E26-8 The Montoye Company's organization chart includes the president; the vice-president of production; three assembly plants—Dallas, Atlanta, and Tucson; and two departments within each plant—Machining and Finishing. Budget and actual manufacturing cost data for July 1987 are as follows:

Finishing Department—Dallas: Direct materials $42,000 actual, $46,000 budget; direct labor $83,000 actual, $82,000 budget; manufacturing overhead $51,500 actual, $49,200 budget.

Machining Department—Dallas: Total manufacturing costs $218,000 actual, $215,000 budget.

Atlanta Plant: Total manufacturing costs $426,000 actual, $421,000 budget.

Tucson Plant: Total manufacturing costs $497,000 actual, $499,000 budget.

The Dallas plant managers office costs were $95,000 actual and $92,000 budget. The vice-president of production's office costs were $132,000 actual and $130,000 budget. Office costs are not allocated to departments and plants.

INSTRUCTIONS

Prepare the reports in a responsibility reporting system for (a) the Finishing Department—Dallas, (b) the plant manager—Dallas, and (c) the vice-president of production. Use the format on page 1033.

E26-9 Meredith Manufacturing produces and sells a single product. On April 1, there were no finished units in inventory. During April, 30,000 units were produced and 27,000 units were sold. The accounting department prepared the income statement below using absorption costing.

MEREDITH MANUFACTURING
Income Statement
For the Month Ended April 30, 1987
Absorption Costing

Sales		$1,080,000
Cost of goods sold		
Inventory, April 1	$ -0-	
Cost of goods manufactured	900,000	
Cost of goods available for sale	900,000	
Inventory, April 30	90,000	
Cost of goods sold		810,000
Gross profit		270,000
Selling and administrative expenses		261,000
Net income		$ 9,000

Fixed manufacturing costs are $240,000 per month, and fixed selling and administrative expenses are $180,000 per month.

INSTRUCTIONS

Prepare an income statement for April using variable costing. Use the CVP income statement format.

E26-10 The Allen-Stuart Equipment Company manufactures and distributes industrial air compressors. The following costs are available for the year ended December 31, 1987. The company has no beginning inventory. In 1987, 1,500 units were produced, but only 1,200 units were sold. The unit selling price was $4,500.

Variable costs per unit	
Direct materials	$ 500
Direct labor	1,500
Variable manufacturing overhead	300
Variable selling and administrative expenses	75
Annual fixed costs and expenses	
Manufacturing overhead	$1,200,000
Selling and administrative expenses	100,000

INSTRUCTIONS

(a) Calculate the cost of one unit of product using (1) absorption costing, and (2) variable costing.

(b) Prepare a 1987 income statement for the Allen-Stuart Company using (1) absorption costing, and (2) variable costing.

PROBLEMS

P26–1 The Barnard Manufacturing Company produces one product, Zebo. Because of wide fluctuations in demand for Zebo, the Assembly Department experiences significant variations in monthly production levels.

The master overhead budget for the year, based on 300,000 direct labor hours, and the actual overhead costs incurred in July in which 28,000 labor hours were worked, and 28,000 hours were expected to be worked, are as follows:

Overhead Cost	Master Budget	Actual in July
Variable:		
Indirect labor	$ 360,000	$32,000
Indirect materials	210,000	20,000
Utilities	90,000	8,000
Maintenance	60,000	5,400
Fixed:		
Supervision	150,000	12,500
Depreciation	120,000	10,000
Insurance and taxes	60,000	5,000
Total	$1,050,000	$92,900

INSTRUCTIONS

(a) Prepare a flexible overhead budget, assuming monthly production levels range from 20,000 to 30,000 direct labor hours. Use increments of 2,500 direct labor hours.

(b) Prepare a budget performance report for July comparing actual results with budget data based on (1) the master budget and (2) the flexible budget. (Hint: For the master budget, assume costs are incurred evenly throughout the year.)

(c) Which comparison is most meaningful in evaluating the department manager's performance? Why?

(d) State the formula for computing the total budgeted overhead costs in the Barnard Company. (Fixed cost plus variable cost per unit.)

(e) Prepare the flexible budget graph showing total budgeted costs at 25,000 and 27,500 direct labor hours. Use increments of 5,000 on the horizontal axis and increments of $10,000 on the vertical axis.

P26-2 The Cullen Company estimates that 240,000 direct labor hours will be worked during 1987 in the Assembly Department. On this basis, the following budgeted manufacturing overhead data are computed:

Variable Overhead Costs		Fixed Overhead Costs	
Indirect labor	$ 72,000	Supervision	$ 60,000
Indirect materials	36,000	Depreciation	30,000
Repairs	24,000	Insurance	9,600
Utilities	12,000	Rent	7,200
Lubricants	9,600	Property taxes	6,000
	$153,600		$112,800

It is estimated that direct labor hours worked each month will range from 16,000 to 24,000 hours.

During January, 19,000 direct labor hours were worked and the following overhead costs were incurred.

Variable Overhead Costs		Fixed Overhead Costs	
Indirect labor	$ 5,700	Supervision	$5,000
Indirect materials	3,200	Depreciation	2,500
Repairs	1,600	Insurance	800
Utilities	900	Rent	700
Lubricants	700	Property taxes	500
	$12,100		$9,500

INSTRUCTIONS

(a) Prepare a flexible manufacturing overhead budget for each increment of 2,000 direct labor hours over the relevant range.

(b) Prepare a manufacturing overhead budget report for January, assuming 19,500 direct labor hours were expected.

(c) Comment on management's efficiency in controlling manufacturing overhead costs in January.

(d) What overhead rate should be used in product costing in (1) January, and (2) February (assuming 22,000 direct labor hours worked)? Why?

P26-3 The Huegera Company uses budgets in controlling costs. The May 1987 budget report for the company's Packaging Department is as follows:

HUEGERA COMPANY
Budget Report
Packaging Department
For the Month Ended May 31, 1987

Manufacturing Costs	Budget	Actual	Difference Favorable F Unfavorable U
Variable costs:			
Direct materials	$ 30,000	$ 32,000	$2,000 U
Direct labor	40,000	43,000	3,000 U
Indirect materials	15,000	15,200	200 U
Indirect labor	10,000	10,500	500 U
Utilities	8,000	7,900	100 F
Maintenance	5,000	5,100	100 U
Total variable	108,000	113,700	5,700 U

Manufacturing Costs	Budget	Actual	Difference Favorable F Unfavorable U
Fixed costs:			
Rent	7,000	7,000	-0-
Supervision	8,000	8,000	-0-
Depreciation	5,000	5,000	-0-
	20,000	20,000	-0-
Total costs	$128,000	$133,700	$5,700 U

The budget amounts in the report were based on the master budget for the year, which assumed that 600,000 units would be produced. (Hint: The budget amounts above are one-twelfth of the master budget for the year.)

The company president was displeased with the department manager's performance. The department manager, who thought he had done a good job, could not understand the unfavorable results. In May, 55,000 units were produced.

INSTRUCTIONS

(a) Prepare a flexible budget for the Packaging Department, assuming monthly production will range from 40,000 to 60,000 units. Use 5,000 unit increments.

(b) Prepare a budget report for May using flexible budget data. Why does this report provide a better basis for evaluating performance than the report based on static budget data? Assume 55,000 units were expected to be produced.

(c) In June, 45,000 units were produced when 46,000 were expected. Prepare the budget report using flexible budget data, assuming (1) each variable cost was 20% less than its actual cost in May, and (2) fixed costs were the same in June as in May.

P26-4 The Marti Marker Company uses a responsibility reporting system. It has divisions in Denver, Seattle, and San Diego. Each division has three production departments: Cutting, Shaping, and Finishing. The responsibility for each department rests with a manager who reports to the division production manager. Each division manager reports to the vice-president of production. There are also vice-presidents for marketing, finance, and personnel. All vice-presidents report to the president.

In January 1987, controllable actual and budget manufacturing overhead cost data for the departments and divisions were as follows:

Manufacturing Overhead	Actual	Budget
Individual costs—Cutting Department—Seattle:		
Indirect labor	$ 73,000	$ 70,000
Indirect materials	46,700	46,000
Maintenance	11,300	12,000
Utilities	19,500	17,000
Insurance	5,000	5,000
Supervision	15,600	15,000
Miscellaneous	10,200	6,000
	$ 181,300	$ 171,000
Total costs:		
Shaping Department—Seattle	$ 158,000	$ 148,000
Finishing Department—Seattle	210,000	208,000
Denver division	676,000	673,000
San Diego division	722,000	715,000
	$1,766,000	$1,744,000

Additional overhead costs were incurred as follows: Seattle division production manager—actual costs $52,500, budget $51,000; vice-president of production—actual costs $65,700, budget $64,000; president—actual costs $75,400, budget $74,200. These expenses are not allocated.

The vice-presidents who report to the president, other than the vice-president of production, had the following expenses:

Vice-president	Actual	Budget
Marketing	$133,600	$130,000
Finance	107,000	105,000
Personnel	116,800	114,000

INSTRUCTIONS

(a) Prepare the following responsibility performance reports:
   1. Manufacturing overhead—Cutting Department manager—Seattle division.
   2. Manufacturing overhead—Seattle division manager.
   3. Manufacturing overhead—vice-president of production.
   4. Manufacturing overhead and expenses—president.
   Use the format on page 1033.

(b) Comment on the comparative performances of
   1. Department managers in the Seattle division.
   2. Division managers.
   3. Vice-presidents.

P26-5 The Ohio Metal Company produces the steel wire that goes into the production of paper clips. In 1987, the first year of operations, Ohio produced 40,000 miles of wire and sold 30,000 miles. In 1988, the production and sales results were exactly reversed. In each year, selling price per mile was $80, variable manufacturing costs were 25% of the sales price, variable selling expenses were $8.00 per mile sold, fixed manufacturing costs were $1,200,000 and fixed administrative expenses were $300,000.

INSTRUCTIONS

(a) Prepare comparative income statements for each year using variable costing.
(b) Prepare comparative income statements for each year using absorption costing.
(c) Reconcile the differences each year in income from operations under the two costing approaches.
(d) Comment on the effects of production and sales on net income under the two costing approaches.

ALTERNATE PROBLEMS

P26-1A The Sherman Company manufactures tablecloths. Sales have grown rapidly over the past two years. As a result, the president has installed a budgetary control system for 1987. The following data were used in developing the master manufacturing overhead budget for the Ironing Department, which is based on an activity index of direct labor hours.

Variable Costs	Rate per Direct Labor Hour	Annual Fixed Costs	
Indirect labor	$.40	Supervision	$27,000
Indirect materials	.50	Depreciation	18,000
Factory utilities	.30	Insurance	12,000
Factory repairs	.20	Rent	24,000

The master overhead budget was prepared on the expectation that 480,000 direct labor hours will be worked during the year. In June, 42,000 direct labor hours were worked and 42,000 were expected. At that level of activity, actual costs were as follows:

Variable—per direct labor hour: Indirect labor $.42, Indirect materials $.50, Factory utilities $.35, and Factory repairs $.12.

Fixed: same as budgeted.

INSTRUCTIONS

(a) Prepare a flexible manufacturing overhead budget, assuming production levels range from 30,000 to 50,000 direct labor hours. Use increments of 5,000 direct labor hours.

(b) Prepare a budget performance report for June comparing actual results with budget data based on (1) the master budget, and (2) the flexible budget. (Hint: For the master budget, assume costs are incurred evenly throughout the year.)

(c) Which comparison is most meaningful in evaluating the department manager's performance? Why?

(d) State the formula for computing the total budgeted overhead costs for the Sherman Company. (Fixed cost plus variable cost per unit.)

(e) Prepare the flexible budget graph, showing total budgeted costs at 35,000 and 45,000 direct labor hours. Use increments of 5,000 direct labor hours on the horizontal axis and increments of $10,000 on the vertical axis.

P26-2A The Mullet Company estimates that 360,000 direct labor hours will be worked during the coming year, 1987 in the Packaging Department. On this basis, the following budgeted manufacturing overhead cost data are computed for the year:

Fixed Overhead Costs		Variable Overhead Costs	
Supervision	$ 90,000	Indirect labor	$144,000
Depreciation	45,000	Indirect materials	90,000
Insurance	27,000	Repairs	54,000
Rent	36,000	Utilities	72,000
Property taxes	18,000	Lubricants	18,000
	$216,000		$378,000

It is estimated that direct labor hours worked each month will range from 24,000 to 36,000 hours.

During October, 28,000 direct labor hours were worked and the following overhead costs were incurred:

Fixed overhead costs: Supervision $7,500, Depreciation $3,750, Insurance $2,225, Rent $3,000, and Property taxes $1,500.

Variable overhead costs: Indirect labor $11,760, Indirect materials $6,400, Repairs $4,000, Utilities $5,900, and Lubricants $1,740.

INSTRUCTIONS

(a) Prepare a flexible manufacturing overhead budget for each 3,000 increment of direct labor hours over the relevant range.

(b) Prepare a flexible budget report for October, when 27,000 direct labor hours were expected.

(c) Comment on management's efficiency in controlling manufacturing overhead costs in October.

(d) What overhead rate should be used in product costing in (1) October, and (2) November (assuming 32,000 direct labor hours were worked)? Why?

P26-3A The Hernandez Company uses budgets in controlling costs. The August 1987 budget report for the company's Assembling Department is as follows:

HERNANDEZ COMPANY
Budget Report
Assembling Department
For the Month Ended August 31, 1987

Manufacturing Costs	Budget	Actual	Difference Favorable F Unfavorable U
Variable costs:			
Direct materials	$ 48,000	$ 47,000	$1,000 F
Direct labor	72,000	68,000	4,000 F
Indirect materials	24,000	24,200	200 U
Indirect labor	18,000	17,600	400 F
Utilities	15,000	14,900	100 F
Maintenance	9,000	9,100	100 U
Total variable	186,000	180,800	5,200 F
Fixed costs:			
Rent	12,000	12,000	-0-
Supervision	15,000	15,000	-0-
Depreciation	7,000	7,000	-0-
Total fixed	34,000	34,000	-0-
Total costs	$220,000	$214,800	$5,200 F

The budget data in the report are based on the master budget for the year, which assumed that 720,000 units would be produced. The Assembling Department manager is pleased with the report and expects a raise, or at least praise for a job well done. The company president, however, is unhappy with the results for August, because only 58,000 units were produced. (Hint: The budget amounts above are one-twelfth of the master budget.)

INSTRUCTIONS

(a) Prepare a flexible budget for the Assembling Department, assuming monthly production will range from 52,000 to 68,000 units. Use 4,000-unit increments.

(b) Prepare a budget report for August using flexible budget data. Why does this report provide a better basis for evaluating performance than the report based on static budget data? Assume 58,000 units were expected to be produced.

(c) In September, 64,000 units were produced when 65,000 were expected. Prepare the budget report using flexible budget data, assuming (1) each variable cost was 10% higher than its actual cost in August, and (2) fixed costs were the same in September as in August.

P26-4A The Gomez Company has three departments in each of its three stores in the Carmel area. The departments are Shoes, Hose, and Accessories. The stores are Oceanside, Mission Valley, and Santa Rio. Each department has a manager who reports directly to the general manager of the store. There are two vice-presidents, one for sales and one for purchasing. They report to the president, and the general managers report to the vice-presidents.

The shoe department of the Oceanside store had the following relevant expense data in June 1987:

Expense	Actual Expense	Budget Difference
Salaries	$13,000	$ -0-
Advertising	1,600	600 Unfavorable
Utilities	1,400	300 Unfavorable
Rent	5,000	-0-
Repairs	1,000	50 Favorable
Miscellaneous	700	550 Unfavorable
Total	$22,700	$1,400 Unfavorable

All expenses are controllable at the departmental level. The other departments at the Oceanside store had the following data: Hose—actual expenses $5,150, budget $4,825; Accessories—actual expenses $3,600, budget $3,950. The general manager of the Oceanside store incurred general and administrative expenses of $3,400 when $3,500 was budgeted. These expenses are not allocated to the departments.

The other stores reported the following results for the month: Mission Valley—actual expenses $33,825, budget $36,175; Santa Rio—actual expenses $20,150, budget $14,500.

The vice-president for purchasing lost the budget data for the three stores but not the differences from budget. The summarized results were:

Store	Actual Purchases	Budget Difference
Oceanside	$57,250	$8,915 Unfavorable
Mission Valley	84,435	7,095 Favorable
Santa Rio	35,885	3,005 Favorable

The general and administrative expenses for the vice-presidents and the president were as follows:

Officer	Actual	Budget
President	$26,500	$28,000
Vice-president, purchasing	16,500.	17,000
Vice-president, sales	18,900	18,200

These expenses are not allocated. The Gomez Company uses a responsibility reporting system.

INSTRUCTIONS

(a) Prepare the following responsibility reports:

1. Expense report for the manager of Shoe Department of the Oceanside store.
2. Expense report for the general manager of the Oceanside store.
3. Expense report for the vice-president, sales.
4. Expense and purchases report for the president.

Use the format on Page 1033.

(b) Comment on the following:

1. The comparative performances of the three departments of the Oceanside store.
2. The comparative performances of the three stores.
3. The comparative efficiencies of the two vice-presidents.

P26-5A The Walton Company manufactures subassembly units for automobile transmissions. On January 1, there was no inventory of finished goods. During January, Walton sold 20,000 units at $6 per unit. On January 31, there were 4,000 units of finished goods on hand. An analysis of January manufacturing costs shows that variable manufacturing costs were $3.15 per unit and fixed manufacturing costs were $32,400. Selling and administrative expenses were $20,000 in January of which 30% were variable.

In February, 18,000 units were produced and 22,000 units were sold at $6 per unit. Variable manufacturing costs per unit and variable selling and administrative expenses per unit were the same as in January. In addition, total fixed costs and expenses remained the same in February as in January.

INSTRUCTIONS

(a) Prepare comparative income statements for each month using variable costing.

(b) Prepare comparative income statements for each month using absorption costing.

(c) Reconcile the differences in income from operations in each month under the two costing approaches.

(d) Comment on the effects of production and sales on income under each of the costing approaches.

DECISION CASE

Parkhill Polytechnic Institute offers continuing education programs in many cities throughout the state. For the convenience of its faculty, the school operates a motor pool. In 1987, the motor pool operated with 15 automobiles, until March when two additional vehicles were acquired. The motor pool furnishes gasoline, oil, and other supplies for its automobiles. A mechanic does routine maintenance and minor repairs. Major repairs are done at a nearby commercial garage.

Each year, the supervisor of the motor pool submits an operating budget to the university administration. Depreciation (using the straight-line method) on the automobiles is recorded in the budget in order to determine the cost per mile of operating the vehicles. The operating budget for 1987 approved by university administration is as follows:

MOTOR POOL
Operating Budget
For the Year Ending December 31, 1987

Basis: 15 automobiles	
Expenses	
Gasoline	$ 18,000
Oil and minor repairs	5,400
Commercial repairs	2,700
Insurance	7,200
Salaries	36,000
Automobile depreciation	40,500
Total expenses	$109,800
Total miles	360,000
Total cost per mile	$ .3050

The annual budget was based on the following assumptions:

1. Annual mileage per car, 24,000.
2. Average miles per gallon of gasoline, 20.
3. Cost per gallon of gasoline, $1.00.
4. Cost per mile for oil and minor repairs, $0.015.
5. Annual cost per automobile for commercial repairs, $180.
6. Annual cost per automobile for insurance, $480.
7. Annual cost per automobile for depreciation, $2,700.

In April, the 17 vehicles were driven 33,000 miles and the following budget report was prepared by the university administration.

MOTOR POOL
Operating Budget Report
For the Month Ended April 30, 1987

	Budget	Actual Costs	Difference Favorable F Unfavorable U
Activity: Mileage	30,000	33,000	3,000 F
Expenses			
Gasoline	$ 1,500	$ 1,600	$ 100 U
Oil and minor repairs	450	480	30 U
Commercial repairs	225	200	25 F
Insurance	600	680	80 U
Salaries	3,000	3,000	-0-
Depreciation	3,375	3,825	450 U
Total expenses	$ 9,150	$ 9,785	$ 635 U

The supervisor is unhappy with the budget report because it is not based on a flexible budget.

INSTRUCTIONS

(a) What type of budget report was prepared by the university administration? Was the supervisor's unhappiness justified? Why?

(b) Prepare a budget report for April using a flexible budget.

(c) Evaluate the supervisor's performance based on the budget report in (b) above. (CMA adapted)

CHAPTER 27

Claremont McKenna College, California

CHAPTER 27

PERFORMANCE EVALUATION THROUGH STANDARD COSTS

STUDY OBJECTIVES

After studying this chapter, you should be able to:

1. Distinguish between a standard and a budget.
2. Identify the advantages of standard costs.
3. Describe how standards are set for direct materials, direct labor, and manufacturing overhead.
4. Indicate the formulas for analyzing direct material and direct labor variances.
5. Explain how manufacturing overhead variances are analyzed.
6. Discuss the reporting of variances and how management uses variance reports.
7. Enumerate the features of a standard cost accounting system.

Suppose you were assigned one of the following responsibilities: manufacturing 10,000 Champion spark plugs, making 500,000 Bruce Springsteen T-Shirts, or printing 200 wedding invitations. How would you want your performance to be evaluated? An important consideration would be whether you accomplished the task. Closely related would be whether or not you met the scheduled completion date and the expected quality control objectives. Collectively, these measures relate to your **effectiveness** in discharging your assigned responsibility.

Your boss would want to use some additional measures to evaluate your performance. These measures would relate to the **efficiency** of your work. Efficiency focuses on the cost of accomplishing the task. Efficiency measures are used to ascertain whether (1) the best cost was obtained in purchasing raw materials, (2) the specified quantities of raw materials were used, and (3) the

anticipated amount and level of skilled labor were utilized. Because most tasks are accomplished with limited resources, efficiency measures are often very demanding.

In this chapter we continue the study of controlling costs by considering additional measures that permit the evaluation of performance. We will first explain the performance measures called **standard costs** and illustrate how they are used. We will then describe a standard cost accounting system.

NEED FOR STANDARDS

Standards are a fact of life. You met the admission standards for the college or university you are attending. The automobile that you drive had to meet certain governmental environment standards. The hamburgers and salads you eat in a restaurant have to meet certain health and nutritional standards before they can be sold. The reason for standards in these cases is very simple: they help to insure that the overall quality of the product produced is high. Without standards, quality control is lost.

Standards are also common in business. Those imposed by government agencies are often called **regulations.** They include the Fair Labor Standards Act, the Equal Employment Opportunity Act, and a multitude of environmental standards. Standards established internally by a company may extend to personnel matters, such as employee absenteeism and ethical codes of conduct, quality control standards for products, and standard costs for goods and services.

Although we will focus on manufacturing operations in the remainder of this chapter, you should recognize that standard costs are also applicable to many other types of businesses. For example, a fast-foods restaurant such as McDonald's knows not only the price it should pay for pickles, beef, buns, and other ingredients, but also how much time it should take an employee to flip hamburgers. If too much is paid for pickles or too much time is taken to prepare Big Macs, the deviations are noticed and corrective action is taken. In addition, standard costs may be used in not-for-profit enterprises such as universities, charitable organizations, and governmental agencies.

DISTINCTION BETWEEN STANDARDS AND BUDGETS

In concept, **standards** and budgets are essentially the same. Both are predetermined costs and both contribute significantly to management planning and control. There is a difference, however, in the way the terms are expressed. A standard is a **unit** amount, whereas a budget is a **total** amount. Thus, it is customary to state that the standard cost of direct labor for a unit of product is $10. However, if 5,000 units of the product are produced, the $50,000 of direct labor is the budgeted labor cost. In this context, a standard is the budgeted cost per unit of product. A standard is, therefore, concerned with each individual cost component that makes up the entire budget.

There are important accounting differences between budgets and standards. Except in the application of manufacturing overhead to jobs and processes, budget data are not journalized in cost accounting systems. In contrast, as will be illustrated later in the chapter, standard costs may be incorporated into cost accounting systems. It is also possible for a company to report its inventories at standard cost in its financial statements but it is not possible to report inventories at budgeted costs.

Computerized standard cost systems present a major challenge to programmers. They are very long programs since they must include the complete general ledger, as well as the data base of standard costs for every product. They must also have the ability to make the variance computations and produce the variance reports like those discussed in this chapter.

WHY STANDARD COSTS?

Standard costs offer the following advantages to an organization.

1. Standard costs facilitate management planning by establishing expected future costs.
2. When properly set, they should promote greater economy and efficiency of operations by making employees more "cost-conscious."
3. They may be useful in setting selling prices for finished goods.
4. They contribute to management control by providing a basis for evaluating the performance of managers responsible for controlling costs.
5. Performance may be evaluated through "management by exception," as deviations (or variances) from standard are highlighted.
6. When standard costs are incorporated into the accounting system, they simplify the costing of inventories and reduce clerical costs.

These advantages will be realized only when standard costs are carefully established and prudently used. Using standards solely as a means of finding fault or placing blame can have a negative effect on managers. In an effort to minimize this effect, many companies offer wage incentives to those who meet their standards.

SETTING STANDARD COSTS—A DIFFICULT TASK

The setting of standard costs to produce a unit of product is a difficult task. It requires input from all persons who have responsibility for costs and quantities. To determine the standard cost of direct materials, the purchasing agents, product managers, quality control engineers, and production supervisors may

have to be consulted. In setting the cost standard for direct labor, pay rate data are obtained from the payroll department, and the labor time requirements may be determined by industrial engineers. The managerial accountant provides input to the standards-setting process through the accumulation of historical cost data and knowledge of the behavior of costs in response to changes in activity levels. The decision as to what the standard cost should be is, of course, a management responsibility.

Standards may be set at one of two levels: ideal or normal. **Ideal standards** represent the optimum level of performance under perfect operating conditions. In contrast, **normal standards** represent an efficient level of performance that is attainable under expected operating conditions.

Some managers believe ideal standards will stimulate the conscientious worker to ever-increasing improvement. However, most managers believe that because these standards are so difficult, if not impossible, to meet, they discourage self-improvement and lower the morale of the entire work force. Very few companies use ideal standards.

Most companies that use standards set them at a normal level. When properly set, normal standards should be **rigorous** but **attainable.** In setting normal standards, allowances are made for rest periods, machine breakdowns, and other "normal" contingencies pertaining to the production process. It will be assumed in the remainder of this chapter that standard costs are set at a normal level.

SETTING STANDARD COSTS—AN ILLUSTRATION

To illustrate the setting of standards, assume that Susan's Chili Factory manufactures and sells chili.[1] The cost of manufacturing Susan's chili consists of the costs of raw materials, labor to convert the basic ingredients to chili, and overhead. We will use material cost as an example. Three standards need to be developed. They are: (1) What should be the formula (mix) of ingredients for one gallon of chili? (2) What should be the normal wastage (or shrinkage) for the individual ingredients? and (3) What should be the standard cost for the individual ingredients that go into the chili? The schedule on the top of the next page indicates these standards and the resulting standard materials cost per gallon (rounded to nearest ounce).

The standard materials cost to make a gallon of chili is $6.85. To develop this standard cost, production and quality control departments should determine the proper formula to be used to make the chili. In addition, the engineering and production departments provide the data for the standard usage and wastage figures. The purchasing department is the main source of information for the standard costs for the ingredients.

Susan's chili factory also provides a good illustration as to how standard costs can be used by management in controlling costs. Suppose that summer droughts have reduced crop yields and, as a result, prices have doubled for beans, onions, and peppers. In such a case, actual costs will be significantly

[1]Illustration adopted from David R. Beran, "Cost Reduction Through Control Reporting," *Management Accounting*, April 1982, pp. 29–33.

Standard Materials Cost for Susan's Chili

Computation of standard materials cost

Item	(1) Per Gallon	(2) Waste	(3) Standard Usage (1) × (2) + (1)	(4) Standard Cost	(5) Standard Cost/Gallon (3) × (4)
Hamburger	32 oz.	6%	34 oz.	$.08/oz.	$2.72
Chili beans	32 oz.	6%	34 oz.	.05/oz.	1.70
Onions	8 oz.	11%	9 oz.	.07/oz.	.63
Peppers	8 oz.	11%	9 oz.	.20/oz.	1.80
Standard materials cost per gallon					$6.85

higher than standard costs, which will cause management to evaluate the situation. Such an evaluation might lead to an increase in the price charged for a gallon of chili, reexamination of the product mix to see if other types of ingredients can be used, or curtailment of production until ingredients can be purchased at or near standard costs. Similarly, assume that poor maintenance procedures caused the onion-dicing blades to become dull. As a result, usage of onions to make a gallon of chili tripled. Because this deviation is quickly highlighted through standard costs, corrective action can be taken.

SETTING STANDARDS—A CASE STUDY

To establish the standard cost of producing a product, it is necessary to establish standards for each manufacturing cost element—direct materials, direct labor, and manufacturing overhead. The standard for each element is derived from a consideration of the standard price to be paid and the standard quantity to be used. To illustrate, we will assume that Xonic, Inc. wishes to use standard costs to measure performance in filling an order for 1,000 gallons of Weedo, a liquid weed killer.

DIRECT MATERIALS

The price standard for direct materials should be based on the purchasing department's best estimate of the **cost of raw materials.** This is frequently based on an analysis of current purchase prices. The price standard should also include an amount for related costs such as receiving, storing, and handling. The materials price standard per pound of material for Xonic's weed killer is:

Setting direct materials price standard

Item	Price
Purchase price, net of discounts	$2.70
Freight	.20
Receiving and handling	.10
Standard direct materials price per pound	$3.00

The **direct materials quantity standard** is expressed as a physical measure, such as pounds, barrels, or board feet. In setting the standard, consideration should be given to both the quality and quantity of materials required to manufacture the product. The standard should include allowances for unavoidable waste and normal spoilage. To illustrate, the standard quantity per unit for Xonic, Inc. is determined as follows:

Setting direct materials quantity standard

Item	Quantity (Pounds)
Required materials	3.5
Allowance for waste	.4
Allowance for spoilage	.1
Standard direct materials quantity per unit	**4.0**

From the price and quantity standards, the standard material cost per gallon of product is $12.00 ($3.00 × 4.0 pounds).

DIRECT LABOR

The **direct labor price standard** is based on current wage rates adjusted for anticipated changes, such as COLAs (cost of living adjustments) included in many union contracts. In addition, the price standard generally includes employer payroll taxes and fringe benefits, such as paid holidays and vacations. For Xonic, Inc., the direct labor price standard, often called the **standard direct labor rate,** is as follows:

Setting direct labor price standard

Item	Price
Hourly wage rate	$ 7.50
COLA	.25
Payroll taxes	.75
Fringe benefits	1.50
Standard direct labor rate per hour	**$10.00**

The objective in setting the **direct labor quantity standard** is to determine the aggregate time required to make one unit of the product. This standard, often called the direct labor **efficiency** standard, is especially critical in labor- (as opposed to capital-) intensive companies. Allowances should be made in setting this standard for rest periods, cleanup, machine setup, and machine downtime. For Xonic, Inc., the direct labor quantity standard is determined as follows:

Setting direct labor quantity standard

Item	Quantity (Hours)
Actual production time	1.5
Rest periods and cleanup	.2
Setup and downtime	.3
Standard direct labor hours per unit	**2.0**

From the price and quantity standards, it is possible to establish the standard labor cost per gallon of Weedo at $20 ($10.00 × 2.0 hours).

MANUFACTURING OVERHEAD

For manufacturing overhead, a **standard predetermined overhead rate** is used in setting the standard. This rate is based on an **expected standard activity index.** For example, the index may be standard direct labor hours or standard direct labor cost. Xonic, Inc., uses standard direct labor hours as the activity index. The company expects to produce 13,200 gallons of Weedo during the year at normal capacity. Since it takes two direct labor hours for each gallon, total standard direct labor hours are 26,400 (13,200 × 2). At this level of activity, overhead costs are expected to be $132,000 of which $79,200 are variable and $52,800 are fixed. The standard predetermined overhead rates, therefore, are computed as follows:

Computing predetermined overhead rates

Budgeted Overhead Costs	Amount	÷	Standard Direct Labor Hours	=	Overhead Rate per Direct Labor Hour
Variable	$ 79,200		26,400		$3.00
Fixed	52,800		26,400		2.00
Total	$132,000		26,400		$5.00

The standard manufacturing overhead rate per gallon of Weedo is determined by applying the predetermined overhead rate per hour ($5) to the standard direct labor hours per gallon (2 hours). The overhead standard, therefore, is $10 per gallon ($5 × 2 hours).

TOTAL STANDARD COST PER UNIT

Now that the standard quantity and price have been established per unit of product for each of the manufacturing cost elements, the total standard cost to produce one gallon of Weedo can be determined. The total cost is $42 per gallon, as shown on the following standard cost card.

Illustration of standard cost card

Xonic, Inc.
Standard Cost Card

Product: Weedo **Unit Measure: Gallon**

Manufacturing Cost Elements	Standard Quantity	×	Standard Price	=	Standard Cost
Direct materials	4 pounds		$ 3.00		$12.00
Direct labor	2 hours		$10.00		20.00
Manufacturing overhead	2 hours		$ 5.00		10.00
					$42.00

The standard cost card provides the basis for determining variances from standards.

DETERMINING VARIANCES FROM STANDARDS

One of the major uses of standard costs is to identify **variances** from the standards. A comparison of actual costs with standard costs reveals the amount of the variance. In producing 1,000 gallons of Weedo in the month of June, Xonic, Inc. incurred the following costs:

Actual costs

Direct materials	$13,020
Direct labor	20,580
Variable overhead	6,500
Fixed overhead	4,400
Total actual costs	$44,500

Total standard costs are determined by multiplying the units produced by the standard cost per unit. The total standard cost of Weedo is $42,000 (1,000 gallons × $42). Thus, the total variance is $2,500, as shown below.

Computation of total variance

Actual costs	$44,500
Standard costs	42,000
Total variance	$ 2,500

When actual costs exceed standard costs, the variance is unfavorable. Thus, the $2,500 variance is unfavorable. An unfavorable variance has a negative connotation. It suggests that too much was paid for one or more of the manufacturing cost elements or that the elements were used inefficiently. If actual costs are less than standard costs, the variance is favorable. A favorable variance has a positive inference. It suggests efficiencies in incurring manufacturing costs and in using direct materials, direct labor, and manufacturing overhead. However, be careful! A favorable variance could be obtained in printing wedding invitations, for example, by using an inferior grade of paper. Similarly, a favorable variance may be achieved in installing tires on an automobile assembly line by tightening only half of the lug bolts. The point should be obvious: a variance is not favorable if quality control standards have been sacrificed. To properly interpret the significance of a variance, you must analyze it to determine the underlying cause(s).

ANALYZING VARIANCES

The analysis of a variance begins with a determination of the cost elements that comprise the variance. For each cost element, a total variance is computed. Then this variance is analyzed into a price variance and a quantity variance. The relationships are shown graphically as follows:

Relationships of variances

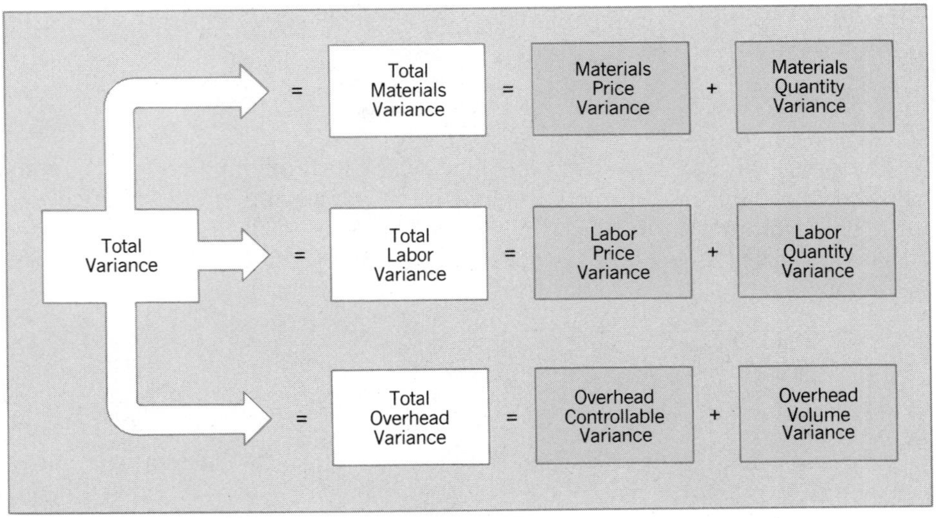

Each of the variances is explained below.

DIRECT MATERIALS VARIANCES

In completing the order for 1,000 gallons of Weedo, Xonic, Inc. used 4,200 pounds of direct materials purchased at a cost of $3.10 per unit. The **total materials variance** is computed from the following formula:

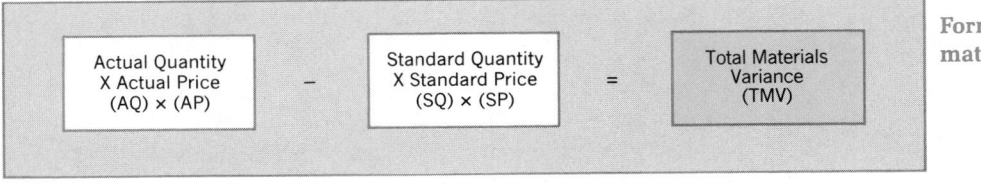

Formula for total materials variance

Actual Quantity X Actual Price (AQ) × (AP) − Standard Quantity X Standard Price (SQ) × (SP) = Total Materials Variance (TMV)

For Xonic, Inc., the total materials variance is $1,020 ($13,020 − $12,000) unfavorable as shown below:

$$(4{,}200 \times \$3.10) \quad - \quad (4{,}000 \times \$3.00) \quad = \quad \$1{,}020 \text{ U}$$

Next, the total variance is analyzed to determine the amount attributable to costs and to quantity (use). The **materials price variance** is computed from the following formula:[2]

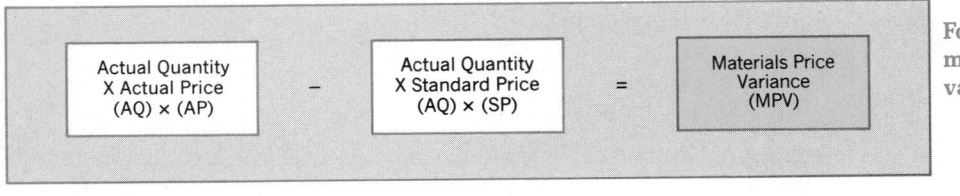

Formula for materials price variance

Actual Quantity X Actual Price (AQ) × (AP) − Actual Quantity X Standard Price (AQ) × (SP) = Materials Price Variance (MPV)

[2]It will be assumed that all materials purchased during the period are used in production and no units remain in inventory at the end of the period.

For Xonic, Inc., the materials price variance is $420 ($13,020 – $12,600) unfavorable as shown below:

$$(4{,}200 \times \$3.10) \quad - \quad (4{,}200 \times \$3.00) \quad = \quad \$420 \text{ U}$$

The price variance can also be computed by multiplying the actual quantity purchased by the difference between the actual and standard price per unit. The computation in this case is 4,200 × ($3.10 – $3.00) = $420(U).

The **materials quantity (or use) variance** is determined from the following formula:

Formula for materials quantity variance

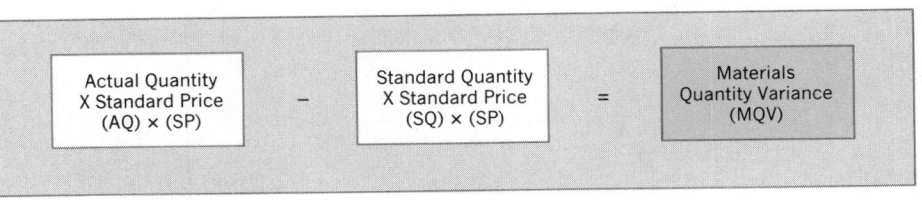

Actual Quantity X Standard Price (AQ) × (SP)	–	Standard Quantity X Standard Price (SQ) × (SP)	=	Materials Quantity Variance (MQV)

For Xonic, Inc., the materials quantity variance is $600 ($12,600 – $12,000) unfavorable, as shown below:

$$(4{,}200 \times \$3.00) \quad - \quad (4{,}000 \times \$3.00) \quad = \quad \$600 \text{ U}$$

This variance can also be computed by applying the standard price to the difference between actual and standard quantities. The computation in this example is $3.00 × (4,200 – 4,000) = $600(U).

The total materials variance of $1,020(U), therefore, consists of the following:

Summary of materials variance

Materials price variance	$ 420 U
Materials quantity variance	600 U
Total materials variance	$1,020 U

Using a Variance Matrix

Some accountants favor the use of a matrix to determine and analyze a variance. When the matrix is used, the formulas are computed first and then the variances. The completed matrix for the direct materials variance for Xonic, Inc. is as follows on the next page. The matrix provides a convenient structure for determining each variance.

The matrix approach can be formatted very nicely into a computer spreadsheet template. Although large firms use customized standard cost software, spreadsheets are used very effectively by small- and medium-sized firms to satisfy their standard cost system needs.

Matrix for direct materials variance

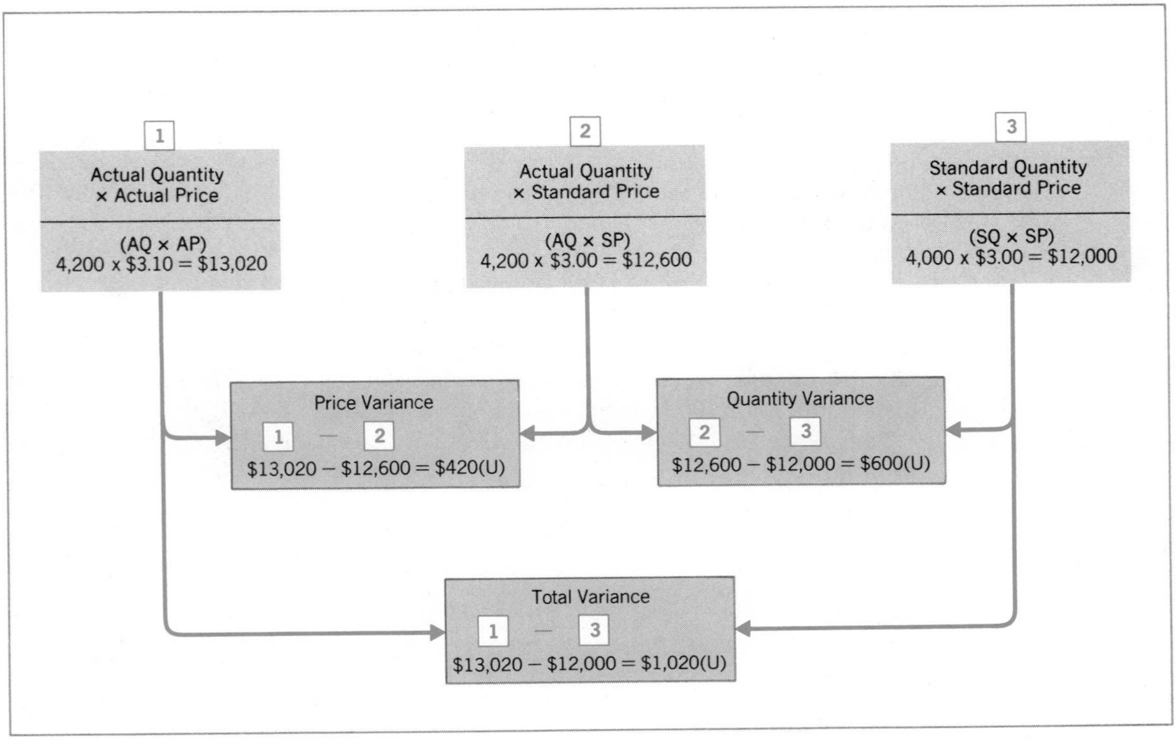

DIRECT LABOR VARIANCES

The process of determining direct labor variances is the same as for determining the direct materials variances. In completing the Weedo order, Xonic, Inc., incurred 2,100 direct labor hours at an average hourly rate of $9.80 when the standard hours allowed for the units produced was 2,000 hours (1,000 units × 2 hours) and the standard rate was $10 per hour. The **total labor variance** is obtained from the following formula:

Formula for total labor variance

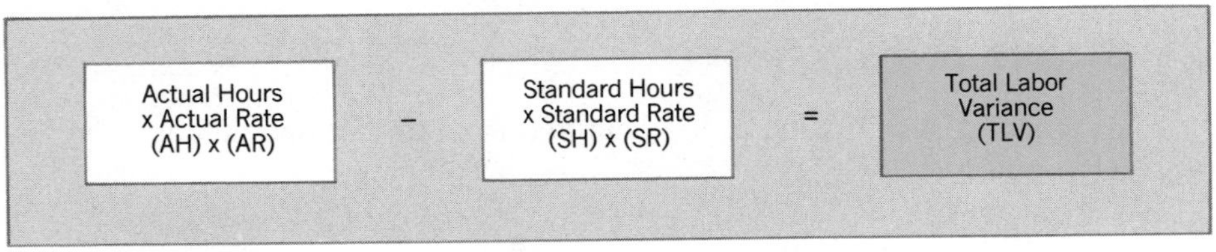

The total labor variance is $580 ($20,580 – $20,000) unfavorable, as shown below:

$$(2{,}100 \times \$9.80) \quad - \quad (2{,}000 \times \$10.00) \quad = \quad \$580\ U$$

The formula for the **labor price (or rate) variance** is:

Formula for labor price variance

Actual Hours x Actual Rate (AH) x (AR)	−	Actual Hours x Standard Rate (AH) x (SR)	=	Labor Price Variance (LPV)

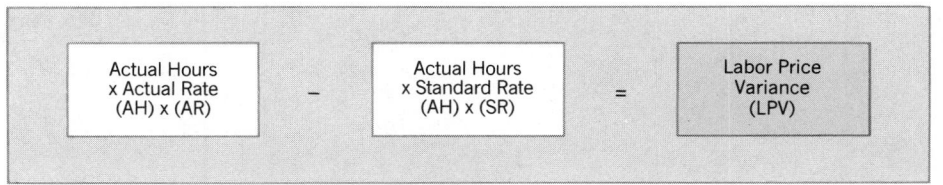

For Xonic, Inc., the labor price variance is $420 ($20,580 − $21,000) favorable as shown below:

(2,100 × $9.80) − (2,100 × $10.00) = $420 F

This variance can also be computed by multiplying actual hours worked by the difference between the standard and actual pay rates. The computation in this example is 2,100 × ($10.00 − $9.80) = $420(F).

The **labor quantity (or efficiency) variance** is derived from the following formula:

Formula for labor quantity variance

Actual Hours x Standard Rate (AH) x (SR)	−	Standard Hours x Standard Rate (SH) x (SR)	=	Labor Quantity Variance (LQV)

For Xonic, Inc., the labor quantity variance is $1,000 ($21,000 − $20,000) unfavorable as shown below:

(2,100 × $10.00) − (2,000 × $10.00) = $1,000 U

The same result can be obtained by multiplying the standard rate by the difference between actual hours worked and standard hours allowed. In this case the computation is $10.00 × (2,100 − 2,000) = $1,000(U).

The total direct labor variance of $580 U, therefore, consists of

Summary of labor variances

Labor price variance	$ 420 F
Labor quantity variance	1,000 U
Total direct labor variance	$ 580 U

The foregoing results can also be obtained from the following matrix on the next page.

MANUFACTURING OVERHEAD VARIANCES

The computation of the manufacturing overhead variances is conceptually the same as the computation of the materials and labor variances. However, the task is more challenging for manufacturing overhead because both variable and fixed overhead must be considered.

Matrix for direct labor variances

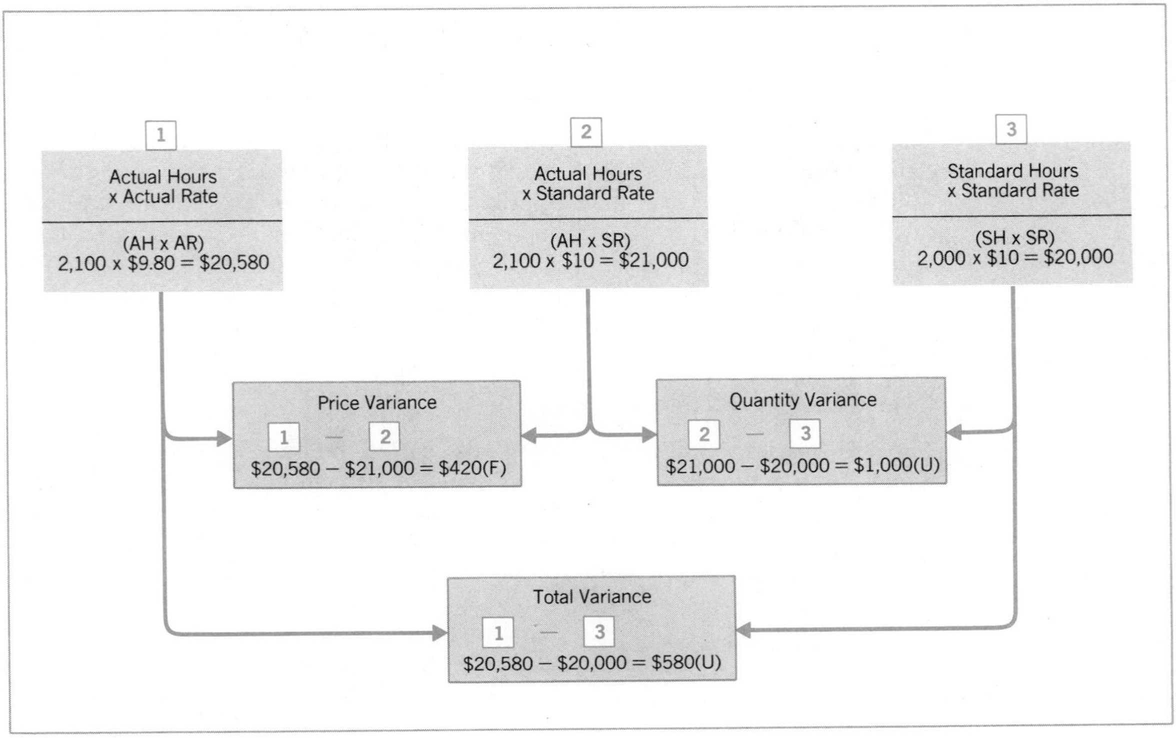

Total Overhead Variance

The total overhead variance is the difference between actual overhead costs and overhead costs applied. As indicated earlier, manufacturing overhead costs incurred were $10,900, as follows:

Actual overhead costs

Variable overhead	$ 6,500
Fixed overhead	4,400
Total actual overhead	$10,900

With standard costs, manufacturing overhead costs are applied to work in process on the basis of the **standard hours allowed** for the work done. Standard hours allowed are the hours that should have been worked for the units produced. For the Weedo order, the standard hours allowed are 2,000 and the predetermined overhead rate is $5 per direct labor hour. Thus, overhead applied is $10,000 (2,000 × $5). Note that the actual hours of direct labor (2,100) are not used in applying manufacturing overhead.

The formula for the total overhead variance is:

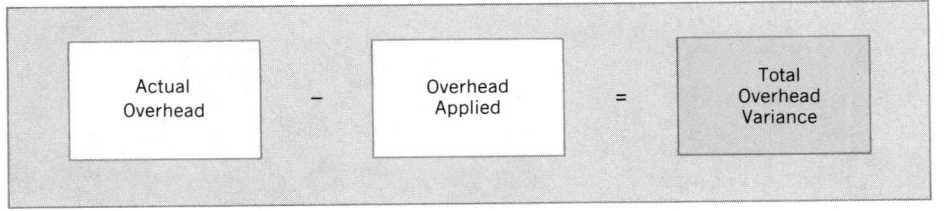

Formula for total overhead variance

Actual Overhead	–	Overhead Applied	=	Total Overhead Variance

Thus, for Xonic, Inc., the total overhead variance is $900 unfavorable as shown below:

$10,900 − $10,000 = $900 U

The analysis of the total overhead variance may be made through either a two- or three-variance approach. We will use the two-variance approach in the chapter; the three-variance approach will be explained in the appendix to this chapter. Under the two-variance approach, the overhead variance can be analyzed through a price variance and a quantity variance. The name usually given to the price variance is the overhead controllable variance whereas the quantity variance is referred to as the overhead volume variance.

Overhead Controllable Variance

The **overhead controllable variance** (also called the **budget** or **spending variance**) is the difference between the actual overhead costs incurred and the budgeted costs for the **standard hours allowed.** The budgeted costs are determined from the flexible manufacturing overhead budget. The budget for Xonic, Inc. is as follows:

Flexible budget using standard direct labor hours

XONIC, INC.
Flexible Manufacturing Overhead Budget

Activity Index				
Standard direct labor hours	1,800	2,000	2,200	2,400
Costs				
Variable costs				
Indirect materials	$1,800	$ 2,000	$ 2,200	$ 2,400
Indirect labor	2,700	3,000	3,300	3,600
Utilities	900	1,000	1,100	1,200
Total variables	5,400	6,000	6,600	7,200
Fixed costs				
Supervision	3,000	3,000	3,000	3,000
Depreciation	1,400	1,400	1,400	1,400
Total fixed	4,400	4,400	4,400	4,400
Total costs	$9,800	$10,400	$11,000	$11,600

As shown, the budgeted costs for 2,000 standard hours are $10,400 ($6,000 variable and $4,400 fixed).[3]

The formula for the overhead controllable variance is:

Formula for overhead controllable variance

Actual Overhead − Overhead Budgeted = Overhead Controllable Variance

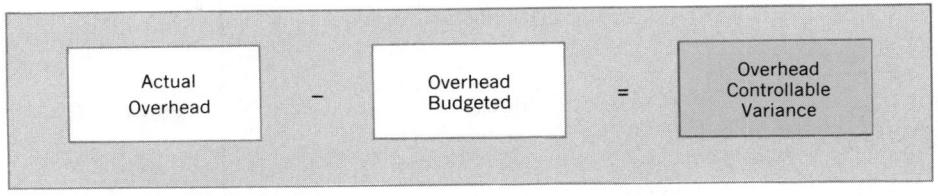

[3]The flexible budget formula is: variable costs $3 per hour plus fixed costs $4,400. Thus, total budgeted costs are ($3 × 2,000) + $4,400, or $10,400.

The controllable overhead variance for Xonic, Inc., is $500 unfavorable as shown below:

$10,900 − $10,400 = $500 U

Most controllable variances are associated with variable costs as fixed costs are usually known at the time the budget is prepared. In Xonic, Inc., the variance is accounted for by comparing the actual variable overhead costs ($6,500) with the budgeted variable costs ($6,000).

If desired by top management, a comparison can also be made for actual and budgeted overhead for each manufacturing overhead cost that contributes to the controllable variance. In addition, cost and quantity variances can be developed for each overhead cost, such as indirect materials and indirect labor.

Overhead Volume Variance

The **overhead volume variance** indicates whether plant facilities were efficiently used during the period. The formula for computing the volume variance is as follows:

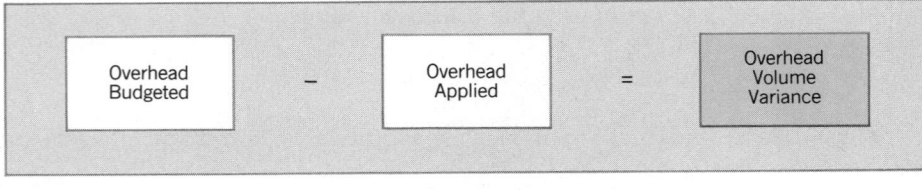

Formula for overhead volume variance

Overhead Budgeted − Overhead Applied = Overhead Volume Variance

Both of the factors in this formula have been explained above. The overhead budgeted is the same as the amount used in computing the controllable variance or $10,400. Overhead applied of $10,000 is the amount used in determining the total overhead variance. For Xonic, Inc., the overhead volume variance is $400 unfavorable as shown below:

$10,400 − $10,000 = $400 U

Further insight into the volume variance can be obtained from a detailed analysis of the two factors. As shown in the flexible manufacturing overhead budget, the budgeted overhead of $10,400 consists of $6,000 variable and $4,000 fixed. As indicated in determining the predetermined overhead rate on page 1061, the rate of $5 consists of $3 variable and $2 fixed. The detailed analysis, therefore, is:

Detailed analysis of overhead volume variance

Overhead budgeted		
Variable costs	$6,000	
Fixed costs	4,400	$10,400
Overhead applied		
Variable costs (2,000 × $3)	6,000	
Fixed costs (2,000 × $2)	4,000	10,000
Overhead volume variance—unfavorable		$ 400

A careful examination of this analysis indicates that **the overhead volume variance relates solely to fixed costs** (fixed costs budgeted $4,400 − fixed costs applied $4,000). Thus, **the volume variance measures the amount that fixed overhead costs are under- or overapplied.**

We have already established that total fixed costs remain the same at every level of activity within the relevant range. Since a predetermined overhead rate based on normal capacity is used in applying overhead, it follows that if the standard hours allowed are less than the standard hours at normal capacity, fixed overhead costs will be underapplied. In contrast, if production exceeds normal capacity, fixed overhead costs will be overapplied.

An alternative formula for computing the overhead volume variance, therefore, is:

Alternative formula for overhead volume variance

Fixed Overhead Rate × (Normal Capacity Hours − Standard Hours Allowed) = Overhead Volume Variance

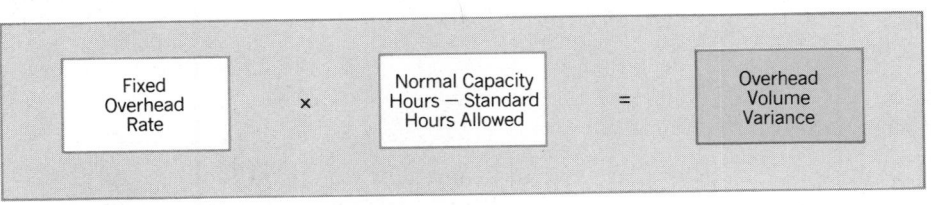

In Xonic, Inc., normal capacity is 26,400 hours for the year or 2,200 hours for a month (26,400 ÷ 12) and the fixed overhead rate is $2 per hour. Thus, the volume variance is $400 unfavorable as shown below:

$$\$2 \times (2{,}200 - 2{,}000) = \$400 \text{ U}$$

The total overhead variance of $900 unfavorable for Xonic, Inc., therefore, consists of the following:

Summary of overhead variance

Overhead controllable variance	$500 U
Overhead volume variance	400 U
Total overhead variance	$900 U

The foregoing results can also be obtained from the following matrix on the next page.

In computing the overhead variances under the two-variance approach, it is important to remember the following:

1. Standard hours allowed are used in each of the variances.
2. Budgeted costs for the controllable variance are derived from the flexible budget.
3. The controllable variance generally pertains to variable costs.
4. The volume variance pertains solely to fixed costs.

REPORTING VARIANCES

All variances should be reported to appropriate levels of management as soon as possible. The sooner management is informed, the sooner problems can be evaluated and corrective actions taken.

Matrix for manufacturing overhead variance

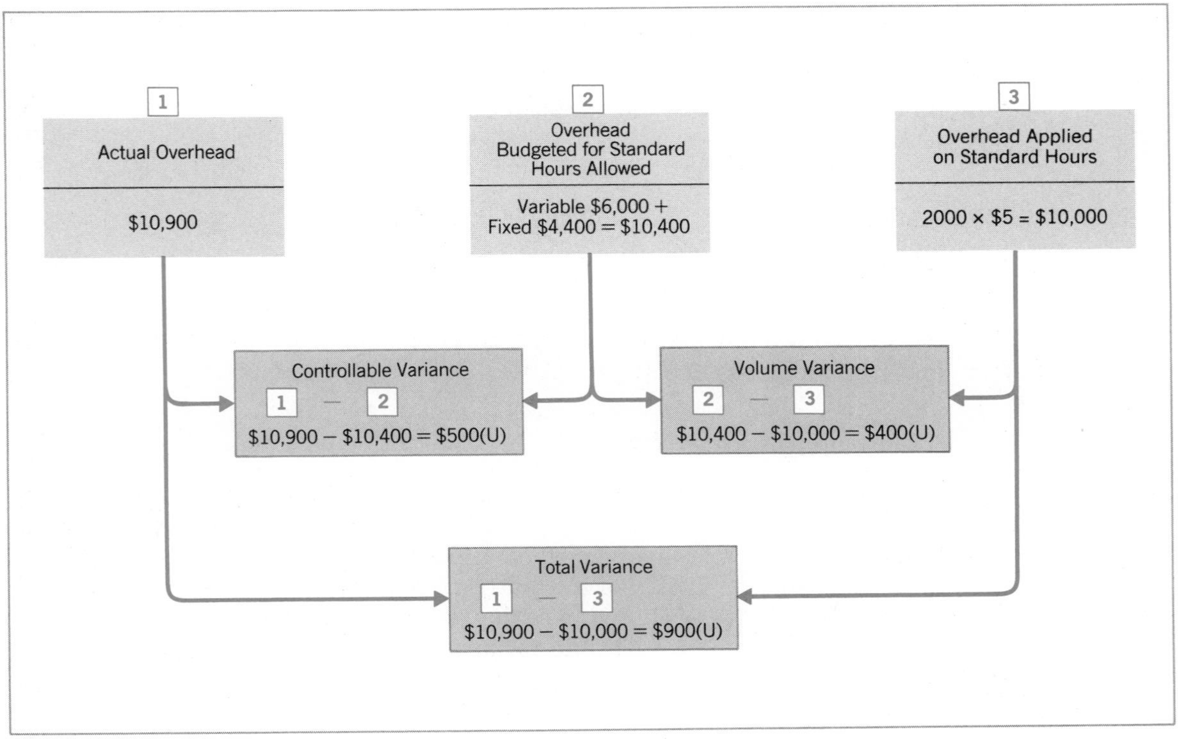

The form, content, and frequency of variance reports vary considerably among companies. One approach is to prepare weekly reports for each department that has primary responsibility for controlling the cost. Under this approach, materials price variances are reported to the purchasing department and all other variances are reported to the production department that did the work. The following report for Xonic, Inc., with the materials for the Weedo order listed first, illustrates this approach.

Materials price variance report

Xonic, Inc.
Variance Report—Purchasing Department
For Week Ended June 8, 1987

Type of Materials	Quantity Purchased	Actual Price	Standard Price	Price Variance	Explanation
X 100	4,200 lbs.	$3.10	$3.00	$420 U	Rush order.
X 142	1,200 units	2.75	2.80	60 F	Quantity discount.
A 85	600 doz.	5.20	5.10	60 U	Regular supplier on strike.
Total price variance				$420 U	

The explanation column is completed after consultation with the purchasing department manager.

Variance reports facilitate the principle of "management by exception." For example, the vice-president of purchasing can use the report illustrated above to evaluate the effectiveness of the purchasing department manager.

Similarly, the vice-president of production can use production department variance reports to determine how well each production manager is controlling costs. In using variance reports, top management normally looks for **significant variances.** The significance of a variance may be judged on the basis of some quantitative measure, such as more than 10% of the standard or more than $1,000.

CAUSES OF VARIANCES

What are the causes of a variance? The causes may relate to both internal and external factors as explained below.

MATERIALS VARIANCES

The investigation of a materials price variance usually begins in the purchasing department. Many factors affect the price paid for raw materials. These include the delivery method used, availability of quantity and cash discounts, and the quality of the materials requested. To the extent that these factors have been considered in setting the price standard, the purchasing department should be responsible for any variances. It should be recognized, however, that a variance may be beyond the control of the purchasing department. In a period of inflation, prices may rise faster than expected. Moreover, actions by groups over which the company has no control, such as the OPEC nations who sharply increased oil prices, may cause an unfavorable variance. There are times when a production department may be responsible for the price variance. This may occur when a rush order forces the company to pay a higher price for the materials.

The starting point for determining the cause(s) of an unfavorable materials quantity variance is in the production department. If the variances are due to inexperienced workers, faulty machinery, and carelessness, the production department would be responsible. However, if the materials obtained by the purchasing department were of inferior quality, then the purchasing department should be responsible.

LABOR VARIANCES

Labor price variances usually result from two factors: (1) paying workers higher wages than expected, and (2) misallocation of workers. In companies where pay rates are determined by union contracts, labor price variances should be very infrequent. When workers are not unionized, there is a much higher likelihood of such variances. The responsibility for these variances rests with the manager who authorized the wage increase. Misallocation of the work force refers to using skilled workers in place of unskilled workers and vice versa. The use of an inexperienced worker instead of an experienced one will result in a favorable price variance because of the lower pay rate of the unskilled worker. An unfavorable price variance would result if the skilled worker were substituted for the inexperienced employee. The production department generally is responsible for labor price variances resulting from misallocation of the work force.

Labor quantity variances relate to the efficiency of workers. An investigation of the causes of a quantity variance generally focuses on the production department. The causes of an unfavorable variance may be worker fatigue, faulty machinery, or carelessness. These causes are the responsibility of the production department. However, if the excess time is due to inferior materials, the responsibility falls outside the production department.

MANUFACTURING OVERHEAD VARIANCES

Since the controllable variance relates to variable manufacturing costs, the responsibility for the variance rests with the production department. The cause of a variance may be (1) higher than expected use of indirect materials, indirect labor, and factory supplies, or (2) increases in indirect manufacturing costs, such as fuel and maintenance costs.

The overhead volume variance is the responsibility of the production department if the cause is inefficient use of direct labor or machine breakdowns. However, when the cause is a lack of sales orders, the responsibility rests outside the production department.

STANDARD COST ACCOUNTING SYSTEM

A **standard cost accounting system** is a double-entry system of accounting in which standard costs are used in making entries and standard cost variances are formally recognized in the accounts. A standard cost system may be used with either job order or process costing. At this point, we will explain and illustrate a standard cost job order cost accounting system. The system includes two important assumptions: (1) variances from standards are recognized at the earliest opportunity, and (2) the work in process account is maintained exclusively on the basis of standard costs. In practice, there are many variations among standard cost systems. However, the system described here should facilitate your transition to a specific company's system.

JOURNAL ENTRIES

The transactions of Xonic, Inc. will be used to illustrate the journal entries. You will note as you study the entries that the major difference between the entries and those for the job order cost accounting system in Chapter 22 is the variance accounts.

1. Purchase raw materials on account for $13,020 when the standard cost is $12,600.

Raw Materials Inventory	12,600	
Materials Price Variance	420	
Accounts Payable		13,020
(To record purchase of materials)		

The inventory account is debited for actual quantities at standard cost. This enables the perpetual materials records to show actual quantities. The price variance, which is unfavorable, is debited to Materials Price Variance.

2. Incur direct labor costs of $20,580 when the standard labor cost is $21,000.

Factory Labor	21,000	
Labor Price Variance		420
Wages Payable		20,580
(To record direct labor costs)		

Like the raw materials inventory account, Factory Labor is debited for actual hours worked at the standard hourly rate of pay. In this case, the labor variance is favorable. Thus, Labor Price Variance is credited.

3. Incur actual manufacturing overhead costs of $10,900.

Manufacturing Overhead	10,900	
Accounts Payable/Cash/Acc. Depreciation		10,900
(To record overhead incurred)		

The controllable overhead variance is not recorded at this time. It is dependent on standard hours applied to work in process, which is not known at the time overhead is incurred.

4. Issue raw materials for production at a cost of $12,600 when the standard cost is $12,000.

Work in Process Inventory	12,000	
Materials Quantity Variance	600	
Raw Materials Inventory		12,600
(To record issuance of raw materials)		

Work in Process Inventory is debited for standard materials quantities used at standard prices. The variance account is debited because the variance is unfavorable. Raw Materials Inventory is credited for actual quantities at standard prices.

5. Assign factory labor to production at a cost of $21,000 when standard cost is $20,000.

Work in Process Inventory	20,000	
Labor Quantity Variance	1,000	
Factory Labor		21,000
(To assign factory labor to jobs)		

Work in Process Inventory is debited for standard labor hours at standard rates, and the unfavorable variance is debited to Labor Quantity Variance. The credit to Factory Labor "clears" the balance in this account.

6. Apply manufacturing overhead to production, $10,000.

Work in Process Inventory	10,000	
Manufacturing Overhead		10,000
(To assign overhead to jobs)		

Work in Process Inventory is debited for standard hours multiplied by the standard overhead rate.

7. Transfer completed work to finished goods, $42,000.

Finished Goods Inventory	42,000	
Work in Process Inventory		42,000
(To record transfer of completed work to finished goods)		

In this example, both inventory accounts are at standard cost.

8. The 1,000 gallons of Weedo are sold for $60,000.

Accounts Receivable	60,000	
Cost of Goods Sold	42,000	
Sales		60,000
Finished Goods Inventory		42,000
(To record sale of finished goods and the cost of goods sold)		

Cost of Goods Sold is debited at standard cost. Gross profit, in turn, is the difference between sales and the standard cost of goods sold.

9. Recognize unfavorable overhead variances: controllable, $500; volume, $400.

Overhead Controllable Variance	500	
Overhead Volume Variance	400	
Manufacturing Overhead		900
(To recognize overhead variances)		

This entry recognizes the overhead variances. The information needed for this entry is often not available until the end of the accounting period.

LEDGER ACCOUNTS

The cost accounts for Xonic, Inc., after posting the journal entries are on the next page. Note that six variance accounts are included in the ledger. The remaining accounts are the same as those illustrated for a job order cost system in Chapter 22 in which only actual costs were used.

STATEMENT PRESENTATION OF VARIANCES

In income statements prepared for management, cost of goods sold is stated at standard cost and the variances are separately disclosed, as shown on page 1077. The statement is based entirely on the production and sale of Weedo and assumes selling and administrative costs of $3,000.

Observe that each variance is shown, as well as the total variances. In this example, variations from standard reduced net income by $2,500.

Cost accounts with variances

Raw Materials Inventory

Debit	Credit
(1) 12,600	(4) 12,600

Factory Labor

Debit	Credit
(2) 21,000	(5) 21,000

Manufacturing Overhead

Debit	Credit
(3) 10,900	(6) 10,000
	(9) 900

Materials Price Variance

Debit	Credit
(1) 420	

Materials Quantity Variance

Debit	Credit
(4) 600	

Labor Price Variance

Debit	Credit
	(2) 420

Labor Quantity Variance

Debit	Credit
(5) 1.000	

Overhead Controllable Variance

Debit	Credit
(9) 500	

Overhead Volume Variance

Debit	Credit
(9) 400	

Work in Process Inventory

Debit	Credit
(4) 12,000	(7) 42,000
(5) 20,000	
(6) 10,000	

Finished Goods Inventory

Debit	Credit
(7) 42,000	(8) 42,000

Cost of Goods Sold

Debit	Credit
(8) 42,000	

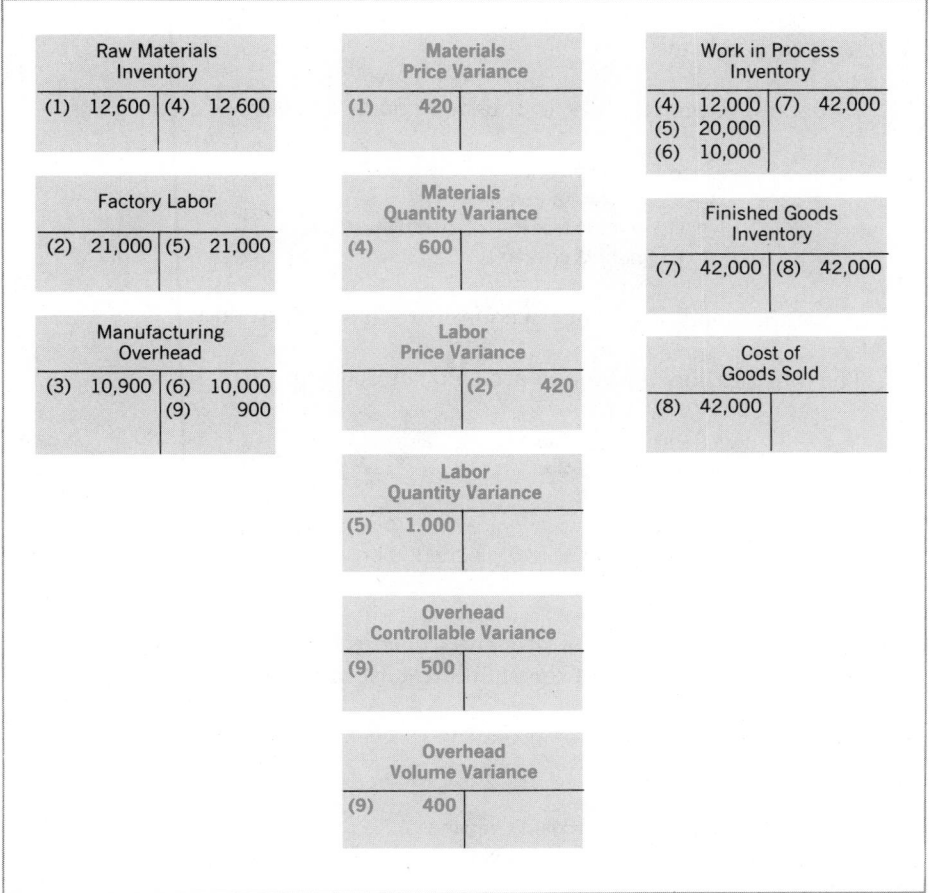

In financial statements prepared for stockholders and other external users, standard costs may be used. The costing of inventories at standard costs is in accordance with generally accepted accounting principles when there are no significant differences between actual costs and standard costs. Hewlett-Packard and Westinghouse Electric, for example, report their inventories at standard costs. However, if there are significant differences between actual and standard costs, inventories and cost of goods sold must be reported at actual costs.

Variances in income statement

XONIC, INC.
Income Statement
For the Month Ended June 30, 1987

Sales		$60,000
Cost of goods sold (at standard)		42,000
Gross profit (at standard)		18,000
Variances		
Materials price	$ 420	
Materials quantity	600	
Labor price	(420)	
Labor quantity	1,000	
Overhead controllable	500	
Overhead volume	400	
Total variances (unfavorable)		2,500
Gross profit (actual)		15,500
Selling and administrative expenses		3,000
Net income		$12,500

SUMMARY OF STUDY OBJECTIVES

1. Both standards and budgets are predetermined costs. The primary difference is that a standard is a unit amount, whereas a budget is a total amount. A standard may be regarded as the budgeted cost per unit of product.

2. Standard costs offer a number of advantages to an organization. They (a) facilitate management planning, (b) promote greater economy and efficiency, (c) are useful in setting selling prices, (d) contribute to management control, (e) permit "management by exception," and (f) simplify the costing of inventories and reduce clerical costs.

3. The direct materials price standard should be based on the delivered cost of raw materials plus an allowance for receiving and handling. The direct materials quantity standard should establish the required quantity plus an allowance for waste and spoilage.

The direct labor price standards should be based on current wage rates and anticipated adjustments such as COLAs. In addition, it generally includes payroll taxes and fringe benefits. Direct labor quantity standards should be based on required production time plus an allowance for rest periods, cleanup, machine setup, and machine downtime.

For manufacturing overhead, a standard predetermined overhead rate is used based on an expected standard activity index such as standard direct labor hours or standard direct labor cost.

4. The formulas for the direct materials variances are:

$$\left(\frac{\text{Actual quantity}}{\times \text{ actual cost}}\right) - \left(\frac{\text{Standard quantity}}{\times \text{ standard cost}}\right) = \text{Total materials variance}$$

$$\left(\frac{\text{Actual quantity}}{\times \text{ actual cost}}\right) - \left(\frac{\text{Actual quantity}}{\times \text{ standard cost}}\right) = \text{Materials price variance}$$

$$\left(\frac{\text{Actual quantity}}{\times \text{ standard cost}}\right) - \left(\frac{\text{Standard quantity}}{\times \text{ standard cost}}\right) = \text{Materials quantity variance}$$

The formulas for the direct labor variances are:

$$\left(\frac{\text{Actual hours}}{\times \text{ actual cost}}\right) - \left(\frac{\text{Standard hours}}{\times \text{ standard rate}}\right) = \text{Total labor variance}$$

$$\left(\frac{\text{Actual hours}}{\times \text{ actual rate}}\right) - \left(\frac{\text{Actual hours}}{\times \text{ standard rate}}\right) = \text{Labor price variance}$$

$$\left(\frac{\text{Actual hours}}{\times \text{ standard rate}}\right) - \left(\frac{\text{Standard hours}}{\times \text{ standard rate}}\right) = \text{Labor quantity variance}$$

5. The formulas for the manufacturing overhead variances are:

Actual overhead − Overhead applied = Total overhead variance

Actual overhead − Overhead budgeted = Overhead controllable variance

Overhead budgeted − Overhead applied = Overhead volume variance

6. Variances are reported in variance reports. The reports facilitate management by exception because significant differences can be highlighted.

7. In a standard cost accounting system, standard costs are journalized and posted and separate variance accounts are maintained in the ledger. When differences between actual costs and standard costs do not differ significantly, inventories may be reported at standard costs.

APPENDIX 27–A

Three-Variance Analysis of Manufacturing Overhead

The three-variance analysis of manufacturing overhead is an expansion or refinement of the two-variance analysis. The similarities and differences between the analyses are:

Two- vs. three-variance analysis

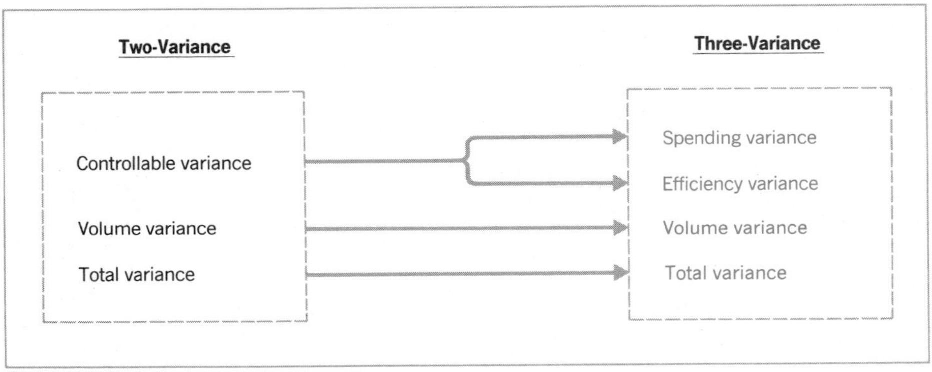

As illustrated, the three-variance method of analysis divides the controllable variance into two variances, a spending variance and an efficiency variance. The expanded analysis provides management with more relevant data for assessing responsibility for deviations from planned objectives. In addition, this analysis eliminates any management misinterpretation of the significance of a controllable variance. It is possible, for example, for a small controllable variance to be the net result of the offsetting effects of a large unfavorable spending variance and a large favorable efficiency variance (or vice versa).

To illustrate the computations of the three variances, we will again use the overhead data for Xonic, Inc., which are summarized below:

Summarized overhead data

Actual overhead incurred	$10,900	Fixed overhead:	
Overhead applied	$10,000	Annual	$52,800
Actual hours worked	2,100	Month	$ 4,400
Standard hours allowed	2,000	Predetermined	
Standard hours at		overhead rates:	
normal capacity	2,200	Variable	$3
		Fixed	2
		Total	$5

It will be recalled that the controllable variance for the month was $500 unfavorable, the volume variance was $400 unfavorable, and the total vari-

ance was $900 unfavorable under the two-variance method. As shown below, the three-variance analysis requires only one more budgeted amount than the two-variance approach. This amount is the **budgeted allowance for actual hours worked** using flexible budget data.

Spending Variance

The **overhead spending variance** is the difference between overhead incurred and overhead allowed for the **actual hours worked.** The overhead allowed is based on the flexible budget formula of variable costs plus fixed costs. At Xonic, Inc., 2,100 actual hours were worked. The computation of the spending variance is as follows:

Computation of spending variance

Overhead budgeted for actual hours worked		
Variable overhead ($3 × 2,100)	$6,300	
Fixed overhead	4,400	$10,700
Overhead incurred		10,900
Spending variance		$ 200 U

In this case, the department manager has spent $200 more than was allowed. The department manager is responsible for this variance because the budget data are based on the activity level actually attained.

Efficiency Variance

This variance involves the comparison of budget allowances for two activity levels: (1) actual hours worked, and (2) standard hours allowed for the work done. For Xonic, Inc., standard hours allowed were 2,000. The computation of the efficiency variance is shown below:

Computation of efficiency variance

Overhead budgeted for actual hours worked		
Variable overhead ($3 × 2,100)	$6,300	
Fixed overhead	4,400	$10,700
Overhead budgeted for standard hours allowed		
Variable overhead ($3 × 2,000)	6,000	
Fixed overhead	4,400	10,400
Efficiency variance		$ 300 U

A study of the computations above will show that the efficiency variance is equal to the difference between actual and standard hours allowed (2,100 − 2,000 = 100) times the variable overhead rate ($3) or $300. This result will always hold since budgeted fixed overhead costs will remain the same, within the relevant range, regardless of the level of production.

The **overhead efficiency variance** reveals the costs added or saved, because the actual level of activity is more or less than the standard activity level for the units produced. This variance may be the responsibility of either the department foreman or a production manager.

For Xonic, Inc., the sum of the spending variance ($200 unfavorable) and the efficiency variance ($300 unfavorable) equals the controllable variance ($500 unfavorable) under the two-variance analysis. This result is achieved because the budgeted overhead for actual hours worked ($10,700 in this case) has an offsetting effect under the three-variance analysis, and this amount is ignored under the two-variance analysis.

Comparative Summary

A summary of the computations and variances under the two- and three-variance analysis is presented below. The additional data required under the expanded analysis is underscored to help you understand the principal difference between the two approaches.

Comparative summary of two- and three-variance analysis

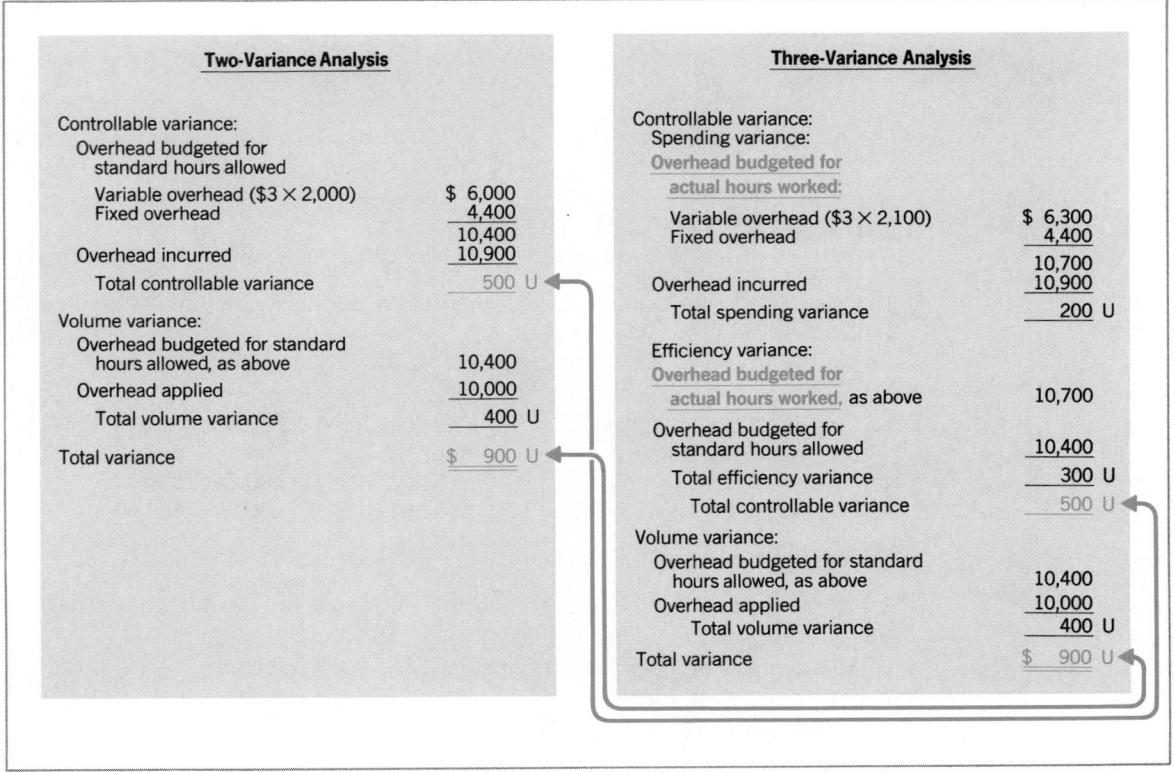

Two-Variance Analysis

Controllable variance:		
Overhead budgeted for standard hours allowed		
Variable overhead ($3 × 2,000)	$ 6,000	
Fixed overhead	4,400	
	10,400	
Overhead incurred	10,900	
Total controllable variance	500 U	
Volume variance:		
Overhead budgeted for standard hours allowed, as above	10,400	
Overhead applied	10,000	
Total volume variance	400 U	
Total variance	$ 900 U	

Three-Variance Analysis

Controllable variance:	
Spending variance:	
Overhead budgeted for actual hours worked:	
Variable overhead ($3 × 2,100)	$ 6,300
Fixed overhead	4,400
	10,700
Overhead incurred	10,900
Total spending variance	200 U
Efficiency variance:	
Overhead budgeted for actual hours worked, as above	10,700
Overhead budgeted for standard hours allowed	10,400
Total efficiency variance	300 U
Total controllable variance	500 U
Volume variance:	
Overhead budgeted for standard hours allowed, as above	10,400
Overhead applied	10,000
Total volume variance	400 U
Total variance	$ 900 U

GLOSSARY

Direct labor price standard, p. 1060

Direct labor quantity standard, p. 1060

Direct materials price standard, p. 1059

Direct materials quantity standard, p. 1060

Ideal standards, p. 1058

Labor price variance, p. 1065

Labor quantity variance, p. 1066

Materials price variance, p. 1063

Materials quantity variance, p. 1064

Normal standards, p. 1058

Overhead controllable variance, p. 1068

Overhead efficiency variance, p. 1080

Overhead spending variance, p. 1080

Overhead volume variance, p. 1069

Standard cost accounting system, p. 1073

Standard costs, p. 1056

Standard hours allowed, p. 1067

Standard predetermined overhead rate, p. 1061

Total labor variance, p. 1065

Total materials variance, p. 1063

Total overhead variance, p. 1067

Variances, p. 1062

DEMONSTRATION PROBLEM

The Manlow Company makes a cologne called Allure. The standard cost for one bottle of Allure is as follows:

	Standard			
Manufacturing Cost Elements	Quantity		Price	Cost
Direct materials	6 oz.	×	$ .90	$ 5.40
Direct labor	0.5 hrs.	×	$12.00	$ 6.00
Manufacturing overhead	0.5 hrs.	×	$ 4.80	$ 2.40
				$13.80

During the month, the following transactions occurred in manufacturing 10,000 bottles of Allure.

1. 58,000 ounces of materials were purchased at $1.00 per ounce.
2. All the materials purchased were used to produce the 10,000 bottles of Allure.
3. 4,900 direct labor hours were worked at a total labor cost of $56,350.
4. Variable manufacturing overhead incurred was $15,000 and fixed overhead incurred was $10,400.

The manufacturing overhead rate of $4.80 is based on a normal capacity of 5,200 direct labor hours. The total budget at this capacity is $10,400 fixed and $14,560 variable.

INSTRUCTIONS

Compute the total variance and the variances for each of the manufacturing cost elements.

SOLUTION TO DEMONSTRATION PROBLEM

Total Variance

Actual costs incurred:	
Direct materials	$ 58,000
Direct labor	56,350
Manufacturing overhead	25,400
	139,750
Standard cost (10,000 × $13.80)	138,000
Total variance	$ 1,750(U)

Direct Materials Variances

Total	=	$58,000 (58,000 × $1.00)	−	$54,000 (60,000 × $.90)	=	$4,000 U
Price	=	$58,000 (58,000 × $1.00)	−	$52,200 (58,000 × $.90)	=	$5,800 U
Quantity	=	$52,200 (58,000 × $.90)	−	$54,000 (60,000 × $.90)	=	$1,800 F

Direct Labor Variances

Total	=	$56,350 (4,900 × $11.50)	−	$60,000 (5,000 × $12.00)	=	$3,650 F
Price	=	$56,350 (4,900 × $11.50)	−	$58,800 (4,900 × $12.00)	=	$2,450 F
Quantity	=	$58,800 (4,900 × $12.00)	−	$60,000 (5,000 × $12.00)	=	$1,200 F

Overhead Variance

Total	=	$25,400 ($15,000 + $10,400)	−	$24,000 (5,000 × $4.80)	=	$1,400 U
Controllable	=	$25,400 ($15,000 + $10,400)	−	$24,400 ($14,000 + $10,400)	=	$1,000 U
Volume	=	$2.00 × 200 (5,200 − 5,000)			=	$ 400 U

***Note:** All **asterisked** Questions, Exercises, and Problems relate to material contained in the appendix to each chapter.

QUESTIONS

1. Maria Mota claims that standards and budgets are essentially the same. What are the reasons for her assertion?

2. Nick Nero claims that there are important accounting differences between standards and budgets. What are the reasons for his assertion?

3. Standard costs facilitate management planning. What are the other advantages of standard costs?

4. Contrast the roles of the management accountant and management in setting standard costs.

5. Distinguish between an ideal standard and a normal standard.

6. What factors should be considered in setting (a) the materials price standard, and (b) the materials quantity standard?

7. The objective in setting the direct labor quantity standard is to determine the aggregate time required to make one unit of product. Do you agree? What allowances should be made in setting this standard?

8. How is the predetermined overhead rate determined when standard costs are used?

9. What is the difference between a favorable price variance and an unfavorable price variance?

10. In each of the following formulas, supply the words that should be inserted for each number in parentheses.
a. (Actual quantity × (1) – ((2) × standard price) = total materials variance.
b. ((3) × actual price) – (actual quantity × (4)) = materials price variance.
c. (Actual quantity × (5)) – (standard quantity × (6)) = materials quantity standard.

11. In the direct labor variance matrix, there are three factors: (1) actual hours × actual rate, (2) actual hours × standard rate, and (3) standard hours × standard rate. Using the numbers, indicate the formulas for each of the direct labor variances.

12. The Dent Company's standard predetermined overhead rate is $8.00 per direct labor hour. For the month of June, 25,000 actual hours were worked and 27,000 standard hours were allowed. Normal capacity hours were 28,000. How much overhead was applied?

13. If the $8.00 per hour overhead rate in question 12 consists of $5.00 variable, and actual overhead costs were $220,000, what is the overhead controllable variance for June? Is the variance favorable or unfavorable?

14. Using the data in questions 12 and 13, what is the overhead volume variance for June? Is the variance favorable or unfavorable?

15. What is the purpose of the overhead volume variance? What is the basic formula for this variance?

16. Helen Holt does not understand why the overhead volume variance indicates that fixed overhead costs are under- or overapplied. Clarify this matter for Helen.

17. Stan Stone is attempting to outline the important points about overhead variances on a class examination. List four points that Stan should include in his outline.

18. How often should variances be reported to management? What principle may be used with variance reports?

19. What circumstances may cause the purchasing department to be responsible for both an unfavorable materials price variance and an unfavorable materials quantity variance?

20. (a) Explain the basic features of a standard cost accounting system. (b) What type of balance will exist in the variance account when (1) the materials price variance is unfavorable and (2) the labor quantity variance is favorable?

21. (a) How are variances reported in income statements prepared for management? (b) May standard costs be used in preparing financial statements for stockholders? Explain.

***22.** Indicate the formulas for computing the overhead spending and overhead efficiency variances.

EXERCISES

E27-1 Roberta Senior manufactures and sells homemade wine, and she wants to develop a standard cost per gallon. The following are required for production of a 50-gallon batch:

3,000 ounces of grape concentrate at $.02 per ounce
55 pounds of granulated sugar at $.30 per pound
60 lemons at $.65 each
50 yeast tablets at $.25 each
50 nutrient tablets at $.15 each
2,500 ounces of water at $.005 per ounce

Roberta estimates that 4% of the grape concentrate is wasted, 12% of the sugar is lost, and 20% of the lemons cannot be used.

INSTRUCTIONS

Compute the standard cost of the ingredients for one gallon of wine. (Carry computations to three decimal places.)

E27-2 The standard cost of Product B manufactured by the Keyo Company includes 3 units of direct materials at $5.00 per unit. During June, 30,000 units of direct materials are purchased at a cost of $4.60 per unit, and 28,000 units of direct materials are used to produce 9,000 units of Product B.

INSTRUCTIONS

(a) Compute the materials price and quantity variances.
(b) Journalize the purchase of the materials and the issuance of the materials, assuming a standard cost accounting system is used.
(c) Repeat (a) and (b), assuming the purchase price is $5.30 and the quantity used is 26,000 units.

E27-3 The Garcia Company's standard labor cost of producing one unit of Product DD is 4 hours at the rate of $12.00 per hour. During August, 41,000 hours of labor are incurred at a cost of $12.20 per hour to produce 10,000 units of Product DD.

INSTRUCTIONS

(a) Compute the labor price and quantity variances.
(b) Journalize the incurrence of the labor costs and the assignment of direct labor to production, assuming a standard cost accounting system is used.
(c) Repeat (a) and (b), assuming the standard is 4.2 hours of direct labor at $12.50 per hour.

E27-4 Plum, Inc., which produces a single product, has prepared the following standard cost sheet for one unit of the product.

Direct materials (8 pounds at $2.50 per pound)	$20.00
Direct labor (3 hours at $10.50 per hour)	$31.50

During the month of April, the company manufactures 240 units and incurs the following actual costs:

Direct materials (1,900 pounds)	$4,940
Direct labor (700 hours)	$7,700

INSTRUCTIONS

(a) Compute the materials and labor variances, using the variance matrix.

(b) Journalize the entries to record the variances.

E27-5 The following direct materials and direct labor data pertain to the operations of Simmons Manufacturing Company for the month of August.

Costs		Quantities	
Actual labor rate	$13.00 per hour	Actual hours incurred and used	4,150 hours
Actual materials price	$126.00 per ton	Actual quantity of materials purchased and used	1,251 tons
Standard labor rate	$12.00 per hour	Standard hours used	4,300 hours
Standard materials price	$130.00 per ton	Standard quantity of materials used	1,200 tons

INSTRUCTIONS

(a) Compute the materials and labor variances.

(b) List several possible explanations for each of the unfavorable variances calculated above and suggest where responsibility for the unfavorable result might be placed.

E27-6 The following information was taken from the annual manufacturing overhead cost budget of the Worby Company:

Variable manufacturing overhead costs	$33,000
Fixed manufacturing overhead costs	$20,625
Normal production level in hours	16,500
Normal production level in units	4,125

During the year, 4,000 units were produced, 16,100 hours were worked, and the actual manufacturing overhead was $53,500. Actual fixed manufacturing overhead costs equaled budgeted fixed manufacturing overhead costs. Overhead is applied on the basis of direct labor hours.

INSTRUCTIONS

(a) Compute the total, fixed, and variable predetermined manufacturing overhead rates.

(b) Compute the total, controllable, and volume overhead variances.

(c) Briefly interpret the overhead controllable and volume variances computed in (b) above.

E27-7 Manufacturing overhead data for the production of Product M by the Parna Company are as follows:

Overhead incurred for 51,000 actual direct labor hours worked	$211,000
Overhead rate (variable $3.00; fixed $1.00) at normal capacity of 54,000 direct labor hours	$ 4.00
Standard hours allowed for work done	52,000

INSTRUCTIONS

(a) Compute the total, controllable, and volume overhead variances (use the matrix).

(b) Journalize the incurrence of the overhead costs and the application of overhead to the job, assuming a standard cost accounting system is used.

(c) Prepare the adjusting entry for the overhead variances.

E27-8 Angella Company uses a standard cost accounting system. During January, Angella Company reported the following manufacturing variances:

Material price variance	$1,250 debit	Labor quantity variance	$ 725 debit
Material quantity variance	700 credit	Overhead controllable	200 credit
Labor price variance	525 debit	Overhead volume	1,300 debit

In addition, 6,000 units of product were sold at $8.00 per unit. Each unit sold had a standard cost of $6.00 each. Selling and administrative expenses were $8,000 for the month.

INSTRUCTIONS

Prepare an income statement for management for the month ending January 31, 1987.

E27-9 The Rosanne Company uses a standard cost accounting system. Some of the ledger accounts have been destroyed in a fire. The controller asks your help in reconstructing some missing entries and balances.

INSTRUCTIONS

Answer the following questions:

1. Materials Price Variance shows a $2,400 favorable balance, and Accounts Payable shows $126,000 of raw materials purchases. What was the amount debited to Raw Materials Inventory for raw materials purchased?
2. Materials Quantity Variance shows a $3,000 unfavorable balance, and Work in Process Inventory shows $121,000 for direct materials used. What was the amount credited to Raw Materials Inventory for direct materials used?
3. Labor Price Variance shows a $1,500 unfavorable balance, and Factory Labor shows a debit of $151,000 for wages incurred. What was the amount credited to Wages Payable?
4. Factory Labor shows a credit of $151,000 for direct labor used, and Labor Quantity Variance shows an $800 unfavorable balance. What was the amount debited to Work in Process for direct labor used?
5. Overhead applied to Work in Process totaled $168,000. If the total overhead variance was $1,200 unfavorable, what was the amount of overhead costs debited to Manufacturing Overhead?
6. Overhead Controllable Variance shows a debit balance of $1,600. What was the amount and type of balance (debit or credit) in Overhead Volume Variance?
7. There was no beginning work in process, and 90% of the work started was finished. What was the amount debited to Finished Goods Inventory?

E27-10 The Millard Company installed a standard cost system on January 1. The bookkeeper was inexperienced and failed to fully understand the system. An explana-

tion of the January transactions and the entries made by the bookkeeper are shown below.

1. Purchased 20,000 units of raw materials at a cost of $3.10 per unit. Standard cost was $3.00 per unit.

Raw Materials Inventory	62,000	
Accounts Payable		62,000

2. Issued 17,000 units of raw materials for jobs which required 17,500 standard units of raw materials.

Work in Process Inventory	52,700	
Raw Materials Inventory		52,500
Materials Quantity Variance		200

3. Incurred 15,100 actual hours of direct labor at an actual rate of $4.90 per hour. The standard rate is $5.00 per hour.

Factory Labor	73,990	
Wages Payable		73,990

4. Performed 15,100 hours of direct labor on jobs when standard hours were 15,300.

Work in Process Inventory	75,500	
Labor Quantity Variance		1,510
Factory Labor		73,990

5. Applied overhead to jobs at the rate of 100% of direct labor cost.

Work in Process Inventory	73,990	
Manufacturing Overhead		73,990

INSTRUCTIONS

Prepare separate correcting entries for each incorrect entry.

*E27-11 To produce 5,000 units of product, John Anderson Inc. has the following standard costs for direct labor and manufacturing overhead:

Direct labor (7,500 hours at $5 per hour)	$37,500
Manufacturing overhead (normal capacity 8,000 hours; budgeted fixed costs at normal capacity are $12,800; budgeted variable costs at normal capacity are $19,200)	

During the month of June, 4,500 units of products were produced and the following actual costs were incurred:

Direct labor (7,750 hours at $5.20 per hour)	$40,300
Manufacturing overhead – Variable costs	$17,500
Manufacturing overhead – Fixed costs	$12,800

INSTRUCTIONS

Compute the manufacturing overhead:

(a) Total variance
(b) Spending variance
(c) Efficiency variance
(d) Volume variance

PROBLEMS

P27-1 The Beman Corporation uses standard costs with its job order cost accounting system. In January, an order (Job No. 12) for 2,000 units of Product B was received. The standard cost of 1 unit of Product B is as follows:

Direct materials	3 pounds at $1.00 per pound	$ 3.00
Direct labor	1 hour at $8.00 per hour	8.00
Overhead	Variable $4.00 per hour; Fixed $2.00 per hour	6.00
Standard cost per unit		$17.00

Normal capacity for the month was 2,100 direct labor hours. During January, the following transactions applicable to Job No. 12 occurred:

1. Purchased 6,100 pounds of raw materials on account at $1.10 per pound.
2. Requisitioned 6,100 pounds of raw materials for Job No. 12.
3. Incurred 2,200 hours of direct labor at a rate of $7.80 per hour.
4. Worked 2,200 hours of direct labor on Job No. 12.
5. Incurred manufacturing overhead on account $12,300.
6. Applied overhead to Job No. 12.
7. Completed Job No. 12.
8. Billed customer for Job No. 12 at a selling price of $40,000.
9. Incurred selling and administrative expenses on account $2,000.

INSTRUCTIONS

(a) Journalize the transactions.
(b) Post to the job order cost accounts.
(c) Prepare the entry to recognize the overhead variances.
(d) Prepare the January income statement for management.
(e) Explain how the income statement would differ if it were prepared for stockholders.

P27-2 The Fabray Manufacturing Corporation accumulates the following data relative to jobs started and finished during the month of June 1987.

Costs and Production Data	Actual	Standard
Raw materials purchases, 10,000 units	$21,000	$20,000
Raw materials units used	10,000	9,600
Direct labor payroll	$122,100	$120,000
Direct labor hours worked	14,800	15,000
Manufacturing overhead incurred	$73,200	
Manufacturing overhead applied		$75,000
Hours expected to be worked at normal capacity		14,500
Budgeted fixed overhead for June		$29,000
Variable overhead rate per hour		$3.00

The jobs were sold for $295,000; selling and administrative expenses were 10% of sales.

INSTRUCTIONS

(a) Prepare an analysis of the variances from standard for direct materials, direct labor, and manufacturing overhead.

(b) Journalize the transactions, assuming a standard cost accounting system is used.
(c) Prepare an income statement for management. Ignore income taxes.

P27-3 The Garver Corporation manufactures a single product. The standard cost per unit of product is shown below:

Direct materials — 1 pound plastic at $7.00 per pound	$ 7.00
Direct labor — 1.5 hours at $12.00 per hour	18.00
Variable manufacturing overhead	9.00
Fixed manufacturing overhead	3.00
Total standard cost per unit	$37.00

The predetermined manufacturing overhead rate is $8.00 per direct labor hour ($12.00 ÷ 1.5). This rate was computed from a master manufacturing overhead budget based on normal production of 60,000 units for the year. The budget consisted of the following costs:

Variable overhead costs		
Indirect labor	$360,000	
Lubricants	90,000	
Utilities	54,000	
Maintenance	36,000	
Total variable		$540,000
Fixed overhead costs		
Supervision	90,000	
Depreciation	60,000	
Rent	30,000	
Total fixed		180,000
Total budgeted overhead costs		$720,000

Actual costs for October in producing 4,800 units were as follows:

Direct materials (5,100 pounds)	$ 37,230
Direct labor (7,100 hours)	88,040
Indirect labor	28,520
Lubricants	8,550
Utilities	3,800
Maintenance	2,900
Supervision	7,500
Depreciation	5,000
Rent	2,500
	$184,040

The Purchasing Department normally buys the quantities of raw materials that are expected to be used each month in production. Raw materials inventories, therefore, can be ignored.

INSTRUCTIONS

(a) Prepare a flexible manufacturing overhead budget for a range of 7,200–8,000 direct labor hours. Use increments of 200 hours.
(b) Compute the materials, labor, and overhead variances.

(c) Prepare an income statement for management for the month ending October 31, 1987, assuming (1) 4,500 units were sold at $55 per unit, (2) selling and administrative expenses were $32,000, and (3) there was no beginning finished goods inventory on October 1. Ignore income taxes.

P27-4 Perkins Manufacturing Company uses a standard cost accounting system. In 1987, 11,000 units were produced. Each unit required several pounds of direct materials at a standard price of $.63 per pound, and 1¼ standard hours of direct labor at a standard rate of $8.40 per hour. Normal capacity was 13,000 direct labor hours. During the year 38,500 pounds of raw materials were purchased and used.

INSTRUCTIONS

Answer the following questions:

1. If the materials price variance was $1,155 favorable, what was the total price paid for the materials?
2. If the materials quantity variance is $3,465 unfavorable, what was the standard quantity per unit?
3. What were the standard hours allowed for the units produced?
4. If the labor quantity variance is $4,620 favorable, what were the actual direct labor hours worked?
5. If the labor price variance is $5,280 unfavorable, what was the actual rate per hour?
6. If total budgeted manufacturing overhead was $78,000 at normal capacity, what was the predetermined overhead rate per direct labor hour?
7. What was the standard cost per unit of product?
8. How much overhead was applied to production during the year?
9. If the overhead volume variance is $3,000 favorable, what was the fixed overhead rate?
10. If the overhead controllable variance is $2,400 favorable, what were the total variable overhead costs incurred?
11. Using selected answers above, what were the total costs assigned to work in process?
12. What was the total variance for the year? Was this variance favorable or unfavorable?

P27-5 Mondale Clothiers is a small company that manufactures women's business suits. For the past several years, the company has used a standard cost accounting system. Mondale Clothiers prepares monthly income statements for management with variances reported within the statement.

In March 1987, 11,250 suits were produced. There were no finished suits on hand at either March 1 or March 31. The selling price per suit was $80.00. Selling expenses were 10% of sales; administrative expenses were 4% of sales plus $25,000.

The following standard and actual cost data applied to the month of March when normal capacity was 14,000 direct labor hours.

Cost Element	Standard (per unit)	Actual
Direct materials	8 yards at $4.50 per yard	$400,928 for 91,120 yards
Direct labor	1.2 hours at $12.75 per hour	$182,000 for 14,000 hours
Overhead	1.2 hours at $6.00 per hour	$49,000 fixed overhead
		$33,500 variable overhead

Overhead is applied on the basis of direct labor hours. At normal capacity, budgeted fixed overhead costs were $49,000.

INSTRUCTIONS

(a) Compute the total, price, and quantity variances for (1) materials, (2) labor, and (3) the total, controllable, and volume variances for manufacturing overhead.
(b) Journalize the entries to record the variances.
(c) Prepare an income statement for management for the month of March.
(d) What variances appear to merit investigation by management?

***P27-6** Norma Lockert Industries employs a standard cost accounting system. Overhead is applied to work in process on the basis of direct labor hours. The following overhead costs were budgeted on the basis of a normal capacity of 15,000 hours.

Budgeted variable overhead costs	$60,000
Budgeted fixed overhead costs	37,500
Total overhead costs	$97,500

In 1987, operating results were as follows:

Actual overhead incurred	$105,000
Actual hours worked	16,000
Standard hours allowed	15,500

INSTRUCTIONS

(a) Calculate the predetermined variable, fixed, and total overhead rates that were used in 1987.
(b) Determine the amount of overhead applied to production in 1987.
(c) Compute the overhead variances using the three-variance approach.
(d) What would the overhead controllable variance have been under the two-variance approach?
(e) Journalize and post the entries to Manufacturing Overhead under the three-variance approach.

ALTERNATE PROBLEMS

P27-1A The Lonned Manufacturing Company decided to use a standard cost accounting system at the beginning of 1987. The purchasing, personnel, engineering, and production departments established the following standards for the company's product:

Direct materials — 1.5 pounds at $4.00 per pound	$ 6.00
Direct labor — 2.0 hours at $9.00 per hour	18.00

As the accountant for the company, you have been given the task of establishing the standard overhead rate. You determine that normal capacity for each month is expected to be 8,500 direct labor hours. At this production level, budgeted fixed overhead is expected to be $42,500 and budgeted variable overhead is expected to be $25,500.

The following transactions occurred during January in producing 4,000 units of product for Job No. 84.

1. Purchased 6,250 pounds of raw materials on account at $3.90 per pound.

2. Requisitioned 6,250 pounds of raw materials for production.
3. Incured 7,900 hours of direct labor at $9.20 per hour.
4. Worked 7,900 hours of direct labor on Job No. 84.
5. Incurred $66,650 of manufacturing overhead on account.
6. Applied overhead to Job No. 84 on the basis of direct labor hours.
7. Transferred Job No. 84 to finished goods.
8. Billed customer for Job No. 84 at a selling price of $270,000.
9. Incurred selling and administrative expenses on account, $61,000.

INSTRUCTIONS

(a) Journalize the transactions.
(b) Post to the job order cost accounts.
(c) Prepare the entry to recognize the overhead variances.
(d) Prepare the income statement for management for January 1987.
(e) Explain how the income statement would differ if it were prepared for stockholders.

P27-2A Monay Manufacturing Company uses a standard cost accounting system. In July, 1987, it accumulates the following data relative to jobs started and finished:

Cost and Production Data	Actual	Standard
Raw materials		
Units purchased	17,500	
Units used	17,500	18,000
Unit cost	$3.20	$3.00
Direct labor		
Hours worked	29,000	30,000
Hourly rate	$11.75	$12.00
Manufacturing overhead		
Incurred	$87,200	
Applied		$90,000

Manufacturing overhead was applied on the basis of direct labor hours. Normal capacity for the month was 28,000 direct labor hours. At normal capacity, budgeted overhead costs were: variable $56,000 and fixed $28,000.

Jobs finished during the month were sold for $700,000; selling and administrative expenses were 15% of sales.

INSTRUCTIONS

(a) Prepare an analysis of the variances for direct materials, direct labor, and manufacturing overhead.
(b) Journalize the transactions.
(c) Prepare an income statement for management. Ignore income taxes.

P27-3A The Joyner Corporation manufactures a single product. The standard cost per unit of product is as follows:

Direct materials – 2 pounds of plastic at $5.00 per pound	$10.00
Direct labor – 2 hours at $12.00 per hour	24.00
Variable manufacturing overhead	12.00
Fixed manufacturing overhead	4.00
Total standard cost per unit	$50.00

The master manufacturing overhead budget for the year based on normal productive capacity of 90,000 units consisted of the following costs:

Variable Overhead		Fixed Overhead	
Indirect labor	$ 540,000	Supervision	$180,000
Lubricants	405,000	Depreciation	60,000
Utilities	72,000	Rent	120,000
Maintenance	63,000		
Total variable	$1,080,000	Total fixed	$360,000

Overhead is applied on the basis of direct labor hours. Actual costs for November in producing 7,500 units were as follows:

Direct materials (14,700 pounds)	$ 72,030	Maintenance	$ 4,100
Direct labor (14,800 hours)	180,560	Supervision	15,000
Indirect labor	46,360	Depreciation	5,000
Lubricants	34,040	Rent	10,000
Utilities	6,200		

The purchasing department normally buys the quantities of raw materials that are expected to be used each month in production. Raw materials inventories, therefore, can be ignored.

INSTRUCTIONS

(a) Prepare a flexible manufacturing overhead budget for a range of 10,000 to 20,000 direct labor hours. Use increments of 2,500 hours.

(b) Compute the materials, labor, and overhead variances.

(c) Prepare an income statement for management for the month ending November 30, 1987, assuming (1) 7,500 units were sold at $85 per unit, and (2) selling and administrative expenses were $72,000. Ignore income taxes.

P27-4A Owens Manufacturing Company uses a standard cost accounting system. In 1987, 33,000 units were produced. Each unit took several pounds of direct materials and 1⅓ standard hours of direct labor at a standard hourly rate of $12.00. Normal capacity was 42,000 direct labor hours. During the year, 130,000 pounds of raw materials were purchased at $.94 per pound. All pounds purchased were used during the year.

INSTRUCTIONS

(a) Answer the following questions:

1. If the materials price variance was $5,200 unfavorable, what was the standard materials price per unit?
2. If the materials quantity variance is $1,800 favorable, what was the standard materials quantity per unit?
3. What were the standard hours allowed for the units produced?
4. If the labor quantity variance is $9,600 unfavorable, what were the actual direct labor hours worked?
5. If the labor price variance is $11,200 favorable, what was the actual rate per hour?
6. If total budgeted manufacturing overhead was $315,000 at normal capacity, what was the predetermined overhead rate?
7. What was the standard cost per unit of product?
8. How much overhead was applied to production during the year?

9. If the fixed overhead rate was $2.50, what was the overhead volume variance?
10. If the overhead controllable variance is $3,000 unfavorable, what were the total variable overhead costs incurred?
11. Using selected answers above, what were the total costs assigned to work in process?
12. What was the total variance for the year? Was this variance favorable or unfavorable?

P27-5A Cass Manufacturing Company is a family-owned firm that produces the pressed cardboard transportation vehicles for 24-bottle cases of beer. For the past three years, Cass Manufacturing has used a standard cost accounting system and prepares its monthly income statement with the variances incurred during the month incorporated into the body of the statement.

In April, 1987, 900,000 cases were sold at $.80 each. There were no beginning or ending inventories of any kind. Selling expenses were 5% of sales, and administrative expenses were $.02 per case plus $12,000.

The following standard and actual costs were in effect for April (normal capacity is 1,000,000 cases):

	Standard (per unit)	Actual
Pressed board	6 square feet at .05 per square foot	$264,435 for 5,185,000 square feet
Labor	.6 minutes at $9.00 per hour	$84,000 for 10,500 hours
Overhead	.6 minutes at $27.00 per hour (fixed rate = $20.00 per hour variable rate = $7.00 per hour)	fixed overhead = $200,000 variable overhead = $55,000

INSTRUCTIONS

(a) Compute the total, price, and quantity variances for (1) materials, and (2) labor, and (3) the total, controllable, and volume variances for manufacturing overhead.
(b) Journalize the entries to record the variances.
(c) Prepare an income statement for management for the month of April.
(d) What variances appear to merit investigation by management?

DECISION CASE

Planning Professionals, a management consulting firm, specializes in strategic planning for financial institutions. Tom Allen and Beth Mears, partners in the firm, are assembling a new strategic planning model for use by clients. The model is designed for use on most microcomputers and replaces a rather lengthy manual model currently marketed by the firm. In order to market the new model Tom and Beth will need to provide clients with an estimate of the number of labor hours and computer time needed to operate the model. The model is currently being test marketed at five small financial institutions. These financial institutions are listed below, along with the number of combined computer/labor hours used by each institution to run the model one time.

Financial Institutions	Computer/Labor Hours Required
Midland National	25
First State	45
Financial Federal	40
Pacific America	30
Lakeview National	30
Total	170
Average	34

Any company that purchases the new model will need to purchase user manuals to access and operate the system. Also required are specialized computer forms that are only sold by Planning Professionals. User manuals will be sold to clients in cases of 20 at a cost of $300 per case. One manual must be used each time the model is run because each manual includes a nonreusable computer accessed password for operating the system. The specialized computer forms are sold in packages of 250 costing $50 per package. One application of the model requires the use of 50 forms. This sum includes two forms that are generally wasted in each application due to printer alignment errors. The overall cost of the strategic planning model to user clients is $12,000. Most clients will use the model 4 times annually.

Planning Professionals must provide its clients with estimates of ongoing costs incurred in operating the new strategic planning model. They would like to provide this information in the form of standard costs.

INSTRUCTIONS

(a) What factors should be considered in setting a standard for computer/labor hours?

(b) What alternatives for setting a standard for computer/labor hours might be used?

(c) What standard for computer/labor hours would you select? Justify your answer.

(d) Determine the standard material cost associated with the user manuals and computer forms for each application of the strategic planning model.

CHAPTER 28

Hunter College, New York

CHAPTER 28

INCREMENTAL ANALYSIS AND CAPITAL BUDGETING

STUDY OBJECTIVES

After studying this chapter, you should be able to:

1. **Identify the steps in management's decision-making process.**
2. **Describe the concept of incremental analysis.**
3. **Identify the relevant costs in accepting an order at a special price.**
4. **Indicate the relevant costs in a make or buy decision.**
5. **Give the decision rule in deciding whether to sell or process materials further.**
6. **Identify the factors to be considered in retaining or replacing equipment.**
7. **Explain the factors that are relevant in deciding whether to eliminate an unprofitable segment.**
8. **Determine which products to make and sell when a company has limited resources.**
9. **Contrast the annual rate of return and cash payback techniques in capital budgeting.**
10. **Distinguish between the net present value and internal rate of return methods.**

An important purpose of management accounting is to provide management with relevant information for decision making. Examples of these decisions might include:

1. Wilson Sporting Goods' decision to sell its golf balls to a Japanese distributor at a special discount price.

2. IBM's decision to discontinue production of its PC (Jr) computers.
3. RCA's decision to buy the picture tubes for its television sets rather than to manufacture them.

In this chapter we will discuss a number of management decisions and consider the information that is relevant to each.

In addition, we will explain management's decision-making process known as capital budgeting. This process pertains to a company's major investments in long-term productive assets.

MANAGEMENT'S DECISION-MAKING PROCESS

Making decisions is an important part of management. Management's decision-making process does not always follow a set pattern, because decisions may vary significantly in their scope, urgency, and importance. It is possible, however, to identify some steps that are frequently involved in the process. These steps are graphically shown below.

Management's decision-making process

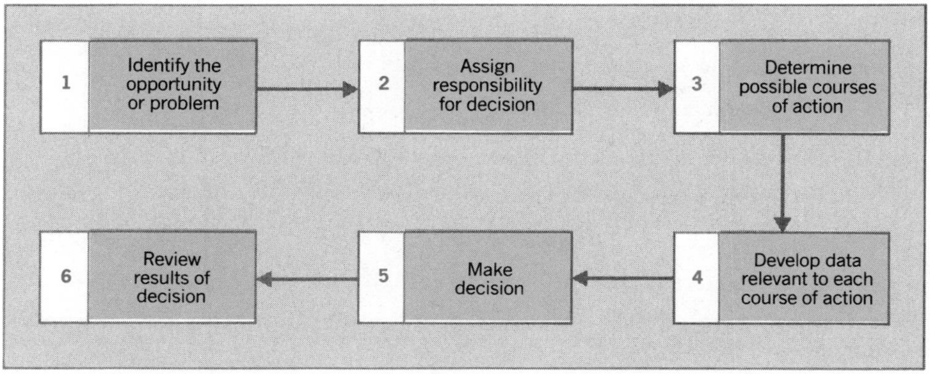

Accounting's contribution to the decision-making process occurs primarily in Steps 4 and 6. In Step 4, for each possible course of action, relevant revenue and cost data are provided to show the expected overall effect on net income. In Step 6, internal reports are prepared that review the actual impact of the decision.

SECTION ONE—INCREMENTAL ANALYSIS

In making business decisions, management ordinarily considers both financial and nonfinancial information. Financial information is related to revenues and costs and their effect on the company's overall profitability. Nonfinancial information relates to such factors as the effect of the decision on employee turnover, the environment, or the overall image of the company in the community. Although the nonfinancial information can be as important

as, and in some cases more important than, the financial information, we will limit our discussion primarily to financial information that is relevant to the decision.

MEANING OF INCREMENTAL ANALYSIS

Decisions involve a choice among alternative courses of action. Suppose that you were deciding whether to purchase or lease an IBM PC for your accounting homework. The financial data relate to the cost of leasing versus the cost of purchasing. For example, leasing would involve periodic lease payments; purchasing would require payment of the purchase price. In other words, the financial data that are relevant to the decision are the data that would vary in the future among the possible alternatives. The process used to identify the financial data that change under alternative courses of action is called **incremental analysis** or **differential analysis.** In some cases, you will find that when you use incremental analysis, both costs and revenues will change; in others, only costs or revenues will vary.

Since management's decision will affect the future, it follows that incremental analysis includes the probable effects of that decision on future earnings. Such data inevitably involve estimates and uncertainty. The accumulation of data for incremental analyses may involve market analysts, engineers, and accountants. In quantifying the data, the accountant is expected to exercise professional judgment to produce the most reliable information available at the time the decision must be made.

HOW INCREMENTAL ANALYSIS WORKS

The basic approach in incremental analysis is illustrated in the following example:

Basic approach in incremental analysis

	Alternative A	Alternative B	Net Income Increase (Decrease)
Revenues	$125,000	$110,000	**$(15,000)**
Costs	100,000	80,000	**20,000**
Net income	$ 25,000	$ 30,000	**$ 5,000**

In this example, alternative B is being compared with alternative A. The analysis shows that incremental revenue will be $15,000 less under alternative B than under alternative A but a $20,000 incremental cost saving will be realized.[1] Thus, alternative B will produce $5,000 more net income than alternative A.

[1]Although income taxes are sometimes important in incremental analysis, they are ignored in the chapter for simplicity's sake.

In incremental analysis, it is also important to recognize that (1) variable costs may not change under the alternative courses of action, and (2) fixed costs may change. For example, direct labor, normally a variable cost, is not an incremental cost in deciding between two new factory machines if each asset requires the same amount of direct labor. In contrast, rent expense, normally a fixed cost, is an incremental cost in a decision to continue occupancy of a building or to purchase or lease a new building.

TYPES OF INCREMENTAL ANALYSIS

A number of different types of decisions may be made by management that involve incremental analysis. The more common types are as follows:

1. Acceptance of an order at a special price.
2. Make or buy.
3. Sell or process further.
4. Retain or replace equipment.
5. Elimination of an unprofitable segment.
6. Allocation of limited resources.

ACCEPTANCE OF AN ORDER AT A SPECIAL PRICE

Sometimes, a company may have an opportunity to obtain additional business if it is willing to make a major price concession to a specific customer. To illustrate, assume that Sunbelt Company produces 100,000 automatic blenders per month, which is 80% of plant capacity. Variable manufacturing costs are $8 per unit, and fixed manufacturing costs are $400,000, or $4 per unit. The blenders are normally sold directly to retailers at $20 each. Sunbelt has an offer from Mexico Co. (a foreign wholesaler) to purchase an additional 2,000 blenders at $11 per unit. Acceptance of the offer would not affect normal sales of the product, and the additional units can be manufactured without increasing plant capacity. What should management do?

If management makes its decision on the basis of the total cost per unit of $12 ($8 + $4), the order would be rejected, because costs ($12) would exceed revenues ($11) by $1 per unit. However, since the units can be produced within existing plant capacity, the special order will not increase fixed costs. The relevant data for the decision, therefore, are the variable manufacturing costs per unit of $8 and the expected revenue of $11 per unit. Thus, as shown below, Sunbelt will increase its net income by $6,000 by accepting this special order:

Incremental analysis—acceptance of an order at a special price

	Reject Order	Accept Order	Net Income Increase (Decrease)
Revenues	$-0-	$22,000	$22,000
Costs	-0-	16,000	(16,000)
Net income	$-0-	$ 6,000	$ 6,000

Two points should be emphasized. First, it is assumed that sales of the product in other markets would not be affected by this special order. If other sales were affected, then Sunbelt would have to consider the lost sales in making the decision. Second, if Sunbelt is operating at full capacity, it is likely that the special order would be rejected. Under such circumstances, the company would have to expand plant capacity, and, the special order would have to absorb these additional fixed manufacturing costs, as well as the variable manufacturing costs.

MAKE OR BUY

When a manufacturer assembles component parts in producing a finished product, management must decide whether to make or buy the components. For example, General Motors Corporation may either make or buy the batteries, tires, and radios used in its cars. Similarly, Zenith Corporation may make or buy the electronic circuitry, cabinets, and speakers for its television sets. The decision to make or buy components should be made on the basis of incremental analysis.

To illustrate the analysis, assume that Baron Company incurs the following annual costs in producing 25,000 ignition switches for motor scooters.

Annual production cost data

Direct materials	$ 50,000
Direct labor	75,000
Variable manufacturing overhead	40,000
Fixed manufacturing overhead	60,000
Total manufacturing costs	$225,000
Total cost per unit ($225,000 ÷ 25,000)	$9.00

Baron Company may purchase the ignition switches from Ignition, Inc. at a price of $8 per unit. The question again is, "What should management do?"

On the one hand, it appears that management should purchase the ignition switches for $8, rather than make them at a cost of $9. However, a review of operations indicates that if the ignition switches are purchased from Ignition, Inc., all of Baron's variable costs but only $10,000 of its fixed manufacturing costs will be eliminated. Thus, $50,000 of the fixed manufacturing costs will remain if the ignition switches are purchased. The relevant costs for incremental analysis, therefore, are as follows:

Incremental analysis—make or buy

	Make	Buy	Net Income Increase (Decrease)
Direct materials	$ 50,000	$ -0-	$ 50,000
Direct labor	75,000	-0-	75,000
Variable manufacturing costs	40,000	-0-	40,000
Fixed manufacturing costs	60,000	50,000	10,000
Purchase price (25,000 × $8)	-0-	200,000	(200,000)
Total annual cost	$225,000	$250,000	$(25,000)

This analysis indicates that Baron Company will save $25,000 by continuing to produce the ignition switches, even though the total manufacturing cost

is $1 higher than the purchase price. The reason is that if the company purchases the ignition switches, it will still have fixed costs of $50,000 to absorb.

The foregoing analysis is complete only if it is assumed that the productive capacity used to make the ignition switches cannot be converted to another purpose. If there is an opportunity to use this productive capacity in some other manner, then this opportunity cost must be considered. **Opportunity cost** may be defined as the potential benefit that may be obtained by following an alternative course of action. To illustrate, assume that through buying the switches Baron Company can use the released productive capacity to generate additional income of $28,000. This lost income is an additional cost of continuing to make the switches in the make or buy decision. This opportunity cost therefore is added to the make column for comparison purposes as shown below:

Make or buy with opportunity cost

	Make	**Buy**	**Net Income Increase (Decrease)**
Total annual cost	$225,000	$250,000	$(25,000)
Opportunity cost	28,000	-0-	**28,000**
Total cost	$253,000	$250,000	$ 3,000

As shown, it is now advantageous to buy the ignition switches. The qualitative factors in this decision include the adverse effect on employees producing the ignition switches. In addition, management must assess how long the supplier will be able to satisfy the company's quality control standards at the quoted price per unit.

SELL OR PROCESS FURTHER

Many manufacturers have the option of selling products at a given point in the production cycle or continuing processing with the expectation of selling them at a higher price. For example, a bicycle manufacturer such as Schwinn could either sell its 10-speed bicycles to retailers unassembled or assembled, and a furniture manufacturer such as Ethan Allen could sell its dining room sets to furniture stores either unfinished or finished. The sell or process further decision should be made on the basis of incremental analysis. The basic decision rule is: **process further as long as the incremental revenue from such processing exceeds the incremental processing costs.**

Assume, for example, that Woodmasters Inc. makes tables. The cost to manufacture an unfinished table is $35, computed as follows:

Per unit cost of unfinished table

Direct material	$15
Direct labor	10
Variable manufacturing overhead	6
Fixed manufacturing overhead	4
Manufacturing cost per unit	$35

The selling price per unit is $50. Woodmasters currently has unused productive capacity that is expected to continue indefinitely. Management concludes that some of this capacity may be used to finish the tables and sell them at $60

per unit. For a finished table, it is anticipated that direct materials and direct labor costs will increase $2 and $4, respectively. In addition, variable manufacturing overhead costs will increase by $2.40 (60% of direct labor). No increase is anticipated in fixed manufacturing overhead. The incremental analysis on a per unit basis is as follows:

Incremental analysis—sell or process further

	Sell	Process Further	Net Income Increase (Decrease)
Sales per unit	$50.00	$60.00	$10.00
Costs per unit			
Direct materials	15.00	17.00	(2.00)
Direct labor	10.00	14.00	(4.00)
Variable manufacturing overhead	6.00	8.40	(2.40)
Fixed manufacturing overhead	4.00	4.00	-0-
Total	$35.00	$43.40	$(8.40)
Net income per unit	$15.00	$16.60	$ 1.60

As indicated from the analysis, it would be advantageous for Woodmaster to process the tables further. In this case, the incremental revenue of $10.00 from the additional processing is $1.60 higher than the incremental processing costs of $8.40.

RETAIN OR REPLACE EQUIPMENT

Management often has to decide whether to continue using an asset or replace it. To illustrate, assume that the Jeffcoat Company has a factory machine with a book value of $40,000 and a remaining useful life of four years. A new machine is available that costs $120,000 and is expected to have zero salvage value at the end of its four-year useful life. If the new machine is acquired, variable manufacturing costs are expected to decrease from $160,000 to $125,000 annually and the old unit will be scrapped. The incremental analysis for the four-year period is as follows:

Incremental analysis—retain or replace equipment

	Retain Equipment	Replace Equipment	Net Income Increase (Decrease)
Variable manufacturing costs	$640,000[a]	$500,000[b]	$140,000
New machine cost		120,000	(120,000)
Total	$640,000	$620,000	$ 20,000

[a](4 × $160,000)
[b](4 × $125,000)

In this case, it would be to the company's advantage to replace the equipment. The lower variable manufacturing costs due to replacement more than offset the cost of the new equipment.

One other point should be mentioned regarding Jeffcoat's decision: **the book value of the old machine does not affect the decision.** Book value is a sunk cost, which is a cost that cannot be changed by any present or future decision. Sunk costs, therefore, are not relevant in incremental analysis. In this example, if the asset is retained, book value will be depreciated over its remaining useful life. On the other hand, if the new unit is acquired, book value will be recognized as a loss of the current period. Thus, the effect of book value on current and future earnings is the same regardless of the replacement decision. Any trade-in allowance or cash disposal value of the existing asset, however, is relevant to the decision, because this value will not be realized if the asset is continued in use.

ELIMINATION OF AN UNPROFITABLE SEGMENT

Our concern here focuses on the relevant data management needs in deciding whether to eliminate an unprofitable segment. To illustrate, assume that Martina Company manufactures tennis racquets in three models: Pro, Master, and Champ. Pro and Master are profitable lines, whereas Champ (highlighted in color) operates at a loss. Condensed income statement data are as follows:

Segment income data

	Pro	Master	Champ	Total
Sales	$800,000	$300,000	$100,000	$1,200,000
Variable expenses	520,000	210,000	90,000	820,000
Contribution margin	280,000	90,000	10,000	380,000
Fixed expenses	80,000	50,000	30,000	160,000
Net income	$200,000	$ 40,000	$ (20,000)	$ 220,000

It might be expected that total net income will increase by $20,000 to $240,000 if the unprofitable line of racquets is eliminated. However, it is possible for income to decrease if the Champ line is discontinued. The reason is that the fixed expenses allocated to the Champ racquets will have to be absorbed by the other products. To illustrate, assume that the $30,000 of fixed costs applicable to the unprofitable segment are allocated 2/3 and 1/3 to the Pro and Master product lines respectively. Fixed expenses will increase to $100,000 ($80,000 + $20,000) in the Pro line and to $60,000 ($50,000 + $10,000) in the Master line. The revised income statement is:

Income data after eliminating unprofitable product line

	Pro	Master	Total
Sales	$800,000	$300,000	$1,100,000
Variable expenses	520,000	210,000	730,000
Contribution margin	280,000	90,000	370,000
Fixed expenses	100,000	60,000	160,000
Net income	$180,000	$ 30,000	$ 210,000

Total net income has decreased $10,000 ($220,000 − $210,000). This result is also obtained in the following incremental analysis of the Champ racquets.

Incremental analysis— eliminating an unprofitable segment

	Continue	Eliminate	Net Income Increase (Decrease)
Sales	$100,000	$ -0-	$(100,000)
Variable expenses	90,000	-0-	90,000
Contribution margin	10,000	-0-	(10,000)
Fixed expenses	30,000	30,000	-0-
Net income	$ (20,000)	$(30,000)	$ (10,000)

The loss in net income is attributable to the contribution margin ($10,000) that will not be realized if the segment is discontinued.

In deciding on the future status of an unprofitable segment, management should consider the effect of elimination on related product lines. It may be possible for continuing product lines to obtain some or all of the sales lost by the discontinued product line. In addition, management should consider the effect of eliminating the product line on employees who may have to be discharged or retrained.

ALLOCATION OF LIMITED RESOURCES

We all have limited resources at our disposal. For a company, the limited resource may be floor space in a retail department store, and raw materials, direct labor hours, or machine capacity in a manufacturing company. When it has limited resources, management must decide which products to make and sell.

To illustrate, assume that Collins Company manufactures deluxe and standard model pen and pencil sets. The limiting resource is machine capacity, which is 3,600 hours per month. Relevant data consist of the following:

Contribution margin and machine hours

	Deluxe Sets	Standard Sets
Contribution margin per unit	$8	$6
Machine hours required	4	2

The deluxe sets may appear to be more profitable since they have a higher contribution margin ($8) than the standard sets ($6). However, note that the standard sets take less machine hours to produce than the deluxe sets. Therefore, it is necessary to find the **contribution margin per unit of limited resource.** This is obtained by dividing the contribution margin per unit of each product by the number of units of the limited resource required for each product. The computation of the contribution margin per unit of limited resource is as follows:

Contribution margin per unit of limited resource

	Deluxe Sets	Standard Sets
Contribution margin per unit (a)	$8	$6
Machine hours required (b)	4	2
Contribution margin per unit of limited resource (a) ÷ (b)	**$2**	**$3**

If the Collins Company is able to increase machine capacity from 3,600 hours to 4,200 hours, the additional hours could be used to produce either the standard or deluxe pen and pencil sets. The units produced would be as follows:

Computation of units produced

	Produce Deluxe Sets	Produce Standard Sets
Machine hours (a)	600	600
Machine hours per unit (b)	4	2
Units produced (a) ÷ (b)	**150**	**300**

The total contribution margin then is computed as follows:

Total contribution margin

	Deluxe Sets	Standard Sets
Units produced	150	300
Contribution margin per unit	$8	$6
Total contribution margin	**$1,200**	**$1,800**

From this analysis, we can see that to maximize net income all of the increased capacity should be used to make and sell the standard sets.

SECTION TWO—CAPITAL BUDGETING

Individuals make a capital expenditure when they buy a new home, car, or television set. Similarly, businesses make a capital expenditure when they decide to modernize plant facilities or to expand operations. Examples include the new terminal being built by United Airlines at O'Hare Airport and the Saturn automobile plant being built by General Motors in Tennessee.

The amounts spent by companies on capital expenditures each year are substantial. For example, in 1985, U.S. businesses spent approximately $387.13 billion on capital expenditures. More specifically, in a recent year, General Motors spent $6 billion and Alcoa spent $2.6 billion. In business enterprises, as for individuals, the amount of possible capital expenditures usually exceeds the funds available for such expenditures. Thus, the resources available must be allocated (or budgeted) among the competing alter-

natives. The process of making capital expenditure decisions in business is known as **capital budgeting.**

Many companies follow a carefully prescribed process in capital budgeting. At least once a year, proposals for projects are requested from each department and plant and from authorized personnel. The proposals are screened by a capital budgeting committee, which submits its findings to the officers of the company. The officers, in turn, select the projects they believe to be most worthy of funding and submit them to the board of directors. Ultimately, the directors approve the capital expenditure budget for the year. The involvement of top management and the board of directors in the process demonstrates the importance of capital budgeting decisions. These decisions often have a significant impact on a company's future profitability. Indeed, poor capital budgeting decisions have led to the bankruptcy of some companies. Accounting data are indispensable in assessing the probable effects of capital expenditures.

APPROACHES TO CAPITAL BUDGETING

To provide management with relevant data for capital budgeting decisions, accountants should be familiar with the quantitative techniques that may be used. The three most common techniques are: (1) annual rate of return, (2) cash payback, and (3) discounted cash flow. To illustrate the three quantitative techniques, assume that Tarply Co. is considering an investment of $130,000 in new equipment. The new equipment is expected to last 10 years and have zero salvage value at the end of its useful life. The straight-line method of depreciation is used for accounting purposes. The expected annual revenues and costs of the new product that will be produced from the investment are as follows:

Annual net income from capital expenditures

Sales		$200,000
Less: Costs and expenses		
Manufacturing costs (exclusive of depreciation)	$145,000	
Depreciation expense ($130,000 ÷ 10)	13,000	
Selling and administrative expenses	22,000	180,000
Income before income taxes		20,000
Income tax expense		7,000
Net income		$ 13,000

ANNUAL RATE OF RETURN

The **annual rate of return technique** is based directly on accounting data. It is the same as using return on investment (ROI) in evaluating the profitability of a segment. The only difference is that the time period involved is much longer in a capital budgeting situation. Annual rate of return is derived from the following formula:

Annual rate of return formula

$$\text{Expected Annual Net Income} \div \text{Average Investment} = \text{Annual Rate of Return}$$

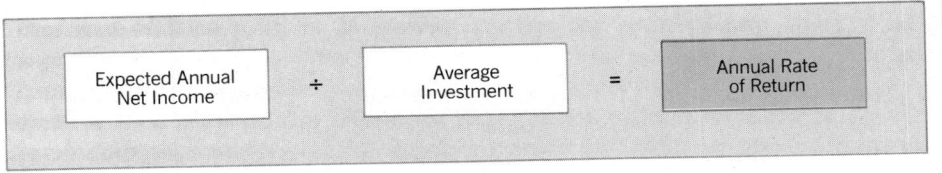

Expected annual net income is obtained from the income statement. Tarply Company's expected annual net income is $13,000. Average investment is based on the following:

Computation of average investment

$$\text{Average investment} = \frac{\text{Original investment} + \text{Investment at end of useful life}}{2}$$

The investment at the end of useful life is equal to the asset's salvage value, if any. For Tarply Company, average investment is $65,000 [($130,000 + $0) ÷ 2].

The annual rate of return for Tarply Company is, therefore, 20%, computed as follows:

$$\$13{,}000 \div \$65{,}000 = 20\%$$

The annual rate of return is then compared with management's required minimum rate of return for investments of similar risk. The minimum rate of return (also called the **hurdle rate** or **cutoff rate**) is generally based on the company's cost of capital. The **cost of capital** is the rate of return that management expects to pay on all borrowed and equity funds. It does not relate to the cost of funding a specific project. The decision rule is: **a project is acceptable if its rate of return is greater than management's minimum rate of return; it is unacceptable when the reverse is true.** When the rate of return technique is used in deciding among several acceptable projects, **the higher the rate of return for a given risk, the more attractive the investment.**

The principal advantages of this technique of analysis are the simplicity of its calculation and management's familiarity with the accounting terms used in the computation. A major limitation of the annual rate of return approach is that it does not consider the time value of money. For example, no consideration is given as to whether cash inflows from the investment will occur early or late in the life of the investment. As explained in this textbook, recognition of the time value of money can make a significant difference between the future value and the discounted present value of an investment.

CASH PAYBACK

The **cash payback technique** identifies the time period required to recover the cost of the capital investment from the annual cash inflow produced by the investment. The formula for computing the cash payback period is:

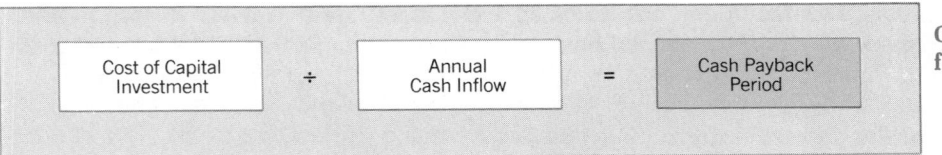

Cash payback formula

Cost of Capital Investment ÷ Annual Cash Inflow = Cash Payback Period

Annual cash inflow, also known as net cash inflow, is approximated by taking net income and adding back depreciation expense. Depreciation expense is added back because depreciation on the capital expenditure does not involve an annual outflow of cash. Accordingly, the depreciation deducted in determining net income must be added back to determine annual cash inflows. In the Tarply Company example, annual cash inflow is $26,000, as shown below.

Computation of annual cash inflow

Net income	$13,000
Add: Depreciation expense	13,000
Annual cash inflow	$26,000

The cash payback period in this example is therefore 5 years computed as follows:

$130,000 ÷ $26,000 = 5 years

The evaluation of the payback period is often related to the expected useful life of the asset. For example, assume that at Tarply Company a project is unacceptable if the payback period is longer than 60% of the asset's expected useful life. The five-year payback period in this case is 50% of the project's expected useful life. Thus, the project is acceptable. It follows that when the payback technique is used to decide among acceptable alternative projects, **the shorter the payback period, the more attractive the investment.** The reason is that the cash payback technique recognizes that: (1) the earlier the investment is recovered, the sooner the cash funds can be used for other purposes, and (2) the risk of loss from obsolescence and changed economic conditions is less in a shorter payback period.

The cash payback technique may be useful as an initial screening tool. It also may be the most critical factor in the capital budgeting decision for a company that desires a fast turnaround of its investment because of a weak cash position. Like the annual rate of return technique, the cash payback technique is relatively easy to compute and understand. However, it should not ordinarily be the only basis for the capital budgeting decision because it ignores the expected profitability of the project. To illustrate, assume that Projects A and B have the same payback period, but Project A's useful life is double the useful life of Project B. Project A's earning power, therefore, is twice as long as Project B's. A further disadvantage of this technique is that it ignores the time value of money.

DISCOUNTED CASH FLOW

The **discounted cash flow technique** is generally recognized as the most informative and best conceptual approach to making capital budgeting deci-

sions. This technique considers both the estimated total cash inflows from the investment and the time value of money. As indicated above, consideration of the time value of money is critical because of the long-term nature of the capital budgeting decision. The expected total cash inflow consists of the sum of the annual cash inflows plus the estimated liquidation proceeds when the asset is sold for salvage at the end of its useful life. Two methods are used with the discounted cash flow technique: (1) net present value, and (2) internal rate of return. Before discussing the methods, we will provide a brief summary of present value concepts.

Present Value Concepts

As explained above, both the annual rate of return and cash payback techniques suffer from an important drawback—they ignore the time value of money. In the Appendix to Chapter 17, we discussed a number of concepts pertaining to the time value of money. These concepts are very important in capital budgeting. The decision to accept or reject a given project often depends on the timing of the cash inflows from the project and the interest rates used in discounting the cash flows. If you need a review of the time value of money concepts, you should reread the Appendix to Chapter 17. Otherwise the short discussion below that highlights the major concepts should be sufficient for capital budgeting.

Present value of a single future amount

TABLE 1
PRESENT VALUE OF A SINGLE FUTURE AMOUNT

(n) Periods	5%	6%	8%	9%	10%	11%	12%	15%
1	.95238	.94340	.92593	.91743	.90909	.90090	.89286	.86957
2	.90703	.89000	.85734	.84168	.82645	.81162	.79719	.75614
3	.86384	.83962	.79383	.77218	.75132	.73119	.71178	.65752
4	.82270	.79209	.73503	.70843	.68301	.65873	.63552	.57175
5	.78353	.74726	.68058	.64993	.62092	.59345	.56743	.49718
6	.74622	.70496	.63017	.59627	.56447	.53464	.50663	.43233
7	.71068	.66506	.58349	.54703	.51316	.48166	.45235	.37594
8	.67684	.62741	.54027	.50187	.46651	.43393	.40388	.32690
9	.64461	.59190	.50025	.46043	.42410	.39092	.36061	.28426
10	.61391	.55839	.46319	.42241	.38554	.35218	.32197	.24719
11	.58468	.52679	.42888	.38753	.35049	.31728	.28748	.21494
12	.55684	.49697	.39711	.35554	.31863	.28584	.25668	.18691
13	.53032	.46884	.36770	.32618	.28966	.25751	.22917	.16253
14	.50507	.44230	.34046	.29925	.26333	.23199	.20462	.14133
15	.48102	.41727	.31524	.27454	.23939	.20900	.18270	.12289
16	.45811	.39365	.29189	.25187	.21763	.18829	.16312	.10687
17	.43630	.37136	.27027	.23107	.19785	.16963	.14564	.09293
18	.41552	.35034	.25025	.21199	.17986	.15282	.13004	.08081
19	.39573	.33051	.23171	.19449	.16351	.13768	.11611	.07027
20	.37689	.31180	.21455	.17843	.14864	.12403	.10367	.06110

There are two present value tables presented here. **The first table is the present value of a single future amount.** This table is illustrated in the Appendix to Chapter 17 and it is reproduced on page 1112 for your convenience. This table contains the amounts that must be deposited now at a specified rate of interest to amount to 1 at the end of a specified number of periods. In other words, these amounts are the present values of receiving $1 at a specified time in the future. For example, what is the present value of $90,000 to be received in five years if a 9% rate of return is anticipated? From Table 1 we find that the discount (or present value) factor for 5 years at 9% is .64993. The present value of $90,000, therefore, is $58,494 ($90,000 × .64993).

The present value of a single future amount is used in capital budgeting decisions when the project will have unequal cash payments over its useful life. It is also used when liquidation proceeds are expected at the end of the project's useful life.

The second table is the present value of a series of future payments. It is often referred to as the present value of an annuity table. This table is also illustrated in the Appendix to Chapter 17 and it is reproduced below for your convenience. The table shows the amounts that must be deposited now at a specified rate of interest to provide for a series of equal payments of 1 over a specified period in the future at equal intervals. In other words, these amounts are the present values of receiving a series of $1 payments at equal intervals in the future. For example, what is the present value of $6,000 to be

Present value of a series of future payments

TABLE 2
PRESENT VALUE OF A SERIES OF FUTURE PAYMENTS

(n) Periods	5%	6%	8%	9%	10%	11%	12%	15%
1	.95238	.94340	.92593	.91743	.90909	.90090	.89286	.86957
2	1.85941	1.83339	1.78326	1.75911	1.73554	1.71252	1.69005	1.62571
3	2.72325	2.67301	2.57710	2.53130	2.48685	2.44371	2.40183	2.28323
4	3.54595	3.46511	3.31213	3.23972	3.16986	3.10245	3.03735	2.85498
5	4.32948	4.21236	3.99271	3.88965	3.79079	3.69590	3.60478	3.35216
6	5.07569	4.91732	4.62288	4.48592	4.35526	4.23054	4.11141	3.78448
7	5.78637	5.58238	5.20637	5.03295	4.86842	4.71220	4.56376	4.16042
8	6.46321	6.20979	5.74664	5.53482	5.33493	5.14612	4.96764	4.48732
9	7.10782	6.80169	6.24689	5.99525	5.75902	5.53705	5.32825	4.77158
10	7.72173	7.36009	6.71008	6.41766	6.14457	5.88923	5.65022	5.01877
11	8.30641	7.88687	7.13896	6.80519	6.49506	6.20652	5.93770	5.23371
12	8.86325	8.38384	7.53608	7.16073	6.81369	6.49236	6.19437	5.42062
13	9.39357	8.85268	7.90378	7.48690	7.10336	6.74987	6.42355	5.58315
14	9.89864	9.29498	8.24424	7.78615	7.36669	6.98187	6.62817	5.72448
15	10.37966	9.71225	8.55948	8.06069	7.60608	7.19087	6.81086	5.84737
16	10.83777	10.10590	8.85137	8.31256	7.82371	7.37916	6.97399	5.95424
17	11.27407	10.47726	9.12164	8.54363	8.02155	7.54879	7.11963	6.04716
18	11.68959	10.82760	9.37189	8.75563	8.20141	7.70162	7.24967	6.12797
19	12.08532	11.15812	9.60360	8.95012	8.36492	7.83929	7.36578	6.19823
20	12.46221	11.46992	9.81815	9.12855	8.51356	7.96333	7.46944	6.25933

received at the end of each of the next four years if a 9% rate of return is anticipated? From Table 2 we find that the discount factor for 4 periods at 9% is 3.23972. The present value of receiving $6,000 each period is, therefore, $19,438 ($6,000 × 3.23972).

The present value of a series of future payments is used in capital budgeting decisions when the project will provide equal cash payments periodically over its useful life. It should be noted that both tables are condensed because of space considerations. However, enough factors are provided for the subsequent material in this chapter and for homework problems.

Net Present Value Method

Under the **net present value method,** cash inflows are discounted to their present value and then compared with the capital outlay required by the investment. The difference between these two amounts is referred to as **net present value.** The interest rate to be used in discounting the future cash inflows is the required minimum rate of return. A proposal is acceptable when net present value is zero or positive, because this means the rate of return in the investment equals or exceeds the required rate of return. When net present value is negative, the project is unacceptable. The following diagram illustrates these points.

Net present value decision diagram

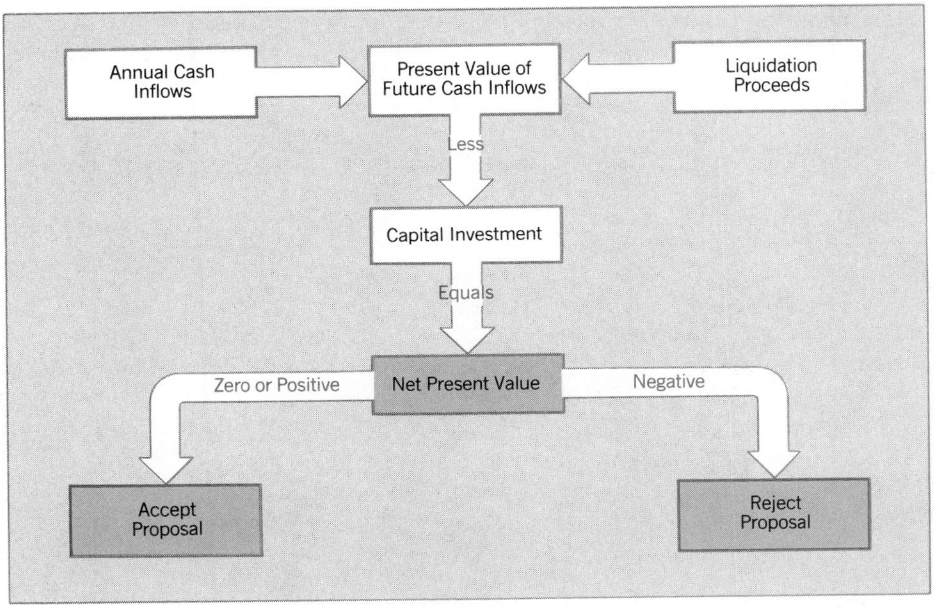

When making a selection among acceptable proposals, **the higher the positive net present value, the more attractive the investment.**[2] The application of this method to two cases is described below.

Equal Annual Cash Inflows. Tarply Company's annual cash inflows are $26,000. If we assume this amount is uniform over the asset's useful life, the

[2]The relationship between net present value and the capital investment is sometimes expressed as the excess present value index, as explained on page 1115.

present value of the annual cash inflows can be computed by using the annuity table (Table 2) based on the present value of 1 to be received periodically for 10 periods. The computations at rates of return of 12% and 15%, respectively, are as follows:

Present value of annual cash inflows

	Present Values at Different Discount Rates	
Discount factor for 10 periods	12%	15%
Present value of cash inflows:	5.65022	5.01877
$26,000 × 5.65022	$146,906	
$26,000 × 5.01877		$130,488

The proposed investment does not have any salvage value. Thus, it is not necessary to determine the present value of the liquidation proceeds. Therefore, the analysis of the proposal by the net present value method is as follows:

Computations of net present values

	12%	15%
Present value of annual cash inflows	$146,906	$130,488
Present value of liquidation proceeds	-0-	-0-
Present value of future cash inflows	146,906	130,488
Capital investment	130,000	130,000
Positive (negative) net present value	$ 16,906	$ 488

The proposed capital expenditure is acceptable at both a required rate of return of 12% and 15% because the net present values are positive.

The findings from the net present value method are often summarized as follows, assuming that the 12% required rate of return is used.

Net present value report

Project: X240 — Life of Project 10 years

Required Investment: $130,000 — Required rate of return 12%

Item	Amount	Years	PV Factor	PV
Cash inflows				
Annual	$ 26,000	1–10	5.65022	$146,906
Salvage				-0-
Total present value				146,906
Cash outflows				
Investment	$130,000	now	1.00000	130,000
Positive net present value				$ 16,906

In some companies, an **excess present value index** is used in ranking acceptable projects. The **excess present value index** indicates the percentage relationship between total present value and the amount of the capital investment. The index is derived from the following formula:

Excess present value index formula

Total Present Value ÷ Capital Investment = Excess Present Value Index

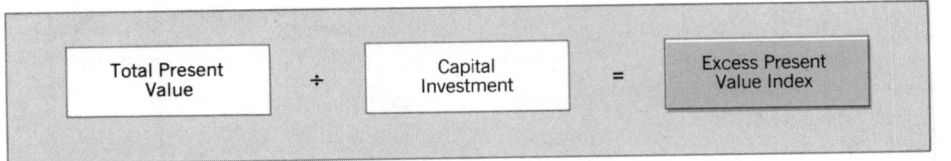

For Tarply Company, the index based on the above report is as follows:

$$\$146{,}906 \div 130{,}000 = 1.13$$

When the excess present value index is used, **the higher the index, the more attractive the investment.** A major advantage of the excess present value index is that investments of different sizes can be compared. For example, we might conclude that an investment that provides a $250,000 total present value is better than an investment that provides only a $100,000 total present value. However, if the first investment required an outlay of $250,000 (excess present value index 1.00) and the second $50,000 (excess present value index 2.00), the latter is the preferred investment.

Unequal Annual Cash Inflows. When annual cash inflows are unequal, it is not possible to use annuity tables to calculate their present value. Instead, tables showing the present value of a single future amount (Table 1) must be applied to each annual cash inflow. To illustrate, assume in the Tarply Company that management expects the same aggregate annual cash inflow ($260,000) but a declining market demand for the new product over the life of the equipment. The present value of the annual cash flows is calculated as follows:

Computing present value of unequal annual cash inflows

Year	Assumed Annual Cash Inflows	Discount Factor 12%	Discount Factor 15%	Present Value 12%	Present Value 15%
	(1)	(2)	(3)	(1) × (2)	(1) × (3)
1	$ 36,000	.89286	.86957	$ 32,143	$ 31,305
2	32,000	.79719	.75614	25,510	24,196
3	29,000	.71178	.65752	20,642	19,068
4	27,000	.63552	.57175	17,159	15,437
5	26,000	.56743	.49718	14,753	12,927
6	24,000	.50663	.43233	12,159	10,376
7	23,000	.45235	.37594	10,404	8,647
8	22,000	.40388	.32690	8,885	7,192
9	21,000	.36061	.28426	7,573	5,969
10	20,000	.32197	.24719	6,439	4,944
	$260,000			$155,667	$140,061

In this example, the present values of the cash inflows is greater than the $130,000 capital investment. Thus, the project is acceptable at both a 12% and 15% required rate of return. The difference between the present values using the 12% rate under equal cash inflows ($146,906) and unequal cash inflows ($155,667) is due to the pattern of the inflows.

Liquidation Proceeds. When a salvage value is expected at the end of the project, it is necessary to include the present value of the liquidation proceeds in determining the present value of future cash inflows. Since the liquidation proceeds are obtained through one transaction, the discount factor is based on Table 1.

To illustrate, assume that the Wilmar Company expects liquidation proceeds of $5,000 on a capital expenditure that has a useful life of 15 years. Assuming a 10% required rate of return, the present value of the liquidation proceeds is as follows:

Computation of present value of liquidation proceeds

Discount factor for 15 periods at 10%	=	.23939
Present value of liquidation proceeds: $5,000 × .23939	=	**$1,197**

The present value of the liquidation proceeds is added to the present total value of annual cash inflows to determine the present value. The total present value is then compared to the investment to arrive at the net present value.

Internal Rate of Return Method

The internal rate of return method, sometimes called the **time-adjusted rate of return,** differs from the net present value method in that it results in finding the **true interest yield** of the potential investment. The true yield corresponds to the effective rate of interest used in Chapter 17 when bonds are issued above or below face value. The true interest rate is the rate that will cause the present value of the proposed capital expenditure to equal the present value of the expected annual cash inflows.

The determination of the true interest rate involves two steps. First, an **internal rate of return factor** is computed. Second, this factor is used with the present value of a series of future payments table (Table 2) to find the true interest rate. The formula for determining the internal rate of return factor is as follows:

Formula for internal rate of return factor

Capital Investment ÷ Annual Cash Inflows = Internal Rate of Return Factor

The computation for the Tarply Company, assuming equal annual cash inflows is:

$130,000 ÷ $26,000 = 5.0[3]

The true interest rate is then found by locating the discount factor in Table 2 that is closest to the internal rate of return factor for the time period covered by the annual cash inflows. In Tarply, the annual cash inflows are expected to continue for 10 years. Thus, it is necessary to read across the period 10 row

[3]When annual cash inflows are equal, the internal rate of return factor is the same as the cash payback period.

to find the discount factor. In this case, the closest discount factor to 5.0 is 5.01877 which represents an interest rate of approximately 15%. The approximate rate can be determined by interpolation, but since we are using estimated annual cash flows such precision is seldom required.

When the internal rate of return has been determined, it is compared to management's required minimum rate of return. The decision rule, therefore, is: **accept the project when the internal rate of return is equal to or greater than the required rate of return, and reject the project when the internal rate of return is less than the required rate.** These relationships are shown graphically below.

Internal rate of return decision diagram

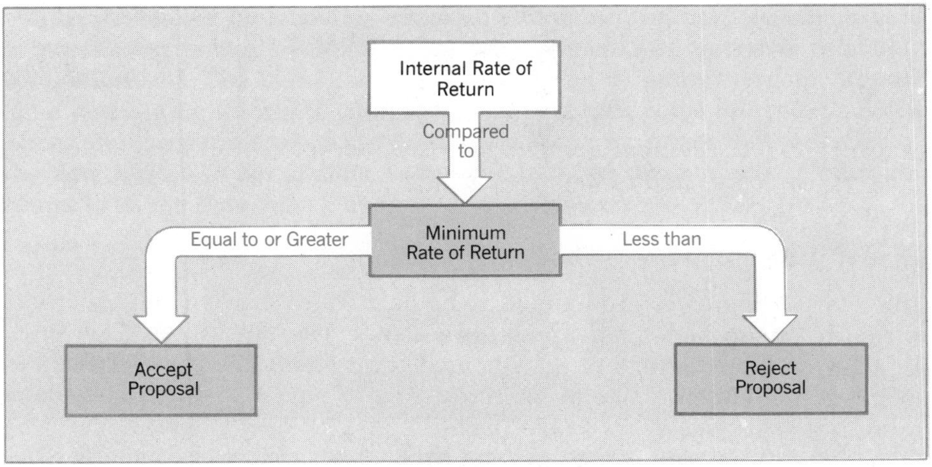

Assuming the minimum required rate of return is 10% for Tarply Company, the project is acceptable because the 15% internal rate of return is greater than the required rate.

The internal rate of return method is widely used in practice. Most managers find the internal rate of return easy to interpret.

COMPARISON OF DISCOUNTED CASH FLOW METHODS

A comparative summary of the two discounted cash flow methods is as follows:

Comparison of discounted cash flow methods

Item	Net Present Value	Internal Rate of Return
1. Objective	Compute net present value.	Compute internal rate of return.
2. Decision rule	If net present value is zero or positive, accept the proposal; if net present value is negative, reject the proposal.	If internal rate of return is equal to or greater than the minimum required rate of return, accept the proposal; if internal rate of return is less than the minimum rate, reject the proposal.

When properly used, either method will provide management with relevant quantitative data for making capital budgeting decisions.

There are software programs available for each of the decision situations described in the incremental analysis and capital budgeting sections of this chapter. Because of their power and flexibility, spreadsheet programs can also be designed to perform any of these calculations. Thus, businesses often face another decision. Should they purchase programs dedicated only to specific tasks (called the canned approach) or will a general purpose application package, like a spreadsheet or data base program, be better? Answers to questions like this are typically studied in information systems courses.

SUMMARY OF STUDY OBJECTIVES

1. Management's decision-making process consists of (a) identifying the problem or opportunity, (b) assigning responsibility for the decision, (c) determining possible courses of action, (d) developing data relevant to each course of action, (e) making the decision, and (f) reviewing the results of the decision.

2. Incremental analysis is the process used to identify financial data that change under alternative courses of action. These data are relevant to the decision because they will vary in the future among the possible alternatives.

3. The relevant information in accepting an order at a special price is the difference between the variable manufacturing costs and expected revenues.

4. In a make-or-buy decision, the relevant costs are (a) the variable manufacturing costs that will be saved, (b) the purchase price, and (c) opportunity costs.

5. The decision rule in deciding whether to sell or process materials further is: process further as long as the incremental revenue from processing exceeds the incremental processing costs.

6. The factors to be considered in determining whether equipment should be retained or replaced are the effects on variable costs and the cost of the new equipment. In addition, any disposal value of the existing asset must be considered.

7. In deciding whether to eliminate an unprofitable segment, it is necessary to determine the contribution margin, if any, produced by the segment and the disposition of the segment's fixed expenses.

8. When a company has limited resources, it is necessary to find the contribution margin per unit of limited resource. This amount is then

multiplied by the units that could be produced to determine which product maximizes net income.

9. The annual rate of return technique is obtained by dividing expected annual net income by the average investment. The cash payback technique identifies the time period to recover the cost of the investment. The formula is: cost of capital expenditure ÷ estimated annual cash inflow equals cash payback period. The shorter the payback period, the more attractive the investment.

10. Under the net present value method, the present value of future cash inflows is compared with the capital investment to determine net present value. The decision rule is: accept the project if net present value is zero or positive; reject the investment if net present value is negative.

Under the internal rate of return method, the objective is to find the true interest yield of the potential investment. The decision rule is: accept the project when the internal rate of return is equal to or greater than the required rate of return; reject the project when the internal rate of return is less than the required rate.

GLOSSARY

Annual rate of return technique, p. 1109

Capital budgeting, p. 1109

Cash payback technique, p. 1110

Cost of capital, p. 1110

Differential analysis (incremental analysis), p. 1101

Discounted cash flow technique, p. 1111

Incremental analysis (differential analysis), p. 1101

Internal rate of return method, p. 1117

Net present value method, p. 1114

Opportunity cost, p. 1104

Sunk cost, p. 1106

DEMONSTRATION PROBLEM

The Juanita Company must decide whether to make or buy some of its components. The costs of producing 50,000 electrical cords for its floor lamps are as follows:

Direct materials	$60,000	Variable overhead	$12,000
Direct labor	30,000	Fixed overhead	8,000

Instead of making the electrical cords at an average cost per unit of $2.20 ($110,000 ÷ 50,000), the company has an opportunity to buy the cords at $2.30 per unit. If the cords are purchased all variable costs and one-half of the fixed costs will be eliminated.

INSTRUCTIONS

(a) Prepare an incremental analysis showing whether the company should make or buy the electrical cords.

(b) Will your answer be different if the released productive capacity will generate additional income of $25,000?

SOLUTION TO DEMONSTRATION PROBLEM

(a)	Make	Buy	Net Income Increase (Decrease)
Direct materials	$ 60,000	$ —	$ 60,000
Direct labor	$ 30,000	—	30,000
Variable manufacturing costs	12,000		12,000
Fixed manufacturing costs	8,000	4,000	4,000
Purchase price		115,000	(115,000)
	$110,000	$119,000	$ (9,000)

This analysis indicates that the Juanita Company will save $9,000 by continuing to make the electrical cords.

(b) Yes, the answer is different because the opportunity cost of $25,000 will result in $16,000 of additional income ($25,000–$9,000) if the cords are purchased.

QUESTIONS

1. Willis Wells claims that management decisions usually follow a set pattern. Is his assertion correct? Explain.

2. How does accounting contribute to the decision-making process of management?

3. Incremental analysis involves the accumulation of information concerning a single course of action. Do you agree? Why?

4. Marla Mason asks your help concerning the relevance of variable and fixed costs in incremental analysis. Help Marla with her problem.

5. What data are relevant in deciding whether to accept an order at a special price?

6. The Rosa Company has an opportunity to buy parts at $7 each which currently cost $9 to make. What manufacturing costs are relevant to this make-or-buy decision?

7. Define the term, "opportunity cost." How may this cost be relevant in a make-or-buy decision?

8. What is the decision rule followed in deciding whether to sell a product or process it further?

9. Your roommate is confused about sunk costs. Explain to your roommate the meaning of sunk costs and their relevance to a decision to retain or replace equipment.

10. Multi-Products Inc. has one product line that is unprofitable. What circumstances may cause overall company net income to be lower if the unprofitable product line is eliminated?

11. How is the contribution margin per unit of limited resources computed?

12. Describe the process a company may use in screening and approving the capital expenditure budget.

13. Your classmate is confused about the factors that are included in the annual rate of return technique. What is the formula for this technique?

14. Jill Jarvis is trying to understand the term "cost of capital." Define the term and indicate its relevance to the decision rule under the annual rate of return technique.

15. Sam Seer claims the formula for the cash payback technique is the same as the formula for the annual rate of return technique. Is Sam correct? What is the formula for the cash payback technique?

16. What are the advantages and disadvantages of the cash payback technique?

17. Two types of present value tables may be used with the discounted cash flow technique. Identify the tables and the circumstance(s) when each table should be used.

18. (a) What items are discounted when the net present value method is used? (b) What is the decision rule followed under the net present value method?

19. What is the excess present value index? How is the index derived?

20. When liquidation proceeds are anticipated, the total proceeds are subtracted from the cost of the investment to determine net present value. Is this true? Explain.

21. The Coles Company uses the internal rate of return method. How is the internal rate of return used in capital budgeting decisions?

EXERCISES

E28-1 The Troy Company manufactures toasters. For the first eight months of 1988, the company reported the following operating results while operating at 75% of plant capacity:

Sales (300,000 units)	$3,000,000
Cost of goods sold	2,100,000
Gross profit	900,000
Operating expenses	400,000
Net income	$ 500,000

Cost of goods sold was 70% variable and 30% fixed; operating expenses were 60% variable and 40% fixed.

In September, Troy Company receives a special order for 10,000 toasters at $7 each from the Amigo Company of Mexico City. Acceptance of the order would result in $2,000 of shipping costs but no increase in fixed operating expenses.

INSTRUCTIONS

(a) Prepare an incremental analysis for the special order.

(b) Should the Troy Company accept the special order? Why or why not?

E28-2 Lonberg Inc. has been manufacturing its own shades for its table lamps. The company is currently operating at 100% of capacity, and variable manufacturing overhead is charged to production at the rate of 50% of direct labor cost. The direct materials and direct labor cost per unit to make the lamp shades are $3.00 and $4.00, respectively. Normal production is 20,000 table lamps per year.

A supplier offers to make the lamp shades at a price of $10.00 per unit. If Lonberg Inc. accepts the supplier's offer, all variable manufacturing costs will be eliminated, but the $30,000 of fixed manufacturing overhead currently being charged to the lamp shades will have to be absorbed by other products.

INSTRUCTIONS

(a) Prepare the incremental analysis for the decision to make or buy the lamp shades.

(b) Should Lonberg Inc. buy the lamps?

(c) Would your answer be different in (b) above if the productive capacity released by discontinuing making the lamp shades could be used to produce income of $24,000?

E28-3 Delphine Ladendorf recently opened her own basketweaving studio. She sells finished baskets in addition to the raw materials needed by customers to weave baskets of their own. Delphine has put together a variety of raw material kits, each including materials at various stages of completion. Unfortunately, owing to space limitations, Delphine is unable to carry all varieties of kits originally assembled and must choose between two basic packages.

The basic introductory kit includes undyed, uncut reeds (with dye included) for weaving one basket. This basic package costs Delphine $10 and sells for $24. The second kit, called Stage 2, includes cut reeds that have already been dyed. With this kit the customer need only soak the reeds and weave the basket. Delphine is able to produce the second kit by using the basic materials included in the first kit and adding one hour of her own time, which she values at $15 per hour. Because she is more efficient at cutting and dying reeds than her average customer, Delphine is able to make two kits of the dyed reeds from one kit of undyed reeds. The kit of dyed reeds sells for $29.

INSTRUCTIONS

Determine whether Delphine's basketweaving shop should carry the basic introductory kit with undyed reeds or the Stage 2 kit with reeds already dyed. Prepare an incremental analysis to support your answer.

E28-4 Maiden Enterprises uses a word processing computer to handle its sales invoices. Lately, business has been so good that it takes an extra three hours per night, plus every third Saturday, to keep up with the volume of sales invoices. Management is considering updating its computer with a faster model that would eliminate all of the overtime processing.

	Current Machine	New Machine
Original purchase cost	$12,000	$20,000
Accumulated depreciation	5,000	—
Estimated operating costs	20,750	15,600
Useful life	5 years	5 years

If sold now, the current machine would have a salvage value of $2,000. If operated for the remainder of its useful life, the current machine would have zero salvage value. The new machine is expected to have zero salvage value after five years.

INSTRUCTIONS

Should the current machine be replaced? (Ignore the time value of money and income taxes.)

E28-5 Jane Sutton, a recent graduate of Slippery Stone's accounting program, evaluated the operating performance of Waldo Company's six divisions. Jane made the following presentation to Waldo's Board of Directors and suggested the Halen Division be eliminated. "If the Halen Division is eliminated," she said, "our total profits would increase by $21,870."

	The Other Five Divisions	Halen Division	Total
Sales	$1,564,200	$ 78,200	$1,642,400
Cost of goods sold	938,520	66,470	1,004,990
Gross profit	625,680	11,730	637,410
Operating expenses	507,940	33,600	541,540
Net income	$ 117,740	$(21,870)	$ 95,870

For the other divisions, cost of goods sold is 75% variable and operating expenses are 60% variable. The cost of goods sold for Halen Division is 20% fixed, and its operating expenses are 70% fixed. None of the Halen Division's fixed operating expenses will be eliminated if the division is discontinued.

INSTRUCTIONS

Is Jane right about eliminating the Halen Division? Prepare a schedule to support your answer.

E28-6 Meridian Company manufactures and sells three products. Relevant per unit data concerning each product are given below:

	Product		
	A	B	C
Selling price	$9	$10	$12
Variable costs and expenses	$5	$ 7	$10
Machine hours to produce	2	1	1

INSTRUCTIONS

(a) Compute the contribution margin per unit of the limited resource for each product.

(b) Assuming 900 additional machine hours are available, which product should be manufactured?

(c) Prepare an analysis showing the total contribution margin if the additional hours are (1) divided equally among the products, and (2) allocated entirely to the product identified in (b) above.

E28-7 Wayne's Service Center just purchased an automobile hoist for $8,000. The hoist has a five-year life and an estimated salvage value of $520. Installation costs and freight charges were $2,500 and $420, respectively. Wayne uses straight-line depreciation.

The new hoist will be used to replace mufflers and tires on automobiles. Wayne estimates that the new hoist will enable his mechanics to replace three extra mufflers per week. Each muffler sells for $60 installed. The cost of a muffler is $35 and the labor cost to install a muffler is $5.00.

INSTRUCTIONS

(a) Compute the payback period for the new hoist.

(b) Compute the annual rate of return for the new hoist. (Round to one decimal.)

E28-8 The Phelan Manufacturing Company is considering three new projects, each requiring an equipment investment of $19,000. Each project will last for three years and produce the following cash inflows:

Year	AA	BB	CC
1	$ 5,000	$ 8,500	$12,000
2	8,000	8,500	8,000
3	14,000	8,500	10,000
Total	$27,000	$25,500	$30,000

The equipment salvage value is $1,000, and Phelan uses straight-line depreciation. Phelan will not accept any project with a payback period over two years. Phelan's minimum required rate of return is 15%.

INSTRUCTIONS

(Round to two decimals.)

(a) Compute each project's payback period, indicating the most desirable project and the least desirable project using this method.

(b) Compute the net present value of each project. Does your evaluation change?

(c) Compute the excess present value index for project CC.

E28-9 Gordi Company is considering a capital investment of $160,000 in additional productive facilities. The new machinery is expected to have a useful life of 5 years with no salvage value. Depreciation is by the straight-line method. During the life of the investment, annual net income and cash inflows are expected to be $16,000 and $48,000 respectively. Gordi has a 15% cost of capital rate which is the minimum acceptable rate of return on the investment.

INSTRUCTIONS

(Round to two decimals.)

(a) Compute (1) the annual rate of return and (2) the cash payback period on the proposed capital expenditure.

(b) Using the discounted cash flow technique, compute the net present value. Present your net present value findings in report form.

E28-10 The Bordine Company is considering five capital expenditure projects. Relevant data for the projects are as follows:

Project	Investment	Annual Income	Life of Project
21A	$150,000	$10,000	4 years
22A	210,000	16,000	6 years
23A	240,000	23,400	8 years
24A	288,000	20,000	9 years
25A	310,000	17,500	10 years

Annual income is constant over the life of the project. Each project is expected to have zero salvage value at the end of the project. Bordine Company uses the straight-line method of depreciation.

INSTRUCTIONS

(a) Determine the internal rate of return for each project. Round the internal rate of return factor to three decimals.

(b) If Bordine Company's minimum required rate of return is 12%, which projects are acceptable?

PROBLEMS

P28-1 Real Sports Inc. manufactures basketballs for the National Basketball Association (NBA). For the first six months of 1988, the company reported the following operating results while operating at 80% of plant capacity.

	Amount	Per Unit
Sales	$4,000,000	$40.00
Cost of goods sold	3,200,000	32.00
Selling and administrative expenses	300,000	3.00
Net income	$ 500,000	$ 5.00

Fixed costs for the period were: cost of goods sold $1,200,000, and selling and administrative expenses $100,000.

In July, normally a slack manufacturing month, Real Sports receives a special order for 10,000 basketballs at $25 each from the Japanese Basketball Association (JBA). Acceptance of the order would increase variable selling and administrative expenses $.25 per unit because of shipping costs but would not increase fixed costs and expenses.

INSTRUCTIONS

(a) Prepare an incremental analysis for the special order.

(b) Should Real Sports Inc. accept the special order?

(c) What is the minimum selling price on the special order to produce net income of $2.00 per ball?

(d) What nonquantitative factors should management consider in making its decision?

P28-2 The management of the Pointer Manufacturing Company is trying to decide whether to continue manufacturing a part or to buy it from an outside supplier. The part, called WISCO, is a component of the company's finished product.

The following information was collected from the accounting records and production data for the year ending December 31, 1987.

1. 6,000 units of WISCO were produced in the Machining Department.
2. Total manufacturing costs applicable to the Machining Department were:

Direct materials	$75,000	Depreciation	$12,000
Direct labor	60,000	Property taxes	4,000
Indirect labor	6,000	Insurance	5,000
Utilities	10,000		

3. Variable manufacturing costs applicable to the production of each WISCO unit were: Direct materials $3.75, Direct labor $4.50, Indirect labor $.25, Utilities $.25.
4. Fixed manufacturing costs applicable to the production of WISCO were:

Cost Item	Direct	Allocated
Depreciation	$1,500	$ 800
Property taxes	300	200
Insurance	900	500
	$2,700	$1,500

All variable manufacturing and direct fixed costs will be eliminated if WISCO is purchased. Allocated costs will have to be absorbed by other production departments.

5. Any equipment and machinery used exclusively to produce WISCO units has a zero salvage value. (All tax effects should be ignored.)
6. The lowest quotation for 6,000 WISCO units from a supplier is $53,000.
7. If WISCO units are purchased, freight and inspection costs would be $.36 per unit, and receiving costs totaling $750 per year would be incurred by the Machining Department.

INSTRUCTIONS

(a) Prepare an incremental analysis for WISCO. Your analysis should have columns for (1) Make WISCO, (2) Buy WISCO, and (3) Net Income Increase/Decrease.

(b) Based on your analysis, what decision should management make?

(c) Would the decision be different if the Pointer Company has the opportunity to produce $5,000 of net income with the facilities currently being used to manufacture WISCO? Show computations.

(d) What nonquantitative factors should management consider in making its decision?

P28-3 Midtown Manufacturing Company has four operating divisions. During the first quarter of 1987, the company reported aggregate income from operations of $85,000 and the following divisional results.

	Division			
	I	II	III	IV
Sales	$400,000	$300,000	$200,000	$100,000
Cost of goods sold	280,000	240,000	180,000	90,000
Selling and administrative expenses	40,000	30,000	25,000	30,000
Income (loss) from operations	$ 80,000	$ 30,000	$ (5,000)	$ (20,000)

Analysis reveals the following percentages of variable costs in each division.

	I	II	III	IV
Cost of goods sold	70%	80%	75%	90%
Selling and administrative expenses	40	50	60	80

Discontinuance of any division would save 50% of the fixed costs and expenses for that division.

Top management is very concerned about the unprofitable divisions (III and IV). Consensus is that one or both of the divisions should be discontinued.

INSTRUCTIONS

(a) Compute the contribution margin for Divisions III and IV.

(b) Prepare an incremental analysis concerning the possible discontinuance of (1) Division III and (2) Division IV. What course of action do you recommend for each division?

(c) Prepare a columnar condensed income statement for Midtown Manufacturing, assuming Division IV is eliminated. Use the CVP format. Division IV's unavoidable fixed costs are allocated equally to the continuing divisions.

(d) Reconcile the total income from operations ($85,000) with the total income from operations without Division IV.

P28-4 The A & L partnership is considering three long-term capital investment proposals. Each investment has a useful life of 5 years. Relevant data on each project are as follows:

	Project Rip	Project Tip	Project Zip
Capital investment	$120,000	$150,000	$200,000
Annual net income:			
year 1	8,000	19,000	28,000
2	8,000	18,000	22,000
3	9,000	14,000	20,000
4	8,000	10,000	17,000
5	7,000	9,000	8,000
Total	$ 40,000	$ 70,000	$ 95,000

Depreciation is computed by the straight-line method with no salvage value. The company's cost of capital is 15%.

INSTRUCTIONS

(Round all computations to the nearest dollar.)

(a) Compute the annual rate of return for each project.

(b) Compute the cash payback period for each project.

(c) Compute the net present value for each project.

(d) Prepare a net present value report for the Zip project.

(e) Compute the excess present value index for each project.

(f) Rank the projects on each of the foregoing bases. Which project do you recommend?

P28-5 Bill Scott is an accounting major at a midwestern state university located approximately sixty miles from a major city. Many of the students attending the university are from the metropolitan area and visit their homes regularly on the weekends. Bill, an entrepreneur at heart, realizes that few good commuting alternatives are available for students doing weekend travel. He believes that a weekend commuting ser-

vice could be organized and run profitably from several suburban and downtown shopping mall locations. Bill has gathered the following investment information:

1. Six used station wagons would cost a total of $60,000 to purchase and would have a 3-year useful life with negligible salvage value. Bill plans to use straight-line depreciation.
2. Ten drivers would have to be employed at a total annual payroll expense of $28,000.
3. Other annual out of pocket expenses associated with running the commuter service would include Gasoline $10,000, Maintenance $2,500, Repairs $3,000, Insurance $3,200, Advertising $1,000.
4. Bill has visited several financial institutions to discuss funding for his new venture. The best interest rate he has been able to negotiate is 10%. Use this rate for cost of capital.
5. Bill expects each station wagon to make 8 round trips weekly and carry an average of 5 students each trip. The service is expected to operate 30 weeks each year, and each student will be charged $10.00 for a round trip ticket.

INSTRUCTIONS

(a) Determine the annual (1) net income, and (2) cash inflow for the commuter service.

(b) Compute (1) the annual rate of return, and (2) the cash payback period.

(c) Compute the net present value of the commuter service. (Round to the nearest dollar.)

(d) Repeat (a)–(c) assuming (1) each station wagon will make 9 round trips weekly and carry 5 students each trip, (2) total salaries will be $35,000, and (3) Bill's cost of capital rate is 12%.

(e) What should Bill conclude from these computations?

ALTERNATE PROBLEMS

P28–1A The Craft Company is currently producing 12,000 units per month, which is 80% of its production capacity. Variable manufacturing costs are currently $9.50 per unit, and fixed manufacturing costs are $45,000 per month. Craft pays an 8% sales commission to its sales people, has $20,000 in fixed administrative expenses per month, and is averaging $240,000 in sales per month.

A special order received from a foreign company would enable the Craft Company to operate at 100% capacity. The foreign company offered to pay 65% of Craft's current selling price per unit. If the order is accepted, Craft will have to spend an extra $1.50 per unit to package the product for overseas shipping. Also, the Craft Company would need to lease a new stamping machine to imprint the foreign company's logo on the product, at a monthly cost of $2,000. The special order would require a sales commission of $1,560.

INSTRUCTIONS

(a) Compute the number of units involved in the special order and the foreign company's offered price per unit.

(b) What is the manufacturing cost of producing one unit of Craft's product for regular customers?

(c) Prepare an incremental analysis of the special order. Should management accept the order?

(d) What is the lowest price that Craft could accept for the special order to earn net income of $1.00 per unit.

(e) What nonquantitative factors should management consider in making its decision?

P28-2A The management of the Walker Manufacturing Company has asked for your assistance in deciding whether to continue manufacturing a part or to buy it from an outside supplier. The part, called Master-mind, is a component of Walker's finished product.

An analysis of the accounting records and the production data revealed the following information for the year ending December 31, 1986.

1. The Machinery Department produced 36,000 units of Master-mind.
2. Each Master-mind unit requires 10 minutes to produce. Three people in the Machinery Department work full time (2,000 hours per year) producing Master-minds. Each person is paid $8.50 per hour.
3. The cost of materials per Master-mind unit is $1.75. Total manufacturing overhead for the Machinery Department was $39,780, broken down as follows: Indirect labor, $18,000; Utilities, $8,000; Depreciation, $9,000; Property taxes and insurance, $4,780.
4. Manufacturing costs directly applicable to the production of Master-minds are: Indirect labor, $4,500; Utilities, $1,200; Depreciation, $1,500; Property taxes and insurance, $680.
5. The lowest price for a Master-mind from an outside supplier is $3.00 per unit. Freight charges will be $.25 per unit, and a part-time receiving clerk at $8,000 per year will be required.
6. If Master-mind is purchased, the excess space will be used to store Walker's finished product. Currently, Walker rents storage space at approximately $.45 per unit stored per year. Approximately 4,000 units per year are stored in the rented space.

INSTRUCTIONS

(a) Prepare an incremental analysis for the make-or-buy decision. Should Walker make or buy the part? Why?

(b) Prepare an incremental analysis, assuming the released facilities can be used to produce $5,000 of net income in addition to the saving on the rental of storage space. What decision should now be made?

(c) What qualitative factors should be considered in the decision?

P28-3A Eastern Manufacturing Company has four operating divisions. During the first quarter of 1987, the company reported total income from operations of $76,000 and the following results for the divisions:

	Division			
	Boston	Syracuse	Hartford	Newark
Sales	$400,000	$700,000	$900,000	$500,000
Cost of goods sold	360,000	450,000	546,000	420,000
Gross profit	40,000	250,000	354,000	80,000
Selling expenses	50,000	133,000	142,000	70,000
Administrative expenses	35,000	74,000	104,000	40,000
Total operating expenses	85,000	207,000	246,000	110,000
Income (loss) from operations	$ (45,000)	$ 43,000	$108,000	$ (30,000)

Analysis reveals the following percentages of variable costs in each division.

	Boston	Syracuse	Hartford	Newark
Cost of goods sold	95%	80%	90%	85%
Selling expenses	90	70	80	75
Administrative expenses	40	30	40	35

Discontinuance of any division would save 60% of the fixed costs and expenses for that division.

Top management is deeply concerned about the unprofitable divisions (Boston and Newark). The consensus is that one or both of the divisions should be eliminated.

INSTRUCTIONS

(a) Compute the contribution margin for the two unprofitable divisions.

(b) Prepare an incremental analysis concerning the possible elimination of (1) the Boston Division and (2) the Newark Division. What course of action do you recommend for each division?

(c) Prepare a columnar condensed income statement using the CVP format for Eastern Manufacturing Company, assuming (1) the Boston Division is eliminated, and (2) the unavoidable fixed costs and expenses of the Boston Division are allocated 30% to Syracuse, 50% to Hartford, and 20% to Newark.

(d) Compare the total income from operations with the Boston Division ($76,000) to total income from operations without this division.

P28-4A The partnership of Harns and Handley is considering three long-term capital investment proposals. Relevant data on each project are as follows:

	Project		
	Blue	Green	Red
Capital investment	$170,000	$220,000	$250,000
Annual net income:			
Year 1	20,000	18,000	28,000
2	16,000	18,000	27,000
3	12,000	18,000	24,000
4	10,000	18,000	20,000
5	8,000	18,000	18,000
6		18,000	17,000
7			14,000
8			12,000

Salvage value is expected to be $10,000 at the end of each project. Depreciation is computed by the straight-line method. The company's minimum rate of return is the company's cost of capital which is 12%.

INSTRUCTIONS

(Round all computations to the nearest dollar.)

(a) Compute the average annual rate of return for each project.

(b) Compute the cash payback period for each project.

(c) Compute the net present value for each project.

(d) Prepare a net present value report for the Blue project.

(e) Determine the excess present value index for each project.

P28–5A Joan Bloomfield is managing director of the Wee-Care day care center. Wee-Care is currently set up as a full-time child care facility for children between the ages of 12 months and 6 years. Joan is trying to determine whether the center should expand its facilities to incorporate a newborn care room for infants between the ages of 6 weeks and 12 months. The necessary space already exists. An investment of $20,000 would be needed, however, to purchase cribs, high chairs, etc. The equipment purchased for the room would have a 5-year useful life with zero salvage value.

The newborn nursery would be staffed to handle 10 infants on a full-time basis. The parents of each infant would be charged $120 weekly, and the facility would operate 52 weeks of the year. Staffing the nursery would require two full-time specialists and five part-time assistants at an annual cost of $45,000. Food, diapers, and other miscellaneous supplies are expected to total $11,500 annually.

INSTRUCTIONS

(a) Determine (1) annual net income, and (2) cash inflow for the new nursery.

(b) Compute (1) the annual rate of return and (2) the cash payback period for the new nursery.

(c) Assuming that Wee-Care can borrow the money needed for expansion at 12%, compute the net present value of the new room. (Round to the nearest dollar.)

(d) Repeat (a)–(c) assuming (1) only 9 infants are cared for in an average week, (2) the weekly fee is $125, the annual cost of support personnel and supplies are $41,000 and $11,250, respectively, and (3) the cost of capital is 12%.

(e) What should Joan conclude from these computations?

DECISION CASE

The Reno Company is considering the purchase of a new machine. The invoice price of the machine is $120,000, freight charges are estimated to be $3,000, and installation costs are expected to be $4,000. Salvage value of the new equipment is expected to be $15,000 after a useful life of 4 years. Existing equipment could be retained and used for an additional 4 years if the new machine is not purchased. At that time, the salvage value of the equipment would be zero. If the new machine is purchased now, the existing machine would have to be scrapped. Reno's accountant, Anna Garcia, has accumulated the following data regarding annual sales and expenses with and without the new machine.

(a) Without the new machine, Reno can sell 10,000 units of product annually at a per unit selling price of $100. If the new unit is purchased, the number of units produced and sold would increase by 20%, and the selling price would remain the same.

(b) The new machine is faster than the old machine, and it is more efficient in its usage of materials. With the old machine the gross profit rate will be 26.5% of sales, whereas the rate will be 28% of sales with the new machine.

(c) Annual selling expenses are $150,000 with the current equipment. Because the new equipment would produce a greater number of units to be sold, annual selling expenses are expected to increase by 20% if it is purchased.

(d) Annual administrative expenses are expected to be $100,000 with the old machine, and $113,000 with the new machine.

(e) The current book value of the existing machine is $30,000. Reno uses straight-line depreciation.

(f) Reno's management wants a minimum rate of return of 15% on its investment and a payback period of no more than 3 years.

INSTRUCTIONS

(Ignore income tax effects.)

(a) Prepare an incremental analysis for the four years showing whether Reno should keep the existing machine or buy the new machine.

(b) Calculate the annual rate of return for the new machine. (Round to two decimals.)

(c) Compute the payback period for the new machine. (Round to two decimals.)

(d) Compute the net present value of the new machine. (Round to the nearest dollar.)

(e) On the basis of the foregoing data, would you recommend that Reno buy the machine? Why?

CHAPTER 29

Boise State University, Idaho

CHAPTER 29

INCOME TAXES AND MANAGEMENT DECISIONS

STUDY OBJECTIVES

After studying this chapter, you should be able to:

1. Contrast the importance of an average tax rate and a marginal tax rate.
2. Identify the filing status that an individual may elect.
3. Give the formula for determining taxable income.
4. Distinguish between the standard deduction and itemized deductions.
5. State the formula for determining the tax refund or balance due.
6. Indicate the principal components in determining taxable income for a corporation.
7. Enumerate circumstances in which income taxes may affect management decisions.

Explanatory Note

This chapter discusses only the new Tax Reform Act of 1986. The magnitude of this new Act cannot be overstated. Familiar concepts and terminology related to the old law are often eliminated, or, in some cases, given different meanings. Thus, students interested in understanding the impact of the tax law on decision making must be aware of the basic provisions of this new Act.

They say there are only two certainties in life: death and taxes. The only difference, according to one senator, is that death doesn't get worse every

time Congress meets.[1] The federal government, most states, and many cities levy an income tax. It follows that income taxes can be a significant expense for individual and corporate taxpayers. It is important, therefore, to recognize the income tax consequences when making business decisions.

In 1986, Congress passed the Tax Reform Act, the most sweeping federal tax legislation in more than 40 years. The Tax Reform Act, hereinafter referred to as the Act, dramatically lowers income tax rates, significantly broadens the tax base, and shifts the tax burden from individuals to corporations. It also renamed the tax law The Internal Revenue Code of 1986.

In this chapter, we first explain the basic structure of the federal income tax system and the major provisions of the Act that pertain to individuals and corporations. Then we consider the effect of income taxes on business decisions.

FEDERAL INCOME TAX SYSTEM

Federal income taxes originated in the Sixteenth Amendment to the Constitution, which was passed in 1913. Since that date, numerous tax acts have been passed by Congress, and these acts (or laws) are summarized in the Internal Revenue Code. Primary responsibility for administering and interpreting the federal income tax laws rests with the Treasury Department, and a division of this department, The **Internal Revenue Service** (IRS). The IRS is charged with the collection of taxes and enforcement of the tax regulations. Final authority for resolving disputes between the federal government and a taxpayer rests with the federal courts.

Originally, levied solely to raise revenue for the federal government, income taxes have become a powerful economic and social force. Considerable reliance is placed on income taxes in fighting inflation and deflation and in attaining full employment.

TAXABLE ENTITIES

Income taxes are imposed on **taxable entities.** A taxable entity and an accounting entity need not be identical. The three major classes of taxable entities are (1) individuals, (2) corporations, and (3) fiduciaries (estates and trusts). **A business operated as a proprietorship or a partnership is an accounting entity but not a taxable entity.** Net income from such a source is reported as income on the proprietor's or partners' individual tax return(s), regardless of whether the net income is actually withdrawn from the business. In contrast, a corporation is both an accounting and a taxable entity. A corporation must file a tax return and pay income taxes on its taxable income.

[1] "Current Accounts," *Money*, October 1986, p. 11.

TAX RELATIONSHIPS

A tax may be proportional, regressive, or progressive. A **proportional tax** occurs when a constant rate (or percentage) is applied regardless of changes in the amount of the tax base. Sales taxes are proportional because the same tax rate is applied irrespective of the amount of the sale. A **regressive tax** is one in which the amount of the tax remains unchanged or the tax rate decreases inversely with increases in the tax base. For example, license taxes imposed for the privilege of engaging in a business, occupation, or profession are usually regressive, since they are not related to sales or net income. A **progressive tax** results when the tax rate becomes higher as the amount of tax base increases. Federal income taxes and most state income taxes are progressive with respect to income.

In considering the effect of income taxes, it is necessary to distinguish between an **average rate** and a **marginal rate.** The average rate is determined by dividing the total tax paid by total taxable income. The marginal rate is the tax rate applicable to the last dollars of taxable income. For example, if the tax rate is 15% on the first $30,000 of taxable income and 28% on all taxable income over $30,000, the marginal tax rate is 28% if the taxpayer has taxable income in excess of $30,000. Under the Act, the highest marginal rate is 28% for most individuals and 34% for most corporations. The marginal tax rate is usually more significant than the average tax rate in making business decisions. For example, in both incremental analysis and in capital budgeting, the anticipated income will be subject to the marginal tax rate.

TAX METHODS

For tax purposes, individual taxpayers generally have the option to use either the cash method or the accrual method in determining taxable income. Most corporations, however, are required to use the accrual method. The choice between the methods relates to the timing of revenues and expenses. Changes from one method to another must be approved by the Internal Revenue Service. The essential features of each method are described below.

ACCRUAL METHOD

The accrual method of accounting has been stressed throughout this textbook. Under this method, revenues are recognized when they are earned, and expenses are recognized when they are incurred. The accrual method is normally used when taxable income is based on business net income.

CASH METHOD

Under the cash method, revenues are recognized when they are realized in cash, and expenses are recognized when they are paid. The cash method

requires a minimum of record-keeping. When taxable income consists primarily of salaries, interest, and dividends, the results under this method may approximate the results under the accrual method. The cash method is normally used by individual taxpayers.

FILING STATUS FOR INDIVIDUALS

Individual taxpayers must elect one filing status from the following options:

1. Single.
2. Head of household.
3. Married filing a joint return.[2]
4. Married filing a separate return.

Filing status is determined on the last day of the taxable year. To qualify as a head of a household, an individual taxpayer who is unmarried or legally separated at the end of the taxable year must have paid more than half the cost of keeping up a home that has been the principal residence of his or her dependents. In most cases, married couples will pay less tax by filing a joint return than by filing separate returns.

SECTION ONE—INDIVIDUALS

The Internal Revenue Service provides specific tax forms and instructions for filing an income tax return. The formula for computing taxable income for an individual taxpayer is as follows:

Taxable income formula for an individual

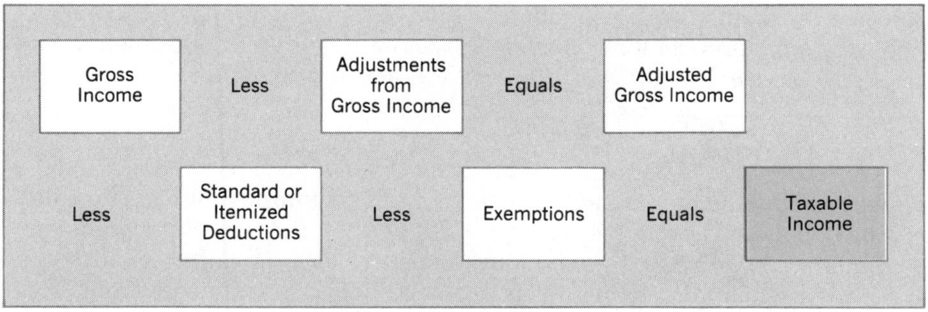

Each of the steps in the formula is explained below.

[2]This status includes qualifying widows and widowers.

GROSS INCOME

Gross income is "all income from whatever source derived." The Act identifies both inclusions and exclusions from gross income. A representative listing of items in each category is presented below.

Gross income inclusions and exclusions

Gross Income

Inclusions	Exclusions
Wages, including salaries, bonuses, commissions, fees, and tips	Interest on certain state and municipal bonds
Dividends, rents, and royalties	State and federal welfare benefits
Interest on bank deposits, bonds, and notes	Gifts, inheritances, and bequests
Business and farm income	Life insurance proceeds received from a person's death
Pensions, annuities, and endowments	Dividends on veterans' life insurance
Gains from sale or exchange of real estate, securities, and personal residence	Child support
Prizes and awards from contests, raffles, and lotteries	
Artistic, scientific, and employee productivity awards	
Unemployment compensation	
Reimbursed business expenses	
Alimony received	

Gross income may be received in the form of cash, property, or services. When cash is not involved, income is measured by the fair market value of the property or services received.

Although most of the items included in gross income are self-evident, three concepts need additional explanation: (1) business income, (2) passive income, and (3) capital gains and losses.

BUSINESS INCOME

Net income from a proprietorship and an individual's share of the net income of a partnership are included in gross income. Conversely, a net loss from a business in which the taxpayer actively participates can be offset against gross income.

Business net income or net loss determined in conformity with generally accepted accounting principles may not be in accord with tax provisions for determining business income. In determining net income for tax purposes, the taxpayer should take advantage of as many favorable tax provisions as possible. For example, a taxpayer would likely adopt the Tax Code's Accelerated Cost Recovery System (ACRS), which provides for rapid write-off of the

cost of depreciable assets. Further consideration is given to this method of depreciation later in the chapter.

PASSIVE INCOME

In the Act, a distinction is made between active and passive income, depending on the nature of the activity and the taxpayer's involvement in generating the income. **Active income** includes salaries and wages earned by the taxpayer, and business and farm income when the taxpayer materially participated in producing the income. **Passive income** relates to income obtained from activities in which the taxpayer does not participate on a regular, continuous, and substantial basis. The Act also recognizes **portfolio income** which includes interest and dividends from securities held as an investment.

All income is reported in gross income and is taxed at regular rates. However, the Act prohibits the taxpayer from using net passive losses to offset the other types of income until the taxpayer's entire interest in the passive activity is terminated. At that time, net passive losses can offset active and portfolio income.

The provisions applicable to passive income and losses substantially reduce the use of tax shelters. A **tax shelter** is an investment that is designed to take advantage of various tax benefits. One objective of the investment is to use losses from the investment as immediate offsets against gross income. In terms of real dollars, the return on a tax shelter was often very high. Typically, investments in rental properties, equipment leasing, and oil and gas ventures have been used as tax shelters. These types of investments are generally considered to be passive activities. Thus, losses from tax shelters must now be deferred, as described above.

CAPITAL GAINS AND LOSSES

A **capital gain or loss** occurs when property classified under tax law as a capital asset is sold or exchanged. A capital asset is any item of property other than (1) inventories, (2) trade receivables, (3) plant assets used in a trade or business, and (4) certain intangible assets such as copyrights and artistic compositions.[3] For an individual, capital assets include all property held for investment and for personal use.

When a capital asset is sold, gain or loss is determined by the difference between the proceeds from the sale and the **tax basis** of the property, which is generally cost or cost less accumulated depreciation. Under the Act, the length of time capital assets are held is irrelevant. Net capital gains are included in gross income and are taxed in the same manner as other types of gross income. A net capital gain results when capital gains exceed capital losses. A net capital loss occurs when capital losses exceed capital gains. Net capital losses are offset against gross income on a dollar-for-dollar basis up to a maximum of $3,000 per year. Losses in excess of $3,000 can be carried forward to future years with the same $3,000 limitation.

To illustrate a net capital gain, assume that Paul Moran sold the following securities in 1988:

[3] In some cases, plant assets used in a trade or business may qualify as capital assets.

Computation of net capital gain

Type of Security	Tax Basis	Selling Price	Capital Gain	Capital Loss
Burlington common stock	$ 4,200	$ 6,000	$1,800	
Newport preferred stock	5,000	5,500	500	
Pacific common stock	2,600	2,000		$600
Totals	$11,800	$13,500	$2,300	$600

Paul Moran has realized a net capital gain of $1,700 (capital gains of $2,300 less capital losses of $600), which is reported under gross income.

COMPUTATION OF GROSS INCOME

To illustrate the computation of gross income, we will assume the following data for Paul Moran:

Assumed income data

Salary and commissions as sales representative for Standard Manufacturing Company	$45,000
Net capital gains (see above)	1,700
Interest from tax-exempt municipal bonds	3,600
Dividends from investments	2,400
Net income from a limited partnership	5,000

Paul Moran's gross income is $54,100, computed as follows:

Computation of gross income

Salaries and commissions	$45,000
Net capital gains	1,700
Dividends	2,400
Partnership income	5,000
Total gross income	$54,100

All of the items except the interest from the tax-exempt municipal bonds must be reported under gross income.

ADJUSTMENTS FROM GROSS INCOME

Adjustments from gross income include (1) reimbursed business expenses, (2) payments to retirement plans, and (3) alimony payments.

REIMBURSED BUSINESS EXPENSES

Reimbursed business expenses are business expenses initially paid by the taxpayer that are subsequently reimbursed by the taxpayer's employer. Reim-

bursed business expenses are an adjustment to gross income to the extent that they are included in gross income. Consequently, these business expenses are offset to the extent of gross income and have no effect on the amount of adjusted gross income.

PAYMENTS TO RETIREMENT PLANS

To encourage individuals to save for retirement, certain types of payments to retirement plans are deductible for tax purposes. In addition, the income earned on the assets invested is not taxed until it is withdrawn. Two of the most common types of personal retirement plans are:

1. Payments to an Individual Retirement Arrangement plan (IRA).
2. Payments to a Keogh H. R. 10 plan (Keogh).

IRAs

All individuals who work are allowed to contribute up to $2,000 annually to an IRA. However, restrictions apply as to the amount the individual may claim as an allowable deduction from gross income. **For individuals who are not covered by a company-sponsored pension plan, the allowable deduction is $2,000.** Married taxpayers filing a joint return may each deduct $2,000 if both individuals **work.** However, if one spouse does not **work,** the allowable deduction for the spouse is $250 per year, or a total deduction of $2,250 for the couple.

For taxpayers covered by a company-sponsored retirement plan, a deduction is permitted if income levels are below certain minimums. For example, when adjusted gross income before an IRA deduction exceeds $25,000 for a single taxpayer and $40,000 for married taxpayers filing jointly, the allowable deduction is phased out proportionately. The deductible amount becomes zero at adjusted gross income of $35,000 for a single taxpayer and at $50,000 for married taxpayers filing jointly.

Keogh Plans

Self-employed individuals can also make retirement payments to a Keogh H.R. 10 plan. The amount deductible for Keogh payments is significantly higher than the amount for IRA payments. Under a defined contribution plan, for example, the maximum deduction is $30,000. The Keogh plan enables self-employed individuals to accumulate retirement funds similar to pension funds for employed taxpayers provided by many employers.

ALIMONY PAYMENTS

Alimony payments made by an individual are an adjustment to gross income. To qualify as alimony, the payment must be made under a divorce or separation instrument and meet certain requirements. For example, (1) the payment must be in cash, (2) the parties must live in separate households, and (3) the payment cannot be treated as child support. Alimony payments represent gross income to the recipient.

ADJUSTED GROSS INCOME

Adjusted gross income is the difference between gross income and adjustments from gross income. To illustrate the computation of adjusted gross income, assume that Jane and Carl Baker are married and filing a joint return. Jane works as a word processor for Hi-Tech Inc., which does not have a company-sponsored retirement plan, and Carl is a self-employed building contractor. In 1988, Jane earned $24,000 in salary and Carl's business income was $40,000. Both individuals made the maximum $2,000 contribution to an IRA plan. In addition, Carl made an allowable contribution to a Keogh plan of $8,000. Adjusted gross income is $52,000, computed as follows:

Computation of adjusted gross income

Gross income		
Salary		$24,000
Business income		40,000
Total gross income		64,000
Deductions from gross income		
IRA contributions	$4,000	
Keogh contribution	8,000	
Total deductions		12,000
Adjusted gross income		$52,000

DEDUCTIONS FROM ADJUSTED GROSS INCOME

Deductions from adjusted gross income consist of either a standard deduction or itemized deductions.

STANDARD DEDUCTION

The **standard deduction** is the amount a taxpayer can claim without supporting documentation. It is the floor for determining whether or not it would be advantageous to itemize deductions. The standard deduction also determines whether an individual must file a tax return. If gross income is equal to or less than the standard deduction and personal exemptions (discussed later), it is not necessary to file a tax return.

The standard deduction varies for each filing status. The deductions for 1988 are as follows:

Standard deductions

Filing Status	Standard Deduction
Single	$3,000
Head of household	4,400
Married filing a joint return	5,000
Married filing a separate return	2,500

Taxpayers who are 65 years of age or older or blind may claim an extra standard deduction of $600 if married or $750 if single.

ITEMIZED DEDUCTIONS

Instead of claiming the standard deduction, the taxpayer may elect to **itemize deductions.** These deductions represent actual expenditures made by the taxpayer during the year. They are itemized in a separate tax schedule, and the taxpayer must be able to provide documentary evidence of each deduction. Itemized deductions are grouped into the following categories:

Itemized deduction categories

(1) Medical expenses and health insurance	(4) Charitable contributions
(2) State and local taxes	(5) Casualty and theft losses
(3) Interest expense	(6) Employee business expenses and miscellaneous deductions

Medical Expenses and Health Insurance

Medical expenses consist of (1) prescription drugs and insulin, and (2) other medical and dental expenses including doctors' fees, hospital care, medical examinations, X-rays, nursing help, medical aids, ambulance service, and other travel costs to obtain medical care. This itemized deduction pertains only to expenses paid by the taxpayer that are not reimbursed by insurance or paid by others. In addition, premiums paid for hospital, doctor, and dental insurance plans are deductible.

The amount of deduction for medical expenses and health insurance is limited to payments in excess of 7.5% of adjusted gross income. The computation of this itemized deduction for Wilbur Kane, using assumed data, is shown below:

Computation of medical expenses and health insurance deduction

Prescription drugs	$ 450
Orthodontic fees	1,200
Blue Cross/Blue Shield premiums	600
Other medical and dental expenses	1,300
Total	3,550
Less: 7.5% of $30,000 adjusted gross income	2,250
Deduction for medical expenses and health insurance	$1,300

Basically, the Act permits the taxpayer to deduct all legitimate major medical and health care expenses above a certain minimum.

State and Local Taxes

The list of state and local taxes that are deductible is much shorter than the taxes that are disallowed. The allowable taxes and examples of taxes that are not allowable are as follows:

Allowable and not allowable taxes

Allowable Taxes	Not Allowable Taxes
State and local income taxes	Federal income, estate, and excise taxes
Real estate taxes	FICA (social security) taxes
Personal property taxes	Sales taxes
	Gasoline taxes
	Automobile, driver's, and marriage license fees

Interest Expense

The Act classifies interest expense as either (1) mortgage interest on a qualified residence, (2) consumer (or personal) interest such as interest on car loans and credit cards, and (3) investment interest. The rules are:

Interest rules

Type of Interest	Tax Rule
Mortgage	Fully deductible
Consumer[4]	Nondeductible
Investment	Deductible to extent of investment income

A qualified residence is the taxpayer's principal residence and one other residence. There is no limit on the amount of interest that can be deducted as long as the total mortgage does not exceed the cost of the home plus improvements. Interest on mortgage indebtedness (up to the fair market value of the residence) incurred for qualified educational or medical expenses is also fully deductible.

The rules on interest expense may affect a taxpayer's use of credit. From a tax standpoint, it is advantageous to maximize the borrowing of money on one's personal residence and to minimize the use of credit for other purposes.

Charitable Contributions

An individual can deduct amounts given to qualified organizations operated for religious, charitable, educational, scientific, or literary purposes. Contributions can be in the form of cash or property such as clothing, furniture, and equipment. The annual deduction for charitable contributions cannot exceed 50% of adjusted gross income. Any contributions in excess of this amount in any year can be carried forward to future years.

Casualty and Theft Losses

A taxpayer generally is allowed to deduct losses caused by vandalism, fire, storm, theft, car and boating accidents, and similar causes (often referred to as casualties). The deductible amount is limited to the uninsured loss, and the taxpayer must file timely insurance claims. If a taxpayer fails to pursue a claim to avoid a rate increase, no deduction is allowed. To determine the

[4]Because consumer interest was allowed as a deduction under prior tax law, the disallowance is phased in over five years, increasing to 100% in 1991 and thereafter.

amount deductible, two tests have to be performed. First, only casualty losses in excess of $100 per loss are deductible. Second, the casualty loss (after subtracting the $100 deduction) is limited to an amount that exceeds 10% of adjusted gross income.

Employee Business Expenses and Miscellaneous Deductions

Unreimbursed business expenses and miscellaneous deductions are allowable as itemized deductions. Some items in this category are not subject to any floor (minimum amount). These include moving expenses, certain work expenses incurred by handicapped employees, and gambling losses to the extent of gambling winnings. All other items in this category are allowed only to the extent they exceed 2% of adjusted gross income. These items include the following:

Travel. Travel expenses include transportation, lodging, and meals incurred on trips away from home for business purposes. No deduction is allowed for travel expenses incurred (1) as a form of education, (2) for charitable purposes that provide personal, recreational, or vacation benefits, and (3) to attend seminars for investment purposes.

Entertainment and Meals. Deductions for entertainment and meals incurred for business purposes are limited to 80% of the amount paid. Further monetary restrictions apply to entertainment expenses. For example, the deduction for theater tickets is 80% of the face value of the tickets, and the deduction for the use of luxury skyboxes at a sports arena is limited to 80% of the cost of regular tickets. However, amounts paid for tickets to charitable events are fully deductible as charitable contributions.

Meals are deductible only if (1) business is discussed before, during, or after the meal, and (2) the meal has a clear business purpose directly related to the active conduct of the taxpayer's trade or business.

Deductible travel, entertainment, and meal expenses must be aggregated with miscellaneous deductions. This total is then deductible only to the extent that it exceeds 2% of adjusted gross income. From a tax standpoint, it is better for an individual to have all business expenses reimbursed by the company. As explained earlier, reimbursed expenses have no effect on adjusted gross income. Moreover, the individual will not be required to defend the deductions for reimbursed business expenses.

Other Individual Items. Expenses for union dues, tools, and uniforms are examples of items included under miscellaneous deductions. These deductions also include subscriptions to trade magazines, membership dues in professional organizations, tax counsel and tax preparation fees, and the cost of pursuing a business that is considered to be a hobby under tax law.

To illustrate the computation of employee business expenses and miscellaneous deductions, we will assume that Mary Norton incurred the following expenses when her adjusted gross income was $36,000: (1) business entertainment, $500 (paid $500 for theater tickets having a face value of $450); (2)

business meals, $400; (3) income tax preparation fee, $250; and (4) membership dues in professional organization, $50.

The allowable deduction is $260 computed as follows:

Computation of allowable business expenses and miscellaneous deductions

Entertainment (80% × $450)	$360
Meals (80% × $400)	320
Income tax preparation fee	250
Membership dues in professional organization	50
Total expenses	980
Less: 2% of adjusted gross income ($36,000 × 2%)	720
Allowable deduction for business expenses and miscellaneous deductions	**$260**

PERSONAL EXEMPTIONS

A taxpayer is allowed a **personal exemption** for himself or herself, his or her spouse, and for each dependent. Specific requirements must be met to qualify as a dependent. In general, a dependent must:

1. Receive less than $1,950 of gross income unless he or she is a child of the taxpayer and under 19 years of age or a full-time student.
2. Receive over one-half of his or her support from the taxpayer.
3. If married, not be filing a joint return with his or her spouse.
4. Be a citizen or a resident of the United States.
5. Be related to the taxpayer by marriage or by blood or have lived in the taxpayer's home for the entire taxable year.

The personal exemption is $1,950 for 1988. High-income taxpayers will lose part or all of this exemption if their taxable income reaches a certain level, as discussed later.

An individual who is eligible to be claimed as a dependent on another taxpayer's return is not permitted a personal exemption on his or her own return. This means, for example, that students who have summer or part-time jobs during the school year cannot claim personal exemptions on their returns if they can be claimed as a dependent on their parents' return.

TAXABLE INCOME AND COMPUTATION OF THE TAX

As indicated in the formula on page 1138, **taxable income** is determined by subtracting deductions and personal exemptions from adjusted gross income. The amount of the tax is derived from two computations: (1) determining the regular tax, and (2) determining the alternative minimum tax. The taxpayer must pay the higher of the two amounts.

DETERMINING THE REGULAR TAX

The regular tax is computed by applying the appropriate tax rate to taxable income. The Act provides for a two-bracket rate structure for 1988 and thereafter.[5] The tax rates are:

1988 tax rates

Taxable Income—Dollars				
Single Taxpayer	**Head of Household**	**Married—Jointly**	**Married—Separately**	**Tax Rate**
Up to $17,850	Up to $23,900	Up to $29,750	Up to $14,875	15%
Above $17,850	Above $23,900	Above $29,750	Above $14,875	28

The computations of the tax on $30,000 of taxable income for a single taxpayer and a married taxpayer filing a joint return are as follows:

Computation of tax

Single Taxpayer			Married Taxpayer Filing a Joint Return		
Taxable Income	Tax Rate	Tax Amount	Taxable Income	Tax Rate	Tax Amount
$17,850	15%	$2,677.50	$29,750	15%	$4,462.50
12,150	28	3,402.00	250	28	70.00
$30,000		$6,079.50	$30,000		$4,532.50

The taxpayer is subject to a 5% surtax at certain levels of taxable income. The reason for the surtax is that Congress wanted to subject higher-income taxpayers to a **flat tax rate** of 28% on all of their taxable income—not just the amount above a certain level. The income ranges in which the surtax applies are as follows:

Surtax income ranges

Filing Status	Surtax Income Range
Single taxpayer	$43,150 to $ 89,560
Head of household	$61,650 to $123,790
Married – filing jointly	$71,900 to $149,250
Married – filing separately	$35,950 to $113,300

To illustrate how the surtax works, assume that a taxpayer with $149,250 of taxable income is filing a joint tax return. The income subject to the surtax is $77,350 ($149,250 − $71,900). The surtax is $3,867.50 ($77,350 × 5%). Because of the surtax, the last dollars of taxable income are being taxed at a marginal rate of 33%. The tax computation is as follows:

Surtax computation

$ 29,750 × 15%	$ 4,462.50
$119,500 × 28%	33,460.00
$ 77,350 × 5%	3,867.50
Total tax	$41,790.00

[5] A five-bracket rate structure is used in 1987 during the phase-in of the new rates.

As a result, the taxpayer pays 28% on all taxable income ($41,790 ÷ $149,250 = 28%). Income above $149,250 for a taxpayer filing jointly is not subject to the 5% surtax, because the benefits of the 15% tax brackets have been totally eliminated at this point.

ALTERNATIVE MINIMUM TAX

The alternative minimum tax is designed to ensure that all taxpayers who have economic resources will pay some income taxes. The minimum tax liability is 21% of the individual taxpayer's alternative minimum taxable income reduced by an allowable exemption. The Act prescribes numerous adjustments and preferences to taxable income in determining alternative minimum taxable income. The computation of the alternative minimum tax is deferred to a tax accounting course.

DETERMINING TAX REFUND OR BALANCE DUE

The remaining steps in the filing of an income tax return result in determining either the tax refund or the balance due. The steps consist of subtracting tax credits and tax payments from the amount of the tax as diagrammed below:

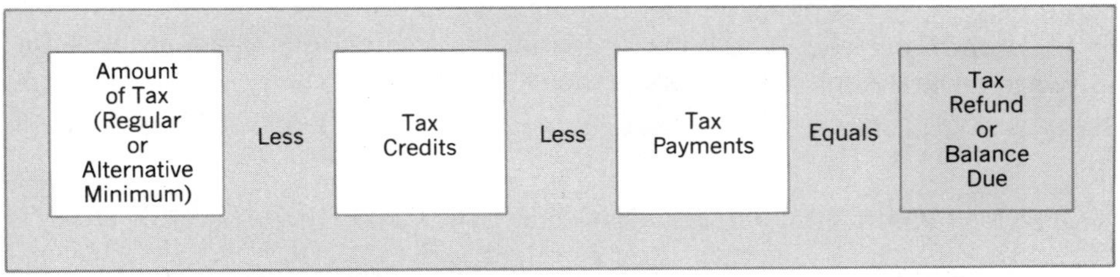

Steps required to determine tax refund or balance due

Each of these steps is explained below.

TAX CREDITS

Tax credits are reductions in the tax liability computed on taxable income. They are more beneficial to a taxpayer than a deduction or an exemption because they are deducted directly from the amount of the tax. A $100 tax credit reduces the tax liability by $100, whereas the effect of a $100 tax deduction on the tax liability depends entirely on the taxpayer's marginal tax rate. For individuals, tax credits may be claimed for (1) child and dependent care, and (2) earned income.

The child and dependent care credit helps certain working parents to defray the cost of caring for children and elderly dependents. The maximum credit is $1,440 for two or more dependents.

The earned-income credit allows low-income families with children to keep more of their earnings. The maximum credit is $800.

TAX PAYMENTS

As explained in Chapter 12, employers are required to withhold income taxes from employees. In addition, a taxpayer with gross income that is not subject to withholding (e.g., dividends and interest) is required to make quarterly estimated tax payments. The withholdings and estimated payments are subtracted from the amount of the tax (less tax credits, if any) to determine either the amount payable to the Internal Revenue Service or the amount to be refunded to the taxpayer. When a refund results, the taxpayer has the option of applying the amount to the estimated tax in the following year.

The total of taxes withheld and estimated taxes paid must be either (1) 100% of the previous year's tax liability, or (2) 90% of the current year's liability. Interest penalties are imposed for any underpayment of estimated taxes.

Individual taxpayers are required to file a tax return on or before the 15th day of the fourth month following the close of the tax year. For individual taxpayers the tax year is generally the calendar year.

Many computerized tax return preparation and planning programs are available. These programs are capable of handling the simplest to the most complex tax situations far less expensively and more accurately than manual systems. As noted in Chapter 28, spreadsheet programs can be designed to handle any business decision model, and this includes tax return preparation and planning as well. Thus, tax practitioners can choose between specific software programs or design spreadsheets to do the work.

ILLUSTRATION OF DETERMINING TAX REFUND OR BALANCE DUE

To illustrate the determination of the tax liability or the amount of the refund, we will make the computation for Sharon and James Moore, who are married and filing jointly. They have two children who are claimed as dependents. Sharon has no income. James is not covered by an employer-sponsored retirement plan. The couple has made the maximum payment to IRA. Their federal income tax computation for the year 1988 is shown on page 1151.

SECTION TWO—PARTNERSHIPS

Although a partnership is not a taxable entity, it is required to file an information return for each taxable year, regardless of the amount of partnership income. The return must state specifically the items composing gross income and the allowable deductions. In addition, the return must include the name of each partner who would be entitled to share in taxable income if distributed, and the dollar amount of the distributive shares of each individual.

Computation of tax due

SHARON AND JAMES MOORE
Federal Income Tax Computation

GROSS INCOME			
James Moore salary		$67,750	
Interest and dividends		4,500	
Total gross income			$72,250
ADJUSTMENTS FROM GROSS INCOME			
Payments to IRA (Sharon $250, James $2,000)			2,250
ADJUSTED GROSS INCOME			70,000
ITEMIZED DEDUCTIONS			
Medical expenses and health insurance			
St. Theresa Hospital – surgery	$5,250		
Orthodontic fees	2,500		
Other medical expenses	500		
Total expenses	8,250		
Less: 7.5% of adjusted gross income (7.5% × $70,000)	5,250		
Deductible amount		3,000	
Taxes			
State income taxes	1,200		
Real estate taxes	2,800	4,000	
Interest			
Interest on home mortgage		2,400	
Charitable contributions			
Church	1,100		
United Fund	200	1,300	
Casualty and theft loss			
Uninsured loss from boat accident	7,500		
Less: Floor ($100 per loss)	100		
	7,400		
Less: 10% of adjusted gross income	7,000	400	
Employee business expenses and miscellaneous deductions			
Income tax preparation fee	200		
Professional dues	50		
Total	250		
Less 2% of adjusted gross income ($70,000 × 2%)	1,400	-0-	
Total itemized deductions			11,100
Adjusted gross income less itemized deductions			58,900
PERSONAL EXEMPTIONS ($1,950 × 4)			7,800
TAXABLE INCOME			**$51,100**
COMPUTATION OF INCOME TAX			
$29,750 × 15%		$4,462.50	
21,350 × 28%		5,978.00	$10,440.50
TAX PAYMENTS			
Income tax withholdings			9,800.00
TAX DUE			**$ 640.50**

The tax law requires that certain specified income, deductions, and credits be separately stated on the partnership return. Segregated presentation is required, because these items may be subject to special treatment on the partners' individual returns. Some of the special items include tax-free interest income, dividend income, charitable contributions, and capital gains and losses.

The IRS has begun a pilot program to allow selected tax preparers to file their clients' returns electronically. The IRS uses the paper version of the tax returns only as a source of data entry into its computer system. Once the data entry is done, there is little need for the paper copy of the return. The purpose of the pilot program is to determine whether it is feasible and practical to consider electronic filing for all returns.

SECTION THREE—CORPORATIONS

A corporation is a taxable entity that is required to file an income tax return annually within 2½ months of the close of its fiscal year. The provisions of the Act for corporations are extensive; many special provisions apply to certain types of corporations, such as banks and insurance companies. Corporation tax law contains no provisions for a standard deduction and personal exemptions. Moreover, the concept of adjusted gross income is not applicable to corporations.

The determination of taxable income for a corporation consists of (1) computing gross income, and (2) subtracting allowable business expenses, as shown below:

Taxable income formula for a corporation

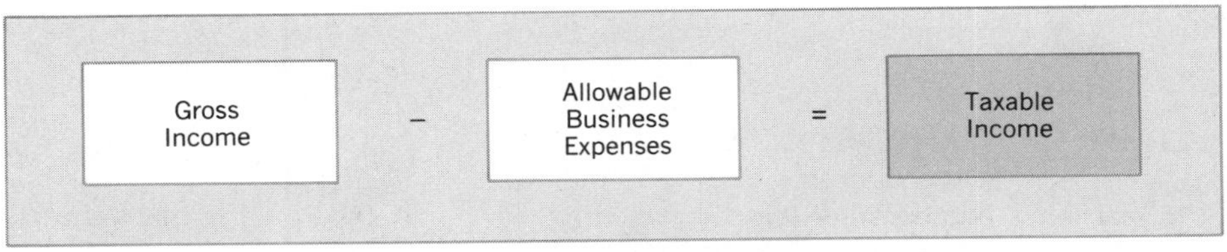

A corporation's income statement is the primary source of information for determining taxable income. Most corporations are required to use the accrual method of accounting in determining taxable income. The Act restricts the use of the cash method to specifically identified types of corporations.

Three areas that merit special attention in discussing corporations are:

1. Tax rates
2. Depreciation
3. Effects on management decisions

TAX RATES

The 1986 Code provides for a graduated rate with a three-bracket rate structure as follows:

Corporation tax rate structure

Taxable Income	Tax Rate
$50,000 or less	15%
$50,001 – $75,000	25
Above $75,000	34

An additional 5% tax is imposed on taxable income between $100,000 and $335,000, which in effect creates a flat tax rate of 34% for corporations with taxable income of $335,000 or more. The 5% surtax results in a 39% marginal rate on taxable income between $100,000 and $335,000. The surtax is designed to recapture the revenue lost by the lower tax rates applicable to the first two tax brackets.

DEPRECIATION

The Act continues the concept of **Accelerated Cost Recovery System (ACRS)** that has been part of tax law since 1981. However, significant modifications have been made to the ACRS system.

All depreciable assets are classified according to class life, as determined by their description (i.e., tools, autos, computers, office furniture, aircraft, etc.) or their asset depreciation range (ADR). All assets fall into one of eight classes, and for each class a specific depreciation method is prescribed. The following schedule lists the classes, the type of assets assigned to each class, and the depreciation method prescribed for each class.

Classes of assets under ACRS

Classes	Illustrative Applicable Assets	Depreciation Method
3-year	Small tools, tractors, horses, and specialized manufacturing devices	200% declining balance
5-year	Computers, automobiles and light trucks, small aircraft, construction equipment, and research and development property	200% declining balance
7-year	Office furniture, fixtures and equipment, commercial aircraft, most machinery	200% declining balance
10-year	Specialized heavy manufacturing machinery and equipment	200% declining balance
15-year	Billboards, service station buildings, telephone equipment	150% declining balance
20-year	Sewer pipes, most utility property, land improvement	150% declining balance
27½-year	Residential real estate property	Straight-line
31½-year	Office and other nonresidential real estate property	Straight-line

Salvage values are ignored, and the declining balance method is applied until the depreciation figured under the straight-line method exceeds the accelerated depreciation. Then the straight-line method is applied to complete depreciating the asset over the class life.

For personal property such as furniture, equipment, and machinery, a "half-year convention" is applied. This convention assumes that the asset is depreciable for one-half year in the year of acquisition and for one-half year in the year of disposition or in the last year of service life. For real property such as a building, a "mid-month convention" is applied. That is, depreciation is taken on a monthly basis beginning in the month the asset is put into service.

To illustrate the application of ACRS, assume that Ruger Company purchases a computer (personal property) for $500,000 on April 19, 1987. According to ACRS rules, a computer is a 5-year class asset that must be depreciated over 6 years, one-half year's depreciation in years one and six, using the 200% declining balance method until the straight-line depreciation for the year exceeds the declining balance depreciation. Separate computations of annual depreciation under the two methods are required to determine the point when straight-line depreciation should be started. The depreciation by year and by method is shown in the following schedule.

ACRS depreciation schedule

Year	Method	Depreciable Basis	Computation	Annual Depreciation
1987	D.B.	$500,000	$500,000 × (20% × 2) × 1/2	$100,000
1988	D.B.	400,000	$400,000 × (20% × 2)	160,000
1989	D.B.	240,000	$240,000 × (20% × 2)	96,000
1990	D.B.	144,000	$144,000 × (20% × 2)	57,600
1991	S.L.	86,400	$ 86,400 ÷ 1.5 yrs.	57,600
1992	S.L.	86,400	($ 86,400 ÷ 1.5 yrs.) × 1/2	28,800

In this example, straight-line depreciation, using the remaining years of life as the period over which to allocate the remaining undepreciated cost, first exceeds the 200% declining balance depreciation in 1991. Under the 200% declining balance method, depreciation would have been $34,560 ($86,400 × 20% × 2) in 1991, in contrast to $57,600 under straight-line.

ACRS is used for income tax purposes only. Annual depreciation under this system generally does not equal the amount of depreciation recorded under generally accepted accounting principles. The effect on net income of this difference between tax depreciation and accounting depreciation was explained in Chapter 17.

It should be noted that the straight-line method may be elected in computing depreciation rather than ACRS. The straight-line election is an annual class election, and the method must be applied to all assets within the class acquired in any year.

EFFECTS ON MANAGEMENT DECISIONS

With a 34% marginal tax rate for most corporations, each $1 deduction saves the company 34 cents. Thus, income taxes are an important factor in most business decisions. Some applications of income taxes to management decisions are explained in the remainder of this chapter.

Determining the Form of Business Organization

A business enterprise may be either unincorporated or incorporated. Income taxes are a significant factor in deciding whether to incorporate. As previously indicated, proprietorships and partnerships are not taxable entities, whereas a corporation is a taxable entity. Moreover, the net income of an unincorporated enterprise is taxable to the owner (or owners), regardless of whether it is withdrawn from the business. In contrast, corporate earnings are taxable to the owners only when they are received in the form of dividends. In addition, salaries paid to owners for services rendered are a business expense only to a corporation. From a tax standpoint, the decision regarding the best form of business organization rests in part on the dividend policy that is expected to be followed by the corporation.

For tax purposes, another alternative is to form an S Corporation. An S Corporation has the legal advantages of a corporation, such as limited liability and transferability of shares. However, an S Corporation's tax liability is similar to that of a partnership under tax law. Thus, the income of an S Corporation is subject to the maximum individual marginal tax rate of 28%, rather than the 34% marginal corporate tax rate.

Deciding on the Type of External Financing

A corporation has three primary sources of external funds: (1) bonds, (2) preferred stock, and (3) common stock. Income taxes may have a significant effect on the choice of external financing, because interest on bonds is fully deductible on the tax return, while dividends on preferred and common stock are not deductible. In making the decision, management should recognize that at the marginal tax rate of 34%, the after-tax expense of issuing 10% bonds is only 6.6% [10% × (1−34%)]. A tabular comparison of the cost of financing bonds and common stock is presented in Chapter 17.

Cost-Volume-Profit Analysis

In Chapter 24, the effect of income taxes in cost-volume-profit analysis was ignored. For a corporation, income taxes may have a significant effect on sales required to earn target net income after income taxes. When management wants an after-tax net income, the desired net income must be divided by **1 minus the income tax rate.** The term "1 minus the income tax rate" equals the amount the business can keep from each dollar earned after deducting income taxes. For example, if a company desires $49,000 after 30% income taxes, the required pretax income is $70,000 [$49,000 ÷ (1 − 30%)]. The formula for computing sales required to earn net income after taxes is:

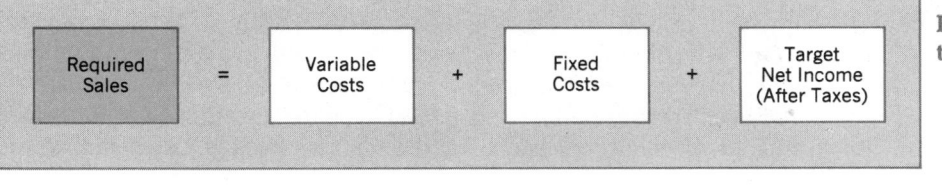

Required Sales	=	Variable Costs	+	Fixed Costs	+	Target Net Income (After Taxes)

Formula for after-tax net income

To illustrate, assume that the Stefan Corporation desires net income of \$132,000 after income taxes of 34%, when it has \$300,000 of fixed costs and variable costs are 60% of sales. The computation is as follows:

Computation of required sales

$$
\begin{aligned}
X &= 60\% X + \$300{,}000 + [\$132{,}000 \div (1-34\%)] \\
.40X &= \$300{,}000 + \$200{,}000 \\
X &= \$1{,}250{,}000
\end{aligned}
$$

This amount can be verified as follows:

Proof of net income after taxes

Sales		$1,250,000
Less: Variable costs	$750,000	
Fixed costs	300,000	1,050,000
Income before income taxes		200,000
Income tax expense (34%)		68,000
Net income		$ 132,000

This final computer note is in the form of a story with a not too futuristic scenario.

It is 5 o'clock in the evening of April 15th, and you decide that you had better file your income taxes. After dinner, you sit down at your computer terminal and link into your confidential IRS file maintained at the National Computer Center. On January 3rd, your employer transmitted your earnings (Form W-2) data to your IRS file. Also, on January 4th, all banks and brokerage firms that you do business with transmitted your other income data (Form 1099) into your IRS file, so all you have to do now is make the transfer from your home accounting system, containing your itemized deductions into the IRS file.

You do this, and the video display shows that you owe \$100. The display also prompts you to accept this sad fact or asks if you would like a hard copy printout of the return computations to review.

You decide to edit the hard copy and find, much to your joy, that, somehow, you failed to get a major deduction into your home accounting software. You enter the change and your IRS file is updated accordingly. The CRT now says that you have a \$100 refund coming.

You push the proper function key on your computer terminal and accept the refund. In 1/10,000 of a second, \$100 is electronically transferred from the IRS depository account at your local bank into your checking account. Your home accounting package is also updated to reflect the additional \$100 in your account. You are happy to see, on the screen, that the IRS has accepted all of your return input and does not anticipate the need to request any other input for audit verification. The session is closed when you acknowledge acceptance of your filed return and refund. This entire process took less than fifteen minutes, and you decide to enjoy the rest of your evening celebrating your refund.

SUMMARY OF STUDY OBJECTIVES

1. The average tax rate is determined by dividing the total tax paid by total taxable income. The marginal tax rate is the rate applicable to the lost dollars of taxable income. The marginal tax rate is usually more significant than the average tax rate in making business decisions.

2. An individual must elect one filing status from the following options: (a) single, (b) head of household, (c) married and filing a joint return, and (d) married and filing a separate return.

3. The formula for computing taxable income is: gross income less adjustments from gross income equals adjusted gross income less the standard or itemized deductions and exemptions equals taxable income.

4. The standard deduction is the amount a taxpayer can claim without supporting documentation. Itemized deductions represent actual expenditures made by the taxpayer during the year.

5. The formula for determining the tax refund or balance due is: amount of tax (regular or alternative minimum) less tax credits and tax payments equals tax refund or balance due.

6. The components in determining taxable income for a corporation are gross income and business expenses.

7. Income taxes may affect management's decisions concerning (1) the form of business organization, (2) the type of external financing, and (3) cost-volume-profit analysis.

GLOSSARY

DEMONSTRATION PROBLEM

Renee and Manuel Ortiz are married and have two children in grade school. Manuel is employed by Baldwin Digital, Inc. as a salesman and he is not covered by the company's retirement plan. Renee is a housewife with no income.

In 1988, Manuel received $52,000 in salary and Renee won $1,000 in the state lottery. The Ortizes made the maximum $2,250 payment to an IRA. Because they had few itemized deductions, the Ortizes elected to use the standard deduction in filing a joint tax return for 1988. Federal income taxes withheld from Manuel's earnings totaled $6,500.

INSTRUCTIONS

Prepare a schedule showing taxable income and income taxes payable or refundable.

SOLUTION TO DEMONSTRATION PROBLEM

RENEE AND MANUEL ORTIZ
Federal Income Tax Computation
For the Year 1988

Gross income		
Manuel Ortiz salary	$52,000	
Renee Ortiz lottery winnings	1,000	
Total gross income		$53,000
Adjustments from gross income		
Payments to IRA (Renee $250, Manuel $2,000)		2,250
Adjusted gross income		50,750
Standard deduction		5,000
Adjusted gross income less standard deduction		45,750
Personal exemptions ($1,950 × 4)		7,800
Taxable income		$37,950
Computation of income tax		
$29,750 × 15%	$ 4,463	
$8,200 × 28%	2,296	6,759
Tax payments		
Income tax withholdings		6,500
Tax due		$ 259

QUESTIONS

1. Sheila Stone claims that taxable entities and accounting entities may not be identical. Is Sheila correct? What are the major classes of taxable entities?

2. Distinguish between an average and a marginal income tax rate. Which rate is more significant in management decisions?

3. Identify and explain the tax methods that may be elected by a taxpayer in determining taxable income.

4. What filing status may be elected by an individual taxpayer?

5. Indicate the formula for computing taxable income.

6. Which of the following items should be included in gross revenue?

(a) Dividends, rents, and royalties
(b) State and federal welfare benefits
(c) Child support
(d) Business and farm income
(e) Unemployment compensation
(f) Gifts, inheritances, and bequests

7. Distinguish between passive and active income. How must passive income or loss be reported for tax purposes?

8. Ryne Richards asks your help concerning a net capital gain or a net capital loss. Explain (a) the steps that are required in determining these amounts, and (b) the tax treatment of the gain or loss.

9. Rhonda Reder is reviewing for a quiz on income taxes. What should Rhonda know about the deductibility of IRA payments by taxpayers not covered by a company-sponsored retirement plan who are married and filing jointly?

10. Distinguish between a standard deduction and itemized deductions. Is the standard deduction the same for each filing status?

11. Identify the categories that are used for itemized deductions.

12. What monetary restrictions must be met to qualify as a dependent?

13. How are high-income taxpayers required to pay a flat rate of 28% on all taxable income in 1988 and thereafter when the first tax bracket is only 15%?

14. What steps are required to determine the tax refund or the tax due?

15. Joan Elbert claims that an itemized deduction and a tax credit are basically the same. Is Joan correct? Why or why not?

16. How is taxable income determined for a corporation? Where is the information generally found to determine taxable income for a corporation?

17. Cindy Sims says that the tax brackets and tax rates for a corporation are different than they are for an individual taxpayer. Is Cindy correct? Explain.

18. How many classes of depreciable assets are recognized under ACRS? What depreciation method predominates under ACRS depreciation?

19. Will tax considerations increase the attractiveness of bonds over stock as a source of external financing? Why?

20. The Cojeen Company wants $133,000 of net income after income taxes. What amount should be used for income before income taxes in determining required sales if the income tax rate is (a) 30%, and (b) 20%?

EXERCISES

E29-1 Tillie Reichenbacher is single and has no dependents. Tillie compiles the following information for her tax return. Tillie's employer has no pension plan.

Gross income	$39,500
Payments to IRA	2,000
Itemized deductions	2,800
Income taxes withheld from salary	6,500

INSTRUCTIONS

(a) Determine the tax refund or liability.

(b) Repeat (a), assuming that Tillie is the head of a household with one dependent.

E29-2 Marlo Meers has the following sources of income in 1988.

Salary	$50,000
Income from rental properties (passive income)	8,000
Capital gain from sale of bonds	10,000
Loss from passive investment in oil and gas properties	6,000
Capital loss from sale of common stock	7,000

Marlo continues to have an interest in the oil and gas properties.

INSTRUCTIONS

(a) Compute gross income for the year.

(b) Repeat (a), assuming that both losses are $5,000 higher.

E29-3 Gross income and other tax data for four taxpayers are presented below:

	Vera	Velda	Wilma	Wanda
Gross income	$25,000	$54,000	$41,000	$53,000
IRA contribution	2,000	4,000	-0-	2,250
Keogh contribution	-0-	-0-	5,000	-0-
Reimbursed business expenses	3,000	-0-	-0-	2,000
Unreimbursed business expenses	800	500	600	-0-

Vera is single; the other taxpayers are married and filing jointly. Vera and Wanda are covered by company-sponsored retirement plans. Velda and her spouse are not covered by company retirement plans; they both have income over $20,000. Wilma is self-employed. Wanda's spouse has no income. Reimbursed business expenses are included in gross income.

INSTRUCTIONS

Compute the adjusted gross income for each taxpayer.

E29-4 Adjusted gross income and other tax data for four taxpayers are presented below:

	Hart	Hill	Vane	Zahn
Adjusted gross income	$28,000	$42,000	$54,000	$65,000
Itemized deductions	3,500	4,000	4,500	7,000
Exemptions	1	3	3	4
Income taxes withheld	3,700	6,000	8,125	9,600

Hart is single with no dependents. Hill is the head of a household with two dependents. Vane is married, has one child, and is filing a joint return. Zahn is married, has two children, and is filing a joint return.

INSTRUCTIONS

Compute the tax due or the tax refund for each taxpayer.

E29–5 Heather Humas is a CPA who specializes in the preparation of tax returns for individuals. For 1988, four clients submit the following information:

Client	Filing Status	Taxable Income
M. C. Burton	Single taxpayer	$ 89,560
R. D. Norris	Head of household	123,790
C. B. Quinn	Married and filing jointly	130,200
A. L. Rice	Married and filing separately	113,300

INSTRUCTIONS

(a) Compute the tax amount for each client.

(b) Prove that there is a flat tax of 28% on all income earned by Burton and Norris.

E29–6 Janice and Toby Meers are married and are filing a joint income tax return for 1988. The couple's adjusted gross income is $32,000, and they have no children or dependent relatives. The Meers's had the following tax-related expenditures during the year:

1. Contributions to church and United Fund	$ 750
2. Membership dues in professional associations	100
3. Interest on home mortgage	2,700
4. State sales tax	600
5. Medical and dental expenses	1,900
6. Unreimbursed business travel and entertainment	2,500
7. CPA fee for tax counseling	200
8. Blue Cross/Blue Shield premiums	800
9. Real estate taxes	2,200
10. Casualty loss in excess of insurance settlement	3,700
11. State income taxes	1,200
12. Interest on car loan	700

INSTRUCTIONS

(a) List the allowable itemized deductions by categories, together with any limitations on the amount deductible.

(b) Compute the tax liability for Janice and Toby Meers.

E29–7 Ruby Howatt spent $400,000 on capital expenditures during the year. Included in this total are two tractors that cost $45,000 each. The tractors are in the 3-year class, and the depreciation method is 200% declining balance. At the end of their useful lives, the tractors are expected to have no salvage value.

INSTRUCTIONS

Prepare a schedule showing the ACRS depreciation for each year on the tractors.

E29–8 Thomas Robinson earned net income (after income taxes) of $120,000 last year. This year it wants to earn net income after taxes of $198,000. The company's fixed

costs are expected to be $320,000, and variable costs are expected to be 60% of sales.

INSTRUCTIONS

(a) Determine the required sales to meet the target net income after taxes of $198,000, assuming an income tax rate of 34%.

(b) Determine the required sales to earn net income after taxes of $140,000, assuming an income tax rate of 30%.

PROBLEMS

P29-1 Warren Crews is a college professor. His dependents consist of his wife Gwen, his mother, who is 65 years of age, and two children, Lee and Kate. Lee is in law school; he earned $1,200 from a summer job. Kate is a 19-year-old junior in the school of nursing. She earned $700 during the year. The Crews's file a joint tax return. Warren Crews provides the following data from his records for the 1988 taxable year:

Income:	
University salary ($47,000 less income taxes withheld $9,000)	$38,000
Royalties from publisher of Crews's textbook	15,000
Dividends from stock investments	700
Consulting fees from business enterprises	6,500
Gain on sale of stock investments	800
Interest on tax-exempt municipal bonds	600
Expenses:	
Unreimbursed business travel expenses	1,000
Medical expenses for mother and health insurance	5,700
Interest on home mortgage	1,200
Interest on purchase of automobile	1,000
State and local income taxes	2,300
Sales taxes on purchase of automobile	600
Charitable contributions	3,000
Income tax preparation fee	200
Membership dues to professional organizations	300

In 1988, Professor Crews made a $2,000 contribution to a Keogh plan on the basis of his royalty income.

INSTRUCTIONS

Prepare a schedule showing the computation of taxable income and the amount of taxes due or refundable. (Round to the nearest dollar.)

P29-2 Joe Kares owns and operates a small proprietorship. He and his wife Ann have three children: Ted, 9 years old, Jan, 6 years old, and Ray, 20 years old. Ray receives over half of his support from his parents. He is a full-time college student who earned $1,000 during the year. Joe and Ann Kares file a joint tax return. The following cash receipts and disbursements were obtained from J. Kares' personal records.

Cash Receipts:	
Withdrawals of income from the business	$18,000
Proceeds from sale of stock purchased as an investment for $800	1,400
Dividends from Mrs. Kares' investments	500
Interest on corporate bonds	300
Inheritance from Mr. Kares' mother's estate	5,000
Cash Disbursements:	
Hospitalization insurance premiums	900
Personal property taxes	1,600
Charitable contributions	1,500
Unreimbursed medical and dental expenses	2,600
Interest on home mortgage	1,100
Real estate taxes	900
State income taxes	1,200
State and local sales taxes	500
Payment to Keogh retirement plan	5,000
Estimated current year's federal income tax payments	4,400

The accounting records of the proprietorship show sales $462,000, cost of goods sold $304,000, operating expenses $108,000, and net income $50,000.

INSTRUCTIONS

Prepare a schedule showing taxable income and income taxes payable or refundable.

P29-3 An inexperienced tax accountant prepared the following tentative joint tax return for Harry and Helen Rush:

HARRY AND HELEN RUSH
Federal Income Tax Computation

Gross income:		
Partnership drawings	$10,000	
Interest on tax-exempt municipal bonds	200	
Prize from church raffle	400	
Dividends from investments	600	
Rents received from rental property	4,200	
Total gross income		$15,400
Deductible expenses:		
Medical expenses		1,200
Charitable contributions		1,500
Property taxes		3,200
Other taxes		300
Utilities		4,000
Depreciation		2,000
Total deductible expenses		12,200
Taxable income		$ 3,200

Analysis reveals the following additional data.

1. The distribution schedule for partnership income in which Harry is an active partner showed:

	Rush, Capital	Moren, Capital
Salaries	$ 7,200	$ 6,000
Interest on capital	1,200	800
Remainder	4,600	4,600
Total net income	$13,000	$11,400
Less: Drawings	10,000	5,400
Increase in capital	$ 3,000	$ 6,000

2. Some items listed under deductible expenses pertained to several activities:

	Partnership Property	Personal Residence
Property taxes	$1,200	$2,000
Utilities	1,000	3,000
Depreciation	1,000	1,000

The partnership expenses were properly recorded on the partnership books.

3. Other taxes consisted of state income taxes $250 and state sales taxes $50.
4. The Rushes have one child, Marion, who is 6 years old.

INSTRUCTIONS

Prepare a schedule showing the computation of taxable income and the amount of taxes due or refundable. (Round to the nearest dollar.)

P29-4 Bonnie Harris Inc. reported income before depreciation and income taxes in the first five years of operations as follows:

Year	Income	Year	Income	Year	Income
1	$60,000	3	$75,000	5	$82,000
2	70,000	4	80,000		

On January 1 of the first year of operations the company purchased depreciable assets at a cost of $85,000. The assets were expected to have a useful life of 5 years and no salvage value.

INSTRUCTIONS

(a) Determine taxable income for each of the five years, assuming (1) straight-line depreciation, and (2) ACRS depreciation (5-year class life).

(b) Determine the income taxes payable each year under each depreciation method.

(c) Determine the aggregate difference in income taxes payable for the five years between the depreciation methods.

ALTERNATE PROBLEMS

P29-1A Jim Kales is the sports editor for the *Daily Chronicle*. His dependents consist of his wife Jill, who is unemployed, and his parents, who are both over 65 years of age. Jim is covered by the newspaper's retirement plan. The Kales's file a joint return based on the following data:

Income:	
Salary ($39,150 less $3,500 federal income taxes withheld)	$35,650
Interest from corporate bonds	800
Loss on sale of common stock held as an investment	1,000
Gain on sale of stamp collection (hobby income)	1,400
Loss from active investment in oil and gas properties	600
Expenses:	
Uninsured automobile collision damage	700
Interest on home mortgage	1,500
Interest on credit card billings	200
State income taxes	1,100
Real estate taxes	1,800
Medical expenses and health insurance	1,600
Charitable contributions	2,075
Unreimbursed business travel and lodging	600
Payments to IRA	2,250

INSTRUCTIONS

Prepare a schedule showing the taxes due or refundable. (Round to the nearest dollar.)

P29-2A Tim Thomas owns and operates a small proprietorship. He and his wife Tina have three small children. Tim and Tina file a joint tax return. The following data were obtained from their records from 1988:

Cash Receipts:	
Withdrawals of income from the business	$24,000
Proceeds from sale of corporate bonds purchased for $2,500	2,000
Interest from tax-exempt municipal bonds	1,000
Dividends from corporation stocks	800
Proceeds from sale of rare coins purchased for $4,000	4,600
Cash Disbursements:	
McCauley Hospital surgery fees	3,000
Dental insurance premiums	500
Charitable contributions	2,000
Interest on home mortgage	1,200
State income taxes	800
Real estate taxes	1,000
Final payment on 1987 federal income taxes	400
Payment to Keogh retirement plan	4,000
Payments on estimated 1988 federal income taxes	3,700

In addition, Tim had a loss of $800 on a passive investment in uranium mine properties, and a gain of $1,000 on a passive investment in oil properties. The accounting records of the proprietorship show sales $660,000, cost of goods sold $440,000, operating expenses $175,000, and net income $45,000.

INSTRUCTIONS

Prepare a schedule showing taxable income and income taxes payable or refundable. (Round to the nearest dollar.)

P29-3A An inexperienced tax accountant prepared the following tentative joint tax return for Edward and Mamie Oslo:

EDWARD AND MAMIE OSLO
Federal Income Tax Computation

Gross income:		
Partnership salary	$15,000	
State lottery award	500	
Interest on tax-exempt municipal bonds	600	
Life insurance proceeds from mother's death	2,500	
Gain on sale of stock held as an investment	700	
Dividends from investments in corporation stocks	400	
Total gross income		$19,700
Deductible expenses:		
Medical expenses and health insurance paid	2,500	
Charitable contributions made	2,000	
Interest on car installment payments	800	
State income taxes	900	
Property taxes	4,000	
Utilities	3,200	
Depreciation	2,800	
Gambling losses in excess of gambling winnings of $800	200	
Total expenses		16,400
Taxable income		$ 3,300

Analysis reveals the following additional data:

(a) The distribution schedule for partnership income in which Edward is an active partner showed:

	Oslo, Capital	Malmo, Capital
Salaries	$15,000	$10,000
Interest on capital	2,400	1,000
Remainder	5,600	5,600
Total net income	23,000	16,600
Less: Drawings	12,000	8,000
Increase in capital	$21,000	$ 600

(b) Expenses related to the following properties are as follows:

	Partnership Property	Personal Residence
Property taxes	$2,500	$1,500
Utilities	2,000	1,200
Depreciation	2,000	800

The partnership expenses were properly recorded on the partnership books.

(c) The Oslos have two children, Marion, who is 6 years old, and Shawn, who is 4 years old.

INSTRUCTIONS

Prepare a schedule showing the taxes due or refundable.

P29-4A Munsen Inc. reported income before depreciation and income taxes in the first five years of operations as follows:

Year	Income	Year	Income	Year	Income
1	$50,000	3	$72,000	5	$88,000
2	64,000	4	81,000		

On January 1 of the first year of operations the company purchased heavy machinery at a cost of $210,000. The assets were expected to have a useful life of 10 years and no salvage value.

INSTRUCTIONS

(a) Determine taxable income for each of the five years, assuming (1) straight-line depreciation, and (2) ACRS depreciation (10-year class life).

(b) Determine the income taxes payable each year under each depreciation method.

(c) Determine the aggregate difference in income taxes payable for the five years between the depreciation methods.

DECISION CASE

Joan Elbert Corporation must raise $8,000,000 to finance a plant expansion program. Management has narrowed its choices to the issuance of either one million shares of $5 par value common stock at the current market price of $8 per share or $8 million ten-year 10% bonds. The new plant is expected to produce income before taxes of $2.5 million, and income taxes are expected to be 34%. Joan Elbert Corporation currently has 1 million shares of common stock outstanding.

INSTRUCTIONS

(a) Which method of financing will produce the higher net income after income taxes?

(b) Which method of financing will produce the higher earnings per share? (Hint: For both (a), and (b) prepare a tabular schedule beginning with income before interest expense and taxes.) Carry per share figures to three decimals.

APPENDIX A

SPECIMEN FINANCIAL STATEMENTS

THE ANNUAL REPORT

Once each year a corporation communicates to its stockholders and other interested parties the financial results of its operation and its plans for the future through its **Annual Report.** Many such **Annual Reports** have become attractive, multicolored, glossy public relations ad pieces containing pictures of corporate officers and directors as well as photos and descriptions of new products and new buildings. Yet, the basic function of every **Annual Report** is to report financial information, almost all of which is a product of the corporation's accounting system.

The content and organization of corporate **Annual Reports** has become fairly standardized. Excluding the public relations part (pictures, products, and propaganda) of the report, the following outline shows the traditional financial portions of the **Annual Report**:

Financial Highlights
Letter to the Stockholders
Management's Report
Auditor's Report
Financial Statements
Notes to the Financial Statements
Supplementary Financial Information

In this appendix we illustrate current financial reporting with a comprehensive set of corporate financial statements that are prepared in accordance with generally accepted accounting principles and audited by an international independent certified public accounting firm. We are grateful for permission to use the actual financial statements and other accompanying financial information from the **Annual Report** of a large, publicly held company, familiarly known to you as PepsiCo, Inc.

FINANCIAL HIGHLIGHTS

The financial highlights section, called the **Financial Summary** by PepsiCo, is usually presented inside the front cover or on the first two pages of the annual report. This section generally reports the total or per share amounts for five to ten financial items for the current year and one or more previous years. Financial items from the income statement and the balance sheet that are typically presented are sales, income from continuing operations, net income, net income per share, dividends per common share, and the amount of capital expenditures. The financial highlights section from PepsiCo's **Annual Report** is shown below.

Financial Summary

($ in millions except per share amounts)		**1985**	1984	**Percent Change**
Net Sales	$	**8,056.7**	7,451.1	**+8**
Income from continuing operations before refranchising credit (charge)	$	**405.2**	337.0	**+20**
Per share	$	**4.35**	3.55	**+23**
Refranchising credit (charge)	$	**14.9**	(62.0)	**–**
Per share	$	**.16**	(.65)	**–**
Income from continuing operations	$	**420.1**	275.0	**+53**
Per share	$	**4.51**	2.90	**+56**
Income (loss) from discontinued operations	$	**123.6**	(62.5)	**–**
Per share	$	**1.32**	(.65)	**–**
Net income	$	**543.7**	212.5	**+156**
Per share	$	**5.83**	2.25	**+159**
Dividends declared	$	**161.2**	156.2	**+3**
Per share	$	**1.76**	1.67	**+5**
Return on average shareholders' equity	%	**22.0**	18.5	**+19**
Property, plant and equipment expenditures	$	**785.9**	555.8	**+41**

As shown above, PepsiCo chose also to present the percent change from last year to the current year for each of the reported items.

LETTER TO THE STOCKHOLDERS

Nearly every Annual Report contains a letter from the Chairman of the Board or the President (or both) to the stockholders. This letter typically discusses the company's accomplishments during the past year and highlights sigificant events such as mergers and acquisitions, new products, operating achievements, changes in officers or directors, financing commitments, expansion plans, and future prospects. The letter to the stockholders signed by the Chairman of the Board and the President of PepsiCo is shown below:

To Our Shareholders

In 1965 Pepsi-Cola and Frito-Lay merged to form PepsiCo. Our objective was to build one of the premier consumer products companies in the world. By any measure, we believe we've succeeded.

Twenty exciting years have passed, and today PepsiCo is in an era of sustained high growth. Strategic reshaping has made our company leaner, more tightly focused and an even more effective competitor:

- We have leadership positions in three very attractive consumer businesses—soft drinks, snack foods and restaurants. Each is very large and very responsive to product, packaging and marketing innovations. As a result, these markets have been growing rapidly and show every sign of continued growth in the future.
- We have the strong brand names, advertising impact and marketing savvy necessary to achieve outstanding results.
- We have the innovative management talent required to outmaneuver our competition.
- And we have the financial strength and flexibility to maintain our impressive momentum.

Although our company is large and complex—with 150,000 employees doing business in more than 120 countries—our management philosophy is quite simple. Our priority is to maximize shareholder value, primarily through internal growth and astute application of our financial resources.

Business Investment

To illustrate our commitment to internal growth, last year we invested $786 million in our existing businesses. We significantly expanded our soft drink operations, added more units to our restaurant system than ever before and built a state-of-the-art snack food manufacturing plant to expand Frito-Lay's markets. In 1986 we plan even higher capital spending to support our aggressive growth objectives.

We also used our financial resources in 1985 to spend $458 million repurchasing more than seven percent of our outstanding common stock. This investment, coupled with the continued growth and vitality of all our businesses, produced earnings per share gains of 23 percent and drove our return on equity to an all-time high of 22 percent. Income of $405 million rose 20 percent, and sales of $8.1 billion increased eight percent. PepsiCo stock outperformed a very strong market; the price of our shares soared 70 percent.

Growth Opportunities

We also took advantage of attractive acquisition opportunities. We purchased for $160 million Allegheny Pepsi-Cola Bottling Company, one of our more important bottlers, and signed agreements for two other key acquisitions. During 1986 we'll complete the $590 million purchase of MEI Corporation, one of the largest and most profitable Pepsi-Cola bottlers. We also intend to purchase for $380 million the worldwide franchise beverage operations of The Seven-Up Company. 7UP is one of the most valuable trademarks in the world. And, based on our success with Pepsi-Cola products, we believe we can significantly build the 7UP brand and strengthen its bottler network.

These acquisitions, which will add nearly $1 billion to our soft drink sales, reflect our continued belief that the greatest growth opportunities lie in our existing businesses. Building on our strengths makes good economic and marketing sense, and is one of the most effective ways to increase shareholder value.

Complementing this commitment to existing lines of business, we'll continue to be alert to growth opportunities in related markets.

Board of Directors

The overall guidance of our company remains in the strong hands of our Board of Directors, which includes some of the most distinguished leaders in the fields of business, law, finance and education.

And we're very pleased to welcome to our Board Sharon Percy Rockefeller. She has demonstrated considerable leadership on the Corporation for Public Broadcasting, including service as its chairman. Mrs. Rockefeller also has been very active in a wide range of political, social and educational programs, and brings valuable insights to our Board.

On a sad note, we mourn the death of Harold R. Lilley, one of the early leaders of our corporation. Mr. Lilley was associated with Frito-Lay for 22 years, and served on our Board for nine years until his retirement in 1978. Harold Lilley was a friend and an able businessman who made major contributions to the success we enjoy today.

Continuing Commitment

The goals we established for ourselves in 1965 have been refined, but never altered. Our success over the past 20 years reflects our continuing commitment to growth and our resolve to focus on those businesses where we can drive that growth ourselves and create our own opportunities.

In the pages that follow, we report on some of the highlights of our dramatic growth. And, more importantly, we discuss the characteristics that shaped our success in the past, that were responsible for our record performance in 1985 and that will guide our continuing growth in the years ahead.

February 27, 1986

Donald M. Kendall

Donald M. Kendall
Chairman of the Board and
Chief Executive Officer

Wayne Calloway

D. Wayne Calloway
President and
Chief Operating Officer

MANAGEMENT'S REPORT

A relatively recent addition to corporate annual reports is the statement made by management about its role in and responsibility for the accuracy and integrity of the financial statements. PepsiCo's management letter is entitled **Report of Chief Financial Officer.** In it the executive vice president and chief financial officer, on behalf of management: (1) assumes primary responsibility for the financial statements and the related notes, (2) outlines and assesses the company's internal control system, (3) declares the financial statements in conformity with generally accepted accounting principles, and (4) comments on the audit by the certified public accountant and the composition and role of the Audit Committee of the Board of Directors. PepsiCo's management report is presented below.

Report of Chief Financial Officer

To Our Shareholders:

Management is responsible for the integrity and objectivity of the financial statements and related notes. To meet this responsibility, we maintain a system of internal control, supported by formal policies and procedures and an internal audit program designed to monitor and report on the adequacy of and compliance with our internal controls, policies and procedures. We believe the established system of internal control provides reasonable assurance that assets are safeguarded, transactions are recorded in accordance with our policies and the financial information is reliable.

The financial statements have been prepared in conformity with generally accepted accounting principles applied on a consistent basis, and include amounts based upon our estimates and judgments, as required. The financial statements have been audited by certified public accountants who have expressed their opinion, presented below, with respect to the fairness of the statements. Their examination included a review of the system of internal control and tests of transactions to the extent they considered necessary to render their opinion.

The Audit Committee of the Board of Directors is composed of non-employee directors. The Audit Committee meets on a regular basis with management, our internal auditors and certified public accountants to review audit plans, results and recommendations, as well as the effectiveness of our system of internal control.

Both our certified public accountants and internal auditors have free access to the Audit Committee.

Michael H. Jordan
Executive Vice President
and Chief Financial Officer

AUDITOR'S REPORT

All publicly held corporations, as well as many other enterprises and organizations (both profit and not-for-profit, large and small) engage the services of independent certified public accountants for the purpose of obtaining an objective, expert report on the financial statements. Based on a comprehensive examination of the company's accounting system and records, and the financial statements, the outside CPA renders the auditor's report.

The standard auditor's report consists of two paragraphs: (1) the scope paragraph, and (2) the opinion paragraph. In the scope paragraph, the auditor indicates who and what was audited and that the examination was conducted in accordance with generally accepted auditing standards. In the opinion paragraph, the auditor renders an informed opinion as to (1) the fairness of the financial statements, (2) the conformity with generally accepted accounting principles, and (3) the consistency in the application of those principles from year to year. The **Report of Certified Public Accountants** appearing in PepsiCo's Annual Report is shown below.

Report of Certified Public Accountants

Board of Directors and Shareholders
PepsiCo, Inc.

We have examined the accompanying consolidated statement of financial condition of PepsiCo, Inc. and subsidiaries at December 28, 1985 and December 29, 1984, and the related consolidated statements of income, changes in financial condition and shareholders' equity for each of the three years in the period ended December 28, 1985, appearing on pages 36, 38, 40 and 42 through 51. Our examinations were made in accordance with generally accepted auditing standards and, accordingly, included such tests of the accounting records and such other auditing procedures as we considered necessary in the circumstances.

In our opinion, the statements mentioned above present fairly the consolidated financial position of PepsiCo, Inc. and subsidiaries at December 28, 1985 and December 29, 1984, and the consolidated results of operations and changes in financial position for each of the three years in the period ended December 28, 1985, in conformity with generally accepted accounting principles applied on a consistent basis during the period.

Arthur Young & Company

277 Park Avenue
New York, New York
February 4, 1986

The auditor's report issued on PepsiCo's financial statements is "unqualified" or "clean"; that is, it contains no qualifications or exceptions. In other words, the auditor conformed completely with generally accepted auditing standards in performing the audit, and the financial statements conformed in all material respects with generally accepted accounting principles consistently applied during all periods reported.

When the financial statements do not conform with generally accepted accounting principles or when the accounting principles are not consistently applied from one period to the next, the auditor must issue a "qualified" opinion and describe the exception. If the lack of conformity with GAAP is sufficiently material, the auditor is compelled to issue an "adverse" or nega-

tive opinion. An adverse opinion means that the financial statements do not present fairly the company's financial condition and/or the results of the company's operations at the dates and for the periods reported.

In circumstances where the auditor is unable to perform all of the auditing procedures necessary to reach a conclusion as to the fairness of the financial statements, a "disclaimer" must be issued. In these rare instances, the auditor must report the reason for failure to reach a conclusion on the fairness of the financial statements.

Companies strive to obtain an unqualified auditor's report. Hence, only infrequently are you likely to encounter anything other than the standard two-paragraph unqualified audit report.

FINANCIAL STATEMENTS AND ACCOMPANYING NOTES

The standard set of financial statements consists of: (1) a comparative balance sheet for two years, (2) a comparative income statement for three years, (3) a comparative statement of cash flows for three years, (4) a statement of retained earnings (or stockholders' equity) for three years, and (5) a set of accompanying notes that are considered an integral part of the financial statements. The auditor's report, unless stated otherwise, covers the financial statements and the accompanying notes. The financial statements and accompanying notes for PepsiCo, Inc. appear on the following pages.

Consolidated Statement of Income—PepsiCo, Inc.

(000 omitted)	Years Ended Dec. 28 1985	Dec. 29 1984	Dec. 31 1983
Net Sales	**$8,056,662**	$7,451,106	$6,899,884
Costs and Expenses			
Cost of sales	**3,148,261**	2,974,458	2,821,816
Marketing, administrative and other expenses	**4,171,339**	3,763,974	3,537,556
Interest expense	**195,378**	205,099	175,232
Interest income	**(96,382)**	(86,117)	(53,614)
	7,418,596	6,857,414	6,480,990
Income From Continuing Operations Before Refranchising Credit (Charge) and Income Taxes	**638,066**	593,692	418,894
Refranchising credit (charge)	**25,900**	(156,000)	–
Income From Continuing Operations Before Income Taxes	**663,966**	437,692	418,894
Provision for federal and foreign income taxes	**243,885**	162,677	140,602
Income From Continuing Operations	**420,081**	275,015	278,292
Discontinued Operations			
Income (loss) from discontinued operations (net of income tax provision (benefit) of $6,716, $(61) and $359 in 1985, 1984 and 1983, respectively)	**9,609**	(47,468)	5,819
Gain (loss) from disposals (net of income tax provision (benefit) of $28,760 and $(500) in 1985 and 1984, respectively)	**114,000**	(15,000)	–
	123,609	(62,468)	5,819
Net Income	**$ 543,690**	$ 212,547	$ 284,111
Net Income (Loss) Per Share			
Continuing operations	**$4.51**	$2.90	$2.95
Discontinued operations	**1.32**	(.65)	.06
Net Income	**$5.83**	$2.25	$3.01
Average shares outstanding used to calculate earnings per share	**93,567**	95,827	95,480

See accompanying notes

Consolidated Statement of Financial Condition—PepsiCo, Inc.

(000 omitted)	Dec. 28 1985	Dec. 29 1984
Assets		
Current Assets		
Cash	**$ 25,738**	$ 27,501
Short-term investments	**886,527**	784,684
Receivable from sale of North American Van Lines	**375,540**	–
Notes and accounts receivable, less allowance: 1985–$30,382; 1984–$30,663	**648,659**	587,373
Inventories	**380,096**	340,689
Prepaid expenses, taxes and other current assets	**477,984**	232,998
Net assets held for disposal	**–**	289,593
	2,794,544	2,262,838
Long-term Receivables and Other Investments	**232,251**	254,184
Property, Plant and Equipment	**2,571,773**	2,115,981
Goodwill	**185,716**	163,904
Other Assets	**76,876**	79,497
	$5,861,160	$4,876,404
Liabilities and Shareholders' Equity		
Current Liabilities		
Notes payable (including current installments on long-term debt and capital lease obligations)	**$ 344,137**	$ 280,796
Accounts payable	**621,993**	487,451
Federal and foreign income taxes	**123,609**	117,736
Other accrued taxes	**64,746**	63,414
Other current liabilities	**681,234**	622,658
	1,835,719	1,572,055
Long-term Debt	**1,035,571**	536,076
Capital Lease Obligations	**127,097**	133,565
Other Liabilities and Deferred Credits	**211,391**	162,732
Deferred Income Taxes	**813,700**	618,600
Shareholders' Equity		
Capital stock, par value 5¢ per share; authorized 135,000,000 shares; issued: 1985–95,898,068; 1984–95,164,331 shares	**4,795**	4,758
Capital in excess of par value	**282,453**	251,915
Retained earnings	**2,061,442**	1,678,912
Cumulative translation adjustment	**(40,931)**	(49,426)
Cost of repurchased shares: 1985–8,191,905; 1984–1,256,768	**(470,077)**	(32,783)
	1,837,682	1,853,376
	$5,861,160	$4,876,404

See accompanying notes

Consolidated Statement of Changes in Financial Condition—PepsiCo, Inc.

(000 omitted)	Years Ended Dec. 28 1985	Dec. 29 1984	Dec. 31 1983
Cash was Generated by (Used for):			
Continuing Operations:			
Income	**$ 420,081**	$ 275,015	$ 278,292
Depreciation and amortization	**290,819**	249,604	232,852
Deferred income taxes	**81,100**	121,300	60,200
Refranchising (credit) charge	**(14,900)**	62,000	–
Changes in operating working capital accounts (see details below)	**(68,694)**	186,600	(9,004)
Other non-cash charges and credits, net	**95,840**	85,360	107,894
Cash generated by continuing operations	**804,246**	979,879	670,234
Discontinued operations:			
Cash generated by (used for) discontinued operations	**16,507**	(63,211)	30,001
Wilson restructuring charge	**–**	59,300	–
Other, net	**(15,147)**	2,872	(29,755)
Cash generated by (used for) discontinued operations	**1,360**	(1,039)	246
Investment activities:			
Purchases of property, plant and equipment	**785,896**	555,802	503,352
Receivable from sale of North American Van Lines	**375,540**	–	–
Proceeds from sale of North American Van Lines	**(368,950)**	–	–
Allegheny Pepsi-Cola acquisition	**160,000**	–	–
Proceeds from the sale of Wilson Sporting Goods	**(134,100)**	–	–
Proceeds from sales of property, plant and equipment	**(49,459)**	(42,210)	(42,910)
Miscellaneous, net	**15,605**	26,828	(89,997)
Cash used for investment activities	**784,532**	540,420	370,445
Financing activities:			
Increase in long-term debt	**689,930**	41,356	62,257
Purchase of capital stock	**(458,171)**	–	–
Reductions of long-term debt and capital lease obligations	**(220,527)**	(197,849)	(135,363)
Cash dividends	**(161,054)**	(154,624)	(151,271)
Deferred income taxes arising from tax leases	**114,035**	115,584	105,347
Increase in notes payable	**63,341**	5,501	87,372
Issuance of capital stock	**51,452**	11,306	5,903
Cash generated by (used for) financing activities	**79,006**	(178,726)	(25,755)
Resulting in:			
Increase in cash and short-term investments during the year	**$ 100,080**	$ 259,694	$ 274,280
Details of Changes in Operating Working Capital Accounts Which Generated (Used) Cash:			
Notes and accounts receivable	**$ (61,286)**	$ (45,005)	$ 1,732
Inventories	**(39,407)**	(80,951)	17,410
Prepaid expenses, taxes and other current assets	**(125,096)**	17,844	(43,433)
Accounts payable	**134,542**	130,489	(74,766)
Other current liabilities	**24,910**	106,958	39,531
Federal and foreign income taxes payable	**5,397**	58,898	34,662
Other accrued taxes	**(7,754)**	(1,633)	15,860
	$ (68,694)	$ 186,600	$ (9,004)

See accompanying notes

Consolidated Statement of Shareholders' Equity—PepsiCo, Inc.

(000 omitted)

	Capital Stock				Capital in Excess of Par Value	Retained Earnings	Cumulative Translation Adjustment	Total
	Issued		Repurchased					
	Shares	Amount	Shares	Amount				
Shareholders' Equity, December 25, 1982	94,916	$4,746	(1,542)	$ (40,219)	$242,154	$1,489,797	$(46,013)	$1,650,465
1983 Net income						284,111		284,111
Cash dividends declared (per share–$1.62)						(151,358)		(151,358)
Shares reissued to TRASOP			116	3,024	886			3,910
Payment of compensation awards and exercise of stock options	53	2			1,640			1,642
Conversion of debentures	17	1			350			351
Translation adjustments (net of income taxes of $25,900)							5,037	5,037
Shareholders' Equity, December 31, 1983	94,986	4,749	(1,426)	(37,195)	245,030	1,622,550	(40,976)	1,794,158
1984 Net income						212,547		212,547
Cash dividends declared (per share–$1.665)						(156,185)		(156,185)
Shares reissued to PAYSOP			169	4,412	2,484			6,896
Payment of compensation awards and exercise of stock options	170	9			4,237			4,246
Conversion of debentures	8				164			164
Translation adjustments (net of income taxes of $18,700)							(8,059)	(8,059)
Amount included in refranchising charge (net of income taxes of $44,500)							(391)	(391)
Shareholders' Equity, December 29, 1984	95,164	4,758	(1,257)	(32,783)	251,915	1,678,912	(49,426)	1,853,376
1985 Net income						543,690		543,690
Cash dividends declared (per share–$1.755)						(161,160)		(161,160)
Shares reissued to PAYSOP			76	3,946	478			4,424
Payment of compensation awards and exercise of stock options	156	8	25	1,316	5,500			6,824
Conversion of debentures	578	29	299	15,615	24,560			40,204
Translation adjustments (net of income taxes of $100)							8,495	8,495
Share repurchases			(7,335)	(458,171)				(458,171)
Shareholders' Equity, December 28, 1985	**95,898**	**$4,795**	**(8,192)**	**$(470,077)**	**$282,453**	**$2,061,442**	**$(40,931)**	**$1,837,682**

See accompanying notes

Notes to Consolidated Financial Statements

Summary of Significant Accounting Policies

Principles of Consolidation. The consolidated financial statements include the accounts of PepsiCo, Inc. and its subsidiaries (all of which are wholly-owned), except for those held as temporary investments, which are accounted for under the cost method. The financial statements and accompanying notes have been reclassified for discontinued operations. All significant intercompany accounts and transactions have been eliminated.

Short-term Investments. Short-term investments are stated at cost, which approximates market, and include time deposits of $269 million and $481 million at year-end 1985 and 1984, respectively, and secured interests in pools of short-term discounted third-party receivables of $203 million in 1985.

Inventories. Inventories are valued at the lower of cost (computed on the average, first-in, first-out or last-in, first-out method) or net realizable value.

Property, Plant and Equipment. Property, plant and equipment, including capital leases, are stated at cost. Depreciation is calculated principally on a straight-line basis over the estimated useful lives of the respective assets.

Goodwill. Goodwill represents the excess of cost over identifiable net assets of companies acquired. Goodwill is amortized over appropriate periods not exceeding 40 years. Amortization was $8 million in 1985, $10 million in 1984 and $8 million in 1983.

Marketing Costs. Costs of advertising and other marketing and promotional programs are charged to expense during the year, generally in relation to sales, and except for materials in inventory and prepayments, are substantially expensed by the end of the year in which the costs are incurred.

Income Taxes. Deferred income taxes arise from the deferral of investment tax credits, which are amortized over the estimated useful lives of the related assets, and from timing differences between financial and tax reporting, principally financing transactions, foreign exchange translation and depreciation.

Taxes that would result from dividend distributions by foreign subsidiaries to the U.S. parent are provided to the extent dividends are anticipated. All other undistributed earnings of subsidiaries operating outside the United States have been reinvested indefinitely and no provision has been made for additional taxes that might be payable with regard to such earnings in the event of remittance.

Net Income Per Share. Net income per share is computed by dividing net income (adjusted for interest expense related to convertible debentures) by the average number of shares and share equivalents outstanding during each year. The conversion of all convertible debentures would not result in a material dilution.

Refranchising Credit (Charge)

In 1984, PepsiCo recorded a $156 million before-tax and $62 million after-tax ($.65 per share) charge for the refranchising of several company-owned foreign bottling operations (the Refranchising Program). This charge was comprised of a $24 million before-tax and $11 million after-tax charge for estimated losses from operations expected to be incurred during the course of the Refranchising Program and a $132 million before-tax and $51 million after-tax charge for estimated net losses upon disposition of the various operations.

Subsequent to the initiation of the Refranchising Program, charges applied to the operating loss reserve totaled $26 million before-tax and $16 million after-tax. Net losses actually incurred to December 28, 1985 upon the disposition of operations refranchised totaled $27 million before-tax (net of a cumulative translation adjustment gain of $50 million) and $3 million after-tax. As of December 28, 1985 all but one of the company-owned foreign bottling operations in the Refranchising Program have been refranchised. As a result of more favorable results than originally estimated from the 1985 refranchisings, the reserve has been reduced and a $26 million before-tax and $15 million after-tax ($.16 per share) credit has been recorded. This credit is reflected in the Consolidated Statement of Income under the caption "Refranchising credit (charge)." The balance of the reserve, $72 million, represents the estimated amount required to complete the Refranchising Program and to provide for other obligations and contingencies related to the completed refranchisings.

In 1985 refranchisings were completed in Belgium, Brazil, Canada, the Philippines and South Africa. In 1984, a refranchising was completed in Mexico.

The remaining net assets of the company-owned foreign bottling operations in the Refranchising Program are carried, net of accruals for future operating and disposition related losses, in the Consolidated Statement of Financial Condition under the caption "Other current liabilities." The net liability arising from the Refranchising Program as of December 28, 1985 and December 29, 1984 is detailed below:

	1985	1984
	(in thousands)	
Current assets	$14,308	$ 47,318
Current liabilities	21,249	39,696
Net current assets	(6,941)	7,622
Property, plant and equipment	23,919	78,888
Other non-current assets	4,406	11,602
Non-current liabilities	1,974	2,001
Net non-current assets	26,351	88,489
Net assets	19,410	96,111
Less:		
Accrued future operating and disposition related losses	72,300	160,606[a]
Net liability for refranchising	$52,890	$ 64,495

[a] Represents the year-end balance of the approximately $201 million of accruals established at the outset of the Refranchising Program in 1984. The accruals were reduced by approximately $45 million of balance sheet translation gains transferred from the "Cumulative translation adjustment" account, resulting in a $156 million before-tax charge to 1984 earnings.

Discontinued Operations

In 1985 PepsiCo sold its Wilson Sporting Goods operation (Wilson). The proceeds from the sale of $134 million consisted of cash and $42 million (face amount) of Wilson 10 percent cumulative preferred stock, valued at $13 million. The loss on the sale of $41 million before-tax and $18 million after-tax ($.19 per share), includes provisions for certain obligations of Wilson assumed by PepsiCo in connection with the sale, and is reflected in the Consolidated Statement of Income under the caption "Gain (loss) from disposals." Of the loss, $12 million before-tax and $9 million after-tax ($.09 per share) was recorded in the fourth quarter, primarily to reflect the currently estimated fair market value of the Wilson preferred stock. The sale proceeds are subject to adjustments arising from the audit of Wilson's balance sheet as of the closing date, which is not yet complete. If PepsiCo and the purchaser are unable to agree upon the adjustments related to Wilson's balance sheet, the contract provides that the differences will be settled by an independent accounting firm agreed upon by the parties. Management believes any change will not have a material adverse effect on PepsiCo's business or financial condition.

PepsiCo has extended Wilson a $10 million line of credit, expiring December 31, 1986. As of February 1986 the line of credit remains unused. PepsiCo is contingently liable as of December 28, 1985 for $14 million of various obligations of Wilson, including $9 million of short-term letters of credit, which decreased to $3 million in February 1986. The letters of credit expire in August 1986.

In 1984 PepsiCo adopted a plan to sell its transportation segment, which was comprised of North American Van Lines, Inc. (NAVL) and Lee Way Motor Freight, Inc. (Lee Way).

The sale of NAVL was completed in 1985 for a $369 million interest-bearing deferred payment due January 2, 1986. On that date, $376 million, including accrued interest, was received. The sale resulted in a gain of $194 million before-tax and $139 million after-tax ($1.49 per share), and is reflected in the Consolidated Statement of Income under the caption "Gain (loss) from disposals."

The sale of Lee Way was completed in 1984 and produced a loss of $16 million before-tax and $15 million after-tax ($.16 per share). This loss is reflected in the Consolidated Statement of Income under the caption "Gain (loss) from disposals." In 1985 PepsiCo made payments and incurred costs under certain guarantees that existed at, or were entered into in connection with, the sale of Lee Way. The purchaser of Lee Way merged into Lee Way in 1985, shortly before filing for bankruptcy. The merged company is now in liquidation. PepsiCo has filed a claim to recover the amounts paid or payable under the guarantees, but any significant recovery is uncertain. As a result, an additional charge of $10 million before-tax and $7 million after-tax ($.08 per share) was recorded in the fourth quarter of 1985. This loss is reflected in the Consolidated Statement of Income under the caption "Gain (loss) from disposals."

The results of operations of NAVL, Wilson and Lee Way are recorded in the Consolidated Statement of Income under the caption "Income (loss) from discontinued operations" and include results of operations through the dates in 1985 and 1984 on which the sales of the respective operations were recorded in the financial statements. Also included under this caption is the $64 million before-tax and $59 million after-tax ($.62 per share) Wilson restructuring charge recorded in 1984, primarily resulting from the write-off of $54 million (without tax benefit) of Wilson's goodwill. The results of NAVL, Wilson and Lee Way are as follows:

	1985	1984	1983
	(in thousands)		
Net sales and operating revenues	$422,240	$ 976,888	$996,052
Costs and expenses	404,802	957,546	988,052
Net interest expense	1,113	2,871	1,822
Wilson restructuring charge	–	64,000	–
	405,915	1,024,417	989,874
Income (loss) before income taxes	16,325	(47,529)	6,178
Income tax provision (benefit)	6,716	(61)	359
Income (loss) from discontinued operations	$ 9,609	$ (47,468)	$ 5,819

The net assets of Wilson and NAVL are carried at their historical cost in the Consolidated Statement of Financial Condition under the caption "Net assets held for disposal" at December 29, 1984 as follows (in thousands):

Current assets	$405,688
Current liabilities	217,566
Net current assets	188,122
Property, plant and equipment	145,887
Other non-current assets	52,529
Non-current liabilities	96,945
Net non-current assets	101,471
Net assets held for disposal	$289,593

Acquisitions

In May 1985 PepsiCo purchased the Allegheny Pepsi-Cola Bottling Company (Allegheny) for $160 million in cash. Allegheny was acquired with the intent of refranchising the operations to other purchasers. Accordingly, the acquisition has been accounted for as a temporary investment under the cost method and is included in the Consolidated Statement of Financial Condition under the caption "Prepaid expenses, taxes and other current assets."

In December 1985 PepsiCo agreed to purchase the soft drink business of MEI Corporation (MEI) for $590 million in cash. The transaction is subject to various conditions, including approval by the shareholders of MEI. MEI is PepsiCo's third largest independent bottler. This acquisition will be accounted for by the purchase method and is expected to be completed in the second quarter of 1986.

In January 1986 PepsiCo agreed to purchase the domestic and international franchise beverage businesses of The Seven-Up Company (Seven-Up) from Philip Morris Incorporated (Philip Morris) for $380 million cash. The transaction is subject to various governmental approvals. Upon transfer of the international business, PepsiCo is obligated to pay the full purchase price, and assume all the risks of ownership, for both the international and domestic Seven-Up businesses, even though governmental approvals for the transfer of the domestic business may not have been received. If, after transfer of the international business, sale of the domestic Seven-Up business to PepsiCo is prohibited under the antitrust laws or if PepsiCo so requests, then Philip Morris is obligated to use its best efforts to sell the domestic business on the same terms and conditions as the proposed sale and to remit the net proceeds to PepsiCo. Management believes that none of the foregoing alternatives will have a material adverse affect on PepsiCo's business or financial condition. This acquisition will be accounted for by the purchase method.

Also, in January 1986 PepsiCo agreed to acquire A & M Food Services, Inc. (A & M) in exchange for PepsiCo Capital Stock. The number of shares of PepsiCo Capital Stock to be received by stockholders of A&M will be between 584,000 and 741,000. The transaction is subject to various conditions, including approval by the shareholders of A & M. A & M is Pizza Hut's largest franchisee. This acquisition will be accounted for by the purchase method and is expected to be completed in the second quarter of 1986.

Share Repurchases

During 1985 PepsiCo announced plans to repurchase up to 9.7 million shares of PepsiCo's Capital Stock. These shares are to be used to fund outstanding convertible securities, employee stock plans and for other corporate purposes.

As of December 28, 1985 PepsiCo had purchased 7.3 million shares at an aggregate purchase price of $458 million and had commitments to purchase 260,000 shares at an aggregate purchase price of $18 million. As of February 4, 1986 PepsiCo had purchased 9 million shares at an aggregate purchase price of $572 million and had commitments to purchase 57,000 shares at an aggregate purchase price of $4 million.

Inventories

Inventories at December 28, 1985 and December 29, 1984 are summarized as follows:

	1985	1984
	(in thousands)	
Finished goods	$163,311	$140,482
Raw materials, supplies and in-process	223,132	208,323
Total (approximates current cost)	386,443	348,805
Excess of current cost over LIFO cost	(6,347)	(8,116)
	$380,096	$340,689

Inventories valued at cost, computed on the last-in, first-out (LIFO) method comprised 57 percent of inventories at December 28, 1985 and December 29, 1984.

Property, Plant and Equipment

Property, plant and equipment at December 28, 1985 and December 29, 1984 are summarized as follows:

	1985	1984
	(in thousands)	
Land	$ 250,671	$ 217,811
Buildings	1,015,068	809,513
Machinery and equipment	2,361,762	1,934,954
Capital leases	170,901	172,535
Bottles and cases	25,048	23,785
	3,823,450	3,158,598
Less accumulated depreciation and amortization	1,251,677	1,042,617
	$2,571,773	$2,115,981

Notes Payable and Long-term Debt

Notes payable and long-term debt (less current maturities) at December 28, 1985 and December 29, 1984 are summarized below:

	1985	1984
	(in thousands)	
Notes Payable		
10⅛% notes due 1986	$150,000	$ –
8¼% notes due 1985	–	100,000
Current maturities on other long-term debt and capital lease obligations	25,284	17,789
Other notes payable, primarily to foreign banks	168,853	163,007
	$344,137	$280,796

	1985	1984
	(in thousands)	
Long-term Debt (less current maturities)		
Commercial paper (7.97% weighted average interest rate)	$ 603,000	$ –
10⅛% notes due 1986	–	150,000
Zero coupon serial debentures, $850 million face value due 1988-2012 (13.91% semiannual yield to maturity)	89,361	78,014
13% notes, 50 million Australian dollars, due 1990 (After interest rate swap: Variable interest based on 90-day Australian Bank Bill rate – 19.6% at year-end)	34,456	–
Zero coupon notes, $100 million face value due 1992 (14.42% semiannual yield to maturity)	42,758	37,213
Zero coupon notes, $125 million face value due 1994 (14.08% semiannual yield to maturity)	41,112	35,896
5¼% bearer bonds, 130 million Swiss francs, due 1995 (After exchange agreement: $50 million principal at maturity, 10.96% semiannual yield to maturity)	47,773	–
8% convertible subordinated debentures due 1996	40,088	73,184
Other (11.9% weighted average interest rate)	137,023	161,769
	$1,035,571	$536,076

The original issue discounts associated with the zero coupon issues listed above are being amortized over the lives of the issues on a yield-to-maturity basis. For tax purposes, the original issue discounts are deductible on a straight-line basis over the lives of the issues, thus reducing the effective costs of these transactions.

At the option of the holder, the convertible subordinated debentures are primarily convertible at a rate of approximately 26 shares for each $1,000 of principal. At December 28, 1985, 1.1 million shares were reserved for issuance upon conversion of the debentures.

During 1985 PepsiCo issued Swiss francs (SFr.) 130 million of 5¼ percent Bearer Bonds, due March 1995. Simultaneously with the issuance of the SFr. Bonds, PepsiCo entered into a currency exchange agreement. The debt issuance and related agreement created a U.S. dollar liability in the amount of $50 million at maturity with a semiannual yield to maturity of 10.96 percent.

Also in 1985 PepsiCo issued Australian dollar 50 million of 13 percent Guaranteed Notes due 1990. Subsequent to the issuance of the notes, PepsiCo entered into an interest rate swap converting the fixed interest rate to a variable interest rate based on the 90-day Australian Bank Bill rate which at year-end 1985 was 19.6 percent.

During 1984 PepsiCo issued $104 million Deutsche mark denominated bearer bonds yielding 7¼ percent, due February, 1994. A major portion of the bond proceeds were used to purchase higher yielding notes of the West German Government that produce cash flows sufficient to meet the interest and principal payments of the bearer bonds. PepsiCo defeased the bonds by depositing the Deutsche mark denominated government notes in an irrevocable trust established for the sole purpose of servicing the bearer bonds. This defeasance resulted in a $2 million ($.02 per share) gain, after related expenses and taxes. The bearer bonds and promissory notes of the West German Government offset each other in the Consolidated Statement of Financial Condition.

At December 28, 1985 PepsiCo had unused credit facilities aggregating $1.52 billion, providing it with domestic and international credit availability and support for the issuance of commercial paper. Of the total, approximately $17 million represents lines of credit and $1.5 billion represents revolving credit agreements covering maximum potential borrowings maturing January 2, 1991. These unused credit facilities of $1.52 billion provide PepsiCo the ability to refinance short-term borrowings and currently support the classification of $603 million of commercial paper as long-term debt, since it is PepsiCo's intent to refinance this commercial paper during 1986 on a long-term basis.

Maturities of long-term debt (excluding capital lease obligations) are as follows: 1986-$165 million; 1987-$6 million; 1988-$46 million; 1989-$14 million; and 1990-$43 million. The debt agreements to which PepsiCo is a party include various restrictions, none of which is presently significant to PepsiCo.

Interest capitalized as an additional cost of property, plant and equipment was $13 million in 1985, $8 million in 1984 and $7 million in 1983.

In February 1986 PepsiCo issued Australian dollar 75 million of 14⅛ percent notes due in 1989. Concurrently with the issuance, PepsiCo has committed to enter into a currency exchange agreement. The debt issuance and related agreement create a U.S. dollar liability in the amount of $51 million at maturity with a floating interest rate based upon the AA Federal Reserve Composite Commercial Paper rate.

Employee Stock Option and Ownership Plans

The shareholder-approved 1979 Incentive Plan (the Plan) provides long-term incentives to certain key employees through the granting of performance shares, stock options, stock appreciation rights (SARs) and incentive stock units. Under the Plan a maximum of 4.6 million shares of PepsiCo Capital Stock may be purchased or paid pursuant to grants by the Compensation Committee of the Board of Directors (the Committee) at prices not less than 100 percent of the fair market value at the date of grant. The Committee is composed of outside directors.

Performance shares and an equal number of stock options have been awarded to senior management employees. Each stock option represents the right to purchase one share of PepsiCo Capital Stock. The Committee sets the period during which an option may be exercised; however, none are exercisable until four years after the option is granted and may not have a term longer than 10 years from date of grant. Stock option activity for the years 1983 through 1985 was as follows:

	Option Exercise Prices	Shares Under Option
Balance, December 25, 1982	$23.88 to $43.06	978,526
1983		
Granted	–	–
Exercised	$28.31	(22,175)
Cancelled or surrendered for SARs	–	(211,259)
Balance, December 31, 1983	$23.88 to $43.06	745,092
1984		
Granted	$37.00	526,590
Exercised	$23.88 and $24.13	(158,082)
Cancelled or surrendered for SARs	–	(237,129)
Balance, December 29, 1984	$23.88 to $43.06	876,471
1985		
Granted	$34.69	1,488
Exercised	$23.88	(101,548)
Cancelled or surrendered for SARs	–	(103,395)
Balance, December 28, 1985	$34.69 to $43.06	673,016

At December 28, 1985 no options for shares were exercisable. Also at year-end 1985, 3,245,613 shares were reserved for issuance under the Plan. In January 1986, 278,349 options were issued at an exercise price of $69.25 per share.

Each performance share is equivalent to one share of PepsiCo Capital Stock. Performance shares are not paid unless PepsiCo achieves earnings per share growth targets established by the Committee for the four-year period following the award. Upon a determination by the Committee that a performance share has been earned, the holder receives the lesser of the fair market value of one share of Capital Stock at the date of award or the fair market value of one share of Capital Stock at the end of the award period. The performance share is paid in cash or Capital Stock or a combination thereof as determined by the Committee. During 1982 and 1984, 1,008,224 performance shares were awarded, of which 694,252 and 804,136 shares were outstanding at December 28, 1985 and December 29, 1984, respectively. In January 1986, 278,349 performance shares were awarded.

Stock appreciation rights (SARs) permit the holder of a stock option to surrender an exercisable option for an amount equal to the appreciation between the option price and the fair market value of Capital Stock on the date the SAR is exercised or expires. The amount is paid in cash or Capital Stock or a combination thereof. SARs expire on the same dates as the related options. In January 1984, 141,352 SARs were granted; and as of December 28, 1985, none was outstanding. In January 1986, 85,385 SARs were granted.

Incentive stock units (Units) are awarded by the Committee as incentives to middle management employees. Each Unit entitles the holder to receive the value of a share of Capital Stock without payment of any amounts to PepsiCo or satisfaction of any performance objectives. Each Unit is valued at the fair market value of the Capital Stock at the end of each vesting period. Currently, 30 percent of each award vests at the end of two years, an additional 30 percent vests at the end of four years, and the remainder vests at the end of six years. Payment of the Units is made in cash or Capital Stock or a combination thereof as determined by the Committee. From 1979 to 1985, 645,497 Units were awarded, of which 233,894 were outstanding at December 28, 1985.

The estimated cost of all awards under the Plan is charged to expense over the applicable terms of the awards. The cost was $19 million in 1985, $11 million in 1984 and $13 million in 1983.

Effective January 1, 1981, PepsiCo established a Tax Reduction Act Stock Ownership Plan (TRASOP) for the benefit of most employees. Beginning January 1, 1983, this plan was changed as a result of the Tax Reform Act of 1982, to a Payroll-based Employee Stock Ownership Plan (PAYSOP). Under these plans, PepsiCo may make a tax creditable contribution of either cash or Capital Stock to a trust on behalf of participating employees. During 1985 and 1984, PepsiCo contributed 75,540 and 169,147 shares, respectively, to the employee trust.

Income Taxes

U.S. and foreign income (loss) from continuing operations before federal and foreign income taxes were as follows:

	1985	1984	1983
	(in thousands)		
U.S.	$440,528	$ 503,592	$509,730
Foreign	197,538	90,100	(90,836)
	638,066	593,692	418,894
Refranchising credit (charge)	25,900	(156,000)	–
	$663,966	$ 437,692	$418,894

The provision for federal and foreign income taxes on continuing operations is comprised of the following:

	1985	1984	1983
	(in thousands)		
Current:			
Federal	$ 82,132	$ 135,609	$ 77,408
Foreign	6,453	13,568	12,294
Deferred (principally federal)			
Current	74,200	(107,800)	(9,300)
Non-current	81,100	121,300	60,200
	$243,885	$ 162,677	$140,602

The provision for state income taxes, which is included in marketing, administrative and other expenses, was $7 million in 1985, $13 million in 1984 and $26 million in 1983.

The differences between the effective and statutory federal income tax rate on continuing operations are comprised of the following:

	1985	1984	1983
Statutory federal rate	46.0%	46.0%	46.0%
Investment tax credits	(2.9)	(3.8)	(3.5)
Losses on refranchising of foreign bottling operations taxed at an aggregate rate different than the statutory federal rate	(0.2)	(5.1)	(4.0)
Earnings and losses of foreign operations taxed at an aggregate rate different than the statutory federal rate	(5.7)	(1.2)	(6.0)
Other-net	(0.5)	1.3	1.1
Effective rate	36.7%	37.2%	33.6%

The effective tax rate on earnings from discontinued operations was 41.1 percent in 1985, zero percent in 1984 and 5.8 percent in 1983. The difference between the effective and the statutory federal income tax rate for 1985 and 1983 is principally due to the amortization of investment tax credits. For 1984 the difference is principally due to the write-off of Wilson goodwill without tax benefit. In 1985 the net before-tax gain of $143 million on the disposal of NAVL and Wilson and the additional costs related to the 1984 sale of Lee Way resulted in an income tax expense of $29 million. The effective tax rate of 20 percent is due to the lower capital gain tax rate and the effect of permanent differences between the book and tax basis of the Capital Stock sold. The $16 million before-tax loss on the disposal of Lee Way in 1984 generated $500,000 of tax benefit due to the difference in the book and tax basis of the Capital Stock sold and the treatment of the sale as a capital loss.

The current portion of deferred federal income taxes of $194 million in 1985 and $176 million in 1984 was included in the Consolidated Statement of Financial Condition under the caption "Prepaid expenses, taxes and other current assets."

Federal and foreign income taxes payable consists of the following:

	1985	1984
	(in thousands)	
Federal	$ 96,810	$ 92,673
Foreign	26,799	25,063
	$123,609	$117,736

Deferred income tax expense on continuing operations arises from the following items:

	1985	1984	1983
	(in thousands)		
Excess of tax over financial statement expense related to depreciable assets (including capital leases)	$ 40,900	$ 38,400	$31,400
Excess of tax over financial statement expense related to financing transactions	6,100	21,500	22,200
Net financial statement effect related to refranchising	55,000	(51,600)	–
Deferral of investment tax credit benefits	13,700	4,700	3,800
Prefunded employee benefits	31,300	–	–
Other-net	8,300	500	(6,500)
	$155,300	$ 13,500	$50,900

Deferred income taxes payable include:

	1985	1984
	(in thousands)	
Deferred taxes—tax leases	$361,500	$247,500
Deferred taxes—other	372,700	305,300
Deferred investment tax credits	79,500	65,800
	$813,700	$618,600

In 1981 and 1982, PepsiCo invested $429 million in tax leases. This investment, reduced by realized tax credits and tax savings from accelerated depreciation deductions, is principally included in the Consolidated Statement of Financial Condition under the caption "Long-term Receivables and Other Investments." The balance of the investment at year-end 1985 and 1984 was $74 million and $78 million, respectively. As a result of these investments, actual current taxes payable for 1985, 1984 and 1983 were reduced by approximately $114 million, $116 million and $119 million, respectively. Certain of the tax benefits that arise from these investments are temporary and will be repaid in future years over the lives of the leases. The benefits of the tax leases are not included in the provision for federal and foreign income taxes in the Consolidated Statement of Income.

Unremitted earnings of subsidiaries operating outside the United States that have been, or are intended to be, permanently reinvested, on which taxes have not been provided, aggregated approximately $314 million at December 28, 1985 and $214 million at December 29, 1984. These unremitted earnings are exclusive of amounts that if remitted in the future would result in little or no tax under current tax laws.

In 1985 PepsiCo reached an administrative settlement with the Internal Revenue Service regarding proposed tax deficiencies of $100 million for the years 1973 through 1978. The proposed deficiencies dealt with the reallocation to the U.S. parent company of a portion of the income of foreign soft drink concentrate manufacturing subsidiaries operating primarily in Puerto Rico and Ireland under tax incentive grants. The settlement was for significantly less than the proposed deficiencies and had no effect on 1985 results of operations.

Leases

PepsiCo and its subsidiaries have noncancellable commitments for rental of restaurant facilities, office space, plant and warehouse facilities, transportation equipment and other personal property under both capital and operating leases. Certain franchised restaurants are leased and a portion have been subsequently subleased to franchisees. Lease commitments on capital and operating leases expire at various dates to 2031. An analysis of leased property under capital leases by major classes at December 28, 1985 and December 29, 1984 is summarized as follows:

	1985	1984
	(in thousands)	
Buildings	$168,060	$168,842
Machinery and equipment	2,841	3,693
	170,901	172,535
Less accumulated amortization	72,885	68,818
	$ 98,016	$103,717

The following is a schedule of future minimum lease commitments and sublease receivables under all noncancellable leases:

	Commitments		Sublease Receivables	
	Capital	Operating	Direct Financing	Operating
	(in thousands)			
1986	$ 25,097	$ 63,053	$ (7,891)	$ (7,601)
1987	24,416	51,433	(7,778)	(7,323)
1988	23,226	41,762	(7,492)	(6,776)
1989	21,310	37,137	(7,176)	(6,386)
1990	20,184	34,473	(6,829)	(5,841)
Later years	126,418	250,269	(61,582)	(48,614)
Total minimum lease commitments (receivables)	$240,651	$478,127	$(98,748)	$(82,541)

The present value of minimum lease payments for capital leases amounts to $137 million after deducting $2 million for estimated executory costs (taxes, maintenance and insurance) and $102 million representing imputed interest. The present value of minimum sublease receivables amounts to $42 million after deducting $57 million of unearned interest income. Total rental expense for all operating leases for years ended December 28, 1985, December 29, 1984 and December 31, 1983 was $117 million, $110 million and $108 million, respectively. Total rental income from all operating subleases for years ended December 28, 1985, December 29, 1984 and December 31, 1983 was $16 million, $15 million and $15 million, respectively.

Employee Benefit Plans

PepsiCo and its subsidiaries have several non-contributory pension plans covering substantially all domestic employees (mostly non-union). The total pension expense for all plans was approximately $37 million, $41 million and $36 million in 1985, 1984 and 1983, respectively, which includes amortization of unfunded past service cost over 30 years for certain defined benefit plans. In accordance with recommendations received from its actuary, PepsiCo changed actuarial cost methods in 1985 for its pay-related plans from the frozen initial liability cost method to the projected unit credit method. Over a period of years, the change is expected to better match pension expense to benefit obligations. The effect of this change was to reduce pension expense by approximately $7 million in 1985.

A comparison of accumulated plan benefits and plan net assets for PepsiCo's domestic defined benefit plans is presented below:

	January 1 1985	1984
	(in thousands)	
Actuarial present value of accumulated plan benefits:		
Vested	$303,338	$268,795
Non-vested	87,009	77,285
	$390,347	$346,080
Net assets available for plan benefits	$469,017	$433,360

PepsiCo changed its funding policy in 1985 from making annual contributions equal to amounts accrued for pension expense to making annual contributions equal to the minimum statutory requirement. As a result, $15 million of the 1984 accrued pension expense has not been currently funded and PepsiCo does not currently expect to fund $18 million of the 1985 accrued pension expense. These amounts are included in the Consolidated Statement of Financial Condition under the caption "Other Liabilities and Deferred Credits."

The rate of return used in determining the actuarial present value of accumulated plan benefits was seven percent for both 1985 and 1984.

In December 1985 the Financial Accounting Standards Board issued Statement of Financial Accounting Standards No. 87, Employers' Accounting for Pensions. None of the provisions of this statement are required to be adopted until fiscal years beginning after December 15, 1986, however, PepsiCo estimates that when adopted, they will have a favorable effect on consolidated income from continuing operations. The estimated impact may be affected by future events, the outcomes of which are not known at this time.

PepsiCo and its subsidiaries provide certain health care and life insurance benefits for retired non-union employees. Substantially all of PepsiCo's employees, including employees in certain foreign countries, may become eligible for those benefits if they reach retirement age while still working for PepsiCo. The cost of retiree health care benefits is recognized as an expense as claims are incurred. PepsiCo recognizes the cost of providing retiree life insurance by expensing the annual insurance premiums for these benefits. The domestic expenditures for retired employees under these programs for the years ended December 28, 1985, December 29, 1984 and December 31, 1983 were $4 million, $3 million and $2 million, respectively. Foreign expenditures under these programs were insignificant.

Contingencies

PepsiCo and its subsidiaries are involved in various litigated matters, but management believes that the resolution of these matters will not have a material effect on PepsiCo's business or financial condition. PepsiCo intends to prosecute or defend vigorously, as the case may be, all such matters.

At December 28, 1985 PepsiCo and its subsidiaries were contingently liable under direct and indirect guarantees aggregating $51 million.

SUPPLEMENTARY FINANCIAL INFORMATION

In addition to the financial statements and the accompanying notes, four items of supplementary financial information typically are presented: business segment information, effects of inflation, five- (or ten-) year summary of related financial data, and quarterly financial data.

BUSINESS SEGMENT INFORMATION

To help financial statement users assess the performance of diversified companies that operate in several different industries and lines of business, segmented financial information is required. The required information for each significant segment includes: revenues, income from operations, capital expenditures, identifiable assets, and depreciation and amortization. This information is generally included in the form of notes and schedules in the notes accompanying the financial statements. PepsiCo's note summarizing its business segment information is shown below:

Business Segments

In 1985 PepsiCo's business segments, formerly referred to as beverages, food products and food service, were renamed soft drinks, snack foods and restaurants to more clearly reflect the products and services of each business.

The soft drinks segment primarily manufactures and markets Pepsi-Cola and its allied brands. The snack foods segment primarily produces salty snacks. The restaurants segment primarily includes the operations of Pizza Hut and Taco Bell.

Sales between segments were not significant, and no single customer accounted for more than 10 percent of sales. Other than North America, no geographic area accounted for more than 10 percent of sales.

Soft drinks amounts for 1985 and part of 1984 exclude the results of company-owned foreign bottling operations in the Refranchising Program. In addition, the 1985 and 1984 soft drinks operating profits exclude a $26 million credit and a $156 million charge, respectively, related to the Refranchising Program described on page 43.

Operating profits exclude net corporate expenses and net interest expense of $221 million, $222 million and $209 million in 1985, 1984 and 1983, respectively.

The operating profits of each business segment include the foreign exchange gains and losses generated by their respective foreign operations. Operating profits in the soft drinks segment have excluded the net foreign exchange gains related to the local currency borrowings of the company-owned bottling operations in the Refranchising Program since that program was initiated in the second quarter of 1984. Foreign exchange gains included in consolidated operating profits were $32 million, $53 million and $17 million in 1985, 1984 and 1983, respectively. Segment operating profits included total research and development expenses of $66 million, $49 million and $40 million in 1985, 1984 and 1983, respectively.

Corporate identifiable assets are principally short-term investments, investment in tax leases, administrative office buildings, the receivable from the sale of North American Van Lines and the investment in the Allegheny Pepsi-Cola Bottling Company.

The following summarizes PepsiCo's business segment information:

	1985	1984	1983
		(in millions)	
Net Sales:			
Soft drinks	$3,128.5	$2,908.4	$2,940.4
Snack foods	2,847.1	2,709.2	2,430.1
Restaurants	2,081.1	1,833.5	1,529.4
Total continuing operations	$8,056.7	$7,451.1	$6,899.9
Foreign portion	$ 951.9	$ 963.9	$1,128.6
Operating Profits:			
Soft drinks	$ 263.9	$ 246.4	$ 126.2
Snack foods	401.0	393.9	347.7
Restaurants	194.0	175.2	154.3
Total segments	$ 858.9	$ 815.5	$ 628.2
Foreign portion	$ 66.7	$ 35.5	$ (99.1)
Capital Spending:			
Soft drinks	$ 160.7	$ 83.6	$ 93.7
Snack foods	286.3	188.9	180.2
Restaurants	331.0	252.5	217.9
Corporate	7.9	30.8	11.6
Total continuing operations	$ 785.9	$ 555.8	$ 503.4
Foreign portion	$ 67.3	$ 36.4	$ 42.4
Identifiable Assets:			
Soft drinks	$1,318.6	$1,038.9	$1,249.0
Snack foods	1,487.1	1,254.5	1,110.1
Restaurants	1,326.7	1,020.7	825.9
Corporate	1,728.8	1,277.0	882.7
Total continuing operations	$5,861.2	$4,591.1	$4,067.7
Foreign portion	$1,054.3	$ 687.5	$ 945.8
Depreciation and Amortization Expense:			
Soft drinks	$ 69.2	$ 71.1	$ 84.9
Snack foods	107.7	93.6	81.9
Restaurants	109.2	75.7	58.0
Corporate	4.7	9.2	8.1
Total continuing operations	$ 290.8	$ 249.6	$ 232.9
Foreign portion	$ 25.3	$ 36.8	$ 51.7

EFFECTS OF INFLATION

Because financial statements are expressed in terms of money, and because the purchasing power or value of money changes, financial statements are affected by changes in price levels. The effects of price-level changes on financial statements are discussed in Chapter 13. While at one time required, the disclosure of supplemental data on the effects of price-level changes is now optional. The following price-level information was disclosed in PepsiCo's **Annual Report.**

Information on the Effects of Inflation (Unaudited)

In accordance with the Statement of Financial Accounting Standards No. 33 as amended, the information presented on this page has been provided under the current cost method in an attempt to measure the impact of inflation on PepsiCo's operations.

The current cost method attempts to measure the effects of specific price changes by reflecting the cost to replace existing property, plant and equipment and inventory with identical property, plant and equipment and inventory today. The amounts were estimated in a number of ways, including direct pricing and indexing.

Also presented is a comparison of the increase in current cost based on specific prices of property, plant and equipment and inventory with the amount of such increase in the general price level. General price level is measured by the movement in the U.S. Consumer Price Index for all Urban Consumers.

PepsiCo's 1985 adjusted financial results reflect a $66 million decrease in income from continuing operations and an increase in net assets of $375 million, which are principally attributable to the cumulative impact of inflation on PepsiCo's property, plant and equipment. The effective tax rate is increased from the historical financial statements because the provision for income taxes is not adjusted for current cost purposes, yet it is compared to reduced pre-tax income.

Since PepsiCo had net monetary liabilities during the year, a net gain in purchasing power of $57 million resulted, which should be viewed as part of the overall impact of inflation on operations.

The five-year comparison of financial data restated into average 1985 dollars, depicts that sales have grown each year, as have reported sales. Income from continuing operations when adjusted for inflation, although always lower than reported earnings, reflects the trends in PepsiCo's reported earnings.

Statement of Earnings Adjusted for the Effects of Inflation For the Year Ended December 28, 1985

(dollars in thousands except per share amounts, unaudited)

	Historical Cost	Current Cost
Net sales	$8,056,662	$8,056,662
Cost of sales, excluding depreciation	3,080,326	3,082,686
Depreciation and amortization	282,405	346,100
Other operating expenses, net	3,956,869	3,956,869
Net interest expense	98,996	98,996
Refranchising credit	(25,900)	(25,900)
Provision for income taxes	243,885	243,885
	7,636,581	7,702,636
Income from continuing operations	$ 420,081	$ 354,026
Per share	$ 4.51	$ 3.81
Effective income tax rate	37%	41%
Purchasing power gain on net monetary liabilities		$ 57,193
Effect of changes in general price level and specific prices on inventories and property, plant and equipment during the year:		
Increase in general price level		$ 58,353
Decrease in specific prices (current costs) [a]		79,968
Excess of increase in general price level over decrease in specific prices		$ 138,321

Five-Year Comparison of Selected Supplementary Financial Data Adjusted for the Effects of Inflation

(dollars in thousands of average 1985 dollars except per share amounts, unaudited)

	1985	1984	1983	1982	1981
Net sales $	8,056,662	7,749,150	7,480,323	7,263,936	7,158,935
Current Cost Information:					
Income from continuing operations $	354,026	209,189	231,519	131,789	223,478
Per share $	3.81	2.22	2.46	1.42	2.44
Excess of increase in general price level over the change in specific prices $	138,321	232,059	128,815	126,814	163,513
Net assets $	2,212,666	2,387,073	2,568,276	2,613,483	2,687,014
Other Information:					
Purchasing power gain on net monetary liabilities $	57,193	51,274	50,676	48,422	108,927
Cash dividends declared per share $	1.755	1.732	1.735	1.768	1.687
Market price per share at year-end $	71.25	42.94	40.78	37.63	41.81
Average consumer price index (1967 = 100)	322.2	311.1	298.4	289.1	272.4

FIVE- OR TEN-YEAR SUMMARY

Usually presented in close proximity to the audited financial statements is a five- or ten-year summary of selected financial data. From such a summary, one can determine trends and growth patterns over a fairly long period of time. PepsiCo presented the following five-year summary that includes operating data, financial position data, and selected statistics and ratios.

Selected Financial Data—PepsiCo, Inc.

(000 omitted)

	1985	1984	1983	1982[c]	1981
Summary of Operations					
Net sales	**$ 8,056,662**	7,451,106	6,899,884	6,492,380	6,025,261
Cost of sales and operating expenses	**7,319,600**	6,738,432	6,359,372	5,881,603	5,454,352
Net interest expense	**98,996**	118,982	121,618	114,409	111,893
	7,418,596	6,857,414	6,480,990	5,996,012	5,566,245
Income from continuing operations before unusual credits (charges) and income taxes	**638,066**	593,692	418,894	496,368	459,016
Unusual credits (charges)	**25,900**[a]	(156,000)[b]	–	(79,400)[d]	–
Income from continuing operations before income taxes	**663,966**	437,692	418,894	416,968	459,016
Federal and foreign income taxes	**243,885**	162,677	140,602	213,467	190,146
Income from continuing operations	**$ 420,081**	275,015	278,292	203,501	268,870
Income per share from continuing operations $	**4.51**[a]	2.90[b]	2.95	2.18[d]	2.92
Average shares and equivalents outstanding #	**93,567**	95,827	95,480	94,904	93,060
Cash dividends declared	**$ 161,160**	156,185	151,358	147,127	129,944
Per share	**$ 1.755**	1.665	1.620	1.580	1.420
Year-End Position					
Total assets	**$ 5,861,160**	4,876,404	4,421,079	4,005,390	3,883,057
Long-term debt [e]	**$ 1,162,668**	669,641	799,765	843,901	804,597
Shareholders' equity	**$ 1,837,682**	1,853,376	1,794,158	1,650,465	1,556,264
Per share	**$ 20.95**	19.74	19.18	17.68	16.99
Shares outstanding	**# 87,706**	93,908	93,561	93,374	91,605
Statistics and Ratios					
Return on average shareholders' equity [f]	**% 22.0**	18.5	16.2	17.6	18.3
Return on revenues [f]	**% 5.0**	4.5	4.0	4.4	4.5
Long-term debt [e] to total capital employed [g]	**% 26.6**	18.7	23.6	28.3	27.0
Total debt to total capital employed [g]	**% 34.5**	26.5	31.7	34.6	40.7
Employees	**# 150,000**	150,000	154,000	133,000	120,000
Shareholders	**# 72,000**	62,000	60,000	48,000	49,000

QUARTERLY FINANCIAL DATA

Nearly all publicly held companies and many nonpublic companies issue financial information on a quarterly basis to stockholders, regulatory agencies, and others. These quarterly reports are referred to as interim financial reports, for which there are prescribed accounting standards. Quarterly financial data are frequently summarized in the Annual Report. PepsiCo summarizes its quarterly data as follows:

Quarterly Financial Data and Information on Capital Stock

(in thousands, except per share amounts and stock prices, unaudited)

		First Quarter (12 weeks)		Second Quarter (12 weeks)		Third Quarter (12 weeks)		Fourth Quarter (16 weeks)		Full Year (52 weeks)	
		1985	1984	**1985**	1984	**1985**	1984	**1985**	1984	**1985**	1984
Net Sales		**$1,626,893**	1,552,072	**1,937,512**	1,815,831	**2,071,752**	1,886,894	**2,420,505**	2,196,309	**8,056,662**	7,451,106
Gross profit from continuing operations	**$**	**982,589**	931,322	**1,180,554**	1,085,161	**1,267,314**	1,136,534	**1,477,944**	1,323,631	**4,908,401**	4,476,648
Income from continuing operations	**$**	**60,529**	47,479	**119,295**	30,334[d]	**135,304**	111,632	**104,953**[a]	85,570	**420,081**	275,015
Income (loss) from discontinued operations	**$**	**2,311**	(326)	**136,998**[c]	(72,880)[e]	**—**	6,661	**(15,700)**[b]	4,077	**123,609**	(62,468)
Net income (loss)	**$**	**62,840**	47,153	**256,293**	(42,546)	**135,304**	118,293	**89,253**	89,647	**543,690**	212,547
Income (loss) per share:											
Continuing operations	**$**	**.64**	.51	**1.25**	.32[d]	**1.45**	1.17	**1.17**[a]	.90	**4.51**	2.90
Discontinued operations	**$**	**.02**	(.01)	**1.47**[c]	(.76)[e]	**—**	.07	**(.17)**[b]	.05	**1.32**	(.65)
Net income (loss) per share	**$**	**.66**	.50	**2.72**	(.44)	**1.45**	1.24	**1.00**	.95	**5.83**	2.25
Dividends per share[f]	**$**	**.420**	.405	**.445**	.420	**.445**	.420	**.445**	.420	**1.755**	1.665
Market price of Capital Stock[f]:											
High	**$**	**52¾**	38⅜	**60⅛**	43	**60½**	45	**75⅜**	45⅝	**75⅜**	45⅝
Low	**$**	**40⅝**	34½	**50½**	36¼	**55¼**	40½	**57⅜**	39⅞	**40⅝**	34½
Close	**$**	**51⅝**	36½	**59**	42⅜	**58⅞**	42⅜	**71¼**	41⅞	**71¼**	41⅞

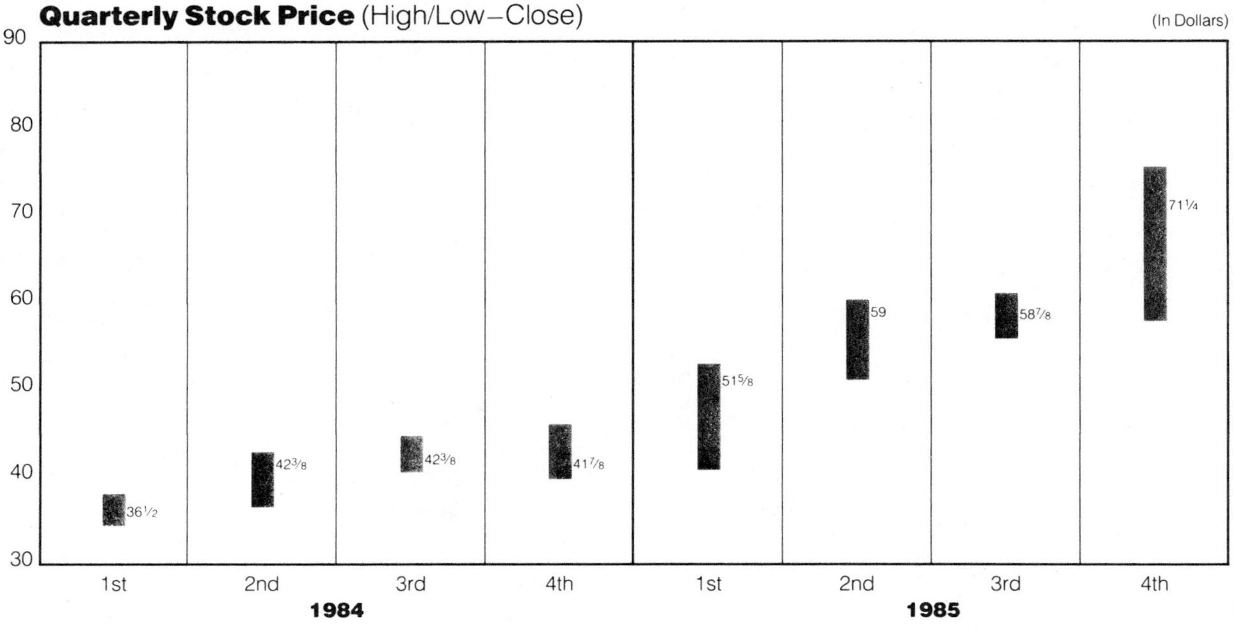

APPENDIX B—GLOSSARY

Absorption costing A costing approach in which all manufacturing costs are charged to, or absorbed by, the product. (26)

Accelerated cost recovery system (ACRS) A system of depreciation in which all depreciable assets are classified according to eight class lives and depreciation is by the declining-balance method. (29)

Active income Income which the taxpayer has materially participated in producing. (29)

Account An individual accounting record of increases and decreases in specific asset, liability, and owner's equity items. (2)

Accounting The process of identifying, measuring, recording, and communicating the economic events of an organization to interested users of the information. (1)

Accounting information system A system that involves data collection, data processing, and information dissemination. (6)

Accounts payable (creditors') ledger A subsidiary ledger that contains accounts with individual creditors. (6)

Accounts receivable (customers') ledger A subsidiary ledger that contains individual customer accounts. (6)

Accounts receivable master file A file in a computerized system that is comparable to the accounts receivable subsidiary ledger in a manual system. (6)

Accounts receivable transaction file A file in a computerized system that is comparable to the sales and cash receipts journals in a manual system. (6)

Accrued expenses (liabilities) Expenses incurred but not yet paid or recorded. (3)

Accrued revenues (receivables) Revenues earned but not yet received or recorded. (3)

Acid-test ratio A measure of a company's immediate short-term liquidity computed by dividing the sum of cash, temporary investments, and receivables by current liabilities. (20)

Activity index The activity that causes changes in the behavior of costs. (24)

Additions and improvements Costs incurred to increase the operating efficiency, productive capacity, or expected useful life of the asset. (10)

Adjunct account An account added to another account. (5)

Adjusted trial balance A list of accounts and their balances after all adjustments have been made. (3)

Adjusting entries Entries made at the end of an accounting period to ensure that the revenue recognition and matching principles are followed. (4)

Adjusted gross income The difference between gross income and adjustments from gross income. (29)

Administrative expenses Expenses relating to such activities as personnel, accounting, management, and store security. (5)

Affiliated companies Companies that are under the common control of a single company. (18)

Aging of accounts receivable The analysis of customer balances by the length of time they have been unpaid. (8)

Amortization The periodic write-off of an intangible asset. (11)

Annual rate of return technique The determination of the profitability of a capital expenditure by dividing expected annual net income by the average investment. (28)

Appropriated retained earnings The portion of retained earnings that is currently unavailable for dividend declarations. (16)

Asset turnover (segments) Sales divided by average operating assets. (21)

Asset turnover ratio A measure of how efficiently a company has used its assets to generate sales that is computed by dividing net sales by average assets. (20)

Assets Future economic benefits owned or controlled by a particular entity as a result of past transactions or events. (1)

Auditing The examination of financial statements by a certified public accountant in order to express an opinion on their fairness. (1)

Authorized stock The amount of stock that a corporation is authorized to sell as indicated in its charter. (15)

Average cost method An inventory costing method which assumes that the cost of goods available for sale are homogeneous. (9)

Average tax rate The total tax paid divided by taxable income. (29)

Balance sheet A financial statement that reports the assets, liabilities, and owner's equity at a specific date. (1)

Bank service charge A fee charged by a bank for the use of its facilities. (7)

Bank statement A statement received monthly from the bank that shows the depositor's bank transactions and balances. (7)

Bearer (coupon) bonds Bonds issued to bearer that are unregistered and holders must send in coupons to receive interest payments. (17)

Bond indenture A legal document that sets forth the terms of the bond issue. (17)

Bookkeeping A part of accounting that involves only the recording of economic events. (1)

Book value The difference between the cost of a depreciable asset and its related accumulated depreciation. (3)

Book value per share The equity a common stockholder has in the net assets of the corporation from owning one share of stock. (15)

Break-even point The level of activity at which total revenues equals total costs. (24)

Budget A formal written summary of management's plan for a specified future time period expressed in financial terms. (25)

Budget committee A group responsible for coordinating the preparation of the budget. (25)

Budgetary control The use of budgets to control operations. (26)

Budgeted balance sheet A projection of financial position at the end of the budget period. (25)

Budgeted income statement An estimate of the expected profitability of operations for the year. (25)

Business combination The acquisition by one entity of part or all of another entity for the purpose of combining resources. (18)

By-laws The internal rules and procedures for conducting the affairs of the corporation. (15)

By-products Products that have a relatively small value in relation to the main product. (23)

Calendar year An accounting period that extends from January 1 to December 31. (3)

Callable bonds Bonds that are subject to call and retirement at a stated dollar amount prior to maturity at the option of the issuer. (17)

Callable preferred stock Preferred stock that grants the issuer the right to purchase the stock from stockholders at specified future dates and prices. (15)

Capital The term used to determine the owner's permanent investment in the business. (1)

Capital budgeting The process of making capital expenditure decisions in business. (28)

Capital expenditures Expenditures that increase the company's investment in productive facilities. (10)

Capital gain or loss The gain or loss resulting from the sale or exchange of property classified under tax law as a capital asset. (29)

Capital lease A contractual arrangement which transfers substantially all the benefits and risks of ownership to the lessee so that the lease is in effect a purchase of the property. (17)

Cash Resources that consist of coins, currency, checks, money orders, and money on hand or on deposit in a bank. (7)

Cash budget A projection of anticipated cash flows. (25)

Cash dividend A pro rata distribution of cash to stockholders. (16)

Cash equivalent price An amount equal to the fair market value of the assets given up or the fair market value of the asset received, whichever is more clearly determinable. (10)

Cash over and short The difference between a cash register tape and the amount of cash in the cash register. (7)

Cash payback technique Identification of the time period required to recover the cost of a capital investment from the annual cash inflow produced by the investment. (28)

Cash payments journal A special journal used to record all cash paid. (6)

Cash receipts journal A special journal used to record all cash received. (6)

Change in accounting principle The use of a principle in the current year that is different from the one used in the preceding year. (16)

Chart of accounts A list of accounts and account numbers that identify their location in the ledger. (2)

Charter A document that creates the corporation. (15)

Check A written order signed by the depositor directing the bank to pay a specified sum of money to a designated recipient. (7)

Check register The journal used to record payments by check in a voucher system. (7)

Classified balance sheet A balance sheet that contains a number of standard classifications or sections. (4)

Classified income statement An income statement that shows various relationships by subdividing the statement into a number of sections. (5)

Closing entries Entries at the end of an accounting period to transfer the balances of temporary accounts to a permanent owner's equity account. (4)

Columnar journal A special journal with more than one column. (6)

Committed fixed costs Costs that are long-term in nature and remain unchanged over extremely wide fluctuations in activity levels. (24)

Comparability Information is comparable when similar methods of measurement and reporting are used by different enterprises. (13)

Complex capital structure A situation where a corporation has securities that may be converted into common stock, which, if converted, would reduce or dilute earnings per share. (16)

Compound entry An entry that involves three or more accounts. (2)

Conceptual framework A coherent system of interrelated objectives and fundamentals that can lead to consistent standards that prescribe the nature, function, and limits of financial accounting and financial statements. (13)

Consistency Use of the same accounting principles and methods from period to period by the same business enterprise. (13)

Consolidated financial statements Financial statements that present the assets and liabilities controlled by the parent company and the aggregate profitability of the affiliated companies. (18)

Constant dollar accounting A type of accounting that restates financial statement items into dollars that have equal purchasing power. (13)

Contingent liability A potential liability that may become an actual liability in the future. (12)

Contra asset account An account that is offset against an asset account on the balance sheet. (3)

Contra revenue account An account reported as a deduction from sales. (5)

Contribution margin The amount of revenue remaining after deducting variable costs. (24)

Control account An account in the general ledger that controls a subsidiary ledger. (6)

Controllable costs Costs that a manager has the authority to incur within a given period of time. (26)

Controlling interest Ownership of more than 50% of the common stock of another entity. (18)

Conversion costs Direct labor and manufacturing overhead costs incurred in converting raw materials into finished goods. (22)

Convertible bonds Bonds that permit bondholders to convert them into common stock at their option. (17)

Convertible preferred stock Preferred stock that provides for the exchange of preferred stock into common stock at a specified ratio. (15)

Copyright A right granted by the federal government allowing the owner to reproduce and sell an artistic or published work. (11)

Corporation A business organized as a separate legal entity under state corporation law having ownership divided into transferable shares of stock. (1) (15)

Correcting entries Entries to correct errors made in recording transactions. (4)

Cost accounting An area of accounting that involves the measuring, recording, and reporting of product costs. (22)

Cost accounting system Manufacturing cost accounts that are fully integrated into the general ledger of a company. (22)

Cost behavior analysis The study of how specific costs respond to changes in the level of activity. (24)

Cost center A segment of an organization that incurs costs but does not directly generate revenues. (21)

Cost method (for investments) An accounting method in which the investment in common stock is initially recorded and then maintained at cost. (18)

Cost principle An accounting principle which states that assets should be recorded at their cost. (1) (13)

Cost of capital The rate of return that management expects to pay on all borrowed and equity funds. (28)

Cost of goods available for sale The sum of the beginning merchandise inventory plus the cost of goods purchased. (5)

Cost of goods purchased The sum of net purchases plus freight-in. (5)

Cost of goods sold The total cost of goods sold during the period, determined by subtracting ending inventory from the cost of goods available for sale. (5)

Cost-volume-profit analysis The study of the effects of changes in costs and volume on a company's profits. (24)

Cost-volume-profit graph A graph showing the relationship between costs, volume, and profits. (24)

Cost-volume-profit income statement A statement for internal use that classifies costs and expenses as fixed or variable and reports contribution margin. (24)

Credit The right side of an account. (2)

Credit memorandum A document issued by the seller for sales returns and allowances. (5)

Cumulative dividend A feature of preferred stock entitling the stockholder to receive current and unpaid prior-year dividends before common stockholders receive any dividends. (15)

Current assets Cash and other resources reasonably expected to be realized or sold or consumed in the business within one year or the operating cycle, whichever is longer. (4)

Current cost The cost of replacing the identical asset owned; a measure of the change in a specific price. (13)

Current cost income from operations The excess of sales revenue over current cost of goods sold and operating expenses. (13)

Current cost net income The total income of a company, based on current costs. (13)

Current liabilities Obligations reasonably expected to be paid from existing current assets or through the creation of other current liabilities within the next year or operating cycle, whichever is longer. (4) (12)

Current ratio A measure that expresses the relationship of current assets to current liabilities by dividing current assets by current liabilities. (20)

Current replacement cost The cost to replace an inventory item by purchase or reproduction. (9)

Debenture bonds Unsecured bonds issued against the credit of the borrower. (17)

Debit The left side of an account. (2)

Debit memorandum A document issued by the purchaser for purchase returns and allowances. (5)

Declaration date The date the board of directors formally declares the dividend and announces it to stockholders. (16)

Declining-balance method A depreciation method that applies a constant rate to the book value of the asset and produces a decreasing annual depreciation amount over the useful life of the asset. (10)

Deferred income taxes Taxes deferred because of differences between accounting income and taxable income. (17)

Deficit A debit balance in retained earnings. (15)

Defined benefit plan A pension plan in which the benefits that the employee will receive at retirement are defined. (12)

Defined contribution plan A pension plan in which the employer's contribution to the plan is defined by the terms of the plan. (12)

Departmental gross profit The difference between a department's net sales and its cost of goods sold. (21)

Departmental income from operations The difference between a department's net sales and the sum of its cost of goods sold and operating expenses. (21)

Departmental margin The excess of a department's net sales and the sum of its cost of goods sold and direct operating expenses. (21)

Departmental payroll summaries A payroll record that is similar to a payroll register. (23)

Depletion The systematic write-off of the cost of natural resources. (11)

Deposits in transit Deposits recorded by the depositor that have not been recorded by the bank. (7)

Depreciable cost The total amount subject to depreciation. (3)

Depreciation The process of allocating the cost of an asset to expense over its useful life in a rational and systematic manner. (3)

Differential analysis See incremental analysis. (28)

Direct approach An approach to preparing a statement of cash flows in which cash revenues and cash expenses are determined. (19)

Direct expenses Expenses that relate specifically to one segment and are incurred for the sole benefit of that segment. (21)

Direct labor The work of factory employees that can be physically and conveniently associated with converting raw materials into finished goods. (22)

Direct labor budget A projection of the quantity and cost of direct labor to be incurred. (25)

Direct labor price standard The rate per hour that should be incurred for direct labor. (27)

Direct labor quantity standard The aggregate time required to make one unit of product. (27)

Direct materials Raw materials that can be physically and conveniently associated with manufacturing the finished product. (22)

Direct materials budget An estimate of the quantity and cost of direct materials to be purchased. (25)

Direct materials price standard The cost per unit of direct materials that should be incurred. (27)

Direct materials quantity standard The quantity of direct materials that should be used per unit of finished goods. (27)

Direct posting The posting of subsidiary accounts directly from a source document, rather than from a journal. (6)

Discontinued operations The disposal of a significant segment of a business. (16)

Discounted cash flow technique A capital budgeting technique that considers both the estimated total cash inflows from the investment and the time value of money. (28)

Discretionary fixed costs Costs that are avoidable within a relatively short period of time such as a month or a year. (24)

Dishonored note receivable A note that is not paid in full at maturity. (8)

Dividend payout ratio Cash dividends paid divided by net income. (16) See payout ratio.

Donated capital Paid-in capital that results from the gift of assets to a corporation. (15)

Double-entry system A system that records the dual effect of each transaction in appropriate accounts. (2)

Drawings Withdrawal of cash or other assets from an unincorporated business for the personal use of the owner(s). (1)

Earnings per share The net income earned by each share of outstanding common stock. (16) (20)

Economic entity assumption An assumption that economic events can be identified with a particular unit of accountability. (1) (13)

Effective interest method of amortization A method of writing off bond discount or bond premium that results in a periodic interest expense equal to a constant percentage of the carrying value of the bonds. (17)

Electronic funds transfer A disbursement system that uses wire, telephone, telegraph, or computer to transfer cash from one location to another. (7)

Elements of financial statements Definitions of basic terms used in accounting. (13)

Employee earnings record A separate record kept for each employee that is updated after each pay period. (12)

Employee's withholding allowance certificate (W-4) An Internal Revenue Service form on which the employee indicates the number of allowances claimed for withholding federal income taxes. (12)

Equity method An accounting method in which the investment in common stock is initially recorded at cost and is then adjusted annually to show the investor's equity in the investee. (18)

Equivalent units of production The work done during the period on the physical units of output expressed in terms of fully completed units.

Expenses The cost of assets consumed or services used in the process of earning revenue. (1)

Extraordinary items Events and transactions that are unusual in nature and infrequent in occurrence. (16)

Federal unemployment taxes A tax imposed on the employer that provides benefits to employees who lose their jobs. (12)

FICA taxes A tax designed to provide workers with supplemental retirement, employment disability, and medical benefits. (12)

Financial Accounting Standards Board (FASB) A private organization that establishes generally accepted accounting principles. (1)

First-in, first-out method (FIFO) An inventory costing method which assumes that the earliest goods acquired are the first to be recognized as cost of goods sold. (9)

Fiscal years Accounting periods that are one year in length. (3)

Fixed costs Costs that remain the same in total regardless of changes in the activity level. (24)

Flexible budget A projection of budget data for various levels of activity. (26)

FOB destination Freight terms indicating that the goods will be placed free on board at the purchaser's place of business, and the seller pays the freight costs. (5)

FOB shipping point Freight terms indicating that goods are placed free on board by the seller, and the buyer pays the freight costs. (5)

Footings Debit and credit totals of an account. (2)

Franchise (license) A contractual arrangement under which the franchisor grants the franchisee the right to sell certain products, or to render specific services, or to use certain trademarks, usually within a designated geographical area. (11)

Full-cost approach The capitalization of both successful and unsuccessful exploration costs. (11)

Full disclosure principle Sufficient information should be provided so that circumstances and events that make a difference to financial statement users are disclosed. (13)

Fully diluted earnings per share An amount that shows the maximum dilution possible in earnings per share. (16)

General journal The most basic form of journal. (2)

General ledger A ledger that contains asset, liability, and owner's equity accounts. (2)

Generally accepted accounting principles (GAAP) A common set of guidelines which indicate how to report economic events. (1)

Going-concern assumption The assumption that the enterprise will continue in operations long enough to carry out its existing objectives and commitments. (13)

Goodwill The value of all favorable attributes that relate to a business enterprise. (11)

Gross income All income from whatever source derived. (29)

Gross profit The excess of sales over cost of goods sold. (5)

Gross profit method A method for estimating the ending inventory by applying a gross profit rate to net sales. (9)

High-low method A mathematical method that uses the total costs incurred at the high and low levels of activity. (24)

Holding gain (loss) The increase (decrease) in an item's value while it is held by the company. (13)

Honored note receivable A note paid in full at its maturity date. (8)

Horizontal analyses A technique for evaluating a series of financial statement data over a period of time to determine the amount and/or percentage increase that has taken place. (20)

Ideal standards Standards based on the optimum level of performance under perfect operating conditions. (27)

Income from operations Income from a company's principal operating activity determined by subtracting cost of goods sold and operating expenses from net sales. (5)

Income ratio The basis for dividing both net income and net loss in a partnership. (14)

Income statement A financial statement that presents the revenues and expenses and resulting net income of a company for a specific period of time. (1)

Income summary A temporary account used in closing revenue and expense accounts. (4)

Incremental analysis The process of identifying the financial data that change under alternative courses of action. (28)

Indirect approach An approach to preparing a statement of cash flow in which net income is adjusted for items that did not affect cash. (19)

Indirect expenses Expenses that relate to the company as a whole and are incurred for the benefit of two or more segments. (21)

Indirect labor Work of factory employees that has no physical association with the finished product, or it is impractical to trace the costs to the goods produced. (22)

Indirect materials Raw materials that do not physically become part of the finished product or cannot be traced because their physical association with the finished product is too small. (22)

Inflation Rising price levels. (13)

Installment method Recognition of revenue and income over time as cash installments are received. (13)

Intangible assets Rights, privileges, and competitive advantages that result from the ownership of long-lived assets that do not possess physical substance. (4) (11)

Intercompany eliminations Eliminations made to exclude the effects of intercompany transactions in preparing consolidated statements. (18)

Intercompany transactions Transactions between affiliated companies. (18)

Interim periods Monthly or quarterly time periods. (3)

Internal accounting control The methods and measures adopted within a business to safeguard its assets and enhance the accuracy and reliability of its accounting data. (7)

Internal administrative control The methods and measures adopted within a business to promote operational efficiency and encourage adherence to prescribed managerial policies. (7)

Internal auditors Company employees who evaluate the effectiveness of the company's system of internal control on a continuous basis. (7)

Internal control A plan of organization and all of the related methods and measures adopted within a business to safeguard its assets, enhance the accuracy and reliability of its accounting data, promote operational efficiency, and encourage adherence to prescribed managerial policies. (7)

Internal rate of return method A method that results in finding the true interest yield of a potential investment. (28)

Intraperiod tax allocation The procedure of associating income taxes with the specific item that directly affects the income taxes for the period. (16)

Inventoriable costs The costs that are assigned to the goods sold and to the goods in ending inventory. (9)

Inventory summary sheets A listing of the quantities and costs of each item of inventory at the balance sheet date. (9)

Inventory turnover A measure of the liquidity of inventory by dividing cost of goods sold by average inventory. (20)

Investment center A segment of an organization that incurs costs, generates revenues, and has control over the investment funds available for use. (21)

Investment portfolio The holding of securities of different corporations. (18)

Itemized deductions Actual expenditures made by the taxpayer during the year, claimed as a deduction. (29)

Job cost sheet A form used to record the costs charged to a job and to determine the total and unit cost of the completed job. (22)

Job order system A cost accounting system in which costs are assigned to jobs or batches. (22)

Joint products Products of significant revenue-generating ability manufactured from a single raw material. (23)

Joint-products Products of significant revenue-generating ability manufactured from a single raw material. (23)

Journal An accounting record in which transactions are initially recorded in chronological order. (2)

Journalizing The procedure of entering transaction data in the journal. (2)

Labor price variance The difference between the actual and standard rates times the actual hours worked. (27)

Labor quantity variance The difference between actual hours worked and standard hours times the standard rate. (27)

Last-in, first-out method (LIFO) An inventory costing method which assumes that the latest units purchased are the first to be allocated to cost of goods sold. (9)

Lease A contractual understanding between a lessor and a lessee that grants the right to use specific property for a period of time in return for cash payments. (11)

Leasehold A lease prepayment that gives the lessee the right to use the property for an extended period of time. (11)

Ledger The entire group of accounts maintained by a company. (2)

Legal capital The amount per share of stock that must be retained in the business for the protection of corporate creditors. (15)

Lessee The renter of leased property. (11)

Lessor The owner of leased property. (11)

Liabilities Obligations arising from past transactions of the entity to transfer assets or services to other entities or individuals in the future. (1)

Liquidating dividend A dividend declared out of paid-in capital. (16)

Liquidity ratios Measures of the short-term ability of the enterprise to pay its maturing obligations and to meet unexpected needs for cash. (20)

Long-range planning The selection of strategies to achieve long-term goals and the development of policies and plans to implement the strategies. (25)

Long-term investments Resources not expected to be realized in cash within the next year or operating cycle. (4)

Long-term liabilities Obligations expected to be paid after one year or the operating cycle, whichever is longer, from sources other than current assets or current liabilities. (4) (17)

Lower of cost or market basis (LCM) (inventories) A basis where inventory is stated at cost or market value, whichever is lower. (9)

Lower of cost or market method (investments) An accounting method in which marketable equity securities are reported at cost or market, whichever is lower. (18)

Lump-sum purchase A single transaction in which more than one type of asset is acquired. (10)

Majority interest The stockholders who own the controlling interest in a subsidiary company. (18)

Maker The party in a promissory note who is making the promise to pay. (8)

Managerial accounting A field of accounting that provides economic and financial information for managers and other internal users. (21)

Manufacturing overhead Manufacturing costs that are indirectly associated with the manufacture of the finished product. (22)

Manufacturing overhead budget An estimate of expected indirect manufacturing costs for the year. (25)

Margin of safety The difference between actual or expected sales and sales at the break-even point. (24)

Marginal tax rate The tax rate applicable to the last dollars of taxable income. (29)

Market (effective) interest rate The interest rate of a bond based on its issue price. (17)

Marketable debt securities Government and corporation bonds that are currently traded in the securities market. (8)

Marketable equity securities Capital stock of corporations that are currently traded in the securities market. (8)

Master budget A set of interrelated budgets that constitutes a plan of action for a specific time period. (25)

Matching principle The principle that efforts (expenses) be matched with accomplishments (revenues). (3) (13)

Materials price variance The difference between the actual price and the standard price times the actual quantity of materials purchased. (27)

Materials quantity variance The difference between the actual quantity of materials used and the standard quantity times the standard price. (27)

Materials requisition slip A document authorizing the issuance of raw materials from the storeroom to manufacturing. (22)

Minority interest The stockholders who are not part of the controlling group in a subsidiary company. (18)

Minutes book A record of decisions made at the annual stockholders' meeting and at meetings of the board of directors. (15)

Mixed costs Costs that contain both a variable and a fixed cost element. (24)

Monetary items Contractual claims to receive or pay a fixed amount of cash. (13)

Monetary unit assumption An assumption stating that only transaction data capable of being expressed in terms of money be included in the accounting records of the economic entity. (1) (13)

Mortgage bond A bond secured by real estate. (17)

Multiple-step income statement An income statement that shows numerous steps in determining net income. (5)

Natural resources Assets that consist of standing timber and underground deposits of oil, gas, and minerals. (11)

Net income The excess of revenues over expenses. (1)

Net loss The excess of expenses over revenues. (1)

Net present value method A method in which cash inflows are discounted to their present value and then compared to the capital outlay required by the capital investment. (28)

Net purchases Purchases less purchase returns and allowances and purchase discounts. (5)

Net realizable value The expected selling price of a unit of inventory less the expected costs to be incurred to dispose of the unit. (9)

Noncontrollable costs Costs allocated to a level of responsibility. (26)

Nonmonetary items Items whose prices change in proportion to changes in the general price level. (13)

No-par value stock Capital stock that has not been assigned a value in the corporate charter. (15)

Normal standards Standards based on an efficient level of performance that are attainable under expected operating conditions. (27)

NSF check A check that is not paid by a bank because of insufficient funds in a customer's bank account. (7)

Operating assets Current assets and plant assets used in operations by a segment. (21)

Operating cycle The average time required to go from cash to cash in producing revenues. (4)

Operating lease A contractual arrangement giving the lessee temporary use of the property with continued ownership of the property by the lessor. (17)

Operating statement Another name for the income statement. (1)

Opportunity cost The potential benefit that may be lost from following an alternative course of action. (28)

Ordinary repairs Expenditures to maintain the operating efficiency and expected productive life of the unit. (10)

Organization costs Costs incurred in the formation of a corporation. (11)

Other expenses and losses A nonoperating section of the income statement that shows expenses from auxiliary operations and losses unrelated to the company's operations. (5)

Other revenues and gains A nonoperating section of the income statement that shows revenues from auxiliary operations and gains unrelated to the company's operations. (5)

Outstanding checks Checks issued and recorded by a company that have not been paid by the bank. (7)

Outstanding stock Capital stock that has been issued and is being held by stockholders. (15)

Overapplied overhead A situation where overhead assigned to work in process is greater than the overhead incurred. (22)

Overhead controllable variance The difference between overhead incurred and overhead budgeted for the standard hours allowed. (27)

Overhead efficiency variance The difference between the overhead budgeted for the hours worked and the standard hours allowed. (27)

Overhead spending variance The difference between overhead budgeted for actual hours worked and overhead incurred. (27)

Overhead volume variance The difference between overhead budgeted for the standard hours allowed and the overhead applied. (27)

Owner's equity The ownership claim on total assets. (1)

Owner's equity statement A financial statement that summarizes the changes in owner's equity for a specific period of time. (1)

Paid-in capital The investment of cash and other assets in the corporation by stockholders in exchange for capital stock. (15)

Par value stock Capital stock that has been assigned a value per share in the corporate charter. (15)

Parent company A company that owns more than 50% of the common stock of another entity. (18)

Partially owned A subsidiary company whose stock is not 100% owned by the parent company. (18)

Participating dividend A feature of preferred stock enabling the stockholder to share ratably with common stockholders in any dividends beyond the rate specified on the preferred stock. (15)

Partners' capital statement The owners' equity statement for a partnership. (14)

Partnership An association of two or more persons to carry on as co-owners of a business for profit. (1) (14)

Partnership agreement A contract expressing the voluntary agreement of two or more individuals in a partnership. (14)

Passive income Income obtained from activities in which the taxpayer did not participate on a regular, continuous, and substantial basis. (29)

Patent An exclusive right issued by the U.S. Patent Office that enables the recipient to manufacture, sell, or otherwise control his or her invention for a period of seventeen years from the date of the grant. (11)

Payee The party to whom payment is to be made. (8)

Payment date (dividend) The date dividend checks are mailed to stockholders. (16)

Payout ratio Measures the percentage of earnings distributed in the form of cash dividends by dividing cash dividends by net income. (16) (20)

Payroll register A payroll record that shows the gross earnings, deductions, and net pay for each employee for each pay period. (12)

Pension plan An arrangement whereby an employer provides benefits to employees after they retire. (12)

Percentage-of-completion method Recognition of revenue and income on a construction project on the basis of costs incurred during the period. (13)

Period costs Costs that are identified with a specific time period and charged to expense as incurred. (22)

Periodic inventory system A system in which detailed records are not maintained and the cost of goods sold is determined only at the end of an accounting period. (5)

Periodicity assumption An assumption that the economic life of a business can be divided into artificial time periods. (3) (13)

Permanent (real) accounts Asset, liability, and owner's capital accounts whose balances are carried forward to the next accounting period. (2)

Perpetual inventory system A detailed inventory system in which the cost of each inventory item is maintained and the records continuously show the inventory that should be on hand. (5) (9)

Personal exemptions Exemptions allowed a taxpayer for himself or herself, his or her spouse, and for each dependent. (29)

Petty cash fund A cash fund used to pay relatively small amounts. (7)

Pooling-of-interests method A method of accounting for a business combination in which the assets of the acquired company are recorded by the acquiring company at book values and no goodwill is recognized. (18)

Portfolio income Income in the form of interest and dividends from securities held as an investment. (29)

Post-closing trial balance A list of permanent accounts after closing entries have been journalized and posted. (4)

Posting The procedure of transferring journal entries to the ledger accounts. (2)

Predetermined overhead rate A rate based on the relationship between estimated annual overhead costs and expected annual operating activity expressed in terms of a common activity base. (22)

Preferred stock Capital stock that has contractual preferences over common stock in certain areas. (15)

Prepaid expenses Expenses paid in cash and recorded in an asset account before they are used or consumed. (3)

Present value The discounted value of a future amount. (17)

Price-earnings ratio An oft-quoted statistic that is computed by dividing the market price of the stock by earnings per share. (20)

Primary earnings per share The amount of earnings per share based on the weighted average common shares outstanding plus common stock equivalents. (16)

Prime costs Direct materials and direct labor. (22)

Prior period adjustment The correction of an error in previously issued financial statements. (16)

Private (or managerial) accounting An area of accounting within a company that involves such activities as cost accounting, budgeting, and accounting information systems. (1) (21)

Privately held corporation A corporation that has only a few stockholders and whose stock is not available for sale to the general public. (15)

Process cost accounting A system of accounting used by companies that manufacture products through a series of continuous processes or operations. (23)

Product costs Costs that are a necessary and integral part of producing the finished product. Also called inventoriable costs. (22)

Production budget A projection of production requirements to meet anticipated sales. (25)

Profit center A segment of an organization that incurs costs and also generates revenues. (21)

Profit margin ratio Measures net income generated by each dollar of sales. (20)

Profit margin (segments) Income from operations divided by sales. (21)

Profitability ratios Measures of the income or operating success of an enterprise for a given period of time. (20)

Program budgeting A technique that requires managers to request funds for specific programs. (25)

Progressive tax A tax where the rate becomes higher as the amount of the tax base increases. (29)

Promissory note A written promise to pay a specified amount of money on demand or at a definite time. (8)

Property, plant, and equipment Assets of a relatively permanent nature that are being used in the business and not intended for resale. (4)

Proportional tax A tax when a constant rate is applied regardless of changes in the amount of the tax base. (29)

Proprietorship A business owned by one person. (1)

Protest fee Reimbursement to the holder of a note for the cost of obtaining an affidavit by a notary public that the maker of a note has refused to pay it. (8)

Public accounting An area of accounting in which the accountant offers expert service to the general public. (1)

Publicly held corporation A corporation that has thousands of stockholders and whose stock is regularly traded on a national securities market. (15)

Purchase invoice A document that supports each credit purchase. (5)

Purchase method A method of accounting for a business combination in which the assets of the acquired company are recorded by the acquiring company at their fair market values, and the excess of cost over the sum of the fair market values of the assets less liabilities assumed is recognized as goodwill. (18)

Purchases budget An estimate of the quantity and cost of goods to be purchased to meet expected sales. (25)

Purchases journal A special journal used to record all purchases of merchandise on account. (6)

Purchasing power The amount of goods and services that can be purchased by a dollar. (13)

Purchasing power gains and losses Gains and losses that result from holding monetary items during periods of price changes. (13)

Quick ratio Another name for acid-test ratio; see acid-test ratio. (20)

Ratio An expression of the mathematical relationship between one quantity and another. The relationship may be expressed either as a percentage, a rate, or a simple proportion. (20)

Receivables turnover A measure of the liquidity of receivables computed by dividing net credit sales by average net receivables. (20)

Record date The date when ownership of outstanding shares is determined for dividend purposes. (16)

Registered bonds Bonds issued in the name of the owner. (17)

Regressive tax A tax where the amount of the tax remains unchanged or the tax rate decreases inversely with an increase in the tax base. (29)

Relevance Information capable of making a difference in a decision. (13)

Relevant range The range over which the company expects to operate during the year. (24)

Reliability The quality of information that makes it dependable. (13)

Research and development costs Expenditures that may lead to patents, copyrights, new processes, and products. (11)

Residual income Income of a segment that is above its minimum required rate of return on average operating assets. (21)

Responsibility accounting A part of management accounting that involves the accumulation of costs on the basis of the individual manager who has the authority to make the day-to-day decisions about the items. (26)

Responsibility reporting system The preparation of reports for each level of responsibility shown in the company's organization chart. (26)

Retail inventory method A method used to estimate the ending inventory by applying a cost to retail ratio to the ending inventory at retail. (9)

Retained earnings Net income retained in a corporation. (15)

Retained earnings statement A financial statement showing the changes in the retained earnings of a corporation during the accounting period. (4)

Return on assets ratio An overall measure of profitability computed by dividing net income by average assets. (20)

Return on investment A measure of the profitability of an investment center (or a company) computed by dividing income from operations by average operating assets. (21)

Revenue expenditures Expenditures charged against revenues as an expense when incurred. (10)

Revenue recognition principle The principle that revenue be recognized in the accounting period in which it is earned. (3) (13)

Revenues The inflow of cash or other assets resulting from the business's major operating activity. (1)

Reversing entry An entry at the beginning of the next accounting period that is the exact opposite of the adjusting entry made in the previous period. (4)

Salaries Specified amounts per month or per year paid to managerial, administrative, and sales personnel. (12)

Sales budget An estimate of expected sales for the year. (25)

Sales forecast The development of potential sales for the industry and the company's expected share of such sales. (25)

Sales invoice A document that provides support for credit sales. (5)

Sales journal A special journal used to record all sales of merchandise on account. (6)

Sales mix The ratio of the number of units of each product sold to the total units of product sold. (24)

Salvage value The expected cash value of an asset at the end of its useful life. (10)

Scatter diagram method The plotting of costs incurred at various levels of activity and fitting a line to determine the average relationship between total costs and the activity levels. (24)

Schedule of cash payments A schedule showing the distribution of cash in the liquidation of a partnership. (14)

Secured bonds Bonds that have specific assets of the issuer pledged as collateral. (17)

Securities and Exchange Commission A governmental agency that requires companies to file financial reports in accordance with generally accepted accounting principles. (1)

Segment Any subunit or activity of an organization for which management information is desired. (21)

Selling and administrative expense budget A projection of anticipated selling and administrative expenses for the year. (25)

Selling expenses Expenses associated with the making of sales. (5)

Serial bonds Bonds that mature in installments. (17)

Short-term liquid assets Cash, temporary investments, and short-term receivables. (8)

Single-step income statement An income statement that shows only one step in determining net income. (5)

Sinking fund Cash or other assets segregated to retire debt.

Solvency ratios Measures of the ability of the enterprise to survive over a long period of time. (20)

Special journal A journal that is used to group similar types of transactions such as all credit sales. (6)

Specific identification method An actual physical flow method in which the cost of the specific unit sold is recognized as cost of goods sold. (9)

Standard cost accounting system A double-entry system of accounting in which standard costs are used in making entries and variances are recognized in the accounts. (27)

Standard costs Predetermined measures of performance. (27)

Standard deduction The amount a taxpayer may claim without supporting documentation. (29)

Standard hours allowed The hours that should have been worked for the units produced. (27)

Standard predetermined overhead rate An overhead rate based on an expected standard activity index. (27)

State unemployment taxes A tax imposed on the employer that provides benefits to employees who lose their jobs. (12)

Stated (contractual) interest rate The interest rate indicated on the bonds. (17)

Statement of cash flows A financial statement that provides information about the cash receipts and cash payments of an entity during a period. (1) (19)

Statement of earnings A document attached to a paycheck that indicates the employee's gross earnings, deductions, and net pay. (12)

Static budget A projection of budget data at one level of activity. (26)

Stock dividend A pro rata distribution of the corporation's own stock to stockholders. (16)

Stock split The issuance of additional shares of stock to stockholders accompanied by a reduction in the par or stated value per share. (16)

Straight-line method A method in which periodic depreciation is the same throughout the service life of the asset. (10)

Subsidiary company A company whose stock is owned by a parent company. (18)

Subsidiary ledger A group of accounts with a common characteristic that is controlled by an account in the general ledger. (6)

Subsidiary plant ledger A ledger that contains records for each plant asset. (11)

Successful efforts approach The capitalization of only the costs of successful exploration efforts. (11)

Sum-of-the-years' digits method A depreciation method that produces decreasing periodic depreciation by applying a decreasing fraction to the depreciable cost of the asset. (10)

Sunk cost A cost that cannot be changed by any present or future decision. (28)

T-accounts The basic form of an account. (2)

Target net income The income objective for individual product lines. (24)

Tax credits Direct reductions of the tax liability. (29)

Tax shelter An investment designed to take advantage of various tax benefits. (29)

Taxable entities May be either individuals, corporations, or fiduciaries (estates and trusts). (29)

Taxable income The excess of adjusted gross income over the sum of deductions and personal exemptions. (29)

Taxation An area of public accounting involving tax advice, tax planning, and preparing tax returns. (1)

Temporary (nominal) accounts Revenue, expense, and drawing accounts whose balances are transferred to owner's capital at the end of an accounting period. (2)

Temporary investments Investments that are readily marketable and intended to be converted into cash within the next year or operating cycle, whichever is longer. (8)

Term bonds Bonds that mature at a single specified future date. (17)

Three-column form of account A form containing columns for debit, credit, and balance amounts. (2)

Tickler file A file in which unpaid vouchers are filed by date of payment. (7)

Time ticket A document indicating the time worked by an employee and the account to be charged. (22)

Total labor variance The difference between actual hours times the actual rate and standard hours times the standard rate for labor. (27)

Total materials variance The difference between the actual quantity times the actual price and the standard quantity times the standard price of materials. (27)

Total overhead variance The difference between actual overhead costs and overhead costs applied. (27)

Trademarks (trade names) A word, phrase, jingle, or symbol that distinguishes or identifies a particular enterprise or product. (11)

Transactions The economic events of the enterprise recorded by accountants. (1)

Treasury stock A corporation's own stock that has been issued, fully paid for, and reacquired by the corporation but not cancelled. (15)

Trial balance A list of accounts and their balances at a given time. (2)

Unappropriated retained earnings The portion of retained earnings that is available for dividend declarations. (16)

Underapplied overhead A situation where overhead assigned to work in process is less than the overhead incurred. (22)

Unearned revenues Revenues received and recorded as liabilities before they are earned. (3)

Units of activity method A depreciation method where service life is expressed in terms of the total units of production or use expected from the asset. (10)

Unsecured bonds Bonds issued against the general credit of the borrower. Also called debenture bonds. (17)

Useful life The length of service of a productive facility. (3)

Variable costing A costing approach in which only variable manufacturing costs are considered to be product costs and fixed manufacturing costs are recognized as period costs when incurred. (26)

Variable costs Costs that vary in total directly and proportionately with changes in the activity level. (24)

Variances The difference between actual costs and standard costs. (27)

Vertical analyses A technique that expresses each item within a financial statement in terms of a percent of a base amount. (20)

Voucher An authorization form prepared for each expenditure in a voucher system. (7)

Voucher register A columnar journal used to record all types of expenditures in a voucher system. (7)

Voucher system An extensive series of prescribed control procedures designed to assure that every disbursement by check is a proper payment. (7)

Wage and tax statement (Form W–2) A form showing gross earnings, FICA taxes withheld, and federal and state income taxes withheld that is prepared annually by an employer for each employee. (12)

Wages Amounts paid to employees based on a rate per hour or on a piecework basis. (12)

Wasting assets See Natural Resources. (11)

Wholly owned A subsidiary company whose common stock is 100% owned by the parent company. (18)

Work sheet A multiple-column form that may be used in the adjustment process and in preparing financial statements. (4)

Working capital Current assets in excess of current liabilities. (4)

Zero-base budgeting A technique which starts at a zero budget level each year and requires each manager to justify all expenditures as though the area of activity were being started for the first time. (25)

INDEX